What Hath God Wrought

The Oxford History of the United States

David M. Kennedy, *General Editor*

ROBERT MIDDLEKAUFF
THE GLORIOUS CAUSE
The American Revolution, 1763–1789

DANIEL WALKER HOWE
WHAT HATH GOD WROUGHT
The Transformation of America, 1815–1848

JAMES M. MCPHERSON
BATTLE CRY OF FREEDOM
The Civil War Era

DAVID M. KENNEDY
FREEDOM FROM FEAR
The American People in Depression and War, 1929–1945

JAMES T. PATTERSON
GRAND EXPECTATIONS
The United States, 1945–1974

JAMES T. PATTERSON
RESTLESS GIANT
The United States from Watergate to Bush v. Gore

WHAT HATH GOD WROUGHT

The Transformation of America, 1815–1848

DANIEL WALKER HOWE

OXFORD
UNIVERSITY PRESS

2007

OXFORD
UNIVERSITY PRESS

Oxford University Press, Inc., publishes works that further
Oxford University's objective of excellence
in research, scholarship, and education.

Oxford   New York
Auckland   Cape Town   Dar es Salaam   Hong Kong   Karachi
Kuala Lumpur   Madrid   Melbourne   Mexico City   Nairobi
New Delhi   Shanghai   Taipei   Toronto

With offices in
Argentina   Austria   Brazil   Chile   Czech Republic   France   Greece
Guatemala   Hungary   Italy   Japan   Poland   Portugal   Singapore
South Korea   Switzerland   Thailand   Turkey   Ukraine   Vietnam

Copyright © 2007 by Oxford University Press, Inc.

Published by Oxford University Press, Inc.
198 Madison Avenue, New York, NY 10016

www.oup.com

Library of Congress Cataloging-in-Publication Data
Howe, Daniel Walker.
What hath God wrought : the transformation of America,
1815–1848 / Daniel Walker Howe.
p. cm. — (Oxford history of the United States)
Includes bibliographical references and index.
ISBN 978-0-19-507894-7
1. United States—History—1815–1861.
2. United States—Foreign relations—1815–1861.
3. United States—Politics and government—1815–1861.
4. United States—Economic conditions—To 1865.
5. Social change—United States—History—19th century.   I. Title.
E338.H69 2007   973.5—dc22   2007012370

2   3   4   5   6   7   8   9
Printed in the United States of America
on acid-free paper

To the Memory of
John Quincy Adams

Whatever the heats of party may be, however the tone of disappointment against Mr. Adams may sometimes rise to something too like hatred, there is undoubtedly a deep reverence and affection for the man in the nation's heart; and any one may safely prophesy that his reputation, half a century after his death, will be of a very honourable kind. He fought a stout and noble battle in Congress last session in favour of discussion of the slavery question, and in defence of the right of petition upon it; on behalf of women as well as of men. While hunted, held at bay, almost torn to pieces by an outrageous majority—leaving him, I believe, in absolute unity—he preserved a boldness and coolness as amusing as they were admirable. Though he now and then vents his spleen with violence when disappointed in a favourite object, he seems able to bear perfectly well that which it is the great fault of Americans to shrink from, singularity and blame. He seems, at times, reckless of opinion; and this is the point of his character which his countrymen seem, naturally, least able to comprehend.

—Harriet Martineau,
Retrospect of Western Travel, 1838

Acknowledgments

This book has been a long time in the making, and many people have helped make it. I should like to thank Peter Ginna, Susan Ferber, Joellyn Ausanka, the late Sheldon Meyer, and the late C. Vann Woodward for their confidence and wise counsel.

David Kennedy, editor-in-chief of the Oxford History of the United States, read my drafts with patience, care, and insight. James McPherson, Daniel Feller, and Richard R. John each read the whole long manuscript, made valuable comments, and saved me from many a mistake. Professor John's unequaled knowledge of the communications revolution proved indispensable. A number of scholars gave generously of their expertise on particular subjects: Joyce Appleby, Gabor Boritt, Michael Holt, Naomi Lamoreaux, Mark Neely, Barbara Packer, William Pencak, Donald Ratcliffe, Timothy Roberts, Kathryn Kish Sklar, Conrad Wright the younger, and John Yoo. Of course, I am responsible for whatever faults may remain—all the more so because I did not always follow advice received.

Research grants supporting the work that made this book possible came from Oxford University's Rothermere American Institute, the Academic Senate of the University of California at Los Angeles, the Institute for the Advanced Study of Religion at Yale University, the Bellagio Study Center of the Rockefeller Foundation, and the R. Stanton Avery Distinguished Fellowship of the Huntington Library. The continued hospitality of the Huntington and the graciousness of its staff have provided an ideal environment for research and writing. For a happy decade I enjoyed the company and intellectual stimulation of the Master and Fellows of St. Catherine's College, Oxford. A series of talented research assistants over the years have included Martin Meenagh and Rebecca Webb at Oxford; Julia Ott at Yale; and Michael Bottoms,, Michael Hawkins, Rebecca Hood, Susan Kim, Anne Lescoulie, and Richard Lester at UCLA. Freddie LaFemina assisted at a critical juncture. India Cooper is the ideal copy editor.

Sandra Shumway Howe and Stephen Walker Howe read the manuscript chapter by chapter as I wrote it, and offered both comments and encouragement over the long haul.

March 2007   D.W.H.

Contents

Maps

Editor's Introduction

In 1844, near the end of the period covered in this volume of *The Oxford History of the United States*, Ralph Waldo Emerson proclaimed that "America is the country of the Future. It is a country of beginnings, of projects, of vast designs and expectations." Emerson spoke a common sentiment in that heady age of what might be called America's national adolescence. In scarcely more than two generations since its founding, the young nation had stretched its domains to the Rocky Mountain crest and stood poised to assert its sovereignty all the way to the Pacific coast. The American people, lustily doubling their numbers every two decades, dreamed without embarrassment of extravagant utopias both spiritual and secular. Their economy, fueled by startling new technologies like the telegraph and the railroad, was growing robustly. Their churches were rocked by revivalism, even as their political system was giving the world an exhilarating lesson in the possibilities of mass democracy.

Yet Emerson's America was already a country with a past. Its history held peril as well as promise—not least the noxious heritage of chattel slavery, a moral outrage that mocked the Republic's claim to be a model of social and political enlightenment and eventually menaced the nation's very survival.

What Hath God Wrought recounts a critical passage in that history. It opens on a note both ironic and prophetic: Andrew Jackson's storied victory over a crack British force at the Battle of New Orleans in 1815. Ironic because the battle was fought some two weeks *after* British and American delegates had signed a formal peace treaty in Ghent, Belgium. Prophetic because, as Daniel Walker Howe conclusively demonstrates, victory owed far less to the derring-do of the buckskin-clad backwoodsmen celebrated in song and fable than to the methodical gunnery of General Jackson's artillery batteries, firing American-forged cannons that were among the early fruits of the onrushing industrial revolution whose gathering force was transforming countless sectors of national life.

As his subtitle declares, transformation is the central theme of Howe's compelling narrative. Few periods in American history have witnessed changes as diverse, deep, and durable as the three decades following the War of 1812. Few historians have explained them as comprehensively, cogently, and colorfully as Howe.

Not the least of those changes transfigured the very nature of politics, in the United States and beyond. Americans in this era became the first people to embrace universal white manhood suffrage, build mass-based political parties, and invent the institutions and practices of democracy for a continent-sized nation. The often raucous spectacle of American democracy in this era fascinated the world, conspicuously including a brilliant young Frenchman, Alexis de Tocqueville. After nine months traversing Andrew Jackson's United States in 1831–32, he wrote: "I confess that in America I saw more than America; I sought there the image of democracy itself, with its inclinations, its character, its prejudices, and its passions, in order to learn what we have to fear or to hope from its progress" (*Democracy in America*, Everyman's Library, 14).

No less an ambition animates Daniel Howe's richly textured account. Like Tocqueville's, his deepest subject is not simply politics—though the pages that follow do full justice to the tumultuous and consequential politics of the era—but the entire array of economic, technological, social, cultural, and even psychological developments that were beginning to shape a distinctively American national identity. Howe brings to bear an impressive command of modern scholarship to explicate topics as varied as the origins of feminism and abolitionism; the Missouri Compromise and the Mexican War; the crafting of the Monroe Doctrine and the clash with Britain over the Oregon country; the emergence of the Whig, Free Soil, and Republican Parties; the Lone Star revolution in Texas and the gold rush in California; the sectional differentiation of the American economy; the accelerating pace of both mechanical and cultural innovations, not least as they affected the organization of the household and the lives of women; and the emergence of a characteristic American literature in the works of writers like Emerson, Henry David Thoreau, James Fenimore Cooper, Margaret Fuller, Frederick Douglass, and Walt Whitman.

With singular deftness, Howe tells the remarkable story of American religion in this formative period, as the Second Great Awakening kindled roaring evangelical revivals and even spawned the new religion of Mormonism. Indeed, few if any other writers have so sensitively explored both the social and the doctrinal dimensions of the astonishing developments that were fracturing American Protestantism into countless sects, with consequences that have persisted to our own time.

Howe also recounts with admirable clarity the story of President Andrew Jackson's notorious "Bank War" and his even more notorious policies of forcible Indian removals. And *What Hath God Wrought* artfully draws out the myriad implications of the homely tale that Jackson traveled to his inaugural in 1829 in a horse-drawn carriage and left the capital at the end of his term eight years later by train—marking in the arc of this one president's tenure in office the pervasive impact of the "transportation revolution" that was one of the era's signature achievements.

The railroad and the telegraph were both the principal causes and the most conspicuous emblems of the deep transformations that are Howe's principal subjects. They catalyzed the phenomenal expansion of the slave South, as planters pushed the "Cotton Kingdom" over the Appalachians and out onto the loamy bottomlands of Alabama and Mississippi and ever onward to the West. The railroad's iron tracks and the telegraph's gossamer filaments tenuously bound together a nation growing ever larger even as it divided ever more bitterly over slavery. And when at last in 1846 Americans made war on Mexico to enlarge their dominions still further, the telegrapher's key clacked war reports among newsrooms in Charleston, Washington, Baltimore, Philadelphia, New York, and Boston. By war's end the first newspaper wire service, the Associated Press, was born—but one example of the "communications revolution" that swept America in the years after Andrew Jackson had battled in ignorance of war's end at New Orleans in 1815.

Howe's history concludes with America's victory in the Mexican War—a bittersweet triumph that both enlarged Thomas Jefferson's vaunted "empire of liberty" in the West and reopened the festering wound of the slavery controversy. "Mexico will poison us," a chastened Emerson presciently declared. That prognosis was bloodily confirmed scarcely a dozen years later when the Civil War engulfed the nation, a tale told with incomparable panache in the volume that chronologically succeeds this one in the Oxford series, James McPherson's *Battle Cry of Freedom*. Like that acclaimed work, *What Hath God Wrought* is another outstanding contribution to *The Oxford History of the United States*, one that will enlighten scholars and general readers alike.

David M. Kennedy

Abbreviations Used in Citations

AHR	*American Historical Review*
JAH	*Journal of American History*
JER	*Journal of the Early Republic*
OED	*Oxford English Dictionary*
WMQ	*William and Mary Quarterly*, 3rd ser.
Collected Works of AL	*Collected Works of Abraham Lincoln*, ed. Roy P. Basler (Princeton, 1953)
Correspondence of AJ	*Correspondence of Andrew Jackson*, ed. John Spencer Bassett (Washington, 1926–35)
Freehling, *Secessionists at Bay*	William W. Freehling, *The Road to Disunion*, vol. I, *Secessionists at Bay, 1776–1854* (New York, 1990)
Meinig, *Continental America*	D. W. Meinig, *The Shaping of America: A Geographical Perspective on 500 Years of History* (New Haven, 1986–2004), vol. 2, *Continental America, 1800–1867*
Presidential Messages	James D. Richardson, ed., *Messages and Papers of the Presidents* (Washington, 1901)
Remini, *Jackson*, I	Robert Remini, *Andrew Jackson and the Course of American Empire* (New York, 1977)

Remini, *Jackson*, II

Robert Remini, *Andrew Jackson and the Course of American Freedom* (New York, 1981)

Remini, *Jackson*, III

Robert Remini, *Andrew Jackson and the Course of American Democracy* (New York, 1984)

TJ: Writings

Thomas Jefferson: Writings, ed. Merrill D. Peterson (Charlottesville, Va., 1984)

What Hath God Wrought

Introduction

On the twenty-fourth of May 1844, Professor Samuel F. B. Morse, seated amidst a hushed gathering of distinguished national leaders in the chambers of the United States Supreme Court in Washington, tapped out a message on a device of cogs and coiled wires:

WHAT HATH GOD WROUGHT

Forty miles away, in Baltimore, Morse's associate Alfred Vail received the electric signals and sent the message back. The invention they had demonstrated was destined to change the world. For thousands of years messages had been limited by the speed with which messengers could travel and the distance at which eyes could see signals such as flags or smoke. Neither Alexander the Great nor Benjamin Franklin (America's first postmaster general) two thousand years later knew anything faster than a galloping horse. Now, instant long-distance communication became a practical reality. The commercial application of Morse's invention followed quickly. American farmers and planters—and most Americans then earned a living through agriculture—increasingly produced food and fiber for distant markets. Their merchants and bankers welcomed the chance to get news of distant prices and credit. The New York *Journal of Commerce,* conceived by Morse himself and published by the famous Christian businessmen and philanthropists Arthur and Lewis Tappan, could put such intelligence carried over the telegraph to good use. The *Journal* has published continuously from 1827 to the present—since 2000 on the Internet as well as in print.

This book is a narrative history of the American republic between 1815 and 1848, that is, from the end of the War of 1812 to the end of the war with Mexico. Along with the traditional subject matter of history—political, diplomatic, and military events—the story includes the social, economic, and cultural developments that have extensively concerned historians in recent years. This reflects my own conviction that both kinds of history are essential to a full understanding of the past.

The invention of electric telegraphy, coming near the close of the period treated here, represented a climactic moment in a widespread revolution of communications. Other features of this revolution included improvements in printing and paper manufacturing; the multiplication of newspapers, magazines, and books; and the expansion of the postal system (which mostly carried newspapers and commercial business, not personal letters). Closely related to these developments occurred a simultaneous revolution in transportation: the introduction of steamboats, canals, turnpikes, and railroads, shortening travel times and dramatically lowering shipping costs. How these twin revolutions transformed American life will be central to the story told here. Their consequences certainly rivaled, and probably exceeded in importance, those of the revolutionary "information highway" of our own lifetimes.

Morse's telegraph had particular importance for a large country with a population spreading into increasingly remote areas. Thomas Jefferson had declared the United States "an empire for liberty" and by his Louisiana Purchase had put the new nation on course to dominate the North American continent. In 1845, the ambition to occupy still more land would be characterized by John L. O'Sullivan's *Democratic Review* as the fulfillment of America's "manifest destiny"—a term that soon became as important as "empire" to describe American nationhood. Samuel F. B. Morse shared this view, which he reinforced with a religious sense of divine providence. Nation-builders awaited news as eagerly as did people selling crops.

Within a few days of the initial demonstration of his invention, Morse was keeping members of Congress in Washington abreast of developments at the Democratic national convention in Baltimore as they happened. The professor felt disappointment when his favorite candidate, the imperialist Lewis Cass of Michigan, missed out on the presidential nomination but was soon reassured to report that it went to another expansionist, James Knox Polk of Tennessee. Polk won the ensuing election and led the country into a war with Mexico. The conquest of that large republic by the small armed forces of the United States, despite formidable geographical difficulties and in the face of a hostile population, constituted one of the most amazing military achievements of the nineteenth century, and the early telegraph lines helped keep the U.S. president and public abreast of events. When the momentous conflict came to a close, the United States stretched from sea to sea, having acquired Texas, California, and everything in between. The electric telegraph then helped integrate this continental empire.

The text of Morse's demonstration message came from the Bible: "It shall be said of Jacob and of Israel, What hath God wrought!" (Numbers 23:23). Credit for applying the verse to this occasion belongs to Nancy Goodrich Ellsworth, who suggested it to her daughter Annie, who in turn provided it to Morse. (The professor was in love with Annie.) The quotation proved the perfect choice, capturing the inventor's own passionate Christian faith and conception of himself as an instrument of providence.

As Morse later commented, the message "baptized the American Tele-graph with the name of its author": God.[1] The American public appreci-ated the significance of the message, for biblical religion then permeated the culture in ways both conventional and sincerely felt. Morse's invoca-tion of the Bible typified that recurrent importance of religion which has long characterized American history.

Morse's synthesis of science and religion represented the predominant American attitude of the time; only a few eccentrics believed there was any conflict between scientific and religious truth. Revelation and reason alike, Americans were confident, led to knowledge of God and His cre-ation. Religious awakening, expansion of education, interest in science, and technological progress all went hand in hand. Evangelists welcomed technological advances along with mass education as helping them spread the good news of Christ. Literature, like education and science, was satu-rated with religious meanings and motivations. The writers of America's literary renaissance took advantage of the improvements in communica-tions technology to market their art and their moral values to larger and more widespread audiences than writers had ever before enjoyed.

A combination of Protestantism with the Enlightenment shaped Amer-ican culture and institutions. Morse's telegraph appealed to both these strains in American ideology, for it fostered what contemporaries called the brotherhood of man and could also be viewed as promoting the king-dom of God. Many Americans interpreted their nation's destiny in reli-gious terms, as preparing the world for a millennial age of free institu-tions, peace, and justice. A Methodist women's magazine explained the role that the electric telegraph would play in this process, revealing both the optimism and the arrogance characteristic of the time:

> This noble invention is to be the means of extending civilization, re-publicanism, and Christianity over the earth. It must and will be ex-tended to nations half-civilized, and thence to those now savage and barbarous. Our government will be the grand center of this mighty in-fluence. . . . The beneficial and harmonious operation of our institu-tions will be seen, and similar ones adopted. Christianity must speedily follow them, and we shall behold the grand spectacle of a whole world, civilized, republican, and Christian. . . . Wars will cease from the earth. Men "shall beat their swords into plough shares, and their spears into pruning-hooks." . . . Then shall come to pass the millennium.[2]

1. Quoted in Samuel Prime, *The Life of Samuel F. B. Morse* (New York, 1875), 494.
2. "The Magnetic Telegraph," *Ladies' Repository* 10 (1850): 61–62; quoted in James Moor-head, *American Apocalypse* (New Haven, 1978), 6.

The first practical application of Morse's invention—to report a political party convention—was no accident. The formation of mass political parties, their organization on local, state, and national levels, the application of government patronage to knit them together, their espousal of rival political programs, and their ability to command the attention of the public all combined to give this period of American history its distinctive, highly politicized quality. The rise of mass parties has often been traced to the broadening of the franchise (the right to vote) to include virtually all adult white males. However, no such parties with mass followings could have come into existence without the revolution in communication. Many newspapers of the time were the organs of a political party, existing to propagate its point of view; influential policymakers might be former journalists.[3] The newspapers quickly enlisted the telegraph in their quest to gather and distribute information; the newspapers of New York City formed the Associated Press wire service "to secure the transmission of news from the South, and particularly from the seat of War in Mexico, in advance of all ordinary channels."[4]

The most common name for the years this book treats is "Jacksonian America." I avoid the term because it suggests that Jacksonianism describes Americans as a whole, whereas in fact Andrew Jackson was a controversial figure and his political movement bitterly divided the American people. Even worse difficulties arise from the familiar expression "Jacksonian Democracy." Our own age finds the limitations on the democracy of that period glaring: the enslavement of African Americans, the abuse of Native Americans, the exclusion of women and most nonwhites from the suffrage and equality before the law. The Jacksonian movement in politics, although it took the name of the Democratic Party, fought so hard in favor of slavery and white supremacy, and opposed the inclusion of nonwhites and women within the American civil polity so resolutely, that it makes the term "Jacksonian Democracy" all the more inappropriate as a characterization of the years between 1815 and 1848. Nor did Andrew Jackson's presidential campaigns constitute a nationwide struggle on behalf of universal white manhood enfranchisement. In most states, white male suffrage evolved naturally and with comparatively little controversy.

3. Jeffrey Pasley has compiled a list, *Printers, Editors, and Publishers of Political Journals Elected to the U.S. Congress, 1789–1861*, found at http://pasleybrothers.com/newspols/images/Editors_in_Congress.pdf (viewed March 2, 2007).
4. Moses Beach in 1853 recalling events in 1846–48, quoted in Menahem Blondheim, *News over the Wires: The Telegraph and the Flow of Public Information in America, 1844–1897* (Cambridge, Mass., 1994), 50.

The *consequences* of white male democracy, rather than its *achievement*, shaped the political life of this period.[5]

Another term that has sometimes been applied to this period—more by historians than by the general public—is "the market revolution." I avoid this expression also. Those historians who used it have argued that a drastic change occurred during these years, from farm families raising food for their own use to producing it for distant markets. However, more and more evidence has accumulated in recent years that a market economy already existed in the eighteenth-century American colonies.[6] To be sure, markets expanded vastly in the years after the end of the War of 1812, but their expansion partook more of the nature of a continuing evolution than a sudden revolution. Furthermore, their expansion did not occur in the face of resistance from any substantial group of people preferring subsistence farming to market participation. Most American family farmers welcomed the chance to buy and sell in larger markets. They did not have to be coerced into seizing the opportunities the market economy presented.

Accordingly, I provide an alternative interpretation of the early nineteenth century as a time of a "communications revolution." This, rather than the continued growth of the market economy, impressed contemporary Americans as a startling innovation. During the thirty-three years that began in 1815, there would be greater strides in the improvement of communication than had taken place in all previous centuries. This revolution, with its attendant political and economic consequences, would be a driving force in the history of the era.

The America of 1848 had been transformed in many ways: by the growth of cities, by the extension of United States sovereignty across the continent, by increasing ethnic and religious diversity as a result of both immigration and conquest—as well as by expanding overseas and national markets, and by the integration of this vast and varied empire through dramatic and sudden improvements in communications. But while the citizens of the giant republic largely agreed in welcoming the growth of their economy, they were very far from uniting in a bland consensus. The *nature* of the expanding economy constituted one of the

5. My interpretation differs from that presented in Sean Wilentz, *The Rise of American Democracy: Jefferson to Lincoln* (New York, 2005), which affirms the democratic role conventionally attributed to Andrew Jackson.

6. The older view was powerfully presented in Charles Sellers, *The Market Revolution: Jacksonian America, 1815–1846* (New York, 1991). For an introduction to the new evidence, see Richard Bushman, "Markets and Composite Farms in Early America," *WMQ* 55 (1998): 351–74.

most frequently debated issues: Should it remain primarily agricultural, with manufactured products imported, or should economic diversification and development be encouraged along with economic growth?

Not all Americans endorsed their country's imperial destiny of territorial expansion. For some people, the Christian religion provided a fulcrum for criticism of American national aggrandizement rather than an endorsement of it. America's national mission should be one of democratic example rather than conquest, they insisted. The government's massive dispossession of eastern Indian tribes in the 1830s aroused bitter protest. Later, a strong political opposition criticized Polk's war against Mexico. Opponents of slavery deplored territorial expansion as a plan (in the words of the poet James Russell Lowell) "to lug new slave states in." Critics of American culture wondered whether Morse's invention was merely an improved means to an unimproved end. "We are in great haste to construct a magnetic telegraph from Maine to Texas," noted Henry David Thoreau, "but Maine and Texas, it may be, have nothing important to communicate."[7]

In fact, the various improved means of communication carried very important messages. The early national period witnessed new and controversial ideas being formulated, publicized, and even in many cases implemented. The history of the young American republic is above all a history of battles over public opinion. The political parties debated serious issues, economic and constitutional; political divisions were sharp and party loyalties fierce. Meanwhile, innovators at least as original as Morse explored novel approaches in law, in education, in popular politics, and in corporate organization.[8] Workers tried to legitimate labor unions in the eyes of public opinion and struck in defiance of the common law. Like technology, politics, and economic development, American religion displayed remarkable originality. Millenarians warned of the imminent Second Coming of Christ. The evangelical movement prompted national soul-searching and argument over the country's goals and the best means to achieve them. Reformers motivated by religion challenged long-held practices relating to the treatment of women, children, and convicts; utopians of every stripe founded communities dedicated to experimenting with new gender roles and family relationships. Manners

---

7. "The Biglow Papers," *Poetical Works of James Russell Lowell*, ed. Marjorie Kaufman (Boston, 1978), 182; Henry David Thoreau, *Walden*, intro. Norman Holmes Pearson (New York, 1964), 42.

8. None of the basic science that the electric telegraph applied originated with Morse.

and customs came under as much criticism as institutions: Cockfighting, dueling, and drinking alcohol (among other traditional pursuits) became controversial. All such reforms were created, discussed, and propagated through the enormously expanded media of print and wire. Through these debates, disparate groups competed to define America's national mission. That America, among the nations of the world, had a mission no one doubted. Whatever America stood for, whether an empire for liberty or a light of virtue unto the nations, the Hand of God had wrought it.

More than any other discussion, the debate over the future of human slavery in an empire dedicated to liberty threatened to tear the country apart. The communications revolution gave a new urgency to social criticism and to the slavery controversy in particular. No longer could slaveholders afford to shrug off the commentary of outsiders. Critics of slavery seized upon the new opportunities for disseminating ideas to challenge the institution in the South itself. Alarmed, the defenders of slavery erected barricades against the intrusion of unwelcome expression. Better communication did not necessarily foster harmony.

In the King James Version of the Bible, an exclamation mark follows the words "What hath God wrought." But when Morse transmitted the message, he left off any closing punctuation.[9] Later, when transcribing the message, Morse added a question mark, and thus it was often printed in accounts of his achievement. This misquotation had its own significance. Morse's question mark unintentionally turned the phrase from an affirmation of the Chosen People's destiny to a questioning of it. What God had wrought in raising up America was indeed contested, in Morse's time no less than it is today. In the title of this book I leave the final punctuation off, as Morse originally did. This allows the title to explore both potential meanings, as the book itself seeks both to affirm and to question the value of what Americans of that period did.

9. The original strip of paper with the dots and dashes of Morse's transmission can be seen at http://memory.loc.gov/ammem/atthtml/morse2.html (viewed Feb. 22, 2007). Modern biblical translations render the expression as "See what God has done" (New Revised Standard Version) or "Yea Israel, what God has planned" (Jewish Study Bible).

Prologue:
The Defeat of the Past

January 1, 1815, dawned faintly through the dense fog over southern Louisiana. Six miles downstream from New Orleans, two hostile armies hid from each other in the enveloping mists. The invaders consisted of eight thousand British soldiers, some still in ships offshore, commanded by Major General Edward Pakenham. To defend the city, the United States had so far gathered no more than four thousand men under Major General Andrew Jackson. Though small by the standards of Napoleonic Europe, these were large armies for North America. A severe winter all over the Atlantic world slowed communication and made transportation difficult. Neither army knew that across the ocean, representatives of their respective countries had signed a treaty of peace eight days earlier. They did know that heavy rains had fallen on them almost every day since the British landing two weeks before and that the nights were frosty and chill. The British had to operate at the end of a tenuous supply line, without tents and on short rations. Suffering especially were the eleven hundred black colonial troops from the British West Indies. Not acclimated to winter weather and still wearing thin tropical uniforms, some of these men died of hypothermia.[1]

Behind the curtain of fog, each army was active. The Americans celebrated New Year's Day with a parade review of their motley army. Jackson's force counted but few regulars. There were Tennessee militia (the component with whom the Tennessee general felt most comfortable), Louisiana militia, mostly French-speaking, and mounted Mississippi dragoons. There was an Irish American regiment called the Louisiana Blues, and two battalions of black men, one made up of African Americans and the other of Haitian immigrants. Some of the black soldiers were slaves on loan from their masters to the army, but most of them were free men. Jackson addressed the blacks as "brave fellow citizens" and had promised them pay and respect the equal of whites'. Up from their hideout at Barataria came the notorious pirate band of Jean and Pierre Laffite—who had cast their lot with the Americans after deciding that a strong presence

1. Robin Reilly, *The British at the Gates* (London, 1974), 258.

by the Royal Navy was not in their best professional interests. Jackson's orders to this heterogeneous army had to be translated not only into French but also into Spanish (for Louisiana had been a Spanish colony as well as a French colony before becoming an American state) and Choctaw, the language of the Native American allies who protected his left flank. The general had assembled these mixed forces behind a parapet of logs and earth constructed along an abandoned watercourse that had once turned a mill wheel. Called the Rodriguez Canal, this served as a defensive moat in front of the breastwork. On Jackson's right flowed the Mississippi River.[2]

But on New Year's Day the invaders were even more active: They were preparing an assault on the American line. Shortly before 10:00 A.M. the fog lifted a bit and the British artillery opened its preparatory bombardment, catching the Americans by surprise. Jackson's headquarters building was demolished, although he and his officers miraculously escaped unhurt. Gradually at first, then with increasing determination, the American artillery replied. Each army had improvised shelters for its cannoneers from items available at nearby plantations; the Americans used cotton bales, and the British hogsheads of sugar. Neither stood up well to the test of battle. The British infantry waited, bayonets fixed, for the signal to charge. Pakenham wanted to silence some of his enemies' guns and punch a hole in their defensive works before ordering the assault. For three hours the artillery duel went on. Eventually, with his guns' ammunition running low, Pakenham ceased the bombardment and called off the attack. Although the British artillery was slightly superior to the American as measured by "throw weight," the American gunners had inflicted more damage on their enemy than they sustained themselves. That afternoon it rained again.[3]

Pakenham decided to wait for reinforcements of men and ammunition before planning another attack. By doing so, however, he accorded Jackson the same opportunity to strengthen his army and its position. Neither general had an inclination to stand on the defensive. Both were tough, seasoned soldiers. Thirty-eight years old, Ned Pakenham had been schooled in the Peninsular War by two of the greatest generals of the age: his patron Wellington and his adversary Napoleon. Unhesitatingly courageous, Pakenham had been twice wounded in action. Andrew Jackson

2. Robert Remini, *The Battle of New Orleans* (New York, 1999), 25–60, 107, 124. Jackson's proclamation "to the free coloured inhabitants of Louisiana," Sept. 21, 1814, is in *Correspondence of AJ*, II, 58–59.
3. Robert S. Quimby, *The U.S. Army in the War of 1812* (East Lansing, Mich., 1997), 875–78, 945.

was forty-seven and in poor health but sustained by indomitable willpower. He told how, as a thirteen-year-old boy during the Revolution, a British officer had struck him in the face with his sword. For the rest of his life, Jackson bore the scars and a bitter hatred of the British. Although he had spent time as a frontier lawyer, cotton planter, and congressman, temperamentally Jackson was always a soldier. Earlier in this war, he had distinguished himself in campaigns against the British, the Spanish, and the Creek Indians. Impatient of restraints, as a military leader Jackson relied as much upon his instinct for command as upon formal authority.

The prize for which the two armies contended was well worth fighting over. The city of New Orleans comprised the second greatest port in the United States (after New York), a position it would retain until surpassed by Los Angeles in the twentieth century. Before the Erie Canal and the railroads, New Orleans constituted the gateway to the world for the whole vast area drained by the Mississippi, Missouri, and Ohio Rivers. The city had much more export than import trade, for until the arrival of the steamboat it was hard to ship goods up the Mississippi against the current. The census of 1810 had enumerated 24,552 people in greater New Orleans, a big city by North American standards. Cosmopolitan in composition as well as metropolitan in size, its population included French and Spanish Creoles (born in the New World of European descent), émigré French planters fleeing the Haitian Revolution, free people of color (*gens de couleur*), and slaves, some of whom had been illegally smuggled in from overseas. There were immigrants from many European countries and Latin America. Along the Gulf Coast lived the Acadians (the name contracted locally into "Cajuns"), French-speaking refugees from the eighteenth-century ethnic cleansing of Nova Scotia. Americans of Anglo descent comprised only 13 percent of the population of New Orleans.[4] The trade carried on in the great seaport included just about every agricultural and manufactured product known, and the consumer goods available made the quality of life enviable. Famous for their sophistication and attractiveness, the women of New Orleans were almost the only ones in the United States to use makeup.[5] The British soldiers downstream, cold and hungry, consoled themselves with dreams of "beauty and booty" once they captured the city.

---

4. Wilburt Brown, *The Amphibious Campaign for West Florida and Louisiana* (University, Ala., 1969), 36. See also Joseph Tregle, *Louisiana in the Age of Jackson* (Baton Rouge, 1999), 23–41.

5. As late as 1834, an Englishwoman commented that "New-Orleans is the only place in the United States where I am aware of having seen a particle of rouge." Harriet Martineau, *Retrospect of Western Travel*, ed. Daniel Feller (1838; Armonk, N.Y., 2000), 116.

New Orleans had been U.S. territory only since 1803, and Louisiana had been admitted to statehood as recently as 1812. Knowing that the dominant French community of New Orleans merchants and Louisiana planters despised the recently arrived Yankees, the invaders hoped to recruit the *ancienne population* to their cause. In fact, the Creoles were mostly Bonapartists who considered the United States a lesser evil compared to England. But Andrew Jackson did not feel altogether sure of their loyalty, which was why he imposed martial law in New Orleans on December 16. The New Year's artillery duel, in which many of the guns were served by French-speakers, reassured him somewhat, but he remained impatient for the two thousand Kentucky militiamen floating down the Father of Waters and expected daily.[6]

Upon their arrival on January 4, the reinforcements proved a disappointment. Freezing in their tattered clothing, the Kentuckians lacked tents or blankets to shelter them from the elements. Worst of all, only 550 of them were armed. Because the ordnance department had been unwilling to pay enough to have supplies sent by the fastest means, their weapons and ammunition did not reach New Orleans until after the big battle had been fought. Jackson joked in disgust that it was the first time he'd ever seen a Kentuckian "without a gun, a pack of cards, and a jug of whiskey."[7] He equipped some of the men with miscellaneous weapons from the armory kept by the city of New Orleans against the possibility of a slave uprising. Pakenham, whose two regiments of reinforcements were meanwhile arriving, had suffered even worse from his government's stinginess. Since the admiralty had not provided the shallow-draft vessels requested, the British had to ferry men and supplies long distances from ships to shore by rowboats—exhausting, slow work for the sailors. As a result, their soldiers suffered shortages of everything, including ammunition and food.[8]

Pakenham could not expect his men to endure these conditions indefinitely; he needed to break through to the shelter and supplies of New Orleans. Jackson, reading the situation the same way, resolved that if he could not defend the city, he would put it to the torch rather than let the British occupy it.[9] Pakenham devised a complicated plan of attack. He would

6. Remini, *Battle of New Orleans*, 31, 58, 132. On the distrust between Jackson and the Creoles, see Joseph Tregle, "Andrew Jackson and the Continuing Battle of New Orleans," *JER* 1 (1981): 373–94.
7. Brown, *Amphibious Campaign*, 133–34; Jackson quoted in Reilly, *British at the Gates*, 287.
8. Quimby, *U.S. Army*, 814–15.
9. Remini, *Battle of New Orleans*, 98.

ferry a substantial force under Colonel William Thornton across the Mississippi to capture the American guns on the right bank and turn them onto Jackson's own lines. At the opposite end of the battlefield, he would send some of his West Indians and other light infantry to infiltrate the swamps and turn the American left flank. Simultaneously he would mount two assaults across the Chalmette plantation against Jackson's main line of defense. To get across the Rodriguez Canal and over the parapet, each assault would be led by troops carrying fascines (bundles of sugar-cane to fill up the ditch) and ladders. It was a plausible plan on paper. Coordinating it all in practice was highly problematic.

The attack on the west bank of the Mississippi got under way late because of the difficulty of transporting troops across the river. On the east bank, the most important of the assault forces had trouble locating the fascines and ladders to use. The commander of the unit assigned to place them, Lieutenant Colonel Thomas Mullins, felt his men were being sacrificed on a suicidal mission, and in his resentment neglected to follow orders and ascertain where the equipment was kept. Perhaps Mullins's suspicions were justified: Because his troops were Irish, they might have been thought expendable. (The other unit assigned to place fascines and ladders was West Indian.) But his neglect of duty was clearly wrong and cost his cause dearly.[10]

At dawn on Sunday, January 8, Pakenham learned of both potential problems with his plan but gave the signal to attack anyway. Having canceled the New Year's Day offensive, he was in no mood to delay further. If he moved out promptly, the morning mist would still provide some cover for the advance. Pakenham had gambled with risky assaults in the Peninsular War, and they had paid off. This time he made the wrong decision.

The main attack, on Jackson's left center, became hopelessly snarled by the failure of Mullins's 44th Regiment to have the fascines and ladders ready. Men arriving at the canal were mowed down by canister and grapeshot while waiting to cross. A few heroes swam the canal and managed to climb the parapet by using their bayonets, only to be captured or killed when they got over. Meanwhile, the attack through the swamps was frustrated by Tennesseans and Choctaws familiar with the terrain. The assault on Jackson's right, where West Indians carried the fascines and ladders, achieved initial success but was left unsupported. In a final mistake, Pakenham shifted the 93rd Highlanders from following up this penetration of the American line into a futile and costly attempt to help the stalled attack on Jackson's left. What he lacked in judgment the British

10. See Quimby, *U.S. Army*, 895–900.

commander tried to make up in bravery. Wounded twice and with his horse shot from under him, Pakenham insisted on being helped to mount another. From his saddle he waved encouragement to the Highlanders; a moment later a round of grapeshot wounded him mortally.[11] Two other British generals and eight colonels also died in the attack. The battle had turned into another Agincourt, with Americans playing the role of the English archers and the British themselves cast as the gallant but luckless French knights. Within a few minutes the British lost 251 killed, 1,259 wounded, and 484 missing. Most of the missing were taken prisoner. When the Americans lifted their fire, some of the men on the ground hesitantly rose with their hands up. Other prisoners were wounded men whom the Americans collected after a temporary truce was agreed. Jackson's army lost but 11 killed and 23 wounded.[12]

Ironically, Colonel Thornton's attack on the other side of the Mississippi, despite its delay, overcame the Kentucky militia and captured the artillery there (too late to affect the main battle). The poorly armed Kentuckians had only just reached the position they were expected to defend, and they behaved the way American militia units often behaved in the War of 1812: They ran away. Jackson made plain his fury at them in his official report to Secretary of War James Monroe. "The Kentucky reinforcement, in whom so much reliance had been placed, ingloriously fled."[13] Thornton's success might have opened up a route to New Orleans if the British had had any stomach for more fighting. But General John Lambert, who succeeded to the British command, declined to exploit the opportunity and chose to evacuate his exhausted and by now dispirited expeditionary force to its ships.

Some of his officers urged Jackson to take the opportunity to counterattack. But for once Old Hickory declined to take the offensive. He had saved New Orleans and was content to leave well enough alone. Jackson owed his victory in large part to good fortune and British mistakes. He decided not to press his luck. Jackson recognized the limitations of his untrained militia. Under his inspirational leadership, they had performed well alongside artillery and behind a parapet. He would not risk them in the open field against professional soldiers.[14]

With the battle over, Jackson ignored his promise to secure equal

11. Reilly, *British at the Gates*, 300.
12. Some sources give British dead as 291; see Quimby, *U.S. Army*, 906.
13. Quoted in Remini, *Battle of New Orleans*, 162.
14. For a judicious estimate of Jackson's generalship, see J.C.A. Stagg, *Mr. Madison's War* (Princeton, 1985), 498.

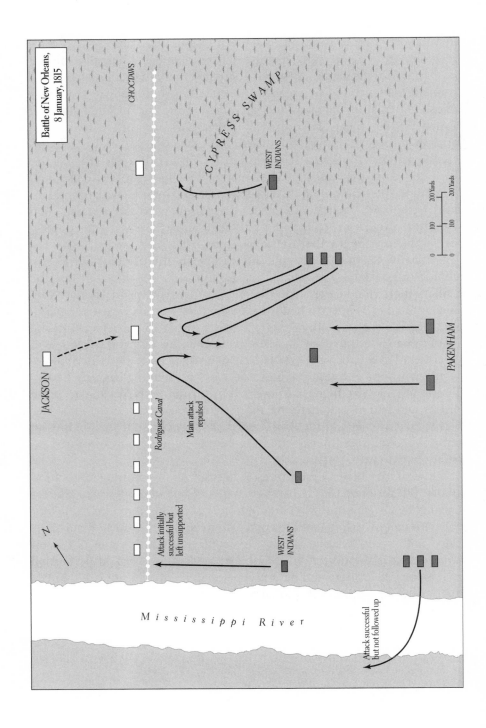

Battle of New Orleans, 8 January, 1815

CHOCTAWS

CYPRESS SWAMP

WEST INDIANS

PAKENHAM

JACKSON

Rodriguez Canal

Main attack repulsed

Attack initially successful but left unsupported

WEST INDIANS

N

Mississippi River

Attack successful but not followed up

0   100   200 Yards

0   100   200 Yards

rewards for the black men who had stood with him at the barricade. Besides twenty-four dollars cash, each soldier was supposed to receive 160 acres of public land, but forty years later, the black veterans were still trying to get their land claims honored. The slaves among them had been returned to their owners, who were not bound by any promises made.[15] On the other hand, Jackson showed solicitude for those masters whose slaves had escaped and taken refuge with the enemy. He repeatedly demanded that the departing British army return them. General Lambert, to his credit, refused and took some two hundred self-emancipated people off to lives of poverty but freedom in Bermuda.[16]

If history were a novel, this episode would end with the dramatic repulse of the invaders on January 8. In real life the British did not abandon their campaign against New Orleans. The day after the great land battle, their fleet sailed up the Mississippi and bombarded Fort St. Philip at Plaquemine for the next nine days, hoping to force a passage, but to no avail. General Lambert's army, having rejoined its ships and recovered its resolve, sailed off to Mobile Bay and there resumed the offensive. After taking Mobile they would be able to march westward to the Mississippi and cut off New Orleans from the north. On February 11, Fort Bowyer, guarding Mobile Bay, surrendered to the British. The city of Mobile would surely have fallen, but the next day news finally arrived that a peace treaty had been signed on December 24. In the language of boxing, Mobile was saved by the bell.

Six months after the Battle of New Orleans, the Irishmen of the 44th Regiment redeemed their military reputation at Waterloo. But Thomas Mullins was court-martialed and cashiered.[17]

II

What did the American victory really mean? The Battle of New Orleans had been fought after the treaty of peace had been signed. Technically, the war ended only with the exchange of treaty ratifications, but in fact the armies ceased hostilities as soon as they learned of the treaty itself. Had

---

15. See Donald Everett, "Emigres and Militiamen: Free Persons of Color in New Orleans," *Journal of Negro History* 38 (1953): 377–402; James Horton and Lois Horton, *In Hope of Liberty* (New York, 1997), 186; Don Fehrenbacher, *The Slaveholding Republic* (New York, 2001), 7–8.
16. Reilly, *British at the Gates*, 320–21; *The Papers of Andrew Jackson*, ed. Harold Moser et al. (Knoxville, Tenn., 1991), III, 290, 316–17.
17. It is remarkable how many high-ranking officers on both sides in the War of 1812 were court-martialed for incompetence or cowardice: Other British officers included Generals Procter and Prevost; on the American side, Generals Hull and Wilkinson.

news of the treaty arrived soon enough, the battle would not have been fought. The bloodshed at the Battle of New Orleans was a particularly tragic result of the slowness of communication at the start of the nineteenth century. In fact, the slow pace at which news crossed the Atlantic had been responsible for the war in the first place: When Congress declared war on Great Britain, June 18, 1812, its members did not know that two days earlier Foreign Secretary Castlereagh had announced in Parliament that the Orders in Council restricting American commerce would be suspended.[18]

In an effort to endow the Battle of New Orleans with strategic significance, Jackson's admirers later claimed that if the British had won the engagement, they might have revoked the Treaty of Ghent by declining to exchange ratifications and seeking a more advantageous settlement.[19] In fact, no such meaning can be derived from the bloodshed of January 8. The prince regent ratified the treaty as soon as he received it and dispatched the ratification to Washington without waiting to hear the outcome of the campaign in the Gulf of Mexico. Far from planning any alteration in ratifying the treaty, Prime Minister Liverpool worried that the other side might "play us some trick in the ratification of it."[20] Hence the quick British ratification. A more plausible possibility is that if the British had captured either Mobile or New Orleans, they might have turned the places over to the Spanish. Neither Britain nor Spain recognized the legality of the Louisiana Purchase, since France had violated the Treaty of San Ildefonso (1800) by selling Louisiana to the United States. The American occupation of the city and environs of Mobile rested on nothing more legitimate than a military seizure from the Spanish in 1813, so the British would have been legally justified in returning them to the Spanish governor at Pensacola. Yet there is no direct evidence the British had such an intention, and they did not deliver Fort Bowyer on Mobile Bay to the Spanish at the conclusion of hostilities. Instead, the evidence suggests that the British were principally motivated to capture New Orleans by the prospect of plunder, and that their occupation of the city, if it had been achieved, would have been short.[21]

18. Madison later confirmed that the declaration "would have been stayed" if he had known about the British concession; Donald Hickey, *The War of 1812* (Urbana, Ill., 1989), 42.
19. Some historians have repeated the claim; see Marshall Smelser, *The Democratic Republic, 1801–1815* (New York, 1968), 281.
20. Lord Liverpool to Lord Castlereagh, December 23, 1814, quoted in Irving Brant, *James Madison, Commander in Chief* (New York, 1961), 372.
21. See James A. Carr, "The Battle of New Orleans and the Treaty of Ghent," *Diplomatic History* 3 (1979): 273–82.

Americans at the time did not see their great victory as meaningless. What they chose to make of it is instructive. They did not emphasize the fact that the battle had been fought after peace had been agreed. They seldom rejoiced in the multiracial, multiethnic nature of the winning army. Neither did they celebrate the technological know-how that enabled their artillery to perform so well. Instead the public seized upon the notion that western riflemen, untrained but sharp-eyed, had defeated the arrogant British. In fact, primary responsibility for the American victory lay with the artillery, not with the frontier marksmen of legend. It was the cannons that wrought most of the slaughter on the Chalmette plantation. A single noteworthy discharge from a thirty-two-pound naval gun crammed with musket balls "served to sweep the centre of the attacking force into eternity," in the words of a British officer.[22] The infantrymen in the center of Jackson's line were under strict orders to hold their fire. Those in his army who got to use their weapons were typically armed not with rifles but with muskets or hunting pieces firing buckshot. The fog and smoke severely limited opportunities for sharpshooting. In any case, the best marksmen were not necessarily frontiersmen: A target contest between Coffee's Tennessee Volunteers and Beale's Rifle Company, composed of middle-class New Orleans citizenry, was won by the latter.[23]

The excellent gunnery that served the American cause so well at New Orleans paralleled the excellent gunnery that stood the U.S. Navy in good stead whenever the outnumbered American ships got the chance to fight the Royal Navy on equal terms. The contrast between the effectiveness of the artillery and the navy with the repeatedly disgraceful performances of the militia in the War of 1812 could scarcely be more glaring. But cannons seemed not altogether satisfactory as a patriotic symbol for the American public. Cannons were products of the industrial revolution and government-sponsored technological development. A predominantly rural people wanted heroes from the countryside. Surely it must be "the *American Husbandman*, fresh from his plough," a congressional orator insisted, who had bested the best Europe had to offer.[24]

22. The definitive study of the effectiveness of the artillery in the battle is Carson Ritchie, "The Louisiana Campaign," *Louisiana Historical Quarterly* 44 (1961): 13–103; Major John Cooke is quoted on 74. See also Smelser, *Democratic Republic*, 280.
23. Ritchie, "Louisiana Campaign," 71–77; John K. Mahon, *The War of 1812* (Gainesville, Fla., 1972), 369; John William Ward, *Andrew Jackson, Symbol for an Age* (New York, 1955), 26.
24. George M. Troup of Georgia in the House of Representatives, quoted ibid., 8; italics in original.

A popular song of the 1820s, "The Hunters of Kentucky," extolled the performance of the Kentucky militia at New Orleans despite the fact that Jackson himself had criticized the Kentuckians harshly and never retracted his condemnation. Exploited for political purposes, the song perpetuated the misperception of what had happened.[25] The Battle of New Orleans came to be regarded by Jackson's many admirers as a victory of self-reliant individualists under charismatic leadership. It seemed a triumph of citizen-soldiers over professionals, of the common man over hierarchy, of willpower over rules.

The reluctance to credit the artillery with the victory partly reflected a reluctance to credit the professional servicemen, ethnic-minority city-dwellers, and pirates who manned the guns rather than the all-American frontiersmen. It also manifested a failure to foresee how much the future of the United States would owe to mechanization and government-sponsored enterprises like the federal armories that made cannons. Jackson's admirers liked to believe theirs was a country where untutored vigor could prevail; to point out that technical expertise mattered seemed undemocratic. Their interpretation of the battle was compatible with Jefferson's vision of "an empire for liberty" stretching to the west, a belief that the nation's destiny lay in the multiplication of family farms and the extension of American power across continental space.

Americans agreed in rejecting the traditional class privilege exemplified by the British army and Europe in general. The Battle of New Orleans symbolized America's deliverance from all that. The past had been defeated. But where did America's future lie? With the individualistic, expansionist values exemplified by frontier marksmen? Or with the industrial-technological values exemplified by the artillery? Which would better serve American security and prosperity: the extension of agriculture across the continent or the intensive improvement and diversification of the economy and its infrastructure? To those great questions the rival political parties of the coming decades, Democrats and Whigs, offered sharply divergent answers.

---

25. See ibid., 13–16. The lyrics were written by Samuel Woodworth, author of another song of rural nostalgia, "The Old Oaken Bucket."

1

The Continental Setting

In the thirty-three years following the Battle of New Orleans, the United States would extend its imperial reach across a continent vast, diverse, and already inhabited. The history of the United States can be understood only in relation to the continental setting within which it unfolded. The human geography of North America in 1815 included peoples of several races, many languages, and sometimes incompatible aspirations. Innumerable tribes of Native Americans maintained de facto independence of three great mainland empires: the United States, Mexico, and British North America. The imposition of U.S. authority all the way to the Pacific, so clear by 1848, represented an astounding transformation when one considers the state of North America in 1815.

Within the United States, the overwhelming majority of the population in 1815 engaged in agriculture. The largest number were family farmers, who lived lives of hardship and toil, conditioned by earnest hopes for a better standard of living. Their agricultural practices husbanded scarce resources and squandered those, like land, that they found plentiful. Sometimes their ambitions included taking the lands of others. A distinctive group of Americans consisted of those enslaved; among the harsh realities of their lives, they nursed aspirations of their own. The United States in 1815 was still an open-ended experiment, mostly potential rather than actuality. Amidst a continent of unrealized possibilities, the various peoples of North America pursued diverging visions of the future.

I

In 1815, as today, the largest metropolis on the North American continent was Mexico City. At that time it held about 150,000 people—almost as many as the two largest cities in the United States (New York and Philadelphia) put together.[1] Beginning in 1521, the Spanish had built it on top of the even more populous Aztec city of Tenochtitlán, founded in 1325. The Catholic cathedral, constructed on the site of the Aztec temple by the central plaza now called the Zócalo, had just been renovated in 1813. "This city is truly a magnificent one," marveled Stephen Austin

---

1. U.S. Census Bureau, www.census.gov/population/documentation/twps0027/tab04.txt (viewed Feb. 24, 2007).

when he arrived in 1822.[2] *La ciudad de México* boasted botanical gardens, an art academy, the world's best mining college, and a distinguished university. Remarkably for cities at the time, it had wide streets lighted at night, paved sidewalks, and a system of public transportation.[3] The newly independent Mexican nation that Stephen Austin visited stretched from Panama to Oregon, occupied an area approximately equal to that of the United States, and included about two-thirds as many people. Yet in 1847, this proud capital city would stand conquered, occupied like a fallen Rome and (as a Mexican government committee warned in 1821 might happen) stripped of half its vast domain by barbarians from the north.[4] After the Treaty of Guadalupe Hidalgo in 1848, the United States would rank far larger than Mexico in both area and population. Through waging war, the United States wrought a momentous transformation in international power.

In 1815, Mexican independence lay six years in the future, and the chief executive occupying the Palacio Nacional was still the viceroy of New Spain. The mother country had recently granted a written constitution, and Mexico sent representatives to the Spanish Cortes (parliament). Fighting for Mexican independence had begun five years earlier, but for the time being Spanish officials seemed to have overcome the rebels and felt confident that royal authority would prevail. Overt disloyalty actually constituted less of a problem to central control than the difficulties of communication and transportation. Lack of roads and restrictive imperial regulations intended to monopolize trade for the benefit of the home country had hindered Mexico's economic development, and strong traditions of regional autonomy prevailed. The newspaper press flourished in the capital, but people who lived in other cities experienced remarkable isolation. A small creole elite of European descent dominated the country; a *mestizo* (mixed-race) middle class supplied its energy; but the Native American peasantry, even within the national heartland, mostly remained outside the mainstream of national life. Throughout their villages, and across the open spaces of the northern borderlands, people had little awareness of the larger world. In some remote areas, especially the far north and south, Indian tribes remained virtually independent of Spanish

2. Quoted in Gregg Cantrell, *Stephen F. Austin, Empresario of Texas* (New Haven, 1999), 112.

3. Michael Meyer and William Sherman, *The Course of Mexican History* (New York, 1990), 361–69; Jonathan Kandell, *La Capital: The Biography of Mexico City* (New York, 1988).

4. Nettie Lee Benson, "Texas Viewed from Mexico," *Southwestern Historical Quarterly* 90 (1986–87): 227.

law, language, and culture, at times indeed waging war against them. Mexico City's lack of effective communication with and control over the vast northern territories would make it difficult to protect them against the ambitions of an expansionist United States.[5]

The most distant of all New Spain's far-flung lands was Alta (Upper) California. In 1815, its northern boundary remained undefined. Spain claimed the coast all the way to the Strait of Juan de Fuca, but British, Russian, and American merchants and explorers had been active in that vicinity for a generation.[6] In 1812, the Russians had established a fur-trading post at Fort Ross on Bodega Bay. From San Diego to San Rafael above San Francisco Bay, the Spanish maintained their authority through a system of military bases (*presidios*) and missions operated by the Franciscan order of friars. Each mission community strove for substantial economic self-sufficiency through a mixture of agriculture and artisan manufacturing. The missions had been located, with the orderliness of absolutism, so that each lay a day's journey away from the next one along the royal highway (*el camino real*).

The California missions provoked controversy, in their own time as well as in ours. The Franciscans intended to Christianize the local Indians and teach them useful skills. If the Natives adopted Western civilization they could become *gente de razón* ("rational people") and taxpayers. Critics in Mexico and Spain claimed that the friars exploited their charges. Worst of all, contemporaries correctly observed, the missions incubated illness, by concentrating vulnerable populations in places where they became exposed to unfamiliar diseases. Between 1769, when Hispanic settlement began, and the end of Spanish rule in 1821, the Indian population of Alta California declined from approximately 300,000 to approximately 200,000.[7]

The disease problem in the California mission communities was all too characteristic of encounters between European and Native American peoples. A population lacking any acquired immunity, either inherited or individual, to unfamiliar diseases can suffer rapid fatalities of catastrophic proportion during what is called a "virgin-soil" epidemic of infectious disease. Europeans themselves suffered virgin-soil epidemics of bubonic

5. See Timothy Anna, *Forging Mexico* (Lincoln, Neb., 1998), 34–76; Brian Hamnett, *Roots of Insurgency: Mexican Regions, 1750–1824* (Cambridge, Eng., 1986).
6. See David Igler, "Diseased Goods: Global Exchanges in the Eastern Pacific Basin, 1770–1850," *AHR* 109 (2004); 693–719.
7. James Sandos, *Converting California* (New Haven, 2004), 113–14; Robert H. Jackson and Edward Castillo, *Indians, Franciscans, and Spanish Colonization* (Albuquerque, N.M., 1995), 44–51; Sherburne Cook, *The Population of the California Indians* (Berkeley, 1976), 43–44; Walter Nugent, *Into the West* (New York, 1999), 35–38.

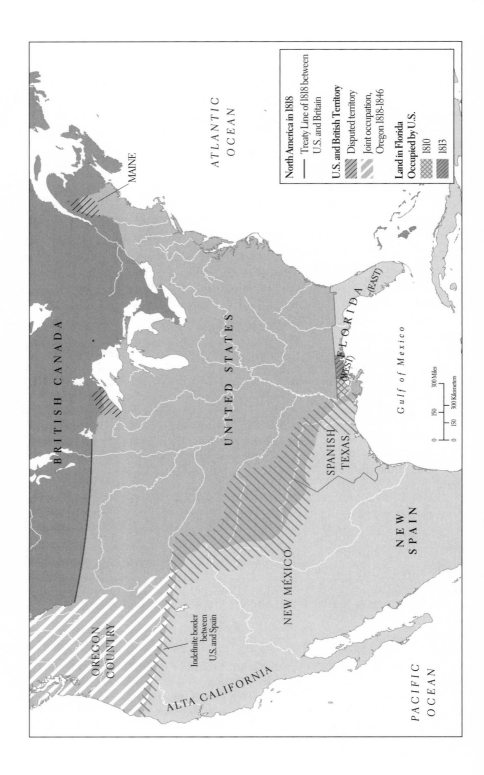

ATLANTIC OCEAN

MAINE

North America in 1818

Treaty Line of 1818 between U.S. and Britain

U.S. and British Territory

Disputed territory

Joint occupation, Oregon 1818–1846

Land in Florida

Occupied by U.S.

1810

1813

BRITISH CANADA

UNITED STATES

FLORIDA (EAST)

FLORIDA (WEST)

Gulf of Mexico

SPANISH TEXAS

NEW MÉXICO

NEW SPAIN

OREGON COUNTRY

Indefinite border between U.S. and Spain

ALTA CALIFORNIA

PACIFIC OCEAN

300 Miles

0   150   300 Kilometers

0   150   300

plague from Asia in the fourteenth century and of syphilis following the return of Columbus's men. The ravages suffered by the inhabitants of the New World from unfamiliar European contagious diseases—including smallpox, measles, and influenza—were compounded by the disruptions of warfare and losses of food-producing land to the intruders. The resulting mortality, considered collectively, constituted one of the most gigantic calamities ever to befall the human race. Population estimates for the Americas on the eve of European contact vary widely, but even the most conservative ones indicate horrific death rates soon thereafter. Within central Mexico, population had bottomed out a hundred years or so after the Spanish conquest and slowly began to rebound, though at about 6 million in 1815 it remained far below the estimated numbers for the subjects of the Aztec Empire, notwithstanding immigration from the Old World.[8]

In the United States, the Constitution exempted "Indians not taxed" from the census. In 1820, however, the federal government engaged Jedidiah Morse, a noted scholar, to undertake a comprehensive examination of the Indian tribes within the United States. Morse's book-length report estimated the Indian population at 472,000, most of them living west of the Mississippi River in the Louisiana Purchase or in the Oregon Territory under joint U.S.-British authority. The original inhabitants of California, Texas, and the other Mexican lands that would be annexed by 1848 probably numbered a third to a half of a million. These figures do not include people of mixed ancestry living with white or black Americans and undifferentiated from them. But they certainly represented a dramatic decline from the Amerindian population of the same area c. 1600, which most scholars currently estimate at around 5 million, perhaps even 10 million.[9] Dispersed, nomadic peoples suffered less from contagion than concentrated village-dwellers like the Mandans, whom recurrent smallpox epidemics reduced from 9,000 c. 1750 to 150 in 1837. Many white contemporaries, even if compassionate, agreed with Alexis de Tocqueville that the Indians were "doomed" to die out entirely.[10]

8. See Russell Thornton, *American Indian Holocaust and Survival* (Norman, Okla., 1987), 15–41; David Jones, "Virgin Soils Revisited," *WMQ* 60 (2003): 703–42; Elinore Melville, "Disease, Ecology, and the Environment," in *The Oxford History of Mexico*, ed. Michael Meyer and William Beezley (New York, 2000), 222–26.

9. Jedidiah Morse, *Report to the Secretary of War on Indian Affairs* (New Haven, 1822), 375; Alan Taylor, *American Colonies* (New York, 2001), 40.

10. Loretta Fowler, "The Great Plains from the Arrival of the Horse to 1885," in *Cambridge History of the Native Peoples of the Americas: Vol. 1, North America*, ed. Bruce Trigger and Wilcomb Washburn (Cambridge, Eng., 1996), pt. 2, 21; Alexis de Tocqueville, *Democracy in America*, ed. Phillips Bradley (1834; New York, 1945), I, 342.

Because of the transatlantic slave trade, Africa too contributed diseases to the deadly mixture. Malaria and yellow fever, transmitted between human hosts by mosquitoes, came to the Western Hemisphere on the slave ships. Yellow fever, widespread in the Caribbean, periodically visited as far north as Philadelphia. In the early nineteenth century, malaria spread from the Atlantic and Gulf Coasts to become endemic throughout the vast Mississippi basin. In the case of these diseases, white people had no more immunity than Native Americans; malaria had killed a high proportion of early English colonists in Virginia, and the "ague," as they called it, remained a curse for many settlers in the swampy lands or river bottoms of the Midwest.[11]

The oldest, most populous, and most economically developed of the Spanish borderlands was New Mexico. There Santa Fe and Taos became important commercial hubs, linked with El Paso and Chihuahua by New Mexico's own *camino real*. Yet relations with the local Indian nations had remained problematic ever since the great Pueblo uprising in 1680. The prolonged war for Mexican independence that began in 1810 prompted the Spanish government to withdraw the troops protecting the province against Apache and Navajo raiders to more critical duties elsewhere, and for self-defense the *nuevomexicanos* contracted their settlements.[12] They remained a potential market for U.S. traders whenever the Spanish mercantile rules could be lifted.

Between the Rio Grande (then usually called the Rio Bravo) and the Nueces River countless cattle grazed. The Mexicans were the first cowboys, called *vaqueros*; they invented the horned saddle and the technique of roping from horseback. The cattle they rounded up for branding in the Nueces strip were longhorns, tough beasts descended from animals brought from Spain, some of which had gone wild and adapted to the dry environment. In 1846, this would constitute the "disputed area" between the United States and Mexico and witness the outbreak of the Mexican–American War. The Mexican *rancheros* would lose their lands and herds, but their successors would retain their occupational terminology: "corral," "remuda," "rodeo," "sombrero," "pinto," "chaps" (*chaparajos*), "mustang" (*mesteño*), "lariat" (*la reata*).[13]

Northeast of the Nueces stretched Texas, or Tejas. Nominally an outpost of New Spain in 1815, this had long been a borderland where Spanish,

11. Gerald Grob, *The Deadly Truth: A History of Disease in America* (Cambridge, Mass., 2002).
12. See David J. Weber, *The Spanish Frontier in North America* (New Haven, 1992).
13. Terry Jordan, *North American Cattle-Ranching Frontiers* (Albuquerque, N.M., 1993), 152–53.

French, British, and American traders, soldiers, and settlers rotated a kaleidoscope of alliances, trade agreements, and wars with each other and the Kiowa, Comanche, Wichita, Jumano, Caddo, Apache, and more. Europeans call such a border region with no functioning sovereign power a "marchland"; American historians term it a "middle ground."[14] Like the whites, some of the Indian tribes had only recently pushed their way into the Texas region. In a strategic borderland, Native peoples enjoyed their ability to play off the competing European powers against one another; conversely, however, whites played off Indian tribes against each other too. Warfare and trade among these diverse peoples coexisted in parallel; a group could buy weapons from one party to make war on another, or steal horses from one to sell to another. In Texas, as in New Mexico and elsewhere in North America, captives taken in war could be turned into trade goods by being held for ransom or sold as slaves; alternatively they might be tortured and killed, adopted, or even married.[15]

Adding fuel to the fierce intergroup rivalries in Texas and the southern Plains was the introduction of the horse, a Spanish contribution even more important than cattle. Like the longhorns, some of these horses had escaped and turned feral, only to be redomesticated by Native Americans. More commonly, however, horses diffused north from Mexico by being stolen or sold from one human owner to another. During the eighteenth century, horses revolutionized hunting and warfare on the Great Plains, as they had done on the steppes of Central Asia five thousand years earlier. The nomadic way of life quickly adopted by the Comanche, Cheyenne, and Sioux, so famous and heroic, would have been impossible without their skillful exploitation of the possibilities created by horses. Other tribes, like the Pawnee, retained permanent villages and used hunting with horses to supplement their agriculture. But the horse shifted the military balance in favor of nomads and against villagers. Horses served as an end as well as a means of warfare, since most battles between tribes originated in raids to capture another's horses. In an economic sense, many of the nomads became primarily pastoral people, that is, herders of their horses, and only intermittently buffalo hunters.[16]

14. Richard White gave us the term in *The Middle Ground: Indians, Empires, and Republics in the Great Lakes Region* (Cambridge, Eng., 1991).

15. See Jeremy Adelman and Stephen Aron, "From Borderlands to Borders," *AHR* 104 (1999): 814–41; James Brooks, *Captives and Cousins: Slavery, Kinship, and Community in the Southwest Borderlands* (Chapel Hill, 2002).

16. Pekka Hamalainen, "The Rise and Fall of Plains Indian Horse Culture," *JAH* 90 (2003): 833–62; Elliott West, *The Contested Plains* (Lawrence, Kans., 1998), 49–71; John Ewers, *Plains Indian History and Culture* (Norman, Okla., 1997), 170–72.

Many misconceptions regarding the American Indians of this period remain prevalent. Their societies were not static, necessarily fixed to particular homelands and lifestyles. They evolved and changed, often rapidly, sometimes as a result of deliberate decisions, both before and after their contact with whites. Native societies did not live in isolation until "discovered" by intruders; they traded with each other, exchanging not only goods but ideas and techniques as well. As early as the year 900, the cultivation of corn (maize) spread from Mexico to the inhabitants of what is now the eastern United States. "For hundreds of years," notes the historian Colin Calloway, "Indian peoples explored, pioneered, settled, and shaped" their environment. Long before the Jacksonian Democrats conceived the program of "Indian Removal" from east of the Mississippi, tribes had migrated of their own volition. When the Native Americans first met whites, they integrated them into their existing patterns of trade and warfare, sometimes allying with them against historic enemies. They welcomed the trade goods on offer, especially those that made life easier like firearms, kettles, and metal tools.[17]

Though their white contemporaries generally thought of them as hunters, the Native Americans were also experienced farmers. Throughout much of the United States they typically grew corn, squash, and beans together, cultivating them with a hoe. East of the Mississippi their crops provided more of their food than hunting and gathering did. Potatoes, tomatoes, and tobacco, indigenous American products eagerly taken up by Europeans, played a less important role in Native agriculture. In most tribes, farming was traditionally women's work and hunting, men's. Well-intentioned whites encouraged Indian men to downplay hunting, take up farming, and use plows pulled by draft animals. By 1815, white agricultural practices had been extensively adopted among several Amerindian nations east of the Mississippi; so had cattle-raising.[18] Some Native communities and individuals had become economically scarcely distinguishable from their white neighbors. On the other hand, the strong economic demand for deerskin and furs encouraged the Indians to pursue deer, beaver, and buffalo with renewed vigor rather than abandon the chase in favor of agriculture.

The numerous Native American nations were at least as diverse as the different European nations (linguistically, they were more diverse), and they adapted to contact with the Europeans in different ways, often quite resourceful. The Navajo transformed themselves from predatory nomads to sheepherders, weavers, and (later) silversmiths. Indians usually adopted aspects of Western culture that they found appealing and rejected others. Individuals did not always choose wisely: Exposed to alcohol, some became alcoholics. (Conversely, whites exposed to tobacco often became addicted to it.) Some Indians converted to Christianity, like the Mohican Hendrick Aupaumut, who preached pan-tribal unity and peaceful coexistence with the whites. Others undertook to revitalize their own religious traditions, as did the Seneca Handsome Lake and the Shawnee prophet Tenskwatawa, whose brother Tecumseh preached pan-tribal unity and

17. Neal Salisbury, "The Indians' Old World," *WMQ* 53 (1996): 435–58; Colin Calloway, *One Vast Winter Count* (Lincoln, Neb., 2003), quotation from 17.
18. See, e.g., James Carson, "The Choctaw Cattle Economy," in *Cultural Change and the Market Revolution in America*, ed. Scott Martin (Lanham, Md., 2005), 71–88; Robbie Ethridge, *Creek Country* (Chapel Hill, 2003).

militant resistance to the whites.[19] Despite the shocking fatalities from unfamiliar diseases, most Native peoples did not despair, nor (whatever whites might think) did they think of themselves as a doomed race. Their history is one of resilience and survival, as well as of retreat and death.

East of the Mississippi, the soggy, swampy Gulf region remained another multiethnic borderland (or "middle ground"), with Florida belonging to Spain, the white population of Louisiana still predominantly French and Spanish, and several powerful Indian nations asserting independence. The "Old Southwest" was a volatile area. Only gradually did it come under U.S. control. During the American War for Independence, the Spanish had allied with the rebels and conquered West and East Florida from the British. (West Florida extended along the Gulf Coast from what we call the Florida panhandle through what is now Alabama and Mississippi into Louisiana; the Apalachicola River divided the two Floridas from each other.) At the peace negotiations in 1783, Spain had been allowed to keep the Floridas as consolation for not having succeeded in capturing Gibraltar from the British. In 1810 and 1813, an ungrateful United States had unilaterally occupied chunks of West Florida. Policymakers in Washington had their eyes on East Florida as well.

The Native Americans of the Old Southwest had been caught in a time of turbulence by the coming of the Europeans. The indigenous Mississippian civilization had declined and left in its wake a variety of competing peoples somewhat analogous to the tribes that migrated around Europe following the disintegration of the Roman Empire. Those who called themselves the Muskogee played a pivotal role; whites named them the Creek Indians because they built their villages along streams. One branch of the Creeks had migrated southward into Florida, where they linked up with black "maroons" escaped from slavery and became known as Seminoles. The main body of Creeks, led by their chief Alexander McGillivray, had negotiated a treaty with George Washington's administration guaranteeing their territorial integrity; they formed a national council and created a written legal code. But a civil war broke out among the Creeks in 1813, and the dissident "Red Stick" faction, who resented the influence of white ways, staged an ill-

19. Rachel Wheeler, "Hendrick Aupaumut," *JER* 25 (2005): 187–220; Anthony Wallace, *Death and Rebirth of the Seneca* (New York, 1972); R. David Edmunds, *The Shawnee Prophet* (Lincoln, Neb., 1983).

advised and bloody uprising against the Americans and their Native supporters.[20]

Around the Great Lakes lay another historic "middle ground" where European empires and Native peoples had long competed with each other. In the eighteenth century, British, French, Americans, and the First Nations (as Canadians today appropriately call the Indian tribes) had all jockeyed for advantage in the rich fur trade and waged repeated wars on each other. Following independence, the Americans had nursed the delusion that Canadians would welcome them as liberators from the British. After two U.S. invasions of Canada, in 1776 and 1812, had both been repulsed, most Americans had given up this fantasy. The border between Canada and the United States began to take on a permanent character. Canada became a place of refuge for former American Loyalists who had experienced persecution in their previous homes and emphatically rejected U.S. identity. To the Catholic Quebecois, Yankee Protestants seemed even worse than British ones and the United States a de facto ally of the godless Napoleon.

By 1815, the land around the Great Lakes was losing its character as a "middle ground" where Native peoples could play off the competing white powers for their own advantage. The once-powerful Iroquois, a confederation of six nations, no longer found themselves in a position to carry out an independent foreign policy. When war came in 1812, the Iroquois north of the border supported their traditional ally, the British. Those to the south attempted neutrality but were compelled to fight for the United States against their kinsmen. The Canadian–U.S. border had taken on stability and real meaning. The Treaty of Ghent brought an end to sixty years of warfare over the Great Lakes region, going back to Braddock's expedition of 1754.[21] Yet contemporaries did not know for sure that the wars were all over. They worried that the area might revert to instability and took precautions against this. In the 1830s, armed rebellions among both Anglophone and Francophone Canadians, coupled with friction between the United States and Britain, would confront American policymakers with that very real possibility.

20. Thomas Clark and John Guice, *Frontiers in Conflict: The Old Southwest, 1795–1830* (Albuquerque, N.M., 1989); L. Leitch Wright Jr., *Creeks and Seminoles* (Lincoln, Neb., 1986). On the Mississippian civilization, see Bruce Smith, "Agricultural Chiefdoms of the Eastern Woodlands," in Trigger and Washburn, *Cambridge History of Native Peoples: North America*, pt. 1, 267–323.

21. Alan Taylor, "Upper Canada, New York, and the Iroquois Six Nations," *JER* 22 (2002): 55–76; David Skaggs and Larry Nelson, eds., *Sixty Years' War for the Great Lakes* (East Lansing, Mich., 2001).

White attitudes toward the Native Americans varied. Some viewed them as hostile savages needing to be removed or even exterminated. More sympathetic observers thought the Natives could and should convert to Christianity and adopt Western civilization. Whether they would then continue to exist as separate communities or be assimilated remained unclear; Washington's administration had assumed the former, but Thomas Jefferson hoped for the latter.[22] Disagreement over "Indian policy" turned out to be an important issue separating the political parties that would emerge during the coming era. Despite all the mutual cultural borrowing between Native and Euro-Americans, neither cultural synthesis nor multicultural harmony achieved acceptance with the white public or government. Indians frequently intermarried with whites, as well as with blacks both enslaved and free, in all "middle ground" areas, and persons of mixed ancestry (sometimes called *métis*, a French term) like Alexander McGillivray often negotiated between their parental backgrounds. As time passed, however, such intermarriage became less acceptable in white society.[23]

In the nineteenth century, two territorially contiguous empires expanded rapidly across vast continental distances: the United States and Russia. The tsarist empire was an absolute monarchy with an established church, yet in one respect surprisingly more tolerant than republican America. The Russians showed more willingness to accept and live with cultural diversity among their subject peoples.[24]

II

The volcano of Tambora on the Indonesian island of Sumbawa erupted in a series of giant explosions commencing on April 7, 1815, and lasting five days. It was the largest volcanic eruption in recorded history, far surpassing that of Krakatoa in 1883 or Mount St. Helens in 1980. The volcano and the tsunami it generated killed some ten thousand people; many more died from indirect consequences. Gases emitted by Tambora included sulfur, which formed sulfuric acid droplets high in the atmosphere. For months, these droplets slowly girdled the Northern Hemisphere, absorbing and reflecting the sun's radiation, lowering the surface temperature of the earth. Sunspot activity compounded the meteorologi-

22. Reginald Horsman, "Indian Policy of an 'Empire for Liberty,'" in *Native Americans and the Early Republic*, ed. Frederick Hoxie et al. (Charlottesville, Va., 1999), 37–61.
23. See Margaret Szasz, *Between Indian and White Worlds* (Norman, Okla., 1994); and Theda Perdue, *"Mixed Blood" Indians* (Athens, Ga., 2003).
24. Cf. Meinig, *Continental America*, 185–88, 195–96.

cal effects. By mid-1816, strange disturbances affected the weather and ocean currents in the North Atlantic. Snow fell in New England in June, July, and August; otherwise little precipitation appeared. South Carolina suffered a frost in mid-May. Widespread crop failures led to food shortages in many parts of North America and Europe. No one who lived through it would forget "the year without a summer."[25]

To people whose lives were governed by the sun—by the hours of daylight and the seasons of the year—the weather mattered a great deal. Even in the best of times life was hard in North America, the climate harsher than that of western Europe and West Africa, its temperatures extreme and storms violent. During what is called "the little ice age" of 1550 to 1850, the growing season shortened by a month, diminishing the size of harvests. A season of bad weather implied not only financial losses but hunger, cold, and curtailed communication. After the harrowing experiences of 1816, many Yankee farm families—particularly in northern New England—despaired of eking out a living where they were and moved west. Some speculated that the bizarre summer that year heralded the approach of Judgment Day and the millennium.[26]

Agriculture provided the livelihood for the overwhelming majority of all Americans, regardless of race. Even people engaged in other occupations usually owned farmland as well. The clergyman had his glebe, the widowed landlady her garden. The village blacksmith supplemented his income with a plot of land. Geography as well as climate imposed constraints on people's livelihoods. Much depended on access to navigable water. With it, one could market a crop nationally or internationally; without it, the difficulty of transporting bulky goods overland could limit one to a local market. Trying to find a product that would bear the cost of wagon transportation, many backcountry farmers hit upon distilling their grain into spirits. As a result, cheap whiskey flooded the country, worsening the problem of alcohol abuse that Dr. Benjamin Rush of Philadelphia had identified.[27]

Life in America in 1815 was dirty, smelly, laborious, and uncomfortable. People spent most of their waking hours working, with scant opportunity

25. R. B. Stothers, "The Great Tambora Eruption of 1815," *Science* 224 (1984): 1191–98; Gregory Zielinski and Barry Keim, *New England Weather, New England Climate* (Hanover, N.H., 2003), 35; John D. Post, *The Last Great Subsistence Crisis in the Western World* (Baltimore, 1977), 1–27.

26. C. Edward Skeen, *1816: America Rising* (Lexington, Ky., 2003), 9–12; Allan Kulikoff, *From British Peasants to Colonial American Farmers* (Chapel Hill, 2000), 80–83; Michael Barkun, *Crucible of the Millennium* (Syracuse, N.Y., 1986), 108–11.

27. Mark Lender and James Martin, *Drinking in America* (New York, 1987), 30–40.

for the development of individual talents and interests unrelated to farming. Cobbler-made shoes being expensive and uncomfortable, country people of ordinary means went barefoot much of the time. White people of both sexes wore heavy fabrics covering their bodies, even in the humid heat of summer, for they believed (correctly) sunshine bad for their skin. People usually owned few changes of clothes and stank of sweat. Only the most fastidious bathed as often as once a week. Since water had to be carried from a spring or well and heated in a kettle, people gave themselves sponge baths, using the washtub. Some bathed once a year, in the spring, but as late as 1832, a New England country doctor complained that four out of five of his patients did not bathe from one year to the next. When washing themselves, people usually only rinsed off, saving their harsh, homemade soap for cleaning clothes. Inns did not provide soap to travelers.[28] Having an outdoor privy signified a level of decency above those who simply relieved themselves in the woods or fields. Indoor light was scarce and precious; families made their own candles, smelly and smoky, from animal tallow. A single fireplace provided all the cooking and heating for a common household. During winter, everybody slept in the room with the fire, several in each bed. Privacy for married couples was a luxury.[29]

In recent years, one would find a similar standard of living only in the third world. The gross domestic product per capita of the United States in 1820 was about the same as that of Ecuador or Jordan in 2002.[30] But although this is an instructive comparison for us, it was of course not one made by contemporaries. They compared their lot with that of European peasants of the time and felt good about it. Most white Americans lived on family farms and worked land that they owned or squatted on. A farm of one's own had been the dream of Old World peasantry; it seemed the key to dignity and economic security. Only a minority of American farmers owed rent to a landlord; none owed tithes to a bishop or abbot; taxes were low. Many did owe mortgage payments to the banker who had advanced them money to buy their farm; resentment that might have fo-

---

28. As an English visitor, William Faux, complained in 1819; quoted in Suellen Hoy, *Chasing Dirt* (New York, 1995), 7–8. The physician is cited in Charles Rosenberg, *The Cholera Years* (Chicago, 1987), 18.

29. See Jack Larkin, *The Reshaping of Everyday Life* (New York, 1988); David Danbom, *Born in the Country* (Baltimore, 1995); Priscilla Brewer, *From Fireplace to Cookstove* (Syracuse, N.Y., 2000).

30. Historical currency conversions provided by www.westegg.com/inflation and 2002 GDP tables at www.studentsoftheworld.info/infopays/rank/PIBH2 (viewed March 8, 2007).

cused on a nobility or an ecclesiastical establishment instead often turned toward banks, indispensable and yet unpopular.

The drastic decline of the Native population left a land-to-population ratio very favorable for the settlers coming in from the Old World. The historian John Murrin has called them the "beneficiaries of catastrophe." They were able to marry earlier than their relatives in Europe, set up housekeeping on their own, and have more children. Because of their high birthrate, the population of the United States approximately doubled every twenty years. By 1815, it had reached almost 8.5 million, even though the Napoleonic Wars had dampened immigration from Europe and the importation of slaves from Africa became illegal in 1808. Vital statistics bore out the benefits of America for its white settlers and their descendants. At five feet eight inches, the average American man was four inches taller than his English counterpart and as tall as his successor who was drafted in World War II. His health reflected the benefits of the land-to-population ratio: abundant food and rural isolation from contagious disease.[31]

The American of 1815 ate wheat and beef in the North, corn and pork in the South. Milk, cheese, and butter were plentiful; potatoes came to be added in the North and sweet potatoes in the South. Fruits appeared only in season except insofar as women could preserve them in pies or jams; green vegetables, now and then as condiments; salads, virtually never. (People understood that low temperatures would help keep food but could only create a cool storage place by digging a cellar.) Monotonous and constipating, too high in fat and salt, this diet nevertheless was more plentiful and nutritious, particularly in protein, than that available in most of the Old World. The big meal occurred at noon.[32]

American farm families generally produced partly for their own consumption and partly for sale or local barter; historians term this practice "composite" farming. Virtually no farm families expected to satisfy all their wants by purchase; neither could any possess the range of skills and tools that would make them entirely self-sufficient. Historians have tried

31. John Murrin, *Beneficiaries of Catastrophe* (Philadelphia, 1991); Peter McClelland and Richard Zeckhauser, *Demographic Dimensions of the New Republic* (Cambridge, Eng., 1982); Robert Fogel, "Nutrition and the Decline in Mortality Since 1700," in *Long-term Factors in American Economic Growth*, ed. Stanley Engerman and Robert Gallman (Chicago, 1986), Table 9.A.1. For the World War II draftee, see David Kennedy, *Freedom from Fear* (New York, 1999), 710.

32. Sarah McMahon, "Laying Foods By," in *Early American Technology*, ed. Judith McGaw (Chapel Hill, 1994), 164–96; Jane Nylander, *Our Own Snug Fireside* (New York, 1993), 96–98, 187–93; Danbom, *Born in the Country*, 99.

to sort out the extent of their market participation under varying circumstances. From the family's own point of view, however, this issue seemed less important than that their activities, taken as a whole, enabled them to survive and prosper.[33] Whether producing for a market or their own consumption, their way of life depended on the practice of thrift. When a husband hammered together a stool and his wife made the children's clothes, they were not being "thrifty" in the same way that someone shopping for groceries today is thrifty by remembering to use a coupon. They were performing their occupations, earning their living, just as much as when the man plowed the field or the woman churned butter to sell in the village. Their thrift was a necessity, not an option. Thrift demanded the family set aside enough corn or wheat to be able to seed next year's crop, feed the animals, and go on farming. Significantly, the very word for their occupation, "husbandry," also meant thrift, as in the expression "to husband resources."

So many and varied were the aspects of farm labor that unmarried farmers were exceedingly rare; to operate a farm household took both a man and woman. And so the word "husband," originally meaning "farmer," came to mean "married man." Typically, American farms were economically individualistic, operated by a single nuclear family, not an extended kin-group or communal enterprise. Families might supplement their own labor with that of a "hired man" or "hired girl" (called a girl because not yet married), but wage labor was relatively expensive, and the employee expected decent treatment. The preferred sources of agricultural labor consisted of family members, neighbors offering reciprocal favors, or (for those who could afford the investment) bound workers, indentured or enslaved. Children could perform many of the necessary errands and tasks: fetching water from the well, feeding chickens, collecting firewood. Foresight, not irresponsibility, prompted farm couples to have many children. In 1800, the white birthrate stood at an average of seven children per woman; by 1860, when it had declined to five, the rural percentage of the population had fallen from 95 to 80.[34]

Although the particular crops grown varied with the local climate, some principles of family farming were common to all regions. Following

33. Among many works, see esp. Richard Bushman, "Markets and Composite Farms in Early America," WMQ 55 (1998): 351–74; Christopher Clark, The Roots of Rural Capitalism (Ithaca, N.Y., 1990).

34. Herbert S. Klein, A Population History of the United States (Cambridge, Eng., 2004), 78; Mark Cairnes and John Garraty, Mapping America's Past (New York, 1996), 94–95. See further Christopher Clark, Social Change in America: From the Revolution Through the Civil War (Chicago, 2006), 141–44.

the principle of "safety first," newly settled agricultural families generally began by growing food for their own consumption, then turned as quickly as possible to supplementing this with something they could market. Their "market" might be a neighbor—or a "factor" who would ship the produce halfway around the world. A composite-farm family could simultaneously live in a local world of barter and engage in international commerce.[35] Market success and a measure of self-sufficiency were not even incompatible goals. Big landowners producing staple crops for export and commanding a large labor force (perhaps enslaved) achieved the greatest degree of self-sufficiency. They could afford to grind their own grain and employ their own artisans like blacksmiths, carpenters, and saddlers. When an ordinary farming family needed something they could neither produce for themselves nor swap with a neighbor, they could visit the local storekeeper. With currency chronically scarce, people seldom paid for their purchases using actual coins or banknotes. Instead, the storekeeper kept an account book, which recorded who owed what. When the husband bought a tool, he was debited; when the wife brought in a surplus cured ham, she was credited. In many little towns, the storekeepers still kept their accounts in shillings and pence fifty years after the Revolution. If customers had been paying cash, it would have made sense to convert to dollars and cents, but since nobody expected this, why not go on using the old-time familiar units of exchange?[36]

Most family farms relied on crude agricultural methods and the natural fecundity of the soil. Their wooden plows differed little from those used at the time of the Norman Conquest. Livestock foraged for themselves, so they bred unselectively and their manure did not accumulate for fertilizer. Fences encircled the cultivated land to keep the animals *out*, not *in*. Clearing land to plow was arduous labor, and a man might leave tree stumps in his fields for years rather than go to the work of removing them, even if this required him to use a hoe instead of a plow. As Virginian James Madison, a critic of prevailing methods, complained in 1819, "Whilst there was an abundance of fresh and fertile soil, it was the interest of the cultivator to spread his labor over as great a surface as he could, land being cheap and labor dear." Madison spoke for an enlightened

35. Gavin Wright, *The Political Economy of the Cotton South* (New York, 1978), 69–72; Martin Bruegel, *Farm, Shop, Landing: The Rise of a Market Society in the Hudson Valley* (Durham, N.C., 2002), 5.
36. Ruth Cowan, *Social History of American Technology* (New York, 1997), 39–43; Nylander, *Our Own Snug Fireside*, 46–47; Benjamin Klebaner, *American Commercial Banking* (Boston, 1990), 12; Larkin, *Reshaping Everyday Life*, 38, 53.

minority of agricultural reformers, often large landowners living in areas long under cultivation, who recommended means of conservation such as crop rotation and fertilization. Their ideas would spread, along with technological improvements in plowing, harrowing, and threshing, during the years after 1815.[37]

Almost all life's activities went on within the household setting: production as well as consumption, birthing and child-rearing, transmitting the rudiments of literacy, caring for the sick and those few persons who lived to old age. Work we would label "manufacturing" took up a lot of a typical housewife's time. A government report in 1810 estimated that two-thirds of all clothing and linens were produced in households. Such production would not necessarily be for the woman's own family, for merchants "put out" spinning, weaving, and sewing to women to do at home for payment. The early industrial revolution would not put an end to such home manufacturing. When women could buy fabrics instead of having to weave them, they did not stop making clothes at home. They welcomed new technology, including eventually sewing machines, as enabling them to clothe their family better or to earn more money.[38]

The man was the "head of the house," by both law and custom, and he could exploit the labor of other family members, as his predecessors had done for centuries. Yet in practice, the other members of the household enjoyed increasing autonomy in white America, and fathers could not control whom their sons or daughters married. In the decades to come, men would lose much of their legal control over the property and labor of their wives and children. Despite the common law of "coverture," which deprived married women of legal independence from their husbands, women almost always looked forward to the prospect of marriage. Only by marriage could a woman acquire a home of her own; as a spinster, she would have to live in some other woman's home. Except for some aspects of dairy farming, custom clearly labeled most work activities as either men's or women's. A family farm worked best when husband and wife cooperated closely and accorded each other mutual respect. Enslaved women, however, could be set tasks otherwise reserved for men.[39]

37. Peter McClelland, *Sowing Modernity: America's First Agricultural Revolution* (Ithaca, N.Y., 1997); Madison quoted on 41. See also Brian Donahue, "Environmental Stewardship and Decline in Old New England," *JER* 24 (2004): 234–41; Steven Stoll, *Larding the Lean Earth: Soil and Society in Nineteenth-Century America* (New York, 2002).
38. Laurel Ulrich, *The Age of Homespun* (New York, 2001), esp. 37–38.
39. See Nancy Osterud, *Bonds of Community* (Ithaca, N.Y., 1991); Hendrik Hartog, *Man and Wife in America* (Cambridge, Mass., 2000); Carole Shammas, *A History of Household Government in America* (Charlottesville, Va., 2002).

It was a young society: The census listed the median age as sixteen, and only one person in eight as over forty-three years old.[40] Women bore children in agony and danger, making their life expectancy, unlike today, slightly shorter than that of men. Once born, infants often succumbed to diseases like diphtheria, scarlet fever, and whooping cough. One-third of white children and over half of black children died before reaching adulthood. The women had enough babies to beat these grim odds. To help them through labor, neighbors and trained midwives attended them. Doctors were in short supply, hospitals almost unknown. This proved a blessing in disguise, for physicians then did as much harm as good, and hospitals incubated infection. The upside of rural isolation was that epidemics did not spread easily.[41]

The widespread distribution of land had powerful consequences, psychological and political as well as economic. Ownership of his own land meant a lot to the American husbandman. It meant that one's livelihood was not dependent on the goodwill of another, as was the case, presumably, with tenants, serfs, indentured servants, wage-workers, or chattel slaves, as well as women and children. Americans affirmed a resolute egalitarianism among white men. The custom of shaking hands, a gesture of social reciprocity, replaced bowing. Not only the widespread ownership of land but also the widespread ownership of horses fostered a rough equality of esteem among free adult males. In the Spanish language, the word for "gentleman" (*caballero*) literally means "horseman." In a society where riding a horse did not signify a special status, neither did the designation "gentleman." The American husbandman nurtured a pride comparable to that of a European gentleman; he defined himself as a citizen rather than a subject, and he did not hesitate to assert his rights as he saw them.

Political leaders had to take account of this yeoman's worldview, especially his aversion to taxes and suspicion of all authority (except, sometimes, that of religion). American republican ideology gave formal expression to the outlook. Thomas Jefferson was the leading formulator of the ideology during the Revolution and also proved its most successful political practitioner afterwards. This republican ideology had intellectual precursors in England: John Locke's social-compact philosophy and the writings of the eighteenth-century "commonwealthmen" who traced

---

40. Bureau of the Census, *Historical Statistics of the United States* (Washington, 1975), I, 19.
41. Larkin, *Reshaping Everyday Life*, 75–76; Donald Wright, *African Americans in the Early Republic* (Arlington Heights, Ill., 1993), 68–70; Laurel Ulrich, *A Midwife's Tale* (New York, 1990).

their lineage to the English Puritan Revolution. Although historians have pointed out intellectual differences between Locke and the common-wealthmen, Americans of Jefferson's generation were interested in what they had in common: their defense of liberty. Besides asserting individual rights and equality, Jefferson's republican ideology celebrated popular virtue and free enterprise, in religion and politics as well as in economic undertakings; it expressed deep suspicion of pretensions to power and privilege.[42]

This was not a relaxed, hedonistic, refined, or indulgent society. For-mal education and family connections counted for comparatively little. The man who got ahead in often primitive conditions did so by means of innate ability, hard work, luck, and sheer willpower. Disciplined himself, he knew how to impose discipline on his family, employees, and slaves. Impatient of direction, he took pride in his personal accomplishments. An important component of his drive to succeed was a willingness— surprising among agrarian people—to innovate and take risks, to try new methods and locations. With an outlook more entrepreneurial than peas-ant, the American farmer sought to engross more land than he could cul-tivate in hopes that its value would rise as other settlers arrived.[43]

For most white men, this proud, willful independence derived from having one's own land. However, one did not actually have to operate a family farm to embrace such an outlook. Thinking of their tools and shop as the equivalent of a family farm, artisans appropriated the yeoman out-look to themselves. So did planters using slave labor, for they did not apply the rights they claimed for themselves to people of other races. Indeed, slaveowning planters like Jefferson wrote the most learned expositions of the yeoman ideology and exploited it most successfully in their political leadership.

Although independent of higher classes of persons, the American hus-bandman remained dependent upon nature. This dependence he from time to time acknowledged to God; more often, his wife acknowledged it. The earthquakes centered along the New Madrid Fault in Missouri dur-ing the winter of 1811–12, the greatest ever recorded in North America, provoked religious revivals. The prevailing versions of Protestantism preached a stern morality and self-control. Such austere religion did not

---

42. The secondary literature on this subject is enormous. See James Kloppenberg, "The Virtues of Liberalism," *JAH* 74 (1987): 9–33; Joyce Appleby, *Liberalism and Republi-canism in the Historical Imagination* (Cambridge, Mass., 1992).

43. For portrayals of this outlook, see Jon Butler, *Becoming America* (Cambridge, Mass., 2000); Joyce Appleby, *Inheriting the Revolution* (Cambridge, Mass., 2000).

foster the traditional high arts of music, painting, and sculpture. It did foster literacy for Bible-reading, broad participation in decision-making, and a sense of equality among the lay members. "Membership" in a church, however, was often a closely guarded privilege, and many more people attended services than attained full membership. The characteristic American religious harvest festival, Thanksgiving Day, spread from New England, where it had been observed since colonial times, to other parts of the young republic. (On the other hand, most Protestants shunned celebrating Christmas as a Catholic corruption of Christianity.)[44]

Their respect for religious tradition reminds us that these Americans displayed less individualism in their culture than they did in their economic activity. Although separate conjugal families each operated their own farm, most people thought of themselves as members of a local community. They usually lived in communities with others of their own background. Euro-Americans already represented a variety of such backgrounds, the Mid-Atlantic states being especially diverse, including substantial Dutch, German, and Swedish minorities. Highland Scots sometimes still spoke Gaelic upon arrival; Germans perpetuated their language for generations in their well-defined enclaves. Immigrants from Ireland, usually Ulster Presbyterians in this period, often settled in remote Appalachian places because earlier arrivals had claimed the more favorable locations. (Though later termed "Scots-Irish," at this time they more commonly called themselves Irish Protestants.) In areas dominated by whites, the remaining Native Americans typically lived in villages of their own. Besides ethnicity, religion constituted a common tie binding local communities. Quakers and Baptists wanted to live where they could worship with others of their persuasion. In New England, descendants of the seventeenth-century Puritans still predominated, their distinctive villages centered on a "green" and a Congregational meetinghouse. These were the people properly called "Yankees," a term that southerners would come to apply to all northerners, and foreigners to all Americans.[45]

Besides the minister, the local community also supplied other occupational specialists like the blacksmith, the storekeeper, and the miller. In some places it might also provide common pastureland and a school.

44. James Penick, *The New Madrid Earthquakes* (Columbia, Mo., 1976); Malcolm Rohrbough, *The Trans-Appalachian Frontier* (New York, 1978), 152; Nylander, *Our Own Snug Fireside*, 261–76.

45. Donald Akenson, *The Irish Diaspora* (Toronto, 1996), 253–54; Edward Grabb, Douglas Baer, and James Curtis, "The Origins of American Individualism," *Canadian Journal of Sociology* 24 (1999): 511–533.

Neighbors bartered with each other and joined in occasional collective efforts like barn raising or corn husking. Their willingness to come to the rescue (if, say, a building caught fire) supplied a primitive kind of insurance. Institutions of local government generally approximated a freeholders' democracy—explicitly so, in New England town meetings. But within the small communities, consensus appeared more often than divisions of opinion. Local pressures to conformity of opinion were substantial. Ordinary people usually regarded outsiders with suspicion, especially those with pretensions to elite status.[46]

For all the political liberty that American institutions and ideology promised to adult white men, in practical terms most lives were disciplined and limited by the economic necessities of a harsh environment and the cultural constraints of a small community. Instead of "freedom" from demands, it might be more accurate to think of the American husbandman as possessing "agency," that is, the ability to act purposefully in the service of goals. The goals might come from family, community, religion, or personal ambition.[47]

In the America of 1815, a network of unpaved short roads connected family farms with nearby towns or docks on navigable streams. Seldom more than rutted trails, littered with boulders and tree stumps, these "country roads" were muddy when it rained, dusty when dry, and frequently impassable. Local authorities supposedly drafted neighboring farmers to work on the roads during the agricultural slack seasons. Such grudging labor under inexpert direction did not maintain the roads beyond the barest minimum. While these pathways permitted farm produce to be hauled a few miles to a local market or place of storage, they were hopeless for extended journeys. Most long-distance travel and commerce went by water, which explains why most cities were seaports—Cincinnati on the Ohio River and St. Louis on the Mississippi being notable exceptions. To transport a ton of goods by wagon to a port city from thirty miles inland typically cost nine dollars in 1815; for the same price the goods could be shipped three thousand miles across the ocean.[48]

---

46. There are many fine studies of particular communities. Examples include John Brooke, *The Heart of the Commonwealth* (New York, 1990); John Faragher, *Sugar Creek* (New Haven, 1986); Randolph Roth, *The Democratic Dilemma* (Cambridge, Eng., 1987); Robert Gross, "Agriculture and Society in Thoreau's Concord," *JAH* 69 (1982): 42–61.

47. An idea explored more fully in James Block, *A Nation of Agents* (Cambridge, Mass., 2002).

48. George Rogers Taylor, *The Transportation Revolution* (New York, 1951), 15–17, 132–33.

Though peace came to the Atlantic world in 1815, *distance* remained for Americans "the first enemy," as it had been for inhabitants of the Mediterranean world of the sixteenth century.[49] If distance is expressed in terms of time of travel, the country was far larger then than now. To get from New York City to Cincinnati on the other side of the Appalachians took nineteen days in 1817. Travel over water was always faster; sailing along the coast, one could get from New York to Charleston in eight days.[50] During the war, the British blockade had cut off the coastal traffic, forcing Americans to rely on difficult overland routes. Slow travel restricted communication as well as commerce, making it difficult to receive news, control armies in the field from Washington, or organize a timely protest against a government action.

The distribution of population reflected the existing realities of transportation and communication. Most Americans lived not far from the coast. Of the 7.23 million people counted in the third census, taken in August 1810, only about 1 million lived in the new states and territories west of the Appalachians. The mean center of population was located in Loudoun County, Virginia, forty miles from Washington, D.C.[51] Extensive American settlement in the continental interior awaited improvements in transportation, both to get the people in and to get their products out. Improvements in communication had perhaps even more far-reaching consequences. For example, they would greatly facilitate the development of mass political parties in the coming years. It is no accident that so many leaders of these parties would be newspapermen, or that the largest source of political party patronage came from the Post Office.[52]

The "frontier" in 1815 was not so much a specific line on a map as any area where it was hard to get produce to market. In such a place, economic self-sufficiency was involuntary, forced upon the settlers. They had traded consumer civilization for land, but they did not want the trade-off to be permanent. With few exceptions, westward migrants worked impatiently to liberate themselves from the oppression of isolation. The exceptions to

49. The apt term of the great French historian Fernand Braudel, in *The Mediterranean and the Mediterranean World in the Age of Philip II*, trans. Sian Reynolds (New York, 1976), I, 355.
50. Menahem Blondheim, *News over the Wires* (Cambridge, Mass., 1994), 11, 17.
51. The mean center of population has moved westward with every decade's census. In 1980 it crossed the Mississippi River. http://www.census.gov/geo/www/cenpop/meanctr.pdf (viewed Feb. 23, 2007).
52. See Richard John, *Spreading the News* (Cambridge, Mass., 1995) and Richard Brown, *Knowledge Is Power* (New York, 1989).

the rule consisted of religious communities like the Pennsylvania Amish, who deliberately insulated themselves from the outside world, and some people, mainly in the milder climate of the South, who seem to have preferred subsistence to market farming as a way of life. Historians now realize that there were fewer of the latter than they once thought. Even farmers in the remote southern piney woods raised cattle and hogs for market.[53]

The simple methods of agriculture limited the number of people the land would support. As a result, explosive population growth prompted migration inland. From the standpoint of the United States as a nation, this westward movement brought expansion and increased power. But from the standpoint of the individuals involved, westward migration did not necessarily constitute a success story. It might well reflect a disappointment in the East, the crop failures of 1816 being the most dramatic example. Often soil exhaustion prompted a move. A Virginian complained in 1818, "Our woods have disappeared and are succeeded, too generally, by exhausted fields and gullied hills."[54] A large landowner could allow some fields to lie fallow until they recovered fertility; a smallholder could not. For him, a move west constituted a resurgence of hope. Families usually stayed in the same general latitude when they moved, so they could keep their accustomed farming practices and use their seed crops. But sometimes farm families would fail and move repeatedly in a recurring cycle of hope and despair. Moving entailed risk. For the first few years in a new location, the family's living standard would probably fall. Unless they simply "squatted" on land they didn't own, the family might well have to borrow money to pay for their new land. People lacking the requisite ambition or access to credit might end up as tenant farmers or, if unmarried, look for wage work.[55]

Unfortunately, although farm families moved west in hope of a better life, in these early years their migration often took them farther away from access to markets, toward less rewarding forms of agriculture, and into

53. Jeremy Atack et al., "The Farm, the Farmer, and the Market," in *Cambridge Economic History of the United States*, ed. Stanley Engerman and Robert Gallman (Cambridge, Eng., 2000), II, 245–84; Bradley Bond, "Herders, Farmers, and Markets on the Inner Frontier," in *Plain Folk of the South Revisited*, ed. Samuel Hyde Jr. (Baton Rouge, 1997), 73–99.

54. Quoted in Stoll, *Larding the Lean Earth*, vii.

55. See Alan Taylor, "Land and Liberty on the Post-Revolutionary Frontier," in *Devising Liberty*, ed. David Konig (Stanford, 1995), 81–108; Richard Steckel, "The Economic Foundations of East-West Migration During the 19th Century," *Explorations in Economic History* 20 (1983): 14–36.

conflict with the Native peoples. In fact, once on the frontier, white settlers did not always pursue a way of life strikingly different from their
Indian neighbors'; both mixed agriculture with hunting. In the Old Southwest, both whites and Indians raised a lot of cattle to sell for their hides
and tallow, more practical to ship a long way than unrefrigerated beef. All
too often both peoples succumbed to alcohol abuse. In sum, the agricultural economy of 1815 contained no necessary tendency toward economic
development or diversification. Instead, the westward movement tended
to perpetuate a dispersed population practicing relatively primitive agricultural methods.[56]

The United States in 1815 resembled the economically developing
countries of today in many ways: high birthrate, rapid population growth,
most people being in the agricultural sector, and surplus rural population
migrating in quest of a livelihood. Poor transportation meant that many
farms in the hinterland operated only just above subsistence level. As
usual in such countries, communication was slow; infectious disease was
prevalent; conflicts among ethnoreligious communities sometimes became violent. Save in New England, free public education represented
the exception rather than the rule. Like developing countries generally,
the United States needed to import manufactured goods and paid for
them with agricultural staples and the export of raw materials like timber,
tar, and fur. Over the next three decades the United States would confront many issues common in developing countries: how to attract or mobilize investment capital; how to provide municipal services (police, water, fire protection, public health) for the suddenly growing cities; how to
create and fund a system of public education capable of delivering mass
literacy; how to combine industrialization with decent labor conditions
and hours of employment; how to arbitrate disputes between indigenous
peoples and white settlers intent on expropriating them. Realizing the
hopes of America's family farmers and the transformation of their under-
developed country awaited the coming of trade, transportation, and communication. With them, everyday life would improve significantly both
for those agriculturalists who could get more produce to market and for
the growing number of townsfolk who bought that produce. For the very
poor and for those enslaved, however, little would change.

56. Christopher Clark, "Rural America and the Transition to Capitalism," *JER* 16 (1996):
223–36; Elliott West, "American Frontier," in *The Oxford History of the American
West*, ed. Clyde Milner et al. (New York, 1994), 114–49; Forrest McDonald and Grady
McWhiney, "The Antebellum Southern Herdsman," *Journal of Southern History* 41
(1975): 147–66.

III

Aaron Fuller of Massachusetts had reason to worry about the future. He had not yet established himself in farming (or any other career), and his wife had just died, leaving him with four small children. In September 1818, Fuller wrote out an account of "The Life I should like." He hoped someday to own a "mercantile business," large enough to "employ two faithful clerks." He also hoped to farm "about fifty Acres of Good Land," not only for economic reasons but also because agriculture was "of the greatest importance to the whole human family—it supports *life & health*." Fuller hoped that his business and farm would keep him out of debt but not bring in so much income that he forgot to "use economy" or became "slothfull & indolent." His vision of happiness hinged, he realized, on finding the right wife—"a partner," "affectionate," "prudent," and a good cook. Aaron Fuller's dream came true. Within two years he had remarried, to Fanny Negus, who took good care of his four children and bore him seven more in the course of their twenty-five years together. The two of them operated a bakery, an inn, and a farm in the Connecticut River valley that sold livestock, cranberries, corn, and dairy products. The historian Catherine Kelly offers their partnership as an example of "companionate marriage," both emotionally fulfilling and economically productive.[57]

Aaron Fuller's dream was the typical American dream of his generation, though it did not come true for everyone. A family farm offered the key to a life of "virtue"—a word then used to mean wholesome, productive, public-spirited independence. What made for independence in this sense was not literal economic self-sufficiency but self-employment, heading a household of one's own, and owning real estate in fee simple, clear of mortgage indebtedness. Aaron Fuller's linking of agrarian virtue with small-scale commercial endeavor was not unusual. When Alexis de Tocqueville visited from France in 1831, he noticed that "almost all farmers of the United States combine some trade with agriculture; most of them make agriculture itself a trade." As early as 1790 the Jeffersonian Albert Gallatin, an astute economic observer, had remarked: "You will scarcely find a farmer who is not, in some degree, a trader."[58] Farming certainly had its commercial aspect. If a farmer could market a good crop

---

57. Catherine Kelly, *In the New England Fashion: Reshaping Women's Lives in the Nineteenth Century* (Ithaca, N.Y., 1999), 93–98, discusses and quotes from Fuller's manuscript.

58. Tocqueville, *Democracy in America*, II, 157; Gallatin is quoted in Bruce Mann, *Republic of Debtors* (Cambridge, Mass., 2000), 209.

and get a merchant's "bill of exchange" in return, he might clear his account with the storekeeper and have enough left to invest in one of the recently invented agricultural implements, like a steel plow. Demand generated by prosperous farmers helped encourage the new industries of New England.[59] Still, as Aaron Fuller's manuscript indicates, many family farmers aspired to competence rather than wealth.

The synthesis of agriculture and commerce such as Aaron and Fanny Fuller practiced had profound cultural as well as economic consequences in the early nineteenth-century United States. The way they and others succeeded in realizing their vision of the good life strengthened their purposefulness and reinforced the dignity of their labor and thrift. The availability of such opportunities on a relatively wide scale fostered individual autonomy, even within the family, weakening patriarchal traditions and encouraging sons and daughters to strike out on their own. Like the early-modern European advocates of free enterprise, Americans of the Fullers' generation thought of their economic careers as making a moral and political statement on behalf of freedom. Despite the continued exclusion of women from the "public sphere" of politics, wives laid (a modest) claim to the gratitude of the commonwealth, for were they not "republican mothers," responsible for rearing future citizens?[60] It is no accident that the word "liberalism" came to have both an economic and a political meaning—although our generation often finds this a confusing ambiguity. In early nineteenth-century America, economic development in regions such as southern New England, western New York and Pennsylvania, or Ohio was associated with the appearance of social reform movements.[61]

The woman of the house often led the way in establishing commercial contact with the wider world beyond the local community, through her desire to introduce amenities into the rustic simplicity of her home. From the peddlers who called with increasing frequency over the years, she could purchase a clock for the mantel, a second book to go with the Bible, and even porcelain cups. The traveling artisan could make furniture better than

59. Naomi Lamoreaux, "Rethinking the Transition to Capitalism in the Early American Northeast," *JAH* 90 (2003): 437–61; David R. Meyer, *Roots of American Industrialization* (Baltimore, 2003), 11, 34–36.
60. Linda Kerber, *Women of the Republic* (Chapel Hill, 1980), 199–200, 228–31, 283–88; Mary Beth Norton, *Liberty's Daughters* (Ithaca, N.Y., 1980), 228–35, 247–50.
61. See Joyce Appleby, "The Vexed Story of Capitalism Told by American Historians," *JER* 21 (2001): 1–18; Thomas Haskell, "Capitalism and the Origins of the Humanitarian Sensibility," in *The Antislavery Debate: Capitalism and Abolitionism*, ed. Thomas Bender (Berkeley, 1992), 107–60.

her husband's best efforts. She might have earned the money to pay for these things herself, with "put out" work. So, despite occasional reproaches from neighbors that she was introducing unbecoming "luxuries," she initiated the democratization of refinement. Sometimes her husband resisted. The famous itinerant preacher Peter Cartwright remembered how, in the 1820s, he had to urge a Methodist layman to spend some of his savings on furnishing his primitive cabin, so as to "give your wife and daughters a chance" at a decent life.[62] More often the husband cooperated in improving the family's standard of living. After all, if he could be addressed as a "gentleman," should not his home reflect gentility? A successful yeoman family looked forward to dividing the downstairs into two rooms (one of them bravely named "the parlor") and adding a full upstairs, perhaps with additional fireplaces and chimneys. In warm climates, a prosperous family would build a separate structure for cooking, to keep from overheating the main house. A few even had their portraits painted by itinerant artists.[63]

Many of the items in the peddler's pack or on the storekeeper's shelves came from overseas: "dry goods" (that is, textiles of wool, linen, and silk), "wet goods" (wine, gin, brandy, and rum), household hardware, cutlery, firearms, tools, and the aptly named China-ware. Besides manufactured products such as these, the United States also imported unfinished iron, citrus fruits, coffee, tea, and cocoa. Even prior to independence, American consumers had played an important role in the economy of the British Empire, which has been called "an empire of goods." The colonists employed for political advantage the leverage this provided them. Before having recourse to arms, they famously collaborated to boycott British imports as a way of protesting against parliamentary taxation.[64] More recently, when the Jefferson administration had embargoed all overseas trade, the impact on the American economy had been very serious. Americans paid for their imports with exports that included wheat, tobacco, rice, lumber, "naval stores" (turpentine, tar, and tall pines for ships' masts), animal hides and pelts—and, by 1815, cotton. Indeed, all the countries bordering on the Atlantic had long been integrated by a complex network of trade routes that, despite the efforts of

62. Allan Kulikoff, *Agrarian Origins of American Capitalism* (Charlottesville, Va., 1992), 49; Peter Cartwright, *Autobiography*, ed. Charles Wallis (1856; New York, 1956), 169–70.

63. David Jaffee, "Peddlers of Progress," JAH 78 (1991): 511–35. More generally, see Richard Bushman, *The Refinement of America* (New York, 1992); John Crowley, *The Invention of Comfort* (Baltimore, 2001).

64. See T. H. Breen, *The Marketplace of Revolution: How Consumer Politics Shaped American Independence* (New York, 2004).

metropolitan governments, often broke the bonds of the mercantile systems of the rival empires. The coming of peace to the Atlantic world in 1815 found the British and French Empires greatly diminished, the Spanish and Portuguese Empires in the final stages of disintegration. International commerce consequently expanded in response to increased freedom of the seas, and so did the opportunities for American agricultural producers to find markets abroad.

Ocean travel was easier than overland travel, and ocean commerce far greater in scope. People had been crossing the Atlantic regularly for more than three hundred years; no one crossed the North American continent above Mexico until Sir Alexander Mackenzie's Canadian expedition in 1793–94; the only Americans to have done so in 1815 were the veterans of Lewis and Clark's expedition of 1805–6. A typical ocean crossing from New York to Liverpool took three or four weeks, but the westward voyage, against prevailing winds and currents, took anywhere from five to eight or even more. (The news that might have prevented the War of 1812 and that which would have prevented the Battle of New Orleans were both carried in westward crossings.) These times had not improved since the middle of the eighteenth century.[65]

New England Yankees made themselves one of the world's great seafaring peoples; they had already traveled around Cape Horn and across the Pacific to open the China trade. They had a remarkable amount in common with the Dutch—another seagoing, predominantly Calvinist people who combined agriculture with commerce, practiced religious toleration, and had no compunction about subjugating native populations. Seaport Americans earned livings not only as merchant sailors but also as fishermen, whalers, and shipwrights. North Atlantic cod flourished in vast numbers off the coasts of Newfoundland, Labrador, Nova Scotia, and New England. The fish could be preserved by drying, for even longer by salting. Yankee men who had not secured land to farm or had spare time on their hands in winter could go out on the fishing boats. In colonial times cod became one of America's important exports, to Europe and to the West Indies. But after the Revolution London clamped down on American rights to fish off the Canadian shore and to sell in the British West Indies. Both would be the subject of diplomatic negotiations after 1815. In the meantime, Yankee fishermen contrived to expand their domestic market.[66]

65. Ian Steele, *The English Atlantic: An Exploration of Communication and Community* (New York, 1986), 273–75; Robert Albion, *The Rise of New York Port* (New York, 1939), 51.
66. Daniel Vickers, *Farmers and Fishermen* (Chapel Hill, 1994), 263–85; Mark Kurlansky, *Cod* (New York, 1997), 78–102.

Until 1815, Americans looked principally eastward, toward the Atlantic and Europe. The Battle of New Orleans encouraged them to face westward toward the continent—but not exclusively: They still needed frequently to glance back over their shoulders, toward the ocean that continued to bring them goods, additional people, and new ideas. Atlantic crossing times and costs would both fall steadily over the next thirty-five years and for the rest of the century, integrating commodity markets, even on the North American frontier, in an early example of what our own era calls "globalization."[67]

Native Americans showed as much willingness as white people to participate in the market economy. Their aptitude for commerce gave rise to one of the fastest-growing "industries" of the late eighteenth and early nineteenth centuries: the fur trade. Tribes all over North America participated, trapping beaver, hunting buffalo, and catching sea otters to sell into what was truly a global market. When the Old Northwest around the Great Lakes ceased to be a "middle ground," the New Northwest on the Pacific Coast took its place, with Americans, British, and Russians all competing to obtain beaver and sea otter furs. Furs from Oregon sold in China, Hawaii, South America, and Europe. No longer do historians believe that white traders laughingly obtained these pelts for a few trifling beads. On the contrary, Native people drove shrewd bargains and received items of use and value to them—even though, in the Pacific Northwest, they sometimes destroyed their profits in spectacular potlatches to win prestige. Among other benefits, the fur trade promoted peace on the frontier. Nevertheless, it proved but a mixed blessing to the Indians, for it not only depleted their ecological resources but spread unfamiliar diseases, including dependency on alcohol, a favorite item of their purchase.[68]

Enthusiasm for the fur trade prompted the most powerful tribes of the Great Plains to conclude a peace agreement with each other in 1840 so they could concentrate on lucrative buffalo hunting instead of warfare. By that time they hunted buffalo not primarily for their own consumption but in order to sell the hides and robes to white traders. Serious overhunting resulted. Meanwhile, the Indians' new herds of domesticated horses competed with the buffalo for grasslands and sheltered winter

---

67. See Kevin O'Rourke and Jeffrey Williamson, *Globalization and History: The Evolution of a Nineteenth-Century Atlantic Economy* (Cambridge, Mass., 1999).

68. James Axtell, "The First Consumer Revolution," in his *Natives and Newcomers* (New York, 2001), 104–20; Robin Fisher, "The Northwest from the Beginning of Trade with Europeans to the 1880s," in Trigger and Washburn, *Cambridge History of Native Peoples: North America*, pt. 2, 117–82. See also Daniel Richter, "A Quaker Construction of Indianness," *JER* 19 (1999): 601–28.

habitats. So did the animals with the wagon trains of white settlers cross-ing the Plains to Utah, Oregon, and California. The great bison herds had begun to diminish even before "Buffalo Bill" Cody and his fellow white hunters slaughtered meat for the workers on the transcontinental railroad. Despite the mythology of "noble savages" in harmony with na-ture, in fact Native Americans collaborated with whites in altering their environment and depleting its resources.[69]

Whites involved in the fur trade followed the examples, sometimes the actual leadership, of French Canadians who had been involved in the en-terprise since long before Jefferson's Louisiana Purchase. Besides buying pelts, whites also trapped beaver on their own. Starting in 1825, the firm of William H. Ashley paid salaries to keep white trapper-traders in the wilderness the year round, departing from the depot-based practice of its British rival, the Hudson's Bay Company. Other "mountain men" worked as free agents or on shares for their creditors. These white men of-ten married Native women, who contributed valuable knowledge as con-tacts, guides, and interpreters. All would hold an annual *rendezvous* with each other and traders from many Indian tribes to pool their catches. The trade in beaver furs declined after about 1840, as beaver became harder to find and the fashion for men's fur hats passed.[70]

After the proclamation of Mexican independence in 1821, the old Span-ish mercantile restrictions on trade with foreigners came to an end. Now, *nuevomexicanos* could exchange Mexican silver, livestock, and beaver pelts for U.S. cotton textiles and manufactured goods. Traders opened up communication between the western United States and the north of Mex-ico. Entrepreneurial Mexicans journeyed as far north as Council Bluffs, Iowa, in search of commercial opportunities. The Santa Fe Trail they and their American counterparts followed between New Mexico and St. Louis was surveyed and marked by the U.S. federal government as far as the in-ternational border, though no actual roadway was ever laid. In 1833, Bent's Fort in what is now southeastern Colorado began to facilitate commerce among Americans, Mexicans, and the Indian tribes of the southern Plains; it became "the capital of the southern fur trade."[71]

69. Andrew Isenberg, *The Destruction of the Bison* (Cambridge, Eng., 2000); Elliott West, *The Way to the West* (Albuquerque, N.M., 1995), 53–83; Dan Flores, "Bison Ecology and Bison Diplomacy," *JAH* 78 (1991): 465–85.
70. David Wishart, *The Fur Trade of the American West* (Lincoln, Neb., 1979); William Goetzmann, *New Lands, New Men* (New York, 1986), 127–45.
71. Howard Lamar, *The Far Southwest* (New York, 1970), 46–55, quotation from 46; David Dary, *The Santa Fe Trail* (New York, 2000), 55–106; Stephen Hyslop, *Bound for Santa Fe* (Norman, Okla., 2002), 47–50.

During its height in the 1820s and '30s, the beaver fur trade added greatly to whites' knowledge of North American geography. The mountain men's commercially motivated expeditions revealed valuable information about the Rocky Mountains and practicable ways to cross them. The most extensive of the explorations of the American fur trade were those of Jedediah Smith. The fourth of twelve children born to a New Hampshire farming family, he went to work for Ashley's fur company in 1821 at the age of twenty-two and retraced much of Lewis and Clark's route up the Missouri in 1822–23. During his short life Smith proved himself a natural leader, an intrepid explorer, and a successful businessman. Taking his Bible and a few companions, this sober, religious young man laid out the route of the future Oregon Trail over South Pass in 1824 and explored the region of the Great Salt Lake. He traveled over the Mojave Desert to Mexican San Diego and returned as the first American (quite possibly the first person) to have crossed the Sierra Nevada and the Great Basin. The next year, he trekked overland a second time to California and thence up the coast by land to Oregon. Along the thousands of miles that he traveled without maps, he fought some Indians, traded with others, survived hunger, thirst, snowstorms, and floods, and got mauled by a grizzly. He successfully challenged the Hudson's Bay Company in the fur business, and with two partners was able to buy out his employer Ashley in 1826. A rich man when he returned to St. Louis in 1830, Smith had seen more of the Rocky Mountain West than anyone else in his time — and more than most since. He decided to make a final expedition, to New Mexico, partly in order to complete a map of the Rockies he was drawing based on his own experiences. Along the Santa Fe Trail in May 1831, he rode by himself away from his well-equipped wagon train, to look for a water hole. He located the water hole, but so did a Comanche hunting party. When his nervous horse wheeled, they interpreted it as a hostile movement and opened fire. His body was never found.[72]

IV

In 1815, Isabella, a slave girl of about seventeen living in Ulster County, New York, married Thomas, an older man who belonged, as she did, to the Dumont family. Over the next eleven years Isabella bore Thomas five children, in between stints of strenuous labor in the fields. New York had recognized the legality of marriages between slaves in 1809, meaning that now the couple and their children could not be sold apart from each other. Isabella herself had been sold away from her own parents at the age

72. Dale Morgan, *Jedediah Smith and the Opening of the West* (Indianapolis, 1953).

of nine for a hundred dollars, when their master died and his estate went up for auction. Isabella's first owner had been a Dutch American, and the child's first language was Dutch. Her next owner, an English-speaker, beat her for not comprehending his commands; her back bore the scars for the rest of her life. By 1810, she had been sold twice more (each owner realizing a profit on the transaction), ending up with the Dumonts.

The state of New York had adopted a program of gradual emancipation, decreeing that slaves born after the Fourth of July 1799 should become free at age twenty-eight (for males) or twenty-five (for females). This would allow the owner who bore the cost of rearing the children reimbursement with several of their prime working years. Isabella, having been born before the cutoff date, would remain in slavery for the rest of her life. But in 1817, the New York legislature sped up the emancipation process and decreed that on July 4, 1827, all remaining slaves, whenever born, should become free. Masters would receive no financial compensation from the state but did have one more decade to exploit their chattels' unpaid labor. Shortly before the final emancipation took effect, Isabella's five-year-old son was sold away from her, south to Alabama. This constituted a violation of New York law; the newly free Isabella took the remarkable step of suing for and obtaining the boy's return, an act that set a pattern for her lifetime of resolute opposition to injustice.[73]

Having developed an active prayer life in childhood under the guidance of her mother, Isabella grew into a fervent "Holiness" Methodist. Once free, she left her husband (who may have been chosen for her by their owner) and became an itinerant preacher. She warned of the Second Coming of Christ and demanded the abolition of slavery throughout the nation. In 1843, she adopted the name Sojourner Truth, appropriate for a traveling herald of the Divine Word. Although illiterate, she spoke powerfully and dictated a financially successful autobiography. Five feet eleven inches tall, with dark skin and a muscular frame, Sojourner Truth commanded attention from an audience. Her resonant voice had a New York working-class accent that never lost traces of the Dutch.[74]

Of all the many aspects of the early-modern global economy, none was more infamous or more wide-ranging in its consequences than the Atlantic slave trade. Both Great Britain and the United States had passed

---

73. For the texts of the New York laws of 1799 and 1817, see *Jim Crow New York*, ed. David Gellman and David Quigley (New York, 2003), 52–55, 67–72.
74. For information on Isabella, I rely on Nell Painter, *Sojourner Truth* (New York, 1996); for Truth's accent, 7–8. Reenactors usually portray her, inaccurately, with a southern accent.

legislation in 1807 outlawing the traffic, already notorious for its cruelty, though the Spanish and Portuguese colonies of Latin America still permitted it, and the French West Indies winked at it. The trade had its origins in the post-Columbian demographic catastrophe, which created a severe labor shortage in the New World. European colonizers filled their demand for cheap labor by importing people from Africa. These consisted primarily of prisoners captured in wars between West African nations, supplemented by convicts and victims of kidnapping. The captives would be transported to the coast and sold to Europeans who had secured permission from local rulers to operate trading posts called "factories." From there they embarked on the horrific transoceanic "middle passage" to the Western Hemisphere. As of 1815, more people had traveled to the New World from Africa via the slave trade than had come from Europe.[75]

In the United States, depopulation of the Native inhabitants left land inexpensive and widely available once British limitations on westward migration had been removed. Most free people preferred to secure a farm of their own rather than work on someone else's land. Accordingly, large landowners had imported unfree laborers, first indentured Europeans and then enslaved Africans. Wars in North America, like those in West Africa, also produced captives to enslave, but not in great numbers. Ironically, America's free land had promoted slavery—for much the same reason that the plentiful lands of Russia promoted serfdom.[76]

In 1815, of about 8.4 million people in the United States, almost 1.4 million were held in hereditary slavery, the personal property of their owners. During the colonial period, slavery had been legal in all the future United States, and challenges to its moral legitimacy were rare. But the Revolution popularized Enlightenment ideas, synthesized them with elements of Christianity, and summed them up in the affirmation that "all men are created equal," in that all possess "unalienable rights." By the early years of the nineteenth century, scarcely anyone outside the Deep South states of South Carolina and Georgia tried to justify slavery in

---

75. David Brion Davis, *In the Image of God* (New Haven, 2001), 64.
76. See Hugh Thomas, *The Slave Trade* (New York, 1997); John Thornton, "The African Background to American Colonization," in Engerman and Gallman, *Cambridge Economic History of the United States*, I, 53–94; Juliana Barr, "From Captives to Slaves: Commodifying Indian Women in the Borderlands," *JAH* 92 (2005): 19–46; Evsey Dornar, "The Causes of Slavery or Serfdom," *Journal of Economic History* 30 (1970): 18–32.

principle. Public opinion in 1815 generally held the institution a regret-table evil, contrary to both Christianity and natural rights. However, in places with large African American populations, the whites worried that general emancipation would jeopardize white supremacy and threaten insurrection, and even where the black population was small, whites worried that freed people might become public charges. Nowhere were whites willing to be taxed to pay compensation to owners for freeing their slaves.

The legal regulation of slavery had been reserved to the states by the Constitution of 1787, and most Americans seem to have assumed that the several states would eventually find ways to eliminate the institution without undue difficulty. Pennsylvania and the New England states, where slavery had never been economically important, had abolished it, either suddenly or gradually, during the Revolution. Thousands also gained their own freedom then, escaping to the British army and sailing to other parts of the empire. Some black men had joined the rebel armed forces too, but in the South they were seldom welcomed as recruits. The Continental Congress prohibited slavery in the Northwest Territory in 1787, so when Ohio was admitted to the Union in 1803 it came in as a free state. New York and New Jersey, having more slaves, had waited until 1799 and 1804 respectively to start their gradual emancipations. According to the census of 1810 they still had twenty-six thousand enslaved residents. New Jersey's process unfolded so slowly that the state contained a few hundred slaves as late as the 1840s. Isabella's little boy was far from the only person illegally sold out of state during these long transition periods; kidnappers as well as unscrupulous masters committed that crime.[77]

The same ideological impulses that prompted northern state emancipations had prompted in the South extensive voluntary manumissions by individual masters, especially in Delaware, Maryland, and Virginia. Reinforcing the appeal of liberty, it must be noted, was the depressed market for tobacco in the 1780s and '90s. Many planters in the Chesapeake region had not yet identified a profitable alternative and found themselves owning more slaves than they knew what to do with. ("I have more working Negros," complained George Washington, "than can be employed to any advantage in the farming system.") Those who manumitted significant

77. Arthur Zilversmit, *The First Emancipation: The Abolition of Slavery in the North* (Chicago, 1967); James Horton and Lois Horton, *In Hope of Liberty* (New York, 1997), 55–76; Joannne Melish, *Disowning Slavery: Gradual Emancipation in New England* (Ithaca, N.Y., 1998), 101–7.

numbers included Washington himself and one of the largest slaveholders in Virginia, Robert Carter III.[78]

By 1815, this first wave of state and individual acts of liberation had largely run its course. Some Chesapeake planters had learned how to put slaves to work growing wheat instead of tobacco. Others sold slaves westward, from the Tidewater to the Piedmont or Kentucky. Delaware undertook no state emancipation program, even though it contained a mere four thousand slaves, three-quarters of its black population being already free. Some Virginians got worried about the number of free blacks in the commonwealth and secured a law requiring any slaves liberated in the future to leave the state. Most disturbing, the shipment of slaves from the existing states into the Louisiana Purchase had been permitted despite a strong effort led by Connecticut senator James Hillhouse to legislate against it. As a result many thousands had been sent off in bondage to Louisiana, even before its admission as a state, to grow sugarcane there.[79] Nevertheless, the line between "free" and "slave" states was not yet sharply drawn in 1815. There were many freedpeople in Virginia, many still enslaved in New York. Hardly anyone would have predicted that no more states would undertake emancipation. For the time being, it seemed as if events could move in either a pro- or an antislavery direction, depending on political decisions.

Meanwhile, in the cities, owners often allowed slaves to "hire their own time" in return for a percentage of their earnings. After a number of years of this, bondsmen might save up enough to buy their freedom and that of their family members. By 1830, four-fifths of Baltimore's black inhabitants were legally free. In the other metropolis of the South, New Orleans, the free proportion was two-fifths. In all American cities, slavery declined. Urban life proved less congenial to slavery than rural largely because masters found it difficult to control every aspect of the slave's life in the city. Urban slaves were far more likely to make successful escapes. The shrewdest contemporaries came to regard the growth of cities as one of the factors undermining the persistence of slavery.[80]

78. Ira Berlin, *Many Thousands Gone: The First Two Centuries of Slavery in North America* (Cambridge, Mass., 1998), 262–85, quotation from 264. Washington manumitted 124 in his will; Carter manumitted 509. Gary Nash, *The Forgotten Fifth: African Americans in the Age of Revolution* (Cambridge, Mass., 2006), 66, 104–05.

79. Roger Kennedy, *Mr. Jefferson's Lost Cause* (New York, 2003), 210–16; Adam Rothman, *Slave Country* (Cambridge, Mass., 2005), 31–35.

80. T. Stephen Whitman, *The Price of Freedom: Slavery and Manumission in Baltimore* (Lexington, Ky., 1997), 1; John Ashworth, *Slavery, Capitalism, and Politics in the Antebellum Republic* (Cambridge, Eng., 1995), I, 101–8; Richard Wade, *Slavery in the Cities* (New York, 1964), 243–81.

The combination of state and individual liberations had given the United States a substantial population of free African Americans— approximately 200,000 by 1815. (Actually, more had been freed by individuals—generous masters, courageous escapees, or thrifty self-purchasers—than by state laws.) The large majority of "free Negroes" both North and South lived in cities, where they worked mostly in service occupations. Ironically, emancipated black workers sometimes found themselves excluded from skilled jobs that they had performed in slavery. In the ports, many went to sea: Twenty percent of the sailors in the U.S. merchant and whaling fleets were black.[81] (Herman Melville would celebrate the racial diversity of the ship's crew in *Moby-Dick.*) The urban African American communities provided their enslaved neighbors both an example of life in freedom and a haven where they might escape and find shelter. Generally excluded from Independence Day celebrations on July 4, the free black communities celebrated historical festivals of their own, observing the abolition of the slave trade, emancipation in New York, and (beginning in 1834) the abolition of slavery in the British West Indies. These communities provided the core audience for antislavery crusaders like Sojourner Truth and her co-workers of both races. Congregations like the African Methodist Episcopal Church, Zion, where Truth worshipped in New York City, became centers of black autonomy. Self-consciously respectable community leaders, often clergymen or businessmen, defended black rights to those outside and preached to those inside the virtues of literacy, hard work, and thrift—both for their own sake and to rebut white racial slurs.[82]

Sojourner Truth was a tall, strong woman, and the statistics that have survived show black Americans, like white Americans, taller on average than their Old World counterparts. They also had a high birthrate that produced a natural increase of 2 percent per annum, almost as high as that of the white population. (Young Isabella was the last of her parents' ten or twelve children.) Alone among New World slave societies, the enslaved population of the United States grew independent of importations from overseas. The rice and sugarcane areas of South Carolina and Louisiana, however, constituted exceptions. There severe working conditions and

81. Lois Horton, "From Class to Race in Early America," *JER* 19 (1999): 631.
82. See Leslie Harris, *In the Shadow of Slavery* (Chicago, 2003); Gary Nash, *Forging Freedom* (Cambridge, Mass., 1988); Elizabeth Bethel, *The Roots of African-American Identity* (New York, 1997); Patrick Rael, "The Market Revolution and Market Values in Antebellum Black Protest Thought," in Martin, *Cultural Change and the Market Revolution*, 13–45.

disease environments resembled those in the West Indies, and the slave population had to be replenished by purchases from elsewhere in the country.[83]

The key factor in explaining both the Atlantic slave trade and the perpetuation of slavery in the United States was profitability. In the South, when a yeoman farmer purchased his first slave it usually signaled a resolve to emphasize production for the market, that is, for profit as opposed to family subsistence. Had short-staple cotton not emerged in the years after 1815 as an extremely profitable employment for slave labor, finding a peaceful, acceptable resolution to the problem of emancipation might not have been so difficult. Economic historians, after prodigious research and argument, have come to general agreement that Americans who invested in slave property usually made a competitive return on their investment. A lively commerce in slaves, both local and interstate, sustained the economic efficiency and profitability of the slave system. During the period 1790 to 1860, some 3 million slaves changed ownership by sale, many of them several times. Almost all slaveowners bought or sold slaves at some point in their lives. Slave ownership was widely dispersed and yet concentrated: One southern white family in three owned at least one slave; one in eight owned at least twenty, and this one-eighth owned well over half of all the slaves. Many whites who did not own slaves expected to acquire them later in life, and in the meantime might rent their services on a short-term or long-term basis. Thus even nonslaveowners could feel a direct interest in slavery as a system. Prices of slaves eventually rose far above their 1815 levels, primarily because of the demand for slave labor in the cotton fields, bringing substantial capital gains to the owners of slaves and demonstrating broad confidence in the security of that form of investment. Slavery became so profitable, in fact, that it crowded out other forms of investment in the South. By 1850, data show southern planters disproportionately numerous among the wealthiest Americans.[84]

Slaves being human beings and not machines, and their masters more than "economic men," the two sometimes related to each other as fellow

83. Robert Fogel, *Without Consent or Contract* (New York, 1989), graphs on 124, 141; Michael Tadman, "The Demographic Cost of Sugar," *AHR* 105 (2000): 1534–75; William Dusinberre, *Slavery in the American Rice Swamps* (New York, 1996).

84. Steven Deyle, *Carry Me Back: The Domestic Slave Trade* (Oxford, 2005), 4–7; Stanley Engerman, "Slavery and Its Consequences for the South," in Engerman and Gallman, *Cambridge Economic History of the United States*, 219–66, esp. 343. For more data, see Fogel's *Without Consent or Contract* and its three accompanying volumes of substantiating analysis.

humans. Such relationships most frequently developed between masters and house servants, occasionally between masters and the elite of trusted, skilled supervisors and artisans. Aristotle, who of course lived amidst the practice of slavery, observed that although masters used their slaves as living tools, it was also possible to have between masters and slaves a limited degree of friendship.[85] Among slaveholding Americans, small children of both races played together. Masters took an interest in their slaves' personal lives and probably did not often realize how frequently their meddling was resented. Slaves took an interest in their masters' personal lives and probably knew more than they let on. Sometimes slaves pretended more affection for the occupants of "the big house" than they felt; sometimes the affection was sincerely reciprocal. Sojourner Truth fondly remembered her former master John Dumont for his "kindness of heart." But close personal relationships could be unpleasant as well as pleasant; Truth also recalled the abuse she secretly suffered from her mistress Sally Dumont with discreet shame and loathing.[86] And always the suspicion lurked that the master (or his teenage son) was taking sexual advantage of the women and girls whose bodies he owned. President Madison's sister commented in disgust that "a planter's wife is but the mistress of a seraglio."[87]

The African Americans had been Christians since the mid-eighteenth-century religious revival known as "the Great Awakening." Most states abolished the importation of African slaves well before the federal government's prohibition took effect in 1808, so African American culture had been evolving on its own for several generations by 1815. The religion of the slaves could underwrite either accommodation or resistance to white authority, but in either case it inspired spiritual strength. Within the Christian tradition as both masters and slaves understood it, they were equal in the sight of God. Many southern churches counted people of both races as members and referred to them in their records alike, as "Sister" or "Brother." Sometimes a common religion helped individuals bridge the gulf separating them. William Wells Brown, who escaped from slavery in 1834, acknowledged "the greatest respect" for the devout planter John Gaines. Many a master echoed the heartfelt wish of Rodah Horton

---

85. *Politics* 1255a–1255b, 1259b–1260b.
86. *Narrative of Sojourner Truth*, intro. William Kaufman (1850; Mineola, N.Y., 1997), 17, 12.
87. Quoted in George Dangerfield, *The Era of Good Feelings* (New York, 1952), 213. There is an excellent discussion of master-slave relations in Peter Kolchin, *American Slavery* (New York, 1993), 111–27.

when an aged slave died in 1836, that "she has gone to a better world I hope." Preachers frequently urged masters to deal justly and mercifully with their slaves (who might be listening to the sermon too). Counteracting whatever tendencies existed toward human relationships between slaves and masters, however, was a substantial body of advice on plantation management discouraging intimacy and fraternization as inimical to discipline and efficiency.[88]

The apologetic attitude toward slavery, common around 1815, soon began to be challenged by a new justification for slavery: planter paternalism. In colonial times, masters had candidly and unflinchingly admitted that they owned slaves for profit and that the institution rested upon force. The notion of paternalism provided a framework for discussing slavery different from both naked self-interest and the violation of natural rights. Slaveowners, in response to moral criticism, sought to explain their relationship to "their people" as one of caring for those who could not look after themselves. Negroes as a race, they insisted, were childlike. Demeaning and offensive as this "domestic" attitude toward slavery was, it at least acknowledged that the slaves were human beings and not beasts of burden. Viewed objectively, paternalism seems less an overall characterization of American slavery than a rationalization on the part of the masters. If there is a kernel of truth in the paternalist legend it may be this: While the average slaveowner was forty-three, the average age of slaves was under eighteen.[89]

Paternalism never extended to include overseers hired by the master. They always had a reputation for cruelty, partly because masters blamed them for whatever went wrong, mostly because of the conflicting expectations placed upon them: to bring in as large a crop as possible, but with as little harm as possible to their employer's valuable slave property. The reasonably good health of the enslaved population by standards of the day, evinced in their height and natural increase, can be attributed to a diet almost as nutritious as the one free farmers ate. Strong, healthy slaves reflected the conjunction of self-interest with paternalist responsibility on the master's part. No one explained this better than the distinguished Virginia planter who admonished his overseer not to overwork "a breeding woman" (his term) but to remember that her healthy baby was worth more money than her extra labor would represent—adding that "in this, as in all other cases, providence has made our interests & our duties coincide perfectly."[90]

Almost half of all slaves lived on plantations with at least thirty others in their situation. In some ways, these slaves were relatively lucky. They had more privacy than an isolated enslaved individual or family could expect as the property of a white small farmer. They enjoyed more opportunities for social life and the nourishment of their own distinctive culture, music, and folktales. They had a better chance to find a marriage partner on their own plantation and thus avoid the inconveniences of having a spouse miles away whom they could only see on weekends. Masters of large plantations often allowed each slave nuclear family a garden of their own behind their living quarters; these could consist of several acres. Such slaves managed to engage in small-scale composite farming, supplementing their allotted rations, trading produce with their neighbors, even earning cash to spend on little luxuries. All such privileges were held, of course, on sufferance of their owners. But in their aspirations for a modicum of personal security, dignity, and tangible reward for hard work, enslaved American families resembled other American families.[91]

Not that slaves felt satisfied with the rewards available to them in their bondage. Some labored diligently for years to buy their own freedom, even though their master could legally take their money and break his promise. Slaves resisted their bondage in countless small ways; they malingered, damaged property, ran away, and in general matched wits with whoever supervised them. The master class labored under no illusions of black contentment. Masters insisted on "pass laws" for slaves found wandering and on "slave patrols" to enforce the laws. (White men were obligated to take a turn on these patrols even if they did not themselves own slaves.) The fear of insurrection haunted the white South; sometimes it is hard for historians to tell real slave conspiracies from ones the whites imagined. This fear profoundly affected all debates over slavery. Although they owned slaves in order to profit, American masters would not even consider a general emancipation in return for financial compensation, such as slaveowners received in the British West Indies in 1833. Most

---

90. Thomas Jefferson to Joel Yancey, Jan. 17, 1819, *Thomas Jefferson's Farm Book*, ed. Edwin Betts (Princeton, 1953), 43.
91. Kenneth Stampp, *The Peculiar Institution* (New York, 1956), 38; Larry Hudson Jr., *To Have and to Hold: Slave Work and Family Life in Antebellum South Carolina* (Athens, Ga., 1997), 177–84.

southern whites, whether they owned slaves or not, feared emancipation would invite black rebellion.[92]

Although united in their support for white supremacy, white southerners varied a great deal in other ways. Yeoman farmers lived much like yeoman farmers in the North, even if the prosperous ones had a slave family sleeping on the floor of the kitchen building. Landless whites lived worse, driven to the margins of the southern economy, taking jobs too temporary to justify an investment in slave labor. Because they moved so frequently, they found it hard to get the credit on which most forms of economic improvement depended and might resort to hunting, fishing, or squatting on public land. Recognizing the plight of wage labor in the South, few free immigrants chose to settle there. The middle class of the scattered towns (the South contained few cities) prayed in similar churches, voted for the same national politicians, and belonged to most of the same voluntary associations as their northern counterparts.[93] The southern planter class, however, constituted a highly distinctive social group. Much of the romantic mythology surrounding them (even then) was fictional. Hardly ever descended from aristocratic European ancestors, the large slaveholders were modern, not medieval, in their sensibilities. Often parvenus, they operated at the very heart of the global market economy and ran their plantations with as much attention to efficient moneymaking as northern merchants showed for their ships and mills.[94]

As the historian Joyce Appleby has pointed out, the plantation owners were "the great consumers of the American economy," with their big houses, their lavish hospitality, their horse races, and hordes of domestic servants.[95] In their printed periodicals they read about attractive transatlantic concepts of "politeness" and good taste. The large planters, America's wealthiest class, were in a position to acquire what others could only sample carefully. In a nation of austerity and thrift, they opted for extravagance, honor, and refinement. Like their exemplar Thomas Jefferson, many American plantation owners lived well and died broke. Americans of the twenty-first century may look back upon them as our precursors in some ways, for like them we too spend even more than our relatively high

92. Stampp, *Peculiar Institution*, 86–140; John Ashworth, *Slavery, Capitalism, and Politics* (Cambridge, Eng., 1995), I, 1–8.

93. Charles Bolton, *Poor Whites of the Antebellum South* (Durham, N.C., 1994), 23–24; Jonathan Wells, *Origins of the Southern Middle Class* (Chapel Hill, 2004).

94. Besides Fogel, *Without Consent or Contract*, see Lawrence Shore, *Southern Capitalists* (Chapel Hill, 1986), 11–15; William Scarborough, *Masters of the Big House* (Baton Rouge, 2003).

95. Joyce Appleby, *Inheriting the Revolution* (Cambridge, Mass., 2000), 59.

average incomes and slide more and more into debt to outside creditors (in their case, northerners and Europeans).

Their strong sense of common interest enabled the slaveowning planters to become the most politically powerful social group in the United States. They dominated southern state governments. The Constitution's three-fifths rule (counting five of their slaves as three free persons) enhanced their representation in Congress and the electoral college. In 1815, they had held the presidency for twenty-two of the past twenty-six years, and they would control it for all but eight of the next thirty-four.[96]

V

Washington, D.C., presented a strange aspect in 1815. The ambitious design of the original city planner, Pierre L'Enfant, had been adopted but not implemented. The Capitol and the White House, monumental in design, looked incongruous in their muddy surroundings, their construction (with slave labor) set back years after the British army burned them in 1814. The community had no economic rationale save the government, but the government's presence in the city remained slight; as a result Washington grew slowly and haphazardly. For decades to come, every visitor would be struck by the discrepancy between its grand ambitions and their limited realization. As late as 1842, Charles Dickens called it a "City of Magnificent Intentions." Few government officials even lived the year round in Washington, its summers notoriously humid and unpleasant. During the months when Congress met in session (winter and spring), the members roomed together in boardinghouses, then fled back to their families, who had remained in their constituencies. The District of Columbia, like the United States as a whole, embodied big plans but remained mostly empty. America and its capital city lived for the future.[97]

In 1815, America was still more potential than realization. The Western world looked upon it as an example of what liberty could achieve for good or ill, but the experiment had not yet unfolded very far. The economy remained preindustrial, though its people's outlook was innovative and ambitious. By 1848, a great deal of development had occurred, often in ways no one would have predicted. Between 1815 and 1848, the United States achieved gigantic expansion from the Atlantic to the Pacific, both in the extension of its sovereignty and in the actual movement of people

96. For more on the slaveholders' political influence, see Robin Einhorn, *American Taxation, American Slavery* (Chicago, 2006).
97. John Mayfield, *The New Nation*, rev. ed. (New York, 1982), 3–5; James Young, *The Washington Community* (New York, 1966).

on the ground. The widespread participation of Americans in a global market economy had long since turned the Atlantic Ocean into a commercial highway; now, the innovations in transportation and communications would enable Americans to traverse and exploit the vast continent to their west as well. Their imperial ambitions brought them into conflict with the people already living athwart their path, Native Americans and Mexicans. Their ambitions also brought white Americans into disagreement with each other. What version of their society would be projected westward: an agricultural one, producing staples for export to the world, often by means of slave labor? Or the mixture of agriculture and commerce typified by the enterprise of Aaron and Fanny Fuller, producing for domestic consumers, some of them urban? Should America expand much as it already was, or should it be a reformed and improved America that rose to continental dominance and moral leadership?

In the years between 1815 and 1848, two rival political programs appeared, reflecting rival sets of hopes. Some Americans felt largely satisfied with their society the way it was, slavery and all, especially with the autonomy it provided to so many individual white men and their local communities. They wanted their familiar America extended across space. Other Americans, however, were beguiled by the prospect of improvement to pursue economic diversification and social reform, even at the risk of compromising some precious personal and local independence. They envisioned qualitative, not just quantitative, progress for America. In the long run, the choice was more than an economic decision; it was a moral one, as the tall, prophetic figure of Sojourner Truth, preaching the coming judgment like a latter-day John the Baptist, reminded her countrymen.

2

From the Jaws of Defeat

Mail coming from New Orleans to Washington, traveling across the Natchez Trace route, usually took about three weeks, but the harsh winter of 1814–15 made it slower. While Washington waited "in awful suspense,"[1] news of the great victory at New Orleans took a full four weeks by the fastest horsemen, arriving on Saturday, February 4. It provoked delirious rejoicing; all that night the District of Columbia blazed with candles and torches, as if to mimic in celebration the horror of the burning of the White House and Capitol by enemy invaders only five months earlier. Never has good news been more badly needed or more anxiously awaited. By act of Congress and presidential proclamation, January 12 had been a day of national prayer and fasting; though they did not know it, the people's prayers had already been answered.[2] On Monday, February 6, President James Madison issued another proclamation: This time, coming after a weekend of festivities, it was a full pardon for the pirates of Louisiana who had rallied to Jackson's call. (Alas, the pirates proved incorrigible, and within the year the president needed to order out the navy against them again.)[3]

To say that Jackson's victory came as an enormous relief to Madison would be an understatement. The previous six months had been probably the most harrowing that any president has ever been called upon to endure. In August the British had landed an expeditionary force in Chesapeake Bay and advanced upon Washington. Secretary of War John Armstrong had belittled the possibility of such an invasion and impeded preparations to defend against it. The president made it clear that he lacked confidence in the secretary and had curtailed his authority without actually replacing him. With the enemy nearing the capital by both

---

1. Washington *National Intelligencer*, Jan. 8, 1815. On communication between New Orleans and Washington, see Leonard Huber and Clarence Wagner, *The Great Mail: A Postal History of New Orleans* (State College, Pa., 1949).
2. "In the present time of public calamity and war," President Madison set aside the day as one "of public humiliation and fasting and of prayer to Almighty God for the safety and welfare of these States, His blessing on their arms, and a speedy restoration of peace." *Presidential Messages*, I, 558.
3. Ibid., 558–60; Irving Brant, *James Madison: Commander in Chief* (New York, 1961), 366.

land and water, American military intelligence was so inadequate, and staff work so nonexistent, that when a scouting party formed to ascertain the position of the redcoats, Secretary of State James Monroe saddled up and led it. For political reasons, the defense of the nation's capital had been entrusted to Brigadier General William H. Winder, an officer of demonstrated incompetence. Winder and Secretary Armstrong were jealous of each other and showed more concern with shifting blame for what was going wrong than with rectifying it.[4]

Even before the scouts located the enemy, the citizens of Washington began to pack up and flee the city, fearful not only of the British army but also of persistent rumors of slave insurrection. In fact, although the British in the Chesapeake campaign did not call upon the slaves to revolt, they did promise freedom for those who would rally to their cause (as they had also done during the Revolutionary War). About three hundred escaped slaves donned the uniform of Royal Marines and—with very little training—showed "extraordinary steadiness and good conduct" in combat against their former oppressors, the British commander reported. Many other escapees helped the British as spies, guides, and messengers. The fear of slave insurrection forced the Americans to divert large numbers of militiamen away from the battlefront into preserving domestic security.[5]

At Bladensburg, Maryland, on August 24, 1814, seven thousand Americans faced forty-five hundred British. With the tactical advantages of the defense as well as numbers, the Americans should have been able to repel the invaders. But the hastily assembled local militia were undisciplined and poorly positioned, and their units uncoordinated. When the British artillery opened up with Congreve rockets—a novel weapon more spectacular than lethal—some of the militia panicked. At this juncture, with battle scarcely joined, Winder ordered a general retreat. The panic spread, the retreat became a rout, and the road back to Washington was littered with unfired muskets thrown away by militiamen in a hurry. The verdict of history terms Bladensburg "the greatest disgrace ever dealt to American arms," and the defense—or rather, nondefense—of Washington "the most humiliating episode in American history."[6] Yet, as at New

4. Harry Ammon, *James Monroe* (New York, 1971), 330; J.C.A. Stagg, *Mr. Madison's War* (Princeton, 1983), 407–16.

5. Frank A. Casell, "Slaves of the Chesapeake Bay Area and the War of 1812," *Journal of Negro History* 57 (1972): 144–55; quotation from Sir George Cockburn on 151. See also John K. Mahon, *The War of 1812* (Gainesville, Fla., 1972), 312–15.

6. Quotations from James Sterling Young, *The Washington Community, 1800–1828* (New York, 1966), 184, and Robert Rutland, *The Presidency of James Madison* (Lawrence, Kans., 1990), 159.

Orleans, the American artillery performed well; its guns covered the flight of the militia. African Americans fought on both sides, and "a large part" of these cannoneers "were tall, strapping negroes, mixed with white sailors and marines."[7]

The crowd of fugitives included the president of the United States. On the field of combat the commander in chief had not even been able to control his horse, much less his army. Madison and his cabinet secretaries, after witnessing the first stages of the farcical "battle," galloped off in different directions and went into hiding, out of touch with each other, leaving the country leaderless. Congress was taking its accustomed summer vacation, its members out of town. In this political vacuum, responsibility for the evacuation of the executive mansion fell to the first lady. Unlike most of those around her, Dolley Madison kept her head and safeguarded some of the national treasures (including Gilbert Stuart's famous portrait of George Washington) in organizing her departure. But when Mrs. Madison sought refuge the next day at a Virginia farmhouse, the housewife cursed her because her husband had been called up for militia service, and threw the first lady and her entourage out. It was all too typical of the disrespect into which military humiliation had cast the country's leaders.[8]

The advancing British columns found their way to the public buildings of central Washington with such ease that contemporaries believed they must have been guided by traitorous informants. At the President's House (not yet called the White House), they found the main dining room set with food and wine for forty guests—a banquet had been scheduled for that evening. The laughing redcoats feasted themselves and drank a sarcastic toast to "Jemmy's health" before putting the torch to the building.[9] Besides the presidential mansion, the British burned the Capitol and the Departments of State, War, Navy, and Treasury. A rainstorm blew up during the night and quenched most of the flames, but not before millions of dollars' worth of damage had been done and thousands of volumes in the original Library of Congress destroyed. Damage was exacerbated by looting, committed not by the enemy but by locals, "knavish wretches about the town who profited from the general distress," a Washington newspaper reported. The burning of the public buildings did not represent the

7. Paul Jennings, "A Colored Man's Reminiscences of James Madison" (1865), *White House History* 1 (1983): 46–51, quotation from 47.
8. Ralph Ketcham, *James Madison* (New York, 1971), 577–78; Virginia Moore, *The Madisons* (New York, 1979), 321. The Madisons' conduct was satirized in a mock-heroic poem, *The Bladensburg Races* (Washington, 1816).
9. Washington *National Intelligencer*, Sept. 2, 1814; Ketcham, *Madison*, 579.

casual vandalism of drunken soldiers; the fires had been set on orders from Vice Admiral Sir Alexander Cochrane, overall British commander in the Chesapeake, who sent a message notifying President Madison that the action constituted a reprisal for earlier outrages committed by the Americans during their invasion of Canada. The most significant of these incidents had been the burning of the parliament house of Upper Canada when the Americans captured York (now Toronto) in April 1813.[10]

The municipal authorities of Georgetown and Alexandria rushed off messengers assuring the British they would capitulate without a fight; Alexandria's surrender was accepted, but the British actually had no intention of occupying Georgetown.[11] Instead the invaders moved on Baltimore. Only the successful defense put up at Fort McHenry on September 13, immortalized by Francis Scott Key in "The Star-Spangled Banner," kept that city from sharing the fate of Washington. The British then evacuated as quickly as they had come, taking with them some twenty-four hundred African American men, women, and children who had seized the opportunity to escape from slavery. In all but a few cases the British kept their promise of freedom to these people, most of whom wound up settling in Nova Scotia. For eleven years after the war the United States pursued Britain to obtain compensation for their former masters, and eventually collected.[12] Strategically, the purpose of the British raid on the Chesapeake had been to distract the Americans from efforts to conquer Canada; psychologically, to discredit the Madison administration. Both objectives were attained. No wonder an October visitor to Octagon House in Washington (at the corner of New York Avenue and Eighteenth Street), where the Madisons lived during the repair of the President's House, found the chief executive looking "miserably shattered and woe-begone."[13]

Madison's troubles were political as well as military, involving his own party, the Jeffersonian Republicans,[14] and his cabinet. Even in defeat,

10. Washington *National Intelligencer*, Aug. 31, 1814; Charles W. Humphries, "The Capture of York," in Morris Zaslow, ed., *The Defended Border: Upper Canada and the War of 1812* (Toronto, 1964), 251–70.

11. Walter Lord, *The Dawn's Early Light* (New York, 1972), 182–83, 197–201.

12. Robin Winks, *The Blacks in Canada* (New Haven, 1971), 114–27; Frank A. Updyke, *The Diplomacy of the War of 1812* (1915; Gloucester, Mass., 1965), 404.

13. William Wirt, quoted in Henry Adams, *History of the United States During the Administration of James Madison* (New York, 1890), VIII, 231.

14. The Republican Party of Jefferson was not the same as the Republican Party of Lincoln, which was founded in the 1850s and still exists today. The Republican Party of Jefferson eventually split, the "Old" Republicans becoming the Democratic Party of today and the "National" Republicans becoming the Whigs.

Secretary of War Armstrong represented a political faction Madison must treat with care, the prowar Republicans of New York. So the president graciously allowed Armstrong to resign instead of firing him; Armstrong repaid Madison's consideration with years of recriminations.[15] Madison transferred Armstrong's rival, James Monroe, to the War Department, creating a vacancy at the State Department that went unfilled, so Monroe handled both jobs until he worked himself to exhaustion. The Treasury and Navy Departments also needed new heads, but again it proved difficult to find appropriate candidates willing to perform such thankless tasks. The prestige of the federal government had sunk so low and the prospects for victory in the war become so doubtful that few politicians cared to identify themselves with the administration. State and local governments, frightened by the prospect of further British raids along the coast, were losing interest in overall war strategy and concentrating on their own defenses, even disregarding federal authority. In a way they had justification for doing so, for the successful defense of Baltimore had been mounted by the Maryland authorities, not by the federal ones.[16]

On September 19, 1814, Congress assembled, summoned into a special session by the president. It met in the only public building in Washington to have escaped destruction, the Post Office *cum* Patent Office. Even though surrounded by the charred evidence of their country's plight, the elected representatives of the people could not bring themselves to meet the urgent needs the president laid before them. He called for universal military conscription, and they responded by authorizing more short-term volunteers and state militia, specifying that the latter would not have to serve outside their own or an adjacent state without the consent of their own governors. Recent Treasury attempts to borrow having failed, the president asked for a new national bank to enable the government to raise money for the war and to restore the collapsed financial system of the country. After long debate the congressmen substituted a paper-money measure that Madison felt compelled to veto. They even quibbled over Thomas Jefferson's generous offer to sell his magnificent library to the federal government as a replacement for the lost Library of Congress. The legislators did conduct a congressional investigation into the fall of Washington and made more trouble for Madison by debating a proposal to move the nation's capital back to Philadelphia on the grounds that it would be more militarily defensible. (The change only narrowly lost in the House, 83 to 74.) In short, Congress put Madison's exemplary

---

15. See C. Edward Skeen, *John Armstrong, Jr.* (Syracuse, N.Y., 1981), 187–213.
16. Stagg, *Mr. Madison's War*, 424–28.

patience to a severe test. "How much distress in every branch of our affairs" resulted from lack of congressional cooperation, he complained to
a fellow ex-president.[17]

Nominally, Madison's Republican Party enjoyed a large majority in
Congress. In fact, little party discipline existed, and the Republicans had
been badly factionalized throughout the war. Once news arrived, in the
summer of 1812, that the British had repealed their Orders in Council restricting American commerce, congressional Republicans divided over
the wisdom of persisting in the war for the sake of resisting impressment
alone. Speaker of the House Langdon Cheves of South Carolina was no
friend of the administration; House Ways and Means Committee chairman John Wayles Eppes, son-in-law of Thomas Jefferson, proved a thorn
in Madison's side. Several of the legislative leaders to whom the president
might have looked for support were absent, in the armed forces or away
on crucial diplomatic missions, like Henry Clay, across the ocean trying
to negotiate a peace. Congressmen calling themselves "Old" Republicans remained such stubborn adherents of their little-government, low-
tax, state-rights philosophy that no national emergency could budge
them, though the president belonged to their own party. Even Madison's
friend and mentor Jefferson sided with his son-in-law and against the proposed second national bank; it was one of the few times Jefferson and
Madison did not cooperate with each other. The minority party, the Federalists, constituted the natural friends of national authority, but in the
present situation they behaved as the most obstructionist of all Madison's
opponents. Bitterly hostile to an administration that had ruined their
commerce and destroyed Alexander Hamilton's financial system, they
were not about to grant assistance to wage a war they deplored.[18]

After the debacle at Washington, Federalist opposition to the war escalated. Federalist Massachusetts and Connecticut withdrew their militia
from federal service. A Federalist-sponsored convention of New England
states met at Hartford, Connecticut, from December 15 to January 5, de-
liberating in secret what steps to take in response to the crisis. A week after its adjournment, the convention's report appeared on January 12—by
coincidence also the day of national prayer, fasting, and humiliation.
Speculation had been rife as to what the convention might decide: Secession and the negotiation of a separate peace with the British seemed

17. James Madison to John Adams, Dec. 17, 1814, quoted in Rutland, *Presidency of Madison*, 181.
18. See Stagg, *Mr. Madison's War*, 438–39; Rutland, *Presidency of Madison*, 173–75, 185;
Ammon, *James Monroe*, 338–41; Young, *Washington Community*, 185–86.

not at all unthinkable. But in fact, moderate Federalists led by Harrison Gray Otis dominated the Hartford Convention, and its outcome, when revealed, proved less threatening than the Republicans had feared. Protesting that the administration had neglected to protect New England while diverting military effort to unsuccessful invasions of Canada, the convention asked that states be allowed to assume responsibility for their own defense, receiving some federal revenues to help pay the cost. Otherwise the delegates simply repeated the standard complaints of Federalist New England and called for amendments to the Constitution to correct them. Their grievances included the constitutional provision allowing the slave states extra representation in Congress for three-fifths of the people they held as property. (Only because of this clause had Jefferson defeated John Adams in the election of 1800, driving the Federalists from power.) Other requested amendments would have required two-thirds congressional majorities to declare war, embargo commerce, or admit new states. Presidents would be limited to one term and could not come from the same state as their predecessor. Federal offices would be restricted to native-born citizens (New England having relatively few immigrants at the time). When he read the recommendations, Madison is said to have laughed aloud[19]—a reflex that might have expressed either his relief or his recognition of the political impossibility of such amendments. Although its Federalist sponsors have received much criticism, both in their own time and since, the resolutions of the Hartford Convention proved in the end less of a long-term danger to the federal Union than the Kentucky and Virginia Resolutions of 1798, which had championed state nullification of federal laws. Only one Hartford action posed even a potential threat: if the war continued until next June, the delegates resolved, a call should go out for another New England convention, presumably to seek more drastic remedies.[20]

Into this context of high anxiety in Washington, news of victory at New Orleans came like a deliverance from purgatory. To be sure, the repulse of the British invasion at Plattsburgh on Lake Champlain the previous September had been strategically more important, prompting the British to abandon their plan to annex part of New England to Canada. But New Orleans was a much bigger battle, and the great disparity in casualties made it especially gratifying. The British army defeated in the Gulf included units that had fought in the Chesapeake, so the events at Bladensburg

---

19. Brant, *Commander in Chief*, 361.
20. Theodore Dwight, *History of the Hartford Convention* (New York, 1833), 352–79; William Edward Buckley, *The Hartford Convention* (New Haven, 1934).

and Washington seemed properly avenged. The success of Jackson's citizen army over professional soldiers seemed to vindicate those who had argued that the militia constituted the most cost-effective means of defense. The victory could therefore be welcomed wholeheartedly, not only by the Republican nationalists, who had wanted the war, but also by the "Old" Republicans, who had not wanted any innovations in the direction of bigger government. Finally, while the uncharismatic Madison had never captured the public imagination as a wartime leader, Jackson perfectly personified a popular war hero.

The curious aftermath of the New Orleans campaign, however, dampened the administration's pleasure in the country's new hero. Infatuated with his own sense of power, General Jackson kept the city of New Orleans under martial law until March 13, long after the first news of peace arrived. During this period his arbitrary rule lost him much of the universal popularity his victory had won him among the local population. On February 21, six militiamen who had tried to leave before their term of service expired were executed in Mobile by his orders, a draconian action at a time when everybody but Jackson considered the war over. When the federal district judge in New Orleans challenged Jackson's dictatorship, the general put him in jail! After the eventual restoration of civil law, Judge Dominick Hall hailed Jackson into federal court and fined him a thousand dollars for contempt. Jackson's admirers chipped in to pay the fine, but the general declined their money and paid it himself. Both the peremptory behavior of the strong-willed Jackson and the way he polarized people by it were premonitory of things to come. (Twenty-nine years later, a Democratic Congress would refund Jackson, by then an ex-president, the fine plus interest.)[21]

II

Not until Monday evening, February 13, did Washington learn that a treaty of peace had been signed by representatives of Great Britain and the United States at Ghent, Belgium (then the Austrian Netherlands), on Christmas Eve of 1814. Because of storms in the Atlantic, this news had taken even longer in crossing the ocean than that from New Orleans had in coming through the forests and rivers of the continent. The delay in receiving the news from Europe had psychological significance. Upon

21. Remini, *Jackson*, I, 308–15; Patrick Kastor, *The Nation's Crucible: The Louisiana Purchase and the Creation of America* (New Haven, 2004), 174–78. For the later repercussions of this episode, see Joseph G. Tregle Jr., "Andrew Jackson and the Continuing Battle of New Orleans," *JER* 1 (1981): 373–93.

first hearing, it seemed to the American public as if Jackson had won a decisive victory, and even when people later learned that the war had ended two weeks before his battle, its effect on their attitude remained.

In the public mind, Andrew Jackson had won the war; the incompetence, confusion, cowardice, and humiliations of the fall of Washington were forgotten. The President's Mansion received a hasty coat of white paint over its stone exterior to hide the black smoke marks, though the interior took years to restore; from this cover dates the new name "White House."[22] The paint job symbolized the country's attitude perfectly. Americans reinterpreted the War of 1812 as a second war for independence, a vindication of their national identity rather than a revelation of its precariousness. "Seldom has a nation so successfully practiced self-induced amnesia!" the historian Bradford Perkins has commented.[23] In the euphoria of nationalism that the messengers from the Hartford Convention found upon arrival in Washington, they did not even dare to present their demands. Later, when the Capitol was rebuilt, Madison enjoyed the satisfaction of commissioning two huge paintings by John Trumbull depicting British defeats in an earlier war to decorate the walls of the rotunda.[24]

Viewing the war with hindsight after the Battle of New Orleans, Americans felt that they had won the respect of Europe in general and Britain in particular. Of much more importance, they had gained self-respect. "The war has renewed and reinstated the national feelings and characters which the Revolution had given," declared Albert Gallatin, informal leader of the American negotiating team at Ghent. "The people . . . are more American; they feel and act more as a nation." For their part, the Canadians too came to regard the war as a defining moment in their national history, and with even more justification. The successful repulse of the U.S. invasions fostered among the inhabitants of Upper Canada a sense of their own identity as a proud people, separate from the Americans.[25]

Like the prince regent, President Madison had no hesitation in accepting the Treaty of Ghent. On February 15, he submitted it to the Senate, which unanimously consented to ratification the following day. When

22. Ammon, *James Monroe*, 396.
23. Bradford Perkins, *The Creation of a Republican Empire, 1776–1865* (Cambridge, Eng., 1993), 146.
24. The paintings are *The Surrender of General Burgoyne at Saratoga* and *The Surrender of Lord Cornwallis at Yorktown*.
25. Gallatin quoted in Rutland, *Presidency of Madison*, 188; J.M.S. Careless, "Introduction" to Zaslow, ed., *The Defended Border*, 6.

news of the British ratification reached Washington on February 17, the president declared the war officially over. But naval engagements on the high seas continued as late as June 30, when the last hostile shots were fired in Sunda Strait near Java.[26]

The terms of the treaty provided for an end to the fighting and little else. "Nothing in substance but an indefinite suspension of hostilities was agreed to," commented one of the American negotiators.[27] The two sides referred some minor boundary disputes to commissions of arbitration. The British conceded nothing on either of the issues for which the United States had gone to war: restrictions on American trade and impressment of American seamen. Indeed, the treaty did not so much as mention these issues. It did require prisoners of war to be returned; among these were over two thousand Americans impressed into the Royal Navy before the war who had refused to fight against their own country. Unconscionable delays in repatriating American POWs occurred simply because the two governments disagreed about who should pay the cost of their transportation. At Dartmoor prison in England, over six thousand frustrated American sailors (eleven hundred of them black) still awaited release months after the treaty. In April 1815, they rioted. The guards fired, killing six and wounding sixty.[28]

Why, one may wonder, did Americans receive the terms of the Treaty of Ghent with such thankfulness? In the first place, people measure events in terms of their expectations. The Madison administration had long since become reconciled to making peace without obtaining recognition of the rights for which war had been declared. As far back as June 1814, the president and his cabinet had instructed their negotiators not to insist on these demands, deciding, in effect, to settle for less than victory in return for peace.[29] The terms of Ghent therefore represented about as much as the American side could have expected after this decision had been reached. That the British had not insisted on any boundary concessions—particularly in the portion of Maine they occupied, where many people had already taken the oath to George III on the supposition that British rule would be permanent[30]—came as good news for the United States and disappointed the Canadian public.

26. See H. Adams, *History*, IX, 73.
27. John Quincy Adams, quoted in William Earl Weeks, *Building the Continental Empire* (Chicago, 1996), 29.
28. Donald Hickey, *The War of 1812* (Urbana, Ill., 1989), 176, 306; James Horton and Lois Horton, *In Hope of Liberty* (New York, 1997), 184–85.
29. Madison and Monroe reaffirmed the instruction in October; Ketcham, *Madison*, 590. See also Stagg, *Mr. Madison's War*, 392–95; Hickey, *War of 1812*, 289.
30. See Hickey, *War of 1812*, 194–95.

The peace also rendered most of the federal government's political problems moot. With no war to fight, the need for conscription vanished, and placing the financial system on a more secure footing could safely wait for the next Congress. The prospects of secession by New England, constitutional crisis, or the breakup of the Republican Party all receded. The administration could safely reject advice to create a coalition government by reaching out to the Federalists with offers of patronage; the opposition could now be isolated and crushed.[31]

Finally, regardless of the terms of the treaty, the public overwhelmingly welcomed peace itself. Indeed, the government would probably have accepted a less favorable treaty, in the interests of restoring peace. Maritime New England had of course wanted peace all along; by now the staple-producing agricultural regions as well were hurting badly from the British blockade and desperately needed peace to market their crops abroad. In fact, the peace came just in the nick of time. If the war and its economic hardships had dragged on much longer, the federal government, the Constitution, and the Republican Party might not have survived intact. With peace, they all did. And with peace the economy rebounded suddenly. The price of imports plummeted and that of export staples rose. Treasury bonds gained 13 percent overnight on the news of peace. What though the terms of the treaty were not all that Americans would have desired? Congressman William Lowndes of South Carolina went to the heart of the matter when he observed to his wife that "the time of making" the peace was "more fortunate" than the treaty itself.[32]

As things turned out, avoiding mention of the issues of the war in the treaty of peace proved convenient. With the end of the Napoleonic Wars, the occasion for British interference in American trade and impressment of American seamen came to an end. This, however, could not have been foreseen at the time. Indeed, Napoleon's return to France from Elba on March 1, 1815, might well have inaugurated another protracted period of European warfare instead of only a short one. With perfect justice, therefore, some thoughtful observers warned that the new peace between the United States and Britain might prove only temporary. Both sides took some precautions against future wars. Throughout the next generation, the British strengthened the fortifications of Quebec.[33]

31. Stagg, *Mr. Madison's War*, 432.
32. Updyke, *Diplomacy of the War of 1812*, 368–69; William Lowndes to Elizabeth Lowndes, Feb. 17, 1815, quoted in Stagg, *Mr. Madison's War*, 500.
33. See C. P. Stacey, "The Myth of the Unguarded Frontier, 1815–1871," *AHR* 56 (1950): 2–12; Kenneth Bourne, *Britain and the Balance of Power in North America, 1815–1908* (London, 1967), 33–52.

Considered as a conflict between Great Britain and the United States, the War of 1812 was a draw. For the Native Americans, however, it constituted a decisive defeat with lasting consequences. For centuries the tribes had been able to retain much autonomy—economic, political, and military—by playing off the British, French, Spanish, and Americans against each other. After 1815, nowhere east of the Mississippi could this strategy remain viable.[34] The call of the Shawnee brothers, Tecumseh and Tenskwatawa ("the Prophet"), for united Native resistance against the encroaching white settlers had been sufficiently successful to bring on widespread frontier race war beginning in 1811, but not successful enough to forge durable pan-tribal cooperation. Tecumseh carried the message of militancy and traditionalism to the Southwest as well as the Northwest, and in both areas it often divided tribes internally. In 1812 Tecumseh and his followers sided with the British as representing the lesser white evil, but several tribes, notably the Cherokee in the South, allied with the United States. Others remained divided or neutral. The defeat and death of Tecumseh at the Battle of the Thames on October 5, 1813, and the slaughter of the traditionalist Red Stick Creeks at Horseshoe Bend on March 27, 1814, marked the end of the serious military power of the American Indians in the Northwest and Southwest respectively.[35]

From the point of view of U.S. expansionism, Andrew Jackson really had been a major architect of victory in the War of 1812, though it was not his triumph at New Orleans but those in the Creek War that possessed strategic significance. In the Southwest, waging the War of 1812 represented part of a larger struggle by the United States to secure white supremacy over a multiracial and multicultural society that included Native Americans, African American maroons, French and Spanish Creoles, and intermixtures of all these peoples with each other and white Americans. Along the Gulf Coast, as in the Chesapeake, the British took advantage of racial divisions; they armed, uniformed, and trained about a thousand African Americans and some three thousand Indians for service with their forces.[36] But the British did not mount a significant effort of their own in

---

34. On the Northwest, see Richard White, *The Middle Ground: Indians, Empires, and Republics in the Great Lakes Region, 1650–1815* (Cambridge, Eng., 1991); on the Southwest, see L. Leitch Wright Jr., *Creeks and Seminoles: The Destruction and Regeneration of the Muscolunge People* (Lincoln, Neb., 1986).

35. The Red Sticks got the name from their red war clubs. See John Sugden, *Tecumseh's Last Stand* (Norman, Okla., 1985); George F. G. Stanley, "The Indians in the War of 1812," *Canadian Historical Review* 31 (1950): 145–65.

36. Wright, *Creeks and Seminoles*, 182. See also Frank Owsley Jr., *The Struggle for the Gulf Borderlands* (Gainesville, Fla., 1981).

the region soon enough to prevent Jackson from crushing the Creek insurgency before he had to turn to defend New Orleans. On August 9, 1814, he imposed the Treaty of Fort Jackson upon the Creeks, forcing the tribe to cede over 22 million acres in Alabama and Georgia, more than half their territory. Among the lands thus seized, much belonged to Creeks who had been friendly to Jackson, for the conflict had begun as a civil war among Creeks. Some of it was not Creek land at all but belonged to Jackson's allies the Cherokees. The eminent nineteenth-century historian John Bach McMaster called the Treaty of Fort Jackson a "gross and shameless" wrong, and the twenty-first century has no reason to alter that judgment.[37]

None of the Indian tribes was party to the Treaty of Ghent. Originally, the British negotiators had called for the creation of a completely independent Native American buffer state in the Great Lakes region, but they backed away from this demand when their U.S. counterparts made clear its unacceptability. By Article Nine of the treaty as agreed, the signatories undertook to make peace with the Indians on the same basis as their settlement with each other, the *status quo ante bellum*. The United States promised to restore to the Native Americans the "possessions, rights, and privileges, which they may have enjoyed or been entitled to in 1811, previous to such hostilities."[38] This might seem to invalidate the Treaty of Fort Jackson, and so the Creeks hoped. In the months immediately following the peace, British agents in Spanish Florida promised refugee Creeks that Britain would make sure they recovered the lands lost at Fort Jackson. At first, the U.S. government itself accepted this interpretation of the requirements of the Ghent agreement. In June 1815, the Madison administration ordered Andrew Jackson to begin to return to the Creeks the lands taken from them by his treaty. But Jackson raged and refused to obey, and the government felt loath to enforce its edict upon a popular hero supported by white public opinion in the Southwest. Would the British make an issue of it? Lord Bathurst, the secretary of state for war, argued that they should, but he could not persuade his cabinet colleagues.[39]

After the Treaty of Ghent, the British left their former allies to the not-so-tender mercies of the United States. A series of U.S. treaties with the northwest tribes in 1814–15, beginning with the Second Treaty of Greenville,

37. John Bach McMaster, *History of the People of the United States, from the Revolution to the Civil War* (New York, 1895), IV, 171.

38. Treaty of Ghent as printed in *Niles' Weekly Register*, Feb. 18, 1815, 397–400.

39. Remini, *Jackson*, I, 302–5; Wright, *Creeks and Seminoles*, 190; Weeks, *Building the Continental Empire*, 40.

forced the Indians to declare themselves allies of the United States. Having complied with the letter of the Treaty of Ghent in the first round of treaties, the U.S. government then felt free to resume the negotiation of cessions of tribal lands in the Northwest, which recommenced in 1816 with the Potawatomi of Illinois. Over the next few years the fur-trading activities that the British had maintained on the American side of the Great Lakes were at last closed down, restricting the economic leverage of the Native Americans. Tenskwatawa, the once formidable prophet of a religious revitalization movement, eked out an obscure existence in Canadian exile.[40]

Tribes like the Cherokees who had allied with the United States during the War of 1812 found little gratitude afterwards. In the Southwest, Andrew Jackson, returning to his primary interest in gaining lands for white occupancy, extorted a fraudulent treaty with unauthorized Cherokees in September 1816, purporting to confirm the loss of the area he had taken from their tribe by the Treaty of Fort Jackson. Not willing to defy his popularity with southwestern voters, the Senate ratified it.[41] By a series of such treaties in the years immediately after 1814, Jackson obtained vast lands for white settlement. A historian has estimated his acquisitions at three-quarters of Alabama and Florida, one-third of Tennessee, one-fifth of Georgia and Mississippi, and smaller portions of Kentucky and North Carolina.[42]

In the racial warfare around the Gulf, the Treaty of Ghent did not bring peace. In July 1816, amphibious expeditions of U.S. soldiers, sailors, and their Indian allies converged against the most powerful of North American maroon communities, the Negro Fort on the Apalachicola River in Spanish East Florida. During their naval bombardment, a red-hot shot hit the fort's powder magazine, destroying the fort and taking more than 270 lives in a gigantic explosion. The leaders of the maroons were captured, tortured, and killed; about sixty surviving followers were rounded up and taken to Alabama and Georgia for sale into slavery (in violation of the federal law of 1807 prohibiting the importation of slaves

40. Francis Paul Prucha, *Sword of the Republic: The United States Army on the Frontier* (New York, 1969), 119–28; Willard Karl Klunder, *Lewis Cass and the Politics of Moderation* (Kent, Ohio, 1996), 20, 32–33; R. David Edmunds, *The Shawnee Prophet* (Lincoln, Neb., 1983), 143–64.

41. William G. McLoughlin, *Cherokee Renascence in the New Republic* (Princeton, 1986), 198–201, 210–11.

42. Michael Rogin, *Fathers and Children: Andrew Jackson and the Subjugation of the American Indian* (New York, 1975), 165. The texts of the treaties are in *American State Papers: Indian Affairs* (Washington, 1834), II, 1–150.

across international boundaries). The victors treated the weapons and property of the maroon colony as booty and confiscated them.[43] This was not the first time that Spanish sovereignty in Florida had been disregarded by the United States, and it would not be the last.

One other epilogue to the War of 1812 remained to be written: the punishment of Algiers. The dey of Algiers had sided with Britain and made war on United States commerce—a foolish decision since, because of the British blockade, there were few American ships then in the Mediterranean for the Algerians to seize. The advent of peace with Britain would bring a resumption of American exports to the Mediterranean and necessitated an immediate resolution of the problem with Algiers. Accordingly, President Madison wasted no time in calling upon Congress on February 23, 1815, to declare war against Algiers and authorize an expedition against that power. Flush with confidence and with a greatly expanded navy now at its disposal, Congress for once promptly complied with the president's request.

Nominally tributary to the Ottoman Empire, Algiers was for all practical purposes independent, and Congress voted its declaration of war against the dey alone, not against the sultan. Like the other states of the Barbary Coast, Algiers had for centuries demanded and received tribute from nations wishing to trade in the Mediterranean. In default of tribute, the Barbary powers preyed upon a country's shipping, capturing vessels, confiscating their cargoes, and either selling the crew as slaves or holding them as prisoners for ransom. Although often called "pirates," the Barbary states were actually hostile governments and their predatory actions a form of warfare, not private crime. Smaller trading nations (such as the United States) suffered more than the great powers, since they found it harder to come up with the necessary protection money. Under the Jefferson administration, the United States had already been involved in several naval campaigns against the Barbary rulers; this time the country was better prepared to exert substantial force. If the Treaty of Ghent had achieved no assurances for American commerce, a war with Algiers might accomplish something more positive.

In May 1815, a ten-ship squadron set sail from New York for the Mediterranean, with an even stronger one to follow. The two squadrons were commanded respectively by Commodore Stephen Decatur and Commodore William Bainbridge, both of whom had had extensive

43. Wright, *Creeks and Seminoles*, 198–99; Joshua Giddings, *The Exiles of Florida* (Columbus, Ohio, 1858), 40–45; David Heidler and Jeanne Heidler, *Old Hickory's War: Andrew Jackson and the Quest for Empire* (Mechanicsburg, Pa., 1996), 62–75.

experience in Jefferson's wars on the Barbary Coast. Decatur's last ship, the frigate *President*, had been captured by the British in January 1815 while trying to run the Royal Navy's blockade off the coast of Long Island.[44] His new assignment offered Decatur the chance to redeem his reputation, and he rose to the occasion. Off Cape de Gata, Spain, on June 17, Decatur caught up with the Algerian corsair Raïs Hamidou, who was killed in the ensuing engagement. Hamidou's battered flagship *Meshouda* surrendered to Decatur's flagship *Guerriere*. After taking another Algerian warship, Decatur entered the harbor of Algiers on June 29 and dictated peace terms. The tribute the United States had been paying Algiers before 1812 would cease but American ships would enjoy full trading privileges anyway; Algiers would return confiscated American property, release the ten Americans currently held captive, and pay them each a thousand dollars in compensation (modest enough for their sufferings).[45] In return Decatur promised to give their captured ships back to the Algerians. The combination of strong force and reasonable demands proved effective: The dey signed. In the follow-up squadron, Commodore Bainbridge, who had spent nineteen months as a prisoner during the earlier Barbary Wars, enjoyed the satisfaction of reminding Algiers, Tunis, and Tripoli, all three, of American might. The other two Barbary governments followed the example of Algiers and renounced their claims to tribute from the United States. But the luckless Americans who had been released from Algerian captivity tragically died on the way home when the ship carrying them sank in a storm.[46]

The following year, the dey tried to renege on the new agreement. But with the Western powers no longer at war with each other, the days when the Barbary rulers could prey upon Mediterranean commerce were numbered. The weakness of Algiers having been revealed by the Americans, an Anglo–Dutch fleet bombarded the city in August 1816, destroying its fortifications and compelling the dey to release all eleven hundred Western captives and renounce permanently the enslavement of Christians. After this

---

44. See H. Adams, *History*, IX, 63–70.
45. Less than $100,000 per victim in today's money. For this and other monetary equivalents, I rely on John J. McCusker, *How Much Is That in Real Money?* (Worcester, Mass., 1992).
46. See Frederick Leiner, *The End of Barbary Terror* (Oxford, 2006); Robert J. Allison, *The Crescent Obscured: The United States and the Muslim World, 1776–1815* (New York, 1995), 209–11; John B. Wolf, *The Barbary Coast: Algiers Under the Turks* (New York, 1979), 149–50, 330–32; Glenn Tucker, *Dawn like Thunder: The Barbary Wars and the Birth of the U.S. Navy* (New York, 1963), 447–65.

episode the dey was in no position to repudiate his treaty with the United States. Thus closed the era of the Barbary Wars. Not until the late twentieth century would the United States again make war against a Muslim ruler.[47]

Commodore Decatur received a hero's welcome home. In Norfolk, Virginia, at one of the many banquets in his honor, he proposed a toast that became famous: "Our country! In her intercourse with foreign nations may she always be in the right; but our country, right or wrong."[48] In the prevailing mood of postwar nationalism, this accurately summed up the feelings of most Americans.

III

James Madison is revered today by political scientists and legal scholars as "the Father of the Constitution," but unlike such other Founders as Washington, Franklin, and Jefferson, there is no popular cult of Madison today and few public monuments to his memory. It was the same even in his lifetime. Madison owed his presidency to the confidence of Jefferson and the other leaders of the Virginia Republican Party rather than to popularity with a mass following. By temperament, Madison was an intellectual rather than an executive. In the Constitutional Convention and the debate over ratification that followed, he had been in his element and earned his place in history. The papers he wrote (along with Alexander Hamilton and John Jay) on behalf of the new national Constitution are rightly judged masterpieces of political argumentation and analysis. Afterwards Madison had drafted the Bill of Rights and led the opposition to his erstwhile collaborator Hamilton in the House of Representatives. He had made Jefferson a loyal secretary of state. But as a wartime president, James Madison did not display dynamic leadership. Andrew Jackson acknowledged Madison "a great civilian," but declared "the mind of a philosopher could not dwell on blood and carnage with any composure," and judged his talents "not fitted for a stormy sea."[49]

Those who met the president often remarked on his small size; Washington Irving called him "a withered little Apple-John."[50] True, Madison's

47. James Madison, "Eighth Annual Message to Congress" (1816), *Messages and Papers of the Presidents*, I, 575; Ray Irwin, *The Diplomatic Relations of the United States with the Barbary Powers* (New York, 1970), 176–86. During the First World War, the United States did not declare war on the Ottoman Empire.
48. Quoted in *Dictionary of American Biography*, ed. Allen Johnson and Dumas Malone (New York, 1931), III, 189.
49. Andrew Jackson to James Monroe, Jan. 6, 1817, *Papers of Andrew Jackson*, ed. Harold Moser et al. (Nashville, Tenn., 1994), IV, 82.
50. Gaillard Hunt, *The Life of James Madison* (New York, 1902), 299–300.

height barely reached five feet six, two inches below the average for those days, but observers were also noticing that the president lacked a commanding presence. Fortunately, the vivacious and strong-willed Dolley Payne Todd Madison supplied some of the social skills her husband needed; she exerted more influence in the administration than any other antebellum first lady save Abigail Adams.[51] The president, patient and fair to a fault, listened to advice and then found it hard to make up his mind. He had allowed himself to be dragged reluctantly into war with Great Britain. In waging it, he showed himself a poor judge of men. No one in politics feared him, and he had never been able to control Congress. He was too nice.

But if James Madison was not a strong chief executive, he remained a conscientious and public-spirited statesman. And in the relief and rejoicing over peace, the president enjoyed a sudden, unaccustomed popularity. His first State of the Union message after the conclusion of peace gave Madison his best chance to leave a lasting mark as president, and he recognized the opportunity. Madison determined to draw the appropriate lessons from the nation's narrow escape from disaster. Accordingly, his Seventh Annual Message to Congress, dated December 5, 1815, sought to turn the war-generated nationalism to constructive purpose. The message laid out a comprehensive legislative program that showed his presidency in its best light. In subsequent years, its elements became known as the "Madisonian Platform."[52]

Following the example of Jefferson rather than that of Washington, Madison sent his annual messages in writing and did not deliver them in person. For the president to open the session of Congress with an address in person seemed to Republicans, if not to Federalists, altogether too reminiscent of the monarch's speech from the throne at the opening of Parliament. Not until Woodrow Wilson did an American president recur to Washington's practice and deliver his State of the Union address in person.

Madison began by pointing with pride to the victory over Algiers, the reestablishment of commercial relations with Great Britain, and the pacification of the Indian tribes. Despite the inevitable reductions in the army, he warned, it was important to retain the general staff, reform the

51. See Catherine Allgor, *A Perfect Union: Dolley Madison and the Creation of the American Nation* (New York, 2006).
52. Almost thirty years later, the Madisonian Platform was still endorsed: John Pendleton Kennedy, *Defence of the Whigs, by a Member of the Twenty-Seventh Congress* (New York, 1844), 12–24.

militia, and provide a system of military pensions that would "inspire a martial zeal for the public service." Coastal defenses and naval ships under construction should be completed, not abandoned. Although peace had restored the government's revenues and credit, Madison remained convinced that a national bank should be reconstituted. Such a bank would not only market government securities and provide credit for an expanding economy but provide a uniform national currency, the lack of which, the president noted, produced "embarrassments." Support for a national bank, originally the brainchild of Jefferson's adversary Alexander Hamilton, represented a major change of policy for the Republican Party. Nevertheless, in three weeks time, Madison's secretary of the Treasury would lay before Congress a detailed plan for a second Bank of the United States.[53]

Madison presented the rest of his domestic program as flowing naturally from his concern with a strong defense posture. The tariff not only provided revenue, he reminded Congress; it could also protect against foreign competition those industries "necessary for the public defense." Such a protective tariff, by making the United States independent of foreign markets or suppliers, would help avoid commercial troubles like those that had led to war in 1812. Where did this leave the principle of *laissez-faire*? "However wise the theory may be which leaves to the sagacity and interest of individuals the application of their industry and resources, there are in this as in other cases exceptions to the general rule." Common sense should mitigate the application of any theory.

The most ambitious part of Madison's address was his plea for "establishing throughout our country the roads and canals which can best be executed under the national authority." The obvious benefits of improved transportation were economic and military; but, he bravely added, there would also be "political" benefits: "binding together the various parts of our extended confederacy." The strict construction of the Constitution, to which Madison's party stood pledged, need not stand in the way of progress. "Any defect of constitutional authority which may be encountered can be supplied" by amendment. Madison was playing upon the patriotic and optimistic postwar mood he sensed in the public. What better way to manifest this self-confidence than through a coherent program of national economic development?

53. *Presidential Messages*, I, 562–69. Madison's Seventh Annual Message to Congress has also been conveniently reprinted in Marvin Meyers, ed., *The Mind of the Founder: Sources of the Political Thought of James Madison* (Hanover, N.H., 1981), 279–306.

In the American legislative process, the president proposes, but Congress disposes. Then, as now, one-third of the senators and all the members of the House of Representatives were newly chosen for each biennial Congress. Elections for the Fourteenth Congress had been held at various times throughout the fall and winter of 1814–15, for there was no nationally standardized date; then, in accordance with the ponderous operation of the Constitution prior to the Twentieth Amendment, the members waited until the first Monday in December 1815 to hold their first session.[54] The Fourteenth Congress reflected choices the electorate had made during some of the darkest days of the war, and its members accordingly inclined toward strong government. They also comprised one of the most talented Congresses in history. The energetic, popular, and visionary Henry Clay of Kentucky returned to the Speakership. The chairman of the House Committee on National Currency was a brilliant and patriotic young South Carolinian named John C. Calhoun. Clay and Calhoun worked closely together; they ate in the same boardinghouse, and in that era when congressmen seldom brought their families to Washington, this relationship counted for a lot.[55] Other capable nationalists included John Forsyth of Georgia, Henry St. George Tucker of Virginia, and Calhoun's fellow South Carolinian William Lowndes. Daniel Webster led the small Federalist minority. Much reduced in numbers and influence, the Old Republican state-righters were typified in the Senate by Nathaniel Macon of North Carolina and in the House by the eccentric John Randolph of Roanoke County, Virginia. As usual in the period, the House displayed more leadership than the Senate, whose members were chosen by state legislatures rather than by direct popular election.[56]

Madison's nationalist program put the Federalists in an embarrassing position; they could not offer consistent opposition to it.[57] The most telling criticisms of it came from the Old Republicans, sometimes called "quids" because of their self-styled role as a *tertium quid* (third element or third force), alongside Federalists and administration Republicans. These Old Republicans claimed to defend their party's original principles against corrupt innovation; they looked upon the nationalism of the

---

54. The Twentieth Amendment (ratified in 1933) moved the date for sessions of Congress forward by eleven months, so that they begin in January rather than December.
55. Young, *Washington Community*, 98–106.
56. George Dangerfield, *The Awakening of American Nationalism* (New York, 1965), 8–9; Norman K. Risjord, *The Old Republicans* (New York, 1965), 163–64; Rutland, *Presidency of Madison*, 194–95.
57. For example, House Federalists split 25 for, 23 against the tariff bill; 15 for, 38 against the Second Bank.

Madison administration with profound suspicion. The quid leader, John Randolph, once a devoted Jeffersonian, then an opponent of the war, had become the harsh critic of an administration he felt had betrayed its principles. Heir of an aristocratic Virginia family, Randolph cut a self-consciously picturesque figure, attending the House with his riding crop in hand, accompanied by his hunting dogs and slave valet. (Appropriately, he named his Virginia plantation Bizarre.) His frail body and high-pitched voice provoked suspicion of sexual impotence.[58] Politically, however, Randolph was far from impotent; his sharp mind and sharper tongue made him a power to be reckoned with. Randolph possessed a gift for apt phrases (he had invented the term "war hawk"), and his gibes at the Republican new nationalism hurt. The Madisonian program encouraged financial speculation and would be "fatal to Republican virtue," he warned.[59]

Randolph spoke for a venerable tradition that grounded republicanism in the honest industry of those practicing agriculture and opposed it to the rapaciousness and luxury of courtier capitalism.[60] Madison's program would cost money, and ever since the 1790s the Republican Party had opposed both taxation and government debt. But Randolph was wrong to see in Madison's program simply a craven betrayal of principle. In fact, aspects of it were legitimately Republican and different from the Federalist program Alexander Hamilton had advocated in the 1790s. Hamilton had presumed the national debt to be permanent, a means to enlist the support of the creditor class behind the federal government. For Madison the debt constituted a temporary means to financing projects for national defense and economic infrastructure. Hamilton's program had been based on a tariff for revenue and American acquiescence in British maritime supremacy. Madison's program was based on a tariff to protect domestic manufacturing, and came in the aftermath of a war demonstrating American unwillingness to submit to dictation by British commercial and naval interests.[61]

Jefferson himself had come around to the new, Madisonian version of Republicanism, at least with regard to the protective tariff. Early in 1816,

---

58. Confirmed by postmortem medical examination; see Michael O'Brien, *Conjectures of Order* (Chapel Hill, 2004), II, 669.

59. John Randolph, Feb. 29, 1816, *Annals of Congress*, 14th Cong., 1st sess., 1111.

60. See Lance Banning, *The Jeffersonian Persuasion* (Ithaca, N.Y., 1978); Robert Dawidoff, *The Education of John Randolph* (New York, 1979), 145–63.

61. On the difference between Hamilton and the Madisonian Republicans, see John Nelson, *Liberty and Property: Political Economy and Policymaking in the New Nation* (Baltimore, 1987); Andrew Shankman, "A New Thing on Earth," *JER* 23 (2003): 323–52.

he declared that circumstances had changed in the thirty years since he had expressed the hope that America might remain forever an agrarian arcadia. "We must now place the manufacturer by the side of the agriculturalist," he declared.[62] And when it came to promoting the development of transportation—"internal improvements," in the language of the day—Republican nationalists went beyond anything Hamilton had envisioned. Where his outlook had been Atlanticist, theirs was continentalist. Internal improvements commended themselves to agrarians wanting to market their crops. Madisonians could invoke precedents for federal aid to internal improvements in the actions of Jefferson and his Treasury secretary Albert Gallatin.[63] John Randolph expressed his bitterness against what he considered Jefferson's apostasy from Old Republican virtue when he called Jefferson "St. Thomas of *Cantingbury*." Alluding to the shrine of St. Thomas Becket at Canterbury, Randolph added sarcastically that "Becket himself never had more pilgrims at his shrine than the Saint of Monticello."[64]

Responding to the Madisonian Platform and its own leadership, the Fourteenth Congress achieved one of the most creditable legislative records in American history. Members appropriated most of what the president recommended for the defense establishment. The landmark tariff they enacted on April 27, 1816, was candidly protectionist in its features. Only articles that could not be produced in the United States were placed on the free list. Those (few) articles that could be produced in the United States in sufficient quantity to satisfy the national market enjoyed the absolute protection of prohibitively high duties. Those that could be produced domestically, but not in sufficient quantity to satisfy demand, were subjected to a modest tariff thought sufficient to allow domestic producers to survive, generally about 25 percent. The protection came none too soon, for with the return of peace British manufacturers had already begun to dump products in the American market below cost, hoping to drive the American producers out of business. Optimistically, the rate-setters decided that after three years the country's infant industries ought to need less protection and no rates should be higher than 20 percent. This decision set the stage for future tariff debates.[65]

62. Letter to Benjamin Austin, Jan. 9, 1816, *TJ: Writings*, 1371.
63. For a provocative interpretation of Gallatin's program, see Steven Watts, *The Republic Reborn* (Baltimore, 1987), 224–39.
64. Quoted in William Cabell Bruce, *John Randolph of Roanoke* (New York, 1922), II, 283.
65. Brant, *Commander in Chief*, 403; John Mayfield, *The New Nation, 1800–1845*, rev. ed. (New York, 1982), 79; Frank Taussig, *The Tariff History of the United States* (New York, 1910), 18–19.

The most eloquent speech on behalf of the tariff came from John C. Calhoun on April 4. Calhoun argued for the encouragement of manufacturing on the grounds that a diversified economy would make the nation more self-sufficient, less dependent on foreign markets, and less vulnerable in time of war. Economic diversification would produce economic interdependence and "powerfully cement" the Union together. In opposition, John Randolph pointed out that a protective tariff was in effect a tax on consumers. "On whom do your impost duties bear?" he demanded. The burden of these taxes on "the necessaries of life" would fall on two classes: "on poor men, and on slaveholders."[66] Randolph had, as usual, cut to the heart of the matter. On this occasion his rhetoric was in vain, and the tariff passed the House, 88 to 54; but Randolph played the part of Cassandra to the new nationalists. Many times in the future, the political alliance of poor men with slaveholders would frustrate the hopes of tariff protectionists.

The same month, Congress passed an act authorizing a Second Bank of the United States, the result of cooperation between Secretary of the Treasury Alexander Dallas and Calhoun, who chaired the relevant House committee. It chartered the Bank for twenty years, with a capital of $35 million, of which $7 million would be provided by the federal government; in return the administration would get to choose five of the twenty-five members of the board of directors. (By comparison, Hamilton's Bank had had a capitalization of only $10 million.) The congressional delegations of the South and West supported the proposed bank even more strongly than those from the Northeast, partly because it was a Republican Party measure, partly because their agricultural constituents looked to the new bank for credit.[67] Scarcely any discussion addressed whether a national bank was constitutional, the issue that had so bitterly divided Hamilton and Jefferson a generation earlier. Madison had indicated in his message that he considered the constitutional question to have been settled by the precedent of the First Bank, and almost everyone in Congress accepted this resolution of the matter. "I seem to be the only person," complained the aging quid Nathaniel Macon, "that still cannot find the authority for a bank in the constitution of the U.S."[68] Madison, after

---

66. Calhoun, *Annals of Congress*, 14th Cong., 1st sess., 1329–36; Randolph, Jan. 31, 1816, ibid., 842; Dangerfield, *Awakening of Nationalism*, 15–16.

67. "If the votes of the two houses be combined, New England and the four middle states gave 44 votes for the Bank and 53 against it; and the southern and western states gave 58 for it and 30 against." Bray Hammond, *Banks and Politics in America from the Revolution to the Civil War* (Princeton, 1957), 240.

68. Nathaniel Macon to Joseph Nicholson, March 3, 1816, quoted in Risjord, *Old Republicans*, 167.

signing the Second Bank's charter on April 10, 1816, happily appointed five Republicans as the government's directors.

Congress also made a start on addressing the country's transportation needs, appropriating $100,000 to build a segment of the National Road through Wheeling, Virginia (now West Virginia). The road represented an ambitious plan, crossing the Appalachian barrier, intended to link Baltimore in the Chesapeake with St. Louis near the confluence of the Mississippi and the Missouri. It was a favorite project with Republican nationalists like Speaker Henry Clay. Madison raised no constitutional objection and signed the bill.[69] The extension of the National Road accommodated the westward movement of white settlement prompted by the defeat of Tecumseh's confederation. In Indiana Territory these settlers had multiplied from 24,520 in 1810 to 63,897 in 1815, according to a specially commissioned census, leading to pressure for Indiana statehood. Accordingly, on April 19, 1816, Madison signed an act enabling Indiana to draw up a state constitution.

Unfortunately the productive Fourteenth Congress ruined itself with the electorate by overreaching. More than two-thirds of its members were defeated for reelection or decided not to run again. The so-called salary-grab bill triggered this massive popular repudiation. Congress had voted itself a pay raise, from six dollars a day while in session to fifteen hundred dollars a year. By no means unreasonable, the new annual salary was less than twenty-eight federal civil servants earned. The president received a munificent salary of twenty-five thousand dollars, out of which he had to pay for running the White House. (Multiply these numbers by 100 for something like present-day equivalents.)[70] Given the nationalist agenda, it made perfect sense to strengthen the national legislature by making service in it more attractive to talent.[71] The electorate, however, would have none of it: Their wrath fell on Federalist and Republican alike. All told, of the eighty-one members who voted for the bill, only fifteen won reelection. Even some who voted against it were punished with defeat, on the grounds that they should not have accepted the money.[72] It was a sad end for one of the most talented of American Congresses and helped perpetuate a pattern of low pay, high turnover, and all too common congressional ineffectiveness.

---

69. See Karl Raitz, ed., *The National Road* (Baltimore, 1996).

70. See McCusker, *How Much Is That in Real Money?*

71. As Calhoun argued. *Annals of Congress*, 14th Cong., 1st sess., 1183–84.

72. C. Edward Sheen, "The Compensation Act of 1816 and the Rise of Popular Politics," *JER* 6 (Fall 1986): 253–74.

What made the Compensation Act such a political liability was the fact that the Fourteenth Congress applied the new salary to itself, rather than only to its successors. A generation earlier, while in the House of Representatives, Madison had proposed an amendment to the Constitution stating, "No law, varying the compensation for the services of the Senators and Representatives, shall take effect, until after an election of Representatives shall have intervened." The amendment had been approved by the First Congress along with the Bill of Rights but not ratified by the states. The prohibition that the state legislatures had neglected, the electorate enforced with a vengeance. The conflict of interest involved in Congress setting its own salary has remained a touchy matter; in 1992, more than two hundred years after its submission, Madison's limitation on the right of Congress to vote itself a raise was finally ratified by a sufficient number of states. What had been intended as the Second Amendment to the Constitution became the Twenty-seventh.

But before it went out of existence, the Fourteenth Congress held one more session, in the winter of 1816–17. This strange practice of bringing the former Congress back after its successor had been elected, allowing legislators who had been repudiated at the polls a final chance to make history, became known as the "lame duck" session. It reflected the slow transportation and communication in the young republic, its rationale being that a month might not be long enough to sort out election returns and for the newly elected members to travel to Washington. The lame duck session long outlived this justification, for it persisted until the adoption of the Twentieth Amendment in 1933.

These particular lame ducks repealed the salary increase for their successors but not for themselves, then resumed work on their nationalist agenda. The Bank of the United States was scheduled to pay $1.5 million to the federal government as a "bonus" in return for its charter. Clay and Calhoun proposed that this bonus, together with the regular dividends the BUS would pay to the government as a stockholder, be earmarked for roads and canals. On behalf of the Bonus Bill, Calhoun waxed eloquent. "We are under the most imperious obligations to counteract every tendency to disunion," he declared. "Let us, then, bind the republic together with a perfect system of roads and canals. Let us conquer space."[73] The conquest of space beckoned to the American spirit in Madison's day no less than in John F. Kennedy's race to the moon.

Marked regional differences in attitude toward the Bonus Bill appeared. New England and much of the South opposed it, feeling that

73. *Annals of Congress*, 14th Cong., 2nd sess., 854.

they had little to gain from encouraging the development of the West and the out-migration of their own people. By contrast the Middle Atlantic states were eager, expecting commercial benefits from a transportation system linking the Hudson and Delaware Rivers with the Ohio and the Great Lakes. In order to maximize support for the Bonus Bill, Clay and Calhoun did not specify which projects would get aid, leaving as many congressmen as possible hopeful. Even with all their legislative skillfulness, the Bonus Bill passed but narrowly, 86 to 84 in the House and 20 to 15 in the Senate. Then it went to the president for signature.

On March 3, 1817, his last day in office, Madison vetoed the Bonus Bill on the grounds that it was unconstitutional. Neither the interstate commerce clause of the Constitution nor the "general welfare" clause, Madison declared, could be stretched enough to authorize federal spending on roads and canals. Clay and Calhoun felt dumbfounded. "No circumstance, not even an earthquake that should have swallowed up one half of this city, could have excited more surprise," commented Clay. As recently as last December 3, the president had urged Congress to create "a comprehensive system of roads and canals, such as will have the effect of drawing more closely together every part of our country."[74] What was the problem? In the first place, Madison wanted an amendment to the Constitution to authorize federal aid to internal improvements; Jefferson had originally called for such an amendment back in 1805. Only thus could the two presidents reconcile their desire for better transportation with a strict construction of the Constitution. Having abandoned his earlier constitutional objections to a national bank, Madison could not bring himself to do the same with internal improvements. In the second place, Madison felt deeply suspicious of the kind of fund the Bonus Bill would create. A pool of money available for whatever roads and canals each Congress wanted would be an invitation to corruption and logrolling. Madison preferred an integrated national plan for internal improvements, such as the $20 million program Secretary of the Treasury Gallatin had drawn up back in 1808.[75]

Intellectually respectable as Madison's conception was, it was politically impractical. The amendment for internal improvements found opponents not only among state-righters but also among broad constructionists who did not want to establish the precedent of having to amend the Constitution

---

74. *Presidential Messages*, I, 561, 569–70; *Annals of Congress*, 15th Cong., 1st sess., 1371.
75. See John Lauritz Larson, "'Bind the Republic Together': The National Union and the Struggle for a System of Internal Improvements," *JAH* 74 (1987): 363–87; Drew McCoy, *The Last of the Fathers* (Cambridge, Eng., 1989), 92–103.

every time someone called a federal power into question. As the congressional salary amendment abundantly demonstrated, amending the Constitution is a protracted and imponderable process. If the advocates of internal improvements threw their weight behind such an amendment and it failed, they would be worse off than before. As for another Gallatin Plan, this ran up against all the local prejudices that have made Americans perennially suspicious of comprehensive national plans in general. The chance of such a program being approved in the first place, and then faithfully carried out over many years, was nil.

In the light of hindsight, Madison's veto of the Bonus Bill seems a mistake. Faced with a choice between theoretical consistency and practical politics, Madison chose theory. By rejecting the "good" because it was not the "best," Madison not only slowed the economic development of the country but, uncharacteristically, missed an opportunity to cement the Union together.[76] With the chance to set the United States firmly on the course of development missed, the country would grope its way toward undefined possible futures.

IV

In those days before national party conventions had been invented, presidential candidates were nominated in Congress. On March 16, 1816, the caucus of Republican members of both houses, meeting together, nominated Secretary of State James Monroe of Virginia over Secretary of War William H. Crawford of Georgia by 65 votes to 54, with 22 absentees. Daniel Tompkins, the governor of New York, received the vice-presidential nomination. Madison, who had been grooming Monroe to be his successor, felt gratified and relieved. Crawford's candidacy showed surprising strength, considering how inhibited he had been about opposing his senior cabinet colleague. Its appeal reflected discontent at the perpetuation of the "Virginia dynasty" of presidents.[77]

A dull presidential campaign ensued, its outcome a foregone conclusion. Senator Rufus King of New York served as standard-bearer of the Federalists' forlorn hope. Like congressional elections, the balloting for president occurred across the calendar, with states choosing their members of the electoral college on different days and by different methods—in ten states by popular vote, in nine by the state legislature. The strength that the Federalists had shown in the middle states during the war years

---

76. See John Lauritz Larson, *Internal Improvement* (Chapel Hill, 2001), 63–69.
77. Lynn W. Turner, "Elections of 1816 and 1820," in *History of American Presidential Elections*, ed. Arthur Schlesinger Jr. et al., (New York, 1985), I, 299–311.

melted away. The congressional and presidential elections occurred with virtually no interaction between them; the Federalist Party did not turn popular dissatisfaction with the "salary-grab bill" to its advantage. And so, while the electorate drastically purged Madison's Congress, his chosen presidential successor won handily in the electoral college, 183 to 34, with King carrying only Massachusetts, Connecticut, and Delaware. The Federalists had not even bothered to nominate a running mate for King, so their electors scattered their vice-presidential votes among several candidates.

Monroe's easy victory reflected the spirit of national self-satisfaction and self-congratulation following the War of 1812, from which the incumbent Republican Party benefited. While the Federalists' quasi-war with France in the 1790s had divided their party between Hamiltonians and Adamsites, the Republicans' War of 1812, once it was over, actually strengthened their party's grip on power. Though Madison's administration could be faulted for incompetence, no one could accuse it, as the Federalists had been accused, of militarism and authoritarianism.[78] The Republican way of waging war on a shoestring, if militarily risky, had been politically safe. The Federalists had taxed; the Republicans had borrowed. The Federalists had recourse to repressive legislation (the Alien and Sedition Acts); the Republicans did not—partly because mobs like that in Baltimore in 1813 did their dirty work for them.[79] However valid Federalist complaints that the War of 1812 had been unnecessary and mismanaged, they were politically futile. The antiwar Federalists found themselves stigmatized as disloyal; the Hartford Convention now looked almost treasonable and became a huge political liability. No one offered an effective rebuttal to Commodore Decatur's toast.

78. See Roger H. Brown, "Who Bungled the War of 1812?" *Reviews in American History* 19 (1992): 183–87.
79. Antiwar Federalists suffered repeated violence. In Baltimore a mob destroyed a press, killed two people, and badly injured several others, including the elderly Revolutionary hero "Light-Horse Harry" Lee, who never recovered from his beating (see Hickey, *War of 1812*, 52–71).

3

An Era of Good and Bad Feelings

Monday, March 4, 1817, was unseasonably warm and sunny in Washington—a stroke of good fortune for the eight thousand spectators who had come to witness the inauguration of the new president. The House and Senate had wrangled over plans for the event, and with the public buildings still not yet fully repaired from their burning two and a half years before, indoor options were limited. So it had been decided to hold the ceremony in the open air on the steps of the Capitol.[1] The site became a tradition, although since inauguration day has been moved back to January 20 the chances of good weather are even less.

James Monroe was the third of the Virginia dynasty of Jefferson, Madison, and Monroe, and the last president to have won fame in the Revolution. He had crossed the Delaware with Washington and been wounded leading a charge against the Hessians at the Battle of Trenton. What's more, he *looked* like a Revolutionary veteran. At a time when male fashions had changed to long trousers, the fifty-eight-year-old Monroe still wore the "small clothes" of the eighteenth century: knee breeches and buckled shoes, with powdered wig and three-cornered hat.[2] (Of course, it was a helpful image to cultivate.) Like all the early presidents, Monroe had served a long political apprenticeship. He had pursued an independent course and in earlier years had often been identified with state rights. Monroe had opposed the ratification of the Constitution and had run against Madison (and lost) for the House of Representatives in the First Congress. In 1808 the quids put him up against Madison again as their candidate for president. But in March 1811, Monroe and Madison achieved a momentous reconciliation and Madison named him secretary of state. From then on Monroe became Madison's right-hand man, and after Armstrong's resignation headed the War Department as well as the State Department. He emerged from the war a convert to nationalism and Madison's chosen successor.

1. Harry Ammon, *James Monroe: The Quest for National Identity* (New York, 1971), 367–68.
2. Lynn W. Turner, "Elections of 1816 and 1820," in *History of American Presidential Elections*, ed. Arthur Schlesinger Jr. et al. (New York, 1985), I, 311.

Monroe's reputation has suffered somewhat by the inevitable comparisons with Jefferson and Madison.[3] Unlike them, he was no intellectual, but he was a hard worker with a thorough understanding of the personalities and political conventions of his age. He had friends and contacts throughout all factions of the Republican Party. He brought to the White House a reputation for strict integrity: "Turn his soul wrong side outwards, and there is not a speck on it," declared Jefferson.[4] At a time that called for conciliation, Monroe conciliated well. In international affairs he possessed a firm grasp of U.S. national interest. In domestic affairs he knew how to wrap innovation in the mantle of respectable tradition. Behind the scenes, he was a more skillful practical politician than many people then or since have realized. Despite Jefferson's confidence in the purity of his soul, Monroe appreciated the value of discretion over candor.

The president's inaugural address emphasized continuity with his Jeffersonian predecessors and the new Republican nationalism, including protection for domestic manufacturing. He endorsed "the improvement of our country by roads and canals" but added "proceeding always with a constitutional sanction"—which seemed to second Madison's Bonus Bill veto message of the day before. National self-congratulation provided the theme of his inaugural. Some of this was legitimate: Monroe gave thanks for peace, prosperity, and abundant natural resources. But in his enthusiasm for American institutions, the incoming president got carried away. "And if we look to the condition of individuals what a proud spectacle does it exhibit! On whom has oppression fallen in any quarter of our Union? Who has been deprived of any right of person or property?"[5] Monroe took it for granted that the answer to these rhetorical questions was negative. If someone had responded by pointing to 1.5 million persons held in chattel slavery, or to white women firmly deprived of rights of person and property, or to expropriated Native Americans, the president would have been startled, then irritated by the irrelevancy. To him and most of those in his audience, such people did not count. But within the next generation, that assumption would be seriously challenged.

Monroe's inaugural address celebrated the people of the United States as "one great family with a common interest." "Discord does not belong to our system." While they may strike us as empty platitudes, these

---

3. Contrasting estimates of his abilities are presented in Noble Cunningham Jr., *The Presidency of James Monroe* (Lawrence, Kans., 1996), and George Dangerfield, *The Era of Good Feelings* (New York, 1952).

4. Thomas Jefferson to James Madison, January 30, 1787, *TJ: Writings*, 886.

5. *Presidential Messages*, II, 4–10, quotations from 5 and 8.

phrases actually embodied a key policy objective of the new administration. Monroe's one-sided electoral victory led friend and foe alike to feel that the Federalists no longer provided a realistic alternative government. Party strife therefore seemed a thing of the past. "The existence of parties is not necessary to free government," the president believed.[6] Monroe wanted to be a president of all the people, to govern by consensus. Accordingly, he set out on a triumphal national tour. He even included far-off New England on his itinerary, something no Virginia president had done since Washington's trip in 1789. Monroe saw all the sights; on the Fourth of July he climbed Bunker Hill. The New Englanders were grateful for this gesture of reconciliation and hoped to be included in the favors of patronage. A Boston Federalist newspaper welcomed the president's visit as evidence of a new "era of good feelings."[7] The administration was happy with the expression, and the name stuck.

The concept of an era of good feelings that would transcend party conflict expressed some of the highest political ideals of the age. It was in keeping with the conventional wisdom of political philosophy, which viewed political parties as an evil. The political philosophers of classical times, including the Greek Aristotle and the Roman Polybius, taught that institutions of balanced government could prevent the rise of political parties and the decline of republicanism that partisanship heralded. Early-modern political theorists like Bolingbroke and the authors of Cato's Letters and The Federalist Papers likewise relied upon balanced institutions of government rather than a balance between two or more political parties to preserve liberty. The framers of the American Constitution, far from favoring parties, had hoped to prevent their emergence.[8] Although political parties had nevertheless developed in the young republic as a result of the bitter policy debates of the 1790s, no one approved of them in principle. In his Farewell Address, Washington had warned his countrymen to beware "the baneful effects of the spirit of party." Monroe felt he enjoyed an unparalleled opportunity to achieve the widely shared aspiration of eliminating parties. Through a quest for political unanimity, the original intention of the Founders could be

6. Ibid., 10; Ammon, *James Monroe*, 371.
7. Boston *Columbian Centinel* [sic], July 12, 1817.
8. There are many books on this subject, including Richard Hofstadter, *The Idea of a Party System* (Berkeley, 1969); Gordon Wood, *The Creation of the American Republic* (Chapel Hill, 1969); and Paul Rahe, *Republics Ancient and Modern* (Chapel Hill, 1992). *Cato's Letters*, published anonymously in England in 1720–23 by John Trenchard and Thomas Gordon, were much admired in America for their political philosophy.

restored. The elimination of party divisions was a goal shared by all of the first six presidents, but most especially sought by James Monroe.[9] Despite all such good intentions, however, much partisanship and bad feeling persisted.

As a practical matter, to bestow patronage on Federalists would anger many Republicans, especially of the older generation, and Monroe was not quite ready for this. When General Jackson, among others, urged him to appoint to his cabinet a Federalist who had supported the recent war, Monroe demurred. What emerged in the new administration was therefore not so much nonpartisanship as one-party rule by a broadly based party.[10]

The closest Monroe came to a concession to the Federalists was to choose as his secretary of state John Quincy Adams, a New Englander and a former Federalist who had left that party back in 1807. This appointment strengthened the Republican Party in the Northeast, but it meant disappointing Henry Clay of Kentucky, who had hoped for the job. The State Department was perceived as a stepping-stone to the presidency, and some politicians already felt that William H. Crawford (his 1816 Republican challenger) should be Monroe's successor. Monroe gave Crawford the Treasury Department. The War Department went to another rising light, John C. Calhoun. Calhoun's ally John McLean of Ohio became postmaster general, a key position though not yet officially one of cabinet rank. It was a strong set of appointees, who made their mark on their respective departments. All save Crawford identified with the nationalist wing of the Republican Party, and all, including Crawford, aspired to the presidency. Throughout his incumbency, Monroe had to be careful to balance the rival ambitions of his cabinet secretaries in order to keep his administration from fragmenting. His triumphant reelection in 1820, winning every electoral vote but one, demonstrates Monroe's measure of political skill.[11]

The administration sought not to absorb the Federalists but to render them irrelevant. At the national level this policy largely succeeded during Monroe's first term. Supporters of a stronger central government, whether

9. Washington, *Messages and Papers of the Presidents*, I, 205–16; Ralph Ketcham, *Presidents Above Party* (Chapel Hill, 1984), esp. 124–30.
10. Andrew Jackson to James Monroe, Nov. 12, 1816, and James Monroe to Andrew Jackson, Dec. 14, 1816, *Correspondence of AJ*, II, 263–65, 266–70. Harry Ammon, "James Monroe and the Era of Good Feelings," *Virginia Magazine* 66 (1958): 387–98.
11. For a sophisticated analysis of Monroe's statecraft, see Stephen Skowronek, *The Politics Presidents Make* (Cambridge, Mass., 1993), 86–109.

for internal improvements, banking, or the tariff, had no longer any need to embrace Federalist politicians. Meanwhile, the defeat and exile of Napoleon in Europe removed the fear of Revolutionary France, which had been an important wellspring of Federalist feeling throughout the country. What sealed the doom of the Federalists was their failure to develop a nationwide coherence, a failure for which their last nominal standard-bearer, Rufus King, must bear a good deal of the responsibility. The Federalists in Congress found it difficult to agree even on individual issues, much less on a program differentiating them from the administration. At the state level the party declined more slowly and continued to make its influence felt even in defeat. In several states serious issues pitted Federalists against Republicans after 1816—including the disestablishment of the Congregational Church in Connecticut and New Hampshire, and state constitutional conventions in Massachusetts and New York—but the Federalists wound up on the losing side of most of these battles. Only in little Delaware did the Federalist Party remain dominant. Such leverage as the Federalists might have exerted at the national level they dissipated by dividing their support among the various Republican presidential aspirants, including Calhoun, Crawford, Clay, Adams, and General Jackson.[12] The Federalists, who had identified themselves so strongly as the friends of national government, proved incapable of reorganizing as an effective national opposition to government. The demise of the Federalist Party had a significant ideological effect, extinguishing in America the tradition of statist conservatism that has been so strong in Europe.[13]

Monroe expected and wanted one-party rule to evolve over time into true nonpartisanship. What actually happened was something different. Since virtually all ambitious politicians joined the Republican Party, the party ceased to have coherence. As these politicians jockeyed for influence and advancement, the internal divisions that had plagued the party during and before the War of 1812 reappeared. Sectional differences superimposed upon these divisions made for an even more complex grid of rivalries. Monroe's Era of Good Feelings proved transitory, and during his second term it led not to nonpartisanship but to factionalism.

12. Shaw Livermore, *The Twilight of Federalism* (Princeton, 1962); James H. Broussard, *The Southern Federalists* (Baton Rouge, 1978), 183–95.
13. This ideological tradition was weakening even among younger Federalists; see David Hackett Fischer, *The Revolution of American Conservatism* (New York, 1965).

II

Monroe made use of his solid base of domestic support to achieve substantial results in foreign policy. Some of these achievements addressed business left unfinished by the indeterminate conclusion to the war with Great Britain. The first one was the agreement of April 1817 signed by Richard Rush for the United States and Charles Bagot for Britain. It provided gradual naval disarmament on the Great Lakes, forestalling a costly arms race between the still mutually suspicious powers. Rush–Bagot was one of the earliest arms limitation agreements and proved remarkably durable. Although the Lincoln administration threatened to abrogate it in retaliation for British help to the Confederacy, it persisted until World War II, when Canada and the United States agreed that the Great Lakes could be used for naval construction and training—no longer, of course, directed against each other.[14] Rush–Bagot did not deal with land defenses, and the U.S.–Canadian boundary on land was not demilitarized until 1871. (The Americans spent three years building a fort at the northern end of Lake Champlain only to discover in 1818 that it stood on the Canadian side of the boundary; it had to be evacuated.)[15]

The Anglo-American Convention signed in London on October 20, 1818, dealt with a variety of subjects. From early colonial days to recent times, fishing rights in the North Atlantic have been a recurrent source of contention between Newfoundland and New England fishermen competing for cod and other marine resources. The Convention of 1818 redefined the rights Yankee fishermen enjoyed along the coasts of Newfoundland and Labrador, though it did not restore all the privileges they had been granted in 1783.[16] The negotiators also fixed the boundary between Canada and the Louisiana Purchase at the 49th parallel, which was considerably more to the advantage of the United States than the natural boundary, the area drained by the Missouri River system, would have been. In another article of the convention, Britain and the United States temporarily resolved their dispute over the Oregon Country by agreeing to treat it as a condominium or jointly occupied territory for the next ten

14. James Morton Callahan, *American Foreign Policy in Canadian Relations* (New York, 1937), 90–102; Arthur L. Burt, *The United States, Great Britain, and British North America* (New York, 1961), 388–95; Stanley L. Falk, "Disarmament on the Great Lakes," *Proceedings of the United States Naval Institute* 87 (1961): 69–73.

15. Reginald Stuart, *United States Expansionism and British North America, 1775–1871* (Chapel Hill, 1988), 91; Kenneth Bourne, *Britain and the Balance of Power in North America, 1815–1908* (Berkeley, 1967), 3–33.

16. See Mark Kurlansky, *Cod* (New York, 1997), 101.

years. (In making their agreement the two countries conveniently ignored the claims of Russia and Spain to the same area.) The claim of the United States to Oregon arose out of the voyage of the *Columbia* in 1792 and the Lewis and Clark expedition of 1804–6. It had been weakened during the War of 1812, when the fur-trading post of Astoria had been sold to the North West Company of Montreal by John Jacob Astor, who feared that otherwise it would be captured by the British and no compensation paid. Finally, the issue of British payment for persons rescued from American slavery during the War of 1812 was referred to arbitration. All in all, the convention constituted a remarkably favorable agreement from the U.S. point of view, and the Senate gave unqualified consent to ratification.[17] It signaled the beginning of a new era of accommodation in Anglo-American relations.

Relations with Spain turned out to be much more problematic than those with Britain. After the Louisiana Purchase of 1803, East and West Florida still belonged to the Spanish Empire, cutting off the United States from access to the Gulf of Mexico east of New Orleans. The Pearl, Perdido, and Apalachicola Rivers of Mississippi and Alabama all flowed into the Floridas before reaching the sea. Because Spanish control over these river mouths stunted the economic development of the American Southwest by limiting access to markets, commercial as well as strategic considerations encouraged the United States to covet the Floridas. But the most pressing motive prompting successive administrations to intervene was that the Spanish had allowed the Floridas to become a haven for African Americans and Native Americans fleeing oppression on the U.S. side of the border. Jefferson had tried in vain to take over West Florida through secret diplomacy and threats without overt military action. Madison had proved more successful, taking advantage of Spain's preoccupations with the Napoleonic Wars and Latin American revolutions to snatch two substantial bites out of West Florida in 1810 and 1813. Monroe's administration pursued this objective of Republican expansionism to its ultimate conclusion, the complete acquisition of both Floridas.[18]

The means by which Republican administrations had carried on their Florida policies never enjoyed unqualified support from American public opinion. Jefferson's designs on West Florida had been frustrated when his behavior was denounced by John Randolph. An attempt by Madison to

---

17. Burt, *British North America*, 399–426; Bradford Perkins, *Castlereagh and Adams: England and the United States, 1812–1823* (Berkeley, 1964), 166, 260, 273.
18. See William Earl Weeks, *John Quincy Adams and American Global Empire* (Lexington, Ky., 1992), 21–36.

gain East Florida by using freebooters from Georgia to stage a pretended revolt in the Spanish colony likewise ended in public embarrassment.[19] The most controversial of all these episodes, however, was the invasion of Florida by Andrew Jackson in 1818.

After the defeat of the Red Stick Creeks at Horseshoe Bend, a renewed migration of Creek refugees flowed into Florida, and since the destruction of the Negro Fort incidents of violence had continued to erupt along the international boundary. On November 12, 1817, troops under the command of General Edmund Gaines burned the Creek village of Fowltown on the Georgia side of the border and killed several of the villagers. The local Indian agent criticized the action as an unwarranted use of force against people who had never been hostile, but Fowltown was located on land claimed by the whites under the terms of the Treaty of Fort Jackson. On November 30, those who had been made homeless hit back hard. Warriors from Fowltown, allied with escaped slaves, attacked a boat carrying forty U.S. soldiers and eleven of their dependents on the Florida side of the border: Four men escaped; one woman was taken prisoner; everyone else was killed. The First Florida War, also called the First Seminole War, had begun.[20]

Upon receiving news of these events, Secretary of War John C. Calhoun issued orders to General Gaines, dated December 16, to demand satisfactory reparations from the Seminoles, as all the refugees of Florida, whether red or black, were called. If atonement was not forthcoming (it is not clear what could have been acceptable), the general was to cross into Florida and attack the Seminoles. But he was specifically forbidden to attack Spanish forts, even if they harbored Seminoles. Ten days later Calhoun diverted General Gaines to lead an expedition against Amelia Island on the east coast of Florida, long a center for smuggling. There was some possibility that the Amelia outlaws might seek an independent Florida, which would complicate U.S. objectives. Gaines captured the island in due course.[21]

The administration decided to turn over the main theater of operations to General Andrew Jackson, who was summoned from Tennessee to Fort Scott, not far from Fowltown. The choice of Jackson showed a disposition

19. See Virginia Bergman Peters, *The Florida Wars* (Hamden, Conn., 1979), 27–45.
20. David Heidler and Jeanne Heidler, *Old Hickory's War: Andrew Jackson and the Quest for Empire* (Mechanicsburg, Pa., 1996), 94–108; Peters, *Florida Wars*, 49–50; Remini, *Jackson*, I , 345–46.
21. Calhoun to Gaines, Dec. 16, 1817, *Correspondence of AJ*, II, 342, n. 2; Ammon, *James Monroe*, 412–18; Weeks, *Global Empire*, 57–58, 64–69.

in Washington for a commander of demonstrated energy and aggressiveness. (He was also known to disobey orders, having refused instructions to return lands to the Creeks in 1815.) There is a letter dated January 30, 1818, in which the president tells Secretary Calhoun to instruct Jackson "not to attack any post occupied by Spanish troops."[22] But Calhoun never sent the order. Perhaps he forgot to send it; perhaps the president changed his mind and told him not to; or perhaps Calhoun believed the order to Gaines did not require restating for Jackson. Maybe the letter was only intended to absolve the president from responsibility. In any case, the limitations placed on Gaines's discretion were never explicitly imposed on Jackson but left to implication. Jackson, however, had been sent a copy of Gaines's orders, and indeed had expostulated over them.

On January 6, 1818, before receiving news of his own appointment, Jackson had already written Monroe stating that he disapproved of the limits imposed on Gaines. Jackson believed "the whole of East Florida [should be] seized and held as an indemnity for the outrages of Spain upon the property of our citizens." He volunteered to carry out such a policy if the president agreed. To preserve the strictest confidentiality, Jackson proposed that the reply be sent through a trusted friend, John Rhea, congressman from Tennessee.[23] Jackson never received a response to this suggestion. But Monroe did compose a letter to Jackson, dated December 28, 1817, giving him vague yet momentous instructions, or rather, exhortations. "Great interests are at issue, and until our course is carried through triumphantly & every species of danger to which it is exposed is settled on the most solid foundation, you ought not to withdraw your active support from it." Quite possibly all Monroe really intended was to urge Jackson not to resign his commission (as he had threatened to do when feeling unappreciated) at a time when the country needed his services. But Jackson seems to have chosen to interpret this letter—even though its date proved it not a reply to his inquiry—as presidential authorization for the conquest of Florida.[24]

What did the Monroe administration really hope for from Jackson? Did they intend him to attack only Seminoles or Spanish forts as well?

22. James Monroe to John C. Calhoun, January 30, 1818, *The Papers of John C. Calhoun*, ed. W. Edwin Hemphill (Columbia, S.C., 1963), II, 104.
23. AJ to James Monroe, January 6, 1818, *Papers of Andrew Jackson*, ed. Harold Moser et al. (Knoxville, Tenn., 1994), IV, 166–67.
24. Remini, *Jackson*, I, 347–49, quoting from the Papers of James Monroe in the New York Public Library. The suggestion regarding Monroe's intention comes from James E. Lewis Jr., *The American Union and the Problem of Neighborhood* (Chapel Hill, 1998), 247, n. 92.

Secretary of State Adams was already negotiating with Don Luis de Onís to see if Spain would cede the Floridas, and the administration was always careful to relate all foreign policy actions to this major objective. Monroe claimed he never saw Jackson's letter of January 6 until a year later, after it had been overtaken by events, although Calhoun and Crawford both admitted reading it when it arrived.[25] Once a decision had been made to entrust a highly sensitive operation to Jackson, the failure of the administration to provide him with a clear response to his proposal would seem culpable negligence—if negligence it was. It is conceivable that the administration deliberately chose ambiguity, leaving the impetuous Jackson to expose the weakness of Spanish authority, while allowing the president to disavow later an intention to wage an undeclared war. This is what Monroe had done in 1811–12, when as Madison's secretary of state he had prompted General George Mathews to intervene in East Florida and then disavowed him when the episode became embarrassing to the government. Many a covert action in the area of foreign policy has been undertaken in such a way as to preserve official deniability. Andrew Jackson, however, proved to be a more dangerous loose cannon than his civilian superiors had foreseen.[26]

Jackson took a thousand volunteer Tennessee militiamen with him and led them by forced marches to Fort Scott. The 450-mile trip, on short rations and across swollen rivers, took forty-six days. On a similar tough march in 1813 his men had called him "Old Hickory"; this time he showed the nickname still appropriate. At Fort Scott, Jackson found reinforcements but little provision for his hungry men. He allowed them but a day's rest before moving south toward Florida on March 10, 1818. In five days they reached the site of the ruined Negro Fort, where they were met by a long-awaited supply boat bearing food. Jackson ordered the fort rebuilt and renamed Fort Gadsden, and gathered further reinforcements, including friendly Creeks under the command of their chief, William McIntosh. McIntosh regarded the campaign as a resumption of the Creek civil war of 1813-14.[27] By now Jackson had about three thousand white soldiers, both regulars and militia, and two thousand Indian allies. He then moved his army toward the east, attacking and destroying village

25. Ammon, *James Monroe*, 416.
26. Samuel Flagg Bemis, *John Quincy Adams and the Foundations of American Foreign Policy* (New York, 1956), 314. For an argument that the president was culpably negligent, see Heidler and Heidler, *Old Hickory's War*, 119–21. For different viewpoints on what the Monroe administration intended, compare Remini, *Jackson*, I, 347–49, 366–68 with Ammon, *James Monroe*, 414–17, 421–25.
27. See George Chapman, *Chief William McIntosh* (Atlanta, 1988), 46–49.

after village of the Miccasukee band of Seminoles. The year before, the Miccasukee had refused General Gaines's demand to allow him to send an expedition to recapture fugitive slaves. Jackson hoped for a decisive confrontation with his enemies, but they melted into the forest and swamps, leaving him to wreak vengeance on their homes and fields. In one of the villages, Jackson's men found the scalps of those slain on the Apalachicola River the previous November.[28]

On April 6, Jackson's army arrived at the Spanish fort of St. Mark's. Here he demanded the commandant to surrender so as to prevent the fort falling into the hands of "Indians and negroes." He promised to respect private property and to provide a receipt for all public property. Lacking the military capacity to resist, Francisco Caso y Luengo complied. As he later explained to Secretary Calhoun, Jackson primarily wanted the fort as a supply base for further operations. He found no hostile Seminoles there, but he did arrest a prominent British trader, Alexander Arbuthnot, whom Jackson blamed for encouraging and supplying his enemies.[29]

Jackson's next objective was the cluster of Seminole villages on the Suwannee River. There he hoped to find Peter McQueen, a former Red Stick, as well as Billy Bowlegs, chief of the Alachua Seminoles. Especially important to Jackson were the hundreds of fugitive slaves living in settlements of their own nearby, among whom two talented leaders, Abraham and Nero, were accounted most dangerous. In the ensuing campaign, Jackson delegated responsibility for attacking the Indians to his Creek allies under McIntosh, while he went after the blacks. In the event, the Suwannee peoples of both races, warned of Jackson's advance by Arbuthnot before his capture, mostly succeeded in escaping. A small force of black men engaged the invading army to cover the retreat of their families and friends. Once again Jackson could only burn houses and seize livestock. But the friendly Creeks rescued the white woman captured on the Apalachicola four months earlier. Jackson arrested another Briton, Robert Ambrister, a soldier of fortune and former royal marine, who had been helping train and equip Seminoles for battle. After a brief pause for his troops to rest and share their booty, Jackson's force returned to St. Mark's.[30]

28. Kenneth W. Porter, *The Black Seminoles* (Gainesville, Fla., 1996), 19–21; James W. Covington, *The Seminoles of Florida* (Gainesville, Fla., 1993), 43; J. Leitch Wright, *Creeks and Seminoles* (Lincoln, Neb., 1986), 204–6.
29. AJ to John C. Calhoun, April 8, 1818, *Papers of Andrew Jackson*, IV, 189–90.
30. AJ to John C. Calhoun, April 20, 1818, ibid., IV, 193–95; Covington, *Seminoles*, 45–46; Peters, *Florida Wars*, 51–53.

Back in St. Mark's, the general convened a court-martial to try Ambrister and Arbuthnot on charges of helping the Seminoles fight against the United States. The two trials took little time (April 26–28); neither defendant was represented by counsel or had opportunity to obtain witnesses in his behalf. Arbuthnot, an idealist as well as a businessman, claimed he had only sought the Natives' welfare and had actually tried to dissuade them from warmaking; this was probably the truth. Ambrister had indeed been helping the Seminoles prepare for war—but against the Spanish, whose rule in Florida he hoped to overthrow. Both defendants were found guilty. The court sentenced Ambrister to flogging and a year at hard labor, Arbuthnot to death. Jackson changed Ambrister's sentence to death also and carried out the executions the next day so there would be no chance of an appeal. A former justice of the Tennessee state supreme court, he must have known the convictions would not stand up to appellate scrutiny. Jackson reported to Calhoun that he hoped "the execution of these Two unprincipled villains will prove an awfull example" to the British government and public.[31]

Meanwhile, an American naval officer had tricked two Seminole chiefs onto his riverboat by flying the Union Jack instead of the Stars and Stripes. They were Himomathle Mico, a former Red Stick, and Hillis Hadjo, also known as Francis the Prophet, who had served with Tecumseh and had sought British help to invalidate the Treaty of Fort Jackson. They too were executed, without a trial.[32]

In May, Jackson heard rumors (which turned out to be false) that Seminoles were gathering at Pensacola. He welcomed the opportunity to move against the capital of Spanish West Florida. Only then did Governor José Masot protest the invasion and declare he would pit force against force, but Jackson warned that if the capital city offered resistance, "I will put to death every man found in arms." Threats by Andrew Jackson had to be taken seriously. Masot evacuated Pensacola and took refuge in nearby Fort Barrancas. There, after a brief exchange of artillery fire, the governor surrendered on May 28, 1818. Jackson proclaimed that American occupation of Florida would continue unless and until Spain could station sufficient military force there to control the borderlands. He sent the Spanish governor and his garrison off to Havana, appointed a U.S. territorial governor and a collector of U.S. customs, thanked his army, and went home

31. Frank Owsley Jr., "Ambrister and Arbuthnot," *JER* 5 (1985): 289–308; Remini, *Jackson*, I, 357–59; AJ to John C. Calhoun, May 5, 1818, *Papers of Andrew Jackson*, IV, 199.
32. Heidler and Heidler, *Old Hickory's War*, 144–46; Wright, *Creeks and Seminoles*, 205–7.

to Tennessee.[33] In Florida the Seminoles, red and black, relocated their communities farther down the peninsula. In Washington there was an uproar.

The administration responded to events in Florida with the slowness typical of the era. In this case, problems of communication were compounded by bureaucratic inefficiency at the War Department and Monroe's habitual deliberateness. The president learned of the execution of Ambrister and Arbuthnot from newspapers in mid-June; Jackson's own reports took even longer to reach him.[34] Much of the press bitterly criticized Jackson. Foreign envoys were demanding explanations. Not until July 15 did Monroe take up the Florida issue with his cabinet. By this time he faced a crisis, both diplomatic and political.

Jackson's occupation of St. Mark's does not seem to have upset official Washington, although it contravened the order given Gaines not to move against Spanish forts. But by now Jackson had evidently gone further than anyone in the administration had expected, executing two British subjects and evicting the whole Spanish government from Pensacola. Within the cabinet, Secretary of War Calhoun had the most at risk as a result of Jackson's behavior. He had the biggest interest in preserving civilian authority over the military and was potentially the most to blame if negligence should be identified as the cause of the problem. He argued that the government should dissociate itself from Jackson's conduct and court-martial him for disobeying orders. Secretary of the Treasury Crawford took the same line; he had experienced Jackson's recalcitrance during his own tenure at the War Department in earlier years. Attorney General William Wirt supported Calhoun and Crawford. But Secretary of State Adams argued that the government could use Jackson's conduct, headstrong and brutal though it had been, to advantage. He proposed to take a hard stand in his discussions with the Spanish envoy Onís, arguing that since Spain could not control what went on in the Floridas, she should sell them to the United States. Monroe deftly adopted a toned-down version of the Adams plan, which avoided antagonizing the general's popular following while denying administration complicity in waging an undeclared war.[35]

---

33. AJ to [Luis Piernas,] Commanding Officer of Pensacola, May 24, 1818, *Papers of Andrew Jackson*, II, 371; Heidler and Heidler, *Old Hickory's War*, 169–76; Remini, *Jackson*, I, 362–65; "Proclamation on Taking Possession of Pensacola" (May 29, 1818), *Correspondence of AJ*, II, 374–75.

34. Remini, *Jackson*, I, 366; Ammon, *James Monroe*, 421, 424.

35. See Ammon, *James Monroe*, 421–23; Bemis, *Foundations*, 315–16; John Niven, *John C. Calhoun and the Price of Union* (Baton Rouge, 1988), 68–70.

The president's resolution of the crisis was initially explained through the Washington *National Intelligencer*, journalistic voice of the administration. The Spanish authorities in Pensacola would be restored. In occupying the Spanish posts General Jackson had acted on his own responsibility, without orders, but out of patriotic motives and on the basis of reliable information. Meanwhile, Monroe wrote personally to Jackson, taking the same position and choosing his language with care. The limits imposed on Gaines had also been intended for Jackson, and he should have understood this, said the president: "In transcending the limit" of your orders, "you acted on your own responsibility."[36]

In the same letter (dated July 19), the president suggested to Jackson that the general might like to have his reports from Florida altered to make sure the written record backed up Washington's interpretation of events, blaming everything on the Spanish authorities. He offered to have someone in Washington make the appropriate changes in the documents. Monroe was already worried about a congressional investigation. Jackson indignantly rejected the favor, for which historians can be grateful. He insisted that his orders had authorized him to do whatever was necessary to eliminate the Seminole threat and that he had nothing to hide or excuse.[37] Monroe's suggestion to Jackson casts some doubt upon the integrity and completeness of the other documentary records relating to the subject. Might Monroe's letter to Calhoun of January 30, 1818, have been a later interpolation? It could have been intended to legitimate the assurances Monroe had provided Congress on March 25, 1818, that "orders have been given to the general in command not to enter Florida unless it be in pursuit of the enemy, and in that case to respect the Spanish authority wherever it is maintained."[38] Perhaps James Monroe's soul had some speck on it that Jefferson did not know about.

When Congress assembled in December 1818, the pressure for inquiry and discussion of the Florida invasion proved irresistible. Interestingly, no one criticized the president; the controversy addressed Jackson's conduct. Both houses took up the subject. The climax of the congressional debate occurred on January 20, 1819, when Henry Clay of Kentucky left the Speaker's chair to address the House of Representatives. This was the first

36. Cunningham, *Presidency of Monroe*, 61–62; Washington *National Intelligencer*, July 27, 1818; James Monroe to AJ, July 19, 1818, *Papers of Andrew Jackson*, IV, 224–28, quotation from 225.

37. Ibid., 227; AJ to James Monroe, Aug. 19, 1818, ibid., 236–39. See also Skowronek, *Politics Presidents Make*, 95–97.

38. *Presidential Messages*, II, 31–32.

of the great speeches that would bring Clay renown. Having been announced in advance, it drew crowds to the galleries; the Senate adjourned so its members could attend too.[39]

Clay began with expressions of personal respect toward President Monroe and General Jackson, then listed the four motions before the House.
The first expressed "disapprobation" of the trial and execution of Ambrister and Arbuthnot; the second would require presidential approval for future executions of military prisoners. The third expressed "disapproval" of
the seizure of the Spanish posts as a violation of orders and an unconstitutional waging of war without congressional authority. The last would
forbid the U.S. military to enter foreign territory without prior Congressional authorization, unless in hot pursuit of an enemy. (The issues were,
of course, not unlike those confronted in later attempts by Congress to exercise oversight of American foreign policy.)

The genesis of the war against the Seminoles, Clay declared, lay in the
unjust Treaty of Fort Jackson, which created a resentful population of
refugees in northern Florida. In actually initiating hostilities, the whites
bore at least as much responsibility as the Indians. Nor had the war been
prosecuted with honor: Hanging the two chiefs captured by deception
was a regression to barbarism. Jackson should have considered himself
bound by the orders to Gaines not to attack Spanish posts. The possible
capture of the forts by the Seminoles, offered by Jackson as his excuse,
was wildly improbable. As to the British prisoners, there was substantial
doubt of the guilt of Arbuthnot if not Ambrister, and the proceedings
against them were indefensible. They had been charged with newly
invented crimes before a court whose jurisdiction was unknown to international law; their trials had been a mockery of due process and their
executions carried out with unseemly haste.[40]

Clay was still resentful that he had not been named secretary of state,
but he had plenty of statesmanlike reasons as well as personal ones for
finding that Jackson's conduct set a dangerous precedent. "Beware how
you give a fatal sanction, in this infant period of our republic, scarcely yet
two score years old, to military insubordination. Remember that Greece
had her Alexander, Rome her Caesar, England her Cromwell, France
her Bonaparte, and that if we would escape the rock on which they split,

39. Merrill Peterson, *The Great Triumvirate: Webster, Clay, and Calhoun* (New York,
    1987), 55–56; Robert Remini, *Henry Clay* (New York, 1991), 162–68.
40. "Speech on the Seminole War" (Jan. 20, 1819), *The Papers of Henry Clay*, ed. James
    Hopkins (Lexington, Ky., 1961), II, 636–62.

we must avoid their errors."[41] Despite Clay's eloquence, however, after three weeks of congressional argument, all the motions critical of Jackson were defeated. (On the most important, the bill to prohibit American troops entering foreign territory without prior Congressional approval, the vote was 42 for, 112 against.)[42] Jackson's confidant, John Rhea of Tennessee, summed up the attitude of the majority: "General Jackson was authorized by the supreme law of nature and nations, the law of self-defense, . . . to enter the Spanish territory of Florida in pursuit of, and to destroy, hostile, murdering savages, not bound by any obligation, who were without the practice of any moral principle reciprocally obligatory on nations."[43] Jackson's critics in the cabinet, their views not having prevailed with the president, supported the Monroe–Adams line in public, though their political followers were not so constrained.

Nor did the foreign powers induce the administration to censure the general. The Spanish had hoped that because of what happened to Ambrister and Arbuthnot, the British would make common cause with them in denouncing the Florida invasion, but this was not to be. Britain was already finding the postwar renewal of commerce with the United States extremely profitable. The trade that the British had carried on for so long with the Native Americans of the borderlands was now dwarfed by the cotton trade with their white enemies. The foreign secretary, Lord Castlereagh, decided not to let the fate of two Scotsmen in a remote jungle interfere with the conduct of high policy, which now dictated good relations with the United States and a severing of those ties with the Indian tribes that had been advantageous before and during the War of 1812. Ignoring the outrage voiced in the British and West Indian press at Jackson's action, he calmly went ahead with implementing the Anglo-American Convention of 1818. Even the indignation of the Spanish cooled when the Americans restored to them Pensacola and St. Mark's—but not, significantly, Fort Gadsden, the former Negro Fort, which remained under U.S. occupation.[44]

Having arrived in Washington near the end of the congressional debate, Old Hickory felt he had been vindicated and was accorded the

---

41. Ibid., 659.
42. Richard W. Leopold, *The Growth of American Foreign Policy* (New York, 1961), 97. See also David S. Heidler, "The Politics of National Aggression: Congress and the First Seminole War," *JER* 13 (1993): 501–30.
43. *Annals of Congress*, 15th Cong., 2nd sess., 867, quoted in Reginald C. Stuart, *War and American Thought* (Kent, Ohio, 1982), 176.
44. Weeks, *Global Empire*, 76–77; Dangerfield, *Era of Good Feelings*, 149–50; Wright, *Creeks and Seminoles*, 208.

treatment of a national hero. More than any other one person, John Quincy Adams had saved him from the disavowal and censure of his civilian superiors, but it was a debt Jackson never acknowledged. Jackson seemed to remember grievances more than favors. He never forgave Henry Clay.

III

John Quincy Adams was a tough negotiator. This Yankee in an overwhelmingly southern administration determined to prove himself worthy of having been entrusted with the State Department. In November 1818, Secretary Adams composed a truculent memorandum, blaming everything in Florida on Spanish weakness and British meddling, while completely ignoring the gross American violations of international law. This he sent to the U.S. minister in Madrid, George Erving, with instructions to show it to the Spanish government. Pensacola and St. Mark's would be returned this time; next time, Adams warned, the United States might not be so forgiving. Actually, the letter was intended at least as much for British and American consumption as for the Spaniards, in order to rebut the critics of Jackson and justify the course the secretary of state was pursuing. Adams saw that it reached all its intended audiences. Jefferson, reading it in his retirement, gave the statement his hearty endorsement.[45]

The United States had been actively negotiating with Spain for the Floridas since before the War of 1812; their acquisition was a top priority within the Monroe administration. Spain at the time was locked in a gigantic and protracted struggle to retain her far-flung New World empire. Revolution had broken out in 1809–10 and spread through most of Latin America. This, Adams knew, was why Ferdinand VII's government could not spare troops for service in Florida, either to control the Seminoles or to resist the United States. The administration did not wish to become involved in this Latin American war, though neither did it prevent some of its citizens from fitting out privateers to aid the revolutionaries and prey on Spanish shipping (as the Spanish government did not prevent the Seminoles from raiding across the border). Adams was not nearly as sympathetic toward the revolutionaries as Clay was; nevertheless, he intended that his own country should profit directly from the Latin

---

45. John Q. Adams to George W. Erving, Nov. 28, 1818, *American State Papers, Foreign Relations* (Washington, 1834), IV, 539–45; Bemis, *Foundations*, 325–29; William Earl Weeks, *Building the Continental Empire* (Chicago, 1996), 45–47.

American independence movements by seizing the opportunity they created to help dismember the empire of the *conquistadores*.[46]

Jackson's invasion of Florida temporarily hindered Adams's negotiations because the Spanish minister, Onís, withdrew from Washington in protest and did not resume direct contact with Adams until October 1818, after the restoration of Spanish rule in Pensacola and St. Mark's. In the meantime, however, Adams communicated with Onís through the French legation. But the lesson of Jackson's invasion had not been lost on the authorities in Madrid, who instructed Onís that it was hopeless to try to retain Florida and to make the best bargain he could for it. The negotiations progressed feverishly throughout the fall and winter.[47]

Adams's ambitions were not confined to Florida. Spain had never recognized the legitimacy of the Louisiana Purchase, because in ceding Louisiana to France in 1800, the Spanish had stipulated that the province could not be transferred to any third power without their prior consent. Besides resolving this long-standing problem, Adams wanted to negotiate a treaty that would establish the boundaries between the United States and New Spain (Mexico) all the way to the Pacific in such a way as to strengthen the American claim to Oregon. Adams had a great interest in the trans-Pacific trade with China and had already been instrumental in recovering the Oregon fur-trading post of Astoria for the United States. At a critical juncture in the negotiations, therefore, Adams widened the scope of the discussions to include defining a boundary between Spanish California and the Oregon Country.[48]

On February 22, 1819, George Washington's Birthday, Adams realized his dream in one of the most momentous achievements in American diplomacy, the signing of the Transcontinental Treaty of Washington. By the terms there set out, Spain not only acquiesced in the earlier American occupations of chunks of West Florida but ceded all the rest of both Floridas to the United States. The Louisiana Purchase was acknowledged and its western boundary fixed along the Sabine, Red, and Arkansas Rivers, and then north to the 42nd parallel of latitude. Adams had stubbornly insisted on the west banks, not the centers, of these rivers as constituting the boundary, so as to monopolize them for American commerce. The 42nd

46. See Charles Carroll Griffin, *The United States and the Disruption of the Spanish Empire* (New York, 1937); Arthur Whitaker, *The United States and the Independence of Latin America*, 2nd ed. (New York, 1964); John Johnson, *A Hemisphere Apart: The Foundations of United States Policy Toward Latin America* (Baltimore, 1990).

47. Bemis, *Foundations*, 317–25, 327–34.

48. Weeks, *Global Empire*, 55–56, 122.

parallel was identified as the limit of Alta California. North of that line Spain relinquished all of her claims in favor of the United States. Coming on top of the joint occupancy agreement recently concluded with Great Britain over Oregon, this Transcontinental Treaty constituted another big step toward making the United States a two-ocean power. (The maps consulted in the negotiations were inaccurate, so the lines that were drawn on them looked different from the way they would appear on a modern map.) At "near one in the morning," Adams wrote in his monumental diary, "I closed the day with ejaculations of fervent gratitude to the Giver of all good. . . . The acknowledgement of a definite line of boundary to the South Sea forms a great epocha [sic] in our history."[49]

Of course, the United States had had to give up something in return for these huge concessions by Spain. The Spanish negotiator was nobody's fool; considering the weakness of his position, Onís did not make a bad bargain for his king.[50] In the first place, the U.S. government agreed to pay off claims by private American citizens against the Spanish government, mainly arising out of events in the Napoleonic Wars, up to a limit of $5 million. More important, the United States relinquished the claim that what is now eastern Texas should have been included in the Louisiana Purchase. At the start, Adams had been demanding the Colorado River of Texas as the boundary, but over the course of the negotiations he had gradually retreated to the Sabine. In making this compromise the secretary had been encouraged by the president. Ever sensitive to American domestic politics, Monroe felt that the acquisition of Florida needed to be paired with gains in the Oregon Country, lest northern congressmen complain. Committed to the ideal of consensus, Monroe did not wish to expose the administration to accusations of sectional favoritism by refusing to make concessions over Texas for gains in the Pacific Northwest.[51]

After the signing of the treaty, two more years of anticlimactic wrangling preceded the exchange of ratifications. Ferdinand VII had secretly granted most of Florida's lands to several court favorites just before the signing, and the treaty bound the United States to respect the rights of private property. If the grants were allowed to stand, there would be little

49. John Quincy Adams, *Memoirs*, ed. Charles Francis Adams (Philadelphia, 1875), IV, 274–75; Bemis, *Foundations*, 334–40.
50. See Philip Coolidge Brooks, *Diplomacy and the Borderlands: The Adams-Onís Treaty of 1819* (Berkeley, 1939).
51. Weeks, *Global Empire*, 123–24, 167–68; Bemis, *Foundations*, 321. The text of the treaty is reprinted in Brooks, *Diplomacy and the Borderlands*, 205–14.

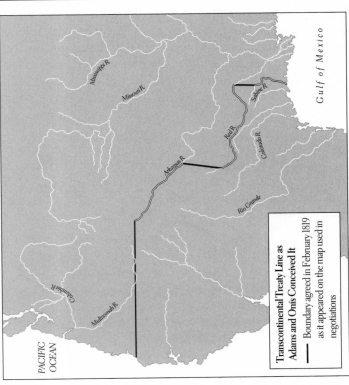

Transcontinental Treaty Line as Adams and Onís Conceived It

—— Boundary agreed in February 1819 as it appeared on the map used in negotiations

PACIFIC OCEAN

Columbia R.

Multnomah R.

Mississippi R.

Missouri R.

Arkansas R.

Red R.

Sabine R.

Colorado R.

Rio Grande

Gulf of Mexico

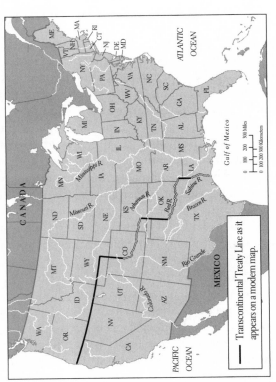

—— Transcontinental Treaty Line as it appears on a modern map.

CANADA

ATLANTIC OCEAN

Gulf of Mexico

MEXICO

PACIFIC OCEAN

0   100   200   300 Miles
0 100 200 300 Kilometers

land left in Florida for white settlers from the United States. Adams was outraged that he had allowed himself to be outsmarted by this maneuver, and the Americans insisted on having the grants annulled. Meanwhile, several countries in South America made good their struggles for independence and awaited international recognition. The Spanish authorities realized that they could deter the United States from according such recognition by threatening not to ratify the treaty. By 1820, the Monroe administration was making thinly veiled threats to occupy Florida anyway—and Texas as well—if the treaty remained unratified much longer. The bitter pill was sweetened by an assurance from Adams that the United States "probably would not precipitately recognize the independence of the South Americans."[52] Finally, the land grants were revoked and ratifications exchanged in February 1821, two years to the day from the signing of the treaty.

The United States waited sixteen months and then, on June 19, 1822, formally received the first envoy from an independent Gran Colombia (which included Colombia, Panama, Ecuador, and Venezuela). The other new nations to the south were recognized soon thereafter—except for black Haiti, independent from France since 1804, which had to wait until 1862 for recognition by the Lincoln administration. Despite the delay, the United States was the first outside power to recognize the independence of the former Spanish colonies. Henry Clay, whose speeches on behalf of recognition had been welcomed in Latin America, could feel gratified.[53] Among the earliest of the Latin American nations to be recognized was Mexico, which as an independent country inherited the boundary that had been negotiated between the United States and Spain such a short time before.

The hemispheric scale of the diplomacy of Monroe and Adams attained explicit statement in the famous Monroe Doctrine. Formulated by Adams and enunciated in Monroe's State of the Union message of December 1823, the doctrine synthesized the administration's concerns with Latin America, the Pacific Northwest, and Anglo-American relations. It was to become a fundamental statement of American foreign policy, though it originated in some very specific concerns of the moment.

During the summer of 1823, rumors circulated in diplomatic circles that the Spanish Bourbons might get help to regain their lost empire. The Holy Alliance, an association of the reactionary powers of continental

---

52. Quoted in Bemis, *Foundations*, 352.
53. Weeks, *Global Empire*, 169–74; Bemis, *Foundations*, 350–62; Henry Clay, "The Independence of Latin America" (March 24, 25, 28, 1818), *Papers*, ed. Hopkins, II, 512–62.

Europe under the nominal leadership of the Russian tsar, might send an expeditionary force to the New World. The possibility could not altogether be dismissed, since the French army had just intervened to restore Ferdinand VII to power in Spain itself. Neither Britain nor the United States welcomed these reports, which seemed inimical to the strategic and commercial interests of both.[54] In August 1823, George Canning, who had become British foreign secretary, suggested that the two countries might issue a joint statement disapproving intervention in the conflict between Spain and its former colonies by any third parties. Canning was continuing the policy Castlereagh had begun, of cordial relations with the United States. Monroe took counsel with ex-presidents Madison and Jefferson, both of whom advised him to cooperate with Canning.[55]

When he raised the matter with his cabinet, however, Monroe found the secretary of state opposed to a joint declaration. Adams believed (correctly) that the chance of intervention by the Holy Alliance was small, and he argued that the United States would look stronger and risk little if it made a pronouncement of its own, rather than appearing to follow in the British wake.[56] Besides a strategy for the United States, Adams was also implementing a personal political strategy that he hoped would make him the next president. This required that he run on his record as a successful vindicator of national self-interest as secretary of state. Being a New Englander and a former Federalist, Adams could not afford the slightest imputation of being pro-British.[57]

Meantime, another threat to American interests had materialized, one also involving the tsar. In the Pacific Northwest, Russia had been extending its claims from Alaska down into the Oregon Country. In 1821, Tsar Alexander I had issued an imperial ukase (edict) warning foreign ships not to come within a hundred miles of the coast of Russian America, as

54. British trade with Latin America was substantial, and from 1822 on, exceeded British trade with the United States. The United States was also hoping to expand commerce with Latin America. See Charles M. Wiltse, *The New Nation* (New York, 1961), 78, 86–87, 218.

55. Bradford Perkins, *The Creation of a Republican Empire, 1776–1865* (Cambridge, Eng., 1993), 155–65. On Canning's policy, see Dangerfield, *Era of Good Feelings*, 249–92. Jefferson's advice to Monroe, dated Oct. 24, 1823, is printed in *TJ: Writings*, 1481–83.

56. For the discussions within the cabinet, see Cunningham, *Presidency of Monroe*, 149–59.

57. See Ernest R. May, *The Making of the Monroe Doctrine* (Cambridge, Mass., 1975), 181–89. This interpretation of Adams's motivation is critiqued in Harry Ammon, "The Monroe Doctrine: Domestic Politics or National Decision?" *Diplomatic History* 5 (1981): 53–70.

Alaska was then called, north of the 51st parallel of latitude. This unilateral assertion of maritime monopoly showed that the Russians were serious competitors for the fur trade and intending to expand their influence in the Pacific Northwest. Both the United States and Britain determined to resist the edict. However, because of their rivalry with each other, it became necessary for the British and Americans to deal separately with the Russians.[58]

Within the administration, Adams carried the day, as he had on Florida; the president took his advice over that of Calhoun and the ex-presidents. The secretary had already delivered a warning to the tsar (July 17, 1823) against any further colonization in Oregon; on November 27 he presented the Russian minister with another note, this time warning the tsar against intervention by the Holy Alliance in Latin America. The president made it all public by incorporating much of Adams's language into his own annual message to Congress on December 2. Meanwhile, across the Atlantic, the issues had been rendered moot. The tsar had already suspended enforcement of his ukase. And in response to pressure from Canning, the French ambassador to Britain, Jules de Polignac, had secretly assured him in October that the continental powers would not meddle in the New World. After Polignac's promise had become public, Canning boasted to the House of Commons, "I called the New World into existence to redress the balance of the Old."[59] While the Latin American revolutionaries themselves deserved primary credit for the achievement Canning claimed, it was clear enough that Monroe's pronouncement had come after its precipitating problems had already been resolved. The tsar was not disposed to undertake risky adventures in the Western Hemisphere, either as leader of the Holy Alliance or on behalf of Russia's own imperial expansion.

The Monroe Doctrine of 1823, as the president set it forth, contained several components.[60] (1) The United States proclaimed that the continents

58. The tsar's ukase and other documents are printed in Charles M. Wiltse, ed., *Expansion and Reform, 1815–1850* (New York, 1967), 46–53. The complicated three–way diplomatic maneuvers are related in Irby Nichals and Richard Ward, "Anglo-American Relations and the Russian Ukase," *Pacific Historical Review* 41 (1972): 444–59.

59. John Quincy Adams, diary entry for July 19, 1823, in his *Memoirs*, VI, 163; Edward P. Crapol, "John Quincy Adams and the Monroe Doctrine," *Pacific Historical Review* 48 (1979): 413–18; Worthington C. Ford, ed., "Some Original Documents on the Genesis of the Monroe Doctrine," Massachusetts Historical Society, *Proceedings*, 2nd ser., 15 (1901–2): 373–436; Canning, Dec. 12, 1826, quoted in Dangerfield, *Era of Good Feelings*, 306.

60. See James Monroe, "Seventh Annual Message" (Dec. 2, 1823), *Presidential Messages*, II, 207–20; the doctrine itself is on 209 and 217–19.

SIBERIA

ARCTIC
OCEAN

Bering Strait

BERING
SEA

RUSSIAN
AMERICA

Ceded by
Russia
to Britain
in 1825

CANADA

54°40'

Russian Treaty Line, 1824

PACIFIC

OCEAN

Oregon Country,
joint Anglo-U.S.
occupation

49° *British Treaty Line, 1818*

42° *Spanish Treaty Line,* 1819

UNITED

STATES

0   250   500 Miles

0   250   500 Kilometers

MEXICO
(Independent, 1821)

**The Alaskan Aspect of
the Monroe Doctrine**

100 mile wide strip within which
only Russian ships were allowed
according to Ukase of 1821

of North and South America "are henceforth not to be considered as subjects for future colonization by any European power." (2) The United
States declared it would regard any European political intervention in
the Western Hemisphere as "dangerous to our peace and safety." (3) In a
gesture of reciprocal isolationism, the United States resolved that it would
not intervene in European wars or "internal concerns." (4) In Adams's
version of the doctrine, the United States also forbade Spain to transfer
any of its New World possessions to any other European power. This "no-
transfer principle," as it has been called, was not included in the president's speech, but it has been treated by U.S. policymakers as being of
equal importance with the other components of the doctrine.[61]

In terms of international power politics, the Monroe Doctrine represented the moment when the United States felt strong enough to assert a
"sphere of influence" that other powers must respect. In terms of national
psychology, the Monroe Doctrine marked the moment when Americans
no longer faced eastward across the Atlantic and turned to face westward
across the continent. The changed orientation was reflected in domestic
political alignments. In the 1790s, different attitudes toward the French
Revolution had been of basic importance in defining the political allegiances of Americans as either Federalists or Republicans. In the second
party conflict that would emerge as Monroe's consensus disintegrated,
different attitudes toward westward expansion, Indian policy, and war
against Mexico would be correspondingly fundamental. In the 1850s, a
third party system would also emerge out of a problem created by westward expansion: the extension of slavery into the territories.

The immediate Russian threat to Oregon was contained when the
Americans and British made separate agreements with the Russians in
1824 and 1825 respectively, defining the southern limit of Alaska as 54° 40'
north latitude, its present boundary.[62] (The agreements did not affect the
Russian trading post at Fort Ross, California, for that was in Mexican territory.) In other areas of the Western Hemisphere, the United States made
no early effort to enforce the noncolonization principle; for example, the
British occupation of the Falkland Islands in 1833 evoked no U.S. response. For years the Latin American countries traded more with Britain
than with the United States and relied more on the Royal Navy than on
the Monroe Doctrine for their strategic security. American relations with

---

61. The no-transfer principle was originally enunciated by resolution of Congress in 1811,
   at a time when it was feared that Spain might transfer West Florida to a country more
   capable of defending it. See Cunningham, *Presidency of Monroe*, 159.
62. Bemis, *Foundations*, 523–27.

Russia soon became the most amicable of any with a major European power. As a result the Monroe Doctrine proved more important in the long run than in the short run. The United States seriously invoked the Monroe Doctrine for the first time only after the Civil War, when it persuaded Napoleon III to withdraw French military support from Maximilian von Hapsburg in Mexico. Thereafter the doctrine loomed increasingly large in the American public imagination.[63]

The Monroe Doctrine was destined to become a durable force in the shaping of U.S. public opinion and foreign policy. A hundred years later, in 1923, Mary Baker Eddy spoke for millions of Americans when she declared, "I believe strictly in the Monroe Doctrine, in our Constitution, and in the laws of God." The doctrine's influence was felt as late as the Cuban missile crisis of 1962, although by then the policy of renouncing U.S. intervention in Europe had been abandoned. The doctrine always remained purely a unilateral policy statement, never recognized in international law. The Latin American nations whom it claimed to protect resented its presumption of U.S. hegemony, especially in the years when the "Theodore Roosevelt corollary" to the Monroe Doctrine asserted a right to intervene militarily in Latin America. In the twentieth century, multilateral pan-American agreements gradually took the place of the Monroe Doctrine and led to the founding of the Organization of American States. But no one doubts that the United States still regards the Western Hemisphere as its special sphere of influence, whether or not the Monroe Doctrine is mentioned when defending it.[64]

IV

The word "nationalism" did not come into usage until the 1830s, but the attitude antedated the name for it. Madison's bank, Monroe's aspiration to one-party government, Jackson's invasion of Florida, and Adams's assertive diplomacy: All displayed in one form or another the American nationalism characteristic of the period immediately after the War of 1812. These public policies paralleled the celebrations on national festivals like presidential inaugurations or the Fourth of July. But for national unity to acquire a tangible meaning, as opposed to a purely ideological one, required the country to become much more integrated economically.

---

63. See Leopold, *Growth of American Foreign Policy*, 41–53; Perkins, *Republican Empire*, 165–69.
64. Dexter Perkins, *A History of the Monroe Doctrine* (Boston, 1963); Mary Baker Eddy is quoted on ix. See also Donald M. Dozer, ed., *The Monroe Doctrine: Its Modern Significance* (Tempe, Ariz., 1976).

Surprisingly, one of the most important achievements of national economic integration came about not through the efforts of the national government, nor from those of private enterprise, but by the initiative of a
single state. This state was New York; its project, the Erie Canal.

The Erie Canal extended from Albany on the Hudson River to Buffalo
on Lake Erie. The veto of the Bonus Bill in early 1817 had dashed any
hope that Congress might make a contribution toward the undertaking;
some were cynical enough to think that Madison's constitutional scruples
against the bill might have been influenced by a reluctance to help New
York in its economic rivalry with Virginia. After Madison's veto, the New
York legislature put together a funding package of its own for the canal.
Planners took advantage of an opening through the Appalachians discovered centuries earlier by the Iroquois, who had made it a trade route. The
canal realized the dream of New York's Governor DeWitt Clinton, formerly mayor of New York City and an admirer of the Iroquois who called
them "the Romans of the western world." Derided by opponents as "Clinton's big ditch," the proposed canal seemed like "madness" to Thomas
Jefferson. A coalition of Federalist and Republican business interests supported the undertaking. The New York City workingmen, organized
through Tammany Hall, feared it would lead to higher taxes and opposed
it. Martin Van Buren, Clinton's arch-rival in the New York Republican
Party, fought against the canal until the last minute; when legislative passage was assured in April 1817, he switched sides. Such sleight-of-hand
gave Van Buren his nickname, "The Little Magician." Once functioning,
the canal became overwhelmingly popular in the state.[65]

DeWitt Clinton called the Erie Canal "a work more stupendous, more
magnificent, and more beneficial than has hitherto been achieved by the
human race." He might be forgiven an excess of rhetorical zeal; most
contemporaries found the canal an extraordinary triumph of human art
over nature. The completed canal ran for 363 miles (the longest previous
American canal extended 26 miles); workers dug it forty feet wide and
four feet deep, with eighteen aqueducts and eighty-three locks to overcome changes in elevation totaling 675 feet.[66] To make use of Lake Ontario for part of the course would have been cheaper, but planners feared
that route would not be militarily secure in case of another war with

65. Evan Cornog, *The Birth of Empire: DeWitt Clinton and the American Experience*
(New York, 1998), 121; Carol Sheriff, *The Artificial River* (New York, 1996), 21–22, 27;
Ronald Shaw, *Erie Water West* (Lexington, Ky., 1966), 62–80.

66. DeWitt Clinton quoted in Daniel Feller, *The Jacksonian Promise* (Baltimore, 1995),
16; Shaw, *Erie Water West*, 87–88.

Britain. Besides, once boats got into Lake Ontario they might be tempted to follow the St. Lawrence to Montreal instead of the Hudson to New York City. So the canal route reflected its designers' policy as well as their technology. To the generation that built it and benefited from it, the canal exemplified a "second creation" by human ingenuity perfecting the original divine creation and carrying out its potential for human betterment. What man had wrought became, indirectly, what God had wrought.[67]

Work began at Rome, New York, at dawn on the Fourth of July 1817. The date was no accident: The canal's promoters saw economic development as fulfilling the promise of the American Revolution. With no adequate engineering training available in the United States, the engineers and contractors learned as they went along. They dug the level central section of ninety-four miles first. When it came time to construct the more challenging eastern and western termini, toll revenues from the completed segments were already more than paying interest on the bonded debt the state had incurred. Contracts were let to local builders, sometimes for only a fraction of a mile of construction, to allow many small businessmen to participate. About three-quarters of the nine thousand laborers were upstate New Yorkers, native born Americans of Dutch or Yankee descent, perhaps surplus workers out of the agricultural sector whose sisters would go off to textile mills. The rest were mostly Irish immigrants, as almost all canal diggers would be within a generation. (On July 12, 1824, a riot erupted at Lockport between rival mobs of Catholic and Protestant Irish workmen.)[68]

The Erie Canal represented the first step in the transportation revolution that would turn an aggregate of local economies into a nationwide market economy. Within a few years the canal was carrying $15 million worth of goods annually, twice as much as floated down the Mississippi to New Orleans.[69] Wheat flour from the Midwest was stored in New York alongside the cotton that the city obtained from the South through its domination of the coastal trade; both could then be exported across the Atlantic. New York merchants began to buy wheat and cotton from their producers before shipping them to the New York warehouses. Soon the merchants learned to buy the crops before they were even grown; that is,

---

67. Sheriff, *Artificial River*, 19; Julius Rubin, "An Innovating Public Improvement," in *Canals and American Economic Development*, ed. Carter Goodrich (New York, 1961), 15–66; David Nye, *America as Second Creation* (Cambridge, Mass., 2003), 151–54.
68. Sheriff, *Artificial River*, 36; Shaw, *Erie Water West*, 132.
69. Charles Sellers, *The Market Revolution* (New York, 1991), 43.

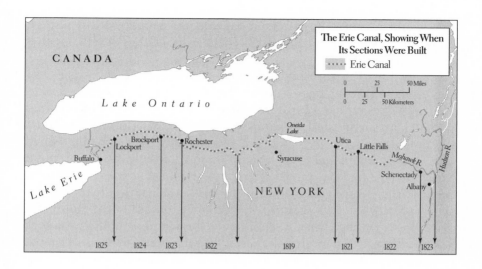

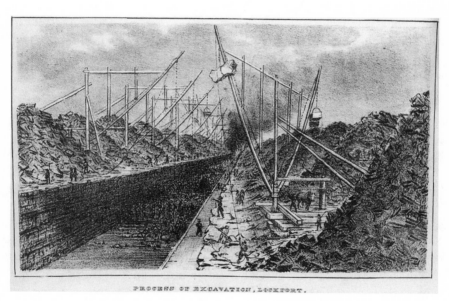

PROCESS OF EXCAVATION, LOCKPORT.

Contemporary depiction of technology devised to dig the Erie Canal. The horse inside the base of the crane supplies power to lift debris blasted out by gunpowder. From Cadwallader Colden, *Memoir Prepared for the Celebration of the Completion of the New York Canals*, 1825. Courtesy of the New York Public Library, Astor, Lenox and Tilden Foundations.

they would advance the grower money on the security of his harvest. Thus the city's power in commercial markets fostered its development as a financial center.

Meanwhile, New York City had adopted (in 1817) an auction system for imports that made it attractive to merchants shipping high-quality textiles from Manchester and Leeds, iron, steel, and tools from Sheffield and Birmingham in England, or wines from continental Europe. Traditionally, passengers had to wait around a port city until their ship's hold filled with cargo. Commencing in January 1818, a transatlantic service from New York to Liverpool provided passengers with scheduled sailings for the first time; people called its ships "packets" because they had a government contract to carry packets of mail. New York also came to outdistance Boston in the China trade. Finally, the founding of the New York Stock Exchange in 1817 made it easier for entrepreneurs to raise capital from investors. When the Erie Canal reinforced all these other developments, together they made New York the most attractive place in the country to do business on a large scale. Jobs multiplied, and as a result the city grew in population from 125,000 in 1820 to over half a million by 1850. New York had redrawn the economic map of the United States and put itself at the center.[70]

V

The modern scholar Benedict Anderson has called nations "imagined communities."[71] Certainly it required some imaginative power to think of the enormous and diverse extent of the United States as constituting a single nation in the days before the railroad and the telegraph. Many orators and politicians exercised their imagination in the creation of American nationalism. But no imagination of a unified national identity would have more lasting significance than the jurisprudence of the United States Supreme Court under Chief Justice Marshall.

In 1815, John Marshall turned sixty years old and had been chief justice for fourteen years. He had already made a huge mark in history through his assertion of judicial review. In *Marbury v. Madison* (1803) he had declared an act of Congress unconstitutional; even more importantly, he had extended this power to state legislation in *Fletcher v. Peck* (1810). Marshall had not been President Adams's first choice for his job, and he had

---

70. John Lauritz Larson, *Internal Improvement* (2001), 73–80. See also Robert G. Albion, *The Rise of New York Port* (New York, 1939); Edwin G. Burrows and Mike Wallace, *Gotham: A History of New York City to 1898* (New York, 1999).

71. Benedict Anderson, *Imagined Communities*, 2nd ed. (London, 1991).

been confirmed without enthusiasm by the Federalist-controlled lame duck Senate of January 1801.[72] But while Federalism withered away as a party, and failed to nurture a conservative political philosophy, Marshall preserved its legacy through his jurisprudence. The values the chief justice defended on the bench were those of the Augustan Enlightenment: He believed in the supremacy of reason over passion, the general welfare over parties and factions, the national government over the states, and the wise, virtuous gentry over the mob. He admired George Washington, under whom he had served at Valley Forge, and made time between court terms to write a multivolume biography of his hero. Marshall felt a deep respect for the rights of property, having worked hard himself to become a man of substance; as late as 1829, he endorsed property qualifications for voting.

His friends among the Virginia gentry found Marshall a hearty companion, enthusiastic sportsman, and appreciative wine-drinker. Unlike his cousin Thomas Jefferson he showed no inclination toward science or philosophy; Marshall preferred lighter reading like Jane Austen novels. Between Jefferson and Marshall there existed a bitter personal enmity of long standing. Ironically, of the two, Marshall possessed more of the common touch.[73]

The most important of Marshall's personal qualities was the respect he commanded among his colleagues on the bench. In thirty-four years on the Supreme Court he almost always persuaded a majority to go along with his point of view. Although the justices spent much of the year "riding circuit" to try cases and hear appeals from federal district courts, when they were in Washington they all lived together in a single boardinghouse. (Their families, like those of congressmen, remained in their homes scattered about the country and did not set up residences in Washington.) In their boardinghouse the justices bonded closely together, which helps explain their tendency to decide cases unanimously. The chief justice approached the law with a practical rather than scholarly aim, relying upon his colleagues on the bench for supplementary learning. The associate justice who would prove Marshall's most valuable coadjutor was the formidably learned Joseph Story of Massachusetts, who had joined the supreme bench in 1811. Appointed by Madison, young

72. Charles Warren, *The Supreme Court in United States History* (Boston, 1923), I, 172–78.
73. See Charles F. Hobson, *The Great Chief Justice: John Marshall and the Rule of Law* (Lawrence, Kans., 1996), 1–25.

Story reflected the new views of the nationalist wing of the Republican Party.[74]

Surprisingly enough, the major constitutional case confronting the Court in the winter of 1815–16 involved John Marshall not as chief justice but as an interested party in the suit. Back in 1793, Marshall, along with his brother and brother-in-law, had invested in 160,000 acres of land on the Northern Neck of Virginia. Their syndicate bought the land from the heir of Lord Fairfax, who had been one of the largest Loyalist landowners at the time of the Revolution. But the title conveyed to the Marshalls by their purchase was open to question. In 1779, the state of Virginia had laid claim to Fairfax's land as part of a policy of confiscating the property of Loyalists. The Marshalls were relying on the 1783 peace treaty between Britain and the United States, which stipulated that confiscations from Loyalists would be restored and their property respected. However, state courts were notoriously unenthusiastic about enforcing the rights of Loyalists, and Virginia had subsequently conveyed some of the Fairfax land to other parties. Another complication was the fact that it was not clear whether Lord Fairfax's will leaving the land to his nephew in England was valid under Virginia common law.

Jay's treaty with Great Britain reaffirmed British and Loyalist property rights in 1795, strengthening the case for the Marshalls. But their local political position was weak, since Federalists had become almost as unpopular in most of Virginia as the Loyalists from whom their title to the land derived, and the landlords compounded their unpopularity by billing their tenants for quitrents, the feudal dues Lord Fairfax had collected in colonial times. In 1796, the state legislature enacted a compromise that divided the Fairfax lands between the Marshall syndicate and the commonwealth. But one legal issue was left unresolved: Had the state of Virginia the right to sell a parcel of the land to David Hunter long before the compromise had been enacted? Title to this part of the former Fairfax estate remained in litigation even after the legislative compromise.[75] In 1809, the Virginia Court of Appeals (state supreme court) found for Hunter, upholding the confiscation act of 1779 and invalidating the Marshalls' title to the tract in question. The opinion was written by Spencer Roane, the leading judicial exponent of state rights, son-in-law of Patrick Henry, and the man Thomas Jefferson would have liked to appoint chief

---

74. G. Edward White, *The Marshall Court and Cultural Change* (New York, 1988), 158–64; R. Kent Newmyer, *Supreme Court Justice Joseph Story* (Chapel Hill, 1985).

75. The complicated reasons why the legislative compromise did not resolve this issue are explained in *The Papers of John Marshall*, vol. 8, ed. Charles F. Hobson (Chapel Hill, 1995), 108–26.

justice of the United States. Because rights involving a federal treaty had been called into question, the Marshalls were able to appeal to the U.S. Supreme Court. Of course John Marshall recused (disqualified) himself from participating in the decision, and the opinion of the court was delivered in 1813 by Story. Story completely reversed Roane's decision, declaring that the state confiscation had been invalidated by federal treaty, Fairfax's will was valid under Virginia's common law, and the Marshalls' title to the disputed tract was confirmed.[76]

The case took an even more surprising turn when the Virginia Court of Appeals refused to obey the decision of the United States Supreme Court. Spencer Roane claimed that final authority to define Virginia law had to rest with Virginia's own highest court, and that the U.S. Supreme Court had no power to review its decisions. He called the Constitution of the United States a "compact" to which the states were parties and cited the favorite proof-text of Jeffersonian state-righters, Madison's Virginia Resolutions of 1798. Roane went so far as to declare that section 25 of the United States Judiciary Act, authorizing appeals from the highest state courts to the U.S. Supreme Court, was unconstitutional! When John Marshall learned of this, he wrote out an appeal petition in his own hand and took it to Associate Justice Bushrod Washington (nephew of George) to endorse for hearing at the next term of the Supreme Court, just weeks away.[77] Since the Virginia court refused to forward the record of the case for review, files on it had to be hastily assembled. This time around, the case bore the name *Martin v. Hunter's Lessee*. (Martin was the person who had sold the land to the Marshalls and whose title they had to validate.)

Once again, Story delivered the opinion. Now he was not so much concerned with the merits of the lawsuit as with defending the jurisdiction of his court. His opinion was a comprehensive vindication of the logical necessity and constitutionality of a single ultimate interpreter of the law. Instead of treating the federal Constitution as a compact among the states, Story characterized it as the act of a sovereign national people.

---

76. *Fairfax's Devisee v. Hunter's Lessee*, 11 U.S. (7 Cranch) 603 (1813); White, *Marshall Court*, 165–67; Newmyer, *Joseph Story*, 106–7; F. Thornton Miller, "John Marshall versus Spencer Roane," *Virginia Magazine of History and Biography* 96 (1988): 297–314; Jean Edward Smith, *John Marshall: Definer of a Nation* (New York, 1996), 426–30. By this time the Marshalls had sold the land; those who had bought from them were confirmed in their possession.

77. An extraordinary act, given that Marshall had recused himself from participation in the case, but the handwriting seems conclusive. See White, *Marshall Court*, 167–73; and the exchange between Charles Hobson and G. Edward White, WMQ 59 (2002): 331–38.

Even William Johnson, a friend of Jefferson and the associate justice with the most sympathy for Roane's point of view, concurred in the decision, though he filed a separate and more restrained opinion. In Richmond, the authorities chose to pretend they were complying with Justice Johnson's opinion rather than Justice Story's. They remained unconvinced of their subordination to the federal tribunal and would raise the jurisdictional issue again in the future.[78]

The judgment of history on the judgments of the courts must be qualified. Of course Story has been absolutely vindicated in asserting the right of the United States Supreme Court to hear appeals from state supreme courts. This, the major point at issue, is fundamental to ensuring legal uniformity throughout the country. On the other hand, Roane had a legitimate point too: the state courts came to be accepted as final arbiters of their own laws, except insofar as these conflict with the federal Constitution, laws, and treaties. Story presumed not only to decide the conflict issue, but also to overrule the state court on the meaning of Virginia's own common law regarding the validity of the Fairfax will, a matter in which no issue of federal law was involved.[79]

Story had echoed the new Republican nationalism. His opinion represented the judicial counterpart of the legislative nationalism of Clay and Calhoun. Nor was Story embarrassed that his kind of Republicanism seemed so similar to John Marshall's Federalism. When the chief saw his opinion, Story felt pleased that Marshall "concurred in every word of it."[80]

Before long, Monroe's Era of Good Feelings would splinter, and the different kinds of nationalism that flourished together briefly in his first term would be at loggerheads. American "nationalism" developed a variety of permutations. The judicial nationalism of Marshall and Story endorsed the legislative nationalist program of banking and internal improvements. But Andrew Jackson would encourage another kind of nationalism, based on territorial expansion, that embraced the strict constructionism of Spencer Roane. In the United States no less than in other nineteenth-century countries, nationalism turned out to be a concept that aroused strong feelings but could mean different things to different people. As communications improved in the years ahead, rival interests and rival leaders seized the opportunity to press their rival nationalisms on the public.

78. *Martin v. Hunter's Lessee*, 14 U.S. (1 Wheaton) 304 (1816); Warren, *Supreme Court*, I, 442–53; Newmyer, *Joseph Story*, 107–11.
79. For a technical legal analysis of the case, see David P. Currie, *The Constitution in the Supreme Court: The First Hundred Years* (Chicago, 1985), 91–96.
80. Story quoted in Newmyer, *Joseph Story*, 111.

4

The World That Cotton Made

The end of the War of 1812 precipitated one of the great migrations of American history. White settlers eagerly took advantage of Andrew Jackson's expropriation of 14 million acres from the Creeks. Shortly after signing the Treaty of Fort Jackson, the general sent his topographical engineer to report on the condition of the Alabama River valley. Along his route, Major Howell Tatum could observe farms with all their improvements that had been abandoned by the dispossessed natives (many of whom, ironically, had been Jackson's allies in the war). The officer concluded in his report that the land was "capable of producing, in great abundance, every article necessary to the sustenance of man or beast." Jackson encouraged white squatters to move onto the lands immediately, without waiting for survey or legal authorization. In December 1815, President Madison ordered them evicted, but his proclamation proved impossible to enforce. When the army moved people off, they came back again as soon as the soldiers had left.[1]

Jackson's victory at New Orleans and his subsequent invasion of Florida further encouraged migration to the Southwest by confirming the strategic security of American control. So did the additional cessions he extorted from the other tribes, beginning with the treaties of September 1816 with the Cherokee and Chickasaw, opening up vast areas adjacent to the Creek Cession. Land-hungry thousands rushed into the Old Southwest, where the new states of Mississippi and Alabama were admitted to the Union in 1817 and 1819 respectively. The migrants included rich and poor, speculators and squatters, slaveholders, slaves, and nonslaveholders, single men, very few single women, and families. The great majority came from upland areas of the nearby states of Georgia, Tennessee, and the Carolinas, but some from as far away as Europe; Scots-Irish seem to have been the most prominent ethnic group. Jackson himself purchased land in the area, and acting on his advice, members of his family made profitable investments in Pensacola real estate.[2] Seldom in human history

1. Harvey H. Jackson III, *Rivers of History: Life on the Coosa, Tallapoosa, Cahaba, and Alabama* (Tuscaloosa, Ala., 1995), 42–43; Daniel Feller, *The Public Lands in Jacksonian Politics* (Madison, Wisc., 1984), 17.
2. Thomas P. Abernethy, *From Frontier to Plantation in Tennessee* (Chapel Hill, 1932), 272. See also David Heidler and Jeanne Heidler, *Old Hickory's War* (Mechanicsburg, Pa., 1996), 128.

has so large a territory been settled so rapidly. Between 1810 and 1820, Alabama's population increased twelvefold to 128,000; Mississippi's doubled to 75,000 even though the Choctaw and Chickasaw Indian tribes still owned the northern two-thirds of the state. The population of Louisiana also doubled to 153,000, as an influx of white American southerners arrived to rival the old multicultural society of colonial New Orleans.[3] Fittingly, when the ambitious settlers of Mississippi established a capital for their state, they called the new little settlement Jackson.

This great migration into the Southwest focused on certain particularly attractive areas, including the Mississippi River valley in the vicinity of Natchez and the Tennessee River valley in northern Alabama. The most important of these was in the Creek Cession: the region of central Alabama called the "black belt" because of its rich dark soil. Thousands of farm families came to the black belt from the Piedmont via the Federal Road connecting Columbia, South Carolina, with Columbus, Georgia. A North Carolina planter viewed the exodus from his neighborhood with dismay: "The Alabama *fever* rages here with great violence and has *carried off* vast numbers of our Citizens."[4] Mississippi, more remote, drew settlers from Kentucky and Tennessee coming downstream along the Father of Waters. From the frenetic activity of the government land offices in this period comes the American folk expression "doing a land office business."

The federal government tried to impose a semblance of order on the process of settlement. Only after public lands had been surveyed were they offered for sale. A public auction then provided an opportunity to bid for those willing to pay more than the minimum price of $2 an acre. Large tracts would be bought up by speculators, sometimes working together in syndicates, for resale. The speculators often benefited from inside information acquired through the land agents and surveyors. Any land left after the auction would be sold privately at $2 an acre, with the minimum purchase being 160 acres; buyers had to put 25 percent down and had four years to pay the balance. Credit was easily available in the immediate postwar years. To make sure that even high-risk borrowers could get loans, Alabama Territory abolished limitations on interest in 1818 by repealing the law against usury. Under these terms, the federal government sold over a million acres of public lands in 1815. (By comparison, before the war sales had averaged 350,000 acres.) In the year ending

3. Thomas P. Abernethy, *The South in the New Nation* (Baton Rouge, 1961), 465–73; Bureau of the Census, *Historical Statistics of the United States* (Washington, 1975), I, 24–37. The population figures do not include tribal Indians.

4. Quoted in Adam Rothman, *Slave Country* (Cambridge, Mass., 2005), 183.

September 30, 1818, the figure reached 2.5 million acres.[5] Reacting to the flood of purchases, incoming president Monroe proposed in 1817 that the minimum price of land be raised so the treasury could realize more benefit from the land boom; Congress turned a deaf ear to the proposal. Instead, the minimum purchase was cut from 160 to 80 acres, to make it easier for small farmers to get a piece of the action. Congress was opting to promote settlement rather than raise revenue. But the pressures of demand bid up the average price of public lands in the Creek Cession to more than $5 an acre in 1818; at the same time they were going for an average of $7.50 an acre in the Tennessee Valley, which had been open to settlement longer. The choicest cotton lands, near water transport, could command $50 an acre at auction.[6]

The situation on the ground was untidy. Squatters who entered on public lands before they had been surveyed and put up for sale faced an uncertain future. From time to time the authorities would relent and allow them to buy the land they occupied for the minimum price; this was called "preemption." On the other hand, the place where they were living might be bought at auction by some other private party who would prove less understanding. Preexisting land titles, arising out of grants made by the Spanish colonial and British colonial governments, and by the notorious corrupt Yazoo land grant of 1795, further complicated matters. The Yazoo claims took years to sort out; in 1816, the federal government paid the claimants $4 million in scrip they could redeem at the land offices.[7] Lawyers found plenty to keep them occupied on the frontier.

Not that everyone settled disputes by legal means. The Old Southwest was a violent society, even by American standards. Institutions of local government could not be set up fast enough to keep pace with needs. In the first few years of settlement, law and order might constitute more an aspiration than a reality. Men fought duels and did not always conduct them according to the conventions of gentlemanly honor; contemporary accounts emphasize brawls, fistfights, shootouts, and knife fights. Natchez and the Natchez Trace road linking it with Nashville had particularly rough reputations for the violence accompanying crime, gambling, drunkenness, and prostitution. The routine cruelty associated with slave discipline and the determination of the whites to maintain their racial supremacy over Indians

5. Meinig, *Continental America*, 242–43; Daniel S. Dupre, *Transforming the Cotton Frontier* (Baton Rouge, 1997), 86–87; Feller, *Public Lands*, 10, 16, 20.
6. Daniel Usner Jr., "American Indians on the Cotton Frontier," *JAH* 72 (1985): 316; Dupre, *Transforming the Cotton Frontier*, 43.
7. Feller, *Public Lands*, 18.

and free Negroes legitimated other forms of violence, including lynchings. Even the folk humor of the Old Southwest featured tall tales and cruel practical jokes that both portrayed and caricatured the violence of the society. "I'm an alligator, half-man, half-horse; can whip any man on the *Mississippi*, by G-d," ran a comic boast that led to a real fight.[8]

What made migration into this hazardous environment so attractive was the high price of cotton. The difficulties in processing short-staple greenseed cotton into textiles had earlier been surmounted through a series of technological innovations culminating in the development of the "saw" cotton gin ("gin" being short for "engine"). The contribution of the Connecticut Yankee Eli Whitney to this long process has been much exaggerated.[9] But the Napoleonic Wars had inhibited international commerce and delayed the mass marketing of cotton for nearly a generation. Now, within a year of the end of hostilities in Europe and North America, the price of raw cotton doubled on the New Orleans market, reaching twenty-seven cents a pound. Wherever the soil was suitable and the farmer could count on two hundred frost-free days in the year, short-staple cotton suddenly became an economically attractive crop. The virgin earth of the New Southwest seemed ideal: While backcountry South Carolina yielded three hundred pounds of cotton per acre, the Alabama black belt could yield eight hundred or even a thousand pounds per acre. In response to an apparently insatiable world demand for textiles, U.S. cotton production soared from seventy-three thousand bales in 1800 to ten times that in 1820—the year the United States surpassed India, long the leading cotton producer.[10] Cotton, fueling an expansion of transatlantic industrial capitalism, enormously enhanced the importance of the United States in the world economy. In 1801, 9 percent of the world's cotton came from the USA and 60 percent from Asia. Half a century later, the United States provided 68 percent of a total world production three times as large.[11] The American South was to be the most favored place for the production of a raw material of global significance, as the Caribbean sugar islands had been in the eighteenth century or as the oil-rich Middle East would become in the twentieth.

8. Elliott Gorn, "Gouge and Bite, Pull Hair and Scratch," *AHR*, 90 (1985): 18–43; D. Clayton James, *Antebellum Natchez* (Baton Rouge, 1968); quotation from Kenneth Lynn, *Mark Twain and Southwestern Humor* (Boston, 1960), 27.
9. See Angela Lakwete, *Inventing the Cotton Gin* (Baltimore, 2003).
10. John Solomon Otto, *Southern Frontiers* (Westport, Conn., 1989), 84–85; David Danbom, *Born in the Country: A History of Rural America* (Baltimore, 1995), 74.
11. Douglas Farnie and David Jeremy, eds., *The Fiber that Changed the World* (Oxford, 2004), 17–18; Leonard Richards, *The Advent of American Democracy* (Glenview, Ill., 1977), 70.

Cotton cultivation required labor-intensive application, but chattel slavery remained legal in the states where the climate was favorable to cotton. The new marketability of short-staple cotton prompted the expansion of slave-plantation agriculture far beyond the areas that would have sustained the traditional export crops, tobacco, rice, and indigo. The spread of cotton cultivation entailed not only the westward migration of free farmers but also the massive forced migration of enslaved workers into the newly acquired lands. Not all cotton planters in the Southwest were self-made pioneers, for some already wealthy men hastened to the area and purchased large holdings, clearing the forest and draining the swamps with slave labor. Whether he owned many slaves or few, a master might bring his bondsmen with him, but sometimes he would go out and select the lands to buy first, returning (or sending agents) later to buy a workforce suited to the property. Most often, the southwestern planter bought slaves who had been transported to that region by a trader. Because the importation of slaves from overseas had been illegal since 1808, the trader's human merchandise could only come from the seaboard slave states. Contemporaries typically observed the transit of a slave coffle with disgust and shame: "a wretched cavalcade . . . marching half naked women, and men loaded with chains, without being charged with any crime but that of being black, from one section of the United States to another, hundreds of miles."[12] Such a procession could number anywhere from a dozen to over a hundred souls, who were expected to walk up to twenty-five miles a day and sleep on the ground. The long trek overland from Virginia to Mississippi or Louisiana would consume six to eight weeks and was usually undertaken in winter, when agricultural labor could best be spared. Coastal vessels, more expensive, absorbed some of the traffic when the great slave marketplace in New Orleans was the destination. Only later, after Kentucky and Tennessee acquired surpluses of slaves and began exporting them, did the phrase "sold down the river" come into common use. The slave traders favored people in the prime of life—late teens or early twenties—since they could withstand the rigors of the march and bring a good price as field hands and (in the case of the women) breeders. Small children accompanying their mothers were placed in the supply wagon. The interstate slave trade was big business;

---

12. Paul Gates, *The Farmer's Age: Agriculture, 1815–1860* (New York, 1960), 140–41; James K. Paulding (1815), quoted in Robert P. Forbes, "Slavery and the Meaning of America" (Ph.D. diss., Yale University, 1994), 23.

the Chesapeake Bay region alone exported 124,000 enslaved workers, mostly across the Appalachians, during the decade following 1810.[13]

Westward migration meant different things to different people. For a white man eager to raise cotton, it could mean a welcome fresh start in life and even a chance at quick wealth—"to hang a crystal chandelier in his frontier log cabin," as one historian put it.[14] For white female participants, the move might be less attractive, which helps explain why fewer women than men made it. Women tended to regret the breakup of their accustomed networks of kinfolk and friends. Once living in an isolated frontier home, they might not have a chance to visit their previous companions, because women rarely traveled alone.[15] Migrating slaves shared these regrets in even more acute form, since they would probably never again even communicate with those they left behind, who could include spouse or child. For African Americans, the move across the mountains constituted a second giant disruption in the generation following the end of forced migration across the ocean. Accordingly, the historian Ira Berlin has called it a "Second Middle Passage."[16] Conditions of slave labor generally worsened in newly settled areas, where there was much backbreaking work to be done clearing the land and little of the paternalism that could soften the brutality of the "peculiar institution" among the planter aristocracy of more stable regions. The most unfortunate were those sent to the sugar plantations of southern Louisiana, where conditions resembled those on the infamous Caribbean islands. Under tight time pressures, sugar planters systematically overworked their slaves during the harvest and grinding season.[17]

The Great Migration to the Gulf States converted thousands of semi-subsistence farmers from the Piedmont into cotton producers. It was not necessary to trade off all the security of agrarian self-sufficiency for the economic opportunity presented by the new staple. Many a small farmer, possessing few or no slaves, mixed cotton-growing with raising corn and

13. Michael Tadman, *Speculators and Slaves* (Madison, Wisc., 1989), 31–41, 70–82; Daniel Johnson and Rex Campbell, *Black Migration in America* (Durham, N.C., 1981), 22–32; Allan Kulikoff, *The Agrarian Origins of American Capitalism* (Charlottesville, Va., 1992), 242. See further Walter Johnson, *Soul by Soul: Life Inside the Antebellum Slave Market* (Cambridge, Mass. 1999).

14. Malcolm Rohrbough, *The Trans-Appalachian Frontier* (New York, 1978), 199.

15. See Joan Cashin, *A Family Venture: Men and Women on the Southern Frontier* (New York, 1991).

16. Ira Berlin, *Generations of Captivity* (Cambridge, Mass., 2003), 161.

17. Gates, *Farmer's Age*, 122–24; David J. Libby, "Plantation and Frontier: Slavery in Mississippi, 1720–1835" (Ph.D. diss., University of Mississippi, 1997), 113–17; Ira Berlin, *Many Thousands Gone* (Cambridge, Mass., 1998), 342–44.

hogs, though they were less profitable. He thus insured against the fluctuations in the price of a single cash crop with products that, come what may, his own family could eat. The agricultural rhythm of cotton production left plenty of time in the year to grow corn. Some settlers took to the piney woods, where there was a living to be earned poaching lumber from the public lands, often with the use of slave lumberjacks. Others raised livestock for sale, as the local Indians did. Squatters generally practiced hunting, grazing, and simple subsistence agriculture, because it made little sense for them to invest much in their farms so long as their legal title was insecure.[18] There were those migrants, mostly men, who loved adventure and their own personal freedom in a new country, but these feelings did not stand in the way of seizing whatever market opportunity presented itself. Versatility and adaptability were at a premium, and a man with five months' schooling, like Gideon Lincecum, who moved from Georgia to Alabama in 1815, could set himself up by turns as a cotton-and-corn farmer, carpenter, surveyor, Indian trader, and (unlicensed) physician.[19] The southwestern humorist Johnson Hooper satirized such men-on-the-make in his character Simon Suggs, who professes the maxim "It is good to be shifty in a new country."[20]

The rapid rise of "the Cotton Kingdom" wrought a momentous transformation. Cotton became a driving force in expanding and transforming the economy not only of the South but of the United States as a whole—indeed of the world. While the growing of cotton came to dominate economic life in the Lower South, the manufacture of cotton textiles was fueling the industrial revolution on both sides of the Atlantic. Most of the exported American cotton went to Britain, in particular to the port of Liverpool, convenient to the textile mills of Lancashire. During the immediate postwar years of 1816 to 1820, cotton constituted 39 percent of U.S. exports; twenty years later the proportion had increased to 59 percent, and the value of the cotton sold overseas in 1836 exceeded $71 million. By giving the United States its leading export staple, the workers in the cotton fields enabled the country not only to buy manufactured goods from Europe but also to pay interest on its foreign debt and continue to import more capital

18. See Gavin Wright, *The Political Economy of the Cotton South* (New York, 1978), esp. 70–71; Usner, "American Indians on the Cotton Frontier," 305, 308; John Hebron Moore, *The Emergence of the Cotton Kingdom in the Old Southwest* (Baton Rouge, 1988), 140–55.
19. "Autobiography of Gideon Lincecum," summarized in Rohrbough, *Trans-Appalachian Frontier*, 200–203. See also Bradley G. Bond, "Herders, Farmers, and Markets on the Inner Frontier," in *Plain Folk of the South Revisited*, ed. Samuel C. Hyde Jr. (Baton Rouge, 1997), 73–99.
20. Johnson Hooper, *Some Adventures of Captain Simon Suggs* (Philadelphia, 1850, c. 1845), 12.

to invest in transportation and industry. Much of Atlantic civilization in the nineteenth century was built on the back of the enslaved field hand.[21]

II

"Whoever says industrial revolution says cotton," observed the great economic historian Eric Hobsbawm.[22] The same short-staple cotton that spread plantation agriculture all over the South gave rise to textile mills. In New England, the War of 1812 climaxed a series of interruptions playing havoc with the maritime trade and fishing that had been the mainstays of the regional economy. American commerce was driven from the seas. Watching their ships rot in port, Yankee investors hit upon a solution. As southern planters solved the problem of worn-out lands and low tobacco prices by shifting their workforce to the new cotton fields, New England merchants solved their own problem by shifting capital from shipping to manufacturing. What they started to manufacture was inexpensive cloth, made from local wool and southern cotton.

In 1813, Francis Cabot Lowell formed a business association with Patrick T. Jackson and Nathan Appleton, subsequently incorporated as the Boston Manufacturing Company with other investors. The purpose was to construct a water-powered loom for the manufacture of cotton textiles. Lowell had recently returned from one of the most successful of all enterprises of industrial espionage, conceived even before the war began. He had spent two years in Britain, where he meticulously observed the textile mills of Manchester. The technology of the power loom invented by Edmund Cartwright remained a scrupulously guarded British national secret. When Lowell left Britain just before war broke out, customs officers searched his luggage twice. They did not realize that the sharp-eyed Lowell had carefully memorized the structure of the loom well enough to replicate it once he got back to the United States. By 1814, Lowell and his brilliant mechanic, Paul Moody, could proudly demonstrate to the company directors an operational water-powered loom in Waltham, Massachusetts.[23]

21. The classic account of the importance of cotton to the American economy is Douglass C. North, *The Economic Growth of the United States, 1790–1860* (Englewood Cliffs, N.J., 1961); data on 75–76. On the international importance of cotton, see also Sven Beckert, "Emancipation and Empire: Reconstructing the Worldwide Web of Cotton Production," *AHR* 109 (2004): 1405–38.

22. Quoted in Sally and David Dugan, *The Day the World Took Off: The Roots of the Industrial Revolution* (London, 2000), 19.

23. Robert F. Dalzell Jr., *Enterprising Elite: The Boston Associates and the World They Made* (Cambridge, Mass., 1987), 5–6.

Yankee merchants were famous for their resourcefulness and enterprise. Frederic Tudor had recently discovered that New England's ice could be exported at a profit to tropical countries, turning a liability into an asset. Nathaniel Wyeth then discovered that the ice could be packed in sawdust, thereby finding a commercial use for this waste by-product of Maine lumber mills. By such practical imagination, New Englanders had overcome their region's paucity of natural advantages.[24] But the vision of Lowell, Jackson, and Appleton went beyond identifying another way to turn a profit; they undertook to create a new industrial order. Their three mills at Waltham having proved successful, the shareholders embarked in 1821 on a still more ambitious project, a custom-built mill town. Jackson and Appleton named it for Lowell, who had died in 1817.

The town of Lowell was created at a point where the Merrimack River drops thirty feet. Irish immigrant laborers dug a canal, and Moody designed a thirty-foot waterwheel to take full advantage of the power. Once their own mill was operational, the associates sold mill sites and water power through the Locks and Canals Company. They had subdued nature to human purposes.[25] For a labor supply, the owners turned to the young women of rural New England. Unlike most parts of the United States, New England had a surplus of women over men because so many of the males had migrated west, while the region received at that time few immigrants from overseas.[26]

Farm women had long supplemented the family income by weaving woolen yarn and cloth, using spinning wheels and hand looms at home. Now cotton from the South provided raw material much more plentiful than local sheep. So young women left home, recruited by company-owned boardinghouses in Lowell. There they put in long hours under unhealthy conditions and contracted not to leave until they had worked at least a year. But twelve to fourteen dollars a month was a good wage, and the new town had attractive shops, social activities, churches, lending libraries, and evening lectures. The "mill girls," as they called themselves, wrote and published a magazine, the *Lowell Offering*. Americans had feared industrialization, lest it create an oppressed, depraved, and turbulent

24. See Elizabeth David, *Harvest of the Cold Months* (London, 1994), 76, 255–64; Carl Seaburg and Stanley Paterson, *The Ice King: Frederic Tudor and His Friends* (Mystic, Conn., 2003).
25. Theodore Steinberg, *Nature Incorporated: Industrialization and the Waters of New England* (Cambridge, Eng., 1991), 38–46, 59–76.
26. On the importance of women as a source of cheap labor, see Claudia Goldin and Kenneth Sokoloff, "The Relative Productivity Hypothesis of Industrialization," *Quarterly Journal of Economics* 99 (1984): 461–87.

Table 1
Ratio of Free White Women to Men, 1820

Five Highest States	
Rhode Island	1.06
Massachusetts	1.05
Connecticut	1.04
New Hampshire	1.04
Vermont	1.00
National Average	**0.97**

proletariat. But because these women typically worked for only a few years prior to marriage, and did so in a morally protected environment, they did not seem to constitute a permanent separate working class. To observers, the community looked like an industrial utopia, more successful than the Scottish models that Francis Lowell and Nathan Appleton had toured years before. Lowell, Massachusetts, boasted the largest concentration of industry in the United States before the Civil War.[27]

Lowell was a stunning innovation in many respects: in its technology, in its labor relations, in the amount of capital raised for it ($8 million), and in the consolidation of all stages of production from raw cotton to finished cloth. Eventually the Lowell capitalists even took over the distribution of their products for sale. Their Locks and Canals Company returned profits on its real estate development averaging 24 percent per annum for twenty years, an even higher rate of return than the manufacturing operations showed. The owners had good reasons to make the mill town a

Table 2
Percentage of Females, 16–44, Among White
Population, 1820

Five Highest States	
Rhode Island	21.41%
Massachusetts	21.4%
Connecticut	21.06%
New Hampshire	20.8%
Vermont	20.61%
National Average	**19.31%**

Source for both tables: Bureau of the Census, *Historical Statistics of the United States* (Washington, 1975).

27. Thomas Dublin, *Lowell: The Story of an Industrial City* (Washington, 1992), 30–40; Edward Everett, "Fourth of July at Lowell" (1830), *Orations and Speeches* (Boston, 1850), I, 47–66.

stable environment for the workers. They wanted Lowell to be a secure investment, less speculative than ocean commerce, one that would return a reliable income to the investors who had pooled their capital. They delegated the day-to-day running of the mills to capable managers like Kirk Boott so that they themselves could turn their attention to traditional upper-class activities like politics, charity, and high culture.[28] These innovative northern capitalists retained some traditional and paternalistic values, just as the southern plantation aristocracy did.

The Waltham-Lowell system presented the most dramatic but by no means the only way that industrialization came to the North. Investment in textile mills, like enthusiasm for the cloths they produced, was widespread. Small capitalists raising money locally could start up mills; they did not need to mobilize large amounts of capital through corporations. These small entrepreneurs would group their activities wherever they found waterpower, at sites either urban or rural. At first these small entrepreneurs might not be much different from master craftsmen. Many of them had immigrated from England or Scotland, trading on the skills they had acquired in the advanced textile industry of their native land. As time went by, consolidation would occur among the businesses, producing a growing differentiation between employers and employees.[29] Smaller textile enterprises often continued "putting out" some of their processes to workers at home. This kind of industrialization did not produce the sharp discontinuities that made Lowell so conspicuous.

For their workers on site, some mills followed the practice of Samuel Slater. Back in 1789, Slater had brought the secrets of Sir Richard Arkwright's spinning frame to America, a transatlantic shift in technological know-how comparable to the one Lowell achieved. Slater contracted with entire farm families to work in and around his mills. Like the proprietors of Lowell, Slater took a paternalistic interest in his workers' morality and religion; unlike them, he enlisted the authority of the husband/father to keep the other members in line. Under his labor system, daughters did not achieve the degree of personal independence that they got by living away from home and receiving their own wages.[30]

28. Walter Licht, *Industrializing America: The Nineteenth Century* (Baltimore, 1995), 22–26; Dalzell, *Enterprising Elite*, 77–78, 225–31.
29. See David Jeremy, *Transatlantic Industrial Revolution* (Cambridge, Mass., 1981); Philip Scranton, *Proprietary Capitalism* (Cambridge, Eng., 1983); Anthony F. C. Wallace, *Rockdale* (New York, 1978).
30. Jonathan Prude, *The Coming of Industrial Order* (Cambridge, Eng., 1983); Barbara M. Tucker, *Samuel Slater and the Origins of the American Textile Industry* (Ithaca, N.Y., 1984).

Though its origins and methods of doing business varied, the textile industry proved central to industrialization in America, as in Europe. And large size became characteristic of the industry even if mills did not necessarily start out that way. Enterprises that began with a few local investors could attract more distant capital if and when they proved themselves. In 1832, textile companies comprised 88 of the 106 largest corporations in the United States.[31]

III

Historians sometimes make use of hypothetical counterfactual cases in order to illuminate what actually happened. In the case of the trans-Appalachian West, however, we do not have to invent cases for comparison; two examples from real life illuminate each other. The Old Southwest was built around cotton and slavery. The Old Northwest grew up differently. By comparing the two regions, we can develop a sense for how much difference cotton and slavery made in shaping the America of the nineteenth century.

The lands north of the Ohio River experienced their own version of the Great Migration. There, however, no one crop predominated to the extent that cotton did in the South, and slavery had been prohibited since the Northwest Ordinance of 1787. After the peace of Ghent, the Great Lakes region was no longer a "middle ground," where Indian tribes could ally with French or British to resist encroaching American settlers. Henceforward U.S. hegemony over the Old Northwest stood unchallenged. Lewis Cass's treaty with the Wyandots and other tribes in 1817 stripped them of almost all the lands they had retained north and west of the Greenville Treaty line of 1795. This set a pattern, and by 1821 most of Indiana and Illinois and even much of Michigan Territory had been ceded. Thereafter the tribes were confined to small reservations, within which Indian agents and missionaries undertook to teach the Natives to become family farmers like the whites. All this contrasted with the South, where the Five Civilized Tribes (as they were called)—Creek, Cherokee, Choctaw, Chickasaw, and Seminole—still retained large territorial bases and considerable corporate autonomy.[32]

Ohio had achieved statehood in 1803, but it continued to grow dramatically, doubling in population from a quarter of a million to half a million in the decade following 1810. By 1820, it had actually become the fourth most

31. François Weil, "Capitalism and Industrialization in New England," *JAH* 84 (1998): 1334–54; Alfred Chandler, *The Visible Hand* (Cambridge, Mass., 1977), 60.
32. See R. Douglas Hurt, *The Ohio Frontier* (Bloomington, 1996); Andrew Cayton, *Frontier Indiana* (Bloomington, 1996); James E. Davis, *Frontier Illinois* (Bloomington, 1998).

populous state, exceeded only by New York, Pennsylvania, and Virginia. Indiana and Illinois, admitted into the Union as states in 1816 and 1818, had respectively 147,000 and 55,000 people in the census of 1820.[33] The southern parts of the three states were settled faster, because the Ohio River provided both a convenient highway for travelers and the promise of access to market. Most early settlers in this area came from the Upland South, the same Piedmont regions that supplied so many migrants to the Southwest. Often of Scots-Irish descent, they got nicknamed "Butternuts" from the color of their homespun clothing. The name "Hoosiers," before its application to the people of Indiana, seems to have been a derogatory term for the dwellers in the southern backcountry.[34] Among the early Hoosiers was Thomas Lincoln, who took his family, including seven-year-old Abraham, from Kentucky into Indiana in 1816. (Abraham Lincoln's future antagonist Jefferson Davis, also born in Kentucky, traveled with his father, Samuel, down the Mississippi River in 1810, following another branch of the Great Migration.) Some of these settlers crossed the Ohio River because they resented having to compete with slave labor or disapproved of the institution on moral grounds; Thomas Lincoln shared both these antislavery attitudes. Other Butternuts, however, hoped to introduce slavery into their new home. In Indiana Territory, Governor William Henry Harrison, a Virginian, had led futile efforts to suspend the Northwest Ordinance prohibition against slavery. In Illinois, some slaveowners smuggled their bondsmen in under the guise of indentured servants, and as late as 1824 an effort to legalize slavery by changing the state constitution was only defeated by a vote of 6,600 to 5,000.[35]

Settlers in the Ohio Valley generally raised corn and hogs, as many of them had done in their previous homes. They found the region too cold for cotton, and by raising their accustomed crops they were able to use seed corn they brought with them and skills they had already mastered. Wooded areas were settled sooner than open country; timber provided building material and fuel, as the settlers well understood.[36] Taking advantage of the river system, they could market their produce in far-off

33. Bureau of the Census, *Historical Statistics of the United States* (Washington, 1960), I, 24–37.
34. Nicole Etcheson, *The Emerging Midwest: Upland Southerners and the Old Northwest* (Bloomington, 1996), 5. There are also other theories for the origin of the name.
35. David Herbert Donald, *Lincoln* (New York, 1995), 24; Cayton, *Frontier Indiana*, 187–93; Davis, *Frontier Illinois*, 165–68.
36. Richard Steckel, "The Economic Foundations of East-West Migration," *Explorations in Economic History* 20 (1983): 14–36; John Faragher, *Sugar Creek: Life on the Illinois Prairie* (New Haven, 1986), 62–63.

New Orleans, especially after the coming of the steamboats made the return trip upstream practical. The first western steamboat had been launched from Pittsburgh in 1811, appropriately named the *New Orleans*. Converting corn to pork made it more efficient to transport. Cincinnati on the Ohio became a meatpacking center nicknamed "Porkopolis," turning hogs into ham and lard for shipment hundreds or thousands of miles by water. In 1837, two immigrant brothers-in-law, William Procter and James Gamble, formed a partnership to use some of Cincinnati's mountain of lard in making soap for market, initiating the replacement of an article of household manufacture with a mass consumer product.[37]

Yankees coming either from upstate New York or New England itself settled across the northern band of the midwestern states. Some came as early as the 1790s to the Western Reserve in Ohio, which Connecticut had long claimed as part of its colonial land grant. But on the whole, the area along the Great Lakes was occupied more slowly than the Ohio Valley; access remained difficult before the Erie Canal opened a water highway across western New York to the Hudson River in 1825. A communal people, the Yankees often moved in families rather than as individuals; sometimes communities of several hundred would migrate together, replicating the name of the town from which they had come. In this way New England place names (deriving ultimately from seventeenth-century East Anglia) came to be repeated across the continent: There are Springfields in Massachusetts, Vermont, Ohio, Indiana, Illinois, Minnesota, Colorado, and Oregon. Wheat was the favorite crop of these settlers; it withstood the severe climate, and they were used to growing it. In the early days wheat and flour floated downstream to New Orleans; only after the Erie Canal opened could the market orientation of the Upper Midwest shift direction. Until the canal barges came, wheat-growers, like corn-growers, depended on the riverboats for access to world markets.[38]

Participants in the Great Migration were not purely "economic men"; they remained loyal, often fiercely loyal, to their cultural heritages and resolved to re-create them on the frontier. As a result, geographically distinct culture zones appeared in the West. Yankees and Butternuts spoke with different accents, ate different foods, and practiced agriculture differently. Yankees supplemented their staple crop with dairying and transplanted fruit orchards; the legendary "Johnny Appleseed" was a Yankee visionary named John Chapman. (Apples could be drunk as well as eaten, and hard cider marketed to communities with unsafe water.) Migrants

37. Andrew Cayton, *Frontier Republic: Ohio, 1780–1825* (Kent, Ohio, 1986), 112–13.
38. Hurt, *Ohio Frontier*, 388–96.

from the Upland South, on the other hand, raised animals for their meat, hides, and tallow. Styles of architecture contrasted, even under primitive conditions. Upland Southerners built log cabins, said to have been invented by the Finnish colonists in Delaware while it was still New Sweden. Yankee pioneers built homes of sod, stone, or clapboard; they were more eager to form villages than to live on isolated farmsteads. When the migrants built churches, their theologies differed: Yankees were characteristically Congregationalists or Presbyterians and espoused the relatively liberal "New School" Calvinism; southern settlers included Baptists, Methodists, and Presbyterians of the "Old School." Institutions of local government differed too: "Extended New England" preferred townships, "Extended Virginia," counties. In this cultural rivalry, the southern portions of Ohio, Indiana, and Illinois counted for many purposes as part of Extended Virginia. Not surprisingly, cultural differences gave rise to political conflicts within those states even after the introduction of slavery had been ruled out. Yankees believed in public education; Butternuts, in individualism and low taxes. Yankees thought the Butternuts lazy; the latter resented Yankee condescension.[39] A contemporary observer recorded their mutual dislike: Southerners believed the "Yankee was a close, miserly, dishonest, selfish getter of money, void of generosity, hospitality, or any of the kindlier feelings of human nature"; northerners saw the Butternut as "a long, lank, lean, and ignorant animal, but little in advance of the savage state; one who was content to squat in a log-cabin, with a large family of ill-fed and ill-clothed, idle, ignorant children."[40]

But the cultural history of the Northwest encompassed more than the rivalry between Yankees and Butternuts. Between their zones of occupancy developed a diverse intermediate zone settled by peoples from the Middle Atlantic states: Pennsylvania Presbyterians, Methodists, and Quakers, Dutch as well as Yankees from New York, and "Pennsylvania Dutch," who were really German-Americans. (Their name for themselves, Deutsch, had been misunderstood as meaning Dutch.) Cincinnati has been called "a Middle States enclave in an Upland South environment."[41] Amidst them all were the remaining Native Americans, the French settlements that antedated U.S. sovereignty, and free Negroes hoping to encounter less hostility in the West. Later decades would find

39. See also Susan Gray, *The Yankee West* (Chapel Hill, 1996); Richard Lyle Power, *Planting Corn Belt Culture* (Indianapolis, 1953).
40. Thomas Ford, *History of Illinois . . . 1818–1847*, ed. Milo Quaife (1857; Chicago, 1945), II, 90.
41. Meinig, *Continental America*, 281.

immigrants from Europe, especially Germany, Scandinavia, and Ireland. Accustomed to cultural pluralism, the settlers from the Middle Atlantic states partially blunted the conflict between Yankees and Butternuts. This conflict did, however, persist at least through the Civil War.[42]

Adding together the Northwest and Southwest, the early nineteenth century witnessed a population movement of stunning magnitude. The census of 1800 identified a third of a million people living beyond the Appalachians; in 1820, the number was over 2 million. Never again did so large a portion of the nation live in new settlements. Later generations of Americans would revere the westward migrants as "pioneers," a word that originally meant the advance guard of an army, who carried tools to enable them to repair roads and bridges or throw up fortifications as needed.[43] It was an apt metaphor insofar as it suggested both occupation of another's territory and construction for later generations. But the settlers of the Great Migration gave little thought to preserving the natural environment for future use. They concerned themselves primarily with short-term advantage. They employed profligate methods of agriculture and land-clearing, heedlessly burning off timber and valuable ground cover, leaving precious topsoil to wash or blow away. Wildlife they destroyed, often deliberately (if they judged it incompatible with agriculture), sometimes through indifference, but also just for the morbid thrill of killing. Decades of wasteful slaughter plus destruction of habitat led to the extinction of the passenger pigeons, which the first settlers found by countless millions in the Ohio Valley.[44]

Northwest or Southwest, the frontier did not always deliver a tangible improvement in the lives of those who moved there. Poorer migrants voluntarily accepted travel conditions not much different from those imposed on the slaves sent west. "A cart and single horse frequently affords the means of transfer, sometimes a horse and pack-saddle," observed Morris Birkbeck along the National Road heading for Ohio in 1817. "Often the back of the poor pilgrim bears all his effects, and his wife follows, naked-footed, bending under the hopes of the family."[45] To be sure, such migrants had been inured to privation in their previous homes. But the trials of the trip itself were only the beginning. Settlers found a land of

42. Andrew Cayton and Peter Onuf, *The Midwest and the Nation* (Bloomington, 1990), 27; Donald Ratcliffe, *Party Spirit in a Frontier Republic: Ohio, 1793–1821* (Columbus, Ohio, 1998), 219.

43. OED.

44. John Mayfield, *The New Nation, 1800–1845* (New York, 1982), 59; Arlie Schorger, *The Passenger Pigeon* (Madison, Wisc., 1955), 199–230.

45. Quoted in Frederick Jackson Turner, *Rise of the New West, 1819–1829* (New York, 1906), 79–80.

hardship and disease. Malaria was endemic in the wet valleys of the Midwest. Amidst a thick woods in Indiana in 1819, a traveler came across "a log house built out of slabs without a nail," with a dirt floor and no chimney. "This small cabin contained a young and interesting female and her two shivering and almost starving children." Though it was November, all were barefoot. The family had a cow and a pig. The husband "was absent in search of bread," the visitors learned. "In this situation the woman was polite, smiled and appeared happy. She gave us water to drink."[46] Pioneers like this woman were living on hope, and little more. Her condition differed little from that of the Lincoln family, who started the winter of 1816–17, upon their arrival in Indiana, in a rude shelter enclosed on three sides and open on the fourth until Thomas could build a regular log cabin. In October 1818, Nancy Hanks Lincoln, wife of Thomas and mother of nine-year-old Abraham, died of brucellosis. A frontier household needed two parents. Thomas soon found a widow who also needed to remarry and brought her to the cabin to bring up his children with her own. Sarah Bush Johnson Lincoln did an excellent job of it.[47]

Absentee speculators who slowed development by withholding their lands from settlement until they had appreciated made themselves understandably unpopular with actual settlers. But settlers North and South, large holders and small, whatever their crop, were speculators too, in the sense that they hoped their lands would increase in value and often held more than they could actually farm. Because the settlers in the Northwest did not invest in slaves, they had even more at stake in their lands than their southern counterparts did; they were "land-lords" but not "labor-lords." Land titles were always more secure in the Old Northwest because the lands there had been properly surveyed from the outset, whereas in the Old Southwest the hope of making quick profits through cotton and slavery led to rapid and often unregulated settlement, with potential confusion over titles. In the hasty southwestern process, wealthy planters ended up with not only more land but also better land, because they could send advance agents out quickly to identify choice parcels. More towns sprouted up in the Northwest, and one of the reasons for this was the greater incentive northern speculators had to sponsor the growth of urban areas and commercial development so their landholdings would appreciate in value. In the Southwest, on the other hand, population remained more dispersed because slaveowners were free to relocate their labor force as they saw fit. Compared with freedom, slavery proved less

46. Richard Lee Mason, 1819, quoted in Rohrbough, *Trans-Appalachian Frontier*, 165–66.
47. Donald, *Lincoln*, 25–28.

favorable not only to urbanization but also to the development of infra-structure like transportation and public education, all of which made real estate more valuable. But southwestern speculators did not mind; cotton lands with access to natural waterways and an enslaved labor force could be yielding quick profits while northerners waited years for their more complicated plans to bear fruit. River transportation—easier downstream than upstream—worked satisfactorily for cotton-growers because the product they sold was so much bulkier than the items they bought.[48]

Speculators sometimes win and sometimes lose. Although the Great Migration was a success story from the point of view of American national aggrandizement, it did not constitute a success story for all its individual participants. Some prospered in their new homes. Those who did not might end up as tenants or hired laborers. But often they simply moved on. Sixty to 80 percent of frontier residents moved within a decade of their arrival, the historian Allan Kulikoff has found, though "the wealthier the farmer, the less often his family moved."[49] Many would fail repeatedly, drifting ever farther westward in the hope that their luck would turn. Hope was what it was all about. Tomorrow was more important than yesterday.

IV

The speculative bubble burst in 1819. By then, Europe had recovered enough from the Napoleonic conflicts that postwar shortages had been made up, and a good harvest in 1818 diminished reliance on American food-stuffs. Most importantly, the rapidly expanded supply of raw cotton temporarily outran the ability of the new mills to absorb it, and its price in Liverpool began to drop in late 1818. The value of cotton in the American seaports fell from a high of 32.5 cents a pound in October 1818 to 24 cents by the end of the year and kept going down to 14 cents.[50] London banks decided there was no longer a need to extend more credit. The Second Bank of the United States, still only two years old, responded by shifting suddenly away from its own expansionist policy. The reversal reflected an effort by Bank president William Jones to protect his institution, but his

48. See Malcolm Rohrbough, *The Land Office Business* (New York, 1968), and Wright, *Political Economy of the Cotton South*.

49. Quotations from Kulikoff, *Agrarian Origins of American Capitalism*, 218. See also Faragher, *Sugar Creek*, 51–52.

50. George Dangerfield, *The Awakening of American Nationalism* (New York, 1965), 73–74. See further Clyde Haulman, "Virginia Commodity Prices During the Panic of 1819," *JER* 22 (2002): 675–88.

clumsiness exacerbated the credit contraction. State banks, in debt to the BUS, had no choice but to call in their own loans. Banks in those days issued paper money, backed by gold and silver. Now specie was draining out of the hinterland into the commercial centers, and from there out of the country altogether. When banks began to suspend specie payment (that is, to stop redeeming their currency in gold and silver), confidence in the banking system evaporated. Investors panicked and tried to liquidate. With everyone trying to sell at the same time, the value of investments plummeted.[51]

Each businessman in the commercial chain was trying to save himself. At the end of the chain, the little people, the farmers and workers, the consumers, had less recourse when *their* debts were called in. They lost their mortgaged homes and farms. As their demand for goods and services shriveled, those who sold to them went bankrupt and laid off their employees. Historians refer to it as "the Panic of 1819," from the behavior of the investors. Contemporaries called it "hard times," reflecting the perspective of the little people.[52] Hard times lasted three to four years, longer in some places.

The Great Migration itself ground to a halt, since people could not afford to buy land, prices of agricultural commodities hit rock bottom, and places like Cincinnati no longer offered jobs. The government discovered it had sold $44 million worth of land since 1790 but had collected only half the money. Overextended westerners were now trying to return unimproved lands to the Treasury in return for debt cancellation. Congress acquiesced in 1820, deciding at the same time to end the sale of public lands on credit. To keep the door open to small purchasers, the basic price of land was lowered from $2 an acre to $1.25.[53]

The Panic of 1819 has been called "a traumatic awakening to the capitalist reality of boom-and-bust."[54] This was the first time that the American public had experienced collectively what would become a recurrent phenomenon, a sharp downward swing of the business cycle. Because it was the first time, people had no perspective from which to judge the events. Previous economic troubles had not been universal and had had more obvious causes in war, natural disaster, or the political paralysis of

51. Murray Rothbard, *The Panic of 1819* (New York, 1962), 11–17; North, *Economic Growth of the U.S.*, 182–88; Ratcliffe, *Party Spirit*, 224.
52. David Lehman, "Explaining Hard Times: The Panic of 1819 in Philadelphia" (Ph.D. diss., UCLA, 1992), 28.
53. Otto, *Southern Frontiers*, 91; Feller, *Public Lands*, 26–38.
54. Charles Sellers, *The Market Revolution* (New York, 1991), 137.

the Articles of Confederation. By 1819, economic relationships had become strongly interconnected; more people were producing for national or international markets rather than home or local consumption. With the advantages of such commercial ties went a corresponding exposure to risk. It was profoundly disturbing that a change in personal fortunes could be unrelated to personal merit, yet the hardworking and honest suffered along with the undeserving. The United States had been hit harder than Europe by the downturn. Today economists recognize that less developed, staple-producing economies are especially vulnerable to the international business cycle. No such frame of reference existed then. Who was to blame?

The Bank of the United States, said some. This was not altogether inaccurate; if the BUS had not been ultimately responsible for the panic, it had certainly made matters worse than necessary. William Jones, who had been culpably lax in extending credit during the boom years, resigned as its president early in the crisis; Langdon Cheves of South Carolina replaced him. Cheves's policy of contraction rescued the Bank's solvency but not its popularity. "The Bank was saved but the people were ruined," a bitter commentator observed.[55] Feeling ran especially high against the Bank in Maryland, where the managers of the Baltimore branch had not only mismanaged the panic but also embezzled something in excess of $1.5 million (the equivalent of $19 million in 2006). Reflecting public outrage, the state legislature levied a tax of fifteen thousand dollars on the Baltimore branch. When the Bank refused to pay, Maryland sued the branch cashier, James M'Culloh, one of the embezzlers, and the tax case went up to the United States Supreme Court. (In their separate, later trial for embezzlement, M'Culloh and his two friends won acquittal by claiming their prosecution was politically motivated.)[56]

John Marshall used the opportunity presented by *McCulloch v. Maryland* to render what may have been the most important of his many important judicial decisions. The first question he had to decide was whether Congress had been within its rights to incorporate the Bank. Endorsing the line of argument used by Alexander Hamilton to justify the first national bank, Marshall held that the power of Congress to charter

---

55. William Gouge, quoted in George Dangerfield, *The Era of Good Feelings* (New York, 1952), 187.

56. Mark Killenbeck, *M'Culloch v. Maryland* (Lawrence, Kans., 2006), 90–94, 184–90. The court reporter misspelled M'Culloh's name, and so have most historians. The spelling "McCulloch" having become common, I use it to refer to the Supreme Court case but not to the person.

corporations, while not explicitly mentioned in the Constitution, was implied. The Constitution enumerates a list of powers of Congress and then authorizes it "to make all laws which shall be necessary and proper for carrying into execution the foregoing powers." Marshall adopted a broad construction of the phrase "necessary and proper," defining it so as to approve not merely "indispensable" measures but whatever means seemed "appropriate," "plainly adapted" to a constitutional objective, and "not prohibited" explicitly. Having confirmed the constitutionality of the Bank, Marshall then went on to ask whether the state had the right to tax it. The power to tax was the power to destroy, as the Bank's lawyer Daniel Webster had argued. States must not be allowed to frustrate the legitimate authority of Congress. "The states have no power, by taxation or otherwise," Marshall concluded, "to retard, impede, burden, or in any manner control, the operations of the Federal Government, or its agencies."[57]

The chief justice had made great law, but in the political context of 1819 he had also inflamed great controversy. His decision demonstrated insensitivity to public resentment of the BUS, and there was difficulty enforcing it. The state of Ohio had just enacted a tax heavier than Maryland's on its own two branches of the Bank, and the Ohio state treasurer seized the money by force—six months after the *McCulloch* decision! This case too reached the Supreme Court—though not until 1824—when Marshall reaffirmed his position.[58] The BUS decided it was the better part of valor to close down its Ohio branches.

Actually, a decision upholding the constitutionality of the Bank did not in itself surprise observers, since the Republican Party had come around to endorsing it in 1816. The controversial parts of Marshall's opinion were the extremely broad interpretation he gave to the powers of Congress, his insistence that the Constitution rested on the sovereignty of the American people as a whole and not on a compact among the states, and his denial that the states possessed any concurrent authority over the BUS. Marshall treated the Bank as if it were entirely a government agency, ignoring the fact that it was also a private corporation operated for profit. Plenty of constitutional lawyers disagreed with his position—including seventy-one-year old Luther Martin, Maryland's chief counsel in the case, who as a young man in 1787 had attended the Constitutional Convention.

---

57. *McCulloch v. Maryland*, 17 U.S. (4 Wheaton) 316–437 (1819); Bernard Schwartz, *History of the Supreme Court* (New York, 1993), 45–47; Charles Hobson, *The Great Chief Justice* (Lawrence, Kans., 1996), 116–24.
58. Cayton, *Frontier Republic*, 132; Ratcliffe, *Party Spirit*, 225–27; *Osborn v. Bank of the United States*, 23 U.S. (9 Wheaton) 738 (1824).

Prolonged criticism of Marshall's opinion in the press led the chief justice himself to respond in print (under a pseudonym). Among those publishing critiques was his old adversary Spencer Roane.[59]

Beyond the question of blame for the panic was the question, Where
do we go from here? Some people argued that the most urgent priority
must be economic recovery. They advocated restoration of business confidence, the reconstitution of the banking system, more tariff protection
for producers, government-sponsored transportation projects, and renewed expansion of credit. Others, however, thought the most important
issue was reform, moral as much as economic, to make sure no more panics occurred. To prevent another round of speculative frenzy, they advocated retrenchment of government spending, called for controls to curb
the irresponsible issue of banknotes, and urged consumers to live within
their means. On the state level, other battles revolved around relief legislation like "stay laws" to postpone the foreclosure of mortgages and the issue of paper money by state banks with no specie reserves. In *Sturges v.
Crowninshield* (1819) the Marshall Court invalidated a New York state law
facilitating bankruptcies as a violation of the constitutional rule against
"impairing the obligation of contracts." Desperate for solutions, people
did not necessarily adopt consistent positions on all these issues. Pro-
debtor politicians might, for example, back inflationary schemes to make
debts easier to pay off and then switch to a "hard money" policy to discourage speculation and fraud.[60]

Probably because this was the first depression in national history, the
citizenry did not assume the administration in Washington could have
prevented it. The blame that attached to the Bank of the United States
did not rub off on the Monroe administration. In any case, no organized
opposition stood ready to provide an alternative government. Monroe was
reelected with no difficulty in 1820. Even the thirty-four Federalist presidential electors (from Massachusetts, Connecticut, and Delaware) backed
him, though they couldn't stomach his running mate, Daniel Tompkins
of New York, and scattered their vice-presidential votes, as they had in
1816, among several candidates. Monroe wound up with every electoral
vote except one, which was cast for John Quincy Adams by a maverick

59. Harold Plous and Gordon Baker, "McCulloch v. Maryland: Right Principle, Wrong
    Case," *Stanford Law Review* 9 (1957), 710–30; G. Edward White, *The Marshall Court
    and Cultural Change* (New York, 1988), 238–40, 544–66; Saul Cornell, *The Other
    Founders* (Chapel Hill, 1999), 278–88.
60. 17 U.S. (4 Wheaton) 122 (1819); Daniel Feller, *The Jacksonian Promise* (Baltimore,
    1995), 40–45; Sellers, *Market Revolution*, 164–71.

New Hampshire elector. (The elector did not do so in order to protect George Washington's record as the only unanimously elected president but simply because he thought Adams would make a better chief executive.)[61] The Panic of 1819 remains the only nationwide depression in American history when the voters did not turn against the administration in Washington.[62]

V

Although the Panic of 1819 did not prevent the reelection of Monroe, another crisis occurred simultaneously that gave the administration a bad scare: the Missouri Controversy.

By 1819, enough settlers had crossed the Mississippi River that Missouri Territory could meet the usual population criterion for admission to the Union. Accordingly, an "enabling act" was presented to Congress authorizing Missouri voters to elect a convention to draft a state constitution. On Saturday the thirteenth of February, a congressman from Poughkeepsie, New York, tossed a bombshell into the Era of Good Feelings. Representative James Tallmadge proposed that as a condition of Missouri statehood, further importation of slaves should be prohibited and all children of slaves born after Missouri's admission to the Union should become free at the age of twenty-five. Tallmadge was an independent-minded Republican, allied at the time with DeWitt Clinton's faction in New York state politics. The year before, he had objected to the admission of Illinois on the (well-founded) grounds that its constitution did not provide enough assurance that the Northwest Ordinance prohibition of slavery would be perpetuated. In 1817, he had helped speed up the gradual emancipation of the remaining slaves in his own state. The number of blacks in Missouri, ten thousand, was about the same as the number remaining in New York in 1817, and the emancipation plan Tallmadge proposed for Missouri resembled the one adopted in New York. Masters could hardly complain that their vested interests were being disregarded; the plan would have freed no one already enslaved. But what might have proved a constructive step toward peaceful emancipation provoked consternation in the House of Representatives.[63]

---

61. See Lynn Turner, "Elections of 1816 and 1820," in *History of American Presidential Elections*, ed. Arthur Schlesinger Jr. (New York, 1985), I, 316–19.
62. After the Panic of 1873, the opposition Democrats won the popular vote in the election of 1876, although the Republicans retained the White House as a result of the Compromise of 1877.
63. *Annals of Congress*, 15th Cong., 2nd sess., 1170; Freehling, *Secessionists at Bay*, 144.

On behalf of the Tallmadge amendment, northern members invoked morality, religion, economics, and the Declaration of Independence. They reminded southerners that their own revered statesmen, led by Thomas Jefferson, had often expressed the hope to find a way out of perpetuating slavery. Yet now, the South presented a virtually solid and implacable opposition (in which the aged Jefferson himself joined) to mandating emancipation in a new state. Through days of rancorous debate, the two sides rehearsed arguments that would be used by the North and South for many years to come. Before it was over, not just the extension of slavery on the frontier but the existence of slavery throughout the whole Union would be challenged. Thomas W. Cobb of Georgia fixed Tallmadge in his gaze: "You have kindled a fire which all the waters of the ocean cannot put out, which seas of blood can only extinguish." But Tallmadge defended his moderate proposition with a steadfastness not at all moderate: "If a dissolution of the Union must take place, let it be so! If civil war, which gentlemen so much threaten, must come, I can only say, let it come!"[64] Like the overture to an operatic drama, the Missouri Controversy prefigured the coming forty-five years of sectional conflict.

The Missouri debate revealed—to the surprise of some observers—that the South had quietly become much more committed to slavery than it had been during the Revolutionary generation. The opening of the Southwest to cotton cultivation, providing a vast new demand for slave labor, had caused the value of slave property to soar. A prime field hand worth four to five hundred dollars in 1814 commanded a price of eight to eleven hundred dollars by early 1819.[65] Though the price then fell back with hard times, everyone expected it would rise again. As tobacco became less profitable, the Chesapeake had come to rely more and more on selling off some of the region's human increase. Slave children represented capital gains. So a respected Virginia planter could advise his son-in-law in 1820: "A woman who brings a child every two years [is] more valuable than the best man of the farm."[66] To restrict the expansion of slavery into the West threatened to snatch away this lucrative market permanently. Missouri was not a cotton-growing region, but slave-exporting

---

64. Glover Moore, *The Missouri Controversy* (Lexington, Ky., 1953), 41; *Annals of Congress*, 15th Cong., 2nd sess., 1204.
65. Roger Ransom, *Conflict and Compromise: The Political Economy of Slavery* (Cambridge, Eng., 1989), 42–47; Ulrich B. Phillips, *American Negro Slavery*, intro. by Eugene Genovese (New York, 1969), 370–71.
66. Thomas Jefferson to John W. Eppes, June 30, 1820, quoted in Steven Deyle, "Origins of the Domestic Slave Trade," *JER* 12 (Spring 1992): 51.

areas like Virginia and South Carolina reacted with horror to what looked like a bad precedent.

Reflective southerners had long regretted the introduction of black slavery but feared that emancipation would invite race war, at least in areas with substantial black populations. To the economic fear of losing western slave markets was added the physical fear of living amidst an ever-increasing population of potential rebels—"dammed up in a land of slaves," as Judge Spencer Roane put it.[67] Southern statesmen on record as deploring slavery, such as ex-president Jefferson, now found themselves having to argue that it would be better if the institution were diffused thinly into newly settled areas rather than concentrated in the older states. "Diffusion" of slaves "over a greater surface," as Jefferson explained it, would "facilitate the accomplishment of their emancipation" by making local white populations more willing to contemplate the possibility of freeing them and by spreading the burden of paying compensation to masters. So the extension of slavery actually would help long-term prospects for bringing an end to slavery! What makes the argument so unconvincing is that it was being used to prevent gradual emancipation in a place where blacks constituted no more than 16 percent of the population. In the last analysis, even those white southerners who regretted slavery and hoped to eliminate it would not tolerate northern participation in planning how to end it.[68]

In one respect the Missouri debates were not representative of later ones: Only a few of the participants actually defended slavery as a positive moral good at this time. Most southern spokesmen preferred to talk about constitutional issues. Jefferson, for example, refused to take northern antislavery professions seriously and defined the issue instead as an attempt to deprive the sovereign (white) people of Missouri of their constitutional equality.[69] But northern legislators did not lack for constitutional arguments of their own. Restrictionists observed that the Constitution authorized Congress to "make all needful rules and regulations" for the territories and to control the "migration" of slaves across state lines after the year 1808. The power to admit new states seemed to imply the power to set conditions for

---

67. Quoted in Harry Ammon, *James Monroe* (Charlottesville, Va., 1990), 455. Roane misspelled the word as "damned," which looks like a Freudian slip.
68. Jefferson to John Holmes, April 22, 1820, in *TJ: Writings*, 1434; see also David Brion Davis, *The Problem of Slavery in the Age of Revolution* (Ithaca, N.Y., 1975), 326–42; Drew McCoy, *The Last of the Fathers* (Cambridge, Eng., 1989), 267–76; Freehling, *Secessionists at Bay*, 150–57.
69. See Peter Onuf, *Jefferson's Empire* (Charlottesville, Va., 2000), 111.

their admission. Some slavery restrictionists also argued that the constitutional duty to "guarantee to each state in this Union a republican form of government" created a presumption against the introduction of slavery into new areas. But southerners replied to all this that once a state had been admitted, it became the equal of the original states, so there would be no constitutional way to prevent it from altering or revoking whatever scheme of gradual emancipation had been imposed by Congress.[70]

The Missouri Controversy also concerned political power. Northern whites were not all humanitarians concerned for the welfare of African Americans, but many of them were increasingly alarmed at the disproportionate political influence of southern slaveholders. The North had come to resent the constitutional clause by which three-fifths of the slave population counted for purposes of representation in Congress and the electoral college. The rule helped perpetuate the Virginia dynasty of presidents that reigned for thirty-two of the first thirty-six years under the Constitution; specifically, it had cost John Adams the presidency in the close election of 1800. In 1819, the three-fifths clause was boosting southern membership of the House by seventeen.[71] To free the slaves in Missouri, or any other state, would not reduce the state's representation in the federal House but potentially add to it, since freedpeople would be fully counted (unless they were colonized elsewhere). But if slavery were on the road to ultimate extinction in Missouri, the state might not vote with the proslavery bloc. In such power calculations, the composition of the Senate was of even greater moment than that of the House. Despite the three-fifths rule, the northern majority in the House of Representatives increased with every census reapportionment. So the South looked to preserve sectional equality in the Senate, where each state had two members regardless of population. The recently approved admission of Alabama would balance the scales at eleven free and eleven slave states.

Voting on the Tallmadge amendment reflected these political realities. The House of Representatives narrowly approved gradual emancipation for Missouri, with the North supporting it 80 to 14 and the South opposing 64 to 2. But in the Senate the slave states had greater strength; furthermore, three of the four senators from Illinois and Indiana reflected Butternut sentiment and voted with the South. The Senate refused to

---

70. William M. Wiecek, *Sources of Antislavery Constitutionalism in America* (Ithaca, N.Y., 1977), 110–22.
71. Freehling, *Secessionists at Bay*, 153; John McCardell, *The Idea of a Southern Nation* (New York, 1979), 23.

accept any restriction on slavery. With the two houses deadlocked, the Missouri statehood bill lapsed when Congress adjourned.[72]

The opponents of slavery extension now took their case to the people. They organized antislavery demonstrations in northern states, though it was hard to mobilize popular sentiment while the panic distracted the public. Rufus King, Federalist senator from New York, rallied other northern members of his party behind the Tallmadge amendment. King had been a critic of the three-fifths clause back in 1787, when he attended the Constitutional Convention as a young man; now, he was a political ally of the African American voters of Manhattan.[73] Republicans accused him of fanning the flames of northern sectionalism to revitalize the Federalist Party. Motives on both sides of this emotional issue were mixed with politics. But it is not clear how much King and other Federalists can have hoped to achieve for their party by exploiting the Missouri Controversy when they were not even contesting the presidency. The election returns of 1820 show no Federalist resurgence at either state or congressional level.[74] A rebirth of the Federalist Party seems to have been a bugaboo that some Republican politicians used to frighten northern voters into appeasing the slaveholders.

The Jeffersonian Republican Party leadership, both in the White House and on Capitol Hill, interpreted Tallmadge's amendment as a challenge to their power, a revolt by northern political outsiders threatening to split the party. They were determined to get Missouri admitted without restrictions on slavery. After the Sixteenth Congress convened in December 1819, the debate over Missouri resumed. The speeches seemed interminable as well as intemperate. When Felix Walker of North Carolina was urged to sit down, he replied that he had to give his speech for the folks back home, "for Buncombe County." Ever since, Americans have called a certain kind of inflated political oratory "buncombe"—or "bunk" for short.[75]

Meanwhile, President Monroe, Representative Henry Clay of Kentucky, and the Senate Republican leaders busied themselves behind the scenes.[76] What is now the state of Maine had been a part of Massachusetts ever since

72. Freehling, *Secessionists at Bay*, 149; Donald L. Robinson, *Slavery in the Structure of American Politics* (New York, 1971), 402–12.
73. Sellers, *Market Revolution*, 129–30; Robert Ernst, *Rufus King* (Chapel Hill, 1968), 369–74, 377–78.
74. Shaw Livermore, *The Twilight of Federalism* (Princeton, 1962), 88–112.
75. *OED*, s.v. "buncombe," also spelled "bunkum."
76. See Noble Cunningham, *The Presidency of James Monroe* (Lawrence, Kans., 1996), 93–104; Ammon, *James Monroe*, 450–55.

colonial times. In June 1819, the Massachusetts legislature consented to separate statehood for what had been "the District of Maine." The Senate leadership promptly linked the admission of Maine and Missouri into a single bill, in effect holding Maine hostage for the admission of Missouri without the Tallmadge amendment. Most of the congressmen from the Maine portion of Massachusetts were thus eventually persuaded to accept Missouri with slavery permitted.

But to bring about the desired result required one further concession. Senator Jesse Thomas of Illinois, who had been voting with the proslavery side (he himself owned what his state euphemistically called "indentured" workers), made the offer. He proposed that slavery should be prohibited, not in Missouri, but in all the rest of the Louisiana Purchase lying north of 36° 30' north latitude, that is, the southern boundary of Missouri. Even then, most northern congressmen would not vote to admit Missouri without the Tallmadge amendment, but enough of them eventually came around to permit enactment of the famous "Missouri Compromise." Considering that slavery on the frontier was remote from the daily lives of most northern whites, and that the country was in the grip of a depression, it is surprising that the antislavery congressmen held their ground as long as they did. In the end, eighteen northern representatives either voted for Missouri without restriction on slavery or else abstained—enough for it to pass with the support of a solid South. The acid-tongued Virginian John Randolph derided the eighteen as "dough faces," and the epithet stuck as a name from then on applied to northerners who betrayed their section. As a group, doughfaces fared badly in the next election.[77]

The Thomas proviso passed the House with the support of 95 out of 100 northern Representatives and even a majority of southern ones, 39 to 37. The Senate considered all the compromise measures together as a package: The South voted 20 to 2 in favor; the North, 18 to 4 against. It is remarkable how many southern Congressmen felt willing, in 1820, to concede a ban on slavery in the greater part of the territories. In general, the slave-exporting states of the Atlantic seaboard insisted more strongly on keeping the territories open to slavery than did the slave-importing

77. As tabulated in Robert Forbes, "Slavery and the Meaning of America, 1819–1837" (Ph.D. diss., Yale University, 1994), 285–90. Randolph, mocking the northerners intimidated by the South, referred to a children's game in which the players daubed their faces with dough and then looked in a mirror and scared themselves. Sean Wilentz, "The Missouri Crisis Revisited," *Journal of the Historical Society* 4 (2004): 397.

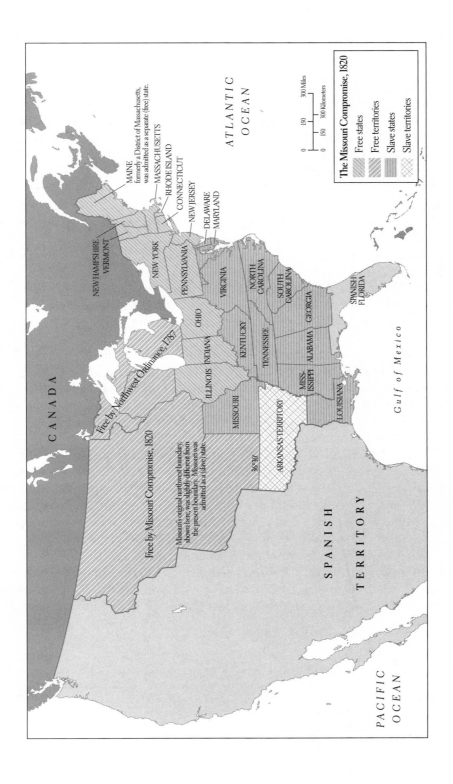

The Missouri Compromise, 1820

Free states

Free territories

Slave states

Slave territories

ATLANTIC
OCEAN

300 Miles

150

300 Kilometers

150

0

0

150

MAINE,
formerly a District of Massachusetts,
was admitted as a separate (free) state.

MASSACHUSETTS

RHODE ISLAND

CONNECTICUT

NEW JERSEY

DELAWARE

MARYLAND

NEW HAMPSHIRE

VERMONT

NEW YORK

PENNSYLVANIA

VIRGINIA

NORTH
CAROLINA

SOUTH
CAROLINA

GEORGIA

SPANISH
FLORIDA

OHIO

KENTUCKY

TENNESSEE

ALABAMA

MISS-
ISSIPPI

INDIANA

ILLINOIS

Free by Northwest Ordinance, 1787

CANADA

MISSOURI

ARKANSAS TERRITORY

LOUISIANA

Free by Missouri Compromise, 1820

Missouri's original northwest boundary,
shown here, was slightly different from
the present boundary. Missouri was
admitted as a (slave) state.

36°30'

Gulf of Mexico

SPANISH

TERRITORY

PACIFIC
OCEAN

states, where masters had less at stake in keeping the price of slaves high. Intense opposition to any prohibition of slavery in the territories came especially from two pockets of "Radicalism" (as proslavery extremism was called): Virginia and Georgia. As time went by, southern Radicalism would become more widespread.[78]

Had the Missouri statehood bill passed Congress with the Tallmadge amendment, Monroe would have vetoed it. Now, the question arose whether he should sign the Thomas proviso. Actually, Monroe favored this concession to northern sentiment, but first he polled his cabinet on the constitutionality of restricting slavery in the territories; this way the president covered himself with the Radicals of his home state. Although tensions between the New Englander Adams and the Georgian Crawford surfaced at the meeting, in the end the cabinet secretaries unanimously endorsed the prohibition of slavery in the territory north of 36° 30'. Secretary of War Calhoun, still in his nationalist phase, went along, and his followers in the South Carolina congressional delegation voted for the Thomas proviso.[79]

At the time, the South felt much better satisfied with the Missouri Compromise than the North. The South had got what its leaders felt was essential: preservation of the principle that there could be no emancipation against the wishes of a local white majority. The compromise also created a new principle out of what had been happening more or less by accident, that states would be admitted in pairs so as not to alter the sectional balance. The South benefited from this custom, because southern territories were often admitted to statehood before achieving requisite population just to keep up the balance.[80] To be sure, the North got by far the largest share of the Louisiana Purchase, but this mattered less in practice than it seems when one looks at a map. The only portion of the purchase actually open to settlement in 1820 was the part open to slavery, Arkansas, which went on to became a slave state in 1836. Settlement of the area above 36° 30' proceeded more slowly. Before the North could realize its full benefits under the compromise, the South would secure repeal of the restriction against slavery by the Kansas-Nebraska Act of 1854.

---

78. William Cooper, *Liberty and Slavery* (New York, 1983), 141. See also Don Fehrenbacher, *Sectional Crisis and Southern Constitutionalism* (Baton Rouge, 1995), 17–21.
79. Cunningham, *Monroe*, 101–3; Sellers, *Market Revolution*, 142; John Niven, *John C. Calhoun and the Price of Union* (Baton Rouge, 1988), 83–85.
80. Leonard Richards, *The Slave Power* (Baton Rouge, 2000), 48–49.

What the Missouri Compromise really prevented was not the rebirth of the Federalist Party but the breakup of the Republican Party along sectional lines.[81] Another effect of the compromise was to confirm the growing power of the Senate, which had prevailed over the House in their conflict over the Tallmadge amendment. In the early years of the Republic, the House had been the more influential branch of Congress; in a few more years the Senate would enter what is called its golden age. A third result was to enhance the reputation of Henry Clay, whose role in effecting the outcome (unlike that of President Monroe) everyone recognized.

But probably the most important outcome of the Missouri Controversy was not the compromise itself but the startling solidity of southern opposition to gradual emancipation in Missouri. Jefferson and the other southern "conditional terminators" (those who favored terminating slavery under the right conditions) had sided not with the restriction of slavery but with those who wanted to extend it. Their essential condition was the consent of the local white population, not obtained in Missouri. Their theoretically antislavery position had become proslavery in practice. Hope for a moderate, peaceful resolution of America's number one social problem dimmed.[82]

The action now shifted to the western frontier, where most white Missourians came from the South. Although Henry Clay let it be known that he hoped they would adopt a gradual emancipation plan of their own, there was never any chance of this.[83] In the election for a Missouri constitutional convention in 1820, the opponents of slavery were routed. The framers of the new state constitution, taking precautions against future settlement coming from the free states, legalized slavery in perpetuity and also forbade "free negroes and mulattoes from coming to and settling in this State."[84] Later, German American immigrants would bring a substantial antislavery vote into Missouri, but in the meantime, the minority of antislavery settlers often found themselves targets of violence.

---

81. Two thought-provoking discussions of this are Major Wilson, *Space, Time, and Freedom, 1815–1861* (Westport, Conn., 1974), 22–48, and Richard H. Brown, "The Missouri Crisis, Slavery, and the Politics of Jacksonianism," *South Atlantic Quarterly* 65 (Winter 1966): 55–72.

82. See Matthew Mason, *Slavery and Politics in the Early American Republic* (Chapel Hill, 2006), 205–7; and, on "conditional termination," Freehling, *Secessionists at Bay*, 121–27.

83. Moore, *Missouri Controversy*, 94–95; *Annals of Congress*, 16th Cong., 1st sess., 1206; Henry Clay to Thomas Wharton, Aug. 28, 1823, Gilder Lehrman Collection, New York, 509.

84. Quoted in Dangerfield, *Era of Good Feelings*, 232.

By their provocative conduct the Missourians almost undid the compromise, for some northerners threatened not to consent to the Missouri constitution when it came back to Congress for final approval. The ban against free blacks conflicted with the clause in the federal Constitution requiring states to respect the "privileges and immunities" of citizens of other states, for a few northern states accorded citizenship to their black residents. Secretary of State Adams made no secret of his outrage. As he told Representative Henry Baldwin: "If acquiesced in, [the Missouri state constitution] would change the terms of the federal compact—change its terms by robbing thousands of citizens of their rights."[85] The southern bloc responded by denying that any review of Missouri's constitution was in order; the admission had already been finalized. This dispute had not been resolved when it came time for a joint session of Congress to count, officially, the votes of the presidential electors. Of course, everyone knew that Monroe had been reelected almost unanimously, but was Missouri entitled to cast three electoral votes? The clerk announced the total both with and without the disputed votes of Missouri, concluding, "But in either case James Monroe is elected President of the United States." This did not prevent the dignity of the occasion from being marred by shouting, disorder, and a walkout by angry senators.[86]

The second Missouri controversy was finally resolved by a second Missouri compromise, largely the work of Henry Clay. The Missouri constitution would be approved provided the state legislature promised not to pass any law violating the "privileges and immunities" clause of the federal Constitution. The promise was redundant, since no state has the right to violate the federal Constitution, but it served its purpose of allowing an exhausted Congress to check Missouri off its agenda. Really at issue in the second Missouri debate was the interpretation of the "privileges and immunities" clause: whether free African Americans could enjoy its protection if they were citizens of their home state. Congress left this issue unresolved, and Missouri proceeded to exclude all free blacks except those who were citizens of their home states. The bad example of Missouri was followed by other states (including some northern ones) legislating against settlement by free Negroes on the assumption that they were not protected by the "privileges and immunities" clause. By 1847,

---

85. JQA diary entry for Nov. 29, 1820, in Charles Francis Adams, ed., *Memoir of John Quincy Adams* (Philadelphia, 1875), V, 209–10.

86. See Dangerfield, *Era of Good Feelings*, 240–41; Robert Remini, *Henry Clay* (New York, 1991), 188–90.

Missouri felt secure in banning all free black settlers, period. The second Missouri compromise proved even less durable than the first.[87]

When it was all over, the most famous comment on the Missouri crisis came from seventy-seven-year-old Thomas Jefferson:

> This momentous question, like a fire bell in the night, awakened and filled me with terror. I considered it at once as the knell of the union. It is hushed, indeed, for the moment. But this is a reprieve only, not a final sentence. . . . I regret that I am now to die in the belief, that the useless sacrifice of themselves by the generation of 1776, to acquire self-government and happiness to their country, is to be thrown away by the unwise and unworthy passions of their sons, and that my only consolation is to be, that I live not to weep over it.[88]

These sad words have often been quoted out of context. Jefferson wrote them in a letter to John Holmes, a Maine Republican who had recruited northern supporters for the compromise. Now Holmes found himself in political trouble for not having fought for the Tallmadge amendment. Holmes showed the letter around, as Jefferson expected he would, to vindicate his conduct as saving the Union. Holmes's invocation of the patriarch's authority worked; he saved his career. Assessing Jefferson's state of mind at this time is not easy. He certainly feared that emancipation, if imposed from outside, would be a disaster for the South. He also worried about the political party he had founded and its continued hegemony. Yet he found other contemporaneous events cheering. He felt extremely pleased with the acquisition of Florida and was encouraging Monroe to acquire Texas as well.[89]

The prospect of the North uniting and using its greater population to force a resolution of the slavery problem upon the South worried Jefferson and his fellow southern politicians for two reasons. Not only did it threaten emancipation, it posed a real danger to the Jeffersonian Republican political ascendancy. Such a united North might use its power for other purposes too, promoting economic policies contrary to southern interests. The stronger the federal government, the greater the potential danger if it fell under hostile northern control.

---

87. Dangerfield, *Era of Good Feelings*, 242. See also Peter Knupfer, *The Union as It Is* (Chapel Hill, 1991), 98–102.

88. TJ to John Holmes, April 22, 1820, in *TJ: Writings*, 1434.

89. See Stuart Leibiger, "Thomas Jefferson and the Missouri Crisis," *JER* 17 (Spring 1997): 121–30; Robert Pierce Forbes, *The Missouri Compromise and Its Aftermath* (Chapel Hill, 2007), 103–6; Freehling, *Secessionists at Bay*, 154–57.

Nowhere did politicians show more acute awareness of this danger than in Jefferson's home commonwealth. There a collection of Old Republican politicians known as the "Richmond Junto" controlled state politics and influenced opinion through Thomas Ritchie's *Richmond Enquirer*. These politicians worried not only about the declining influence of the South as a section but more particularly about the declining influence of Virginia. Once "the Prussia of the American confederation," Virginia was no longer even the most populous state; New York had taken the lead and would hold it for over a century. Prompted by declining fertility of the soil, too many of Virginia's sons and daughters migrated out of state—about a million of them in the antebellum era, by far the most from any state. By 1850, 100,000 former Virginians would live in Kentucky and Tennessee; 150,000 in the Old Northwest. These numbers do not include their children, lost to the Old Dominion. In 1820, cotton had already replaced tobacco as the country's leading export. The Virginia dynasty of presidents had clearly come to an end with Monroe. Like some embittered New England Federalists, the politicians of the Richmond Junto sought refuge from their declining national influence behind the barricades of state rights.[90]

In 1820 the Virginia House of Delegates passed two resolutions affirming state rights, one denouncing the Tallmadge amendment and the other denouncing John Marshall's decision in *McCulloch v. Maryland*. In 1821, Marshall would provoke another jurisdictional confrontation with Spencer Roane in the case of *Cohens v. Virginia*, affirming the right of the U.S. Supreme Court to hear criminal appeals from the highest state courts when a federal issue is involved. This was one more judicial humiliation for state rights as the Virginians understood them. Once again Spencer Roane took up the cudgels in the public press, this time writing under the pen name of a seventeenth-century defender of English liberty, Algernon Sidney.[91]

But in the hands of the Virginians of the 1820s, the strict construction of the Constitution, which Jefferson had originally conceived as a defense of liberty, was becoming identified with the defense of slavery. The transition can be observed in a volume called *Construction Construed and Constitutions Vindicated*, published in 1820 by John Taylor, a planter, philosopher, and statesman of Caroline County, Virginia. Over the years,

90. David Fischer and James Kelly, *Bound Away: Virginia and the Westward Movement* (Charlottesville, Va., 2000), 137; Mason, *Slavery and Politics*, 198–99; Feller, *Jacksonian Promise*, 55–58.
91. 19 U.S. (6 Wheaton) 254 (1821); White, *Marshall Court*, 504–24.

Taylor had been a prolific exponent of Jeffersonian Republicanism of the old school. He had attacked the Hamiltonian doctrine of "implied powers"; he had subjected to searching criticism John Adams's defense of an aristocratic component in government; he had maintained the superior virtue of agriculture as compared with commerce, manufacturing, and finance. While Republican nationalists had waged war and established banks, Taylor had kept alive the flame of pure limited government. Like Spencer Roane invoking Sidney, Taylor respected the tradition of the English "commonwealthmen" who had protested against the growth of government power, executive influence, and finance capitalism in eighteenth-century Britain; like Jefferson, he synthesized their views with Enlightenment faith in individual rights. It has been well said that Taylor treated political theory as "a mode of indignation."[92] His discernment of the conspiratorial power of high finance anticipated Charles Beard's analysis of the Constitutional Convention. Not surprisingly, Taylor's new book denounced John Marshall's *McCulloch* decision as well as the depression-induced proposals for more tariff protection; he charged that both of these were power grabs by the moneyed interests.

Like many southern thinkers of his generation, Taylor had earlier expressed regret at the introduction of slavery. But now he marshaled his intellectual weapons against efforts to tamper with the institution. He denounced the Tallmadge amendment, along with other attempts to broaden the interpretation of the Constitution, as hypocritical frauds designed to subject the South and the country as a whole to a conspiracy of bankers, manufacturers, and government pensioners.[93] The Virginia legislature rewarded the author with election to the U.S. Senate. John Taylor of Caroline showed how the Old Republican political thought and strict constitutional construction now provided a rationale for the new proslavery Radicalism. (The name Radicalism was intended to connote a friend of the constitution, for it was taken from the Radical party in France who defended the charter granted by Louis XVIII.)[94]

Virginians, however, were not the only ones to ponder carefully the meaning of the Missouri controversies. John Quincy Adams entered the

---

92. Michael O'Brien, *Conjectures of Order: Intellectual Life and the Old South* (Chapel Hill, 2004), II, 798.

93. John Taylor, *Construction Construed and Constitutions Vindicated* (Richmond, Va., 1820), 298; Duncan MacLeod, "The Political Economy of John Taylor," *Journal of American Studies* 14 (1980): 403; Robert Shalhope, *John Taylor of Caroline* (Columbia, S.C., 1980), 188–202; Andrew C. Lenner, "John Taylor and the Origins of American Federalism," *JER* 17 (1997): 417–20.

94. Norman Risjord, *The Old Republicans* (New York, 1965), 229–30.

most perceptive, profound, and far-sighted of such contemporary reflections in his diary on November 29, 1820:

> If slavery be the destined sword of the hand of the destroying angel which is to sever the ties of this Union, the same sword will cut in sunder the bonds of slavery itself. A dissolution of the Union for the cause of slavery would be followed by a servile war in the slave-holding States, combined with a war between the two severed portions of the Union. It seems to me that its result might be the extirpation of slavery from this whole continent; and, calamitous and desolating as this course of events in its progress must be, so glorious would be its final issue, that, as God shall judge me, I dare not say that it is not to be desired.[95]

When Adams's prophecy came to fulfillment, Abraham Lincoln too saw the hand of God in it, for as he pointed out in his Second Inaugural, "If we shall suppose that American Slavery is one of those offences which, in the providence of God, must needs come, but which, having continued through His appointed time, He now wills to remove, and that He gives to both North and South, this terrible war, as the woe due to those by whom the offence came, shall we discern therein any departure from those divine attributes which the believers in a Living God always ascribe to Him?"[96]

VI

Denmark Vesey, a free black man in his fifties, practiced the carpenter's trade in Charleston, South Carolina. A man of the world who could read and write, and who spoke several languages, Vesey had led a life of adventure and excitement. He spent his childhood in slavery on the island of St. Thomas, in what was then the Danish West Indies, and as a youthful sailor visited Africa as well as various Caribbean ports. At the age of fourteen he had been sent to the living hell of a sugar plantation on Haiti; luckily the French planter found the boy unsatisfactory and returned him to the slave dealer for a refund. In 1785, Vesey had come to Charleston, where like many other enslaved urban workers he was allowed to hire his own time so long as he turned over most of his earnings to the man who owned him. Late in 1799 Denmark Vesey got lucky again: he won fifteen hundred dollars in the lottery, enough to buy his freedom and open a carpenter's shop of his own. He joined a free Negro community in Charleston County that numbered 3,615 persons in 1820. Vesey worked

95. *Memoir of John Quincy Adams*, V, 210.
96. *Collected Works of AL*, VIII, 333.

hard and saved his money; by 1822 his net worth was eight thousand dollars. A proud man, Vesey hated the whites for what they had done to him and his people. Charismatic, determined, and by some accounts ruthless, he meant to do something about it.[97]

During the Missouri Controversy, southern spokesmen accused the slavery restrictionists of encouraging, inadvertently if not on purpose, the violence of insurrection. Such fears were not altogether groundless. To the alarm of southern whites, blacks living in the District of Columbia, both slave and free, crowded into the galleries of Congress to listen to the debates.[98] By word of mouth as well as by print among the literate black minority, news of the Missouri debates and their criticism of slavery spread through African American communities. Among those who took an interest was Denmark Vesey, who cherished a copy of Rufus King's speech denouncing slavery in the name of natural rights.[99] But Vesey had other sources of inspiration too. Informers claimed he originally scheduled his revolt for Bastille Day: July 14, 1822. Firsthand reports circulated in South Carolina of the only successful slave uprising in history, the Haitian Revolution of the 1790s. Most important of all, Vesey had his Bible with the Book of Exodus. Vesey was a class leader in the local African Methodist Episcopal (AME) church. When preaching religion, he usually came around to the injustice of slavery.[100]

Vesey's leading co-conspirators included an awesome African-born conjurer named Gullah Jack, a number of craftsmen and sailors, and two trusted household servants of the state governor. Vesey's lieutenants visited the countryside to make recruits on the plantations, but it is difficult to know the extent of their success; his claim that nine thousand were ready to rise was surely an exaggeration meant to steel the nerves of his urban followers. Their plan, as investigators later pieced it together, relied on complete surprise and simultaneous coordinated actions for success. It called for attacks on the city's arsenal, gun stores, and other places where

---

97. See John Lofton, *Denmark Vesey's Revolt* (Kent, Ohio, 1983); the population figures are on 80.

98. *Annals of Congress*, 15th Cong., 2nd sess., 1179, 206; 16th Cong., 1st sess., 1016–17; Taylor, *Constructions Construed*, 301; Moore, *Missouri Controversy*, 91.

99. Confession of Jack Purcell, quoted in David Robertson, *Denmark Vesey* (New York, 1999), 121.

100. Testimonies of William Paul and Benjamin Ford, quoted in Douglas Egerton, *He Shall Go Out Free*, 2nd ed. (Lanham, Md., 2004), 115–16. For Vesey's opportunity to learn about the Haitian Revolution, see Robert Alderson, "Charleston's Rumored Slave Revolt of 1793," in *The Impact of the Haitian Revolution in the Atlantic World*, ed. David P. Geggus (Columbia, S.C., 2001).

weapons were held; these were known to be guarded lightly if at all. Taking their masters' horses, some rebels would form a cavalry unit. All whites in the city were to be killed, along with any blacks who refused to join the cause. To those who expressed moral qualms, Vesey invoked a God of wrath. Charleston should suffer the fate of Jericho: "And they utterly destroyed all that was in the city, both man and woman, young and old" (Joshua 6:21). Revolution was not for the faint of heart.[101]

As the size of the conspiracy grew, so did the risk of revealing it to someone who could not be trusted. On May 25, 1822, a slave informed his master that a conspirator had attempted to recruit him. The authorities began an investigation. But so tight was the conspirators' security and so convincing their denials that for weeks the investigation went nowhere. On June 14, a slave who had been sent out as a spy reported back that the Hampstead neighborhood AME church was the center of the conspiracy and that the rising was now slated for midnight June 16. Galvanized, the authorities mobilized troops, forestalled any action by would-be rebels, and commenced a serious crackdown. A special tribunal met in secret. Suspects were held without bail. Vesey himself was not apprehended until June 22, when about to flee the city; Gullah Jack, not until July 5, as he was attempting to carry out the uprising.

Such is the story the investigating tribunal claimed to uncover. The special tribunal arrested 135 persons, of whom 35 were executed, 43 transported and sold (an especially severe punishment for those who left families behind), 15 tried and acquitted, and 38 questioned and not charged. Four white men were convicted of encouraging the rebels and sent to prison. Two slave and two free black traitors to the plot received handsome rewards for informing. Vesey himself and most of his principals remained faithful to their cause and met their deaths with courage. The last words of one of them, Peter Poyas, were "Die silent, as you see me do."[102] This silence, and the fact that the conspirators had the chance to destroy evidence, makes the historian's task difficult. Two prominent contemporaries criticized the tribunal for procedural irregularities: South Carolina's Governor Thomas Bennett and Associate Justice of the U.S. Supreme Court William Johnson, a Charleston resident speaking in his private, not judicial, capacity. Some slaveowners refused to believe in the involvement of their own bondsmen and defended them before the tribunal earnestly but in vain.

---

101. Lofton, *Denmark Vesey's Revolt*, 141–42.
102. The sentences are tabulated in Robert S. Starobin, ed., *Denmark Vesey* (Englewood Cliffs, N.J., 1970), 60; Poyas is quoted in Lofton, *Denmark Vesey's Revolt*, 169.

Modern historians have reached differing conclusions about the investigation and trial.[103] Some believe the tribunal's findings, so far as they went, substantially accurate, but others question the credibility of the coerced confessions and view the tribunal's prosecutions as revealing more about white fears than black intentions. Surely Vesey was indeed at the center of an antislavery cell in the AME church, but the form his movement took, the extent of his contacts, and the specifics of their plans we shall never know for certain. If Vesey and his fellows had been simply victims of white paranoia, it is hard to see why they steadfastly went to their deaths silently instead of protesting their innocence. The congregation of Charleston's African Methodist Episcopal church know enough to have revered Vesey ever since as a hero of resistance to oppression. Whether he planned to massacre the whites of Charleston or not, Vesey faced his executioners convinced that he died in a "glorious cause."[104]

Denmark Vesey's rebellion had surprisingly far-reaching consequences for a nonevent. It convinced white Charlestonians that "our NEGROES are truly the *Jacobins* of the country."[105] It led not only to tighter security measures but also to stricter limitations on black religious gatherings and on the ability of free Negroes to communicate out of state. Fearing subversives from outside, the state authorities decided to keep any arriving free black sailor locked up until his ship prepared to weigh anchor. This rule, when applied to British subjects, violated a treaty, and, when applied to northern citizens, violated the national Constitution. Defying repeated protests and the federal judiciary, Charleston harbor enforced the rule until the Civil War, and other southern port cities imitated it.[106] In South Carolina politics, Vesey's conspiracy had profound implications, which included influencing the momentous transformation of John C. Calhoun from a nationalist into the most famous champion of state rights.

---

103. For conflicting viewpoints, see William Freehling, *The Reintegration of American History* (New York, 1994), 34–58; Michael P. Johnson, "Denmark Vesey and His Co-Conspirators," WMQ 58 (2001): 915–76; the Forum on "The Making of a Slave Conspiracy," WMQ 59 (2002): 135–202; Robert Paquette, "From Rebellion to Revisionism," *Journal of the Historical Society* 4 (2004): 291–334; Egerton, *He Shall Go Out Free*, Appendix II, 233–60.

104. Reported by Mary Beach, quoted by Michael P. Johnson, "Reading Evidence," WMQ 59 (2002): 195–96.

105. Edwin C. Holland, quoted in William Freehling, *Prelude to Civil War* (New York, 1965), 59.

106. See W. Jeffrey Bolster, *Black Jacks: African American Seamen in the Age of Sail* (Cambridge, Mass., 1997), 192–214. In those days federal judges did not have the authority to issue habeas corpus writs to state courts.

5

Awakenings of Religion

When the state of Connecticut disestablished religion in 1818, the prominent revival preacher Lyman Beecher fell into depression and apprehension. He had fought hard to protect his faith from political defeat, and he had lost. "It was as dark a day as ever I saw," he recalled. "The injury done to the cause of Christ, as we then supposed, was irreparable. For several days I suffered what no tongue can tell *for the best thing that ever happened to the State of Connecticut.* It cut the churches loose from dependence on state support. It threw them wholly on their own resources and on God."[1] As Beecher came to realize, the change in status proved an advantageous trade-off for organized religion.

Americans eventually came to think of the separation of church and state as one of the achievements of the Revolution, and as guaranteed by the Bill of Rights. Actually, these common beliefs are but half-truths. The Revolution separated church and state in those places where the Church of England had been established in colonial times. But in several New England states, Congregationalist religious establishments remained in place. Unlike the Anglican establishments, those of the Congregationalists had been on the winning side of the Revolution and did not seem discredited by American independence. The Bill of Rights, added to the national Constitution in 1791, read: "Congress shall make no law respecting an establishment of religion or prohibiting the free exercise thereof." Applying specifically to Congress, this First Amendment restricted the federal government only, not the states.[2] The Congregational Standing Orders (as these establishments were called) persisted in Vermont, Connecticut, New Hampshire, and Massachusetts. In Vermont the Baptists, resenting discrimination against their denomination, forced disestablishment in 1807, but in the other three the connection between church and state persisted. With slight variation from state to state, these establishments

---

1. *The Autobiography of Lyman Beecher*, ed. Barbara M. Cross (Cambridge, Mass., 1961), I, 252–53.
2. States no longer have the right to maintain establishments of religion. In the twentieth century, the U.S. Supreme Court held that the Fourteenth Amendment (adopted in 1867) "incorporated" freedoms of the Bill of Rights and made them applicable to the states.

created a presumption that all citizens belonged to the Congregational Church and could be taxed for its support, unless they filed a statement that they were active members of a different Christian congregation in their locality.[3]

Any establishment of religion, even as democratic a religion as Yankee Congregationalism, violated the tenets of Jeffersonian Republicanism. The Republican Party in New England embraced the goal of disestablishment, which proved good politics as well as sound ideology. After the War of 1812, rallying a coalition of secularists and religious minorities, Republicans used the issue successfully to overcome the normal Federalist majorities in New Hampshire and Connecticut. The Episcopalians (as the Anglicans were called after the Revolution) had usually voted Federalist like the Congregationalists, but the disestablishment issue won them over, along with the other religious minorities, to the Republicans. By strengthening the Republican Party in New England, the politics of disestablishment made New England more like the rest of the country and helped set the stage for the "era of good feelings." Under Republican leadership, New Hampshire separated church from state in 1817, and Connecticut in 1818, leaving Massachusetts the only state with an establishment of religion, which would endure until 1833.[4]

Ever since Constantine the Great had made Christianity the established religion of the Roman Empire, the Western world had typically connected church and state. Now, the Americans undertook to experiment with their separation: Religion would be purely voluntary. The results astonished both friends and foes of Christianity. "They say ministers have lost their influence; the fact is, they have gained" by disestablishment, Beecher observed. "By voluntary efforts, societies, missions, and revivals, they exert a deeper influence than ever they could by queues, and shoe-buckles, and cocked hats, and gold-headed canes."[5] Far from hindering religion, the American model of voluntarism hugely facilitated it, liberating powerful religious energies. Religion, which had played such an important part in the life of the American colonies, was reinvigorated and reawakened in the life of the American republic. Religious denominations

3. The state laws providing for these establishments did not actually specify the Congregational denomination as the recipient of public support, only Protestantism; in practice, however, the support went to Congregationalism.
4. See William G. McLoughlin, *New England Dissent, 1630–1833: The Baptists and the Separation of Church and State* (Cambridge, Mass., 1971), II, 877–911 (on New Hampshire), 1025–62 (on Connecticut), 1189–1262 (on Massachusetts).
5. Beecher, *Autobiography*, I, 253.

and religious action organizations multiplied beyond number. Americans of this generation experienced widespread direct democracy through the creation, administration, and financing of churches and other voluntary societies. Indeed, the religious institutions they created sometimes displayed more democracy than the nation's civic ones. Women, African Americans, and newly arrived poor immigrants were all participating in religion, often in leadership roles, before they participated in politics. The churches and other voluntary associations nurtured American democracy.[6]

II

No one illustrated the power of religious voluntarism better than the indefatigable Lyman Beecher. Son of a blacksmith, reared on his uncle's Connecticut farm, Beecher's attendance at the local Yale College did not get rid of the homespun rusticity of his accent and manner. But Lyman Beecher made himself one of the most influential of the many who labored to build Christ's Kingdom in the young republic. His sermons proclaimed the universal appeal of the Risen Christ to people of every race, nation, sex, and class. From small-town pastorates in Connecticut and Long Island he moved to the big city (Boston in 1826) and then to the West (Cincinnati in 1832) to carry the message of the gospel. Wherever he went, his preaching manifested his physical vigor, sense of humor, and passionate conviction. Beecher took as his mission not simply the winning of individual souls but the transformation of society as a whole. "The great aim of the Christian Church in its relation to the present life is not only to renew the individual man, but also to reform human society," he declared. Accordingly, Beecher not only preached revivals, he founded reform movements and the organizations needed to implement them. One who knew him well commented, "He had no small ambitions."[7]

Beginning in 1812, Beecher embraced the cause of temperance, infusing it with his religious zeal. The problem he addressed was a real one. For centuries, alcohol had mitigated hardship, cold, and pain, helped celebrate harvests and festivals, and provided periodic relief from hard work. Along with the comforts of alcohol went its abuse and the toleration of its

---

6. See Nathan Hatch, *The Democratization of American Christianity* (New Haven, 1989); Mark Noll, *America's God* (New York, 2002).

7. Quoted in *Autobiography*, II, 399. See Vincent Harding, *A Certain Magnificence: Lyman Beecher and the Transformation of American Protestantism* (Brooklyn, 1991); Robert H. Abzug, *Cosmos Crumbling: American Reform and the Religious Imagination* (New York, 1994), 30–56.

abuse. Americans in the early nineteenth century quaffed alcohol in prodigious quantities. In 1825, the average American over fifteen years of age consumed seven gallons of alcohol a year, mostly in the form of whiskey and hard cider. (The corresponding figure at the start of the twenty-first century was less than two gallons, most of it from beer and wine.) Workers typically took a midmorning break and a midafternoon break, both accompanied by alcohol, as well as liquor with every meal. To entertain guests meant to ply them with several kinds of alcohol until some fell down. All social classes drank heavily; college students, journeyman printers, agricultural laborers, and canal-diggers were especially notorious. Schoolchildren might face an inebriated teacher in the classroom. Although socially tolerated, drunkenness frequently generated violence, especially domestic violence, and other illegal behavior. In such a society, intemperance represented a serious issue of public health, comparable to the problems of drug abuse experienced in later generations.[8]

Making temperance a Christian cause constituted an innovation, for traditional Christianity had not discouraged drinking. Indeed, Beecher recalled, ministerial conferences during his youth had been occasions for heavy convivial drinking. Unlike a later generation of crusaders, Beecher never thought the legal prohibition of alcohol a practical solution; he relied purely on changing public attitudes. This was no mean feat. To take a stand against the strong social pressures to drink took real courage, especially for young men. To help them, temperance workers paid reformed alcoholics to go on speaking tours, published temperance tracts, put on temperance plays, and drove the "water wagon" through towns encouraging converts to jump on. Publicists and organizers like Beecher struck a nerve with the public. The temperance cause resonated among people in all walks of life, rural and urban, white and black. Although it began in the Northeast, temperance reached the South and West and exerted powerful and lasting influence there.[9] At first the temperance advocates restricted themselves to encouraging moderation (hence the name "temperance"); in this phase they condemned only distilled liquors, not beer and wine. At the grassroots level, however, it became apparent that total abstinence made a more effective appeal. Beecher endorsed this shift in *Six Sermons on Intemperance* (1825). Those who signed a temperance pledge were

8. See W. J. Rorabaugh, *The Alcoholic Republic* (New York, 1979), 1–146; Joyce Appleby, *Inheriting the Revolution* (Cambridge, Mass., 2000), 204–15; Mark Lender and James Martin, *Drinking in America* (New York, 1987), 205–6.

9. See John Quist, *Restless Visionaries: The Social Roots of Antebellum Reform in Alabama and Michigan* (Baton Rouge, 1998).

encouraged to put a *T* after their names if willing to take the extra step of pledging total abstinence; from this derives our word "teetotaler."[10]

This campaign to alter age-old habits and attitudes proved amazingly successful: consumption of alcohol, especially of hard liquor, declined steadily and dramatically after 1830, falling to 1.8 gallons per person over fifteen by the late 1840s.[11] As important as this success, however, was the example the reformers set of organizing voluntary societies to influence public opinion. Beecher conceived the societies as forming "a disciplined moral militia."[12] The American Temperance Society, founded in 1826, served as a model for other movements. Through such issue-oriented organizations, reformers transcended geographical and denominational limitations to wage nationwide campaigns. The voluntary associations became a conspicuous feature of American society from that time forward. They distributed Bibles and tracts, supported missions foreign and domestic, and addressed such varied social problems as poverty, prostitution, and the abuse of women, children, animals, convicts, and the insane. Most momentous of all their activities would be their crusade against slavery.[13]

Lyman's wife, Roxana Foote Beecher, ran a school for girls. Her academy made an essential contribution to supporting their large family, for then as now the clerical profession was generally underpaid. The school also demonstrated the Beechers' commitment to developing the intellectual potential of women. The five daughters in the family included Harriet Beecher Stowe, the novelist, Isabella Beecher Hooker, the woman suffragist, and Catharine Beecher, the founder of home economics. Among the eight sons were Edward, who worked for the abolition of slavery, Henry Ward, the most famous American preacher in the next generation, and Thomas, an innovative urban pastor.[14] The elder Beechers taught their children to think for themselves, and in adulthood the daughters and sons staked out their own theological positions. But in a variety of ways they continued their parents' work of trying to reshape American society along moral and religious lines.[15]

---

10. Beecher, *Autobiography*, I, 179. See also Ian R. Tyrell, *Sobering Up: From Temperance to Prohibition in Antebellum America* (Westport, Conn., 1979), 54–87.
11. Rorabaugh, *Alcoholic Republic*, 8, 233.
12. Quoted in Abzug, *Cosmos Crumbling*, 45, from Beecher, *A Reformation of Morals Practicable and Indispensable* (1813).
13. See John G. West, *The Politics of Revelation and Reason* (Lawrence, Kans., 1996), 84–129; James W. Fraser, *Pedagogue for God's Kingdom* (Lanham, Md., 1985), 25–48.
14. Isabella and Thomas were children of Lyman's second wife, Harriet Porter Beecher.
15. The best study of the family as a whole is Marie Caskey, *Chariot of Fire: Religion and the Beecher Family* (New Haven, 1977).

Taken together, the members of the Beecher family demonstrate how the heirs of the Puritans coped, not simply with the disestablishment of religion, but also with the demise of the Federalist Party and New England's shrinking political influence in a growing Union. They devised new means of influencing public opinion outside of politics: education, literature, magazines, religious revivals, and organized reform. They engaged the energies of people in all walks of life, not simply a privileged elite. As a result their evangelical movement exerted a powerful social, moral, and cultural influence over the United States during the critical transition to industrialization and urbanization.[16]

When Lyman and Roxana were courting, they engaged in theological discussion. Lyman had taken up a strict form of Calvinist thought developed by Samuel Hopkins. Hopkins taught that God should be loved for His own sake, not for the sake of reward; therefore the highest and most disinterested virtue must consist in being willing to be damned to hell, if God so wished. Hopkinsianism provoked much discussion at the time, engaging as it did both the high seriousness and the love of logical argument characteristic of old-time Yankees. Lyman tried it out on Roxana, to no avail. "The disinterested love to God which you think is alone the genuine love, I see not how we can be certain we possess," she replied; "our love of happiness and love of God are so inseparably connected." Roxana's was the conventional Christian position: One is not required to welcome the prospect of damnation. "Could any real Christian rejoice if God should take from him the mercy bestowed?" she demanded.[17]

Roxana had made her point. Lyman turned away from Hopkins to a different theological mentor, Nathaniel William Taylor of Yale. Taylor addressed problems of human moral responsibility in a way that many revival preachers found helpful. He reinterpreted the Reformation doctrine of original sin to mean that sinning was universal but not causally necessary. Although all human beings sinned, they possessed "power to the contrary," that is, the moral power to refrain from sinning if they chose. Taylor designed his formulation to facilitate revivals, by encouraging the preacher to emphasize the importance of making a conscious choice for Christ. Applied by Beecher and other revivalists, Taylor's teachings became known as "New School Calvinism." In wrestling with the problem of reconciling human responsibility with divine foreknowledge and

---

16. See Daniel Walker Howe, ed., *Victorian America* (Philadelphia, 1976).
17. Roxana Foote to Lyman Beecher, Sept. 1, 1798, quoted in Beecher, *Autobiography*, I, 56. See also Joseph Conforti, *Samuel Hopkins and the New Divinity Movement* (Grand Rapids, Mich., 1981).

omnipotence, Taylor participated in a dialogue that stretched across centuries of Christian history. The answers he came up with, reconciling the free choices of the autonomous individual with the intellectual heritage of the Reformation, reflected concerns typical of his own time and place. Taylor's New School of thought largely replaced Hopkins's doctrines among the next generation of Calvinist revivalists in the North.[18]

Roxana Foote Beecher died of consumption (as tuberculosis was then called) in 1816 at the age of forty-one. She had borne nine children in seventeen years; with her dying breath she consecrated them all to God's service, a charge they could never forget.[19] Although Lyman remarried (twice, since he outlived his second wife too) he mourned for Roxana the rest of his life. He kept on trying to rally the diverse Protestant denominations in one crusade after another, first to prevent the spread of Unitarianism in the East, then to compete with the Catholics in founding colleges in the West. Theological conservatives called Old School Calvinists put him on trial for heresy in 1835. Beecher claimed his opponents were out to get him because of his antislavery stands; in any case, he won acquittal. Meanwhile, he had become president of Lane Seminary in Ohio. Beecher did not retire until 1850, at the age of seventy-five. When visiting the church of his son Henry Ward Beecher in Brooklyn, the old man remained as strong in spirit as ever: "If God should tell me that I might choose . . . whether to die and go to heaven, or to begin my life over again and work once more (straightening himself up, and his eye kindling, with finger lifted up), I would enlist again in a minute!"[20]

III

Early in the morning of October 10, 1821, alone in the woods outside the little town of Adams in western New York state, Charles Grandison Finney was born again in Christ. It was a transforming experience for the twenty-nine-year-old apprentice lawyer. Upon walking back to the law firm, Finney told a would-be client, "Deacon Barney, I have a retainer from the Lord Jesus Christ to plead his cause, and I cannot plead yours." With that, the young man left the practice of law and embarked upon his

18. Bruce Kuklick, *Churchmen and Philosophers* (New Haven, 1985), 94–111; Leo P. Hirrel, *Children of Wrath: New School Calvinism and Antebellum Reform* (Lexington, Ky., 1998), 26–40, 63–64; William R. Sutton, "The Influence of Nathaniel W. Taylor on Revivalism in the Second Great Awakening," *Religion and American Culture* 2 (Winter 1992): 23–48.
19. Harding, *Certain Magnificence*, 101.
20. *Autobiography*, II, 414.

famous career as an evangelist.[21] Although lacking formal theological training (or even a college education), Finney obtained a license to preach from the Presbyterian regional authority. Like Abraham Lincoln and many other Americans of his generation, Finney was largely self-educated but not badly educated.

An identifiable conversion experience, accompanied by a once-and-for-all decision for Christ, was the central event in the spiritual life of Christians in the evangelical Reformed tradition into which Finney had been born. Based on New Testament accounts like the conversion of St. Paul, the tradition had been particularly important in America through the influence of the New England Puritans and their Yankee descendants. In the revivals that he conducted, Finney would play an important role in perpetuating this tradition and spreading it throughout the United States and Britain. The revivalists of Finney's generation saw themselves as carrying on the work of such eighteenth-century evangelicals as Jonathan Edwards and George Whitefield. They called the revivals that Edwards and Whitefield had participated in "the Great Awakening" and their own work "the Second Great Awakening." The terms have stuck.[22]

Many observers, both in Finney's time and since, have been struck by the differences between Finney and Jonathan Edwards rather than the similarities. Old School Calvinists considered Finney's theology a betrayal of Edwardsean intellectual consistency. In at least one respect the difference between the two great evangelists was explicit. Edwards had regarded religious revivals as ultimately mysterious, the action of divine grace. By contrast Finney boldly proclaimed, "A revival of religion is not a miracle" but a human work, a "result of the right use of the constituted means." The evangelist's job was to employ these means effectively in the effort to save souls. A good evangelist should be as self-conscious about his methods as a good farmer about scientific agriculture, Finney declared. If all the farmers waited upon the sovereignty of God "to give them a crop only when it pleases him," the world would starve.[23] By putting evangelical preaching on a scientific basis, Finney and his co-workers hoped to transcend the cycle of revivals and declensions, creating

21. Charles Hambrick-Stowe, *Charles G. Finney and the Spirit of American Evangelicalism* (Grand Rapids, Mich., 1996), 1–21; Charles G. Finney, *Autobiography* (Westwood, N.J., 1908; orig. pub. as *Memoirs*, 1876), 21–24.

22. One of the most influential books about Edwards and Whitefield, and still one of the best, was written by a scholarly evangelical clergyman of this generation: Joseph Tracy, *The Great Awakening* (Boston, 1842).

23. Charles G. Finney, *Lectures on Revivals of Religion*, ed. William G. McLoughlin (1835; Cambridge, Mass., 1960), 13–14.

a continuous downpour where once there had been but intermittent showers of grace. In their new theology of how revivalism should be organized, the evangelists turned themselves into early psychologists of the techniques of persuasion.

While he held settled pastorates in several places during his career, Finney's fame rested on his role as a traveling evangelist. The "new measures" he popularized but did not invent defined the practices of modern revivalism. Upon arriving in town, he would hold prolonged revival meetings and continue them for several days. Sometimes he singled out individuals, praying for them by name to encourage their conversion. Persons who seemed promising candidates might be seated in front of the church on what was called "the anxious bench," especially if they were prominent citizens whose conversion would encourage others. Finney benefited from a charismatic personality and an intuitive sense of his audience. He always preached extemporaneously, never from a prepared script. He used colloquial, forthright language. America enjoyed a free marketplace in religion, and through his *Lectures on Revivals of Religion* (published in 1835) Finney instructed preachers on how to market their message.[24] In years to come, both political and commercial applications would be found for his principles.

Finney's innovations in promoting revivals provoked controversy, even among Christians who shared his objectives. Although he hoped for the cooperation of the settled clergy in the areas he visited, they sometimes regarded him as an interloper and a threat. He couched his message in terms of making a personal decision for Christ, not in terms of waiting for the grace of God. "Instead of telling sinners to use the means of grace and pray for a new heart, we called on them to make themselves a new heart," he explained.[25] Christians loyal to the theology of the Reformation believed such an appeal left too little role for divine initiative. Some of them reproached Finney for excessive emotionalism, as other revivalists have been reproached before and since. But the feature of Finney's revivals most criticized in his own day was the role played by women. Not only did women organize the religious and benevolent activities that surrounded and followed the revivals, they participated in the actual meetings, sometimes speaking and praying in public. Defending himself against critics of women's public participation, Finney declared, "I had

---

24. Ibid. See also William G. McLoughlin, *Modern Revivalism: Charles G. Finney to Billy Graham* (New York, 1959).
25. Finney, *Autobiography*, 189.

no agency in introducing the practice," when it first appeared in Utica.[26] This rings true: The Christian women of western New York took the initiative, and Finney accepted it. His wife, Lydia Finney (from Whitestown near Utica), encouraged the women to organize and assert themselves. In the western New York town of Seneca Falls the women's suffrage movement would be born in 1848.[27]

Finney's early clerical critics included Lyman Beecher. Beecher, however, wanted to forge an ecumenical evangelicalism that could unite evangelicals to combat the influence of Unitarianism on the one hand and Roman Catholicism on the other. Accordingly, Beecher arranged for Finney and his supporters to meet with more conservative evangelicals at a conference in New Lebanon, New York, for a week in July 1827. Both sides wanted to encourage revivals. The Finneyites agreed not to call their colleagues "cold," "unconverted," or "dead"; the other side consented not to call the Finneyites "heretics," "enthusiasts," or "mad." On the rights of women to religious participation they had to agree to disagree. Later, Beecher invited Finney to preach at his Park Street Church in Boston as a gesture of conciliation and cooperation.[28]

Finney's career took him to many places, including Philadelphia, Wilmington, and Providence, as well as Boston, west to Ohio, and across the Atlantic to England and Wales.[29] He preached in the notorious, crime-ridden Five Points neighborhood of Manhattan, where he had a theater converted for his use. But he will always be primarily associated with the area of western New York state where he enjoyed his greatest revival triumphs, particularly in young Rochester. This is the area that became known as "the burned-over district," because the fires of religious zeal swept across it.[30] The region owed its growing population and prosperity to the Erie Canal. Its people were mostly Yankee migrants from New England. Among this potentially responsive audience, Finney felt "most at home," according to his biographer, "with young and middle-aged

26. Ibid., 178. On the role of women in organizing Finney's revivals, see Mary P. Ryan, *Cradle of the Middle Class* (Cambridge, Eng., 1981), 81–98.
27. See Nancy Hardesty, *Your Daughters Shall Prophesy: Revivalism and Feminism in the Age of Finney* (Brooklyn, 1991). Leonard Sweet, *The Minister's Wife* (Philadelphia, 1983), is a broader study than the title may suggest; on Lydia Finney, see 113–27, 159–72.
28. Harding, *Certain Magnificence*, chap. 14; Hambrick-Stowe, *Finney*, 71.
29. On his British trips, see Richard J. Carwardine, *Transatlantic Revivalism* (Westport, Conn., 1978).
30. Whitney R. Cross, *The Burned-Over District* (New York, 1950), 3; for Finney's own use of the term "burnt district," see his *Autobiography*, 78.

business and professional people, upwardly mobile master craftsmen, and women from the better families"—that is, with the middle classes responding to the opportunities presented by the new canal. They included residents of the surrounding countryside as well as those of the town itself. These people seized opportunities for bettering themselves socially and personally as well as commercially.[31]

Like Beecher, Finney saw social implications in the Christian message. He preached against the evils of alcohol and tobacco. He ran greater risks by his active opposition to slavery. Although New York had begun a process of gradual emancipation, some persons remained in bondage there until 1827. When Finney was preaching at Chatham Street Chapel (the remodeled Manhattan theater), he refused the sacrament of communion to slaveholders on the grounds that they were unrepentant sinners. In October 1833, he offered the chapel to a meeting of the New York Anti-Slavery Society. Their demands for immediate, uncompensated abolition met a hostile reception in New York, a city heavily dependent on the cotton trade. When a mob stormed the building, the leaders of the society barely escaped—among them the evangelical businessmen Arthur and Lewis Tappan, Finney's chief financial backers in New York City. A series of disorders followed, all deriving from the church's support for the antislavery cause. After the Broadway Tabernacle was built for Finney's use to replace the theater-turned-chapel, arsonists burned it down. Finney's undaunted New York supporters raised more money and rebuilt it; the auditorium could seat three thousand people.[32]

In 1835, Finney went to Ohio to teach theology at the exciting newly founded Oberlin College. Oberlin had been created by one of the major student rebellions in American history. Seventy-five radical antislavery students left Lane Seminary in Cincinnati en masse, protesting racist practices by the seminary trustees. Led by Theodore Dwight Weld, a Finney convert, the former Lane students cooperated with the philanthropic Arthur Tappan to found Oberlin and invited Finney to come teach there. Ironically, Lane's president was the antislavery Lyman Beecher, who had admitted a former slave as a Lane student. Beecher had been out of town when the campus crisis came to a head. Explosive

---

31. Hambrick-Stowe, *Finney*, 107. On the social characteristics of Finney's converts, see also Paul E. Johnson, A *Shopkeeper's Millennium: Society and Revivals in Rochester, New York, 1815–1837* (New York, 1978), partially corrected by Mary P. Ryan, *Cradle of the Middle Class*, esp. 103; Curtis D. Johnson, *Islands of Holiness: Rural Religion in Upstate New York, 1790–1860* (Ithaca, N.Y., 1989).
32. Hambrick-Stowe, *Finney*, 142–62.

rumors circulated among the Cincinnati townspeople that Lane students were associating with free blacks as social equals. Fearing attacks on the school by white supremacist mobs, the trustees acted in Beecher's absence to regulate social contact between the races and discourage discussion of antislavery. When Beecher got back, he found it all he could do to keep Lane from disintegrating completely.[33]

Finney taught at Oberlin College for the rest of his life, using it as a base from which to travel on revival tours. He also held revival meetings in the town of Oberlin, speaking to overflow crowds in a huge tent that flew a banner inscribed "Holiness to the Lord." Finney was both a theology professor and minister of the local First Church, for many years the largest building west of the Appalachians. In 1851, he would become president of the college. During Finney's years there, Oberlin defined the cutting edge of social and religious innovation. At a time when women could find little higher education open to them, it was the first coeducational college in the world. It trained Christian missionaries and antislavery activists of both sexes. Its early graduates included Antoinette Brown, Lucy Stone, and other early crusaders for women's rights. The college was racially desegregated on more than a token basis; indeed, before he accepted his professorship Finney stipulated that "we should be allowed to receive colored people on the same conditions that we did white people."[34] Oberlin became a safe haven on the underground railroad for slaves escaping to freedom in Canada. Finney's impact on history derives not only from his own efforts but also from the work of those he converted and trained. For some of them, the reforms that for him were ancillary to Christianity would become primary goals.

Meanwhile, Finney's theological views evolved further away from the Reformation creeds. In 1836, he left the Presbyterians and affiliated with Congregationalism, a more decentralized denomination that left him theologically freer. More and more he emphasized the freedom of the will and the doctrine of sanctification, that is, the duty of Christians after their conversion experience to improve their conduct and purify their lives. He called the process "Christian perfection."[35] Many shook their heads at this apparent presumptuousness. Still, Finney's great disciple Theodore Dwight Weld could well ask, "When shall we look on his like again?"[36] For widespread

33. Benjamin P. Thomas, *Theodore Dwight Weld* (New Brunswick, N.J., 1950), 11–16, 70–88; Lawrence T. Lesick, *The Lane Rebels* (Metuchen, N.J., 1980), 132.
34. Finney, *Autobiography*, 333.
35. Ibid., 340–41.
36. Quoted in Hambrick-Stowe, *Finney*, 197.

influence, personal integrity, social conscience, and spiritual power, few American evangelists of a later age could equal Charles G. Finney.

IV

The revivalism of Beecher and Finney was interdenominational and ecumenical in purpose. The revivalism of the early Methodists, by contrast, focused on building a particular denomination. In fulfilling their mission, the Methodist circuit riders achieved unparalleled collective success. These men, generally artisans, shopkeepers, or small farmers by background, volunteered to ride through the remote backcountry, bringing the message of the gospel to otherwise isolated settlers. Although practically none of them possessed formal theological training, they would preach sermons and offer pastoral counseling, refute freethinkers and heretics in debate, and convert sinners and Indians. Lacking much benefit of education themselves, they nevertheless encouraged literacy and schooling for others and would give away Bibles and sell other uplifting books for the profit of their movement. In the early days they usually observed celibacy, for the Methodist leadership believed single men more suited to the endless travel and hardship of life on the circuit. (The circuit riders sometimes resembled Catholic priests in other ways too, addressed as "Father" and clothed in black.)[37]

Peter Cartwright, one of the most renowned of the Methodist itinerants in Tennessee and Illinois, described their life in his *Autobiography:*

> A Methodist preacher in those days, when he felt that God had called him to preach, instead of hunting up a college or Biblical institute, hunted up a hard pony of a horse, and some traveling apparatus, and with his library always at hand, namely, Bible, Hymn Book, and [Methodist] Discipline, he started, and with a text that never wore out nor grew stale, he cried, "Behold the Lamb of God, that taketh away the sin of the world." In this way he went through storms of wind, hail, snow, and rain; climbed hills and mountains, traversed valleys, plunged through swamps, swam swollen streams, lay out all night, wet, weary, and hungry, held his horse by the bridle all night, or tied him to a limb, slept with his saddle blanket for a bed, his saddle or saddle-bags for his pillow, and his old big coat or blanket, if he had any, for a covering. . . . Under such circumstances, who among us would now say, "Here am I, Lord, send me?"[38]

37. T. Scott Miyakawa, *Protestants and Pioneers* (Chicago, 1964), 109–16; Jon Butler, *Awash in a Sea of Faith: Christianizing the American People* (Cambridge, Mass., 1990), 237.
38. Peter Cartwright, *Autobiography*, ed. Charles Wallis (1856; New York, 1956), 164.

The circuit rider—in effect a Christian Lone Ranger—stands among America's most heroic western frontiersmen. He received a miserable stipend and often had difficulty collecting even that. The Discipline that Cartwright notes he carried and taught represented a code of behavior that reinforced family and community values in a violent society. The Discipline laid down rules against swearing, drunkenness, sexual license, and ostentatious dress and enforced John Wesley's maxim, "Cleanliness is next to godliness." It provided a way for ordinary people to reorder their lives, even when living in hardship conditions. A man of the people, the circuit-rider brought moral order and civilization to the people.[39]

Methodism was still a new movement in the early national period, having originated in the eighteenth century within the Church of England under the leadership of an Anglican priest, John Wesley. Aided by the magnificent hymns of his brother Charles (most of them celebrations of Christ's expected return), Wesley won many followers in all walks of life, but especially among skilled workers (artisans). His devotional regimen, called the Wesleyan "method," gave his followers their name. At the time of the Revolution, Wesley's Tory politics made his movement unpopular in the United States, and at the close of the war scarcely fifteen thousand Methodists worshipped in the new republic. American Methodism was rescued by the devotion and organizational ability of Francis Asbury, who died in 1816. During his lifetime Methodism established itself as a denomination entirely separate from Anglicanism, with bishops of its own (hence the name Methodist Episcopal Church). Building upon his legacy, the next generation of Methodist preachers made their institution the largest religious denomination in the United States. By 1850, Methodists in the United States numbered 2.7 million, including children.[40]

Soon after the beginning of the nineteenth century, the Methodists began to make use of "camp meetings." These gatherings would last for several days, to make it worthwhile for rural families to spend a day or more traveling to attend. Obviously such events required extensive planning, organization, and publicity. Camp meetings took place not only on the western frontier but in rural areas throughout the United States. American Methodists held three to four hundred of them annually, drawing an attendance reliably estimated at about a million people a year. They provided welcome opportunities for socializing and the exchange of news to

39. See John H. Wigger, *Taking Heaven by Storm: Methodism and the Rise of Popular Christianity in America* (New York, 1998), 48–79, 98–103.
40. Russell Richey, *Early American Methodism* (Bloomington, 1991); Roger Finke and Rodney Stark, *The Churching of America* (New Brunswick, N.J., 1992), 113.

people leading lives of isolation. They also proved extraordinarily success-ful in winning converts to Methodism and were widely imitated by others—including Finney.[41]

To carry on between camp meetings or visits by a circuit rider, the Methodists organized their followers into "classes" of about thirty persons each. In 1815, some seven thousand of these classes met in the United States. They provided the indispensable grassroots structure of Method-ism. The class leaders, responsible laypersons, led worship, collected fi-nancial contributions, and enforced discipline. Once every three months all the classes in a circuit would hold a quarterly meeting, a spiritual as well as administrative occasion. The Methodist system of organization demonstrated impressive effectiveness; no other association of any kind in the United States grew so dramatically and over so large an area in so short a time as Methodism. Membership of Methodist classes soared from 175,000 in 1810 to 1,247,000 by 1850, increasing by 168 percent between 1810 and 1820, and by 86.5 percent in the decade of the 1830s.[42]

Becoming a Methodist class leader could be an invaluable leadership experience for a person of humble origin. Circuit riders usually arose from the ranks of male class leaders. Women and African Americans could be class leaders; they could also become exhorters, the term for the laypeople who delivered what were in effect mini-sermons.[43] African American men, free or slave, could also become licensed Methodist preachers, even in the South. Black preachers usually worked locally rather than on circuit—an obvious necessity in the case of those who were enslaved.[44] Many early Methodists disapproved of slavery and even emancipated their own slaves at financial sacrifice. They did not gener-ally agitate the issue publicly, however, until the 1840s.[45]

One of the most famous of the Methodist exhorters in this period was Phoebe Palmer, daughter of an English immigrant who had been con-verted by Wesley himself. In 1835, she began addressing a typical Methodist women's prayer meeting in her living room in New York City; four years later, she opened her "Tuesday Meeting for the Promotion of

---

41. Wigger, *Taking Heaven by Storm*, 96–97; Hatch, *Democratization of American Chris-tianity*, 49–56.

42. Membership table in David Hempton, *Methodism* (New Haven, 2005), 212. See also Donald Matthews, "The Second Great Awakening as an Organizing Process," *Ameri-can Quarterly* 21 (1969): 23–43.

43. Wigger, *Taking Heaven by Storm*, 81–83.

44. Randy Sparks, *On Jordan's Stormy Banks: Evangelicalism in Mississippi, 1773–1876* (Athens, Ga., 1994), 66.

45. See, for example, Peter Cartwright's *Autobiography*.

Holiness" to the public, including men. Palmer brought the practices of the Methodist class to bear upon the evangelical movement as a whole, for leading evangelicals of all denominations came to hear her. She always refused to hold the Tuesday meetings anywhere but in a home (her house had to be enlarged to accommodate them). She did, however, travel widely in the United States and Britain, and she addressed many a camp-meeting revival. Like Finney, she preached Christian perfectionism and "entire sanctification." She continued her work until her death in 1872. Phoebe Palmer came to be recognized as a founder of the Holiness branch of evangelicalism and a precursor of the Pentacostal movement.[46]

The early Methodists devoted more attention to organization than they did to the study of theology. Most Methodist preachers declared the Bible to be self-explanatory, requiring no learned exegesis. Following Wesley, the great majority embraced Arminianism, that is, belief in free will, rather than the philosophical determinism of Calvinism. Early Methodist Arminianism was less an intellectual system than an affirmation of the competence and autonomy of the average person, in religion and life in general. Sometimes heated debates pitted Arminian against Calvinist spokesmen, and they attracted a widespread following that Americans today may find surprising. In evangelical practice, however, the distinction between Calvinism and Arminianism appeared less sharp than in doctrinal logic. Both taught that God extended grace to human beings, which they were morally responsible for accepting. John Wesley, for all his Arminianism, greatly admired his Calvinist evangelical contemporaries George Whitefield and Jonathan Edwards. There were even a few Calvinist Methodists, mainly from Wales, who took Whitefield as their theological mentor. (Historians still disagree about whether to classify Charles Finney as a Calvinist or an Arminian.)[47]

While Beecher's and Finney's kind of revival activity led to the formation of benevolent associations and reform movements, Methodist exhorters and preachers concentrated on creating classes, congregations, and churches. As a result of its enormous growth during the first half of the nineteenth century, Methodism gradually succeeded in replacing the

46. Charles Edward White, *The Beauty of Holiness: Phoebe Palmer as Revivalist and Feminist* (Grand Rapids, Mich., 1986).

47. Paul Conkin, *The Uneasy Center: Reformed Christianity in Antebellum America* (Chapel Hill, 1995), xii, 63–89; Richard B. Steele, *"Gracious Affection" and "True Virtue"* (Metuchen, N.J., 1994); Allen Guelzo, "Charles Grandison Finney and the New England Theology," *JER* 17 (1997): 61–94.

system of itinerancy with local clergy. Many a circuit rider eventually settled down to married life in a conventional ministry. Methodists erected church and chapel buildings, making class meetings in houses unnecessary. The fifty Methodist congregations at the time of the Revolution became twenty thousand by the time of the Civil War.[48]

Starting in the 1820s, Methodists also founded colleges and theological seminaries, which began to train a more professional clergy. The nature of the laity evolved over time too. Early Methodists had come mainly from the ranks of skilled artisans and small farmers. As the decades went by, these people's hard work and self-discipline paid off, and more and more Methodist laity joined the ranks of the middle class. When they did so, their characteristically austere way of life softened. The gradual refinement of Methodist homes and churches manifested personal and denominational success, but there were always "croakers" who mourned the transition and looked back fondly on the good old days of circuit riders and extreme simplicity. In the 1840s, some of those dissatisfied with the increasingly respectable character of the Methodist movement seceded to form the Wesleyan Methodist Church.[49] Most Methodists, however, welcomed the innovations and saw them as the fulfillment of their (and their parents') labors. The transformation of Methodism mirrored changes in other areas of American life, as it lost some of its rough-hewn pioneer edges.

Other Christian groups picked up where the Methodists left off, notably the Baptists. It is not easy to make generalizations about the Baptists, for they had a strong tradition of congregational independence and splintered into innumerable factions: Separate Baptists, Regular Baptists, United Baptists, General Baptists, Particular Baptists, Calvinist Baptists, Free-Will Baptists, Primitive Baptists, Anti-Mission Baptists, Two-Seed-in-the-Spirit Baptists. But all these groups did agree in rejecting infant baptism and insisting that the rite be performed on consenting adults by immersion, not merely the sprinkling or pouring of a small amount of water. Adult baptism by immersion reinforced the dramatic importance of the conversion experience that revival preachers worked to provoke. Some of the divisions among Baptists reflected social class differences; middle-class Baptists were more likely to support interdenominational cooperation on behalf of temperance, for example, while the Primitive Baptists (also called "Hard Shell" Baptists) warned that such reform activities were distractions and corruptions of the pure gospel message. While New

48. Butler, *Awash in a Sea of Faith*, 270.
49. Wigger, *Taking Heaven by Storm*, 173–95.

England Baptists supported institutions of higher learning (beginning with Brown University in colonial times), Baptist groups in other areas could be unashamedly anti-intellectual. Anti-Mission Baptists took the Calvinist doctrine of predestination so seriously that they declared missions to the heathen a waste of effort: If God intended to save a person, He would do so.[50]

The Baptists shared many characteristics with the early Methodists, except for the latter's centralized organization. Like the Methodists, they provided scope for lay leadership, recruited from the common people, and numbered women and African Americans among their leaders as well as followers. They too enforced discipline among members of their churches. They too had their itinerant preachers, as heroic if less well organized, such as John Leland, who led the Baptist fight for religious disestablishment, first in Virginia against the Episcopalians and then in New England against the Congregationalists.[51] While the Methodists evolved from a working-class to a middle-class constituency, the Baptists consistently recruited among all classes, but most especially among the rural poor. Many Baptist ministers in rural areas served as unpaid volunteers and earned their living as farmers. Among the most energetic in seeking converts on the frontier were Baptists from Virginia, who had a long tradition of resistance to the Anglican gentry of the tidewater. By 1850, it is estimated, the different kinds of Baptists together counted about 1.6 million members.[52]

The Baptists were the largest of many "restorationist" religious movements seeking to recover the New Testament faith and practice that they considered had been lost or corrupted. One of the most remarkable and successful restorationist movements emerged from the labors of Barton Stone, Elias Smith, and Alexander Campbell, among others. Stone had participated in the famous early camp meeting at Cane Ridge, Kentucky, in 1801. Smith came out of a New England Baptist background; Campbell, from a Scottish Presbyterian one. Since doctrinal disputes had led to such bigotry and cruelty over the centuries, these leaders reached the

---

50. See Gregory Willis, *Democratic Religion: Freedom, Authority, and Church Discipline in the Baptist South* (New York, 1997); Sparks, *On Jordan's Stormy Banks*; Bertram Wyatt-Brown, "The Antimission Movement in the Jacksonian South," *Journal of Southern History* 36 (1970): 501–29.

51. Hatch, *Democratization of American Christianity*, 95–102.

52. For the sake of consistency, this includes children, although Baptists themselves count only those baptized after the age of discretion. See Roger Finke and Rodney Stark, "Estimating 19th-Century Church Membership," *Journal for the Scientific Study of Religion* 25 (1985): 185; Finke and Stark, *Churching of America*, 113.

conclusion that all theological and creedal formulations must be wrong; Christians should confine themselves to the language of the New Testament and affirm or deny no religious doctrines beyond that. They hoped by this means to transcend and indeed eliminate denominationalism altogether. For this reason, they rejected ecclesiastical organization in favor of local autonomy and refused any name save "Christian." The rebirth of the primitive church was their objective; "no creed but the Bible," their slogan. Well under way by 1815, the Christian movement won many converts in the South and West, particularly among people impatient with Calvinist theology; by mid-century it claimed more than 200,000 of them.[53] The eventual outcome of the movement, however, renders a sobering judgment on human endeavors. The scriptures require interpretation, and restricting religious assertions to those of scripture proved no solution to the scandal of disagreement and division. In the end, the antidenominational Christian movement added to the number of denominations; indeed, they even wound up creating several: the Christian Connection, the Disciples of Christ, and the Churches of Christ.[54]

Among the new churches of the young republic were those of the free black people. Philadelphia, with a closely knit black community of twelve thousand in 1820, led the way. The first black Episcopal church (1794), the first black Methodist church (also 1794), the first black Presbyterian church (1809), and the first black northern Baptist church (also 1809) all appeared in that city. Often these congregations would remain part of their national denomination. But in 1816 the trustees of Philadelphia's Bethel Methodist Church, after years of property disputes with the central Methodist authorities, secured legal recognition of their independence. Thus they created a separate denomination, the African Methodist Episcopal Church, the one institution in the United States at the time entirely under black control. In 1817, the AME Church adopted its own Discipline. Soon another independent African American denomination joined it, the AME Zion Church, founded in New York City.[55]

At the time of the American Revolution, a slave in Kent County, Delaware, named Richard Allen had undergone a classic conversion

---

53. Alexander Campbell, quoted in Edwin Scott Gaustad, *Historical Atlas of Religion in America* (New York, 1962), 64.
54. See David Harrell Jr., *Quest for a Christian America* (Nashville, Tenn., 1966); Richard Hughes and Leonard Allen, *Illusions of Innocence: Protestant Primitivism in America* (Chicago, 1988).
55. Gary B. Nash, *Forging Freedom: The Formation of Philadelphia's Black Community* (Cambridge, Mass., 1988), 127–30, 199–202.

experience. "I cried to the Lord both night and day," he recalled; "all of a sudden my dungeon shook, my chains flew off, and, glory to God, I cried." From then on he felt confident: "The Lord, for Christ's sake, had heard my prayers and pardoned all my sins." The Methodists were already active in Delaware, and Allen's owner, Stokely Sturgis, allowed him to join them. One day he even permitted Allen to bring them into the master's house. There Sturgis heard a sermon by one of the greatest early Methodist preachers, Freeborn Garrettson. Sturgis too converted as a result, and expressed his new faith by allowing Allen to hire himself out and purchase his own freedom for two thousand dollars in depreciated Continental currency. It took five years of hard work and thrift, but Allen made the final payment in 1786. He had already begun to cooperate with Bishop Francis Asbury to spread Methodism among African Americans, and in 1794 founded Bethel Church in Philadelphia. When the AME Church declared its independence, Allen became its first bishop.[56]

Clergymen like Allen and his friend Absalom Jones, founding priest of St. Thomas's Episcopal in Philadelphia and like him a self-made former slave, established themselves as leaders and spokesmen for their community—a role the black clergy have never lost. In a world where they were shut out from so much else, African Americans found their churches a source of mutual strength and spiritual fulfillment. In a world where black talent was undervalued, their churches provided scope for it. African Americans formed evangelical moral reform associations analogous to their white counterparts, to support temperance and suppress vice, but with the added urgency of a desire for the collective "uplift" of the race as well of individuals.[57] Friend and foe alike recognized the free black churches as bastions of opposition to slavery and havens for those escaping from it.

As Richard Allen's account of his spiritual awakening illustrates, evangelical Christianity resonated powerfully among the slaves. The German philosopher Friedrich Nietzsche declared Christianity a religion well suited to slaves because of its emphasis on humility. Nietzsche ignored the liberating strain in the Christian message, but many African Americans heard it. Allen's religious metaphor expressed it well: "My chains flew off." Missions to the plantations were among the many missions organized

56. Albert J. Raboteau, *A Fire in the Bones* (Boston, 1995), 79–102; Allen is quoted in Carol George, *Segregated Sabbaths: Richard Allen and the Rise of Independent Black Churches* (New York, 1973), 26.
57. See Frederick Cooper, "Elevating the Race," *American Quarterly* 24 (1972), 604–25.

by the interdenominational evangelicals; however, Baptist and Methodist itinerants got there earlier and to greater effect. Ever since the First Awakening there had been preachers and exhorters among the slaves themselves, so the religion of the great antebellum revival did not come to them as an alien "white" intrusion. Slaves embraced evangelical Christianity as an affirmation of hope and self-respect, of moral order and justice in circumstances where these were scarce and precious.

Where a critical mass of participants could be assembled, as on large plantations, slaves often worshipped on their own, thereby provoking anxiety among whites who did not share Nietzsche's estimate of Christianity. Despite such misgivings, black preachers and exhorters, both free and slave, continued to be licensed and black congregations to be organized in the antebellum South. Of course, many slave congregations existed informally and do not show up in ecclesiastical records. The semisecret, potentially subversive network of religious associations among the enslaved has been termed an "invisible institution."[58]

In southern cities, slaves could also belong to congregations organized by free Negroes. One of these was the AME church in Charleston where Denmark Vesey and two of his closest associates served as class leaders; most of those executed with him belonged to it. The congregation traced its origins to Francis Asbury's visits to Charleston between 1785 and 1797. Drawing inspiration and instruction from the new AME church in Philadelphia, in 1817 Charleston's black Methodists founded an AME congregation of their own with over four thousand members, the majority of whom were enslaved. The harassment of this church by the local authorities could have pushed Vesey toward a decision to rebel.[59]

By 1820, one Methodist in five was black, and the percentage of black Baptists was probably even higher. In the South, most congregations held biracial services, with blacks and whites usually seated separately. Members of the two races heard each other's preaching and caught each other's forms of prayer and praise. The Second Great Awakening in the South fostered an extraordinary religious synthesis of African American

58. Albert Raboteau, *Slave Religion* (New York, 1978), 151–210; Donald Mathews, *Religion in the Old South* (Chicago, 1977), 185–236; Eugene Genovese, *Roll, Jordan, Roll: The World the Slaves Made* (New York, 1974), 161–284. The term "invisible institution" was invented by the African American sociologist E. Franklin Frazier and has been widely used since his time.

59. Peter Hinks, *To Awaken My Afflicted Brethren: David Walker and the Problem of Antebellum Slave Resistance* (University Park, Pa., 1997), 25–37; John Lofton, *Denmark Vesey's Revolt* (Kent, Ohio, 1983), 52–53.

and European American cultures. Preachers at camp meetings, of either race, might chant their sermons, punctuated with cries from the congregation: "Amen!" "Hallelujah!" "Lord, have mercy!" Out of this synthesis came a distinctive musical expression. From the European tradition came the practice of "lining out" the psalms: A leader sings a line, the congregation echoes it. The practice dovetailed readily with the "call-and-response" pattern of African music. It suited a society possessing more singers than hymnbooks—and where not everyone could read music or words. A northern visitor to a camp meeting in Mississippi in 1816 observed, "They sung in ancient style, lineing [*sic*] the Psalm, and uniting in every part of the house, both white and black."[60] American Christians drew inspiration from the great European tradition of evangelical hymnody, of Charles Wesley and Isaac Watts. But the extraordinary creativity of the Second Great Awakening also stimulated the production of American folk music of unparalleled power: the black spirituals and the gospel music of both races. Richard Allen, who emancipated himself first from sin and then from slavery, expressed the spirit of the awakening in one of the Methodist hymns he wrote:

> What poor despised company
> Of travellers are these,
> That's walking yonder narrow way,
> Along that rugged maze?
>
> Why they are of a royal line,
> They're children of a King,
> Heirs of immortal crown divine
> And loud for joy they sing.
>
> Why do they then appear so mean
> And why so much despised?
> Because of their rich robes unseen
> The world is not appriz'd.
>
> Why some of them seem poor distress'd
> And lacking daily bread.
> Heirs of immortal wealth possess'd
> With hidden Manna fed.[61]

---

60. Quoted in Sparks, *On Jordan's Stormy Banks*, p. 28.
61. Mechal Sobel, *Trabelin' On: The Slave Journey to an Afro-Baptist Faith* (Westport, Conn., 1979), 97–98, 140, 153, 160, 203; Raboteau, *Slave Religion*, 243–66; Hatch, *Democratization of American Christianity*, 146–61, quoting Allen's hymn on 157–58.

V

The closer one looks for the Era of Good Feelings in American politics the harder it is to find. By contrast, when one looks for evidence of religious awakening in this period, one finds it everywhere: not only in the astonishing variety of religious sects, both imported and native, but also in literature, politics, educational institutions, popular culture, social reforms, dietary reforms, utopian experiments, child-rearing practices, and relationships between the sexes.[62] In terms of duration, numbers of people involved, or any other measure, the Second Great Awakening dwarfed the First. Because of its diversity, perhaps it should be called a multitude of contemporaneous "awakenings."

While the number of religious options multiplied, so did the number of congregations and individual believers. The physical landscape reflected the formation of new congregations: Americans were erecting church buildings at the rate of a thousand a year.[63] While the U.S. population increased from 7.2 million in 1810 to 23.2 million in 1850, the number of church members increased even faster—although since the census did not enumerate people by religious groups, their numbers have to be extrapolated from other data. By the middle of the nineteenth century, an estimated one-third of the population affiliated with organized religion, twice the percentage of 1776, even though church membership was often deliberately demanding and difficult to achieve.[64] To be sure, this still represented a minority, and the evangelical movement would always be resisted in many quarters. But the Second Great Awakening put religious practice in the United States on an upward trajectory that would continue through the twentieth century. The contrast with Europe, where religious faith declined in the same era, is striking.

The evangelical revival inevitably provoked controversy. Even many religious people criticized its methods as manipulative and overly emotional, its theology as shallow and unorthodox. Major denominations that argued over the legitimacy of revivalism included the Presbyterians, Lutherans, and Episcopalians. And of course many people disliked religion altogether. From their point of view all the awakenings represented so much error, superstition, and meddlesome intrusion. Even the evangelists themselves disagreed with each other over issues of doctrine and

---

62. A provocative commentary on the broad significance of this awakening is Perry Miller's unfinished classic, *The Life of the Mind in America from the Revolution to the Civil War* (New York, 1965), 3–95.
63. Butler, *Awash in a Sea of Faith*, 270.
64. Finke and Stark, *Churching of America*, 16.

practice. Some evangelical sects, including the Disciples of Christ and the Anti-Mission Baptists, promoted revivals of their own but disapproved of the interdenominational benevolent associations. Fundamental doctrinal differences excluded other religious bodies from interdenominational evangelical cooperation: Roman Catholics, Jews, and Unitarians. As time went by, disagreements over slavery would increasingly embitter relations among the evangelicals.[65]

Assessing the implications of such a diverse and wide-ranging phenomenon as the Second Great Awakening is complicated and therefore difficult. The Awakening had an uneven impact; for example, religious adherence seems to have been higher in small towns than in either rural areas or big cities. Some of the consequences of the Awakening seem ambiguous. For people to have so many choices about which religion to embrace (if any) enhanced individualism. On the other hand, religion also strengthened community ties among church members. Religion stimulated innovation in society, as believers tried to bring social practice more into conformity with religious precepts. On the other hand, religion also exerted a conservative influence, reinvigorating cultural heritages that various social groups were trying to preserve in a New World. The revivals sometimes encouraged interdenominational cooperation and a sense of collective moral responsibility, but they were also a divisive force that split denominations and even tore individual congregations apart. The sects could be authoritarian, yet many people found them personally liberating. It is not even obvious to what extent we should define the Awakening as American. Although the evangelical movement was unusually successful and varied in the United States, it had its counterparts all over the world, and evangelicals and revivalists in Britain and the United States cooperated closely.

American religion flourished in a society with a thinly developed institutional structure, enlisting the energies of the people themselves. The most important social consequences of the Awakening in America derived from its trust in the capacities of ordinary people. In the early American republic, the most significant challenge to the traditional assumption that the worth of human beings depended on their race, class, and gender came from the scriptural teachings that all are equal in the sight of God and all are one in Christ. Different revivals appealed to different constituencies, but taken together, the Second Great Awakening

65. See James Bratt, ed., *Anti-revivalism in Antebellum America* (New Brunswick, N.J., 2006).

was remarkable for embracing (in the words of the Book of Common Prayer) "all sorts and conditions of men." Including women, the poor, and African Americans among the exhorters and exhorted, the revivals expanded the number of people experiencing an autonomous sense of self. They taught self-respect and demanded that individuals function as moral agents. In this way the Awakening empowered multitudes.

The decision for Christ that the revivalists demanded had to be made voluntarily and responsibly. Having taken this decision, the believer, regardless of denomination, should accept self-discipline while also engaging in long-term moral self-improvement, sometimes called "sanctification." The preachers urged people to search the scriptures for themselves and apply the lessons they found there to their own lives. In short, the believer was expected to remake himself or herself into a new person—to be "born again." The new personal identity thus attained was both follower of Christ and rational, autonomous individual—paradoxical as that may seem.[66]

The evangelical movement brought civilization and order, not only to the frontier but throughout the rural and small town environments in which the vast majority of Americans then lived. Evangelical revivals rolled through the canal towns where Finney enjoyed his famous successes, through rustic Vermont, and through the booming cotton lands of Mississippi. All over the country, farmers and townspeople expressed by innumerable voluntary activities their commitment to republicanism and religious toleration along with their desire for spiritual sustenance and stable values. Some evangelicals committed themselves to the moral reformation of society as a whole; these tended to be the ones concerned with interdenominational cooperation. Others concentrated attention on the moral standards of their own membership as "islands of holiness" in a sea of infidelity and immorality. This distinction would turn out to be important when evangelicals chose sides in politics.[67]

Social classes were more sharply defined in the cities and new industrial towns than in most of rural America, and this reality affected evangelical activity. Despite Beecher's working-class origins and Finney's common touch, their versions of evangelicalism appealed primarily to middle-class people. But evangelical religion also appealed to the working class. Finney and a Methodist minister held revival meetings together

66. See Daniel Howe, *Making the American Self* (Cambridge, Mass., 1997), 114–17.
67. Randolph Roth, *The Democratic Dilemma: Religion, Reform, and the Social Order in the Connecticut River Valley of Vermont* (Cambridge, Eng., 1987); Johnson, *Islands of Holiness*; Sparks, *On Jordan's Stormy Banks*.

in a textile mill on Oriskany Creek in 1826 where about fifteen hundred converted, many of them mill girls. In this case, the revivalists enjoyed the support of the mill owner, who stopped production to allow the revival to take place. Evangelical religion inculcated virtues that employers generally approved, especially temperance—though there is no indication that heavy drinking among the mill girls had been a problem for this employer.[68]

In general, evangelical religion was not foisted upon the industrial working classes, whether artisans or factory employees. When they embraced it, they did so voluntarily and for reasons that did not conflict with their self-interest. Hardworking journeymen who joined the Methodist Church did not find its social ethics particularly different from the behavior endorsed by the Mechanics' Society. If some employers saw the temperance movement as a means to discipline workers, some of the workers themselves viewed it as a means of "mutual improvement" and a way of retaking control over their lives.[69] When workers challenged their employers in collective protest, they could draw strength from their religion. Antebellum American labor organizers did not forget that Jesus had been a carpenter. In Finney's Rochester, working-class people held their own version of the Awakening and did not allow employers or the middle class to monopolize the Christian message. Rochester's artisan organizations and periodicals combined Christianity with labor agitation and a working-class legislative agenda of mechanics' lien laws and an end to imprisonment for debt. Methodist and Presbyterian church members appeared prominently in the leadership of the Rochester labor movement. Evangelicalism played a part in the making of the working class, as it did in shaping middle-class consciousness as well.[70]

The economic teachings of evangelical preachers contained much the same message whether their congregation was rural or urban, working or middle class, Calvinist or Arminian, white or black. Serve God in your calling. Work hard, be thrifty, save your money, don't go into debt. Be honest in business dealings; don't screw down the wages of those who

68. Hambrick-Stowe, *Finney*, 53–54. The role of employers in promoting Finney's revival is emphasized in Johnson, *Shopkeeper's Millennium*.

69. William R. Sutton, *Journeymen for Jesus: Evangelical Artisans Confront Capitalism in Jacksonian Baltimore* (University Park, Pa., 1998); David G. Hackett, *The Rude Hand of Innovation: Religion and Social Order in Albany* (New York, 1991), 90–99, 119–21, 156; Roth, *Democratic Dilemma*, 300–302.

70. Jama Lazerow, *Religion and the Working Class in Antebellum America* (Washington, 1995); Teresa Anne Murphy, *Ten Hours' Labor: Religion, Reform, and Gender in Early New England* (Ithaca, N.Y., 1992).

work for you to the lowest possible level. (In that society, even people of very modest means might have a "hired man" helping on the farm or "hired girl" helping in the kitchen.) If you manage a surplus, be faithful stewards of your bounty, that is, be generous to the church and other good causes. It wasn't bad personal advice, then or later. The message presupposed private property and a commercial order but not ruthless competition; it attempted to infuse the marketplace with moral meaning. In the South, the ministers admonished masters not to overwork or abuse their slaves and to respect their family ties. In other respects their teachings were the same as in the free states.[71]

Of all the social groups involved in the Awakening, perhaps none was affected more profoundly than women. Besides Phoebe Palmer, many other women evangelists emerged, despite the reluctance of most denominations to ordain them as ministers. Jarena Lee of the AME Church succeeded in getting permission from Bishop Richard Allen to become an itinerant preacher; she traveled as much as two thousand miles a year in the 1820s and published her spiritual autobiography.[72] The best-known women itinerants included Clarissa Danforth, Nancy Towle, and Harriet Livermore; they all came from the "Christian movement" but preached in other churches too—Methodist, Free-Will Baptist, wherever they could get a hearing. Livermore attained such fame that she preached before a joint session of Congress and President John Quincy Adams in January 1827, taking as her text "He that ruleth over men must be just." By defending the right of women to speak in public, the female evangelists took a preliminary but essential step in the direction of the next generation of women's-rights activists.[73]

More typically, however, women occupied the pews rather than the pulpits. Joining in church activities with their "sisters in Christ" could be socially as well as spiritually rewarding, especially for women in isolated farm households. Often, wives and mothers led the way in joining a church and then encouraged male family members to convert too. A woman might welcome the discipline of a church community over the

---

71. See Mark Noll, ed., *God and Mammon: Protestants, Money, and the Market* (New York, 2002); Kenneth Startup, *The Root of All Evil: Protestant Clergy and the Economic Mind of the Old South* (Athens, Ga., 1997).

72. Jarena Lee, *Religious Experience and Journal* (Philadelphia, 1836, 1849), has been reprinted in *Spiritual Narratives*, ed. Sue Houchins (New York, 1988), 1–97.

73. Catherine A. Brekus, "Harriet Livermore, the Pilgrim Stranger," *Church History* 65 (1996): 389–404. See further the readings in Elizabeth B. Clark, "Women and Religion in America, 1780–1870," *Church and State in America*, ed. John F. Wilson (New York, 1986), I, 365–413.

family as a limitation on the discipline of a tyrannical husband. Women outnumbered men by two to one in most antebellum congregations, regardless of denomination.[74] (Women typically outnumber men in almost all churches, Catholic, Protestant, and Orthodox, everywhere in the world.)

Countless thousands of women participated in church-related benevolent associations that acted as a training ground for fuller citizenship. Women distributed Bibles, tracts, and material help to the poor of cities and countryside. Frequently their organizations were officially "auxiliaries" to male associations, but middle-class women often had more time and energy to devote than their men. While men could be active in civic, political, and occupational associations, all women's associations before the mid-1830s were religious in nature. "No other avenue of self-expression besides religion," the historian Nancy Cott has written, "at once offered women social approbation, the encouragement of male leaders (ministers), and, most important, the community of their peers." Religious benevolence could perform constructive social functions for women from a variety of social groups. For upper-class women, it might confirm their social position. For black or working-class women, it lent substance to their claims of respectability. Benevolent associations became important to middle-class women in somewhat the same way that getting paid employment mattered to working-class women, as a way of getting out of the house and into the larger world, taking responsibility and making decisions. The temperance movement in particular helped pave the way for the assertion of women's rights because it so often took up the cause of wives against the abuse of alcoholic husbands.[75]

The laity, women and men together, saw to it that the Second Great Awakening exerted much of its influence through purposeful voluntary associations, typically headed by boards of directors on which laypersons appeared prominently. Because the associations were interdenominational and run by the laity, women could exercise many leadership functions even when clerical ordination remained closed to them. The list of evangelical benevolent associations is long and bewilderingly varied.

74. Butler, *Awash in a Sea of Faith*, 283; Hackett, *Rude Hand of Innovation*, 141–44; Ryan, *Cradle of the Middle Class*, 77–81; Johnson, *Islands of Holiness*, 53–66.
75. Nancy F. Cott, *The Bonds of Womanhood* (New Haven, 1977), 126–59, quotation from 141; Carroll Smith Rosenberg, *Religion and the Rise of the American City* (Ithaca, N.Y., 1971), 97–124; Nancy Hewitt, *Women's Activism and Social Change* (Ithaca, N.Y., 1984), esp. 228; Ryan, *Cradle of the Middle Class*, 210–81.

They included the American Board of Commissioners for Foreign Missions (which also handled missions to Native Americans), American Home Missionary Society, Bible Society, Peace Society, Sunday School Union, Tract Society, Temperance Society, and the different societies into which the antislavery movement eventually split. Some, like the Peace Society, participated in international cooperation; others were distinctively American, like the Society for the Promotion of Theological Education at the West. Some had a wide remit, like the Society for Bettering the Condition and Increasing the Comforts of the Poor; others were highly specialized, like the American Seamen's Friend Society, the Protestant Half Orphan Society, or the Ladies' Association for the Benefit of Gentlewomen of Good Family, Reduced in Fortune Below the State of Comfort to Which They Have Been Accustomed. Many were local, like the New York Anti-Tobacco Society or the Society for the Encouragement of Faithful Domestic Servants in New York. The Seventh Commandment Society and the Society for Returning Young Women to Their Friends in the Country both addressed the problem of prostitution. A few of the associations now strike us as grotesque (the Evangelical Alliance to Overthrow the Papacy) or ludicrous (the National Truss Society for the Relief of the Ruptured Poor).

Contemporaries called the interlocking, interdenominational directorates of these organizations "the Evangelical United Front" or "the Benevolent Empire." It is scarcely an exaggeration to say that the United Front aspired to transcend America's sectarian diversity and create the functional equivalent of an established church. Its advocates declared that bringing souls to Christ and ushering in His Kingdom took precedence over the theological differences dividing the various Protestant sects. They therefore embraced interdenominational ("ecumenical") cooperation in the service of a general "reformation of manners" both personal and institutional. Of course, their conception of cooperation did not include "unevangelical" denominations like Catholics and Unitarians.

The efforts of this benevolent empire had remarkable impact on American culture. The activities of the American Bible Society and American Sunday School Union, for example, held more importance than may at first appear. The American version of Protestantism was a religion of a book, and to practice the religion required being able to read the book. In many a log cabin, parents taught their children by candlelight the rudiments of reading in the only book they had: a Bible from the American Bible Society. In many a frontier community, the Sunday school arrived well before the more expensive public school, and in the meantime provided children with weekly instruction in literacy.[76] The wide variety of voluntary organizations themselves provided their members practice in exercising civic responsibilities. What is more, the collection of small donations from far-flung contributors, which then had to be accounted for and safely invested so as to yield an income, actually pioneered techniques for pooling capital in a society with a chronic shortage of capital. Nonprofit corporations as well as business enterprises helped shape the development of American capitalism, and women participated fully in the nonprofit sector.[77]

The social reforms embraced by the Evangelical United Front characteristically involved creating some form of personal discipline serving a goal of redemption. Prison reform serves as an example: No longer would the prison be intended only as a place to hold persons awaiting trial, coerce debt payment, or inflict retributive justice. Reformers reconceived the prison as corrective in function, as a "penitentiary" or "reformatory," in the vocabulary they invented. Besides prisoners, other people who did not function as free moral agents might become objects of the reformers' concern: alcoholics, children, slaves, the insane. The goal of the reformers in each case was to substitute for external constraints the inner discipline of morality. Some historians have interpreted the religious reformers as motivated simply by an impulse to impose "social control," but it seems more accurate to describe their concern as redemptive, and more specifically the creation of responsible personal autonomy.[78] Liberation and control represented two sides of the redemptive process as they conceived it. Christians who had achieved self-liberation and self-control through conversion not surprisingly often turned to a concern with the liberation and discipline of others.

The Evangelical United Front had no more able servant or advocate than Robert Baird. After training for the Presbyterian ministry at Princeton Theological Seminary, Baird spent the rest of his life in the service of benevolent associations. He labored to distribute Bibles, to fund a state

76. Peter Wosh, *Spreading the Word: The Bible Business in Nineteenth-Century America* (Ithaca, N.Y., 1994); Paul Gujahr, *An American Bible* (Stanford, 1999); Anne Boylan, *Sunday School* (New Haven, 1988).

77. Lori Ginzburg, *Women and the Work of Benevolence* (New Haven, 1990); Kathleen D. McCarthy, *American Creed: Philanthropy and the Rise of Civil Society* (Chicago, 2003), 50–54, 81–82.

78. See Lois Banner, "Religious Benevolence as Social Control: A Critique," *JAH* 60 (1973): 34–41; Martin Wiener, ed., "Humanitarianism or Control?" *Rice University Studies* 67 (1981): 1–84; Daniel Howe, "The Evangelical Movement and Political Culture," *JAH* 77 (1991): 1216–39.

public school system in New Jersey, and to establish Sunday schools throughout the nation. Beginning in 1834, he spent most of the next thirty years in Europe as an agent for the American and Foreign Christian Union, working to promote literacy and the temperance movement and to secure rights for Protestants in countries with Roman Catholic governments. Baird crossed the Atlantic eighteen times in an age when few leaders felt at home, as he did, on both sides of the ocean. In response to requests from European colleagues, he wrote his monumental book, *Religion in America*, first published in Scotland in 1843, then in New York in 1844, and subsequently translated into French, German, Dutch, and Swedish. Baird intended it to introduce European Protestants of his time to American religion; the book remains to expound the worldview of the nineteenth-century Evangelical United Front to us. In it Baird explained religious freedom, the separation of church and state, and America's extraordinary religious diversity for the benefit of readers to whom all these seemed strange. He defended revivalism (though taking account of its abuses) and the voluntary benevolent associations. While broad-minded by the standards of his day, he did not hesitate to rank-order other religions, rating Catholicism superior to Unitarianism and Judaism superior to Mormonism.[79] Like many others of his generation, Baird saw evangelical Protestantism as the legatee of Puritanism, the core of American culture, the source of American democratic institutions, the primary engine of economic and political progress, and ultimately the hope of the world. The American version of evangelical Protestantism represented, for him, what God hath wrought.

The religious awakenings of the early nineteenth century marshaled powerful energies in an age when few other social agencies in the United States had the capacity to do so. Baird's Evangelical United Front organized its voluntary associations on a national, indeed international, level, at a time when little else in American society was organized, when there existed no nationwide business corporation save the Second Bank of the United States and no nationwide government bureaucracy save the Post Office. Indeed, the four major evangelical denominations together employed twice as many people, occupied twice as many premises, and raised at least three times as much money as the Post Office. The extent to which evangelical religion dominated communication in the early republic is most vividly exemplified by the fact that, per capita, twice as

---

79. Robert Baird, *Religion in the United States of America* (New York, 1969, rpt. from the 1844 ed.), 612–13.

many Methodist sermons were heard in 1840 as there were letters received.[80] The historian Richard Carwardine, after carefully estimating that about 40 percent of the U.S. population was "in close sympathy with evangelical Christianity" (not the same thing as belonging to a church), concludes, "This was the largest, and most formidable, subculture in American society."[81] It could only be a matter of time before the energies generated by religion began to make themselves manifest in politics.

VI

Old Elias Hicks had a farm on Long Island. When a young man he had traveled as an itinerant Quaker evangelist between Vermont and the Chesapeake, preaching the Inner Light, "that lighteth every man that cometh into the world" (John 1:9). His sermons were spontaneous, their emotional power reinforced by his transparent sincerity. A decade after his death they would still tell the story of how, in Virginia, he courageously called upon a planter who had threatened to shoot him for preaching against the sin of slavery, and after repeated visits persuaded the man to set his people free.[82] Throughout his life Hicks rigorously defended the right as he saw it: the austere Quaker tradition of refusing to compromise with worldliness. He insisted that principled persons should avoid consuming the products of slave labor, such as sugar, rice, or cotton textiles. Besides slavery, he denounced banks, politics, and the Erie Canal. ("If the Lord had intended there should be internal waterways, he would have placed them there.") As for scientific learning, he considered it as "trivial" as "ribbons on a young woman's head."[83] Elias Hicks had little time for the modern world; nothing really mattered to the old man except moral integrity. In the 1820s, he became the focal point of a controversy that irreparably split the American Society of Friends.

Ever since the seventeenth century, the Society of Friends (nicknamed "quakers" for their occasional emotional trances) had conceived themselves as a people apart. Within Protestantism, they were super-Protestants. Where Protestants demystified and simplified the Eucharist, Quakers did not observe it at all, nor did they practice baptism. Their silent meetings

---

80. Statistics from Noll, *America's God*, 201: in 1840, only 2.9 letters per person per year, but six Methodist sermons heard per person per year.
81. Richard Carwardine, *Evangelicals and Politics in Antebellum America* (New Haven, 1993), 44.
82. Lydia Maria Child, "An Anecdote of Elias Hicks," *Liberty Bell* (Boston, 1839), 65–68.
83. Quotations from Robert Doherty, *The Hicksite Separation* (New Brunswick, N.J., 1967), 28. On Hicks, see also H. Larry Ingle, *Quakers in Conflict* (Knoxville, Tenn., 1986), 39–47.

had no order of service. They wrote no systematic theology. Since both women and men possessed the divine Spirit, the Inner Light, they practiced a substantial degree of gender equality. They did not ordain clergy, though they "recorded" the fact that God's Spirit particularly spoke through designated individuals. They dressed plainly and spoke plainly, using "thee" and "thou," the familiar form of address, instead of "you," considered more polite. They refused to serve in the armed forces. They refused to take oaths in court, on the grounds that one should tell the truth all the time, not just in special circumstances. But the international evangelical movement affected them in ways that two hundred years of persecution had never done. First in England, then in the United States, nineteenth-century Quakers began to share in the religious currents of their age. They started associating with non-Quakers in philanthropic organizations. Sometimes they seemed more interested in cooperating with other white evangelicals than in bearing uncompromising witness against slavery. They emphasized evangelical biblical teachings more and the Inner Light of individual conscience less. They began to speak of Jesus as Redeemer, to celebrate his atonement for sin, and even considered adopting a creedal confession of faith similar to that of other evangelical Protestants. Elias Hicks stood out against these trends. He also criticized those Quakers, chiefly in Philadelphia, who had adapted sufficiently to the ways of the world to become successful merchants and entrepreneurs.[84]

In April 1827, dissension wracked the Philadelphia Yearly Meeting (analogous to a synod in Presbyterianism). The followers of Hicks walked out and set up their own Philadelphia Yearly Meeting. Other yearly meetings had to decide which of the two Philadelphia meetings to recognize, and in doing so they precipitated a schism throughout American Quakerism. The more evangelical branch took the name Orthodox; the Hicksites eventually called themselves the Liberal branch. The British Friends sided unequivocally with the Orthodox. In the United States, about 40 percent of the 100,000 Quakers, mainly Friends living in rural areas of the Mid-Atlantic states and Ohio, became Hicksites.[85]

The Hicksites continued to record ministers, as the orthodox Quakers did, and they commissioned "Public Friends" to spread the Word among non-Quakers. Sometimes these evangelists addressed camp meetings.

84. Ingle, *Quakers in Conflict*, 3–15; Thomas Hamm, *The Transformation of American Quakerism* (Bloomington, 1988), 15–28.

85. Thomas Hamm, *The Quakers in America* (New York, 2003), 42–43.

But the Hicksite movement also represented a religious "revival" in another, perhaps more fundamental, sense. It revived the original kind of anti-institutional, "come-outer" Quaker piety, resembling that of the founder George Fox and the seventeenth-century Friends. Surprisingly, however, though Hicks himself despised the modern world, some of his followers turned out to constitute the cutting edge of modernity. If Lyman Beecher's followers represented the conservative wing of evangelical reform and Charles Finney's its liberal one, those of Elias Hicks contributed the radical vanguard, what contemporaries called "ultraism." All three of these evangelical groups could agree on many issues, such as temperance, prison reform, and public support for elementary schools. But the Hicksites displayed a willingness to pursue causes that others thought quixotic. Hicksite Quakers provided a disproportionately large number of recruits to the immediate, uncompensated abolition of slavery. And when at last a movement endorsing equal rights for women surfaced, the little minority of Hicksite Quakers would make themselves conspicuous in its support.[86]

VII

In 1815 John Carroll, Bishop of Baltimore and the first Roman Catholic bishop in the United States, died. A native-born American and cousin to Charles Carroll, signer of the Declaration of Independence, he had been elected bishop by his clerical colleagues in 1789, the same year his friend George Washington was elected the first president. Rome (preoccupied with more momentous events closer to home) went along with the strange procedure. Bishop Carroll undertook to demonstrate to a skeptical public that his church could reconcile itself to republicanism. Staunchly patriotic and Federalist, Bishop Carroll made it clear that American Catholics embraced freedom of religion, which he grounded in natural law. To represent his irenic and rational faith, Carroll commissioned Benjamin Latrobe, architect of the U.S. Capitol in Washington, to design a neoclassical cathedral for Baltimore.[87] The first Catholic Bishop of Boston, consecrated in 1810, was another cultivated gentleman, the French émigré Jean Cheverus. Respected even in that ultra-Protestant city as a broad-minded and conciliatory liberal, Cheverus remained at heart a European conservative, and in 1823 the restored Bourbon monarchy welcomed him back home, where he become Archbishop of Bordeaux and eventually a cardinal. In 1820, the pope appointed as Bishop of

86. See Brooks Holifield, *Theology in America* (New Haven, 2003), 320–27.
87. Jay Dolan, *In Search of an American Catholicism* (New York, 2002), 22–25.

Charleston an Irishman named (ironically) John England. Bishop England carried the effort to Americanize the Catholic Church still further, creating a written constitution for his diocese that included participation by elected delegates, clerical and lay, in an annual convention. This experiment in representative government did not outlive the bishop who created it. But reciprocating such overtures, the houses of Congress invited Bishop England to address them in 1826 and in 1832 chose a Roman Catholic priest as their chaplain.[88]

The social situation faced by the Catholic church in the young republic resembled in many respects that faced by the Protestant denominations: dispersed populations, perhaps recently migrated from other parts of the country or the Atlantic world, and often long out of touch with organized religion. The church responded with what has been called "Catholic revivalism." Priests of several religious orders (notably, Jesuits and Redemptorists) became traveling missionaries, carrying the divine word and sacraments to the thinly scattered 150,000 Catholics living in the United States in 1815. Like their Protestant counterparts these preachers warned of the flames of hell and encouraged hymn-singing; then they would exhort their hearers to the sacraments of penance and holy communion. The Catholic itinerants did not have to take their cue from Protestants; such missions had been known for centuries in Europe (where monarchs had sometimes banned them as subversive). Like the evangelical movement among Protestants, Catholic revivalism was an international movement, but one that matched the needs of the American environment particularly well. To observe the jubilee proclaimed by Leo XII, a Catholic evangelist from Ireland rallied crowds in frontier Kentucky that resembled those at Protestant camp meetings. The emotional nature of such Catholic revivalism contrasted with the genteel piety exemplified by Carroll and Cheverus. To help the faithful carry on once the missionary had left, he would distribute prayer books containing devotions the laity could perform, privately or collectively, even without a priest.[89]

The extent to which the church should adapt to the American situation became a controversial issue among Catholics. In many areas the

88. David Gleeson, *The Irish in the South* (Chapel Hill, 2001), 77–80; Charles Morris, *American Catholic* (New York, 1997), viii. For more on Bishop England, see Patrick Carey, *An Immigrant Bishop* (Yonkers, N.Y., 1982).

89. Jay Dolan, *Catholic Revivalism* (Notre Dame, 1978); Dale Light, *Rome and the New Republic* (Notre Dame, 1996), 248–49; Ann Taves, *The Household Faith: Roman Catholic Devotions in Mid-Nineteenth-Century America* (Notre Dame, 1986).

laity had taken the initiative in forming a parish and requesting a priest. In the meantime, laymen led public services (not the mass, of course). Sometimes they expected to be able to choose their priest. Furthermore, the laws of many states, reflecting Protestant assumptions, mandated that parish church property be held in the name of lay trustees, not by the clergy. Bishop England tolerated this system up to a point, but the other bishops did not, and meeting at their first council in 1829 they insisted that church property should rightfully be vested in the diocesan bishop. The lay trustees throughout the country did not always give up without a fight, however; conflicts between bishops and trustees occurred in Philadelphia, New York City, New Orleans, and Buffalo. Philadelphia had a particularly messy wrangle, which included the excommunication of a priest whom the lay trustees supported against his bishop. The trustee system had still not been entirely purged by 1848; its eventual elimination demonstrated the limits of Roman Catholic accommodation to American republican practices.[90]

A leading opponent of the trustee system was the redoubtable John Hughes, appointed bishop coadjutor (associate bishop) of New York in 1837, succeeding Jean Dubois as diocesan bishop in 1842, and promoted to archbishop in 1850. Very different from his aristocratic French predecessor, Hughes had immigrated from Ireland in 1817 and worked as a gardener to finance his education. Firmly asserting his ecclesiastical authority, the new bishop set a pattern for the American episcopate in the era of Catholic expansion. Hughes became known as "Dagger John," ostensibly because the bishop's cross he drew after signing his name resembled a dagger; more subtly, as an expression of respect for his militant toughness.

John Hughes labored to bring a largely working-class Irish constituency into a meaningful relationship with Catholic Christianity. Many of the immigrants had had scarcely any contact with the persecuted Catholicism of their homeland. At the same time, the bishop worked to conciliate middle-class Catholics and Protestant well-wishers whose financial support he needed for his amazingly ambitious program of building. Hughes conceived and commenced the great St. Patrick's Cathedral on Fifth Avenue, hiring America's leading architect of the Gothic Revival, James Renwick (a Protestant). Although no theologian, John Hughes ranks high for political judgment and in the significance of his accomplishments among nineteenth-century American statesmen,

90. See Patrick Carey, *People, Priests, and Prelates* (Notre Dame, 1987); on Philadelphia, Light, *Rome and the New Republic*.

civil as well as ecclesiastical. He successfully coped with fierce party competition in New York, bitter battles over the public school system, revolutions in Europe, the rise of nativism across the United States, and soaring rates of immigration after the Irish Potato Famine. He encouraged his people to hard work, personal discipline (including temperance), acceptance of the American way of life, and upward social mobility. Reconciling Catholicism with Americanism presented no problem to the bishop; the church had always been the "schoolmistress of Liberty," he declared. Hughes backed the nation's war effort against Catholic Mexico and later the Union's war effort against a Confederacy that had many sympathizers in both New York City and the Vatican. Crucially, he combined his staunch American patriotism with staunch devotion to a nineteenth-century papacy deeply suspicious of all liberalism, especially Americanism.

In the end, by knowing how and when to promote both assimilation and minority group distinctiveness, John Hughes succeeded in fostering a strong Irish American identity, one centered on the Catholic faith rather than on the secular radicalism of the Irish nationalists who competed with him for community leadership. While making the Irish Americans into Catholics, Hughes and other Irish bishops like England and Francis Kenrick of Philadelphia simultaneously made the American Catholic Church dominated by the Irish. They achieved this, however, at the cost of losing to the Irish-American community the Irish Protestant immigrants, some of whom even became nativists, a term for those who sought to limit Catholic and/or immigrant political influence.[91]

Thanks to the energetic devotion of the religious orders and the ecclesiastical statesmanship of Hughes and other bishops, the church kept pace with Catholic (or more accurately, potentially Catholic) immigration. Most immigrants during this period came from the British Isles and the German-speaking lands, with only a minority of them Catholic by heritage. Even in the case of Ireland, before 1840 a majority of migrants were Protestant—either Scots-Irish Presbyterians or Anglo-Irish Anglicans. Still, a quarter of a million prospective recruits for the Catholic Church arrived in the United States during the 1830s and three times that number in the 1840s. Largely because of its success in ministering to this

91. See Martin Meenagh, "John J. Hughes, First Archbishop of New York" (D.Phil. thesis, Oxford University, 2003), quotation from 55; Lawrence Moore, *Religious Outsiders and the Making of Americans* (New York, 1986), 48–79; Kevin Kenney, *The American Irish* (Edinburgh, 2000), 72–116.

immigrant constituency, the American Catholic Church grew (according to the best estimate) by 1850 to a million members, about the same as the Presbyterians. By comparison, the Methodists then counted 2.7 million and the Baptists 1.6 million. Not until after the Civil War did Roman Catholicism surpass Methodism to become the largest single denomination in the country.[92]

In the final analysis, the success of Roman Catholicism in spreading among immigrants to the United States reflected the way it met the needs of the immigrants themselves. It did so despite, rather than because of, the nineteenth-century papacy's lack of sympathy for the American political experiment. History gets made from the bottom up as well as from the top down. Belonging to the church helped immigrants adjust to a new and unfamiliar environment while affirming the dignity of their own ancestral group and preserving an aspect of its heritage. Most of all, through the church they found fortifying grace, communion with the saints throughout the ages, and the presence of Christ in the sacrament of the altar.

VIII

The evangelists of the various religious awakenings, Protestant and Catholic, adapted their message of salvation to different races, classes, occupations, regions, ethnic groups, and genders. As much as any previous generation of Christian missionaries, they followed the admonition of St. Paul to be "all things to all men." The awakenings of religion in the antebellum United States took many forms. Revivalism was by no means the only method employed, despite its importance as a characteristically American type of Christianity. Indeed, a number of American religious leaders formulated critiques of the revival model and preferred such alternative evangelical approaches as Christian education, Christian nurture in childhood, reliance upon traditional institutions and creeds, dissemination of Christian literature (including fiction), and work for social justice. The variations and implications of Christian zeal will recur throughout our story. But whatever the differences in the evangelists' methods and theology, and however momentous or complicated the temporal consequences of their undertakings, their goal was ultimately to bring souls to Christ. A great historian of American religion, Sydney Ahlstrom, put it this way:

92. Finke and Stark, *Churching of America*, 110–15.

Our final conclusion regarding all of these social results—good, bad, and questionable—is that in one sense they are only side effects of efforts that were ineffable and beyond mundane measuring, for the missionaries and church founders came above all to minister the consolations of religion—to bring word of amazing grace to wretched souls. In what measure they succeeded in that primary task God only knows.[93]

93. Sydney E. Ahlstrom, *A Religious History of the American People* (New Haven, 1972), 471.

6

Overthrowing the Tyranny of Distance

No sooner was President Monroe reelected in 1820 than campaigning began for the election of 1824. By the spring of 1822, a journalist could already comment that the "electioneering begins to wax hot."[1] All the rival presidential candidates called themselves Republicans, and each claimed to be the logical successor to the Jeffersonian heritage. Ironically, what the campaign produced was the breakup of the party and the traditions everyone honored. One-party government proved an evanescent phase in American history.

The presidential campaign of 1824 reflected a clash of personal ambitions, to which issues of region, class, and political philosophy were secondary. Three of the five leading contenders belonged to the cabinet. The power brokers favored William H. Crawford of Georgia, secretary of the Treasury under both Madison and Monroe. A big man physically, Crawford had a jovial manner that disguised a strong mind and an even stronger ambition. He had deferred that ambition by standing aside and preserving party unity when Monroe was anointed in 1816. Now the Republican establishment felt Crawford's rightful turn had come. Despite his embarrassing conflicts of interests, Jefferson and Madison supported him, perhaps influenced by his birth in Virginia. To reassure proslavery politicians alarmed by the Missouri controversies, Crawford pitched his campaign as a return to the virtues of Old Republicanism—state sovereignty, economy in government, and strict construction of the Constitution. To solidify their proslavery credentials, the Crawfordites succeeded in blocking implementation of a treaty Secretary of State Adams negotiated with the British to cooperate in suppressing the Atlantic slave trade.[2] But Crawford's candidacy turned out to have little popular appeal outside southern Radical circles. Only Martin Van Buren's prototypical political machine in New York state loyally backed Crawford out of devotion to party regularity as the highest good.[3]

1. Quoted in James F. Hopkins, "Election of 1824," in *History of American Presidential Elections*, ed. Arthur M. Schlesinger Jr. (New York, 1985), 363.
2. See Bradford Perkins, *Castlereagh and Adams* (Berkeley, 1964), 275–77.
3. See Chase Mooney, *William H. Crawford* (Lexington, Ky., 1974), 213–48; James S. Chase, *Emergence of the Presidential Nominating Convention* (Urbana, Ill., 1973), 48–50.

Secretary of War John C. Calhoun offered a clear ideological alternative. The South Carolinian was an energetic proponent of the new Republican nationalism and an architect of the Second BUS, the Tariff of 1816, and the vetoed Bonus Bill that would have promoted internal improvements. A lawyer and planter like Crawford, Calhoun had a more cosmopolitan background, having been educated at Yale and the famous law school in Litchfield, Connecticut (Lyman Beecher's hometown). A "war hawk" in 1812, he remained convinced that defense imperatives dictated nationalist policies and internal improvements. At Monroe's War Department he undertook fortifications and western exploration and had upgraded the Military Academy under the leadership of Superintendent Sylvanus Thayer. In person Calhoun was all business, dour, analytical, and intense.[4]

While the previous two candidates defined themselves in terms of policy, the next two defined themselves as regional favorites. Secretary of State John Quincy Adams of Massachusetts enjoyed a solid power base in the East, as New England was then called, with additional support extending along the band of Yankee settlement across upstate New York. Legend has portrayed Adams as aloof and impractical; in reality he was an active and capable player in the political game. Though he started public life as a Federalist like his president-father, he had long since become a Republican, and the anti-British stands he had taken during his tenure at the State Department could not be exploited by an opponent trying to use his early past against him. Adams had wide experience in foreign affairs even before becoming secretary of state. Now, with his Transcontinental Treaty and the Monroe Doctrine as monumental achievements, Adams could lay a solid claim to the nation's attention and respect. Although everyone found him austere and moralistic, these qualities did not hurt Adams much with the Yankee voters of his time.[5]

As Adams was the candidate of the East, Henry Clay of Kentucky proclaimed himself the candidate of the West. The resolution of the Missouri controversies had showcased his political talents. On economic issues, Clay of course embraced the new Republican nationalism just as Calhoun and Adams did. In sharp contrast to them, Clay was outgoing, charming,

4. See John Niven, *John C. Calhoun and the Price of Union* (Baton Rouge, 1988), 75–88, 93–101; John Larson, *Internal Improvement: National Public Works and the Promise of Popular Government* (Chapel Hill, 2001), 127–28.
5. Melba Porter Hay, "Election of 1824," in *Running for President*, ed. Arthur M. Schlesinger Jr. (New York, 1994), I, 77–99; Daniel Howe, *The Political Culture of the American Whigs* (Chicago, 1979), 44–45.

and witty, the life of any party. With so many contenders in the presidential race, most observers expected that no one would secure a majority in the electoral college, throwing the race into the House of Representatives for final decision. Clay welcomed this eventuality. As Speaker of the House, he expected to be in a strong position there.[6]

The one candidate running as an outsider was General Andrew Jackson, famous from Horseshoe Bend, New Orleans, and Pensacola, and since 1823 senator from Tennessee. Jackson possessed an appeal not based on issues; it derived from his image as a victor in battle, a frontiersman who had made it big, a man of decision who forged his own rules. Anyone with a classical education knew to regard such men as potential demagogues and tyrants; the word for the danger was "caesarism." Jefferson delivered a straightforward opinion of Jackson's presidential aspirations: "He is one of the most unfit men I know of for such a place."[7] In fact, no one liked Jackson for president except the voting public. Many of the latter, however, found in him a celebrity hero. The fact that only men could vote probably helped Jackson. Many men of voting age had served in local militia units and took pride in Jackson's exploits as a commander of militia.[8]

At first, the established politicians did not take Jackson's candidacy seriously. Adams wanted Jackson to take second place on his own ticket, figuring that he would balance its geography nicely. He expected Jackson would be grateful because Adams had saved his authority after the Florida invasion of 1818 and had sided with him again in 1821 when Jackson, during a short term as governor of Florida Territory, had characteristically defied another federal judge.[9] The high point in Adams's courtship of Jackson was the ball Louisa Adams staged on January 8, 1824, to celebrate the ninth anniversary of the Battle of New Orleans. A thousand guests attended the Adamses' house on F Street for the climax of the Washington social season. The general, however, had no interest in becoming a junior partner in someone else's enterprise.

Jackson nursed a special grudge against Crawford and Clay for opposing his Florida actions. (Calhoun's opposition remained a government secret.) When other candidates organized stop-Crawford movements, they

6. See Merrill Peterson, *The Great Triumvirate: Webster, Clay, and Calhoun* (New York, 1987), 116–31.
7. Quoted in Michael Heale, *The Presidential Quest* (London, 1982), 55.
8. For sympathetic insight into Jackson's appeal, see Charles Sellers, *The Market Revolution* (New York, 1991), 174–81; Robert Remini, *Jackson*, II, 71–75.
9. See Robert Remini, *Jackson*, I, 409–17.

sometimes enlisted Jackson for that purpose, since they did not feel threatened by him. Jackson was originally nominated for president by a resolution of the Tennessee legislature in 1822; ironically, this represented a stratagem by Clay supporters to stymie Crawford in their state. Once Jackson's popularity became apparent, his nominators recoiled in horror, but it was too late.[10] Calhoun made the same mistake in North Carolina. Jackson's unexpected popularity there and in Pennsylvania, two states crucial to Calhoun, derailed the latter's campaign. Early in 1824, Calhoun decided that he would settle for the vice presidency this time around; he was still young (forty-two) and could afford to wait for the big prize. Pleased to have him out of the race and hoping to pick up his supporters, both Jackson and Adams agreed to take him as their running mate. In the end, therefore, Calhoun received an overwhelming electoral vote for vice president.

Customarily, the Jeffersonian Republican Party selected its presidential candidate by a joint caucus of party members in the two houses of Congress. In the absence of a functional opposition, this nomination had become tantamount to election, as in Monroe's case. Conventional wisdom held that Crawford, the insider, would prevail in the caucus. The other candidates denounced the caucus as a method of choosing the Republican nominee, both out of self-interest and because it seemed a system that did not necessarily reflect national public opinion. They boycotted it. Then fate intervened: Crawford suffered a mysterious illness, perhaps a stroke, in September 1823, though he was but fifty-one years old. The treatments of his doctors only made him worse. The seriousness of his condition was kept quiet, but it became unclear how well he would recover. His backers, not knowing what else to do, went ahead and nominated him at a caucus in February 1824. But only 66 out of 240 members showed up, shattering the myth that Crawford's men controlled Congress. This proved the last such nominating caucus ever held. The American political community did not allow the congressional caucus to preempt the means of choosing the president.[11]

To have three members of his cabinet running for president against each other proved awkward for Monroe, who remained scrupulously neutral. The rivals sought to embarrass each other by planting scandal

10. This intrigue is unraveled in Charles Sellers, "Jackson Men with Feet of Clay," *AHR* 62 (1957): 537–51.
11. Noble Cunningham, "The Jeffersonian Republican Party," in *History of U.S. Political Parties*, ed. Arthur M. Schlesinger Jr. (New York, 1973), 268–71; Chase, *Presidential Nominating Convention*, 41–50.

stories anonymously. Particularly troublesome was Crawford's campaign, based on a state-rights Radicalism that clearly contrasted with the Republican nationalism of the administration as a whole. But Crawford had expected Monroe's full support and felt betrayed. Relations between the president and his secretary of the Treasury gradually soured, though for the appearance of party unity Monroe did not remove him and even helped cover up the extent of his incapacity in the winter of 1823–24.[12]

In the nineteenth century it was not customary for presidential candidates to campaign overtly.[13] Their supporters made speeches and wrote articles on their behalf; the candidates themselves directed matters by private correspondence but in public preserved the fiction that the presidential office sought the man, not the man the office. Jackson's chief campaign document appeared anonymously under the pseudonym "Wyoming"; it was largely the work of his aide John Eaton. The *Letters of Wyoming* called for the election of Jackson to restore accountability and public spirit (then called "virtue") to a republic whose government allegedly had lost touch with the people and become corrupt. While all the other candidates were intriguing in the capital, Jackson alone, claimed Wyoming, remained in touch with the "honest yeomanry" of the country. Jackson's campaign marked the debut of a common and effective tactic in American politics: running against Washington, D.C. It took advantage of the unfocused resentments of people who had suffered from the hard times after 1819.[14]

The campaign of 1824 fell in the midst of a transition from one system of electing presidents to another. In the early days of the republic, the presidential electors had been chosen by state legislatures. However, public opinion throughout the country was shifting in favor of having the electors chosen by the voters, and since the last presidential contest in 1816, several more states, including all the newly admitted ones, had adopted a popular vote for presidential electors. Generous franchise laws, including the popular election of presidential electors, constituted one of the ways that new states bid for settlers. Old states, worried about losing population, felt pressure to adopt similar rules. By 1824, the number of states following the popular practice had grown to eighteen out of twenty-four. (Later in the century, a similar mechanism would spread women's

---

12. See Noble Cunningham, *The Presidency of James Monroe* (Lawrence, Kans., 1996), 126–30.
13. The most conspicuous exceptions to this rule were Stephen A. Douglas in 1860 and William Jennings Bryan in 1896; neither was an incumbent.
14. *The Letters of Wyoming to the People of the United States* (Philadelphia, 1824).

suffrage from west to east.) Meanwhile, a tradition was developing that presidential electors should pledge themselves in advance instead of exercising their individual discretion. But not all states cast their electoral votes as a block; five states awarded them by congressional district to the candidate who carried that district.[15] The election of 1824 was the first in which it is possible to tabulate a popular vote for president, although it does not include all the states. Jackson's cause, based on his personal popularity, exemplified and benefited from the changing nature of presidential campaigns and the more direct role of the electorate. All the other candidates were still playing the political game the old-fashioned way, assuming that opinion leaders could speak for their followers and act as power brokers.

As the returns gradually accumulated in the absence of a common date for states to choose their electors, it became apparent that Jackson had won a plurality of both popular and electoral votes, but no candidate had the required majority in the electoral college. Of popular votes, Jackson had 152,901 (42.5 percent), Adams 114,023 (31.5 percent), Clay 47,217 (13 percent), and Crawford 46,979 (13 percent).[16] The small numbers indicate a low turnout, plus the fact that six states had no popular votes for president. The electoral votes stood as follows: Jackson 99, Adams 84, Crawford 41, and Clay 37. Jackson had undercut Clay in the West, just as he had hurt Crawford among Old Republicans. Jackson owed his electoral college lead to the three-fifths clause of the Constitution, which inflated the voting power of slaveholding states. Without it, he would have received 77 electoral votes and Adams 83.[17]

Under these circumstances, the Twelfth Amendment to the Constitution provided that the House of Representatives should choose a president from among the three top contenders, with the delegation from each state casting one vote. Since Crawford was so far behind the other two, and his health still a question mark, Jackson and Adams were clearly the two most credible candidates. Adams had no intention of bowing out just because Jackson was the front-runner. Now came the round of lobbying congressmen, when Adams came into his own. He understood well this kind of politics, based on an "old-boy" network and implicit understandings. Adams held on to the delegations from the seven states he had carried in the general election and won over three more as well. In Illi-

---

15. Remini, *Jackson*, II, 81.
16. The figures given in Robert Remini, *Henry Clay* (New York, 1991), 249.
17. Calculated by Robert Forbes, "Slavery and the Meaning of America" (Ph.D. diss., Yale University, 1994), 499.

nois, the chief issue in state politics at the time was whether or not to introduce slavery. Illinois's sole congressional representative, Daniel Cook, strongly antislavery, found no difficulty in preferring Adams to Jackson. To firm up support in Maryland, Adams promised not to exclude Federalists from the patronage. Meanwhile, Congressman James Buchanan of Pennsylvania, a Jackson supporter, was trying to broker a deal in which Jackson would make Clay secretary of state in return for Clay's support. Buchanan's plan got nowhere; in fact, Clay had already made up his mind to support Adams.[18]

Originally, Clay had hoped to use his influence in the House to benefit his own candidacy; as things turned out, he could be only kingmaker, not king. Adams and Clay had rubbed each other the wrong way in the past, especially when they had been colleagues in the American negotiating team at Ghent, but now they proved capable of reaching a momentous understanding in a three-hour private meeting on Sunday evening, January 9, 1825.[19] Their alliance was quite logical: Clay and Adams agreed on the issues, both being nationalists who wanted the government to promote economic development, and their different sectional power bases complemented each other. Besides, Clay thought a military hero with a record of defying civilian authority a dangerously inappropriate choice for president.

"Harry of the West" had three states he could deliver in the House: Kentucky, Ohio, and Missouri (whose lone member was grateful for Clay's role in getting the state admitted).[20] Added to the ten states already in Adams's camp, they made thirteen: a majority of the twenty-four states. Jackson, although he had carried eleven states in the electoral college, received the votes of only seven state delegations in the House; he was less popular inside the political community than he was with the public at large. On a snowy ninth of February 1825, John Quincy Adams was elected sixth president of the United States by the House of Representatives on its first ballot. Back home in Quincy, Massachusetts, his eighty-nine-year-old father felt overwhelmed with emotion when the news arrived.[21] Not until George Bush would another former president see his son in the White House.

18. See Peterson, *Great Triumvirate*, 148.
19. *Memoirs of John Quincy Adams, Containing Portions of His Diary*, ed. Charles Francis Adams (Philadelphia, 1874–77), VI, 464–65; Samuel Flagg Bemis, *John Quincy Adams and the Union* (New York, 1956), 40–41; Remini, *Henry Clay*, 255–58.
20. Robert Seager II, "Henry Clay and the Politics of Compromise and Non-Compromise," *Register of the Kentucky Historical Society* 85 (1987): 8.
21. John Adams to John Quincy Adams, Feb. 18, 1825, *Memoirs of JQA*, VI, 504.

The outcome stunned the political community. Most observers had supposed that Jackson's popularity in the West would force Clay to throw his support in that direction. (Indeed, Kentucky's legislature had "instructed" Clay and the rest of the state's House delegation to vote for Jackson.) It might have made sense in general ideological terms for the Crawford supporters to switch to Jackson, but they were not sure they could trust the general. The extraordinary personal bitterness between the two principals inhibited Crawford's followers from allying with Jackson too readily. So they waited, expecting the process to require several ballots; if a deadlock between Adams and Jackson developed, they could hope that Crawford might emerge as a compromise choice.[22]

It was Adams himself who made the quick resolution of the contest possible. By successfully winning over the delegations of three states Jackson had carried in the general election (Maryland, Illinois, and Louisiana), he had created a situation in which an alliance with Adams was the only winning option for Clay. Clay's decision to support Adams was therefore, in the words of one historian, "the only reasonable and responsible one, the only one that could avert a long drawn-out battle leading to constitutional crisis."[23] But however rationally and constitutionally defensible, the outcome outraged the Jacksonians, who saw their popular and electoral pluralities frustrated. The election of 1824–25 marked the last time the constitutional machinery of Jeffersonian republicanism, defined in the Twelfth Amendment of 1804, would prevail over the politics of mass democracy. The House of Representatives has never again chosen a president.[24]

While the election of 1824 marked the end of nonparty politics, it also laid the foundation for the party system that was to come. The alliance of Adams and Clay formed the basis of what would be called first the National Republican and later the Whig Party. Before long, Jackson's and Crawford's followers would coalesce into the Democratic Republican, later named the Democratic Party. Of the five presidential contenders in 1824, only Calhoun did not manage to find any comfortable home in the second party system. Among the larger public, diligent historical research

22. Crawford himself would have considered Adams the lesser evil to Jackson. Mooney, *William H. Crawford*, 295. On Crawford's chances as a compromise candidate, see Thomas Jefferson to Richard Rush, June 5, 1824, *Writings of Thomas Jefferson*, ed. John Leicester Ford (New York, 1899), X, 304–5.

23. Peterson, *Great Triumvirate*, 129.

24. There was a disputed election resolved by a special commission in 1876, a disputed election resolved by the Supreme Court in 2000, and one other case, in 1888, when the winner of the popular vote did not win the electoral vote.

has shown substantial continuity in voting alignments between 1824 and subsequent elections.[25]

What Clay himself wanted in return for supporting Adams was, of course, to be designated his heir. The State Department had served as the stepping-stone to the presidency in early republican history: Jefferson, Madison, Monroe, and now Adams had all been secretaries of state. When Adams appointed Clay secretary of state, everyone knew what it meant. Whether there had been an explicit prior agreement between the two men to this effect we shall never know; most historians today think not. But Andrew Jackson's comment epitomized the bitterness he felt: "The Judas of the West has closed the contract and will receive the thirty pieces of silver. His end will be the same."[26]

II

The issues the incoming president would face were intimately bound up with what historians have called "the transportation revolution." People throughout the United States recognized the need for a better transportation system. The Great Migration had increased the number of agricultural producers wanting to get their crops from the interior to national or international markets. While some people moved westward, others were migrating to the coastal cities to work in the merchant marine and its many ancillary occupations, from shipbuilding to insurance. These city people had a need to be fed even more urgent than that of the farmers to market their crops. Pressure for improvements in transportation came at least as much from cities eager to buy as from farmers seeking to sell. Urban merchants hoped to funnel as much farm produce as possible from as large a hinterland as possible into their own market, either for consumption or transshipment elsewhere.[27] Technology, new or newly applied, made available improvements in transportation, but constructing "internal improvements" posed problems not only physical but also economic, legal, and political. Who should be responsible for addressing the needs and funding the solutions? Private enterprise, local, state, or national government? Adams, Clay, and Vice President Calhoun all supported

25. See Donald Ratcliffe, *The Politics of Long Division: The Birth of the Second Party System in Ohio, 1818–1828* (Columbus, Ohio, 2000), esp. p. 331.

26. Andrew Jackson to William B. Lewis, Feb. 14, 1825, *Correspondence of AJ*, III, 276. On whether there had been an explicit agreement, see Remini, *Henry Clay*, 258; Charles Sellers, *The Market Revolution* (New York, 1991), 199.

27. See Meinig, *Continental America*, 216–23.

spending federal money on transportation, but many other political leaders disagreed.[28]

The pressure of the great westward movement itself first made it clear that locally maintained country roads would be insufficient. In preparation for admitting Ohio to statehood, Congress had agreed back in 1802 to devote some of the proceeds from the sale of public lands there to the construction of a gravel road to facilitate trans-Appalachian travel, communication, and commerce. Begun in 1811 at Cumberland, Maryland, on the Potomac, the National Road (also called the Cumberland Road) reached Wheeling on the Ohio in 1818, fulfilling a dream of linking those two river systems. Thereafter the road was extended piecemeal to the west across Ohio, Indiana, and Illinois. It constituted one of the few portions of Albert Gallatin's vast scheme for a national system of internal improvements that the federal government actually ever implemented. The road profited the construction industry wherever it went and raised land values. Thanks to the traffic it generated, Baltimore temporarily surpassed Philadelphia to become the nation's second-largest city in the 1820s.[29] In the early twentieth century the National Road was extended east to Atlantic City and west to San Francisco and renamed Highway 40; later, portions of it were incorporated into Interstate 70.

Despite widespread clamor for better transportation and its manifest tangible benefits, doubts remained in some quarters whether the Constitution delegated power to the federal government to construct internal improvements. These doubts, combined with disputes over which routes the government should favor, proved strong enough to ensure that the National Road had no counterparts. And when Congress passed a bill in 1822 to authorize the collection of tolls on the National Road, thereby making it self-funding, Monroe vetoed it. Along with his veto he transmitted to Congress a 25,000-word explanatory essay arguing the same position Madison had enunciated in 1817, that the country needed internal improvements financed by the federal government, but that only a constitutional amendment could authorize them. Yet Monroe proved no more consistent than Madison had been on the issue of internal improvements. At the last minute he inserted into his document a qualification

28. See Carter Goodrich, *Government Promotion of American Canals and Railroads* (New York, 1966); John Lauritz Larson, "Jefferson's Union and the Problem of Internal Improvements," in *Jeffersonian Legacies*, ed. Peter Onuf (Charlottesville, 1993), 340–69.

29. Joseph S. Wood, "The Idea of a National Road," in *The National Road*, ed. Karl Raitz (Baltimore, 1996), 93–122.

that the constitutional power to levy taxes for "the general welfare" might authorize spending federal money on certain internal improvements even without an amendment. Later, the president requested an advisory opinion from the U.S. Supreme Court on the subject. Modern lawyers will be surprised to learn that he got one. In an opinion written by Associate Justice William Johnson of South Carolina and kept confidential by Monroe, the Court advised the president that federally funded internal improvements were constitutional.[30] Emboldened, Monroe signed a bill to extend the National Road and another authorizing a "General Survey" of possible routes and estimated costs for a number of other roads and canals.

While the federal government dithered, arguing over routes and the meaning of legal texts, resourceful state and local authorities moved to encourage the building of turnpikes. Some of these, like the Lancaster Turnpike in Pennsylvania, antedated the War of 1812. Typically, a state legislature chartered a corporation and granted it the exclusive franchise to build a certain road and charge tolls for its use. (In those days obtaining a corporate charter required special legislative action.) To help raise the necessary capital, state and local governments would often subscribe some of the stock in the turnpike company, creating a "mixed" public-private enterprise. The private stockholders often included hundreds of small investors, local boosters motivated not only by the promise of dividends but even more by hope of rising land values for themselves and their kinship groups in the area where the turnpike would pass. The political popularity of turnpikes and the large number of small investors in them testify to the extent of grass-roots enthusiasm for improved transportation.[31]

Despite their popularity, turnpikes provided only slow and uncertain transportation. Stagecoaches usually went six to eight miles an hour, though on an unusually fine road, such as that between New York and Philadelphia, they could make over eleven miles an hour.[32] In the event, turnpikes proved more helpful in moving people into the hinterland than in bringing their produce back out. Wagon transportation of goods could seldom compete with river boats and canal barges for distances over a hundred miles. While turnpikes did benefit the communities they served, not least in higher property values, they never paid much in the way of

---

30. Donald G. Morgan, *Justice William Johnson* (Columbia, S.C., 1954), 122–25.
31. See John Majewski, *A House Dividing: Economic Development in Pennsylvania and Virginia Before the Civil War* (New York, 2000), 49–58.
32. George Rogers Taylor, *The Transportation Revolution* (New York, 1966), 142.

dividends. For one thing, it was too easy to avoid the tollbooths (paths around them came to be so well known they were called "shun-pikes"). Had the roads been financed by bonds, the bondholders would have had a legal claim to payment. Financing them instead by taxes and stock sales meant many a small farmer lost a hundred dollars or so of savings, but the benefits were widely distributed among local users whether they had invested or not. Small investors, then as now, seldom pick the most profitable stocks.

The invention of the steamboat enhanced the comparative advantages of water transportation. In 1787, John Fitch had built the first American steamer, but he could not obtain financial backing and died in obscurity. The first commercially successful steamboat, Robert Fulton's *Clermont*, plied the Hudson River starting in 1807. Steamboats proved most valuable for trips upstream on rivers with powerful currents, of which the Mississippi was the ultimate example. In 1817, a twenty-five day steamer trip up the Mississippi from New Orleans to Louisville set a record; by 1826, the time had been cut to eight days. Pre-steamboat traffic on the Mississippi had been mostly one-way downstream; at New Orleans, boatmen broke up their barges to sell for lumber and *walked* back home to Kentucky or Tennessee along the Natchez Trace road.[33]

Early steamboats, with side or rear paddlewheels, navigated rivers, lakes, and the coastal trade. They were built with drafts as shallow as possible to avoid obstacles in the water. The joke ran that they could float on a heavy dew, and it was literally true that one of them could carry eighty passengers with forty tons of freight in two feet of water.[34] Even so, the dredging of rivers and harbors became one of the most important kinds of internal improvement that state and federal authorities undertook in this period.

For all their utility, nineteenth-century steamboats were dangerous. Between 1825 and 1830 alone, forty-two exploding boilers killed 273 people. Commenting on steamboat accidents, Philip Hone of New York City, one of the great diarists of the period, observed in 1837, "We have become the most careless, reckless, headlong people on the face of the earth. 'Go ahead' is our maxim and pass-word, and we do go ahead with a vengeance, regardless of consequences and indifferent to the value of human life."[35] In 1838, an enormous boiler explosion in Charleston took 140 lives.

33. Brooke Hindle, *Emulation and Invention* (New York, 1981), 25–57; Feller, *Jacksonian Promise*, 24; Thomas Clark and John Guice, *Frontiers in Conflict* (Albuquerque, N.M., 1989), 258.
34. Sellers, *Market Revolution*, 132.
35. *Diary of Philip Hone*, ed. Bayard Tuckerman (New York, 1889), entry for May 22, 1837, I, 260.

Congress responded that year with the first federal regulation, warranted by the interstate commerce clause. From then on, every steamboat boiler had to bear a certificate from a government inspector. Steamboats continued to blow up. In 1845 Congress extended the jurisdiction of federal courts to include cases arising on inland waterways.[36]

Even after the invention of steamboats, merchants continued to favor sailing ships for ocean voyages because they did not have to devote a lot of precious cargo space to carrying fuel for a long voyage. The famous American clipper ships that traded between New England and China in the 1850s were sailing vessels. In general, seaborne commerce needed improvement less urgently than land and river commerce; indeed, the oceans had constituted the highways of traffic for generations. The first ocean vessels to find steam practical were warships. They used steam power to enable them to maneuver independently of the wind and bring their guns to bear. But even they kept full sailing rigging, so they could conserve fuel for times when it was most needed. A Canadian named Samuel Cunard pioneered the development of transatlantic commercial steamships starting in 1840. Instead of wood fuel, his ships burned coal, which took up less space in the hold; they cut the westward crossing time from thirty to fourteen days. In 1847, Congress awarded a subsidy to Edward Collins to create an oceangoing steamship line under the U.S. flag, but the Collins Line did not compete successfully with the Cunard Line and went bankrupt after a decade.[37]

Besides carrying goods and passengers, ocean vessels also hunted whales and fish. For two decades beginning in 1835, four-fifths of the world's whaling ships were American. New Bedford, Massachusetts, dominated American whaling (as Nantucket had done in the eighteenth century). The demand for whale oil, used for lighting, increased as more people left the farms and moved to cities. Other whale products included whalebone, used much as we use plastic; ambergris, used in perfume; and spermaceti, used as candle wax. In sharp contrast to textiles, whaling ships employed an all-male labor force. The historian William Goetzmann has aptly called the bold navigators who added to geographical

36. Ruth Cowan, *Social History of American Technology* (New York, 1997), 111; Harry Scheiber, "The Transportation Revolution and American Law," in *Transportation and the Early Nation* (Indianapolis, 1982), 15–16.

37. Robert Post, *Technology, Transport, and Travel in American History* (Washington, 2003), 18–20; Stephen Fox, *Transatlantic: Samuel Cunard and the Great Atlantic Steamships* (New York, 2003), xii, 6.

knowledge in their pursuit of the leviathan the "mountain men of the sea." The forty years beginning in 1815 represented the golden age for the American whaling industry; its fleet peaked at mid-century, just before the new petroleum industry began to replace whale oil.[38]

Canals further extended the advantages of water transport. Canals might connect two natural waterways or parallel a single stream so as to avoid waterfalls, rapids, or obstructions. Locks raised or lowered the water level. Horses or mules walking along a towpath moved barges through the canal; an animal that could pull a wagon weighing two tons on a paved road could pull fifty tons on the towpath of a canal.[39] In Europe, canals had been around a long time; the Languedoc Canal connected the Mediterranean with the Bay of Biscay in 1681. In North America, canal construction had been delayed by the great distances, sparse population, and (embarrassing as it was to admit) lack of engineering and management expertise.[40] During the years after 1815, a society eager for transportation and open to innovation finally surmounted these difficulties. Because canals cost more to construct than turnpikes, public funding proved even more important in raising the capital for them. Energy and flexibility at the state level got canal construction under way when doubts about constitutional propriety made the federal government hesitate. Many canals were built entirely by state governments, including the most famous, economically important, and financially successful of them all, the Erie Canal in New York.[41]

Astonishingly, this ambitious artificial waterway from Albany to Buffalo was completed in eight years. On October 26, 1825, Governor DeWitt Clinton boarded the canal boat *Seneca Chief* in Lake Erie and arrived at Albany a week later, having been cheered in every town along the way. He then floated down the Hudson to New York harbor, where, surrounded by a flotilla of boats and ships of all kinds, he poured a keg of Lake Erie water into the Atlantic. On shore, the city celebrated with fireworks and a parade of fifty-nine floats. The canal had contributed might-

38. William Weeks, *Building the Continental Empire* (Chicago, 1996), 67; William Goetz-mann, *New Lands, New Men: America and the Second Great Age of Discovery* (New York, 1986), 231–46; Lance Davis, Robert Gallman and Karin Gleiter, *In Pursuit of Leviathan* (Chicago, 1997).
39. Philip Bagwell, *The Transport Revolution from 1770* (London, 1974), 13.
40. Noticed by Michel Chevalier, who included much information on the transportation revolution in his *Society, Manners, and Politics in the United States*, trans. T. Brad-ford (Boston, 1839), 272.
41. See Nathan Miller, *The Enterprise of a Free People: Economic Development in New York during the Canal Period* (Ithaca, 1962).

ily to the prosperity of New York City (which in those days meant simply Manhattan). Even the urban artisans, who had originally opposed it in fear of higher taxes, had become enthusiastic about the Erie Canal. Because it facilitated transshipment of goods from New York City inland, the canal encouraged the extraordinary growth of the port of New York. One day in 1824 some 324 vessels were counted in New York harbor; on a day in 1836 there were 1,241.[42]

The Erie Canal's effects elsewhere were at least as dramatic as those in New York City. Across western New York state, construction of the canal mitigated the hard times following the Panic of 1819, and its operation stimulated both agriculture and manufacturing. The Erie Canal made New York the "Empire State." Within nine years, the $7,143,789 it had cost the state to construct the canal had been paid off in tolls collected; by then its channel was being expanded to accommodate more traffic.[43] The canal initiated a long-term boom in the cities along its route, including Albany, Utica, Syracuse, Rochester, and Buffalo. Between 1820 and 1850, Rochester grew in population from 1,502 to 36,403; Syracuse, from 1,814 to 22,271; Buffalo, from 2,095 to 42,261.[44]

The canal transformed the quality as well as the quantity of life in western New York state. Where earlier settlers had been to some extent "self-sufficient"—eking out a subsistence and making do with products they made themselves or acquired locally—people now could produce for a market, specialize in their occupations, and enjoy the occasional luxury brought in from outside. When fresh Long Island oysters first appeared on sale in Batavia, a western New York town, it made headlines in the local newspaper. The cost of furnishing a house fell dramatically: a clock for the wall had dropped in price from sixty dollars to three by midcentury; a mattress for the bed, from fifty dollars to five. Although some of this saving was due to mass production, much of it was due to lower transportation costs.[45] Changes from the rustic to the commercial that had taken centuries to unfold in Western civilization were telescoped into a generation in western New York state. While some people moved to

---

42. Feller, *Jacksonian Promise*, 17–18; Ronald Shaw, *Erie Water West: A History of the Erie Canal* (Lexington, Ky., 1966), 184–92; Christopher Clark, *Social Change in America: From the Revolution Through the Civil War* (Chicago, 2006), 155.
43. Ronald Shaw, *Canals for a Nation* (Lexington, Ky., 1990), 42, 49.
44. Shaw, *Erie Water West*, 263.
45. *Republican Advocate*, Nov. 5, 1825, quoted in Carol Sheriff, *The Artificial River* (New York, 1996), 3; Donald Parkerson, *The Agricultural Transition in New York State* (Ames, Iowa, 1995), 10.

cities, other families moved to new farms where they could maximize their contact with markets. The value of land with access to transportation rose; that of farmland still isolated fell. The social and cultural effects of these changes were particularly felt by women, causing some to turn from rural household manufacturing to management of middle-class households based on cash purchases.[46] The religious revivals of the burned-over district reflected in part a longing for stability and moral order amidst rapid social change. They began with efforts to tame the crudity and vice of little canal towns and went on to bring a spiritual dimension to the lives of the new urban middle and working classes.

Meanwhile, by the shores of the Great Lakes, the canal facilitated the settlement of northern Ohio, Indiana, and Illinois by people of Yankee extraction moving west by water and sending their produce back east the same way. Without the canal, the pro-southern Butternuts would have dominated midwestern politics, and the river route down to New Orleans would have dominated the midwestern economy.[47]

Canals were more exciting for shippers and engineers than for passengers. Long-distance travel by canal boat proved effective in moving large numbers of people, but it was not much fun. The speed limit on the Erie Canal was four miles an hour, and travelers like the writer Nathaniel Hawthorne commented on the "overpowering tedium" of the journeys. Catherine Dickinson of Cincinnati, the aunt of Emily Dickinson, complained like many others of sleeping quarters so "crowded that we had not a breath of air." Still, canal travel was safe and suitable for families, and passengers relieved their boredom with singing and fiddles. Harriet Beecher Stowe summed it up: "Of all the ways of travelling, the canal boat is the most absolutely prosaic."[48]

Others rushed to imitate New York's canal success. Ohio complemented the Erie Canal with a system of its own linking Lake Erie and Cleveland with the Ohio River and Cincinnati. The canals brought the frontier stage of Ohio history to a rapid close and integrated the state into the Atlantic world of commerce.[49] The Canadians constructed the Welland Canal, bypassing Niagara Falls for vessels going between Lake

46. Parkerson, *Transition*, 146; Mary Patricia Ryan, *Cradle of the Middle Class: The Family in Oneida County, New York* (New York, 1981).

47. See Douglas North, *The Economic Growth of the United States* (New York, 1961), 102–11.

48. These and other reports are quoted in Shaw, *Canals for a Nation*, 178–86.

49. Andrew Cayton, *Frontier Republic: Ohio, 1780–1825* (Kent, Ohio, 1986), x. See also R. Douglas Hurt, *The Ohio Frontier* (Bloomington, 1996), 388–96.

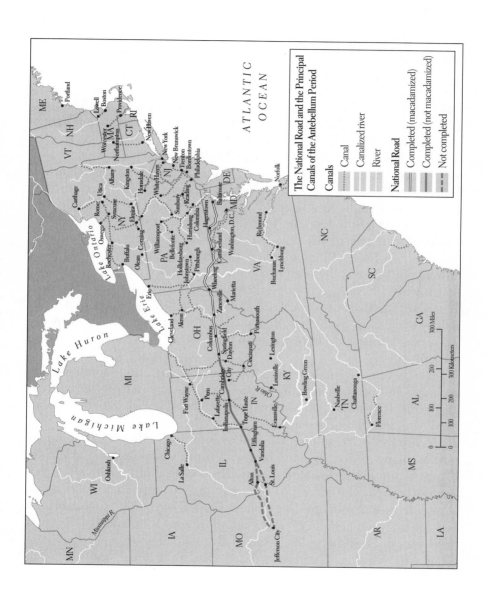

The National Road and the Principal
Canals of the Antebellum Period

Canals
Canal
Canalized river
River

National Road
Completed (macadamized)
Completed (not macadamized)
Not completed

Erie and Lake Ontario. Pennsylvania undertook the most extensive canal system of any state. Jealous of New York City, Philadelphia businessmen wished to expand their own city's commercial hinterland beyond the 65-mile-long Lancaster Turnpike. A group of them led by Matthew Carey persuaded the Pennsylvania legislature to commence in 1826 the Mainline Canal, going all the way to Pittsburgh and the Ohio River. The Mainline Canal was an even more impressive engineering feat than the Erie: 395 miles long, it rose 2,322 feet over the Alleghenies and had 174 locks and an 800-foot tunnel.[50] Its backers hoped that the Mainline Canal would compete successfully with the Erie because, being farther south, it would be blocked by ice for a shorter time in winter. But inevitably, it cost more time and money to surmount Pennsylvania's more formidable geographical barriers, and the planners of the Mainline Canal compounded their difficulties by dissipating resources on too many feeder canals. As a result, Pennsylvania's canal system came into operation just a little too late. The advent of a startling new technology spoiled the hopes of the state's canal builders. When the Mainline Canal finally linked Philadelphia with Pittsburgh in 1834, it included a railway portage over the crest of the mountains. By this time it was clear that it would have been more efficient to build a railroad all the way. The Mainline Canal's advocates had not wanted to wait for railway technology to develop, so they pressed ahead with a program that quickly became obsolescent.[51] In transportation projects, as in love and war, timing was critical.

Yet even internal improvements that did not earn a profit for their owners could still be economically valuable to their region by lowering shipping costs. Improved transportation made a big difference to daily life in rural America. Not only could farmers sell their crops more readily, they could also buy better implements: plows, shovels, scythes, and pitchforks, now all made of iron. Even sleighs with iron runners became available. Clothing and furniture could be purchased instead of homemade. Information from the outside world was more readily available, including advertisements that told of new products, helpful or simply fashionable. As early as 1836, the *Dubuque Visitor*, far off in what is now Iowa (then part of Wisconsin Territory), advertised ready-made clothing and "Calicoes, Ginghams, Muslins, Cambricks, Laces, and Ribbands." And instead of

50. Larson, *Internal Improvement*, 86.
51. Julius Rubin, "An Imitative Public Improvement," in *Canals and American Development*, ed. Carter Goodrich et al. (New York, 1961), 67–114.

bartering with neighbors or the storekeeper, rural people increasingly had cash to facilitate their transactions.[52]

Did internal improvements benefit everybody? No. Sometimes local farmers or artisans went bankrupt when exposed to the competition of cheap goods suddenly brought in from far away. Northeastern wheat-growers were hurt once the Erie Canal brought in wheat from more productive midwestern lands. Some of them could switch from grains to growing perishable vegetables for the nearby cities, but others had to abandon their farms. Generations later, travelers could find the ruins of these farmhouses among the woods of New England. Before the great improvements in transportation, such farms, however inefficient on their infertile and stony soil, could yield a living producing for a nearby market. There were also people, mostly in the South, who didn't expect to use internal improvements and therefore didn't want to have to pay for them. These included not only the lucky owners of farms or plantations located on naturally navigable waterways but also subsistence cultivators who were almost self-sufficient, perhaps supplementing what they grew by hunting and fishing as their Native American precursors had done. If these people felt content with their lives—as some of them did—they would not care to have internal improvements changing things. Similarly isolated were certain ethnic enclaves in the North such as the Pennsylvania Amish, whose members traded little and mainly within their own community. People like that could afford to be indifferent to internal improvements. But the lives of most Americans were powerfully affected, and usually for the better.

Finally, internal improvements could be opposed for reasons that had nothing to do with their economic effects. There were those who felt their stake in the status quo threatened by any innovation, especially innovation sponsored by the federal government. All slaveholders did not feel this way, as Clay and Calhoun clearly demonstrated, but some did. North Carolina's Nathaniel Macon confided their fears to a political ally in 1818: "If Congress can make canals, they can with more propriety emancipate." Northern enthusiasm for internal improvements needed to be checked, he cautioned. "The states having no slaves may not feel as strongly as the states having slaves about stretching the Constitution, because no such interest is to be touched by it." The strident John Randolph

---

52. Ronald Shaw, "Canals in the Early Republic," *JER* 4 (1984): 117–42; William Gilmore, *Reading Becomes a Necessity of Life* (Knoxville, Tenn., 1989), 110; Gary Nash et al., *The American People*, 3rd ed. (New York, 1994), 350.

of Roanoke made this logic public: "If Congress possesses the power to do what is proposed in this bill," he warned in 1824 while opposing the General Survey for internal improvements, "they may emancipate every slave in the United States."[53] Men like Macon and Randolph were willing to block the modernization of the whole country's economy in order to preserve their section's system of racial exploitation. Clay made the opposite choice, and for the time being he could count on the trans-Appalachian West, free and slave states alike, to back internal improvements. Calhoun, however, was about to change his mind.

III

As part of the celebration of the Erie Canal's completion, cannons were placed within earshot of each other the entire length of its route and down the Hudson. When Governor Clinton's boat departed from Buffalo that October morning in 1825, the first cannon of the "Grand Salute" was fired and the signal relayed from gun to gun, all the way to Sandy Hook on the Atlantic coast and back again. Three hours and twenty minutes later, the booming signal returned to Buffalo.[54] Except for elaborately staged events such as this, communication in early nineteenth-century America usually required the transportation of a physical object from one place to another—such as a letter, a newspaper, or even a message attached to the leg of a homing pigeon. This was how it had been since time immemorial. But as transportation improved, so did communications, and improved communications set powerful cultural changes in motion.

Because of the scheduled packets, news from Europe almost always arrived in New York City first. Competition among the packets placed a greater emphasis on speed, and these sailing vessels out of Liverpool shaved the average westward crossing time from fifty days in 1816 to forty-two days a decade later. Beginning in 1821, arriving ships would send semaphore signals of the most important messages to watching telescopes on shore, saving precious hours in transmitting information. During the 1830s, two New York commercial papers, the *Journal of Commerce* and the *Courier and Herald*, starting sending schooners fifty to a hundred

---

53. Nathaniel Macon to Bartlett Yancey, April 15, 1818, quoted in Larson, *Internal Improvement*, 105; Macon to Yancey, March 8, 1818, in *James Sprunt Historical Monographs*, no. 2 (Chapel Hill, 1900), 49; John Randolph in the House of Representatives (1824), quoted in Larson, *Internal Improvement*, 143.
54. Shaw, *Canals for a Nation*, 43.

miles out to sea to meet incoming ships and then race back to port with their news, trying to scoop each other.

From New York City, information dispersed around the country and appeared in local newspapers. In 1817, news could get from New York to Philadelphia in just over a day, traveling as far as New Brunswick, New Jersey, by steamer. To Boston from New York took more than two days, with the aid of steamboats in Long Island Sound. To Richmond the news took five days; to Charleston, ten.[55] These travel times represented a great improvement over the pre-steamboat 1790s, when Boston and Richmond had each been ten days away from New York, but they would continue to improve during the coming generation. For the most important news of all, relay express riders were employed. In 1830. these riders set a record: They carried the presidential State of the Union message from Washington to New York in fifteen and a half hours.[56]

Communications profoundly affected American business. For merchants eagerly awaiting word of crop prices and security fluctuations in European cities, the advantage of being one of the first to know such information was crucial. New Yorkers benefited because so many ships came to their port first, even though Boston and Halifax, Nova Scotia, were actually closer to Europe. The extra days of delay in receiving European news handicapped merchants based in Charleston, Savannah, or New Orleans. The availability of information affected investors of all kinds, not only commodity traders. No longer did people with money to invest feel they needed to deal only with their relatives or others they knew personally. Through the New York Stock Exchange, one could buy shares in enterprises one had never seen. Capital flowed more easily to places where it was needed. Information facilitated doing business at a distance; for example, insurance companies could better assess risks. Credit rating agencies opened to facilitate borrowing and lending; the first one, the Mercantile Agency, was established by the Tappan brothers, who also created the New York *Journal of Commerce* and bankrolled much of the abolitionist movement.[57] In colonial times, Americans had needed messages from London to provide commercially relevant news. Now, they could get their news from New York and get it faster. Improved communications stimulated economic growth.[58]

55. Taylor, *Transportation Revolution*, 145; Allan R. Pred, *Urban Growth and the Circulation of Information, 1790–1840* (Cambridge, Mass., 1973), 31, 36–48.
56. Pred, *Urban Growth*, 13.
57. Conference on "Risk and Reputation: Insecurity in the Early American Economy" at the Library Company of Philadelphia (2002).
58. See Robert Wright, *The Wealth of Nations Rediscovered* (Cambridge, Eng., 2002), 18–25.

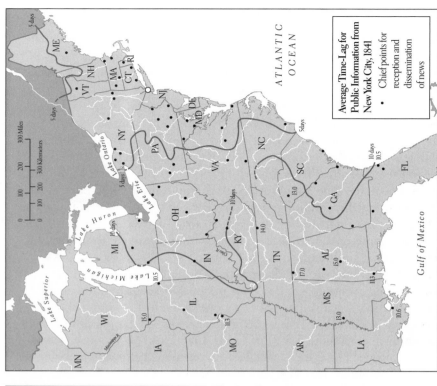

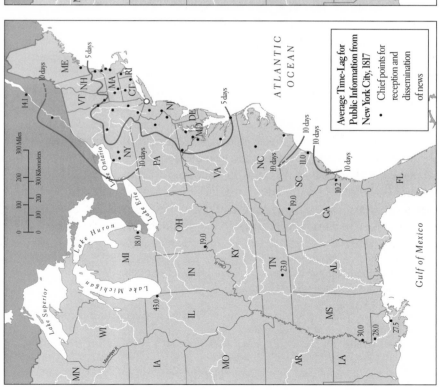

Source for both maps: Allan Pred, *Urban Growth and the Circulation of Information* (Harvard University Press, 1973).

Among the lessons learned from the War of 1812, the military importance of communication seemed clear. Better communications would have made the Battle of New Orleans unnecessary; indeed, faster communication between Parliament and Congress might well have avoided the declaration of war in the first place. If war did have to be waged in North America, better communications would enable the high command in Washington to maintain military command and control better than it had along the Great Lakes frontier in 1812–13. Events in Florida in 1818 underscored this need. Influenced by defense considerations as well as by the economic interests of those who needed to keep abreast of the market, the federal government played a central role in the "communications revolution" which accompanied the "transportation revolution." Together, the two revolutions would overthrow the tyranny of distance.[59]

The United States Post Office constituted the lifeblood of the communication system, and it was an agency of the federal government. The Constitution explicitly bestowed upon Congress the power "to establish post offices and post roads." Delivering the mail was by far the largest activity of the federal government. The postal service of the 1820s employed more people than the peacetime armed forces and more than all the rest of the civilian bureaucracy put together. Indeed, the U.S. Post Office was one of the largest and most geographically far-flung organizations in the world at the time. Between 1815 and 1830, the number of post offices grew from three thousand to eight thousand, most of them located in tiny villages and managed by part-time postmasters. This increase came about in response to thousands of petitions to Congress from small communities demanding post offices. Since mail was not delivered to homes and had to be picked up at the post office, it was a matter of concern that the office not be too distant. Authorities in the United States were far more accommodating in providing post offices to rural and remote areas than their counterparts in Western Europe, where the postal systems served only communities large enough to generate a profitable revenue.[60] In 1831, the French visitor Alexis de Tocqueville called the American Post Office a "great link between minds" that penetrated into "the heart of the wilderness"; in

59. See Richard John, "American Historians and the Concept of the Communications Revolution," in *Information Acumen*, ed. Lisa Bud-Frierman (London, 1994), 98–110.
60. Harry Watson, *Liberty and Power: The Politics of Jacksonian America* (New York, 1990), 26; Richard John, *Spreading the News: The American Postal System from Franklin to Morse* (Cambridge, Mass., 1995), 3–5, 50–52.

1832, the German political theorist Francis Lieber called it "one of the most effective elements of civilization."[61]

The expansion of the national postal system occurred under the direction of one of America's ablest administrators, John McLean of Ohio. McLean served as postmaster general from 1823 to 1829, under both Monroe and John Quincy Adams. Like just about everybody in Monroe's cabinet, he nursed presidential ambitions. Waiting for his chance at the big prize, he allied himself politically with John C. Calhoun and shared the young Calhoun's nationalistic goals. While European postal services were run as a source of revenue for the government, McLean ran the U.S. Post Office as a service to the public and to national unification. He sought to turn the general post office into what one historian has described as "the administrative headquarters for a major internal improvements empire that would have built and repaired roads and bridges throughout the United States."[62] But John McLean proved no more able to make himself a transportation czar than Albert Gallatin. Congressmen were not willing to delegate such authority, since it would have sacrificed their own power over favorite projects and "pork barrel" appropriations.

Not only did improved transportation benefit communication, but the communication system helped improve transportation. Even without a central plan, the post office pushed for improvements in transportation facilities and patronized them financially when they came. The same stagecoaches that carried passengers along the turnpikes also carried the mail, and the postmaster general constantly pressed the stages to improve their service (though, because the federal government subsidized the means of conveyance but seldom the right of way over which they traveled, passengers complained bitterly about the wretched roads). Contracts for carrying mail helped finance the early steamboats as well as nurture the stagecoach industry. Bidders for the contracts competed feverishly with each other—which did not hurt the political influence of the postmaster general. When a two-party system came to American politics, it would be predicated upon the existence of an enormous Post Office, both as a means of distributing mass electoral information such as highly partisan newspapers and as a source of patronage for the winners.[63]

Newspapers, not personal letters, constituted the most important part of the mail carried by the Post Office. Printed matter made up the

61. Quotations from Richard John, "The Politics of Innovation," *Daedalus* 127 (1998), 188–89.
62. John, *Spreading the News*, 108.
63. Ibid., 90–98; John, "Politics of Innovation," 194.

overwhelming bulk of the mail, and it was subsidized with low postal rates while letter-writers were charged high ones. Editors exchanged complimentary copies of their papers with each other, and the Post Office carried these free of charge; in this way the provincial press picked up stories from the metropolitan ones. The myriad of small regional newspapers relied on cheap postage to reach their out-of-town, rural subscribers. As early as 1822, the United States had more newspaper readers than any other country, regardless of population. This market was highly fragmented; no one paper had a circulation of over four thousand. New York City alone had 66 newspapers in 1810 and 161 by 1828, including *Freedom's Journal*, the first to be published by and for African Americans.[64]

The expansion of newspaper publishing resulted in part from technological innovations in printing and papermaking. Only modest improvements had been made in the printing press since the time of Gutenberg until a German named Friedrich Koenig invented a cylinder press driven by a steam engine in 1811. The first American newspaper to obtain such a press was the *New York Daily Advertiser* in 1825; it could print two thousand papers in an hour. In 1816, Thomas Gilpin discovered how to produce paper on a continuous roll instead of in separate sheets that were slower to feed into the printing press. The making of paper from rags gradually became mechanized, facilitating the production of books and magazines as well as newspapers; papermaking from wood pulp did not become practical until the 1860s. Compositors still set type by hand, picking up type one letter at a time from a case and placing it into a handheld "stick." Until the 1830s, one man sometimes put out a newspaper all by himself, the editor setting his own type. The invention of stereotyping enabled an inexpensive metal copy to be made of set type; the copy could be retained, and if a second printing of the job seemed warranted (such as a second edition of a book), the type did not have to be laboriously reset.[65] More important than innovations in the production of printed matter, however, were the improvements in transportation that facilitated the supply of paper to presses and then the distribution of what they printed. After about 1830, these improvements had reached the point where a national market for published material existed.

64. Richard Kielbowicz, *News in the Mail* (Westport, Conn., 1989), 3, 71; Joyce Appleby, *Inheriting the Revolution: The First Generation of Americans* (Cambridge, Mass., 2000), 100.

65. Ronald Zboray, *A Fictive People* (New York, 1993), 9–11; William Huntzicker, *The Popular Press* (Westport, Conn., 1999), 165. On papermaking, see Judith McGaw, *Most Wonderful Machine* (Princeton, 1987).

About half the content of newspapers in this period consisted of advertising, invariably local. (Half of daily newspapers between 1810 and 1820 even used the term "advertiser" in their name.) The news content, however, was not predominantly local but rather state, national, and international stories. Many if not most newspapers of the 1820s were organs of a political party or faction within a party, existing not to make a profit but to propagate a point of view. Since custom inhibited candidates for office from campaigning too overtly (especially if running for the presidency), partisan newspapers supplied the need for presenting rival points of view on the issues of the day. Such papers relied on subsidies from affluent supporters and government printing contracts when their side was in power.[66] The newspapers of the early republic often printed speeches by members of Congress, a particularly valuable service since Congress itself did not publish its own debates until 1824. The papers also published periodic "circular letters" from the members to their constituencies. Newspapers played an essential role in making representative government meaningful and in fostering among the citizens a sense of American nationality beyond the face-to-face politics of neighborhoods.[67]

It did not require much capital to publish one of the small papers typical of the day. Even a limited circulation made the enterprise viable, and papers often catered to a specific audience. One kind of newspaper specialized in commercial information, especially commodity and security prices; a business and professional readership avidly devoured such periodicals, while many planters and farmers took an interest in their subject matter too. The party-political press and the newspapers published for profit competed with each other for advertisers and readers, and over the next generation the distinction between them blurred. In 1833, the *New York Sun* reached out for a truly mass audience by charging only a penny a copy and selling individual copies on the street instead of by subscription only; soon it had many imitators. The *New Orleans Picayune*, founded in 1837, took its name from the little coin that defined its price. The drop in prices quickly produced a dramatic rise in circulation; between 1832 and 1836, the combined circulations of the New York dailies

66. Bernard Weisberger, *The American Newspaperman* (Chicago, 1961), 70; John, *Spreading the News*, 41.
67. On this subject, see Michael Schudson, "News, Public, Nation," *AHR* 107 (2002): 481–95; Richard D. Brown, *The Strength of a People: The Idea of an Informed Citizenry* (Chapel Hill, 1996).

quadrupled from 18,200 to 60,000.[68] The growing commercialization of the press entailed both positive and negative effects. News reporting and editing became more professionalized and the newspapers less blatantly biased. On the other hand, the number of newspapers, the variety of their viewpoints, and the detail with which they covered politics all gradually declined. These developments, however, remained in their early stages during the first half of the nineteenth century.

On the frontier, pioneer newspaper editors performed a function similar to the schoolteachers and religious evangelists: They brought civilization. At the age of twenty, Eber D. Howe moved from Buffalo to the Western Reserve area of Ohio, following a typical path of Yankee migration. There he started the *Cleveland Herald* and later the *Painesville Telegraph*. In the early days, he had to rely on once-a-week mails to fill his papers with news. After writing the articles and setting them in type, he would mount his horse to deliver the papers himself to scattered farmhouses, sometimes taking payment in kind. He kept the settlers in touch with what was happening in the world, even though the news was forty-some days old from Europe and ten days old from New York.[69] To people at the time, of course, this did not seem slow.

Despite its admirable function of helping keep the citizenry informed, the typical local post office did not present a very edifying scene. Except in the handful of cases where a postmistress was in charge, it was a purely male environment where the occasional woman who ventured in was considered fair game. Most postmasters were also storekeepers selling liquor by the drink on the premises. The federal government mandated that post offices open every day, and this overrode whatever state and local laws might require Sunday closings. The post office thus became a conspicuous exception to general Sabbath observance in small-town America. On Sundays many men would flock to the local post office after church to pick up their mail and have a drink. Christian reformers, including Lyman Beecher and Senator Theodore Frelinghuysen of New Jersey, called for the suspension of transportation and sorting of mail on Sunday, and for postmasters to have the option of closing their offices that day. The reformers argued that the government's rules were effectively preventing conscientious observers of the Sabbath from working for the Post Office.

---

68. Gerald Baldasty, *The Commercialization of News in the Nineteenth Century* (Madison, Wisc., 1992), 11–35; Menahem Blondheim, *News over the Wires* (Cambridge, Mass., 1994), 25; Huntzicker, *Popular Press*, 1–6.
69. Appleby, *Inheriting the Revolution*, 100–101.

The sabbatarians mounted concerted campaigns to change postal rules in 1810–17 and again in 1827–31; antisabbatarians rallied to oppose them. With the communications revolution, it became possible to wage a nationwide contest over public opinion. Both sides used the mails to enlist support for their view on how the mails should be treated; the debate proved a training ground for organizing grassroots politics. The sabbatarians pioneered mass petition drives, a tactic later exploited by the antislavery movement, which included many of the same people. The sabbatarian postal cause won more supporters among Presbyterians and Congregationalists than other Christian denominations, and fewest on the frontier where information was precious. As long as the transmission of urgent news remained slow, the antisabbatarians were able to prevail, pressing the needs of the military and of merchants in remote business centers. After the invention of the electric telegraph these arguments carried less weight, and much of the transportation of the mails on Sunday was discontinued. In 1912, after a hundred years of recurrent agitation, the sabbatarians, aided now by organized postal workers, finally succeeded in closing U.S. post offices on Sundays. This antebellum reform, like temperance and women's suffrage, at last achieved its big victory in the Progressive era.[70]

In spite of the sabbatarian controversy, it would be a mistake to assume that the churches opposed improved communication. In fact, the evangelical movement seized upon the communications revolution, exploited it, and even fostered it. Religious publishers took advantage of advances in the technology of printing to turn out Bibles and tracts by countless thousands, many of which they distributed free of charge. The churches also contributed heavily to a new genre of printed matter, the magazine. Magazines, even more than newspapers, tended to be published for specialized audiences with similar interests and opinions. Literary and scientific magazines had existed in America for more than a generation. The most influential included Boston's *North American Review*, founded in 1815 and modeled on Scotland's *Edinburgh Review* in its wide-ranging subject matter, and Richmond's *Southern Literary Messenger*, which began in 1834. Agricultural journals appealed to sophisticated farmers and planters. But most of the periodicals with national circulations and successful publishing histories before 1840 were religious. They included the *Christian Spectator* (Congregationalist), the *Christian Register* (Unitar-

---

70. John, *Spreading the News*, 162–64, 173, 178, 201; John G. West, *The Politics of Revelation and Reason* (Lawrence, Kans., 1996), 137–70. For more, see Wayne Fuller, *Morality and the Mail in Nineteenth-Century America* (Urbana, Ill., 2003).

ian), the *Watchman-Examiner* (Baptist), *Zion's Herald* (Methodist), and the *United States Catholic Miscellany*. In 1829, the Methodist *Christian Advocate* claimed twenty thousand subscribers, at a time when no secular periodical had as many as five thousand. The religious press was certainly as authentically popular a medium as the political press.[71]

In democratizing American political life, the transportation and communications revolutions played an even more important role than did changes in state laws and constitutions. While states in the 1820s were abolishing remaining property qualifications for voting, and providing that presidential electors should be chosen by the voters instead of the legislators, the spread of information kept the voters politically informed and engaged, especially since so many of the periodicals existed for this express purpose. Improved roads made it easier for rural farmers to come into the polling place, typically the county courthouse. The turnout of eligible voters increased markedly in the generation from 1820 to 1840, and foreign visitors marveled at the extent of public awareness even in remote and provincial areas of the country.[72] A periodical of particular value in creating an informed public was *Niles' Register*, published in Baltimore from 1811 to 1849. This weekly constituted the closest thing to a nonpartisan source and provided, as it boasted, "political, historical, geographical, scientifical, statistical, economical and biographical" information. Historians as well as contemporaries have reason to be grateful to Hezekiah Niles.

Besides newspapers and magazines, the production and distribution of books also changed. A new book publishing business developed out of the old craft of printing. These early publishing companies typically acted as printers, wholesalers, and even retailers of their own books.[73] In the 1820s, the modest American book publishing industry was scattered among a number of cities, each serving a regional market. As transportation improved, publishing gradually concentrated in Philadelphia, New York, and Boston, with Cincinnati as a smaller western center. Few books were published south of the Potomac, where population was dispersed and literacy rates lower; however, the South's river transportation network facilitated the distribution of books brought in from outside. Conversely,

---

71. Candy Gunther Brown, *The Word in the World: Evangelical Writing, Publishing, and Reading* (Chapel Hill, 2004), esp. 155; Leonard Sweet, ed., *Communication and Change in American Religious History* (Grand Rapids, Mich., 1993); David Nord, *Evangelical Origins of Mass Media in America* (Columbia, S.C., 1984).
72. Ronald Formisano, *The Transformation of Political Culture: Massachusetts, 1790s–1840s* (New York, 1983), 16.
73. See Rosalind Remer, *Printers and Men of Capital* (Philadelphia, 1996).

Boston was able to remain in the publishing business even without access to the kind of river transport system New York and Philadelphia enjoyed, because New England's high literacy rate made it a fine regional book market. Although concentrated in fewer cities, the publishing industry expanded steadily; the value of books manufactured and sold in the United States rose from $2.5 million in 1820 to five times that by 1850 even while the price of individual books fell sharply.[74]

A historian named William Gilmore has studied the distribution of printed matter in the Upper Connecticut River Valley of Vermont and New Hampshire during the early nineteenth century. Thousands of newspapers, magazines, pamphlets, almanacs, advertisements, and books of all kinds, including hymnals, children's books, and textbooks, circulated among the inhabitants. As a consequence, he found, "landlocked rural residents in areas such as the Upper Valley kept up with many recent intellectual trends in the North Atlantic Republic of Letters."[75] The printed media were overcoming geographical isolation and providing consumers with unprecedented choices in what to read.

The expansion of publishing enabled a few American authors to earn a living, for the first time, by writing. One of the earliest writers to take advantage of this new opportunity was New York's Washington Irving. Irving's *Sketch Book* (1819), a collection of short stories and essays, proved an instant success with the public. Some of its tales, including "Rip Van Winkle" and "The Legend of Sleepy Hollow," found an enduring place in the hearts of American readers. "Rip Van Winkle," about a man who goes to sleep for twenty years and awakens to find his world utterly transformed, spoke to the feelings of a generation acutely aware of the quickening pace of change. Yet Irving's writings owed much of their popularity to the fact that they were comfortable and comforting. They affirmed traditional values, sentimental favorites, and picturesque local color; they poked fun at people who were too serious, like Ichabod Crane in "The Legend of Sleepy Hollow." Irving went on to a celebrated career, wrote commercially successful histories and biographies, was rewarded by the government with diplomatic posts in Britain and Spain, and became recognized internationally as an American "gentleman of letters."[76]

74. Michael Bell, "Conditions of Literary Vocation," in *The Cambridge History of American Literature*, ed. Sacvan Bercovitch (Cambridge, Eng., 1995), II, 13–17; William Charvat, *Literary Publishing in America, 1790–1850* (Philadelphia, 1959).

75. Gilmore, *Reading Becomes a Necessity of Life*, 205.

76. See Bell, "Conditions of Literary Vocation," 17–24; Ralph Aderman, ed., *Critical Essays on Washington Irving* (Boston, 1990).

A contemporary and rival of Irving, less polished but more profound, was James Fenimore Cooper. Cooper's father, William, a large-scale land speculator and Federalist congressman, had founded Cooperstown, New York. When the elder Cooper died he left Fenimore and his five siblings each assets worth fifty thousand dollars. Unfortunately he also left tangled legal affairs that led ultimately to the family estates having to be auctioned off at depressed prices after the Panic of 1819. Cooper found himself unable to live his expected life of a gentleman landowner and turned to his pen for a livelihood. When Walter Scott's *Ivanhoe*, set in medieval England, attained great success upon its appearance in the United States in 1819, Cooper decided that romances based on American history could be popular too.

The most memorable of Cooper's books were the five novels called "the Leatherstocking Tales." The first of these, *The Pioneers*, appeared in 1823. The story takes place in a town called Templeton, presided over by a landed magnate named Marmaduke Temple. Contemporaries and posterity alike have found Temple and Templeton fictionalized versions of William Cooper and Cooperstown. In the complex character of Judge Temple, the author worked through his ambivalent feelings toward the dead father whose aristocratic values Fenimore Cooper shared but whose commercial dealings had betrayed the son's trust. The novel also explores Cooper's ambivalent feelings toward the westward movement, which was spreading not only the high civilization the author prized but also the mercenary greed he loathed. What seems at first a conventional romance actually grapples with fundamental moral questions of Cooper's time and place. Three years later, Cooper produced *The Last of the Mohicans*, based on the siege of Fort William Henry during the French and Indian War. Here the heroic woodsman Leatherstocking, a marginal character in *The Pioneers*, becomes central. He and his Mohican Indian friends, Chingachgook and Uncas, exemplify the natural virtues that the westward movement was destroying. In Leatherstocking, Cooper had created an enduring American mythic figure, the manly hero who relates to nature rather than women, who stands outside society but not outside morality, who resorts to violence to do right. The myth sold well, both in Cooper's time and since.[77]

Irving and Cooper both lived in Britain for several years, enabling the two authors to claim royalties on British editions of their works. Returning

77. See Alan Taylor, *William Cooper's Town* (New York, 1995); Henry Nash Smith, introduction to James Fenimore Cooper, *The Prairie* (New York, 1950) v–xxi; Richard Slotkin, *Regeneration Through Violence* (Middletown, Conn., 1974), 466–513.

to America in 1833, Cooper repurchased his father's mansion and tried to settle down to the life of a country squire. But he quarreled with his neighbors and his countrymen in general and soon found himself again embroiled in lawsuits. Cooper came to feel ever more estranged from the American society whose paradoxes he probed in his fiction. He identified with the old landed gentry rather than with the commercial world he inhabited. Ironically, he particularly despised the mass printed media that facilitated his own success. This bitterness is most evident in his novel *Home as Found* (1838), with its savage portraits of the unscrupulous journalist Steadfast Dodge and the demagogic politician Aristabulus Bragg. Cooper's sense of alienation from bourgeois society would be typical of a host of later American intellectuals.

The extension of secondary education to many (not all) women in the years since American independence had created a new audience for printed matter. With female literacy rates rising, especially in the North, a majority of the audience for creative writing now consisted of women, for middle-class women had more leisure than their men. Women relished reading as a way to broaden their horizons, the more so since their everyday lives were so often constrained by home and children. Female writers sometimes found it easier to address this wide new audience than male writers did. In spite of the prevailing attitude that earning money was inappropriate for middle-class married women, some professional women writers and editors emerged. The best known of the American women writers of this generation was Catharine Maria Sedgwick, a New Englander. Sedgwick started out writing about young heroines who triumphed over adversity, then moved into historical romance with *Hope Leslie*, and finally developed a formula for didactic stories that reached a mass working-class audience. In her lifetime Sedgwick achieved both critical and commercial success, though she was then forgotten and has only recently been rediscovered. Disenchanted with the Calvinist theology of her cultural inheritance, Sedgwick turned to storytelling to convey her message of liberal spirituality. She exemplified the type of writer, especially common among women authors, who treated literature as a form of religious and moral suasion. This literary enterprise would achieve its high point in Harriet Beecher Stowe's *Uncle Tom's Cabin* (1852).[78]

In 1820, Daniel Boone died in Missouri at the age of eighty-five. The old frontiersman had been a model for Cooper's Leatherstocking. Boone

---

78. Mary Kelley, ed., *The Power of Her Sympathy: The Autobiography and Journal of Catharine Maria Sedgwick* (Boston, 1993); David Reynolds, *Faith in Fiction* (Cambridge, Mass., 1981), 50–55.

had fought in the Revolution and opened Kentucky to white settlement; his passing seemed to mark the end of an era. Even before he died Boone had been transformed into a legendary figure. Timothy Flint, a Cincinnati journalist-printer, completed that process in his account of Boone's life, the best-selling biography of the nineteenth century. In Flint's hands Boone became a model for young Americans, courageous and self-reliant, a harbinger of progress. With the aid of mass communications, a hero from the past could help the coming generation cope with the future in a rapidly changing world.[79]

IV

Innovations in technology often pose new questions in law. The steamboat company that employed Robert Fulton was owned by the powerful Livingston clan of New York; the state legislature rewarded them for their technological breakthrough with a monopoly over the steamboat trade in New York. The Livingstons then licensed Aaron Ogden to carry on the trade between New York City and the Jersey shore. Thomas Gibbons, a former business partner of Ogden, hired Cornelius Vanderbilt as his boat captain and Daniel Webster as his lawyer and challenged the monopoly. The case of *Gibbons v. Ogden* reached the U.S. Supreme Court in 1824. There Chief Justice Marshall ruled that because the Constitution grants Congress power to "regulate commerce among the several states," the monopoly granted by the state of New York could not be applied to commerce with New Jersey.[80] Unlike the Court's decision in the Bank case, this one was widely welcomed, for the steamboat monopoly had become unpopular even within New York and was soon repealed.

Even more important than the interpretation of the federal Constitution was interpretation of the common law by state courts. Unlike continental European lawyers, fascinated by Enlightenment reason and the law codes of Napoleonic times, the American legal profession venerated a heritage peculiar to English-speaking people, based on popular customs first recorded by the traveling royal judges of King Henry II. Fiercely defended by Anglo-American colonists before independence, respect for common law was reaffirmed in the federal Constitution's Seventh Amendment. Common law provided the foundation for the legal system of every state save the former French colony of Louisiana. In the words of

79. John Mack Faragher, *Daniel Boone: The Life and Legend* (New York, 1992).
80. *Gibbons v. Ogden*, 22 U.S. (9 Wheaton) 1 (1824); Taylor, *Transportation Revolution*, 56–69.

Justice Joseph Story, common law constituted "the watchful and inflexible guardian of private property and public rights."[81]

The use of common law implied a system based on custom and precedent, yet American judges established their independence of English decisions and shaped their rulings to evolving American needs. By no means unchanging, common-law jurisprudence, being derived from community experience, valued flexibility. Within its framework antebellum judges balanced the interests of society and the individual, of debtors and creditors, of freedom and regulation, of innovation and stability. Judges became increasingly self-conscious of their role as lawmakers for society. They restricted the scope of jurors' discretion to finding matters of fact, reserving legal decisions for themselves. Two legal maxims often helped guide their opinions: *salus populi suprema lex est* ("the welfare of the people is the supreme law") and *sic utere tuo* ("so use your right that you injure not the rights of others").[82] Judges gradually reinterpreted law on such subjects as eminent domain, water use, and patent rights in ways that facilitated entrepreneurship and technological innovation. This did not necessarily mean choosing between public and private interests, for in an age of many "mixed" public-private institutions, their opposition did not seem so sharp as it later appeared. Nor did the federal government's jurisdiction over interstate commerce always preclude state legislation, as it had in the case of the steamboat monopoly. States exercised extensive "police powers" even in areas affecting interstate commerce, the Supreme Court acknowledged repeatedly.[83] A litigious people even then, Americans provided their state courts with plenty to do. The decisions of state jurists like the eminent Chief Justice Lemuel Shaw of Massachusetts created the basis for an American common law jurisprudence.[84]

---

81. Joseph Story, *Discourse as Dane Professor of Law in Harvard University* (Cambridge, Mass. 1829), 6. Even in Louisiana, the common law came to predominate in the long run; Mark Fernandez, *From Chaos to Continuity: The Evolution of Louisiana's Judicial System, 1712–1862* (Baton Rouge, 2001).

82. Morton Horwitz, "The Emergence of an Instrumental Conception of American Law," *Perspectives in American History* 5 (1971): 287–326; William Novak, *The People's Welfare: Law and Regulation in Nineteenth-Century America* (Chapel Hill, 1996), 9, 44.

83. *Willson v. Blackbird Creek Marsh Company*, 27 U.S. (2 Peters) 245 (1829); *New York v. Miln*, 36 U.S. (11 Peters) 102 (1837); *License Cases*, 46 U.S. (5 Howard) 504 (1847).

84. See Leonard Levy, *The Law of the Commonwealth and Chief Justice Shaw* (Cambridge, Mass., 1957); William Nelson, *Americanization of the Common Law*, 2nd ed. (Athens, Ga., 1994).

V

Among the many aspects of life affected by the transportation and communications revolutions, politics was conspicuous. The availability of information coming from outside liberated people from the weight of local tyrannies, whether that of a local elite or a local majority. (Local authorities "were no longer the information gatekeepers for their neighbors," as the historian Richard D. Brown has put it.)[85] People could now read newspapers and magazines for themselves and could join organizations led by people who lived elsewhere, just as they could invest their money in distant enterprises. Politics, which had long seemed a game of personal rivalries among local leaders, became a battle over public opinion conducted through political organizations and the medium of print. The change occurred first, appropriately enough, in the state that built the Erie Canal. New York politics became a microcosm of the future of national politics. To understand these changes will require some attention to the state's complex power struggles, particularly those between DeWitt Clinton and Martin Van Buren.

Governor DeWitt Clinton was a survivor of the Byzantine intrigues characteristic of the old New York state politics. But through all the kaleidoscopic recombinations of factions and clans, Clinton had nurtured a vision of strong government, a government acting in partnership with private enterprise to promote public prosperity and enlightenment. From 1815 on, the Erie Canal provided the centerpiece for this vision. In his youth Clinton's friends dubbed him "Magnus Apollo" for his handsome physique and the diverse accomplishments of a Renaissance man; later critics used the nickname to satirize his pride and love of classical culture. In 1812, at the age of forty-four, Clinton had had the audacity to challenge Madison's reelection as president, carrying the northeast. Thereafter the Virginia dynasty had no use for him, even though he was the nephew of Jefferson's vice president. An innovator, DeWitt Clinton introduced economic and reform issues into the clannish political culture of New York. His long agenda included, besides internal improvements, aid to education, libraries, and manufacturing, prison reform, scientific agriculture, and the abolition of both chattel slavery and imprisonment for debt.[86]

---

85. Richard D. Brown, *Knowledge Is Power* (New York, 1989), 294.
86. Evan Cornog, *The Birth of Empire: DeWitt Clinton and the American Experience* (New York, 1998), 135; Steven Siry, *DeWitt Clinton and the American Political Economy* (New York, 1990), 255–71; Craig Hanyan and Mary Hanyan, *DeWitt Clinton and the Rise of the People's Men* (Montreal, 1996), 94–99.

Clinton's most successful philanthropic enterprise was the Savings Bank of New York, chartered in 1819. The idea that a bank could gather up small deposits from ordinary people and invest them seemed novel at the time. Clinton explained in a gubernatorial address that if working men had a secure place to save some of their wages, it would "prevent or alleviate the evils of pauperism." The SBNY turned out to be a huge success, both with the saving public and financially. It played a key role in financing the Erie Canal, for the bank purchased twelve times as much of the canal's bonded indebtedness as the second biggest investor.[87]

The popularity of Clinton's great canal portended a period of Clintonian dominance in New York. To block this eventuality, Clinton's political rival Martin Van Buren deployed his own faction of Republicans, called "Bucktails" for the emblems they wore in their hats to party meetings. Van Buren determined to trump Clinton's appeal by changing the dominant electoral issue in the state from economic prosperity to political democracy. The Bucktails began to call for revision of the New York state constitution of 1777 to do away with the unpopular property qualifications for voting. By this time the legal voting requirements were more honored in the breach than in the observance. Clinton did not oppose doing away with the requirements; indeed, he enjoyed political support among propertyless Irish immigrants thanks to his own Irish ancestry. But he hoped to delay calling a constitutional convention until it could include on its agenda a reapportionment of legislative seats based on the census of 1820. This would improve the representation of the western part of the state, which thanks to the Erie Canal was both growing fast and pro-Clintonian. The Bucktails, however, succeeded in getting the convention held quickly and in stigmatizing the Clintonians as reluctant democrats for seeking delay.[88]

When the convention met in August 1821, Bucktails dominated it. James Kent, chancellor of the state's highest court of equity and an elderly Federalist, made a forlorn defense of property requirements to vote for the state senate, though their demise was a foregone conclusion. But even Kent did not oppose the removal of property qualifications in voting for governor and the assembly.[89] Actually, Van Buren and his close associates would have preferred to retain a modest property qualification, but some

---

87. Kathleen McCarthy, *American Creed: Philanthropy and the Rise of Civil Society* (Chicago, 2003), 88–90, quotation from Clinton on 90.
88. Cornog, *Birth of Empire*, 143; Siry, *DeWitt Clinton*, 239.
89. Kent's speech is reprinted in Merrill D. Peterson, ed., *Democracy, Liberty, Property: The State Constitutional Conventions of the 1820s* (Indianapolis, 1966), 190–97.

of their supporters got the bit in their teeth and ran out of control. The property qualification for voting was abolished for white men, though the Bucktails pandered to racist sentiment by requiring that black voters have a net worth of $250, over the opposition of Clintonians. The convention also made various institutional changes and legislative redistricting ("gerrymanders," critics charged) that weakened the Clintonians. As a slap at Clinton himself, the gubernatorial term was reduced to two years and a year sliced off the current term Clinton was already serving. When the governor naturally protested, he was made to seem the opponent of the new constitution in general, including its democratic features. Even today, some historians continue to accept the claims of Van Buren's Bucktails to have scored a dramatic victory for democracy at the New York constitutional convention of 1821. On the whole, however, partisan advantage rather than philosophical disagreement over democracy explains the differences between Bucktails and Clintonians at the convention.[90]

As a result of these tactics and an advantageous alliance with a group of so-called high-minded Federalists led by Rufus King, Van Buren's followers gained control of the state government in 1822, creating a patronage machine nicknamed "the Albany Regency." The Bucktails did not consistently support popular democracy, even for white men. When the presidential election of 1824 approached, the two factions of New York Republicanism reversed their roles as friends of democracy. The Bucktails wanted to keep the state legislature, which they controlled, in charge of choosing presidential electors, thinking to benefit Crawford. A new organization called "the People's Party," demanding a popular presidential election in New York, rallied all those who favored Jackson, Adams, or Clay to their banner. The Clintonians now embraced democracy as their cause and won with it in November 1824. As the candidate of the People's Party, Clinton rode back into the governor's mansion with a landslide victory in time to lead the celebrations of the canal's completion. His running mate, the antislavery hero James Tallmadge, won election as lieutenant governor by an even larger majority. Although the new constitution increased the number of men who could legally vote for the state

90. The view that the constitutional convention witnessed the triumph of Bucktail democracy over Clintonian aristocracy is presented in Dixon Ryan Fox, *The Decline of Aristocracy in the Politics of New York* (New York, 1919), 264–68, and repeated, albeit with significant qualifications, in Sean Wilentz, *The Rise of American Democracy* (New York, 2005), 189–96. More persuasive analyses are those of Alvin Kass, *Politics in New York State, 1800–1830* (Syracuse, N.Y., 1965), 81–89; and Donald Cole, *Martin Van Buren* (Princeton, 1984), 66–82.

assembly by 56 percent, the Clintonians remained competitive in New York politics.[91]

Despite the Clintonian victory in the state election of 1824, the presidential election took place, one last time, under the old rules: The lame duck legislature got to choose New York's presidential electors. The Adams and Clay followers in the legislature formed an alliance that presaged the one their chiefs would forge at a later stage. But at the last minute, Van Buren succeeded in holding Clay's New York electoral vote below the threshold the Kentuckian needed to finish in the top three candidates and qualify for consideration in the House of Representatives.[92] When the contest then moved to the House, New York's large delegation seemed split evenly between Crawford and Adams. Van Buren strove to keep it that way, in effect denying the state its vote for president, because he hoped for a deadlock in which he could barter New York's vote to the highest bidder.

The Little Magician's plan was foiled when Stephen Van Rensselaer, one of the "high-minded" Federalists who had been temporarily allied with Van Buren, decided to vote for Adams. Many years later, after Van Rensselaer had died, Van Buren told a story of how the old man had found an Adams ballot lying on the floor and took it as a sign from heaven. Van Buren, of course, had every reason to trivialize Van Rensselaer's choice. The great patroon (as proprietors of Dutch land grants were called) might have decided to vote as he did for any number of causes. His constituents and the rest of his clan were for Adams, he had been lobbied by Daniel Webster and Henry Clay, and he was a longtime supporter of internal improvements. A month after the election, Van Rensselaer gave his own explanation in a letter to DeWitt Clinton. He had become convinced that Adams was bound to win eventually, and to cut short "the long agony" voted for him on the first ballot.[93]

In 1826, DeWitt Clinton was reelected to another two-year term as governor of New York, this time—amazingly—with the support of the Bucktails, for both Clinton and Van Buren were now backing Jackson for

91. Hanyan and Hanyan, *DeWitt Clinton*, 13–14.
92. The legislature had distributed New York's electoral vote thus: Adams 25, Clay 7, Crawford 4. When the electors met, Van Buren managed to detach three votes from Clay. See Cole, *Van Buren*, 136–37.
93. *Autobiography of Martin Van Buren*, ed. John Fitzpatrick (Washington, 1920), 152; Stephen Van Rensselaer to DeWitt Clinton, March 10, 1825, quoted in William Fink, "Stephen Van Rensselaer and the House Election of 1825," *New York History* 32 (1951): 323–30. See also Shaw Livermore, *The Twilight of Federalism* (Princeton, 1962), 180–81.

president. Both men aspired to become Jackson's designated heir. Clinton, who had been backing his old friend and fellow Royal Arch Mason longer than Van Buren had, might well have enjoyed the advantage in the contest. The choice would be important in determining the nature of Jackson's political agenda. DeWitt Clinton had come to personify political enthusiasm for economic development and transportation in particular. His rival Van Buren, on the other hand, typified a kind of politician willing to play the economic issues whichever way seemed momentarily advantageous. Van Buren reached out to forge an alliance with Calhoun and arrange for him to be named Jackson's 1828 running mate in order to make sure that Clinton was not chosen for the number two place.[94] Had Clinton become Jackson's confidant and designated heir, would Old Hickory have embraced Clinton's faith in planned economic development? It would have made a dramatic difference to the course of American history, but we shall never know. For on February 11, 1828, Magnus Apollo died, the victim of a heart attack at the age of fifty-eight. If Jackson wanted an alliance with a major New York political figure, Martin Van Buren was now the obvious choice. Van Buren would bring to the national arena all the skills in party organization and flexibility in economic issues that he had learned in the demanding school of New York state intrigue. His career represented not the triumph of the common man over aristocracy but the invention of machine politics.

DeWitt Clinton, on the other hand, leader of the People's Party, was an authentic but largely forgotten hero of American democracy. His Erie Canal liberated many farm families from commercial and political isolation. The public schools he supported provided the basis for mass literacy; his Savings Bank mobilized the thrift of small savers for investment capital. The infrastructure he worked to create would transform American life, enhancing economic opportunity, political participation, and intellectual awareness.

VI

Late in 1833, a twenty-seven-year-old French engineer named Michel Chevalier arrived in the United States. American canals, bridges, steamboats, and railroads fascinated him. During his two-year tour of the country, he concluded that improvements in transportation had democratic implications. In former times, he remarked, with roads rough and dangerous, travel required "a long train of luggage, provisions, servants, and

94. Bartlett, *Calhoun*, 138.

guards," making it rare and expensive. "The great bulk of mankind, slaves in fact and in name," had been "chained to the soil" not only by their legal and social status but also "by the difficulty of locomotion." Freedom to travel, the ability to leave home, was essential to the modern world and as democratic as universal suffrage, Chevalier explained:

> To improve the means of communication, then, is to promote a real, positive, and practical liberty; it is to extend to all the members of the human family the power of traversing and turning to account the globe, which has been given to them as their patrimony; it is to increase the rights and privileges of the greatest number, as truly and as amply as could be done by electoral laws. The effect of the most perfect system of transportation is to reduce the distance not only between different places, but between different classes.[95]

As Chevalier realized, improved transportation and communications facilitated not only the movement of goods and ideas but personal, individual freedom as well. Americans, a mobile and venturesome people, empowered by literacy and technological proficiency, did not hesitate to take advantage of the opportunity provided (as he put it) to turn the globe to their account.

In traditional society, the only items worth transporting long distances had been luxury goods, and information about the outside world had been one of the most precious luxuries of all. The transportation and communications revolutions made both goods and information broadly accessible. In doing so, they laid a foundation not only for widespread economic betterment and wider intellectual horizons but also for political democracy: in newspapers and magazines, in post offices, in nationwide movements to influence public opinion, and in mass political parties.

95. Michael [sic] Chevalier, *Society, Manners, and Politics in the United States*, trans. T. G. Bradford (Boston, 1839), quotations from 208–10.

7

The Improvers

On the Fourth of July 1826, Americans celebrated their nation's Golden Jubilee, the fiftieth anniversary of the Declaration of Independence. They observed the occasion with a holiday, speeches, toasts, and cannon salutes. Most remarkably, however, the day was hallowed by an unforeseeable combination of events. At fifty minutes past noon Thomas Jefferson, eighty-two-year-old author of the Declaration and third president, died at Monticello, his home in Albemarle County, Virginia. His last words had been, "Is it the Fourth?" Five hours later ninety-year-old John Adams, congressional advocate of the Declaration and second president, likewise died at his home in Quincy, Massachusetts. Friends in youth, the two men had become political adversaries, only to resume their friendship in old age and engage in a philosophical correspondence. Adams's last words were "Thomas Jefferson still survives," though in fact he was mistaken. Couriers traveling by steamboats and relays of galloping horses carried the news of the deaths north from Virginia and south from Massachusetts. Compounding the coincidence, the riders bearing these tidings met in Philadelphia, where it had all started at Independence Hall fifty years before. In Washington, John Quincy Adams, sixth President of the United States, learned of Jefferson's death on the sixth; he learned of his father's on the ninth in Baltimore, having started north to visit the old man. The president pronounced the juxtaposition of events a "visible and palpable mark of Divine favor" to the nation, and most of his countrymen agreed.[1]

With the deaths of Jefferson and Adams, only one signer of the Declaration of Independence, eighty-nine-year-old Charles Carroll of Maryland, remained alive. As the Founders of the republic passed from the scene, Americans were left to carry on their legacy with the help of their example. John Quincy Adams could not have felt more keenly the responsibility to preserve that "precious inheritance." The United States demonstrated to the world the merits of "representative democracy" (the

---

1. Lyman Butterfield, "The Fourth of July, 1826," *Virginia Magazine of History and Biography* 61 (1953), 117–40; Merrill Peterson, *The Jefferson Image in the American Mind* (New York, 1960), 3–4; James Morton Smith, *The Republic of Letters* (New York, 1995), III, 1973–74.

term was still novel, and Adams the first president to use it). The president believed that knitting the Union together, strengthening it economically and culturally, fulfilled the promise of the Revolution. The whole point of liberation from foreign domination, Adams asserted, was so that Americans could pursue the goal of human improvement, for their own benefit and that of mankind.[2]

The deceased patriarchs had been obvious examples of the talent and virtue that the Founders believed should characterize leadership in a republic. But they were also examples of personal improvement. Through hard work and study they had developed their potential and then turned it to the betterment of their countrymen. "Improvement," in its early nineteenth-century sense, constituted both an individual and a collective responsibility, involving both the cultivation of personal faculties and the development of national resources. Representative government and the Erie Canal improved society. The printing press and public education improved both society and individuals. To improve something was to turn it to good account, to make use of its potential. Thus, one could "improve" an occasion, that is, take advantage of it. A system of "internal improvements" would take advantage of the nation's opportunities and develop its resources, just as a woman might "improve herself by reading." Whether individual or collective, the word "improvement" had a moral as well as a physical meaning; it constituted an obligation, an imperative. Many an American, rural as well as urban, poor as well as middle-class, embraced the ethos of material and intellectual improvement. The young Abraham Lincoln with his book by the firelight shared this outlook, both as applied to himself and as applied to navigable waterways in Illinois. Improvement, personal and social, had not only a secular but also a religious appeal, as evangelical reformers like Beecher and Finney showed. To this culturally powerful conception John Quincy Adams dedicated his presidency.[3]

II

John Quincy (pronounced "Quinzy") Adams represented another man of talent and virtue, a worthy son of his father. His intellectual ability and

---

2. John Quincy Adams, "Inaugural Address," *Presidential Messages*, II, 294, 296; Daniel Howe, *The Political Culture of the American Whigs* (Chicago, 1979), 44–50.

3. *OED*, VII, 118; Daniel Howe, *Making the American Self* (Cambridge, Mass., 1997), 123; Allen Guelzo, *Abraham Lincoln* (Grand Rapids, Mich., 1999), 43–49. See also Nicholas Marshall, "The Power of Culture and Tangible Improvements," *American Nineteenth-Century History* 8 (207: 1–26.

courage were above reproach, and his wisdom in perceiving the national interest has stood the test of time. In an age when presidents were typically well prepared by prior public service, he came to the office the best prepared of all. He had been professor at Harvard, senator from Massachusetts, and "minister plenipotentiary" to the Netherlands, Prussia, Britain, and Russia (the United States did not use the title "ambassador" until the 1890s). More recently, Adams had served his country as peace negotiator at Ghent and as one of the greatest secretaries of state. Despite all this, Adams was not fated to enjoy a successful presidency. The limitations on his effectiveness lay partly beyond his control, but some of the responsibility rested with contradictions in Adams's own conception of his presidential role.

Contemporaries considered John Quincy Adams the quintessential New England Yankee: serious, hardworking, devout, with integrity of granite. Yet his time in Europe had given him a cosmopolitan perspective (and thanks to childhood years in Paris, fluency in French). Though his ancestors had been Puritans, Adams belonged to the liberal wing of the Congregational Church, much influenced by Enlightenment concepts of human rights and freedom. In both public and private life, Adams devoted himself to "improvement," which for him meant the painstaking regulation of all activities. Every day he made time for diary-writing and exercise; during his presidential term this included swimming naked in the Potomac at dawn. (He almost drowned there on June 13, 1825, in a rowboat that suddenly filled with water; the president didn't have time to take off his clothes, which weighed him down.)[4] A lifelong student of Cicero and the moral philosophers of eighteenth-century Scotland, Adams envisioned the American republic as the culmination of the history of human progress and the realization of the potential of human nature. Drawing an analogy between technological and political improvement, he once called the United States government "the steamboat of moral and political being."[5] Adams was the most learned president between Jefferson and Wilson but, like many intellectuals, felt ill at ease in society. He could not learn to welcome public appearances. Portly and balding by the time of his inauguration at the age of fifty-seven, he had lost his youthful good looks; charisma he had never possessed. Brooding, critical of those around him, Adams was most unsparing of all toward himself. First

---

4. Samuel Flagg Bemis, *John Quincy Adams and the Union* (New York, 1956) is still unsurpassed; for this episode, see 121.

5. John Quincy Adams, "Report on Manufactures," U.S. Congress, *Register of Debates*, 22nd Cong., 1st sess. (1833), VIII, pt. III, 83.

Lady Louisa Catherine Johnson Adams of Maryland, charming and musical, had been a major asset to her husband's election campaign. In the White House, however, her health and spirits declined.[6]

Adams came into office acutely conscious of his vulnerability as a minority president. "Less possessed of your confidence in advance than any of my predecessors," he pleaded in his inaugural address for the "indulgence" of the public.[7] The contrast between the all-but-unanimous election of Monroe in 1820 and the protracted, divisive election of 1824–25 could not have been greater. Accordingly, the new president took every possible step to underscore the continuity between Monroe's administration and his own. He stayed in close contact with the outgoing president during the transition, praised Monroe's achievements, and promised to pursue his initiatives. Indeed, Adams probably had been Monroe's favored candidate, though it is characteristic of the Virginian's politic discretion that he never made any such public acknowledgment.

Upon assuming the presidency, Adams refused to admit that the Era of Good Feelings could not be perpetuated. His inaugural address rejoiced that the "baneful weed of party strife was uprooted." He avowed as his goal a truly nonpartisan approach to government and sought to create an administration based on "talents and virtue," not party politics or sectionalism—which he declared even "more dangerous" than party. The role of an executive above party was dictated by political theory (Adams had long admired Bolingbroke's treatise *The Idea of a Patriot King*), by Monroe's example, and by the constraints of his situation as a minority president with little natural support outside his own section.[8] Accordingly, Adams left most of Monroe's officeholders in place, although some of them had backed his rivals in the recent election. He even offered to allow William H. Crawford to remain at the Treasury, though he must have been relieved when Crawford declined. Forgiving DeWitt Clinton his support for Jackson, Adams offered Clinton the premier diplomatic post at London. But Magnus Apollo was unwilling to forgo his governorship and the coming Erie Canal ceremonies, which he understandably relished. Adams then turned to the Federalist elder statesman, Rufus King, who had been minister to Britain many years before. Old

6. Lyman Butterfield, "Tending a Dragon Killer," *Proceedings of the American Philosophical Society* 118 (1974): 165–78; Jack Shepherd, *Cannibals of the Heart* (New York, 1980), 259–69.
7. *Presidential Messages*, II, 299.
8. Ibid., 296, 297. See Ralph Ketcham, *Presidents Above Party* (Chapel Hill, 1984), 130–36.

Republicans howled in protest against the nomination of a Federalist, and Adams actually made few other Federalist appointments.[9] He filled the vacancy at the Treasury with Richard Rush of Pennsylvania and gave the War Department, Calhoun's former office, to James Barbour of Virginia. Monroe's attorney general, postmaster general, and secretary of the navy all stayed put. In the end, Adams hoped he had laid the basis for government by consensus, or what his British contemporaries called a government of "all the talents."

Of course, Henry Clay's nomination as secretary of state represented the most momentous appointment. Apart from the role Clay had played in Adams's election, it was a logical choice, both to give the West a seat in the cabinet and to recognize Clay's concern with Latin American policy. Adams consulted with Monroe before making the offer, and the outgoing president did not advise against it. In later years Clay came to regret accepting the office, as seeming to confirm the accusation that he had traded his support in the presidential race for it. At the time, however, Clay felt that to decline would be to concede the justice of the accusation even more clearly. Clay had been disappointed when Monroe had not appointed him secretary of state, and now it seemed that Adams had recognized his deserts. Even if Clay had not joined the administration, his enemies would very likely still have gone into opposition.[10] However logical the Adams-Clay alliance in terms of their agreement on future policies, in 1825 it startled observers that the leading policymaker in the Monroe administration should join up with that administration's most outspoken congressional critic. Jackson rallied the disappointed of several factions to his cause with the cry that a "corrupt bargain" had been consummated.

The accusation of a "corrupt bargain" proved one of the most effective political weapons ever forged; it harassed the Adams administration and would haunt Henry Clay for the rest of his life. Today its effectiveness seems puzzling. In a multifactional election, a coalition government is inevitable, and an Adams-Clay coalition was as logical as any other (except Adams-Jackson, now no longer an option). But the political culture of the time did not acknowledge that the Jeffersonian Republican party had indeed fragmented into a multifactional system, nor even that candidates sought the presidency. Adams's appointment of Clay seemed to confirm the charge of "Wyoming" that all the candidates but Jackson were intriguers. Furthermore, the word "corruption" had a special resonance.

9. Shaw Livermore, *The Twilight of Federalism* (Princeton, 1962), 187–94.
10. Mary Hargreaves, *The Presidency of John Quincy Adams* (Lawrence, Kans., 1985), 43–47.

In the eighteenth century, British monarchs bestowed offices in return for support in Parliament, and colonial governors often tried the same tactic with their legislatures. Critics had called the practice "corrupting" the legislature.[11] The parallel, while not exact, was close enough to imply that Adams and Clay were not only dishonest but un-American.

In the Senate, the vitriolic Old Republican John Randolph led the opposition to the administration. Of all possible critics, this flamboyant Virginia aristocrat was surely the most to be feared. Randolph hated Clay's nationalism, envied his successful career, and for years had contrived ways to torment him. In the first session of Congress he delivered a characteristically inflammatory speech full of ingenious insults, calling the Adams-Clay administration "the coalition of Blifil and Black George—the combination, unheard of till then, of the puritan with the blackleg." His listeners gasped, then roared with laughter. Everyone recognized the allusion to the popular culture of the time. In Henry Fielding's novel *Tom Jones*, Blifil was a sanctimonious hypocrite, Black George an irresponsible scamp. A "blackleg" meant a cardsharp.[12] Poor Clay had been trying to live down his early reputation as a gambler and high liver and cultivate an image of statesmanlike moderation. Coming on top of the "corrupt bargain" charges, Randolph's insult seemed one too many, and Clay challenged the Virginian to a duel. Dueling was a feature of the southern code of manly honor, but two years earlier Clay had foresworn the practice, in support of Lyman Beecher's movement to abolish it. His good resolution was forgotten in the heat of the moment.[13]

On April 8, 1826, the two men, accompanied by their seconds and doctors, met and exchanged shots at a distance of ten paces. In spite of coming from Kentucky, Clay was a fumbling incompetent with firearms and missed both times, though his second bullet put a hole in Randolph's coat. Randolph was a better marksman and came with a pistol set on hair-trigger. Still, he too missed the first time (apparently aiming at Clay's leg) and then fired into the air. Honor satisfied, the two shook hands and went home. Clay had embarrassed the Adams administration, which depended on evangelical reformers opposed to dueling as part of its core constituency. To his own core constituency of plantation masters, Randolph had shown himself a chivalrous gentleman. He had counted on Clay's

---

11. See Bernard Bailyn, *Origins of American Politics* (New York, 1968), chap. 2.
12. There is a good account of the speech in Merrill Peterson, *The Great Triumvirate* (New York, 1987), 140–41.
13. On the frequency of dueling in this period, see Joyce Appleby, *Inheriting the Revolution* (Cambridge, Mass., 2000), 41–45.

poor marksmanship and had never intended to kill him. The theatricality of it all, speech and duel alike, appealed to Randolph.[14]

In the House of Representatives the administration initially enjoyed the support of a modest majority and secured the Speakership for John Taylor of New York, who had been a strong supporter of the Tallmadge amendment. The Senate presented more difficulty, but the presiding officer there was Vice President Calhoun, who assumed the right to appoint committee members.[15] Calhoun and Adams had long been close associates in Monroe's cabinet and had worked together in support of a nationalist agenda. In 1821, Adams had confided to his diary that Calhoun seemed "above all sectional and factious prejudices more than any other statesman of this Union with whom I have ever acted."[16] Now, however, far from aiding the administration, Vice President Calhoun used his influence in the Senate to distance himself more and more from President Adams. What had gone wrong with their partnership?

When Adams first indicated an intention to appoint Clay secretary of state, Calhoun tried desperately to dissuade him.[17] Calhoun thought he should be Adams's successor and felt betrayed. Adams did not feel he had made such a commitment to Calhoun—and anyway, Calhoun had not delivered South Carolina to Adams in the election, so Adams didn't owe him as he did Clay. But if Adams served two terms and Clay then succeeded him, Calhoun could see his own presidential hopes receding into a remote, imponderable future.

The estrangement of the two former colleagues derived from more than personal ambition. The political climate in South Carolina had changed significantly since Denmark Vesey's aborted uprising of 1822. Moderation and nationalism were becoming unpopular in the white community. James Hamilton, who as mayor of Charleston had rooted out the plotters, gained election as a Radical state-rights congressman; Justice William Johnson, who had questioned the propriety of the measures

---

14. See Andrew Burstein, *America's Jubilee* (New York, 2001), 181–204; Kenneth S. Greenberg, *Honor and Slavery* (Princeton, 1996), 53–65; Robert Dawidoff, *The Education of John Randolph* (New York, 1979), 255–59.

15. No other vice president has exercised this power. In 1823, the Senate had delegated the right to its "presiding officer," who at the time was its president pro tempore in the absence of Vice President Tompkins. Calhoun, when he took up his duties as vice president, appointed the Senate committees. Restive at having a nonsenator possess this power, the Senate later in the session resumed control over its own committees.

16. John Quincy Adams, *Memoirs*, ed. Charles Francis Adams (Philadelphia, 1874–79), V, 361.

17. Ibid., VI, 506–7.

taken in the wake of the conspiracy, came to feel so uncomfortable he moved to Philadelphia. As secretary of state, Adams had angered South Carolina by urging repeal of preventive detention for visiting black sailors. While he was president-elect, the state legislature emphatically rebuffed his proposal.[18] Even if Calhoun had wanted to cooperate with Adams, it would have been politically awkward for him to do so. A sudden fall in cotton prices from thirty-two cents a pound to thirteen cents during 1825 compounded South Carolinians' growing sense of insecurity. Rather than blame overproduction on the rich soils of the Gulf states, Carolinians complained about the unfairness of the tariff (raised in 1824 against their wishes), which condemned cotton producers to buy in a protected market and sell in an unprotected one. Calhoun decided he could no longer support a nationalist agenda of internal improvements and a protective tariff in the face of such dissatisfaction in his home state. After the Missouri Compromise, Calhoun and his lieutenant, George McDuffie, had beaten back a challenge from South Carolina Old Republican Radicals who had refused to accept the restriction of slavery. But by 1825, Radicals were starting to call the shots in South Carolina politics. That year the legislature passed a resolution condemning internal improvements and a protective tariff as unconstitutional. Calhoun spent seven months in his home state then, his first extended stay there in eight years, and he came to realize that he would jeopardize his political base if he continued to defy the state-righters. The new vice president accordingly commenced what has been called a "breathtaking reinvention" of his political self, from nationalist to particularist.[19]

As the running mate of both Jackson and Adams in 1824, Calhoun had been officially neutral between the two. In office he made clear his independence from the Adams administration. By 1826, he was actually debating against an administration spokesman in the newspapers—both parties using pseudonyms, of course.[20] In June of that year Calhoun offered Jackson his unequivocal support for president in the next election.

18. David Robertson, *Denmark Vesey* (New York, 1999), 108–16; Philip Hamer, "Great Britain, the United States, and the Negro Seamen Acts," *Journal of Southern History* 1 (1935): 3–28.

19. Quotation from John Larson, *Internal Improvement* (Chapel Hill, 2001), 176. See also William Freehling, *Prelude to Civil War* (New York, 1966), 89–122; Charles Sellers, *The Market Revolution* (New York, 1991), 143–45.

20. Calhoun used the pen name "Onslow"; the defender of the administration was Philip Fendall, writing as "Patrick Henry." Many contemporaries assumed "Patrick Henry" was the president himself. See Irving Bartlett, *John C. Calhoun* (New York, 1993), 132–35.

The two reached an understanding, brokered by Van Buren, that Calhoun would again be Jackson's running mate. Calhoun could still hope to become Jackson's heir, if not Adams's. Encouragingly, Jackson had said presidents should serve but one term.[21] At this point, it remained unclear in what policy directions either Jackson or Calhoun would move.

The Crawfordites too eventually rallied to the standard of the military hero who claimed to represent the voice of the people, unfairly shut out by a bargain among corrupt insiders. The Richmond Junto took longer than the Albany Regency to be persuaded to accept this rank outsider.[22] Jackson himself resigned his Senate seat and went back to Nashville, where planning his next run at the White House became his full-time job. In October 1825—before Adams's first Congress had even met—the Tennessee legislature nominated Jackson for president. With the caucus now discredited as a system of choosing nominees, and national party conventions not yet invented, this seemed a logical way of putting Old Hickory's candidacy before the public, though it was three years early.

As the Republican Party drew apart into two contending divisions, the press groped for terms to describe them. Most often it simply referred to "Adams men" and "Jackson men." Everyone felt reluctant to admit publicly the splintering of Jefferson's great party. For a president who had aspired to govern by consensus, the reality of polarization, whether avowed or not, showed that things were not working out.

III

While the opposition to his administration gathered its forces, John Quincy Adams was formulating a program for American economic development. Adams laid out his vision both broadly and specifically on December 6, 1825, in his First Annual Message to Congress—what later generations would call a "State of the Union" message.[23] Where the president had been conciliatory in his inaugural address, this time he was bold. His message represented the logical fulfillment of John C. Calhoun's exhortation of 1816: "Let us conquer space."[24] Adams celebrated the benefits of improved transportation and communication and

21. John Niven, *John C. Calhoun and the Price of Union* (Baton Rouge, 1988), 118.
22. Robert Forbes, "Slavery and the Meaning of America" (Ph.D. diss., Yale University, 1994), 486–88.
23. Although the Constitution directs that the president "shall from time to time give to the Congress information on the state of the union," in the antebellum years people referred simply to the President's "annual message."
24. *Annals of Congress*, 14th Cong., 2nd sess., 854. Also see above, p. 87.

undertook to marshal the resources of the federal government to further them. The time had come to implement the projects planned by the General Survey enacted under Monroe, and the Army Corps of Engineers should be expanded to aid in the process. One of the president's favorite Scottish philosophers, Adam Smith, had declared that where private enterprise needed help, government should supply economic infrastructure and public education; this would be especially important in the early stages of economic development.[25] Adams agreed. With the national debt about to be retired, Adams looked forward to the time when "the swelling tide of wealth" generated by the sale of the public lands "may be made to reflow in unfailing streams of improvement from the Atlantic to the Pacific." What made it particularly appropriate to spend the proceeds from public land sales on transportation projects was that these improvements would raise land values, benefiting the government and private landowners alike. Land sales under this policy would eventually generate enough money for the federal government to run all its programs, Adams hoped, without having to take anything from the people in taxes. In this climactic document of Republican nationalism, Adams proposed a federal version of DeWitt Clinton's program for the state of New York, singling out the Erie Canal as an example of what could be done by an involved government.[26]

The president's vision of expanded American commerce did not stop at the water's edge. He endorsed negotiating free-trade agreements based on reciprocity and "most favored nation" clauses with as many countries as possible, meanwhile building up the navy to protect American ocean commerce. Other proposals to help American business included a standard national bankruptcy law and the adoption of the metric system, a fulfillment of the massive *Report on Weights and Measures* Adams had prepared while secretary of state. Both of these were explicitly authorized by the Constitution but had not yet been carried out. Adams's forward-looking proposals included a Department of the Interior (it would be created in 1849) and a federal organization to coordinate the state militias (not really implemented until 1903). The president waxed most eloquent over his plans for exploration, science, and education, which included a national university in Washington, D.C., and at least one astronomical

25. Adam Smith, *The Wealth of Nations*, ed. R. H. Campbell and A. S. Skinner (Indianapolis, 1981), II, 723.
26. John Quincy Adams, "First Annual Message," *Presidential Messages*, II, 299–317, quotation from 305; Daniel Feller, *The Public Lands in Jacksonian Politics* (Madison, Wisc., 1984), 56, 76.

observatory (of which, he pointed out, there were 130 in Europe and not one in all North America). The inclusion of these subjects demonstrates that his objectives were not only material but also intellectual, including personal as well as public improvement. Indeed, there is a striking analogy between Adams's plan for national improvement and his own careful, rigorous program of individual self-improvement.[27]

After enumerating the Constitution's grants of power to the federal government, the president concluded that "to refrain from exercising them for the benefit of the people" would be "treachery to the most sacred of trusts." Adams interpreted the Constitution as defining duties as well as rights. He had a positive rather than a negative conception of liberty; freedom properly exercised was not simply a limitation on authority but an empowering of human initiative. "Liberty is power," he declared. American citizens had a responsibility to use their freedom, to make the most of their God-given faculties. Their officials had a corresponding duty to facilitate improvement, both public and private. "The spirit of improvement is abroad upon the earth," Adams pointed out in his peroration. Let not foreign nations with less liberty exceed us in "public improvement," the president exhorted his countrymen. To do so would "cast away the bounties of Providence" and doom what should become the world's most powerful nation "to perpetual inferiority."[28]

When Adams laid the draft of this message before his cabinet, all save Richard Rush considered it too ambitious. But the president stuck to his guns. He felt that even if his program could not all be attained immediately, it would be worthwhile to have it before the public as a long-term goal, provoking discussion and influencing opinion. Adams's explicit presentation contrasted sharply with the consummate ambiguity of his predecessor. Adams had no taste for Monroe's hidden agendas, advanced through patient private consultation. Long before Theodore Roosevelt, John Quincy Adams determined to use the White House as a "bully pulpit." How could the American people reject his compelling vision of national destiny and mission?[29]

In fact, upon delivery, Adams's famous message provoked no hostile outcry from the public at large. Internal improvements were not unpopular,

---

27. See also Daniel Howe, *The Political Culture of the American Whigs* (Chicago, 1979), 43–68.
28. "First Annual Message," quotations from 316. Adams's message is well analyzed by John Larson, "Liberty by Design," in *The State and Economic Knowledge*, ed. Mary Furner and Barry Supple (Cambridge, Eng., 1990), 73–102.
29. See John Quincy Adams, *Memoirs*, VII, 58, 63.

and the president's program deliberately included a lot for the South, including a second national road to link Washington with New Orleans. The formation of an opposition to the administration had more to do with the Adams-Clay alliance and consequent frustration of Jackson, Crawford, and Calhoun than it did with internal improvements. Criticism of Adams's national program originated with the strict constructionists of the Richmond Junto, among whom old man Jefferson seemed particularly irreconcilable.[30] The opposition mocked Adams's rhetoric not only where it was weak (his tactless admonition to Congress not to be "palsied by the will of our constituents") but also where it was strong (his felicitous metaphor for astronomical observatories as "lighthouses of the skies"—which called attention to the applicability of astronomy to celestial navigation).

In Congress, of course, members did not want to surrender control over pork-barrel legislation to planners in the Executive Branch. The same reaction had stymied the plans of Albert Gallatin and John McLean. The result this time was not a blanket rejection of internal improvements but a multitude of individual projects with no overall plan. Back in 1817, James Madison had vetoed the Bonus Bill rather than allow congressional logrolling to define priorities in internal improvements. Adams proved more flexible. Even piecemeal federal aid to internal improvements was better than none at all, he decided, approving more internal improvements than all his predecessors put together. By 1826, the federal government had become the largest entrepreneur in the American economy. The bottleneck of presidential reluctance to sanction internal improvements without a constitutional amendment had finally been uncorked.[31]

Conspicuous among the internal improvements Congress approved during the Adams administration, the Chesapeake and Ohio Canal fulfilled the dream of George Washington long before. Centerpiece of the system of national works laid out in the General Survey Act of 1824, the canal was built by a mixed public-private enterprise in which the states of Maryland and Virginia, several municipalities, and the federal government all cooperated. On the Fourth of July 1828, the president participated in the ceremonial groundbreaking. When he took spade in hand to dig the first earth, the tool struck a hard root and bounced ineffectually off. Rising to the occasion, Adams threw off his coat and renewed his

30. See Joseph Harrison, "*Sic et Non*: Thomas Jefferson and Internal Improvements," *JER* 7 (1987): 335–50.
31. Larson, *Internal Improvement*, 67–68, 149–50, 165–66; William Appleman Williams, *Contours of American History* (Cleveland, 1961), 211.

assault with such vigor that soon he was able to hold up a shovelful of dirt. The friendly crowd of two thousand cheered the president's resolution. It was one of the few times that Adams felt good about a public appearance.[32] Eventually the Chesapeake and Ohio, like many other canals, was overtaken by the development of railroads. In 1850, the canal reached Cumberland, Maryland, where it connected with the National Road. Thereafter construction ceased, and in 1852 the Baltimore & Ohio Railroad made the link to the Ohio River at Wheeling, Virginia (now West Virginia), that the canal had originally been intended to create. But until it finally closed in 1924, the C&O Canal performed a useful function as a broad waterway from upcountry to tidewater.

Adams's "spirit of improvement" addressed not only transportation but also communications. His innovative and successful postmaster general, John McLean, completed the postal network and reinvested the profits of the postal system in it. An expanded stagecoach industry received federal subsidies for carrying the mail, strengthening both communication and transportation. But McLean's political ambitions complicated the picture. His alliance with John C. Calhoun had made good sense during the latter's nationalist years. As Calhoun became estranged from the administration, however, McLean had to choose. Secretly, he remained loyal to the vice president, rather than to the president. When this came to light, Clay urged Adams to fire McLean, but Adams refused. Having been accused already of "corruption" in bestowing cabinet office as a reward for political support, Adams did not want to lay himself open to another such charge by a dramatic removal. Besides, there was a philosophical issue. The chief executive wanted the federal government to operate as a nonpartisan meritocracy even at the highest levels. McLean exemplified the talent Adams hoped the government would recruit. To dismiss him for political reasons would concede the failure of government by consensus and the conception of office as a public trust.[33]

The president's grand program for economic development was by no means the only serious challenge he faced. Additional problems arose for the Adams administration from Indian affairs. During the Monroe administration, Secretary of War Calhoun had been responsible for Indian policy. He had encouraged gradual resettlement of the southern tribes across the Mississippi, while simultaneously promoting the assimilation of some of their members into white society. This dual policy failed to

32. *Memoirs*, VIII, 49–50.
33. Richard R. John, *Spreading the News: The American Postal System from Franklin to Morse* (Cambridge, Mass., 1995), 64–111.

satisfy white settlers eager to seize the Natives' lands; in particular, it led
to a conflict between Calhoun and Governor George M. Troup of Georgia. Back in 1802, Georgia had relinquished her claim to what is now
Alabama and Mississippi in return for a promise by the Jefferson administration that the federal government would seek voluntary removal of the
Indian tribes remaining within her boundaries. The Georgians now felt
they had waited long enough for the federal government to make good on
what they saw as a binding commitment. They were eager to take possession of the lands retained by the Creek and Cherokee nations. Crawford
had exploited these feelings in his presidential campaign. The Georgians
also complained that Calhoun seemed too ready to treat the Native
Americans as racial equals.[34]

In the closing days of the Monroe administration, leaders of the Creek
tribe signed a treaty at Indian Springs agreeing to sell their Georgia lands
and move west of the Mississippi. Seeing in the treaty a convenient end to
a troublesome issue, the lame duck Senate swiftly consented to ratification. Within two months, however, serious problems came to light. Chief
William McIntosh, head of the Creek delegation and Andrew Jackson's
old ally against the Seminoles, had apparently been bribed. The federal
commissioners who negotiated the treaty had colluded with Georgia officials. The Creeks refused to ratify the treaty, and outraged fellow tribes-
men assassinated McIntosh as a traitor. Adams concluded that the Treaty
of Indian Springs was a nullity and that the Creeks remained the rightful
possessors of their lands. Yet the state of Georgia, led by Governor Troup,
insisted on implementing the treaty and surveying the Creek lands.
Adams's secretary of war, James Barbour, maintained federal authority
against the claims of state rights with a firmness all the more commend-
able in a Virginian. Andrew Jackson, however, egged on the Georgians.
The stage seemed set for a serious federal-state confrontation. At the last
minute the Creek tribe got the administration off the hook by agreeing to
sell the lands in another treaty, one more favorable to them. Whites
throughout the South drew the conclusion that Jackson, but not Adams,
could be counted on to secure the complete expropriation of the Five Civilized Tribes. Adams's annulment of the Treaty of Indian Springs would remain unique in the history of the government's Indian relations.[35]

---

34. Niven, *Calhoun*, 111; Bartlett, *Calhoun*, 95–98; Lynn Parsons, "John Quincy Adams
    and the American Indian," *New England Quarterly* 46 (Sept. 1973): 352.
35. Benjamin Griffith, *McIntosh and Weatherford, Creek Indian Leaders* (Tuscaloosa,
    Ala., 1988), 234–52; Lynn Parsons, *John Quincy Adams* (Madison, Wisc., 1998), 182;
    Michael Green, *The Politics of Indian Removal* (Lincoln, Neb., 1982), 125.

Foreign policy proved most troublesome of all for Adams's presidency — an irony indeed for this great diplomatist. Adams integrated his foreign policy with his domestic policy and designed both to promote commercial expansion. In his First Message to Congress, he recommended appointment of delegates to attend the first pan-American conference, scheduled to meet in Panama City. The conference had been conceived by the great Latin American liberator Simón Bolívar. Secretary of State Clay felt the United States should play an active role in inter-hemispheric affairs. He wanted to take advantage of the breakup of the Spanish New World Empire to promote U.S. trade with Latin America. Otherwise, he feared, the newly independent republics would gravitate into the British commercial orbit. The location of the conference in Panama had particular relevance to the potential of Central America for a canal linking Atlantic and Pacific, a possibility that already interested the Adams administration.

Martin Van Buren, senator from New York, hit upon the idea of criticizing participation in the Panama conference as an issue that could rally opposition to the administration. Van Buren was smarting from the resounding defeat his Bucktails had sustained at the hands of the New York People's Party in 1824 and looking for a way to make a comeback. Vice President Calhoun seized the opportunity to join with him. Calhoun hoped to discredit Clay's foreign policy leadership and force the president to remove him as secretary of state. Van Buren looked farther ahead, to the next presidential election; he had already decided to throw in his lot with Jackson. To lead the charge against the administration in the Senate, they enlisted two redoubtable orators: Robert Y. Haynes of South Carolina and Thomas Hart Benton of Missouri. The Panama conference might compromise the country's avoidance of entangling alliances, the senators argued. To win over the South, they played the race card. Participation in the conference would require associating with mixed-race regimes that had in most cases already abolished slavery. Discussion of the slave trade appeared on the agenda; who knew where this could lead? What if delegates from the black nation of Haiti showed up? Eventually Congress approved participation in the conference, 27 to 17 in the Senate and 134 to 60 in the House. But prolonged debate had delayed the delegates past their optimum departure time. One delegate refused to set out during the malaria season; the other, more foolhardy, died on the way. Having postponed its meetings in the hope of securing U.S. participation, the Panama conference finally came to little. Clay's hopes for expanding trade with Latin America were not fulfilled.[36]

36. Bartlett, *Calhoun*, 130; Bemis, *Adams*, 76–77; Forbes, "Slavery and the Meaning of America," 470–79.

A mere six months after Spain and the United States exchanged ratifications of the Transcontinental Boundary Treaty, Mexico achieved her
hard-won independence from Spain in the Treaty of Córdova, signed August 23, 1821. It occurred to Adams that the new regime in Mexico City
might be willing to renegotiate the boundary, so he instructed Joel Poinsett, the first U.S. minister (in effect, ambassador) to Mexico, to learn
what concessions might be forthcoming. Poinsett, a diplomat with broad
Latin American experience and fluency in Spanish, got nowhere with
this. He tried to strengthen the hand of Mexican liberals in domestic politics and counteract the influence of the British, but his efforts backfired,
and a conservative Mexican government eventually requested his recall.
Poinsett returned to his native South Carolina to lead the Unionist Party
there and cultivate his botanical interests, developing the poinsettia from
a flower he had found in Mexico. His *Notes on Mexico, Made in the Autumn of 1822*, remain a classic account by an outside observer.

Another problem for U.S. policymakers was presented by Cuba, still a
Spanish colony after almost all the rest of Spain's once great American
empire had achieved independence. Latin Americans discussed the possibility of Mexico and Colombia mounting an expeditionary force to encourage a Cuban revolution and liberate the island. The prospect of an
independent Cuba provoked great anxiety in the United States, which
coveted the island but could only hope to purchase it so long as Spanish
rule continued. Moreover, an independent Cuba would probably abolish
slavery and set another bad example. Perhaps the worst eventuality, from
the U.S. point of view, would be for Spain to transfer Cuba to France or
Britain, for in the hands of a major power the island would pose a strategic threat. Accordingly, the United States employed its diplomatic leverage to dissuade all other countries, both Latin American and European,
from intervention in Cuba.[37]

The final big diplomatic issue of the Adams years also involved the Caribbean: the American attempt to recover the trade with the British West
Indies, which had been so profitable before the Revolution. When the
United States achieved independence, it was at the cost of losing imperial
preferences in trading with the British Empire. To recover the West Indian export trade would help American farmers and fishermen; to have it
carried in American vessels would help Yankee shipowners. In 1823,
the United States began to threaten retaliations in an effort to pry open the
BWI. From 1826 on, mutual retaliations diminished the remaining trade

37. See Piero Gleijeses, "The Limits of Sympathy," *Journal of Latin American Studies* 24
    (1992): 481–505.

to the vanishing point. Adams was paying a price for not having cooperated with Canning's overtures at the time of the Monroe Doctrine; the British did not trust him. The deadlock in negotiations hurt the administration politically and (to a lesser extent) the United States economically. It overshadowed the administration's successes in nine trade agreements with other foreign powers. The British West Indian trade stalemate was not resolved until after Adams had left office.[38]

As the midterm congressional elections of 1826 and 1827 approached, Adams and his secretary of state disagreed over tactics. With each state setting its own election date, the voting was staggered across the months, like presidential primaries today. Clay thought it time to abandon nonpartisanship and purge the government of officials who were not backing the administration, but Adams did not feel ready to give up on government by consensus. The president had been trying to use patronage to win over critics rather than to reward friends, but his policy had not proved effective. The politics Adams understood was the old-fashioned kind, based on courting regional leaders who could deliver their followings. Van Buren and the men around Jackson's Nashville headquarters were forging a new politics that worked from the grass roots up, based on patronage, organization, and partisan loyalty. When the elections came, they revealed the administration's organizational weakness. All too often its supporters could not agree on a single congressional candidate and consequently split their vote, especially in places where there were Federalists as well as Adams Republicans. The opposition gained control of both houses of Congress, producing the country's first experience with divided government. One of the few consolations for the administration was the Virginia legislature's decision to replace John Randolph in the U.S. Senate. His successor, John Tyler, seemed willing to work with the administration.

Adams's difficulties did not simply result from his crotchety temperament, nor from any refusal on his part to engage in political calculation. They stemmed most obviously from the determination, ruthlessness, and skill of his opponents, especially Martin Van Buren. Adams's program of government activism had a fighting chance for adoption on the strength of its merits and was not inevitably doomed. But his administration suffered from an incompatibility between the president's means and ends. Adams wanted to govern by consensus, as Monroe had done, but at the same time he wanted to press an agenda of major policy innovations. The

38. Hargreaves, *Presidency of Adams*, 91–112; George Dangerfield, *The Era of Good Feelings* (New York, 1952), 367–81.

president's goals, openly avowed, proved too controversial to permit implementation by consensus. The Monroe model of governance did not fit with Adams's bold program in domestic and foreign affairs.[39]

IV

In February 1816, a Massachusetts merchant sea captain named Paul Cuffe sailed his brig *Traveller* across a stormy Atlantic to the west coast of Africa with a cargo of tobacco, flour, and tools to trade for camwood. Cuffe was unusual among New England shipowners in being the son of a West African father and a mother from the Wampanoag Indian tribe; he staffed his ships with all black crews. Cuffe had made similar voyages before, but this time he also carried thirty-eight African American passengers intending to make new homes in Sierra Leone, Senegal, and the Congo. Cuffe sought to implement a dream that had been nursed by a few black Americans for more than a generation: emigration away from racist oppression to the ancestral homeland. He hoped this would be the first of many such trips and had worked to create an institutional network to promote emigration as a means to a better life for black people. A practicing Quaker, Cuffe also intended his enterprise to promote Christianity in Africa, help stifle the slave trade, and, God willing, turn a profit.[40]

After Cuffe's return to New England, white sympathizers contacted him. Cuffe welcomed their involvement, for he wanted congressional support for his cause. He attracted two groups of whites, one centered in Virginia and the other in New Jersey. The Virginians were led by Congressman Charles Fenton Mercer, the Princetonians by the Rev. Robert Finley. Mercer enlisted an impressive range of supporters, including not only Federalists like himself but staunch Republicans like John Randolph and John Taylor of Caroline. As Mercer proposed it, voluntary migration to West Africa would help Virginia deal with what whites saw as the problem of a growing free black population. Proslavery whites regarded free Negroes as a bad example to the slaves, and even antislavery whites feared them as potential incendiaries.

The most common objection offered to emancipation in the South was that it would create a subordinate population who could neither be admitted to political participation nor any longer be effectively controlled. White southern critics of slavery professed themselves baffled by

---

39. See Stephen Skowronek, *The Politics Presidents Make* (Cambridge, Mass., 1993), 110–28.
40. Floyd Miller, *The Search for a Black Nationality* (Urbana, Ill., 1975), 21–44; Lamin Sanneh, *Abolitionists Abroad* (Cambridge, Mass., 1999), 88–98.

this conundrum. In Jefferson's eloquent metaphor, "we have the wolf by the ears, and we can neither hold him, nor safely let him go."[41] Presented as a solution to Jefferson's dilemma, the African colonization movement initially attracted widespread support in Virginia. The commonwealth had passed a law requiring newly manumitted freedpeople to leave within a year. But other states were reluctant to accept them; Missouri had set the example by banning the settlement of free Negroes. Perhaps a foreign destination would work. Mercer's own long-range goal was that Virginia should industrialize and shift away from reliance on enslaved labor. But he carefully phrased his endorsement of colonization in such a way as to make it appealing as well to proslavery whites who simply wanted to get rid of those blacks already free. Back in 1807-8, humanitarians had realized their hope to abolish the importation of slaves from overseas by cooperating with slaveholders who wanted to protect the value of their property against cheap foreign imports. Mercer had been active in the anti-slave-trade movement; now, he hoped to forge an analogous alliance behind his new cause. His strategy paid off when the Virginia state legislature overwhelmingly endorsed colonization in December 1816.[42]

Robert Finley seems to have learned of colonization from Mercer and Cuffe but gave it his own spin. His version of colonization was more clearly antislavery than Mercer's. Finley saw it as a way of solving both the slavery problem and the race problem, encouraging manumissions by individual masters and, in the long run, gradual emancipation by states. No longer would southern whites have to fear that emancipation would create a class of embittered freedpeople ripe for rebellion. This vision did capture the imagination of certain self-consciously enlightened moderates in the Upper (and occasionally even in the Lower) South. Some slaveholders were willing to promise emancipation to certain slaves at a future date on condition they then left for Africa. Such action, while partly altruistic, also helped ensure the good behavior of the slave and deterred escape. Slaves might even negotiate under these circumstances, agreeing to emigrate only if family members could accompany them.[43]

Finley's followers operated colonization as a voluntary fund-raising charity, while Mercer's treated the cause as a political lobby. The two groups cooperated within a nationwide American Colonization Society,

41. Jefferson to John Holmes, April 22, 1820, *TJ: Writings*, 1434.
42. Douglas Egerton, "A New Look at the American Colonization Society," *JER* 5 (1985): 463–80.
43. Many such cases of masters, mistresses, and slaves are described in Eric Burin, *Slavery and the Peculiar Solution* (Gainesville, Fla., 2005).

headed at first by Associate Justice Bushrod Washington and later by ex-president Madison. (Ex-president Jefferson, though on record as supportive of colonization, remained aloof from the movement.)[44] In the next few years, the legislatures of Maryland, Kentucky, Tennessee, and six northern states followed Virginia's example in endorsing colonization; so did the national governing bodies of the Presbyterian, Methodist, Baptist, and Episcopal denominations. The Maryland legislature was the most forthcoming with funds. In an age of great migrations, when many people responded to a wide range of problems by leaving home, plans to address the problems of race and slavery through migration commanded serious support down to the time of the Civil War and even afterwards.[45]

In 1819, Mercer succeeded in getting an appropriation from the Monroe administration to subsidize the ACS; more help would come later. The American Colonization Society operated, like the national bank and so many other institutions in this period, as a mixed public-private enterprise. The society decided to follow the example of the British philanthropist Granville Sharp. He had founded Sierra Leone on the west coast of Africa in 1787 as a haven for blacks migrating from England and the empire, some of whom had originally been liberated by the British army during the American Revolution.[46] In 1821–22, the U.S. Navy helped the ACS purchase from indigenous Africans land adjacent to Sierra Leone in order to found Liberia, with its capital of Monrovia named in the president's honor. After Andrew Jackson became president, the federal government sharply reduced the financial support it had been providing.[47] Still, by 1843, African Americans to the number of 4,291, most of them former slaves, had migrated to Liberia; over ten thousand more would come before the Civil War. Disease exacted a heavy toll and deterred others from coming. At first it was supposed Liberia might be a U.S. colony, but in 1847 the nation declared its independence. The settlers saw themselves as freedom-loving black Americans, enabled by migration to realize their dream of opportunity, seldom as Africans returning from exile. For over a century these settlers and their descendents would

---

44. See Thomas Jefferson to Jared Sparks, Feb. 4, 1824, *TJ: Writings*, 1484–87.
45. See Katherine Harris, *African and American Values: Liberia and West Africa* (London, 1985); William Freehling, *The Reintegration of American History* (New York, 1994), 138–57.
46. See Simon Schama, *Rough Crossings* (London, 2005).
47. Some of this support had actually lacked congressional authority; see Douglas Egerton, "Averting a Crisis," *Civil War History* 43 (1997), 142–56.

rule the indigenous African inhabitants through the Liberian True Whig Party.[48]

The minority of Colonization Society migrants who took an interest in African cultural roots were generally first- or second-generation African expatriates. Among these was Abdul Rahahman, born into a wealthy noble family in Timbo (now part of Guinea), captured in war as a young man, enslaved, and shipped across the ocean to New Orleans. Eventually Rahahman was recognized in a Natchez market by a white mariner who had known his family in Africa and had been aided by them. With the help of this man and the ACS, Rahahman's cause attracted publicity and contributions. He finally secured his own liberation and that of eight family members. Rahahman returned to Africa in 1829 after an absence of forty-one years. When he died (sadly, soon afterwards) he donated his writings to the library of the Timbo school where he had been educated as a child.[49]

In the meantime, Paul Cuffe had died prematurely in 1817, and other black leaders sympathetic to his cause, such as AME Bishop Richard Allen, began to have second thoughts. Could not locations for black self-development be found less distant than Africa—such as Haiti or the American West? And if the talent and resources of the black community were drained off into emigration, would not the plight of the remaining African Americans worsen? While reaching out to whites, the colonization movement began to lose some of its early appeal among the free Negro elite. Colonization gathered support from an unstable coalition, and it was difficult to strike the right balance among the different aims of its supporters. The great majority of free African Americans firmly decided that their future lay in the United States. Still, historians have estimated that about 20 percent of free blacks remained favorably disposed to emigration during the years from 1817 to the Civil War. During the 1850s, the black nationalist Martin R. Delaney would advocate a "Back to Africa" program of his own.[50]

48. James Wesley Smith, *Sojourners in Search of Freedom* (Lanham, Md., 1987); Amos Beyan, *The American Colonization Society and the Creation of the Liberian State* (Lanham, Md., 1991); Antonio McDaniel, *Swing Low, Sweet Chariot: The Mortality Cost of Colonizing Liberia* (Chicago, 1995), 60.

49. James Horton and Lois Horton, *In Hope of Liberty* (New York, 1997), 189–91. Terry Alford, *Prince Among Slaves* (New York, 1977), treats the name Abdul Rahahman used by contemporaries as a form of Ibrahima (Abraham).

50. See Gary Nash, *Forging Freedom: The Formation of Philadelphia's Black Community* (Cambridge, Mass., 1988), 233–45; Donald Wright, *African Americans in the Early Republic* (Arlington Heights, Ill., 1993), 171–78; Mary Frances Berry and John Blassingame, *Long Memory: The Black Experience in America* (New York, 1982), 400.

One of the most committed leaders in the American Colonization Society was Secretary of State Henry Clay. Although Clay operated his plantation of Ashland in Kentucky with the labor of fifty slaves, he consistently advocated gradual emancipation for his home state from 1799 until his death half a century later. Self-consciously moderate, Clay saw colonization as a responsible middle ground between abolitionism and the defense of slavery as a positive good. His enthusiasm for it was typical of his faith in active government and his optimism that solutions could always be found that offered something to everybody. Colonizationists like Clay took the existence of white racism as a given and tried to work around it to achieve emancipation. It would not be necessary to transport *all* black Americans to Africa; Clay advocated colonization as a way of reducing the black population in America to the point where the whites would not feel threatened by the prospect of emancipation. Although the number of people transported to Liberia was very small, Clay insisted that colonization constituted a realistic program. He estimated in 1825 the annual increase in the slave population of the United States at fifty-two thousand. If each year fifty-two thousand healthy young slaves could be freed and persuaded to go to Liberia, this would keep the slave population static or slowly declining, at a time when the white population was doubling every generation. Eventually, Clay argued, the black percentage of the American population would fall to the point where southern whites would feel comfortable with the abolition of slavery. There was nothing fantastic about Clay's numbers: The illegal international slave trade of the 1820s was still transporting more than fifty-nine thousand people a year across the Atlantic in the opposite direction, mostly to Brazil and Cuba, in spite of efforts by the Royal Navy to interdict it.[51] President Adams never shared Clay's enthusiasm for African colonization, but he allowed his secretary of state to promote it and continued the modest level of financial support commenced by the Monroe administration.

When Rufus King was about to leave the Senate to accept Adams's appointment as minister to Britain in 1825, he laid out a program of African colonization to be funded by the government's western land sales. It was similar to ideas advanced earlier by Jefferson and Madison. Nevertheless King's proposal angered many southern politicians, for they had come to feel that the slavery question must be left to the southern white public

---

51. "Speech Before American Colonization Society" (Jan. 20, 1825), *Papers of Henry Clay*, ed. Mary Hargreaves and James Hopkins (Lexington, Ky., 1981), VI, 83–97; David Brion Davis, "Reconsidering the Colonization Movement," *Intellectual History Newsletter* 14 (1992): 13, n. 1.

alone. Radicals like George Troup of Georgia and William Smith of South Carolina used the issue to strengthen their local power base and inflame resentment against the Adams administration.[52] Meanwhile, the Ohio state legislature had recently (in January 1824) passed an even more far-reaching resolution, proposing colonization linked with gradual emancipation, the whole package to be accomplished at federal expense. Within a year this proposal was seconded by the legislatures of seven other free states plus Delaware, the southern state with the fewest slaves. In reaction, six other southern state legislatures passed resolutions deploring outside interference with slavery.

Despite the hopes of King and others to use land sales for emancipation and colonization, the Great Migration to the West both undercut colonization plans and facilitated the expansion of slavery. The early white support for colonization in Virginia and the rest of the Upper South largely rested on a desire to shrink the black percentage of the population. But the export of people through the interstate slave trade could serve much the same purpose—the "diffusion" (as it was called) of the blacks so they would pose less of a danger in the case of rebellion. As it became clear that the New Southwest beyond the Appalachians would absorb them, masters found it more attractive to sell surplus workers out of state than to pay for their manumission and transport to Africa. African colonization was then revealed more clearly as a means of facilitating emancipation, and therefore became more alarming to states of the Deep South whose economy clearly rested on the exploitation of enslaved labor. These states had never embraced colonization; now, their politicians denounced it harshly. They feared involving the federal government in any solution to the problem of slavery, even on a voluntary basis, lest it move in more threatening directions later.[53]

African colonization constituted one of the most grandiose schemes for social engineering ever entertained in the United States. Improvers of this era did not think small. The colonization program provided a means for questioning the merits of slavery that remained discussible in many slave states until the 1850s. At least in the Upper South, the American Colonization Society could function along with temperance organizations, Sunday schools, and Bible societies, as part of the network of Christian reform movements.[54] Despite considerable support, the colonization

52. See Richard H. Brown, "The Missouri Crisis, Slavery, and the Politics of Jacksonianism," *South Atlantic Quarterly* 65 (1966), 66–67.
53. Freehling, *Secessionists at Bay*, 157–61; Egerton, "Averting a Crisis."
54. See, for example, Elizabeth Varon, "Evangelical Womanhood and the African Colonization Movement," in *Religion and the Antebellum Debate over Slavery*, ed. John McKivigan and Mitchell Snay (Athens, Ga., 1998), 169–95.

plan was ultimately killed by resistance from two opposite quarters: southern masters and African-Americans themselves.

In the event, many more black Americans in search of a better life would move to Canada than to Liberia. Slavery had been ended in the colonies of British North America by a series of executive, legislative, and judicial actions in the late eighteenth century. As a result, Canada attracted both fugitive slaves and free Negroes from the United States. There they joined the descendants of black Loyalists from the Revolution, African American refugees from the War of 1812, and Jamaican maroons transported to Nova Scotia. In one migration of 1829, a thousand free African Americans, after violent persecution in Cincinnati, obtained refuge in Canada. Although Canadian whites were seldom eager to welcome large numbers of black settlers, by 1860 the black population of Canada numbered about forty thousand.[55] An escaped slave named Joseph Taper, who settled on a farm in St. Catharines, Ontario, in 1839, wrote this letter back to a white Virginian, instructing him to pass it on to his former master:

> Dear Sir,
>
> I now take this opportunity to inform you that I am in a land of liberty, in good health. . . . Since I have been in the Queens dominions I have been well contented, Yes well contented for Sure, man is as God intended he should be. That is, all are born free & equal. This is a wholesome law, not like the Southern laws which puts man made in the image of God, on level with brutes. . . .
>
> We have good schools, & all the colored population supplied with schools. My boy Edward who will be six years next January, is now reading, & I intend keeping him at school until he becomes a good scholar. . . .
>
> My wife and self are sitting by a good comfortable fire happy, knowing that there are none to molest [us] or make [us] afraid. God save Queen Victoria.[56]

V

On the evening of September 12, 1826, a stonecutter named William Morgan languished in the jail of Canandaigua, New York, where he was being held for an alleged two-dollar debt. Morgan had been subject to a

---

55. Wright, *African Americans*, 136; Robin Winks, *The Blacks in Canada*, 2nd ed. (Montreal, 1997), 233–40.

56. Quoted in John Hope Franklin and Loren Schweninger, *Runaway Slaves* (New York, 1999), 294–95.

series of persecutions by local authorities and mysterious mobs ever since he had undertaken to publish the secret rituals of Freemasonry. His home in nearby Batavia had been ransacked in search of the manuscript. An attempt to burn down the shop where his work awaited printing had been foiled. Two days earlier he and his printer had both been transported to this jail on trumped-up charges. The printer had been released by a magistrate, and Morgan expected he would be too as soon as his case was called. Suddenly, the prisoner learned that someone had paid his bail. Morgan found himself released into the custody of strangers who forced him into a waiting carriage. "Murder! Murder!" he cried out. The renegade former Mason was never again seen alive.

The investigation of Morgan's disappearance was hampered at every turn by the cover-up of strategically placed Freemasons. Although his wife and dentist identified a partly decomposed body, three inquests did not make an official finding. Juries were packed with Masonic brothers; accused conspirators fled before testifying. Eventually the sheriff of Niagara County served thirty months for his central role in the kidnapping conspiracy, but otherwise prosecutors had little to show after twenty trials. Enough came to light, however, that the public felt outrage and the Masonic Order (whose leaders never denounced the crimes committed against Morgan or dissociated the order from the perpetrators) was badly discredited.[57]

Freemasonry, introduced into America from Britain in colonial times, had been an important force in the young republic. Its members had constituted a kind of republican elite, with Benjamin Franklin and George Washington prominent among them. The international Masonic brotherhood satisfied longings for status, trust, and metropolitan sophistication in an amorphous new society; its hierarchies and secret rituals offered a dimension lacking in the stark simplicity of much of American Protestantism. Freemasonry promoted the values of the Enlightenment and new standards of politeness. Its symbols of the pyramid and the eye had been incorporated into the Great Seal of the United States. Its ceremonies graced many public occasions, including the dedication of the United States Capitol and the construction of the Erie Canal. But in the Morgan episode, Masonic commitments of secrecy and mutual assistance led to disastrous consequences. To be sure, the Masonic brotherhood succeeded in the short run, protecting members from legal punishment

57. Paul Goodman, *Towards a Christian Republic: Antimasonry and the Great Transition in New England* (New York, 1988), 4; Ronald Formisano and Kathleen Kutalowski, "Antimasonry and Masonry," *American Quarterly* 39 (1977): 139–65.

and preventing Morgan from publishing all but the first three degree rituals, which appeared in print a month after his disappearance. But, as
American Masonry's most recent historian has shown, "it lost the larger
battle in the court of public opinion." During the decade after the Morgan affair, thousands of brothers quit the order and hundreds of lodges
closed. Although Freemasonry recovered its numbers after the Civil War,
it never recovered the influence it had wielded in the first fifty years of
independence.[58]

Reaction against the Morgan crime and (even more) its cover-up led to
the formation of an Antimasonic movement. Concerned citizens pressed
for judicial investigations of Morgan's disappearance and more information about Freemasonry. But Antimasonic speakers were harassed and
their publishing outlets persecuted by local authorities who belonged to
the order. Masons and Antimasons disrupted each other's meetings and
vandalized each other's property. The conflict soon acquired a political
dimension. Since the Morgan episode had occurred in western New York
state, the Antimasonic movement arose in an area of strong support for
DeWitt Clinton, the People's Party, and John Quincy Adams. President
Adams and his New York campaign manager, Thurlow Weed, showed
clear sympathy with the Antimasons; Martin Van Buren and his Albany
Regency, on the other hand, treated the movement as a threat. Governor
Clinton, a prominent active Mason, could not afford to alienate the Antimasons and trod a fine line, mostly leaving the problem to local authorities.
Andrew Jackson was a Mason, but so were a few of the Adams Republican
leaders, including Henry Clay. Eventually, the Antimasonic movement
organized as a third party but supported Adams in the presidential race of
1828. The party elected members to the New York legislature and spread
to neighboring states, notably Pennsylvania, Ohio, Vermont, and Massachusetts.[59]

The Antimasons became the first third party in American history. Once
organized as a political party, Antimasonry developed a political image
and stands on other issues. The participants saw themselves as restoring
moral order and transparent democracy, defending the little people
against a secret cabal with ties to machine politics. Antimasonry appealed
to the same attitudes that had been fostering increased democratization of

58. Steven Bullock, *Revolutionary Brotherhood* (Chapel Hill, 1996), 277–79, 313–16, quo-
    tation from 278; *Illustrations of Masonry, by One of the Fraternity* (New York, 1827).
59. Michael Holt, *Political Parties and American Political Development* (Baton Rouge,
    1992), 90–94; Donald Ratcliffe, "Antimasonry and Partisanship in Greater New En-
    gland," *JER* 15 (1995): 199–239.

American politics, such as the elimination of property requirements for voting and the popular election of presidential electors. The Antimasons took advantage of the opportunities for influencing public opinion provided by the growth of the printed media. Strongest in rural areas and small towns, their movement nurtured a provincial suspicion of metropolitan and upper-class values (Masonry was strongest in the cities). In their own time and since, the Antimasons have been accused of fanaticism, demagogy, and "paranoid delusions."[60] It seems more accurate to see them as responding to real provocation and reviving a tradition of popular political participation going back to the American Revolution and the English "commonwealthmen." The Antimasons often supported tenant farmers against landlords. They welcomed the participation of women in their movement, contrasting it with Masonry, which was then all male. (When the Masons created their own women's branch, the Order of the Eastern Star, in 1852, it helped defuse such criticism.) Many Antimasons eventually moved into antislavery. Antimasonry would remain an identifiable force in American politics for years to come.[61]

Despite historians' efforts to correlate Antimasonry with economic interests, the movement in fact cut across economic lines. Including middle-class townsmen as well as poor farmers and residents of areas both prospering and declining, newly settled and long established, Antimasons had in common an ideological commitment to democracy and Protestant Christianity. In many ways the movement was a political precipitation from the evangelical religious awakenings, embracing a variety of denominations.[62] Antimasons referred to their cause as "the blessed spirit." They accused Freemasonry of corrupting Christianity, of being in effect a rival religion. They showed some continuity with the sabbatarian opposition to Sunday mails, though Antimasonry enjoyed broader support. Antimasonry represented a Christian grassroots version of the impulse to "improvement."

In 1831, the Antimasons would be the first political party to hold a national convention, a practice that evangelical reform movements had pioneered. The convention seemed a more democratic means of selecting a nominee than the congressional caucus, and the other political parties quickly adopted it. While Martin Van Buren has often been credited with creating the modern American political party, in fact his rivals the

60. Goodman, *Toward a Christian Republic*, 245.
61. For more on the Antimasonic Party, see Ronald Formisano, *The Transformation of Political Culture: Massachusetts Parties, 1790s–1840s* (New York, 1983), 197–221.
62. See Kathleen Kutalowski, "Antimasonry Reexamined," *JAH* 71 (1984): 269–93.

Antimasons made an important contribution too.[63] Van Buren's concept of party was primarily concerned with organization and patronage. The lasting contribution of the Antimasonic movement to America was a concept of party politics that combined popular participation with moral passion. Antimasonry proved to be a precursor of the Republican Party of the 1850s, devoted to halting the spread of slavery. It can also be likened to the Progressive movement at the beginning of the twentieth century, which would favor popular participation against corruption and secrecy in government and would share something of the same Protestant moral tone.

VI

Henry Clay's hometown of Lexington, Kentucky, was a thriving commercial crossroads with a diversified economy. Located in the fertile Bluegrass country, it boasted the first newspaper and the first library west of the Appalachians, as well as Transylvania University, founded in 1798. There the aspiring young Clay had earned fame as a trial lawyer and money as counsel to banks and insurance companies. On his plantation, Ashland, just outside town, Clay grew hemp with a labor force of some fifty slaves. He also invested in the rope factory at Louisville that used his raw material. His wife, Lucretia Hart Clay, the daughter of a prominent local merchant and manufacturer, made the perfect plantation mistress, combining social graces with financial good sense. Henry Clay's political philosophy was his private life writ large. As his own career synthesized commerce, agriculture, and industry with public service, so the Kentuckian aspired to create a harmony of varied economic interests in the United States as a whole. Clay called his program for the nation "the American System." "I am executing here [at Ashland], in epitome, all my principles of Internal improvements, the American System, &c.," he correctly observed. Clay's American System was a full-blown systemization of the Republican nationalism that had found expression in Madison's message to Congress after the War of 1812.[64]

As Clay envisioned it, the American System constituted the economic basis for social improvement. It would create, not division between haves and have-nots, but a framework within which all could work harmoniously to improve themselves both individually and collectively. To

---

63. On Van Buren, see Richard Hofstadter, *The Idea of a Party System* (Berkeley, 1969); for the Antimasonic Party, see Robert O. Rupp, "Antimasonry in New York Reconsidered," *JER* 8 (1988): 253–79.

64. Daniel Howe, *The Political Culture of the American Whigs* (Chicago, 1979), 123–49; Clay quotation from Stephen Aron, *How the West Was Lost* (Baltimore, 1996), 134.

achieve this goal, Harry of the West was more than willing to enlist the power of government. Through sale of its enormous landholdings, the federal government could well afford to subsidize internal improvements. By levying protective tariffs, the government should foster the development of American manufacturing and agricultural enterprises that, in their infancy, might not be able to withstand foreign competition. The promotion of industry would create a home market for agricultural commodities, just as farms provided a market for manufactured products. Farmers and planters would benefit not only from increased sales to the cities and towns that would grow up around industry but also from the increased value of their lands as internal improvements connected them with markets. Clay could see that the policy of cheap land and rapid settlement favored by westerners like Thomas Hart Benton would multiply agricultural producers and production faster than existing markets could absorb, leading to cycles of overproduction and more panics like that of 1819.[65]

Clay's system was "American" in a triple sense. Obviously, it purported to promote the welfare of the nation as a whole. But it was also "American" in its assertion of national independence against the "British system" of unregulated free trade. The Kentuckian feared that a passive policy of economic laissez-faire would leave America in a neocolonial relationship to Britain, the economic giant of the day. Britain, Clay pointed out, protected her own domestic interests with tariffs like the "corn laws" while pressuring other countries to practice free trade.[66] In a third sense, Clay also used the term "American System" to apply to his hemispheric trade policy. He was willing, indeed eager, to include Latin America as part of his home market. Clay wanted to synthesize the Madisonian Platform with the Monroe Doctrine. The American System was directed against European, particularly British, commercial hegemony, not against sister republics of the New World.[67]

In 1824, Clay succeeded in getting the average tariff rates set in 1816 increased from 20 to 35 percent. The Panic of 1819 and ensuing depression had illustrated the dangers of dependence on foreign markets for trade and capital. Reapportionment following the census of 1820 had increased the political power of the Middle Atlantic and Ohio Valley states, where

65. See Maurice Baxter, *Henry Clay and the American System* (Lexington, Ky., 1995).
66. "Speech on the Tariff," March 30–31, 1824, *Papers of Henry Clay*, ed. James Hopkins (Lexington, Ky., 1963), III, 683–730.
67. On this use of the term "American System," see Robert Remini, *Henry Clay: Statesman for the Union* (New York, 1991), 174–75.

tariff protection commanded popular support. Monroe's last Congress included many members elected on protariff pledges. The debate in Congress was conducted at a high intellectual level, with free-traders invoking Adam Smith and the classical economists, while protectionists challenged them with arguments about the need to maintain full employment, encourage infant industries, prevent foreign dumping, and secure the national defense. Free-traders argued that individual profit maximization would promote the general welfare, but protectionists declared that republican virtue sometimes demanded short-term sacrifice by the public in the long-run national interest.[68] At the end, protection prevailed; among those voting for Clay's tariff of 1824 was Andrew Jackson, then senator from Tennessee.

In New England, the growth of the textile mills encouraged protectionist sentiment, which by the 1820s overcame the traditional free-trade sentiment of the region's maritime shipping interests. New England's most famous congressional spokesman, Daniel Webster, converted from free trade to protectionism while also abandoning the moribund Federalist Party for the "National" Republicans (i.e., the Republicans supporting the national administration). In 1827, Webster pressed for a further increase in the duty on woolen textiles, and the administration supported it. After passing the House, Webster's bill was defeated in the Senate by the casting vote of Vice President Calhoun. This dramatic action publicly affirmed Calhoun's break with the Adams-Clay administration and his own protectionist past. Martin Van Buren, eager to underscore the break, arranged for a tie to occur by absenting himself from the Senate chamber so the vice president would have to vote.[69]

Calhoun's change of heart on the issue of the tariff reflected the South's loss of interest in developing a textile industry of its own. In the early years of the cotton boom, it had seemed plausible to suppose that mills might be built near the fields where the cotton was grown. Occasionally a wealthy planter would erect a mill to spin and weave some of his own cotton production, operating it with slave labor, or hire out slaves to work in a neighbor's mill. But early textile mills depended on waterpower, and sometimes the fall line was inconveniently located far upstream from the best cotton-growing lands. More importantly, it was usually more profitable to keep the enslaved labor force in the fields. During the pre–Civil War years, southern investors complained they found it hard to recruit diligent mill workers among southern poor whites, but after the war they certainly found them. In the final analysis, cultivating the short-staple cotton so well suited to the climate with the gang labor of slaves proved a far more attractive investment opportunity than building factories. For most of the antebellum South, what economists call its comparative advantage was encapsulated in the slogan "cotton is king."[70]

New England, with its stony soil and short growing season, had needed to industrialize; most of the South did not. Manufacturing enabled the Yankees to make use of female labor, but the planters found plenty of work for their female slaves in agriculture. The relationship between the planters and the Yankee processors of their raw cotton proved by no means altogether compatible. Two-thirds of the cotton crop was exported, mainly to Britain, giving its producers an interest in free trade. But the American cotton mills needed a tariff to stay in business. Even with its protection, they could only compete in the cheaper lines of product; the finer goods required a skilled workmanship that was prohibitively expensive in the United States.[71] The kind of coarse textiles that American mills made from cotton and wool was the kind in which southern masters clothed their slaves. The protective tariff raised the price of textiles and thus diminished the demand for southern cotton at the same time as it increased the cost of maintaining slaves. The cotton planters were morally wrong about slavery, but they were economically right to complain that the tariff did not serve their interest.[72] Only three islands of protectionist sentiment remained in the South: the sugarcane growers of Louisiana, Clay's hemp growers in Kentucky and Missouri, and the Appalachian valleys of eastern Tennessee and western North Carolina, where the predominantly nonslaveholding population continued to hope for industrial development of their natural resources and water power.

70. Randall Miller, "Slavery in Antebellum Southern Textile Mills," *Business History Review* 55 (1981), 471–90; Carole Scott, "Why the Cotton Textile Industry Did Not Develop in the South Sooner," *Agricultural History* 68 (1994): 105–21.

71. Mark Bils, "Tariff Protection and Production in the Early U.S. Cotton Textile Industry," *Journal of Economic History* 44 (1984): 1033–45; Knick Harley, "International Competitiveness of the Antebellum American Cotton Textile Industry," ibid. 52 (1992): 559–84.

72. John James, "Welfare Effects of the Antebellum Tariff," *Explorations in Economic History* 15 (1978): 231–46, esp. 249; Knick Harley, "The Antebellum American Tariff," ibid. 29 (1992): 375–400.

President Adams allowed Clay and his secretary of the Treasury, Richard Rush of Pennsylvania, to take the lead in pressing for tariff protection. He thus deferred just a bit to what was left of the old free-trade sentiment in maritime New England. However, no one had any doubt where the president's sympathies lay on the tariff question. Protectionism embodied the conscious encouragement that Adams wanted the federal government to give to economic development. Clay encouraged protariff forces to hold a convention in Harrisburg, Pennsylvania, during the summer of 1827. Because of its popularity in strategic places like Pennsylvania (already appropriately nicknamed "the Keystone State"), protectionism potentially provided a winning issue for the Adams administration.

Martin Van Buren began to worry about the groundswell of opinion building up in favor of a tariff increase. Van Buren realized that he needed to neutralize Clay's efforts politically, lest the tariff issue help reelect Adams. In theory, Van Buren was a strict constructionist of the Old Republican school. In practice, however, he recognized the strength of protectionism in the Middle Atlantic region, including his own New York state. Accordingly, Van Buren determined to construct a tariff that could be turned to the advantage of the Jackson presidential campaign. Led by Silas Wright of New York and James Buchanan of Pennsylvania, Van Buren's followers in Congress took control of the administration's tariff initiative. They reshaped it to add benefits for pivotal regions that Jackson sought to carry, cynically disregarding the interests of regions whose electoral votes were not in doubt: New England (sure to go for Adams) and the cotton South (sure to go for Jackson). To help sheep raisers (like Van Buren himself), raw wool got high protection, though it increased the price masters would have to pay for "slave cloth." The transformed bill sharply increased tariffs on other raw materials like molasses, hemp, and iron, to the disadvantage of New England distillers, ropemakers, and shipbuilders, not to mention consumers. The result was the well-named "Tariff of Abominations." John Randolph's witticism got repeated often: The tariff bill had been designed to promote not the manufacture of broadcloths and bed blankets but the manufacture of a president. Van Buren was happy for the bill to pass in the form he had given it, "ghastly, lopsided, and unequal" though it was.[73]

---

73. This is the characterization of the historian who has studied the passage of the act most thoroughly, Robert Remini (*Henry Clay*, 329). Many contemporaries and later historians were reluctant to believe that Van Buren could really have intended the Tariff of Abominations to pass, but Remini has proved he did (*Martin Van Buren and the Making of the Democratic Party*, 170–85).

Southern Jacksonians hoped that Van Buren's bill had become so objectionable to New England that Yankee congressmen would join them in voting against its final passage. They therefore prevented it from being amended in the House of Representatives. In the Senate, however, amendments were added making the tariff slightly less unpalatable to New England. It then finally passed by the combined votes of Van Buren's followers plus the administration supporters, who accepted the general principle of protection while deploring particular features of the bill. The act served the Little Magician's purpose of allowing Jacksonians in the middle states to board the tariff bandwagon. Jackson backers in the South felt bitter and betrayed but had nowhere else to turn, since Adams was the only alternative. They consoled themselves that Calhoun would be Jackson's running mate and hoped the South Carolinian could exert more influence on the next administration. Embarrassing the hope of Adams and Clay for government-promoted economic development, Van Buren's Tariff of Abominations demonstrated how government intervention in the economy could be manipulated for political advantage.

VII

The campaign for the presidential election of 1828 lasted the whole four years of John Quincy Adams's administration. Eventually defenders of the national administration started calling themselves "National" Republicans, while the supporters of the man who claimed the popular mandate called themselves "Democratic" Republicans, later simply "Democrats." The terms came into use only very slowly. For Adams and his followers, to recognize the emergence of partisanship was to confess failure. Jackson and his followers saw themselves as the legitimate Jeffersonian Republican party and referred to their opponents as a corrupt clique of "federalists." Accustomed as we are to a two-party system, we seize upon labels that contemporaries hesitated to employ. By the time the new party names gained acceptance, the election was over.

What came to be called the National Republicanism of Adams and Clay represented a continuation of the new Republican nationalism that had arisen out of the experience of the War of 1812. The Democratic Republicans of Jackson, Van Buren, and the recently transformed Calhoun recruited the proslavery Radicals of William H. Crawford and embraced the state-rights tradition of Old Republicanism. Despite the role played by Van Buren in putting together the opposition coalition, Jackson always controlled his own campaign, operating it from his headquarters in Nashville, Tennessee. The few remaining Federalists generally joined the

Adams party in New England, the Jackson party in the South, and divided between them in the middle states.

Each side embraced its own version of modernity. The administration's supporters endorsed economic modernization and appealed for votes on the basis of their improvement program. The Jacksonians emphasized their candidate rather than a program but developed a very modern political organization with attendant publicity and rallies. The one step they did not take was to hold a national party convention, but they did sponsor many state conventions. The Adams supporters followed suit; in the face of Jackson's political machine, their aspiration to classical nonpartisanship could not practically be maintained. Taking advantage of improvements in communications, both sides relied heavily on partisan newspapers to get across their message, though Jackson's followers kept theirs under tighter control. Handbills and campaign biographies also made use of the new opportunities for printed propaganda. Mindful of ethnic divisions, both sides published some campaign literature in German.[74] The techniques of electioneering reflected the increased public participation in the election of the president. By 1828, all but two states (Delaware and South Carolina) chose their presidential electors by popular vote. Most states opted for electing them at large, since that maximized the state's influence, although it would have been more democratic (that is, reflected public opinion more accurately) to choose the electors by congressional district.[75]

As in 1824, Jackson campaigned against Washington insiders. He himself described the contest as a "struggle between the virtue of the people and executive patronage"—an ironic expression indeed, in view of his party's exploitation of the spoils of office once in power, but there is no reason to suppose it not sincerely felt.[76] Rather than debate policy, Jacksonians harped on the "corrupt bargain" that had robbed the people of their preferred candidate. The charge played well in provincial America, where Yankees like Adams were often unpopular peddlers and storekeepers, notorious for cheating farm wives with wooden nutmegs and driving many a small "corrupt bargain."[77] (Through much of the Ameri-

74. Sample election documents are reprinted in Arthur Schlesinger Jr., *History of American Presidential Elections* (New York, 1985), II, 437–91.

75. On the transition in the method of electing presidents, see Michael Heale, *The Presidential Quest, 1787–1852* (London, 1982).

76. AJ to James Hamilton Jr., June 29, 1828, *Papers of Andrew Jackson*, ed. Harold Moser et al. (Knoxville, Tenn., 2002), VI, 476–77.

77. Pointed out by Harry Watson, *Liberty and Power* (New York, 1990), 93.

can hinterland, Yankees were the functional equivalent of Jews in rural Europe.) Contrasted with such a figure of metropolitan guile appeared the Old Hero Jackson, a leader of stern virtue, a frontiersman who had made his own legend. To celebrate his victory at New Orleans, Jackson's campaign marketed the song "The Hunters of Kentucky"—in defiance of the historical record, which showed that Jackson had reproached the Kentucky militia for their conduct in the battle. Where Adams exhorted his countrymen to a program of deliberate "improvement," the Jacksonians celebrated their unrefined "natural" leader. Old Hickory was portrayed as a straightforward man of action, a hero the common man could trust.[78]

The Adams press responded that Jackson's personal attributes actually disqualified, rather than qualified, him for the presidency. He possessed a notoriously fiery temper and had repeatedly displayed vindictive anger. Adams partisans reminded the public that Jackson had been involved in several brawls and duels, killing a man in one of them. The "coffin handbill" distributed by Philadelphia newspaperman John Binns called sympathetic attention to the six militiamen executed by Jackson's orders in February 1815. (In retaliation, pro-Jackson mobs persecuted Binns and his wife.)[79]

The Adams-Clay supporters also indicted Jackson's character on the basis of his sex life. Back in 1790, young Jackson had set up housekeeping with Rachel Robards, a woman married to another man. Though divorce was difficult and rare, Rachel's husband, Lewis Robards, successfully divorced her on grounds of desertion and adultery. In 1794, after learning of the divorce, Andrew and Rachel underwent a marriage ceremony; prior to that time they had been "living in sin," as respectable nineteenth-century opinion understood it. (On the eighteenth-century frontier, people did not inquire closely into such matters; Andrew and Rachel had simply been accepted as Mr. and Mrs. Jackson.) This juicy story was resurrected by an Adams newspaper, the *Cincinnati Gazette*, on March 23, 1827. Jackson's Nashville campaign office responded with an elaborately contrived narrative claiming that Andrew and Rachel had participated in an earlier marriage ceremony in 1791 under the mistaken belief that Lewis Robards had obtained a divorce then, so their adultery had been inadvertent and merely technical. No evidence has ever been found of this alleged wedding, and Jackson's scrupulous biographer Robert Remini

78. See John William Ward, *Andrew Jackson: Symbol for an Age* (New York, 1955).
79. Robert Remini, *The Election of 1828* (Philadelphia, 1963), 156.

must be right in concluding that no 1791 ceremony took place, and that in any case Andrew and Rachel were living together as husband and wife as early as 1790.[80]

Raising the subject of adultery related to the larger issue of Jackson's character, the charge that he was so willful, impetuous, and impatient of restraint that he could not be trusted with supreme responsibility. In the vocabulary of the time, it was said that Jackson's "passions" ruled him. The general almost played into his critics' hands during the campaign. When Samuel Southard (Adams's secretary of the navy) suggested at a dinner party that Secretary of War Monroe might have been entitled to some of the credit for the New Orleans victory, Old Hickory wrote a furious message to him preparing the way for a duel. Jackson's friend Sam Houston managed to get the letter rephrased.[81]

The Jackson campaign did not confine its falsehoods to defenses of the candidate's honor but invented others to attack his rival. The scrupulous, somber Adams might not seem to offer much of a target for salacious arrows, but Jacksonians did not let this inhibit their imagination. Jackson's New Hampshire supporter Isaac Hill retailed the libel that while U.S. minister to Russia, Adams had procured an American girl for the sexual gratification of the tsar. Less preposterous, and therefore perhaps more dangerous, was the accusation that Adams had put a billiard table in the White House at public expense. In truth, Adams did enjoy the game and had bought such a table, but paid for it out of his own pocket. Adams's religion was not exempt from attack: The Presbyterian Ezra Stiles Ely denounced the president's Unitarian theological views as heresy and called on all sound Christians to vote for Jackson. Taken together, the accusations against Adams were designed to show him as aristocratic, intellectual, and un-American.[82]

The hope that Adams and Clay had entertained that the election might constitute a referendum on the American System evaporated. Instead, the presidential campaign of 1828 was probably the dirtiest in American history. It seems only fair to observe that while the hostile stories circulated about Adams were largely false, those about Jackson were

80. Norma Basch, "Marriage, Morals, and Politics in the Election of 1828," *JAH* 80 (1993): 890–918; Remini, *Jackson*, I, 64–67.

81. Michael Birkner, "The General, the Secretary, and the President," *Tennessee Historical Quarterly* 42 (1983): 243–53.

82. Edwin Miles, "President Adams' Billiard Table," *New England Quarterly* 45 (1972): 31–43; Ezra Stiles Ely, *The Duty of Christian Freemen to Elect Christian Magistrates* (Philadelphia, 1828).

largely true. An exception was the charge appearing in an Adams paper that Jackson's mother had been a prostitute.[83] However, shifting the focus of the campaign from program to personalities generally benefited the Jacksonians. They were only too willing to see the choice posed as a popular ditty had it: "Between J. Q. Adams, who can write/And Andy Jackson, who can fight." Depressed by the turn the campaign was taking, Adams stopped recording events in his diary in August and did not resume until after the election.

The bitterness with which the campaign was waged manifested the intensity of the feelings it aroused. For beyond the mudslinging, important national issues were at stake. Adams stood for a vision of coherent economic progress, of improvement both personal and national, directed by deliberate planning. Instead of pursuing improvement, Jacksonians accepted America the way it was, including its institution of slavery. They looked upon government planners as meddlesome, although they were more than willing to seek government favors on an ad hoc basis, as when a particular internal improvement or tariff rate gratified a particular local interest. They did not publicize a comprehensive program as the national administration did. But they too had a vision of the future, and theirs centered not on economic diversification but on opening new lands to white settlement, especially if those lands could be exploited with black labor. Jackson the frontier warrior personified this vision, and it had potential appeal not only to the slaveholders of the South but also among the common white men of both sections.

Martin Van Buren set out the strategic logic behind the Jackson campaign in a letter he wrote to Thomas Ritchie on January 13, 1827. Editor of the *Richmond Enquirer*, Ritchie was a key opinion-maker in the southern Radical circles that had supported Crawford in 1824. Van Buren wanted Ritchie to swing his influence behind Jackson in 1828. But this time the Little Magician had more than just a temporary, tactical purpose in mind; he aspired to forge a fundamental realignment in American politics. Van Buren despised the nonpartisan, meritocratic ideal of James Monroe and John Quincy Adams; he wanted to re-create the party system that had divided Republicans from Federalists. Van Buren wrote to persuade Ritchie of the merits of a political alliance "between the planters of the South and the plain Republicans of the North." This alliance around Jackson should claim the mantle of the Jeffersonian Republican party and stigmatize its opponents as Federalists. Political parties are inevitable,

83. Remini, *Election of 1828*, 153.

Van Buren argued, so it behooved the Jackson supporters not only to embrace partisanship openly but also to define the parties in as advantageous a way as possible. If a second party system were not created, Van Buren believed, the result would be a politics based on sectionalism. In the absence of strong party distinctions, "prejudices between free and slave holding states will inevitably take their place," he warned Ritchie. The Missouri debate illustrated the danger, he pointed out. The senator from New York did not scruple to appeal to the southern Radical's desire to preserve slavery from northern interference. "Party attachment in former times furnished a complete antidote for sectional prejudices by producing counteracting feelings." Van Buren held out the creation of the Jacksonian Democratic Party as a promised means of containing antislavery. Ritchie was persuaded.[84]

As Van Buren's letter foretold, the campaign saw the commencement of a novel acceptance of parties in American political life. And not surprisingly, given the commitment of Van Buren and most other Jacksonians to protecting slavery, the campaign also shaped up as highly sectional. For the only time in American history, the two sides presented the electorate with opposing sectional tickets. To run with him against the two southerners, Jackson and Calhoun, President Adams picked his Treasury secretary, Richard Rush of Pennsylvania, creating an all-northern team. In the South, Jackson's popularity was enhanced by the feeling that only he could be relied upon to maintain white supremacy and expand the white empire, to evict the Indian tribes, to support and extend slavery.

In the North, the race was tight. Appeals to defend slavery would not work for Old Hickory, and the Adams-Clay economic development program enjoyed widespread support. Moreover, the populistic, egalitarian Antimasons were opposing Jackson. Without Van Buren's brilliant strategy, his party organization, and his tariff abominations, it is hard to see how the all-southern ticket could have won, even given Jackson's legend. Van Buren gave the effort his all, even sacrificing his Senate seat to run for governor of New York in 1828, so as to hold back the tide of Antimasonry in the state.

The election returns, as they gradually came in, gave Jackson the victory, 178 to 83 in the electoral college. His 56 percent of the popular vote set a record that was not surpassed until the twentieth century. His followers

---

84. The classic analysis of this letter is Richard H. Brown, "The Missouri Crisis, Slavery, and the Politics of Jacksonianism," *South Atlantic Quarterly* 65 (1966): 55–72. The letter itself is in *Martin Van Buren Papers* (Library of Congress microfilm), ser. 2, reel 7, rpt. in Robert Remini, ed., *The Age of Jackson* (New York, 1972), 3–7.

also won control of both houses of Congress, by a particularly impressive 138 to 74 in the House of Representatives. Jackson racked up awesome majorities across the South and West—except, ironically, in Louisiana, scene of his greatest battle. There his high-handed conduct was remembered, he was unpopular with the French Creoles, and the sugarcane planters needed a tariff. The Jacksonians, who believed in partisan politics wholeheartedly, not surprisingly had waged it more effectively than the Adamsites, some of whom engaged in it only grudgingly. Everywhere outside New England and New Jersey, Jackson benefited from more effective organization. In Georgia, where Indian Removal was the big issue, Adams got no popular votes at all. Calhoun's record on Indian Removal did not satisfy Georgians either, so seven of the Georgia electors cast their vice-presidential votes for the South Carolina Radical William Smith, Calhoun's longtime rival.

As in 1824, Adams carried his core constituency: New England, the Antimasonic and evangelical areas of New York state, the shores of the Great Lakes. He also won New Jersey, Delaware, and some of the congressional districts of Maryland. Under his leadership, New England had emerged from Federalist particularism and embraced Republican nationalism. The attack on his theology did not hurt Adams among Christians of the Universal Yankee Nation (as the New England zone of settlement was called). In the South, Adams showed pockets of strength in the towns and commercial areas like the Kentucky Bluegrass. But his running mate Rush failed to deliver Pennsylvania, and Clay failed to deliver any electoral votes in the Ohio Valley. The Tariff of Abominations had effectively counteracted the political appeal of the American System in those areas.

The popular vote tripled in size from 1824, partly because of states changing their method of choosing electors, but mostly because of heightened public interest and organized get-out-the-vote efforts. A two-way race captured the public imagination more clearly than a five-way race had done. Participation of eligible voters, 57.5 percent overall, was generally highest in states where the race was close, like New York and Ohio, and where good local transportation made it not too inconvenient to get to the polling place.[85] Where state offices were more hotly contested than the presidency, turnout was higher in those races. Legal enfranchisement of new voters did not represent a significant factor in increasing the size of the turnout, although some states were in the process of removing the remaining property and religious tests for voting. The

85. Voter participation figures are given at www.multied.com/elections/1828.html (viewed March 1, 2007).

great majority of adult white males had long enjoyed the legal right to vote.[86]

Did Jackson's victory constitute the coming of democracy to America? Certainly the Jackson political machine tried to persuade voters to see it that way. But continuities with an earlier time are evident: Jackson's campaign slogans celebrated antique agrarian virtue and promised to restore Old Republicanism. His personal popularity rested to a large extent on military prowess, which of course is the oldest political appeal of all, and by no means democratic. If Jackson was the candidate of the "common man," as he was so often described, it was specifically the common *white* man, and one not bothered by slavery or the abuses of Freemasonry. The Jacksonians cultivated an antielitist image. How far this corresponded with the reality of their support has not been easy for historians to document. Most voters in antebellum America, on both sides of the political divide, were farmers. The few industrial wage-earners who were male often voted for the American System, not Andrew Jackson, in the belief that a tariff protected their jobs. Adams did well among people living along commercial routes. Jackson did well in economically undeveloped regions, among non-English white ethnic groups, and among first-time voters (young men, immigrants, or the previously apathetic). But Jackson's leading newspaper editor, the ardently proslavery Missourian Duff Green, knew how to exploit the communications revolution: He distributed his *United States Telegraph* through the mails using the franking privilege of Jackson congressmen. Jackson's successful campaign owed as much to improvements in communications as to the democratization of the electorate.[87]

The vote displayed striking sectional characteristics. Jackson managed a bare majority in the free states (50.3%) while racking up 72.6 percent in the slave states. The South provided most of his electoral votes. Thanks to the peculiarities of the Electoral College (with the notorious three-fifths clause inflating the power of the slaveholding states), the 400,000 popular votes Jackson got in the North brought him only 73 electoral votes, while the 200,000 southerners who voted for him produced 105.[88] There is no justification for claiming that the states Jackson carried were more democratic

86. See Richard P. McCormick, *The Second American Party System* (Chapel Hill, 1966).

87. For careful analyses of the election of 1828, see Richard R. John, "Affairs of Office," in *The Democratic Experiment*, ed. Meg Jacobs et al. (Princeton, 2003), 50–85; and Lee Benson, *Toward the Scientific Study of History* (Philadelphia, 1972), 40–50.

88. Leonard Richards, "The Jacksonians and Slavery," *Antislavery Reconsidered*, ed. Lewis Perry and Michael Fellman (Baton Rouge, 1979), 101.

than the ones Adams carried; indeed, in some tangible ways state governments in the North, where Adams ran better, were the more democratic.[89]
To be sure, Jackson and his supporters had successfully encouraged and
exploited broadening political participation. They had laid the ground-
work for a new two-party system. But much of what they had done could
as fairly be called demagogy as democracy. In the words of an antebellum
newspaperman, the Adams campaign had "dealt with man *as he should
be*," while the Jackson campaign had "appealed to him *as he is*."[90]

The election of 1828 proved a pivotal one; it marked the end of one
kind of politics and the beginning of another. During the so-called Era of
Good Feelings, presidential politics had been unstructured by party rivalry and had been driven less by issues than personal ambitions. In 1828,
the incumbent, Adams, had boldly based his campaign on a national economic program. The challenger, Jackson, had run on a combination of
personal popularity, organization, and the evocation of symbolism. The
Jackson campaign, while claiming to be anti-politics, had in practice created a new and far more potent political machinery. Having won, Jackson
did not feel content to bask in the glory of his record as a military hero
vindicated by the electorate. He became an activist president. His administration would witness novel assertions of presidential power, rancorous
debate over issues, and the rebirth of political parties. After 1828, the classical ideal of nonpartisan leadership, which Adams and Monroe had
shared with Washington and countless political philosophers, was dead—
killed in battle with Old Hickory as surely as General Pakenham.

There was another aspect of the outcome, less often noticed by historians
but no less important. The National Republican improvement program of
planned economic development would have encouraged a diversified economy in place of reliance on the export of slave-grown agricultural staples.
Its strong central government would have held long-term potential for
helping the peaceful resolution of the slavery problem, perhaps in connection with some kind of colonization program, while weaning portions
of the South, especially in the border states, away from plantation agriculture toward mixed farming, industry, and commerce.[91] Whatever such
promise Adams's program held had been frustrated, to a large extent by

89. E.g., Robin Einhorn, "Institutional Reality in the Age of Slavery: Taxation and
    Democracy in the States," *Journal of Policy History* 18 (2006): 21–43.
90. Thomas B. Stevenson, quoted in Peter Knupfer, *The Union as It Is* (Chapel Hill,
    1991), 156.
91. See Richard John, "Governmental Institutions as Agents of Change," *Studies in Amer-
    ican Political Development* 11 (1997): 347–80.

defenders of slavery who recognized in it a vision of America's future incompatible with their own. Still, the Adams-Clay vision of government-sponsored national economic development, though temporarily checked, lived on. The second American party system, originating in the election of 1828, was strongly issue-oriented. It would be characterized by fierce debates over both economic policy and the enforcement of white supremacy.

8

Pursuing the Millennium

Many people shared John Quincy Adams's view of America as the country where God would bring His plans for humanity to fulfillment. But the blueprints for realizing this providential destiny could be far bolder and more presumptuous than Henry Clay's American System. Some Americans actually hoped to cooperate in hastening the Second Coming of Christ, which would usher in the end of history. Almost all Americans regarded their country as an example and a harbinger of popular government to the rest of the world, and even non-church-members found millennial expectations an appropriate metaphor for this destiny. To appreciate the seriousness with which Americans of the early nineteenth century took the millennium, one must enter a world many readers will find alien and full of arcane lore. Millions of twenty-first-century Americans, however, still live in that world.

Traditional Judaism and Christianity both have much to say about the end of history. Chapters 20 and 21 of the New Testament book of Revelation speak of a thousand-year Kingdom of Christ on earth, after which all the dead will be resurrected, Satan defeated, a final judgment passed, and the world replaced by a new creation. The blessed thousand-year epoch has been named the millennium, and Christians identify it with the messianic age of peace and justice foretold by the Jewish prophets. Theologians have interpreted the prophecy in various ways, two of which—surprisingly enough—contributed to shaping events in the young American republic. One view of the millennium sees it as the climax and goal of human progress, with human effort contributing to the realization of God's providential design. This is called *post*millennialism, because the Second Coming of Christ occurs at the end of the millennium. The other view sees the millennium as requiring God's supernatural intervention to initiate it. The Second Coming of Christ must occur before the millennium; hence this interpretation is called *pre*millennialism. Where postmillennialists regard the millennium as part of history, premillennialists do not. While premillennialists (looking to divine intervention for deliverance) often feel alienated from their surrounding society and culture, American postmillennialists have typically celebrated theirs.

Both kinds of millennial expectations had flourished in America since the earliest European settlements. The colonial Puritans conceived their relationship to God on the model of ancient Israel's covenant and their relationship to the nations of the world as that of "a city upon a hill, the eyes of all people upon us."[1] Some of them also believed that they were living near the end of history and that their efforts to restore the purity of New Testament Christianity hastened the millennium. The Puritan diarist Samuel Sewell, for example, persuaded himself that the New Jerusalem, the capital of Christ's millennial kingdom, would be located in the New World. The Puritan polymath Cotton Mather tried to predict the year of the Second Coming; he chose by turns 1697, 1716, and 1736. The greatest of American Puritan intellectuals, Jonathan Edwards, observing in 1742 the awakening of religion that he and other revivalists fostered, interpreted it as evidence that the millennial age approached and might well begin in America.[2] The series of eighteenth-century wars against Catholic France and, even more, the Revolution itself, preached as a crusade from many a patriot pulpit, nurtured American Protestant millennial nationalism. Of the minister Samuel Hopkins, who carried Edwardsean piety into the Revolutionary cause and the abolition of slavery, a contemporary wrote: "The millennium was more than a belief to him; it had the freshness of visible things. He was at home in it."[3]

The Second Great Awakening of religion, more widespread and diverse than the First, inflamed renewed outbursts of chiliasm, that is, belief that the millennium will occur soon.[4] Postmillennialism in particular flourished, for material improvements, political democratization, and moral reform all provided encouraging signs that history was moving in the right direction, as did the spread of Christianity to the four corners of the globe. Americans seemed a "chosen people" not only because they enjoyed a covenanted relationship with the God of Israel but also because they were destined to prepare the way for the return of His Messiah and Son. William Sprague, a prominent spokesman for New England's neo-Puritan tradition, declared: "We know—for God has told us—that there is a period of universal moral renovation approaching, and there is much in the

---

1. Words from "A Model of Christian Charity," John Winthrop's famous address to the settlers aboard the *Arbella* in 1630. I have modernized his spelling. Winthrop was invoking Matthew 5:14.
2. Brooks Holifield, *Theology in America* (New Haven, 2003), 77, 123. See also Ruth Bloch, *Visionary Republic: Millennial Themes in American Thought, 1756–1800* (Cambridge, Eng., 1985).
3. William Ellery Channing, *Works* (Boston, 1888), 427–28.
4. The word "chiliasm" is derived from the Greek word for thousand, as "millennium" is derived from the Latin one.

aspect of Providence, which seems to indicate that our country is to have a prominent—may I not say—a principal instrumentality in the introduction of that period."[5] The postmillennial role that Sprague envisioned for America was underscored by countless evangelists. "The stated policy of heaven is to raise the world from its degraded condition," declared the revivalist-reformer Lyman Beecher. Beecher had political and material, as well as moral and spiritual, elevation in mind; he saw the United States as the example to uplift the rest of the nations. Postmillennial expectations extended well beyond the New England heirs of the Puritans; the Dutch Reformed and Presbyterians in the middle states and the South overwhelmingly endorsed them too.[6] The tolerant and humane evangelist Alexander Campbell led his disparate Christian movement into faith in postmillennial progress through his journal, the *Millennial Harbinger*. Charles Finney, however, exceeded all others in the urgency of his rhetoric. Once, in a burst of enthusiasm, Finney told his congregation that if evangelicals applied themselves fully to the works of mission and reform they could bring about the millennium within three years.[7]

John Quincy Adams invoked postmillennial aspirations in support of his political program. "Progressive improvement in the condition of man is apparently the purpose of a superintending Providence," he declared. Adams saw himself as working for the establishment of the messianic age foretold by the second Isaiah ("the sublimest of prophets"). His First Message to Congress called a system of internal improvements "a sacred duty" imposed by God to elevate America in the scale of civilization. He recommended U.S. conversion to the metric system of weights and measures on the ground that it implemented "the trembling hope of the Christian" for the unity of humanity, the binding of Satan in chains, and the promised thousand years of peace. The political policies of his rivals, Adams complained, "led us back to the savage state" and away from the millennium.[8]

Postmillennialism provided the capstone to an intellectual structure integrating political liberalism and economic development with Protestant Christianity. One of the most powerful statements of this worldview was

5. Sprague's Fourth of July address in 1827 is quoted in Jonathan Sassi, *A Republic of Righteousness* (New York, 2001), 150.
6. Quotation from Lyman Beecher, *A Plea for Colleges* (Cincinnati, 1836), 11; Fred Hood, *Reformed America: The Middle and Southern States* (University, Ala., 1980), 68–87.
7. Charles Finney, *Lectures on Revivals of Religion*, ed. William McLoughlin (Cambridge, Mass., 1960), 306. On another occasion he supposedly said three *months*: Paul Johnson, *A Shopkeeper's Millennium* (New York, 1978), 3–4.
8. Quotations from J. Q. Adams in Daniel Howe, *The Political Culture of the American Whigs* (Chicago, 1979), 59.

delivered in 1825 by Francis Wayland, Baptist clergyman, later president of Brown University and the country's most widely read economist. Wayland began with the salient characteristic of his age, the increased awareness and self-confidence of the middle and lower classes throughout the Western world. The two engines driving this momentous transformation toward modernity, he explained, were Protestantism as a force for literacy and the mass production of cheap printed media enabling the common people to take advantage of their literacy. Improved transportation supplemented these effects by facilitating the flow of commerce and information across national boundaries and raising living standards. Without using those names, Wayland had described the transportation and communications revolutions.

Opposing these constructive developments, however, stood the autocratic regimes united in the Holy Alliance, together with the Roman Catholic Church, which had cast its lot with them in reliance upon intolerance and persecution for protection against modern ideas. If one looked at Europe alone, the division between the Catholic autocracies and the Protestant countries where political liberalism was on the rise seemed like a fine balance. Fortunately, the influence of the United States would tip that balance in favor of progress and Protestantism. The ideological conflict might even become a violent war, but if it did, Wayland predicted, the United States would end up leading a world coalition to save freedom and civilization.

To his prescient interpretation of the forces shaping his age, Wayland added a moral imperative. American citizens had the duty to promote the "means for elevating universally the intellectual and moral character of our people." Of these means, the most obvious was education, but the most essential was knowledge of the Bible, for "man has never correctly understood nor successfully asserted his rights, until he has learned them from the Bible." At the end, Wayland spelled out America's postmillennial mission: "The dim shadows of unborn nations . . . implore this country to fulfill the destiny to which she has been summoned by an all-wise Providence, and save a sinking world from temporal misery and eternal death." Millennial expectations by no means implied simply optimism. The scriptures foretold terrible suffering and catastrophes before God would finally bring good out of evil. Americans must work and pray hard to bring about the millennium. "Ye who love the Lord, keep not silence, and give him no rest, until he establish this his Jerusalem, and make her a praise in the whole earth."[9] A century later, the postmillennial liberal-

---

9. Francis Wayland, *The Duties of an American Citizen* (Boston, 1825), quotations from 19, 34, 44.

ism so effectively summarized by Wayland would influence Woodrow Wilson.

A minority position in earlier generations, postmillennialism became the most widely held viewpoint on eschatology (the study of last things) among Protestants in antebellum America. It synthesized the faith in progress characteristic of the Enlightenment with biblical Christianity. Postmillennialists, as their most acute historian, James Moorhead, has pointed out, planted one foot firmly in the world of steam engines and telegraph while keeping the other in the cosmos of biblical prophecy.[10] Theirs was a happy compromise, typical of the middle-class mainstream intellectual life of that period. Postmillennialism celebrated reformers, inventors, and Christian missionaries. Faith in progress toward the millennium synthesized readily with revival-based religion, holding out the promise that revivals could be made perpetual, without periodic declines in fervor. Psychologically, postmillennialism replicated on a cosmic scale the individual believer's struggle to free himself from sin and embrace the Lord's coming into his heart. Finally, postmillennialism legitimated American civil religion, that durable fusion of patriotism, nondenominational Protestantism, and belief in America's responsibility to conduct an experiment in free government. Though postmillennialism may seem naive to our own chastened century, it flourished in a time and place, as Alfred North Whitehead observed, where even "wise men hoped."[11]

II

In September 1814, the British army had massed overwhelming strength to drive south from Canada in its most serious invasion of the War of 1812. But after a naval battle at Plattsburgh on nearby Lake Champlain, their commander suddenly ordered the army to withdraw. General George Prevost's astonished and angry superiors summoned him back to Britain to face a court-martial. On the American side, Captain William Miller could only attribute his country's amazing salvation to divine intervention. This evidence of providence in history persuaded the young officer to turn his back on fashionable deism and join a Baptist church. On his farm after the war, Miller helped runaway slaves escape to Canada and studied the Bible every chance he got. Undeterred by his lack of training in biblical studies and ignorance of Hebrew and Greek, he applied a mixture of ingenuity

10. James Moorhead, *World Without End: Mainstream American Protestant Visions of the Last Things* (Bloomington, 1999), 2.
11. Quoted in Sidney Mead, *The Lively Experiment: The Shaping of Christianity in America* (New York, 1963), 90.

and common sense to the task, dignified in Protestant tradition, of individual interpretation of scripture. Daniel 8:14 gave him his key to predicting the future: "Unto two thousand and three hundred days; then shall the sanctuary be cleansed." Miller read "days" to mean years and the cleansing of the sanctuary to mean the Second Coming of Christ to judge the world. His calculations convinced him that this Advent would occur sometime between March 1843 and April 1844.[12] Although shy and lacking any natural charisma, Miller experienced a calling from God to share his breathtaking news with the world and began to preach it in 1831, when the pudgy farmer was almost fifty years old.

Miller's message of premillennialism seemed to have nothing going for it save his naive earnestness, but it resonated with a powerful strand in Anglo-American culture. The popularity of postmillennialism proved quite compatible with consideration for premillennial proposals. Indeed, the respect accorded millennialism in general predisposed people to take premillennialism (also called millenarianism) seriously. Expectations of Christ's imminent miraculous return by no means appealed solely to the unlettered. Prominent intellectuals like Timothy Dwight, president of Yale, and John Livingston, president of Rutgers, shared them. In 1827, a conference at Albury Park in England, attended by many leading clerics and respectable laymen, applied methods of calculation similar to Miller's and concluded that the judgment day was close at hand.[13]

Miller reached a large audience once his publicity was taken over by Joshua Himes, a minister and social reformer who made use of the new means of communication to spread the millennial warning. Millions of pages of Millerite tracts were distributed; camp meetings in an enormous but portable tent attracted a total of half a million auditors in the three summers of 1842–44. Millerite preaching prominently featured laypeople; the movement especially encouraged women to speak in public. Many evangelical clergy gladly accorded Miller's views a hearing because he shook people up and interested them in religion. The Millerites, like many other American millenarians, combined their "ideological archaism" with "organizational modernity."[14] When newspapers published elaborate refutations of Miller, as the *New York Tribune* did on March 2,

---

12. The Millerite calculations are contextualized and explained in Paul Conkin, *American Originals: Homemade Varieties of Christianity* (Chapel Hill, 1997), 111–21.

13. Ernest Sandeen, *Roots of Fundamentalism* (Chicago, 1970), 18–20.

14. Catherine Brekus, *Strangers and Pilgrims: Female Preaching in America, 1740–1845* (Chapel Hill, 1998), 318–29. Quotation from Michael Barkun, *Crucible of the Millennium* (Syracuse, N.Y., 1986), 128.

1843, it brought him still more attention. By then Miller and Himes had anywhere from twenty-five to fifty thousand Americans, mostly in New England and upstate New York, thoroughly convinced and a much larger number hedging their bets; Millerism also won converts in Britain. Sociological theory long held that persons attracted to millenarian causes would be the marginalized and despairing, looking for compensatory consolation. The historians who have studied William Miller's Adventist movement, however, are unanimous in concluding that it was made up of average rural and small-town Americans, the solid middle class and respectable working class, a few blacks along with whites, generally coming from an evangelical background, usually Baptist or Methodist.[15]

When the target year expired on April 18, Miller publicly apologized for his evident mistake. But his followers were not all ready to give in. One of them, Samuel Snow, recalculated and decided that the correct day for Christ's return would be the next Jewish Day of Atonement: October 22, 1844. (Snow used the ancient Jewish calendar of the Karaite sect, thinking it the one Daniel had used, not the calendar of modern mainstream Judaism.)[16] Miller had never been willing to pinpoint a specific day, but eventually he went along with Snow's prediction because it aroused so much renewed enthusiasm among his followers.

How would people behave if they were convinced the world was coming to an end on a known day only months away? In 1844, many paid their debts, quit their jobs, closed their businesses, left their crops unharvested in the fields. Some who felt guilty about past frauds and cheats turned over money to banks or the U.S. Treasury. Others simply gave away money, keeping no accounting of it. There was a rush to get baptized. On the appointed night, thousands gathered in many locations outdoors to watch the sky. But Jesus did not appear to them, and October 22 became known among Adventists as "the Great Disappointment." The legend that Miller's people had donned ascension robes for the occasion was one of many humiliations heaped on the Adventists over the next year by a laughing public that had not quite dared risk scorning them until after the fact.[17]

15. See David Rowe, "Millerites," in *The Disappointed: Millerism and Millenarianism*, ed. Ronald Numbers and Jonathan Butler (Bloomington, 1987), 1–15; Richard Rogers, "Millennialism and American Culture," *Comparative Social Research* 13 (1991): 105–36. Estimating the number of Miller's followers is very difficult because they did not yet belong to a separate denomination.

16. Conkin, *American Originals*, 121.

17. See Everett Dick, "The Millerite Movement," in *Adventism in America*, ed. Gary Land (Grand Rapids, Mich., 1986), 1–35.

William Miller had never formed a denomination while expecting Christ in 1843, for there would have been no point in any long-term planning. But after the Great Disappointment his followers, many of them expelled from their previous churches, kept their movement alive by differentiating themselves more sharply from mainline evangelicalism. The largest group organized as the Seventh-Day Adventists, under the new leadership of Joseph Bates, who declared Sunday observance an unwarranted innovation and restored the Jewish Sabbath, and Ellen Harmon White, an inspired visionary who instituted dietary reforms opposing tobacco, alcohol, coffee, and meat. The denomination reinterpreted Daniel's prophecy and decided that Christ had entered a new "heavenly sanctuary" on October 22, 1844, in preparation for an early but unspecified return to earth. In the Civil War and subsequent conflicts its members have been conscientious objectors. Miller himself never got over his great embarrassment and retired quietly, but the Seventh-Day Adventists survive to this day.[18]

III

While the postmillennial mainstream of American Protestantism identified the whole country as God's new Israel and a model for the other nations, a host of sectarian movements proclaimed their own little communities as examples to mankind. Scholars call these exemplary planned communities "utopias," a term that does not necessarily have a derogatory connotation, although Marx and Engels used it disparagingly to distinguish "utopian" socialism from their own allegedly "scientific" socialism. In the early republic, many utopian communities flourished, religious and secular, imported and native, each struggling to demonstrate the millennium, literal or figurative, here and now. As one utopian participant put it in 1844: "Our ulterior aim is nothing less than Heaven on Earth."[19]

We would err to dismiss these aspirations as a trivial, lunatic fringe. In a time of rapidly changing means of communication and systems of production, when everything from race relations to banking practices came under challenge, there was no sharp distinction between the mainstream and the marginal. The utopians simply carried even further the perfectionism that mainstream evangelists like Charles Finney preached. Typically, they did not so much reject American society as wish to elaborate

---

18. For their later history, see Douglas Morgan, *Adventism and the American Republic* (Knoxville, Tenn., 2001).
19. Charles Dana, quoted in Barkun, *Crucible of the Millennium*, 67.

upon it, to carry its innovative qualities to extremes. Their communities attracted attention out of all proportion to their size. Contemporaries took the communities seriously, whether they sympathized with them or not, as potential alternatives for religious, social, and economic life. Of particular interest are the ways the communities addressed gender issues before there was a women's movement addressing them in the world at large. Collectively, the communities underscore the experimental nature of American life, its idealism and ambition, its independence from the givens of custom and tradition.

Once again, the story begins with cotton. Robert Owen, a self-made man from Wales, gained a fortune operating cotton textile mills in the mushrooming industrial city of Manchester, England. In 1800, he moved to Scotland and undertook to make a mill town called New Lanark an example of industrial efficiency. A thoroughgoing Enlightenment rationalist who took the technological progress of the age as his analogy, Owen felt confident he knew how to reshape social relations. Such optimism, of course, was not peculiar to freethinkers in that age but shared by many varieties of Christians.

On New Year's Day 1816, Owen proposed a model community of no more than twenty-five hundred people that could serve as an example to Britain and the world. Each community would be self-governing and hold its property in common. Within its environment a new human nature could be created: healthy, rational, and tolerant. Owen propagated his ideas through a journal appropriately entitled *The New Moral World*. When his Christian wife, Ann Dale Owen, pointed out the analogy between his new moral world and that of the Christian millennium, Robert took to quoting scripture on behalf of his ideas and warning that the end of the existing commercial world was imminent. His own version of behavioral science he labeled "the Great Truth," acceptance of which would constitute the coming of "the Messiah."[20]

As if in imitation of the seventeenth-century Puritans, European visionaries continued to come to America to implement their millennial aspirations. One of these was Robert Owen. At first the American press accorded him a favorable reception. As a successful industrialist, Owen enjoyed credibility; his goal of reaping the advantages of the industrial revolution without its accompanying misery was generally shared. When Owen arrived in the United States in 1824, he met not only starry-eyed reformers but President Monroe, ex-presidents Jefferson and Madison,

20. J.F.C. Harrison, *Quest for the New Moral World* (New York, 1969), 84, 92–102.

DeWitt Clinton, Justice Joseph Story, New York and Philadelphia society, and the chiefs of the Chickasaw and Choctaw. In February 1825, he delivered, by special permission, two public lectures in the U.S. Capitol, both attended by president-elect Adams. After moving into the White House, Adams put on display there a six-foot-square architectural model of Owen's ideal community—also displaying by implication his own sympathies for social engineering.[21] Only after Owen publicly confessed his disbelief in the scriptures and denounced the institution of marriage did he put himself beyond the pale of acceptable American opinion.

Robert Owen's community of New Harmony, Indiana, begun in 1825, lasted only two years. In it not only work but also recreation and meditation were communal and regimented. "I am come to this country," Owen announced upon his arrival, "to introduce an entire new system of society; to change it from an ignorant, selfish system to an enlightened social system which shall gradually unite all interests into one and remove all causes for contest between individuals."[22] But Owen and his aides made no attempt to match the training of their prospective members with what a frontier community needed to make itself self-supporting; they ended up with many intellectuals and freeloaders but not enough skilled workers. Owen's community never reconciled his paternalist control with its goals of rational self-determination, and its members never developed much sense of commitment. Owen collectivized cooking, child care, and other domestic work, all still assigned to the women; in practice, the women members experienced his program as an unwelcome imposition. The most viable aspect of New Harmony turned out to be its school, run by the geologist William Maclure, which continued to function and serve as a model into the 1840s. The workingmen's library that Maclure founded still survives in New Harmony, Indiana.[23]

Robert Owen soon returned to Britain, there to attempt other communal utopias, none of which lasted long. In the United States, eighteen other utopian experiments drew in varying degrees upon Owenite principles; the last one, Modern Times, on Long Island, closed in 1863. Owen's talented sons and daughters (the most famous being Robert Dale Owen) remained in the United States, became citizens, and continued into the next generation their father's secular humanitarianism, active in such

21. Donald Pitzer, "The New Moral World of Robert Owen," in *America's Communal Utopias*, ed. Donald Pitzer (Chapel Hill, 1997), 96.
22. Quoted in Mark Holloway, *Heavens on Earth* (London, 1951), 104.
23. Carol Kolmerten, *Women in Utopia* (Bloomington, 1990), 90–101; Arthur Bestor, *Backwoods Utopias* (Philadelphia, 1970), 199–200.

fields as public education, women's rights, and birth control. Owenism provided a welcome alternative ideology to religion for embattled American freethinkers like Abner Kneeland and the feminist Ernestine Rose. Invoking the paternalist side of Owenism, Jefferson Davis's older brother Joseph applied the Welshman's principles of scientific management to slaves on his plantation at Davis Bend, Mississippi, and succeeded admirably in maximizing production.[24] In Britain, where Owen's followers invented the term "socialism" in 1827, his movement became one of the precursors of the Labour Party.

In the 1840s, another form of utopian socialism attracted even more widespread interest in the United States: the Associationism of Albert Brisbane. Brisbane was an American disciple of the French social theorist Charles Fourier. At the beginning of the nineteenth century, Fourier had become disillusioned with the inefficiencies and conflicting interests characteristic of competitive commerce. He believed he had found the solution in collectivism practiced on a small scale: planned communities called "phalanxes," each of exactly 1,620 people, representing all occupations, living on six thousand acres of land. There, work would be fulfilling as well as socially useful. The Frenchman's meticulous plan sought to match jobs with aptitudes—for example, since children like to play in dirt, he reasoned, they should be the trash collectors. A few such communities, once established, would set so compelling an example that they would gradually convert the rest of world. In this pre-Marxian vision, socialism would be achieved without revolution or violence.

Brisbane adapted Fourier's scheme for an American audience, carefully avoiding Owen's mistake of attacking religion and marriage. He presented the phalanx as an example of applied Christianity. It would not be necessary to ban private property; each member of the phalanx would own shares in it and participate in its profits. Brisbane was willing to experiment with phalanxes of only a few hundred people. His program was as much about town planning as about the redistribution of wealth. At present, Brisbane remarked, "there is no adaptation of architecture to our wants and requirements; our houses are as little suited to our physical welfare, as our social laws are to our attractions and passions." To remedy this, Associationist architects planned to bring members of the phalanx together in central buildings, called "phalansteries," with generous communal spaces.[25]

24. Janet Hermann, *Pursuit of a Dream* (New York, 1981), 3–34.
25. Quotation from Albert Brisbane, *The Social Destiny of Man* (Philadelphia, 1840), 78. See also Dolores Hayden, *Seven American Utopias* (Cambridge, Mass., 1981).

In all, some twenty-eight phalanxes were established in the antebellum United States. Unlike Owen's New Harmony, they successfully recruited displaced artisans, though they did not get enough farmers. In 1843, Associationism became an even more widespread popular fad than Adventism, reflecting prevalent working-class discontent during economic hard times. Brisbane and other national publicists for the movement never controlled it; to their dismay phalanxes sprang up spontaneously. Associationism was mainly a northern phenomenon, although two Louisiana utopians conceived of gradual emancipation with the freedpeople living in Fourierist communities—plans of course never implemented. But grassroots enthusiasm proved no substitute for investment capital and careful planning. Like New Harmony, the phalanxes assembled too hastily. They overpromised quick material results, could not sustain a common identity, and suffered from internal schisms. None endured more than a dozen years. Their members, never very isolated from the American mainstream, readily reentered it as prosperity returned and the job market improved.[26]

The intellectual influence of Fourier and Brisbane outlasted the cooperative communities that invoked their name. Though now forgotten, Fourierism, like Owenism, exerted an effect upon American social thinkers throughout the nineteenth century. Horace Greeley, the political journalist and founder of the planned community of Greeley, Colorado, the feminist Elizabeth Cady Stanton, the city planner Frederick Law Olmsted, who designed Central Park, and the utopian novelist Edward Bellamy illustrate the diversity of Associationism's impact. The cooperative movement, initiated by Brisbane, remains another part of his legacy, one still visible.[27]

The interest aroused by communitarian social experiments in the United States on the eve of the industrial revolution revealed something about the mood and temper of the American public, its willingness to entertain a broad range of social and economic possibilities. The seeming boundlessness of America's prospects and the open-mindedness of its people encouraged the formation of big plans of all kinds, whether for an integrated transportation network, African colonization, utopian communities, or the Second Coming of Christ. Yet the very illimitability and openness of the society that accorded such plans a hearing made it difficult in the last analysis to impose them—as Albert Gallatin, John Quincy Adams, and Henry Clay learned, as well as Robert Owen. "The tendency of American

26. See Carl Guarneri, *The Utopian Alternative: Fourierism in Nineteenth-Century America* (Ithaca, N.Y., 1991), esp. 176–77, 264.
27. Carl Guarneri, "Brook Farm and the Fourierist Phalanxes," in Pitzer, *America's Communal Utopias*, 174.

conditions, as well as the inclination of its people, was for diffusion rather than discipline, toward self-determination and away from supervision, however benign," the historian Daniel Feller has observed.[28]

Utopian communities founded for religious motives tended to last longer than secular ones. Like the secular communities, they often addressed issues of particular concern to women. One movement followed a former Quaker named Ann Lee, a charismatic visionary who came to America from England in 1774. Mother Ann's followers worshipped her as a second incarnation of Christ; as Jesus had been the Son of God, Ann was the Daughter. God the Father they reinterpreted as both Father and Mother. Members called themselves "the United Society of Believers in Christ's Second Appearing" but are better known as the Shakers, from a famous ritual dance they performed. In keeping with their theology of gender equality and androgyny, the Shakers adopted a kind of ascetic feminism and accorded leadership positions to women equally with men.[29] Like many millennial sectarians, the Shakers rejected mainstream culture and isolated themselves from "the world." They practiced celibacy to purge themselves from sin in preparation for the end of the world and relied on converts to propagate their sect. (They did, however, adopt orphans and rear them in their communities.)

The Shakers would attend camp meetings organized by more conventional evangelicals and seize the opportunity to spread their own gospel among rural Christians. Mother Ann had been illiterate, but by 1823 her followers and successors had embraced the written word with formal organization and theology, their lives governed by 125 "Millennial Laws." In that year there were something over four thousand Believers scattered among nineteen villages stretching from Maine to western Kentucky.[30] Although Shaker villages were not without their rivalries and strifes, overall their cohesion and commitment contrast markedly with the bickering and evanescence of the Owenite communes. More than twenty thousand Americans have been Shakers at one time or another, some of whom found a spiritual and material security that seemed a "heaven on earth."[31]

While taking economic self-sufficiency as their goal, in practice the Shakers marketed seeds, crops, and handicrafts to buy things they could

28. Feller, *Jacksonian Promise*, 83.
29. See J.F.C. Harrison, *The Second Coming* (New Brunswick, N.J., 1979), 164–76; Suzanne Thurman, *"O Sisters Ain't You Happy?" Gender, Family and Community Among the Shakers* (Syracuse, N.Y., 2002).
30. Stephen Stein, *The Shaker Experience in America* (New Haven, 1992), 87–89, 114.
31. Priscilla Brewer, *Shaker Communities, Shaker Lives* (Hanover, N.H., 1986), 203.

not produce themselves. Through hard work and simple living, Shaker villages accumulated considerable property, much as medieval monastic communities did. The Believers consistently welcomed new technology and employed it, for example, in their mills. The buildings and furniture they made have endured as masterpieces of American folk art.

Central to Shaker doctrine and life was the notion of "gift" — a divinely given talent or revelatory insight. The song "Simple Gifts," probably composed by the Shaker Joseph Brackett in 1848 and sung in the quick tempo of Shaker dances, was borrowed by Aaron Copland in the twentieth century for his *Appalachian Spring* suite.

> 'Tis the gift to be simple, 'tis the gift to be free,
> 'Tis the gift to come down where we ought to be;
> And when we find ourselves in the place just right,
> 'Twill be in the valley of love and delight.
> When true simplicity is gain'd,
> To bow and to bend we shan't be asham'd
> To turn, turn, will be our delight,
> Till by turning, turning we come round right.[32]

Few of the orphans adopted by the Shakers chose to remain in the community upon adulthood, and after the Civil War the society commenced a long, slow decline in numbers. The movement had always attracted more female than male members; by 1900, three-quarters of the surviving Shakers were women. At the beginning of the twenty-first century a handful of practicing Shakers still inhabited their one remaining village of Sabbathday Lake, Maine, their culture if not their theology revered by the American society that their predecessors sought to escape.

Similar to the Shakers in some ways were several pietistic religious communities that migrated from Germany in the eighteenth and nineteenth centuries. In 1804, George Rapp arrived in America with six hundred followers who had separated from the established Lutheran Church of Württemberg during the German counterpart to the Great Awakening in America. Peasants and artisans well suited to the pioneer life, thirty miles north of Pittsburgh they set up a community called Harmony. There they practiced celibacy, farmed their property in common, and enjoyed the music of their German band, while their premillennialist leader tried to calculate the date of the Second Coming of Christ with reference to biblical prophecies. He expected it soon. In 1814, Rapp led his people into Indiana, where, on the banks of the Wabash River, they built another com-

---

32. Stein, *Shaker Experience*, 190–91.

munity also called Harmony. Rapp sold the land and improvements at this New Harmony to Robert Owen in 1824 and went back to Pennsylvania, where his faithful followers built still another village, this time named Economy. Rapp was much surprised to die in 1847 without having led his people into the millennial kingdom. The Rappites continued to prosper greatly in financial terms, making donations to other millennial communities, including the Shakers and Mormons, and pioneering the Pennsylvania petroleum industry. But, having ceased to recruit new members, their celibate community died out at the end of the nineteenth century.[33]

The experience of several other communitarian colonies of German pietists in America roughly paralleled that of the Rappites. One group that has survived to the present, however, is the Amana Society, or the Community of the True Inspiration. Drawn from much the same social base as other German pietists, the Inspirationists did not have a tradition of authoritarian leadership, although they accepted the teachings of *Werkzeuge*, who were men and women inspired by the Holy Spirit. Beginning in 1843, about seven hundred Inspirationists migrated from Hesse to western New York state, where they established a colony called Ebenezer. In the 1850s, as their numbers swelled with additional immigrants, they found more room by moving to southeastern Iowa. There they live to this day in seven villages known collectively as the Amana Colonies (the name Amana comes from the Song of Solomon). Not celibate as the Shakers and Rappites were, the Inspirationists obeyed until 1932 the law of "all things in common," following the example of the primitive Christian church recorded in the New Testament (Acts 2:44 and 4:32). Today the Amanans continue the practice of their religion with very little change. Their temporal affairs prosper through a balanced combination of agriculture, tourism, and the manufacture of Amana refrigerators.[34]

Most of the many communities of German pietists who came to the young American republic practiced versions of Lutheranism and did not hold their property in common. They thus contributed to the enormous growth of Lutheranism in many varieties throughout the United States but especially in the Midwest. One group of six hundred, fleeing from Saxony to St. Louis in 1838, became the origin of what is now a large and separate denomination. Their migration occurred under the leadership of Martin Stephan of Dresden, a charismatic preacher and critic of the established

33. Karl Arndt, "George Rapp's Harmony Society," in Pitzer, *America's Communal Utopias*, 57–87.

34. Jonathan Andelson, "The Community of True Inspiration from Germany to the Amana Colonies," ibid., 181–203.

Lutheran Church in Saxony. Stephan had to be deposed shortly after arrival in America for misappropriations of both money and women; his dismayed community might well have returned to Germany if there had been any funds left to pay their way. Instead they found a new pastor, C.F.W. Walther, under whose forceful leadership the Lutheran Church–Missouri Synod was organized in 1847. Religious services remained in German until the First World War. Walther's durable dedication to vested authority, the historic creeds of Lutheranism, and the verbal inerrancy of the Bible gave Missouri Synod Lutheranism a distinctive character it has never lost.[35]

Catholic monasticism, the oldest form of religious communal life, also appeared in a still predominantly Protestant America. The parallels with other communitarian movements were considerable, including celibacy, self-discipline, and the rejection of worldly selfishness for alternative lifestyles. In Europe, the early nineteenth century marked a low point in Catholic monasticism, for the Henrician Reformation in England and the Napoleonic era on the Continent had suppressed hundreds of religious houses. Antebellum America represented an opportunity for the orders to begin a comeback. By 1830, eleven Roman Catholic communities functioned in the United States, with women's orders more prominent than men's. As they had in founding Protestant communes, German immigrants played a prominent role in American Catholic monasticism, particularly among the Benedictines. However, one order of nuns was founded by a noteworthy American-born woman, Elizabeth Seton, the first citizen of the republic to be canonized as a saint. Well educated, a widow with five children, and a convert from High Church Episcopalianism, Seton had honed her leadership skills in a Protestant benevolent association whose mission she understood at first hand, the Society for the Relief of Poor Widows with Small Children. Mother Seton won the approval of Archbishop John Carroll for the Sisters of Charity in 1812 and ran their convent in Emmitsburg, Maryland, until her death in 1821. Fund-raising, managing a legal corporation, running a school, and combining charity with remunerative work, the sisters nurtured Catholic female talents in somewhat the same way that voluntary associations did among Protestants. The life of Mother Seton's male counterpart, Isaac Hecker, illustrated the parallel between utopian communities and Catholic religious orders. A former participant in the Brook Farm community during the period in 1843 when it was adopting Fourierist principles, Hecker converted to Catholicism in 1844, retained his concern with the nurture of community

---

35. See Mary Todd, *Authority Vested: Identity and Change in the Lutheran Church–Missouri Synod* (Grand Rapids, Mich., 2000).

in American society, and founded in 1858 the Paulist Fathers, the first American-based order of priests.[36]

Both pre- and postmillennial Christians have typically been interested in the restoration of the Jews to the Holy Land, since that is one of the events prophesied as heralding the Second Coming.[37] One of the early Jewish Zionists, Mordecai Manuel Noah, took advantage of sympathy among American Christians in his call for Jews from all over the world to come establish a community in western New York state. He issued his "proclamation to the Jews" in September 1825 at a ceremony in St. Paul's Episcopal Church, Buffalo. Noah hoped to create a Zionist haven named Ararat on Grand Island in the Niagara River, where Jews might study agriculture and plan the recovery of Palestine from the Ottoman Empire. European Jewish opinion was not prepared to entertain his plan, however. Noah resumed his career as newspaper editor and playwright, but he never abandoned his faith in the restoration of the Chosen People to their promised land.[38] Several Jewish agricultural colonies were actually established in the United States prior to the massive Jewish immigration from the tsarist lands in the 1880s. In 1846 Isaac Mayer Wise came from Bohemia to the United States, where he developed in the ensuing years not only the Reform Movement of Judaism but also a kind of Enlightenment millennialism, envisioning roles for both the Jews of the Diaspora and a democratic America in hastening a messianic age to benefit all humanity.

Meanwhile, a down-and-out former carpenter named Robert Matthews, impressed by Mordecai Noah's Zionism, had decided that he himself must be Jewish too and adopted the role of Prophet Matthias, Spirit of Truth. In the 1830s, he attracted a band of followers (rich and poor, white and black, but all gentiles) with a message featuring millenarianism, female subordination, and professed affinity with the Jews. The commune disintegrated when its leader, after several sensational trials (he won acquittal on a murder charge), went to jail for beating his daughter. The prophet's bizarre career may have inspired Herman Melville to write *The Confidence-Man*.[39]

36. On Seton, see Ann Boylan, *The Origins of Women's Activism* (Chapel Hill, 2002), 101–9, 118–24; Kathleen D. McCarthy, *American Creed: Philanthropy and the Rise of Civil Society* (Chicago, 2003), 68–74. For Hecker, see *Hecker Studies*, ed. John Farina (New York, 1983).

37. See Sandeen, *Roots of Fundamentalism*, 9–13.

38. "Ararat Proclamation and Speech" (1825); "Discourse on the Restoration of the Jews" (1844), "Address to Aid in the Erection of the Temple at Jerusalem" (1849), in *Selected Writings of Mordecai Noah*, ed. Michael Schuldiner and Daniel Kleinfeld (Westport, Conn., 1999), 105–59.

39. See Paul Johnson and Sean Wilentz, *The Kingdom of Matthias* (New York, 1994).

One of the most radical and yet surprisingly successful of utopias in antebellum America was the "Perfectionist" community established by John Humphrey Noyes in the 1840s. Noyes's career illustrates the smooth continuum between mainstream evangelical reform and utopianism. The son of a U.S. congressman, converted by Charles Finney in 1831, young Noyes felt called to the ministry and trained at Andover Theological Seminary and Yale. He elaborated Finney's perfectionist doctrine and claimed a state of "perfection" for himself, provoking revocation of his preaching license in 1834. Now on his own theologically, Noyes developed a distinctive theory of eschatology. Christ's Second Coming had occurred already, he decided, back in A.D. 70, during the lifetime of some of the original disciples. The overdue Kingdom of God could be established if only a few committed Christians with a "perfected" outlook would set the right example. Noyes studied the Owenites, the Associationists, and the Shakers to learn from their experiments. By 1841, he had collected a small group of his own followers in Putney, Vermont. When William Miller came preaching his own version of the millennium, Noyes denounced this rival more emphatically than did the mainstream clergy.[40]

Noyes's Perfectionists shared everything: not only their property, which they held in common, but also their spouses. Noyes candidly explained it all in his book, *Bible Communism* (1848). According to their practice of "complex marriage," all the men in the Perfectionist community considered themselves husbands to all the women, and each woman the wife of every man. After Noyes was indicted by the state of Vermont for adultery and fornication, he fled to Oneida, New York, followed by thirty-one adults and fourteen children. There for many years the authorities left them alone; antebellum New York tolerated diversity. Noyes's community soon grew to more than two hundred adults, some of whom contributed substantial property. The Perfectionists required consent of their whole community before any couple engaged in sexual relations, and community consent had to be given again before the conception of children. Noyes insisted on "intelligent, voluntary control over the propagative function."[41] (His publications were among the first public discussions of methods of birth control; another was *Moral Physiology* [1832] by Robert Dale Owen, a son of Robert Owen.) Perfectionists employed as their method of contraception *coitus reservatus*, which Noyes called "male

---

40. Michael Barkun, "John Humphrey Noyes and the Rise of Millerism," in Numbers and Butler, *The Disappointed*, 153–72.

41. Quoted in Lawrence Foster, *Religion and Sexuality: Three American Communal Experiments of the Nineteenth Century* (New York, 1981), 94.

continence." Experienced older women initiated young men into the practice. As a means of birth control, it evidently worked. "During the community's first twenty-one years," writes a scholar who has studied Oneida thoroughly, "an average of only about one accidental pregnancy a year" occurred among its two hundred sexually active members.[42] It was the ultimate application of the Victorian virtue of self-control.

Economically Oneida flourished, at first by manufacturing animal traps. The Perfectionists shared their labors and rotated the most unpleasant tasks. The women took to cutting their hair neck-length (short by the standards of the age) and wearing "bloomer garments" (loose trousers under skirts, invented by Amelia Bloomer to allow more freedom of movement than the current fashions). As one of the Perfectionist women expressed it, "We believed we were living under a system which the whole world would sooner or later adopt."[43] But in 1879, responding to both outside pressure and internal dissension, John Humphrey Noyes recommended an end to "complex marriage." A year later the experiment in economic socialism ended too with the formation of Oneida Community, Ltd., a joint-stock company whose shares were parceled out among the former Bible communists. Oneida silverware remains a highly esteemed product.

Most antebellum utopian communities were not fleeing the industrial revolution. Some (like Owenites and Associationists) explicitly endorsed it, while others (like Shakers and Perfectionists) seized the chance to make whatever use of it they could. The only communities that really did reject industrialization were two German Mennonite sects: the Amish, who had settled in Pennsylvania during colonial times, and the Dakota Hutterites, who came in the 1870s.[44] In the eyes of many Americans the mill town of Lowell constituted an industrial utopian community of sorts: a planned and supervised experiment, aspiring to a model role. Still, the most common and popular utopia of all was simply a family farm. There the average white American could enjoy the dignity of a freehold, exchange help with neighbors during stressful seasons, entertain the expectation of a good harvest, and hope to build a competence that would see a couple through old age with something to pass on to their children. By comparison with what was available in Europe, such a place indeed seemed God's promised land. The openness of the American prospect allowed many groups to try

42. Spencer Klaw, *Without Sin: The Life and Death of the Oneida Community* (New York, 1993), 177.
43. Pierrepont Noyes, *My Father's House* (New York, 1937), 17.
44. The Amanans are sometimes confused with the Amish and the Hutterites.

their hand at building utopias. But the availability of land for individual cultivators, whether in fact or in popular imagination, undercut the appeal of the more collectivist social planners.

IV

Contemporaries viewed not only utopian communities but all America as an experimental society, an example to the world of popular rule. The United States had the widest suffrage of any nation at that time, and the American expectation of social equality among white men made its example still more emphatically democratic. Even people who would never have accepted the idea that America was God's favorite nation or destined to play a role in Christ's Second Coming thought their country performed a special mission as exemplar of freedom. American "exceptionalism," the term often applied to this role, constituted a secularized version of America's millennial destiny. Both the religious and the secular versions of American exceptionalism seemed to imply that America was exempt from the kind of history that other nations experienced and had, like ancient Israel, a destiny all its own. "Exceptionalism" is an unfortunate term, however, since if America were thoroughly exceptional, its experience would be irrelevant to other countries. In fact, even during the nineteenth century, when the United States might seem most isolated from the rest of the world, she was part of a global community of peoples who observed each other closely. America showed them how popular sovereignty worked, as Britain showed how the industrial revolution worked.

Americans put on display their self-image as an example to the world when they hosted the sixty-seven-year-old Marquis de Lafayette on his triumphal visit to the United States in 1824-25. At the invitation of President Monroe, the Frenchman who had served as a major general in the Continental Army toured the country, feted everywhere amid mass expressions of national gratitude. A consistently courageous advocate of constitutionalism and human rights against tyrannies of both left and right, Lafayette had sent Washington the key to the Bastille to display at Mount Vernon. All contemporaries on both sides of the Atlantic saw him as an emissary of liberal values between New and Old Worlds; Americans regarded him as an agent of their international mission. The president had invited Lafayette in order to affirm his Monroe Doctrine's defiance of the Holy Alliance and to celebrate his Era of Good Feelings. The event succeeded beyond his dreams.

Eighty thousand people turned out to welcome Lafayette when his ship landed in New York City on August 16, 1824. Congress voted him $200,000 and twenty-three thousand acres of public land where now stands Tallahassee, Florida; Samuel F. B. Morse painted his portrait. When the visitor laid the cornerstone of Bunker Hill Monument in Boston before forty thousand onlookers, Daniel Webster gave one of his great orations. For thirteen months Lafayette traveled about the United States by stagecoach and steamboat, resolutely hewing to his schedule despite swollen rivers and typically poor roads; solicitous, however, of sabbatarian scruples among his hosts, the Frenchman did not travel on Sundays. His boat ran aground in the Ohio River and sank, carrying all his effects and six hundred unanswered letters to the muddy bottom.[45]

The occasion of Lafayette's Second Coming evoked rhetoric usually reserved for that of Christ. It had been forty years since the Frenchman last set foot on American soil; now he seemed "like one arisen from the dead." "Benefactor of the world" and "Redeemer of posterities," he was termed; "he shed his blood for all mankind!" Speakers repeatedly declared that the real significance of Lafayette's visit lay in what it showed Americans about themselves and in the opportunity it presented to demonstrate their national virtues to a European audience. "Might the Potentates of Europe but behold this Republican spectacle in America!" called out one welcomer.[46] On the occasion of his address to a joint session of Congress, Lafayette offered this toast to the Union: "One day it will save the world."[47] Inspired by his example, a few Americans went off to join the Greeks in their revolution against the Ottoman Empire.

Americans were by no means alone in thinking of their country as an example from which others could learn. Foreign observers also often viewed the United States as an indicator of future developments in their own countries. The German philosopher Hegel called America "the land of the future" and predicted that "in the time to come, the center of world-historical importance will be revealed there."[48] Such an attitude characterized the most famous of all European commentators on America, Lafayette's fellow countryman and fellow nobleman Alexis de Tocqueville. Tocqueville came to the United States in 1831 at the age of twenty-five with his young friend Gustave de Beaumont. The liberal French monarchy of Louis Philippe, interested in reform, had authorized the two to study

45. Anne Loveland, "Lafayette's Farewell Tour," in Stanley Idzerda et al., *Lafayette, Hero of Two Worlds* (New York, 1989), 63–90.
46. Quotations from the account of Lafayette's visit in Fred Somkin, *Unquiet Eagle* (Ithaca, N.Y., 1967), 131–74.
47. Quoted in Harlow Unger, *Lafayette* (New York, 2002), 357.
48. G.W.F. Hegel, *Introduction to the Philosophy of History*, trans. Leo Rauch (Indianapolis, 1988), 90. Hegel died in 1831; this work was first published posthumously in 1840.

American prisons and report back on innovations in penology. Tocqueville secured useful letters of introduction from Lafayette, although the two men were not close and their temperaments differed significantly. Where Lafayette endorsed the American example with the enthusiasm of a partisan, Tocqueville regarded it with the detachment of a born social theorist. He spent less than ten months traveling about the United States and Canada with Beaumont before their government recalled them, yet he returned with a multitude of lessons for the French audience of his generation as well as impressions that have intrigued analysts of American society ever since. "In America I saw more than America," Tocqueville explained; "I sought there the image of democracy itself, with its inclinations, its character, its prejudices, and its passions, in order to learn what we [in France] have to fear or to hope from its progress."[49] After he and Beaumont had written up their required report on American prison experiments, Tocqueville turned his attention to an examination of the general subject of democracy as America revealed it. The volumes entitled *De la démocratie en Amérique* appeared in Paris in 1835 and 1840, with translations published in the United States almost immediately.

What Tocqueville meant by "democracy" was not simply political ("one man, one vote") but broadly social: "equality of condition." He considered increasing equality—of dignity, influence, wealth, and political power— an irrepressible tendency in the modern world. In Tocqueville's own moral system, the highest value was neither democracy nor equality but liberty. Just as aristocratic regimes had sometimes interfered with liberty, he worried that democracies might do so too, in their own ways. He called attention to the danger of "the tyranny of the majority," by which he meant not only overt repression but also conformity of opinion. Accordingly, he took special interest in how liberty of thought and action could be preserved within a democratic order. He hoped American institutions of local government might provide one means of achieving this. A lawyer and magistrate who regarded respect for the law as a bulwark of liberty, he rejoiced in the unique power of the judiciary in the United States and called the legal profession "the American aristocracy." The prevalence and freedom of the printed media impressed him; "there is scarcely a hamlet that has not its newspaper," he marveled. He praised the post roads, which he saw kept the citizenry informed and helped consolidate the Union.[50]

49. Alexis de Tocqueville, *Democracy in America*, ed. Phillips Bradley, trans. Henry Reeve and Francis Bowen (New York, 1945), I, 14.
50. Ibid., 3, 258, 278, 186, 404–5.

Above all, Tocqueville recognized the crucial importance of America's numerous and diverse voluntary associations. They mediated between the individual and mass society; they provided opportunities for self-improvement and civic involvement; they could influence public opinion and public policy. The most prominent voluntary associations, of course, were the churches. This struck Tocqueville forcibly, as it usually did foreign visitors, for it contrasted with the European tradition of church establishment. As a consequence European religions generally allied with conservatism and social privilege. By contrast, American churches manifested American freedom. "The Americans combine the notions of Christianity and of liberty so intimately in their minds," he noted, "that it is impossible to make them conceive the one without the other."[51] As a Catholic liberal, Tocqueville welcomed the American religious situation and used it to argue that European liberals should not assume religion their adversary.

Tocqueville was very quick to generalize from his experiences, and for all his insight, his interpretations have their limitations. In praising America's strong traditions of local self-government, he seemed not to notice how often local democracy tyrannized individuals. An aristocrat himself, he saw more of elite and middle-class life than of the working classes. His impression that wealth exerted minimal influence in American politics probably derived from uncritical acceptance of the complaints of wealthy informants. Though he never freed himself from his European perspective, Tocqueville shared the belief of most Americans that the growth of the Great Democracy was "a providential event," in which he detected "the hand of God."[52] Unlike those of many other foreign commentators, his writings were well received in the United States—particularly by the critics of President Jackson, who could read with grim satisfaction Tocqueville's characterization of him as "a man of violent temper and very moderate talents."[53]

Tocqueville's traveling companion Beaumont also wrote a book upon returning to France: a novel called *Marie*, a searing indictment of American racism, focused not on the South but on the North. Though it sold well in France, sadly the book had no impact in the United States, probably because it dealt with the sensitive subject of interracial marriage; it was not even translated into English until 1958.[54]

51. Ibid., 306.
52. Ibid., 398. Tocqueville admired the Puritan millennial historian Cotton Mather (ibid., II, 345–48).
53. Ibid., I, 289.
54. Gustave de Beaumont, *Marie*, trans. Barbara Chapman (Stanford, 1958); see also Louis Masur, *1831* (New York, 2001), 40–46.

Several of the most interesting and widely read foreign observers of the United States were women, a circumstance all the more remarkable in view of the fact that single women travelers were so unusual that few inns were set up to accommodate them. Harriet Martineau, an earnest, inquiring Englishwoman mocked for her intellectuality and the ear trumpet that mitigated her deafness, has been called "the first woman sociologist." She spent almost two years in the United States in 1834–36, longer than Tocqueville, and saw more of the country and a greater variety of its people. Her social background in the provincial bourgeoisie was less alien to America than Tocqueville's noble birth. "Miss Martineau," as she was always called, had an eye for picturesque detail. Her three-volume work *Society in America* (1837), supplemented with the anecdotal *Retrospect of Western Travel* (1838), contains more empirical data than Tocqueville provided, along with no less interest in generalizations. She paid more attention than he did to such important topics as transportation and education, as well as to the groups she called "sufferers," such as the insane, the handicapped, and the poor.[55] Like Tocqueville, however, she wrote primarily for an audience in her home country and used America as an example instructive to them. A "radical" as that term was then used in England and one of the early feminists, Martineau strongly sympathized with America's avowed principles of liberty and equality. Where democracy to Tocqueville was a practical inevitability, to her it was a moral imperative. She criticized the United States for not living up to its ideals, in particular in its oppression of black people and in the "political nonexistence" of women.[56] She therefore rendered a mixed verdict in the end: Americans "have realized many things for which the rest of the world is still struggling," yet "the civilization and the morals of the Americans fall far below their own principles."[57]

Harriet Martineau typified a class of reformist foreign visitors who tried to help America improve, not only for its own sake but also because it could then provide a better model for their home countries. A more extreme example of the type was the Scotswoman Frances Wright. Tall, striking, and self-confident, Wright first visited the United States in 1818 at the age of twenty-three. Out of her travels came a book entitled *Views of Society and Manners in America* (1820), an idealized portrayal of the country as a radical's utopia. The work brought her to the attention of

55. Harriet Martineau, *Society in America* (London, 1837), III, 179–205.
56. Ibid., I, 193–207.
57. Ibid., III, 299–300.

Lafayette, and in 1821 she journeyed to France to meet him. Young enough to be his granddaughter, Fanny quickly formed an emotionally intense relationship with the widowed elder statesman; rumor had her his mistress.[58] When Lafayette left for America in 1824, Wright followed him. But when the marquis returned to France, she stayed in the United States with the intention of making it an even better model society. Wright had become involved in antislavery and in Robert Owen's communal experimentation in Indiana. She hit upon a plan to start an Owenite commune in the South, staffing it with slaves. The profits it earned would pay off the masters, the freedpeople would be learning skills, and eventually they could go off to establish other Owenite communities. Lafayette broached the subject to Jefferson, Madison, and Jackson. Madison and Jackson warned that it all depended on southern "collaboration"; Jefferson declined to participate.[59]

In 1825, Wright published a pamphlet describing her *Plan for the Gradual Abolition of Slavery in the United States without Danger of Loss to the Citizens of the South,* hoping to elicit federal aid and private contributions. With her own money she purchased a few second-rate acres at Nashoba, Tennessee. Leaving nine adult slaves and some children there under the direction of an untrained overseer, she departed for Britain to fund-raise. In 1827, Wright returned to Nashoba, bringing not money but a friend named Frances Trollope. The wife of an ineffectual country gentleman, Trollope had fallen for Fanny Wright's exaggerated promises of an idyllic plantation life. Upon arrival, "one glance sufficed to convince me that every idea I had formed of the place was as far as possible from the truth," Trollope later wrote. "Desolation was the only feeling" inspired by Nashoba.[60] Wright soon torpedoed whatever chance of success her undercapitalized experiment might have had by endorsing Owenite principles of free love, to which she added an interracial dimension. She left Tennessee for good in 1828; Nashoba's slaves eventually obtained their freedom in Haiti.

Forgiving her friend Wright for having been blinded by idealism, Frances Trollope headed for Cincinnati to meet her husband. She had heard much of America's foremost inland city, "its beauty, wealth, and unequaled prosperity," but found "the flatness of reality" there in 1828 disappointing. She conceived an ambitious plan to make Cincinnati a more

---

58. For a sensitive analysis of their relationship, see Celia Eckhardt, *Fanny Wright: Rebel in America* (Cambridge, Mass., 1984), 71–77.

59. Lloyd Kramer, *Lafayette in Two Worlds* (Chapel Hill, 1996), 160–63.

60. Frances Trollope, *Domestic Manners of the Americans,* ed. Donald Smalley (New York, 1949), 27.

lively, cosmopolitan city by constructing a building something like a modern shopping mall plus cultural center and ballroom, which she called a "Bazaar." Like many another entrepreneur in America, Frances Trollope found difficulty raising enough capital to realize her grandiose ambition, and her enterprise ended in bankruptcy. But the resourceful Mrs. Trollope recovered her family's fortunes by writing a successful account of her travels: *Domestic Manners of the Americans* (1832). Unlike Martineau and Wright, Trollope felt no sympathy for democracy or equality, and unlike Tocqueville, she wanted Europe to stay clear of them. Her vividly written story sold well in Britain, where it was cited by opponents of Parliamentary Reform, infuriated Americans, and launched the fifty-three-year-old mother of five into a career that included 113 other books—a torrent of print that would be continued by her still more famous novelist son Anthony.

It is easy to put down Frances Trollope as a Tory embittered by her American business failure. But her observations on American manners, confirmed by many other observers foreign and domestic, actually provide a sharply drawn picture of daily life in the young republic. Most observers at the time agreed with her in finding Americans obsessively preoccupied with earning a living and relatively uninterested in leisure activities. Not only Tories but reformers like Martineau and Charles Dickens angered their hosts by complaining of the overwhelmingly commercial tone of American life, the worship of the "almighty dollar."[61] Americans pursued success so avidly they seldom paused to smell the flowers. A kind of raw egotism, unsoftened by sociability, expressed itself in boastful men, demanding women, and loud children. The amiable arts of conversation and cooking were not well cultivated, foreigners complained; Tocqueville found American cuisine "the infancy of the art" and declared one New York dinner he attended "complete barbarism."[62] Despite their relatively broad distribution of prosperity, Americans seemed strangely restless; visitors interpreted the popularity of the rocking chair as one symptom of this restlessness. Another symptom, even more emphatically deplored, was the habit, widespread among males, of chewing tobacco and spitting on the floor. Women found their long dresses caught the spittle, which encouraged them to avoid male company at social events. Chewing tobacco thus reinforced the tendency toward social segregation

---

61. Dickens's term: Charles Dickens, *American Notes* (1842; Boston, 1867), 211.
62. Tocqueville to Abbé Lesueur, May 28, 1831, quoted in George Pierson, *Tocqueville and Beaumont in America* (New York, 1938), 90.

of the sexes, with each gender talking among themselves about their occupations: the men, business and politics; the women, homemaking and
children.[63]

Hypersensitive to foreign opinion, the American public resented any
criticism from outsiders, especially women. Even the sympathetic Harriet
Martineau found enough faults to render her unpopular in the States.
Years later, Mark Twain would declare that "candid Mrs. Trollope" deserved American gratitude for her forthrightness. "She knew her subject
well, and she set it forth fairly and squarely." But his observation, made in
Life on the Mississippi, was suppressed.[64]

An Anglican, Frances Trollope criticized aspects of American religion
as well as manners. She disliked the proliferation of religious sects and
missed "the advantages of an established church as a sort of headquarters
for quiet, unpresuming Christians, who are content to serve faithfully,
without insisting upon having each a little separate banner." After witnessing a religious revival in Cincinnati, she commented that "I think the
coarsest comedy ever written would be a less detestable exhibition for the
eyes of youth and innocence."[65]

Mrs. Trollope concurred with most other foreign visitors, whatever their
political or religious views, in deploring American slavery and the
hypocrisy that sanctioned it in a land dedicated to freedom. One Englishwoman whose repugnance for slavery affected her life profoundly was
the beautiful stage star Fanny Kemble. She married an American named
Pierce Butler without realizing that the source of his fortune was a Georgia cotton and rice plantation. Upon her visit to his estate in 1838, what
she found distressed her deeply. When she carried slaves' complaints to
their master, he assured her that it was "impossible to believe a single word
any of these people said." But she believed the women who told her they
had been impregnated by a former overseer. (The overseer's wife believed
them too: She had them flogged.) Kemble's revulsion against the slave system and her condemnation of Butler's part in it led to the couple's estrangement and eventual divorce, in which her husband, as was customary
at the time, gained custody of their two daughters. Fanny Kemble's frank,
unsparing journals of plantation life, published in 1863 in an effort to

63. Harriet Martineau, *Retrospect of Western Travel*, ed. Daniel Feller (London, 2000), 24;
    Trollope, *Domestic Manners*, 16, 18, 58, 421–23.
64. Marcus Cunliffe, "Frances Trollope," in *Abroad in America*, ed. Marc Pachter (Read-
    ing, Mass., 1976), 40.
65. Trollope, *Domestic Manners*, 108, 81.

influence British public opinion against the Confederacy, remain a valuable antidote to conventional accounts of planter paternalism.[66]

American opposition to slavery owed a good deal to encouragement from overseas. Lafayette on his grand tour sometimes used his American platforms to reproach his hosts for their oppression of blacks; in several southern cities the authorities accordingly forbade blacks to attend the rallies in his honor.[67] Tocqueville treated the oppression of the nonwhite races as the worst example of the tyranny of the majority. Both he and Lafayette actively opposed slavery in the French overseas empire. The relationship between the British and American antislavery movements was even closer because of their common language, Protestantism, and (often) millennial hopes. The example of the Englishman William Wilberforce, the earnest evangelical Anglican who persuaded Parliament to make the Atlantic slave trade illegal and then went on to attack slavery itself, inspired reformers on both sides of the ocean. Harriet Martineau and her Boston friend Maria Weston Chapman fostered the development of a transatlantic network of antislavery women. British evangelicals like George Thompson visited the United States on antislavery speaking tours; American abolitionists like Frederick Douglass toured Britain raising money. When the British Empire abolished slavery in 1833, and the Second French Republic followed suit in 1848, their actions served as encouraging examples to antislavery Americans. This was not the way American exceptionalism was supposed to work; Americans expected to set the example. But on the subject of slavery, white Americans needed foreigners to remind them of the full implications of their country's millennial aspirations.

V

"They draw near to me with their lips while their hearts are far from me, and mine anger is kindling against the inhabitants of the earth to visit them according to their ungodliness." So spoke Jesus Christ, reported by a young man in the "burned-over district" of western New York state who claimed to have seen Him in a vision. Christ's Second Coming, thus ominously proclaimed, would not be long delayed. "Behold and lo I come quickly as it [is] written of me in the cloud clothed in the glory of my Father."[68] For Joseph Smith Jr., of Palmyra on the Erie Canal, this vision led

---

66. *Fanny Kemble's Journals*, ed. Catherine Clinton (Cambridge, Mass., 2000), quotation from 111.

67. Somkin, *Unquiet Eagle*, 170–72.

68. *The Papers of Joseph Smith*, ed. Dean Jessee (Salt Lake City, 1989), I, 7. This record dates from 1832; the vision allegedly occurred in 1820, when Joseph was fifteen years old.

not merely to his personal conversion but to revelations prompting him to found the Church of Jesus Christ of Latter-day Saints. If Jesus was returning "quickly," then the people of the 1830s were already living in the "latter days" of history. Joseph Smith, like William Miller, felt called to preach an urgent premillennial warning. Smith's prophecies, however, contained a far more elaborate and novel message than Miller's calculations.[69]

Joseph Smith's background was perfectly ordinary, even humble. He came from a close-knit farming family who had moved to western New York along with thousands of other Vermonters after the disastrously cold and snowy summer of 1816. To feed eight children and make mortgage payments, they pursued the typical strategy of mixing subsistence farming with selling products on the local market; notwithstanding all their hard work, however, the mortgage on their New York farm was foreclosed in 1825. Pressed for cash, Joseph and his father earned some money by advising farmers on the location of buried treasure. The region contains relics of the prehistoric Mound Builders, and local lore, nourishing local hope, encouraged belief that there would be gold among the artifacts. In his divinations, young Joseph employed a "seerstone," a form of folk magic that had been common among New Englanders for generations. Such peepstones also helped find lost belongings and identify places to dig wells.[70]

An angel named Moroni appeared to Joseph in a series of visions beginning in 1823. The angel delivered similar warnings of the Second Coming but also told the youth that at the Hill Cumorah, not far away, was buried a lost scripture inscribed on golden plates in an unknown language known as Reformed Egyptian. Joseph claimed to unearth the golden plates in 1827 and read them by looking through two seer-stones fastened into a breastplate and named Urim and Thummim, which miraculously translated the inscriptions into English. After a while Smith could use one of his own seer-stones instead of the Urim and Thummim to translate. (Meanwhile, across the sea, Jean-François Champollion was deciphering the Egyptian hieroglyphics on the Rosetta Stone, and the news appeared in the American press.)[71] Over the next two years, Smith dictated the contents of the plates to a scribe while sitting behind a screen to shield the sacred records from profane eyes. When the translation was complete, the

---

69. See Grant Underwood, *The Millenarian World of Early Mormonism* (Urbana, Ill., 1993).

70. See John Brooke, *The Refiner's Fire: The Making of Mormon Cosmology* (Cambridge, Eng., 1994), esp. 152–53.

71. *Niles' Register* 33 (Dec. 1, 1827): 218.

angel took the golden plates along with the Urim and Thummim away to heaven. In 1830, a printer in Rochester, New York, published *The Book of Mormon*, with Joseph Smith, Jr. listed on the title page as author.[72]

The Book of Mormon purports to chronicle the history of an ancient people who once inhabited the American continent. The Nephites, a Hebrew kinship group, made their way to the New World on the eve of the Babylonian captivity. There one branch of the family, the Lamanites, rebelled. As the generations passed, the Nephites and the apostate Lamanites grew into rival nations and fought war after war. The Nephites represented the authentic faith of Israel, had prophets of their own, and were even visited by Jesus Christ. The Book of Mormon is named for the prophet Mormon, who recorded much of it. Eventually the wicked Lamanites prevailed, and Nephite civilization, having lost touch with its religious roots, became extinct. The last of the Nephite prophets, a man named Moroni, buried the records of his people after their final battle with the Lamanites, which took place at the Hill Cumorah. Centuries later, this same Moroni, as a resurrected angel, revealed the plates to Joseph Smith. To the Latter-day Saint, this is scripture, a supplement to the Old and New Testaments. To the unbeliever, it is a fantastic tale invented by the imaginative Joseph Smith.

True or not, the Book of Mormon is a powerful epic written on a grand scale with a host of characters, a narrative of human struggle and conflict, of divine intervention, heroic good and atrocious evil, of prophecy, morality, and law. Its narrative structure is complex. The idiom is that of the King James Version, which most Americans assumed to be appropriate for a divine revelation. Although it contains elements that suggest the environment of New York in the 1820s (for example, episodes paralleling the Masonic/Antimasonic controversy), the dominant themes are biblical, prophetic, and patriarchal, not democratic or optimistic. It tells a tragic story, of a people who, though possessed of the true faith, fail in the end. Yet it does not convey a message of despair; God's will cannot ultimately be frustrated. The Book of Mormon should rank among the great achievements of American literature, but it has never been accorded the status it deserves, since Mormons deny Joseph Smith's authorship, and non-Mormons, dismissing the work as a fraud, have been more likely to ridicule than read it.[73]

72. For Mormon accounts of this, see Richard Bushman, *Joseph Smith and the Beginnings of Mormonism* (Urbana, Ill., 1984), 43–114; Tyrrel Givens, *By the Hand of Mormon* (New York, 2002), 19–42. Urim and Thummim are mentioned in the Bible, e.g., Exodus 28:30.

73. The leading Mormon historian Richard Bushman, if I understand him correctly, credits the prophet's literary skills as well as his divine inspiration; see his *Joseph Smith: Rough Stone Rolling* (New York, 2005), 71–74, 291–92.

In a society where religious doctrine aroused so much interest as western New York in 1830, Smith's purported revelation was of course subjected to elaborate examination, refutation, and satire. Alexander Campbell, leader of the Christian movement, made serious criticisms; no doubt he recognized Smith as a potential rival because both preached the restoration of authentic New Testament religion and the coming millennium.[74] Despite such opposition, by the end of 1830, some two hundred people, including Joseph's own large family, had been baptized Latter-day Saints, commonly nicknamed "Mormons" from their holy book. Their tall, magnetic young leader, styled "Joseph the Prophet, Seer, and Revelator" as well as president of the church, ruled his little community firmly. He combined personal charisma with a talent for organizational innovation. He cast out devils and cured the sick. He continued to receive revelations from God (sometimes using a seer-stone) that amplified what was in the Book of Mormon and provided guidance to the faithful; these the LDS Church has codified as their *Doctrine and Covenants*.

Under the prophet's guidance, in 1831 the Saints moved into the Western Reserve area of northeastern Ohio, to a town called Kirtland. There Sidney Rigdon, a Campbellite millenarian minister influenced by Robert Owen, had converted to Mormonism along with members of his local utopian socialist community. In Kirtland the Mormon church set up a communal experiment of its own under a Law of Consecration, holding property given to it by the members. (Joseph and his wife Emma had lived in Harmony, Pennsylvania, former hometown of the Rappite millennial community.) Converts swelled the ranks of the LDS Church; by 1835 they may have numbered four thousand, half of them in Kirtland.

Joseph Smith was winning followers in the same time and region as Charles Finney, but while Finney's converts tended to be from the middle class, early Mormons usually came from among small farmers and the small-town working class. Although it is tempting to try to fit them into theories about premillennialism appealing to the disinherited of this world, the first generation of Mormons were actually defined more by their culture than by socioeconomic attributes. They tended to be people of New England birth or heritage, carrying the cultural baggage of folk Puritanism (as distinguished from Calvinist theology): communalism, chiliasm, identification with ancient Israel, and the practice of magic. Often they had been involved in other Christian restorationist movements, but

74. Alexander Campbell, *Delusions: An Analysis of the Book of Mormon* (Boston, 1832), with a preface by Joshua Himes, William Miller's future promoter. Another influential early critique was Eber D. Howe, *Mormonism Unvailed* [sic] (Painesville, Ohio, 1834).

no particular denominational background predominated. The prophet and his followers perpetuated traditions of a culture, Richard Bushman explains, "in which the sacred and the profane intermingled and the Saints enjoyed supernatural gifts and powers as the frequent blessing of an interested God."[75] Many people shared this culture, among them some jealous neighbors who tried to steal Smith's golden plates. Seeking to build a new Zion, Mormon missionaries claimed to be "looking for the blood of Israel": They assumed their converts would be descended from one of the tribes of Israel. They meant it literally, but one may also see "the blood of Israel" as a graphic, physical metaphor for the inherited biblical cosmology that predisposed converts to accept the Mormon gospel.

For all its affinities with Yankee folk culture, in years to come Mormonism proved able to reach out to even wider audiences. Like the prophet himself, many converts were young males who had moved repeatedly.[76] Some, including the Smith family members, had been religious "seekers" unattached or only marginally attached to any organized congregation. To rootless people confronting a bewildering diversity of sects and movements on offer, or to those of any background who felt spiritually starved, Mormonism presented itself as an authoritative and authoritarian solution. Within a few years, Mormon missionaries took their gospel successfully across the Atlantic to the working classes of Britain and Scandinavia.

The Mormons did not passively await Christ's millennial kingdom but worked to prepare for it. Their brand of premillennialism was as activist as any postmillennialism, and even more certain of a special millennial role for America. Prophet Joseph dispatched missionaries to western Missouri to convert the Indians as part of his plan to create a Mormon haven there, a New World counterpart to the Old World Jerusalem, where the Saints could gather and await the Second Coming in security. He called this American haven "Zion" and applied the biblical prophecies relating to Zion to it. The Mormons embraced a particularly extreme version of American exceptionalism.

Smith's missionaries to the Indians received a warm welcome from the Delaware tribe, especially when they promised that restoration of Native lands formed part of God's plan along with restoration of the Jews to Palestine. But soon the government's Indian agent expelled the missionaries,

---

75. Bushman, *Joseph Smith and the Beginnings of Mormonism*, 184; see also Brooke, *Refiner's Fire*, and Michael Quinn, *Early Mormonism and the Magic World View* (Salt Lake City, 1987).

76. See Marvin Hill, "The Rise of Mormonism in the Burned-Over District," *New York History* 61 (1980): 411–30, esp. 426–27.

and the prophet decided to rely on white converts to build up Zion in Missouri.[77] In the summer of 1831, he and Rigdon journeyed west and consecrated the site for a Zion temple at what is now Independence, Missouri, returning afterwards to Ohio. For the next several years there would be two centers of Mormon settlement, one in Ohio and one in Missouri.

The Book of Mormon never explicitly asserts that the Native Americans of modern times are descended from the Lamanites; however, readers of the book invariably drew that conclusion, and Joseph Smith himself evidently shared it.[78] The speculation that American Indians constituted some of the Lost Tribes of Israel had been expressed by many writers over the years and was current in Smith's milieu. Native Americans themselves sometimes endorsed the Lost Tribes theory of their origins.[79] Early Mormons accordingly hoped to convert the Indians—or rather, reconvert them back to the authentic faith their ancestors had known in ancient times. When the Lamanites converted en masse, the Book of Mormon promised, they would once again become a "white and delightsome people" as their Hebrew ancestors had been.[80]

In February 1833, the prophet received his famous revelation, "the Word of Wisdom," which came to him after his wife had complained about men smoking and spitting tobacco juice in their house. It enjoined abstinence from "wine or strong drink," from tobacco, and from "hot drinks" (interpreted to mean tea and coffee). Meat and poultry should be eaten only "sparingly." The advice was typical of contemporary dietary reform and temperance, but the revelation couched it in poetic biblical eloquence. Saints who followed the rule were promised "health in their navel and marrow in their bones." They "shall run and not be weary, and shall walk and not faint. And I, the Lord, give unto them a promise, that the destroying angel shall pass by them, as the children of Israel, and not slay them."[81] Originally considered advisory, keeping the Word of

77. St. John Stott, "New Jerusalem Abandoned: The Failure to Carry Mormonism to the Delaware," *Journal of American Studies* 21 (1987): 71–85.

78. "The Book of Mormon is a record of the forefathers of our western Tribes of Indians," he declared in a letter to N. C. Saxton, Jan. 4, 1833. Dean Jessee, ed., *Personal Writings of Joseph Smith*, rev. ed. (Salt Lake City, 2002), 297.

79. A Methodist Pequot espoused the theory in his 1829 autobiography rpt. as William Apess, *On Our Own Ground*, ed. Barry Connell (Amherst, Mass., 1992), 53, 74–94. Joseph Smith may have been familiar with *Views of the Hebrews; or, The Ten Tribes of Israel in America* (Poultney, Vt., 1823), by Ethan Smith (no relation).

80. 2 Nephi 30:6, to employ the Mormon method of citing their scriptures. In 1981, the LDS Church declared that the phrase "white and delightsome" should read "pure and delightsome," and subsequent editions of the Book of Mormon show it thus.

81. *Doctrine and Covenants*, sect. 89, verses 18–21. Cf. Proverbs 3:8.

Wisdom became mandatory in the twentieth century for Latter-day Saints.

The Kirtland community eventually disintegrated as a result of external hostility and internal dissension. In 1834, the community decided to divide up its common property, although the Missouri Mormons continued to follow the Law of Consecration. The economic boom in Ohio during the years of Jackson's presidency facilitated the construction of a fine Mormon temple, which still stands in Kirtland. Early in 1837, however, the unchartered bank set up by church leaders failed, taking with it some of the faithful's savings, and other Mormon enterprises headed toward bankruptcy amid the general economic crash of that year. Pursued by lawsuits and a criminal prosecution for banking fraud, Smith lit out for the Mormon haven in Missouri, denounced by disillusioned dissidents but followed in due course by at least six hundred Saints who remained loyal.

The move from Ohio to Missouri proved a flight from the frying pan into the fire. The Mormon community in Missouri had already been subjected to a campaign of frontier terror including robberies, floggings, and burnings, going well beyond anything that had happened in the Western Reserve, whose gentiles (as the Mormons call non-Mormons) were at least fellow Yankees. In Missouri, the unpopularity of the Mormons' religion was compounded by resentment of their Yankee ethnicity, their mutual economic cooperation, their suspicious overtures to the Indians, and the presence of a few free black Latter-day Saints in a slave state that wished to exclude free black settlers. Mormon preaching of the gathering of the Saints in Zion alarmed their neighbors, who feared being crowded out by these strange intruders. Western Missouri remained a frontier area where vigilantes made up their own law and then took it into their own hands. Organized, purposeful citizen bands, not just criminal gangs, attacked the Mormons. Driven out of the area around Independence, many of the Saints took refuge at a town called Far West. Yet persecution did nothing to stem the flow of converts; by this time there were more than ten thousand Mormons in Missouri.

Encouraged by the reinforcements from Kirtland, some of the Mormon men in Missouri organized a paramilitary group called the Danites for self-defense and reprisals. When a Mormon was denied the right to vote at a polling place in August 1838, a riot broke out. A series of violent encounters between Danites and gentiles ensued, collectively termed the Mormon War of 1838. Once it became clear that the Mormons had started to fight back, the alarm of the Missourians knew no bounds. Governor Lilburn Boggs, who had ignored years of recurrent violence so long as the victims were all Mormons, now called up state troops, not so much to restore law and order as to crush what he considered a Mormon rebellion. His notorious order to the militia of October 27, 1838, reads: "The Mormons must be treated as enemies, and must be exterminated or driven from the State if necessary for the public peace."[82] Rather than face the might of the state, on November first the prophet ordered his people to lay down their arms. The brief "war" had cost the lives of one gentile and at least forty Mormons. Now, the Danites watched as the gentiles looted their homes and slaughtered their livestock. Mormons sold their farms for a fraction of their worth and departed; speculators resold them at great profit.[83] The militia commander ordered Joseph Smith shot after a brief illegal court-martial, but the officer charged with the execution refused to carry it out. Turned over to the civil authorities, the prophet escaped custody five months later and joined his refugee people on the Illinois side of the Mississippi River. There they immediately turned their faith and talents to building up another new community, larger and more beautiful, which they named Nauvoo.

VII

Alone among major religious denominations in the antebellum United States, the Roman Catholic Church did not teach the doctrine of the millennium. The church followed St. Augustine of Hippo in interpreting the Book of Revelation as an allegory of the spiritual conflict between Christ and the powers of evil. The Second Coming and the Last Judgment, Catholic authorities taught, will occur supernaturally and not be accompanied by a literal earthly messianic age. Nevertheless, chiliastic movements, common in the early centuries of the Christian era, appeared sporadically in the Middle Ages despite the church's teaching, and they flared up again after the Protestant Reformation, particularly in England during the 1640s and '50s.[84] The Puritan-pietistic religious tradition so powerful in America had perpetuated and disseminated millennialism in the United States. Catholic rejection of the doctrine of the millennium affected the attitude of the church in America in at least two ways. It meant that the church lacked the millennial sense of urgency, widespread

---

82. Quoted in Stephen LeSueur, *The 1838 Mormon War in Missouri* (Columbia, Mo., 1987), 152. Several days later Governor Boggs reaffirmed the order, again using the word "exterminate" (ibid., 230).
83. Ibid., 238–39.
84. J. P. Kiersch, "Millennium and Millennialism," *The Catholic Encyclopedia* (New York, 1907–1914), X, 307–10; R. Kuchner, "Millenarianism," *The New Catholic Encyclopedia* (Washington, 2003), IX, 633–37.

among evangelical Protestants, to remake the world and fit it for Christ's return; it also meant that Catholics did not share in the belief that the United States had a special role, analogous to that of ancient Israel, as an example of divine providence to the rest of the world. While Protestant churches synthesized Christianity with the Enlightenment's science, individual rights, and faith in progress, the nineteenth-century Church of Rome did not. In an age when Americans' belief in progress was typically associated with millennial hopes, Catholic doctrine accepted neither the idea of secular progress nor the millennium.[85]

Many American Protestants had an interpretation of their own for the Book of Revelation. The Antichrist whose downfall it seems to predict they identified with the Roman Catholic Church. The overthrow of the papacy would be one of the events heralding either a premillennial or a postmillennial Second Coming. This vision of the Last Things, coupled with the identification of Roman Catholicism with royal absolutism in Anglo-American historical tradition, and reinforced by the very real hostility manifested by the nineteenth-century papacy toward political liberalism and "modern" ideas of many kinds, combined to foster an ideological hostility toward Catholicism that went well beyond the interdenominational rivalry among Protestant sects. The growth of the Roman Catholic Church, deriving chiefly from immigration but also manifested in efforts to win converts, seemed to some Protestants to threaten American democratic institutions. In their minds, modern liberalism blended with millennial religion to reach a single conclusion: Catholicism could not be allowed to flourish in America if America were to fulfill her mission to the world.[86]

Antebellum Catholic evangelism by no means reached out only to immigrants or others of Catholic background. The religious orders in particular seized upon American freedom of religion to seek converts from Protestantism; means to this end included holding high-profile public theological debates and founding educational institutions. Some 57,400 American Protestants converted to Roman Catholicism between 1831 and 1860, among them the prominent lay theologian Orestes Brownson, as well as Isaac Hecker and Elizabeth Seton.[87] Protestants reacted strongly

85. For more on the contrast between Catholicism and Protestantism in nineteenth-century America, see John McGreevy, *Catholicism and American Freedom* (New York, 2003).

86. Bernard McGinn, "Revelation," *The Literary Guide to the Bible*, ed. Robert Alter and Frank Kermode (Cambridge, Mass., 1987), 523–41; Bloch, *Visionary Republic* (cited in n. 2), esp. 5–10.

87. Brooks Holifield, "Oral Debate in American Religion," *Church History* 67 (1998), 499–520; Jay Dolan, *In Search of American Catholicism* (Oxford, 2002), 61.

to such Catholic proselytizing. They attributed the Catholics' success in part to the cultural appeal of their imagery and art. Accordingly, Protestants began to make use themselves of the symbol of the cross (though not the crucifix), of sacred music performed by organ and choir in church to supplement congregational singing, and of Gothic architecture. Protestants also redoubled their own evangelical and educational initiatives to compete with the Catholics. As Lyman Beecher put it, "The Catholics have a perfect right to proselyte the nation to their faith if they are able to do it. But I too have the right of preventing it if I am able."[88]

When a politically conservative association in the Austrian Empire set about raising funds to proselytize for Catholicism in the United States, it set off alarm bells among certain American evangelicals. America was supposed to redeem monarchical Europe, not the other way around. Those most worried included the prominent painter Samuel F. B. Morse, son of the geographer and Indian demographer Jedidiah Morse. A fervent nationalist and Calvinist like his father, Morse the younger had begun to tinker with the idea of an electric telegraph. Starting in 1835, he led the Native American Democratic Association in New York, a city which already contained substantial Irish Catholic neighborhoods. (In those days, "Native American" meant whites born in the United States, not American Indians.) In letters to the *Journal of Commerce* that year, soon published in pamphlet form, Morse complained that Jesuit missionaries, emissaries of Europe's reactionary Holy Alliance active among the immigrants, dangerously exploited American freedom on behalf of "superstition and ignorance." In 1836 and 1841, he ran unsuccessfully as a candidate for mayor on a platform of limiting the political influence of immigrant Catholics.[89] Morse's strident warnings were among the earliest expressions of a movement known as nativism that would become more powerful after Catholic immigration increased during the late 1840s.

Sometimes opposition to Catholic evangelism betrayed the very democratic ideals that it professed to protect. The most dramatic responses to the expansion of Catholicism took violent form. On the night of August 11, 1834, a well-organized mob burned down the Ursuline Convent outside Charlestown, Massachusetts (the site is now in Somerville). The Order of

88. Lyman Beecher, "A Plea for the West" (1835), rpt. in *The American Whigs*, ed. Daniel Howe (New York, 1973), 144.
89. Benjamin Blied, *Austrian Aid to American Catholics, 1830–1860* (Milwaukee, 1944); Kenneth Silverman, *Lightning Man* (New York, 2003), 139–42; Samuel F. B. Morse, *Imminent Dangers to the Free Institutions of the United States Through Foreign Immigration* (1835; New York, 1969), quotation from 23.

St. Ursula, founded in Italy, came to the United States from French Canada. Specialists in women's education, the Ursuline nuns had been running a boarding school on Mount Benedict for girls aged six to eighteen. The mother superior and about half the sisters were converts from Protestantism. The students' parents, mainly well-to-do Boston Unitarians, sought a good education for their girls and didn't worry about exposing them to Catholicism. To the farmers and workers of Charlestown, however, it looked like young Protestants being corrupted by an un-American ideology. In January 1832, a nineteen-year-old local farmer's daughter and convert to Catholicism left the convent, where she had spent several months as a "special student," denounced the nuns' practices, and then renounced her conversion. Rebecca Reed's story, eventually published as *Six Months in a Convent* (1835), told of severe penances imposed on a sick novice by the mother superior and of nuns prostrating themselves before superiors, kissing their feet and licking the floor—monastic practices that shocked non-Catholic Americans. Then, in July 1832, a second woman left the convent: Sister St. John, assistant to the mother superior. Although she soon relented and returned, her action revived charges that the convent held people against their will. On August 11, Lyman Beecher spoke in Charlestown on the need for Protestant educational institutions in the West to counteract the influence of Catholic ones. By that time, however, conspirators had already plotted the destruction of the convent on Mount Benedict.

Men of Charlestown had recently celebrated the Boston Tea Party of 1775, and many of them concluded that it was time for another patriotic mob to take the law into their own hands. Fears of the incompatibility of Roman Catholicism with liberty, rooted in Anglo-American tradition since the days of Elizabeth I and the Spanish Armada, lived on in the 1830s—despite, ironically, the British Parliament enacting Catholic Emancipation in 1829. In their own eyes, the conspirators acted as Americans rather than Protestants, protecting their country and its mission against alien subversive influence. As their most prominent apologist declared, the Patriots of 1775 "thought not that within sight of Bunker Hill, where the blood of heroes flowed, a Convent would be established, and their granddaughters become its inmates."[90] The bravado of the mother superior, who bravely declared that "twenty thousand Irishmen" would defend her community, did not deter the plotters. The burning of the convent had been thoroughly planned, and the volunteer fire companies

---

90. Charles Frothingham, *The Convent's Doom*, quoted in Jenny Franchot, *Roads to Rome* (Berkeley, 1994), 142.

summoned to the scene made no effort either to interfere with the perpetrators or to put out the flames. The ten nuns and forty students all escaped unharmed. A second night of rioting wrecked the nuns' garden. One vandal, bent on sacrilege, found the consecrated communion wafers and put them in his pocket; uninterested in mere theft, he threw away the silver ciborium that contained them. Twenty-four hours later he committed suicide. The authorities had not defended the convent by force, but upon the insistence of the Boston mercantile community they did promptly investigate and indict twelve men. Local juries acquitted all but one defendant, whom the governor soon pardoned (at the request of prominent Catholics as a gesture of conciliation). A bill to pay state compensation to the religious order failed to pass the legislature. But the Ursulines eventually recovered their ciborium, which remains a precious possession.[91]

VIII

In the wee hours of Monday, August 22, 1831, a trusted family slave climbed through the window of his master's house and unbarred the door for six companions armed with axes. The intruders proceeded to kill Joseph and Sally Travis, her twelve-year-old son, and an apprentice boy, also twelve, hacking them to death in their beds. After leaving the house, they remembered a baby in a cradle and came back to kill him too. So began the greatest slave rebellion in United States history.

The man who opened the door, and the leader of the uprising, was a mystic religious visionary named Nat Turner. By day a field hand, at night and on weekends Turner prophesied, baptized, and healed. Turner learned to read from his parents and had absorbed the Bible's imagery and power. None of his owners tried to discourage his religious activities. As an exhorter revered by blacks and respected among whites, Turner moved about Southampton County in southeastern Virginia, a region of modest landholdings, diversified agriculture, and masters who worked in the fields alongside their bondsmen. The 1830 census of the county showed whites to be a minority and free blacks a significant element. The population of 16,074 was 41 percent white, 48 percent enslaved, and 11 percent free colored.[92]

91. See Nancy Schultz, *Fire and Roses: The Burning of the Charlestown Convent* (New York, 2000); and three articles by Daniel Cohen: "The Respectability of Rebecca Reed," *JER* 16 (1996), 419–62; "Alvah Kelley's Cow," *New England Quarterly* 74 (2001): 531–79; and "Passing the Torch," *JER* 24 (2004): 527–86.
92. Census of 1830, *United States Historical Census Data Browser* http://fisher.lib.virginia .edu/census (viewed May 11, 2007).

Nat Turner listened to "the Spirit that spoke to the prophets in former days" and interpreted signs of divinity in the world around him. Like Isaiah, he heard the Spirit tell him to "proclaim liberty to the captives" and "the day of vengeance of our God" (Isaiah 61:1–2). Turner decided that "the great day of judgment was at hand," when he would become God's instrument. The Spirit instructed him to "fight against the Serpent, for the time was fast approaching when the first shall be last and the last shall be first."[93] An eclipse of the sun in February 1831 signaled him to usher in the millennium with its great role reversal. The date first set for the new revolution was the Fourth of July, but when Turner fell ill, it had been postponed until August 21 (the fortieth anniversary of the Haitian Revolution). Starting from the Travis household, Turner and his band moved from one farm to another, killing all the whites they found on their march toward Jerusalem, as the Southampton county seat was portentously named.[94] (Meanwhile, in western Missouri, Joseph Smith was planning another new Jerusalem, dedicating the site for a Mormon temple there.)

The leader of the uprising prepared himself for his destiny by prayer and fasting. Once the rebellion began, he showed no relish for leading a death squad. Turner killed only one person with his own hands, when she would otherwise have escaped and raised the alarm. After that experience he brought up the rear of his party, arriving at each farm after the killing was finished. At some households, slaves joined Turner's cause, and eventually about sixty participated, along with several free blacks. But not all bondsmen jumped at the chance to participate in a bloody and hopeless enterprise; one, Aaron Harris, tried to talk Turner into abandoning his mission. Some helped their owners hide. Over the two days that the rebellion lasted, some fifty-seven whites were killed, forty-six of them women and children. According to African American tradition, Turner admonished his followers, "Remember that ours is not a war for robbery, nor to satisfy our passions; it is a *struggle for freedom*." None of the victims was raped or tortured, though their bodies were usually decapitated. Outside of Turner's presence, a few of his men looted and got drunk on captured brandy.[95]

---

93. *Confessions of Nat Turner . . . fully and voluntarily made to Thos. C. Gray* (1831; Petersburg, Va., 1881), 6, 10, 11.

94. See Herbert Aptheker, *Nat Turner's Slave Rebellion* (New York, 1966); and Stephen Oates, *The Fires of Jubilee* (New York, 1975).

95. Quotation from Vincent Harding, *There Is a River* (New York, 1981), 95. Estimates of the total number of white victims range from fifty-five to sixty-three.

The uprising was put down by a combination of vigilantes, state militia, and federal troops from the U.S. Navy base at Norfolk. In the final shootout at Simon Blunt's plantation, six white civilians with sixty loyal slaves repulsed twenty attacking rebels. Fear and rage turned the white vigilantes into armed mobs, wreaking vengeance on luckless black people, whether Turner's followers or not. "Some of these scenes are hardly inferior in barbarity to the atrocities of the insurgents," confessed a Virginia journalist witness.[96] The vigilantes too beheaded those they killed, displaying the severed heads on poles. No one knows how many African Americans lost their lives as a consequence of Nat Turner's Uprising. Twenty, including three free Negroes, were tried and legally executed; ten others, convicted and transported for sale. Fifteen defendants were judicially cleared. Perhaps a score were killed fighting in the uprising itself, and about a hundred massacred afterwards. Over twenty additional blacks were executed elsewhere in Virginia and North Carolina during the wave of hysteria that followed.[97]

Nat Turner himself eluded capture for six weeks, until October 30. The authorities took care to prevent his being lynched. He was tried on November 5 in Jerusalem and hanged six days later. In accordance with Virginia law, Turner was represented by counsel, and the commonwealth paid $375 to the estate of his late owner as compensation for executing him. His body, like that of most condemned criminals, was used for anatomical dissection. While in custody, Turner talked with a white man named Thomas Gray, who published his account of the interview as *The Confessions of Nat Turner*. Turner explained to Gray his moral and religious premises and eschatological vision. Marveling at the prisoner's "calm, deliberate composure," Gray asked him, "Do you not find yourself mistaken now?" But defeat and impending death did not shake Nat Turner's faith. "Was not Christ crucified?" he responded.[98]

Turner's Uprising provoked a huge debate among white Virginians over what lessons they should draw from it. Some warned of more rebellions and argued that the best way to forestall bloody racial strife would be a program of compensated emancipation coupled with colonization. Most of the support for this policy of gradual reform came from the western part of

96. John Hampden Pleasants, quoted in Eric Foner, *Nat Turner* (Englewood Cliffs, N.J., 1971), 16.
97. Casualties on both sides of this race war can only be estimated. Many of the sources relating to the uprising have disappeared from the archives. See Mary Kemp Davis, *Nat Turner Before the Bar of Judgment* (Baton Rouge, 1999), 55–61.
98. *Confessions of Nat Turner*, 11.

the commonwealth, where slaveholding was not of central importance. In opposition ranged the large plantation owners of the tidewater, to whom slavery seemed essential for their economy and way of life. Legislative apportionment favored the proslavery eastern part of the state, but even so, the two sides were about evenly balanced. Governor John Floyd, himself a westerner, occupied a pivotal position. A Calhoun Democrat, like his Carolina mentor he had long backed public funding for internal improvements. Floyd saw gradual emancipation as promoting Virginia's economic development, and he planned to endorse it when the state legislature met. His surprising failure to do so is probably explained by a visit he received from Calhoun not long before the session began. No record of their conversation exists, but very likely the vice president persuaded Floyd that emancipation would play into the hands of Yankee politicians and agitators. A new Calhoun, devoted to slavery and state rights, had replaced the old one, and turned Governor Floyd around as well.[99]

Without the governor's support, the emancipation-colonization program stalled in Virginia's House of Delegates. Thirty-nine-year-old Thomas Jefferson Randolph, grandson of the late president, gave it cautious endorsement. So did the editors of the state's two leading newspapers, Thomas Ritchie of the *Richmond Enquirer* and John Hampden Pleasants of the *Richmond Constitutional Whig*. Both sides in the debate agreed that Virginia should be a white person's country and that a substantial free colored population constituted a security risk. (Much was made of the fact that some free Negroes had joined Turner.) Conservatives conceded that the state would be better off with fewer slaves and a more industrial-commercial economy, but argued that the domestic slave trade would suffice to drain off surplus black laborers from Virginia to the trans-Appalachian Southwest, without legislative intervention. After prolonged debate, on January 25, 1832, the House voted 67 to 60 that "further action for the removal of slaves should await a more definite development of public opinion." By this fateful procrastination, Virginian statesmanship abdicated responsibility for dealing with the state's number one problem. When the Civil War came thirty years later, Virginians would still be divided; the great slavery debate of 1831 foreshadowed the bifurcation of the Old Dominion into Virginia and West Virginia.[100] In the short term, reaction prevailed over reform. Instead of emancipation, Virginia's

---

99. Oates, *Fires of Jubilee*, 136–38.
100. See Alison Freehling, *Drift Toward Dissolution: The Virginia Slavery Debate of 1831–32* (Baton Rouge, 1982); and W. Freehling, *Secessionists at Bay*, 178–96.

lawmakers sought security through increased repression: tighter pass rules for slave travelers and more patrols to enforce them, further restraints on the free colored population, and, specifically to inhibit the emergence of more Nat Turners, restrictions on slave literacy and religious gatherings. A slave society could not afford to allow those in bondage to pursue a millennial vision in which the last would be first.

9

Andrew Jackson and His Age

Dressed in deepest mourning black, Andrew Jackson presented a somber figure at his presidential inauguration on March 4, 1829. His beloved wife, Rachel, had suffered a heart attack on December 17 and died five days later at the age of sixty-one. She had been much upset when the propriety of her relationship with Andrew had been made an issue in the campaign. Her husband blamed her death on his political enemies, who had "maligned that blessed one who is now safe from suffering and sorrow, whom they tried to put to shame for my sake!"[1] His resentment may well have been exacerbated by guilt, since Rachel had begged him to retire to private life. Unfashionably stout and self-conscious about her provincial manners, she had been dreading the role of White House first lady. Now she would not have to perform it. A depressed and bitter president-elect managed to avoid the celebration that had been planned to welcome him to Washington at the end of his three-week trip from Nashville. He refused to pay the customary courtesy call on the outgoing president, who reciprocated by not attending the inaugural. Public speaking had always been an ordeal for Jackson even in the best of times. Under the circumstances, the incoming president kept his inaugural address brief and almost entirely ambiguous. Few could hear his words, but thousands watched with pleasure when he bowed to the crowd in a sign of respect for popular sovereignty.[2]

The symbolic gesture expressed an irony at the very heart of Jackson's presidency. Despite the bow, Jackson brought to his task a temperament suited to leadership rather than deference. Although he invoked a democratic ideology, the new president had profoundly authoritarian instincts. Tall, ramrod straight, with piercing eyes and an air of command, the hero of New Orleans was not a man to be crossed. He had come up the hard way, born in a remote area on the border between North and South Carolina to the log-cabin poverty of a migrant Scots-Irish family and tragically orphaned at an early age. Jackson had sought and made his fortune in frontier Tennessee, with an eye on the main chance and just enough

---

1. Andrew Jackson, Dec. 24, 1828, quoted in Remini, *Jackson*, II, 154.
2. Donald Cole, *The Presidency of Andrew Jackson* (Lawrence, Kans., 1993), 33.

book learning to practice law. A man's man, he fought Indians, gambled, and dealt successfully in lands and cotton. Even by frontier standards, Jackson possessed a particularly touchy sense of honor. He participated in several duels and fights, killing a man during one in 1806. The chronic pain of the wound he sustained then, and other bullet wounds from a barroom brawl in 1813, did nothing to help his disposition. Quick to sense a criticism or slight, he never apologized, never forgave, and never shrank from violence. His towering rages became notorious.[3]

Slaves Jackson bought and sold in substantial numbers; in 1817, he disposed of forty at one time for $24,000 (an economy of scale for the purchaser, his friend Edward Livingston). Jackson is said to have wagered his slaves on horse races. However, he indignantly denied ever having been a professional slave trader.[4] Old Hickory was capable of patriarchal generosity to dependents; he even adopted a Creek Indian boy whose parents Jackson's soldiers had massacred. "He is a savage, but one that fortune has thrown in my hands," Jackson explained to his wife. (Adoption of captives was common in frontier warfare. The boy, who never renounced his tribal heritage, died of tuberculosis at sixteen.)[5] But if someone challenged Jackson's authority or he felt his honor questioned, he became implacable. After one of his slaves dared run away, Jackson offered a fifty-dollar reward for his recapture, "and ten dollars extra for every hundred lashes a person will give to the amount of three hundred."[6] Three hundred lashes risked beating the man to death, but perhaps revenge outweighed financial interest.

Jackson's religion was a stern Scots-Irish Presbyterianism. His wife turned increasingly pious in middle age, and although Andrew was never as devout as she became, he took some aspects of the faith seriously. During his short term as governor of Florida Territory, he imposed (at Rachel's urging) strict Protestant sabbatarian regulations on the Catholic population.[7] Once, when a young lawyer in Tennessee tried to argue in his presence

3. See Bertram Wyatt-Brown, "Andrew Jackson's Honor," *JER* 17 (1997): 1–36. Psychological interpretations of Jackson's irascible temperament are offered in Andrew Burstein, *The Passions of Andrew Jackson* (New York, 2003) and James C. Curtis, *Andrew Jackson and the Search for Vindication* (Boston, 1976).
4. Curtis, *Andrew Jackson and the Search for Vindication*, 136; Robert Gudmestad, *A Troublesome Commerce* (Baton Rouge, 2003), 147–52.
5. Andrew Jackson to Rachel Jackson, Dec. 29, 1813, *Papers of Andrew Jackson*, ed. Harold Moser et al. (Nashville, Tenn., 1984), II, 516. The boy was named Lyncoya.
6. Nashville *Tennessee Gazette*, Sept. 26, 1804, rpt. in *Plantation and Frontier*, ed. Ulrich Phillips (New York, 1910), II, 86–87.
7. Remini, *Jackson*, I, 408.

against the existence of hell, Jackson roared, "I thank God that there is such a place of torment as hell." Asked why, the general responded: "To put such d——d rascals as you are in!" The young man fled the room.[8]

Politically influential in Tennessee even before the Battles of Horseshoe Bend and New Orleans made him a national hero, Jackson had served in the state constitutional convention of 1796, in the U.S. House of Representatives and Senate (briefly), and on the state supreme court. His career as frontier warrior and self-made plantation magnate exemplified aspirations that were widely shared by American men of his time. He was the first president with whom many ordinary Americans could identify and the first to have a nickname. That nickname, "Old Hickory," invoked his stature as a tough leader of men in an age when only men could vote. Jackson's success in life personified the wresting of the continent from alien enemies, both Native and European, white supremacy over other races, and equal opportunity for all white males, without preference for birth or education, to enjoy the spoils of conquest. A visitor to his plantation house, the Hermitage outside Nashville, would find the log cabins of his youth standing alongside the stately mansion with its Greek columns and imported French wallpaper. Like many another plantation owner, Jackson enjoyed an expensive lifestyle; he entertained lavishly both at the Hermitage and the White House.[9]

Although ironic, Jackson's combination of authoritarianism with a democratic ideology, his identification of his own will with the voice of the people, worked well for him politically. He defined himself as defender of the people against special interests and advocated—unsuccessfully—a constitutional amendment to abolish the electoral college and choose the president by direct popular vote. The populist rhetoric of Jackson and his political associates combined ceaseless condemnation of elite corruption with the antigovernment political ideology they had taken over from Randolph, Taylor, and the Old Republicans. A large segment of the American electorate shared Jackson's belief in the legitimacy of private violence and the assertion of male honor, his trust in natural rather than acquired abilities, and his impatience with limitations on one's own will.[10]

---

8. Related in Peter Cartwright, *Autobiography*, ed. Charles Wallis (1856; New York, 1956), 134.

9. Remini, *Jackson*, II, 7, 346.

10. Charles Sellers, *The Market Revolution* (New York, 1991), 174–81, provides a sympathetic statement of how and why Jackson's life appealed to many rural Americans. But see also Michael O'Brien, *Conjectures of Order: Intellectual Life and the American South, 1810–1860* (Chapel Hill, 2004), II, 836–49.

But Jackson's values and suspicion of government were far from commanding universal assent, and they were to prove exceptionally divisive in the years ahead. The "age of Jackson" was not a time of consensus. It is unfortunate that the adjective "Jacksonian" is often applied not only to Jackson's followers but to all Americans of the period.

The one unambiguous commitment in Jackson's inaugural address was to what he called *"reform"*: the purging of federal offices.[11] Duff Green, the editor of the Jacksonian *United States Telegraph*, had announced this goal during the campaign itself. Jackson would "REWARD HIS FRIENDS AND PUNISH HIS ENEMIES" through patronage, Green's newspaper trumpeted. This was not just a prediction; it was a threat. Green was deliberately prodding officeholders (customs and land officers, U.S. attorneys and marshals, postmasters and others) to declare for Jackson, on the premise that if Adams won, it would not matter whom they had supported, but if Jackson won, they faced dismissal unless they had endorsed him.[12] Adams had tried to put the federal patronage on a meritocratic basis. For his pains, the opposition press had vilified him as dealing in special privilege. Now, the pro-Jackson journalist Amos Kendall could not help observing that what the Old Hero's supporters really wanted was "the privilege of availing themselves of the very abuses with which we charge our adversaries."[13]

A horde of office-seekers attended Jackson's inauguration. It was they who turned the inaugural reception into a near-riot, damaging White House furnishings until they were diverted outside onto the lawn. Later historians have cast this event in an aura of democratic exuberance; contemporary observers of every political stripe expressed embarrassment at it. "The throng that pressed on the president before he was fairly in office, soliciting rewards in a manner so destitute of decency, and of respect for his character and office," observed a New England Jacksonian, was "a disgraceful reproach to the character of our countrymen."[14]

The largest part of the federal government's patronage lay in the Post Office. Since Postmaster General John McLean remained committed to nonpartisanship and meritocracy, Duff Green insisted that the president replace him. This proved a delicate matter, for both Green and McLean

11. *Presidential Messages*, II, 438. Italics in the original.
12. Green's slogan is quoted and analyzed in Richard R. John, *Spreading the News: The American Postal System from Franklin to Morse* (Cambridge, Mass., 1995), 210–11.
13. Kendall to Francis P. Blair, Feb. 14, 1829, quoted ibid., 212.
14. Henry Orne (1829), quoted in Robert Forbes, "Slavery and the Meaning of America" (Ph.D. diss., Yale University, 1994), 522.

had close ties to Vice President Calhoun. As a solution, Jackson elevated a reluctant McLean to the U.S. Supreme Court and turned over the patronage-rich Post Office to William Barry. Barry allowed the quality of the postal service to deteriorate while a clique of Jacksonian journalists led by Amos Kendall divvied up the spoils in his department. This informal but powerful group of patronage dispensers evolved into what became known as Jackson's "kitchen cabinet." The central role of journalists testifies to the importance the administration attached to the communications revolution and public opinion. While political factions controlled key newspapers, in return newspapermen played key roles in politics and patronage.[15]

The kitchen cabinet had no institutional identity or even permanent membership; it was simply a term (originally derogatory) for a group of presidential favorites operating outside the formal cabinet. Martin Van Buren belonged to both cabinets for a time. No previous president had had such a group of advisors, and they were naturally the objects of suspicion. The kitchen cabinet has sometimes been described as the precursor of the modern presidential White House staff, or alternatively as the precursor of the national party organization, but both these models are anachronistic. The kitchen cabinet had no table of organization, and its members performed only such functions as the president directed. During his military career, Jackson had heard advice from his aides but did not convene councils of war; as president he did not want to be bound by the official cabinet, even after appointing an all-new one in 1831. An informal, flexible group of advisors with no power base other than his favor suited his executive style, allowing him to keep power in his own hands, and, as the historian Richard Latner has pointed out, "to dominate his surroundings."[16]

With the partial exception of John Quincy Adams, every president beginning with Washington had made appointments to office from among his supporters. The early republic had no civil service system, and federal employees enjoyed no legal security of employment. Nevertheless the

---

15. See Richard John, "Affairs of Office: The Executive Departments, the Election of 1828, and the Making of the Democratic Party," in *Democracy in America: New Directions in American Political History*, ed. Julian Zelizer et al. (Princeton, 2003), 51–84. Jeffrey Pasley, *Printers, Editors, and Publishers of Political Journals Elected to the U.S. Congress, 1789–1861*, found at http://www.pasleybrothers.com/newspols/images/ Editors_in_Congress.pdf (viewed May 2, 2007), shows how often journalists went into electoral politics themselves.

16. Richard Latner, "The Kitchen Cabinet and Andrew Jackson's Advisory System," *JAH* 65 (1978): 267–88.

prevailing custom was to leave one's predecessor's appointees in office (except for the top tier of policymaking posts), replacing them gradually through attrition. Even Jefferson, eager as he was to replace Federalists with Republicans, had generally followed this practice. The novelty in the Jacksonian patronage policy lay not in appointments but in removals. According to one set of statistics, Jackson removed 919 federal officials during his first year; this represented about 10 percent of all government employees. The precise number removed is subject to confusion, but it was more than all his predecessors had done in the previous forty years. By the time Congress assembled in December 1829, Jackson had already removed thirteen district attorneys, nine marshals, twenty-three registers and receivers, and twenty-five customs collectors, replacing them all with recess appointments. The removal policy hit the Post Office hard. Within the first year, the new administration dismissed 423 postmasters, many with long and creditable records of service.[17]

At first these removals were routinely justified with accusations of malfeasance. In this way the Jackson leaders dressed up their patronage policy as "reform" of the corruption they alleged had prevailed under Monroe and Adams. In a few cases, those removed were indeed crooks: Tobias Watkins, army surgeon, literary magazine editor, and friend of John Quincy Adams, went to prison for four years for misappropriating three thousand dollars while a Treasury auditor. Others were superannuated and deserved to be retired. But in most cases, straightforward politics dictated the removals. Those in the Post Office were concentrated in the Northeast, where the Jacksonians needed help in building their political party. In fact, however, the mail service there was most efficient and least in need of a managerial shake-up.

After several months, it became obvious that the charges against incumbent officeholders were all too often fabricated. To preserve credibility the administration fell back upon its other rationale, the principle of "rotation in office" as good in itself. Jackson explained this policy in his Message to Congress of December 1829: "The duties of all public officers are, or at least admit of being made, so plain and simple that men of intelligence may readily qualify themselves for their performance." Having thus rejected any need to recruit a meritocracy in public service, he went on to examine the issue purely as the distribution of favors among the citizenry. "In a country where offices are created solely for the benefit of the

17. I owe some of these figures to Daniel Feller, who generously shared his research with me; others come from Cole, *Presidency of Jackson*, 41–42, and John, *Spreading the News*, 223–33.

people no one man has any more intrinsic right to official station than another." Qualifications and experience were just excuses invoked to justify the perpetuation of privilege.[18]

The issues involved in allocating public office and employment have been repeatedly debated ever since, first with civil service reform and more recently in connection with affirmative action and term limits. The arguments were no less contested in Jackson's time than now. But the spoils system, as it was soon named, had come to stay. Once the Jacksonian Democrats had established the new pattern of partisan removals, it remained whichever party won office, until gradually mitigated by civil service reform after the Civil War. Those whom the Jackson administration appointed to office did not differ in their economic class from previous appointees, though they were more often self-made men or born into provincial rather than cosmopolitan elites.[19] Jackson showed no reluctance to appoint former Federalists to office once they had become his supporters; indeed, he appointed more of them than all his Republican predecessors put together. Nor, despite the rhetoric of "reform," did Jackson's appointees represent any improvement in probity; corruption that came to light in the Land Office, the Post Office, and Indian affairs under his administration dwarfed that under his predecessors. Samuel Swartwout, a crony whom the president personally selected for the lucrative post of collector of the port of New York, absconded in 1839 with his accounts over a million dollars in arrears. More rapid turnover in the bureaucracy led to officeholders who were less experienced and less motivated. Over the long term the spoils system diminished both the competence and the prestige of public service.[20]

Under the Federalists and Jeffersonian Republicans, the American administrative system had served as an example of honesty and efficiency to would-be administrative reformers in Britain. However, in the years after 1829, the quality of British administration gradually improved while that of the U.S. federal government declined, until by the 1880s, American civil service reformers opposing the spoils system took Britain as their model.

18. "First Annual Message to Congress" (Dec. 8, 1829), *Presidential Messages*, II, 448–49.
19. Sidney Aronson, *Status and Kinship in the Higher Civil Service* (Cambridge, Mass., 1964), 82, 90.
20. Shaw Livermore, *The Twilight of Federalism* (Princeton, 1962), 241; Cole, *Presidency of Jackson*, 46; Leonard D. White, *The Jacksonians: A Study in Administrative History* (New York, 1954), 327–32.

II

Once John McLean left, only one cabinet member remained with significant political stature: Secretary of State Martin Van Buren. Van Buren had just been elected governor of New York, but having run for the office to ward off the Antimasonic threat to his state power base, the Little Magician felt little interest in the job itself. When offered the State Department, he jumped at the chance to get back to Washington, where his presence would counterbalance that of Vice President Calhoun. With Jackson's ill health and avowed intention to serve but a single term, the Calhoun–Van Buren competition for the succession got under way quickly.[21]

The other cabinet secretaries were little-known figures who appealed to Jackson in large part because they all hated Henry Clay.[22] The worst choice proved to be John Henry Eaton, senator from Tennessee, an old friend who had been Jackson's campaign manager. As secretary of war he would be in charge of Indian Removal, a subject on which he and the president saw eye to eye.[23] But the most significant thing about Eaton turned out to be his recent marriage to Margaret O'Neale Timberlake.

The daughter of a Scots-Irish innkeeper in Washington, young Peggy O'Neale tended bar and had already attracted many suitors before marrying at the age of sixteen. Her husband, John Timberlake, was a purser in the navy and away at sea for long periods, during which Peggy seldom seems to have been lonely. She bestowed her favors widely, becoming in due course good friends with John Eaton and probably his mistress. Eaton gave money to Peggy's father and managed the Timberlake family finances so as to facilitate her husband's absences. People questioned the paternity of her two children. In April 1828 John Timberlake died suddenly on board ship, apparently by suicide. It is still unclear whether his despair was caused by his wife's infidelities, financial difficulties, or bad asthma. On New Year's Day 1829, twenty-nine-year-old Margaret (she preferred that name to the more commonly used Peggy) married the middle-aged widower John Eaton. Remarriage within a year of a spouse's death was considered poor taste, but the couple responded to the wishes of their friend and patron, Andrew Jackson. Jackson told them to marry "forthwith,"

21. Six weeks before the inauguration, a young Democrat noticed that "the friends of Van Buren and those of Calhoun are becoming very jealous of each other." James Buchanan to Benjamin Porter, Jan. 22, 1829, quoted in Richard Latner, "The Eaton Affair Reconsidered," *Tennessee Historical Quarterly* 36 (1977): 333–34.
22. Cole, *Presidency of Jackson*, 31.
23. Harry Watson, *Liberty and Power* (New York, 1990), 100.

in order to forestall gossip. It didn't. The typical reaction of Washington insiders was that "Eaton has just married his mistress, and the mistress of eleven doz. others!"[24]

When the president named John Eaton secretary of war, most of the women in the capital refused to associate with his wife. Led during the past generation by such powerful matrons as Dolley Madison and Margaret Bayard Smith, the women of official Washington had developed a strong collective identity and sense of purpose in transforming their raw young city into a capital worthy of a great nation.[25] A woman who was sexually notorious had no place in their vision. At the inaugural ball, no woman spoke to the new Mrs. Eaton. Floride Calhoun, the aristocratic wife of the vice president, received her when she came calling, but refused to return the call. Soon thereafter the Calhouns departed for South Carolina so Floride could give birth at home, a move that also tactfully avoided further contact with the Eatons.

The newly arrived women who had accompanied Jackson's other appointees proved no more willing to tolerate the presence of Peggy O'Neale Eaton than were the long-established women. (There is reason to believe that Rachel Jackson, during her lifetime, had been unwilling to acknowledge her.)[26] Brash, demanding, and voluptuous in appearance, Margaret Eaton did nothing to reassure those who met her. None of the wives of Jackson's other cabinet members would associate with her except Catherine Barry, wife of the postmaster general who had replaced McLean. Most awkward of all for the president, his own official White House hostess supported the boycott. Years before, First Lady Elizabeth Kortright Monroe had closed the White House to Margaret Timberlake, and now Emily Donelson decided to continue that policy. Her husband, Andrew Jackson Donelson, was the president's private secretary and nephew of his late wife. The Eaton Affair (as it came to be called) put the Donelsons into an excruciating bind, and eventually Jackson sent them back to Tennessee to think about where their loyalties should lie. Although he later recalled them, the Donelsons never regained their former standing in the eyes of their great patron. Some of the foreign diplomats' wives were willing to socialize with Margaret Eaton because they took for granted the behavior of European courts and the need to set aside morality in the interest of politics. American women were not so trained.

24. Louis McLane to James A. Bayard, Feb. 19, 1829, quoted in Catherine Allgor, *Parlor Politics* (Charlottesville, Va., 2000), 200.
25. See ibid., 190–238.
26. John Marszalek, *The Petticoat Affair* (New York, 1997), 79, 81.

Andrew Jackson did not countenance defiance. How could his cabinet members work together when the wife of one was shunned by the wives of others? He insisted that Margaret Eaton must be an innocent victim of slander, the same position he had taken in response to the accusations against Rachel. His argument was deductive rather than based on evidence: John Eaton and John Timberlake were both Freemasons like Jackson, and it would be unthinkable for one Mason to cuckold another.[27] Two Presbyterian ministers close to the president tried in vain to persuade him of Margaret Eaton's guilt. One of them was Ezra Stiles Ely, who had written the pamphlet supporting Jackson as the "Christian" candidate against the Unitarian Adams. On September 10, 1829, the president of the United States summoned his entire cabinet save Eaton, plus his two private secretaries (Donelson and William Lewis) and the two clergymen, to a dramatic meeting to evaluate the sexual morality of Margaret Eaton. Jackson was clearly not open to persuasion: "She is as chaste as a virgin!" he exclaimed, a memorable phrase that became common knowledge. The meeting changed no minds.[28]

The Eaton Affair continued to preoccupy Washington and took up more of the president's time in his first year than any other issue. John Eaton issued dueling challenges to both the secretary of the Treasury and the pastor of the Presbyterian church in Washington (neither accepted). It is difficult for a twenty-first-century person to understand the meaning of the Eaton Affair in nineteenth-century terms. If Margaret Eaton seems appealing in her defiance of prudish convention, one may be disposed to see Jackson's defense of her as an endorsement of women's liberation. In its historical context, however, nothing could be further from the truth.

Jackson was not trying to revise the prevailing code of sexual morality but defending his honor as a patriarch. He expected to be able to control his cabinet members and thought they in turn should be able to control their wives. When the cabinet secretaries expostulated that there was a social sphere within which women enjoyed autonomy, Jackson showed no sympathy with women's rights. "I did not come here to make a cabinet for the Ladies of this place," he declared.[29] Women had no business meddling in politics. If the president vouched for her, Mrs. Eaton should be accepted and normal social life resumed.

---

27. Andrew Jackson to Ezra Stiles Ely, March 23, 1829, in James Parton, *The Life of Andrew Jackson* (New York, 1861), III, 188.
28. Parton, *Life of Jackson*, III, 204.
29. Quoted in Kirsten Wood, "Gender and Power in the Eaton Affair," *JER* 17 (1997): 238.

To understand the women's viewpoint may require even more historical imagination than to understand Jackson's. The women who ostracized Margaret Eaton did not act out of mere snobbish rejection of a tavern-keeper's daughter; social mobility was not despised in the Jackson administration. The women saw themselves defending the interests and honor of the female half of humanity. They believed that no responsible woman should accord a man sexual favors without the assurance of support that went with marriage. A woman who broke ranks on this issue they considered a threat to all women. She encouraged men to make unwelcome advances. Therefore she must be condemned severely even if it meant applying a double standard of morality, stricter for women than for men. This conviction was widespread among women, not only in the middle class and regardless of political party. The women who had the courage to act upon it, standing up to Andrew Jackson and risking their husbands' careers, insisted that expedient politics must not control moral principle. They believed that women acting collectively could advance the moral state of society. Theirs was the attitude that justified women's role in contemporary moral reform causes like temperance and antislavery. And although most or all of them would have been shocked if had been pointed out, theirs was the attitude that would lead in a few more years to an organized movement on behalf of women's rights.[30]

Whether the president really believed in Margaret Eaton's sexual fidelity is doubtful and not even altogether relevant. He insisted that her case paralleled that of his late wife. Yet he would have known his protestations of Rachel's innocence of adultery to be untrue. For Jackson, such matters were issues not of fact but of his authority. Jackson demanded loyalty, and to him this meant acceptance of his assertions, whether he was insisting on Peggy Eaton's chastity or (as he did in the course of another tirade) that Alexander Hamilton *"was not in favor of the Bank of the United States."*[31] In the same spirit of privileging his will over truth, Jackson claimed in 1831 that he had received a message from President Monroe through John Rhea (pronounced "Ray") authorizing his conduct in the invasion of Florida. Historians working over a period of half a century have carefully proved the story a complete fabrication. Nevertheless, Old Hickory persuaded John Rhea to vouch for its truth![32] After all, Jackson had prevailed upon his

30. See ibid., 237–75.
31. James Hamilton, Alexander's son, reported the latter statement and said it was made to him. Quoted in Robert Remini, *Andrew Jackson and the Bank War* (New York, 1967), 49, italics in original.
32. James Schouler, "Monroe and the Rhea Letter," *Magazine of American History* (1884): 308–22; Richard Sternberg, "Jackson's 'Rhea Letter' Hoax," *Journal of Southern History* (1936): 480–96.

friends to endorse the story of his 1791 marriage to Rachel in Natchez. And in 1829–30, with no issue save Indian Removal yet defining the administration's position, personal loyalty to the president meant everything.

One big winner emerged from the Eaton Affair: Martin Van Buren. He understood perfectly Jackson's conception of loyalty as well as how to exploit the Old Hero's vanity. A widower like Jackson, Van Buren had no wife to interfere with his pursuit of political advantage. Accordingly, the secretary of state made a point of cultivating the secretary of war and calling upon his wife, thereby scoring many points with the president. Van Buren secured for himself Jackson's favor as his successor. On the eve of the Civil War, James Parton could write that "the political history of the United States, for the last thirty years, dates from the moment when the soft hand of Mr. Van Buren touched Mrs. Eaton's knocker."[33]

Eventually Van Buren even figured a way out of the seemingly intractable social deadlock. Eaton and his wife would have to go, in order for the administration to get on with the business of government. But the only way the president could save face would be for *all* the cabinet to resign, including the husbands of Mrs. Eaton's detractors. Van Buren was willing to lead the way, confident that he had secured his place in the president's esteem. The other cabinet members were harder to persuade (Margaret Eaton urged her husband not to cooperate), but of course they had no real choice. The *Washington Globe*, the administration's organ, announced the resignations on April 20, 1831, though they were not all consummated until June. The *New York Courier* commented: "Well indeed may Mr. Van Buren be called 'The Great Magician' for *he raises his wand, and the whole Cabinet disappears.*"[34]

William Barry was exempted from the purge, officially on the grounds that the postmaster general was not then technically part of the cabinet, unofficially as a reward for keeping his wife in line. (He would serve until 1835, when, following congressional investigations into malfeasance in the Post Office, he would resign under a cloud.) The Donelsons resumed their previous positions with the president's blessing. Mass resignation of a presidential cabinet was unprecedented but came as something of a relief. The opposition had watched the whole fracas with a mixture of disgust and amusement. Upon Margaret Eaton's departure from Washington, Henry Clay quipped, "Age cannot wither nor time stale her infinite virginity."[35]

33. Parton, *Life of Jackson*, III, 287.
34. Quoted in Allgor, *Parlor Politics*, 208.
35. Quoted in Clement Eaton, *Henry Clay and the Art of American Politics* (Boston, 1957), 167. Clay was parodying Shakespeare's description of Cleopatra.

Not until the 1990s would another national administration be so absorbed by a sex scandal.

Jackson at first charged that the opposition to Margaret Eaton came from Henry Clay and his "hired slanderers."[36] In reality, of course, the president's problem lay not so much with National Republicans as with Democratic Republicans—specifically, Democratic women—but this he could not admit. Opposition to his will could only derive from a conspiracy against him. Before the end of 1829, Jackson had decided that Vice President Calhoun must mastermind the anti-Eaton conspiracy.[37] True, Calhoun had hoped that the War Department would go to a South Carolinian and so might have taken satisfaction if John Eaton had to resign. But he could only lose by a confrontation with the president over the matter. Floride Calhoun, a forceful leader in Washington society, probably made her own decision not to associate with Peggy Eaton, and the other women involved certainly did. The most that can be said is that once Van Buren aligned himself with the Eatons, free-traders who detested Van Buren's Tariff of Abominations tended to gravitate to the opposite camp, whether they were Calhoun partisans or not.[38] Active opposition to the Eatons always remained with women, supported by some clergymen, and not with any male politicians or journalists. (The press, in fact, did its best to hush the story up; not until the mass resignation of the cabinet did the rest of the country learn what had long been the talk of Washington.) By late 1829, however, Van Buren and his agents had poisoned Jackson's mind against the absent Calhoun.

While the Donelsons were out of favor, William Lewis emerged as the president's most trusted private secretary, and his wife took over as White House hostess. Lewis was John Eaton's brother-in-law and became a confidante of Martin Van Buren. Knowing how much importance the Old Hero still attached to vindicating his actions in the Florida War, the crafty Lewis obtained from William H. Crawford a letter confirming what had gone on in Monroe's top-secret cabinet meetings: Calhoun had criticized Jackson's conduct. Crawford had recuperated from the illness that wrecked his presidential ambitions and seized the chance to play the role of high-level insider once again. The Georgian found it gratifying to frustrate the presidential hopes of his old rival Calhoun while helping those

---

36. AJ to Robert Call, July 5, 1829, *Correspondence of AJ*, IV, 51.
37. AJ to John C. McLemore, Nov. 24, 1829, *Correspondence*, IV, 88–89.
38. Michael Holt, *Political Parties and American Political Development* (Baton Rouge, 1992), 45; John Niven, *John C. Calhoun and the Price of Union* (Baton Rouge, 1988), 167–68; Latner, "Eaton Affair," 330–51.

of Martin Van Buren, a longtime ally. Upon receiving Crawford's message, Jackson declared, "I have this moment" seen that which "proves Calhoun *a villain*." Jackson never attributed his discovery to the machinations of his secretary of state. "Van Buren glides along as smoothly as oil and as silently as a cat," observed one insider with a nose for intrigue.[39]

As vice president, John C. Calhoun served under two different presidents, and he suffered the peculiar fate of falling out with both of them quickly and irrevocably. His good relations with Jackson lasted only a little longer than had those with John Quincy Adams. Eventually he found himself waging a public pamphlet war against the dominant element in the administration, just as he had done under Adams. This time he was defending his role as Monroe's secretary of war more than a decade earlier. Crawford had been as critical of Jackson as anyone at the time of the Florida invasion, so it was bizarre for the president now to rely on Crawford's testimony to discredit Calhoun's role. Even at this late date Calhoun refrained from attacking the president personally; instead he blamed a sinister cabal for turning Jackson against him.[40] Calhoun's accusations were better founded than Jackson's; it was the vice president, not the president, who was the victim of a conspiracy.

Van Buren's victory in the competition for Jackson's favor could not have been more complete. The president laid it out in a letter to an old friend while reorganizing his cabinet. "I *now know* both Van Buren and Calhoun: the first I know to be a pure republican who has laboured with an eye single to promote the best interests of his country, whilst the other, actuated alone by selfish ambition, has secretly employed all his talents in intrigue and deception, to destroy them, and to disgrace my administration. The plot is unmasked."[41] As a result of Jackson's decision that Van Buren should succeed him, the administration cut loose from Duff Green's *United States Telegraph*, which had sided with Calhoun in the intraparty conflict, and in December 1830 established the *Washington Globe*, edited by Francis Blair, as its official organ. Green took his newspaper into opposition.

Besides its political fallout, the designation of Van Buren as heir apparent to Jackson, the Eaton Affair had other, more subtle resonances. It took place at a time when sexual behavior was undergoing reexamination by

---

39. Remini, *Jackson*, II, 240–46. AJ to Andrew J. Donelson, Dec. 25, 1830, quoted ibid., 246. Amos Kendall to Francis Blair, April 25, 1830, quoted in Charles Sellers, *James K. Polk, Jacksonian* (Princeton, 1957), 148. On Crawford, see Sellers, *Market Revolution*, 295.
40. Niven, *John C. Calhoun*, 175.
41. AJ to John Coffee, April 24, 1831, *Correspondence of AJ*, IV, 269.

standards we now term "Victorian," which laid increased emphasis on impulse control and strict personal accountability. Jackson did not directly challenge conventional sexual morality; he cast himself as a defender of female purity. Nevertheless, his stand on behalf of Margaret Eaton, coming after his own relationship with Rachel Robards had come under questioning, tended to align the Democratic Party with those (mostly men) who resisted the demands being made in the nineteenth century (mostly by women) for a stricter code of sexual morality. Only occasionally did issues directly involving sex come into the political arena, but even so the associations were not lost on contemporaries. They may help explain why Jackson's opposition, in the years to come, could count on more support from women's groups than the Democrats could. Women, although legally disfranchised, were not necessarily politically apathetic or inert.

III

Indian Removal constituted the major substantive issue the Jackson administration addressed in a first year otherwise largely preoccupied with patronage and personalities. Although Jackson had avoided committing himself on the tariff or internal improvements, his strong stand in favor of rapid Removal was well known and accounted for much of his popularity in Georgia, Alabama, and Mississippi. The issue involved Indian tribes all over the country, but the ones with the most at stake were the Five Civilized Tribes of Cherokee, Creek, Choctaw, Chickasaw, and Seminole. These peoples practiced agriculture and animal husbandry much as their white neighbors did and still possessed substantial domains in the Deep South states plus Tennessee, North Carolina, and Florida Territory. The eminent geographer Jedidiah Morse had been commissioned by the federal government to prepare a comprehensive report on the nation's Indian tribes. His report, issued in 1822, waxed eloquent about the economic and educational progress of the five tribes and advised that they be left in peace to continue it. Morse's advice was not taken. White settlers bitterly resented the Natives' presence; besides occupying good cotton land, they traded with free blacks and sometimes provided a haven for runaway slaves.[42] State and federal governments responded to the wishes of the settlers, not to the advice of experts. Among the numerous racial conflicts that ensued, the one between Georgia and the Cherokee Nation attracted the most national attention and led to a dramatic confrontation with serious constitutional implications.

42. See Kenneth Porter, *The Negro on the American Frontier* (New York, 1971), 182–327.

The earliest European intruders into what later became the southeastern United States had encountered a thriving people called the Cherokees
living in a large area of the southern Appalachians. Like many other Native Americans, the Cherokees sided with the British at the time of the
Revolutionary War, recognizing that while the imperial authorities
wanted to trade, the white settlers wanted their land. Four years after their
British allies surrendered at Yorktown, the Cherokees too conceded defeat
in the Treaty of Hopewell, South Carolina (1785). By its terms, the Cherokees yielded the larger part of their accustomed territory. What remained
acquired for the first time clear boundaries, which were further restricted
by treaties after Tennessee became a state. For a decade there continued to
be sporadic unauthorized raids and reprisals by both sides, but the Cherokee Nation never again made war against the United States. Indeed, the
tribe allied with Andrew Jackson against their old enemies the Creeks and
played a major part in his victory at Horseshoe Bend in 1814. Celebrated as
a triumph at the time, in the long run this campaign against the Creeks
may have been a mistake, since it foreclosed any possibility of intertribal
collective resistance. Jackson's goodwill, which the Cherokees imagined
they had earned, proved short-lived; at the Treaty of Fort Jackson, he extracted land cessions not only from the Creeks but also from his Cherokee
allies. (The willingness of Crawford, then Madison's secretary of war, to
compensate the Cherokees for these lands initially provoked the long-
standing bitterness between him and Jackson.)[43]

The half century following 1785 might be called the golden age of the
Cherokee Nation. As defined by 1819, the nation occupied the northwest
corner of Georgia and adjacent portions of what are now Alabama, Tennessee, and North Carolina. The people had always practiced agriculture
(as their Green Corn Dance testifies), and within their restricted boundaries they increasingly turned to farming as a substitute for hunting and
gathering. Trade with the whites flourished, and permanent towns grew
up. Decades of evolution in the direction of more centralized and for-
malized political institutions reached their climax with the adoption of a
written constitution for the nation in 1827.[44] In these and other ways, the
Cherokees showed an ability to synthesize elements borrowed from Western civilization with their Native culture. A prosperous elite emerged,

---

43. Grace Woodward, *The Cherokees* (Norman, Okla., 1963), 131–33; Thomas P. Aber-
    nathy, *From Frontier to Plantation in Tennessee* (Chapel Hill, 1932), 239.
44. See William McLoughlin, *Cherokee Renascence in the New Republic* (Princeton, 1986);
    Duane Champagne, *Social Order and Political Change: Constitutional Governments
    Among the Cherokee, the Choctaw, the Chickasaw, and the Creek* (Stanford, 1992).

among whom some had received a Western education at mission schools and converted to Christianity. There were Cherokees who intermarried with whites, took up cotton cultivation, and bought slaves. By 1835, about 8 percent of Cherokee families owned slaves. Most of the slaveowners were "mixed bloods," as those with some white ancestry were called.[45] A census taken in 1825 counted 13,563 Cherokees, plus 147 white men and 73 white women who had married into the nation, and 1,277 black slaves. While surely an undercount, the census indicated a growing and cohesive population.[46]

As remarkable as the economic and political history of the Cherokee golden age was its intellectual history. Far away from the mission schools, a disabled Cherokee veteran of the Creek War went off to live in Arkansas. Sequoyah knew no English, but he pondered deeply over bits of paper with little marks on them, called the white people's "talking leaves." How could one make leaves that spoke in the Cherokee language? The solution Sequoyah found workable came to him in a flash of insight in 1821. Within six weeks he devised a system of eighty-six characters, each representing a syllable in the Cherokee language. He rushed back to Georgia with the news. Sequoyah's syllabary could be mastered by an adult Cherokee-speaker within a week and caught on quickly. By 1828 special type had been cast so that a newspaper, the *Cherokee Phoenix*, could be published in the nation, with parallel columns in English and Cherokee using the new system. Sequoyah turned his attention to applying his system to the Choctaw language, but he never learned English. Sequoyah remains the only identifiable person in human history to have invented a system for writing his own language without first being literate in another.[47]

The national development of the Cherokees, undertaken at their own initiative, occurred along lines the federal government had approved and professed to encourage. In the Treaty of Holston (1791), the United States had undertaken to assist the Cherokee Nation to "be led to a greater degree of civilization, and to become herdsmen and cultivators, instead of remaining in a state of hunters." In 1806, President Jefferson had urged the Cherokees "to go on learning to cultivate the earth." Jefferson had

45. Theda Perdue, *Slavery and the Evolution of Cherokee Society* (Knoxville, Tenn., 1979), 60.
46. The census did not include those Cherokees who had migrated beyond the Mississippi with government encouragement. Ulrich B. Phillips, *Georgia and State Rights* (Washington, 1902), 71.
47. See Grant Foreman, *Sequoyah* (Norman, Okla., 1938).

welcomed intermarriage, hoping it would lead to the assimilation of the Natives into the dominant culture. ("In time you will be as we are," the third president had told a delegation of chiefs in 1809; "your blood will mix with ours: and will spread with ours over this great land.")[48] Others, seeing the havoc wrought in the New World by European diseases, predicted that the Indians would simply die out. Significantly, Jefferson's vision of absorption and the less benign expectation of extinction shared a common consequence: The lands of the Natives would become available for white settlement.[49] The government had promoted commerce to encourage the tribes to adopt a white way of life, operating its own Indian trading posts, called "factories," between 1796 and 1822. Beginning in 1815, it subsidized Christian missionaries to set up schools (with no one voicing a concern about church-state relations). The emergence of a commercially and politically viable Cherokee Nation with a growing Christian minority, borrowing Western technology as needed, forced the white majority to decide what they really wanted for and from the Native Americans. In the past, whites had justified taking aboriginal lands on the grounds that the Indians were not fully utilizing them. Now, Cherokee economic development was rapidly eliminating that excuse.

The problem—from a white point of view—was that the success of efforts to "civilize the Indians" had not yielded the expected dividend in land sales. On the contrary, the more literate, prosperous, and politically organized the Cherokees made themselves, the more resolved they became to keep what remained of their land and improve it for their own benefit. The council of chiefs, urged by federal commissioners in 1823 to sell out and migrate beyond the Mississippi, replied, "It is the fixed and unalterable determination of this nation never to cede *one foot* more of our land."[50] Where whites had contemplated such possibilities for them as assimilation, eviction, or extinction, the Cherokees envisioned a different future, built in what remained of their ancestral homeland. A delegation to Washington in 1824 presented the tribe's case with straightforward dignity. "The Cherokees are not foreigners, but original inhabitants of America; they now inhabit and stand on the soil of their own territory; and the limits of their territory are defined by the treaties which they have

48. "Address to the Chiefs of the Cherokee" (1806), *TJ: Writings*, 562; Jefferson (1809) quoted in Meinig, *Continental America*, 80.
49. See Anthony Wallace, *Jefferson and the Indians* (Cambridge, Mass., 1999). The Treaty of Holston is quoted in John West, *The Politics of Revelation and Reason: Religion and Civic Life in the New Nation* (Lawrence, Kans., 1980), 182.
50. Walter Lowrie and Walter Franklin, eds., *American State Papers: Indian Affairs* (Washington, 1834), class 2, vol. II, 469.

made with the Government of the United States."[51] The Monroe administration accorded the delegation diplomatic courtesy, provoking protest from racists.[52]

There was a third party to the debate over the Cherokee lands: the state of Georgia, which had both Creek and Cherokee territory within her boundaries. Georgia's political leaders had concentrated first on pushing out the Creeks; now, they turned against the Cherokees. Governor George Troup, who had been a Crawfordite in 1824, supported state internal improvements and public education. He could logically have rallied to support John Quincy Adams had that upright New Englander winked at defrauding the Creeks. But when President Adams resisted Georgia's high-handed methods of dispossession, Troup decided to capitalize on the Indian Removal issue, issuing inflammatory denunciations of Adams. Troup's demagogic tactics worked: He not only occupied all the Creek lands but also gained reelection as governor in 1825. In 1827, John Forsyth, equally committed to Indian Removal, succeeded Troup as governor and delivered a unanimous Georgia popular vote to Jackson for president in 1828.[53]

In December 1828, with Jackson safely elected, the Georgia state legislature proceeded against the Cherokees, confident that the incoming administration would not interfere. The legislature unilaterally declared that starting in June 1830, state laws would extend over the Cherokee Nation, notwithstanding the federal treaties of 1785 and subsequent years. To justify its presumptuous action, the legislature asserted that the United States could never have meant to accord autonomy to "barbarous and savage tribes," and that the Indians were only Georgia's "tenants at will."[54] When the Cherokees discovered gold on their lands in the spring of 1829 and outsiders found out about it, a horde of impatient whites, unwilling to wait even until June 1, 1830, rushed in and began prospecting. What should have been an economic advantage to the Cherokee Nation turned into a political liability, as violent clashes between Cherokees and intruders ensued. At the request of Governor Forsyth, Secretary of War Eaton

---

51. Ibid., 474.
52. Phillips, *Georgia and State Rights*, 70.
53. Anthony Carey, *Parties, Slavery, and the Union in Antebellum Georgia* (Athens, Ga., 1997), 20–23.
54. Phillips, *Georgia and State Rights*, 71–72. On the origins of this claim, see Stuart Banner, *How the Indians Lost Their Land* (Cambridge, Mass., 2005), 205–6; Lindsay Robertson, *Conquest by Law: How the Discovery of America Dispossessed Indigenous Peoples of Their Lands* (Oxford, 2005), 95–116.

withdrew federal troops from the area and after June 1829 allowed the Georgia Guard to assume responsibility for law and order. The aggressiveness of the Georgia political establishment, compounded by outside pressure on the Cherokee gold fields, lent urgency to the issue of Indian Removal when Jackson's first Congress assembled in December 1829.[55]

The Indian Removal Bill constituted the highest priority in the new president's legislative agenda. Both the passage of the law and its subsequent enforcement engaged Jackson's attention to the fullest. "There was no measure, in the whole course of his administration, of which he was more exclusively the author than this," commented Martin Van Buren (who would know).[56] Indian Removal held the place in Jackson's vision that internal improvements occupied in that of John Quincy Adams: the key to national development. Jackson's concerns were geopolitical as well as economic. In his eyes, the tribes not only occupied rich land, they threatened American sovereignty as the British and Spanish had done and, like the free black maroon communities of Florida, challenged white supremacy. Jackson shared the attitude of the Georgians toward the original inhabitants. To him, the practice of dealing with Indian tribes through treaties was "an absurdity"; the government should simply impose its will on them.[57] Nevertheless, the administration's Indian Removal Bill called for another round of treaty-making, intended to secure the complete removal of the Native Americans to west of the Mississippi River.

This grandiose program had been discussed ever since the early days of the Monroe administration. Jackson had commended it; the president had responded with characteristic ambiguity. Monroe seemed to endorse both emigration and assimilation but did not apply pressure on the Native Americans to adopt either. Instead, he allowed Secretary of War Calhoun to continue supporting education and economic progress within existing tribal domains.[58] In the succeeding administration, both President Adams and his secretary of war, James Barbour, were convinced that assimilation and U.S. citizenship represented the only just long-term policy toward the Indians. But having tried in vain to defend the legal rights of the

55. McLoughlin, *Cherokee Renascence*, 430–33; Tim Garrison, *The Legal Ideology of Removal* (Athens, Ga., 2002), 103–14, 120–21.
56. *Autobiography of Martin Van Buren*, ed. John Fitzpatrick (Washington, 1920), 295.
57. AJ to James Monroe, March 4, 1817, *Papers of Andrew Jackson*, IV, 93–98. Jackson relied on the legal concept of "eminent domain"; see Banner, *How the Indians Lost Their Land*, 202–4.
58. See Thomas Clark and John Guice, *Frontiers in Conflict* (Albuquerque, N.M., 1989), 238–40; James P. Ronda, "Race, Geography, and the Invention of Indian Territory," *JER* 19 (1999): 739–55.

Creeks against Georgia, the two left office gloomy about the prospects of the Native Americans. As Barbour put it in 1826, "They see that our professions are insincere, that our promises are broken, that the happiness of the Indian is a cheap sacrifice to the acquisition of new lands." By the end of his term, Adams had reluctantly concluded that removal probably constituted the only alternative to a lawless destruction of the tribes and the death or subjugation of their members at the hands of the states. He came to view the dispossession of the native inhabitants by the whites as an inevitable tragedy, one that constituted "a perpetual harrow upon my feelings." But he still wanted the process to respect law and order and federal supremacy.[59]

Jackson's State of the Union message claimed that Indian Removal would be "voluntary." In reality, everyone knew that no stone would be left unturned to extract such "voluntary" migrations. Jackson was personally well experienced in the techniques of bribery, intimidation, and fraud through which treaties were imposed on reluctant peoples, having been active in securing a series of land cessions by the Civilized Tribes since 1816. To make it clear what he really meant, the president stated that the federal government would not protect the Indians in their present locations whenever states extended jurisdiction over them. This announcement was a clear departure from policy under Adams. Jackson told the Native Americans "to emigrate beyond the Mississippi or submit to the laws of those States." Submission to the laws of Georgia for a Creek or Cherokee meant not being able to vote, sue, own property, testify against a white person, or obtain credit. For Sharp Knife (as the Indians called Jackson) to pretend that such submission represented a viable option offering the Natives the chance to "become merged in the mass of our population," was disingenuous, to say the least. ("I was satisfied that the Indians could not possibly live under the laws of the state," Jackson admitted privately.) In fact, when an earlier federal treaty (1819) for a Cherokee land cession had guaranteed citizenship and property rights to those Natives who chose to remain, Georgia had refused to accept the stipulations.[60]

The president's Indian Removal Bill provoked a fierce debate, producing alignments that proved remarkably durable in defining support and

59. Lynn Parsons, "'A perpetual Harrow upon my Feelings': John Quincy Adams and the American Indian," *New England Quarterly* 46 (Sept. 1973), 339–79; quotation from Barbour on p. 358.
60. Jackson, "First Annual Message," *Presidential Messages*, II, 458–59; AJ to John Pitchlynn, Aug. 5, 1830, *Correspondence of AJ*, IV, 169; Phillips, *Georgia and State Rights*, 69.

opposition to the Jackson administration. Since the Native Americans themselves were outside the political community, they had to rely on white sympathizers in Congress and society at large. Beyond the doors of Congress, the most conspicuous groups involved in the movement against Removal consisted of Protestant clergy and women. At the head of the movement stood Jeremiah Evarts, corresponding secretary of the American Board of Commissioners for Foreign Missions (ABCFM), an interdenominational organization sponsoring most of the Christian missionaries to the Indians. The attitude of the missionaries must be characterized carefully if we are to understand their role. Passionately devoted to the propagation of Protestant Christianity and Western civilization, they took scarcely any interest in Native culture. Yet at the same time they believed implicitly in the rationality, moral responsibility, and equal human worth of their Indian hosts. Proud of the Cherokee Christian minority and supportive of the tribe's economic development, the missionaries welcomed Sequoyah's accomplishments. Dispossession and deportation of the Indians they condemned as a cruel betrayal. Evarts lobbied strenuously, organized protest meetings and petitions, and wrote powerful tracts defending aboriginal rights, using the pseudonym "William Penn." The Penn essays were reprinted in over a hundred newspapers and read, according to a contemporary estimate, by half a million people.[61]

Catharine Beecher, the redoubtable daughter of Lyman Beecher and sister of Harriet Beecher Stowe, led the women's opposition to Removal. Working anonymously, she organized a drive to deluge Congress with petitions from women opposing Removal. "Women are protected from the blinding influence of party spirit," argued her circular letter. Not being voters, but defenders of morality, charity, and family values, women were free to "*feel* for the distressed." A typical petition, the one from Hallowell, Maine, denounced Removal as undercutting efforts to "enlighten and christianize" the Indians. "We are unwilling that the church, the schools, and the domestic altar should be thrown down before the avaricious god of power."[62] Through language such as this, Beecher and her fellow petitioners shrewdly avoided a head-on challenge to male supremacy and sought to wrap their protest in the protective nineteenth-century doctrine

61. Jeremiah Evarts, *Cherokee Removal*, ed. Francis Prucha (Knoxville, Tenn., 1981); John Andrew, *Jeremiah Evarts* (Athens, Ga., 1992); Michael Coleman, *Presbyterian Missionary Attitudes Toward American Indians* (Jackson, Miss., 1985) 139–42, 177.

62. Beecher is quoted in Mary Hershberger, "Mobilizing Women, Anticipating Abolition: The Struggle Against Indian Removal in the 1830s," *JAH* 86 (1999): 26; the petition is quoted in John West, *The Politics of Revelation and Reason* (Lawrence, Kans., 1996), 185.

of "separate spheres" for women and men. Even so, Democratic politicians like Senator Thomas Hart Benton of Missouri mocked them and their male associates.[63] Unprecedented as a mobilization of women's opinion on a public issue, Catharine Beecher's petition drive against Removal set a pattern that would be followed by the antislavery movement in years to come.

Both female and male opponents of Removal made use of the network of evangelical colleges and organizations as well as the communications system to mobilize their followers. This time the moral reformers mounted a much bigger campaign than they had for sabbatarianism. Their activities and support were not confined to New England neo-Puritan strongholds; the largest of the women's petitions, bearing 670 signatures, came from Pittsburgh. Martin Van Buren felt startled when his own niece denounced Indian Removal to his face and told him she hoped he and Jackson would lose the election of 1832.[64] A popular play called *Metamora*, based on King Philip's War of 1675–76, opened in New York City to foster and exploit white sympathy for the Indians. America's leading actor, Edwin Forrest, played the title role of the Wampanoag sachem who fought courageously against encroaching settlers. When the play went on tour to Augusta, Georgia, a boycott forced its closure.[65] But even within the South courageous opponents of Removal spoke up, like the lawyer Robert Campbell of Savannah, who warned his fellow Georgians that they would bring "enduring shame" on their state. "In modern times in civilized countries there is no instance of expelling the members of a whole nation from their homes or driving an entire population from its native country," he declared.[66]

Within Congress, the most eloquent critic of Jackson's Removal Bill was Senator Theodore Frelinghuysen of New Jersey, a prominent supporter of the ABCFM and other benevolent associations like the American Temperance Union and the American Bible Society. Frelinghuysen proposed an amendment to the bill that would have reaffirmed the government's obligation to protect the tribes in their existing locations unless and until they signed new treaties; this would have continued the policy of Monroe and Adams. On behalf of this amendment he spoke for six

63. *Register of Debates*, 21st Cong., 1st sess. (Feb. 2, 1830), 108–9.
64. Randolph Roth, *The Democratic Dilemma: Religion, Reform, and the Social Order* (Cambridge, Eng., 1987), 164–68; Van Buren, *Autobiography*, 293.
65. Jill Lepore, *The Name of War: King Philip's War and the Origins of American Identity* (New York, 1998), 191–226.
66. Robert Campbell, "From *The Georgian*," *Niles' Weekly Register*, Aug. 30, 1828, 14.

hours over a period of three days. One after another, the senator demolished the arguments offered to justify unilateral expropriation, beginning with the claim that the needs of white society justified taking the Natives' lands. He condemned the "high-handed" conduct of Georgia in defying the Treaty of Hopewell. Frelinghuysen did not shrink from using the U.S. Army to protect the Cherokees against Georgia's intrusion if necessary. "Let such decided policy go forth in the majesty of our laws now, and sir, Georgia will yield. She will never encounter the responsibilities or the horrors of civil war. But if she should, no stains of blood will be on our skirts; on herself the guilt will abide forever." This unflinching high principle won Frelinghuysen the nickname he bore ever after: "the Christian statesman."[67]

The grassroots protest movement organized by Evarts and Beecher succeeded in defining Removal as a moral issue. It served to awaken anti-Jackson politicians less morally committed than Frelinghuysen to their opportunity to resist the president. Henry Clay, who had expressed precious little sympathy for the Indians earlier in his career, now decided to rally to their side.[68] With the opposition invoking moral principle, the administration felt impelled to find philanthropic arguments of its own. The Indians might be better off in the West, farther away from the alcohol and contagious diseases of the whites. There, the administration claimed, the Indians could become "civilized" in peace. One of the administration spokesmen espousing this argument was Isaac McCoy, a former Baptist missionary who was now a government surveyor of Indian lands. The Baptist missionary board and denominational organ repudiated McCoy's statements.[69] Many advocates of Removal, particularly southerners, scorned to employ the philanthropic argument. "I do not believe that this removal will accelerate the civilization of the tribes," Georgia's John Forsyth, now a senator, told his colleagues. "You might as reasonably expect that wild animals, incapable of being tamed in a park, would be domesticated by turning them loose in the forest." The administration's effort to arouse popular support for Removal on a philanthropic basis quickly fizzled.[70]

67. Theodore Frelinghuysen, "The Cherokee Lands," *Register of Debates*, 21st Cong., 1st sess. (April 6, 1830), 309–20.
68. Henry Clay to Jeremiah Evarts, Aug. 23, 1830, *Papers of Henry Clay*, ed. Robert Seager (Lexington, Ky., 1984), VIII, 255.
69. Hershberger, "Mobilizing Women," 29–30.
70. *Register of Debates*, 21st Cong., 1st sess. (April 13, 1830), 327; Herman Viola, *Thomas L. McKenny* (Chicago, 1974), 221–22.

To mobilize support in Congress, the administration relied less on persuasive argument than on party loyalty, though this was still a novel concept in a country not long removed from the Era of Good Feelings. While complaining that their opponents were motivated primarily by partisanship, administration leaders made no secret of their own determination to make support for Removal a test of fealty to the president. Despite Frelinghuysen's oratory, the Jacksonian majority in the Senate passed the Removal Bill by a party-line vote, 28 to 19. In the House it proved a different story. Representatives elected as Jackson supporters from districts with many Quaker, Congregationalist, or New School Presbyterian voters found themselves in an awkward crossfire. The difficulty northern congressmen had in swallowing the betrayal of treaty obligations was compounded by their fear for the future of internal improvements. Indian Removal would be expensive, and Jackson said he wanted to retire the national debt. Even if the government avoided frontier wars, the money spent to buy out the tribes, round up their members, and transport them hundreds of miles would not be available for internal improvements. Beset by these concerns, northern Jacksonian congressmen defected in large numbers. The Indian Removal Bill only barely passed the House, 102 to 97, with 24 Jacksonians voting no and 12 others not voting. On some of the preliminary tests of strength the votes had been even closer, Speaker Andrew Stevenson having to break ties three times. At the last minute the administration managed to press three wavering Pennsylvania Democrats back into the party line, saving the bill. The vote had a pronounced sectional aspect: the slave states voted 61 to 15 for Removal; the free states opposed it, 41 to 82. Without the three-fifths clause jacking up the power of the slaveholding interest, Indian Removal would not have passed. Yet sectionalism did not determine positions so much as political loyalties and moral values. The trans-Appalachian West did not by any means display solid support for the bill; its congressmen voted 23 in favor, 17 opposed. Those opposed included a West Tennessee frontiersman named Davy Crockett, who characterized the bill as "oppression with a vengeance." Like most critics of Indian Removal, Crockett went on to become a permanent opponent of Jackson. The president signed Indian Removal into law on May 28, 1830.[71]

Jackson wasted no time implementing his favorite measure. While the nation's attention was focused on Georgia and Cherokees, he sent his

71. Tabulations of party voting on the bill vary slightly because party designations were not clear in every case. Crockett's statement against Indian Removal was printed in *Speeches on the Passage of the Bill for the Removal of the Indians,* ed. Jeremiah Evarts (Boston, 1830), 251–53.

trusted friend John Coffee and Secretary of War Eaton to Mississippi to obtain the removal of the Choctaws. The efforts they commenced secured the Treaty of Dancing Rabbit Creek on September 27, 1830, against the wishes of the majority of the tribe, by excluding the Indians' white counselors from the negotiations and then bribing selected tribal leaders. While some Choctaws in the forests of eastern Mississippi contrived to elude the government's attention until 1918 (!), the majority were compelled to move to Oklahoma. The first large party of Choctaws crossed the Mississippi River during the severe winter of 1831–32, the French observer Tocqueville noting the hardships of their passage.[72]

While some of the whites placed in charge of the migration, particularly the career army officers, were honest and conscientious, others were political appointees out to get rich quick. The financial aspect of this first dispossession embarrassed the administration, for it cost over $5 million to expel the Choctaws—$2 million more than Jackson had claimed would suffice to deport *all* the tribes east of the Mississippi. The high cost reflected mismanagement and corruption, while the migrants themselves were frequently victims of parsimony.[73]

Meanwhile, Jackson had been applying pressure to the rest of the tribes. Recognizing the missionaries as key adversaries, he withdrew federal funding from mission schools. The administration stopped making the promised annuity payments to the Cherokee Nation and put the money into escrow until the tribe should remove.[74] Existing treaties should have remained in force unless and until tribes consented to alter them, and even the Indian Removal Act as passed did not state otherwise.[75] But the president, far from defending existing U.S. treaty obligations, proved only too willing to turn over federal authority in the tribal lands to the states whenever they claimed it. With his encouragement, Alabama and Mississippi followed Georgia's example and extended state jurisdiction over their own Native populations. And in February 1831, Jackson notified the Senate that he would no longer enforce the Indian Intercourse Act of 1802, a law protecting Indian lands against intruders. Thomas McKenney, the knowledgeable superintendent of Indian affairs,

72. Alexis de Tocqueville, *Democracy in America*, ed. Phillips Bradley (New York, 1945), I, 340.
73. See Arthur DeRosier Jr., *The Removal of the Choctaw Indians* (Knoxville, Tenn., 1970), 100–147; Ronald Satz, *American Indian Policy in the Jacksonian Era* (Lincoln, Neb., 1975), 64–96; Cole, *Presidency of Andrew Jackson*, 109–12.
74. John Andrew, *Jeremiah Evarts*, 232–33; McLoughlin, *Cherokee Renascence*, 438.
75. "Indian Removal Act," *Documents of United States Indian Policy*, ed. Francis Prucha (Lincoln, Neb., 2000), 52–53.

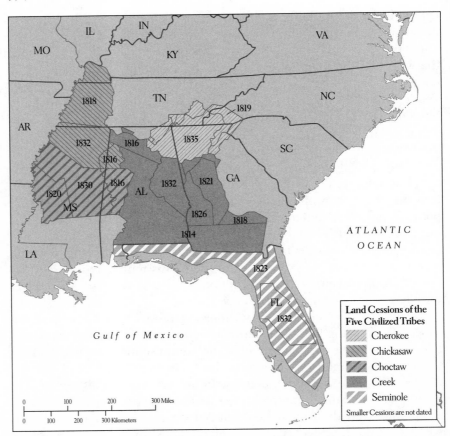

Adapted from Thomas Dionysius Clark and John D.W. Guice, *Frontiers in Conflict: The Old Southwest, 1975–1830* (University of New Mexico Press, 1989).

was a Calhoun protégé and holdover from the Monroe and Adams administrations who had become convinced that Removal was in the tribes' best interests. But when he tried to carry out the policy with honesty and some consideration for Native rights, an impatient Jackson dismissed him in August, 1830.[76]

The Cherokees turned to the federal courts for protection. Georgia was clearly defying their rights as guaranteed by federal treaty, which according to the Constitution should be "the supreme law of the land." Hiring two of the best constitutional lawyers in the country, John Sergeant and

76. Richard Latner, *The Presidency of Andrew Jackson* (Athens, Ga., 1979), 91.

William Wirt (who had been attorney general under Monroe and Adams), the tribe brought a suit in the United States Supreme Court, *Cherokee Nation v. Georgia*, to restrain the state from extending its authority over them. In March 1831, the justices voted 4 to 2 to sidestep the issue. Speaking for the majority, Chief Justice Marshall made clear his sympathy for the Indians' case, but he held that the Cherokees constituted a "domestic dependent nation" and did not satisfy the definition of a sovereign "state" entitled to bring a suit over which the Supreme Court would have original jurisdiction.[77] The expression "domestic dependent nation" was destined to influence subsequent federal law on Indian tribes, but its first use enabled the Court to avoid an unwanted confrontation with state power and the executive branch. The Court may have been influenced by Jackson's announcement the month before that he would not protect the Choctaws against the state of Mississippi in an analogous situation. Georgia served notice that it had extended its jurisdiction by trying and convicting in state court an Indian named Corn Tassel of the murder of another Indian in the Cherokee Nation. When the Supreme Court called for arguments on appeal, the state ignored the writ and executed the prisoner. Meanwhile, extreme state-righters introduced into Congress a bill to repeal section 25 of the Judiciary Act of 1789, the law authorizing the Supreme Court to hear appeals from state courts. Although defeated, the bill seems to have intimidated the Court, for it took no action on the contumacious behavior of the Georgia authorities.[78]

A year later the Cherokee-Georgia crisis confronted the Supreme Court with another case, this time one the justices felt they had to address. Since Christian missionaries were among the most effective opponents of Removal, Governor George Gilmer of Georgia decided in January 1831 to expel them from the Cherokee lands.[79] Two of the missionaries, Samuel Worcester and Elizur Butler, refused to leave and were sentenced to four years at hard labor. Subjected to brutal treatment intended to crack their will to resist, while simultaneously offered pardons if they would acknowledge Georgia's legal authority, the men courageously refused and appealed their convictions to the U.S. Supreme Court. The same lawyers who had appeared for the Cherokee Nation took their case, and by now both were leading political adversaries of Jackson, for in 1832 John Sergeant was vice-presidential

77. *Cherokee Nation v. Georgia*, 30 U.S. (5 Peters) 1–80 (1831).
78. Cole, *Presidency of Jackson*, 111.
79. Annie Heloise Abel, *History of Events Resulting in Indian Consolidation West of the Mississippi River* (Washington, 1908), 397.

candidate of the National Republicans and William Wirt presidential candidate of the Antimasonic Party. Georgia refused to acknowledge that the U.S. Supreme Court had jurisdiction. The state sent surveyors into the Cherokee Nation to prepare its lands for expropriation and tried to intimidate the missionaries' wives and single white female schoolteachers into leaving. But these Christian women were made of stern stuff; they stuck to their posts and urged their men to continue defiance of the state.[80]

In March 1832, when the two missionaries had endured eight months' imprisonment, John Marshall delivered the opinion of the Court: The Cherokee Nation was protected by federal treaty within its own territory, "in which the law of Georgia can have no right to enter but with the assent of the Cherokees." Georgia's argument that the state possessed sovereignty over Indian lands by "right of discovery," inherited from the British Crown (which the state had not deigned to present in person), was rejected. The act of Georgia under which the missionaries had been convicted and imprisoned was declared "void, as being repugnant to the constitution, treaties, and laws of the United States." The decision represented the legal vindication of all the Cherokees had maintained.[81] Embarrassingly for Jackson, the nationalist former postmaster general John McLean, whom he had recently appointed to the Court, wrote a concurrence. The lone dissenter was Jackson's other appointee, Henry Baldwin, who filed no opinion. The new justice feared doing so would only encourage Georgia to defy the Court, whose authority he respected even when he disagreed with it.[82] Everyone knew that enforcing the decision would not be easy.

Seeking the fundamental impulse behind Jacksonian Democracy, historians have variously pointed to free enterprise, manhood suffrage, the labor movement, and resistance to the market economy. But in its origins, Jacksonian Democracy (which contemporaries understood as a synonym for Jackson's Democratic Party) was not primarily about any of these, though it came to intersect with all of them in due course. In the

80. Ann O. Worcester to David Greene, Dec. 7, 1831, and May 17, 1832, and other ms. correspondence in Houghton Library, Harvard Univ., reproduced on the website *Women and Social Movements in the United States*, ed. Kathryn Sklar and Thomas Dublin.
81. *Worcester v. Georgia*, 31 U.S. (6 Peters) 515–97 (1832). Dealing with the "right of discovery" posed a serious problem for Marshall because of an earlier decision of his that accepted it, *Johnson v. M'Intosh* (1823). For legal analyses see Banner, *How the Indians Lost Their Land*, esp. 220–21; and Robertson, *Conquest by Law*, esp. 133–35.
82. Lindsay Robertson, "Justice Henry Baldwin's 'Lost Opinion' in *Worcester v. Georgia*," *Journal of Supreme Court History* 23 (1999): 50–75.

first place it was about the extension of white supremacy across the North American continent. By his policy of Indian Removal, Jackson confirmed his support in the cotton states outside South Carolina and fixed the character of his political party. Indian policy, not banking or the tariff, was the number one issue in the national press during the early years of Jackson's presidency. But in his enthusiasm for Indian Removal, Jackson raised up an angry reaction, not only among evangelical Christians but also from constitutional nationalists, provoking them into an alliance with his political opponents that would shape party alignments for a generation. Claiming to be the champion of democracy, Jackson provoked opposition from the strongest nationwide democratic protest movement the country had yet witnessed. And a statistical analysis of congressional behavior has found that, as the second party system took shape, voting on Indian affairs proved to be the most consistent predictor of partisan affiliation.[83]

IV

The Jacksonian leadership pushed Indian Removal through the House of Representatives with unseemly haste. On May 27, the day after the House voted, the president vetoed a major internal improvements measure, the Maysville Road Bill. The Maysville Road through Lexington, Kentucky, had been intended as a link in a nationwide transportation network, connecting the National Road to the north with the Natchez Trace to the south and the Ohio with the Tennessee river systems. Robert Hemphill of Pennsylvania, a Jackson supporter and proponent of internal improvements, having narrowly failed to win passage of a bill authorizing the entire road, had secured the Maysville segment as a more modest but promising start. Many such Jacksonian congressmen felt outraged that the president had pressured them to back Indian Removal, only to betray their interest in internal improvements. Some demanded a reconsideration of Indian Removal but found that the bill had reached the president's desk and was beyond their recall. Now the significance of the deadline for passing Indian Removal became clear: The president could hold back his veto of the Maysville Road only ten days, and the White House realized that Indian Removal would lose if the veto message arrived on Capitol Hill before the vote.[84]

83. Fred S. Rolater, "The American Indian and the Origin of the Second American Party System," *Wisconsin Magazine of History* 76 (1993): 180–201.
84. See Pamela Baker, "The Washington National Road Bill," *JER* 22 (2002): 438–64; Latner, *Presidency of Jackson*, 94, 102.

Van Buren had urged the veto on the president. The Sly Fox of Kinderhook figured out that a stand against federal internal improvements would play well with state-rights Radicals in the South, thereby preventing Crawford's old constituency from bolting to Calhoun. Furthermore, since New York already enjoyed the benefit of the Erie Canal, built with its own money, Van Buren's home state stood to gain little from federally funded internal improvements elsewhere. Not that Jackson needed much persuasion: He was only too happy to veto a road that would pass through Henry Clay's hometown. "I had the most amusing scenes in my endeavors to prevent him from avowing his intentions before the bill passed the two houses," Van Buren confided to Francis Blair.[85] Working in secrecy, Jackson and Van Buren composed a veto message with the aid of James Knox Polk, a Tennessee Democrat, one of the few western congressmen suspicious of federal internal improvements.

The Maysville Veto Message attracted wide attention and remains a key document for understanding the subtleties of the Jacksonian attitude toward the transportation revolution. The message admitted that federal funding for national schemes of internal improvement had long been practiced, but also pointed out that constitutional doubt had never been altogether overcome and concluded that it would be safer to authorize it by a constitutional amendment. Pending the adoption of such an amendment, however, the president claimed to apply the test of whether the proposal was "general, not local, national, not State," in character. Ignoring the fact that the Maysville Road would be a segment of an interstate highway system, Jackson declared that it failed this test. But while he criticized the Maysville Road for being insufficiently national, Jackson did not wish to be misunderstood as favoring federal funding for a more truly national transportation system. Instead, he warned that expenditures on internal improvements might jeopardize his goal of retiring the national debt—or, alternatively, require heavier taxes. Interestingly, Jackson did not set his face against economic development or the expansion of commerce in general. Far from decrying the effects of the transportation revolution, Jackson fully conceded the popularity and desirability of internal improvements. "I do not suppose there is an intelligent citizen who does not wish to see them flourish," he assured his countrymen. But he felt that these projects were better left to private enterprise and the states. Analysis of the Maysville Veto Message and the

---

85. Quoted in Edward Channing, *History of the United States* (New York, 1921), V, 397.

evidence of Jackson's economic policies in general do not sustain the claim made by some historians that he expressed resistance to market capitalism.[86]

Politically, the Maysville Message was a masterstroke. Sure enough, Old Republicans welcomed the veto. "It fell upon the ears like the music of other days," said John Randolph of Roanoke.[87] Yet it managed to avoid alienating the frontier. To their surprise, western Jacksonian congressmen who had voted in favor of the road, such as Thomas Hart Benton and Kentucky's Richard Mentor Johnson, found the Old Hero's popularity with their constituents undiminished. The Maysville Veto Message had been crafted to endorse what we would call the transportation revolution while condemning what we would call big government. Though the followers of Henry Clay declared this a contradiction in terms, there were plenty of westerners willing to take Old Hickory's word for it that they could have both economic opportunity and republican simplicity. The message tended to firm up Jackson's strength with his supporters while still further estranging his opponents. This comported well with Van Buren's long-term objective, which (as he had explained to Thomas Ritchie in 1827) was to harden party lines.[88]

Jackson vetoed several other internal improvements bills, in two cases exercising his "pocket veto" power over legislation passed in the last ten days of a congressional session. The pocket veto seemed high-handed to contemporaries; among Jackson's predecessors, only Madison had used it.[89] Yet the president signed many other bills for aid to transportation and ended up spending twice as much money on internal improvements as all his predecessors combined, even when adjusted for inflation. Some of the projects he approved were built in territories rather than states, which made them constitutionally safer. Jackson's administration showed more sympathy for improving natural waterways (used by cotton producers) than for canals (more often used by grain producers). Mixed public-private corporations in which the federal government owned some of the stock, a favorite method of subsidy during the Monroe and Adams administrations, found no favor under Jackson. On the other hand, the

---

86. "Veto Message" (May 27, 1830), *Presidential Messages*, II, 483–93. Jackson and his party are interpreted as a popular movement opposed to market capitalism in Sellers, *Market Revolution*. For an interpretation better grounded in evidence, see John Lauritz Larson, *Internal Improvement* (Chapel Hill, 2001).
87. Quoted in Sellers, *Market Revolution*, 316.
88. Martin Van Buren to Thomas Ritchie, Jan. 13, 1827, discussed above on 279–80.
89. U.S. Senate Library, *Presidential Vetoes* (Washington, 1979), 5.

National, or Cumberland, Road, which had received appropriations of $1,668,000 from previous administrations, received $3,728,000 under Jackson's—perhaps because it facilitated the settlement of the Old Northwest by Butternuts from the Upland South who voted Democratic. A Jacksonian Congress preserved state-rights principles by turning the completed sections of the National Road over to the states through which it passed.[90]

Jackson was fortunate that his time in office coincided with a wave of prosperity. Government revenues from tariffs and land sales soared, which made money available for both internal improvements and Indian Removal, even while retiring the national debt. The president and his party managed to reap the political benefits of a reputation for thrift and constitutional probity while at the same time passing "pork-barrel" legislation on a scale unprecedented. Both contemporaries and historians have noted the inconsistency (or, more charitably, the ambiguity) in Jackson's policy on internal improvements. Adams had signed all bills for internal improvements in order to affirm their constitutionality and build support for economic development. Jackson, however, contrived to leave himself free to approve whatever projects he decided were "national" and veto those he decided were "local," without any clear guidelines for distinguishing between them.[91] The one unambiguous consequence of the Maysville Road Veto was the doom of any comprehensive national transportation program. In the absence of such an overall plan, the Jackson administration felt free to distribute its favors where they would do the most political good. What Van Buren had learned fighting Clinton in New York, about how to posture as a friend of democracy while maintaining a tightly knit party machine and remaining completely flexible on economic issues, he put to use in Washington.

The internal improvements Jackson favored with federal appropriations included seacoast projects that might be called "external improvements": dredging harbors and building lighthouses. Far from being suspicious of markets, the president sought to facilitate international commerce and promote the overseas marketing of American crops. One of the early achievements of his administration was the restoration of trade with the British West Indies. Adams, with his New England Federalist background, had to avoid any appearance of softness in dealing with

90. Cole, *Presidency of Jackson*, 67; Carlton Jackson, "The Internal Improvement Vetoes of Andrew Jackson," *Tennessee Historical Quarterly* 25 (1966): 261–80, statistics on 266.
91. As explained in Daniel Feller, *The Public Lands in Jacksonian Politics* (Madison, Wisc., 1984), 136–42.

Britain. Jackson, by contrast, could afford to be conciliatory. In pursuit of commercial benefits, America's most famous Anglophobe courted British opinion: "Everything in the history of the two nations is calculated to inspire sentiments of mutual respect," he now declared, with some exaggeration.[92] Advised by Secretary of State Van Buren and the Baltimore merchant-senator, Samuel Smith, Jackson and his emissary in London, the former Federalist Louis McLane, worked out a compromise accommodation that opened Canada and the British West Indies to U.S. goods. Democratic Republicans, including Old Republicans like Thomas Ritchie and South Carolina nullifiers like Robert Hayne, rejoiced at the commercial opportunities opened to American exports. National Republicans complained that Jackson had given up on trying to gain access to the West Indian carrying trade and noted that Adams could have had the same agreement if he had been willing to accept it. Indeed, the agreement partially sacrificed the interests of Yankee shipowners to those of agricultural exporters. The administration also signed a treaty obtaining more commercial advantages in the British Isles themselves. Of course, by far the most important of American export staples was cotton, and Britain was by far the best customer for American cotton.[93] When Britain took over the Falkland Islands off the coast of Argentina in 1833, the Jackson administration winked and did not allow this violation of the Monroe Doctrine to disturb cordial commercial relations.

On aspects of Anglo-American relations touching slavery, however, Jackson remained implacable. He refused to discuss any international cooperation to suppress the Atlantic slave trade, though all other maritime powers approved of it. He made no effort to accommodate British protests against the treatment of black West Indian sailors in southern ports. Indeed, whereas Monroe's attorney general, William Wirt, had found the preventive detention of black seamen unconstitutional, Jackson's attorney general, Berrien, declared it a constitutionally permissible exercise of state police power.[94]

The Jackson administration sought out new markets in Russia, East Asia, and the Middle East for U.S. cotton, tobacco, and grain; it pursued

---

92. Jackson, "First Annual Message," 443. Although contained in a message to Congress, these words were written with an overseas audience in mind.

93. See John Belohlavek, *"Let the Eagle Soar": The Foreign Policy of Andrew Jackson* (Lincoln, Neb., 1985), 53–60.

94. Hugh Soulsby, *The Right of Search and the Slave Trade* (Baltimore, 1933), 41–46; Philip Hamer, "Great Britain, the United States, and the Negro Seamen Acts," *Journal of Southern History* 1 (1935): 3–28.

Federal Government Expenses for Internal Improvements, 1789–1858

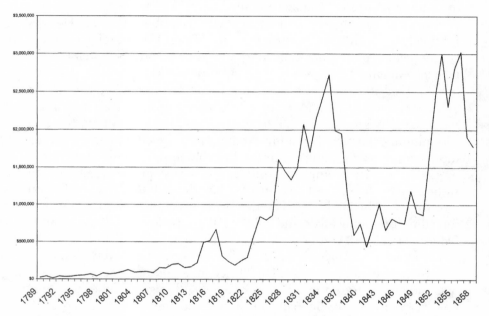

This graph shows how much the federal government spent each year on transportation infrastructure, such as canals, roads, dredging of rivers and harbors, and lighthouses. It indicates a flurry of activity right after the War of 1812, then a marked increase during John Quincy Adams's administration, which soared even higher during the administrations of Jackson and Van Buren until the Panic of 1837 curtailed government revenues and consequently expenses.

Graph prepared by Julia Ott from U.S. Congress, *Statement of appropriations and Expenditures . . . Public works* (Washington, 1882), 47th Congress, 1st session, Senate Executive Documents, vol. 7, no. 196 (U.S. Serial Set number 1992). Data here tabulated do not include expenses for public buildings, forts, armories, arsenals, or mints.

the same objective with less success in Latin America. The navy was expanded, the better to protect American commerce. Responding to the killing of two American merchant sailors by a gang of thieves on Sumatra, Jackson dispatched the USS *Potomac* to the scene with 260 marines. In February 1832, Captain John Downes destroyed the Sumatran town of Quallah Batoo and killed over two hundred of its people, though he did not find the actual perpetrators of the crime. Many critics in the United States felt this an overreaction. In accordance with the wishes of the whaling industry, the administration also authorized the ambitious naval expedition commanded by Charles Wilkes that explored the South Pacific and Antarctic, although because of various delays the flotilla did not set sail until Jackson's successor, Van Buren, had come into office.[95]

Jackson did not hesitate to pursue belligerent foreign policies on behalf of American commercial interests, even against major powers. His envoys gained over $7 million for American merchants in settlements of spoliation claims, mostly against France, dating back to the Napoleonic Wars. When the French Chamber of Deputies in the young July Monarchy balked at paying such a large bill, Jackson raged and threatened to license privateers to prey upon French shipping. Ex-president John Quincy Adams patriotically backed military preparations, but most of Jackson's opponents were appalled. The French put their Caribbean fleet on a wartime basis and demanded that Jackson apologize, an unlikely occurrence. At the last minute (December 1835) the president's advisors found a face-saving formula in which Old Hickory stated that he had not intended "to menace or insult the Government of France." Satisfied, Louis Philippe's ministry authorized payment. Whether tough or gentle, Jackson's foreign policy was usually dictated by commercial interests, especially those of commercial agriculture—which Jackson the cotton planter understood at first hand. During the eight years of his nurturing administration, U.S. exports increased by 70 percent, imports by 250 percent.[96]

The ambiguity or contradictions in the Jacksonians' internal improvements record cannot be explained entirely by the hypocritical machinations of politicians. The mixed signals the administration sent apparently suited the mixed feelings of the American public toward the dramatic changes being wrought by the transportation and communications revolutions. On the one hand, the new economic opportunities were generally

95. William Weeks, *Building the Continental Empire* (Chicago, 1996), 74–77.
96. Belohlavek, *"Let the Eagle Soar,"* 101–25; William Weeks, "Economic Sources of American Foreign Policy in the Early Republic," paper presented to the Society of Historians of American Foreign Relations, June 1994.

welcomed and widely seized. On the other, there were those with reason to fear economic transformations. Artisans, small farmers, and small merchants might find their accustomed local markets disturbed by the sudden intrusion of cheap goods from faraway places. Even some of those benefiting from economic development might worry about threats to local communities and traditional values.[97] Jackson's mixture of appropriations and vetoes affirmed Old Republican principles of limited government while not requiring too much sacrifice of material advantages by his supporters in particular cases. Although unsympathetic to those who wanted the government to help create an integrated *national* market, his policies fostered *international* markets for American commerce. This distinction probably represented the clearest division in economic policy between Jackson and his opposition.

To judge by the views contemporaries expressed, misgivings about government involvement in the economy were much more widespread than misgivings about economic development itself. When Andrew Jackson visited Lowell, Massachusetts, he admired the technology of the textile mills and showed no concern over the social consequences of industrialization.[98] Perhaps his unconcern reflected the fact that the proletariat being created there was female. In any case, economic enterprise generally became controversial only when government became involved. Jackson's election campaigns in 1824 and 1828 had warned against corruption, favoritism, and the perversion of democratic institutions; in office he continued to play upon these fears to discourage federal involvement in economic policymaking. In practice, however, the withdrawal of the federal government from transportation planning did nothing to prevent corruption or inefficiency at the state and local level; indeed, it made them even more likely. Involvement of government—local, state, or federal—in transportation projects helped in a society where large-scale mobilization of capital could be a problem. Most of the debate actually focused not on government intervention as opposed to free enterprise, but on whether only state and local authorities should promote the economy or the federal government play a role too. Doubts over the constitutionality of federal aid to internal improvements persisted throughout the antebellum era, often voiced by slaveholders determined to keep the central government weak lest it interfere with their peculiar institution. Those slaveholders who produced cotton had an additional motive for opposing federal internal

97. The classic discussion of such ambivalent feelings is Marvin Meyers, *The Jacksonian Persuasion* (Stanford, 1957).
98. Watson, *Liberty and Power*, 135.

improvements: If its expenditures could be held down, the government would have less need for tariff revenue. "Destroy the tariff and you will leave no means of carrying on internal improvement," South Carolina's free-trade advocate Senator William Smith declared in 1830; "destroy internal improvement and you leave no motive for the tariff."[99]

The Jackson–Van Buren practice of generous ad hoc appropriations coupled with professions of Old Republican strict construction pleased the friends of particular projects while reassuring slaveholders and staple exporters that the federal government was not being strengthened in principle or undertaking long-term, expensive commitments. Meanwhile, those who continued to believe in the benefits of central economic planning rallied to the opposition. But unfortunately for Adams and Clay, the very popularity of internal improvements hampered federal planning for them. With each region vying with every other for economic advantage, it seldom proved possible to forge the kind of coalitions necessary to legislate in favor of transportation at the national level. Responding to geographical competitions, the expenditures of state and local government to subsidize internal improvements dwarfed those of the federal government, even under Jackson. For the entire period before the Civil War, state governments invested some $300 million in transportation infrastructure; local governments, over $125 million. Direct expenditures by the federal government on such projects came to less than $59 million, though this does not count the substantial indirect help the federal government gave to internal improvements through land grants, revenue distributions, and services rendered by the Army Engineers.[100]

In his first two years in office, President Jackson had already begun to lay the foundations for the future strength of the Democratic Party and to define its character and policies for a long time to come. The spoils system became a powerful instrument for motivating political participation at the grassroots level. The Eaton imbroglio established the pattern that the Democratic Party would resist those who tried to impose their moral standards on the public—whether these related to sexual conduct, Indian affairs, slavery, or war. Indian Removal set a pattern and precedent for geographical expansion and white supremacy that would be invoked in years to come by advocates of America's imperial "manifest destiny." Harder to pin down was Jackson's attitude toward economic development,

---

99. Quoted in Feller, *Public Lands*, 136.
100. Carter Goodrich, *Government Promotion of American Canals and Railroads* (New York, 1960), 268.

but it seemed that he supported the expansion of American commerce and markets, so long as this did not require partnership between the federal government and private enterprise in mixed corporations or long-term, large-scale economic planning. Jackson's hostility to mixed corporations would become much clearer shortly, in his dramatic conflict with the National Bank. His ambiguity on the issue of federal aid to economic development would remain characteristic of the Democratic Party and lead eventually to fierce internal squabbles that pitted the dominant southern wing, determined to keep the central government limited and inexpensive, against northern Democrats eager for internal improvements and tariff protection. But as long as Jackson himself was in the White House, he remained very firmly in charge of both his party and the executive branch.

10

Battles over Sovereignty

All the major political controversies of Andrew Jackson's two terms in the White House involved issues of authority. Jackson exercised presidential authority in new ways, removing competent officeholders and vetoing more bills than all his predecessors put together. (The contrast with his immediate predecessor was particularly striking, since Adams had vetoed no bills at all.) Jackson engaged in contests of authority with Congress and barely avoided one with the Supreme Court. The Eaton Affair showed that even social intercourse could be a matter for the assertion of presidential authority. Ultimate authority, that is, sovereignty, became the subject of explicit and bitter debate during Jackson's administrations. Rival claims of sovereignty for the states and the nation found expression in legal theory, rhetorical eloquence, and finally in political crisis. The president believed in the sovereignty of the American people and in himself as the embodiment of that sovereignty. The conflict between Jackson and the Second Bank of the United States escalated into a "war" waged in defense of both national and popular sovereignty. By the end of his presidency, Jackson had defended federal supremacy in the crisis with South Carolina even while encouraging neighboring Georgia to assert state sovereignty. In the last analysis, it was his personal authority, rather than that of the federal government or even the presidential office, which Jackson zealously maintained.

II

Jacksonians justified Indian Removal as a prerequisite to the westward extension of white settlement. But from the standpoint of Jackson's western supporters, cheap land seemed just as important as the expulsion of the Native population. Western settlers and land speculators wanted to buy cheap from the government and sell dear to later arrivals. Missouri's Thomas Hart Benton, spokesman for the frontier, proposed the price of unsold public lands drop automatically over time until they found a buyer. After four years on the market, their price would reach a mere twenty-five cents an acre. "The public lands belong to the People, and not to the federal government," he thundered.[1] Benton termed his policy "graduation." To achieve more rapid settlement of the West, his plan would severely

---

1. *Register of Debates*, 19th Cong., 1st sess. (May 16, 1826), 727.

curtail the potential value of the lands to the government. It meant abandoning hope of using revenue from the public lands for internal improvements or education and leaving the government without much leverage on the economy. It had therefore been opposed by the Adams administration. Anticipating a more sympathetic response from Jackson, Benton had supported him for president, in spite of the fact that they had once been such bitter personal enemies that Old Hickory still carried a bullet in his body from a shootout with Benton and his brother Jesse in 1813.

In reality, there was plenty of land for all, so much that the price stayed low. Land Office auctions in the 1820s seldom raised much more than the $1.25 minimum even for the best new acres. The Native Americans were dispossessed faster than their lands could be sold. Georgia didn't even try to sell the Cherokee lands it seized; the state raffled them off in a lottery. In New England and the Chesapeake, people complained of depressed property values and abandoned farms because of the abundance of land in the West. Not surprisingly, some argued that Americans would be better off pushing industrialization and developing their infrastructure, instead of trying to expand the agricultural sector with more and more land. As Adams's Treasury secretary, Richard Rush, had put it, "The creation of capital is retarded rather than accelerated by the diffusion of a thin population over a great surface of soil." The growth of cities and towns would eventually provide commercial farmers with a better market. In the meantime, the government's policy of keeping land prices low meant that farms were uneconomically large and too many people worked in the agricultural sector.[2]

When Jackson's first Congress met in December 1829, land sales as well as Indian policy demanded the attention of the members. Senator Samuel Foot of Connecticut, speaking for the East, proposed a temporary moratorium on new lands being offered for sale until more of the existing stock of available land had found buyers. Benton responded on January 18, 1830, with a speech accusing Foot and New Englanders in general of trying "to check the growth and to injure the prosperity of the West." Easterners wanted to keep "the vast and magnificent valley of the Mississippi for the haunts of beasts and savages." Benton suspected a plot by northeastern industrialists, who "want poor people to do the work for small wages," to prevent the masses from having the option of cheap land. He cried out for the South to come to the aid of the West.[3]

2. Annual Report of the Secretary of the Treasury, Dec. 1827, quoted in Daniel Feller, *The Public Lands in Jacksonian Politics* (Madison, Wisc., 1984), 92; James Henretta, "The 'Market' in the Early Republic," *JER* 18 (1998): 289–304.
3. *Register of Debates*, 21st Cong., 1st sess. (Jan. 18, 1830), 25–27.

The rising star of South Carolina politics, Senator Robert Y. Hayne, responded to the call. A protégé of John C. Calhoun, Hayne, like his mentor, had shifted from nationalism to particularism. In the past Hayne had never supported cheap land, but now he endorsed it in a state-rights version: The federal government should cede the public lands to the states where they were located. Western states would surely sell them cheaply, in a race with each other to entice settlers. Jackson was turning the Indian tribes' lands over to the states; why not do the same with the rest of the public lands? The speeches of Benton and Hayne seemed to point the way toward a political alliance of South and West under Jacksonian auspices, directed against New England.

Then Daniel Webster spoke up. "Sir, I rise to defend the East." Earlier a congressman from New Hampshire, Webster was now senator from Massachusetts. "Black Dan" (so called for his dark complexion) had changed more than his constituency, for he was undergoing a political transformation the mirror image of Calhoun's. Formerly a free-trader who had invoked New England state rights in opposition to the War of 1812, Webster emerged as a leading defender of nationalism and a protective tariff when industrialization and cotton textile manufacturing in particular changed the economy of New England. Like Calhoun, Webster nursed presidential ambitions that would be forever frustrated. Unlike the South Carolinian, however, Webster had broad interests outside politics. He was the nation's most famous trial lawyer, a man of letters and bon vivant. Though his private integrity was not above suspicion, his public persona impressed observers. The senator had a feeling for the theatrical; on public occasions he still dressed in the fashion of an eighteenth-century gentleman, with knee breeches and waistcoat.[4] To his cult following, Webster represented the values of civilization, learning, and law that they found wanting in Andrew Jackson.

In this battle of words, Webster chose his adversary carefully: It would be Hayne, not Benton. New England had always been the friend of the West, Webster insisted. The American System of internal improvements and protective tariffs served the mutual interests of West and Northeast. A New Englander had authored the famous Ordinance of 1787, opening up the Old Northwest to settlement and ensuring its prosperity by excluding slavery, he pointed out. In accordance with the policy then established, sale of the public lands, with some of the proceeds going to education, "spreads about benefits and blessings which all can see and all can feel." It "opens channels of intercourse, augments population, enhances the value of property, and diffuses knowledge."

4. Robert Dalzell, *Daniel Webster and the Trial of American Nationalism* (Boston, 1973), 3.

But the "godlike Daniel" (a nickname his admirers used without irony) deliberately broadened the scope of his oration beyond land policy. In reaction to the Tariff of Abominations, South Carolina's legislature had encouraged (without actually yet adopting) the theory that a state could nullify the enforcement of a federal law within its borders. The strident state-righter Thomas Cooper, president of South Carolina College, had even warned in 1827 that "we shall, before long, be compelled to calculate the value of our union," in which "the South has always been the loser and the North always the gainer." In reaction, Webster seized the opportunity to "deprecate and deplore" the conception of the Constitution as a mere compact among states that they were free to interpret or restrict. "I am a unionist, and in this sense a national republican," he declared. The spokesman for New England had thrown down the gauntlet.[5]

Hayne rose to the challenge. The Yankee "has invaded the State of South Carolina, is making war upon her citizens, and endeavoring to overthrow her principles and institutions," he proclaimed. Hayne defended slavery and deplored the "false philanthropy" that criticized both it and Indian Removal. He denounced the tariff and justified state nullification of federal laws.[6] Vice President Calhoun, exercising his duty to preside over the Senate, could be seen passing notes down to prompt his younger friend's wide-ranging response. But the Carolinians had played into their adversary's hands. Webster longed for just such an opportunity to make an eloquent statement on behalf of the Union. His political goal was to identify New England with American nationalism so emphatically as to erase the memory of his section's particularism in the previous generation. Ironically, Webster's famous plea for the Union was every bit as sectional in motive as Hayne's rationalization of state rights.[7]

Webster's "Second Reply to Hayne" laid out a nationalist doctrine of constitutional origin and interpretation. The Constitution had not been created by the states, he declared, but by the people of the Union as a whole, who had distributed their sovereign powers among both state and

5. Webster is quoted in Merrill Peterson, *The Great Triumvirate: Webster, Clay, and Calhoun* (New York, 1987), 173–74; Cooper is quoted in William Freehling, *Prelude to Civil War* (New York, 1965), 130.
6. *Register of Debates*, 21st Cong., 1st sess. (Jan. 25, 1830), 43–58, quotations from 46, 48, 58.
7. See Harlow Sheidley, "The Webster-Hayne Debate," *New England Quarterly* 67 (1994): 5–29; Peter Parish, "Daniel Webster, New England, and the West," *JAH* 54 (1967): 524–49.

federal agencies. The states thus possessed no logical right to determine the extent of federal sovereignty. Ultimately, however, the most salient feature of Webster's address was not its argument but its evocation of patriotic feeling. In a society where elocution was practiced as an art form and oratory constituted a branch of literature, Webster displayed his mastery of the genre.

> When my eyes shall be turned to behold for the last time the sun in heaven, may I not see him shining on the broken and dishonored fragments of a once glorious Union, on States dissevered, discordant, belligerent; on a land rent with civil feuds, or drenched, it may be, in fraternal blood! Let their last feeble and lingering glance rather behold the gorgeous ensign of the republic, now known and honored throughout the earth, still full high advanced, its arms and trophies streaming in their original lustre, not a stripe erased or polluted, nor a single star obscured, bearing for its motto, no such miserable interrogatory as "What is all this worth?" nor those other words of delusion and folly, "Liberty first and Union afterwards"; but everywhere, spread all over in characters of living light blazing on all its ample folds, as they float over the sea and over the land, and in every wind under the whole heavens, that other sentiment, dear to every true American heart,—Liberty *and* Union, now and forever, one and inseparable![8]

Benefiting from some last-minute revisions made after its actual delivery, newspaper reprints and pamphlet versions of Webster's "Second Reply to Hayne" circulated more widely than any previous speech in history. The communications revolution magnified the power of the spoken word: At least one hundred thousand copies sold. In fact, this and the other famous political orations of the time were delivered more for the sake of their distribution in print than in the hope of persuading their actual auditors. Webster's peroration would be recorded in schoolbooks and memorized by the young for one hundred years and more.[9]

At first, Democratic newspapers scorned the address, but once Jackson had taken a stand against nullification they found themselves seconding Webster's veneration of the Union. Hayne himself in later years acknowledged Webster "the most consummate orator of either ancient or modern times." The New Englander's eloquence helped forge the broad consensus of northern opinion that by 1861 was ready to wage war for the integrity of the Union. Abraham Lincoln called Webster on Liberty and

---

8. "Second Reply to Hayne (Published Version)," *Papers of Daniel Webster: Speeches and Formal Writings*, ed. Charles M. Wiltse (Hanover, N.H., 1986), I, 347–48.
9. As the author remembers from East Denver High School in the 1950s.

Union "the very best speech that was ever delivered" and drew upon it in composing his own First Inaugural.[10]

The rest was anticlimax. In May the Senate finally shelved the resolution by Senator Foot that had provoked the great debate. But neither did Benton's plan prevail. At the close of the congressional session, the House of Representatives defeated a watered-down version of his graduation scheme. The president himself refrained from endorsing graduation, reflecting the influence of Van Buren's wing of the party and freeing Jacksonian congressmen from the Mid-Atlantic states to vote their section's interest against the bill. In a close roll call, graduation lost because Ohio cast 8 out of 12 votes against it. Representing the most populous and economically developed state west of the Appalachians, Ohio's delegation no longer identified with the frontier.[11]

During the Webster-Hayne Debate, people generally assumed that President Jackson would sympathize with his fellow southern slaveholder in opposition to a Yankee Federalist. Probably he did up to a point, but once South Carolina challenged the fundamental nature of the Constitution, Jackson felt impelled to affirm the sovereignty of the federal government and show that, like Webster, he deplored the doctrine of state nullification. Unlike Indian Removal, the tariff issue did not seem to him of such overriding importance as to justify pitting state authority against that of the federal government.

On April 13, 1830, the Democratic Republican Party (now starting to call itself the Democratic Party) celebrated the birthday of its late founder, Thomas Jefferson. The president and all the rest of the party's Washington officeholders attended a banquet with twenty-four formal toasts, typical of that hard-drinking and long-winded society. Robert Hayne gave the longest speech of all, celebrating Jefferson's state-rights principles and concluding with a toast to "the *Union* of the States, and the *Sovereignty* of the States." After the formal toasts came the "volunteer" toasts, and it was the president's prerogative to offer one of these. In consultation with Van Buren beforehand, Jackson had resolved to rebuke the nullifiers by proposing a toast to "our federal Union." In the heat of the moment, however, he rose and called out an even more forceful toast: "Our Union: *It must be preserved.*" He glared directly at the vice president. Calhoun, his

---

10. Hayne, quoted in Peterson, *Great Triumvirate*, 179; Lincoln, quoted in David Donald, *Lincoln* (New York, 1995), 270. See also William R. Taylor, *Cavalier and Yankee* (Cambridge, Mass., 1961, rpt. 1979), 109; Maurice Baxter, *One and Inseparable: Daniel Webster and the Union* (Cambridge, Mass., 1984), 188.

11. Feller, *Public Lands*, 132–33.

voice strong but the hand holding his glass shaking with emotion, responded, "The Union. Next to our liberty, the most dear. May we always remember that it can only be preserved by respecting the rights of the states and by distributing equally the benefits and the burdens of the Union." To observers, it was a duel through toasts, and it attracted nation-wide comment.[12]

Jackson's performance at the Jefferson birthday dinner displayed several characteristic features of his presidency: his confidence in Van Buren, his hostility to Calhoun, his impetuousness, his relative indifference to the tariff as an issue, and, above all, his determination to maintain the sovereign authority of the national government, which was the basis of his own authority as its president.

III

That the modern twenty-dollar Federal Reserve Note should bear Andrew Jackson's portrait is richly ironic. Not only did the Old Hero disapprove of paper money, he deliberately destroyed the national banking system of his day. What is called "the Bank War" came about through a clash between two forceful personalities, Andrew Jackson and Nicholas Biddle, president of the Second Bank of the United States. Once the conflict had been provoked, popular prejudices came into play and a dramatic conflict ensued. The sharply contrasting images of Jackson and Biddle appealed to different social constituencies, polarizing public opinion. The United States of America was not big enough for both Andrew Jackson and Nicholas Biddle to play the role that each envisioned for himself. In the end, their conflict had major consequences for the country's economic development.

Nicholas Biddle had been born into an old Philadelphia family of respectability and prominence. Intellectually precocious, he studied at the University of Pennsylvania and Princeton between the ages of ten and fifteen. At eighteen he was private secretary to the American minister in Paris. Back in Philadelphia he edited the leading American literary magazine, the *Port-Folio*, and wrote a history of the Lewis and Clark expedition using the explorers' own notes. As a patron of the arts, he encouraged the Greek Revival architectural style. In the Pennsylvania state senate during the War of 1812 Biddle helped the federal government float war loans and backed Madison's efforts to re-create the Bank of the United

---

12. Remini, *Jackson*, II, 233–36; John Niven, *John C. Calhoun and the Price of Union* (Baton Rouge, 1988), 173. Before publication, Jackson consented to having the word "federal" reinserted into his toast.

States. After Congress agreed to charter a Second Bank for twenty years starting in 1816, President Monroe appointed Biddle one of the government's five members on the BUS board of directors. There he quickly demonstrated both an academic and a practical mastery of economics and finance. In 1823, following the retirement of Langdon Cheves, the stockholders elected thirty-six-year-old Biddle president of the Bank. From then on he dominated the board of directors much as John Marshall did his colleagues on the bench. Brilliant, versatile, public-spirited, and a gracious host, Nicholas Biddle seemed Philadelphia's answer to Virginia's Thomas Jefferson.[13]

The Second Bank of the United States was the largest corporation in the country; indeed, it was the only really nationwide business. Modeled on its precursor, the Bank Hamilton had founded, the Second BUS held the Treasury's tax receipts on deposit and handled the federal government's financial transactions. Like most other banks of the time, it issued its own paper currency; unlike most of theirs, its notes were legal tender and could always be exchanged for gold and silver. The government itself issued no paper money, only coins. By presenting the paper money of state banks for redemption, the national bank could limit their extensions of credit. The BUS made loans to other banks as well as to other businesses and individuals; unlike the Federal Reserve Bank of today, which is the debtor of its member banks, the Second Bank of the United States was the creditor of state banks. Like the Federal Reserve Bank of today, it marketed the Treasury's securities to buyers from all over the world. The BUS handled virtually all foreign exchange transactions, a vital function for a debtor country with a chronically unfavorable trade balance. During the 1820s, the Bank rapidly expanded its practice of making commercial loans. Because its branches had a degree of autonomy, the Bank could accommodate the varying financial needs of different regions. The BUS was evolving into a modern central bank; that is, it could expand or contract the money supply so as to mitigate (within limits imposed by the gold standard) the swings of the business cycle. Under Biddle's direction it did this at times, though usually it was content to police the currency of the state banks, making sure they had adequate specie reserves to back up their note issues.[14]

13. See Thomas Govan, *Nicholas Biddle* (Chicago, 1959).
14. See Peter Temin, *The Jacksonian Economy* (New York, 1969), 44–58; Bray Hammond, *Banks and Politics in America from the Revolution to the Civil War* (Princeton, 1957), 300–325, corrected in some respects by Richard Timberlake, *Origins of Central Banking in the United States* (Cambridge, Mass., 1978), 27–41.

The way in which the national bank combined public functions with private profit inevitably exposed it to criticism. Yet the BUS compared favorably with the contemporary Bank of England in this regard. The most authoritative and impartial expert on American finance at the time, Albert Gallatin, secretary of the Treasury under both Jefferson and Madison and now president of John Jacob Astor's bank in New York City, assessed the performance of the BUS favorably. But if the Bank had done a good job under Biddle, it had not always done so under his predecessors. No real safeguards prevented the Bank misusing its power. Probably the worst feature of the national bank was its practice of lending money to prominent politicians and editors. This created at least the appearance of impropriety, even though the borrowers included not only its defenders like Clay and Webster (the latter the Bank's retained counsel) but also critics like Jackson's postmaster general, William Barry, and his successor, Amos Kendall.[15] Conflict-of-interest rules lay far in the future.

The Second Bank of the United States had not been an issue in the election of 1828; indeed, Biddle had voted for Jackson. Times were prosperous, the BUS was helping them stay that way, and the unpopularity of the institution subsided after the Panic of 1819 had died down. Yet the Bank retained a hard core of adversaries, and among these, it turned out, was the new president. Years before, Jackson had speculated extensively in land and promissory notes. When some of the complicated deals soured, he narrowly escaped financial ruin. From these youthful experiences the old man derived his distrust of banks and promissory notes and his horror of debt. That he found it impossible to live without recourse to banks did not affect these attitudes. Early in their relationship the president told his national banker, "I do not dislike your bank any more than all banks."[16]

But in the White House, Old Hickory's distrust of banks in general was soon overshadowed by his hostility toward the BUS in particular. Amos Kendall and Francis Blair, whose animosity to the national bank went back to their early careers in Kentucky, fanned these flames in their chief's breast. His First Annual Message in December 1829 raised the subject of whether the Bank's charter should be renewed, although it had until 1836 to run. Jackson complained that the Bank had "failed in the great end of establishing a uniform and sound currency." This was simply

15. Albert Gallatin, *Considerations on the Currency and Banking System* (Philadelphia, 1831); Glyndon Van Deusen, *The Jacksonian Era* (New York, 1959), 63.
16. Jackson to Biddle, Nov. 1829, quoted in Ralph Catterall, *The Second Bank of the United States* (Chicago, 1902), 184.

untrue; the Bank's currency circulated at or very near par in all parts of the country. Though it sounded like the president wanted the national bank to be the only one issuing paper money, in fact, Jackson didn't want any banknotes at all. A strict adherent to the gold standard, he believed that only precious metals should circulate as money. When Congress did not respond, he raised the subject again in his Second Annual Message, urging that a different national bank should be created, "shorn of the influence which makes that bank formidable." Jackson proposed to make the national bank an arm of the Treasury itself.[17] A better solution would have been to institute more effective government regulation of the BUS; a national bank under direct political control would have been an even more powerful and potentially dangerous institution than Biddle's.

The Bank of the United States was the largest example in the country of a mixed public-private corporation, and Jackson criticized both its public and private aspects. Sometimes he waged his war on the Bank as an agency of overcentralized government, but more often he attacked it as a private enterprise that had received unjust privileges, an artificial monopoly unresponsive to government or public. What Jackson minded most about the national bank was that it constituted a rival power center. Biddle, self-confident to the point of arrogance, did nothing to hide his institution's potential. Asked by a congressional committee if the BUS ever oppressed state banks, he responded, "Never," adding candidly, "There are very few banks which might not have been destroyed by an exertion of the power of the Bank."[18] To Biddle this testified to his responsibility and restraint, but in the eyes of Jackson and his friends, it was a frank confession. Even if not exercised, such power was incompatible with the sovereignty of the people. The Jacksonian Senator Thomas Hart Benton warned that the Bank could "subjugate the government." Jackson himself habitually referred to the Bank as "the Monster," a word that implied unnatural and enormous power. The president's confidant Amos Kendall predicted, "It will come to this: that whoever is in favor of that Bank will be against Old Hickory."[19]

Although some people felt strongly about it, the public as a whole was not sharply divided into pro- and anti-Bank factions during the 1820s and early '30s. Until the two leaders polarized opinions, most Americans were

17. *Presidential Messages*, II, 462, 529.
18. Quoted in Hammond, *Banks and Politics*, 297.
19. Benton quoted in Walter Buckingham Smith, *Economic Aspects of the Second Bank of the United States* (Cambridge, Mass., 1953), 234; Kendall quoted in Charles Sellers, *The Market Revolution* (New York, 1991), 322–23.

probably ambivalent or complacent in their attitude toward the Bank. Many leading Democrats in both the executive and legislative branches wanted the government to avoid a confrontation with Biddle's institution. In Congress, the president's anti-Bank proposals got nowhere. Intermediaries tried to work out some sort of modus vivendi between the two jealous chieftains. When Jackson reconstituted his cabinet in 1831 to resolve the Peggy Eaton problem, he appointed as his new Treasury secretary Louis McLane, the successful negotiator of the recent trade agreement with Britain. McLane was friendly toward the Bank. Biddle welcomed this action as good news. The bad news from his point of view was that Jackson, despite ill health, resolved to run for reelection. (The president's chronic pain had been somewhat relieved when a surgeon finally removed from his left arm the bullet Jesse Benton had fired at him nineteen years before.)

The national banker faced a difficult situation. His institution's charter would expire in 1836 unless renewed. The administration had sent him mixed signals, the public presidential denunciations mitigated recently by private equivocations from Jackson and reassurances from other high-ranking sources. In August 1831 Martin Van Buren left Washington as chief envoy ("minister plenipotentiary") to Britain, a logical move for the former secretary of state; in his absence no clear presidential favorites emerged. The reconstituted official cabinet was mostly pro-Bank; Jackson's unofficial kitchen cabinet, still anti-Bank. (Biddle confided his fear "that the kitchen would predominate over the parlor.")[20] So the bank president sought to be conciliatory. When Jackson complained that BUS branches in Kentucky had exerted influence against local Democratic candidates, Biddle investigated and tried to reassure Old Hickory. He appointed Democrats to the boards of directors of branch banks and made plans to hasten the retirement of the national debt, a project he knew to be close to the president's heart.[21]

Meanwhile, in England, Van Buren enjoyed the cordial Anglo-American relations that followed the resolution of the West Indian trade dispute. He particularly admired the Tory military hero Wellington, who reminded him of Jackson.[22] But in the Senate, Clay and Calhoun lay in wait to ambush the Fox. In January 1832, Van Buren's nomination as minister plenipotentiary to Britain came up for confirmation. The Senate was

20. Quoted in Govan, *Nicholas Biddle*, 170.
21. See Donald Cole, *The Presidency of Andrew Jackson* (Lawrence, Kans., 1993), 95–100.
22. *The Autobiography of Martin Van Buren*, ed. John Fitzpatrick (Washington, 1920), 463–64.

closely divided between administration supporters and the opposition, and a tie vote was easily arranged. This gave Vice President Calhoun the satisfaction of casting the deciding vote against the man who had supplanted him in Jackson's favor. Van Buren would have to return from London. "It will kill him, sir, kill him dead," Benton overheard Calhoun exult to a friend. "He will never kick, sir, never kick." Events proved Calhoun wrong, as they so often did. The Senate's action cast Van Buren as a victim of political spite and endeared him to the president and Democratic faithful. When Jackson was informed of it in the middle of a dinner party, he jumped to his feet. "By the Eternal! I'll smash them!" Rejection by the Senate has been rightly judged the best thing that ever happened to Van Buren. Benton's warning to a National Republican senator proved accurate: "You have broken a minister and elected a Vice-President."[23] In due course, Van Buren would advance to the presidency itself.

That same month, January 1832, Nicholas Biddle decided to apply for a renewal of the national bank's charter four years early. Assured that the BUS possessed popularity enough to get such a bill passed, he hoped Jackson would defer to Congress and Secretary McLane rather than risk a fight with the Bank and its supporters in an election year. Once the president was safely reelected, Biddle reasoned, the odds would worsen: Then Jackson would feel he could indulge his prejudices and veto recharter. It was a gamble for high stakes. McLane advised Biddle against it: "If you apply now, you assuredly will fail," he warned; "if you wait, you will as certainly succeed."[24] But Biddle suspected otherwise, and not without reason. The most probable explanation for the lull in White House criticism is that the president did not want his showdown with the Bank to come in an election year; but it would have been uncharacteristic for Jackson to back away entirely from a position held long and deeply.[25] Henry Clay, National Republican candidate for president, welcomed Biddle's decision. He hoped that Jackson *would* veto recharter and hand Clay a potential winning issue. Headquartered on Chestnut Street in Philadelphia, the BUS enjoyed wide popularity in Pennsylvania, and the Keystone State was expected to be pivotal in the election.

23. Remini, *Jackson*, II, 349–50; Thomas Hart Benton, *Thirty Years View* (New York, 1854), I, 219, 215.
24. Quoted in Louis Masur, *1831: Year of Eclipse* (New York, 2001), 141.
25. The biographer who has studied Jackson the most thoroughly, Robert Remini, supports this view. *Andrew Jackson and the Bank War* (New York, 1967), 75–77. On the other hand, Sean Wilentz has recently argued the viability of McLane's hopes for a compromise recharter. *The Rise of American Democracy* (New York, 2005), 367–68.

Some pro-Bank Jacksonians on Capitol Hill tried to delay the recharter bill until after the election, hoping to avoid having to make an awkward choice between their leader and the popular Bank. Anti-Bank Jacksonians initiated a congressional investigation of the Bank but turned up nothing that changed minds. Memorials poured into Congress from all over the country, especially the West, supporting recharter. Most state banks supported it.[26] In July 1832, Congress passed a measure to extend the Bank's charter for fifteen years after its expiration in 1836. Many Democrats from the commercial North joined the opposition members in support; others would have liked to support the Bank but were dissuaded by the party leadership. Although Democrats dominated the House, 141 to 72, recharter passed by 107 to 85. Congressional voting correlated closely with that on Indian Removal two years earlier.

The president had made up his mind to veto the measure. He interpreted Biddle's bid for early recharter as a declaration of war. When Van Buren returned from England and hurried over to the White House, he found Jackson pale as a "spectre" but steely with resolve. "The bank is trying to kill me," the old warrior glowered, *"but I will kill it!"*[27] The Bank did not have the votes in Congress to override a veto. All the cabinet secretaries except Attorney General Roger Taney (pronounced "Tawney") advised the president to leave room in his veto message for some possible compromise in the future.[28] But Jackson wanted to make an uncompromising, ringing statement that would rally voters. He enlisted a team of anti-Bank loyalists to help him compose his veto message, including Taney and Amos Kendall from the kitchen cabinet.

On July 10, 1832, Andrew Jackson issued the most important presidential veto in American history. The economic criticisms the veto message made of the Bank were necessarily weak. Jackson and his close advisors, "hard-money" advocates themselves, needed the support of "soft-money" supporters of paper currency and easy credit to kill the Bank; hence a discussion of economic issues had to be ambiguous. The message complained about the dangerous influence of foreign stockholders in the Bank, although they were not allowed to vote their shares, and it was actually to the advantage of the United States to attract overseas investment. (Of 350,000 shares, 84,055 were owned by foreigners.)[29] In spite of Marshall's repeated

26. Jean Wilburn, *Biddle's Bank: The Crucial Years* (New York, 1967); John McFaul, *The Politics of Jacksonian Finance* (Ithaca, N.Y., 1972), 16–57.
27. Van Buren, *Autobiography*, 625.
28. Remini, *Jackson*, II, 365.
29. Catterall, *Second Bank*, 508.

Supreme Court decisions, Jackson rehashed arguments against the constitutionality of the Bank, taking the position that the executive and legislative branches were not bound by the judiciary and could judge constitutional questions for themselves. Jackson made at least one valid point: Considering how much the value of its shares was expected to increase as soon as recharter passed, the government should have charged the Bank more than $3 million for the renewal.[30]

Yet for all its deficiencies the veto message was a masterstroke. Jackson attacked the Bank more on political than economic grounds, as a threat to the sovereignty of the American people. The most memorable part of the message came near the end.

> The rich and powerful too often bend the acts of government to their selfish purposes. Distinctions in society will always exist under every just government. Equality of talents, of education, or of wealth can not be produced by human institutions. In the full enjoyment of the gifts of Heaven and the fruits of superior industry, economy, and virtue, every man is equally entitled to protection by law; but when the laws undertake to add to these natural and just advantages artificial distinctions, to grant titles, gratuities, and exclusive privileges, to make the rich richer and the potent more powerful, the humble members of society—the farmers, mechanics, and laborers—who have neither the time nor the means of securing like favors to themselves, have a right to complain of the injustice of their Government.

As the historian Arthur Schlesinger Jr. has pointed out, the "resounding and demagogic language" of this passage "diverted attention" from the inability of the Bank's critics to agree on a substitute for it.[31] Jackson cast himself as defender of the natural social order and the artificial Monster Bank as its corrupter. But he coupled his appeal to the "humbler members of society" with an invocation of state rights.

> Nor is our Government to be maintained or our Union preserved by invasions of the rights and powers of the several States. In thus attempting to make our General Government strong we make it weak. Its true strength consists in leaving individuals and States as much as possible to themselves.[32]

Jackson was capitalizing on a combination of populist resentment of the rich with faith in limited government and local autonomy. This repre-

---

30. The veto message is in *Presidential Messages*, II, 576–91.
31. See Arthur Schlesinger Jr., *The Age of Jackson* (Boston, 1945), 90.
32. *Presidential Messages*, II, 590.

sented a distinctively American political tradition going back to colonial times, expressed most notably in the Revolution and more recently by Antifederalists and Old Republicans. It reflected an advantageous ratio between land and population and the widespread attitude that if people were left to themselves they could improve their lot by their own efforts.

Jackson's personal hostility toward the Bank resonated with much in American culture. He was obsessed with vigilance against enemies; Americans had a long-standing suspicion of conspiracies against them. Their recurrent fear of conspiracy had manifested itself in some ways well justified and others less well justified, against such varied targets as George III's ministries, deistic "Bavarian illuminati," rebellious slaves, and, most recently, Freemasonry.[33] Throughout his public career, Jackson positioned himself as the champion of the people against a variety of conspiratorial adversaries. He had denounced a "corrupt bargain" for the presidency, dismissed privileged officeholders, and exposed Calhoun's conspiracy against him. Now he was protecting American integrity against foreign influence, maintaining a strict construction of the Constitution against an activist Supreme Court, and, most of all, defending ordinary people against a conspiratorial Bank. The "virtue" of which Jackson spoke, and on which he believed the republic depended, belonged to the common people, not to a public-spirited elite. "The Jackson cause," a Democratic newspaper summed up, "is the cause of democracy and the people, against a corrupt and abandoned aristocracy."[34]

Nicholas Biddle, upon reading the veto message, commented that "it has all the fury of a chained panther biting the bars of his cage" and called it "a manifesto of anarchy."[35] When the Senate received the message, the debate turned nasty. Clay taunted Benton by reminding him of his gunfight with Jackson years before, and soon the two angry senators, shouting accusations at each other, needed to be restrained.[36] All across the country, the veto message raised passions. At first, the Bank's supporters actually distributed copies of the message in the belief that it confirmed their warnings about Jackson's demagogy and irresponsibility. National Republicans accused him of waging class war, setting the poor against the rich. In the twentieth century, some of his historical admirers would

---

33. See David Brion Davis, *The Slave Power Conspiracy and the Paranoid Style* (Baton Rouge, 1969).
34. Quoted in Robert Remini, "The Election of 1832," *History of American Presidential Elections*, ed. Arthur Schlesinger and Fred Israel (New York, 1971), I, 509.
35. Nicholas Biddle to Henry Clay, Aug. 1, 1832, quoted in Govan, *Nicholas Biddle*, 203.
36. Robert Remini, *Henry Clay* (New York, 1991), 400.

cheerfully plead him guilty to that charge.[37] Jackson did indeed take advantage of popular resentments against banks in general in his campaign against the Bank of the United States. But the Bank War was not a class war of labor against capital or the propertyless against the propertied. Jackson gave voice to the feelings of farmers and planters who resented their creditors as much as they needed their financial services. But he was also supported by elements of the business community who had reasons of their own to join in an attack on the BUS. These included New York bankers who wanted Wall Street to replace Philadelphia's Chestnut Street as the nation's financial center; "wildcat" bankers operating on a shoestring, mainly in the West, who resented the way the BUS monitored their behavior; and soft-money entrepreneurs who hoped that without a national bank it would be easier to obtain credit. At the same time Jackson also drew support from people at the opposite pole of public opinion: those who sympathized with his own hard-money views and wanted to abolish paper currency.

The unpopularity of banks among working people derived not only from their age-old suspicion of the wealthy but more immediately from the uncertainty of paper money. When antebellum banks made loans, they lent out their own paper notes, which then circulated as currency. If the bank of issue was far away, its currency might circulate at a discount. With transportation difficult and communication slow, it could be quite inconvenient to redeem the currency and not even easy to learn whether it was creditworthy at all. Unscrupulous businessmen paid workers or other unsophisticated creditors with discounted notes and pocketed the difference. With so many different kinds of notes in circulation, in denominations varying from ten thousand dollars to five cents, counterfeiting was easy. No wonder that many citizens, especially wage-earners, distrusted paper currency in general and preferred hard money—gold and silver. A ten-dollar gold piece, called an eagle, was certainly safer than the note of an overextended, remote, or nonexistent bank. Hard money seemed to provide the many with protection from the unscrupulous few.[38]

The advocates of hard money did not condemn banks as agents of capitalism. They condemned them as recipients of government favor, because their charters granted them the privilege of creating currency, which gave investors in banks of issue an unfair advantage over other entrepreneurs.

37. See in particular Schlesinger, *Age of Jackson*; Sellers, *Market Revolution*.
38. See James Huston, *Securing the Fruits of Labor* (Baton Rouge, 1998), 219–31.

Hard-money Democrat Robert Rantoul protested that "it is wrong and unjust that a set of individuals who make it a business to let money, should be allowed to enjoy privileges which would be denied to men in other business." As the economic historian Naomi Lamoreaux explains, "The crucial point was government intervention"—specifically, government favoritism.[39] To the supporters of hard money, the BUS looked like the greatest of all recipients of such favoritism.

In their attack on the Bank of the United States, Jackson and his followers exploited hard-money sentiments. But in the event, Jackson's victory over Biddle's Bank did nothing to reform the abuses from which the average person suffered. The elimination of the national bank removed restraints from regional and local banks, enabling them to behave more irresponsibly than ever. Getting rid of the BUS, whose notes had constituted the most reliable form of paper money, only exacerbated the difficulties that continued to plague the currency until the Civil War. On the other hand, improvements in communication and transportation helped stabilize the currency as well as minimize price differentials around the country.

Where the election of 1828 had pitted a candidate against a program, that of 1832 pitted the same candidate with his organization against an institution. For all his charm, Henry Clay had much less public appeal than the Old Hero, though the Bank had a strong constituency. The National Republicans accordingly deplored the Bank veto and Indian Removal more than they celebrated their candidate. The Democrats exploited the patronage they had built up while in office and continued to refine their get-out-the-vote techniques. Their party did not issue any statement of principles but allowed the Bank veto message to suffice. The National Republican platform condemned Jackson's "character" as well as his policies.[40] In the last analysis, the election constituted a referendum on Jackson himself. Was he a tyrant ("King Andrew the First," as a famous National Republican cartoon called him) or a popular tribune?

The failure of the National Republicans to incorporate the Antimasons hurt the opposition in the campaign. Clay, a nominal but inactive Mason, refused to repudiate the order in terms that would make him acceptable to the followers of the "blessed spirit." Antimasonic leaders hoped to persuade former postmaster general John McLean to head a third-party ticket:

39. Naomi Lamoreaux, *Insider Lending: Banks, Personal Connections, and Economic Development in Industrial New England* (Cambridge, Eng., 1994), 38, where she also quotes Rantoul.
40. Michael Holt, *The Rise and Fall of the Whig Party* (New York, 1999), 15.

His combination of probity and Methodist piety fit perfectly with their movement. When McLean declined, sensing a hopeless cause, the Antimasons held (in September 1831) the first national political party convention to nominate a presidential candidate. Voluntary benevolent and reform associations had held such conventions; the Antimasons thought of their own movement as similar. By this time they had succeeded dramatically in reducing the size and influence of Freemasonry. Confronted with so much unfavorable publicity, most Masons apparently abandoned their order. The number of lodges represented at the New York State Grand Lodge meeting plummeted from 228 in 1827 to 52 in 1832, and some of the remaining ones were kept alive only by a handful of Masonic brothers.[41] Having gained its point, the Antimasonic tide had begun to ebb by 1832. Its convention's nominee, former attorney general William Wirt, carried Vermont's seven electoral votes and 8 percent of the popular vote.

The Antimasons' procedural innovation proved more successful than their candidate. They had correctly judged that holding a national convention would give a party publicity and its candidate the legitimacy that went with a public selection process. The two major parties (as they may now be termed) rushed to follow the Antimasons' example by holding national conventions to anoint Clay and Jackson their respective leaders. Clay's running mate, John Sergeant, attorney for the BUS and like Wirt a legal counsel for the Cherokee Nation, demonstrated that both of the anti-Jackson parties sought to enlist the opponents of Indian Removal. When the Democrats met in Baltimore, Jackson let it be known that he wanted Van Buren for vice president, and his convention complied. The first Democratic National Convention adopted a two-thirds rule for nominations, initiating a policy that gave the South a veto over Democratic candidates for the next hundred years. (In 1860, this rule denied Stephen A. Douglas the Democratic nomination at Charleston, setting the stage for secession.) The Democratic convention also instituted the "unit rule," under which each state cast its votes as a bloc and minorities within state delegations were squelched.

Biddle's recharter bid failed as a National Republican campaign strategy. Jackson was reelected in triumph, with 219 electoral votes. Clay did worse than John Quincy Adams four years before, winning only 49 electoral votes. Though the anti-Jackson vote was divided, Wirt did not cost Clay the election, and tactical alliances between Antimasons and National Republicans were achieved in some states, including New York.

41. Steven Bullock, *Revolutionary Brotherhood* (Chapel Hill, 1996), 312–13. "When Masonry began to revive after 1840," notes Bullock, "it shed many of the elements that had made it so troubling" (313).

The election proved Jackson more popular than the national bank—even in Pennsylvania, though by a much reduced margin.[42] It also marked a stage in the gradual transition from the personal presidential campaigns of the 1820s to the party presidential campaigns that were to come.

The election returns of 1832, like those four years earlier, showed Old Hickory a markedly sectional candidate. South of Kentucky and Maryland he racked up 88 percent of the popular vote; no Clay ballots at all were recorded in Georgia, Alabama, and Mississippi, where Indian Removal overshadowed everything else. Voter turnout (55.4 percent) fell slightly from 1828.[43] The Bank issue cost Jackson some votes, although the veto message held his losses down and allowed the Democrats to make inroads in New England. Jackson's 54.2 percent of the popular vote overall, though impressive, was 1.8 percentage points below his previous record, which disappointed him.[44] (This is the only time that a president has been reelected to a second term with a smaller popular vote percentage than in his first election.)[45] Further limiting the scope of Jackson's victory, his party lost control of the Senate.

Most historians have concluded that Biddle's decision to press for early recharter was unwise, although there is no reason to think that Clay would have done any better in the election if the Bank had not been an issue. Biddle's only real hope to salvage something for his institution lay in trying to compromise with Jackson. Several of the criticisms that Jackson made of the Bank could have been accommodated if Biddle had been more flexible (for example, it would have been worth phasing out foreign stock ownership as the price of recharter). Instead of allying with Clay, Biddle could have urged Martin Van Buren to put in a good word for the BUS. Van Buren went along with the Bank War only reluctantly, viewing it as an unwelcome complication in his project of becoming Jackson's White House successor.[46] But to pull a charter renewal out of the hat may have been a trick beyond even the famous Magician. There is no assurance that Jackson would have accepted any accommodation with

42. See John Belohlavek, "Dallas, the Democracy, and the Bank War," *Pennsylvania Magazine of History and Biography*, 96 (1972), 377–90, esp. 388.
43. Paul Nardulli et al., "Voter Turnout in U.S. Presidential Elections," *PS: Political Science and Politics* 29 (1996): 481, graph 1.
44. James Curtis, *Andrew Jackson and the Search for Vindication* (Boston, 1976), 131.
45. Entire confidence should not be placed in the popular vote figures for 1832; see Remini, *Jackson*, II, 391.
46. See Edward Perkins, "Lost Opportunities for Compromise in the Bank War," *Business History Review* 61 (1987): 531–50; Frank Gatell, "Sober Second Thoughts on Van Buren, the Albany Regency, and the Wall Street Conspiracy," *JAH* 53 (1966): 19–40.

Biddle. Given the personalities of its two hostile protagonists, the Bank War probably could not have been avoided.

Jackson's Bank War reinforced the political lines already established by Indian Removal and the Maysville Road veto. Taken together, the three issues shaped the party politics of the next generation. Indian Removal set the pattern for Jacksonian Democratic support for continental imperialism and white supremacy. The Maysville veto and the Bank War defined the Jacksonian attitude on economic issues. In both these cases the president struck down a highly visible symbol of centralized economic activity only to turn around and encourage the same kind of economic activity (internal improvements in the one case, banking in the other) on a decentralized, unplanned basis. It was economic planning, not economic progress or even government aid to individual enterprises, that Jacksonian Democracy characteristically opposed. In his annual message of December 1832, the newly reelected president rejoiced that "the free enterprise of our citizens, aided by the State sovereignties, will work out improvements and ameliorations which can not fail to demonstrate the great truth that the people can govern themselves."[47] The dual essence of Jackson's Bank Veto—the defense of the people against the unfairly privileged and the strict construction of the Constitution—would remain the message of the Democratic Party for a long time to come.

IV

Jackson interpreted his reelection as "a decision of the people against the bank."[48] But the BUS was not abolished because public opinion demanded it. Just as quite a few congressional Democrats had supported recharter, there were many voters—especially in Pennsylvania—who had backed Old Hickory in spite of, rather than because of, his Bank Veto. Martin Van Buren himself believed that nothing but Jackson's personal popularity could have carried the day against the widespread support for the Bank. The historian Robert Remini has summed it up well: "The killing of the BUS was primarily the work of one man, and that man was Andrew Jackson."[49] The president of the United States was convinced that the Bank concentrated too much power in private hands. The ensuing "Bank War," in origin a struggle over sovereignty, turned out to inflame hostilities of party and class.

47. *Presidential Messages*, II, 606.
48. Ibid., III, 7.
49. John S. Bassett, *The Life of Andrew Jackson* (New York, 1911), II, 650; Remini, *Andrew Jackson and the Bank War*, 43.

On March 19, 1833, the president polled his cabinet and advisors on the wisdom of removing the government's deposits from the BUS. This would hit the institution's capital hard, for the federal government had almost $10 million in the Bank, almost half of its total deposits.[50] The president intended to retaliate for the role the Bank had played in the election and limit its influence during the remaining years of its life. (He seems to have feared the Bank might persuade Congress to reconsider the recharter issue, though his veto could certainly not be overridden.) Only Kendall and Taney responded to his proposal with enthusiasm; to most it seemed gratuitously provocative, since the Bank's charter would expire anyway during Jackson's second term. Particularly significant was the opposition of Treasury Secretary Louis McLane. By law, the deposits could only be removed from the Bank if the secretary of the Treasury made an official finding that they were unsafe there and communicated this finding to Congress. However, a Treasury inquiry had just shown that the BUS had $79 million in assets and $37 million in liabilities—clearly a solvent and safe bank. The House of Representatives had recently concluded an investigation of its own, undertaken at the president's behest, by voting 109 to 46 to affirm the safety of the government's deposits.[51] Jackson had anticipated McLane's reluctance to carry out removal and had a solution in mind. He reshuffled his cabinet, shifting McLane over to the State Department, where his views coincided with the president's more closely, sending Livingston to be diplomatic envoy in Paris and appointing William J. Duane secretary of the Treasury on June 1. Duane was a known critic of the BUS, and Jackson assumed he would cooperate with removal.

To Jackson's surprise, Duane proved no more willing to remove the deposits than his predecessor. Although the new secretary opposed renewal of the Bank's charter, he informed the president in a letter of July 10 that he considered the deposits perfectly safe there in the meantime. Duane warned that removing the deposits to other banks would encourage the latter in reckless extensions of credit. The secretary took the position that he had to use his own judgment in finding the deposits unsafe in the Bank and could not simply defer to the wishes of the White House. "You called on me, sir," he said to the president in a dramatic conversation on July 15, "to do an act for which I might be impeached." When the president

50. Cole, *Presidency of Andrew Jackson*, 197. The amount fluctuated considerably as tax receipts were not uniform throughout the year.
51. William McDonald, *Jacksonian Democracy* (New York, 1906), 220; Catterall, *Second Bank*, 289.

declared, "A secretary, sir, is merely an executive agent, a subordinate, and you may say so in self-defense," Duane responded, "In this particular case, Congress confers a discretionary power, and requires reasons if I exercise it. Surely this contemplates responsibility on my part."[52]

Failing to persuade Duane to change his mind, on September 23 a frustrated Andrew Jackson summarily dismissed the secretary of the Treasury and put Roger Taney in his place. Taney's was an interim appointment, allowing him to take over immediately without waiting for Senate confirmation; he retained the office of attorney general as well until replaced there by Benjamin Butler, Van Buren's law partner. Taney promptly initiated a process designed as a fig leaf to legitimate removal: Rather than a sudden gigantic withdrawal of funds, the Treasury made no more deposits but continued to pay its bills with drafts on the BUS, thus gradually running down its account to zero by the end of 1833. Instead of putting its tax receipts in the BUS, the Treasury placed them in state banks scattered throughout the Union. Dubbed the "pet banks," these were selected more for their political friendship to the administration than for their financial soundness, which was certainly no improvement over that of the BUS. The reasons for removal submitted by Taney to Congress related more to the Bank's antiadministration activities than to its financial condition. Demonstrating the Jackson administration's solicitude for overseas markets, Taney directed the pet banks to give merchants engaged in foreign trade preference when extending credit.[53]

Jackson had defied the wishes of Congress and most of his cabinet; he had violated the spirit, perhaps the letter, of the law. McLane and Cass, the secretaries of state and war, both tendered their resignations, which the president persuaded them to withdraw by publicly declaring that removal of the deposits was his personal decision, for which they shared no responsibility. Vice President Van Buren stayed out of town, distancing himself both literally and figuratively from the removal policy, which he feared would divide the Democratic party and jeopardize his hopes to succeed Jackson. The political and business communities were shocked. No parallel episode would occur again until 1973, when President Nixon fired two attorneys general in order to find one who would obey his order to dismiss the special prosecutor Archibald Cox.

---

52. Duane's account is quoted in James Parton, *Life of Andrew Jackson* (New York, 1861), III, 519, 530.
53. *Senate Documents*, 23d Cong., 1st sess., no. 2; Taney's directions to the banks of deposit are quoted in Richard Timberlake, *Origins of Central Banking in the United States* (Cambridge, Mass., 1978), 45.

William J. Duane, savaged in Francis Blair's *Washington Globe* and the rest of the Democratic press as proud, petty, and stubborn, retired quietly to private life, taking with him a clear conscience. A hard-money Democrat like the president, he had steadfastly resisted a policy of taking the taxpayers' money out of a solvent bank in defiance of the law and scattering it among doubtful institutions over which the government had even less control than over the BUS.[54]

After Congress came back into session in December, the Senate refused Taney confirmation and declared the reasons he had given for deposit removal "unsatisfactory and insufficient." Impeachment of the popular president was not politically viable, given Democratic strength in the House. The Senate, however, was dominated by Jackson's opponents, notably the National Republicans Henry Clay and Daniel Webster and the nullifier John C. Calhoun. These three eloquent statesmen, dubbed "the great triumvirate," led the Senate into what is universally recognized as its golden age.[55] A fourth spokesman should in fairness be added to their number: the redoubtable Jacksonian Thomas Hart Benton. Crowds flocked to the Senate galleries to witness their debates, for it was a generation that appreciated public speaking as an art form and relished the drama unfolding.

Under Clay's leadership, the Senate debated and finally passed (on March 28, 1834) by a vote of 26 to 20 a motion of censure on the president—the only one in American history. Jackson, the censure read, had "assumed upon himself authority and power not conferred by the Constitution and laws." When Clay first introduced his censure motion, the Old Hero wanted to challenge him to a duel. "Oh, if I live to get these robes of office off me, I will bring the rascal to a dear account," he raged. After censure passed, the president chose a more appropriate response. He sent an indignant protest addressed to the Senate, defending his right to remove cabinet officers and arguing that impeachment was the only constitutional recourse against presidential malfeasance. Wisely, Jackson emphasized presidential prerogatives rather than the substance of the financial issue in his remonstrance.[56] Posterity would vindicate the right of

---

54. [William J. Duane,] *Narrative and Correspondence Concerning the Removal of the Deposites* (Philadelphia, 1838); Sellers, *Market Revolution*, 334–36.
55. Merrill Peterson has written *The Great Triumvirate: Webster, Clay, and Calhoun* (New York, 1987).
56. Jackson quoted in Parton, *Life of Jackson*, III, 542. Clay's speech calling for censure and Jackson's remonstrance against it are reprinted in Harry Watson, ed., *Andrew Jackson vs. Henry Clay* (Boston, 1997), 214–31.

a president to dismiss cabinet members who refuse to follow his orders, but his right to order an officer to break the law (in this case, to remove the deposits without finding them unsafe) is another matter.[57]

As Van Buren had feared, the war Jackson waged against the Bank in his second term drove a substantial number of prominent men out of the Democratic Party. Those alienated included some of the president's own associates, among them Gulian Verplanck, Willie Magnum, John Bell, Hugh Lawson White, and even his close friend John Eaton, for whom Jackson had sacrificed so much. Defections were particularly conspicuous among the business community and in the South, where large cotton planters appreciated the usefulness of a sophisticated banking system and the potential dangers to them of a strong presidency. As Davy Crockett of Tennessee put it, "If Jackson is sustained in this act, we say that the will of one man shall be the law of the land."[58] By 1836, twenty-eight of the Democratic congressmen who had voted to recharter the Bank had left the party.

Encouraged by such recruits, in the spring of 1834 Jackson's opponents adopted the name Whig, traditional term for critics of executive usurpations. James Watson Webb, editor of the New York *Courier and Enquirer*, encouraged use of the name. Clay gave it national currency in a speech on April 14, 1834, likening "the whigs of the present day" to those who had resisted George III, and by summer it was official. To the complaints of the Democrats that the BUS constituted a rich men's conspiracy against the public, the Whigs responded with their own accusations of conspiracy. The Jackson administration, they charged, represented a conspiracy by a few political favorites typified by the kitchen cabinet and pet bankers to substitute executive tyranny for the balanced government of the Founders.[59] The Antimasons came around to join with National Republicans in the new Whig Party (though in Massachusetts they temporarily allied with the Democrats);[60] for a time the nullifiers also cooperated with the Whigs on some issues. For the next twenty years Whigs and Democrats would constitute the two major parties of what historians call "the second party system."

57. Congress challenged President Andrew Johnson's right to remove cabinet officers without Senate consent by the Tenure of Office Act of 1867 and subsequent impeachment proceedings. Johnson was acquitted and the Tenure of Office Act eventually declared unconstitutional by the Supreme Court.
58. David Crockett to John Durey, April 4, 1834, in *The Boisterous Sea of Liberty*, ed. David Brion Davis and Steven Mintz (New York, 1998), 375.
59. Remini, *Henry Clay*, 458–61; Major Wilson, "The 'Country' versus the 'Court': Republican Consensus and Party Debate in the Bank War," *JER* 15 (1995): 619–48.
60. Holt, *Rise and Fall of Whig Party*, 37–38.

In response to the deposits' removal, America's leading banker was not disposed to roll over and play dead. "This worthy President thinks that because he has scalped Indians and imprisoned Judges he is to have his way with the Bank," Biddle declared. "He is mistaken." During the recent election campaign, Biddle had extended credit generously in an effort to make the Bank popular. Now he resolved to use its power over the economy differently. The loss of up to half of all its deposits would impel the Bank to curtail its loans considerably. Biddle chose to impose an even sharper economic downturn than strictly necessary on the country, to make sure that Jackson's deposit removal would be noticed and deplored. The change from his previous easy money policy came swiftly, forcing some firms to curtail expansion plans and others into bankruptcy. Layoffs of workers followed. "All the other banks and all the merchants may break, but the Bank of the United States shall not break," Biddle resolved.[61]

At first Biddle's credit contraction had its desired effect: Memorials poured into Congress from all over the country pleading for the restoration of the deposits to the BUS. But when the petitioners waited upon the White House, the president responded to them: "Insolvent do you say? What do you come to me for, then? Go to Nicholas Biddle. We have no money here, gentlemen. Biddle has all the money." Jackson did not exaggerate: During the thirteen months from August 1833 to September 1834, the specie reserves of the BUS increased from $10 million to $15 million, while at the same time the bank was diminishing its loans by 25 percent.[62] Eventually the public—even including the business community, Biddle's core of support—heeded the president and began to blame high short-term interest rates on the BUS. The national banker had overplayed his hand. He had confirmed in the minds of all observers the correctness of Jackson's accusation: Nicholas Biddle wielded too much power.

In the end, Biddle's contraction failed to help his cause. With the House controlled by Democrats and the Senate by Whigs, Congress did nothing either to restore the federal deposits or to define an alternative to the pet banks. As for recharter, Clay, Calhoun, and Webster had not even been able to agree among themselves on a strategy to pursue, though the cause was hopeless anyway. Under the urging of Whig leaders, Biddle relented, and the country was soon recovering from his artificial contraction, the only (brief) interruption in the otherwise continuous prosperity and economic expansion of the Jackson years. Actually, the recession had

61. Quotations of Biddle from Harry Watson, *Liberty and Power* (New York, 1990), 157; Thomas Govan, *Nicholas Biddle* (Chicago, 1959), 253.
62. Parton, *Life of Jackson*, III, 549–50; Catterall, *Second Bank*, 324.

been mild as well as short. State banks partly compensated for Biddle's contraction by extending their own credit, and capital continued to flow into the country from Europeans investing in American transportation projects and state bonds. Biddle's "panic," as contemporaries called an economic downturn, was to some extent the creation of the press and opinion-makers in exaggerating the effects of Biddle's contraction.[63] The public's response demonstrated the influence of the media in a time of expanding communications. Biddle proved to have less economic power than either he or his critics had believed, but he waged a battle for public opinion and lost. In the midterm elections of 1834-35, the state legislatures returned control of the Senate to the administration.

At the conclusion of its federally chartered existence, the BUS could have wound up its affairs with assets of $70 million (1.25 billion 2005 dollars) and outside liabilities of $26 million (including $21 million in circulating currency). Biddle, however, chose to seek a new lease on life for his institution with a state charter from Pennsylvania. The BUS repurchased its own shares of stock from the federal government for $7,866,145.49. But the great days of the Bank were over, and the state charter proved unwise. Biddle led the Bank into speculation in cotton futures that turned out badly, and in 1839 he retired to Andalusia, his home in the country. In 1841, the renamed United States Bank of Pennsylvania declared bankruptcy. Its creditors and depositors received partial compensation; the stockholders (by then predominantly foreigners) lost everything. When Biddle died in 1844 at the age of fifty-eight, his fortune had gone the way of his popularity.[64]

A comprehensive alternative to the doomed BUS had been the goal of William J. Duane's brief time at the Treasury. He had advised Jackson to wait for Congress to reconvene and then draw up a plan in conjunction with the legislators. But Jackson's impatience to remove the deposits from the BUS left no time to organize such an alternative plan and forced him to resort to the pet bank scheme, though he felt no real enthusiasm for it. Pet banks had been used before, during the interval between the end of the First BUS and the charter of the Second, and occasionally since in areas where the BUS had no branch, never with great success. Taney persuaded Jackson that the pet bank "experiment," as he called it, deserved trying again.[65] Events confirmed Duane's doubts rather than Taney's hopes.

63. Jacob Meerman, "The Climax of the Bank War: Biddle's Contraction," *Journal of Political Economy* 71 (1963): 378–88; Walter Buckingham Smith, *Economic Aspects of the Second Bank* (Cambridge, Mass., 1953), 171–72.
64. Catterall, *Second Bank*, 371, 375; Smith, *Economic Aspects*, 178–230.
65. Fritz Redlich, *The Molding of American Banking* (New York, 1947), 174.

On the whole, the state banks did not welcome Jackson's destruction of the BUS. Where regional or state banking systems were strong, as in New York (whose banks contributed to a statewide "safety fund"), New England, and Virginia, state banks could be relatively indifferent to the BUS; elsewhere all but the most reckless wildcat bankers accepted the necessity of its policing functions. The capital-hungry West relied heavily on the resources of the national bank. The administration was genuinely worried that it might not be easy to find enough state banks willing to accept government deposits transferred from the BUS and felt relieved when Amos Kendall identified seven of them—not surprisingly institutions run by loyal Democrats.[66]

The pet banks responded to the government's largesse by expanding their loans, not only quickly counteracting Biddle's contraction but exacerbating the speculative boom that characterized the closing years of Jackson's administration. The one that behaved the worst was Baltimore's Union Bank, of which Secretary Taney was both legal counsel and a stockholder. By the time Taney was forced out of the Treasury by the Senate, he had been deeply embarrassed by the conduct of the pets in general and Baltimore's Union Bank in particular. Taney's successor, Levi Woodbury, made serious efforts to regulate the pet banks by threatening to withhold further deposits. But Woodbury's sincere efforts were undercut by political pressures to multiply the number of pet banks so as to spread the federal money around. Pet banks became an additional form of Democratic Party patronage. Their number rose from seven to twenty-two, to thirty-five, and eventually to over ninety. It was impossible not to compromise standards of financial integrity in bringing so many banks into the fold, especially when almost all banks run by Whigs were kept off the list.[67]

The most important consequences of Jackson's Bank War were unintended by the participants. The safety fund of the New York banks, together with the commissioners of the Erie Canal, had intervened at a critical junction to make funds available to counteract Biddle's contraction.[68] With the demise of the BUS, New York City, already the nation's center of commerce, replaced Philadelphia as the center of finance, but Van Buren, New York's leading administration spokesman, had not foreseen

66. McFaul, *Politics of Jacksonian Finance*, 16–48. Kendall avowed his preference for "politically friendly" banks; see Remini, *Andrew Jackson and the Bank War*, 117.
67. Frank Gatell, "Secretary Taney and the Baltimore Pets," *Business History Review* 39 (1965): 205–27; idem, "Spoils of the Bank War," *AHR* 70 (1964): 35–58; McFaul, *Politics of Jacksonian Finance*, 147–56.
68. Edwin Burrows and Mike Wallace, *Gotham* (New York, 1999), 575.

this and had been distinctly unenthusiastic about the Bank War. Meanwhile, Jackson and the hard-money advocates in his administration presided to their growing discomfiture over a speculative economy and a dangerously unstable banking system. High cotton prices and the inflow of capital from overseas prompted the founding of many new banks, a process further stimulated by the hope of attracting federal deposits. Jackson, who had declared his dislike for "all banks," witnessed the total number of banks in the country double between 1832 and 1837.[69]

The administration tried to implement hard-money principles, encouraging people to bring gold to the mints for coinage (by slightly overvaluing it) and forbidding the pet banks to issue paper currency in small denominations. But the currency of other banks continued to circulate because most of the public found its convenience outweighed its risk, and when the Van Buren administration abandoned the pet bank scheme, the government lost what leverage it had had on the supply of paper money. Bank notes remained the typical American currency until the Civil War. The failure of the Jacksonians to replace paper with specie was on balance no bad thing, for an all-metallic circulation would have entailed problems even worse than those of bank notes. When the value of gold or silver rose on the world market, American coins would have been exported and the country left to suffer deflation. The consensus of modern economists is that had Jacksonian metallism been effectively adopted, the American money supply would have been significantly constrained and the economic expansion of the rest of the antebellum period inhibited.[70]

The outcome of the Bank War represented a symbolic victory for the president and the Democrats, but it brought little if any tangible benefit to the plain folk who constituted the party's most faithful followers. The influence of wealth on American politics was not lessened, nor the opportunity for speculation decreased, by Jackson's destruction of the Bank. It was America's misfortune that the future of the national bank could not have been resolved through compromise and a larger measure of government supervision. Jackson and Biddle were both too headstrong for the country's good. The great Bank War turned out to be a conflict both sides lost. The government ended up without the services of a central bank, with an uncontrolled and fluctuating paper currency, and powerless to mitigate the swings of the business cycle. The Bank of the United States ended up with

69. Benjamin Klebaner, *American Commercial Banking: A History* (Boston, 1990), 14.
70. David Martin, "Metallism, Small Notes, and Jackson's War with the BUS," *Explorations in Economic History* 11 (1973–74): 227–47.

a far inferior Pennsylvania charter and on a road that led to bankruptcy. Not until the National Banking Act of the Lincoln administration did the government issue paper currency of its own, and not until the establishment of the Federal Reserve System in 1913 did the United States have a central bank in the modern sense to which Nicholas Biddle aspired.

V

Vice President Calhoun observed the election of 1832 in brooding isolation, totally estranged from the rest of Jackson's administration. The Bank was popular in his home state and had been so ever since the presidency of Langdon Cheves; South Carolinians owned more of its shares than citizens of any other state save Pennsylvania.[71] Calhoun's close associate George McDuffie led the fight for recharter in the House of Representatives. Yet Calhoun, reborn as a state-righter, could not swallow the rest of Clay's program, the American System with its faith in protective tariffs. So the former nationalist found himself cut off from both major parties even while he consolidated his political position at home. South Carolina, the only state where the legislature still chose presidential electors, cast its eleven votes as a solitary protest. They went to John Floyd, the Virginia governor who had disappointed the advocates of gradual emancipation during the 1831–32 debate following Nat Turner's Rebellion.

The political isolation of South Carolina and its leading statesman came about during prolonged debates over the protective tariff. The bizarre features of the 1828 Tariff of Abominations had been arranged to put Andrew Jackson in the White House, but once he got there, they presented a problem. The cotton South resented the tariff bitterly but lost its chief free-trade advocate within the administration when Calhoun fell from favor. Pressure to adjust the tariff then arose from a different consideration. Prosperity was filling the Treasury with revenues and the proceeds from land sales. The government expected to pay off the national debt by 1833, at which time either tariff revenues should be reduced or the federal government find ways to spend more money. Jacksonians dreaded the latter prospect since it would invite Henry Clay to exercise his imagination. Revenue could be reduced either by lowering the duties charged or by raising them so high that fewer items were imported. The new president's views were carefully ambiguous (when elected, he was on record as favoring a "judicious" tariff). Far from crusading against the growth of a diverse market economy, Jackson mildly supported tariff rates

71. Catterall, *Second Bank*, 508.

that would nurture industrialization, especially defense industries.[72] But tariff rates did not stir his feelings as did Indian Removal or the Bank.

While Jackson delayed addressing their problem, the planters' resentment over the tariff seethed, most of all in South Carolina, where cotton producers were having difficulty squeezing a profit out of lands less fertile than those of the Creek Cessions to the west. South Carolina's Piedmont had never recovered from the hard times following the Panic of 1819, and its people departed in droves, seeking better opportunities farther west. (By 1840, a third of all the people born in South Carolina were living in other states.) Radical state-righters like William Smith and Thomas Cooper blamed South Carolina's woes on the tariff and made threats of secession if no redress were forthcoming. Calhoun's good friend George McDuffie virtually became one of the Radicals. He harangued the U.S. Senate on how a tariff that imposed duties averaging 40 percent robbed cotton planters of the value of 40 percent of their crop—forty bales out of every hundred. McDuffie's economic reasoning was flawed, but his "forty-bale theory" fell upon receptive ears in South Carolina. (A modern economist has calculated that a 40 percent tariff cost antebellum planters 20 percent of their real income from cotton—less than McDuffie claimed but still very significant.)[73] After the enactment of the Abominations in the spring of 1828, Calhoun felt under serious pressure to do something. He needed a plan that would keep the Palmetto State in the Union while reclaiming control of his state's protest from extremists. Calhoun's patriotic love for the Union, which had earlier impressed John Quincy Adams, had not evaporated—and besides, he still nurtured the hope to succeed Jackson in the White House. As the historian Michael O'Brien has put it, Calhoun hoped to steer between "the Charybdis of Thomas Cooper's radical idea of state nationality and the Scylla of Henry Clay's Unionism."[74]

Calhoun's solution to the problem appeared in an elaborate treatise called *The South Carolina Exposition*, where he laid out a program to force a lowering of the tariff. Calhoun composed it in the summer and fall of 1828, in response to a request from a committee of the state legislature. He commenced with the assertion that protective tariffs were

---

72. *Presidential Messages*, II, 449–50, 523–25.
73. The "forty-bale theory" is analyzed in Freehling, *Prelude to Civil War*, 193–96. The modern calculation comes from John A. James, "The Optimal Tariff in the Antebellum United States," *American Economic Review* 71 (1981): 731.
74. Michael O'Brien, *Conjectures of Order: Intellectual Life and the American South* (Chapel Hill, 2004), II, 827.

unconstitutional, despite long-standing practice. The Constitution says, "The Congress shall have Power To lay and collect Taxes, Duties, Imposts and Excises, to pay the Debts and provide for the common Defence and general Welfare of the United States" (Article II, section 8). Calhoun believed that this should be read as granting the power to tax *in order to* pay the debts, etc. Thus only tariffs for revenue were authorized; tariffs for protection were unconstitutional since they served a particular, rather than the "general," welfare. Other interpreters, however, claimed there was no such limitation on the taxing power; they read the phrase "to pay the Debts" as a separate, additional grant of power to Congress. (Even if Calhoun's grammatical interpretation be granted, the difficulty of deciding when a tariff is "for revenue" and when "protective" seems insuperable, since all tariffs have both elements, and the congressmen who voted for it probably did not all have the same motive. The Supreme Court has never drawn the distinction.) Calhoun marshaled arguments that the tariff hurt the agricultural exporting sector of the economy and that it was dividing the American public into hostile political camps. In his original draft, Calhoun warned that a protective tariff would divide not only South from North but "capitalists" from "operatives," thus provoking not only sectional but also class warfare. This passage, however, was cut from the version that the committee presented to the legislature and published.[75]

Calhoun went on to describe a procedure by which an individual state could force a decision on matters of constitutional interpretation. The people of a state could elect a special convention to decide whether a certain federal law was constitutional. The convention would be empowered to declare an allegedly unconstitutional law null and void within the state; hence the term "nullification." This state convention could also issue a call for a national convention to meet and clarify the issue, proposing amendments to the Constitution, if necessary. The Constitution does provide for supplementary constitutional conventions (none has ever been held), but only if two-thirds of the states, not just one, request it. Calhoun's plan thus required multistate cooperation.

Calhoun's entire scheme rested on the assumption that sovereignty resided in the people of the separate states and not in the national people. The logical strength of his argument resided in the fact that state conventions had originally ratified the U.S. Constitution. Calhoun believed that

---

75. Both versions of the *Exposition* are printed in *The Papers of John C. Calhoun*, ed. Clyde Wilson and Edwin Hemphill (Columbia, S.C., 1977), X, 442–534.

the same parties who had adopted the Constitution in the first place should possess the final power to interpret it. The sovereignty of these parties was indivisible and could not be shared. The federal government could perform functions of sovereignty, but only acting as an agent of the states. When the federal authority abused its trust, a state could "interpose" its sovereignty and arrest the enforcement of the offending law. What happened if, in the end, the Constitution was amended to give the federal government the power the aggrieved state had challenged? By the logic of Calhoun's position, the state would still have the right to secede. Yet here Calhoun held back, displaying the residuum of his former nationalism and perhaps unwilling to indulge the Radicals that far. He concluded that after a definitive resolution of the constitutional question, any further resistance by the state would constitute "rebellion."[76] Nullification was Calhoun's device to render secession unnecessary, to enable the planters to preserve their interests without it.

Taken as a whole, the *South Carolina Exposition* is an impressive argument on behalf of an unworkable proposal. (In an America where nullification prevailed, there might be scores of federal statutes whose operation was suspended in various states, while each awaited resolution in an endless succession of constitutional conventions.) Calhoun and most of the Carolina legislators hoped at the time that Jackson's election would suffice to ensure a downward revision of the tariff, so the *Exposition* concludes with an admonition to wait and see. The vice president did not publicly reveal his authorship, sensing that it would surely offend Jackson. The South Carolina legislature was not yet ready to endorse the *Exposition*, but instead issued a brief official "Protest" against the tariff, perhaps also composed by Calhoun, which asserted the unconstitutionality of a protective tariff but described no nullification plans. Five thousand copies of the *Exposition* were printed for distribution in the hope of winning converts elsewhere in the South. If it proved popular enough, Calhoun could avow the authorship and use it to campaign for president later on a state-rights platform. Meanwhile, the *Exposition* would keep up the pressure for tariff reform. In January of 1830, its doctrine of sovereignty was defended by Hayne and attacked by Webster.

By the summer of 1831, Calhoun reluctantly concluded the time had come to go public with his views, even though doing so risked his long-term presidential hopes. He wanted to head off talk of secession, and he certainly no longer had anything more to lose by angering Jackson. On

76. Ibid., 528–29.

July 26, he published in a South Carolina newspaper what is called "the Fort Hill Address" (named for his plantation outside Clemson), an eloquent defense of state sovereignty and state rights. In it he rejected the federal judiciary as the arbiter of the Constitution, something he had not done in the *Exposition*. Conscious of a nationwide audience, he had less to say this time about the evils of a protective tariff. He emphasized that he was not opposed to industrialization and technological progress but welcomed them, not only for economic reasons but also "as laying the solid foundation of a highly improved condition of society, morally and politically." Very likely this showed Calhoun's wish to protect his standing with an American public that supported modernization, but of course his nationalist past justified the claim. If he worried that improved communication increased the likelihood that a consolidated national majority would emerge, resolved to impose its will, he did not make such a concern explicit. But clearly Calhoun no longer trusted, as James Madison had argued in *The Federalist*, that the sheer size of the United States would protect it against tyranny. Calhoun now wrote as a political theorist proposing state rights as a check on what would otherwise be the "unlimited and despotic" power of a national majority. He endorsed the concept of nullification while avoiding use of the word.[77]

Calhoun deserves his reputation as a brilliant political logician. His tragedy, and America's, was that he turned his talents to immobilizing the federal government in the service of a slave economy. But he could not have done otherwise and retained his political base in his home state. As things turned out, Calhoun's careful reasoning did less to encourage enthusiasm for state rights in South Carolina than news of Nat Turner's Uprising a few days later. Governor Floyd of Virginia wrote the governor of South Carolina warning him of a widespread slave conspiracy led by literate blacks who found anti-slavery principles in the Bible and preached that "God was no respecter of persons; the black man was as good as the white; that all men were born free and equal." This letter fanned flames of hysterical reaction in white South Carolina. The master of Fort Hill plantation shared in the renewed determination to assert the authority of the ruling race. One of his house slaves, named Aleck, chose these anxious times to escape; he was recaptured fifty miles away. Calhoun wrote an instruction that the man should be kept in the local jail for a week on bread and water, then given "30 lashes well laid on at the end of the

77. Calhoun to Frederick W. Symmes, July 26, 1831, ibid., XI, 413–40, quotations from 436, 438.

time." Such punishment, he explained, was "necessary to our proper security." Probably it did not occur to Calhoun that this order illustrated the problem of "unlimited and despotic" power even more graphically than his arguments in the Fort Hill Address.[78]

In both the *Exposition* and the Fort Hill Address, Calhoun invoked the authority of Jefferson's Kentucky Resolutions and Madison's Virginia Resolutions to the effect that states could interpose their sovereignty and nullify unconstitutional federal legislation. Jefferson was dead, but Madison still lived. The "Father of the Constitution," last surviving member of the Philadelphia convention of 1787, had long since embraced the new Republican nationalism, and when the *South Carolina Exposition* was published, Madison repudiated it, insisting that the Virginia Resolutions had meant nothing of the kind. Madison asserted that the Constitution had in fact created a system of divided sovereignty, whatever philosophers might say about sovereignty being indivisible, and that no individual state could nullify a federal law. It is hard not to conclude, however, that Calhoun was fairly entitled to cite the Jefferson and Madison of 1798 in defense of his position on the Constitution as a compact among sovereign states. Like most politicians of that era, Madison did not like to admit that he ever changed his mind.[79] Calhoun never admitted that he himself had changed his views on state rights, the tariff, or any other subject. He attached an exaggerated importance to logical consistency and always claimed to be entirely governed by deduction from first principles rather than any consideration of practicality or political advantage.

A solution to the Jackson administration's tariff quandary presented itself when John Quincy Adams returned to Washington in 1831 to take a seat in the House of Representatives from his home district in Massachusetts. The Democratic majority in the House offered him the chairmanship of the Committee on Manufactures. Ostensibly a courtesy to an ex-president, in reality this enabled the administration to delegate public responsibility for the necessary adjustments in the tariff.[80]

Adams characteristically relished both the task and the responsibility.

78. Quotations in this paragraph are from Niven, *John C. Calhoun*, 183.
79. Madison's principal statements on nullification between April 1830 and March 1833 are in *Writings of James Madison*, ed. Jack Rakove (New York, 1999), 842–66. On their inconsistency with his position in 1798–1800, see Kevin Gutzman, "A Troublesome Legacy: James Madison and 'the Principles of '98,'" *JER* 15 (1995): 569–89. For a sympathetic exposition of Madison's thinking in 1830–33, see Drew McCoy, *The Last of the Fathers* (New York, 1989), 138–51.
80. Samuel Flagg Bemis, *John Quincy Adams and the Union* (New York, 1956), 240–47.

Consulting with Secretary of the Treasury McLane and resisting pressure from Clay to expand the scope of protection, he drafted a measure that successfully resolved the complexities of the problem. Duties were moderately reduced on items not produced in the United States, though key domestic industries such as iron and cotton textiles retained sufficient protection. In a special gesture to conciliate plantation owners, duty on the cheap woolens in which slaves were clothed was slashed from 45 percent to 5 percent; this was Adams's own idea. The outcome was a major legislative achievement for the New Englander, which should be remembered to balance his legislative failures as president. His bill passed with handsome majorities from both sections in the House and won in the Senate the votes of most northerners and exactly half the southerners.[81] The northern business community had come to recognize that their enlightened self-interest lay in tariff rates that could endure rather than ones that inflamed southern agitation. Most southerners saw the measure as a significant amelioration of their grievance and were now content to back Jackson for reelection rather than pursue any more drastic remedy such as the one South Carolina was touting. Hailed as a *"bill of compromise,"* Adams's Tariff of 1832 largely removed the issue from the presidential election of that year. Adams felt satisfied to have resolved a national problem in such a way as to avoid a confrontation between the sections, even though the outcome produced an electoral benefit to Jackson.[82]

In South Carolina, however, many refused to accept the Tariff of 1832 as the resolution that it seemed elsewhere. South Carolina politics were distinctive. It was the only state that had successfully resisted political democratization in the years since independence. By a compromise agreed in 1808, the tidewater controlled one house of the state legislature and the more populous up-country the other; large planters dominated both houses through property qualifications and local custom. The legislators in turn chose the governor and most other state officers as well as the presidential electors. South Carolina's plantation aristocracy lived in a world of conspicuous consumption, male rivalry, and a heightened sense of personal and family honor. To these haughty patriarchs, tariffs represented an insult as well as an injury.

---

81. *Register of Debates*, 22nd Cong., 1st sess. (June 28, 1832), 3830–31 (House); (July 13, 1832), 1293 (Senate). South Carolina and Virginia were the only states both of whose senators opposed the bill.

82. The best account of the Tariff of 1832, correcting confusions in some others, is in Donald Ratcliffe, "The Nullification Crisis, Southern Discontents, and the American Political Process," *American Nineteenth-Century History* 1 (2000), 1–30.

Within South Carolina's peculiar polity competed three political factions: Calhoun's own following, who included Robert Hayne; state-rights Radicals, led by William Smith and Thomas Cooper; and the Unionists, who despite their opposition to protectionism did not countenance nullification as a remedy. Although led by planter magnates like the other factions, the Unionists numbered among their followers up-country yeoman farmers and Charleston merchants.[83] Earlier Calhoun had allied with the Unionists, but since 1825 he had sometimes cooperated with the Radicals, and in 1828 both Calhounites and Radicals had backed Jackson. Taking up the cause of nullification enabled Calhoun to firm up his alliance with the Radicals, whose political strength in the state was growing. In the state elections of October 1832, the Radicals and Calhounites together gained the two-thirds majority in the legislature that they needed to call for a nullification convention, finally overcoming the long resistance of the Unionists. Seizing the opportunity, they ordered a quick special election for November 12, and the voters returned a convention overwhelmingly in favor of nullification.

Why did South Carolina's political community insist on pursuing nullification when the rest of the South felt comfortable with Jackson and thought it could live with the Tariff of 1832? Fears for slavery, while widespread in the South, alarmed whites the most in the state with the highest proportion of the population enslaved (54 percent in 1830). Ever since the Missouri Compromise, those in South Carolina called the Radicals had felt apprehensive regarding the future of slavery. In 1827, a powerfully argued pamphlet called The Crisis appeared in South Carolina under the pseudonym "Brutus," linking the protective tariff and internal improvements with the slavery issue. The American Colonization Society, the author warned, constituted a stalking-horse for the general abolition of slavery. Brutus (whose real name was Robert J. Turnbull) declared that in the face of growing northern strength and ever-broadening constitutional interpretation, only consistent insistence on state sovereignty could forestall eventual emancipation by Congress.[84] With such anxieties in the back of their minds, Calhoun and the Radicals with whom he now cooperated wanted to try out nullification as a means of pressuring the majority into making concessions. If they could make the procedure work in the case of the tariff, they would have the tactic to use whenever needed, and the

---

83. On Charleston's division between nullifiers and Unionists, see William and Jane Pease, The Web of Progress (New York, 1985), 71–82.

84. The Crisis; or, Essays on the Usurpations of the Federal Government. By Brutus (Charleston, S.C., 1827).

protection of slavery would be that much more secure. Proud of his invention, Calhoun hoped that he could demonstrate nullification's effectiveness and hush rash talk of secession. For the Radicals, the tariff provided an occasion for testing a novel weapon on behalf of a state-rights philosophy they had long held. Unlike Calhoun, they had no qualms about secession as another option to exercise.[85]

That South Carolina's nullification was intended as much to defend slavery as to bring down the tariff is clear in the intertwined motives of the low-country growers of rice and long-staple cotton. Like the up-country producers of short-staple cotton, they sold their crops on the international market. Compared with the growers in the Piedmont, the great coastal planters of rice and luxury cotton suffered less from the competition of more fertile lands to the west and consequently felt less squeezed financially. But the tariff, by reducing the supply of dollars in foreign hands, limited the overseas market for their crops and encouraged their customers to look for alternative sources of supply. Rice producers suffered more from the tariff than cotton producers because the world demand for rice was more economically "elastic."[86] Furthermore, with over 50 percent of their total wealth invested in human beings, these particular large-scale capitalists felt that they had the greatest stake in the slave system of anyone in America. The swamps where their rice grew bred mosquitoes. Workers of African descent, carrying partial immunity to malaria along with traditional knowledge of rice culture from their homeland, seemed ideally suited to tend the rice crop. The aristocrats spent much of the year in Charleston, away from their plantations, leaving their holdings to slaves performing pre-assigned "tasks" (typically a half acre of rice land per worker) under the supervision of enslaved overseers called drivers.[87]

Ironically, the South Carolina low country was simultaneously the area where slaves enjoyed the greatest autonomy and the area where masters were most fanatically devoted to slavery. In parts of the low country the ratio of blacks to whites reached ten to one, and no place were the barriers

---

85. The classic study of nullification in South Carolina is William Freehling, *Prelude to Civil War* (New York, 1965).

86. Knick Harley, "The Antebellum American Tariff," *Explorations in Economic History* 29 (1992): 375–400.

87. Philip Morgan, "Work and Culture: The Task System and the World of Lowcountry Blacks," *WMQ* 39 (1982): 563–99; Peter Coclanis, "How the Low Country Was Taken to Task," in *Slavery, Secession, and Southern History*, ed. Robert Paquette and Louis Ferleger (Charlottesville, Va., 2000), 59–78; Judith Ann Carney, *Black Rice: African Origins of Rice Cultivation in the Americas* (Cambridge, Mass., 2001).

against any criticism of slavery more formidable. South Carolina had been founded in the seventeenth century by colonists from Barbados and had long maintained ties of trade and culture with the British West Indies; now, planters read in their newspapers that Parliament would soon abolish slavery in the British Empire. Nullification might be a useful resource if Congress should ever try to follow that example.

On November 24, 1832, South Carolina's Nullification Convention passed an ordinance declaring that the tariffs of 1828 and 1832 were both unconstitutional and that "it shall not be lawful" after February 1, 1833, "to enforce payment of duties imposed by the said acts within the limits of this state." The deadline was later extended; its purpose was to provide time for Congress to repeal the protective features in the tariff under this new ultimatum. The ordinance concluded with a threat to secede if the federal government attempted to coerce the state.[88] Carrying out the mandate of the ordinance, South Carolina's state legislators commenced preparations for resistance to federal authority, including raising twenty-five thousand volunteer militiamen, though they expected to avoid armed conflict. They summoned Robert Hayne back from Washington to become governor of the state and elected Calhoun to replace him in the Senate, showing that (despite the threat of secession) the most extreme Radicals would not be in charge. Accordingly, Calhoun resigned his lame duck vice presidency on December 28, 1832, and took his seat on the Senate floor.[89]

The nullifiers felt encouraged by Jackson's support for South Carolina's Negro Seamen Law and for the Georgians in their defiance of the Cherokees' treaty rights, both of which might well be considered forms of nullification. But they were wrong to think he would support them this time. Jackson was the last person to back away from a confrontation, and he took nullification as a patriotic and personal challenge from a man he had already come to distrust and loathe. The president regarded the nullification movement the same way he did the national bank, as a conspiracy against republican liberty prompted and led by a demagogue's ambition. Though he and Calhoun were both Scots-Irish cotton planters born in South Carolina, and both considered themselves heirs of Jeffersonian Republicanism, they actually differed significantly in temperament and outlook. Calhoun represented a mature slaveholding aristocracy and conceived himself its philosopher-statesman. Jackson thought and spoke as

---

88. The Ordinance of Nullification is printed in Benton, *Thirty Years View*, 297–98.
89. The only other vice president to resign has been Spiro Agnew in 1973.

an outsider to aristocracy. He typified the slaveholding man-on-the-make made good, an old soldier rather than a philosopher. Like Calhoun he was preoccupied with sovereignty, but to him it represented not a theory but a matter of deeply felt personal authority. As commander in chief, Old Hickory would not tolerate mutiny. Calhoun and Jackson shared an old-fashioned concept of manly honor that required vindication at any cost. The most serious constitutional crisis faced by the American republic between the adoption of the Constitution and the Civil War was also a showdown between two resolute individual men.

Jackson's response to the nullification crisis stands as his finest hour. He combined firmness with conciliation. The firmness appeared unmistakably in his historic presidential proclamation on December 10. Nullification, the president told the people of South Carolina, was "in direct violation of their duty as citizens of the United States" and "subversive of its Constitution." In Jackson's straightforward logic, nullification was tantamount to secession. The president must execute the law; resistance to such execution would have to be forcible. Calhoun's arguments for peaceful nullification were specious, Jackson declared. "Do not be deceived by names. Disunion by armed force is *treason*."[90]

The proclamation drew upon the legal acumen of Secretary of State Edward Livingston, who had faced the foe with Jackson eighteen years before at New Orleans. Besides exposing the impracticality of nullification, it defended the constitutionality of protective tariffs and refuted Calhoun's theory that states retained complete sovereignty within the Union. To many contemporaries, including the dying John Randolph, it seemed Jackson had forsaken the Old Republican faith and endorsed the nationalism of Daniel Webster and John Marshall. Back in 1830, as senator from Louisiana, Livingston had endorsed a synthesis of nationalism and state rights based on a theory of divided sovereignty, shared by both state and national authority; this was the standard doctrine in the Democratic Party and would remain so for many years to come. But in December 1832, Jackson insisted that his proclamation endorse the unqualified principle of national sovereignty.[91]

In the face of South Carolina's challenge, Jackson responded with both toughness and responsibility. The commander in chief reinforced the garrisons of Fort Moultrie and Castle Pinckney in Charleston harbor and

90. *Presidential Messages*, II, 640–56, quotations from 640, 654; italics in original.
91. Richard Ellis, *The Union at Risk: Jacksonian Democracy, States' Rights, and the Nullification Crisis* (New York, 1987), 11–12, 81–88.

dispatched two armed revenue cutters to the scene. People both within and without South Carolina started to fear civil war. Eight thousand armed South Carolina Unionists enrolled, ready to answer a presidential call to oppose the state militia. The president ordered General Winfield Scott to prepare for military operations, but like Lincoln a generation later he cautioned that if violence broke out, the federal forces must not be the aggressors.[92] To deter the nullifiers from attacking the Unionists in their midst, Jackson warned a South Carolina congressman that *"if one drop of blood be shed there in defiance of the laws of the United States, I will hang the first man of them I can get my hands on to the first tree I can find."* When Robert Hayne ventured, "I don't believe he would really hang anybody, do you?" Thomas Hart Benton replied, "Few people could have believed that he would hang Arbuthnot and shoot Ambrister . . . I tell you, Hayne, when Jackson begins to talk about hanging, they can begin to look out for ropes!"[93] In January 1833, the president asked Congress for power to deal with the emergency, notably by shifting the collection point for customs duties to offshore federal ships and forts, beyond the range of the nullifiers' control. Angry Carolinians dubbed it "the Force Bill," though the measure actually rendered an armed clash between state and federal authorities less likely. At the same time Representative Gulian C. Verplanck of New York, a Democratic free-trader, introduced a drastic tariff reduction backed by the administration, which would immediately cut duties in half. Jackson wanted to make sure of the loyalty of the rest of the cotton South, and on the tariff issue he was willing to compromise.

The really critical aspect of the situation would be the response of the other southern states to South Carolina's initiative. Only with their support could a single state make nullification a viable precedent. In the end, this support did not come. Not even Mississippi and Louisiana, where the percentage of slaves in the population was almost as high as in South Carolina, came to their sister state's aid, for neither shared her attitude toward the Tariff of 1832. Enjoying newly cultivated, rich soil, southwestern cotton-growers did not feel as hard pressed as those in South Carolina, while Louisiana sugar-growers actually favored protectionism. So no call went out for a new constitutional convention to settle the validity of tariff protection. Instead, legislatures in eight southern states passed

---

92. See documents rpt. in William Freehling, *The Nullification Era* (New York, 1967), 170–71, 175–80.
93. Augustus Buell, *History of Andrew Jackson* (New York, 1904), II, 244–45; italics in original.

resolutions condemning South Carolina's nullification. Most disappointing of all to the nullifiers, Virginia's Governor Floyd, Calhoun's longtime friend, failed to persuade that commonwealth's legislature to support them. Sharply divided along the same East-West line revealed by the post–Nat Turner debate, the Virginia legislature ended up passing a compromise resolution critical of both nullification and the president's proclamation against it.

During the crisis, vice president–elect Van Buren exerted less influence than usual over administration policy. As architect of the Tariff of Abominations, Van Buren had much to answer for. Ironically, the state legislature that gave Jackson the hardest time was that of New York. Van Buren's Bucktail Democrats proved such ardent state-righters that the president wound up depending for support in New York on Antimasons, National Republicans, and dissident Democrats.[94]

While Jackson's willingness to coerce South Carolina if necessary undoubtedly worried southerners and doughfaces, his new support for tariff reduction, his record on Indian Removal, his professions of faith in strict construction, and his undoubted devotion to slavery and white supremacy combined to reassure them. His Force Bill provoked eloquent congressional oratory on state and national sovereignty, but little serious opposition. The Force Bill passed the House with more than a three-quarters majority (149 to 48) and the Senate with but one dissenting vote (though nine southern senators, including those from South Carolina, stayed away).[95] For the time being at least, the slaveholding South appeared content to rely for protection on normal politics, with a sympathetic president representing the will of a majority of the electorate, rather than on a novel and drastic theory about state sovereignty. The Carolinian pursuit of nullification as a remedy for hypothetical future injustices seemed to most southerners, however much they disliked protectionism, a quixotic quest after an abstraction. The way Calhoun operated as South Carolina's ambassador in the negotiations that followed vindicated this judgment. For the sake of abstractions, honor, and promises about the future, he would forgo many of the tangible tariff concessions he could have extracted.

Calhoun scorned to accept Verplanck's bill because it came from the administration. Instead, he preferred to work out a settlement with Henry Clay, although this meant dealing with someone far more seriously

94. Ibid., 122–57.
95. *Register of Debates*, 22nd Cong., 2nd sess. (Feb. 20, 1833), 688 (Senate); (March 1, 1833), 1903 (House).

committed to the tariff than Jackson. Clay took Adams's tariff as their basis for discussion. To placate northern sheep raisers and mill owners, he removed Adams's major concession to the South and put the duties on raw wool and cheap woolen cloth back up again. The resulting tariff he agreed to lower by tiny increments over the next eight years, then finally in 1842 lowering it substantially to 20 percent across the board. What did Calhoun get out of this? He was promised that the process would eventually lead to a tariff where all rates would be fixed ad valorem, so no particular products were being "protected," and one could claim that the whole tariff structure existed for revenue only. In fact, however, many articles that did not compete with domestic producers were allowed in entirely free of duty, which would hardly have been the case if the tariff had really been for revenue only. Calhoun signed off on the deal, although South Carolinians earlier had claimed a 12.5 percent tariff should suffice for revenue. Instead of the Verplanck bill, the nullifiers got Adams's compromise measure minus its most important concession, plus promises—which, however, a future Congress might rescind. Clay had driven a successful bargain, granting (as he explained privately) "a nominal triumph" to Calhoun, "whilst all the substantial advantages have been secured to the Tariff States."[96]

Congress passed both Jackson's Force Bill and Clay's Compromise Tariff of 1833 on the same day, March 1. Together they resolved the nullification crisis. Jackson and Clay were both strong nationalists, but they demonstrated very different styles of political leadership. Jackson's deserved reputation for violence, often an embarrassment, had in this case served the national interest when combined with his responsible actions. Henry Clay's consummate skills as a negotiator proved as valuable in the end. Together, the two leaders presented the "olive branch and sword" (or, less elegantly, the "carrot and the stick") to the nullifiers. A substantial body of northeastern congressmen, led by Daniel Webster, voted against the compromise tariff, on the grounds that the Force Bill alone sufficed and that South Carolina was not in a strong enough bargaining position to deserve even a symbolic reward for its conduct. In Columbia the Nullification Convention reconvened on March 11, declared victory, repealed nullification of the federal tariff duties, and then, in a final gesture of defiance, nullified the (now moot) Force Act.[97]

96. Henry Clay to Nicholas Biddle, April 10, 1833, *Papers of Henry Clay*, ed. Robert Seager II (Lexington, Ky., 1984), VIII, 637. My interpretation of the compromise follows that of Ratcliffe, "Nullification Crisis."

97. See Merrill Peterson, *Olive Branch and Sword: The Compromise of 1833* (Baton Rouge, 1982).

Clay also got another measure through Congress on March 1, his Distribution Bill. This, an early example of revenue-sharing, "distributed" federal revenues to the states for internal improvements, education, and African colonization, with the money to come from public land sales. The Distribution Bill would have enacted a major portion of the American System, and also operated indirectly to prevent the tariff from being reduced below 20 percent, since without land proceeds, the federal government would need the tariff revenue. Whether the Distribution Bill was an integral part of the compromise settlement depended on whom one asked. Clay viewed it so, as a measure to help reconcile northerners to future tariff reductions. Jackson decided it was not, and pocket-vetoed it. Earlier in his presidency, he had favored distribution, but that was before the plan carried Clay's label. Jackson's previous support for distribution had reconciled his sympathy for farmers needing internal improvements with his strict interpretation of the Constitution. Now, however, to sign the Distribution Bill would acknowledge that Clay deserved credit for a comprehensive resolution of the nullification crisis. This was too much to bear, so Old Hickory chose another way to please the West: selling the public lands to settlers as cheaply as possible. His new stance aligned him with Benton, who had been so loyal an administration supporter. Calhoun had been bitterly opposed to the Distribution Bill; its veto meant he emerged from the settlement with a somewhat better deal. Internal improvements would be left to the private sector and unplanned, ad hoc subsidies; the cause of African colonization, having missed its best funding opportunity, withered away.[98]

Objectively, in terms of national politics, the nullifiers had lost. The other southern states had not rallied to their side. Both the legislative and executive branches of the federal government had demonstrated their resolve to suppress nullification. And the tariff that came out of it all would not significantly lower rates until nine years in the future. Yankee farmers expressed their impression that nullification was mere bluster by calling their scarecrows "calhouns."[99] But in South Carolina it was an altogether different story. There the alliance between Calhoun and the Radicals became permanent. Unrepentant, the nullifiers solidified their control of state politics and from then on provided their great spokesman with an unchallenged local power base. The biggest losers from the crisis, in fact, were the South Carolina Unionists; starting in 1834, they were virtually precluded

98. See John Larson, *Internal Improvement* (Chapel Hill, 2001), 187–193; John Van Atta, "Western Lands and the Political Economy of Henry Clay's American System," *JER* 21 (Winter 2001): 633–65.
99. Peterson, *Olive Branch and Sword*, 55.

from holding state office by a test oath swearing primary loyalty to the state and only conditional loyalty to the federal government.[100] Henceforth the aristocratic South Carolina state-righters played a lone hand for high stakes in national politics, from time to time allying with the Democratic Party only to bolt it, sometimes courting Whig allies, more often trying to rally the South as a section to embrace their own extremist agenda. The president recognized that the nullifiers had not been destroyed, and privately warned that they would make trouble again. Next time, he predicted, they would seize upon "the negro, or slavery question."[101] But never again would Calhoun's theory of nullification be taken seriously enough to be tried. Instead, the doctrine of secession, which Calhoun had hoped to preempt, lived on, now endorsed more strongly than ever by the ardent defenders of slavery.

In the wake of the crisis, Jackson enjoyed a brief period of cross-party popularity, as National Republicans acknowledged his veneration for the Union. Webster in particular reached out to embrace his fellow nationalist. At his second inauguration on March 4, 1833, the president instructed Americans on the necessity of Union to their trade, communications, prosperity, and peace.

> You have been wisely admonished to "accustom yourselves to think and speak of the Union as of the palladium of your political safety and prosperity" [an allusion to Washington's Farewell Address]. Without union our independence and liberty would never have been achieved; without union they can never be maintained. Divided into twenty-four, or an even smaller number, of separate communities, we shall see our internal trade burdened with numberless restraints and exactions; communication between distant points and sections obstructed or cut off; our sons made soldiers to deluge with blood the fields they now till in peace. . . . The loss of liberty, of all good government, of peace, plenty, and happiness, must inevitably follow a dissolution of the Union.[102]

That summer Jackson toured New England, where he was greeted with acclamations, delivered a patriotic address at Bunker Hill, and received an honorary LL.D. from Harvard (despite objection from John Quincy Adams, a member of the Board of Overseers). The story that he was asked to address the degree ceremony in Latin and replied, "*E pluribus unum*, my friends, *sine qua non!*" is apocryphal.[103]

100. Ellis, *Union at Risk*, 180.
101. AJ to Andrew J. Crawford, May 1, 1833, *Correspondence of AJ*, V, 72.
102. *Presidential Messages*, III, 4.
103. Remini, *Jackson*, III, 79.

11

Jacksonian Democracy and the Rule of Law

Although Andrew Jackson defended his own authority with resolute determination, he did not manifest a general respect for the authority of the law when it got in the way of the policies he chose to pursue. This character trait, already apparent in his military career, continued to manifest itself during his years in the White House. Jackson's removal of the federal deposits from the Bank of the United States proved but one of a number of presidential actions illustrating his impatience with legal restraints. His reactions to the Supreme Court's decision on Cherokee rights, to abolitionist use of the mails, and to the epidemic of public violence that raged during his presidency all contribute to the pattern. Old Hickory's admirers, in his own time and since, have extolled his willpower and leadership. Yet, although he set an example of an activist presidency, Jackson's administration was also an unusually divisive one. He remains the only president to have been formally censured by the Senate. No wonder the opposition party took up the name that traditionally stood for resistance to abuses of executive authority: "Whigs."

Jackson's personal attitude toward the law bore a decided congruence to the broader relationship of his party to the American legal tradition. Where Whigs voiced reverence for the supremacy of the law, Democrats more typically celebrated the autonomy of the sovereign people. When they were being careful, Democrats would specify that they meant the people of the several states, distinguishing their position from that of Webster and Marshall once the nullification crisis had passed. When they were being careless, Democrats could close their eyes to the problems of pervasive lawlessness and violence that plagued American society in their time. In the words of the historian Richard Hofstadter, violence in the Jacksonian period expressed "the pathology of a nation growing at a speed that defied control, governed by an ineffective leadership, impatient with authority, bedeviled by its internal heterogeneity, and above all cursed by an ancient and gloomy wrong": slavery.[1]

1. Richard Hofstadter and Michael Wallace, eds., *American Violence: A Documentary History* (New York, 1971), 477.

II

The nullification crisis impacted immediately upon the Cherokee Nation. The case of *Worcester v. Georgia* had set the stage for a confrontation between the authority of the Supreme Court and the state of Georgia. Having consistently denied the Court's right to hear the case at all, Georgia took no steps to release Samuel Worcester and Elizur Butler from their confinement despite the decision in their favor. Under the cumbersome legal procedures of the time, there was nothing that could be done about this until the Supreme Court reconvened early in 1833, at which time the two missionaries could officially inform the Court of their difficulty and request a writ. Since the Georgia legislature had forbidden any state officer to obey such a writ, the Court would surely have to call upon the president to exercise his constitutional duty to "take care that the laws be faithfully executed." But no one imagined that Old Hickory intended to enforce the Court's judgment in a case where his sympathies lay so solidly with the other side. An oft-told story goes that when he learned of the Supreme Court's ruling in *Worcester v. Georgia*, Jackson scoffed, "John Marshall has made his decision: *now let him enforce it!*"[2]

By the winter of 1832–33, the situation had changed significantly from the previous March when the original decision was handed down. Clay had been defeated in the election, removing the Cherokees' hope that he would be in a position to enforce Marshall's ruling. At a time when Jackson already faced one contumacious state, neither the administration nor the National Republican opposition wanted to risk antagonizing its neighbor, driving Georgia into alliance with South Carolina; Alabama and Mississippi might well follow suit. The problem called for the skills of the Little Magician. Accordingly, vice president–elect Van Buren brokered an arrangement in December 1832 to defuse the situation. Reluctantly, Worcester and Butler announced they would not seek an order from the Court to enforce their release but would instead accept a pardon from the Georgia governor. The Georgia legislature repealed the law under which the missionaries had been convicted (though not the rest of the code that discriminated oppressively against the Indians), so they could return to their missions in the Cherokee Nation. Governor Wilson Lumpkin almost wrecked the deal by insisting on every possible ounce of

---

2. Horace Greeley, *The American Conflict* (Hartford, Conn., 1864), I, 106, citing the memory of George Briggs. Although the story rests on a recollection long after the fact, it is consistent with Jackson's behavior and quite in character. He wrote to John Coffee: "The decision of the Supreme court has fell still born, and they find that it cannot coerce Georgia to yield to its mandate" (April 7, 1832), *Correspondence of AJ*, IV, 430.

rhetorical satisfaction for state rights but finally issued the pardon on January 14. The nullifiers' hopes to recruit Georgia to their side were frustrated; the Supreme Court avoided the public embarrassment of issuing a writ that proved unenforceable. The big losers, of course, were the Cherokees, whose legally validated rights would now be ignored. Samuel Worcester had never been sanguine about the chances of saving the Cherokee Nation, but (he had reflected two years earlier) "still it appears to me that the effort ought to be made, though it ends in defeat."[3] The two missionaries had endured seventeen months in harsh imprisonment and had been willing to serve a four-year sentence for their cause; they were not willing to jeopardize the national interest for it. Worcester spent the rest of his life with the Cherokees, accompanied them to Oklahoma, and translated much of the Bible into Sequoyah's script.

Hostile confrontation between them safely averted, the president hosted the justices of the Supreme Court at the White House for dinner on January 25, 1833. The great nationalist Justice Joseph Story (whom Jackson had once called "the most dangerous man in America") reported to his wife that "the President specially invited me to drink a glass of wine with him. Since his last proclamation and message [denouncing nullification], the Chief Justice and myself have become his warmest supporters, and shall continue so just as long as he maintains the principles contained in them. Who would have dreamed of such an occurrence?"[4]

At least two other cases before the Supreme Court may have been influenced by the nullification crisis. One of them was *New Jersey v. New York*, a boundary dispute in which Van Buren's home state argued that the Court had no jurisdiction. Since this was the same position that Georgia was taking against Worcester, this case too became potentially explosive in the context of nullification. Chief Justice Marshall prudently halted arguments in March 1832 and postponed their resumption until February 1833. By the time that date rolled around, the parties had set up a commission to negotiate a settlement, which was reached in 1834. Once again Van Buren's sleight-of-hand was evident in the outcome.[5]

Of more long-lasting significance was *Barron v. Baltimore* (1833), which presented the question whether the city of Baltimore, in damaging

3. Quoted in John G. West Jr., *The Politics of Revelation and Reason* (Lawrence, Kans., 1996), 172. See also Edwin Miles, "After John Marshall's Decision," *Journal of Southern History* 39 (1973): 519–44.
4. Quoted in G. Edward White, *The Marshall Court and Cultural Change* (New York, 1991), 739.
5. Michael Birkner, "The New York–New Jersey Boundary Controversy, John Marshall, and the Nullification Crisis," *JER* 12 (1992): 195–212.

a privately owned wharf, had violated the "takings" clause of the Fifth Amendment ("nor shall private property be taken for public use, without just compensation"). The wharf owner had won a judgment of $4,500, which the Maryland Supreme Court set aside on the grounds that the Fifth Amendment did not apply to the state of Maryland (and its municipal corporation Baltimore) but limited only the federal government. Appeal to the U.S. Supreme Court threatened to replay the hostilities that had been aroused when Marshall had ruled against Maryland in *McCulloch* fourteen years before. At that time, legal textbooks and state court precedents around the country revealed no particular pattern, some applying Amendments Two through Nine to the states and some not. (Amendments One and Ten explicitly limit only the federal government.) So devoted a supporter of nationalism as Marshall might have been expected to find that the Fifth Amendment did restrict the states. But no, Marshall spoke for a unanimous Court and ruled otherwise without even waiting to hear oral argument for Baltimore. In his last major opinion on constitutional law, the aged chief justice held that the Bill of Rights restricted only the federal government, not the states. It would take the Fourteenth Amendment and much elaborate reasoning in the twentieth century for the Supreme Court to undo (at least partially) the consequences of Marshall's uncharacteristic decision in favor of state rights. But in the political climate of its January 1833 term, it is unlikely that the Court would have issued an opinion alarming the states.[6]

III

Back on the ground in the Cherokee Nation, the rejoicing at the decision in *Worcester v. Georgia* passed as it became apparent that neither state nor federal authorities would obey it. Starting July 1, 1830, state law had been extended over the Cherokee Nation. Although the federal government usually took over lands relinquished by Indian tribes, in this case the state received them. The mood of Georgia's white populace was captured in a popular song of the day:

> All I want in this creation
> Is a pretty little wife and a big plantation
> Away up yonder in the Cherokee nation.[7]

6. *Barron v. Baltimore*, 32 U.S. (7 Peters) 243 (1833); Walker Mayo, "The Federal Bill of Rights and the States Before the Fourteenth Amendment" (D.Phil. thesis, Oxford University, 1993).
7. Joel Chandler Harris, *Stories of Georgia* (New York, 1896), 216.

To gratify such longings, in 1832 Georgia held a lottery and raffled off all unoccupied Cherokee lands to lucky white ticket holders. For the time being, the Native people themselves were permitted to remain, on plots where they had built improvements, pending their ultimate Removal. Georgia's Jacksonian Democrats, led by Governor Lumpkin, took an even harder line against the Indians than the State Rights Party of Governor Gilmer (who also endorsed Jackson for president in 1828 and '32), though the difference was not striking. The lottery was the idea of Lumpkin's party; Gilmer's party would have preferred deriving a state revenue from the Cherokee lands. While almost all white Georgians hoped the Indians would go away, not all approved of how they were treated. Some state court judges showed a modicum of respect for Cherokee property rights.[8]

In the face of extreme state pressure, tribal unity eventually gave way. Most Cherokees, led by Principal Chief John Ross, resolutely stayed put, but a small minority of the tribe decided that it would be better to sign a removal treaty and try to salvage something from the wreckage. On December 29, 1835, a party led by John Ridge and Elias Boudinot (publisher of the *Cherokee Phoenix*) signed the Treaty of New Echota, consenting to trade the tribe's ancestral homeland in return for $5 million and land in Oklahoma. The treaty party derived its support mainly from mixed-bloods and slaveowners; Ross, although a mixed-blood and slaveowner too, was supported by the overwhelming majority of full-blood yeoman farmers. A mediator between cultures and a Christian himself, Ross numbered among his conservative party followers of the traditionalist sage White Path. The members of the treaty party may be characterized as a rising middle class within Cherokee society, eager for commercial advantage and frustrated by the conservatism of both Ross's elite and the multitude.[9] Notwithstanding Cherokee protests that the treaty signatories lacked authorization, and the eloquent opposition of Daniel Webster and Henry Clay, the U.S. Senate consented to ratification on May 23, 1836, by 31 to 15: one vote over the constitutionally minimum two-thirds.

---

8. H. David Williams, "The Cherokee Nation and Georgia's Gold and Land Lotteries of 1832–33," *Georgia Historical Quarterly* 73 (1989): 519–39; Mary Young, "The Exercise of Sovereignty in Cherokee Georgia," *JER* 10 (1990): 43–63.
9. Theda Perdue, "The Conflict Within: Cherokees and Removal," in *Cherokee Removal: Before and After*, ed. William Anderson (Athens, Ga., 1991), 55–74. For more on Cherokee internal politics, see Gary Moulton, *John Ross, Cherokee Chief* (Athens, Ga., 1978); Duane Champagne, *Social Order and Political Change: Constitutional Governments Among the Cherokee, the Choctaw, the Chickasaw, and the Creek* (Stanford, 1992).

Members of the treaty party now departed for Oklahoma, but most Cherokees still did not abandon their homes voluntarily. Starting in May 1838, the majority of the tribe were rounded up by the U.S. Army and sent to detention camps to await Removal; others fled to neighboring states. Widespread bloodshed at this point was averted by the moderation and good sense of Chief Ross and General Winfield Scott.[10] But incompetence, indifference, and policy disagreements among civilian authorities had frustrated the efforts of General John Ellis Wool to prepare properly for the massive evacuation. Conditions in the unsanitary detention camps and the harsh weather along the notorious "Trail of Tears" westward in the fall and winter of 1838–39 led to a tragically high death rate; the usual estimate is that four thousand people died out of the twelve thousand participants in the forced migration. Among the dead was Chief Ross's wife. Once in Oklahoma, the tribe suffered long recriminations over Removal; John Ridge and Elias Boudinot were assassinated (justly executed, said some) for having signed the Treaty of New Echota.[11]

By this time the Creek and Chickasaw tribes had undergone their own coerced Removals, accompanied by similar hardships, from Alabama and Mississippi, respectively. These states imitated Georgia and extended their own laws over the land guaranteed to Indian tribes by federal treaty. The Creeks, once the most powerful of the southern tribes, suffered perhaps the worst of all during Removal. Their treaty, signed in Washington, D.C., on March 24, 1832, surrendered all tribal lands east of the Mississippi in return for a place in Oklahoma, but also promised that those Creek families who chose to remain in Alabama would be assigned modest "allotments" to own and farm there. But the Creek lands were quickly overrun by whites whom neither state nor federal authorities had the will to evict, and their erstwhile occupants driven off to wander as refugees. In seizing Native American lands, Alabamans made the Georgians look diffident. The many ways of defrauding the Indians of their allotments were varied, ingenious, often brazen, and conducted by large speculative consortia as well as individual cheaters. When the commissioner of Indian affairs investigated, he declared, "It is shocking to reflect on the disclosures elicited. Persons heretofore deemed respectable, are implicated in the

---

10. See Mary Young, "Conflict Resolution on the Indian Frontier," *JER* 16 (1996): 1–19.
11. Anthony Wallace, *The Long, Bitter Trail* (New York, 1993), 88–94. Estimates of Cherokee deaths in connection with Removal range from 1,600 to 8,000. The controversy is summarized in Ronald Satz, "The Cherokee Trail of Tears," *Georgia Historical Quarterly* 73 (1989), 431–32; Russell Thornton, *The Cherokees: A Population History* (Lincoln, Neb., 1990), 73–77.

most disgraceful attempts to defraud." The historian Paul Prucha has commented: "The frauds were spectacular and widespread, making a mockery of the treaty intentions, and the government seemed impotent to stem the speculators' chicanery."[12] Other historians, however, infer that the government actually foresaw these events and signed the treaty as "a clever administration ploy to expedite Indian removal by opening the door to white speculation in Creek lands."[13] Creek tribal law vested land ownership in the woman of the house, but whites insisted on dealing with the man of the house, who might well think he had cheated the strangers by selling what he didn't own—until they came back with guns to evict him and his family. Not surprisingly, some of the Creeks, goaded beyond endurance, put up violent resistance in the spring of 1836, called the Second Creek War. Secretary of War Lewis Cass of Michigan, who had replaced John Eaton but who was equally committed to Removal, rushed in the army. The troops that could not be spared to maintain order against whites now quickly subdued the Creeks, who were escorted en masse to Oklahoma, "hostiles" and "friendlies" alike, without further regard for the treaty. A few escaped to Florida to join the Seminoles, whose language and culture they shared. Mortality due to Creek deportation may have run as high as 50 percent.[14]

The Chickasaws of Mississippi tried to spare themselves some suffering by quickly accepting the inevitable and consenting to move west. Then it turned out that the administration had neglected to identify anyplace for the tribe to relocate. Eventually the Chickasaws themselves purchased a section of the Choctaw domain in Oklahoma in order to escape from the persecutions to which they were being subjected by intruders on their lands in Mississippi.

The Seminoles in Florida Territory proved the most difficult of the southeastern tribes to expel. Willing to fight for their homes, they put up a resolute resistance and benefited from a remote defensible bastion and the assistance of runaway slaves. A treaty consenting to Removal, extorted from a group of Seminoles in 1833 when they visited Oklahoma, was

12. Both quotations are from Paul Prucha, *The Great Father: The United States Government and the American Indians* (Lincoln, Neb., 1984), I, 222. The frauds practiced on the Creeks are thoroughly documented in Mary Young, *Redskins, Ruffleshirts, and Rednecks: Indian Allotments in Alabama and Mississippi, 1830–1860* (Norman, Okla., 1961), 3–98.

13. Ronald Satz, *American Indian Policy in the Jacksonian Era* (Lincoln, Neb., 1975), 105.

14. Michael Doran, "Population Statistics of Nineteenth-Century Indian Territory," *Chronicles of Oklahoma* 53 (1975–76): 497–500.

Tribes were sent not only to Oklahoma, but also to Kansas and Nebraska.

repudiated by the tribe but accepted as binding by the administration. In December 1835, a hundred soldiers under Major Francis Dade were annihilated by a combined force of Indians and blacks. When Jackson left office in March 1837, the federal government had undertaken a serious war effort, and the fate of the Seminole tribe was still unresolved. Before it was through, the government would spend ten times as much on subjugating the Seminoles alone as it had estimated Removal of all the tribes would cost.[15]

The administration's Removal policy applied to all Indians east of the Mississippi, not only those of the Deep South. In the Northwest it led to a

15. Satz, *American Indian Policy*, 103.

tragic conflict known as Black Hawk's War. In April 1832, Black Hawk led between one and two thousand people of the Sac and Fox tribes to cross the Mississippi and return to land in northern Illinois where their right of occupancy was now disputed. Black Hawk had long advocated inter-tribal resistance to white encroachment and had sided with the British during the War of 1812; more recently he had been losing influence to his rival leader, Keokuk, an advocate of accommodation with the settlers. On this occasion, Black Hawk and his band were seeking not conflict but refuge from their traditional enemies, the Sioux; a war party would not have included women and children. Illinois governor John Reynolds nevertheless interpreted their move into his state as hostile. As soon as Black Hawk realized that he could persuade neither other tribes nor Canadian traders to support his venture into Illinois, he tried to surrender. On May 14, a delegation of Indians seeking to negotiate under a flag of truce was fired upon by state militiamen; in the battle that followed, the disorganized militia were routed.[16]

Secretary of War Cass seized this opportunity. He summoned federal troops, requested more Illinois militia to support them, and rushed himself to Detroit so as to be closer to the scene. Among the men assembled for service in the brief campaign were future presidents Abraham Lincoln (whose grandfather had been killed by Indians on the Kentucky frontier), Zachary Taylor, and Jefferson Davis. Jackson pressed the local commander for action, and the hastily gathered army then drove Black Hawk's band away, pursuing them into what is now Wisconsin, and massacring several hundred men, women, and children at Bad Axe on August 2, 1832, as they were trying to flee back across the Mississippi. Those who made it across were killed by Sioux allied with the government. Of all Black Hawk's band, scarcely 150 survived. The administration's seeming overreaction paid off: Peace treaties followed, depriving the Sac and Fox and Winnebago tribes of more lands. The government exhibited the prisoner Black Hawk around the country, as the imperial Romans did with captive monarchs; by his dignity and eloquence, the old warrior won the lasting admiration of the American public.[17]

Only belatedly did the Jackson administration address the fact that shoving eastern tribes onto the Great Plains would require the tribes who

16. Anthony Wallace, "Introduction," *The Black Hawk War*, ed. Ellen Whitney (Springfield, Ill., 1970).

17. William Klunder, *Lewis Cass* (Kent, Ohio, 1996), 68–69; William Hagan, *The Sac and Fox Indians* (Norman, Okla., 1958), 153–91. Also see *Black Hawk: An Autobiography*, ed. Donald Jackson (Urbana, Ill., 1955).

already lived there to turn over some of their historic lands to newcomers. In 1835, the government authorized a commission chaired by Montfort Stokes of North Carolina to seek suitable agreements. Expeditions by cavalry and dragoons based at Fort Leavenworth and Fort Scott, Kansas, eventually persuaded some of the Plains tribes to sign the required treaties, though friction among the different tribes of original inhabitants and relocated easterners would remain, one more tragic aspect of Indian Removal. In 1841, a conscientious investigation of the government's treatment of the exiles, by Major Ethan Allen Hitchcock of the Regular Army, revealed widespread corruption by white contractors.[18]

Andrew Jackson mobilized the federal government behind the expropriation and expulsion of a racial minority whom he considered an impediment to national integrity and economic growth. Before the end of his two terms, about forty-six thousand Native Americans had been dispossessed and a like number slated for dispossession under his chosen successor. In return Jackson had obtained 100 million acres, much of it prime farmland, at a cost of 30 million acres in Oklahoma and Kansas plus $70 million ($1.21 billion in 2005, insofar as such equivalents can be calculated).[19] Little of the money ended up with the American Indians, but its expenditure seriously compromised Jackson's pledges of strict republican economy. Of course, the blame for the dispossession and expulsion of the tribes must be widely shared among the white public, and even a sympathetic administration found it difficult to protect Indian rights, as John Quincy Adams's experience proved. But Jackson's policies encouraged white greed and made a bad situation worse. In some places where the administration did not resort to force to expel them, modest numbers of tribal Indians succeeded in remaining east of the Mississippi, including Iroquois in New York and Cherokee in North Carolina.

Nor did the fault lie simply with the inefficient and corrupt implementation of Removal, rather than with Jackson's policy itself. The Indian Removal Bill called for renegotiating treaties and (assuming what the outcome of the negotiations would be) funding deportation. The treaty-making process was notorious for coercion and corruption, as Jackson knew from firsthand experience, and the new treaties concluded under his administration carried on these practices. Jackson's favorite

18. See Ethan Allen Hitchcock, A *Traveller in Indian Territory*, rpt. with foreword by Michael Green (Norman, Okla., 1996).
19. Donald Cole, *The Presidency of Andrew Jackson* (Lawrence, Kans., 1993), 116. Currency equivalent calculated using the Consumer Price Index in Bureau of the Census, *Historical Statistics of the United States* (Washington, 1975).

negotiator, John F. Schermerhorn, despite much contemporary criticism for his chicanery, was reappointed and rewarded by the president. Firmly believing that "Congress has full power, by law, to regulate all the concerns of the Indians,"[20] Jackson found it convenient to pretend that the states had authority to extend their laws over the tribes because he knew the states would make life intolerable for the Natives. After the white populace and their state governments had looted and defrauded the helpless minority group, Jackson (as the historian Harry Watson has put it) "struck a pose as the Indians' rescuer," offering deportation as their salvation.[21] During the Removal process the president personally intervened frequently, always on behalf of haste, sometimes on behalf of economy, but never on behalf of humanity, honesty, or careful planning. Army officers like General Wool and Colonel Zachary Taylor who attempted to carry out Removal as humanely as possible or to protect acknowledged Indian rights against white intruders learned to their cost that Jackson's administration would not back them up.[22]

Indian Removal reveals much more about Jacksonian politics than just its racism. In the first place it illustrates imperialism, that is, a determination to expand geographically and economically, imposing an alien will upon subject peoples and commandeering their resources. Imperialism need not be confined to cases of overseas expansion, such as the western European powers carried on in the nineteenth century; it can just as appropriately apply to expansion into geographically contiguous areas, as in the case of the United States and tsarist Russia. *Imperialism* is a more accurate and fruitful category for understanding the relations between the United States and the Native Americans than the metaphor of *paternalism* so often invoked by both historians and contemporaries (as in treaty references to the "Great White Father" and his "Indian children"). The federal government was too distant and too alien, too preoccupied with expropriation rather than nurture, for a parental role to describe the relationship, save perhaps as a sinister caricature. Paternalism might be invoked with more justice to characterize the attitude of the Christian missionaries to the Indians.

Besides eagerness for territorial expansion, Jackson's Indian policy also demonstrates impatience with legal restraints. The cavalier attitude

---

20. Andrew Jackson to James Monroe, March 4, 1817, quoted in Robert Remini, *The Legacy of Andrew Jackson* (Baton Rouge, 1988), 49.
21. Harry Watson, *Liberty and Power: The Politics of Jacksonian America* (New York, 1990), 109.
22. See, e.g., Klunder, *Lewis Cass*, 70.

toward the law expressed by Jackson (who was, after all, a Tennessee lawyer and judge) was widespread among his fellow countrymen. The rule of law obtained only in places and on subjects where local majorities supported it. At times during the Georgia gold rush, for example, neither the Cherokee Nation, the state authorities, nor the federal government could enforce law and order. The restoration of legal order to the gold fields came as a result of a desire for secure property titles. Relations with the Indian tribes turned out to be one area of American law where John Marshall's Supreme Court did not make good on its attempt to set binding precedent. When more cases involving Indian rights came before the Court after Marshall's death, the new majority of Jackson appointees disregarded *Worcester v. Georgia* and instead restored the doctrine of *Johnson v. M'Intosh* (1824), affirming white sovereignty over aboriginal lands based on a "right of discovery."[23] During the generations to come, state governments all over the country repeatedly asserted their supremacy over Indian reservations, state courts enforced it, and the federal government, including the judiciary, acquiesced. Even after tribes had relocated to the west of the Mississippi River, their ability to remain on their new domain was no more secure than it had been on their old. In 1831–32, the state of Missouri expelled its Shawnee residents and turned their farms and improvements over to white squatters.[24]

The president's stated goals in Indian Removal included the spread of white family farming, for "independent farmers are everywhere the basis of society, and the true friends of liberty."[25] But Jackson's insistence on opening up the Indian lands quickly, in advance of actual white population movement, played into the hands of speculators with access to significant capital, who engrossed the best lands. Not until his Specie Circular of 1837, issued just before he left office, did Jackson give any indication of wishing to discourage speculation in expropriated Indian lands. Of course, when small farmers got the chance, they too participated in land speculation to the extent that their resources permitted; even actual settlers commonly chose their sites with an eye to later resale.[26]

Martin Van Buren correctly predicted that the issue of Indian Removal would "occupy the minds and feelings of our people" for generations

23. Explained in detail by Lindsay Robertson, *Conquest by Law: How the Discovery of America Dispossessed Indigenous Peoples of Their Lands* (Oxford, 2005).

24. Tim Garrison, *The Legal Ideology of Removal* (Athens, Ga., 2002), 234–45; John Farragher, "From Ethnic Mixing to Ethnic Cleansing," in *Contact Points*, ed. Andrew Cayton and Fredrika Teute (Chapel Hill, 1998), 304–26.

25. "Fourth Annual Message" (Dec. 4, 1832), *Presidential Messages*, II, 600.

26. See Young, *Redskins, Ruffleshirts, and Rednecks*, 172–90.

to come.[27] Today Americans deplore the expropriation and expulsion of racial minorities, a practice now called "ethnic cleansing." The state of Georgia repealed its Cherokee laws in 1979 and exonerated Worcester and Butler in 1992, calling their imprisonment "a stain on the history of criminal justice in Georgia."[28] The federal government has set up markers along the Trail of Tears, which an American of today may observe with shame at the country's past offenses, leavened with at least some pride at the nation's willingness to confess them.

IV

White supremacy, resolute and explicit, constituted an essential component of what contemporaries called "the Democracy"—that is, the Democratic Party. Jackson's administrations witnessed racial confrontation not only between whites and Native Americans but also between whites and blacks. In the case of African Americans, however, the government did not embark on an initiative of its own like Indian Removal but responded to actions by the blacks themselves and their handful of radical white supporters.

Six months after Jackson's inauguration appeared the most incendiary political pamphlet in America since Tom Paine's *Common Sense*. It bore a long title: *An Appeal to the Colored Citizens of the World, But in Particular, and Very Expressly, to Those of the United States of America*. The author, a self-educated free black man named David Walker, owned a used clothing store near the Boston waterfront. Active in the AME Church and an admirer of its Bishop Richard Allen, Walker contributed to the New York–based black newspaper *Freedom's Journal*. Walker's *Appeal*, published on September 28, 1829, deployed a wide range of learning marshaled in the service of moral outrage. It denounced not only the institution of slavery but also the indignities to which all black people, free as well as slave, were subjected.

> Show me a page of history, either sacred or profane, on which a verse can be found, which maintains, that the Egyptians heaped the *insupportable insult* upon the children of Israel, by telling them that they were not of the *human family*. Can the whites deny this charge? Have they not, after having reduced us to the deplorable condition of slaves under their feet, held us up as descending originally from the tribes of *Monkeys* or *Orang-Outangs*? . . . Has Mr. Jefferson declared to the

27. Martin Van Buren, *Autobiography*, ed. John Fitzpatrick (Washington, 1920), II, 295–96.
28. *New York Times* (national ed.), Nov. 11, 1992, A-7.

world, that we are inferior to the whites, both in the endowments of our bodies and our minds? It is indeed surprising, that a man of such great learning, combined with such excellent natural parts, should speak so of a set of men in chains. I do not know what to compare it to, unless, like putting one wild deer in an iron cage, where it will be secured, and hold another by the side of the same, then let it go, and expect the one in the cage to run as fast as the one at liberty.[29]

Both by precept and example, Walker's *Appeal* stressed education as a vehicle for black liberation. In this respect, the author reflected mainstream opinion in the African American middle class. Less conventional aspects of Walker's message made a mark on public attitudes. His denunciation of the colonization movement turned the northern black community decisively against it and to supporting racial equality within American society as the alternative to separation. Walker's insistence that the literate minority spread his message to the rest of the African American community formed part of his call for black solidarity against oppression. Most shockingly of all, at least to those whites who encountered his pamphlet, Walker called for resistance on the part of the slaves. "Never make an attempt to gain our freedom or *natural right*, from under our cruel oppressors and murderers, until you see your way clear—when that hour arrives and you move, be not afraid or dismayed; then be you assured that Jesus Christ the King of heaven and of earth who is the God of justice and of armies, will surely go before you." Walker spoke in the biblical prophetic tradition. Unless white America changed its ways, the country was doomed to the wrath of an avenging God.[30]

David Walker had spent several years in Charleston, South Carolina, where he may well have been involved with Denmark Vesey's circle. Now, Walker made use of his waterfront contacts to distribute his pamphlet to southern ports, hoping its message would reach an audience that included slaves. To evade southern censorship, he sometimes stitched copies into the coats he sold black sailors. Worcester and Butler, the missionaries to the Cherokees whose cause was vindicated by the Supreme Court, may have carried Walker's pamphlet. In the months following its publication, authorities in Georgia, Virginia, the Carolinas, and Louisiana confiscated copies of the *Appeal* wholesale. They also passed new laws against circulating seditious literature, isolated black sailors on ships coming

29. *David Walker's Appeal, in Four Articles*, ed. Sean Wilentz (New York, 1995), 10. Walker's allusion to Thomas Jefferson is based on the latter's *Notes on the State of Virginia* (London, 1787), Query XIV.
30. *David Walker's Appeal*, 11–12.

into port, and tightened restrictions on black religion and literacy. Rumor had it that southern planters put out a contract on Walker's life. No wonder that when David Walker died suddenly on August 6, 1830, many suspected poison.[31]

Walker's work as a Boston antislavery publicist with a national audience was carried on by a white man named William Lloyd Garrison. Garrison's sailor father had walked out when the boy was twelve; his mother, a cleaning woman, could give her son little but love and Baptist devotion. Born in Newburyport, Massachusetts, a few yards from the tomb of the great revival preacher George Whitefield, Garrison grew to manhood poor, talented, and "all on fire" with religious zeal to set the world aright in preparation for the Second Coming of Christ.[32] After experience working in Baltimore for the Quaker Benjamin Lundy on a periodical called *The Genius of Universal Emancipation*, twenty-five-year-old Garrison returned to Boston; with encouragement and help from the black community there he set up his own antislavery newspaper. The first issue of the *Liberator* appeared in January 1831, bearing a statement of editorial policy that became famous.

> I am aware that many object to the severity of my language, but is there not cause for severity? I *will be* as harsh as truth, and as uncompromising as justice. On this subject, I do not wish to think, or speak, or write, with moderation. No! no! Tell a man whose house is on fire to give a moderate alarm; tell him to moderately rescue his wife from the hands of the ravisher; tell the mother to gradually extricate her babe from the fire into which it has fallen;—but urge me not to use moderation in a cause like the present. I am in earnest—I will not equivocate—I will not excuse—I will not retreat a single inch—AND I WILL BE HEARD.[33]

Within six months, the *Liberator* had a firm circulation base in the black neighborhoods of northern cities as well as financial support from the New York businessmen Lewis and Arthur Tappan, who also supported Charles Finney's revivals. Defying conventional journalistic practice, Garrison opened his paper's columns to black and female writers. For the next thirty-five years, the weekly publication of the *Liberator* kept

31. Clement Eaton, "A Dangerous Pamphlet in the Old South," *Journal of Southern History* 2 (1936): 323–34; Peter Hinks, *To Awaken My Afflicted Brethren* (University Park, Pa., 1997), 25–40, 127–31. Boston city records list Walker's cause of death as consumption; modern historians disagree over the likelihood of foul play.
32. For Garrison's postmillennialism, see Henry Mayer, *All on Fire: William Lloyd Garrison and the Abolition of Slavery* (New York, 1998), 125, 225.
33. *Liberator* 1 (Jan. 1, 1831): 1.

Garrison's promise of protest until the ratification of the Thirteenth Amendment purged slavery from the Constitution.

Garrison's *Liberator* became the most prominent voice of a distinctive antislavery position known as abolitionism, whose platform demanded that emancipation should be immediate, not gradual, without compensation to the masters, and without the deportation or "colonization" of the freedpeople. On January 6, 1832, in the basement of Boston's African Meeting House, he and others founded the New England Anti-Slavery Society, dedicated to the principles of abolitionism. Within a few years a nationwide American Anti-Slavery Society had been formed, with a network of abolitionist associations operating throughout the North, despite periodic violent harassment from racist mobs. It is conventional for historians to emphasize what a small minority abolitionism constituted. Yet its expansion actually reflected a remarkably successful effort of communication, organization, and influence on the state of opinion. By 1835, the AASS boasted 200 auxiliaries (local chapters), and by 1838, a remarkable 1,350, representing some 250,000 members. This number, the historian Kathleen McCarthy points out, is 2 percent of the U.S. population at the time—making the American Anti-Slavery Society larger, in relation to its American public, than the Boy Scouts of America or the National Wildlife Federation or the National Rifle Association in the year 2000.[34] Whether accurate or not, AASS numerical claims carried enough conviction to arouse serious alarm in southern political circles.

While Garrison, like Walker, scorned the Colonization Society, he deliberately courted the constituency that had opposed Indian Removal and associated their cause with his own. In his *Thoughts on African Colonization* (1832), he declared that black organizations were "as unanimously opposed to a removal to Africa, as the Cherokees from the council-fires and graves of their ancestors."[35] Indeed, the controversy over Removal, by demonstrating the evils of expulsion as a way to treat a racial minority, helped discredit African colonization in the eyes of northern reformers. Garrison's fundamental objection to the colonization movement was its failure to stress the moral evil of slavery. Though regularly condemned as an impractical fanatic, Garrison actually had a sound understanding of the nature of the antislavery cause. It was a battle for public opinion. If a

34. Kathleen D. McCarthy, *American Creed: Philanthropy and the Rise of Civil Society* (Chicago, 2003), 135. The AASS membership statistics are given in Louis Filler, *The Crusade Against Slavery* (New York, 1960), 67.

35. William Lloyd Garrison, *Thoughts on African Colonization* (Boston, 1832), pt. ii, p. 5.

critical segment of public opinion could be brought to recognize slavery as a moral evil, the institution's days would be numbered.

Failing to capture the imagination of the rising generation of Yankee philanthropists, the colonization movement increasingly fell under the control of southerners. The great debate in Virginia following Nat Turner's Rebellion represented the best chance that the colonization movement ever had of large-scale implementation. Yet the impulse fell apart when it became apparent that western Virginians supported colonization as a means to get rid of emancipated slaves, whereas eastern Virginians only cared about it as a way to get rid of blacks who were already free. Free black Virginians were rarely interested in voluntary emigration, and western white Virginians were unwilling to deport them forcibly.[36] Meanwhile, the Jackson administration decided that the colonization program constituted an implied critique of slavery and curtailed its modest federal funding. Lydia Maria Child's influential abolitionist *Appeal in Favor of that Class of Americans called Africans* (1836) declared colonization impractical, as indeed it was without government support. The decline of colonization as a viable option contributed over the long run to the polarization of positions on the slavery issue.

Through his discussion of Walker and his impact, Garrison positioned the *Liberator* as heir to the *Appeal*. Unlike Walker, however, Garrison was a thoroughgoing pacifist and drew the line at violent insurrection. This did nothing to reassure southerners, however, since he also disapproved of government-sponsored violence such as the suppression of insurrection. Sometimes southern editors reprinted *Liberator* articles with their own rebuttals—thereby magnifying Garrison's fame/notoriety. Nat Turner's Uprising in the summer of 1831 gave a new immediacy to the issue of whether slavery justified violent resistance. Did northern criticism of slavery incite bloodshed? Had Nat Turner read David Walker? The most likely answer is given by the historian Vincent Harding. Without needing to read Walker, "Nat Turner had long been convinced that the God of Walker's *Appeal* had always been in Southampton."[37] Yet, rather than admit that slaves inevitably resented their oppression, white southerners usually blamed insurrection on outside agitators.

For quite a while after Turner's Uprising, the new northern abolitionist organizations refrained from pushing their literature on the South. The debate in the Virginia House of Delegates suggested that southerners themselves might take steps against slavery, even if not the ones that

36. Allison Freehling, *Drift Toward Dissolution* (Baton Rouge, 1982), 177–95.
37. Vincent Harding, *There Is a River* (New York, 1981), 94.

Garrison would find morally sound. However, when nothing had come of Virginia's debate over slavery by the summer of 1835, it seemed clear that the colonization movement had demonstrated its bankruptcy. Garrison and his New York City counterpart, Elizur Wright, then decided to undertake a major southern propaganda offensive. Their target audience consisted of twenty thousand influential southern whites, including many who had previously criticized slavery in conventional Jeffersonian terms as an unfortunate legacy from previous generations, a problem that could be solved with the help of colonization when the time was ripe. The abolitionists intended to persuade such southern moderates that further procrastination was pointless: The time for emancipation was now, and the colonization movement offered no hope. Their program took advantage of the latest mass-production printing technology and relied on the U.S. mails for distribution. The federal Post Office would not be legally bound by the censorship that southern states had enacted in response to David Walker and Nat Turner.[38]

The abolitionists printed up 175,000 tracts and would have a million ready by the end of the calendar year, but no more than a handful ever reached their addressees. Southern local authorities had vainly urged the mayor of Boston to crack down on Walker's *Appeal* and Garrison's *Liberator*; when the first abolitionist tracts showed up in their local post offices, they took the law into their own hands. Regardless of the fact that the literature was addressed to prominent white citizens, most southerners seemed convinced that it could fall into the hands of literate blacks and incite rebellion. On June 29, 1835, a group of burglars broke into the Charleston, South Carolina, post office and made off with a bag of abolitionist publications that the postmaster had (not coincidentally) sorted out and labeled for their convenience. The next night the contents of the mailbag were burned before a crowd of two thousand.[39]

In the abolitionists' fight to influence public opinion, access to the mails was crucial. Postmasters from all over the country began to ask Jackson's newly appointed postmaster general, Amos Kendall, how they should deal with abolitionist literature. Did they really have to obey the law and deliver the mail? A member of the kitchen cabinet who had ghostwritten some of Jackson's major state papers, Kendall consulted his chief on August 7, proposing to allow local postmasters to leave antislavery mail

---

38. Mayer, *All on Fire*, 195–200.
39. Sherman Savage, *The Controversy over the Distribution of Abolitionist Literature* (New York, 1938), 1–26, updated by Richard R. John, *Spreading the News: The American Postal System from Franklin to Morse* (Cambridge, Mass., 1995), 257–63.

undelivered. Old Hickory concurred, calling the abolitionists "monsters" guilty of stirring up "the horrors of a servile war," who deserved "to atone for this wicked attempt with their lives." Whereas Kendall expressed the hope to resolve the matter "with as little noise and difficulty as possible," Jackson characteristically took the issue public. At the next session of Congress, he called for legislation authorizing federal censorship "to prohibit, under severe penalties, the circulation in the Southern States, through the mail, of incendiary publications intended to instigate the slaves to insurrection." Until Congress met, Jackson hit upon a scheme to stifle the distribution of abolitionist material. "Direct that those inflamatory [sic] papers be delivered to none but who will demand them as subscribers," he told the postmaster general, and then publish their names as supporters of "exciting the negroes to insurrection and to massacre." This, the president confidently predicted, would bring them "into such disrepute with all the South, that they would be compelled to desist, or move from the country."[40] Kendall went further. He not only deferred to local sentiment in the South, he even instructed postmasters in the North that although there was no legal authority for them to do so, they were "justified" if they refused to dispatch abolitionist mailings into the South. To shield the administration from legal action, he carefully added that postmasters acted on their own responsibility when they did this.[41]

Where Jackson had proposed the federal government should define and exclude "incendiary" materials from the mail, Calhoun introduced a bill in the Senate to require the federal Post Office to enforce whatever censorship laws any state might enact. At one point in its consideration, Vice President Martin Van Buren saved this measure by his casting vote, but eventually Calhoun's proposal was defeated. Seven slave-state senators, including Henry Clay and Thomas Hart Benton, joined with northerners to vote it down. Concern for civil liberties, even those of unpopular minorities, counted for more in the halls of Congress than within the Jackson administration. In 1836, an opposition representative from Vermont named Hiland Hall persuaded Congress to pass a law affirming the responsibility of postmasters for delivering all mail to its destination.[42] In practice, however,

---

40. Amos Kendall to Andrew Jackson, Aug. 7, 1835, and Andrew Jackson to Amos Kendall, Aug. 9, 1835, *Correspondence of AJ*, V, 359–61; "Message to Congress" (Dec. 7, 1835), *Presidential Messages*, III, 1394–95.
41. Kendall's instructions to the New York City postmaster were printed in *Niles' Weekly Register*, Sept. 5, 1835.
42. See Richard R. John, "Hiland Hall's Report on Incendiary Publications," *American Journal of Legal History* 41 (1997): 94–125.

Kendall found ways to allow southern postmasters to continue deferring to the censorship laws of their states. As he put it in a letter to the Charleston postmaster, "We owe an obligation to the laws, but a higher one to the communities in which we live." What Calhoun and Van Buren would have required, Kendall and his successors managed to permit. And as Jackson had foreseen, no southern addressee—no matter how respectable, moderate, or Jeffersonian—dared challenge the policy and demand his mail. Instead, the prominent men whom the abolitionists had targeted led public meetings across the South, demanding the Post Office ban abolitionist mailings, and often demanding as well that northern states crack down on their antislavery societies.

The southern practice of ignoring inconvenient federal laws in order to preserve white supremacy was established long before the Civil War. Jackson, who had stood up to South Carolina so firmly over the tariff, cooperated with the state's defiance of federal law when the issue was race.[43] The refusal of the Post Office to deliver abolitionist mail to the South may well represent the largest peacetime violation of civil liberty in U.S. history. Deprived of access to communication with the South, the abolitionists would henceforth concentrate on winning over the North.

V

April 8, 1834, was the first of three days of voting in a hotly contested race for mayor and city council of New York. The Bank War, then at its height, inflamed partisan rancor. In the predominantly Democratic Sixth Ward, armed men drove the Whig Party observers away from the polling place. The next day a Whig parade was attacked when it passed through the Sixth Ward. The coverage of these events by the local partisan press exacerbated passions rather than encouraging order. The Whigs resolved to challenge the Democratic "bullies" who for years had intimidated prospective voters, helping keep the city under the control of Tammany Hall. On the third day of voting, the rioting involved thousands; the mayor himself was clubbed to the ground as he tried to restore order; and only the mobilization of twelve hundred soldiers separated the antagonists. The election returned a Democratic mayor (by 180 out of 35,000 votes cast) and a Whig council. Although many were injured in the disorders,

---

43. Amos Kendall to Alfred Huger, Aug. 4, 1835, *Charleston Courier*, Aug. 14, 1835. See also Clement Eaton, *The Freedom-of-Thought Struggle in the Old South*, rev. ed. (New York, 1964), 196–212; Susan Wyly-Jones, "The 1835 Anti-Abolition Meetings in the South," *Civil War History* 47 (2001): 289–309.

Table 3
Riots Reported in *Niles' Register*

1830	1 incident reported
1831	3
1832	1
1833	4
1834	20
1835	53
1836	16
1837	3
1838	4

Source: Leonard Richards, *Gentlemen of Property and Standing* (New York, 1970), 12. *Niles' Register* did not attempt to cover all riots, and the actual number of incidents was perhaps three times as large, but the figures above give a sense of public perceptions and relative frequency.

only one person had been killed, probably because the riot was halted just as the participants began to arm themselves with guns.[44] The April election riot commenced a year of recurrent mob violence in New York City and heralded an explosion of such violence across the whole United States for the next three years. In August 1835, at the peak of the disorders, the *Richmond Whig* deplored "the present supremacy of the Mobocracy," while the Philadelphia *National Gazette* declared, "Whenever the fury or the cupidity of the mob is excited, they can gratify their lawless appetites almost with impunity."[45]

Party politics was by no means the only cause of rioting in Jacksonian America. Ethnic, racial, and religious animosities provided the most frequent provocation to riot. The growing cities seemed vulnerable to anyone exploiting group resentments among the increasingly diverse urban communities, though small settlements certainly demonstrated their share of mob violence, as the Mormons found out in Missouri and Illinois. The absence of effective law enforcement in both urban and rural areas permitted inflammatory situations to get out of hand. The largest riots, surprisingly, were those directed against theaters where prominent British actors accused of anti-American remarks were performing. New York City appearances by actor Joshua Anderson were repeatedly called off in 1831–32, despite audiences paying to see him, because of unchecked

---

44. *Hazard's Register of Pennsylvania* 14 (Oct. 1834): 164–65; David Grimsted, *American Mobbing, 1828–1861* (New York, 1998), 200–203.
45. Quoted ibid., 3.

violent demonstrations by self-styled patriots seeking excitement. Other actors subjected to the same treatment included Edmund Kean and William Charles Macready. The worst of many riots of this kind occurred in 1849 at the Astor Place Opera House in New York, in which as many as thirty-one people may have died.[46]

Rioting, rather than crime by individuals, primarily precipitated the creation of police forces as we know them. There were no professional city police forces before 1844, when New York began the process of creating one in imitation of London's, founded by Sir Robert Peel in 1829 (hence called "Bobby's" or "bobbies"). In pre-police days, the only recourses of beleaguered officials consisted of night watchmen (primarily looking out for fires), courtroom marshals, a few part-time, politically chosen constables, ad hoc sheriff's posses, and the military. Uniforms for the new police forces were introduced only slowly, beginning in the 1850s, because many in America felt they smacked of militarism.[47] The nickname "copper" or "cop" came from the copper badges that antedated uniforms.

The most common targets of mob violence in the 1830s were the abolitionists and the free black communities that supported them. In fact, the appearance of organized abolitionism explains much of the dramatic rise in the number of riots. In October 1833, an elite-led mob forced the prominent evangelical philanthropists Arthur and Lewis Tappan to relocate the founding meeting of their New York Anti-Slavery Society. New Yorkers, with so much of their city's business dependent upon the cotton trade, felt understandably suspicious of interference with southern slavery. Even members of the American Colonization Society, offended by the uncompromising rhetoric of the abolitionists, joined the mob. After intimidating the abolitionists into a change of venue, the crowd conducted their own meeting according to rules of order.[48]

The great abolitionist undertaking of 1835, their mass mailing of pamphlets to southern addresses, provoked the largest number of riots. The communications revolution, by empowering social critics on the one hand and fanning conservative fears on the other, catalyzed the violence. Future president John Tyler, addressing an antiabolition crowd at Gloucester Courthouse, Virginia, in August 1835, focused his remarks on the

---

46. Paul Weinbaum, *Mobs and Demagogues: The New York Response to Collective Violence in the Early Nineteenth Century* (Ann Arbor, 1979), 37–39. Another account sets the death toll at twenty-two.

47. J. F. Richardson, *The New York Police* (New York, 1970), 27–28; Eric Monkkonen, *Police in Urban America* (Cambridge, Eng., 1981), 42–46, 162–68.

48. *Niles' Weekly Register*, Oct. 12, 1833.

sensationalism of the antislavery tracts, their wide circulations, and "the cheap rate at which these papers are delivered." He pointed with horror to the novel involvement of women in the abolitionist movement, particularly in the circulation of mass petitions, and to the "horn-books and primers" aimed at "the youthful imagination." Tyler viewed the abolition crusade as an assault not only on slavery but on the entire traditional social order. Not only in the South, but even in the North, the early antiabolitionist mobs sometimes enjoyed the respectable leadership of "gentlemen of property and standing" like Tyler.[49] On October 21, 1835, such a mob in Boston almost killed William Lloyd Garrison; the mayor of the city saved his life by locking him up in jail. Two years later, an abolitionist editor named Elijah Lovejoy was not so fortunate; he died defending his press against a mob in Alton, Illinois. Lovejoy remained the only abolitionist killed in the North; he was shot after killing one of his assailants. The editor became a martyr to his cause, and his death was held up as a shameful interference with free speech. Thereafter respectable opinion in the North swung away from mob action, whether against abolitionists or others.

The 1830s witnessed a transition in the composition of mobs from elite-led, politically motivated, and relatively restrained collective actions to impromptu violence, sometimes perpetrated as much for the sheer venting of emotion as for any planned objective, in which people were more likely to be injured or killed.[50] In the summer of 1834, the newer, less restrained, kind of mobs spread a more awesome terror in New York City. African American celebrations of the seventh anniversary of the end of New York slavery on July 4, 1827, triggered a massive reaction. For three days and nights starting on July 9, mobs vandalized, looted, and burned the homes, shops, and churches of the free black community and white abolitionists. More than sixty buildings were gutted or destroyed, six of them churches, including St. Philip's African Episcopal Church on Centre Street. Only when it looked like the rioters would turn on the property of the wealthy in general did Democratic mayor Cornelius Lawrence (the one elected by 180 votes) instruct the militia to get serious about enforcing the law. "As long as Negroes and a few isolated white men were the targets, he had not cared," one historian has observed.[51] The local press

49. Leonard Richards, *"Gentlemen of Property and Standing": Anti-Abolition Mobs in Jacksonian America* (New York, 1970). Tyler's speech is quoted at length on 55–58.
50. See Michael Feldberg, *The Turbulent Era: Riot and Disorder in Jacksonian America* (New York, 1980).
51. Bertram Wyatt-Brown, *Lewis Tappan and the Evangelical War Against Slavery* (Cleveland, 1969), 119.

too experienced a change of heart, and suddenly deplored the violence it had earlier shamelessly exacerbated. The rioters seem to have been largely working-class whites motivated (so far as one can tell) by fears of racial intermarriage and black competition for jobs, education, and housing.[52]

The most notorious of 1834 riots, the burning of the convent at Charlestown, Massachusetts, seems to have been an example of the old-fashioned kind of rioting; it involved both middle-class and working-class conspirators and spared the persons of the sisters. Increasingly, however, mob violence expressed the varied discontents of the working classes. Many of the other disturbances of 1834 document the shift. In January, near Hagerstown, Maryland, Irish canal workers from County Cork fought against other Irish canal workers from County Longford, and dozens died before troops arrived from Fort McHenry. The next month, two volunteer fire companies in New York City engaged each other in a pitched battle. In April, a Democratic Party mob looted the branch of the BUS in Portsmouth, New Hampshire. Philadelphia suffered a race riot in August, prompted by white workers' fears of blacks taking their jobs, followed by an election riot in October. Elsewhere Protestant workingmen attacked Catholic immigrants. November saw forty Irish immigrant workers laying track between Baltimore and Washington for one of the newly invented locomotives attack their supervisors and kill two of them in an action with both ethnic and class dimensions.[53]

Workingmen in Baltimore rioted in August 1835 against the defunct Bank of Maryland, ruined by the speculations of Taney's crony Thomas Ellicott, of which many had been depositors or creditors. While their action expressed understandable feelings, it only delayed winding up the bank's affairs (and provoked bitter condemnation from Taney, who was no friend of the working class).[54] An acute analysis of rioting in this period concludes that although immigrant and working-class groups had plenty of legitimate grievances, their rioting was frequently counterproductive and more often than not misdirected against scapegoats.[55]

52. Paul Gilje, *The Road to Mobocracy: Popular Disorder in New York City, 1763–1834* (Chapel Hill, 1987), 162–70; Tyler Anbinder, *Five Points* (New York, 2001), 7–13.
53. Daniel Cohen, "Alvah Kelley's Cow and the Charlestown Convent Riot," *New England Quarterly* 74 (2001): 531–79; Carl Prince, "The Great 'Riot Year'," *JER* 5 (1985): 1–20.
54. Taney's reactions are printed in Frank Otto Gatell, ed., "Roger B. Taney, the Bank of Maryland Rioters, and a Whiff of Grapeshot," *Maryland Historical Magazine* 59 (1964): 262–67.
55. David Grimsted, "Rioting in Its Jacksonian Setting," *AHR* 77 (1972): 361–97.

Frontier vigilantes enforced a venerable version of quasi-respectable violence in America. Vigilantes conceived of their violence as a supplement to, rather than a rebellion against, the law. The vigilante tradition did not die down as soon as an area became settled; in 1834, a mob in Irville, New York, took direct action against prostitution. But the heightening level of violence in vigilantism shocked observers. A mob in St. Louis lynched a black man accused of murder by roasting him over a fire in 1835. The same year, when the people of Vicksburg, Mississippi, decided to rid their town of gamblers, instead of riding the culprits out of town on a rail, they hanged them—along with several other outsiders who were simply in town on business.

Southerners seemed readier to resort to violence, inured as they were to it by the beatings and other brutal punishments routinely inflicted by masters, overseers, and slave patrols. Many riots of the antebellum era manifested the southern attempt to stifle criticism of slavery, just as so many riots of the postbellum era reflected southern determination to keep the freedpeople in subjection. (Vicksburg would become the site of one of the most notorious race riots after the Civil War.) Another category of mob was peculiar to the South: those generated by fear of slave insurrections, real or imagined. Not only did the slave states generate more mobs, their mobs attacked persons more than property, and in consequence killed more people. In the peak year of 1835, the seventy-nine southern mobs counted by historian David Grimsted killed sixty-three people, while the sixty-eight northern mobs killed eight.[56] And in the South, the legal authorities showed even less capacity or interest in controlling mob violence.

The southern penchant for violence was individual as well as collective. The sense of male personal honor that historians have found so much stronger in the South than in the North often led to violence. A virile man was expected to fight if insulted, an expectation shared by southern women as well as men. Some historians have traced this penchant for violence to the folk culture of the Celtic clans (Scots, Irish, Scots-Irish, and Welsh) from which so many southern whites descended. Inherited rural folkways changed more slowly in the South, as the effects of the transportation and communications revolutions were felt more slowly there. The *code duello* and the related practices of private violence in defense of manly honor, such as family feuds, hung on longer in the South, state legislation notwithstanding. Duels sometimes had a political dimension. When Thomas Ritchie Jr., son of the editor of the Democratic

---

56. Statistics from Grimsted, *American Mobbing*, 13.

Richmond Enquirer, accused John Hampden Pleasants, editor of his partisan rival, the *Richmond Whig,* of being an abolitionist, Pleasants, though a critic of dueling, felt constrained to challenge him. In their ensuing encounter, Pleasants was killed; Ritchie was tried and acquitted.[57] When violence marred Congress itself, it was usually southerners who perpetrated it. In April 1832, Congressman William Stanberry of Ohio was waylaid and clubbed by Sam Houston, a former congressman from Tennessee, after Stanberry alluded to Houston's rigging of an Indian contract. Houston was fined five hundred dollars by a District of Columbia court, but President Jackson remitted the fine, and prominent members of his party defended Houston's behavior.[58] Unseemly acts of violence repeatedly disgraced the Capitol over the next generation, leading up to the most notorious incident, the beating of Charles Sumner of Massachusetts on the floor of the Senate by Congressman Preston Brooks of South Carolina in 1856.

President Jackson himself was not immune to the violence of the society around him. In May 1833, Robert Randolph, a formal naval lieutenant who had been dismissed from the service on Jackson's order, assaulted the president, intending to tweak his nose. In the southern code of honor, to tweak a man's nose was to call him a liar. Randolph believed he had been framed on a charge of embezzlement in order to protect Peggy O'Neale's husband, John Timberlake. Randolph succeeded in giving the president a bloody nose, and bystanders restrained Jackson from beating the assailant with his cane. The Old Hero insisted that Randolph must have been part of a conspiracy whose real goal was his assassination, though no evidence substantiated this claim.[59] Later, Jackson did become the object of the first assassination attempt on an American president. On January 30, 1835, Richard Lawrence, an English immigrant and unemployed house painter, pointed two pistols at the president on the east portico of the Capitol from a distance of eight feet and pulled their triggers. Amazingly, both weapons misfired. Jackson once again took after his assailant with upraised cane, but others separated the two men and delivered Lawrence into custody. The would-be assassin turned out to be a madman who thought Jackson had killed his father; appropriately, he was

---

57. Bertram Wyatt-Brown, *Southern Honor* (New York, 1982), 35–39, 350–61; Dickson Bruce, *Violence and Culture in the Antebellum South* (Austin, Tex., 1979); John Hope Franklin, *The Militant South* (Cambridge, Mass., 1956), 33–62.

58. Parton, *Life of Jackson,* III, 385–92.

59. For an account of the episode and an explanation of the significance of nose-tweaking, see Kenneth Greenberg, *Honor and Slavery* (Princeton, 1996), 16–22.

found not guilty by reason of insanity and confined for the rest of his life in St. Elizabeth's mental hospital in Washington. So bitter was the partisanship of the time, however, that Jackson insisted Lawrence must be the hired tool of his political opponents—specifically, of Senator George Poindexter of Mississippi. Two witnesses came forward claiming to have seen Poindexter with Lawrence, but a Senate inquiry demolished their credibility. The historian who has examined the issue concludes the witnesses were suborned by Democratic Party agents but doubts the president's own complicity.[60] Unfortunately, Jackson's temperamental inclination to believe himself the victim of conspiracy was legitimated by the Old Republican ideology that American politicians of the time so often invoked. In the poisoned political atmosphere of 1835, the assassination attempt deepened rather than bridged the gulf of feeling separating the two parties.

Sadly, Jackson himself was part of the problem of violence. He realized that the "spirit of mob-law is becoming much too common and must be checked, or ere long it will become as great an evil as servile war." Yet having said that to his postmaster general, he went on in the same letter to urge Amos Kendall to break the law and cooperate with the mob to prevent delivery of abolitionist tracts.[61] During the Washington race riot of August 1835, the president called out troops to contain the riot but did not seek to protect the free black community from white aggressors. Old Hickory's own image and record, as a hero who stood outside and above the law, typified a strain in American frontier culture that encouraged violence. Nor did his party take a stand against it. Democratic Party rhetoric sometimes actually prompted rioting, as it did against the abolitionists in Utica, New York, in October 1835, when the mob was led by Jacksonian congressman Samuel Beardsley.[62] More often, by harping on the supremacy of popular sovereignty over legal rules, the Democrats simply fostered a climate of opinion that undervalued minority rights and the rule of law. Mike Walsh, a leading Democrat among New York City's Irish working class, headed a youth gang named "the Spartan Band" who carried clubs and roughed up political opponents in the 1840s. As Jackson remitted Houston's fine, a Democratic Congress refunded, with interest, Jackson's own fine for

60. Richard Rohrs, "Partisan Politics and the Attempted Assassination of Andrew Jackson," *JER* 1 (1981): 149–63.
61. Andrew Jackson to Amos Kendall, August 9, 1835, *Correspondence of AJ*, V, 359–61.
62. Grimsted, "Rioting," 394, 376, n. 34; Donald Cole, *Martin Van Buren and the American Political System* (Princeton, 1984), 271.

contempt of court when he jailed the New Orleans federal judge back in 1815.[63]

It is no accident that questions of sovereignty were so important in American politics. Leaders preoccupied with sovereignty and authority sensed a very real problem in America: the danger of anarchy. Significantly, when Martin Van Buren was in England at the time of the Great Reform Bill of 1832, his comments on it had to do not with improving the quality of representative government but with his fears for maintaining order. John Quincy Adams noted in his diary the ironic coexistence of humanitarian movements to abolish capital punishment with brutal lynchings of defendants accused of minor crimes or no crimes at all. Respect for legal authority had declined, he reflected.[64]

Thoughtful contemporaries worried a lot about the strain of violence in American life. Revulsion against violence helped the antislavery movement and Indian rights supporters make their cases; concern about violence within the family helped fuel the temperance movement. Dueling fell out of favor in the North. One of the most remarkable comments on the threat posed by the rising violence came from a young Illinois lawyer named Abraham Lincoln, who addressed the Springfield Lyceum on January 27, 1838. "Accounts of outrages committed by mobs form the everyday news of the times," the speaker noted grimly. Mob rule constituted a greater threat to American liberty and institutions than any foreign tyrant could ever pose, he warned.

> Whenever the vicious portion of the population shall be permitted to gather bands of hundreds and thousands, and burn churches, ravage and rob provision-stores, throw printing-presses into the river, shoot editors, and hang and burn obnoxious persons at pleasure and with impunity, depend on it, this government cannot last.

Lincoln distinguished the mobs of his own day from those of the Revolution. Then, the passions of the crowd were enlisted in the service of liberty. Now, however, Americans must be guided by "reason," not "passion," he insisted. If they allowed themselves to be governed by their passions, they could become prey to ambitious demagogues who would subvert republican institutions. Driving home the lesson of his secular sermon, Lincoln cast himself as an evangelist of obedience to the law: "Let every

---

63. On Walsh, see Arthur Schlesinger Jr., *The Age of Jackson* (Boston, 1945), 410. On Jackson's contempt citation, see above, p. 70.

64. *Autobiography of Martin Van Buren* (Washington, 1920), 463; *Memoirs of John Quincy Adams* (Philadelphia, 1874–77), diary entry for Sept. 1, 1835, IX, 260.

American, every lover of liberty, every well-wisher to his posterity swear by the blood of the Revolution never to violate in the least particular the laws of the country."[65] Though both men were frontier lawyers, the Whig Lincoln revealed an attitude toward the law far different from Jackson's.

VI

On July 6, 1835, the Great Chief Justice died, a few months short of his eightieth birthday. Although John Marshall's nationalism had become unfashionable in his home state of Virginia, he remained personally popular there and found opportunity there to express his deeply felt Burkean conservatism. Serving as a delegate from Richmond to the Virginia state constitutional convention of 1829–30, this self-made man had opposed the democratization of the suffrage and defended the power of the tidewater aristocracy. Modest to the last, he asked that his tombstone bear only the bit of information of which he was proudest: that he was the husband of Mary Willis Ambler. Marshall died at peace with himself but despairing of the American experiment he had tried so hard to perpetuate. He wrote his confidante Joseph Story, "I yield slowly and reluctantly to the conviction that our constitution cannot last." His death came in Philadelphia, where he had gone in search of medical aid for an enlarged liver. The giant Bell at Philadelphia's Independence Hall bore inscribed around its circumference a quotation from Leviticus: "Proclaim liberty throughout all the land unto the inhabitants thereof." The Bell had announced the first public reading of the Declaration of Independence on July 8, 1776. Now, tolling for Marshall's funeral, the Liberty Bell cracked. If a portent, this was ominous.[66]

With the chief justice gone, Associate Justice Story remained to carry on the defense of American nationalism and judicial conservatism. Like Marshall and most other American lawyers, Story venerated the common law. More of a scholar than Marshall, Story labored across many years and many cases, both in the Supreme Court and on circuit, to synthesize English and American precedents from a wide time span into a system of common law appropriate for federal jurisprudence. His impressive

---

65. "Address Before the Young Men's Lyceum of Springfield" (Jan. 27, 1838), *Collected Works of AL*, I, 108–15.

66. John Marshall to Joseph Story, Sept. 22, 1832, quoted in Kent Newmyer, *John Marshall and the Heroic Age of the Supreme Court* (Baton Rouge, 2001), 386. Attempts to continue using the Liberty Bell worsened the crack; it has not been rung since Washington's Birthday of 1846.

Commentaries on the Constitution (1833) presented a nationalistic and Burkean interpretation of that instrument, grounding its authority, as Webster had done, in American society as a whole. James Kent, chancellor of New York's highest court of equity, spread the influence of Story's judgments through his own famous *Commentaries on American Law* (1826–30). Kent became known as the "American Blackstone," a reference to the great eighteenth-century English juridical commentator.[67]

In the 1820s, certain Jeffersonian Old Republicans voiced criticism of the common law as an alien, undemocratic system that should be replaced by simpler legal codes, more readily comprehensible to laymen. The Jacksonian Democrats continued this criticism, though more often they simply endorsed the popular election of state judges to remind those Tocqueville described as "the aristocracy of America" of their true sovereigns. Led by Story and Kent, the legal profession closed ranks in a successful defense of the common law, arguing that since it derived ultimately from the habits of the people, it presupposed their consent.[68] Though some states and the federal government eventually codified their law, the codes embodied common-law principles. But Whig lawyers did not have it all their own way; Jacksonian political philosophy exerted great potency as well. Most states wrote or rewrote their constitutions during the antebellum period, and in doing so demonstrated concepts of natural rights and popular sovereignty congenial to the Democratic Party. While Whig principles stood forth strongly in many a judicial opinion, Democratic ones usually prevailed in elected constitutional conventions.[69]

Marshall had hoped that Henry Clay would win the election of 1832 and appoint Story his successor, but this was not to be. The choice lay with Andrew Jackson. Jackson made five Supreme Court appointments late in his presidency, in addition to two others in his first term. Two of the second-term appointments were made on his last day in office (March 3, 1837), when an obliging Democratic Congress expanded the

67. Joseph Story, *Commentaries on the Constitution of the United States* (Boston 1833), vol. I, bk. III, chap. 3. See also Kent Newmyer, *Supreme Court Justice Joseph Story* (Chapel Hill, 1985); Carl Stychin, "The Commentaries of Chancellor James Kent and the Development of an American Common Law," *American Journal of Legal History* 37 (1993): 440–63.

68. On this controversy, see Marshall Foletta, *Coming to Terms with Democracy* (Charlottesville, Va., 2001), 159–72.

69. See Laura Scalia, *America's Jeffersonian Experiment: Remaking State Constitutions, 1820–1850* (DeKalb, Ill., 1999).

Supreme Court from seven to nine justices. All five of his last round of appointees came from the slave states, although if representation on the Court had been proportional to free population or litigation there would have been but three southern justices. When one of Jackson's last-minute appointees declined, Van Buren plugged in another southerner. Even so, Jackson made more Supreme Court appointments than any other president between Washington and Taft.

To replace Marshall as chief justice, Jackson nominated his former attorney general Roger Taney, whom he had already tried earlier to appoint an associate justice. The Whig Senate that censured Jackson for removal of the deposits had refused to confirm Taney, the instrument of deposit removal, as either secretary of the Treasury or Supreme Court justice. But this time the Democrats controlled the Senate, and on March 15, 1836, they confirmed Taney as Marshall's successor. The ascetic Taney, hollow-chested and stooped, contrasted physically with the bluff outdoorsman image his predecessor maintained even in old age. Born into the Catholic tobacco-planting aristocracy of Maryland, Roger Brooke Taney had begun his political career, like Marshall, as a Federalist. He achieved distinction as a practicing lawyer, particularly for his mastery of civil procedure. Director of a state bank and chair of Maryland's Jackson-for-president campaign, he made a plausible choice when Old Hickory appointed him U.S. attorney general in the cabinet reshuffle of 1831. Taney accepted with the understanding that he would continue his private legal practice. The age displayed a surprising unconcern for what we would consider a clear conflict of interest. Acting in this private capacity, Taney filed the brief for Baltimore in *Barron v. Baltimore*, arguing that the Bill of Rights did not apply to the states.[70]

In Jackson's cabinet Taney early exemplified some of the legal views that would later characterize his chief justiceship. Although he shared the typical lawyer's respect for the common law, he also embraced the strong view of popular sovereignty characteristic of Jacksonian Democrats. Taney believed that law originated in the will of the sovereign. He shared Calhoun's view that sovereignty in the American system resided in "the people of the several states" and that the federal government was only an agent of this sovereign. Jacksonians had invoked this legal doctrine in support of Indian Removal, assuming that the sovereign people must be white. Taney himself had declared that the power of the BUS constituted an intolerable infringement upon popular sovereignty. As

---

70. See Bernard Steiner, *Life of Roger Brooke Taney* (Baltimore, 1922), 139–43.

chief justice, he would rely on his doctrine of state sovereignty in several of his major opinions, notably the *License Cases* (1847) and *Luther v. Borden* (1848).[71]

The most interesting of Taney's opinions as attorney general is probably one he delivered on May 28, 1832, regarding South Carolina's law authorizing imprisonment of any free Negro sailors who came ashore while their ships were in port. Adams's attorney general, William Wirt, had found South Carolina's conduct unconstitutional, but Jackson's previous attorney general, John Berrien, had countenanced it. Taney agreed with Berrien. His reasoning is revealing:

> The African race in the United States even when free, are every where a degraded class, and exercise no political influence. The privileges they are allowed to enjoy, are accorded to them as a matter of kindness and benevolence rather than of right. . . . And where they are nominally admitted by law to the privileges of citizenship, they have no effectual power to defend them, and are permitted to be citizens by the sufferance of the white population and hold whatever rights they enjoy at their mercy. They were never regarded as a constituent portion of the sovereignty of any state. . . . They were not looked upon as citizens by the contracting parties who formed the Constitution.[72]

Excluding African Americans from the sovereign people of the United States, this argument does not address the issue of black foreigners penalized by the law in question. What makes the attorney general's opinion interesting is the way it prefigures a judgment he rendered twenty-five years later as chief justice. In his infamous *Dred Scott* decision of 1857, Taney would rule that, under the Constitution, African Americans had "no rights which the white man was bound to respect." Roger Taney quietly supported the colonization movement and had manumitted his own slaves. Yet, like most southern critics of slavery including Thomas Jefferson, he was determined that neither national majorities nor black people themselves should ever infringe on the absolute power of masters or the sovereign supremacy of the white race.[73]

---

71. *Ohio Life Insurance Co. v. Debolt*, 57 U.S. (16 Howard) 428 (1853); *License Cases*, 46 U.S. (5 Howard) 504 (1847); *Luther v. Borden*, 48 U.S. (7 Howard) 1 (1848). Taney's doctrine of sovereignty is analyzed in Charles W. Smith Jr., *Roger B. Taney: Jacksonian Jurist* (Chapel Hill, 1936).

72. Roger Taney to (Secretary of State) Edward Livingston, May 28, 1832, ms. quoted in Carl Swisher, *Roger B. Taney* (New York, 1935), 154.

73. *Dred Scott v. Sandford*, 60 U.S. (19 Howard) 393 (1857), quotation at 407; Swisher, *Taney*, 154–59.

On the Supreme Court, Taney did not implement an antimarket agenda. Opportunities for him to put his views into the law books came as early as January 1837, while Jackson was still in office. In *Briscoe v. Bank of Kentucky* the former state bank director joined a majority in support of an opinion written by Justice McLean vindicating the right of state banks to issue paper money. The U.S. Constitution declares emphatically that "no state may issue bills of credit," but the Court ruled that states could charter banks to do so, even if the bank in question was wholly owned by the state! The decision represented a huge victory for "soft money."[74] In the same Court term, Taney struck another legal blow in favor of the entrepreneurial wing of the Jacksonian movement in *Charles River Bridge v. Warren Bridge*, and this time delivered the opinion himself.

In 1786, a bridge had been built over the Charles River to link Boston with Charlestown. The Commonwealth of Massachusetts had granted the company that built and operated the bridge the right to collect tolls for seventy years. Although the Charles River Bridge represented an improvement over the old ferry, by 1828 Charlestown had grown considerably, and its businessmen felt the tolls as a constriction on further growth. They successfully lobbied the legislature to charter another bridge company. The new Warren Bridge would charge tolls only until 1836 and then become free. No compensation was offered the proprietors of the Charles River Bridge for infringing on their franchise. They brought a lawsuit charging the legislature had violated the provision in the federal Constitution against states "impairing the obligation of contracts." After losing in the Massachusetts Supreme Judicial Court, the Charles River Bridge company appealed to the U.S. Supreme Court.

Delivering the Court's judgment in favor of the new Warren Bridge, Chief Justice Taney cast his opinion as a vindication of both state sovereignty and economic development. Sovereign states could not be assumed to yield "any portion of that power over their own internal police and improvement, which is so necessary to their well-being and prosperity." Since Massachusetts had made no explicit promise in the Charles River Bridge Company's charter not to charter other bridges, no contract had been impaired. The pressing needs of economic expansion and technological improvement dictated that vested interests might sometimes have to make room for progress. If the Charles River Bridge claims prevailed, Taney warned, who could predict how many old turnpike companies might sue the canals and railroads that had replaced them?

---

74. *Briscoe v. Bank of the Commonwealth of Kentucky*, 36 U.S. (11 Peters) 257 (1837).

We shall be thrown back to the improvements of the last century, and obliged to stand still, until the claims of the old turnpike corporations shall be satisfied, and they shall consent to permit these States to avail themselves of the lights of modern science, and to partake of the benefit of those improvements which are now adding to the wealth and prosperity, and the convenience and comfort of every other part of the civilized world.[75]

Most contemporaries hailed Taney's decision as legitimating strong state government and active state intervention to promote economic growth. Justice Story dissented, writing on behalf of himself and Smith Thompson (the only remaining pre-Jackson members of the Court). Of course, he did not wish to stand in the way of progress either. Story claimed that Taney had compromised the rights of property, without which neither justice nor economic development would prevail. Taney's argument won out, not only on this occasion but on countless others, for state as well as federal courts embraced his point of view. Taney's opinion in the Charles River Bridge Case became a major policy document of its age.[76]

Local Democratic leaders in places like the Alabama hill country could exploit the fears subsistence farmers sometimes entertained about entering the market economy. Nevertheless in Washington, the Democratic-dominated Supreme Court promoted the expansion of commerce, as indeed the Jackson administration itself often did. In *Bank of Augusta v. Earle* (1839), Taney and his Court upheld the right of state-chartered banks to do business outside their home state unless specifically excluded; Whigs welcomed the decision. And though westerners who mortgaged their farms often supported the Democratic Party, they got little sympathy from Taney's Court. Two Illinois laws attempting to protect debtors whose creditors put their farms up for auction were struck down by the Court as impairments of the obligation of contracts.[77]

Some historians have interpreted Taney's chief justiceship as the taming of Jacksonian democracy, rendering its populist agrarianism relatively

75. *Proprietors of the Charles River Bridge v. Proprietors of the Warren Bridge*, 36 U.S. (11 Peters) 420 (1837).

76. See Stanley Kutler, *Privilege and Creative Destruction: The Charles River Bridge Case* (Philadelphia, 1971), 133–54; Morton Horwitz, *The Transformation of American Law* (Cambridge, Mass., 1977), 130–39.

77. Mills Thornton III, *Politics and Power in a Slave Society: Alabama, 1800–1860* (Baton Rouge, 1977); *Bank of Augusta v. Earle*, 38 U.S. (13 Peters) 519 (1839); *Bronson v. Kinzie*, 42 U.S. (1 Howard) 311 (1843).

inoffensive to capitalism.[78] Looked at another way, however, the Taney Court provided a logical fulfillment of Jacksonianism. Taney's blend of state sovereignty, white racism, sympathy with commerce, and concern for social order was typical of Jacksonian jurisprudence. Under Taney the Court strengthened the police power of the states and helped facilitate the transportation revolution. The two issues were closely related, since following Jackson's Maysville Veto the states more than ever exerted leadership over internal improvements. If Marshall embodied the legacy of the Federalists for thirty-five years, Taney did the same for the Democratic Party in the next generation. Ironically, his devotion to state sovereignty and white supremacy in the long run contributed to the dissolution of the Union Andrew Jackson loved. However, a Whig lawyer with an intellect disciplined through the study of Blackstone, Story, and Kent emerged from the Illinois frontier to save it. Abraham Lincoln would rise to the crisis and preserve the Union, invoking both the sovereignty of the nation and the common-law principle that no party to a compact can unilaterally withdraw from it.[79]

78. E.g., Schlesinger, *Age of Jackson*, 329.
79. Austin Allen, *Origins of the Dred Scott Case: Jacksonian Jurisprudence and the Supreme Court* (Athens, Ga., 2006); Perry Miller, *The Life of the Mind in America* (New York, 1965), 116.

12

Reason and Revelation

In April 1829, Cincinnati, the city Frances Trollope found so dull and unsophisticated, hosted a week of intellectual excitement. The famous British rationalist Robert Owen, back in the United States again following the failure of his Indiana utopia, had offered to prove in debate "that all the religions of the world have been founded on the ignorance of mankind." The popular Irish-born postmillennial evangelist Alexander Campbell took up Owen's challenge. For eight days the two debated before an audience averaging twelve hundred people. Each debater spoke for thirty minutes every morning and another thirty in the afternoon. Inveterate controversialists, both of them loved the publicity such events provided; they treated each other with courtesy. Owen argued that planned communities would undergird social morality more effectively than did religion. Campbell defended Christianity as essential to human dignity and social progress. At the end, Campbell asked everyone in the audience who believed in Christianity or wished it to "pervade the world" to stand up. All but three members of the audience rose. Campbell claimed victory and proceeded to publish the full text of the debate as a vindication of Christianity; he invited the reader to "reason, examine, and judge, like a rational being, for himself." The historian Daniel Feller comments, "Owen and his freethinkers were left aside, prophets of a discarded future, as Americans by the thousands decided for a Christian destiny." The episode sums up much about the Christianity characteristic of antebellum America: its commitment to social progress, its confidence in popular judgment, and, most of all, its faith in rational discourse.[1]

Alexander Campbell believed in the Bible—believed that it comprehended all religious truth and constituted a sufficient guide to Christian practice in the present. He also believed it perfectly compatible with reason, history, and science. "The Bible contains more real learning than all the volumes of men," he declared. Although Campbell gave the scriptures his own distinctive interpretation, his attitude toward them typified

---

1. Alexander Campbell, ed., *Debate on Evidences of Christianity . . . held in the City of Cincinnati, Ohio from the 13th to the 21st of April, 1829* (Bethany, Va., 1829), 5; Daniel Feller, *The Jacksonian Promise* (Baltimore, 1995), 105; Mark Noll, *America's God* (New York, 2002), 243.

the faith of evangelical Americans in general. The American Bible Society distributed 21 million copies of the Good Book during the fifty years after its founding in 1816 (in a country whose entire population in 1860 was 31 million). The Reformation principle of *sola scriptura*, that the Bible contained all things necessary for salvation and could be properly interpreted by any conscientious believer, lived on and heavily influenced American culture. It helped promote universal literacy, democratic politics, and art that emphasized verbal expression. Respect for the Bible conditioned national identity, social criticism, natural science, the educational system, and the interpretation of authoritative texts like the Constitution.[2]

The Owen-Campbell debate was not unique. Frequent public debates over religion, like those over politics, attracted large crowds and attention from the national press. Debaters addressed infant baptism, universal salvation, and many other theological subjects. Catholics debated Protestants. Religious issues, like political ones, aroused widespread interest in antebellum America. The young Abraham Lincoln enjoyed debating religious questions before he took up political ones. Historical inquirers have long wrangled about which doctrines he ultimately embraced; what is beyond dispute is that he, like so many other reflective Americans of his generation, thought, read, and argued about them a good deal.[3]

Learned theological reflection flourished in the antebellum United States. Its professional practitioners numbered among the leading American intellectuals of their day. The Protestant majority included Nathaniel William Taylor of Yale, Henry Ware of Harvard, Moses Stuart of Andover Seminary, Charles Hodge of Princeton (the theological seminary, not the university), John W. Nevin of Mercersburg Seminary, James Henley Thornwell of South Carolina College, and Horace Bushnell (who was based not in an academic institution but in a parish, the North Congregational Church in Hartford, Connecticut). All were philosophically sophisticated and determined to apply reason to religion. All save Nevin and Bushnell shared a commitment to religious individualism, the empirical basis of knowledge, the Scottish philosophy of common sense, and an understanding of the Bible as historically accurate, its claim to divine authority confirmed by miracles. Nevin and Bushnell embraced a more

2. See Nathan Hatch and Mark Noll, *The Bible in America* (New York, 1982); Paul Gutjahr, *An American Bible* (Stanford, 1999); James T. Johnson, ed., *The Bible in American Law, Politics, and Rhetoric* (Philadelphia, 1985), Campbell quoted on 62.
3. Brooks Holifield, "Oral Debate in American Religion," *Church History* 67 (1998): 499–520; Richard Carwardine, *Lincoln* (London, 2003), 28–40.

Germanic philosophical outlook, a more organic social theory, and a stronger sense of the evolution of Christianity through history. Like Henry Ware and his "liberal" party, they criticized revivalism and its demand for a conversion experience. All these theologians argued with each other over many issues, including freedom of the will, original sin, atonement, and even whether Catholics could be considered Christians.[4] Among the Roman Catholic minority, the scholarly Bishop Francis Kenrick of Philadelphia (later archbishop of Baltimore), who translated the Bible, and the lay Protestant convert Orestes Brownson were noteworthy thinkers. Within the even smaller Jewish minority, Isaac Harby of Charleston sought to adapt Judaism to American life in ways that prefigured the growth of Reform after Rabbi Isaac Mayer Wise arrived from Bohemia in 1846.[5]

Disputes over theology could have institutional consequences. The "Old School" of Hodge and Thornwell expelled the "New School" of Taylor from the Presbyterian Church in 1837, partly because the New School seemed too sympathetic to social reform. In Massachusetts, the "liberal" and "orthodox" Calvinist wings of the Congregational Church, theologically centered at Harvard and Andover Seminary respectively, split after decades of tension. Because Congregationalism had constituted a state religious establishment since Puritan times, often tax supported, this division entailed a legal controversy. In a case arising from the town of Dedham, the Supreme Judicial Court of Massachusetts ruled in 1820 that the "parish"—that is, the congregation as a whole—had the right to name a clergyman for the town even against the wishes of most members of the "church"—that is, the (typically much smaller) group of persons who had experienced conversion and received communion. Since the parish paid the minister's salary, the decision was just, but it also had theological implications. "Liberal" views prevailed more among parish members than among church members; indeed, many liberals did not believe in "conversion experiences" and took little interest in the sacrament of communion. The decision facilitated the takeover of about a hundred Massachusetts Congregational churches by the liberals (eventually named Unitarians because they rejected the doctrine of the Trinity). Disillusioned with this outcome, orthodox Congregationalists saw no

---

4. See Leonard Allen, "Baconianism and the Bible," *Church History* 55 (1986): 65–80; more generally, Brooks Holifield, *Theology in America* (New Haven, 2003).

5. On Kenrick, see Gerald Fogarty, *American Catholic Biblical Scholarship* (San Francisco, 1989), 14–34; on Brownson, Holifield, *Theology in America*, 482–93; on Harby, Michael O'Brien, *Conjectures of Order* (Chapel Hill, 2004), II, 1076–82.

reason to continue paying taxes for the support of parishes whose theology they no longer endorsed. They allied with religious dissenters (Baptists, Methodists, Episcopalians) to separate church and state in Massachusetts in 1833, ending the last of the state religious establishments. Congregationalists and Unitarians continued as two different denominations.[6]

II

Writing to the lieutenant governor of Kentucky in 1822, James Madison had to admit that Virginia's educational system did not constitute a fit model for the younger commonwealth to follow; instead, Kentuckians should look to the New England states.[7] New England's township-based system of primary schools was the daughter not of the Enlightenment but of the Reformation; it had been created in colonial times to comply with the precept that all good Christians should be able to read the Bible for themselves. In the early republic, Protestant religion remained an important spur to literacy and New England a leader in education.[8] In principle, the American Enlightenment typified by Jefferson and Madison also endorsed universal literacy in the interest of an informed citizenry. Jefferson himself had drafted a plan in 1817 for Virginia to provide free white children with three years of primary education, but the state legislature rejected even this minimal proposal. In practice, Jefferson's political followers generally made their top priority low taxes, and public education accordingly suffered, not only in Virginia but in many other states as well.[9]

The churches of the American republic stepped into the breach left by the states. One of their educational initiatives, the Sunday school, provided one day a week of instruction in basic literacy for 200,000 American children by 1827. Only after public primary education became more widespread did Sunday schools concentrate exclusively on religious instruction.[10] As Yankees moved from New England into the Old Northwest,

6. See Conrad Wright, *The Unitarian Controversy* (Boston, 1994); for the Dedham decision, 111–36.

7. James Madison to W. T. Barry, *The Writings of James Madison*, ed. Gaillard Hunt, IX (New York, 1910), 103–9.

8. See David Paul Nord, "Religious Reading and Readers in Antebellum America," *JER* 15 (1995): 241–72; David Tyack, "The Kingdom of God and the Common School," *Harvard Educational Review* 36 (1966): 447–69.

9. Much of this section is adapted from Daniel Howe, "Church, State, and Education in the Young American Republic," *JER* 22 (2002): 1–24. For more on Jefferson's views, see James Gilreath, ed., *Thomas Jefferson and the Education of a Citizen* (Washington, 1999).

10. Carl Kaestle, *Pillars of the Republic* (New York, 1983), 45; Anne Boylan, *Sunday School* (New Haven, 1988).

they replicated the publicly funded weekday primary schools with which they had been familiar. This project could be seen as hastening Christ's Second Coming. The Connecticut state legislature issued a remarkable exhortation promising westward migrants who established schools a celestial reward. "How great will be your happiness," it assured them, "to look down from heaven" in future centuries and behold your "enlightened and pious and happy" descendants, living under "the mild reign of the PRINCE of peace," who will have returned and established his thousand-year kingdom.[11]

Much of the innovation in secondary education, too, came from religious impulses. In the absence of state-supported high schools, academies under religious auspices flourished. In the early days they hardly ever boarded students but drew them from their own vicinity. Usually coeducational, the academies played a role in opening up secondary education to girls. Of course, their students had to pay tuition. Only after 1840 did public high schools gradually supplant most of these academies.[12]

Secular authorities did not necessarily mind saving the taxpayers money by letting religious groups deal with educational needs. The educational goals of Christian and secular educators dovetailed conveniently. In traditional republican political thought, free institutions rested on the virtue of the citizenry, that is, on their devotion to the common good. Religious educators inculcated that respect for the social virtues which republicanism considered indispensable. Christian and Enlightenment moral philosophy alike taught that young people needed conscientious training to form a properly balanced character in which reason and the moral sense could prevail over baser motives. An educated Protestant laity provided the basis for an educated citizenry.[13] Under the circumstances, public authorities sometimes granted religious educational institutions favors and subsidies to keep them functioning, rather than spend more money to create secular alternatives. Despite Jefferson's famous allusion to a "wall of separation" (he used the phrase in a private letter, not a public document, and with reference to the federal government, not the states), strict separation of church and state, as later

11. Connecticut General Assembly, *An Address to the Emigrants from Connecticut* (Hartford, Conn., 1817), 18.
12. James McLachlan, *American Boarding Schools* (New York, 1970), 35–48; Theodore Sizer, *The Age of the Academies* (New York, 1964); J. M. Opal, "Academies and the Transformation of the Rural North," *JAH* 91 (2004): 445–70.
13. See Stephen Macedo, *Liberal Virtues* (Oxford, 1991); Daniel Howe, *Making the American Self* (Cambridge, Mass., 1997).

generations came to understand that principle, did not characterize the young republic.[14]

For African Americans, religion was even more important as a source of education than it was for the whites. The "invisible institution" of religion in the slave quarters profoundly influenced African American culture.[15] What little interest the state took in the education of black people was mainly negative: In a number of states the law prohibited schools for slaves, intending to insulate them against abolitionist propaganda. However, individual masters were often allowed to teach their own slaves. In fact, between 5 and 10 percent of adult slaves must have possessed some informally taught literacy and numeracy, useful in the skilled and supervisory occupations performed by the top echelon of enslaved workers. Some masters and mistresses also felt a religious obligation to teach their slaves to read. As late as Reconstruction times, northern religious philanthropy worked in tandem with the Freedmen's Bureau to support the newly established schools for southern black children.[16] In the free Negro communities schools existed—almost always segregated, even in the North. These schools had usually been created by white religious philanthropy and/or black self-help, seldom by local public authorities. In Connecticut, the authorities actually opposed Prudence Crandall's efforts to provide secondary education for black girls.[17]

Religious-sponsored education for Native Americans figured prominently in the Cherokee Removal crisis. The American Board of Commissioners for Foreign Missions and other Christian missionaries had established schools in the Cherokee Nation, promoting knowledge of Western civilization. Sometimes such mission schools enjoyed a measure of federal support. Acting with the blessing of the Jackson administration, however, the state of Georgia determined to interrupt this educational process and expel the

14. See Daniel Dreisbach, "Thomas Jefferson, a Mammoth Cheese, and the 'Wall of Separation Between Church and State,'" in *Religion and the New Republic*, ed. James Hutson (Lanham, Md., 1999), 65–114.

15. See, for example, Thomas Webber, *Deep like the Rivers: Education in the Slave Quarter Community* (New York, 1978); Paul E. Johnson, ed., *African-American Christianity* (Berkeley, 1994).

16. There are no hard data on slave literacy. The most commonly given estimate is 5 percent, but the most thorough study to date concludes 10 percent is closer to the truth. Janet Cornelius, *"When I Can Read My Title Clear": Literacy, Slavery, and Religion in the Antebellum South* (Columbia, S.C., 1991), 8–9, 62–67. See also Beth Barton Schweiger, *The Gospel Working Up* (New York, 2000), 73.

17. Kaestle, *Pillars of the Republic*, 171–75; Brown, *Strength of a People*, 170–83. Jennifer Rycenga has a book on Prudence Crandall in progress.

missionaries, provoking the Supreme Court case of *Worcester v. Georgia*. An educated Indian population, determined to retain their land and develop its resources, could have blocked white intruders more effectively.[18]

But schools are not the only vehicles for literacy. Many youngsters learned how to read at home. Beth Schweiger's studies of literacy among the southern yeomanry show that while only 40 percent of southern white children went to school, 80 percent of southern white adults could read. That indicates a lot of people acquiring at least rudimentary literacy at home. Why did farm parents, tired at the end of a day's work, make time to teach their children? The primary motive seems not to have been commercial or political, still less to facilitate the children's upward social mobility. It was religious. Although Protestant piety did not produce free common schools in the rural and individualistic South, the way it did in the villages of New England, Protestantism still promoted literacy in the South.[19] Unlike reading, the ability to write did not have religious significance. Reading was more widely taught than writing, and many people—especially females—who could read at least a little had no experience with writing.

In its broadest definition, education is the entire process of cultural transmission. The rapidly expanding communications of the antebellum period enabled people to be better informed about the world than ever before from magazines, newspapers, and books; mail service integrated commercial and civic life. The Second Great Awakening both exploited and fostered these developments.[20] Voluntary associations, such as foreign missions, the Sunday-School Union, and the sabbatarian, temperance, antislavery, and peace movements, educated a broad public in the issues of the day. The educational function of the evangelical associations seems particularly important in the case of women. Excluded from political institutions, their increasing literacy nevertheless enabled them to read the news and organize benevolent societies, acquiring further skills in the process.[21]

The commercialization and diversification of the economy multiplied

18. For a contemporary source sharing the missionaries' outlook, see Jedidiah Morse, *Report to the Secretary of War on Indian Affairs* (New Haven, 1822). William McLoughlin has written two contrasting assessments: *Cherokees and Missionaries* (New Haven, 1984) and *Champions of the Cherokees* (Princeton, 1990).
19. Schweiger, *Gospel Working Up*, 67 and 202.
20. See Richard D. Brown, *Knowledge Is Power* (New York, 1989); Richard John, *Spreading the News* (Cambridge, Mass., 1995), esp. chaps. 5 and 7; and the works cited in chap. 6, n. 71.
21. See, for example, Nancy Hardesty, *Your Daughters Shall Prophesy: Revivalism and Feminism in the Age of Finney* (Brooklyn, N.Y., 1991); Nancy Hewitt, *Women's Activism and Social Change* (Ithaca, N.Y., 1984); Stuart Blumin, *The Emergence of the Middle Class* (Cambridge, Eng., 1989).

jobs requiring literate and numerate skills; continued economic development would demand still more of them. American society needed an
educational program synthesizing the civic objectives of Jefferson's Enlightenment with the energy and commitment of the religious Awakening.
Such a movement appeared in the educational reforms embraced by the
Whig Party in the 1830s. The greatest of the Whig educational reformers
was Horace Mann, who became secretary of the newly created Massachusetts State Board of Education in 1837. From that vantage point Mann
tirelessly crusaded on behalf of "common schools"—that is, schools that
the whole population would have in common: tuition-free, tax-supported,
meeting statewide standards of curriculum, textbooks, and facilities,
staffed with teachers who had been trained in state normal schools, modeled on the French école normale. In Massachusetts, Mann could build
on the strongest tradition of public education in any state. There, local
communities had become accustomed to taxing themselves to support education. Mann had no hesitation about employing the resources of the
state; he was a political disciple of John Quincy Adams. The normal
schools that he created (beginning with Lexington in 1839) constituted
Mann's most important innovation, the precursors of teacher training colleges. The normal schools turned out to be the avenue through which
women in large numbers first entered any profession. Since they were paid
less than men, women teachers provided a human resource agreeable to
legislators worried about the cost of Mann's ambitious plans.[22]

   As envisioned by Mann and his successors until long after the Civil
War, the common schools embodied a common ideology. The ideology
of the American common schools included patriotic virtue, responsible
character, and democratic participation, all to be developed through intellectual discipline and the nurture of the moral qualities. It would never
have occurred to Mann and his disciples that such an educational program should not include religion, but since they wanted above all to
achieve an education common to all, this necessitated a common religious instruction. In the days of more local autonomy, school districts had
taught the religion of the local majority. Now, the Massachusetts School
Board prescribed that only those doctrines should be taught on which all
Protestants agreed.

22. On Mann in his context, see Jonathan Messerli, *Horace Mann* (New York, 1972);
    Daniel W. Howe, "The History of Education as Cultural History," *History of Educa-
    tion Quarterly* 22 (1982): 205–14; Susan-Mary Grant, "Representative Mann: Horace
    Mann, the Republican Experiment, and the South," *Journal of American Studies* 32
    (1998): 105–23.

The Whig governor, Edward Everett, gave Mann solid support in appointments to the Board and helped him overcome opposition from jealous local authorities, doctrinaire Christian groups, and pedagogically conservative schoolmasters. When a Democrat, Marcus Morton, was elected governor by a margin of one vote in 1839, he proved unable to persuade the Massachusetts legislature to abolish Mann's Board of Education and its new normal schools.[23] Democrats throughout the country remained suspicious of educational programs like Mann's as the creation of a remote elite; they preferred to leave schools under local control as much as possible. What probably tipped the scales in favor of states assuming some responsibility for education was the growth of cities and towns. With apprenticeship programs declining, the new urban working class embraced common schools as their children's guarantor of opportunity — besides keeping them off the street. In rural areas, schools always competed with the need for children to work on the farm. The older ones could only attend a few months during the winter, when their labor and that of their part-time teacher could best be spared; the younger ones could also be taught in the summer after planting and before harvesting.[24]

At the top of Mann's agenda stood the education of the immigrants, especially the children of migrant laborers. But nondenominational Protestant schools proved to be unacceptable to the growing Irish immigrant community. In New York, the conflict between Protestant-public schools and the Catholic minority led by Bishop (later Archbishop) John Hughes embarrassed the enlightened Whig governor, William H. Seward. Seward tried vainly to bridge the gap between the two sides with an unsuccessful proposal for state subsidies to Catholic schools, as Protestant educational enterprises had often been subsidized. Instead the legislature ruled that no public money should go to any school in which religion was taught.[25] The lesson for the rest of the country was clear: Where public aid to Protestant institutions had been within the bounds of political acceptability, such aid to Catholic institutions was not. When faced with a

23. Messerli, *Horace Mann*, 326–31; Carl F. Kaestle and Maris Vinovskis, *Education and Social Change in Nineteenth-Century Massachusetts* (Cambridge, Mass., 1980), 221–28.

24. W. J. Rorabaugh, *The Craft Apprentice* (New York, 1986), 113–27; Joel Perlmann et al., "Literacy, Schooling, and Teaching Among New England Women," *History of Education Quarterly* 37 (1997): 117–39.

25. See Glyndon Van Deusen, "Seward and the School Question Reconsidered," *JAH* 52 (1965): 313–19; Vincent P. Lannie, *Public Money and Parochial Education* (Cleveland, 1968).

charge of inconsistency, public authorities would cut off aid to Protestants rather than extend it to include Catholics.

To be sure, many public, or common, schools would retain features of nondenominational Protestantism for a good many years to come. Horace Mann hoped that passages from the Bible, read without interpretation, might offer a nonsectarian common religious ground. Although Catholics and even some of the Protestant sects did not find this acceptable, Bible-reading in the common schools remained a widespread and even increasing practice in nineteenth-century America. Probably over half of American common schools practiced Bible reading at the end of the nineteenth century.[26]

In 1840, the U.S. census takers for the first time asked questions about literacy. They recorded 9 percent of adult American whites as illiterate, a rate comparable with that of Prussia, whose educational system, run by the established church, was much admired. Even when the African American population was included, U.S. illiteracy at 22 percent compared favorably with the 41 percent illiteracy in England and Wales recorded by their census of 1841. American literacy varied widely by region. In New England no state had less than 98 percent literacy, which equaled Scotland and Sweden, the two countries where energetic programs sponsored by Protestant established churches had forged the world's highest literacy. The American state with the highest white illiteracy in 1840 was North Carolina: 28 percent. The public school system called for in the North Carolina state constitution of 1776 had never been implemented. However, in 1839 the Whigs gained control of North Carolina's legislature and put through a long-delayed law authorizing common schools in counties that consented to them. As a result, white illiteracy in North Carolina fell to 11 percent over the next twenty years.[27]

III

Like school systems, higher education in the antebellum period reflected the energy of religious bodies and the frequent reluctance of civil authorities to spend money or expand the sphere of government. George Washington had conceived of a national university in the District of Columbia

26. R. Laurence Moore, "Bible Reading and Nonsectarian Schooling," *JAH* 86 (2000): 1581–99.

27. See Lee Soltow and Edward Stevens, *The Rise of Literacy and the Common School in the United States* (Chicago, 1981), 11–22; Brown, *Strength of a People*, 141–48; Carl Kaestle, "History of Literacy and Readers," in *Perspectives on Literacy*, ed. Eugene Kintger (Carbondale, Ill., 1988), 105–12.

but had never been able to persuade Congress to implement his vision. He had gone so far as to will a portion of his estate to form a core endowment for such a university. But Congress ignored his bequest, and in 1823 the fund became worthless when the company in which it was invested went bankrupt. Jefferson had originally supported a national university but eventually decided that an amendment to the Constitution would be required to authorize it. Madison and John Quincy Adams both recommended a national university; neither could budge Congress. Opposition came from existing colleges that feared being overshadowed, from strict construction of the Constitution, and from sheer parsimony. Under the Jacksonians the project of a national university vanished.[28]

As an alternative to a university created by the federal government, Thomas Jefferson founded the University of Virginia, intended as a model of public secular education. Drawing upon his network of political influence, the ex-president was able to get himself named rector and its site located in Charlottesville, close enough to Monticello that he could oversee every detail. The versatile elder statesman designed its architecture and mode of governance, named the professors, and even presumed to prescribe the curriculum—at least in sensitive subjects like politics and religion. After his death in 1826, Jefferson's tombstone proclaimed the three achievements of which he was proudest: "Author of the Declaration of American Independence, of the Statute of Virginia for religious freedom; & Father of the University of Virginia."[29]

Jefferson made the University of Virginia an architectural masterpiece. As an institution of higher learning, however, its distinction was not immediately apparent. In the first functioning academic year, 1825–26, the only one the founder lived to see, the students took advantage of Jefferson's permissive discipline to get drunk, gamble, skip classes, and misbehave; among those who had to be expelled for participation in a riot was the founder's own great-grandnephew.[30] The shortcomings of the student body reflected the legislature's failure to establish a proper system of preparatory secondary schools. Funding remained perennially problematic; the recruitment of both faculty and students, difficult. Sadly, Jefferson's own vision for his beloved university had contracted over time.

28. This section is adapted from Howe, "Church, State, and Education."
29. Merrill Peterson, *Thomas Jefferson and the New Nation* (New York, 1970), 976–88; Philip Bruce, *History of the University of Virginia* (New York, 1920), I; James Morton Smith, *The Republic of Letters* (New York, 1995), III, 1883–1951.
30. Robert McDonald, "Thomas Jefferson's Image in America, 1809–1826" (master's thesis, Oxford University, 1997). Cf. Bruce, *University of Virginia*, II, 300.

Originally he had imagined it drawing students from all over the Union, but after his political vision narrowed during the Missouri controversy, his plans for the university changed too. In the end, he conceived it as a bastion of southern sectionalism.[31]

The University of Virginia was by no means the only example of a disparity between promise and realization in American higher education during the early national period. In some states, the gap was greater. The so-called University of the State of New York had been created in 1784 as part of a grandiose plan intended to coordinate all levels of education, primary, secondary, and higher, in the state. In practice, however, this "University" exerted little control over the activities nominally subject to it, some of them private and sectarian. Not until after World War II did New York actually create a state university that would engage directly in teaching and research. The contrast between dream and reality appears again in the case of Michigan. Augustus Woodward, whom Jefferson appointed chief justice of Michigan Territory, projected the "University of Michigania." However, for a long time the state only implemented primary and secondary levels of instruction; the Ann Arbor campus did not open until 1841, although the present University of Michigan proudly declares the date of its founding to be 1817. Finally, one might note the 1816 constitution of Indiana, which called for "a general system of education, ascending in regular gradation from township schools to state university, wherein tuition shall be gratis, and equally open to all." It took more than thirty years for the Indiana legislature to begin to implement this promise. In the meantime, a Presbyterian seminary-turned-college operated in Bloomington.[32]

At the time of independence the United States contained nine colleges, all with religious connections. The status that these colleges would enjoy in the republic only gradually achieved definition. At first they seemed "mixed corporations," privately owned but subsidized in return for serving public functions, like some banks and turnpikes of the time. The instability of such a status appeared in the Dartmouth College case of 1819. This lawsuit originated in a dispute between the president of the college and the trustees. Both sides were Federalist and Calvinist, but a majority of the trustees supported organized revivals and novel moral reforms like temperance. The president of the college had no sympathy

---

31. Thomas Jefferson to James Breckinridge, Feb. 15, 1821, *TJ: Writings*, 1452; Peterson, *Thomas Jefferson*, 981.
32. Lawrence Cremin, *American Education, The National Experience* (New York, 1980), 150–53, 160–63, 171–72.

with this program, and the trustees dismissed him. The Republican-controlled state legislature intervened on the side of the president, trying to make a mixed public-private institution more responsive to religious diversity. But the trustees resisted. Daniel Webster, a Dartmouth alumnus, took their case before the U.S. Supreme Court, arguing that the state legislature had no business tampering with Dartmouth's royal charter. Webster won, and by his victory he set Dartmouth on a course of transformation from a mixed public-private institution into a completely private college.[33]

If the New Hampshire Republicans lost their battle against the Dartmouth trustees, they won the war on another front. The same Jeffersonian legislature that tried to alter the Dartmouth charter took advantage of the division among Federalists to strip the Congregational Church of its favored status in New Hampshire. Republican secularists allied with Baptists and other dissenters to pass what they called a "toleration act" that (in effect, if not in theory) disestablished religion in New Hampshire.[34] The disestablishment of the New England state churches foreshadowed the disestablishment of what we call the Ivy League colleges, though the separation of college and state occurred more gradually. Eventually all but one of the colonial foundations became private and, if they did not need to fear for their autonomy, neither could they look to their state governments for financial assistance.[35] The College of William and Mary in Virginia, alone among the nine colleges predating independence, ended up a state institution. The secularization of the colonial colleges is another story, one that takes place after the Civil War.

The most successful example of a state-founded, state-supported venture in higher education in the early national period was South Carolina College, founded in 1801. Although roiled by some of the same early problems with discipline as the University of Virginia, the college surmounted them to become the only institution of higher learning in the United States generously supported by annual legislative appropriations.

---

33. See Steven Novak, "The College in the Dartmouth College Case," *New England Quarterly* 47 (1974), 550–63; Donald Cole, *Jacksonian Democracy in New Hampshire* (Cambridge, Mass., 1970), 30–41; Lynn Turner, *The Ninth State: New Hampshire's Formative Years* (Chapel Hill, 1983), 334–43.

34. Turner, *Ninth State*, 352–56.

35. See John Whitehead, *The Separation of College and State* (New Haven, 1973), 53–88. The nine colleges predating independence are Harvard, William and Mary, Yale, Princeton, Columbia (originally King's College), Rutgers (originally Queen's College), Dartmouth, Brown, and Pennsylvania. All save Rutgers and William and Mary constitute, along with Cornell, the modern Ivy League.

Since the state did not support public schools, they did not compete with the college for funds.[36] Thomas Cooper, an expatriate Englishman, accepted the presidency of South Carolina College in 1821. Cooper combined proslavery politics with anti-clericalism; Jefferson declared him "the greatest man in America, in the powers of mind," and had tried desperately to recruit him to head the University of Virginia.[37] In South Carolina, Cooper won popularity with his ardent state-rights rhetoric during the nullification crisis, only to lose it soon afterwards by his tactless denunciations of Christianity. Under fire from a combination of Presbyterian clergy and political Unionists, Cooper found it necessary to resign in 1834. The one example of successful state-sponsored higher education in the country also illustrated the unacceptability of state-sponsored secularism.[38]

Disestablishment did not dismay New England's Congregationalists. Looking for ways to reassert their influence, they founded educational institutions. Yankees moving west created a host of Congregationalist colleges across their band of settlement, including Western Reserve University and Oberlin College in Ohio, Illinois College, Beloit College in Wisconsin, and Grinnell College in Iowa. Some of these institutions were in effect daughter colleges of Yale, founded by Yale graduates and imitating the Yale curriculum.[39] But in the enthusiasm of the Second Great Awakening, the denominations that had never been established proved even more prolific in founding colleges than did Congregationalists and Episcopalians. By 1848, the Presbyterians had founded the most colleges (twenty-five), followed by Methodists and Baptists (with fifteen each), Congregationalists (fourteen), and Episcopalians (seven). Presbyterian Princeton had an academic empire in the South comparable to Yale's in the North.[40] Since denominational affiliation mattered little to the college curriculum in most cases, student bodies typically included youths from the area across denominational lines. These numerous little colleges were serving the purposes of their local communities, not just their

---

36. Michael Sugrue, "South Carolina College, the Defense of Slavery, and the Development of Secessionist Politics," *History of Higher Education Annual* 14 (1994): 39–71.
37. Jefferson to Joseph Cabell, quoted in Robert P. Forbes, "Slavery and the Evangelical Enlightenment," in *Religion and the Antebellum Debate over Slavery*, ed. John R. McKivigan and Mitchell Snay (Athens, Ga., 2001), 88.
38. Daniel Hollis, *South Carolina College* (Columbia, S.C., 1951), 74–119.
39. The classic account is Richard Power, "A Crusade to Extend Yankee Culture," *New England Quarterly* 13 (1940), 638–53.
40. Statistics based on Donald Tewksbury, *The Founding of American Colleges and Universities Before the Civil War* (1932; New York, 1972), 32–46. See also Mark Noll, *Princeton and the Republic, 1768–1822* (Princeton, 1989).

Allegheny	Meadville, Pa.	1815	Methodist
Amherst	Amherst, Mass.	1821	Congregational
Beloit	Beloit, Wisc.	1846	Congregational
Bethel	McKenzie, Tenn.	1842	Presbyterian
Brown	Providence, R.I.	1765	Baptist
Bucknell	Lewisburg, Pa.	1846	Baptist
Cincinnati, Univ. of	Cincinnati, Ohio	1819	Nondenominational
Colby	Waterville, Maine	1813	Baptist
Colgate	Hamilton, N.Y.	1819	Baptist
Charleston, Coll. of	Charleston, S.C.	1770	Anglican
Columbia (orig. King's College)	New York, N.Y.	1754	Anglican
Cumberland	Lebanon, Tenn.	1842	Presbyterian
Dartmouth	Hanover, N.H.	1769	Congregational
Denison	Granville, Ohio	1831	Baptist
Duke	Durham, N.C.	1838	Methodist
Earlham	Richmond, Ind.	1847	Quaker
Emory	Atlanta, Ga.	1836	Methodist
Fordham	Fordham, N.Y.	1841	Roman Catholic
George Washington	Washington, D.C.	1821	Nondenominational
Georgetown	Washington, D.C.	1789	Roman Catholic
Georgia, Univ. of	Athens, Ga.	1785	Secular
Gettysburg	Gettysburg, Pa.	1832	Lutheran
Greensboro*	Greensboro, N.C.	1838	Methodist
Grinnell	Grinnell, Iowa	1846	Congregational
Hampden-Sydney	Hampden-Sydney, Va.	1775	Presbyterian
Harvard	Cambridge, Mass.	1636	Congregational; after 1805 Unitarian
Holy Cross	Worcester, Mass.	1843	Roman Catholic
Illinois College	Jacksonville, Ill.	1829	Congregational
Kenyon	Gambier, Ohio	1824	Episcopal
Lafayette	Easton, Pa.	1826	Presbyterian
Louisiana, Univ. of	New Orleans, La.	1845	Secular
Marietta	Marietta, Ohio	1797	Congregational
Maryland, Univ. of	Baltimore, Md.	1812	Secular
Maryville	Maryville, Tenn.	1819	Presbyterian
Miami Univ.	Oxford, Ohio	1809	Secular
Mississippi, Univ. of	Oxford, Miss.	1844	Secular
Missouri, Univ. of	Columbia, Mo.	1839	Secular
Mount Holyoke*	South Hadley, Mass.	1837	Congregational
Mount Union	Alliance, Ohio	1846	Methodist
New York Univ.	New York, N.Y.	1831	Nondenominational
North Carolina, Univ. of	Chapel Hill, N.C.	1789	Secular

(continued)

Table 4 (continued)

Notre Dame	Notre Dame, Ind.	1842	Roman Catholic
Oberlin*	Oberlin, Ohio	1833	Congregational
Ohio Univ.	Athens, Ohio	1804	Secular
Pennsylvania, Univ. of	Philadelphia, Pa.	1740	Nondenominational
Princeton (orig. the College of New Jersey)	Princeton, N.J.	1746	Presbyterian
Rutgers (orig. Queen's College)	New Brunswick, N.J.	1766	Dutch Reformed
St. Louis Univ.	St. Louis, Mo.	1818	Roman Catholic
Tennessee, Univ. of	Knoxville, Tenn.	1794	Secular
Transylvania	Lexington, Ky.	1780	Disciples of Christ
Trinity	Hartford, Conn.	1823	Episcopal
U.S. Military Academy	West Point, N.Y.	1802	Secular
U.S. Naval Academy	Annapolis, MD	1845	Secular
Union College	Schenectady, N.Y.	1795	Presbyterian with Congregational
Vermont, Univ. of	Burlington, Vt.	1791	Nondenominational
Villanova	Villanova, Pa.	1842	Roman Catholic
Wake Forest Coll.	Wake Forest, N.C.	1833	Baptist
Wesleyan Univ.	Middletown, Conn.	1833	Wesleyan Methodist
Western Reserve Univ.	Cleveland, Ohio	1826	Congregational
Wheaton*	Norton, Mass.	1834	Nondenominational
William and Mary	Williamsburg, Va.	1693	Anglican
Williams	Williamstown, Mass.	1793	Congregational
Wisconsin, Univ. of	Madison, Wisc.	1848	Secular
Xavier	Cincinnati, Ohio	1831	Roman Catholic
Yale	New Haven, Conn.	1701	Congregational

Institutions marked with an asterisk admitted women before 1848. Some institutions that began as colleges later became universities.

particular sects. But they existed on the margin of financial viability and frequently succumbed to the same economic downturns that claimed business and financial enterprises.[41]

41. See David Potts, "American Colleges in the Nineteenth Century," *History of Education Quarterly* 11 (1971): 363–80; idem, " 'College Enthusiasm!' as Public Response, 1800–1860," *Harvard Educational Review* 47 (1977): 28–42.

In 1815, thirty-three colleges existed in the United States; by 1835, sixty-eight; and by 1848, there were 113. Sixteen of these were state institutions, which by then were generally distinguishable from private religious ones. Eighty-eight were Protestant denominational colleges; the remaining nine, Roman Catholic.[42] Catholic educational initiatives in the United States were largely the work of religious orders. They included George-town and Fordham (both Jesuit), Notre Dame (Order of the Holy Cross), and Villanova (Augustinian). All these were founded in advance of heavy Catholic immigration; they aimed initially at proselytizing, not simply catering to an existing Catholic population. Protestants like Lyman Beecher correctly interpreted the Catholic institutions as an ideological challenge.

American higher education responded to pressure for vocational utility at the graduate level. The early national period witnessed the foundation of professional schools, starting with medicine, law, and divinity. At the undergraduate level, however, Protestant, Catholic, and public colleges all emphasized a liberal education—that is, one designed to develop the student's intellectual powers rather than to provide vocational training. It was termed "liberal" because designed to be liberating and thus suitable for a free man (*liber* meaning "free" in Latin).[43] The Yale Report of 1828, issued by the faculty of what was then the country's largest and most influential institution of higher learning, defended the traditional conception of a liberal education against its critics. The curriculum centered on the classics, particularly Latin. Advocates of curricular innovation succeeded in introducing modern history, modern literature, and modern foreign languages, but classics remained the core discipline, along with some mathematics and science. Colleges generally required some Latin for entrance, which in turn influenced secondary school curricula. Undergraduates had few elective subjects. Classical study inculcated intellectual discipline and provided those who pursued it, the world over, with a common frame of reference. The use of Latin marked one as educated and gave weight to one's arguments. Physicians wrote their prescriptions in Latin; lawyers sprinkled their arguments with Latin phrases. American statesmen defended their principles of "classical republicanism" with arguments drawn from Aristotle, Publius, and Cicero. Sculptors flattered

---

42. These numbers could vary slightly because of the existence of evanescent and marginal institutions. See Tewksbury, *Founding*, 32–46.

43. *OED*, s.v. "liberal."

public figures by portraying them in togas. Congress met in a Roman-style Capitol.[44]

A distinctive feature of antebellum American colleges was the course on moral philosophy, typically taught to seniors by the president of the college. The capstone of an undergraduate education, it treated not only the branch of philosophy we call ethical theory but also psychology and all the other social sciences, approached from a normative point of view. The dominant school of thought was that of the Scottish philosophers of "common sense," Thomas Reid and Dugald Stewart, plus Adam Smith (whom we remember mostly for his work in economics, then a branch of moral philosophy). These philosophers were valued for their rebuttal to the atheistic skepticism of David Hume, their reconciliation of science with religion, and their insistence on the objective validity of moral principles. They sorted human nature into different "faculties" and explained the difficult, yet important, task of subordinating the instinctive and emotional faculties to the higher ones of reason and the moral sense. Moral philosophy as taught in the colleges reflected American middle-class culture's preoccupation with character and self-discipline. This course, very similar at all public and Protestant colleges, substituted for the study of sectarian religious doctrine, which moved into the professional divinity schools and seminaries for training ministers.[45]

The colonial Puritans had included educational provision for girls as well as boys in their primary schools, and in the early nineteenth-century United States, secondary education opened up to girls with little controversy. The finest girls' secondary school, Troy Female Seminary, founded in 1821 by Emma Willard, offered college-level courses in history and science. By the middle of the century, the United States had become the first country in the world where the literacy rate of females equaled that of males. At least as startling, the first few higher educational opportunities appeared for women. Religious motivations remained important in this, illustrated by the Calvinism of Mount Holyoke College, the evangelical abolitionism of coeducational Oberlin, and the Wesleyan Methodism of

44. Jack Lane, "The Yale Report of 1828," *History of Education Quarterly* 27 (1987): 325–38; Daniel Howe, "Classical Education and Political Culture in Nineteenth-Century America," *Intellectual History Newsletter* 5 (Spring 1983): 9–14; Carl Richard, *The Founders and the Classics* (Cambridge, Mass., 1994).

45. See D. H. Meyer, *The Instructed Conscience* (Philadelphia, 1972); Daniel Howe, *The Unitarian Conscience: Harvard Moral Philosophy, 1805–1861*, 2nd ed. (Middletown, Conn., 1988); Allen Guelzo, "The Science of Duty," in *Evangelicals and Science in Historical Perspective*, ed. David Livingstone et al. (New York, 1999), 267–89.

Georgia Female College, all of them founded in the 1830s. No individual did more to apply the Second Great Awakening to women's education than Catharine Beecher, eldest daughter of the evangelist Lyman Beecher.[46]

The United States pioneered higher education for women, and by 1880 one-third of all American students enrolled in higher education were female, a percentage without parallel elsewhere in the world.[47] Scholars have often debated how far American history is "exceptional" by comparison with the rest of the world. No better example of American exceptionalism exists than higher education for women. Through the efforts of Christian missionaries, the American example of higher education for women has influenced many other countries.

IV

As this chapter is written in the early twenty-first century, the hypothesis that the universe reflects intelligent design has provoked a bitter debate in the United States. How very different was the intellectual world of the early nineteenth century! Then, virtually everyone believed in intelligent design. Faith in the rational design of the universe underlay the worldview of the Enlightenment, shared by Isaac Newton, John Locke, and the American Founding Fathers. Even the outspoken critics of Christianity embraced not atheism but deism, that is, belief in an impersonal, remote deity who had created the universe and designed it so perfectly that it ran along of its own accord, following natural laws without need for further divine intervention. The commonly used expression "the book of nature" referred to the universal practice of viewing nature as a revelation of God's power and wisdom. Christians were fond of saying that they accepted two divine revelations: the Bible and the book of nature. For deists like Thomas Paine, the book of nature alone sufficed, rendering what he called the "fables" of the Bible superfluous. The desire to demonstrate the glory of God, whether deist or — more commonly — Christian, constituted one of the principal motivations for scientific activity in the early republic, along with national pride, the hope for useful applications, and, of course, the joy of science itself.[48]

46. Barbara Solomon, *In the Company of Educated Women* (New Haven, 1985); Kathryn Sklar, "The Founding of Mount Holyoke College," in *Women of America*, ed. Carol Berkin and Mary Beth Norton (Boston, 1979), 177–201; idem, *Catharine Beecher* (New Haven, 1973).

47. Solomon, *In the Company of Educated Women*, 63.

48. I discuss belief in intelligent design during this period more fully in *Unitarian Conscience*, 69–82.

One such demonstration of divine purpose appeared in the widely used textbook *Natural Theology* (1805 and ten subsequent American editions by 1841), written by the English clergyman William Paley. Paley presented innumerable cases to illustrate the teleological argument for the existence of God (that is, the argument that we find apparent design in nature and can infer from this a purposeful designer). For example, Paley argued, the physiology of the human eye shows as much design as a human-made telescope.[49] Though a popularizer, Paley did not misrepresent the attitude of most scientists of his time. Natural theology, the study of the existence and attributes of God as demonstrated from the nature He created, was widely studied and Paley's book used as its text. A synthesis of the scientific revolution with Protestant Christianity viewed nature as a law-bound system of matter in motion, yet also as a divinely constructed stage for human moral activity. The psalmist had proclaimed, "The heavens declare the glory of God, and the firmament showeth his handiwork." The influential Benjamin Silliman, professor of chemistry and natural history at Yale from 1802 to 1853, affirmed that science tells us *"the thoughts of God."*[50]

Silliman and other leading American scientists like Edward Hitchcock and James Dwight Dana harmonized their science not only with intelligent design but also with scripture. They insisted that neither geology nor the fossils of extinct animals contradicted the book of Genesis. They interpreted the "days" of creation as representing eons of time and pointed out that Genesis had been written for an ancient audience, with the purpose of teaching religion, and not to instruct modern people in scientific particulars. Scientists varied in the importance they attached to identifying approximate parallels between science and scripture, such as comparing geologic evidence of past inundation with Noah's flood. The most widely held theory explaining the emergence of different species over time, that of the great French biologist Georges Cuvier, held that God had performed successive acts of special creation. When the Scotsman Robert Chambers published *Vestiges of the Natural History of Creation* in

49. William Paley, *Natural Theology; or, Evidences of the Existence and Attributes of the Deity, Collected from the Appearances of Nature* (Boston, Mass., 1831), 19–38. For context, see John Hedley Brooke, *Science and Religion* (Cambridge, Eng., 1991), 192–225; D. L. LeMahieu, *The Mind of William Paley* (Lincoln, Neb., 1976), 153–83.
50. Quotation from John C. Greene, "Protestantism, Science, and the American Enlightenment," in *Benjamin Silliman and His Circle*, ed. Leonard Wilson (New York, 1979), 19; idem, *The Death of Adam* (New York, 1961), 23. See also Chandos Brown, *Benjamin Silliman* (Princeton, 1989), the first volume of a projected two.

1844, anticipating Darwin's theory of evolution, he still argued that evolution was compatible with intelligent design. The scientific community rejected this theory of evolution until Charles Darwin supplied a theory of natural selection to explain how it worked. But Louis Agassiz of Harvard, the renowned discoverer of past ice ages, defended the theory of special creation even after Darwin published his *Origin of Species* in 1859. His Harvard colleague botanist Asa Gray led the American fight to accept the theory of evolution, but argued (contrary to Darwin's own opinion) for evolution's compatibility with intelligent design.[51]

The early nineteenth century distinguished two branches of science: natural history (biology, geology, and anthropology, all then considered mainly descriptive) and natural philosophy (physics, chemistry, and astronomy, more mathematical in nature). Scientific activity in the United States emphasized natural history, the collection of information about flora, fauna, fossils, and rocks. Exploring parties like those of Lewis and Clark in 1804–6, Army Major Stephen Long across the Great Plains in 1819–23, and Navy Lieutenant Charles Wilkes through the Pacific in 1838–42 contributed to this knowledge. Many scientists were actually amateurs who earned their living in other ways, frequently as clergymen, physicians, or officers in the armed forces. Science figured in the standard curriculum of both secondary and higher education, and the subject enjoyed a broad base of interest in the middle class. Science, like technology, benefited from the improving literacy and numeracy of nineteenth-century Americans. Popular magazines carried articles encouraging interest in the natural history of the New World. The perceived harmony between religion and science worked to their mutual advantage with the public. As the industrial revolution reflected the ingenuity of innumerable artisans, so early modern natural history profited from the dedicated curiosity of many nonprofessional observers and collectors—women as well as men.[52]

51. John C. Greene, "Science and Religion," in *The Rise of Adventism*, ed. Edwin Gaustad (New York, 1974), 50–69; A. Hunter Dupree, *Asa Gray* (Cambridge, Mass., 1959), 288–303, 358–83; idem, "Christianity and the Scientific Community in the Age of Darwin," in *God and Nature*, ed. David Lindberg and Ronald Numbers (Berkeley, 1986), 351–68.
52. See Margaret Welch, *The Book of Nature: Natural History in the United States, 1820–1875* (Boston, 1998); Sally Kohlstedt, "Education for Science in Nineteenth-Century America," in *The Scientific Enterprise in America*, ed. Ronald Numbers and Charles Rosenberg (Chicago, 1996), 61–82; John C. Greene, *American Science in the Age of Jefferson* (Ames, Iowa, 1984).

The careers of several prominent figures in American natural science illustrate the unspecialized quality of their intellectual life and times. Henry Schoolcraft, son of a farmer and glass manufacturer, never went to college. As a government Indian agent with the Ojibwa (also called Chippewa), he described his hosts' language, folklore, and customs with the aid of his wife, who was half Ojibwa and half Irish. In this way he became one of the earliest anthropologists to live with the people he studied. The immigrant Constantine Rafinesque combined prolific identification of new plants and flowers with the study of the Mound Builders and other Amerindian peoples. Some of the leading figures in American natural history are remembered today as both scientists and artists, such as John James Audubon and Charles Willson Peale. Books like Audubon's *Birds of America*, Jedidiah Morse's *American Universal Geography*, and Alexander Wilson's *American Ornithology*, along with Peale's museum in Philadelphia, displaying its celebrated mastodon skeleton, brought natural history to a broad public. Only two American women of this period considered themselves professional scientists: Emma Willard, who taught mathematics and natural philosophy at Troy and published on physiology, and Maria Mitchell, who discovered a comet in 1847 and later became professor of astronomy at Vassar.[53]

It was an age when scientists, like other scholars, placed a premium on organizing, classifying, and presenting their discoveries in readily intelligible form. Taxonomy (the classification of biological species) was understood as reflecting the rationality of the Creator rather than a process of natural selection. The exploration of the globe went hand in hand with improvements in cartography (mapmaking) as well as the discovery of species and varieties. The introduction of the metric system rendered measurements uniform. The organization of scientific data into statistics and graphs accompanied the development of accounting and bookkeeping. Dictionaries, encyclopedias, and law codes excited the imagination. Just as Americans formed voluntary organizations and publications to promote religious, benevolent, and political causes, they also formed scientific ones. The American Philosophical Society and the American Academy of Arts and Sciences had been founded before 1815; they were joined over the years by a host of societies, institutes, and lyceums, often local or regional in nature, and frequently concerned with the presentation of science to the lay public. Silliman's *American Journal of Science* appeared in 1818, devoted to the publication of new research for a professional

53. Nina Baym, *American Women of Letters and the Nineteenth-Century Sciences* (New Brunswick, N.J., 2002).

audience. In short, scientific activity reflected the dramatic improvements taking place in communications and information retrieval, as well as the increased public interest in accessing information.[54]

The antebellum federal government played a somewhat larger role in scientific research than in education, as its three great exploring expeditions demonstrate. Another federal enterprise producing much scientific knowledge was the U.S. Coast Survey, which charted the oceanography of the expanding American empire. Conceived during the Jefferson administration, it was reinvigorated during Jackson's. Designed to facilitate ocean commerce, the Coast Survey reflected the interest of the Jeffersonians and Jacksonians in international trade. Even John Quincy Adams's much maligned call for a federal astronomical observatory gained implementation before long. The Jackson administration found money within the Navy Department to construct a small observatory in 1834 as an aid to celestial navigation, and the first Whig Congress passed an appropriation for a larger one in 1842, to Adams's delight. The U.S. Naval Observatory remains today in Washington, D.C.[55]

But one of the most significant federal scientific undertakings, the Smithsonian Institution, was thrust upon the government from outside. A wealthy English scientist named James Smithson willed his estate to the U.S. government to found "an establishment for the increase and diffusion of knowledge." President Jackson denied that he had authority to accept the gift and referred the matter to Congress, where Calhoun opposed it as unconstitutional. After Congress agreed to take the money, the bequest came across the Atlantic in a packet ship laden with half a million dollars' worth of gold coins, arriving in New York harbor on August 28, 1838; a Democratic administration would not accept mere paper. A dozen years of further wrangling ensued over what to do with the endowment, and not until 1846 did Congress create the Smithsonian Institution, with a museum, laboratory, library, and art gallery. Among those in Congress deserving credit for the outcome were Benjamin Tappan of Ohio (brother of the abolitionists Lewis and Arthur), Robert Dale Owen of Indiana (son of Robert Owen), and John Quincy Adams.[56]

54. Alexandra Oleson and Sanborn Brown, eds., *The Pursuit of Knowledge in the Early American Republic* (Baltimore, 1976); Daniel Headrick, *When Information Came of Age* (New York, 2001).

55. A. Hunter Dupree, *Science in the Federal Government*, 2nd ed. (Baltimore, 1985), 29–33, 62–63.

56. David Madsen, *The National University* (Detroit, 1966), 60; William Rhees, ed., *The Smithsonian Institution: Documents* (Washington, 1901), I.

The new Smithsonian was fortunate to get as its secretary (chief executive officer) America's leading physicist, Joseph Henry, professor of natural philosophy at the College of New Jersey (later Princeton University) since 1832. Henry's researches into electromagnetism had already helped prepare the way for both the electric motor and Morse's telegraph, though Henry had not realized how close his "philosophical toys" were to marketable applications and had taken out no patent. A devout Old School Presbyterian, Henry believed in the intelligent design of the universe and in the compatibility of reason with revelation; he enjoyed a close friendship with the conservative Calvinist theologian Charles Hodge of Princeton Theological Seminary. A capable administrator, Henry concentrated the Smithsonian's endeavors on scientific research and publication and turned its book collection over to the Library of Congress. Together with Alexander Dallas Bache, the head of the Coast Survey, Henry led in the formation of a self-conscious American scientific community and founded the American Association for the Advancement of Science in 1848, modeled on the British Association for the Advancement of Science.[57]

The young American republic enjoyed a Protestant Enlightenment that bestowed an enthusiastic religious endorsement upon scientific knowledge, popular education, humanitarianism, and democracy. The most widespread form of Christian millennialism added faith in progress to this list. The spread of literacy, discoveries in science and technology, even a rising standard of living, could all be interpreted—and were—as evidences of the approach of Christ's Second Coming and the messianic age foretold by the prophets, near at hand.[58]

V

Improvements in travel and transportation had their downside: the spread of contagious disease. Endemic in the Ganges River Valley of India, cholera moved along trade routes in the early nineteenth century to Central Asia, Russia, and across Europe from east to west. In the summer of 1832, it crossed the Atlantic with immigrants to Canada and the United States. Cholera hit the great port cities of New York and New Orleans

---

57. Theodore Bozeman, *Protestants in an Age of Science* (Chapel Hill, 1977) 41, 201; Albert Moyer, *Joseph Henry* (Washington, 1997), 66–77; quotation on 73. On Bache, see Hugh Slotten, *Patronage, Practice, and the Culture of American Science* (Cambridge, Eng., 1994).

58. James Moorhead, *World Without End: Mainstream American Protestant Visions of the Last Things* (Bloomington, 1999), 2–9.

hardest, but the disease spread along river and canal routes, exacting a heavy toll wherever crowded and unsanitary conditions (polluted water in particular) prevailed. Of course, the poor suffered the most.[59]

In response to the epidemic, the Senate passed a resolution introduced by Henry Clay calling upon the president to declare a day of national "prayer, fasting, and humiliation." Jackson, following the example of Jefferson rather than that of Washington, Madison, and the elder Adams, decided that compliance would violate the separation of church and state. The Evangelical United Front supported the resolution, but some denominations backed the president, including Roman Catholics and Antimission Baptists. To Jackson's relief, the resolution did not pass the House of Representatives. Most churches observed the day anyway, on their own authority, and twelve state governments endorsed it. The political issue remained alive, a partisan one. When another cholera epidemic occurred in 1848–49 and both houses requested such a day, Whig president Zachary Taylor issued the proclamation. Whatever the effect of the prayers, at least they did no harm to the victims of the disease—more than one can say for the remedies of the physicians: bloodletting and massive doses of poisonous mercury.[60]

Of all major branches of science in this period, possibly the least well developed was medicine. Vaccination against smallpox constituted one of the few valid medical interventions practiced. The germ theory of disease had been suggested (under the name "animalcular theory") but remained untested, an eccentric speculation. That rotting garbage and excrement fostered disease had long been recognized, blame focusing on their evil-smelling fumes ("miasma"). Recurrent epidemics prompted cities to start to improve sanitation provisions, but they did not act decisively until much later in the nineteenth century. Physicians practiced neither asepsis nor antisepsis and often infected a patient with the disease of the last one they had seen. In 1843, Oliver Wendell Holmes the elder, professor of medicine at Harvard, published a paper showing that unhygienic doctors bore grave responsibility for spreading puerperal fever among women in childbirth.[61]

---

59. Charles Rosenberg, *The Cholera Years* (Chicago, 1987); Sheldon Watts, *Epidemics and History* (New Haven, 1997), 167–212.

60. Rosenberg, *Cholera Years*, 47–52, 66, 121–22; Adam Jortner, "Cholera, Christ, and Jackson," *JER* 27 (2007): 233–64.

61. Joel Mokyr, *Gifts of Athena* (Princeton, 2002), 94. So reluctant was the medical community to accept Holmes's findings that he republished the paper in 1855. It appears in his collected *Medical Essays* (Boston, 1889), 103–72.

Physicians like Jacob Bigelow of Harvard Medical School, looking for *materia medica* (medicinal drugs), classified large numbers of plants and herbs for the benefit of natural history, but in practice the pharmacopoeia chiefly consisted of laxatives and opiates. Holmes remarked with a candor uncommon among his profession that if the entire *materia medica* of his time could be thrown into the sea, it would be "all the better for mankind, and all the worse for the fishes." Physicians acted as their own pharmacists, selling the medicines they prescribed. The invention of the stethoscope in France in 1819 helped diagnosis, but there was little doctors could do to help even a correctly diagnosed patient. Few therapies of the day had any efficacy beyond symptomatic relief. "Heroic," that is, drastic, measures of bloodletting, purging, and blistering found favor with physicians for a wide variety of diseases. They carried the endorsement of Benjamin Rush, still America's leading medical authority long after his death in 1813, despite criticism from Bigelow in 1835. One of the few therapeutic improvements was the isolation of quinine from cinchona bark in 1820 and its gradual application to treating malaria.[62]

Reacting to the futility of scientific medicine, many patients resorted to a variety of alternatives: homeopathy, hydropathy, Thomsonianism, Grahamism, phrenology, spiritualism, and folk remedies (Euro-American, African American, and Native American).[63] To defend their turf, a group of leading orthodox physicians founded the American Medical Association in 1847. But, like religion, American popular medicine reflected the free marketplace of ideas. Though unorthodox practitioners could be unscrupulous charlatans, some of them had sounder ideas and did less harm than the M.D.s. The unorthodox included Sylvester Graham, a Presbyterian minister who combined millennial preaching with advice on health. He advocated temperance, vegetarianism, and avoiding tobacco, heavily salted food, and "stimulating beverages" like coffee. He claimed that most diseases could be prevented by a wholesome diet, exercise, and cleanliness, both personal and public. Graham's teachings made virtues of ordinary Americans' necessities. With heating water so inconvenient that it discouraged bathing, Graham recommended washing in cold water. With most households having a scarcity of beds, he endorsed sleeping

62. John S. Haller, *American Medicine in Transition* (Urbana, Ill., 1981), 36–99; Holmes, *Medical Essays*, 203; Alex Berman, "The Heroic Approach in 19th-Century Therapeutics," in *Sickness and Health in America*, ed. Judith Leavitt and Ronald Numbers (Madison, Wisc., 1978), 77–86.

63. James Cassedy, *Medicine in America* (Baltimore, 1991), 33–39; John Duffy, *From Humors to Medical Science* (Urbana, Ill., 1993), 80–94. On African American folk medicine, see Sharla Fett, *Working Cures* (Chapel Hill, 2002).

on a hard surface. With finely ground flour expensive, he promoted the coarse-grained flour of his famous Graham cracker. With many women hoping to limit the size of their families, he cautioned men that frequent sex would debilitate them. Graham's lectures and writings on physiology exerted influence and provoked controversy throughout the 1830s and '40s. The Seventh-day Adventists perpetuated Graham's dietary program after the Civil War; one of them, John Kellogg, invented corn flakes.[64]

As the country grew, medical schools multiplied but remained small, unlicensed, and sometimes poorly equipped. Many practitioners never attended one anyway, but learned their profession through apprenticeship. (According to one estimate, in 1835 only 20 percent of Ohio physicians held a medical degree.) Gross anatomy was the aspect of medicine then best understood; yet, facing a chronic shortage of cadavers, anatomists made themselves unpopular by grave-robbing. Medical students who wanted the best training went overseas.[65] The only recognized medical specialty was surgery, long regarded as an occupation altogether different from that of the physician; most doctors engaged in general practice.

The benevolent causes of the period included medical philanthropies like hospitals, insane asylums, and care for the deaf and blind. But in the absence of effective therapies, hospitals did not do their patients much good. They generally treated only the poor and recruited convalescents to "nurse" those sicker than themselves; professional schools for training nurses did not yet exist. People who could afford to pay for treatment usually received it at home, with care from family members between the doctor's visits. The medical care of slaves reflected their masters' financial stake in their productive and reproductive capacities but suffered from their often unsanitary living conditions and, of course, from the poor state of therapeutic knowledge. Sometimes physicians experimented on slave patients in ways they would not have done on free white ones.[66]

Not only cholera but other infectious diseases like typhoid spread more readily than in earlier years, as more people traveled and population

64. See Robert Abzug, *Cosmos Crumbling* (New York, 1994), 163–82; Jayme Sokolow, *Eros and Modernization* (London, 1983), 161–68; Stephen Nissenbaum, *Sylvester Graham and Health Reform* (Westport, Conn., 1980), 152–54.

65. William Rothstein, *American Medical Schools and the Practice of Medicine* (New York, 1987), 15–53; Ohio data on 50.

66. For hospitals, see Charles Rosenberg, *The Care of Strangers* (New York, 1987), 15–46. For slaves, see Marie Jenkins Schwartz, *Birthing a Slave* (Cambridge, Mass., 2006); Deborah McGregor, *From Midwives to Medicine* (New Brunswick, N.J., 1998), 33–68.

density increased, especially in unhygienic commercial centers. Schools transmitted disease as well as literacy to children. Even rural families came under increased risk when they moved into the malarial lowlands of the Mississippi and Ohio river basins. Endemic contagions like tuberculosis (then called "consumption") and malaria ("ague") actually constituted a graver health threat than startling unfamiliar epidemics like those of cholera and yellow fever.[67] With medical science unable to understand, prevent, or cure most of these illnesses, the health of the nation deteriorated during the first half of the nineteenth century. Between 1815 and 1845 the average height of native-born white males dropped from 173 to 171.6 centimeters; life expectancy at age 10, from 52 to 47 years. Increasing democracy and economic productivity, even rising real wages, did not offset the spread of contagious diseases, which stunted the growth of young people even if they survived. Economic development outran medical science, and those who lived through this era paid a real physical price.[68]

Dentistry provided a bright spot in the generally gloomy picture. Although the transportation revolution had harmful consequences in contagious disease, the spread of commercial society, advertisements in the printed media, and the widespread aspiration to a better life stimulated desire for dental care and products. Dental fillings, extractions, and prostheses (false teeth) improved in quality in response to consumer demand and competition among providers. The expanding middle class adopted tooth brushing, a major step in the improvement of health. A New Orleans dentist named Levi Parmly recommended his patients floss their teeth with silk thread as early as 1815, though flossing did not become common until after the invention of nylon in the twentieth century. In Europe dentistry had often been considered a trade rather than a profession, but in the United States its status improved. Leading dentists held M.D. degrees. In 1840 the first American dental school opened in Baltimore, and within a generation American dentistry had become recognized as the best in the world.[69]

---

67. Gerald Grob, *The Deadly Truth* (Cambridge, Mass., 2002), 96–101, 108–15, 121–32; Thomas Cuff, *The Hidden Cost of Economic Development* (Burlington, Vt., 2005), xv.
68. Richard Steckel, "Stature and Living Standards in the United States," in *American Economic Growth and Standards of Living Before the Civil War*, ed. Robert Gallman and John Wallis (Chicago, 1992), 265–310; Robert Fogel, *The Fourth Great Awakening* (Chicago, 2000), 139–51, graphs on p. 141; Robert Fogel, *The Escape from Hunger and Premature Death* (Cambridge, Eng., 2004), 35.
69. Malvin Ring, *History of Dentistry* (New York, 1992), 197–228; Suellen Hoy, *Chasing Dirt: The American Pursuit of Cleanliness* (New York, 1995), 5, 89; Bridget Travers, ed., *The World of Invention* (New York, 1994), 635.

One major medical innovation did occur in the United States: the demonstration of anesthesia in 1846. Until then, only alcohol and versions of opium mitigated the agony of surgery. In the absence of anesthesia, patients were reluctant to undergo operations for any but the most serious of reasons, limiting surgeons' opportunities to learn new procedures. Nevertheless, amputation of limbs was tragically common, because in unsanitary surroundings, wounded extremities often developed septicemia or gangrene. Without anesthesia, surgeons placed a great premium on getting their procedures over with quickly, although their haste increased the risk of errors. About a quarter of amputees died from shock or infection.[70]

On October 16, 1846, William Morton (significantly, a dentist by profession) successfully administered ether during an operation by Dr. John C. Warren for the removal of a neck tumor at the Massachusetts General Hospital in Boston. Others had been engaged in parallel research on anesthetic, including Morton's former dental partner, Horace Wells, and a Georgia surgeon, Crawford Long. Morton's public demonstration at one of America's leading hospitals brought anesthesia international attention, but his efforts to obtain patent rights brought him only litigation and controversy—especially with Wells and a Harvard chemistry professor named Charles T. Jackson, who had provided advice. A farmer's son dreaming of riches and fame, Morton neglected his practice to pursue his court actions. He died twenty-two years later in embittered poverty. Meanwhile, ether, chloroform, and other varieties of anesthesia, despite justified concern about their safety, had gained applications in surgery, dentistry, and obstetrics throughout the Western world. Besides its medical impact, anesthesia stimulated philosophical and religious debate over the function of pain in human existence. With the invention of anesthesia, medical science intersected with the humanitarian reform impulse that sought to minimize the infliction of physical pain in a wide variety of contexts, including corporal punishment of schoolchildren, wives, convicts, slaves, and members of the armed forces.[71]

70. James Cassedy, *American Medicine and Statistical Thinking* (Cambridge, Mass., 1984), 87; Elaine Crane, "The Defining Force of Pain in Early America," in *Through a Glass Darkly*, ed. Ronald Hoffman et al. (Chapel Hill, 1997), 370–403. Thomas Dormandy, *Worst of Evils: The Fight Against Pain* (New Haven, 2006) came into my hands too late for me to use.

71. G. B. Rushman et al., *A Short History of Anaesthesia* (Oxford, 1996), 9–19; Martin Pernick, *A Calculus of Suffering* (New York, 1985).

VI

The Bible occupied an even more prominent position in discussions of morality than it did in education and science. Pre–Civil War Americans debating moral issues almost always appealed to biblical authority. This practice extended to the most divisive of all arguments over social morality, the debate over slavery. In 1837, Theodore Dwight Weld published *The Bible Against Slavery*. Like other abolitionists, he quoted St. Paul's great speech in Athens, that God "hath made of one blood all nations of men for to dwell on all the face of the earth" (Acts 17:26). One did not enslave kinfolk. But the defenders of slavery answered by quoting Noah: "Cursed be Canaan; a servant of servants shall he be unto his brethren" (Genesis 9:25). In rebuttal, Weld responded that no evidence showed Africans descended from Canaan. For abolitionists like Weld, slavery clearly violated a precept of Mosaic Law that Jesus had declared one of God's greatest commandments: "Love thy neighbor as thyself" (Leviticus 19:18; Mark 12:28–31). To this, the redoubtable Southern Baptist Thornton Stringfellow pointed out that many other passages in the Pentateuch indicate God's Chosen People practiced chattel slavery and that God, far from issuing a blanket condemnation of the institution, prescribed legal rules for it (as in Exodus 21). Rabbi M. J. Raphall of New York City vouched for the legality of slavery under the Torah.[72] Abolitionists retorted that the patriarchs practiced polygamy too, but this did not legitimate it for Christian men. When opponents of slavery appealed to the Golden Rule in Jesus' Sermon on the Mount, proslavery writers pointed out that Paul's Epistle to Philemon proved that the church of New Testament times, like the Israel of Old Testament times, had included slaveholders and recognized their rights.[73]

Although David Strauss published his *Life of Jesus* in Germany in 1835, on the western side of the Atlantic American Christians carried on their debates without reference to the "higher criticism" of the Bible that Strauss's book exemplified. Nevertheless a difference marked the two sides' use of biblical references. Southerners seized upon specific and literal textual examples, while the advocates of antislavery invoked the general tenor of the Bible, for example, that "God is no respecter of persons" (Acts 10:34). The abolitionist Angelina Grimké declared the real issue not whether Jesus had ever explicitly condemned slavery but whether one

---

72. Raphall is quoted in Mark Noll, *America's God* (Oxford, 2002), 393–94.
73. A recent anthology of primary documents from the debates over slavery is *A House Divided*, ed. Mason Lowance (Princeton, 2003); see 63–67, 92–96. See also Stephen Haynes, *Noah's Curse* (New York, 2002).

could imagine Him owning a slave.[74] The debate over the scriptural status of slavery did not involve only the extremists on both sides. One of the most comprehensive exchanges on the subject occurred in a series of letters between two Baptist clerical moderates, Francis Wayland (president of Brown University and author of the most widely used American textbook on moral philosophy) and Richard Fuller (pastor of a large Baltimore congregation and a leader of the new Southern Baptist Convention).[75] Who "won" the biblical debate depends on whom you ask. At the time, each side felt it had the better of the argument. Some American historians have ruled in favor of the proslavery controversialists, but most contemporary Protestant foreign observers found the antislavery side more convincing—as would most American Christians today. To Jesuit commentators in Rome, the debate demonstrated the chaotic consequences of Protestants' lack of a single religious authority.[76]

After the great debate over slavery by the Virginia legislature in 1831–32 had concluded, Thomas R. Dew, a professor at William and Mary College, published a *Review of the Debate* (1832) that commanded great attention throughout the South. Demonstrating the broad intellectual range of the moral philosophers of his time, he drew upon classical economics and the demography of Malthus. Dew sought to prevent further agitation of the slavery question in the southern states because it would indicate to the slaves that insurrections such as Turner's might pay off. He concentrated his fire on the colonization proposals that had been advanced by legislators from western Virginia and constituted the most widespread version of antislavery in the South. Compensated emancipation and/or colonization would add prohibitively to the tax burden, he argued; uncompensated emancipation he dismissed as manifestly unjust. Dew did not shrink from defending slavery on economic grounds as an efficient and profitable system. Colonization programs would create a labor

74. Daniel McInerney, "The Political Gospel of Abolition," *JER* 11 (1991): 371–94; Richard W. Fox, *Jesus in America* (San Francisco, 2004), 206. Among all U.S. biblical scholars, only Theodore Parker found any merit in Strauss's approach; see Dean Grodzins, *American Heretic* (Chapel Hill, 2002), 186–90.

75. Francis Wayland and Richard Fuller, *Domestic Slavery Considered as a Scriptural Institution* (New York, 1847) is a tribute to the confidence of the participants in reasoned argument.

76. After an extended discussion, Elizabeth Fox-Genovese and Eugene Genovese declare the proslavery side victors in *The Mind of the Master Class* (Cambridge, Eng., 2005), 473–527, though they dismiss the Curse of Ham argument as weak. On foreign observers, see Noll, *America's God*, 400–401, 408. An excellent brief summary of the debate is Holifield, *Theology in America*, 494–504.

shortage and deprive the state of its valuable export of surplus slaves to the Southwest, he warned. Dew did not go so far as to claim slavery superior to free labor, but he included philosophical and biblical defenses of slavery in his presentation to show that it was not necessarily an immoral system. Dew belonged to a generation that readily believed in the providential identity of morality and profitability. If at some future time slavery ceased to be profitable in Virginia (an eventuality he thought quite possible), then would be the just time to reconsider emancipation. Although not flawless, Dew's arguments hurt the cause of colonization in the South at the same time it also came under fire in the North from abolitionists. In the first half century of independence, comparatively few intellectual defenses of slavery had appeared. Dew's skillful and wide-ranging presentation commenced a new era of boldness on the part of slavery's defenders. Not many of them, however, followed him in emphasizing the economic case.[77]

In the early years of the republic, critics of slavery had by no means all come from the North, nor were its few defenders necessarily southerners. Indeed, the existence of opposition to slavery within the South had reassured northerners that the task of emancipation could safely be left in state hands. By the 1830s, however, debates over slavery, often conducted between clergymen and highlighting the biblical arguments, had taken on an overwhelmingly sectional character, although northern biblical scholars like Moses Stuart and Charles Hodge occasionally supplied ammunition their southern colleagues could use to effect.[78] Within the South, criticism of slavery was dampened down by the severe controls imposed in reaction against the abolitionist petition campaign of 1835. Dedicated southern abolitionists like James Birney and Angelina Grimké found they had to move to the North. Defying all threats, Cassius Clay (cousin of Henry Clay) managed to stay in Kentucky and maintain an antislavery movement there. Meanwhile, the increasing world demand for cotton made slavery ever more attractive economically, and the felt need to justify the system against its outside critics all the more urgent following emancipation in the British West Indies (1833). Southern intellectuals

---

77. Thomas R. Dew, *Review of the Debate in the Virginia Legislature of 1831 and 1832* (Richmond, Va., 1832); William Shade, *Democratizing the Old Dominion* (Charlottesville, Va., 1996), 205; John Daly, *When Slavery Was Called Freedom* (Lexington, Ky., 2002), 34–56.

78. See Kenneth Minkema and Harry Stout, "The Edwardsean Tradition and the Antislavery Debate," *JAH* 92 (2005): 47–74.

rallied to their section's defense. Of possible arguments on behalf of slavery, they most often employed the biblical.[79]

The evangelical churches in the South had been a source of antislavery agitation in the eighteenth century. As late as 1818 the nationwide Presbyterian Church had declared slavery "utterly inconsistent with the law of God," without any southern objection voiced. But southern evangelicals gradually made their peace with their section's "peculiar institution" as the price for continuing undisturbed with their preaching and voluntary activities. By the 1830s, their clergy typically endorsed the biblical warrants for practicing slavery. They directed their reform efforts to temperance and combating the high level of violence in southern society, while providing religious instruction to slave and free alike and reminding slaveholders of their paternalistic responsibilities to their dependents. "Masters, give unto your servants that which is just and equal; knowing that ye also have a Master in heaven" (Colossians 4:1). The very clergy who would quote scripture to defend the slave system against outside critics also admonished masters, sometimes in the presence of their slaves, against breaking up families or preventing slaves from hearing or reading for themselves the divine word. The most distinguished South Carolina theologian, James H. Thornwell, justified slavery from the Bible but advocated state legislation during the 1840s to protect slave marriages and repeal restrictions on slave literacy. The Georgia Presbyterian clergyman Charles Colcock Jones, owner of three plantations and one hundred slaves, devoted his ministry to *The Religious Instruction of the Negroes* (title of his 1842 book), sometimes working in collaboration with black preachers. Jones saw himself as a social reformer trying to humanize the institution of slavery.[80]

The South's evangelical clergy did not usually claim that slavery was "a positive good" (as Calhoun and some southern Jacksonian politicians began to do), but they certainly denied its intrinsic immorality. Chiefly, they resented the imputation that slaveholders were necessarily evil people. In 1844, when the national Methodist Church refused to accept as a bishop a man whose wife had inherited slaves, the Southern Methodist Church se-

79. See Jan Lewis, "The Problem of Slavery in Southern Political Discourse," in *Devising Liberty*, ed. David Konig (Stanford, 1995), 265–97; Drew Faust, *Southern Stories* (Columbia, Mo., 1992), 72–87; Ralph Morrow, "The Proslavery Argument Revisited," *Mississippi Valley Historical Review* 48 (1961): 79–94.

80. William Freehling, *The Reintegration of American History* (New York, 1994), 59–81; O'Brien, *Conjectures of Order*, II, 1149–57. On Jones, see Erskine Clark, *Dwelling Place: A Plantation Epic* (New Haven, 2005), esp. 135–39.

ceded. The following year the Southern Baptists likewise created their own denomination. The Presbyterians, who had split along Old School/New School theological lines in 1837, split again on sectional lines just before the Civil War. Emancipation and colonization at some undefined future time allotted by divine providence, when "conditions are ripe," remained a vague but not uncommon hope among antebellum southern evangelicals. The earthly millennium would bring deliverance from slavery.[81]

The Roman Catholic Church in the United States adopted a position not far removed from that of southern evangelical Protestants—if anything, more conservative. In 1839 the otherwise arch-conservative Pope Gregory XVI forbade Catholics to participate in the Atlantic slave trade (by then largely in the hands of the Spanish and Portuguese) but did not condemn slavery itself. Scripture and natural law (going back to Aristotle) sanctioned the institution so long as masters permitted slaves to marry and receive religious instruction. Even when masters did not live up to their obligations, the church taught it preferable to suffer the wrong than to risk social turmoil, perhaps even race war, by immediate emancipation. Abolitionist rhetoric invoked principles derived from Protestantism and the Enlightenment, and emphasized the urgency of the slavery problem; it conveyed little appeal to antebellum American Catholics. Their religion honored the spiritual discipline of patient suffering and submission more than Protestantism did, and valued individual autonomy less. Sometimes individuals had to sacrifice for the sake of public order or community welfare, even to the point of accepting enslavement. In Europe, the Roman Catholic Church generally set its face against liberalism, modernism, and republicanism. It had not embraced the Enlightenment as Anglophone Protestantism had. Most of the American Catholic bishops who came after John Carroll were Europeans and shared that predominantly conservative outlook. Social engineering, such as planned colonization, seemed anathema to such men. Postmillennial expectations, which gave theological underpinning to Protestant Americans' faith in progress, had no Catholic analogue. Anti-Catholicism among Protestants and anti-Protestantism among Catholics, both of them strong and mutually reinforcing, prevented cooperation in antislavery (or, indeed, any other enterprises).[82]

81. Christine Heyrman, *Southern Cross* (New York, 1997), 5–6; Anne Loveland, *Southern Evangelicals and the Social Order* (Baton Rouge, 1980), 191–219; Daly, *When Slavery Was Called Freedom*, 61–72.

82. John McGreevy, *Catholicism and American Freedom* (New York, 2003), 49–56. See also Madeleine Rice, *American Catholic Opinion in the Slavery Controversy* (New York, 1944).

Socioeconomic factors underscored the alienation of Catholics from antislavery. Most American Catholics were also immigrants and poor. They despised what they saw as the hypocrisy of those abolitionists who deplored the plight of distant slaves while ignoring that of the hungry newcomers on their doorstep. Sadly but understandably, poor Catholic immigrants, especially the Irish, treasured the whiteness of their skin as their one badge of privilege over the free Negroes who competed with them for jobs as laborers. Abolitionists, especially black abolitionists, deeply resented the attitude of Irish Americans and their church, contrasting it with the sympathy American antislavery received in Ireland itself from nationalists like Daniel O'Connell. As a result, abolitionists sometimes allied with the cause of nativism.[83]

But not even Catholics argued that slavery was a "positive good" and the best way to organize a society. Those who wished to make that case generally found it necessary to invoke secular rather than religious ideologies to justify their position. John C. Calhoun, theorist of southern sectional unity and constitutional interpretation, made himself the most widely known exponent of the "positive good" of slavery. On February 6, 1837, the South Carolinian addressed the Senate to oppose reception of petitions calling for the abolition of slavery in the District of Columbia. (Since Congress had no power to abolish slavery in the states, the District of Columbia became a favorite target for abolitionists wishing to focus national attention on their cause.) In his speech Calhoun abandoned the conventional Jeffersonian doctrine of slavery as an unfortunate legacy that the South must be left to deal with on its own. "I take higher ground," he declared. "I hold that in the present state of civilization, where two races of different origin, and distinguished by color, and other physical differences, as well as intellectual, are brought together, the relation now existing in the slaveholding States between the two, is instead of an evil, a good—a positive good." Without the coercion of slavery, Calhoun foresaw, white supremacy would be at risk; "the next step would be to raise the negroes [sic] to a social and political equality with the whites." Slavery's virtue lay not in its mere profitability but in its broad social consequences. It prevented both race and class conflict in the South, Calhoun claimed. "There is and always has been in an advanced stage of wealth and civilization, a conflict between labor and capital," he insisted. But southern slavery "exempts us from the disorders and dangers resulting

---

83. See David Roediger, *The Wages of Whiteness* (London, 1991); Noel Ignatiev, *How the Irish Became White* (New York, 1995), 10–31; Charles Morris, *American Catholic* (New York, 1997), 63–80.

from this conflict." This speech prompted the historian Richard Hofstadter to label Calhoun "the Marx of the Master Class."[84]

Proslavery propagandists seized with delight upon the Census of 1840, conducted by the Van Buren administration. Data which that census collected for the first time included statistics on the number of the insane. The census returns wildly inflated the number of insane free Negroes (in some communities it exceeded the total colored population). Southern politicians cited these numbers, seemingly indicating far higher rates of insanity among free than enslaved blacks, to demonstrate that African Americans could not handle freedom. Calhoun himself used the statistics in public statements on behalf of expanding and protecting the beneficent institution of slavery. Meanwhile, however, the absurdity and contradictions contained in the data had been exposed by Edward Jarvis, a northern statistician. John Quincy Adams secured a congressional resolution calling for an inquiry into how the mistakes had occurred. One William Weaver of Virginia had been in charge of the census, and (as secretary of state under Tyler) Calhoun appointed him to head the investigation too, thus assuring a cover-up. Weaver succeeded in delaying the inquiry and obfuscating its outcome; proslavery politicians continued to exploit the returns. How the erroneous data got into the census remained a mystery until the detective work of historian Patricia Cline Cohen, who traced it to small print and confusingly labeled columns on the forms the collectors filled out. The census of 1840, the first to show the United States surpassing Great Britain in population and the first to collect information on literacy, was also the last of the amateurish ones. The census of 1850, conducted by a Whig administration, took advice from Jarvis and made considerable advances in the collection and processing of social statistics.[85]

The hothouse political atmosphere of South Carolina nurtured the attitude that slavery was a "positive good." William Harper, enthusiastic supporter of nullification and chancellor of the state's high court of equity, joined Calhoun in repudiating Jefferson's principles; he explicitly rejected the assertion that "all men are created equal" in the Declaration of Independence as well as its doctrine of natural rights. A disciple of Edmund Burke, Harper distrusted those who would rebuild society on theoretical

---

84. John C. Calhoun, "Speech on the Reception of Abolition Petitions," in his *Works* (New York, 1851–55), II, 625–33, quotations from 631–33; Richard Hofstadter, *The American Political Tradition* (New York, 1948), 68.

85. Patricia Cohen, *A Calculating People* (Chicago, 1982), 175–204; James Cassedy, *Medicine and American Growth* (Madison, Wisc., 1986), 124–26; Frederick Merk, *Slavery and the Annexation of Texas* (New York, 1972), 61–68, 85–92, 117–20.

principles. Though slavery had its evils, so too did "free society," and who could say that there was more happiness or less immorality in England or the northern states than there was in the South?[86] In the years between 1848 and the Civil War, other South Carolinians, including William Smith and James Henry Hammond, would elaborate this proslavery ideology. But the process reached its apogee during the 1850s in the writings of a Virginian. George Fitzhugh repudiated individualism and natural rights entirely in favor of a theory of universal social subordination: children to parents, wives to husbands, subjects to rulers. Abolitionists pointed out that by Fitzhugh's logic, all workers, white as well as black, would be better off enslaved.[87]

Most often, however, the "positive good" school of slavery apologists followed Calhoun and based their arguments on race. They asserted that Negroes were inherently intellectually "defective" and therefore naturally suited to enslavement by their superiors. Josiah Nott, a Mobile physician, took this line to its farthest extreme in the 1840s. Black Africans represented an entirely different species, he claimed, created separately by God from whites. Racial interbreeding produced hybrid offspring inferior to either parent. Nott's theory (called "polygenesis") found some supporters among naturalists of the day but ran into trouble because it contradicted the creation account in Genesis, which clearly affirmed the descent of all human beings from a single original couple ("monogenesis"). The failure of Nott's theory to win over southern public opinion—even though it pandered to popular prejudices and despite its claims to scientific respectability—testified to the strength of the prevailing conception of harmony between reason and revelation.[88]

Bible-centered Protestantism, synthesized with the Enlightenment and a respect for classical learning, helped shape the culture, determine the patterns of intellectual inquiry, and define the terms of debate in the antebellum American republic. On the slavery issue, the synthesis was ambiguous; in most other ways it underwrote democratic values. It supplied a young and rapidly changing society with a sense of stability. Without resolving moral controversy, it endowed moral standards and rational discourse with each other's authority, strengthening both.

---

86. William Harper, *Memoir on Slavery* (Charleston, S.C., 1838); O'Brien, *Conjectures of Order*, II, 946–59.

87. See Eugene Genovese, *The World the Slaveholders Made* (New York, 1969), 118–244; O'Brien, *Conjectures of Order*, II, 972–91.

88. Reginald Horsman, *Josiah Nott* (Baton Rouge, 1987), 81–103, quotation ("defective") from 88. See also George Fredrickson, *The Black Image in the White Mind* (Middletown, Conn., 1971), 78–82.

13

Jackson's Third Term

"Andrew Jackson strengthened the presidency," it is often claimed. True, Old Hickory extended the circle of presidential advisors, expanded the patronage to be dispensed, and broadened use of the veto power. He successfully combined the office of the presidency with leadership of his political party. He triumphed in confrontations with his rivals Biddle and Calhoun. Yet the power of President Jackson remained to a large extent a function of his personal popularity, that is, charismatic rather than institutional. He did not succeed in transferring all of his own power to his successors. Indeed, the second party system that resulted from his rule proved to be a period of weak presidents. (James Knox Polk was the only exception, and even he served but one term.) Jackson did not so much strengthen the institution of the presidency as set an example that later popular presidents could invoke. Martin Van Buren, however, did not make himself one of these. Adept at gaining power, he proved largely unsuccessful in wielding it. Jackson's heir was fated to preside ineffectually over a time of economic hardship and bitter conflicts.

A son of Dutch innkeepers, Martin Van Buren of New York was the first president of non-British ancestry and the first to have been born a citizen of the United States. (His predecessors, all born before the Revolution, started life as British subjects.) Because he was Jackson's chosen successor, Van Buren's presidency has been dubbed Jackson's third term. In most personal respects, of course, the New Yorker seemed utterly unlike Old Hickory: A small, dapper man, ingratiating, flexible, one who got his way through craft rather than assertiveness, he was famously evasive. A senator who made a bet that he could get the Little Magician to commit himself to an assertion once asked Van Buren if it was true that the sun came up in the East. "I invariably sleep until after sunrise," replied the Fox of Kinderhook.[1] Van Buren did, however, commit himself to "tread generally in the footsteps of President Jackson," and in most respects he did so, retaining not only Jackson's cabinet but the kitchen cabinet as well. In his inaugural address, Van Buren defined his goal as preserving the legacy of the Founders. He then humbly deferred to "his illustrious

---

1. Van Buren told this story on himself: *Autobiography*, ed. John Fitzpatrick (Washington, 1920), 199.

predecessor." The personality of the outgoing president continued to dominate the occasion; "for once," Thomas Hart Benton commented, "the rising was eclipsed by the setting sun."[2]

Van Buren's genial social skills impressed everyone, even his political enemies. A master of the new popular brand of party politics based on publicity, patronage, and organization, in private life he loved the traditional arts of conversation and hospitality. In combining political shrewdness with gracious living, Van Buren resembled the Republican patriarch Thomas Jefferson, whom he admired perhaps even more than he did Jackson. Van Buren played politics as a game, and he played it to win. He practiced a popular version of the game because the American playing field so dictated, but his instincts and tastes were deeply conservative. As U.S. envoy in England at the time of the great Parliamentary Reform Bill of 1832, he showed no sympathy for its modest extension of the suffrage. The personalities and mechanics of British politics interested him more than substantive issues.[3] When she met Van Buren as president, Harriet Martineau observed, "His public career exhibits no one exercise of that faith in men and preference of principle to petty expediency by which a statesman shows himself to be great." In fairness to Van Buren, however, if his brand of politics held little of high principle, neither did it evince the jealousy, spitefulness, and obsessive preoccupation with personal honor that characterized so many American politicians of the previous generation, including Alexander Hamilton, John Randolph, John C. Calhoun, and Jackson himself.[4]

In his appreciation for the role of party in politics, Van Buren went well beyond his model Jefferson. The Magician's election as president put the final nail in the coffin of Monroe's Era of Good Feelings, which John Quincy Adams had tried to perpetuate, and buried the Founders' aspiration to nonpartisanship. A defender as well as a practitioner of the new politics, Van Buren pioneered the modern analysis of political parties as a legitimate feature of government instead of considering them (as all conventional political philosophers then did) a dangerous perversion. "It has always therefore struck me as more honorable and manly, and more in harmony with

2. Quotations from Major Wilson, *The Presidency of Martin Van Buren* (Lawrence, Kans., 1984), 37; Thomas Hart Benton, *Thirty Years View* (New York, 1857), I, 735.

3. Donald Cole, *Martin Van Buren and the American Political System* (Princeton, 1984), 223–24.

4. Harriet Martineau, *Retrospect of Western Travel*, ed. Daniel Feller (1838; Armonk, N.Y., 2000), 25. On the role of personal honor in the politics of the early republic, see Joanne Freeman, *Affairs of Honor* (New Haven, 2001).

the character of our People and of our Institutions, to deal with the subject of Political Parties in a sincerer and wiser spirit—to recognize their necessity, [and] to give them the credit they deserve," he wrote in his autobiography.[5] The Bucktail faction that he led in New York state politics, nicknamed the Albany Regency once it gained power, exemplified the techniques of party manipulation and control that Van Buren transferred to the national stage. And it was a prominent member of the Albany Regency, William Marcy, who, when defending Van Buren's New York state patronage policies, coined the famous phrase: "To the victor belong the spoils."[6]

Party itself became a partisan issue in the presidential election of 1836. The Democrats held a national convention at Baltimore a year early in 1835, ostensibly to assemble representatives of their party's faithful to choose their national ticket. In practice, the convention demonstrated the effectiveness of Jackson's control over the party. Van Buren won nomination easily enough, but the Virginia delegation challenged Jackson's choice for vice president, Richard Mentor Johnson of Kentucky. A fellow Indian fighter, reputed killer of the Shawnee chief Tecumseh during the War of 1812, Johnson enjoyed the favor of Old Hickory and his kitchen cabinet. He gained popularity with antievangelical voters through a congressional committee report (ghostwritten by postal clerk Obadiah Brown) resisting sabbatarian demands on the Sunday mail issue.[7] He had also championed the abolition of imprisonment for debt, a favorite cause of eastern artisans. But the unmarried Johnson had kept an enslaved mulatto mistress named Julia Chinn and acknowledged his two children by her, making him persona non grata in some genteel southern circles. As a vice-presidential alternative Virginia fielded William C. Rives, a respectable planter and diplomat who gained enough support to prevent Johnson from getting the two-thirds vote he needed for nomination. Party leaders rode roughshod over Rives's candidacy. Tennessee was one of four states that had sent no delegates to the Democratic convention; its state organization had been taken over by Jackson's opponents. Jackson's people simply brought in a man from Tennessee off the street and empowered him to cast all that state's fifteen votes for Richard Mentor Johnson, putting the Kentuckian over the top. The statement issued instead of a

5. *Autobiography*, 125.
6. Quoted in Richard Hofstadter, *The Idea of a Party System* (Berkeley, 1970), 250.
7. Both Brown and Johnson were Baptists who, like many others of that faith, distrusted efforts to remake the world and especially those enlisting cooperation between church and state. See Richard R. John, "Hiland Hall's Report on Incendiary Publications," *American Journal of Legal History* 41 (1997): 94–125.

platform identified the party with Old Republican principles of state rights and strict construction.[8] Whigs declared the Democratic convention a mockery, deplored "the excesses of party" and pointed with pride to their own failure to hold any party convention at all. The Democrats, they charged, substituted party loyalty for independent judgment on issues.[9]

The Bank War had provoked defections from Jackson's support in all parts of the country except New England, where the Democratic Party started out weak. As a result, Jackson's top-heavy majorities in the South and West disappeared in 1836, and Van Buren faced serious opposition everywhere. However, disillusionment with Jackson did not immediately translate into a well-disciplined opposition party. Not all critics of Jackson and Van Buren even embraced the name "Whig"; Antimasons and Nullifiers maintained separate identities. A national convention of Whigs proved impossible to organize. Northern economic nationalists and southern state-rights Whigs could not get along; Calhoun refused altogether to join their cause. Absence of federal patronage to dispense compounded the opposition's difficulties. The Whigs, in origin a congressional coalition, lacked the tangible basis for building a national party from the ground up that the Democrats possessed. Organizing a party was more difficult when one was out of power and critical of most of the methods by which the Democratic Party had been built. Mass politics as we know it developed only gradually, and the election of 1836 represented a stage in the process.

But while lacking a national organization, the opposition did have a constituency in all parts of the country. And so independent regional campaigns challenged Van Buren. William Henry Harrison, former governor of Indiana and victor over Tecumseh's intertribal alliance at the Battle of Tippecanoe in 1811, received the nomination of several state conventions and legislatures; he broke with tradition by actively campaigning. "Old Tippecanoe" gradually defined himself as the choice of most Whigs in the North and West. Deploring executive usurpation and expressing support for internal improvements and revenue sharing, Harrison gained Clay's grudging endorsement.[10] In the South, Jackson's

8. Thomas Brown, "The Miscegenation of Richard Mentor Johnson as an Issue," *Civil War History* 39 (1993): 5–30; Wilson, *Presidency of Van Buren*, 16; Cole, *Martin Van Buren*, 267.

9. Quotation from John Bell, speech at Nashville in July 1835, rpt. in Arthur Schlesinger Jr. et al., eds., *History of American Presidential Elections* (New York, 1971), I, 639.

10. Michael Holt, *The Rise and Fall of the American Whig Party* (New York, 1999), 38–45. Harrison's statement of principles is printed in Schlesinger et al., *History of American Presidential Elections*, I, 608–13.

longtime Tennessee friend Hugh Lawson White had been antagonized by Old Hickory's abuses of power and defined his own candidacy as a crusade to restore moral responsibility in government. White ran more as a disaffected Democrat than as a Whig. He exploited southerners' fears that no northerner could be trusted on the slavery issue. Outside South Carolina itself, those who had sympathized with nullification generally backed White.[11] Making the best of their lack of organization, some opposition leaders decided that sectional campaigns actually provided a promising strategy; if Van Buren could be kept from getting an electoral college majority, the contest would be thrown into the House of Representatives.[12]

The election took place between November 4 and 23, and by the end of the month the results showed that the Whigs' ideological appeal had gained them votes over Clay's showing in 1832, but not enough to win. Van Buren got only 50.9 percent of the popular vote; if South Carolina had held a popular vote for president, he presumably would have received less than half the nationwide popular tally. But he won the electoral college, 170 to 124 for his combined opponents. Harrison got 73 electoral votes and showed strength in the Ohio Valley, Upper South, and Antimasonic areas. White carried the previous Jackson strongholds of Tennessee and Georgia. Massachusetts voted for its favorite son Daniel Webster, and South Carolina's legislature obeyed Calhoun, casting the state's electoral votes for Willie Magnum of North Carolina. Compared with Jackson, Van Buren ran better in New England, worse in the South and West, showing the effects of having a Democratic candidate from the Northeast. On the whole, however, Democratic partisanship substituted satisfactorily for Jackson's personal stature and delivered Van Buren the victory. Virginia's Democratic electors withheld their votes from Richard Mentor Johnson, so he ended up one vote short of a majority in the vice-presidential contest. The race was therefore decided by the Senate, in accordance with the Constitution, for the only time in history. To no one's surprise, the Democratic Senate elected Johnson. The percentage of eligible males participating in the popular vote rose from 55.4 in 1832 to 57.8 in 1836; most new voters cast their ballots for one of the opposition candidates.[13]

11. Richard P. McCormick, *The Presidential Game* (New York, 1982), 166–74; William Cooper, *The South and the Politics of Slavery* (Baton Rouge, 1978), 54–58.
12. For example, Samuel Southard to Joseph Randolph, Dec. 30, 1835, cited in Michael Birkner, *Samuel L. Southard* (London, 1984), 164.
13. Holt, *Rise and Fall of Whig Party*, 45.

The outcome of the election of 1836 proved to contemporaries that partisanship trumped sectionalism as a basis for political effectiveness; the Whigs resolved to be better organized the next time. The Bank War, dominating Jackson's second term, had polarized the voting public. Despite the Whigs' inability to agree on a single presidential candidate, the election of 1836 provided a referendum on the administration's financial policies. Opposition centered among the business community, which included not only industrialists and merchants but also the larger commercial farmers and planters producing export staples, all of whom relied on banking services and a stable credit system.[14] Although the new incumbent hoped to put economic conflicts behind him, in fact they would dominate Van Buren's presidency.

Former president John Quincy Adams contemplated a third term for the Jacksonians with deep forebodings:

> The American Union as a moral Person in the family of Nations, is to live from hand to mouth, to cast away, instead of using for the improvement of its own condition, the bounties of Providence, and to raise to the summit of Power a succession of Presidents the consummation of whose glory will be to growl and snarl with impotent fury against a money broker's shop, to rivet into perpetuity the clanking chain of the Slave, and to waste in boundless bribery to the west the invaluable inheritance of the Public Lands.[15]

II

Andrew Jackson's greatest legacy to posterity was the Democratic Party. His popular appeal had created it; the decisions he reached in the White House became its policies. Where John Quincy Adams, like the framers, had believed in balanced government, Jackson believed in popular virtue—and in himself as its embodiment. A later admirer described the relationship well: "[Jackson's politics] rested on the philosophy of majority rule. When a majority was at hand Jackson used it. When a majority was not at hand he endeavored to create it. When this could not be done in time, he went ahead anyhow. *He* was the majority pro tem. Unfailingly, at the next election, the people would return a vote of confidence, making his measures their own."[16] Until the Civil War transformed America, the

---

14. Joel Silbey, "Election of 1836," in Schlesinger et al., *History of American Presidential Elections*, I, 577–600.
15. John Quincy Adams to Charles Upham, Feb. 2, 1837, "Ten Unpublished Letters of John Quincy Adams," *Huntington Library Quarterly* 4 (1941): 383.
16. Marquis James, *Andrew Jackson* (New York, 1937), 430.

Democratic Party continued along the trajectory Jackson had set, endorsing popular sovereignty, opposing a national bank and national economic planning, promoting continental expansion, and protecting slavery. Although it responded to the democratization of American life, the Democratic Party was not the spontaneous creation of a mass movement from the bottom up. There were "bottom up" movements in the young republic—among them Antimasonry, nativism, sabbatarianism, and the early labor movement—but the Democratic Party was not among them. The national party convention, for example, invented by the Antimasons, was adopted by the Democrats and later the Whigs in order to unify the respective parties and validate their leadership, not because of grassroots demand for it.

Where Jackson had created the party, Martin Van Buren served it and owed his presidency to it. Van Buren made himself the party's strategist, tactician, and official apologist. Ever since his rivalry with DeWitt Clinton, Van Buren had defined his public life in terms of party loyalty and limited government. John Quincy Adams having outraged him on both accounts, Van Buren had climbed aboard the Jackson wagon. As he explained in his letter to Thomas Ritchie of 1827, Van Buren envisioned the Democratic Party resting upon an alliance between "the planters of the South and the plain Republicans of the North." Van Buren realized that an Old Republicanism of strict construction appealed both to common folk suspicious that government economic intervention advantaged special interests and to slaveowners fearing an activist government might some day move against the South's "peculiar institution."[17]

The American politics Van Buren understood so well reflected the broadening of the franchise in the generation following the War of 1812 and the communications revolution that made political information widely available. During the years after 1815, state after state abolished property requirements for voting; the actions of Massachusetts in 1820 and New York in 1821 attracted particular attention. Historically, such qualifications had been defended as ensuring that voters possessed enough economic independence to exercise independent political judgment. Now, voting increasingly came to be seen as the right of all adult males, at least if they were white. Reflecting the new attitude toward the suffrage, none of the states admitted after 1815 set property requirements. The change in opinion largely antedated industrialization and typically

---

17. Martin Van Buren to Thomas Ritchie, Jan. 13, 1827, Van Buren Papers, microfilm ed., ser. 2, reel 7.

occurred before a significant population of white male wage-earners had appeared. Proponents of the change saw it as enfranchising tenant farmers and squatters on the public domain, small shopkeepers, and craftsmen. They usually excluded free black men from the broadened suffrage. They did not realize that their new rules would enfranchise an industrial proletariat and the large influx of immigrants who would begin to arrive in the 1840s, for they did not foresee the appearance of either. As a result, suffrage liberalization occurred in many places with relatively little controversy. Rhode Island constituted an exception to the pattern of peaceful enfranchisement. There the issue was not confronted until 1842, after a significant degree of industrialization and immigration had occurred, and suffrage reform would come only after the state constitutional crisis known as the Dorr Rebellion. Virginia, reflecting the power of her tidewater aristocracy, withstood pressure to eliminate the property qualification until 1850. South Carolina, whose planter aristocracy remained the strongest of all, hung on to property qualifications until the Civil War.[18]

The widespread change in the conception of the suffrage, from a privilege bestowed on an independent-minded elite to a right that should be possessed by all male citizens, reflected in part the success of the American Revolution and general acceptance of its natural-rights ideology. The process may be compared with the decline of religious qualifications for voting or the progress of state-by-state emancipation of northern slaves, both of which had likewise reflected the triumph of natural-rights ideology where self-interested opposition was not very powerful. Broadening the suffrage also represented one aspect of a long-continuing process of gradual modernization in American society that antedated the Declaration of Independence. The franchise had been relatively widespread even in colonial times, because the property that qualified a man to exercise it was also relatively widely distributed. Compared with Europe, America had seemed democratic for a long time.[19]

Practical as well as principled considerations operated to broaden the suffrage in the young republic. Eager to attract settlers (who boosted land values), the newer states saw no reason to put suffrage obstacles in their path. Some of them even allowed immigrants to vote before becoming citizens. This in turn put pressure on the older states, which worried about losing population through emigration westward. For the most part, property restrictions on voting declined before the rise of the Democratic Party, which benefited from, rather than fought for, the liberalization of

---

18. See Alexander Keyssar, *The Right to Vote* (New York, 2000), 26–52, 67–76.
19. See, for example, Jon Butler, *Becoming America* (Cambridge, Mass., 2000).

the suffrage. Taxpaying qualifications sometimes remained after the elimination of property ones, and the Democratic Party did generally oppose these, while their Whig opponents often agreed in removing these restrictions too by the end of the antebellum period.[20]

Paralleling the extension of the suffrage, another nationwide development also responded to white male democracy: the decline of the militia. Jeffersonians of the founding generation had reposed great confidence in the militia as an alternative to a standing army that could be used against the liberties of the people it supposedly protected. This militia, organized in each locality, consisted of all physically fit white males of military age, who would supply their own arms and donate as much of their time as necessary to keep in training and readiness when called upon to deal with insurrection or invasion. This was the "well regulated militia" postulated in the Second Amendment of the Bill of Rights and prescribed by the federal Militia Act of 1792. The militia had proved ineffective on many occasions in both the Revolutionary War and the War of 1812 (George Washington never put much trust in it), but its gradual disappearance in the generation after 1815 had nothing to do with its military shortcomings. The militia gradually ceased to function because most male citizens resented it as an imposition, and hated serving in it so much that they either refused to show up for the periodic musters and drills, or if they came made a mockery of the occasion. Since the men who defied the militia laws also constituted the electorate, politicians dared not attempt to coerce service. White male democracy could successfully defy the law, as squatters defied landlords or Indian treaties. Militia units continued to function only in those few places where the men took pride in participating in them. When the war with Mexico came in 1846, the administration made little use of the militia and relied instead on its small professional army plus volunteers trained and equipped at government expense.[21]

The development of political parties represented a response not only to legal definitions of the suffrage but also to the conditions of its exercise. The typical antebellum American polling place displayed many of the worst features of all-male society: rowdy behavior, heavy drinking, coarse language, and occasional violence. (This rude ambience, in fact, was one of the reasons offered for excluding women from voting.) Commonly, two or three weekdays would be set aside for each election and declared

20. Keyssar, *Right to Vote*, 51–52.
21. See Richard Uviller and William Merkel, *The Militia and the Right to Arms* (Durham, N.C., 2002), 109–24; Richard Winders, *Mr. Polk's Army* (College Station, Tex., 1997), 66–69.

holidays so men could come to the polling place and vote. With terms of office short and separate elections held for local, state, and federal offices, most communities underwent two elections a year, each preceded by publicity and demonstrations. Since election days varied from state to state, electioneering somewhere in the Union was more or less constant. Although public opinion polls did not exist, politicians had no difficulty keeping a finger on the public pulse at all times. Voting was sometimes oral and seldom secret. Even where written ballots were used, they were printed by the rival parties, each on paper of a distinctive color to make it easy for poll-watchers to tell which one a voter placed in the ballot box. A ballot would only list the names of the candidates of the party that printed it. To cast anything other than a straight party vote, a man had to "scratch his ticket"—line out a name and write in a different one. Challenging a voter could lead to physical conflict. When some states proposed requiring voters to register in advance, the Democratic Party generally opposed it. The prevailing electoral practices encouraged a large turnout, party-line voting, and various forms of partisan cheating, including vote buying and intimidation. Absence of secrecy encouraged most men in each community to vote the same way. This tendency toward local political homogeneity appeared strongest in rural areas, where everyone knew everyone else and where he lived, and threats of political retaliation carried strong conviction. The introduction during the late nineteenth century of the "Australian ballot" (printed at government expense and listing all candidates) was accounted a great reform.[22]

In light of the nature of the voting experience, it is not surprising that men voted from a mixture of motives. The issues themselves certainly did arouse many a voter for substantive reasons. Jackson's Indian Removal and cheap land policies enjoyed wide approval in the West, helping account for his popularity there. The transportation revolution created new economic opportunities, leading some to welcome and others to fear economic intervention by local, state, or national governments. Beginning in 1819, fluctuations in the business cycle created constituencies for hard and soft money, the National Bank, free banking, or no banks of issue at all. The events of Van Buren's administration would heighten the importance of economic issues in party politics that had arisen from Jackson's Bank War.

In general, Van Buren's Democratic Party appealed to people who for whatever reasons preferred limited government and free trade. Often

22. See Richard Bensel, *The American Ballot Box in the Mid-Nineteenth Century* (Cambridge, Eng., 2004), ix–xiii, 14–25; David Grimsted, *American Mobbing* (New York, 1998), 181–89.

these people saw themselves as "outsiders" suspicious that an active government would bestow favoritism upon "insiders." Such outsiders included recent immigrants (generally the most strongly Democratic constituency of all), dwellers in provincial geographical areas bypassed by the arteries of commerce, and critics of the influential, activist Evangelical United Front. These outsiders felt more comfortable leaving matters to local communities where their views counted, rather than trusting remote (to them) cosmopolitan power centers. But in some parts of the country, those supporting the Democrats could be definite "insiders." Many large cotton and tobacco planters and New York export merchants, for example, supported the Democratic Party because they had a vested interest in free trade. Representative James K. Polk of Tennessee encapsulated the desires of those who produced agricultural staples in a toast that became a Democratic slogan: "Sell what we have to spare in the market where we can sell for the best price; buy what we need in the market where we can buy cheapest."[23] Finally, those who felt most zealously committed to preserving white supremacy and expanding slavery, whether insiders or outsiders, found the Democratic Party safe and worried that the Whig Party's program of expanding the federal government might make trouble at some point.

The centrality of the banking issue in party politics was no accident. A banking system that provided an effective source of credit constituted a necessary condition for the economic development of the United States. Banks also performed other essential financial services, mobilizing capital, providing information to prospective investors about risks and rewards, and facilitating financial transactions.[24] Those most committed to promoting economic development supported the Whigs. Those who felt threatened by the prospect of economic change supported the Democrats.

Underscoring the issues themselves in arousing political interest was the communications revolution, with its mass of cheap, intensely partisan publications. Political pamphlets had been around for a long time, and there were also political books, for campaign biographies appeared of every presidential hopeful; but the most influential segment of the political media was the newspaper press. By 1836, both administration and opposition newspapers flourished in all parts of the country. So long as they exempted slavery from criticism, they enjoyed freedom of political expression

---

23. Quoted in Charles Sellers, *James K. Polk, Jacksonian* (Princeton, 1957), 149.
24. See Robert Wright, *The Wealth of Nations Rediscovered: Integration and Expansion in American Financial Markets, 1780–1850* (Cambridge, Eng., 2002).

everywhere. Despite the harshness of the partisan press, no one attempted to revive the Sedition Act of 1798.

On occasion the communications revolution could itself become the subject of partisan debate. In 1832 the Senate spent a week debating a measure to grant all newspapers free postage. Supporters argued that it would promote political awareness among the electorate and help unify the nation. Opponents complained that it would enable people in the countryside to subscribe to big-city newspapers and undercut the local markets of the small-town press. The proposal went down to a narrow defeat, 22 to 23, with all Jacksonian senators voting no. Then as now, those who defined themselves as outsiders distrusted the influence of metropolitan opinion-makers.[25] This attitude did not prevent the Jacksonians from creating big-city newspapers of their own and developing a sophisticated understanding of the role of the media of communication.

The newspaper editors of the time offer fascinating examples not only of colorful personalities but also of the interaction between politics and the press. Francis Blair came out of Kentucky, where he won his spurs as a spokesman for debt relief after the Panic of 1819. Chosen to run the *Washington Globe* as organ of the Jackson administration, Blair displayed across its masthead the slogan "The World Is Governed Too Much" and put out a paper that appealed not only to small farmers but also to recent immigrants and aspiring businessmen impatient with the national bank. The *Globe*, it has been said, served "the army of minor officeholders" as "a kind of continuing communique from national headquarters."[26] Blair was rewarded with the contract to print the record of Congressional debates, which he renamed the *Congressional Globe*. On occasion, he exploited this vantage point to suppress speeches by critics of the administration.

The new media opened new opportunities to talent and imagination. James Gordon Bennett, a self-made immigrant from Scotland, created the *New York Herald* and turned it into America's best-selling newspaper. A Catholic who sometimes criticized his church's clerical hierarchy, Bennett did much to define the Democratic Party's urban constituency. Mordecai Noah, playwright, diplomat, and would-be founder of the Jewish community called Ararat, was rewarded for his Jacksonian journalism with an appointment as surveyor of the Port of New York. Alienated from the Democrats by the Bank War, Noah lost his patronage job, switched to

25. Richard Kielbowicz, "Modernization, Communication Policy, and the Geopolitics of News, 1820–1860," *Critical Studies in Mass Communication* 3 (1986): 21–35.

26. Bernard Weisberger, *The American Newspaperman* (Chicago, 1961), 83.

the Whig Party, and founded the innovative, high-quality *New York Evening Star* in 1833.[27]

Anne Royall, forced to support herself as a fifty-four-year-old widow, established her reputation first as a traveling journalist and then as the incisive editor of a small Washington newspaper. She supported Jacksonian Democracy on the issues of her day, including the Bank Veto, Sunday mail transportation, and state-rights protection of slavery. Though he often disagreed with her, John Quincy Adams admired her spirit and called her "a virago errant in enchanted armor."[28] (The story of her securing an interview with a naked president while Adams was swimming in the Potomac is, alas, apocryphal.) At a time when many women found outlet for their talent and energy in church activities, Anne Royall pointed the finger of scorn at evangelical Christianity. The women of the First Presbyterian Church in Washington complained that she verbally harassed them on their way to church. Tried for the crime of being a "common scold," Royall protested her freedom of speech. Political party lines were sharply drawn at her trial, for the Presbyterian women had ties to the outgoing Adams administration, while Jackson's incoming secretary of war, John Eaton (husband of the controversial Peggy), appeared as a character witness for the defense. Upon Royall's conviction, the judge imposed, instead of the traditional ducking stool, a fine, which sympathetic fellow journalists paid for her. Royall resumed her acerbic denunciations of the churches.[29]

The most important of Jacksonian journalists, however, was undoubtedly Amos Kendall. Gaunt, sallow, and prematurely white-haired, Kendall excited an almost superstitious awe among Washington insiders as the mysterious power behind the throne.[30] Although Lucretia and Henry Clay had befriended him as a poor youth, Kendall broke with the Clays in 1826 and embraced the cause of Andrew Jackson, helping Old Hickory to carry Kentucky in 1828. From then on he enjoyed Jackson's confidence as did no one else save Van Buren. Kendall's newspaper experience had honed his sense of how to shape a political message for the public. Within the kitchen cabinet, he formulated the rationale for the spoils system as "rotation in office" and ghostwrote the Bank Veto Message as well as several of Jackson's other major state papers.

27. Jonathan Sarna, *Jacksonian Jew: The Two Worlds of Mordecai Noah* (New York, 1981).

28. John Quincy Adams, *Memoirs*, ed. Charles Francis Adams (Philadelphia, 1874–79), VII, 321.

29. Elizabeth Clapp, "Anne Royall's 1829 Trial as a Common Scold," *JER* 23 (2003): 207–32.

30. Martineau, *Retrospect*, 55.

In his nurture of the Democratic Party, Kendall synthesized the power of the press over public opinion with the power of patronage to create a network of self-interest. Although the customs offices, land offices, and Indian agencies all provided federal jobs, the postal system dominated the patronage machine that made the national Democratic Party work. The expansion of the Post Office thus fostered both the communications revolution and the development of a modern party system. Even before becoming its formal head, Kendall largely controlled appointments to branch post offices. Once postmaster general, he found a way to censor antislavery opinion from the mail. Kendall understood the potential of the communications revolution as well as anyone in America—as he would also demonstrate later as Morse's partner in the telegraph industry. A man of stern financial probity and a modern sense of responsible management, he strove to impose order and accountability on what was generally a lax and informal postal administration. Kendall's biographer rightly portrays him as a central figure in the communications revolution: "a newspaper editor, party organizer, political propagandist, postmaster general, telegraph builder, and [in the post–Civil War era] promoter of language for the deaf."[31]

In spite of all the parties did, some eligible voters were inevitably neither well informed nor strongly motivated. Local political leaders realized that popular interest in the issues of the day and the propaganda of the party press required supplementing in order to "rouse the sluggish to exertion."[32] The electorate was a mobile population. Especially in the cities or west of the Appalachians, a significant percentage of the voters might have arrived in their community only recently. The core of longer-term residents used national party affiliation to reach newcomers not yet familiar with local issues. Local party leaders came from much the same social background whether they supported the Jacksonian or opposition cause. Seldom simple farmers, they were typically prosperous business and professional men, often with a personal stake in the outcome, either as officeholders or as a result of government economic policies.[33] The leaders worked hard to bring out the party faithful, whether to sign petitions,

31. Matthew Crenson, *The Federal Machine: Beginnings of Bureaucracy in Jacksonian America* (Baltimore, 1975), 140–43, 157; Richard R. John, *Spreading the News* (Cambridge, Mass., 1995), 219–23, 269–72; quotation from Donald Cole, *A Jackson Man: Amos Kendall and the Rise of American Democracy* (Baton Rouge, 2004), 301.

32. Martin Van Buren, quoted in Ralph Ketcham, *Presidents Above Party* (Chapel Hill, 1984), 144.

33. Kenneth Winkle, *The Politics of Community* (Cambridge, Eng., 1988), esp. 176–78; Edward Pessen, *Jacksonian America* (Homewood, Ill., 1969), esp. 180–84.

attend local caucuses and rallies, or visit the polling place at election time. Their methods of political mobilization—the free drinks, the parades, the corruption and illegalities—have been satirized and criticized by contemporaries and historians alike. The French tourist Michel Chevalier, more reflective than many observers, thought American political demonstrations the counterparts of folk holidays and religious processions in his own Catholic country.[34] Antebellum party campaigns fostered a spirit of group loyalty not unlike that associated with sports teams in our day. Get-out-the-vote practices may well have been more necessary to the Jacksonian campaigns of 1824 through 1836 than to their opponents because Democratic voters tended to be people less touched by the communications revolution.[35] Contemporary complaints seemed to focus more on Democratic behavior. When the Whig Party finally mobilized effectively in 1840, it did so with techniques adapted to its own constituency, for each party devoted itself more to energizing its own supporters than to persuading the undecided. One way or another, by fair means or foul, the party leaders did their job effectively enough that voter turnouts increased to the point where they compare favorably with those of today, despite longer hours of work and the difficulties of getting from the family farm to the polling place.[36]

The less the right to vote came to depend on economic criteria like property ownership or taxpaying, the more clearly it depended on race and gender. Those few women in New Jersey who had once exercised the franchise had been deprived of it in 1807. Now, there appeared a movement to roll back the enfranchisement of black men, so as to identify the suffrage clearly with white manhood. Black males lost the right to vote in Connecticut in 1818, in Rhode Island in 1822, in North Carolina in 1835, and in Pennsylvania in 1838. When New York removed its property qualifications for white voters in 1821, it retained one for blacks. Of the states admitted after 1819, every one but Maine disenfranchised African Americans.[37] The United States was well on its way to becoming a "white republic." The issue of black suffrage consistently divided the political

34. Michel Chevalier, *Society, Manners, and Politics in the United States,* trans. T. Bradford (Boston, 1839), 316–21.

35. See, for example, Michael Foley, "The Post Office and the Distribution of Information in Rural New England," *JER* 17 (1997): 611–50.

36. The unsavory practices endured for the rest of the century; see Glenn Altschuler and Stuart Blumin, *Rude Republic: Americans and Their Politics in the Nineteenth Century* (Princeton, 2000).

37. Keyssar, *Right to Vote,* 54–58, Table A4; Harry Watson, *Jacksonian Politics and Community Conflict* (Baton Rouge, 1981), 61.

parties: Federalists supported it and Jeffersonians opposed; Whigs supported it and Jacksonians opposed. Not surprisingly, wherever black men had the power to do so, they voted overwhelmingly against the Democrats. The English visitor Edward Abdy thought it virtually impossible to find an African American who was not "an anti-Jackson man."[38]

III

After the election of 1836, Jackson's administration still had several months to run and important business to conduct. At the top of the outgoing president's own agenda stood personal vindication. Jackson and his friends wanted the censure passed against his removal of the deposits not merely repealed or rescinded but "expunged" from the Senate's journal. Thomas Hart Benton of Missouri led the fight to achieve this remarkable rewriting of history; with the Democrats controlling the Senate, 33 to 16, he led from strength. The Whigs argued that while the Senate could change its collective mind, the integrity of its journal as a record of events should not be violated. Calhoun reminded senators that the Constitution mandates each house to keep a journal of its proceedings, which implies that it should not be mutilated. After thirteen hours of eloquent debate, a vote of 24 to 19 decided the issue. The secretary of the Senate drew black lines around the censure motion passed three years earlier and wrote across its face: "*Expunged by order of the Senate, this 16th day of January, 1837.*" The page was not torn out, and the original censure remains legible. But the Old Hero felt gratified.[39]

Sixty-nine years old, weakened by illness and his physicians' bloodletting, Andrew Jackson now looked upon America with increasing misgivings despite his political victories. The problem, ironically, arose from the country's prosperity. The price of cotton, backbone of the national economy, rose on global markets. Europeans put their capital to work in American development. An influx of Mexican silver into U.S. banks stimulated the economy further. State governments invested money in internal improvements; state banks lent money to private corporations and individuals for capital investments of their own. Jobs multiplied. Prosperity of this kind helped Van Buren's election, but it worried Andrew Jackson.

38. See Leonard Richards, "The Jacksonians and Slavery," in *Antislavery Reconsidered*, ed. Lewis Perry and Michael Fellman (Baton Rouge, 1979), 99–118; Abdy is quoted on 103.

39. Thomas Hart Benton, *Thirty Years' View*, I, 727–31. Benton accidentally gives March 16, 1837, as the date for expunging; January 16 is the correct date.

Jackson's economic views were simple and heartfelt. He believed people should get ahead through hard work and thrift. Speculation and indebtedness bothered him. He associated the paper money that banks issued with speculation and preferred a currency based entirely on gold and silver. He wanted to apply to the government's finances the same precepts of thrift and debt avoidance that he would advise an individual to follow. Jackson had thought that getting rid of the Bank of the United States would be a step toward the implementation of his principles, but it hadn't worked out that way. Now, state bankers fought to get on the approved list to receive deposits of the federal government's revenues so they could issue more paper. Jackson had insisted that the federal government must retire its own debt. Accordingly, in January 1835 the national debt had been paid off for the only time in history. But the revenues kept piling up, since land sales continued strong and the proceeds from the Tariff of 1833 reflected Americans' yearning for imported goods. What should be done with the money? Jackson distrusted big government.

Henry Clay, as usual, had a plan. He revived his proposal for distribution of the federal government's surplus revenue to the states, enabling them to expand both the transportation network and their public school systems, while avoiding constitutional difficulties about the exercise of federal power. Clay added that the proceeds of land sales should be earmarked permanently for distribution to the states for these purposes—an economically sound action to ensure that the proceeds from the nation's major asset would be devoted to capital improvements and not current expenses. But Jackson feared distribution would only contribute to the speculative boom he so distrusted. Besides, it was Clay's project. Jackson had vetoed Clay's Distribution Bill of 1833 and remained skeptical.

Many congressional Democrats did not share Jackson's misgivings. Although they didn't want to make distribution a permanent policy, it seemed a plausible approach to the immediate problem of the federal surplus. So they joined with Whigs to pass, by a veto-proof margin, the Deposit-Distribution Act of 1836, a distribution measure applying only to the current surplus. Increasing the number of state banks in which the federal government kept its funds ("pet banks"), it ordered them to "deposit" some of those federal funds with the states. The $37 million federal surplus would be distributed to each state according to its electoral votes (thus including three-fifths of the slaves). Theoretically the money was a loan, to differentiate the measure from Clay's own distribution scheme, but everybody knew the federal government would never ask for the money back (and it never has). Rather than split his party, the ailing president uncharacteristically went along with others' wishes and signed the bill, though he did extract a concession in the form of a provision forbidding the pet banks to issue paper money in small denominations. The overwhelming support for the Deposit-Distribution Act in Congress demonstrated the widespread eagerness for internal improvements that permeated both parties. But the *Washington Globe* reflected Old Hickory's personal sentiments in its denunciation of the measure.[40]

Jackson had some fight in him still, and he showed it in his Specie Circular of 1836. Disillusioned with the pet banks and their currency, Jackson ordered federal land offices to stop accepting paper money in payment except from actual settlers. Speculators would have to pay in gold or silver. The president had struck a blow against confidence in the economy: If the government wouldn't accept bank notes, who should? "I found the people excited" by the circular, a western banker reported to the secretary of the Treasury. "They appear to distrust all Banks, they think Govt. has no confidence in them." Fearful that Jackson's financial Luddism would sabotage the whole credit system, Congress passed a bill revoking the Specie Circular.[41] On the last day of his presidency, Jackson killed their revocation with a pocket veto.

The outgoing president wished to imitate George Washington and leave his countrymen with a parting admonition. He commissioned Chief Justice Taney to ghostwrite one for him. Although it is called Jackson's Farewell Address, he never delivered it orally but simply approved it, signed it, and sent it off to the publisher. No eloquent speaker, Jackson entrusted his message — as the early presidents usually did — to the printed media.[42]

His Farewell Address reflected Jackson's views as they had taken shape after eight years in the White House. First, he pointed with pride to his accomplishments, notably Indian Removal. Then, he identified two principles requiring vigilant protection: the Union of the states and popular sovereignty. He warned against sectionalism, which might lead to the breakup of the Union into "a multitude of petty states, without commerce, without credit," the pawns of European intervention. He identified two specific dangers to the Union: nullification and abolitionism. The latter, interestingly, received his harsher condemnation; "nothing

---

40. Richard Latner, *The Presidency of Andrew Jackson* (Athens, Ga., 1979), 191.

41. Quotation from John McFaul, *The Politics of Jacksonian Finance* (Ithaca, N.Y., 1972), 188. The Luddites were English workingmen who opposed the industrial revolution that was taking away their jobs; they made themselves notorious by smashing machinery.

42. Remini, *Jackson*, III, 414.

but mischief can come from these improper assaults upon the feelings and rights of others." Turning to popular sovereignty, Jackson found the chief menace to it in "the moneyed power." The populist spirit of his Bank Veto Message reappeared. "Corporations and wealthy individuals" seek a protective tariff, which will weigh heavily upon "the farmer, the mechanic, and the laboring classes." The moneyed power multiplies its leverage through banks and their paper currency, which produce "sudden fluctuations" in the economy and "engender a spirit of speculation injurious to the habits and character of the people."

Despite this populist, anti-Bank rhetoric, Jackson did not attack capitalism in general. Nor did he hope for America to return to some mythic Arcadia of subsistence farming. Instead he praised America's "rich and flourishing commerce" and rejoiced at her progress "in numbers, in wealth, in knowledge, and all the useful arts which contribute to the comforts and convenience of man." Jackson and the Democratic Party valued laissez-faire as a guarantee that economic competition would take place fairly, without the intervention of government favoritism. In his closing, Jackson recommended building up coastal defenses and the navy, for "we shall more certainly preserve peace when it is well understood that we are prepared for war."[43]

For the rest of the antebellum era, the Democratic Party retained the philosophy Jackson expressed, especially his willingness to nurture the Union by sheltering slavery from criticism. Van Buren divorced the government from banks altogether, with Jackson's hearty approval. Faith in the people's rustic virtue continued to coexist with pride in their economic development. Since the Democrats suspected that special interests would inevitably dominate government, they often protested that strong government meant favoritism to the few at the expense of the many. Yet in practice they showed no hesitation in using the power of government to promote interests they favored, particularly the perpetuation and extension of slavery. Popular sovereignty remained a favorite Democratic slogan, while Jackson's endorsement of westward expansion and a strong defense establishment would be magnified into imperialism and conquest.

IV

Moving into the White House, Martin Van Buren realized a goal he had long dreamed of and for which he had schemed ceaselessly. His daughter-in-law, the beautiful, aristocratic southerner Angelica Singleton

---

43. "Farewell Address" (March 4, 1833), *Presidential Messages*, III, 292–308.

Van Buren, served as official hostess for the long-widowed president, winning from even a critical French diplomat the admission that she would qualify "in any country" as a woman of "graceful and distinguished manners."[44] But events quickly frustrated Van Buren's inclination to rest on his laurels and enjoy the presidency as a reward. Though he boasted in his March inaugural address of prosperity and the expansion of commerce, he had inherited an unstable economy and a party divided between hard-money and soft-money advocates. Before the month was over, a New Orleans cotton broker failed, then others followed. By April their New York City creditors were failing too, including even the House of Joseph, an arm of the Rothschild financial empire. On May Day the New York mercantile house of Arthur Tappan and Company, founder of the *Journal of Commerce*, collapsed, taking away the source of much antislavery philanthropic funding, although the *Journal* itself survived. The Panic of 1837 had begun.[45]

The crisis had causes both foreign and domestic. It reflected the chronic shortage of capital in the United States and the country's dependence on inflows of foreign money. By paying off the national debt, Jackson had returned capital to Europe, and by destroying the BUS, he had made it harder to control the domestic money supply. (Jackson was overreacting against the shocking example of Great Britain, where servicing the national debt in this period consumed 70 percent of the government's revenues.)[46] Like the boom that preceded it, the panic manifested the extent to which America, even then, was enmeshed in a global economy.

The United States imported silver from Mexico, where it was mined, and customarily sent it on to China to pay for our unfavorable balance of trade with that country. But in the 1830s Chinese merchants preferred bills of credit on British banks over silver; these proved convenient in paying for Chinese imports of opium from India. American traders could provide these bills of credit because the British were lending us money. Silver then accumulated in the vaults of American banks, constituting a legitimate basis for their expanded issues of paper currency. With more money in circulation, domestic prices rose, including the price people paid the government for western land.[47] On the international market, the

---

44. Adolphe Fourier de Bacourt, quoted in Cole, *Martin Van Buren*, 346.

45. Edwin Burrows and Mike Wallace, *Gotham: A History of New York City* (New York, 1999), 611–16.

46. James Huston, *Securing the Fruits of Labor* (Baton Rouge, 1998), Table 15 on 140.

47. See Peter Temin, *The Jacksonian Economy* (New York, 1969), as modified by Richard Sylla, "Review of Peter Temin's *Jacksonian Economy*," *Economic History Services*, Aug. 17, 2001, http://eh.net/bookreviews/library/sylla.

prices of cotton and other U.S. export staples soared in the 1830s. Yet the American appetite for European, particularly British, manufactured goods increased even faster. In 1836, U.S. imports totaled $180.1 million, $45.7 million more than the combined value of exports and the earnings of our carrying trade.[48] For a while British investors made up the difference by extending credit to cotton factors and buying American securities. But then England suffered a poor harvest and had to import grain suddenly from the Continent. Needing money in early 1837, the Bank of England began to curtail the credit of British firms with large American investments. They in turn pressed their transatlantic debtors. The American financial system could not take the pressure.

Contemporaries reacted to the Panic of 1837 in terms of their political allegiances. Democrats blamed the banks. Whigs blamed Jackson, and especially his Specie Circular. For a long time historians agreed with the Democrats and said that the pet banks had irresponsibly overextended their loans during the boom of 1836.[49] But now we know that, monitored by the Treasury, the state bankers showed appropriate caution and that, except for Taney's friends in Baltimore, the pet banks were generally responsibly managed.[50] There is more truth in the Whig argument.

Jackson's Specie Circular—which Van Buren left in force—did not set the panic in motion but (in the words of an economic historian) "rendered the panic inevitable." The need to pay the Treasury for land purchases in specie drained specie out of the banking system. Between September 1, 1836, and May 1, 1837, the specie reserves of the major New York City banks fell from $7.2 million to $1.5 million, leaving them vulnerable to sudden shifts in the wind. Having destroyed the national bank and, with it, the paper currency in which people had the most confidence, Jackson then planted, through his Specie Circular, the seed of fear in the public mind that state bank paper was not safe either. Bank note holders therefore quickly became frightened by the string of failures triggered among international cotton brokers when the Bank of England contracted credit.[51] The holders started a "run" on New York banks. On May 8 and 9

48. Douglass North, *The Economic Growth of the United States, 1790–1860* (New York, 1961), Tables A-VIII, B-VIII, C-VIII on 233–34.

49. For this point of view, see Reginald McGrane, *The Panic of 1837* (Chicago, 1924).

50. See Stanley Engerman, "A Note on the Economic Consequences of the Second Bank of the United States," *Journal of Political Economy* 78 (1970): 725–28; Marie Sushka, "The Antebellum Money Market and the Economic Impact of the Bank War," *Journal of Economic History* 36 (1976): 809–35 and 39 (1979): 467–74.

51. Peter Rousseau, "Jacksonian Monetary Policy, Specie Flows, and the Panic of 1837," *Journal of Economic History* 62 (2002): 457–88, quotation from 457.

they withdrew a million dollars in gold and silver. No bank could withstand such pressure. On May 10, the New York banks, acting in concert, had to suspend specie payments, and within a few days the rest of the country's banks had followed suit. By 1837, several years of hard-money agitation had born fruit. Everybody was trying to hoard gold and silver: the banks, the states, the public, even the federal government, through the Specie Circular. Yet the federal mints never produced enough coins for circulation, and the public resorted to foreign coins (like the tiny Spanish silver "picayune"). Farmers went on growing crops for lower prices, but outside the agricultural sector, economic activity declined. Faced with falling revenues, the Van Buren administration had to borrow money. The national debt, which Jackson thought he had eliminated permanently, reappeared and has been with us ever since.[52]

The Deposit-Distribution Act of 1836 compounded the banks' difficulties by forcing them to pay out substantial sums to the states. Fortunately, many states simply deposited their money in the same bank that had been keeping it on behalf of the federal government. After the banks had suspended specie payments, they kept up their scheduled distributions to the accounts of the states the only way they could, in nonconvertible funds, and the states accepted this.[53] Virtually all of the states spent their windfalls quickly. With the aid of the states' expenditures, the economy started a tentative rebound in 1838. Some banks cautiously resumed the redemption of their notes. In May 1838, an alliance of Whigs and soft-money Democrats in Congress repealed the Specie Circular, and Van Buren bowed to their will. But then another serious economic blow fell: the Panic of 1839.

Southwestern frontiersmen had speculated as irresponsibly as any city-slicker banker. Lured by rising prices for agricultural commodities, especially cotton, land speculators overextended themselves recklessly, while planters hastened to expand production. By 1839, a cotton glut appeared in Liverpool, and the world price began to drop. The fall continued until cotton sold for less than half its 1836 price. The trade by which the United States had paid its way in the world no longer did so. The sale of public lands virtually ceased, and speculators found themselves stuck with inventory worth a tenth of what they had paid for it. The price of field hands fell, and the interstate traffic in enslaved workers shriveled. The Jacksonian destruction of the national bank had left the country without a

---

52. John Mayfield, *The New Nation* (New York, 1982), 125; Herbert Sloan, *Principle and Interest* (New York, 1995), 216.
53. Temin, *Jacksonian Economy*, 128–36, 147.

lender of last resort.[54] It was 1819 all over again. Only this time, the depression lasted longer, until 1843.

Repercussions of the panic extended throughout the economy. As businesses cut back production or failed altogether, workers lost their jobs. The infant industries of the Northeast, shoes and textiles, laid off thousands of employees. The banks' resumption of specie payment in 1838 proved brief. The Deposit-Distribution Act had created many new pet banks all over the country, scattering the government's deposits among them, making it harder to mobilize what was left of the specie reserves. As a result the American banking system buckled under the pressure from British creditors after 1839. Eventually many banks failed, especially those involved in the cotton trade. Among these was Nicholas Biddle's United States Bank of Pennsylvania, formerly the national bank and still the largest bank in the country, insolvent in 1841. The Panic of 1837 merged with that of 1839 into a prolonged period of hard times that, in severity and duration, was exceeded only by the great depression that began ninety years later, in 1929.[55]

Hard times blighted Van Buren's entire term. Yet the president offered his suffering country nothing by way of relief. "Those who look to the action of this Government for specific aid to the citizen to relieve embarrassments arising from losses by revulsions in commerce and credit lose sight of the ends for which it was created and the powers with which it is clothed," he told Congress. All the public could expect from the government was "strict economy and frugality," and a warning not "to substitute for republican simplicity and economical habits a sickly appetite for effeminate indulgence." The president rehearsed these stern platitudes not so much because they held out any economic hope as because they identified him as loyal to Andrew Jackson's legacy. Like John Quincy Adams, Van Buren wanted to emphasize his embattled administration's continuity with a more popular predecessor. But while hard money and little government had affirmed republican virtue during the prosperity of Jackson's years, they lost some of their appeal during hard times. "It was one thing to invite the people to thrive on their own," the historian Daniel Feller has observed, "another to tell them to suffer on their own."[56] By the end of his administration, the president had acquired the nickname "Martin Van Ruin."

---

54. Rousseau, "Jacksonian Monetary Policy," 487.
55. North, *Economic Growth*, 201–3, Table A-VII on 232.
56. "Third Annual Message" (Dec. 4, 1839), *Presidential Messages*, III, 554; Daniel Feller, *The Jacksonian Promise* (Baltimore, 1995), 193.

From a modern point of view, Van Buren's embrace of laissez-faire seems paradoxical. The hard-money Jacksonian constituents he was courting did not oppose government intervention in the economy out of any preference for commercial values. On the contrary, they deeply distrusted large businesses, especially banks, and wanted to make sure government did them no favors. The only kinds of government intervention they knew about seemed to them to reinforce the privileges of the wealthy, not to counteract them. In another irony, the notoriously evasive Van Buren ended up far more rigidly committed to a particular economic and banking policy than the famously willful Jackson had ever been. Meanwhile, the Whigs, the party of the business community, reminded people that they favored government planning. Henry Clay deplored Van Buren's "cold and heartless insensibility" and invoked his own American System of integrated development as a pathway to economic recovery. "We are all—people, States, Union, banks—bound up and interwoven together, united in fortune and destiny, and all, all entitled to the protecting care of a paternal government." The depression gave the Whig Party a new lease on life. To their goal of rescuing the country from executive tyranny the Whigs now added the restoration of prosperity. "We have many recruits in our ranks from the pressures of the time," observed William Henry Harrison.[57] This was true at the level of leaders as well as voters. A number of soft-money Democratic politicians, calling themselves Conservative Democrats, gave up on Van Buren and went over to the Whigs. In the midterm elections the Whigs gained enough congressional seats that, by striking a temporary alliance with the Calhounites, they were able to install R.M.T. Hunter, an antiadministration state-rights Virginian, in the Speaker's chair.

The system in which the federal government deposited its funds in "pet" state banks had originated in haste when Jackson removed the deposits from the BUS. Jackson had always regarded it as an "experiment." Although Treasury Secretary Woodbury had dutifully regulated the pets, an administration committed as a general principle against federal regulation and planning did not find the task congenial. When the pets along with other banks suspended specie payment for a year starting in May 1837, hard-money Democrats complained that the public trust had been betrayed. It was time to rethink the government's relationship with banking. With Jackson's blessing, Van Buren summoned a special session of Congress in September 1837 and asked for legislation to authorize

---

57. Henry Clay, "Speech on the Sub-Treasury" (Sept. 25, 1837), in his *Life, Correspondence, and Speeches*, ed. Calvin Colton (New York, 1857), VI, 74; William Henry Harrison, quoted in Holt, *Rise and Fall of Whig Party*, 64.

removing the taxpayers' money from all banks, placing it in an Independent Treasury. (The term was used to signify not only independence from banks but also independence from British capital, which had invested heavily in the old BUS.) Each major city would have a Sub-Treasury for local convenience. In the meantime, Van Buren removed the government's deposits from the pet banks by executive action on the grounds that they did not pay specie as required by law. But his request for a statutory Independent Treasury stalled in Congress, where Whigs and soft-money Democrats pointed out that removing federal deposits from state banks had a deflationary effect and worsened the depression. Not until July 1840, nearly three years later, did Congress finally enact the Independent Treasury law the president wanted. Van Buren's relaxed style in the White House, emphasizing gracious living, did not make for effective legislative management. It took the additional round of bank failures in 1839 and the need for Democrats to present a unified party in the coming election to prompt congressional action.[58]

Once the federal government legally "divorced" its pet banks (as the saying went), responsibility for bank regulation fell to the states. At the state level, Democrats pursued a variety of banking policies. "Politically the Jacksonians were happiest and most united when they were hunting down the dreaded bank enemy, but once they had their adversary cornered they never knew quite what to do," one historian has noted. Some Democratic state governments opted to regulate banks, some for a state-run monopoly bank, while some merely banned bank notes below ten or twenty dollars. In New York state, the Albany Regency protected the interests of its favored banks against popular demands to charter additional ones. In the Old Northwest, on the other hand, Democrats came to agree with Whigs that "free banking" provided the solution: Any group who could meet certain standard requirements could incorporate a bank. Democratic politicians throughout the country were primarily interested in building their political party, not in pioneering government regulation of the banking industry. In Massachusetts, the Whigs established a state commission to oversee banks after the failure of a Democratic-owned pet, the Commonwealth Bank; when the Democrats came into power, however, they abolished the commission.[59]

---

58. Wilson, *Presidency of Van Buren*, 99, 114; Cole, *Martin Van Buren*, 359.
59. McFaul, *Politics of Jacksonian Finance*, 96–102, 211, quotation from 96. Also see William Shade, *Banks or No Banks: The Money Issue in Western Politics* (Detroit, 1972); Edwin Dodd, *American Business Corporations Until 1860* (Cambridge, Mass., 1954), 276–309.

The depression dealt harshly with state-sponsored internal improvements, and state-run banks suffered even more. Before the downturn had run its course, eight states plus Florida Territory defaulted on interest payments of their bonded indebtedness. All were in the South or West except for Pennsylvania, two-thirds of whose bonds were held overseas. The federal government not only refused to bail out the states but did not even come to the rescue of Florida Territory. American international creditworthiness sustained a heavy blow. The English poet William Wordsworth, whose family had invested in Pennsylvania securities, declared the state's "high repute, with bounteous Nature's aid, / Won confidence, now ruthlessly betrayed."[60]

After prosperity returned, Pennsylvania and most of the other states resumed interest payments, but Arkansas, Mississippi, and Florida (a state after 1845) repudiated the principal itself, as did Michigan in part. The federal government suffered a loss of its own, since it had invested the original endowment of the Smithsonian Institution in Arkansas bonds. This repudiation had long-term effects on the credit rating of states in the South. A generation later, when the Confederacy tried to market securities in London, British banks remembered that their worst credit experiences had been with southern states and that Jefferson Davis of Mississippi had defended repudiation. Accordingly, they limited their commitment.[61]

V

From the Executive Mansion, Martin Van Buren continued to apply the maxim he had expounded in his 1827 letter to Thomas Ritchie, that the Democratic Party must rest upon an alliance of the plain republicans of the North with the slaveowning planters of the South. The president felt comfortable with such an alliance. In New York politics, his faction had shown less enthusiasm than DeWitt Clinton's for the state enacting emancipation. Van Buren's family had owned slaves before New York's emancipation law took effect, and he himself had owned at least one person as late as 1814. Possessing no moral feelings on the subject, the president justified his solicitude for slavery as preserving the Democratic Party and the Union of the states. In waging his campaign in 1836, Van Buren had bent over backward to reassure southern politicians that, although a northerner,

60. William Wordsworth, "To the Pennsylvanians" (1845), in his Poetical Works (Oxford, 1947), IV, 132.
61. William Graham Sumner, History of Banking in the United States (New York, 1896), 395; Jay Sexton, "Debtor Diplomacy: Finance and American Foreign Relations in the Civil War Era, 1837–1873" (D.Phil. thesis, Oxford University, 2003), chap. 1.

he could be trusted to protect their "peculiar institution." He supported censorship of the mails and pledged himself to oppose any effort to abolish slavery in the District of Columbia (where Congress possesses plenary legislative power), a promise he repeated in his inaugural address. When a newspaper in Oneida, New York, backed both Van Buren and abolitionism, his campaign dealt with this embarrassment by instigating a mob (led by a Democratic congressman) to destroy the paper's office.[62] In the House of Representatives, Van Buren's supporters secured passage of a "gag rule" forbidding even the discussion of petitions addressing the subject of slavery either in the District or anywhere else. On the strength of such assurances, the Red Fox had carried several slave states, including Virginia, where he enjoyed the support of Ritchie's Richmond Junto.[63]

Van Buren faithfully fulfilled his proslavery promises once in the White House. His secretary of war, Joel Poinsett of South Carolina, went so far as to demand universal military training for able-bodied white males in their state militias, making sure force would always be available to suppress slave uprisings. (Whigs denounced the proposal as creating a "standing army," and it got nowhere.)[64] Even John C. Calhoun's state could find no fault with the president's dedication to slavery. The radical nullifier Thomas Cooper assured Van Buren that the South Carolina political establishment endorsed him: "Your pledges on the abolition question are felt and approved," he wrote; "they will tell greatly in your favor in the South." When Van Buren ran for reelection in 1840, Calhoun returned to the Democratic fold and supported him. Reversing his long-standing support for national banking, Calhoun embraced the Independent Treasury. In actuality, defending slavery trumped economic policy for the South Carolinian. With his characteristic zeal for abstractions, Calhoun insisted on the Senate passing six resolutions in favor of the "stability and security" of slavery in the South. Well might John Quincy Adams comment in his diary that Van Buren's presidency illustrated the successful synthesis (first achieved, he noted, by Thomas Jefferson) of "the Southern interest in domestic Slavery with the Northern riotous Democracy."[65]

62. Cole, *Martin Van Buren*, 271; David Grimsted, "Rioting in Its Jacksonian Setting," *AHR* 77 (1972): 376, n. 34.

63. See William G. Shade, "Martin Van Buren, Slavery, and the Election of 1836," *JER* 18 (1998): 459–84.

64. John Niven, *Martin Van Buren* (New York, 1983), 464–65; Cole, *Martin Van Buren*, 366–67.

65. Thomas Cooper to Martin Van Buren, March 27, 1837, quoted in W. Cooper, *South and the Politics of Slavery*, 99; John Quincy Adams, Jan. 1, 1840, *Memoirs*, ed. Charles Francis Adams (Philadelphia, 1874–79), X, 182.

White supremacy remained central to Jacksonian Democracy throughout the second party system, no less pervasively than economic development was to Whiggery. Virtually every aspect of the Democratic political outlook supported white supremacy and slavery in particular one way or another: Indian Removal, local autonomy and state sovereignty, respect for property rights, distrust of government economic intervention, criticism of early industrial capitalism, and (as will become evident) Texas annexation.[66] The Democratic Party endorsed slavery and condemned antislavery explicitly and often, not only in the South but in the North. "The whole democracy of the north," declared the *Washington Globe*, national party organ, "are opposed upon constitutional principle, as well as upon sound policy, to any attempt of the abolitionists" to accomplish their purposes.[67] Where congressional Whigs would divide along sectional lines when votes involved slavery, northern Democrats could usually be found supporting their southern colleagues. A study of 1,300 antebellum politicians has identified 320 of them as "doughfaces," that is, northern congressmen who voted with the South on critical issues involving slavery. All but ten of these doughfaces turned out to be Democrats.[68] Van Buren's early strategic decision to ally with slaveholders, like the decisions of local party politicians to play to northern working-class racism, helped make the Democratic Party more proslavery than its rival. But probably the most important determinant of party attitudes existed at the grassroots level. Many Whig voters, particularly those in the northern evangelical, Antimasonic wing of the party, wanted to improve the moral quality of American life and disapproved of slavery. Northern Democratic voters, on the other hand, concerned themselves less with moral issues outside their own local community. Slavery seemed somebody else's problem, one they were content to let their politicians deal with expediently so long as they could rest assured that blacks would not be moving into their neighborhood and competing with them for jobs. From their standpoint, slavery had the virtue of keeping most African Americans in the South.[69]

66. Jean Baker, *Affairs of Party: Political Culture of the Northern Democrats* (Ithaca, N.Y., 1983), esp. 177; John Gerring, *Party Ideologies in America* (Cambridge, Eng., 1998), esp. 165; more generally, Don Fehrenbacher, *The Slaveholding Republic* (Oxford, 2001).

67. *Washington Globe*, May 18, 1835.

68. Leonard Richards, *The Slave Power* (Baton Rouge, 2000), 109–112.

69. See John McFaul, "Expediency or Morality: Jacksonian Politics and Slavery," *JAH* 62 (1975): 24–40; Joel Silbey, *The Partisan Imperative: Dynamics of American Politics Before the Civil War* (New York, 1985), 87–115.

Both Democratic and Whig parties committed themselves to nation-wide organization, and in both cases, the party's felt need to maintain a southern wing inhibited criticism of slavery. But there was an important difference. The Whigs tolerated antislavery among their northern supporters, while the Democrats did not. Congressional voting statistics bear out the generalization that whereas the Whigs divided over slavery, Democratic members, even in the North, toed the party's proslavery line.[70] Democrats who nursed antislavery sentiments were silenced or required to recant as the price of party loyalty. "No man, nor set of men," promised the Democratic Party's *Address to the People of the United States* in 1835, can "even wish to interfere" with southern slavery "and call himself a Democrat."[71] One of the very few Democrats to dare express any sympathy for the abolitionist movement was the journalist William Leggett. Leggett worked for the Democratic *New York Evening Post*, and when its editor, William Cullen Bryant, went to Europe in 1835, he left Leggett temporarily in charge of the paper. Leggett exercised his authority to run editorials condemning the censorship and mob violence directed against abolitionists. The administration, furious, disowned Leggett; Bryant came home to fire him and reclaim control of the *Post*. Leggett, despite years of service to the party, found himself blackballed and his attempt to gain a Democratic nomination for Congress in 1838 thwarted.[72] Another example illustrates the same point. The Christian philanthropists Arthur and Lewis Tappan had a brother named Benjamin who was, like them, a critic of slavery, but, unlike them, a Democrat and a rationalist. When Benjamin Tappan ran for the U.S. Senate from Ohio in 1838, he had to repudiate antislavery as the price of getting the Democratic nomination. Tappan justified his conduct to himself with the reflection that Van Buren's Independent Treasury was more important than the slavery issue.[73] By contrast, in 1838 Ohio's Whig Party elected the ardent abolitionist Joshua Giddings to Congress. Antislavery sentiment was as strong in Massachusetts as in any state of the Union. Marcus Morton, a Massachusetts Democrat, had cautiously expressed antislavery views during his political career. His party required him, however, to repudiate antislavery before confirming him as Collector of the Port of Boston—"thus

---

70. Thomas Alexander, *Sectional Stress and Party Strength* (Nashville, 1967).

71. Quoted in Silbey, *Partisan Imperative*, 90.

72. After Leggett died, the party revoked his excommunication and placed his statue in Tammany Hall. Walter Hugins, *Jacksonian Democracy and the Working Class* (Stanford, 1960), 48.

73. Daniel Feller, "A Brother in Arms: Benjamin Tappan and the Antislavery Democracy," *JAH* 88 (2001): 48–74.

demonstrating," in the words of a historian sympathetic to Morton, "how little room then existed in the Massachusetts (or for that matter, the Northern) Democracy for an antislavery politician."[74] Meanwhile the two-thirds rule at Democratic National Conventions made sure that no one could receive the party's presidential nomination without southern support. The Whigs had no such rule, and sometimes the northern wing of their party got the nominee it wanted. In shaping the Democratic Party the way they did, Andrew Jackson and Martin Van Buren forged the instrument that would transform the minority proslavery interest into a majority that would dominate American politics until 1861. The "slave power" of which abolitionists and free-soilers complained was no figment of their imagination.[75]

VI

Political opposition to the slave power in these years came chiefly over the so-called gag rule. With their mass mailings to southern addresses shut out, abolitionists had turned to circulating antislavery petitions to Congress. The gag rule, preventing the discussion of these petitions in the House of Representatives, represented another aspect of southern politicians' continuing efforts to prevent the abolitionists from influencing public opinion. "The moral power of the world is against us," Francis Pickens of South Carolina warned his fellow southerners. "England has emancipated her West Indies islands. France is also moving in the same direction." In an age of improved communication, only an intellectual blockade could resist the spread of the idea of freedom. "Sooner or later, we shall have to contend" with abolitionism; better to stifle its expression now, before it gets any stronger, he insisted.[76] Abolitionists exercised the right "to petition the government for a redress of grievances" guaranteed by the Bill of Rights. No one dared prohibit them from composing, circulating, or signing their petitions, but southerners like Pickens wanted to deny abolitionists the chance to use Congress as a forum to publicize their views.

The gag rule complemented the censorship of the mails and, like that policy, originated with the extremists of South Carolina. James H.

---

74. Jonathan Earle, "Marcus Morton and the Dilemma of Jacksonian Antislavery in Massachusetts," *Massachusetts Historical Review* 4 (2002), 60–87, quotation from 63.

75. See Silbey, *Partisan Imperative*, 87–93; and Leonard Richards, *The Slave Power* (Baton Rouge, 2000).

76. Francis Pickens in the House of Representatives, Jan. 21, 1836, quoted in Freehling, *Secessionists at Bay*, 311.

Hammond, a young Carolinian hothead, conceived the idea that the Houses of Congress should refuse to receive petitions touching slavery on the grounds that Congress had no authority over the subject. The whole Calhoun clique picked up on the notion, hoping it would further their long-term strategy of uniting the South under their leadership; perhaps thus Calhoun could realize the White House ambitions he still nursed. The project required them to make two constitutional arguments: one, that Congress lacked legal authority to abolish slavery anywhere, even in the District of Columbia; and two, that the freedom of petition guaranteed by the Bill of Rights did not imply that the government would pay any attention to petitions once delivered. The Carolinians were on much stronger ground in the second of these arguments than in the first, but both issues got debated at length. In the Senate, Calhoun's proposal for a gag rule ran into opposition from Henry Clay and others. An informal practice soon substituted for a formal gag. As soon as a senator introduced an abolitionist petition, another would move that "the question of its reception be laid on the table." A motion to table an issue is not debatable. The motion would carry and the petition be quietly buried without discussion, action, or even official reception. This practice prevailed from 1836 to 1850. The Senate, despite its fame as a chamber indulgent of long debate, contrived thus to stifle debate over slavery.[77]

However, most petitions in those days went to the House of Representatives, because it was the people's chamber, senators being chosen by state legislators. The House scheduled a considerable amount of time for members to present petitions and had rules governing the process. With its larger, more disparate and disorderly membership, elected directly and every two years, the House could not resolve the petition issue as readily as the Senate.

The House Democratic leaders of 1836 refused to let the pariah Calhoun seize credit with southerners for resolving this issue. They picked up on a rival version of the gag, suggested by another South Carolinian, Henry Pinckney. Pinckney's rule resembled the Senate's practice. It would allow antislavery petitions to be received but then immediately "table" them—that is, lay them aside with no discussion. This process still effectively insulated Congress from the petitioners' opinions, while not raising the awkward constitutional questions of the Calhounite approach.

---

77. William Lee Miller, *Arguing Against Slavery* (New York, 1996), 115–19; Lonnie Maness, "Henry Clay and the Problem of Slavery" (Ph.D. diss., Memphis State University, 1980), 153–61; Daniel Wirls, "The Overlooked Senate Gag Rule," *JER* 27 (2007): 115–38.

The southern followers of Hugh Lawson White, originally attracted by the Hammond-Calhoun proposal, climbed on board Pinckney's bandwagon. The House adopted Pinckney's version of the rule on May 26, 1836, 117 to 68, with most southerners and northern Democrats voting for the gag over the opposition of northern Whigs. With a presidential election pending, the Van Buren and White campaigns had together successfully preempted Calhoun's little band as protectors of slavery.[78]

The instigators of the gag had reckoned without John Quincy Adams. The elder statesman of the House persistently criticized, evaded, subverted, and undermined the gag rule. He presented himself as defending, not the substance of the abolitionists' views, but their constitutional right of petition. (He himself supported gradual emancipation, not the immediate abolition of slavery, and introduced a constitutional amendment to that effect, knowing, of course, that it had no chance of passage.) As great a master of parliamentary procedure as any member of Congress in history, Adams invented innumerable devices for getting around the gag. He introduced petitions at the start of each session before the rules had been officially adopted, then would challenge the continuation of the gag and force a vote on it. He would inquire of the Speaker whether a certain petition was permissible and then read from it. He would ask if a petition could be referred to a committee instructed to explain why it could not be granted. People sent him petitions not only from his constituency but from all over the country, cleverly worded so as not quite to fall under the ban. Many of the petitions now asked for the repeal of the gag rule. It was he, of course, who named it "the gag." In his dogged battle, Old Man Eloquent earned the respect of his bitterest foes. The Virginia state-righter Henry Wise called him "the acutest, the astutest, the archest enemy of Southern slavery that ever existed."[79]

Although Adams did not share the abolitionists' belief in immediate, uncompensated emancipation, his efforts proved of incalculable benefit to them. They responded by circulating more petitions than ever. Many of their petitions were signed by people who could not otherwise participate in the political process: women and free blacks from states where they could not vote. Southern members expressed contempt for women signatories, but the son of Abigail Adams defended them. Why should women be "fitted for nothing but the cares of domestic life?" he demanded. "Women are not only justified, but exhibit the most exalted virtue when they do depart from the domestic circle, and enter on the

78. George Rable, "Slavery, Politics, and the South," *Capitol Studies* 3 (1975): 69–87.
79. Quoted in Miller, *Arguing Against Slavery*, 356.

concerns of their country, of humanity, and of their God." He cited biblical heroines like Esther and Deborah. Adams contrived to present petitions from white women and—though it caused consternation—from free black women. Then, on February 6, 1837, he came into the House with "a petition from twenty-two persons, declaring themselves to be slaves," provoking a huge uproar, even though the document purported to endorse slavery. (It was probably a hoax perpetrated by racists to embarrass Adams, but he turned it to good account.) The House promptly passed a new rule: "*Resolved*, that slaves do not possess the right of petition secured to the people of the United States by the constitution."[80]

The attempt to gag abolition petitions proved massively counterproductive. The debates over the gag rule and Adams's tactics to get around it made much more news than abolitionist petitions left to themselves ever would. The press covered it all in greatest detail, newspapers often printing in full the speeches in Congress. Frustrated in his attempt to shape government policies, Adams now bid to influence public opinion and scored a success.[81] The constitutional right of white people to petition aroused more widespread interest and sympathy among the northern public than did the hope of black slaves for emancipation. Aided by all this publicity, the number of petitions coming to the House ballooned. Historians have tried to count the antislavery petitions remaining in the congressional archives from this period, though their efforts are still fragmentary. The House of Representatives, for the four-month session during the winter of 1838–39, had 1,496 petitions relating to antislavery on file, bearing 163,845 signatures from 101,850 different people. As the abolitionists became more adept at circulating them, the number of signatories per petition increased; between 1836 and 1840 the average rose from 32 per petition to 107. An all-female petition from Massachusetts against slavery in the District of Columbia set a record in 1836–37 with the signatures of 21,000 women.[82] The petition drive represented a remarkable achievement for the abolition movement and, thanks to Adams, an embarrassment to the slave power.

---

80. Ibid., 321, 230, 271; *Speech of John Quincy Adams upon the Right of the People, Men and Women, to Petition* (Washington, 1838), 64–81. See further Susan Zaeske, *Signatures of Citizenship* (Chapel Hill, 2003).
81. On Adams and public opinion, see Richard R. John, "John Quincy Adams" in *Reader's Companion to the American Presidency*, ed. Alan Brinkley and Davis Dyer (Boston, 2000), 83–90.
82. Dwight Dumond, *Antislavery* (Ann Arbor, Mich., 1961), 245–46; Edward Magdol, *The Antislavery Rank and File* (Westport, Conn., 1986), 55–56.

VII

Van Buren sealed his white supremacist policy by carrying out Jackson's Indian Removal. The notorious forced march of the Cherokees along the Trail of Tears occurred on Van Buren's watch. In trying to implement Removal, Van Buren also renewed Jackson's conflict with the Seminoles and wound up fighting the Second Florida War, the longest and most costly of all the army's Indian Wars. The issues Jackson had faced, the Seminoles' independence and the refuge they offered to fugitive black slaves, persisted. Whites said the Seminoles kept the runaways as slaves of their own; this would facilitate reenslaving the blacks while sending the Native Americans off to Oklahoma. In reality, however, the African Americans lived in separate villages with their own farms and animals as tenants, paying a portion of their crop to the local Seminole chief. Only a minority of them were slaves of the Indians in any sense, and even they were permitted to live largely autonomously. Sometimes the African Americans intermarried with the Seminoles, and some of them achieved positions of high influence, particularly linguists who could interpret among English, Spanish, and Muskogee.[83]

So few were the Seminoles in number (some five thousand men, women, and children, plus perhaps a thousand blacks), and so remote and inhospitable their lands, that the government could well have ignored their refusal to remove to Oklahoma. That it did not do so was mostly owing to pressure from slaveholders who resented the refuge available to runaways. As General Thomas Jesup accurately declared, "This, you may be assured is a negro and not an Indian war."[84] Once begun, the war dragged on through seven years (1835–42) and six army commanders; repeated promises of victory in sight proved premature. Early in the conflict the Seminoles raided plantations, where they recruited slaves to join their cause; later, however, they waged a defensive guerrilla war. The army—with help from the navy along Florida's coasts, rivers, and swamps—ended up waging economic warfare against the Natives' villages, farms, and herds. The soldiers' morale became a major problem, not only because of disease, insects, and the dangerous sawgrass, but also because many of them agreed with Major Ethan Allen Hitchcock, who wrote in his diary that the treaty the government was trying to impose constituted "a fraud on the Indians: They never approved of it or signed

---

83. George Klos, "Blacks and the Seminole Removal Debate," *Florida Historical Quarterly* 68 (1989): 55–78.
84. Thomas Jesup to Roger Jones, March 6, 1837, quoted in Kevin Mulroy, *Freedom on the Border: The Seminole Maroons* (Lubbock, Tex., 1993), 29.

it. They are right in defending their homes and we ought to let them alone."[85]

A significant turning point in the war came with the capture of Osceola, leader of a combined Indian and black band and an irreconcilable opponent of Removal, along with ninety-four other Seminoles on October 22, 1837. When the American public learned that the capture had been effected by treachery under a flag of truce, there was an outcry leading to a debate on the floor of Congress. Far from letting this reaction deter him, General Jesup violated a flag of truce again the following spring to seize over five hundred more Seminoles, 151 of them warriors. Osceola did not survive long in the dungeon at Fort Moultrie, Charleston; he died there of malaria in January 1838. Admired by friend and foe alike, Osceola is honored today in the names of twenty towns, three counties, two townships, one borough, two lakes, two mountains, a state park, and a national forest.[86]

In August 1842, the federal government granted the army's request to announce that the war had been won and leave Florida, although about 600 irreconcilable Seminoles remained at large with no peace treaty.[87] The black Seminoles succeeded in getting the government to promise that they would not be reenslaved by the whites but would remove to freedom in Oklahoma. In the event some five hundred did so, though others—perhaps as many as four hundred—found themselves enslaved.[88] The war had cost between $30 million and $40 million (half to three-quarters of a billion in our terms) as well as the lives of 1,466 servicemen, three quarters of whom died of disease. Other war deaths included fifty-five militiamen, more than one hundred white civilians, and at least several hundred Seminoles.[89]

Van Buren encountered difficulties not only along the southern but also along the northern frontier, although the problems there were quite different in origin. Chastened by the experience of the Seminole War and

85. Journal entry for Nov. 4, 1840, in Ethan Allen Hitchcock, *Fifty Years in Camp and Field*, ed. W. A. Croffut (New York, 1909), 122.
86. John K. Mahon, *History of the Second Seminole War* (Gainesville, Fla., 1991), 214–18, 237.
87. James Covington, *The Seminoles of Florida* (Gainesville, Fla., 1993), 108–9.
88. Jill Watts says that records show nine hundred blacks registered for removal, and since only five hundred reached Oklahoma, most likely the others were sold. "Seminole Black Perceptions and the Second Seminole War," *UCLA Historical Journal* 7 (1986): 23. Certainly some were returned to white or Creek Indian masters.
89. Covington, *Seminoles of Florida*, 72.

the embarrassment it brought his administration, the president decided against pressuring the Iroquois to leave New York.[90] Even so, his home state gave him plenty of trouble. This arose in 1837 from abortive rebellions against British rule in Canada. In Quebec (then called Lower Canada), the rebellion fed upon long-standing French–Canadian grievances, but in Ontario (Upper Canada), the rebels were often migrants from the United States who wanted the Canadian government to be more like the American; some even nursed hopes of American annexation. Their Scottish-born leader, William Mackenzie, admired Andrew Jackson and blamed the Panic of 1837 (from which Canada suffered too) on the bankers. Invoking memories of the American Revolution, the rebels called themselves "Patriots." When pro-British Canadians quickly put down their uprising, some of the Upper Canada rebels found refuge and sympathy across the border in the United States. In Buffalo, Mackenzie won over followers for his cause, many of them laborers thrown out of work by the panic, promising them homesteads in Ontario after his victory. Led by an upper-class demagogue named Rensselaer Van Rensselaer, hundreds of would-be liberators of Canada occupied an island on the Canadian side of the Niagara River about a mile above the Falls, from which they threatened to renew the rebellion. On December 29, 1837, an American steamboat, the *Caroline*, carried reinforcements and supplies to the island; that night fifty Canadian militiamen came over to the U.S. side, drove off the *Caroline*'s crew, killed a bystander, set fire to the ship, and sank her in the middle of the river. This constituted a major international incident, and passions ran high on both sides of the border.[91]

Six days later, news of the *Caroline* reached the White House, intruding on a dinner party the hospitable president was giving for his Whig congressional opponents. Van Buren resolved to continue Jackson's policy of good relations with Britain rather than go to the aid of Canada's rebellious Jacksonians. He conferred then and there with Henry Clay to ensure bipartisan support for a conciliatory policy. Statesmanlike, he declined to exploit the strain of Anglophobia in American public opinion, particularly strong among Democratic voters; instead he drew upon the British goodwill he had cultivated while minister in London. The president sent the commander of the army, General Winfield Scott, to Buffalo to enforce "peace with honor" (Van Buren's term). Scott had no military force at his disposal, since the small U.S. Army was tied down in Florida, and it

90. Niven, *Martin Van Buren*, 465–66, 674 n. 42.
91. Gerald Craig, *Upper Canada: The Formative Years* (1963; Toronto, 1984), 241–51; Colin Read, *The Rising in Western Upper Canada* (Toronto, 1982).

did not appear that New York state militia would be reliable. By sheer energy and willpower Scott calmed the public and persuaded Van Rensselaer to evacuate his island bastion, though at one point the general had to face down an angry American crowd by drawing a line and telling them that they would cross it only over his dead body. It was one of the era's few triumphs of law and order over mob action. But the militant Patriot sympathizers on the U.S. side of the border went underground into secret societies (called "Hunting Lodges") to pursue the overthrow of British authority in Canada. "Filibustering"—private armed interventions in other nations—was common in the antebellum United States, usually directed against Latin American countries, but in this case aimed to the north.[92]

In May 1838, a party of American "Hunters" got revenge for the *Caroline* by burning a Canadian vessel, the *Sir Robert Peel*, while it was in U.S. waters. In November and December of that year, two filibustering expeditions invaded Ontario with about fourteen hundred armed Patriots. Canadian militia and a few British regulars overpowered the attackers, leaving at least twenty-five of them dead and virtually all the rest captured. Of the prisoners, seventeen were executed and seventy-eight transported to the British penal colony in Van Dieman's Land (Tasmania); the rest were released back into the United States.[93] It became clear that Canada had a stable government able to defend itself, and the Hunter movement began to lose its appeal. American authorities jailed Mackenzie for violations of U.S. neutrality laws; Van Buren released him after he had served ten months of an eighteen-month sentence. Eventually popular passions subsided somewhat, with full diplomatic resolution of outstanding issues (notably the *Caroline*) wisely left for high-level discussions after the presidential election of 1840. In surmounting the Canadian crisis, Van Buren gave a more creditable performance than he generally managed in domestic affairs, though at some political cost to the New York Democratic Party. The Americans forgot about Canada (as they usually do), but north of the border the episode reinforced memories of U.S. invasions in 1776 and 1812 and nurtured the fear of American imperialism. In 1849, William Mackenzie was allowed to return home to Upper Canada and reenter political life there.[94]

---

92. For Van Buren's perspective, see Wilson, *Presidency of Van Buren*, 157–62; Cole, *Martin Van Buren*, 321–25.

93. Albert Corey, *The Crisis of 1830–1842 in Canadian–American Relations* (New Haven, 1941), 121.

94. The fullest account of all these events is Kenneth Stevens, *Border Diplomacy* (Tuscaloosa, Ala., 1989). See also Reginald Stuart, *United States Expansionism and British North America* (Chapel Hill, 1988), 126–47.

VIII

Sengbe Pieh, a twenty-five-year-old farmer, lived in the Upper Mende country of what is now Sierra Leone in West Africa. Married, the father of three children, he came from a prominent local family. One day in late January 1839, four assailants kidnapped Sengbe as he tended his fields. Turned over as a slave to the son of the Vai King Manna Siaka, he was marched to the coast and sold to a Spanish slave trader named Pedro Blanco. Sengbe's plight illustrated the efficiency of the flourishing West African slave business. After captivity in one of the forbidding slave prisons (called "factories") of Lomboko on the Gallinas coast, he and five hundred other men, women, and children found themselves loaded onto the Portuguese slave ship *Tecora* for shipment to the Spanish colony of Cuba in April. Their ensuing ordeal illustrated all too well the horrors of the notorious Middle Passage: In suffocatingly close confinement under unsanitary conditions, with a shortage of water and no protection against contagious diseases, over a third of the captives died on the two-month trip.[95]

Instead of sailing openly into Havana, the *Tecora* unloaded its human cargo quietly at night in a secret cove, from which the survivors marched across country in June to the barracoons (slave pens) of Havana for auction. This back door entry into Cuba reflected the fact that although slavery was legal in the Spanish Empire, the importation of slaves from Africa was not. Officially, the Spanish government had followed the example of Britain and the United States in outlawing the Atlantic slave trade. Royal Navy cruisers patrolled both the African and Cuban coasts and from time to time seized a ship engaged in the slave trade, confiscating the vessel and liberating its cargo. (The U.S. Navy did a little patrolling against slavers too, but less effectively.) Unfortunately, this evil commerce yielded profits so high that traders could afford to write off the loss of an occasional ship as a business expense. In Cuba, high slave mortality on the sugar plantations necessitated continued importation, so the colonial authorities ignored Madrid's pronouncements and notoriously collaborated with the smugglers of slaves in return for unofficial payoffs. The local authorities issued fake documents indicating that the *Tecora*'s Africans were Cuban-born slaves and giving each one a Spanish name. Singbe Pieh became José Cinquez (later rendered Joseph Cinque in U.S. records). In the barracoon, a Cuban plantation owner named Pepe Ruíz

---

95. The following account is based largely on Howard Jones, *Mutiny on the Amistad*, rev. ed. (New York, 1988), with additional information from Arthur Abraham, *The Amistad Revolt* (Freetown, Sierra Leone, 1987).

bought Cinque and forty-eight other men (sugar planters preferred males) for $450 each; Pedro Montes bought four children (three girls and a boy). The two agreed to send their new chattels together along the Cuban coast to Puerto Principe, where their plantations were.

On the night of June 18, 1839, a coasting vessel called the *Amistad* (built in Baltimore, where she had been christened the *Friendship*) took on board the fifty-three Africans, their two owners, and a small crew. The captain expected the trip to take three days but storms slowed them down. On the third night, Cinque picked the lock on his collar-chain with a nail, then freed his companions. They found knives for cutting sugarcane in the hold. Bursting onto the deck, the mutineers quickly overpowered the crew, killing the captain and the cook. They left Ruíz, Montes, and the black cabin boy alive to navigate the ship, ordering them to set course for Africa. Cinque took charge, doling out the precious water and food (he allowed the children more, and took the smallest ration for himself). But Montes managed to trick the Africans by sailing slowly eastward during the day (when they could tell direction from the sun) and more rapidly northwest at night. By August 25, when the *Amistad* wound up in Long Island Sound desperately short of provisions, ten of the Africans had died. Cinque had no choice but to lead a party ashore to buy supplies with Spanish gold doubloons. There the *Amistad* was apprehended and seized by the USS *Washington*, commanded by Lieutenant Thomas Gedney, who took her into the port of New London, Connecticut. Her passengers were confined to the jail in New Haven until the courts could sort out what to do about them.

The Spanish government demanded that the Africans be returned to Cuba, both as slaves who should be restored to their owners and as accused criminals who should be extradited. The Van Buren administration, wanting to demonstrate abhorrence of slave uprisings with a presidential election a year away, seemed only too eager to comply with Spain's wishes. It looked like Cinque and his companions would end up on a hangman's rope in Havana as an example to slaves considering rebellion. But a committee of abolitionists headed by Lewis Tappan arranged for a skilled legal team to aid them. To solve the problem of communicating with their clients, the lawyers turned to Yale's professor of linguistics. Professor J. W. Gibbs correctly identified the language the Africans spoke (Mende) and after a search of New York and Connecticut wharves found an African-born sailor who could interpret. When the case went to trial in November, the defense could argue that Cinque and the others had never been rightfully enslaved; they were free people kidnapped and sold in violation of Spain's own laws. To underscore this point, the lawyers brought charges in a New York state court against Ruíz and Montes for kidnapping. Arrested, the two Spaniards jumped their bail, fled to Cuba, and did not appear in the U.S. courts again.

The issue was tried (as an admiralty case, without a jury) before federal District Judge Andrew Judson. United States District Attorney William Holabird argued that Ruíz and Montes legally owned the prisoners, relying on their Cuban documents. Judge Judson, a lifelong Democrat appointed to the bench by Van Buren, had earlier led the movement to shut down Prudence Crandall's high school for black girls in Connecticut. Everyone now expected him to rule against the prisoners. The administration went to the extraordinary lengths of having a navy schooner await the verdict in New London's dangerously icy harbor, ready to spirit them away to Cuba before an appeal could be lodged. But the dramatic testimony of Cinque and other Africans, given through an interpreter and substantiated by an Englishman resident in Havana who knew how widely the laws against importing slaves were flouted, demolished the credibility of the false documents. On January 13, 1840, Judson ruled that the Africans were legally free and had therefore been justified in resisting their captivity. The judge ordered the government to send Cinque and his companions back to the Mende country. The district attorney, upon orders from the president, appealed.[96]

The federal circuit court affirmed the district court's decision in May 1840. Again the administration appealed. The United States Supreme Court heard argument in January 1841; by then the presidential election was over. All this time Cinque and the other Africans awaited the outcome in New Haven jail, suffering unfamiliar diseases and cold temperatures, trying to keep up their spirits, studying English and Christianity. More of them died. To reinforce the abolitionist legal team, Tappan persuaded seventy-three-year-old former president John Quincy Adams to participate. A lawyer in his youth, Adams had last appeared before the High Court in 1809. Roger Baldwin, who had ably represented the Africans throughout, covered the legal issues in oral argument. Adams used his appearance to denounce the conduct of the administration, which had denied documents to the defense, misrepresented the case to congressional committees, and tried to take control of it away from the judiciary. A hearer interpreted Adams's speech as one president putting another president on trial.[97]

---

96. On legal aspects of the case, see Don Fehrenbacher, *The Slaveholding Republic* (New York, 2001), 191–95; on Van Buren's role in it, see Wilson, *Presidency of Van Buren*, 155–56.

97. *Argument of John Quincy Adams, Before the Supreme Court of the United States, in the Case of the United States, Appellants, vs. Cinque, and Others, Africans* (New York, 1841).

Joseph Story delivered the opinion of the Supreme Court on March 9, 1841. By a vote of 6 to 1, with one justice not participating and another having recently died, the Court declared the Mendeans free. Only Antonio the cabin boy had been legally a slave of the ship's captain. (Rather than accept return to Cuba, Antonio escaped along the underground railway to Montreal.) The chief difference between Story's decision and the original verdict in district court was that the Supreme Court did not order the government to take the Africans home.[98] Instead, the abolitionists faced one more responsibility: raising money to hire transatlantic transportation. The four African children had become fond of their Connecticut foster-parents (the jailer and his wife) and did not wish to leave, but were forcibly separated from them. On November 27, 1841, the bark *Gentleman* set sail for Africa, bearing thirty-five of her lost people back, along with James Covey, the Mendean sailor who had acted as their interpreter, and five Christian missionaries, two of them African Americans. Shortly before their departure, Cinque and two other Mendeans wrote a letter to John Quincy Adams revealing, among other things, their progress in English.

> Most Respected Sir,—the Mendi people give you thanks for all your kindness to them. They will never forget your defence of their rights before the great Court of Washington. They feel that they owe to you in a large measure, their delivery from the Spaniards, and from slavery or death. They will pray for you as long as you live, Mr. Adams. May God bless and reward you.
>
> We are about to go home to Africa. . . . We will take the Bible with us. It has been a precious book, in prison, and we love to read it now we are free.[99]

Tragically, Cinque returned to find his home village ruined by war and his family missing. It was all too typical of the turmoil in West Africa during the era of the slave trade. But with Cinque's help, the American Missionary Association founded a Mendi Mission. The association exerted a lasting influence with its schools for Africans and (after the Civil War) for African Americans in the South.[100]

98. *United States v. Claimants of the Amistad*, 40 U.S. (15 Peters) 518 (1841).
99. Cinque, Kinna, and Kale to John Quincy Adams, Nov. 6, 1841, in John Blassingame, ed., *Slave Testimony: Two Centuries of Letters, Speeches, Interviews, and Autobiographies* (Baton Rouge, 1977), 42–43.
100. The assertion made by some historians that Cinque became a slave trader after his return home rests on no evidence. See Howard Jones, "Cinque of the *Amistad* a Slave Trader? Perpetuating a Myth," *JAH* 87 (2000): 923–39.

Despite the Supreme Court's decision, the Spanish government continued to press the American government, not to return the slaves themselves (now obviously impossible), but for financial compensation to their owners. The Spanish invoked precedent: When American ships engaged in the coastwise slave trade had blown off course from time to time into the British West Indies, the British had freed the slaves but, after strenuous representations by the Van Buren administration, paid compensation for them.[101] The administrations of Tyler and Polk recommended appropriations to reimburse the Spanish owners of the *Amistad* and its human cargo, but faced with strong northern Whig opposition, Congress never acted.

To a large extent Van Buren's term played out events that Jackson had set in motion. Andrew Jackson succeeded in stamping his character upon the Democratic Party, which remained loyal to the policies he had defined even after he left the White House. The party proclaimed itself the tribune of the common white man, as against all other groups in the society, whether of class, race, or gender. In particular, it defined itself, even in the North, as the protector of slavery. Jackson's opposition to abolitionism turned out to be of more long-term significance to the Democratic Party than his opposition to nullification. Jackson's loyal follower, the prominent Pennsylvania Democrat James Buchanan, future president, spoke for the whole next generation of his party. "All Christendom is leagued against the South upon this question of domestic slavery," he acknowledged; slaveholders "have no other allies to sustain their constitutional rights, except the Democracy of the North." Democrats from the North, Buchanan proudly proclaimed, "inscribe upon our banners hostility to abolition. It is there one of the cardinal principles of the Democratic Party."[102] Some of the shortcomings in the party's policies became apparent during the term of Jackson's chosen successor: in limitations on debate that exacerbated debate, in prolonged and unpopular war to enforce Indian Removal, in futile litigation to return kidnapped Africans into illegal slavery. Most important in turning public opinion against Jacksonianism in 1840 was the economic crisis that, arising to a considerable extent out of Jackson's actions, cast a shadow over the term of his genial heir. The talent for manipulation that had served Van Buren so well in pursuit of his presidential ambition proved no help in the face of economic depression. Meanwhile, beyond the swings of the business cycle, long-term economic developments were transforming America in directions that Jacksonians did not always approve and certainly did not wish the federal government to foster.

101. Wilson, *Presidency of Van Buren*, 154.
102. *Congressional Globe*, 27th Cong., 3rd sess. (Aug. 19, 1842), appendix, 103.

The Varied Talents of Professor Morse

Samuel Finley Breese Morse claimed to be "the inventor" of the telegraph, although others contested this claim and rival systems of electric telegraphy also existed. *Courtesy of the Smithsonian Institution.*

Portrait of James Monroe, painted during his presidency by Samuel F. B. Morse. *White House Historical Association (White House Collection).*

Original telegraph receiver, used in Baltimore to receive Morse's message on May 24, 1844. *Courtesy of Cornell University College of Engineering.*

Believers in Improvement

James Madison, as he looked while president. *White House Historical Association (White House Collection).*

John Quincy Adams, painted while Secretary of State by Gilbert Stuart. *White House Historical Association (White House Collection).*

DeWitt Clinton, Governor of New York, responsible for the Erie Canal. Painted by Rembrandt Peale. *Courtesy of The Historical Society of Pennsylvania Collection, Atwater Kent Museum of Philadelphia.*

Henry Clay in 1842, as leader of the Congressional Whig majority, advocate of the "American System." *Library of Congress.*

Religious Leaders

Rev. Charles Grandison Finney, when he went to Oberlin College in 1835. *Courtesy of Oberlin College Archives, Oberlin, Ohio.*

Bishop Richard Allen, founder of the African Methodist Episcopal Church. *National Portrait Gallery, Smithsonian Institution /Art Resource, NY.*

Joseph Smith, Jr., president of the Latter-day Saint Church, prophet, seer, revelator. Based on a portrait painted in Nauvoo, Illinois. *Library of Congress.*

Lucretia Coffin Mott, Hicksite Quaker minister, abolitionist, advocate for women's rights. *Library of Congress.*

Gender Roles in Religion and Politics

This lithograph of a camp meeting in 1830 shows mostly women attending to a male preacher. Some auditors are strongly affected by the revival; others seem merely curious. Tents are pitched in the background, for people would come long distances and stay for several days. *Courtesy of the Library Company of Philadelphia.*

Engraving of George Caleb Bingham, *The County Election*, shows the all-male polling place where voting would go on for two or three days to allow farmers to come in to the county seat. Both the strengths and weaknesses of democracy appear: some men discuss politics earnestly, others get drunk. Voting is not secret. *Courtesy of Saint Louis Art Museum, Friends Fund.*

The Nobility of Industry

And the gospel must first be published among all nations.

An allegorical celebration of the printing press as an aid to the conversion of the world to Christianity, produced by the American Tract Society. *Courtesy of the American Antiquarian Society.*

Pat Lyon at the Forge, by John Neagle (1829). Starting out as a blacksmith, Patrick Lyon turned his mechanical and technological talents to advantage. He had become a wealthy man when he commissioned this heroic portrait of himself in his youth. *Courtesy of the Pennsylvania Academy of the Fine Arts, Gift of the Lyon Family.*

The Transportation Revolution

Early steamboats, like early trains, had horrific safety records. The steamer *Ben Sherod* exploded and burned on the Mississippi River, May 8, 1837. *Library of Congress.*

The first railroad cars sometimes resembled stagecoaches, just as the first automobiles looked like horse-drawn carriages. This locomotive and two passenger cars operated on the Baltimore & Ohio Railroad in 1832. *Library of Congress.*

Images of Andrew Jackson and His Adversaries

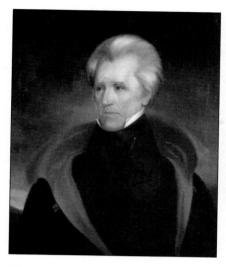

The painter Ralph Earl portrayed President Jackson as a saddened, dignified patriarch in 1835. *White House Historical Association (White House Collection).*

The sculptor Clark Mills celebrated Jackson as a military hero in this famous bronze statue he began in 1847. Three identical casts exist: in Washington, New Orleans, and Nashville. *From* Conjectures of Order: Intellectual Life and the American South, 1810–1860, Vol. 2, *by Michael O'Brien (Chapel Hill: University of North Carolina Press, 2004).*

Nicholas Biddle, President of the Bank of the United States, was depicted by the famous artist Thomas Sully in 1826 as a romantic idealist. *Courtesy of the Andalusia Foundation.*

John C. Calhoun, nationalist-turned-nullifier, portrayed in a Roman toga by the neoclassicist sculptor Hiram Powers in 1835. *Courtesy of Yale University Art Gallery. Given by the fellows and associates in memory of Stanley Thomas Williams, B.A. 1911, M.A. 1914, Ph.D. 1915, to Calhoun College.*

Native Americans Encounter Invaders

Printed version of the syllabary Sequoyah invented for the Cherokee language, based on the model of a language he never learned. *Courtesy of the Boston Athenaeum.*

John Ross, Principal Chief of the Cherokees, defended his homeland through legal and political means but lost in the end. *Library of Congress.*

Osceola, Seminole warrior, defended his homeland in battle, but also lost. *Courtesy of Smithsonian American Art Museum, Washington, DC / Art Resource, NY.*

Political Cartoons

Jackson's opponents viewed him as a tyrant trampling on the Constitution, internal improvements, and the national bank. Later, they adopted the name "Whigs," a traditional term for opponents of royal power. *Library of Congress.*

Jackson's followers saw him as defending republican virtue and his removal of federal deposits from the national bank as the destruction of a corrupt monopoly. The papers scattered on the ground are all pro-bank periodicals. "Major Jack Downing," a comic representation of the common man, cheers Jackson on, speaking in dialect and using a racial epithet. *Courtesy of the American Antiquarian Society.*

Antislavery

The Greek Slave by Hiram Powers (1845) depicts a nude Christian bound for a Turkish slave market. Intended as support for Greek independence, abolitionists made it a statement against slavery all over the world and a reminder of the sexual exploitation to which slave women were exposed. The statue helped legitimate the artistic display of nudity in puritanical America. *Courtesy of the Yale University Art Gallery, Olive Louise Dann Fund.*

Most pictures of William Lloyd Garrison show him in advanced years; this one portrays the thirty-year-old editor of *The Liberator. Library of Congress.*

This drawing of the millenarian antislavery crusader Sojourner Truth appeared as the frontispiece to her autobiography. *Women's History Website.*

The Post-Jackson Presidents

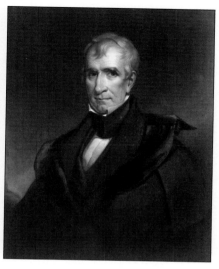

Martin Van Buren. This portrait hints at the ingratiating politeness which charmed even the President's political opponents. *White House Historical Association (White House Collection).*

William Henry Harrison. His long career in public life was capped by a tragically short time as president. *Library of Congress.*

John Tyler. Last of a long line of aristocratic Virginian presidents before the Civil War. *Courtesy of the National Portrait Gallery, Smithsonian Institution / Art Resource, NY.*

James Knox Polk. Photography, invented by the Frenchman Louis Daguerre in 1839, was just beginning to be practiced in the United States during Polk's term. *Library of Congress.*

Nationalists

John Marshall, as he looked the year he decided *Cherokee Nation v. Georgia* (1831). *Courtesy of the National Portrait Gallery, Smithsonian Institution / Art Resource, NY.*

Daniel Webster, nicknamed "Black Dan" for his dark hair, eyebrows, and complexion, at the time of the Nullification Crisis (1832–33). *Library of Congress.*

Abraham Lincoln, as he looked when running for Congress in Illinois (1846). *Library of Congress.*

Zachary Taylor, as a war hero running for president in 1848. When elected, he took a strongly nationalist position in a confrontation with Texas (1850). *Library of Congress.*

Intellectuals of the American Renaissance

William Ellery Channing, pioneer of the American Renaissance, a hero to believers in human dignity, both in the United States and abroad. *Courtesy of the National Portrait Gallery, Smithsonian Institution / Art Resource, NY.*

Ralph Waldo Emerson, most popular of the writers and lecturers known as the Transcendentalists. *Library of Congress.*

Margaret Fuller developed a theoretical basis for feminism out of Transcendentalist principles. *Library of Congress.*

Frederick Douglass denounced slavery and affirmed the equality of all human beings, regardless of race or gender. *Courtesy of National Portrait Gallery, Smithsonian Institution / Art Resource, NY.*

The War with Mexico

This lithograph of the Battle of Monterey, idealizing the heroism of the American attackers, portrays the fierce house-to-house fighting. *Library of Congress.*

This engraving, based on a painting by Richard Caton Woodville, shows how eagerly the public awaited news from the front during the war. Two African Americans and a woman, wanting to hear too, are relegated to the margins of the crowd. A single periodical or book often served many persons, and reading aloud was common practice. *Courtesy of the American Antiquarian Society.*

Scott's Entrance into Mexico City

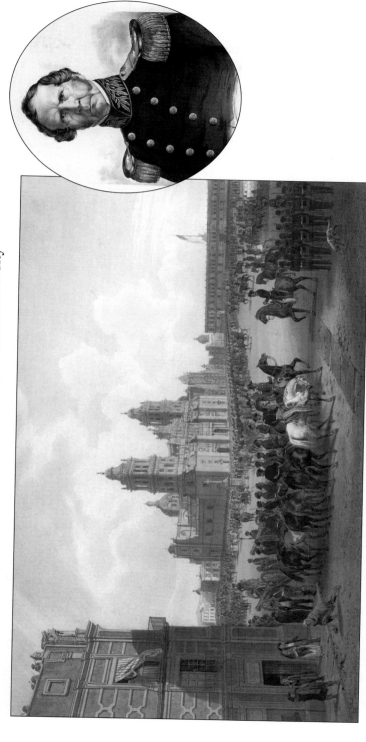

Carl Nebel's painting shows General Winfield Scott's dramatic entrance into Mexico City. In the foreground, a Mexican reaches for a stone to hurl at the invaders, but a U.S. officer, turned in his saddle, has seen him. *Courtesy of the University of Texas at Arlington Libraries.* Inset: General Winfield Scott. *Library of Congress.*

The California Gold Rush

The contemporary depiction of mining operations along the Sacramento River in 1848–49 shows Indians, Mexicans, and recent arrivals from various places and backgrounds all scrambling for gold. *Courtesy of the Beinecke Rare Book and Manuscript Library, Yale University.*

William Sidney Mount's painting *California News* shows the improved access to information from all over the world and its effects. An agent is booking passage by ship to San Francisco in a post office, where most people pick up their newspapers. *Courtesy of the Long Island Museum of American Art, History & Carriages. Gift of Mr. and Mrs. Ward Melville, 1955.*

14

The New Economy

When John Ball reached his twenty-first birthday in 1815, he finally felt free to leave home, his father's semi-subsistence farm atop a thousand-foot hill near Plymouth, New Hampshire. The youngest of ten children, he had worked on the farm from his earliest memories. He looked back on the time of his growing up matter-of-factly but not fondly. "With me it was all work and no play." Sunday brought surcease from physical labor, but Calvinist strictness made it "the dullest day of all." What he minded most was "having so limited an opportunity for an education." Eventually his father had allowed the youth to walk four miles to the home of a clergyman who tutored him, not only in English and history but also in Latin, a prerequisite for college. Soon John knew enough to teach school in the winter, when his work could be spared from the farm. By the time he could gain admission to Dartmouth he was much older than most of the undergraduates, and his father warned him that "you must not look to me for help." Still he managed to graduate in 1820. John Ball went on to a career as a lawyer in New York. Meanwhile, John's sister Deborah, a woman of "vigorous body and mind, quite self-reliant," had also left home, learned the tailoring trade, and married a man named William Powers, who founded a factory in New York making oil cloth. When William died, Deborah carried on the business, and John suspended his law practice to become her factory foreman. After Deborah's factory got on a firm footing, John Ball departed for a well-publicized trip to Oregon, speculated in Michigan land, and despite the hard times following 1837 found both fortune and a happy late marriage there. Remembering his own early struggles, he played an influential role in creating the Michigan public school system.[1]

The experience of John Ball and Deborah Ball Powers—as well as two other Ball brothers who also left their home—was replicated countless thousands of times during these years, if not always with such happy outcomes. Many an American yearned to escape the painful thrift and drudgery of a small farm, growing some necessities of life and trading with neighbors for others, once alternatives presented themselves. Most

1. Quotations from *The Autobiography of John Ball* (Grand Rapids, Mich., 1925), 7, 13, 14, 16. See also Joyce Appleby, *Inheriting the Revolution* (Cambridge, Mass., 2000), 59–62.

felt eager to improve their standard of living, either through increased production for the market or by leaving the agricultural sector altogether. In those days, fathers enjoyed a legal claim on the earnings of sons who had not yet come of age; nevertheless, many sons contrived to "buy their labor from their fathers" and leave home. The drop in market prices for agricultural commodities after 1839 prompted some people to leave their family farm and go to town. Overall, in the years between 1820 and 1850 the sector of the population considered "urban" (residing in places with more than 2,500 people) multiplied fivefold and increased its share of the total population from 7 percent to 18 percent—commencing the period of the most rapid urbanization in American history. In 1820, there were but five cities in the country with more than 25,000 people, and only one—New York—with over 100,000. Thirty years later, there were twenty-six cities with populations over 25,000, and six that exceeded 100,000.[2]

Though John and Deborah responded to the "pull" of the city, some migrants also felt a "push" to leave the farm. Some people came to the cities and towns of the young republic for much the same reasons that people in countries like Brazil and Mexico migrate away from the rural areas today. With improvements in agricultural productivity, farmers in Europe and the United States needed fewer hands even while more of their children were surviving to adulthood. While some grown children went west to start farms of their own, others moved to towns and cities to look for jobs there. Increased farm productivity and improved transportation made it easier to feed people not engaged in agriculture, raising the ceiling on the number of people who could occupy a given urban area. Ironically, even when northern agriculture became more successful economically, it shrank as a sector of society.[3]

The transportation revolution also made it easier for the surplus agricultural population to move around, both within the continent and across the ocean. So American cities and towns received migrants not only from the farms of their own hinterland, but also from those of Europe. Although the nineteenth century witnessed enormous urban growth throughout the Western world, it occurred most dramatically in the United States. During the 1820s and '30s, more than 667,000 overseas immigrants entered the United States—three-quarters of them through the

---

2. Bureau of the Census, *Historical Statistics of the United States* (Washington, 1975), I, 11–12.
3. Winifred Rothenberg, *From Market-Places to a Market Economy* (Chicago, 1992), 244; David R. Meyer, *Roots of American Industrialization* (Baltimore, 2003), 36.

port of New York. (This does not include people who came overland from Canada, nor illegally imported slaves.) These numbers, while significant, came to seem low by comparison with later ones. After years of gradually improving harvests, Europe's most dramatic crop failure prompted enormous migration. When blight wiped out a third of the Irish potato crop in 1845 and nearly all of it the following year, the human tide reaching North American shores suddenly became a flood. The 1840s and '50s saw 4,242,000 immigrants arrive from overseas, and three-quarters of them still came through New York. Enough of them stayed there, joining the migrants from American farms, that the city tripled in size during the first half of the nineteenth century, growing twice as fast as Liverpool and three times as fast as Manchester.[4]

In the South, cities and towns grew less rapidly. There, the surplus in agricultural laborers could be handled differently. The farm laborers were not free to seek jobs on their own. Enslaved laborers sold off by their owners were more likely sent to plantations on the frontier than to urban areas. Immigrants from overseas did not relish the prospect of having to compete for jobs with slave labor. Yet they did not avoid the South altogether: The port of New Orleans received 188,000 immigrants in the decade of the 1840s, and its population included 40 percent foreign born, the same percentage as New York City.[5]

Most of the cities and towns of this period grew up more oriented to commerce and its ramifications (including professional, financial, and artisan services) than to industry. Along the inland waterways, new cities like Cincinnati, Chicago, and Buffalo developed, and older ones like St. Louis and Louisville (eighteenth-century foundations named for French kings) expanded. They were *entrepôts*, places for the collection and shipment of staple commodities in exchange for provisions, equipment, and services. In a way, the city itself formed a commercial commodity, the sale of its own urban real estate being vital to its prosperity. Developers eager to make sales did not differentiate between commercial and residential areas; they reserved little land for public uses like schools and parks. Traders gathered to negotiate and stayed to pool information about mercantile conditions. In the city, ships bearing news docked, the news got printed, and businessmen could talk over lunch. The cities became nerve

4. Edwin G. Burrows and Mike Wallace, *Gotham: A History of New York City to 1898* (New York, 1999), 735–37; Sean Wilentz, *Chants Democratic: New York City and the Rise of the American Working Class* (New York, 1984), 109.
5. Mary Ryan, *Civic Wars: Democracy and Public Life in the American City during the Nineteenth Century* (Berkeley, 1997), 22.

centers, not only of transportation but also of the communications revolution.[6] Prosperous residents and businesses concentrated in the city centers. Unlike today, the poor lived on the outskirts of town, where the absence of public transportation made getting to work less convenient. Rapid urban growth far outpaced the development of all municipal services, including police forces, firefighting, sanitation, and water supplies.

Although the waves of rioting in the 1830s posed the most critical threats to urban law and order, unpunished individual crimes also undermined personal security in the days before police forces. More common than murder and robbery were assaults and batteries.[7] Working-class urban neighborhoods now rivaled the southwest frontier as centers of violence. In the all-too-numerous taverns, youths proved their manhood by drinking, fighting each other, attacking members of different ethnic groups or political parties, and beating up or gang-raping women. A culture of violence prompted working-class males to preserve their honor in the face of hardship and uncertainty by acting tough. Walt Whitman celebrated their feelings of gender pride in his poetry: "O the joy of a manly self-hood! / To be servile to none, to defer to none." A less romantic New York diarist complained in 1839 that "the City is infested by gangs of hardened wretches . . . brought up in Taverns." Tavern gang members most often victimized, next to each other, African Americans and working-class women. Urban mob violence manifested this male tavern culture on a larger scale.[8]

In some of the burgeoning cities, commercialized vice constituted a big business. It is said that ten thousand prostitutes plied their trade in New York City in 1844, though estimates varied. Young women from the countryside, originally hoping for either domestic or factory employment, might find an alternative in a brothel—particularly during economic hard times. Although prostitution per se was not yet illegal in New York, streetwalkers could get arrested for vagrancy. Working in a brothel was safer. Otherwise respectable landlords found whorehouses profitable lessees. Notoriously, theater galleries served as places of assignation. Formerly confined to certain neighborhoods and a hard core of professionals, prostitution

6. See Meinig, *Continental America*, 352–74.
7. The murder rate in pre–Civil War New York City (the only American place for which we have a comprehensive modern study) was lower than at the end of the twentieth century, though it rose in times of major riots; Eric Monkkonen, *Murder in New York City* (Berkeley, 2001), 12–19.
8. Michael Kaplan, "New York City Tavern Violence and the Creation of a Working-Class Male Identity," *JER* 15 (1995): 591–617, quotations from 617, 595.

spread to become one of the urban working-class options exercised by women and girls. Not all of these prostitutes thought of themselves as degraded and oppressed. The historians Christine Stansell and Patricia Cline Cohen have emphasized the opportunities commercial sex provided women: It paid well and offered them a measure of independence. (At a time when a journeyman in the building trades earned twelve dollars a week, a working girl in a fancy brothel could earn fifty dollars.) Apparently they were not always victimized by pimps. Urban philanthropists like the Tappan brothers sought to rescue women from sin and shame, only to find that many prostitutes felt content with their occupation.[9] Immoral by any standard, however, were the houses of prostitution that made use of enslaved women. Evidence survives of a thriving commerce in "fancy maids" to supply the sex trade in New Orleans and other southern cities.[10]

The most terrifying danger to urban life and property had always been fire. Early attempts to respond by creating volunteer fire companies produced mixed results. In their firehouses, the volunteers gloried in manly fraternity and public respect. Sometimes they performed heroically, but they might be more eager to race each other to the scene than to fight the fire once they got there. Too often fire companies constituted rival gangs, wielding political influence sometimes Democratic and sometimes Whig, waging violent turf wars. In the worst cases, fire raged while companies battled each other for the chance to loot the burning buildings.[11] When New York City encountered the great fire of December 16, 1835, its volunteer firefighters still insisted on showing off their strength by pulling their own fire engines through the streets instead of using horse-drawn engines or steam-powered ones such as London had employed since 1829. Worse, bitter cold weather froze the water with which they tried to quench the flames. The conflagration only stopped spreading when they obtained gunpowder to blow up buildings in its path. By the time the fire burned itself out, 674 structures, including almost everything south of Wall Street and east of Broad, had been damaged or destroyed. The remains of Dutch

9. J. F. Richardson, *The New York Police* (New York, 1970), 25–27; Christine Stansell, *City of Women* (New York, 1986), 171–92; Patricia Cline Cohen, *The Murder of Helen Jewett* (New York, 1998), 74, 111; Timothy Gilfoyle, *City of Eros* (New York, 1992), 29–61.

10. Edward Baptist, "Rape, Commodification, and the Domestic Slave Trade in the United States," *AHR* 106 (2001): 1619–50.

11. See, e.g., Amy Greenberg, *Cause for Alarm: The Volunteer Fire Department in the Nineteenth Century* (Princeton, 1998); Bruce Laurie, "Fire Companies and Gangs in Southwark," in *Peoples of Philadelphia*, ed. Allen Davis and Mark Haller (Philadelphia, 1973), 71–88.

colonial New Amsterdam disappeared forever. When cities began to replace wells with municipal water mains and hydrants, they did so more for
the sake of firefighting than as a convenience to householders.[12]

City air had always been polluted by the flames used every day for
cooking, heating, and lighting, and of course tobacco smoking was widespread. Coal- and steam-powered factories now added their soot to the
unhealthy pall of smoke hanging over urban areas. But the most hazardous feature of life in the expanding cities was neither crime nor fire
nor polluted air but the lack of hygiene. Municipal authorities seldom
supplied water to urban residents; people dug wells in their backyards, despite the contamination from nearby outhouses. When it rained, the pits
below outhouses could overflow, spreading stench and filth. Even in dry
weather, horse manure littered the streets. Beginning in the 1830s, horse-
drawn omnibuses carrying commuters facilitated urban growth but added
their droppings to those of horse-drawn delivery wagons, taxis, and private
carriages. To get rid of garbage, city authorities loosed hogs and geese into
alleys where dogs, rats, and vultures joined them in scavenging. Warnings
appeared that unattended infants were in danger of being eaten.[13]

Those who sought out such an unsafe urban environment put themselves at no small risk of life and health. Male children born in cities grew
up to be shorter than those born on farms, an indication of diminished
physical well-being during their formative years.[14] The death rate in the
cities was not only higher than the countryside but also higher than the
urban birthrate. Only a constant influx of new arrivals kept the urban
population from falling. American cities compared unfavorably with European ones; New York's death rate was nearly twice that of London. In
Philadelphia and New York, the life expectancy of newborn babies averaged only twenty-four years during the 1830s and '40s, six years less than
that of newborn southern slaves. The horrendous death rate in the growing cities contributed to the declining overall American life expectancy
during these years.[15] Thomas Jefferson's warning that large cities would

12. Burrows and Wallace, *Gotham*, 596–98; Maureen Ogle, *All the Modern Conveniences* (Baltimore, 1996) 36.
13. George Rogers Taylor, *The Transportation Revolution* (New York, 1951), 390–92;
Ryan, *Civic Wars*, 40.
14. Demonstrated statistically from the records of Pennsylvania men who served in the
Civil War by Timothy Cuff, *The Hidden Cost of Economic Development* (Burlington,
Vt., 2005).
15. Robert Fogel, "Nutrition and the Decline in Mortality Since 1700," in *Long-term Factors in American Economic Growth*, ed. Stanley Engerman and Robert Gallman
(Chicago, 1986), Table 9.A.1; Taylor, *Transportation Revolution*, 392.

constitute "great sores" on the body politic seemed well on its way to grim fulfillment. The most putrid urban carbuncle of all was the "Five Points" slum neighborhood of Manhattan, overcrowded with poor people from a variety of origins, native born and immigrant, notorious for its filth, disease, gangs, crime, riots, and vice. Charles Dickens, no stranger to urban wretchedness, expressed horror when he visited Five Points. "From every corner as you glance about you in these dark retreats," he wrote, "some figure crawls as if the judgement hour were near at hand, and every obscure grave were giving up its dead. Where dogs would howl to lie, women and men and boys slink off to sleep, forcing the dislodged rats to move away in quest of better lodgings."[16]

In the face of such conditions, why did the cities continue to attract newcomers? In some ways the urban standard of living seemed preferable. Urban wages compared favorably, on average, with the earnings of farm laborers.[17] Migrants found most city jobs less arduous than the heavy physical labor of premechanized agriculture. In town, even poor people usually sat on chairs instead of stools at home and ate off plates instead of straight from the common pot; stoves took the place of open fireplaces for heat and cooking. For those with middle-class incomes, a carpet on the floor symbolized their achievement. Unmarried people, whether middle or working class, could live conveniently in urban boardinghouses. (Boardinghouses met a real need: With hours of labor long, employed people had to come home to a prepared meal.) Some of the disincentives to urban life, like crime and communicable infections, were not so bad in provincial towns as in big cities and ports. In all cities and towns, theaters, processions, and public markets provided spectacles unavailable elsewhere; and one could choose from a wider variety of churches than in the countryside. During the late 1840s, running water finally came to middle-class dwellings in New York and Philadelphia. Such attractions, combined with excitement, opportunity, and the broad range of careers open to talent, evidently outweighed urban disadvantages in the eyes of many. And beginning in the 1840s, life insurance companies began compiling statistics on public health and using them to lobby with municipal governments to spend more money on clean water and refuse collection in the interest of urban longevity.[18]

16. Charles Dickens, *American Notes*, ed. John Whitley and Arnold Goldman (1842; Harmondsworth, Eng., 1972), 137–38. See also Tyler Anbinder, *Five Points* (New York, 2001).
17. Economists have termed this factor a "bribe" to attract workers to accept the health risks of city life; Robert Fogel, *The Escape from Hunger and Premature Death* (Cambridge, Eng., 2004), 35, 131–33.
18. James Cassedy, *Medicine and American Growth* (Madison, Wisc., 1986), 197.

Finally, and often decisively, there was the autonomy of urban life. Personal independence from the patriarchal household counted heavily with young adults. In Europe, people had fled to the cities for generations; the German aphorism *Stadtluft macht frei* ("city air makes one free") referred to more than freedom from feudal dues. Young Americans and their immigrant counterparts voted with their feet against staying on their fathers' farms. Among northerners, migration patterns exposed the unpopularity of subsistence agriculture as a life option. Those who moved to the Midwest to take up new farms there concentrated more on cash crops than did eastern farmers. Together, urban places and the western areas opened up to markets by waterways received adventuresome souls fleeing the backbreaking toil, the patriarchal authority, and the stultifying isolation of semi-subsistence farming.[19]

II

Near a dam in Whitneyville, Connecticut (a suburb of New Haven), stands today a small but precious relic of the industrial revolution in America: the machine shop of Eli Whitney's gun factory. There, between 1798 and his death in 1825, Whitney struggled to apply the principle of standardized and interchangeable parts in order to fulfill an arms contract for supplying muskets to the federal government. Whitney never quite managed to achieve the mass production he promised Uncle Sam. Unable to enforce the monopoly on manufacturing southern cotton gins that he tried to achieve, he did not succeed in his northern enterprise either, although his name became legendary. In identifying interchangeable parts as his goal, Whitney had put his finger on the manufacturing technique that would transform the North and, in due course, the world.[20]

Armories like that of Whitney—and the less well known but more technologically sophisticated Simeon North—proved a major contributor to the industrial revolution, for the armed forces represented an extreme case of a market for a large number of identical products. The armories owned by the government itself, as at Springfield, Massachusetts, and Harpers Ferry, Virginia, carried the concept of interchangeable parts still farther

19. Cf. Joyce Appleby, *Inheriting the Revolution: The First Generation of Americans* (Cambridge, Mass., 2000), 170–74.
20. Whitney's status as popular icon is embodied in Constance Green, *Eli Whitney and the Birth of American Technology* (Boston, 1956); for more sober estimates, see Merritt Roe Smith, "Eli Whitney and the American System of Manufacturing," *Technology in America*, ed. Carroll Pursell (Washington, 1979), 49–65; Angela Lakwete, *Inventing the Cotton Gin* (Baltimore, 2003).

forward; since they did not have to show a profit, they could invest more in pursuit of what seemed like perfection. Their goal was parts that would be so uniformly interchangeable that soldiers in the field could take two damaged weapons and reassemble them to make one that worked. Private industry quickly learned about such techniques whenever skilled mechanics left the armories to take up jobs elsewhere.[21]

In the private sector, manufacturers discovered that the components of their consumer products did not have to be standardized to nearly so fine a tolerance as military firearms required. By mixing a degree of standardization with a certain amount of hand fitting and finishing, a serviceable compromise could be obtained. The market for which they produced consisted of middle-class Americans, most of whom lived in rural areas. These customers wanted inexpensive products, unlikely to break down and easy to repair without a long trip to find a craftsman. Finely finished products that would impress observers seemed less important than functionality, since few people visited an isolated farmhouse. The earliest businessman to respond to this market opportunity was Eli Terry, a craftsman-turned-industrialist who mass-produced inexpensive clocks with wooden movements. (An amazed visitor to the West commented, "In Kentucky, in Indiana, in Illinois, in Missouri, and in every dell in Arkansas, and in cabins where there was not a chair to sit on, there was sure to be a Connecticut clock.")[22] American manufacturers supplemented their own ideas with ones freely borrowed from the government armories as well as from European technology, adapting it all to their own commercial objectives. The British, then world experts on industrial technology, took note and named mass production "the American system of manufactures." Henry Clay and Eli Terry each represented a meaning for the phrase "American System." In the end, the large private sector proved more important than the small public sector in determining the course of American industrialization.[23]

Whitney had built his armory next to a source of water power, the chief determinant for the location of most early industry. Just as the cities had more to do with commerce than industry, early factories could be located

21. David Hounshell, *From the American System to Mass Production, 1800–1932* (Baltimore, 1984), 15–46.

22. Quoted in William Gienapp, "The Myth of Class in America," *Journal of Policy History* 6 (1994): 247.

23. See Nathan Rosenberg, "Why in America?" in *Yankee Enterprise: The Rise of the American System of Manufactures*, ed. Otto Mayr and Robert Post (Washington, 1981), 49–63; for Eli Terry, see Donald Hoke, *Ingenious Yankees* (New York, 1990), 52–99.

in small towns or the countryside just as well as in cities, provided cheap labor—often that of rural women and children—could be assembled. Manufacturers didn't even need to have all their work done in the same place; they understood well the advantages of what we call "outsourcing," which they called "putting out." Integrated industrial sites like Lowell came to dominate textile production, but in some other industries like shoemaking the putting-out system could prevail. Not until after the Civil War did the word "factory" come to mean exclusively a place where "manufacturing" went on. Before that it could also mean a marketplace where traders (termed "factors") conducted business, including such varied activities as gathering up the results of put-out work, purchasing pelts from Indian tribes, or buying slaves in West Africa.[24]

A farmer's son, Eli Whitney had saved and worked his way through Yale only to find that his mechanical aptitude, not higher education, constituted his real asset. Other innovators of his time tended to be skilled workmen rather than college graduates, which may help explain why they were more commercially successful. Ichabod Washburn, a blacksmith from Worcester, Massachusetts, founded American wire manufacturing in 1831. Charles Goodyear of New Haven helped his father run a hardware store; in 1844, he patented the process for vulcanizing rubber. Elias Howe, a journeyman machinist in Boston, patented a sewing machine in 1846. Such inventors typified a culture of innovation especially characteristic of southern New England, heartland of the new industrialization. "Every workman seems to be continually devising some new thing to assist him in his work," a British visitor remarked, "there being a strong desire, both with masters and workmen, throughout the New England states, to be 'posted up,' in every new improvement."[25] Though college was superfluous at this stage of industrial innovation, basic literacy was not. One of the reasons why New England led the way in inventions was its system of universal public education.

Starting in 1836, a reorganized federal Patent Office carefully vetted every application before granting a patent. Despite its increasing strictness, the office got busier and busier. Where the government had granted 23 patents a year per million residents during the decade after the War of 1812, the number rose to 42 a year in the 1830s. The statistic at that time for southern New England stood at 106. All across the country, patenting

24. OED, s.v. "factory."
25. See Kenneth Sokoloff and Zorina Khan, "The Democratization of Invention," *Journal of Economic History* 59 (1990): 363–78. Quotation from Richard D. Brown, *Modernization: The Transformation of American Life* (New York, 1976), 144.

activity flowed along the waterways that sustained commerce and provided power for industry.[26]

Inventions revolutionized not only manufacturing but the age-old methods of farming. Cyrus McCormick, twenty-two-year-old son of a Virginia blacksmith-farmer, made his first reaper in 1831, a two-wheeled, horse-drawn chariot that harvested grain; out on the Illinois frontier, a blacksmith named John Deere forged a plow from steel instead of wood in 1837. New approaches to production and the division of labor sometimes turned out even more important than physical inventions, and often they too originated with imaginative mechanics. Arial Bragg, an apprenticed shoemaker from rural Massachusetts, turned his whole industry around by showing how shoes could be ready-made instead of custom-made.[27]

At first American industry flourished most in southern New England, taking advantage of that region's plentiful water power. Use of steam power instead of water promised industry more flexibility to locate near customers or suppliers; it also avoided interruptions from winter freezing or summer droughts. As more applications for power from steam developed in the 1830s and '40s, the geographical center of industrialization shifted to Pennsylvania. Europeans, running low on timber, had learned that coal could fire up a bigger head of steam than wood. Pennsylvania possessed plentiful coal and iron deposits that could be exploited with the aid of British expertise (valuable again, as it had already proved in creating the American textile industry). A Welshman came from Swansea to show the men of Allentown how to set up a blast furnace fueled with anthracite. Hordes of English, Scottish, Welsh, and Cornish miners and ironworkers contributed their skills when they learned of the wages paid in Pennsylvania. The enlightened conservationists of the time urged Americans to burn coal instead of wood. But despite their advice and Pennsylvania's resources, wood still abounded in the New World, and Americans continued to use more of it than Europeans did, as a fuel, as a building material, and even to make machinery. Wooden machines didn't last as

---

26. Steven Usselman and Richard R. John, "Patent Politics," *Journal of Policy History* 18 (2006): 101; Kenneth Sokoloff, "Invention, Innovation, and Manufacturing Productivity Growth," in *American Economic Growth and Standards of Living Before the Civil War*, ed. Robert Gallman and John Wallis (Chicago, 1992), 353; idem, "Patenting Activity in Early Industrial America," *Journal of Economic History* 48 (1988): 813–50.

27. Appleby, *Inheriting the Revolution*, 77–78. See also Kenneth Sokoloff, "Investment in Fixed and Working Capital During Early Industrialization," *Journal of Economic History* 44 (1984): 545–56.

long as iron ones, but by the time they needed replacing perhaps an improved model might have appeared. American industrialization took place in an environment of generally inexpensive material resources and high costs for skilled labor.[28]

In pre-industrial society "manufactured" goods had been made—as the derivation of the word itself implied—by hand. Skilled workers specialized in crafting particular products and usually made them to order. An artisan's skill took years to master; it conferred a proud identity, which is why so many surnames dating from that period identify artisan occupations: Taylor, Draper, Sawyer, Mason, Cooper (barrel-maker), Chandler (candlemaker), Wright (maker of complex structures, as in cart-wright, plow-wright, wheel-wright), or—most common of all—Smith. Almost always males, artisans often handed down their skills, like surnames, from father to son. Society recognized three ranks of artisan: the apprentice learning the "art and mystery" of his calling, the fully qualified journeyman, and the master, who owned his own business where he could instruct apprentices and hire journeymen. Women's dressmakers and milliners (hat-makers) constituted an exception to the rule that skilled artisan callings were male. Often the daughters of artisan fathers, they too served apprenticeships to learn their trade and aspired to become proprietors.[29]

The master artisan combined the roles of workman and small businessman, as does an independent garage mechanic today. In early modern Europe artisans usually belonged to a craft guild, which set prices and quality standards and limited the number of apprenticeships in order to protect the livelihood of its members. In America, where a chronic shortage of skilled labor prevailed instead of a danger of too much competition, guilds did not take root. But each craft had its own organization for mutual aid and marched with its own flag in civic parades. American artisans (also called "mechanics") cherished the memory of their collective action during the Revolution and nursed a strong political consciousness of Jeffersonian Republicanism.

The transportation revolution and the concentration of population in cities greatly increased the number of customers to whom a commodity could be marketed, paving the way for mass production. Imaginative master mechanics found ways to create efficiencies by the division of labor

---

28. Meinig, *Continental America*, 382; Priscilla Brewer, *From Fireplace to Cookstove* (Syracuse, N.Y., 2000), 65. See also Sean Adams, "The Political Economy of Coal," *Journal of Policy History* 18 (2006): 74–95.

29. Wendy Gamber, *The Female Economy: The Millinery and Dressmaking Trades* (Urbana, Ill., 1997), 12, 71.

even before there was much new technology to apply. Though textile mills required substantial capital investment, many other kinds of "manufactories" (or machineless factories) could be started up on a shoestring. When a product previously crafted by hand was produced in this new way, its price fell and consumers benefited. Sometimes the manufactories even improved the quality of the product. Traditional shoes had been made on a straight last by craftsmen called "cordwainers" because they worked in Cordovan leather. The new mass-produced shoes distinguished for the first time between the left and right foot. Shoe manufacturers also discovered how to "put out" various stages of the shoemaking process to farming and fishing families, who could perform the tasks during their off-seasons. The transition from artisan shop to manufactory and putting-out production had progressed a long way by the time Secretary of the Treasury Louis McLane compiled a report on industrialization for Congress in 1832.[30]

Industrialization played havoc with the artisan system of production, though its effects on individuals varied according to their trade and rank. In a manufactory, the employer seemed much more remote than the old-time master craftsman, who had worked alongside his helpers. To a craftsman accustomed to the traditional shop, the manufactory seemed to practice a "bastard artisan system."[31] The more specialized jobs created by industrialization could be less skilled, less interesting, and less well paid. The communications revolution fragmented the printer's trade, as presses specialized in either books, magazines, or newspapers, and the craft itself subdivided into compositors and press operators. While furniture for the upper and middle classes continued to be made by fine craftsmen, new lines of cheap furniture came into factory production by monotonous, low-skilled labor. In the clothing industry, as in furniture, specialization of labor preceded rather than followed mechanization. The new manufactories for ready-made clothing drew new distinctions among tailors; cutters far outranked sewers. Manufacturers outsourced cheaper lines of clothing to female seamstresses working under conditions comparable to those of twenty-first-century East Asian sweatshops.[32] The sewing machine

---

30. Alan Dawley, *Class and Community: The Industrial Revolution in Lynn* (Cambridge, Mass., 1976), 54; U.S. Congress, House of Representatives, *Documents Relative to the Manufactures in the United States, Collected . . . by the Secretary of the Treasury* (Washington, 1833), 2 vols.
31. Wilentz, *Chants Democratic*, 115.
32. Bruce Laurie, *Artisans into Workers* (New York, 1989), as modified by Richard Stott, "Artisans and Capitalist Development," *JER* 16 (1996): 257–71.

boosted production further when it appeared in the 1840s. Although mechanization tended to depress the status and pay of the seamstresses who made men's shirts and pants, women's dressmakers and milliners, relatively well paid female occupations, increased in numbers with the growth of their urban market.[33]

Eighteen forty was a landmark year in American growth, for the census of that year showed that the population of the United States, 17 million, had reached approximate equality with that of Great Britain. Yet the British economy remained substantially larger, reflecting the further advance of the industrial revolution there. The U.S. economy was catching up, however, for the gross national product grew at a long-term rate of 3.9 percent per annum, reflecting the combined effects of population and productivity increases, compared with a 2.2 percent growth rate for Britain.[34]

Despite the commentaries of foreign travelers on America's relative social equality, wealth was by no means evenly distributed. Free adult males in the South held greater wealth on average than in the North, mostly due to slave ownership, although less than 20 percent of them owned slaves.[35] Most historians believe that the early industrial revolution widened inequalities in the standard of living; that is, while average per capita income doubled between 1820 and 1860, property owners and the rich benefited more than wage-earners and the poor. But the evidence is not entirely clear; early data are fragmentary, and occasionally historians have used the household rather than the individual as their unit of comparison, which masks the effects of slavery and restrictions on women's property rights. Some research even suggests that the degree of inequality between rich and poor remained relatively constant during early American industrialization.[36] Rich men were much more likely to be planters,

33. Gamber, *The Female Economy*, 67, 79.

34. Robert Gallman, "Growth and Change in the Long Nineteenth Century," in *Cambridge Economic History of the United States*, ed. Stanley Engerman and Robert Gallman (Cambridge, Eng., 1996–2000), II, 2–8.

35. Clayne Pope, "Inequality in the Nineteenth Century," *Cambridge Economic History of U.S.*, II, 120; U.S. census data for 1860, http://fisher.lib.virginia.edu/census. The percentage of southern white men owning slaves varied between states but showed remarkable consistency over time between 1830 and 1860.

36. Donald Adams, "Prices and Wages," in *Encyclopedia of American Economic History*, ed. Glenn Porter (New York, 1980), 229–46; Lee Soltow, "Inequalities in the Standard of Living in the United States, 1798–1875," in *American Economic Growth and Standards of Living Before the Civil War*, ed. Robert Gallman and John Wallis (Chicago, 1992), 121–72; Carole Shammas, "A New Look at Long-Term Trends in Wealth Inequality," *AHR* 98 (1993), 412–31, esp. 427.

merchants, or bankers than manufacturers, though perhaps for a time industrialization opened new avenues for social mobility, as it had done in Britain. If inequality did increase in this period, it may have been due to the arrival of immigrants without property, or to the secession of young adults like the Balls from their propertied fathers' households, rather than a direct consequence of industrialization. In any case, the substantial degree of economic inequality, even if not caused by industrialization, exacerbated working-class discontents. In the largest American cities of the 1840s, the richest 5 percent of free males owned 70 percent of the real and personal property. The visibility of a small group of super-rich is attested by the invention of the word "millionaire" around 1840.[37]

Social anxieties were more important than economic ones in fueling discontent among workers in the early American industrial revolution. Under the artisan system, workingmen had embraced not only the party of Jeffersonian Republicanism but its ideology, which celebrated the small property owner's political independence and social worth. Journeymen often resented the end of the old system, feeling that it had offered them more dignity and a better chance to become a master than they had now of becoming an employer. Instead of owning his tools and selling what he made with them, the mechanic now feared being left with nothing to sell but his labor. A lifetime as a wage-earner seemed a gloomy prospect to men who had imbibed the political outlook of Old Republicanism, who identified themselves with independent farmers or shopkeepers and looked upon wage labor as a form of dependency. Beginning in Philadelphia, Working Men's political parties sprang up in various places during the 1820s and early '30s, fed by the discontents of journeymen under the impact of industrialization.[38]

The Working Men's political parties espoused a number of causes important to their constituents. These included free public schools, mechanics' lien laws (helping workers recover wages if their employer went bankrupt), reform of compulsory militia service, abolition of imprisonment for debt, and laws requiring wages to be paid in hard currency and defining a day's work as ten hours' labor unless otherwise contracted. In a process often repeated in American politics, the two major parties co-opted the policies of the "Workey" Parties, made them their own and, except for

37. Edward Pessen, *Riches, Class, and Power Before the Civil War* (Lexington, Mass., 1973), 32, 70; James McPherson, *Battle Cry of Freedom* (New York, 1988), 25. On immigrants, see Joseph Ferrie, *Yankeys Now* (New York, 1999); for "millionaire," Christopher Clark, *Social Change in America* (Chicago, 2006), 196.
38. Wilentz, *Chants Democratic*, 61–103.

the ten-hour-day rule, often got them implemented. Sometimes politicians from the major parties even infiltrated the decision-making process of the Workeys.[39]

Meanwhile, more radical programs also bid for the support of the working class. Cornelius Blatchly, a physician and former Quaker, denounced private property as selfish and preached a version of communitarian socialism that integrated efforts to improve the lot of workers with millennial Christianity. Frances Wright, undeterred by the failure of her antislavery enterprise at Nashoba, toured the country speaking on behalf of a philosophy synthesizing Robert Owen's deist socialism with Jeremy Bentham's utilitarianism and Mary Wollstonecraft's feminism. One of the charismatic personalities of her time, Wright presented stage-managed performances in striking costumes to audiences that had never before witnessed any woman speak in public. She founded no movement, but many of the artisans who heard her then read the articles Albert Brisbane published in Horace Greeley's *New York Tribune* and went out to try their hands at building Fourierist phalanxes in the 1840s.[40]

The American mechanics themselves found an authentic voice in the machinist Thomas Skidmore, the most radical agitator of all. In his tract *The Rights of Man to Property* (1829), Skidmore equated the position of the wage-worker with slavery. He demanded the confiscation of all existing property and its equal redistribution by the authority of popular sovereignty working through state constitutional conventions. Once property had been equalized, Skidmore had no objection to talented, hardworking individuals increasing their share, but upon their deaths it should revert to the state for redistribution to those who had just come of age. He also supported equal rights for women and blacks.[41] But when Skidmore died at the age of forty-two in the cholera epidemic of 1832, his program died with him.

Skidmore's views comprised what his contemporaries called—generally with horror—"agrarianism." George Henry Evans, a British immigrant printer, gave agrarianism a more politically plausible form than Skidmore's. As editor of the first labor newspaper, New York's *Working Man's Advocate* (founded in 1829), Evans supported free public education, but beginning around 1834 he turned his attention to land reform. Evans agreed with Skidmore that everyone should be entitled to his own property, but instead of redistributing what already existed, he called for drawing

---

39. Walter Licht, *Industrializing America* (Baltimore, 1995), 48–57.
40. Wilentz, *Chants Democratic*, 158–62, 176–78.
41. Thomas Skidmore, "The Rights of Man to Property" (1829), in *The Perfectionists*, ed. Laurence Veysey (New York, 1973), 83–92.

upon the unclaimed national domain, giving away free homesteads of 160 acres to any actual settler over the age of twenty-one. Evans respected the Indians' rights to land provided they cultivated it; America had room enough for them and settlers too, he insisted. The radical aspects of Evans's program included a limitation on the amount of land any one person could own and a prohibition against mortgaging or selling the homestead. He envisioned the homesteads being grouped around planned villages with land set aside for parks and public buildings.[42]

Evans promoted a kind of individualist utopianism that resonated with Jeffersonian and artisan republicanism. In its early years, Evans's movement sometimes cooperated with British Chartists and radical American utopians (his brother Frederick became a prominent Shaker), but ultimately his program appealed to American aspirations for a democratic capitalism. Employing a catchy slogan, "Vote Yourself a Farm," Evans's National Reform Association gained wide publicity, much of it through Greeley's *New York Tribune*, which accorded a sympathetic presentation to many proposed reforms. Although Evans himself died in 1856, his vision of free homesteads lived on. The Free Soilers endorsed a moderate version of it in 1848, and so did the new Republican Party, which implemented it (shorn of his nonalienation rule and other social engineering features) in 1862. The more popular the idea became, the less close its connection remained to the labor movement. Homesteading, which seemed so radical when Evans first proposed it, turned out to resonate with the aspirations of ordinary Americans, urban and rural, middle and working class, native born and immigrant.[43]

The Working Men's Parties disappeared as quickly as they had appeared. The decline of the antebellum Workey Parties and various associated radical movements reflected changing attitudes among the artisans. Most artisans adapted surprisingly quickly to the new industrial order, and once they did, it ceased to seem threatening. In the nineteenth century, skilled mechanics fitting items to gauges could craft interchangeable parts to tolerances as fine as machine tools could, and consequently mechanics retained an important role even in mass production.[44] A journeyman

---

42. Paul Conkin, *Prophets of Prosperity* (Bloomington, 1980), 237–52; Shelley Streeby, *American Sensations* (Berkeley, 2002), 178–83.
43. For the broad impact of the National Reform movement, see Mark Lause, *Young America* (Urbana, Ill., 2005). Also see Jamie Bronstein, *Land Reform and Working-Class Experience in Britain and the United States* (Stanford, 1999).
44. See Robert Gordon, "Realizing the Ideal of Interchangeability," in *The Industrial Revolution in America*, ed. Gary Kornblith (Boston, 1998), 88–98.

mechanic's expertise often enabled him to become, if not a part owner, then a factory foreman. Another journeyman might prefer to move out west, to a small town where industrialization had not yet penetrated and he could continue to ply his trade. Luck especially favored workers in the building trades. The expansion of the cities created an endless supply of jobs for carpenters, bricklayers, stonemasons, and related crafts. Innovations such as "balloon" framing (so called because of its lightness) and prefabricated doors facilitated rapid, low-cost housing construction, but many building trades, like plastering and shipbuilding, were not adversely affected by industrialization. Other craft skills also remained strong for generations more, such as those of the butcher and the watchmaker. Meanwhile, the industrial revolution created many new skilled occupations including plumber, machinist, telegrapher, and locomotive engineer.

The relatively small scale of antebellum manufacturing often permitted master mechanics to become owners of a manufactory, perhaps by pooling capital with others. (Retail shopkeepers as well as artisans sometimes took this route.) Only in the largest enterprises was industrial management separated from ownership; more typical factories were operated by the same people who owned them. The early industrial revolution in the United States permitted this kind of opportunity for social mobility and thus blurred the line between capitalist and working classes. In the final analysis, the industrial revolution was not simply thrust upon a hostile, sullen mechanic class; to a considerable extent it was their own creation, through their inventions, innovations, and resourcefulness. The human resources of the American working class proved even more critical in fostering the early industrial revolution than did the material resources of a rich continent. The versatile skilled artisan played a key role in America's economic development.[45]

Apprenticeships did not work as well in industry as in the old artisan system, though some building trades retained modified apprenticeships. To substitute for apprenticeships in obsolete crafts, journeymen now sought to place their children in the public schools where they could get an education suitable for the clerical jobs proliferating in the industrialized and urbanized society. In the next generation, the children of American artisans often went on to middle-class occupations, while immigrants

---

45. See Thomas Cochran, *Frontiers of Change: Early American Industrialization* (New York, 1981); Stott, "Artisans and Capitalist Development"; Zorina Khan and Kenneth Sokoloff, "Entrepreneurship and Innovation Among 'Great Inventors' in the United States, 1790–1865," *Journal of Economic History* 53 (1993): 289–307.

who had been peasants in the Old World filled the ranks of the new industrial proletariat.[46] Where public schools did not yet exist, northern working-class organizations campaigned to establish them. Like all political factions of the time, labor had its own newspapers, and these supported free public education, often reprinting statements by middle-class reformers like William Ellery Channing and Horace Mann. As the New York *Working Man's Advocate* declared in 1835, "The man who pretends that an ignorant and vicious people can long remain free, is a fool or a knave."[47] Besides parental concern for their children's welfare, workers had an additional motive for supporting public schools: If children went to school, they stayed out of the labor market, and adult labor did not have to compete with that of low-paid children.

The artisans' interest in education and self-improvement continued after they left school. More durable than Working Men's political parties were the Mechanics' Associations, with their adult education programs, their endowed libraries, lectureships, and encouragement for applied science. These associations represented an area of cooperation between artisans-turned-employers and those who now worked for wages. The artisans also participated in the religious revivals of their time. The evangelical movement and the Working Men's Parties supported much the same values of autonomy, responsibility, and self-respect. A movement for "free churches" in working-class neighborhoods began to erode the practice of having pews assigned to families who owned them in return for money given to erect the church or rented them in return for annual contributions. The cause of temperance spread from its small-town religious origins to the cities. Employers endorsed it because they preferred a sober workforce, but the reform enjoyed the most success when led by tough-minded working-class men called Washingtonians. Their movement included a branch for women: the Martha Washingtonians. Combating alcohol abuse was not treason to the working class; it helped mitigate some of the worst features of life in the antebellum city.[48]

After the disappearance of the Working Men's Parties, some of their former supporters became Whigs, a logical choice in terms of that party's positions on tariff protection and public schooling. American cities in all

46. See Richard Stott, *Workers in the Metropolis* (Ithaca, N.Y., 1990).
47. Quoted in C. K. McFarland and Robert Thistlethwaite, "Labor Press Demands Equal Education," *Journalism Quarterly* 65 (1988): 600–608. See also William Rorabaugh, *The Craft Apprentice* (New York, 1986), 113–27.
48. See William Sutton, *Journeymen for Jesus* (University Park, Pa., 1998); 270–87 deal with the Washingtonians.

parts of the country generally returned anti-Jackson majorities through the 1830s, which must indicate something about the voting of the working class. But in the long run, a majority of the industrial working-class vote ended up captured by the Democrats.[49] This was not due to any special interest the party took in labor unions. Andrew Jackson, for example, never mentioned them as far as we know, though in 1834 he did dispatch federal troops to the Chesapeake and Ohio Canal to deter a strike by construction workers.[50] His postmaster general defended exclusion of abolitionist writings from the mails by warning that without such censorship, English labor radicals would be free to incite the American "laboring population" to organize.[51] But much in the Democratic Party's rhetoric resonated with the journeymen's outlook, especially hard money and opposition to government favoritism toward a national bank or other mixed corporations. The ambiguity of the Jacksonians on the tariff helped them recruit workers in protectionist areas like the Pennsylvania iron industry while not driving away all the cotton and tobacco planters devoted to free trade.

The Democratic and Whig Parties took very different stands on the subject of class. Echoing Jackson's Bank Veto, Democrats called upon the working classes—a term they generally used in the plural and defined to include farmers and planters—to oppose the machinations and oppressions of nonproducers. Whigs insisted that there was no such thing as class conflict, that the different economic classes, like the sections of the Union, were interdependent, and in any case, class membership was fluid. Rhetoric of class conflict they deplored as demagogic.[52] To some extent, urban workingmen chose their political party according to which analysis of class relations they found persuasive. Where industrialization had de-skilled and proletarianized workers, and where workers felt alienated from their employers because of ethnic differences, labor voted Democratic. Where workers felt that the system worked and that they enjoyed an opportunity to better themselves, they voted Whig.

The success of the Democratic Party among white wage-earners owed more than a little, unfortunately, to the emphasis it placed on white

49. On support for the Whigs, see John Brooke, *The Heart of the Commonwealth* (Cambridge, Eng., 1981), 316; on support for the Democrats, Randolph Roth, "Did Class Matter in American Politics?" *Historical Methods* 31 (1998): 5–25.

50. The C&O at the time was headed by Jackson's friend John Eaton. See Richard Morris, "Andrew Jackson, Strikebreaker," *AHR* 55 (1949): 54–68.

51. Amos Kendall, *Report of the Postmaster General*, 24th Cong., 1st sess. (1835), quoted in Richard John, *Spreading the News* (Cambridge, Mass., 1995), 272.

52. See John Ashworth, *'Agrarians' and 'Aristocrats': Party Political Ideology in the United States, 1837–1846* (London, 1983).

supremacy. Democratic politicians found an effective way to synthesize their party's appeal to two disparate groups, the northern working class and the southern planter class. They declared that solicitude for southern slaves distracted attention from the plight of northern "wage-slaves," who, they insisted, were actually worse off. The artisan radical John Finch declared it a "well-known fact that the blacks of the South enjoy more leisure time and liberty and fare quite as well as the operatives in the northern or eastern manufacturing districts." Boston's Democratic labor leader Theophilus Fisk called upon "the philanthropist and christian to advocate and demand the immediate emancipation of the white slaves of the North." Orestes Brownson, one of the Democratic Party's most influential intellectuals, admonished abolitionists to redirect their efforts: "You have enough work for all your philanthropy north of Mason and Dixon's line."[53] Only rarely did anyone make what might seem the obvious point that sympathy for exploited northern workers did not preclude compassion for oppressed southern slaves; when William Leggett tried to do so, the Democratic Party shut him down. Not even Fanny Wright combined the two causes. Once she began seeking audiences of workingmen, she phased out her antislavery activity, denounced the abolitionists as sanctimonious hypocrites, and embraced the party of Jackson and Van Buren.[54]

The journeymen mechanics' political movement was white, male, Protestant, and skilled, and certainly not immune to appeals based on race, gender, and religion. White workers generally regarded black workers, whether free or enslaved, as unfair competitors and forbade them to join their associations.[55] Toward the institution of slavery white mechanics manifested deep ambivalence. On the one hand, slavery associated manual labor with servility, thereby degrading white workers. But wage-earners in the free states, native and immigrant alike, also worried that emancipated slaves might flock north, depressing wages and living conditions. The northern Democratic Party proved adept at manipulating these feelings.[56] Nevertheless, the loyalty of northern industrial labor to the Democratic Party was never entirely sure (except for the Irish). Over the years some workingmen repeatedly jumped ship to support other movements,

53. Finch is quoted in David Roediger, *The Wages of Whiteness* (New York, 1991), 77; Fisk and Brownson in Gerald Henig, "The Jacksonian Attitude Toward Abolitionism," *Tennessee Historical Quarterly* 28 (1969): 53–54.
54. Celia Eckhardt, *Fanny Wright* (Cambridge, Mass., 1984), 243–50.
55. Lois Horton, "From Class to Race in Early America," *JER* 19 (1999): 629–49.
56. See, for example, Anthony Gronowicz, *Race and Class Politics in New York City Before the Civil War* (Boston, 1998).

among them the Locofoco dissidents, homesteads, nativism, Free Soil, and finally the nascent Republican Party.

The Locofocos emerged within the workingmen's wing of the Democratic Party in New York City, but they did not always support trade unionism and should not be confused with the Working Men's Parties.[57] They got their name from a meeting on October 29, 1835, in Tammany Hall, New York Democratic headquarters even then. The party regulars nominated their slate of candidates for the coming municipal election and declared the meeting adjourned; when disaffected workers' delegates tried to prolong the meeting in order to contest the outcome, the organization turned out the gaslights. But the insurgents had come prepared with candles and newly invented sulfur friction matches, called "locofocos" (or "lucifers"). Able to proceed with their meeting, they fielded a slate of their own candidates, though the regular Democrats still won the ensuing election. By 1837, the Locofocos had gained enough concessions from the regulars to return to the party fold, while retaining an identity of their own.[58] Though sarcastically called "locos" ("mad" in Spanish) by their critics, the Locofocos took pride in their name.

III

Lucy Larcom and Sarah Bagley both went to work in the Lowell mills to help out their families. Lucy—a precocious, literary child, dutiful and hardworking—was only twelve when, in 1836, she became a "doffer" of bobbins. Her widowed mother ran one of the many boardinghouses in town. A decade later Lucy departed for Illinois to become a schoolteacher; she eventually gained a modest living and greater fame as a writer. The account she left of her years at Lowell emphasizes the positive, though at the time she hated the confinement, noise, and lint-filled air, and regretted the time lost to education.[59] (Like Lucy Larcom, my own mother, Lucie Walker, became a doffer at age twelve to help with the family budget. She worked at a carpet factory in Halifax, Yorkshire, during the First World War and had very much the same complaints.)

Sarah Bagley, on the other hand, was already an adult when she entered the mills in 1837. There she organized the Lowell Female Reform Association, in effect a labor union with broad social concerns; she allied with

57. Wilentz, *Chants Democratic*, 235.
58. Walter Hugins, *Jacksonian Democracy and the Working Class* (Stanford, 1960), 39–48.
59. Lucy Larcom, *A New England Girlhood*, ed. Charles T. Davis (1889; New York, 1961); Shirley Marchalonis, *The Worlds of Lucy Larcom* (Athens, Ga., 1989), 29–34.

male labor leaders in the struggle for a ten-hour day. To the argument that the mill girls had voluntarily accepted a twelve-hour day, she replied:

> The whip which brings us to Lowell is NECESSITY. We must have money; a father's debts are to be paid, an aged mother is to be supported, a brother's ambition to be aided, and so the factories are supplied. Is this to act from free will? . . . Is any one such a fool as to suppose that out of six thousand factory girls of Lowell, sixty would be there if they could help it?[60]

(These illustrations of typical mill girls' motives do not include the need to feed themselves or their children, reminding us that they were single and came from farms.) In 1846, Sarah Bagley became America's first woman telegraph operator. But when she tried to join the utopian community at Northampton in 1848, they turned her down, perhaps put off by her abrasive manner. In the end, the mill owners responded to the growing militancy of Yankee women by recruiting more of the Irish immigrant women who had a weaker bargaining position.[61]

Despite Sarah Bagley's insistence that mill girls were driven by necessity, the pre-eminent historian of Lowell concludes that the working experience there fostered autonomy, analogous to the experience of young men moving to the frontier or the city. For all their differences, Larcom and Bagley concurred in emphasizing the dignity of the female operatives, manifested (all observers agreed with surprise) in how well the mill girls dressed. As they earned their own money and became less dependent on their menfolk, the women's self-respect increased, a process both Larcom and Bagley encouraged. Both grounded their reformist social views in the Christian tradition. Although often contrasted with each other, very likely what the two women agreed on was more important.[62]

Most workers in the new industrial world did not come to it from artisan shops and did not therefore use the shop as a basis for comparison. There had been few women artisans, yet women constituted more than a third of workers in manufacturing during the 1830s; in textiles the figure was 80 percent.[63] Where some journeymen had been attracted (briefly) to

60. Sarah Bagley, "Voluntary?" *Voice of Industry*, Sept. 18, 1845, in *The Factory Girls*, ed. Philip Foner (Urbana, Ill., 1977), 160.

61. Thomas Dublin, *Women at Work: Lowell, Massachusetts, 1826–1860*, 2nd ed. (New York, 1993), 116–22, 138–40, 199–207; Teresa Murphy, *Ten Hours' Labor: Religion, Reform and Gender in Early New England* (Ithaca, N.Y., 1992), 203–12.

62. Dublin, *Women at Work*, 57. See also Jama Lazerow, "Religion and the Mill Girl," *New England Quarterly* 60 (1987), 429–53.

63. Licht, *Industrializing America*, 58.

Working Men's political parties, more typically industrial wage-earners, whether former artisans or not, formed labor unions. During the burgeoning prosperity of the Jackson years, prices increased faster than wages, prompting some employees to organize and even strike. Unions attracted attention more because of their novelty than because of their numbers. The most reliable estimate of the size of the Jacksonian labor movement puts union membership at 44,000—about 2.5 percent of the nonagricultural free labor force. In 1830, the New York–Brooklyn metropolitan area, with a population of 218,000, held 11,500 union members.[64]

Besides wage demands, a movement to limit working hours to ten a day gathered support. The rigid work discipline enforced in factories seemed onerous to people accustomed to the more elastic hours of preindustrial production; punctuality, for example, was more critical in a factory than it had been in an artisan shop. We should not forget, however, that nature imposes strict temporal imperatives on farmers: A crop must be planted and harvested on time; the cows must be milked on schedule. Plantations operated with slave labor were even more "mastered by the clock" than farms using free labor.[65] The widespread distribution of clocks in rural America demonstrated not only an achievement of manufacturing and distribution but also the time-consciousness of the consumers. In general, employees with prior experience as mechanics showed more inclination to strike than did workers who came off the farms.

Labor strife became particularly sharp in Pennsylvania, where workers in textiles, coal, and iron included many English immigrants who brought with them memories of labor militancy, of machine-breaking and Lancashire trade unionism.[66] In the most impressive labor action of the period, Philadelphia workers united in a general strike (then called a "turnout") that included not only mechanics of many skills from blacksmiths to bakers but also the unskilled coal heavers on the docks, clerks in the dry-goods stores, and municipal employees. Within three weeks of June 1835, the strikers had won a ten-hour day across the board. (A typical ten-hour day of the time ran from six to six, with an hour off for breakfast and an hour for "dinner" in the early afternoon).[67]

64. Maurice Neufeld, "The Size of the Jacksonian Labor Movement," *Labor History* 23 (1982): 599–607; and the same author's statistics in *Labor History* 10 (1969): 10.
65. See Mark M. Smith, *Mastered by the Clock: Time, Slavery, and Freedom in the American South* (Chapel Hill, 1997).
66. Jonathan Prude, *The Coming of Industrial Order* (Cambridge, Eng., 1983), 143, 150–54; Cynthia Shelton, *The Mills of Manayunk* (Baltimore, 1986), 120, 147–48.
67. Leonard Bernstein, "The Working People of Philadelphia," *Pennsylvania Magazine of History and Biography* 74 (1950): 336–39.

Strikes constituted illegal conspiracies under common law, exposing labor union members to criminal prosecution. Sometimes local authorities called out the militia to intimidate strikers, as New York's Democratic mayor Cornelius Lawrence did in February 1836. At the state level, labor law gradually began to be mitigated through both legislation and judicial decisions. New Hampshire in 1847 and Pennsylvania in 1848 were the first states to enact maximum-hours laws. The case of *Commonwealth v. Hunt*, decided in 1842, attracted considerable attention. Chief Justice Lemuel Shaw of Massachusetts there ruled that the Boston Society of Journeymen Bootmakers was not a criminal conspiracy and that its members had the right to press for what we would call a closed shop. Shaw declared labor unions to be as legitimate as other kinds of voluntary associations (he compared them to temperance organizations). Other jurisdictions did not necessarily accept his line of reasoning, however, and management retained the right to seek court injunctions against strikes.[68]

With their option to strike limited, workers might simply quit. Through the 1820s and '30s, turnover remained high among the early industrial labor force. In response, textile mills tried to get employees to sign yearlong contracts. Such contracts were common in agriculture to prevent workers from demanding high pay during harvest season. Under the law of the time, employers could refuse to pay a worker anything unless the entire contract was fulfilled. Apprentices under the age of twenty-one and immigrants who had contracted to work in return for their passage could be prosecuted under the criminal law if they quit in violation of their indentures; this legal rule diminished in importance as apprenticeships declined and indentured servitude disappeared in the 1830s. In practice, the depression of the Van Buren years curtailed the option to quit. When unemployment rose, workers became less mobile and more grateful for jobs under almost any terms. And though prosperity returned in the mid-1840s, impoverished Irish immigrants began arriving in large numbers, undercutting labor's bargaining position again. Despite struggles and sacrifices, the labor movement enjoyed very limited success in antebellum labor disputes.[69]

One small achievement for labor came thanks to President Van Buren: By executive order he mandated a ten-hour day for laborers on federal

---

68. Christopher Tomlins, *Law, Labor, and Ideology in the Early American Republic* (Cambridge, Eng., 1993), 180–219.
69. Jonathan Prude, *Working-Class America* (Urbana, Ill., 1983); Robert Steinfeld, *Coercion, Contract, and Free Labor in the Nineteenth Century* (Cambridge, Eng., 2001).

public works (March 11, 1840). Resisting pleas from some northern Democratic leaders like John L. O'Sullivan to create jobs for the unemployed, Van Buren permitted himself only this more modest gesture toward workingmen.[70] His action probably helped win some votes for the Democratic Party, though it did not apply to all federal wage-earners. Treasury Secretary McLane reported in 1832 that the average working day in manufacturing was eleven hours and twenty minutes. By the eve of the Civil War it had fallen to ten hours and thirty minutes.[71]

Labor for the American industrial revolution came not only from former artisans, surplus farm workers, and immigrants from overseas. Industry also exploited slave labor where available. Although the antebellum South never developed a large textile industry (and sometimes used free white labor in the mills it had), the region did not lack other industrial uses for enslaved labor. Southern employers preferred slave labor in coal, iron, and gold mines, salt works, grist mills, lumber mills, rope factories, sugar refineries, tobacco processing, leather tanning, turpentine extraction, housing construction, and railroad building. The most extensive industrial use of slave labor occurred in the Tredegar Iron Works at Richmond, Virginia. In 1842, Joseph Reid Anderson, the "commercial agent" (chief operating officer) of the company, began a program to train slaves for the most highly skilled work in the mill: "puddling." Five years later, when he was about to turn over a new rolling mill to the now fully trained slave puddlers, the white workers went out on strike in protest, but to no avail. Anderson fired the strikers and replaced them with slaves, and within three years two-thirds of his labor force was owned by the company.[72] In years to come, the Tredegar Iron Works would play an important role in the Confederate armaments industry.

Besides manufacturing, slave labor also found employment in public works such as digging canals, building levees, laying railroad track, cleaning streets, and lighting the gas lamps that illuminated nighttime cities. Business corporations, municipalities, and state and even federal government agencies all owned or hired slaves. In 1842, the Army Corps of Engineers and Quartermaster Corps reported to Congress their regular hiring

---

70. Donald Cole, *Martin Van Buren and the American Political System* (Princeton, 1984), 367–68.

71. Robert Margo, "The Labor Force in the Nineteenth Century," in *Cambridge Economic History of U.S.*, II, 229–30.

72. Robert Starobin, *Industrial Slavery in the Old South* (New York, 1970), 125–28; Ronald Lewis, *Coal, Iron, and Slaves* (Westport, Conn., 1979), 31–34; Patricia Schecter, "Free and Slave Labor in the Old South," *Labor History* 35 (1994), 165–86.

of slaves from willing masters. Surprisingly, the City of Savannah hired slaves as firefighters.[73] Insurance companies underwrote the risk that valuable slave property would be injured or killed by industrial accidents. (Free workers, unlike slaves, had no "worker's compensation" coverage; employers therefore found it prudent to employ free workers for the most dangerous tasks.)

Officially, 5 percent of southern slaves worked in industrial occupations. But the statistic understates the reality. It does not include artisans who worked on plantations making articles for use on that plantation, and thus ignores countless enslaved blacksmiths, masons, cabinet-makers, cordwainers, saddle-makers, plow-wrights, and other craftsmen. Nor are the products of such artisans' labor included in the calculation that the South contributed 11 percent of U.S. industrial output.[74] Even when all such allowances have been made, the South did not industrialize as much as modern economists think would have been cost-effective. When and where they existed, southern industries earned profits comparable to those available in agriculture. The question therefore arises, why did the South not industrialize more?

The price of slaves correlated with that of slave-produced agricultural staples, especially cotton. As a rule of thumb, "the price of slaves could be determined by multiplying the price of cotton by ten thousand (seven cents per pound for cotton yielding seven hundred dollars per slave)," according to the historian Walter Johnson. The world demand for more and more cotton drove up the price of slaves, especially from the 1840s on. Certain kinds of agricultural labor, notably gang labor in the fields, virtually required slaves, because free workers would have demanded astronomical wages to perform it. (After emancipation, gang labor soon fell into disuse, and cotton had to be produced in other, less efficient ways.) When the price of slaves was low, slaves could be diverted into manufacturing and urban commerce, although free labor could perform these jobs too. When the price of slaves rose, their owners pulled them out of marginal economic activities like industry and concentrated them where they were most needed, in gang labor on agricultural staples.[75]

Noneconomic factors probably also contributed to the reluctance of the South to invest in industry. Perhaps the southern planter class felt

73. Lewis, *Coal, Iron, and Slaves*, 33.
74. Licht, *Industrializing America*, 35–38.
75. Walter Johnson, *Soul by Soul: Life Inside the Antebellum Slave Market* (Cambridge, Mass., 2000), 6. See also Claudia Goldin, *Urban Slavery in the American South* (Chicago, 1976).

averse to taking certain kinds of risks. Growing cotton in the new lands of the West was a risky business, to be sure, but southerners understood those risks; investing in manufacturing enterprises seemed mysterious as well as risky. Industrialization became politically controversial in the South. Some planters feared that it would be harder to perpetuate slavery in a diversified economy than in an agricultural one, while a few argued eloquently that the South should industrialize to make itself less dependent on the North. The Democratic Party in the South continued to preach the superiority of the Jeffersonian agrarian ideal and the evils of city life. No other occupation conferred as much social status as the ownership of land and slaves. Most planters found little incentive to pursue industrial innovation when large-scale staple production brought them not only profits but prestige and political leadership as well.[76]

IV

However important the early industrial revolution, the fact remains that most of the workforce in antebellum America—North as well as South—labored in agriculture. Although the independent family farm was the American ideal, in reality the Middle Atlantic states had always made extensive use of nonproprietary farm labor: indentured, enslaved, or tenant. In Pennsylvania some immigrant farm laborers still worked under contracts as late as the 1830s.[77] With the passing of indentured servitude and the emancipation of their slaves, the big landowners of upstate New York had to rely primarily on tenant farmers to operate their holdings. But beginning in the 1830s, their tenants began to express their own form of labor unrest.

The trouble began on the largest of the estates, the Manor of Rensselaerwyck, dating back to a Dutch colonial land grant, which covered 436,000 acres, that is, most of Albany and Rensselaer Counties. The lord of the manor, Stephen Van Rensselaer III, had been a very model aristocrat. He served his country as a general in the War of 1812 and as a congressman from 1822 to 1829 (casting, in 1825, the vote that made John Quincy Adams president). An enlightened philanthropist, he established at Troy in 1824 a school for "the sons and daughters of farmers and mechanics" that became Rensselaer Polytechnic Institute. "The Good Patroon" (as

---

76. Many outstanding social and economic historians have addressed this issue. For a concise, judicious, but somewhat technical analysis, see Fred Bateman and Thomas Weiss, *A Deplorable Scarcity: The Failure of Industrialization in the Slave Economy* (Chapel Hill, 1981).

77. David Montgomery, *Citizen Worker* (Cambridge, Eng., 1993), 31–32.

he was called) specified as terms of tenancy not only rents determined by the price of wheat but also feudal dues that seemed anachronistic in the nineteenth-century United States, such as a day's work with a team of oxen. Yet Van Rensselaer persuaded thousands of Yankee settlers to sign such contracts by offering them free rent for the first seven years, and he kept them on his lands by the indulgence with which he tolerated it if their payments fell into arrears. Then the Erie Canal, which Van Rensselaer had supported, undercut the market for the wheat his tenants produced. Some turned to wool-growing as an alternative; Van Buren was bidding for their support with his Tariff of Abominations in 1828. But before long many tenants fell behind in their rent, and the Panic of 1839 hit farm incomes badly. Also in 1839, the Good Patroon died. In his will he specified that the debts he had piled up should be paid by collecting the $400,000 in back rents he was owed. All of a sudden, the old paternalistic structure no longer seemed viable.[78] What ensued was the largest farm protest movement in pre–Civil War America.

Confronted with demands for outstanding rents that some of them had no means of paying, Van Rensselaer's tenants declared a rent strike and organized to prevent collections. They demanded the right to buy their farms (usually they themselves had paid for all the improvements), but the new landlord, Stephen Van Rensselaer IV, refused the price they offered. The anti-rent movement spread to other estates. The newly elected Whig governor, William H. Seward, sympathized with the tenants' wish to obtain title to their farms, which was congruent with his party's vision of America as a country of middling property owners. Reasoning that only as freeholders could the tenants obtain the credit they needed to switch from raising wheat or sheep to more profitable dairy farming, Seward proposed to use the state's power of eminent domain to buy out those landlords who refused reasonable offers. His plan, however, rested on a reconstituted national bank providing New York state with credit and the distribution of federal land receipts to the states. When the national Whig victory in 1840 did not fulfill these hopes and the state's highest court ruled against such use of eminent domain, Seward's plan died. Meanwhile, he had no alternative but to call out the militia to enforce the law against the anti-renters in December 1839. The tenants credited Seward's intentions rather this action: Their elected state legislators entered into an alliance with the Whigs. While awaiting redress from the legislature,

---

78. David Maldwyn Ellis, *Landlords and Farmers in the Hudson-Mohawk Region* (Ithaca, N.Y., 1946), esp. 227, 233.

bands of anti-rent militants, masked and disguised as Indians, continued to harass process servers and to intimidate any tenant who broke ranks. The Whigs, as the party of law and order, were embarrassed by the behavior of their anti-rent allies and reluctant to press for further help to them. The federal constitutional prohibition against states impairing the obligation of contracts severely limited options.[79]

Although Stephen Van Rensselaer III had been a Whig, most other landlords, including their spokesman, the novelist James Fenimore Cooper, belonged to the Democratic Party, identifying their political interests with the planter aristocracy of Virginia. Nevertheless, when the Democrats gained control of both the statehouse and the legislature in 1844, Governor Silas Wright conceived a secret plan to help the tenants: a law authorizing them to pay to convert leaseholds into freeholds upon the death of a landlord. Wright, however, subordinated this policy to partisanship; he wanted to bring the anti-rent voters over to the Democrats. He did not lay out his plan in his initial annual message for fear the Whig legislators would simply endorse it too, depriving his party of exclusive credit. But later in the session, the complicated scenario he had devised to pass it did not work out when conservative Democrats defected. Wright went down to defeat in 1846 at the hands of a Whig who enjoyed anti-renters' support.[80] George Henry Evans's National Reform Association continued to point to the anti-rent protests as an example of why America needed a homestead act.

The return of agricultural prosperity in the mid-1840s undercut the militancy of the anti-rent movement (as returning prosperity has been wont to do to American farm protests). Although public opinion generally sympathized with the tenants, it also supported the rights of contract. Neither the legislative nor the legal system responded effectively to the demands of the anti-rent movement for relief. Yet antebellum economic reality and the lack of coercive power in the hands of authority favored the will of white settlers on the ground, in this case as in that of squatters on the public lands or the Georgia-Cherokee controversy. Sheriffs elected in anti-rent districts seldom showed much enthusiasm for pressuring their constituents to pay back rent. Sporadic rent strikes continued into the postbellum period. Worn down, the landlords tired of the game and grudgingly consented to sell their holdings, parcel by parcel, as a way of realizing

---

79. Reeve Huston, *Land and Freedom: Rural Society, Popular Protest, and Party Politics in Antebellum New York* (New York, 2000), esp. 45–76.

80. On Wright's failed stratagem, see Charles McCurdy, *The Anti-Rent Era in New York Law and Politics* (Chapel Hill, 2001), 234–59.

needed cash. In the end, Stephen Van Rensselaer IV accepted terms less favorable than those he had rejected in 1839. The New York constitutional convention of 1846 outlawed feudal leases and any agricultural leases running more than twelve years, but these prohibitions applied only to the future, not to existing contracts. To this day, it is said, people who buy homes in the Albany area may find themselves "required every year to pay a nominal rent charge to some remote assignee of Stephen Van Rensselaer."[81]

V

A huge labor force unrecorded in the economic statistics consisted of women and children working at home or on the farm for their own families. In Europe, middle-class households typically included one or more live-in servants, but visitors to the antebellum United States often commented on the scarcity of domestic help available for hire. The census of 1840 recorded only about 5 percent of the total U.S. labor force engaged in domestic service, compared with the British 13 percent in live-in domestic service in 1851, the earliest year for which information is reliable.[82] In both countries, domestic service was an overwhelmingly female occupation. A Philadelphia man spoke for middle-class America in 1822: "In these United States nothing would be wanting to make life perfectly happy (humanly speaking) had we good servants." In the South, the situation resembled that in Europe: 16 percent of the enslaved workforce engaged in domestic service in 1840. There, even nonslaveowning white families could hire slave women from their owners to perform the heavier domestic tasks. But in the North, middle-class women had to do more of their family's housework, cooking, and child care.[83]

Even more than the scarcity of domestic workers, their attitudes surprised observers. As Catharine Maria Sedgwick correctly explained in her didactic novel *Home* (1835), native-born American farm girls preferred to be called "help" rather than "servants." Women willing to work in someone else's home could demand decent treatment and pay. Often they ate

81. Ibid., 336.
82. Bureau of the Census, *Historical Statistics of the United States* (Washington, 1975), I, 139; Leonard Schwarz, "English Servants and Their Employers," *Economic History Review* 52 (1999), 245.
83. Daniel Sutherland, *Americans and Their Servants, 1800–1920* (Baton Rouge, 1981), quotation from 9. Faye Dudden, *Serving Women: Household Service in Nineteenth-Century America* (Middletown, Conn., 1983), 72–79; Keith Barton, "Slave Hiring, Domestic Labor, and the Market in Bourbon County, Kentucky," *JAH* 84 (1997): 436–60.

with the family; sometimes they chose to preserve more independence by living out. When Catharine Beecher published her *Treatise on Domestic Economy* in 1841, she advised employers of domestic employees to treat them as fellow citizens and responsible agents. Domestics simply expected the market value for their services, she explained. "Why is it not right for domestics to act according to a rule allowed to be correct in reference to all other trades and professions?"[84]

Industrialization, competing for the labor of working-class women, sharpened the shortage of domestic help. Increasingly, native-born white women found alternative employment, leaving domestic service to immigrants and African American women. Only the great waves of immigration from Europe that commenced in the mid-1840s would address what middle-class Americans called "the servant problem."

The new economic conditions fostered a new defining characteristic for a proper household. Instead of being a household with servants, a proper household became one where the wife did not need to earn money. The household continued to survive on the basis of a mixture of paid and unpaid work, with the husband now concentrating more on market activities and the wife, ideally, on activities outside the market, named with the new word "housework."[85] Although working-class and farm women more often than not still participated in market production (for example, through put-out piecework or preparing butter, eggs, and chickens for sale), within the urban middle class a married woman was expected to be a full-time mother and homemaker. In midcentury America, while 11 percent of free females over the age of sixteen worked for wages, less than 5 percent of married women did.[86] Men, on the other hand, more often left daily for employment elsewhere, in a factory or office building, rather than working at home as artisans, farmers, and shopkeepers did. The new model household became a unit of consumption rather than production.

Working-class families by no means escaped the influence of such ideas about gender roles. Journeymen mechanics, insisting on a "family wage" for themselves and that their wives belonged at home, simultaneously asserted their claim to respectability and resisted competition from women's lower wages. The wage-earning husband thus asserted claim to

84. [Catharine Maria Sedgwick], *Home* (Boston, 1835), 72; Catharine Beecher, *Treatise on Domestic Economy* (Boston, 1841), 198.

85. *Supplement to the OED* (Oxford, 1976), s.v. "housework"; Ruth Schwarz Cowan, *More Work for Mother* (New York, 1983), 16–19.

86. Margo, "The Labor Force in the Nineteenth Century," 210.

the dignity of a household head, a status that wage-earners had generally been denied in colonial and Jeffersonian America, but one compatible with his standing now as a voter. For her part, the housewife's role came to be recognized as a responsible and versatile occupation in both middle and working classes, the subject of instruction manuals like Lydia Maria Child's *American Frugal Housewife* (1836). The Victorian ideology of separate gender "spheres," a private one for women and a public one for men, while never fully realized in practice, reflected the consequences of industrialization and its separation of workplace and home.[87]

VI

Although the hard times after 1837 produced calls for economic action by the federal government, at the state level the depression acted to discourage rather than encourage government intervention in the economy. Many mixed public-private corporations in the transportation and banking industries lost money for their public investors and even went bankrupt. The economy paid a price for the absence of any national infrastructure scheme, such as Henry Clay's American System or Albert Gallatin's Plan of 1808. Competitive rather than coordinated, responding to their constituents' hopes, the state legislatures had placed some bad bets. Once burned, twice shy: Reflecting a chastened public opinion, state governments now felt reluctant to gamble again on stock ownership, and indeed some states rewrote their constitutions in the 1840s to forbid it. The federal government did not pick up the slack. Jackson's Maysville Veto Message, rather than his internal improvements expenditures on rivers and harbors, stuck in the public memory and shaped his party's policies in the coming years. Significantly, the Maysville Road Company had been a mixed corporation in which the federal government would have purchased stock if Jackson had signed the bill. Few mixed corporations were chartered anymore. For the time being, the responsibility for raising the capital for infrastructure development remained mostly with private enterprise or municipal governments, chartered by the states.[88]

87. In a large historiography, see esp. Amy Dru Stanley, "Home Life and the Morality of the Market," in *The Market Revolution in America*, ed. Melvyn Stokes and Stephen Conway (Charlottesville, Va., 1996), 74–96; Nancy Cott, *The Bonds of Womanhood* (New Haven, 1977); Mary Ryan, *Cradle of the Middle Class: The Family in Oneida County, New York* (New York, 1981).

88. John Majewski, "Toward a Social History of the Corporation," in *The Economy of Early America*, ed. Cathy Matson (University Park, Pa., 2006), 294–316; Michael Lacey, "Federalism and National Planning: The Nineteenth-Century Legacy," in *The American Planning Tradition*, ed. Robert Fishman (Washington, 2000), 89–146.

The decline of mixed corporations in the United States was accompanied and followed by gradual changes in the nature of private corporations facilitating their use to mobilize capital. Corporations could be either civic (such as municipalities with rights to self-government conferred by their state), philanthropic (such as universities), or for business purposes. Defined as a "legal person," a corporation could own property, make contracts, borrow money, and file suit in court. The principle of limited liability for the stockholders of a business corporation, as distinguished from the unlimited liability of members of a partnership, had already been established. Surprisingly to us, business corporations only gradually adopted the uniform principle that stockholders' voting rights depended on how much money they had invested. Antebellum corporations sometimes treated their shareholders like the citizens of a commonwealth, each having one vote. Of course, this rule enhanced the influence of small investors.[89]

Throughout our period, the corporate form of organization remained a privilege conferred by the state in return for what were considered services to the public interest. The sense that corporations received special favors did not enhance their universal popularity. Banks of issue were not the only corporations to encounter resentment on such grounds. Defenders of the old artisan system of manufacturing long remained suspicious of any incorporated business as well as the factory system of production. In 1835, for example, the journeymen cordwainers of Newark, New Jersey, passed this resolution at a meeting:

> We entirely disapprove of the incorporation of Companies, for carrying on manual mechanical business, inasmuch as we believe their tendency is to eventuate and produce monopolies, thereby crippling the energies of individual enterprise, and invading the rights of smaller capitalists.[90]

In an effort to avoid favoritism while also allowing the multitude of small investors their chance, various states enacted general laws of incorporation that conferred corporate status upon any business applicant(s) who complied with certain rules. Connecticut is usually credited with having passed the first such act in 1837, though New York had enacted one in 1811 that applied only to manufacturing companies. States also responded to

89. Colleen Dunlavy, "From Citizens to Plutocrats: Nineteenth-Century Shareholder Voting Rights and Theories of the Corporation," in *Constructing Corporate America*, ed. Kenneth Lipartito and David Sicilia (Oxford, 2004), 66–93.
90. Quoted in Susan Hirsch, *Roots of the American Working Class* (Philadelphia, 1978), 86.

the misgivings of people like the New Jersey cordwainers by imposing
various regulations on corporations, even sometimes specifying the composition of the board of directors.[91] But in the first half of the nineteenth
century, most business corporations were still chartered by special acts of
state legislatures, and most were still in transportation and financial services, not manufacturing. Unlike today's corporations, they might exist
only for a limited term: like the first and second national banks, each
chartered for twenty years. Meanwhile, municipal corporations also multiplied in response to increasing urbanization, and states delegated broad
powers to some of them over public utilities, public health, and law enforcement. These corporations too played an active economic role, exercising the power of eminent domain and, like the states themselves, imposing
innumerable regulations on business enterprises.[92]

Subtle changes in the law of contracts may have proved as significant
as the evolution of corporate structure in determining the climate for private investment. In the eighteenth century, the essence of a contract had
been the concept of *consideration*—that is, the contract as a promise
made in return for money or some other advantage. Judges felt free to invalidate contracts in cases where the consideration seemed inadequate.
The nineteenth century saw judges becoming more concerned with the
concept of *free will*—that is, the contract as an agreement freely entered
into by both sides, with the implication that if one chose to make a promise one should keep it. The general legal maxim for purchases was *caveat
emptor*, "Buyer beware." Legal scholars have argued that the new attitude
helped reassure investors, creditors, and employers and hence fostered
the transportation and industrial revolutions.[93] It would not be surprising
if the judges' outlook reflected the respect for free will that nineteenth-
century thinkers generally demonstrated, not only in law but also in theology, psychology, and moral philosophy.

The rising Christian humanitarianism manifested in the benevolent
reforms of the period also influenced judges, especially in the law of torts

91. Naomi Lamoreaux, "Entrepreneurship, Organization, Economic Concentration," in
    Cambridge Economic History of U.S., II, 410–11; idem, "Partnerships, Corporations,
    and the Limits of Contractual Freedom in U.S. History," in *Constructing Corporate
    America*, 29–65.
92. William Novak, *The People's Welfare: Law and Regulation in Nineteenth-Century
    America* (Chapel Hill, 1999), 105–11. See also Hendrik Hartog, *Public Property and
    Private Power* (Ithaca, N.Y., 1983).
93. Morton Horwitz, *The Transformation of American Law, 1780–1860* (Cambridge,
    Mass., 1977); P. S. Atiyah, *The Rise and Fall of Freedom of Contract* (Oxford, 1979);
    Barbara Black, "A Tale of Two Laws," *Michigan Law Review* 79 (1981): 929–46.

(personal injuries). Particularly from the 1830s on, judge-made legal innovations often reflected increased compassion for underdogs like children hurt by trolleys while playing in the street or persons injured by defective bridges. Even contract law was tampered with in the interests of workers who quit before their entire labor contract had expired. Judicial opinions of this nature often cited "the common feeling of mankind" or the Bible itself in justification for their compassion.[94]

But humanitarian benevolence impacted the law of slavery only marginally, mainly affecting slaves who had some claim to freedom. In general, legal innovations on the subject of slavery seem to have facilitated commercial considerations at the expense of human values. Like other property, slaves could be sold, mortgaged, bequeathed, insured, and hired out. Professional slave traders commanded little respect in southern society, perhaps reflecting moral embarrassment at their occupation but also for much the same reasons that used car dealers do in our society. Though most slave dealerships were small operations, a few like Franklin & Armfield, with offices in Alexandria and New Orleans, were large, sophisticated enterprises. Law courts supervised almost half of all slave sales, as part of estate or bankruptcy proceedings, and no one questioned the probity or dignity of judges for exercising this function. Congress never regulated the interstate slave trade, though it possessed the right to do so. Louisiana had elaborate consumer protection laws to help slave purchasers, reflecting the outlook of a major slave-importing state. Under the law of all states, slaves had a dual character as both property and persons; for example, slaves could be tried in court for crimes, and the unjustified killing of a slave was legally murder (a rule hardly ever enforced against the slave's owner). But down to the middle of the nineteenth century, the evolution of state law in the South tended to make the jurisprudence of slavery more responsive to liberal capitalist and contract notions, favoring the master's free market in slave transfers "at the expense of the slaves and their families," notes historian Thomas Morris.[95] Slavery represented one area within which it is impossible for us to accept that economic rationality was really a good thing.

94. Based on a very thorough study of private law at the state level: Peter Karsten, *Heart Versus Head: Judge-Made Law in Nineteenth-Century America* (Chapel Hill, 1997), quotation from 10. Some legal theorists held that the common law embodied Christianity; see Daniel Blinka, "The Roots of the Modern Trial," *JER* 27 (2007): 293–334.
95. Thomas Morris, *Southern Slavery and the Law* (Chapel Hill, 1996), 434. See also Jenny Wahl, *The Bondsman's Burden: An Economic Analysis of the Common Law of Southern Slavery* (Cambridge, Eng., 1998); Ariela Gross, *Double Character: Slavery and Mastery in the Antebellum Southern Courtroom* (Princeton, 2000).

With state and federal governments holding off on making economic commitments, and in the absence of a national bank, recovery from the depression of the Van Buren years came slowly. The textile mills of Lancashire and New England gradually worked through their glut of American cotton and began to place new orders. This emboldened state and local bankers to make countless small decisions to resume lending money to agricultural producers. Of course, before banks could print banknotes and lend them out, the banks had to exist. Chartering new banks often provoked controversy within a state between soft-money and hard-money factions. The decision of some states, notably New York in 1838, to adopt "free banking," granting bank charters to all comers in accordance with general laws of incorporation, multiplied the sources of credit. Without banks, borrowers (especially in the West) would have found it difficult to negotiate loans from savers (mostly located in the East), and more of the country's capital would have remained unproductively stored up in unused land or inventories of livestock and agricultural produce. Without bank notes, frontier and rural America would have been thrown back on "a rag-tag mixture of foreign and domestic coins, land warrants, tobacco warehouse receipts, even animal pelts"—inefficient substitutes that increased the cost of transacting business.[96] So desperate was the eagerness for currency that counterfeit circulated widely with very little attempt to suppress it, alongside the notes of distant and insolvent banks. Retail traders routinely accepted almost anything resembling money and passed it along, following the maxim "If you buy the devil, the sooner you sell him, the better."[97] The resumption of bank lending in the 1840s produced not inflation but expanded national product. In fact, during the antebellum period the American price level never stayed far out of line from the British.[98] While the opportunities for fraud provoked hard-money criticism, the plain commercial truth was that America needed banks and banknotes. The soft-money advocates were right. The disorderly banking that followed the demise of the BUS proved better than no banking at all.

Despite the anarchic state of the money supply, the nineteenth-century United States did not represent the age of pure laissez-faire that many people imagine. This widespread misconception does not square with the economic role actually played by state and local governments. The

---

96. Howard Bodenhorn, *History of Banking in Antebellum America* (Cambridge, Mass., 2000), quotation from 215. See also Paul Gilje, "The Rise of Capitalism," *JER* 16 (1996): 159–81.
97. Quoted in Appleby, *Inheriting the Revolution*, 86.
98. Noted by Marvin Meyers, *The Jacksonian Persuasion* (Stanford, 1960), 114.

decline of mixed corporations provoked by the depression of the Van Buren years proved permanent, but the decline in state promotion of internal improvements turned out to be very temporary. The coming of the railroads encouraged a new wave of economic interventions by most of the states, many localities, and eventually the federal government as well. Rather than waiting for prosperity to return in the 1840s, American governments actively promoted it through their investments in the newly invented steam railroads.[99]

VII

George Stephenson operated a steam-powered pump that sucked water out of a mineshaft near Newcastle-upon-Tyne in the North of England. In 1814, he invented a steam locomotive that could pull coal from the mine shaft to a nearby dock for loading onto a barge; over the next decade he built similar machines for other local mining companies. Wider applications for the invention became apparent. In 1825, Stephenson demonstrated a locomotive that could pull thirty-six wagons of coal and flour along a level track for nine miles in two hours. Four years later Stephenson's "Rocket" won a competition to pull trains for passengers as well as freight on a railway between Liverpool and Manchester. The intercity track opened in 1830 with Prime Minister Wellington riding the first train. The unschooled son of a mechanic had changed the world. Like its American counterpart, the British industrial revolution was to a large extent the creation of the working class.

Across the Atlantic, an American named John Stevens constructed a prototype locomotive in 1825. Born into a prominent family, Stevens was an exception to the rule that inventors came from artisan origins, but he still couldn't raise enough funding for the railway he planned across New Jersey. The first functioning railroads in the United States were much more modest: They moved animal-drawn cars for short distances, as did the one in Quincy, Massachusetts (1826), which carried stone for three miles from quarry to dockside. An English-built steam locomotive imported in 1828 turned out too heavy to be serviceable on the uneven American terrain. When twenty-three miles of track opened on what was optimistically named the Baltimore & Ohio Railroad that same year, the cars had to be pulled by horses pending the construction of a locomotive. Even so, at the ceremony when construction of the B&O rails began on

99. See further in Richard Sylla, "Experimental Federalism," in *Cambridge Economic History of U.S.*, II, 483–541.

the Fourth of July, 1828, ninety-one-year-old Charles Carroll, sole surviving signer of the Declaration of Independence, turned the first spadeful of earth and told the crowd, "I consider this among the most important acts of my life, second only to my signing the Declaration of Independence, if even it be second to that."[100]

An American coach-maker turned master manufacturer, Peter Cooper, designed a locomotive with a shorter wheelbase and smaller wheels than British models so it could negotiate inclines and sharp curves. Because of its small size, he nicknamed it "Tom Thumb." As a publicity event in 1830, the Tom Thumb raced a horse-drawn wagon. The horse won when the locomotive slipped a drive belt, but Cooper's steam engine impressed the B&O's representatives enough that they adopted it. Peter Cooper's "contrivance," one of them later recalled, proved instrumental "in making available, in America, that vast system which united remote peoples and promotes that peace on earth and good will to men which angels have proclaimed."[101]

Most early American railroads, like Baltimore's, reflected the ambition of cities to engross the trade of a hinterland before some municipal competitor did so. They expressed the same geographical rivalries that canal-building had. Charleston, worried about the competition of Savannah, completed in 1833 a railroad to Hamburg, South Carolina, that was actually the world's longest at that time, 136 miles. Boston tried to get a piece of the trade generated by the Erie Canal with a railroad through Worcester to Albany completed in 1842. Both the Charleston and Boston railways relied predominantly upon public funding.[102]

Andrew Jackson arrived in Washington in 1829 in a carriage and left eight years later on a train. Throughout the United States, people welcomed the steam locomotive as a heaven-sent deliverance from the tyranny of distance. The heady prosperity of the early 1830s encouraged construction, though the ensuing depression slowed it down. By the end of the 1830s, there were 450 locomotives in the country, only 117 of them imported from Britain, and 3,200 miles of track—as much as the total canal mileage and, amazingly, more than twice the track in all Europe. Railroad building proceeded more quickly in the United States not only because of the greater felt need but also because of the availability of

100. http://cprr.org/Museum/First_US_Railroads_Gamst.html (viewed May 25, 2007). Carroll is quoted in Louis Masur, 1831 (New York, 2001), 173.

101. John Latrobe, *The Baltimore and Ohio Railroad* (Baltimore, 1868), 18.

102. John Larson, *Internal Improvement* (Chapel Hill, 2001), 225–55; Ruth Schwarz Cowan, *Social History of American Technology* (New York, 1997), 113–14.

land. Where European railways had to spend a lot of time and money acquiring their rights-of-way, American ones got theirs cheaply or in free
land grants. Even fuel was inexpensive: American locomotives burned
wood rather than coal, as European ones did, because wood was so
cheap.[103] The generosity of public authorities further helped the exceptionally rapid growth of U.S. railways. A comparative study of the economic policies of the United States and Prussia in the nineteenth century
concluded that while the Prussian government contributed only 7 percent of the capital needed for that country's early railroads, American
state governments contributed 45 percent of early railroad capital.[104]

When prosperity began to return around 1842, railroad construction resumed at full throttle. The depression did leave one lasting mark on the
railroad industry, the demise of the mixed public-private corporation as
an investment vehicle. Yet public support continued in a variety of other
forms, including land grants, cash subsidies, loan guarantees, and the
purchase of corporate bonds. Cities as well as states eagerly threw their
money at the new technology. Even the federal government helped out
some, providing free surveys for routes and tariff refunds on iron imported
for rails. Public financial support proved particularly important for railroads in the South, where it was hard to tempt private capital away from
investment in plantations and slaves. The famous subsidies that southern
states granted to railroads during Reconstruction actually had plenty of
precedent in the antebellum years. Without owning stock, the public entities providing support to internal improvements could no longer share
in any profits, but the hoped-for economic benefits to their citizens—plus
an occasional payoff to a relevant officeholder—constituted sufficient
motivation. Mixed corporations were abandoned on the grounds that
they lent themselves to corruption, but in fact the other forms of subsidy
proved no less liable to dishonest exploitation. By fair means or foul, railway mileage had more than doubled to 7,500 by the end of the 1840s.[105]

Railroads dramatically shortened travel times. When Henry Clay first
went to Washington from Lexington, Kentucky, in 1806, his trip took
three weeks; by 1846, he could do it on a train in four days. Despite their

103. Albert Fishlow, "Transportation in the 19th and Early 20th Centuries," in *Cambridge Economic History of U.S.*, II, 572–74, 611–12; Taylor, *Transportation Revolution*, 134–44.
104. Colleen Dunlavy, *Politics and Industrialization: Early Railroads in the United States and Prussia* (Princeton, 1994), 51–55.
105. Richard Sylla, "The Economy of American Government, 1789–1914," in *Cambridge Economic History of U.S.*, II, 483–541; Fishlow, "Transportation," 575.

speed, however, trains by no means immediately rendered canals obsolete. For shippers not in a hurry, canal transportation, with ton-mile charges generally less than those of a railroad, might well remain advantageous. The Erie Canal, granddaddy of them all, continued to expand its traffic until after the Civil War. Weighing the comparative importance of canals and railroads is not easy, and canals may well have been the more critical improvement in transportation. But, of course, their impact was cumulative; the effects of the railroads came on top of those of canals. Perhaps more important than the speed of the railroads was the fact that they offered year-round transportation, since, unlike canals, they did not freeze up in winter.

Railroads had an enormous impact on Americans' lives. They allowed the cities to keep growing by bringing them ever greater quantities of food. The efficiency with which railroads could transport freight meant that inventories and storage costs could be reduced in many parts of the economy. By facilitating long-distance travel, the railroads also made the labor market more responsive. Cultural consequences of the railroads included the proliferation of reading matter and the ability to take regular vacations in distant places, a custom that began with the wealthy and gradually extended to include the middle class. In response, resorts grew up and a tourist trade developed. Railroads increased reliance on the newly mass-produced watches and clocks. Even more than factories and farms, the operation of railroads depended on close attention to accurate timepieces.

Railroads did not come as an unalloyed blessing; they were dirty, noisy, and dangerous. Until after the Civil War, different railroads sometimes had incompatible gauges (track widths), hampering long-distance shippers. Like steamboats, the early trains had abysmal safety records, in large part because of the high-pressure boilers both used; hasty, cheap construction and excessive speeds didn't help either. On November 8, 1833, a passenger train carrying John Quincy Adams ran off the track near Amboy, New Jersey. The train had been speeding at "one mile in one minute thirty-six seconds," he noted. The car ahead of his overturned, leaving "men, women, and a child scattered along the road, bleeding, mangled, groaning." All but one of those in the car were injured, three (including the child) fatally. Adams successfully demanded a coroner's inquiry.[106]

Because of the multiple and cumulative effects of the railroads supplementing canals, the years from 1843 to the Civil War have sometimes

---

106. John Quincy Adams, *Memoirs*, ed. Charles Francis Adams (Philadelphia, 1874–79), IX, 29–32.

been called America's economic "take-off." Whether this is an apt term depends on what one means by it. The U.S. economy before railroads was neither static, anti-entrepreneurial, nor isolated from the rest of the world. What the railroads changed was not American hopes but the material conditions for fulfilling them. Railroads did not produce a "market revolution" any more than canals did; instead they introduced a new phase in a long-range process of economic development. The American economy expanded more or less constantly from 1820 (that is, from before the introduction of the railroads) to the Civil War except for the depression of 1837–42, not only in the aggregate but also per capita; returns to capital over that period constituted a remarkably long-term bull market.[107]

More relevant to railroad history than the concept of a "market revolution" is "industrial revolution." If the railroads did not initiate the industrial revolution, they certainly speeded it up. They stimulated the mining, processing, and importing of iron and steel (and, after the eventual switch in fuel, coal). They created vast primary industries in the manufacture of rails, locomotives, and rolling stock. They encouraged the workforce to continue to leave agriculture and move into other occupations. They multiplied new jobs as engineers, firemen, brakemen, switchmen, conductors, and roundhouse mechanics. (The gendering of so many of these occupational titles was, of course, no accident.) Since their public subsidies so often took the form of land grants, railroads became large-scale land speculators, promoting settlement along their routes and urban development at major railheads.

The sheer size of the railway companies altered the American economy. The major railroads came to dwarf the antebellum manufacturing concerns, even the Lowell mills. Railroads became the largest corporations since the demise of the BUS, and the first nationwide secular enterprises under entirely private control. When these big players went into the capital markets of New York and London, they necessitated the creation of new kinds of financial services to meet their needs. Perhaps most importantly, being too large and technical to operate through the conventional arrangement of an owner and a foreman, the railroads developed a

---

107. Thomas Weiss, "Economic Growth Before 1860," in *American Economic Development in Historical Perspective*, ed. Thomas Weiss and Donald Schaefer (Stanford, 1994), 11–27; Richard Sylla, Jack Wilson, and Charles P. Jones, "U.S. Financial Markets and Long-Term Economic Growth," ibid., 28–35. The term "take-off" originated with Walt Rostow, *Stages of Economic Growth* (Cambridge, Eng., 1963; 3rd ed., 1990).

whole new profession: business management. Yet, throughout the nineteenth century, the skilled machinist remained a key figure in industry alongside the newer white-collar salaried manager.[108] The career of Peter Cooper, builder of the Tom Thumb, is instructive. This former artisan combined iron manufacturing, railroads, and telegraphy in a highly successful business career before turning, as Robert Owen had done, to philanthropy and politics.

The railroads had particularly portentous consequences for settlers in the newer states of the Old Northwest: Illinois (1818), Michigan (1837), and Wisconsin (1848). The space-binding technology of the trains magnified the opportunities for farmers in those places to ship their crops to distant destinations, encouraging market production rather than local consumption. Farmers who migrated into these areas typically concentrated more on commercial staples like wheat than they had done in their previous homes. More small farmers entered the market, where the large ones had been all along. The drop in farm prices after the Panic of 1839 hurt these new commercial farmers and prompted a temporary reversion to diversified production, some of which could be consumed locally.[109] But once transportation improved, both farm prices and land values climbed. Many a midwestern farmer realized a handsome profit reselling land he had obtained cheaply from the government. The coming of the railroad affected farm families in their role as consumers too, widening the choice of clothing and household goods available from the country store. Railroads also facilitated the emergence of towns and cities in the West. The extraordinarily rapid growth of Chicago, from a population of less than one hundred in 1830 to thirty thousand in 1850 and far greater heights thereafter, would have been inconceivable if the city had had to depend entirely on water transportation without the railroad.[110]

In 1845, a poet addressing the Mercantile Library Association of Boston celebrated the effects of the railroad in knitting the country together with a poem that also likened the trains to giant textile looms:

108. The classic account of the rise of management is Alfred Chandler Jr., *The Visible Hand: The Managerial Revolution in American Business* (Cambridge, Mass., 1977). On the continued importance of skilled workers, see Herbert Gutman, *Work, Culture, and Society in Industrializing America* (New York, 1976), 221; John K. Brown, *The Baldwin Locomotive Works* (Baltimore, 1995).

109. Susan Gray, *The Yankee West: Community Life on the Michigan Frontier* (Chapel Hill, 1996), 48–65.

110. Helen Jeter, *Trends of Population in the Region of Chicago* (Chicago, 1927), 7, 21.

América's Railroads in 1840

Here magic Art her mighty power reveals,
Moves the slow beam, and plies her thousand wheels,
Through ponderous looms the rapid shuttle flies,
And weaves the web which shines with varied dyes.
Here, gliding cars, like shooting meteors run,
The mighty shuttle binding States in one.[111]

Railroads did indeed have political as well as economic consequences, but they turned out to be sectional rather than simply strengthening the Union. Their network reinforced east–west ties at the expense of north–south ones. Their resources, added to those of the Erie and related canals, further encouraged the Old Northwest to ship its produce eastward rather than southward along the river system to the Gulf, affecting the balance of political power both regionally and nationally. The geographical competition that the railroads stimulated for westward routes, fostered by politicians like Illinois's Stephen Douglas, was destined to exacerbate sectional tensions in the years leading up to the Civil War.

111. Robert C. Waterston, *Poem Delivered Before the Mercantile Library Association* (Boston, 1845).

15

The Whigs and Their Age

A cold and blustery March wind chilled the ceremonies for the presidential inauguration of 1841. But the old soldier at the center of attention spoke for an hour and a half. In an era when people took oratory seriously, William Henry Harrison delivered the longest inaugural address of any president ever, full of learned classical allusions. In implied but clear reproach to the Democrats, he promised to exercise executive restraint, serve but one term, and use the veto sparingly—the last not too risky a commitment since his party controlled both houses of Congress. He condemned hard money, the spoils system, and "the spirit of party." He warned of the dangers of demagogues claiming to speak "in the name of democracy," who perverted the commonwealth and stripped the people of their liberties. He cited Caesar and Cromwell as his examples, but all understood these as coded references to Andrew Jackson. The Whig victory had averted, just in time, the corruption of American republican institutions—"a calamity so awful, not only to our country, but to the world."[1]

In claiming for the Whigs the toga of Roman virtue, Harrison's inaugural address aimed at personal as well as national vindication. His background and lifestyle having been subjected to considerable distortion during the campaign by friend and foe alike, Harrison felt it time to start looking presidential. He had written his inaugural speech himself, though he allowed Daniel Webster to edit it; the senator jested that in abridging it he had "killed seventeen Roman proconsuls."[2] The erudition of Harrison's address demonstrated that the incoming president was no humble denizen of a log cabin but a distinguished Virginia gentleman like Washington, Jefferson, and Madison. And by delivering such a long speech in the cold with no overcoat, the author would demonstrate his hardy vigor—despite being, at sixty-eight, the oldest president inaugurated up to that time.[3] Harrison's opponents had made his age an issue, ridiculing him as "granny." His proud defiance of their jibes may have proved literally fatal.

1. "Inaugural Address" (March 4, 1841), *Presidential Messages*, IV, 5–21, quotation from 20.
2. Quoted in Robert Remini, *Daniel Webster* (New York, 1997), 516.
3. Harrison's record stood until the inauguration of sixty-nine-year-old Ronald Reagan in 1981.

William Henry Harrison brought to the White House creditable qualifications. Born into a prominent family, the son of Benjamin Harrison V, signer of the Declaration of Independence and governor of Virginia, William attended Hampden-Sydney College, entered the army, and distinguished himself in several important battles against Indians and British, including Fallen Timbers (1794), Tippecanoe (1811), and the Thames (1813).[4] Chosen by the legislature of the Northwest Territory their non-voting representative in Congress, he made himself the most influential such territorial delegate in history, crafting the major federal land legislation of 1800. Governor for a dozen years of Indiana Territory (larger than the later state), he nursed further political ambitions. Moving to Ohio, he served that state as legislator, U.S. representative, and senator, demonstrating sympathy for banking, tariff protection, and the extension of slavery. Secretary of State Clay sent him on a mission to Colombia as part of the effort to increase trade with South America. In 1828, he was mentioned as a possible running mate for John Quincy Adams, though in earlier years Harrison, with the hauteur of the Virginia aristocracy, had privately looked down on the "clownish" dress and manner of the merely bourgeois Adams.[5] Having shown himself the strongest Whig candidate in the presidential election of 1836, Harrison challenged Clay for the party's nomination four years later.

This time around, the Whigs resolved to hold their first national convention. They called it early to give their nominee plenty of exposure, meeting at Harrisburg, Pennsylvania, in December 1839. Harrison arrived already bearing the nomination of the Antimasonic Party, whose supporters preferred him to Henry Clay because of the latter's nominal Masonic membership. At the Whig convention, Harrison gained support from a number of nervous northern politicians who suspected that a military hero could outpoll Clay, by now carrying a lot of contentious baggage from previous years. Clay showed up with most of the southern delegates and a significant minority of northern ones behind him. The convention adopted a "unit rule" that state delegations would vote as blocs; this smothered the Clay votes in states where he did not command a majority. Disgusted at his convention delegates for allowing this rule, Clay later grumbled that they were "not worth the powder and shot it would take" to blow them up.[6] General Winfield Scott, whose role in preventing war

---

4. The family's eminence continued; in 1889 William Henry's grandson Benjamin Harrison also became president of the United States.
5. William Henry Harrison to James Findlay, Jan. 24, 1817, quoted in Donald Ratcliffe, *The Politics of Long Division* (Columbus, Ohio, 2000), 225.
6. As reported by Henry A. Wise, in *Seven Decades of the Union* (Philadelphia, 1881), 171.

along the Canadian border had won favorable attention, attracted support as a possible compromise candidate. The wily Thaddeus Stevens, Pennsylvania Antimason, contrived to turn a key group of Virginia delegates away from Scott and toward Harrison by leaking a document that aroused their fears for the security of slavery. Stevens somehow obtained a letter that Scott had written courting antislavery New Yorkers and deliberately dropped it where he knew the Virginians would find it. (In the light of Stevens's later career as an architect of Radical Reconstruction, his role at the Harrisburg convention is ironic in the extreme.) With Daniel Webster backing Harrison and Scott no longer viable, the Whig convention nominated Old Tippecanoe on the third ballot, 148 to 90 for Clay and 16 for Scott.[7]

The victorious Harrisonians now offered the vice-presidential nomination to Clay himself or a candidate of his choice. But the despondent Kentuckian did not reply to their inquiry. It proved a costly fit of pique. Other Clay followers whom they approached, such as Senator John Clayton of Delaware, would not accept without his permission.[8] In the end the Harrisonians turned to John Tyler of Virginia, who did accept. Tyler had been supporting Clay's candidacy at the convention, but he felt no commitment to Clay's nationalist program. An eccentric Virginia staterighter, Tyler had joined the Whig Party because he found Andrew Jackson high-handed. Surprisingly, Clay might even have been considering Tyler as his own possible running mate.[9] If so, presumably Clay's motive was to solidify support among southern sympathizers with nullification who had backed Hugh White in 1836 and who now appeared slow to identify with the Whig Party. The vice-presidential nomination is customarily dictated by concern to "balance the ticket." But the Whigs' choice of Tyler turned out to be one of the worst mistakes ever made by any political party.

Before the Whig convention adjourned, Clay recovered the good grace to give the party nominees his endorsement. The Harrison campaign moved quickly into high gear, borrowing techniques from the current experts on mass persuasion, the revival preachers. Harrison himself, deferring to nineteenth-century sensibilities, stopped actively campaigning once he received the Whig nomination and relied on supporters to elec-

7. Michael Holt, *The Rise and Fall of the American Whig Party* (New York, 1999), 102–3.
8. Major Wilson, *The Presidency of Martin Van Buren* (Lawrence, Kans., 1984), 194.
9. Robert Seager, "Henry Clay and the Politics of Compromise," *Register of the Kentucky Historical Society* 85 (1987): 14.

tioneer for him. His missionaries would come to a town on his behalf and hold a torchlight parade to whip up popular interest the evening before their main event. During the night, they would pitch a tent on the outskirts of town. The next morning a "barker" standing outside would begin encouraging people to enter and hear the speeches, punctuated by music and songs like "Van, Van, Van Is a Used-up Man," or most famously, "Tippecanoe and Tyler Too." The historian Ronald Formisano has aptly called these activities "a form of political revivalism."[10] In the tent, the speaker would lambaste the administration, particularly its passivity in the face of economic disaster and public hardship. When the crowd had been wound up emotionally, they would be asked to make a commitment, in this case not to Christ but to the Whig ticket. It all must have had a familiar ring, because we know that the Whig Party appealed to many members of evangelical religious bodies. (In later years, Phineas T. Barnum would adapt the same techniques to his traveling circus.) Harrison's campaigners also exploited new technology, moving their speakers from place to place via railroads and attracting attention with a giant transparency displaying Whig emblems.[11]

No incumbent president campaigned overtly for himself before Theodore Roosevelt in the election of 1904.[12] Van Buren's re-election campaign was headed by Amos Kendall, who resigned as postmaster general to devote full time to the effort, and Francis Blair of the *Washington Globe*, who formulated the Democratic case as follows: "The issue, then, is Martin Van Buren, a sound currency, and independence of the honest producing classes, against a spurious and fictitious bank currency, dependency, venality, and servility to the non-producers and aristocrats, the representatives of their available G. Harrison."[13] Kendall and Blair often invoked ex-president Jackson and the necessity to carry on his legacy—an approach that would have been more effective if Clay had been the Whig candidate. Seeking to outdo the earlier Whig convention, the Democratic convention issued the first official party platform in history. Of its nine clauses, six renounced any federal power to implement the American System or interfere with slavery; one endorsed the separation of bank

---

10. Ronald Formisano, *The Birth of Mass Political Parties* (Princeton, 1971), 128–36. Over one hundred pages of Whig song lyrics are printed in A. Banning Norton, *Tippecanoe Songs of the Log Cabin Boys and Girls of 1840* (Mount Vernon, Ohio, 1888).

11. Donald Cole, *Martin Van Buren and the American Political System* (Princeton, 1984), 368–69.

12. President Andrew Johnson, however, conducted a "swing around the circle" to campaign on behalf of Democratic congressional candidates in the 1866 midterm elections.

13. *Washington Globe*, May 5, 1840.

and state; one promised "the most rigid economy" in government; and the last one opposed any curtailing of the rights of immigrants to citizenship. The theme running throughout this negativist document was fear of change. The statement said nothing about the depression.[14] The Democratic convention proved unable to agree to renominate Richard Mentor Johnson, who seemed out of his depth in the vice presidency. But since no one else in the party then had the nerve to challenge the president's choice, that crusty Kentuckian wound up on Democratic ballots again simply by default.

The Van Buren campaign of 1840 is remembered mostly for a blunder. A Democratic newspaper correspondent in Baltimore, intending to mock Harrison's advanced age and suggest he was a better candidate for retirement than for the presidency, wrote, "Give him a barrel of hard cider, and settle a pension of two thousand a year on him, and my word for it, he will sit the remainder of his days in his log cabin by the side of a 'sea coal' fire, and study moral philosophy."[15] Although the suggestion of moral philosophy was probably the most plausible part of this fantasy, since Harrison read seriously, it did not become famous. Instead, the Whigs seized gleefully upon the log cabin and hard cider images, as providing their candidate with precisely that common touch he needed. From then on, cider barrels and miniature log cabins adorned every Whig banner and parade. Temperance advocates of course regretted the "hard cider" symbol but, interestingly, were not alienated from Harrison's candidacy by it.[16]

The populistic, emotionally evocative campaign methods of 1840 by no means precluded a discussion of the issues. The medium was *not* the whole message the parties wanted to convey. In fact, 1840 was the first election in which both parties clearly and forcefully articulated their positions on the issues of the day—the most urgent of which was the depression. The Whigs campaigned for soft money and government intervention in the economy, adding executive restraint to remind people of Jackson's presumptuousness. The Democrats defended hard money and laissez-faire. Evidence of the level of intellectual seriousness in the campaign is provided by such Whig pamphlets as Calvin Colton's *The Crisis of the Country*, Henry C. Carey's *Answers to the Questions*, and the historian Richard Hildreth's *The Contrast: William Henry Harrison versus Martin Van Buren*. (Hildreth declared that the American farmer was no

---

14. *National Party Platforms*, comp. Kirk Porter and Donald Johnson (Urbana, Ill., 1970), 2.
15. [John de Ziska], *Baltimore Republican*, Dec. 11, 1839.
16. Richard Carwardine, *Evangelicals and Politics in Antebellum America* (New Haven, 1993), 61–62.

longer the self-sufficient yeoman "described by poets" but "must have a *market* for his produce.")[17] On the Democratic side, Orestes Brownson asserted the existence of American class conflict in his provocative essay *The Laboring Classes*. The two parties' stated policies were underscored by the programs they actually implemented, which voters could observe in action at the state level. There, Whigs supported chartering banks and subsidizing internal improvements; Democrats generally opposed these.[18] One issue only the parties tacitly agreed to avoid: slavery. Both dissociated themselves from abolitionism.

As month after month of 1840 ticked by, the economy descended deeper and deeper into the tank, taking with it the hopes of the man Whigs now called "Martin Van Ruin." The Magician had run out of magic. The Whigs won the state and local elections that gradually led up to the big contest in the fall. As a Whig presidential victory came to seem inevitable, the significance of the early date of the Whig convention became apparent. Some Whig politicians, particularly in the North, had supported Harrison for prudential reasons but would actually have preferred Clay as the true embodiment of the party's principles. Now it seemed clear that Clay too could have won election—and that he would have gained the nomination had the convention been held later when the full impact of the Panic of 1839 had been felt. Clay himself commented bitterly that he had been "always run by my friends when sure to be defeated, and now betrayed for a nomination when I, or any one, would be sure of an election."[19]

When the results came in, the Whigs indeed swept all before them: Harrison won 234 electoral votes to 60 for Van Buren; the Whigs would have majorities of thirty-one in the House and seven in the Senate. It was the only time in the party's history that the Whigs won control of both the executive and legislative branches of government. Yet 1840 was no fluke; it had long-lasting significance. In fact, the election of 1840 has been rightly judged more important than that of 1828 in defining the Whig–Democratic political party system and the parties' positions on issues.[20] In earlier times, election campaigns had often focused on praising prominent local leaders as candidates for office. Jackson's campaigns, which emphasized his personal popularity, did not altogether depart from this

---

17. Quoted in Wilson, *Presidency of Van Buren*, 199.
18. Holt, *Rise and Fall of Whig Party*, 108–12.
19. Wise, *Seven Decades*, 172.
20. Richard P. McCormick, "New Perspectives on Jacksonian Politics," *AHR* 65 (1960): 288–301.

tradition. From now on, however, elections—state as well as national—focused unmistakably, on both sides, on parties and issues.

For too long historical accounts have attributed Harrison's election to mindless hoopla. A Democratic contemporary came closer to the truth when he wrote Van Buren that "the second revulsion" (meaning the Panic of 1839 coming on top of that of 1837) "and no other cause whatever, has elected your opponent and would have elected any other man."[21] The most judicious modern scholarship concludes, however, that the voters did not just lash out at the incumbent party but rendered a judgment on which party's policy they trusted to get the country out of hard times. The Whig campaign possessed "reason as well as rhyme," as one historian has put it.[22]

A conspicuous feature of the 1840 election was the massive voter turnout of 80.2 percent of the qualified electorate, a dramatic increase over the 57.2 percent turnout four years earlier. It stands as one of the three highest national election turnouts in American history, all of them in the nineteenth century.[23] The Whigs did particularly well among the many voters participating in their first election. The high voter participation of 1840 and the rest of the nineteenth century in general reflected the effectiveness of the parties' efforts to get out the vote as well as the high state of public interest in politics by comparison with more recent American history.

"The spirit of the age," the English visitor Frances Wright observed, was "to be a little fanatical."[24] She described American politics fairly. The Whig and Democratic parties took sharply differentiated positions on policy. Typically, they each endeavored to maximize their appeal, not by moderating their stands so as to win over people in the middle, but by energizing and mobilizing their own core supporters. Organizing the partisan endeavor were men with a personal stake in the outcome: officeholders and those who hoped to hold office. The broad reach of the patronage, with a postmastership in every little community up for grabs, tended to diffuse this kind of strong motivation throughout the public.

---

21. C. C. Cambreling to Martin Van Buren, Dec. 15, 1840, quoted in John Niven, *Martin Van Buren and the Romantic Age of American Politics* (New York, 1983), 471–72.
22. Quotation from Wilson, *Presidency of Van Buren*, 197. See also Holt, *Rise and Fall of Whig Party*, 76–82, 108–12.
23. The others were 1860 (81.2) and 1876 (81.8), both times when momentous sectional issues needed resolution.
24. Quoted in Bertram Wyatt-Brown, *Lewis Tappan and the Evangelical War Against Slavery* (Cleveland, 1969), 63.

The newspapers of the communications revolution, widely distributed and strongly partisan, prodded men to vote while also rousing general popular interest in political events. Some voters, somewhere in the Union, were casting ballots just about all the time, with the press avidly predicting or reporting the results. Aided by the disguised government subsidy of cheap postage rates, the partisan newspapers provided effective propaganda to their respective sponsors with only very modest party subsidies. Rank-and-file Democrats and Whigs paid subscriptions to their respective party newspapers, and advertisers paid to reach them. The general high level of political awareness maintained by the press meant that the parties could depend on a broadly based mass of donors; they also kept their financial costs to a minimum by receiving many contributions in kind, that is, free services from their supporters. Businesses (especially banks) gave money and favors to politicians, but except for the BUS most businesses were small. Political parties of the day, like the philanthropies of the evangelical "benevolent empire," chiefly relied on pooling many modest contributions, not on soliciting a few large ones. We should not read the current political apathy of the American public back into the antebellum past. The public was not yet jaded then, and fewer rival sources of mass entertainment diverted popular attention and loyalty away from the political parties.[25]

Even more than the Democrats, the Whigs depended on literacy and the printed media. Whig support usually came from environments providing good access to information and an awareness of people and events beyond the immediate horizon.[26] Of the many Whig journalists, the greatest undoubtedly was Horace Greeley, editor of the *Log Cabin* and other campaign periodicals. A self-made man who came from a hardscrabble New Hampshire farm, Greeley combined a practical, methodical business sense with idealistic politics (much as did Benjamin Franklin, with whom contemporaries compared him). Starting in 1838, Greeley hitched his talents to the reform-minded cause of New York Whigs William H. Seward and Thurlow Weed. In 1841, he founded the *New York Tribune*, which went on to become one of America's great newspapers, with a circulation

25. On the parties' strenuous efforts to get out the vote, see Glenn Altschuler and Stuart Blumin, *Rude Republic: Americans and Their Politics in the Nineteenth Century* (Princeton, 2000). On the high general level of interest in politics then, see Mark Neely, *American Political Culture in the Civil War Era* (Chapel Hill, 2005).
26. See Thomas Alexander, "The Basis of Alabama's Antebellum Two-Party System," *Alabama Review* 19 (1966): 276. Based on Alabama data, his finding is applicable more generally.

that reached 200,000 before the Civil War; its spin-off, the *Tribune Weekly*, reprinted its articles for a nationwide readership.[27]

No strong sectional pattern emerged in the election of 1840. Harrison carried both North and South, though by an overall popular margin of 53 percent to 47 percent—nowhere near as great as his preponderance in the electoral college. Of the seven states Van Buren carried, five were in the South. But, overall, the New Yorker's long courtship of the slaveholders seems to have been neutralized by Harrison's Virginia background and record in favor of the expansion of slavery into both Missouri and, earlier, the Northwest Territory itself. Whereas the National Republicans had been weak in the South, the Bank War had brought the Whigs considerable recruits in that section, especially among larger planters who recognized the benefits of a strong financial system for commercial agriculture. North and South, a relatively small percentage typically separated winners from losers in 1840, and this remained a striking characteristic of the second party system over the next decade. In antebellum times, more than half the seats in the federal House of Representatives were genuinely competitive, a striking difference from today when more sophisticated voter analysis enables the parties to protect their incumbents, leaving few "swing" congressional districts.[28] Whigs and Democrats had created not only the first mass political parties in the world but also the only truly nationwide party system in America prior to the rebirth of the southern Republicans late in the twentieth century.

Contemporaries generally assumed men with greater income, education, and respectability more likely to vote Whig. But there were innumerable exceptions to such social categories, highlighted when prominent brothers made different political choices. The Whig James Barbour, senator from Virginia and John Quincy Adams's secretary of war, was the brother of Democrat Philip Barbour, member of Thomas Ritchie's Richmond Junto, rewarded by Andrew Jackson with a seat on the Supreme Court. Benjamin Tappan, Democratic senator from Ohio, was the brother of Arthur and Lewis Tappan, abolitionist admirers of John Quincy Adams. Data from North Carolina show virtually the same party breakdown between voters who could meet the fifty-acre freehold qualification to vote for state senators and voters who could not.[29]

---

27. See Robert C. Williams, *Horace Greeley* (New York, 2006); for a brief assessment, Daniel Howe, *The Political Culture of the American Whigs* (Chicago, 1980), 179–97.
28. Joel Silbey, *The American Political Nation, 1838–1893* (Stanford, 1991), 155–56.
29. Richard P. McCormick, "Suffrage Classes and Party Alignments," in *Voters, Parties, and Elections*, ed. Joel Silbey and Samuel McSeveney (Lexington, Mass., 1972), 79.

Easier for historians to categorize than individuals are the voting patterns of geographical entities like counties. In 1840 and other elections, Whig majorities typically came from commercial areas where all classes had been hurt by the depression; Democratic majorities, from less economically developed regions where farmers practicing "safety first" agriculture could fall back on their subsistence crops and local barter to tide them over.[30] The pattern would remain for the duration of the second party system. Occasionally, however, relatively poor areas would back the Whigs, hoping for government-sponsored development projects; such a region was eastern Tennessee. Cities and towns generally yielded Whig majorities. The most important exception to this rule was New York City, where both parties competed vigorously. The Democratic strength there reflected devotion to international free trade arising from the city's role in cotton export, as well as ethnic bloc voting by immigrant groups.[31] In 1840, embarrassingly, Van Buren failed to carry his home state, and the capable Whig governor William Seward won reelection.

The Whig adoption of publicity methods pioneered by evangelical preachers reflected an important dimension of the party's constituency and program. Indeed, evangelical preachers, like the Whig campaigners, had been calling attention to the depression. The preachers saw it as a divine punishment visited upon the people for their sins both individual and collective, including cupidity, fraud, violations of the Sabbath, and injustice to the Indians. Americans, the preachers warned, were not living up to their high destiny to usher in the millennium.[32] Harrison specifically courted evangelical voters with assurances of his sabbatarian, Antimasonic, and temperance principles. Despite having won fame as an Indian fighter, in the election year he published a sympathetic history of the Northwest tribes and carefully distinguished his own record toward them from Jackson's injustices.[33]

With so many of the political issues of the age involving moral judgments, it is hardly surprising that different ethnic and religious groups

30. See Michael Holt, *Political Parties and American Political Development* (Baton Rouge, 1992), 151–92, esp. 181.

31. See Amy Bridges, *A City in the Republic: Antebellum New York and the Origins of Machine Politics* (New York, 1984); Anthony Gronowicz, *Race and Class Politics in New York City Before the Civil War* (Boston, 1998).

32. George Duffield, *A Thanksgiving Sermon* (Detroit, 1839); Richard Carwardine, "Evangelicals, Whigs, and the Election of William Henry Harrison," *Journal of American Studies* 17 (1983): 47–75.

33. William Henry Harrison, *Discourse on the Aborigines of the Valley of the Ohio* (Boston, 1840).

often viewed such issues differently. The distinction between evangelicals and nonevangelicals proved particularly important. Supporters and opponents of evangelical revivalism generally lined up on opposite sides of the Whig–Democratic political debate. The moral and reforming outlook of evangelicals like Lyman Beecher and Charles Finney found the Whig ambition to improve America congenial. Indeed, the evangelical modernization of religion proved both a precursor and a model for the modernization of the economy that Whig political leaders embraced. Many of the skills and virtues promoted by the evangelical awakening helped establish preconditions for economic development: literacy, thrift, impulse control, respect for diligent work, honesty and promise-keeping, moral involvement with the world outside one's local community. Not surprisingly, those whose Christianity prompted them to redeem the world, to agitate for penitentiaries instead of jails, insane asylums to replace locked cellars, or common schools instead of home instruction during the parents' spare time, came to ally with politicians committed to an activist state and a developed economy. The interrelated benevolent projects of the Evangelical United Front bear a strong analogy to the integrated economic program of the American System. The Whig Party benefited from evangelicals who decided to enlist the power of the state on behalf of reform.[34]

To be sure, many good Christians followed the Baptist preacher John Leland and the Methodist itinerant Peter Cartwright in supporting the Democratic Party. The Democrats appealed more to those sects that remained outside the reformist Evangelical United Front. These were particularistic, liturgical, "confessional" groups like Roman Catholics and Missouri Synod Lutherans, concerned to bear witness to their traditional sacraments and creeds ("confessions" of faith) rather than to remake society at large through interdenominational voluntary associations. The Whigs exemplified a political postmillennialism, seeking to improve the world so as to render it fit for Christ's return, endorsing a form of social progress that they believed was a collective version of redemption. Premillennialists, on the other hand, suspicious of worldly elites and looking to providential intervention for deliverance from suffering and oppression, often endorsed the austere tenets of hard-money Jacksonianism.[35]

34. Thomas Haskell, "Capitalism and the Origins of the Humanitarian Sensibility," *AHR* 90 (1985): 339–61, 547–66; Howe, *Political Culture of the American Whigs*, 150–80.

35. Robert Swierenga, "Ethnoreligious Political Behavior in the Mid-Nineteenth Century," in *Religion and American Politics*, ed. Mark Noll (New York, 1990), 146–71, summarizes a large body of historical writing on this subject.

Reflecting such distinctions, some denominations acquired deserved reputations for partisan voting. Congregationalists constituted a Whig voting bloc, Antimission Baptists a Democratic one. Other denominations split: Low Church (evangelical) Episcopalians Whig, High Church (antievangelical) Episcopalians Democratic; New School (prorevival) Presbyterians Whig; Old School (antirevival) Presbyterians Democratic. Even some denominations kept outside the Evangelical United Front by their particular doctrines usually voted Whig out of support for the moral reform agenda: Quakers, Unitarians, and Reform Jews. Anticlericals and avowed secularists like Abner Kneeland (convicted of the crime of blasphemy under Massachusetts common law) worried about the power of the Evangelical United Front and found the Jacksonian party more congenial. Democratic leaders occasionally catered to their preferences, as Richard Mentor Johnson did when he rejected the sabbatarian petitions and Jackson did in resolving not to proclaim a day of prayer and fasting in response to the cholera epidemic of 1832.[36]

Denominations with a particular ethnic character seemed all the more likely to vote as a bloc in the presence of neighboring rivals. Thus New York state politics saw Dutch Reformed voters support the Democratic ticket against Yankee Presbyterian Whigs, despite a common Calvinist heritage; the two denominations also took opposing sides on the legitimacy of revivalism. Irish Catholics, resentful of Protestant evangelicalism even though somewhat analogous movements flourished within their own church, voted Democratic by nineteen to one. Scots-Irish Presbyterians who had been voting Democratic sometimes switched over to the Whig Party when Irish Catholic immigrants showed up nearby. Historians and sociologists call communities with such mutual animosity "negative reference groups." In a world where people often defined themselves in religious and ethnic terms, negative reference voting was common.[37] But evangelicals and the various antievangelical communities constituted the largest pattern of negative reference groups.

Then as now, voters acted out of various motives and did not necessarily sort them all out and classify them. Ethnoreligious and negative reference group voting influenced politics more in the North than in the South, since the North had greater ethnic and religious diversity. Southern politics

36. Daniel Howe, "The Evangelical Movement and Political Culture in the North During the Second Party System," *JAH* 77 (1991): 1216–39.
37. The classic study of negative reference group voting is Lee Benson, *The Concept of Jacksonian Democracy: New York as a Test Case* (Princeton, 1961). See also Robert Kelley, *The Cultural Pattern in American Politics* (New York, 1979).

more often reflected geographical regions defined by their dominant lo-cal economies. Historians have come to accept that, overall, the political loyalties of the second party system involved both economic and ethno-cultural alignments.[38] Both kinds of concern could be perfectly legiti-mate; to vote on the basis of moral principle or ethnic identity was no less rational than to vote one's economic interest. In most cases, no doubt, several different kinds of consideration all pointed toward the same action at the polling place.

In debate, Democrats and Whigs alike employed the rhetoric of Amer-ican republicanism, invoking popular "virtue" against "corruption," though Democrats used it to denounce the money power and Whigs to denounce executive usurpation.[39] Democrats more often invoked Lock-ean natural rights; Whigs, Anglo-American traditions of resistance to monarchical misrule. Both parties traced their origins to Jeffersonian Re-publicanism: Democrats to the Old Republicanism of Macon and Craw-ford; Whigs to the new Republican nationalism of Madison and Gallatin. (In 1832, Madison and Gallatin both supported Clay for president against Jackson.) For all that they had in common as American republicans, how-ever, the Whigs and Democrats differed markedly in their conception of America's future. They disagreed not simply over means but also over ends. The goals of the two parties' voters added up to rival visions of the national destiny.

Democrats basically approved of America the way it was. They wanted to keep it economically homogeneous in the sense that they believed agriculture should remain the predominant occupation, though their party had nothing against the expansion of commercial opportunities for planters and farmers. Democrats enjoyed their greatest party strength in the South, where agriculture predominated even more than in the North. They expressed disapproval of government favors for privileged elites, of which a national bank seemed to them the prime example. Democrats celebrated "popular sovereignty" and the equal rights of common white men. They hoped America would remain culturally (that is, morally) het-erogeneous, so that a variety of religious options could be exercised and local communities of common white men could govern themselves freely. This meant deciding for themselves whether to practice slavery, whether to fund education and internal improvements, whether to toler-

---

38. See, for example, Daniel Feller, "Politics and Society: Toward a Jacksonian Synthe-sis," *JER* 10 (1990): 135–61.
39. Major Wilson, "Republican Consensus and Party Debate in the Bank War," *JER* 15 (1995): 619–48.

ate Native neighbors, and, for that matter, how to deal with deviants like criminals and the insane. The Democrats' vision of America did not require central planning, since most matters could be left either to the marketplace or to state and local decisions. Jacksonians did, however, want a government strong enough to extend their agrarian empire across the continent, expelling or conquering any who stood in their way and protecting slaveowners from interference.

Whigs had a different vision. They wanted to transform the United States into an economically developed nation, in which commerce and industry would take their places alongside agriculture. While the Democrats favored economic uniformity and cultural diversity, Whigs favored economic diversity and cultural uniformity. They wanted to impose cultural (moral) homogeneity because they strongly believed in a society that would nurture and respect conscientious individual autonomy, in contrast to the Democrats, who valued the autonomy of the small white community. Much more than Democrats, Whigs worried about lawlessness, violence, and demagogy. Duties seemed to them as important as rights, and both individuals and the nation had a responsibility to develop their potential to the fullest. Causes like temperance and public education fostered these values and also helped produce a population ready for the demands of a developed economy. Whigs had a *positive* conception of liberty; they treasured it as a means to the formation of individual character and a good society. Democrats, by contrast, held a *negative* conception of liberty; they saw it as freeing the common (white) man from the oppressive burdens of an aristocracy.

The Whigs had the more imaginative program, requiring the transformation of America by conscious effort and therefore needing economic planning and strong government. Twenty-first-century readers will inevitably note with surprise that the party of the business community should be the party most sympathetic to central planning and government intervention in the economy, the reverse of the usual pattern in our own day. But the businessmen of that period realized the difficulty of mobilizing capital and just how little chance existed that private enterprise alone could create the needed infrastructure of transportation and education—particularly in the absence of a central bank. Whig ambitions to transform America were more *qualitative* than *quantitative*; sheer geographical extension of the nation's boundaries appealed to them little unless it promised economic development.

A comparison between the parties does not reveal a perfect symmetry. The Whigs possessed a more coherent program: a national bank, a protective tariff, government subsidies to transportation projects, the public lands treated as a source of revenue, and tax-supported public schools. The Democrats of course denounced the Whig plans, but beyond this, they often displayed a set of generalized attitudes rather than a specific program of their own. Jackson's program of Indian Removal, ambitious and centrally directed, was an exception, to be sure, but often the Jacksonians led by establishing an "emotional bond" with their followers rather than by policy initiatives.[40] Democratic politicians, following the example of Martin Van Buren, learned how to evoke partisan feelings in the electorate while retaining considerable flexibility with regard to policy. The variation in their tariff and banking policies—indeed, the division among them between hard and soft money—manifested this. Accordingly, the Democratic leaders relied on invoking loyalty to the party rather than to a coherent program. They largely succeeded in transferring to their party the personal loyalty Jackson had aroused and wrapped it in his mantle as defender of the people.[41]

By contrast, the Whigs never came around to Martin Van Buren's view that political parties were good things in principle, even in the heat of their campaign of 1840. Rather, they took the view that partisanship had been forced on them by the other side. As the Illinois Whig Abraham Lincoln put it, "*They* set us the example of organization, and we, in self-defence, are driven to it."[42] Although Harrison condemned Jackson's spoils system, his postmaster general soon busied himself replacing Democrats with Whigs throughout the country. Fundamentally, however, the Whigs saw their party not as an end in itself but as a means to set policy. When they deplored what they called "the spirit of party," it was not because they themselves had no party but because they resented a partisanship that substituted for policy. No doubt they resented all the more the fact that the Democrats' practice proved so successful at the polls.

One policy that the Democratic Party embraced consistently was white supremacy. The centrality of white supremacy in Democratic policymaking helps explain that party's hostility toward Clay's American System. Democratic suspicion of government aid to internal improvements reflected *not* a horror of the market revolution but a fear that such a program might threaten the institution of slavery. The danger, from the slaveholders' point of view, was twofold. In the first place, national plans

40. Matthew Crenson, *The Federal Machine: Beginnings of Bureaucracy in Jacksonian America* (Baltimore, 1975), 29.
41. See Thomas Brown, "From Old Hickory to Sly Fox: The Routinization of Charisma in the Early Democratic Party," *JER* 11 (1991): 339–69.
42. *Collected Works of AL*, I, 205.

for internal improvements might be designed to wean areas in the Border States or Upper South away from slave-based agriculture toward a diversified economy in which slavery would become vulnerable to gradual emancipation. In the second place, national plans for internal improvements set a precedent for federal activity that might encourage interference with slavery—for example, by exercising the interstate commerce power over the interstate slave trade. Jacksonians welcomed transporting farm products to market, so long as it could be done without the centralized planning that raised the specter of emancipation.

As he did so often, the perceptive former president Adams saw to the heart of the matter. Solicitude for slavery constituted the real obstacle to federal internal improvements, he told his constituents.

> If the internal improvement of the country should be left to the legislative management of the national government, and the proceeds of the sales of public lands should be applied as a perpetual and self-accumulating fund for that purpose, the blessings unceasingly showered upon the people by this process would so grapple the affections of the people to the national authority that it would, in process of time, overshadow that of state governments, and settle the preponderancy of power in the free states; and then the undying worm of conscience twinges with terror for the fate of *the peculiar institution*. Slavery stands aghast at the prospective promotion of the general welfare.[43]

Significantly, the constitution of the Confederate States adopted in 1861 forbade the central government to sponsor internal improvements.

Of course, the Whig Party too had to compromise with slavery if it were to remain a nationwide party. Unlike its successor, the Republican Party of Lincoln, the Whig Party was committed to a presence in the South. The attitude of both Whigs and Democrats to race and slavery varied from one geographical area to another, but with one constant: In every region, even the Deep South, the Whig Party took the less stridently racist position. For example, in the Alabama "black belt," although most of the large slaveowners voted Whig, it was the Democrats who beat the drums most insistently for protecting slavery from the dangers of abolitionism and strong central government.[44] In the great debate over slavery in Virginia following Nat Turner's Uprising, a majority of Jacksonians defended the institution, and a majority of future Whigs sympathized with gradual

43. John Quincy Adams, "Address to his Constituents," Sept. 17, 1842, in *Selected Writings of John and John Quincy Adams*, ed. Adrienne Koch and William Peden (New York, 1946), 392.

44. J. Mills Thornton, *Politics and Power in a Slave Society* (Baton Rouge, 1978), 133, 137.

emancipation, although the division was primarily geographical. "While both parties practiced the politics of slavery in their partisan rhetoric, Whigs and Democrats stood in distinctly different places on the spectrum of attitudes and behaviors that constituted the slavery issue," writes the historian of Virginia politics in this period.[45] Throughout the South, the Whigs showed significantly less enthusiasm for the expansion of slavery than the Democrats. In the North, Whigs, who tended to accept social differentiation, could easily adopt a condescending paternalism toward nonwhites. Ironically, the Democrats' great insistence on the natural equality of all white men prompted them to make a more glaring exception of non-whites. Taking seriously the motto "all men are created equal," Democrats called into question the very humanity of nonwhites in order to keep them unequal.

Henry Clay as a young man had backed gradual emancipation for Kentucky at the state constitutional convention in 1799. Remarkably, he remained critical of slavery even as a national party leader. In 1827, as secretary of state, he told the American Colonization Society that he would be proud if he could help "in ridding this foul blot," slavery, from both Kentucky and Virginia. Addressing the U.S. Senate in 1832, he expressed the hope that "some day" the country as a whole "would be rid of this, the darkest spot on its mantle," though of course he added that it was entirely up to the states.[46] But when making his bid for the Whig nomination in 1839, Clay determined to solidify his southern support. He decided this required a major policy address disavowing the abolitionists and distinguishing his own antislavery position from theirs.

Clay made his statement in the Senate on February 7, 1839. In it, he reasserted his lifelong conviction that slavery was evil and should not have been introduced into America. Abolitionists exercised their constitutional rights when they petitioned against it, he affirmed; Congress should receive their petitions but not grant them. The evil of slavery must be tolerated at the national level, he asserted, while waiting for it to be addressed at the state level. Slaves represented $1.2 billion in capital, Clay estimated conservatively, and the abolitionists made no provision to cushion the

45. William Shade, *Democratizing the Old Dominion* (Charlottesville, Va., 1996), 12, quotation from 221. See also Lacy K. Ford Jr., "Making the 'White Man's Country' White," in *Race and the Early Republic*, ed. Michael Morrison and James B. Stewart (New York, 2002), 135–58.

46. *Life, Correspondence, and Speeches of Henry Clay*, ed. Calvin Colton (New York, 1857), I, 189, 191. See also Harold Tallant, *Evil Necessity: Slavery and Political Culture in Antebellum Kentucky* (Lexington, Ky., 2003), 49–52.

economic impact of sudden emancipation. Ultimately, Clay, like Jefferson, framed the issue in terms of the dangers of emancipation to the white race. In many places in the South, blacks were so numerous that emancipation risked either black domination or race war. Most whites in the South would cling to slavery despite its evils, as a guarantee of white supremacy, he declared. Should southerners have to choose, Clay predicted, they would value slavery above the Union.[47]

By rejecting gradualism, compensation, and colonization, those Clay called the "ultra-abolitionists" made the resolution of the slavery question more difficult. By endorsing equal rights for all, they made intermarriage ("amalgamation") inevitable. By inveighing against the wickedness of slavery they arrayed section against section and threatened the Union. Without their heedless agitation, Clay supposed, the causes of gradual emancipation and colonization would still be alive and well in Kentucky. In a political climate favoring partisan extremism, in a society entertaining millennial hopes, Clay offered sober moderation, a sense of limitations, and watchful waiting.

> I am, Mr. President, no friend of slavery. The searcher of all hearts knows that every pulsation of mine beats high and strong in the cause of civil liberty. Wherever it is safe and practicable, I desire to see every portion of the human family in the enjoyment of it. But I prefer the liberty of my own country to that of any other people; and the liberty of my own race to that of any other race. The liberty of the descendants of Africa in the United States is incompatible with the safety and liberty of the European descendants.[48]

The speech shows Clay loyal to the Jeffersonian moral position on slavery—probably more faithful to it, in fact, than Jefferson himself had been in old age. Like the Sage of Monticello, Clay looked to providence and posterity to find a solution. The outlook he expressed, for all its tragic limitations, would represent the starting point for Abraham Lincoln's evolving views on slavery.[49]

The most remarkable thing about Clay's speech is that it served its political purpose in the South. Southern Whigs accepted its logic. They did not insist, as Calhoun and other southern Democrats already did, that

---

47. "On Abolition" (Feb. 7, 1839) in *The Works of Henry Clay*, ed. Calvin Colton (New York, 1857), VIII, 139–59.
48. Ibid., 158.
49. Lincoln quoted extensively from Clay's views on slavery in his speech at Edwardsville, Illinois, on Sept. 11, 1858. *Collected Works of AL*, III, 93–94.

slavery must constitute a "positive good," a benefit to both races. They expressed satisfaction with Clay's position, and Harry of the West went off to the Whig convention with the solid backing of southern delegates.[50] In the South, the difference between the parties on slavery remained the difference between endorsing the "peculiar institution" as right and advantageous, and accepting it as an unfortunate social system to which there seemed no feasible alternative.

In the North, however, Clay's speech did him no good. There, some Whig politicians diminished the distance between themselves and the abolitionists—for example, by supporting their right to petition Congress. The northern Whig propagandist Calvin Colton, writing as "Junius" in 1844, declared, "We do not yield to the Abolitionists a whit in our opposition to slavery; we differ from them only as to the mode of getting rid of the evil."[51] In the mean time, Clay's anti-abolitionist speech prompted northern Whigs to consider Harrison and Scott as alternatives for the nomination. When the convention came, Clay received the votes of no northern state save little Rhode Island. The effects of Clay's antiabolitionist speech illustrate the supreme difficulty of bridging the sectional gap on the slavery question within the Whig Party—even for so skillful and principled a moderate as Henry Clay.

There is an ironic footnote to this speech of Clay's. When warned by a sympathetic fellow senator that this remarkably full exposition of his position would make an inviting target for extremists on both sides of the slavery issue, perhaps jeopardizing his presidential campaign, Clay responded, "I had rather be right than be president."[52] It became probably his most famous quotation. One can only wish that this profession of virtue had been voiced on behalf of a more morally courageous statement. Still, though never president, Clay *was* often right.

II

"There never was a President elected who has a more difficult task imposed upon him than General Harrison," observed one cautious Whig. "Too much is expected of him."[53] The public did have strong expectations, and the new President Harrison confronted his challenge head on. He appointed a capable cabinet, headed by Daniel Webster as secretary

50. William J. Cooper, *The South and the Politics of Slavery* (Baton Rouge, 1978), 123–24.
51. [Calvin Colton], *Political Abolition, by Junius* (New York, 1844), 2.
52. *Papers of Henry Clay*, ed. Robert Seager (Lexington, Ky., 1988), IX, 283.
53. J. Mitchell to John McLean, Nov. 28, 1840, quoted in William Brock, *Parties and Political Conscience* (Millwood, N.Y., 1979), 72.

of state. He summoned a special session of Congress to deal with the depression and enact the Whig economic program. His meetings with Henry Clay, who would be the dominant power in the legislative branch, revealed that the two men had not yet transcended their rivalry for the Whig nomination. At one point, when the senator pressed advice upon him too presumptuously, Harrison snapped, "You forget, Mr. Clay, that *I* am the president."[54] But their personal feelings could probably have been subsumed within their broadly common goals. Harrison would have been a mainstream Whig president, enjoying cordial relations with many northern party leaders, if not with Clay, and in any case committed on principle to respecting the will of Congress. He held meetings of his full cabinet and had confidence in its collective judgment.

But within days, Harrison fell ill. At first it seemed a bad cold, presumably caught when chilled at his inauguration. Then it turned to pneumonia. Being president, he of course received the best medical care available—perhaps the worst thing that could have happened to him. His doctors administered the "heroic" treatments of the age: "topical depletion," harsh laxatives, and blistering. Their favorite remedy, bloodletting, they postponed.[55] It was all too much for the veteran of many a battle. Exactly one month after his inauguration, President Harrison died. The Whig electoral triumph had turned to ashes.

It was the first time a president had died in office. "When a Christian people feel themselves to be overtaken by a great public calamity, it becomes them to humble themselves under the dispensation of Divine Providence," declared his successor, in proclaiming May 14, 1841, a day of national prayer and fasting. Charles Finney preached one of his greatest sermons for the occasion, calling on the bereaved country to repent of its sins, which ranged from slavery and the treatment of the aborigines to desecration of the Sabbath, mercenary values, intemperance, and political corruption.[56]

Vice President John Tyler, also a Virginia governor's son, came like Harrison from the tidewater aristocracy. The running mates shared little else in common. Where Harrison had been the oldest chief executive, Tyler at fifty-one became the youngest so far. Rejecting the title "acting president," Tyler successfully insisted that he had fallen heir to the presidency itself.

---

54. Quoted in Norma Peterson, *The Presidencies of William Henry Harrison and John Tyler* (Lawrence, Kans., 1989), 34.
55. "Report of the Physicians" (April 4, 1841), *Presidential Messages*, IV, 31.
56. Charles Hambrick-Stowe, *Charles G. Finney and the Spirit of American Evangelicalism* (Grand Rapids, Mich., 1996), 198–203.

Six feet tall and slender, when his ailing wife, Letitia, died in 1842 he wasted no time courting the beautiful twenty-four-year-old New York heiress Julia Gardiner. Their wedding, the first of an incumbent president, initiated a period of virtually regal luxury in the White House.[57] Like other vice presidents who have succeeded to the presidency, Tyler came into power on short notice and unprepared. At first he retained Harrison's cabinet; perhaps he would defer to their advice, some supposed. They were wrong.

It would be easy to demonize Tyler as a sinister frustrater of the popular will, wrecker of the Whig Party's only clear mandate, and the president who prostituted the Constitution to evade the requirement that the Senate ratify treaties. But the historian's duty is to understand, not simply condemn. In his own mind, John Tyler exemplified high principles. He had entered politics at the age of twenty-one and served as both governor and senator from Virginia. He was a dedicated Old Republican and a faithful disciple of Thomas Jefferson, devoted to both state rights and national expansion. He construed the Constitution strictly in defense of state rights and broadly in asserting executive authority to extend American sovereignty and commercial interests. Like Jefferson, he owned slaves while professing regret for the institution of slavery; like the master of Monticello, he left behind black people claiming descent from him.[58]

Tyler had joined the Whig Party because he objected to Jackson's strong response to nullification and to his withdrawal of the deposits from the BUS. In 1836, the Virginian had been Hugh White's running mate. Tyler's views on public policy, however, left him in a highly anomalous position within the Whig Party. Many of the former sympathizers with nullification, such as members of the old State Rights Party in Georgia, had not only joined the Whig Party but also had embraced Clay's views on a national bank. As major producers of commodities for export, these planters understood the importance of banking, currency, and credit. They preferred a revived national bank to continued dependence on New York City financiers.[59] Government intervention in the economy did not fill all southerners with horror; many of them wanted public funding to dredge river channels or construct railroads, for example. Of those

57. Robert Seager, *And Tyler Too* (New York, 1963), 243–66.
58. See Dan Monroe, *The Republican Vision of John Tyler* (College Station, Tex., 2003); Edward Crapol, *John Tyler, the Accidental President* (Chapel Hill, 2006). On the issue of Tyler's slave children: Crapol, 64–67.
59. For how former nullifiers turned into Whigs, see J. Mills Thornton, *Politics and Power in a Slave Society* (Baton Rouge, 1978).

southerners who still shared Tyler's views on strict construction, most had followed John C. Calhoun back into the Democratic Party once Jackson himself had retired. Indeed, in Tyler's own Virginia, most tidewater Old Republicans had never left the Democratic Party. A large majority of Virginia's Whigs sided with Clay, not Tyler, when the choice had to be made.

John Tyler was also a politician. Throughout his four years in the White House, he assiduously pursued election to a term in his own right. His isolation within the Whig Party complicated matters, but Tyler stuck with his goal and displayed remarkable ingenuity in furthering it. In the end the odds against it were simply too great, but in the course of pursuing it he inflicted huge damage on the Whig Party.

Harrison had called the special session of Congress to meet on May 31, the earliest date practicable in that age of slow communication and travel. "We come here to relieve the country," declared a Whig from New York when the Congress had assembled. "The eyes of the nation are bent upon us with an intensity which has never before been experienced."[60] Clay and the other Whig congressional leaders knew what they wanted and they wanted it quickly. (Democrats suspected that Whig haste betrayed a fear that the economy might begin to recover before their program could take effect; in the event, no such early recovery occurred.) The Whigs repealed Van Buren's Independent Treasury Act, then drew up legislation to establish a third national bank. Tyler signed the repeal, but his reaction to the other bill remained the subject of much speculation as it moved through Congress. The new president offered no alternative proposal. Secretary of the Treasury Thomas Ewing, trying to fill the void, suggested a bank of limited powers. Clay preferred to press ahead with his original plan, making, however, two concessions to strict construction: the bank would be based in the District of Columbia, and states would enjoy a limited right to refuse the establishment of its branches. Clay believed the Whigs had a mandate from the electorate, which was true, and persuaded himself that "Tyler dare not resist"[61]—which was wishful thinking. Tyler waited the full ten days allowed by the Constitution, whether out of indecision or secret pleasure in making Clay squirm, then vetoed the bank bill on August 16, 1841. Unpersuaded by the existence of two previous national banks for a total of forty years, or by the opinion of the Supreme Court, Tyler insisted that such an institution was unconstitutional.[62]

60. Representative Christopher Morgan, quoted in Holt, *Rise and Fall of Whig Party*, 130–31.
61. Quoted in Peterson, *Presidencies of Harrison and Tyler*, 57.
62. "Veto Message" (Aug. 16, 1841), *Presidential Messages*, IV, 63–68.

The Whigs did not have the two-thirds majority necessary to override a veto, but they did pass another bank bill, this time in the form that Secretary Ewing had proposed, in the hope that Tyler would accept it. They gave the revised bank a euphemistic name, "fiscal corporation," and forbade it to establish any branches in states without their consent. Tyler's fellow Virginian, Whig congressman John Minor Botts, who represented the urban-industrial constituency of Richmond, declared that although he would vote for it, Ewing's bank was so weak that investors would shun it, making the plan unworkable and exposing Tyler's economic ignorance. Botts's claim both infuriated and convinced Tyler. He vetoed the Ewing bank bill as well—thus denying the financial community the chance to fulfill Botts's prediction. In the last analysis, Tyler had no interest in reaching an accommodation with Clay. If a compromise bank bill passed, Clay would remain leader of the Whig Party and its next presidential nominee. Tyler was challenging Clay for leadership of the party. No longer possessing either Van Buren's Independent Treasury or a reconstituted BUS, the federal government once again resorted to placing its money in private banks. The solution of the soft-money Democrats prevailed by default over those of the hard-money Democrats and the Whigs.

Despite the deadlock over the national bank, the Whigs managed to pass some items of their program. One of these was the Land Act of 1841, which Whigs hoped would stimulate land sales and strengthen their party in the West. It provided that settlers on government-owned lands would from now on enjoy the right to buy 160-acre homesteads at the minimum price without having to compete in an auction. This made permanent the "preemption" privilege that squatters had been granted from time to time retroactively. The law gave preemption rights to any male citizen over twenty-one or heading a family, and also to widowed women, provided the settler already owned no more than 320 acres of other land. It constituted a long step toward the altogether free homesteads for settlers that the new Republican Party would enact a generation later. Indeed, a careful scholar of federal land policy has declared the Land Act of 1841 even more important than the later law in encouraging western settlement by farmers of modest means.[63] For years, the Jacksonian Thomas Hart Benton had struggled for such a "prospective preemption" law. Ironically, when it finally passed, it did so on a party-line vote with Whigs supporting and Democrats opposing. The reason for Democratic opposition was that the bill included "distribution" of the proceeds of land sales to the states.

63. Roy Robbins, *Our Landed Heritage*, 2nd ed. (Lincoln, Neb., 1976), 91.

Whigs intended the distribution of funds to the states to stimulate internal improvements without running afoul of any constitutional scruples. They had been waiting for this measure ever since Jackson vetoed Clay's distribution bill of 1833. But Tyler, like Calhoun and most Democrats, wanted the proceeds from land sales to go to the federal government so tariffs could remain as low as possible. He therefore insisted that distribution of land proceeds not occur if any tariffs exceeded 20 percent, the ceiling set by the old Compromise of 1833.

The president also approved a depression-relief measure, the Bankruptcy Act of 1841. The Constitution specifically empowers Congress to pass uniform national bankruptcy legislation, so even a strict constructionist could not object. The law applied to individuals, not banks or other corporations, allowing them to declare bankruptcy and start financial life over. No previous federal legislation permitted individuals to seek the protection of bankruptcy, and only a Whig Congress would have passed such a law. Democrats disapproved of voluntary bankruptcy for somewhat the same reasons that they disliked bank notes; they saw it as encouraging people to borrow beyond their means and then defraud their creditors. During the one year the law operated (1842–43), forty-one thousand persons took out bankruptcy under it. The experience chastened some of them (as Democrats thought it should); others plunged back into the whirl of commercial life (as Whigs hoped they would).[64]

The depression had brought hard times to American manufacturing while simultaneously so reducing federal revenues that the surplus of Jackson's day had given way to a deep deficit and the national debt reappeared. As a result, both the impulse to protect domestic industry and the government's need for revenue indicated that the Compromise Tariff of 1833 should be terminated (or reinterpreted) at the close of its nine-year time frame. Twice Tyler vetoed Whig bills to increase the duties; eventually, however, persuaded by the need for revenue if not by its protective features, he signed the Tariff of 1842.

But when the Tariff of 1842 breached the 20 percent ceiling on duties, the distribution of land revenues to the states automatically ceased. Whigs tried to get Tyler to relent and change the law, but he was adamant. Southern Whigs had relied upon distribution to get money for internal improvements and to sweeten the bitter pill of higher tariff duties to their cotton-growing constituents; New York's Governor Seward had

64. Charles Warren, *Bankruptcy in United States History* (Cambridge, Mass., 1935), pt. II; Edward Balleisen, *Navigating Failure: Bankruptcy and Commercial Society in Antebellum America* (Chapel Hill, 2001).

hoped for distribution to enable him to help the anti-rent movement. Southern Whigs also felt especially disappointed at the failure to establish a national bank; northerners had stronger state and regional banks of their own and needed a third BUS less urgently. Tyler hoped the disaffected southerners and New Yorkers would blame their troubles on Clay and rally behind his own banner.

But the president underestimated the Whig Party's cohesion and dedication to its program. In protest against his bank vetoes, in September 1841 the entire cabinet resigned, save Secretary of State Daniel Webster, who was involved in serious negotiations with Britain over the Maine boundary. The same month, a caucus of Whig members of Congress took an extraordinary action unparalleled in American history: They expelled a sitting president from his political party. But Tyler would not abandon his bid for Whig Party leadership. Webster had fancied himself Harrison's prime minister and hoped to become his heir; when the old man died, Webster was reluctant to give up on this aspiration. Tyler exploited the New Englander's vanity to prolong ties with his branch of the party. But by the summer of 1842, Tyler's attempt to turn the Whig Party around had clearly failed. At this point the president switched to a new strategy: He would form a party of his own. With this in mind, he undertook a wholesale purge of the Whig appointees from federal offices, replacing them with state-rights men, most of them Democrats.

The midterm elections of 1842–43 inflicted terrible reprisals upon the Whigs. Their Senate majority was trimmed and their majority in the House lost altogether; the number of Whig representatives plummeted dramatically from 133 to 79. The depression continued, the party had not made good on its promises, and despite its repudiation of him, Tyler had muddied the waters enough so that many voters viewed the Whigs as a party rent by internal division and incapable of governing. The first-time voters whom the Whigs had recruited in 1840 now felt disillusioned and stayed away from the polls in droves. Furthermore, by purging the Whigs from their patronage, Tyler had robbed the party's local leaders of the usual incentives and opportunities to mobilize supporters. Reapportionment following the census of 1840 compounded these effects and cost the Whigs many seats in states where Democratic legislatures had redrawn the constituencies.[65]

Tyler continued to delude himself that he could create a third party by the use of patronage, though as a practical matter he needed support from the congressional Democrats. The latter rested content to apply the

---

65. Statistics presented in Holt, *Rise and Fall of Whig Party*, 140–60.

principle of laissez-faire and wait for the country to struggle out of the depression as best it might. The Democrats showed no interest in Tyler's Exchequer Plan, his belated attempt to craft a substitute for Van Buren's Independent Treasury and the Whigs' national bank—despite the plan's
intrinsic merits.[66] In the spring of 1843 Webster, his treaty with Britain
safely concluded and his dream of using the State Department as a
springboard to the White House finally abandoned, resigned from the
cabinet and returned to the Whig Party. Contrary to Black Dan's advice,
Tyler had begun to pursue the annexation of Texas.

III

Campaigners for Harrison in Illinois throughout the months of 1839–40
included the thirty-one-year-old Whig state legislator Abraham Lincoln.
Though a strong admirer of Clay, Lincoln had backed Harrison even before the party convention. Much in demand during the campaign, Lincoln spoke before many audiences in varied circumstances—in the state
assembly wearing his best sixty-dollar suit, out on the stump dressed in
jeans, or traveling about the state debating against a young Democrat
named Stephen Douglas, as the two men would do again in their more
famous confrontations eighteen years later. Lincoln denounced Van Buren's Independent Treasury and demanded a third national bank to replace it. The partisan presses reported that he also told jokes, poked fun at
local Democrats, and matched wits with hecklers. The Democratic papers wrote him off as a "traveling missionary" for Harrison; Whig papers
found him effective.[67]

Still a frontier agricultural state in 1840, with many Butternut settlers
from the South, Illinois went for Van Buren in spite of Lincoln's efforts.
In Lincoln's hometown of Springfield, however, voters engaged in commerce, industry, and the professions delivered a majority to the Whigs.[68]
Lincoln's political party reflected his choice of occupation and way of
life, as well as, in a larger sense, his personal values. The son of a farmer,
Lincoln had left home like countless other young Americans and struck
out on his own. First he tried his luck in the tiny village of New Salem,
clerking in a store. But New Salem never managed to get connected to

66. On the Exchequer Plan, see Peterson, *Presidencies of Harrison and Tyler*, 96–98.
67. Robert Gunderson, *The Log-Cabin Campaign* (Lexington, Ky., 1957), 212–16; Rein-
    hard Luthin, *The Real Abraham Lincoln* (Englewood Cliffs, N.J., 1960), 54–55; *Col-
    lected Works of AL*, I, 159–79.
68. Kenneth Winkle, "The Second Party System in Lincoln's Springfield," *Civil War
    History* 44 (1998): 267–84.

any transportation that could sustain its commerce; Lincoln moved away to Springfield and helped it become the state capital. New Salem ended up one of the West's countless ghost towns.

Lincoln took the experience of New Salem to heart; he early became and long remained an ardent supporter of internal improvements. The revolutions in transportation and communications captured his imagination. On one occasion, to demonstrate the potential of the Sangamon River as an artery of commerce, he took charge of a steamboat himself and piloted it along the stream from Beardstown to Portland Landing. Later, he even tried inventing a device to enable steamboats to float themselves off when they stuck on shoals; although he actually got a patent for the idea, he never marketed it. (Lincoln envisioned buoyant air chambers, collapsed when not needed and inflated to raise the boat and diminish its draft.)[69] But mostly Lincoln worked through the political process to provide subsidies for canals and railroads. Remembering what the Erie Canal had done for New York state, he confided to his best friend his ambition to become "the DeWitt Clinton of Illinois."[70]

Like a good Whig, Lincoln would have preferred to see federal money spent for internal improvements, but when this was not forthcoming, he heartily endorsed state funding: "the Illinois System," his plan was called, a small-scale American System. During the legislative session of 1836–37, by now Whig minority leader, Lincoln worked with the Democratic majority in the legislature, led by Stephen Douglas, to achieve this end, showing that Democrats too were happy to enable farmers to market their crops. When the Panic of 1837 ruined the economy of Illinois, however, Lincoln demonstrated much more reluctance than the Democrats to give up on the Illinois System.[71] He differed from the Democrats even more in his insistence that the West needed credit and that a third national bank constituted the safest and most practical source of such credit. In the absence of a national bank, Lincoln defended the Illinois state bank against the Democrats. In a famous incident, while trying to protect the state bank, Lincoln and some other Whig legislators jumped out the window of the statehouse in a vain attempt to prevent a quorum.

69. David Donald, *Abraham Lincoln* (New York, 1995), 43–44; "Application for a Patent," *Collected Works of AL*, II, 32–36.

70. Abraham Lincoln to Joshua Speed, quoted in Richard Carwardine, *Lincoln* (London, 2003), 12.

71. For Lincoln and the Illinois System, see Gabor Boritt, *Abraham Lincoln and the American Dream* (Memphis, Tenn., 1978), 13–39. For Lincoln and the Illinois Whig Party, see Joel Silbey, "Always a Whig in Politics," *Papers of the Abraham Lincoln Association* 8 (1986): 21–42.

Most fundamentally, Lincoln differed with the Democrats in broad political outlook. Democrats thought primarily in terms of local white communities; their nationalism consisted of a desire to extend across the continent the area where these communities could flourish. Lincoln and the Whigs thought in terms of an integrated nation, its diverse occupations, classes, and regions harmonized in economic complementarity. The protective tariff, a subject to which Lincoln devoted much attention and study, seemed to him to guarantee home markets for both agriculture and industry while saving on transportation costs. Within an economically developed and integrated nation, Lincoln believed, individual autonomy could flourish as never before. As his biographer David Donald sums it up, the Whig Party embodied for Lincoln "the promise of American life," an opportunity for people to make something of themselves. For Whigs like Lincoln, this involved more than material betterment or upward social mobility. It meant a whole new kind of life away from the farm, the chance "to escape the restraints of locality and community," as the historian Allen Guelzo puts it, "to refashion themselves on the basis of new economic identities in a larger world of trade, based on merit, self-improvement, and self-control."[72] To Lincoln, then, his membership in the Whig Party typified the new life he had made for himself. He remained an active and loyal Whig until the newly organized Republican Party absorbed most northern Whigs in the mid-1850s. This new party represented for Lincoln a continuation of the same aspirations as the Whigs, for the modernization of American society and the creation of new opportunities for personal self-fulfillment.[73]

An important part of Lincoln's life as a Whig was his marriage to Mary Todd. Daughter of a prominent Whig family in Lexington, she had known Henry Clay personally all her life. Mary made no secret of her political opinions. She and her husband shared a strong loyalty to the Whig Party, though in the mid-1850s they briefly disagreed on what that implied: She backed Fillmore for president in 1856 when Abraham backed Frémont. Mary was a devout Christian (Episcopalian until 1850; thereafter Presbyterian), while Abraham never joined a church — not an uncommon pattern, for many more wives than husbands belonged to churches. Nevertheless, Abraham had absorbed biblical culture and a Calvinist sense of fatalism from his Baptist upbringing.

72. Donald, *Abraham Lincoln*, 110; Allen Guelzo, *Abraham Lincoln, Redeemer President* (Grand Rapids, Mich., 1999), 57.
73. See "Address to the Wisconsin State Agricultural Society" (Sept. 30, 1859), *Collected Works of AL*, III, 471–82.

When the Civil War came, his spirituality would deepen profoundly.[74] In the meantime, he participated in some of the same redemptive reforms as the Evangelical United Front. One of these was the temperance movement.

While the Democrats celebrated the natural man and held up Andrew Jackson as his prototype, Whigs like Lincoln celebrated the artificial—that is, self-constructed—personality. An address Lincoln delivered to the local chapter of the Washingtonian Temperance Society in Springfield's Second Presbyterian Church reveals much about his ideal of the self-controlled, autonomous personality. A teetotaler himself, Lincoln declared forthrightly, "The world would be vastly benefited by a total and final banishment from it of all intoxicating drinks." Nevertheless, he spent the first part of his speech criticizing temperance advocates for their self-righteous denunciations. The strength of the Washingtonian movement, he declared, was that it comprised reformed alcoholics, who understood at first hand the meaning of resolve and self-control. They should lead the "temperance revolution," a worthy successor to "our political revolution of '76." In this new revolution, "we shall find a stronger bondage broken, a viler slavery manumitted, a greater tyrant deposed." Like so many other American reformers of his day, Lincoln roused millennial expectations. "Happy day," he concluded, "when, all appetites controlled, all passions subdued, all matters subjected, mind, all conquering mind, shall live and move the monarch of the world. Glorious consummation! Hail, fall of Fury! Reign of Reason, all hail!" Lincoln's version of the millennium was the supremacy of rationality over impulse and passion. And, like most other American millennialists, he made a special place for his own country: "When the victory shall be complete—when there shall be neither a slave nor a drunkard on the earth—how proud the title of that *Land*, which may truly claim to be the birth-place and the cradle of both those revolutions."[75] Temperance and antislavery partook of the same moral impulse, for both sought to redeem humanity from bondage, whether to the passions of others or to those of oneself.

74. For recent interpretations of Lincoln's religion, see Carwardine, *Lincoln*, 28–40; Guelzo, *Abraham Lincoln*, 149–58, 312–24; Ronald White, *Abraham Lincoln's Greatest Speech* (New York, 2002), passim; and Stewart Winger, *Lincoln, Religion, and Romantic Cultural Politics* (DeKalb, Ill., 2003).

75. "Temperance Address" (Feb. 22, 1842), *Collected Works of AL*, I, 271–79, quotations from 276, 278, 279. I say more about Lincoln's conception of the constructed personality in *Making the American Self* (Cambridge, Mass., 1997), 138–49.

IV

Under Jackson, the Democratic Party celebrated popular sovereignty and expressed relative indifference to the rule of law when this conflicted with the will of "the people" as defined by the party. Even violence had been shrugged off when directed against unpopular minorities. Whigs, on the other hand, emphasized that the people had imposed legal limitations on their own sovereignty; in controversies like deposit removal they cast themselves as upholders of the law. The late 1830s saw a continuation of this pattern. Both Arkansas and Michigan drew up state constitutions without waiting for legal authority from Congress. Democrats and Whigs disagreed about whether to accept such behavior and admit the territories as states, but the Democratic predilection for popular sovereignty eventually carried the day. More worrisome was the Democratic proposal to circumvent amendment in favor of popular sovereignty as a method of changing the constitution of Maryland in 1836; Maryland voters, however, opted for the legal procedure by a large margin. In 1838, a Pennsylvania mob inflamed by Democratic editorials burst into the capitol building in Harrisburg, sending the state senators fleeing. Although the Van Buren administration refused the governor's request for aid, state militia managed to restore order.[76] Then, in 1842, the bizarre episode in Rhode Island known as the Dorr Rebellion (or, more hyperbolically, as the "Dorr War") provoked both Democrats and Whigs to reaffirm their principles in the light of experience.

Alone among American states, Rhode Island had not drawn up a new constitution since the Revolution, and as late as 1842 operated under its colonial charter of 1663. Extraordinarily democratic by seventeenth-century standards, the charter had been rendered anachronistic by the industrial revolution. The charter conveyed "freemanship" (the right to vote, sue in court, and serve on juries) to native-born adult white males who either owned real estate or were the eldest sons of freemen. What fraction of Rhode Island men could meet these archaic qualifications in the 1840s is unclear; modern estimates range from 40 percent to two-thirds.[77] The system favored farmers at the expense of residents in the new textile mill towns, not only in the voting requirements but also in the apportionment of the state legislature. While the city of Providence had one-sixth of the state's population and contributed two-thirds of its taxes, it chose only one-twentieth of the state representatives.[78] Rhode Island's

---

76. David Grimsted, *American Mobbing* (New York, 1998), 205–9.
77. George Dennison, *The Dorr War* (Lexington, Ky., 1976), 14 (40 percent); Grimsted, *American Mobbing*, 209 (two-thirds).
78. Peter Coleman, *The Transformation of Rhode Island* (Providence, R.I., 1963), 270.

old charter endured for reasons both procedural and substantive. In the first place, the document contained no provision for its own amendment. (Originally, it had been assumed that the Privy Council in London could change it; now that was out of the question.) Second, the two major parties had come to terms with the charter. The Democrats won the state in 1836; the Whigs in 1840. Would-be reformers disagreed about what changes to make. The textile mills had recruited French Canadian and Irish immigrants, mostly Catholic in religion; a free Negro population dated back to the days when Rhode Island had been a center of the Atlantic slave trade. If the suffrage were to be expanded, Democrats wanted to include immigrants but not black men; Whigs preferred the opposite.

In 1834, a Rhode Island state assemblyman named Thomas Dorr formed a Suffragist movement calling for a new constitution on the basis of universal manhood suffrage. The Suffragists contested the annual state elections as a third party but never gained more than 10 percent of the vote. Dorr himself seemed a quintessential patrician reformer: from a wealthy family, a graduate of Phillips Exeter and Harvard, antislavery, a Whig. His diverse followers included disfranchised workers and artisans, the labor leader Seth Luther, and also middle-class men who objected to the archaic amateurism of the state courts under the charter and the legislature's power to intervene in judicial cases.

The Rhode Island Whig Party became impatient with Dorr's third-party activities and expelled him for splitting the Whig vote. The Democrats then recruited him, not because the local politicians liked him (they didn't) but at the urging of out-of-state party leaders who saw in Dorr's cause a way for the Democratic Party to show its support for popular sovereignty. In 1841, with working-class discontent exacerbated by hard times, Dorr's Suffrage Association held an unauthorized convention that drew up a document called the "People's Constitution" of Rhode Island. This People's Constitution was "ratified" by a referendum in which all white men in the state could vote. Of course, this referendum had no legal status, although the authorities allowed it to take place. The Dorrites asserted that more than fourteen thousand men voted for their constitution, but without any impartial monitoring this result cannot be trusted.[79] The number was critical, since it represented just over half of the adult men in the state and gave the Suffragists their claim to constitute the popular majority.

Events moved rapidly in April 1842. An election for state officials under the charter occurred; seven thousand men voted in it. The reformers staged a parallel poll of their own even though the state legislature this

---

79. Grimsted, *American Mobbing*, 212.

time declared it illegal. Some six thousand voters, Suffragists claimed, unanimously elected Thomas Dorr state governor. Dorr announced that his followers would seek to enforce the outcome of this election rather than that of the authorized one. He addressed cheering thousands in rallies and appeared in public with hundreds of armed men. He listened to Democratic politicians in other states, such as Silas Wright and Mike Walsh of New York, Thomas Hart Benton of Missouri, and former Treasury secretary Levi Woodbury, encouraging him to bold action. Ex-presidents Jackson and Van Buren expressed support. Francis Blair of the *Washington Globe*, leading organ of the Democratic Party, warned the charter government that if it dared try to suppress the rival state government, force would be met with force.[80]

Rhode Island governor Samuel King felt sufficiently alarmed to request military help from President Tyler in maintaining law and order. Tyler did not rush to support a Whig governor against a movement enjoying Democratic Party support at a time when he too was courting Democrats. On the other hand, he could hardly appear unsympathetic to a state's plea for aid against insurrection, the southern white nightmare scenario. So Tyler ruled King's request premature, adding, however, that in the event an insurrection materialized, he would intervene to sustain constituted authority, without any inquiry into "the real or supposed defects of the existing government."[81] (Tyler would have been mindful that his own Commonwealth of Virginia at this time retained a state constitution with property voting qualifications and a malapportioned legislature.)

On May 3, Thomas Dorr's supporters inaugurated him as governor of Rhode Island, along with a "People's Legislature" that met in a deserted factory. This convinced Tyler that the time to dispatch a few federal troops had come. It turned out they were not needed. The eighty would-be legislators in Dorr's shadow government had no real stomach for confrontation. They met for only two days before adjourning and laid no plans for a resort to force. The constituted authorities, by contrast, displayed organization and decisiveness. On May 18, Dorr foolishly led some armed men in an attempt to capture a state arsenal under cover of fog. When the mist lifted, it revealed the arsenal bristling with defenders. Dorr's followers wasted no time fleeing; the authorities then clamped down on his movement. Democratic politicians, national as well as state,

---

80. John Ashworth, *'Agrarians' and 'Aristocrats': Party Political Ideology in the United States, 1837–1846* (London, 1983), 116–27.

81. John Tyler to Samuel King, April 11, 1842, printed in "The Recent Contest in Rhode Island," *North American Review* 58 (1844), 398.

sensed that the Rhode Island public was not really ripe for revolution and did not attempt to intervene on behalf of the Suffrage Association. Dorr found himself arrested, convicted of treason against the state of Rhode Island, and sentenced to life imprisonment.

The charter government meanwhile summoned a legal constitutional convention; the document it drew up became known as the "Law and Order Constitution." In November a referendum ratified this constitution, 7,032 to 59, with the Dorrites boycotting. Surprisingly little differentiated this constitution from the "People's" one. The legally proposed document gave the right to vote to all native-born men who paid at least a dollar a year in taxes and to any immigrants who could meet the traditional property requirements. Like the "People's Constitution," it reapportioned the legislature, providing substantial equity of representation in the lower house, though not in the state senate. Both basic laws included a bill of rights and left the judiciary subordinate to the legislature. The most important difference between them was that the "People's" document had not required a property qualification of immigrants. On the other hand, the "Law and Order" constitution enfranchised taxpaying black men, where the "People's" constitution had restricted voting to whites.[82]

After he had served a year in prison, the state legislature ordered Thomas Dorr released; his conviction was annulled in 1854, not long before he died. Although Dorr had succeeded in intimidating an unresponsive system to change its constitution, much in Rhode Island politics went on as before. The two political parties in the state found no difficulty adjusting to the new system. James Fenner, a bitterly anti-Dorrite Democrat, ran as the "law and order" candidate with Whig support and won the state governorship in the first election held under the new constitution. Although more men were enfranchised, the turnout of qualified voters remained the lowest of any northern state's.[83]

Outside Rhode Island, both political parties pointed to the Dorr Rebellion to illustrate their respective political philosophies. The Democratic press proclaimed Dorr a hero and martyr of popular sovereignty. Whigs, on the other hand, accepted the judgment of Henry Clay that Dorr's uprising typified the dangers to "the permanency and stability of our institutions" along with nullification, Jacksonian illegalities, and the repudiation

---

82. Both constitutions are reprinted in Arthur Mowry, *The Dorr War* (Providence, R.I., 1901), 322–46, 367–90.

83. William Gienapp, "Politics Seem to Enter into Everything," in *Essays on American Antebellum Politics*, ed. Stephen Maizlish and John Kushma (College Station, Tex., 1982), table on 22.

of state bonds.[84] Clay might well have added mob violence and the anti-rent movement to his list. In 1845, well after the issue had become moot, Democrats forced a vote in the U.S. House of Representatives on resolutions endorsing Dorr's claim to the Rhode Island governorship and condemning his imprisonment. Democrats voted 107 to 7 in favor; Whigs voted 67 to 7 against. The uprising highlighted the different political philosophies of the two parties, popular sovereignty versus constitutional order and restraint.[85]

When a case involving a dispute over legal authority in Rhode Island came up before the U.S. Supreme Court, Daniel Webster defended the charter government's actions; his argument constituted a classic statement of Whig constitutional philosophy.[86] While the high court was hearing the case in 1848, revolutions by disfranchised townsmen and workers rebelling against archaic, undemocratic political systems swept across Europe. What Americans called "the Dorr War" in their smallest state seemed a miniature counterpart to these revolutions. If other states had waited until after industrialization to liberalize their voting requirements, they too might have undergone similar crises. Popular sovereignty had explosive implications in the world of the 1840s. Under these circumstances, and perhaps reflecting that his home state practiced slavery, Chief Justice Taney ruled against the "People's Constitution" and validated the charter government. Despite his party's rhetorical affirmations of popular sovereignty, the chief justice preferred prescriptive authority.[87]

V

A week after the first day of spring, Atlantic seaboard weather still felt wintry on March 28, 1841. In Washington, President Harrison had fallen ill. In East Cambridge, Massachusetts, a thirty-nine-year-old unmarried schoolmarm visited the county jail to give a Sunday school class, substituting for the regular teacher. She noticed (along with the debtors, minor

84. Henry Clay, "Address at Lexington, Ky." (1842), in his *Works* (New York, 1904), IX, 359–84.

85. Ashworth, *'Agrarians' and 'Aristocrats,'* 230. See also Sean Wilentz, *The Rise of American Democracy* (New York, 2005), 539–45; William Wiecek, "Popular Sovereignty in the Dorr War," *Rhode Island History* 32 (1973): 35–51.

86. "The Rhode Island Government," *Writings and Speeches of Daniel Webster* (Boston, 1903), XI, 217–42.

87. *Luther v. Borden,* 48 U.S. (7 Howard) 1–88 (1849). The case involved interpreting the "republican form of government" guarantee in the U.S. Constitution. Taney ruled that enforcing the guarantee belonged to the federal executive and legislative branches, not the judiciary.

criminals, and defendants awaiting trial) the local "lunatics" confined in an unheated cell. Dorothea Dix not only took it upon herself to provide them with some warmth, she kept coming back, reading up on the situation of the indigent insane, and composing a petition to the state legislature. When published, her *Memorial to the Legislature of Massachusetts* proved a bombshell. *"I tell what I have seen!"* she proclaimed—and much of it she found "revolting." She had seen people *"Chained, naked, beaten with rods,* and *lashed* into obedience!"[88] Miss Dix had found her true vocation, combining the talents of a publicist who mobilized public opinion with those of a lobbyist who could make things happen.

The treatment of the indigent insane in Massachusetts was actually relatively enlightened, Dix discovered, compared with what went on in other states. Typically, societies at the time incarcerated the indigent insane under whatever conditions cost the least; this could mean private basements or cages. Dix took her crusade on the road. Tall, slender, with angular features and her hair pulled back severely, Dorothea Dix embodied the Victorian image of female dignity and rectitude. She appealed to both heart and head. Her impassioned humanitarian outrage could move audiences, while her writings marshaled statistics and evidences of neglect. Dix spent time at the York Retreat in England, where she saw the Quakers apply principles of faculty psychology to the treatment of mental disorders. She cited the latest scientific papers by "alienists" (as psychiatrists were then called) about the efficacy of "moral" (that is, psychological) treatment as compared with traditional physical remedies for insanity (mainly bloodletting and blistering—the same as the remedies for almost every illness). Herself a Unitarian disciple of William Ellery Channing's doctrine of the perfectibility of human nature, she could preach Christian compassion with an evangelical power that transcended denominations. "Raise up the fallen, console the afflicted, defend the helpless, minister to the poor, reclaim the transgressor, be benefactors of mankind!"[89]

Dix's solution to the problem of the indigent insane was to place them in state-run asylums. The word "asylum," of course, means "haven," and she envisioned asylums as homelike places of tranquility and treatment. Those who recovered could be released; the others would at least be treated humanely. For years Dix traveled all over the United States and Canada, taking her campaign to one legislature after another with remarkable effectiveness. Since states confined the insane in a variety of

---

88. Dorothea Dix, *Memorial to the Legislature of Massachusetts* (Boston, 1843), 3–4.
89. Dorothea Dix, *A Review of the Present Condition of the State Penitentiary of Kentucky; Printed by Order of the Legislature* (Frankfort, Ky., 1846), 36.

institutions, she sometimes needed to address issues involving prisons and almshouses. But two issues she scrupulously avoided. By not mentioning women's rights, she got politicians to take her seriously; and by staying well clear of antislavery, she brought southern state legislatures on board.[90] Dix proved instrumental in founding a multitude of asylums for the mentally ill.

Dix's core support came from Whigs, who found her cause compatible with their disposition toward redemptive reform and positive government. Like the reformers of schools and prisons, she addressed the shaping of human character. She maintained a long friendship and correspondence with Millard Fillmore, the New York Whig who became Zachary Taylor's vice president and successor. Dix also cultivated Democratic politicians whenever she could. But when she shifted her attention to the federal level, a Democratic president frustrated what would have been her greatest achievement. In 1854, after years of lobbying by Dix, a bill setting aside 10 million acres of public lands to fund insane asylums finally passed Congress, only to fall before the veto of Franklin Pierce, a neo-Jacksonian strict constructionist. "I cannot find any authority in the Constitution for making the Federal Government the great almoner of public charity," he explained.[91]

Dix's career illustrates a general principle of the growth of women's political participation in nineteenth-century America. As women achieved more education, as the transportation and communications revolutions broke down their isolation, as the evangelical movement reached out to them, and as the industrial revolution enabled more and more of them to earn their own money (both within and without the home), women became increasingly active in public life. In the South as well as in the North, in free Negro communities as well as among whites, religious and benevolent causes benefited early from women's energies and talents. These kinds of activity seemed most compatible with prevailing assumptions about women's roles. A good "republican mother" could there exert leadership without appearing to break out of her proper "sphere" and challenge male authority. While men were acknowledged to be self-seeking, aggressive, and competitive, a woman like Dix could assume responsibility for making society compassionate and providing the helpless

---

90. This discussion of Dix draws upon that in Daniel Howe, *Making the American Self* (Cambridge, Mass., 1997), 167–75, as well as two recent biographies: David Gollaher, *Voice for the Mad* (New York, 1995); and Thomas Brown, *Dorothea Dix* (Cambridge, Mass., 1998).
91. "Veto Message" (May 3, 1854), *Presidential Messages*, V, 249.

with a home away from home in the form of an asylum. Female reformers could also address, with some show of legitimacy, problems directly affecting women and children, such as intemperance, prostitution, prison
reform—and, ultimately, slavery.[92] Nudging their way into political controversy, women had participated in the sabbatarian movement and in
opposition to Indian Removal. They had signed abolitionist petitions to
Congress.

Of the two major parties, the Whigs did more to encourage women's
political participation than did the Democrats. As the party of evangelical
benevolence and government activism, the Whigs found it made sense to
enlist the support of women even though they could not vote. In recruiting women and then relying on them to influence their men, the Whigs
followed the example of the evangelical revivalists. Contemporaries commented on the presence of women in a presidential campaign for the first
time in the Harrison demonstrations of 1840. Women not only cheered
from the sidelines and of course prepared the food and decorations for
the rallies, they marched in the parades themselves. The Whig women of
Richmond invited Daniel Webster to come address them; twelve hundred of them turned out to hear him. "Though it be out of the common
course for you to take part in the political strife," the Mississippi Whig
Sergeant Prentiss told the Whig women of Portland, Maine, "yet it is your
right and your duty to come forward at a time like this, and say by the interest your presence manifests, how much you have at stake." Occasionally women defied prevailing custom enough to make the speeches. One
Jane Field roused the Whigs of Lincoln's Springfield with her rhetoric,
calling out that "Every hill, and vale, and mountain crag shall echo the
heart cheering shout of Harrison and Liberty."[93] Lucy Kenney of Freder-
icksburg, Virginia, published, under her own name, several Harrison
tracts, including one entitled *The Strongest of All Governments Is that
Which Is Most Free*. (Kenney, who was nothing if not entrepreneurial, offered her campaign services to the Democrats as well, but Van Buren
spurned them, while the Whigs paid her a thousand dollars.)[94]

92. There is an enormous scholarly literature on this process and its ramifications; a good
    introduction to the subject is Paula Baker, "The Domestication of Politics: Women
    and American Political Society, 1780–1920," *AHR* 89 (1984): 620–47.
93. Elizabeth Varon, *We Mean to Be Counted: White Women and Politics in Antebellum
    Virginia* (Chapel Hill, 1998), 71–81; quotations from A. Banning Norton, *Reminis-
    cences of the Great Revolution of 1840* (Dallas, 1888), 243, and Gunderson, *Log Cabin
    Campaign*, 136.
94. Varon, *We Mean to Be Counted*, 75.

The extent to which the Whigs mobilized women dismayed their rival party: "This way of making politicians of their women is something new under the sun," admitted a Georgia Democrat. "We have been pained," declared a Democratic newspaper, "to see our fair countrywomen unsex themselves" by getting involved in politics.[95] Democrats continued to lag behind Whigs in organizing women in the election of 1844. They did enlist women in the movement to secure clemency for Thomas Dorr, but this and the journalism of Anne Royall remained exceptions within the insistent masculinity of Democratic ranks. The Democratic Party's principal constituencies—small farmers, immigrants, and the working class—held more cautiously traditional attitudes toward women's political involvement than did the commercial middle class. On the whole, the Democratic Party would remain less responsive to women's rights than its opponents until long after the Civil War.[96]

Recognizing that theirs was the party of the middle class, the Harrisonians presented their candidate as the custodian of the domestic values cherished by the middle class, as the guardian of hearth and home. The symbol of the log cabin, handed to them by the Democrats, suited this strategy to perfection. Women supporting Harrison could see themselves as acting within the bounds of Victorian conventions, not necessarily as social rebels. They discussed the legitimacy of certain tactics: Should a woman threaten to break off her engagement if her boyfriend would not promise to vote right? Whig women seem to have supported their party for much the same reasons that men did—economic, religious, cultural—and not to score points for their gender. The Harrison campaign shows women taking an active interest in the public, civic sphere, though not yet in their own rights as such. But that would not be long in coming. In 1840, six-year-old Abigail Scott climbed a tree and called out to the other children her enthusiasm for Old Tippecanoe; as an adult, Abigail Scott Duniway crusaded for women's suffrage.[97]

The involvement of women in the public arena owed much to the printed media, just beginning to discover women as a potential audience.

95. Quotations from Gunderson, *Log Cabin Campaign*, 135, and Robert Dinkin, *Before Equal Suffrage* (Westport, Conn., 1995), 32.
96. For women's participation in Tennessee political campaigns, both Whig and Democratic, see Jayne DeFlore, "Come and Bring the Ladies," *Tennessee Historical Quarterly* 51 (1991): 197–212.
97. Ronald and Mary Zboray, "Whig Women, Politics, and Culture in the Campaign of 1840," *JER* 17 (1997): 277–315; Rebecca Edwards, *Angels in the Machinery* (New York, 1997), 19.

The magazines of the day not only printed articles for and about women, they hired women to write them; and before long women appeared in editorial offices as well. A modern scholar has identified over six hundred female magazine and newspaper editors in nineteenth-century America.[98] The greatest of them, undoubtedly, was Sarah Josepha Buell Hale, editress (she always insisted on the gendered form of her title) of the Boston *Ladies' Magazine* from 1828 to 1836, the first magazine directed entirely to women; and then, in Philadelphia, of *Godey's Ladies' Book* from 1837 to 1877. At the eve of the Civil War, *Godey's* had a circulation of 150,000, making it the most widely read magazine in the United States, and certainly one of the most influential.[99] The roster of authors whom Hale's magazines published included most of the famous and popular American writers of the day, among them Edgar Allan Poe, James K. Paulding, Lydia Sigourney, and Catharine Maria Sedgwick.

A small-town New Hampshire girl, Sarah Josepha Buell had been brought up by parents who believed in equal education for the sexes and saw that she acquired at home the equivalent of a college education. She married a promising lawyer, David Hale, who shared her intellectual interests. For nine happy years they pursued mutual self-improvement and parenting. Then, in 1822, David suddenly died, four days before the birth of their fifth child. Like Queen Victoria after the death of Prince Albert, Sarah Hale wore black for the rest of her life. A widow with a family to support, Hale turned to her only asset—her literary skills. In a year a volume of poetry appeared; in five years, a successful novel, *Northwood*, established her reputation and created the chance to edit the *Ladies' Magazine*. In 1830 she published a book of verses for children aimed at the Sunday school market; it included the enduring classic, "Mary's Lamb."

A profound irony characterized Sarah Hale's career: this hardheaded successful businesswoman put out magazines that defined and celebrated female domesticity. A full participant in the market economy herself, she imagined a female world apart from it, a separate sphere. Hale made herself the arbiter of taste for middle-class women in matters of dress, housing, cooking, child-rearing, literature, and morality. Through the medium of print, she constructed and disseminated that polite culture to which her readers aspired. But Hale also wanted to enrich and expand the women's sphere. She labored early and consistently for women's education and helped found Vassar College. Her magazines promoted concern for women's health, property rights, and opportunities for public

98. Patricia Okker lists them in *Our Sister Editors* (Athens, Ga., 1995), 167–220.
99. William Huntzicker, *The Popular Press, 1833–1865* (Westport, Conn., 1999), 82.

recognition—though not suffrage. By reading her magazine, which reached one hundred pages per issue in the 1840s, women all over the country kept in touch with what seemed to them the wider women's world. Respecting the wishes of Louis Godey, her magazine's owner, Hale avoided explicit references to party politics. But she found other ways to get across her message of pro-Union Whiggery, and her nationalism has been usefully compared to that of Daniel Webster.[100] She attached much importance to her efforts on behalf of the construction of Bunker Hill Monument and the preservation of Washington's plantation home, Mount Vernon, as patriotic shrines that North and South could agree to honor. Her most important legacy for Americans today is the holiday of Thanksgiving, originating in New England, which she worked for many years to nationalize and which finally achieved presidential sanction under Lincoln.[101] Hale believed that women had a special role in American society, to counterbalance the harsh competitiveness of male-dominated capitalism and to reconcile sectional conflict through the invocation of sentiment. If Dorothea Dix represented the moral reform side of Whiggery, Sarah Josepha Hale gave voice to its conciliatory, national unionist aspect.

VI

John Quincy Adams and other northern antislavery Whig congressmen like William Slade of Vermont and Joshua Giddings of Ohio deeply embarrassed the southern Whigs. In the South, the Whig Party felt vulnerable to the charge that it was soft on abolitionism, much as, in the 1950s, the Democratic Party worried about being thought soft on Communism. William Cost Johnson's gag rule of 1840 represented a southern Whig attempt to prove the Whig Party's loyalty to southern interests. Representative Johnson, a Maryland Whig, had few slaves in his district and supported colonization and gradual emancipation for his state, but he insisted as strongly as any member from the Deep South that the slavery question was one for southern whites only to sort out. In January 1840, Johnson reintroduced the extreme version of the gag rule, the one Calhoun had originally demanded, under which the House of Representatives would not even receive antislavery petitions. Calhoun had by now rejoined the Democratic Party, and it was an election year, as it had been when the

---

100. William R. Taylor, *Cavalier and Yankee* (Garden City, N.Y., 1961), 92–119.
101. See Angela Howard Zophy, "A True Woman's Duty 'To Do Good,'" in *The Moment of Decision*, ed. Randall Miller and John McKivigan (Westport, Conn., 1994), 155–72.

first gag was adopted. So the House Democratic leadership refused to be outbid for the support of slaveholders. They accepted Johnson's proposal and implemented it: The House adopted the tighter version of the gag rule by a close vote, 114 to 108. But this version was harder for northern members to swallow; over half the northern Democrats voted against it, and not a single one of the northern Whigs followed their Maryland colleague's lead.[102]

When Harrison's Whig-dominated Congress assembled in 1841, antislavery members seized the opportunity to raise the question of the gag rule. Two weeks of the bitterest wrangling and parliamentary snarls ensued. Three times the House voted to repeal the gag rule and three times then reversed itself—all by narrow margins. The problem came down to this: Although the Whigs had a majority of forty in the House, forty-five of their members were southerners. Eventually, faced with the urgency of the economic crisis, the exhausted Whigs abandoned their effort to deal with the gag rule so they could take up the rest of their program. The Democratic minority supported the gag, partly because it tied up the Whig majority. Later, when Tyler split from the Whigs, his little band of southern state-righters led by Henry Wise of Virginia continued as they had always done to join with the Calhounites in support of the strictest enforcement of the gag.

In January 1842, John Quincy Adams presented a petition from fortytwo residents of Haverhill, a town in his constituency, requesting the dissolution of the Union (to free the petitioners from complicity in slavery). Of course Adams disagreed thoroughly with the petition that he thought it his duty to lay before the House. But Henry Wise demanded the former president be censured. Adams turned his ensuing trial before the House into a vindication. Seventy-four years old, unintimidated by threats and hate mail or the invective of outraged southern members, he spoke brilliantly for a week in his own defense, embarrassing his prosecutors (ruining the political career of his chief prosecutor, Thomas Marshall of Kentucky) and rallying enthusiastic support among northern Whigs. The press treated it as a sensation. Rather than let this go on for another week, his adversaries threw in the towel and "tabled" the censure motion. Adams, in a gesture of triumph, laid two hundred other petitions before his stunned colleagues. Afterwards the old man toured the North, feeling somewhat awkward in his unaccustomed role of popular hero.[103]

102. Freehling, *Secessionists at Bay*, 345–52.
103. I tell about the censure motion in a little more detail in *The Political Culture of the American Whigs* (Chicago, 1979), 60–62.

By this time northern Democratic congressmen had become anxious; the signatures on antislavery petitions now included not only Yankee evangelical spinsters (as Jacksonians had alleged) but working-class people and Democratic voters, especially in the "Upper North" above Pennsylvania. Even some southerners, beginning with Wise, could see that the gag rule (like the war against the Seminoles) was costing more than it was worth and should be abandoned.[104] The number of northern Democrats in the House voting to continue the gag steadily declined. Finally, in December 1844, the House voted 108 to 80 to repeal the gag rule. Northern Whigs as usual voted unanimously for repeal, and this time they got strong support from northern Democrats, who voted 54 to 16 to get rid of a rule that had become a clear liability. Old Man Eloquent had won his long fight to vindicate democratic freedom of expression. The cause he had embraced out of conviction had proved an effective vehicle for shaping public opinion. Characteristically, he gave credit to the Almighty: "Blessed, forever blessed, be the name of God!"[105]

VII

The Whig Party, despite its strength in the electorate, its talented leadership, and the coherence of its program, was robbed by a cruel fate and its own appalling blunder (the death of Harrison and the choice of Tyler as his running mate) of the chance to carry out the mandate it had received in the election of 1840. As a result a national bank was not reconstituted, nor Clay's comprehensive American System enacted. And never again did the party control the presidency and both houses of Congress at the same time. Still the Whigs had their impact on American society, although in ways less direct than national political control would have permitted. Through reform movements like that of Dorothea Dix, through influencing the culture as Sarah Hale did, by working for literacy and economic development at the state level as Abraham Lincoln did in Illinois, and by holding up moral wrong to public examination as John Quincy Adams did in Congress, the Whigs brought their distinctive value system to bear. The Dorr Rebellion in Rhode Island, where the Democrats' felt urgency regarding white manhood suffrage conflicted with the Whigs' commitment to law and order, illustrated one of the contrasts between the parties' priorities. The common characterization of this period

104. Edward Magdol, *The Antislavery Rank and File* (Greenwood, Conn., 1986), 102–13; Leonard Richards, *The Slave Power* (Baton Rouge, 2000), 143–48.
105. Diary entry for Dec. 3, 1844, *Memoir of John Quincy Adams*, ed. Charles Francis Adams (Philadelphia, 1874–77), XII, 116.

as "the age of Jackson" has obscured the contribution of the Whigs. Yet, as economic modernizers, as supporters of strong national government, and as humanitarians more receptive than their rivals to talent regardless of race or gender, the Whigs deserve to be remembered. They facilitated the transformation of the United States from a collection of parochial agricultural communities into a cosmopolitan nation integrated by commerce, industry, information, and voluntary associations as well as by political ties. From the vantage point of the twenty-first century, we can see that the Whigs, though not the dominant party of their own time, were the party of America's future.

16

American Renaissance

A sermon could make big news in the young republic, as one did in Baltimore, Maryland, on May 5, 1819. William Ellery Channing, minister of the Federal Street Church in Boston (today the Arlington Street Church) had come to town for the ordination of his young protégé Jared Sparks as minister of a newly erected church dedicated to "Unitarian and anti-Calvinistic worship." Working within a New England tradition of learned preaching and catering to the taste of the age for eloquence, Channing spoke for ninety minutes. He offered a distinctive synthesis of Protestant Christianity with the Enlightenment. Science and the Bible he declared perfectly compatible, for God "never contradicts in revelation what He teaches in his works." Channing and his followers interpreted the Bible not literally but broadly, as a progressive revelation—much as lawyers interpreted the Constitution, he explained. Indeed, there was a parallel between Channing's approach to the Bible and the broad interpretation Chief Justice Marshall had given the Constitution in the Baltimore case of *McCulloch v. Maryland* earlier the same year. While Marshall empowered the federal government to encourage economic development, Channing found in the Bible inspiration for the moral betterment of humanity. A generation later, Abraham Lincoln would synthesize their commitments to strong government, economic progress, and humanitarianism. For the time being, Channing's and Marshall's impulses proceeded on separate but parallel tracks, toward a goal then usually termed "improvement."[1]

Channing's sermon found no justification in either reason or revelation for the traditional doctrine of the Trinity, so he rejected it and called his own teaching "Unitarian Christianity." The heart of his discourse consisted of his rejection of the Calvinist doctrine of predestination. The idea that God would actually intend the damnation of the wicked, as opposed to merely foreseeing it, Channing declared a contradiction of divine moral perfection. In a country where Calvinism represented the dominant cultural heritage and where theological logic carried conviction, this was strong meat. Channing's sermon reflected long-simmering dissatisfaction

---

1. David Brion Davis called attention to the parallel between Channing and Marshall in *Challenging the Boundaries of Slavery* (Cambridge, Mass., 2003), 49–52.

with traditional Calvinist theological formulations among the Congregational clergy and laity of eastern Massachusetts. His speech became what it was intended to be, a manifesto for his religious viewpoint. It provoked prolonged debate between "orthodox" Calvinists and "liberal" Unitarians, prompted considerable rethinking among theologians, and aroused popular interest. When printed, Channing's sermon enjoyed the widest circulation of any American pamphlet between Thomas Paine's *Common Sense* in 1776 and Webster's *Second Reply to Hayne* in 1830.[2]

Although small of stature and plagued by illness, "the saintly Dr. Channing" exuded charisma and captured the imagination of a generation of religious liberals, reformers, and literary intellectuals. Channing inherited from his Puritan precursors an image of the clergyman as an intellectual and moral leader of the community; he lived up to it. As a Fellow of the Harvard Corporation (one of the university's governing bodies) he led the founding of Harvard Divinity School in 1816 to train liberal ministers. His "Remarks on National Literature" (1830) inspired Americans to respond to the challenge of the Englishman Sydney Smith's taunting question: "In all the world, who reads an American book?"[3] Channing's social ideas derived from his religious ones. He supported "the education of the laboring classes" (the title of one of his most popular addresses) and famously opposed both slavery and imperialism. Although the women's movement emerged only after his death in 1842, Channing admired Mary Wollstonecraft's early *Vindication of the Rights of Woman* and enjoyed the esteem of such antislavery feminists as Julia Ward Howe and Lydia Maria Child. Although he criticized revivals for what he thought a shallow emotionalism, Lyman Beecher and Charles Finney respected his personal Christianity, if not his theology.[4]

Channing's philosophy is best characterized as a form of Christian humanism. Like the humanists of the European Renaissance, he affirmed the values of a classical education and believed in realizing the potential divinity in human nature. Channing proclaimed the "self-culture" of our human faculties and powers to be the truest form of worship and celebrated human dignity as what he called our "likeness to

2. Channing's address, with many other documents of early Unitarianism, is contained in *An American Reformation*, ed. Sydney Ahlstrom and Jonathan Carey (Middletown, Conn., 1985), 90–117; the ensuing theological debate has been reprinted in two volumes: *The Unitarian Controversy*, ed. Bruce Kuklick (New York, 1987).

3. *Edinburgh Review* 33 (Jan. 1820), 78–80.

4. William Ellery Channing, "Remarks on National Literature," in his *Complete Works* (London, 1872), 103–15; Charles G. Finney, *Autobiography* (Westwood, N.J., 1908; [orig. pub. as *Memoirs*, 1876]), 356–57.

God." (Channing's outlook differed from that of Hosea Ballou, the theologian of the Universalist denomination that would unite with Unitarianism in 1961; Ballou relied on God's goodness, not humanity's divinity, to guarantee universal salvation.) To his Christian humanism Channing added an Enlightenment faith in individual rights and in reasoning from empirical evidence similar to that of most other American Protestants.[5]

Channing and his Unitarian associates thought of themselves as leading New England away from Calvinism much as Renaissance humanists thought of themselves as leading Europe out of the Middle Ages. The humanistic spirit that they nurtured affected many aspects of American intellectual life and social reform. One sees it in Dorothea Dix's campaign for insane asylums, in Horace Mann's labors for public schools, in the abolitionism and feminism of Samuel J. May, and in Channing's obstetrician brother Walter's application of ether to mitigate the pain of childbirth. It figured in the antebellum debates over whether to abolish capital punishment (or, as more commonly resulted, to cease performing executions in public). Unitarian humanism also provoked a remarkable literary flowering that includes the unique outburst known as Transcendentalism. The widespread influence of this humanism, and particularly its manifestation in artistic expression, justifies the term made famous by the literary historian F. O. Matthiessen: "American Renaissance."[6]

A striking example of the humanism of the American Renaissance is the education of Laura Bridgman. Born in 1829, Laura Bridgman had been rendered both blind and deaf by scarlet fever at the age of eighteen months. Nevertheless she had learned to sew and otherwise help her mother around the house by the age of seven, when she went to live at Boston's Perkins School for the Blind, under the care of its director, Samuel Gridley Howe. Howe regarded young Laura's education not only as a humanitarian undertaking but also as a scientific one, to research the nature of the human faculties. Laura Bridgman became the first blind-and-deaf person to learn language, anticipating the more famous achievement of Helen Keller. Her success satisfied Howe that the human mind was not a "blank sheet," but contained innate capacities and conceptions, including morality, logic, and curiosity. He published scientific papers on her case, claiming to have refuted the psychology of John Locke and to

---

5. Channing, "Self-Culture" and "Likeness to God," in his *Complete Works*, 10–29, 230–39; Daniel Howe, *Making the American Self* (Cambridge, Mass., 1997), 130–35.
6. Amelie Kass, *Midwifery and Medicine in Boston* (Boston, 2002); Stuart Banner, *The Death Penalty* (Cambridge, Mass., 2002), 124–31; Francis Otto Matthiessen, *American Renaissance* (New York, 1941).

confirm that of the Scottish philosophers of innate common sense. A Unitarian, Howe believed that Laura would also refute the Calvinist doctrine of human innate depravity. He particularly wished to discover what kind of "natural religion" the girl would manifest as she learned about the wonders of science. A nurse ruined this aspect of Howe's experiment by telling Laura about the love of Jesus. Howe fired the nurse, but Laura Bridgman remained a devout Baptist for the rest of her life.[7]

Laura Bridgman's triumph over what seemed insurmountable difficulties attracted widespread attention and made her famous. The spirit of self-improvement that she exemplified was widely shared in American society. Increasingly it focused, as in her case, on the acquisition and use of literacy. The spread of public schooling, originally justified as necessary to a Protestant laity and an informed citizenry, also encouraged economic productivity and equal opportunity in a market society where few people rested content with subsistence agriculture as a livelihood. Ambitious souls who did not have public education available, such as the young Abraham Lincoln, applied themselves to the task of self-improvement with whatever reading matter they found at hand—in his case, Bunyan's *Pilgrim's Progress*, Defoe's *Robinson Crusoe*, Aesop's *Fables*, Watts's *Hymns*, and, of course, the King James Bible. They did so partly to enhance their vocational opportunities but also to develop their personal potential. In the industrializing cities, Mechanics' Institutes offered workers and managers in manufacturing the common pursuit of self-improving knowledge.[8] We have already seen how strongly the desire for self-improvement affected American social, economic, and political life; it also impacted literature and the arts. Even the resentment that the ethic of self-improvement provoked would find its own form of cultural expression in satire.

The Unitarian denomination that Channing promoted through theological debate and then helped organize never penetrated much beyond eastern New England and a few other outposts that included Baltimore, Lexington (Kentucky), New York City, and Charleston. Ballou's Universalist denomination spread more widely, but also very thinly. Although the arguments that Unitarians and Universalists marshaled against Calvinist determinism and in favor of human free will won few converts

7. Ernest Freeberg, *The Education of Laura Bridgman* (Cambridge, Mass., 2001); Elisabeth Gitter, *The Imprisoned Guest* (New York, 2001).
8. M. L. Houser, *The Books that Lincoln Read* (Peoria, Ill., 1929). William Gilmore, *Reading Becomes a Necessity of Life* (Knoxville, Tenn., 1989), and Joseph Kett, *The Pursuit of Knowledge Under Difficulties* (Stanford, 1994), 81–83, discuss Channing's ideal of self-culture.

to either denomination, they resonated broadly with the attitudes of the growing urban middle class and the ethos of self-improvement. They had a cumulative effect, across the course of the nineteenth century, in greatly diminishing the influence of Calvin's theology within American Christianity. Their consequences may be observed in a variety of ways, beginning with the religious modernism that became dominant in the mainline Protestant denominations during the first half of the twentieth century.[9] Encouraging a view of education as a process of development rather than discipline, Unitarianism produced a disproportionate number of American educators as well as writers and reformers involved in the antislavery and women's rights movements. The changes initiated at antebellum Harvard under Unitarian auspices would eventually culminate under President Charles William Eliot in its transformation into America's preeminent university. In short, the Unitarianism of Channing's time remains not only interesting for its own sake but, even more, important for the developments it prompted or portended.[10]

II

On Independence Day of 1837, the citizens of Concord, Massachusetts, dedicated a monument to the "Fight" (as they usually termed the battle) between Minutemen and Redcoats that had occurred there on April 19, 1775. A local poet had written an ode for the occasion, and slips of paper with his poem were passed out to those assembled on the riverbank. A choir sang the new words to New England's most familiar tune, the one used for Psalm 100 in sixteenth-century English rhymed meter, "Old Hundred." The Minutemen themselves had sung psalms to keep up their spirits before the battle. Ralph Waldo Emerson's "Concord Hymn" went like this:

> By the rude bridge that arched the flood,
>   Their flag to April's breeze unfurled,
> Here once the embattled farmers stood,
>   And fired the shot heard round the world.
>   . . .
>
> O Thou, that made these heroes dare
>   To die, and leave their children free,
> Bid Time and Nature gently spare
>   The shaft we raise to them and thee.

9. See David Robinson, *The Unitarians and the Universalists* (Westport, Conn., 1985); Anne Bressler, *The Universalist Movement in America* (Oxford, 2001).
10. Channing, "The Moral Argument Against Calvinism," *Complete Works*, 370–78; Conrad Wright, ed., *A Stream of Light* (Boston, 1975), 3–61; Paul Conkin, *American Originals* (Chapel Hill, 1997), 57–95.

Ten years later Emerson would change the words "O Thou" to "Spirit," for he had by then distanced himself from traditional piety. But at Concord on that July Fourth, no one present would have doubted that the Christian God of the Minutemen was being invoked again. Either way, Emerson saw the monument as raised to more than the memory of Minutemen themselves: also to the spirit of liberty, or to God.[11]

Concord in the 1830s stood on the brink of its second wave of historical fame. The first one had derived from its role at the outbreak of the American Revolution. The second came from its role in the golden age of American literature. Emerson's Concord neighbors included Henry David Thoreau, Nathaniel Hawthorne, Louisa May Alcott, Margaret Fuller, Elizabeth Peabody, and a host of other writers and sages. No description of the environment can fully explain an extraordinary outburst of genius. (Why did so much creativity appear in sixteenth-century Florence, or in Athens in the fifth century before Christ?) But Concord did combine several characteristics that facilitated its literary "flowering." A village of about two thousand people, some of them still farmers, it preserved enough of a rural ambiance, and retained woodland close enough, that the Romantic school of writers could indulge their fondness for nature. At the same time, however, the town was also close enough to academic Cambridge and metropolitan Boston (particularly after the railroad connected them in 1844) that these writers could benefit from the intellectual stimulation and publishing opportunities on offer there.[12] Concord represented the kind of mixed agricultural, commercial, manufacturing, and professional economy that, in antebellum America, often produced the most innovative activities; Oberlin, Ohio, and Seneca Falls, New York, serve as other examples.

Most of the Concord writers belonged to an informal "club" (their term) called the Transcendentalists. Their critics had fastened the name on them as a sign of contempt (the labels "Quaker," "Shaker," "Methodist," and "Mormon" had originally been derogatory too), but the writers came to accept it, for it signified their desire to transcend appearances and perceive the underlying reality. Like so much else in

11. *Complete Works of Ralph Waldo Emerson*, ed. E. W. Emerson (Boston, 1904), IX, 158; Robert A. Gross, "The Celestial Village," in *Transient and Permanent*, ed. Charles Capper and Conrad E. Wright (Boston, 1999), 251–81, esp. 273–74. The usual statement that the ode was first performed on April 19, 1836, is erroneous; see Ralph Rusk, *Life of Ralph Waldo Emerson* (New York, 1949), 274.

12. Mary Cayton, *Emerson's Emergence* (Chapel Hill, 1989), 163–64; Gross, "Celestial Village," 267.

pre–Civil War American culture, literary Transcendentalism derived from a religious impulse. Transcendentalism was one of the many forms of religious awakening characteristic of the period, and its members aspired to revive what they accounted true piety—a kind of personal spirituality they believed the organized churches and their creeds inhibited rather than nurtured. The Transcendentalists shared in the millennial mood of their times—not in a biblical or Christian way, but in the sense that they saw themselves initiating a new order of the ages, democratic and free, in harmony with the divine. Like the evangelist Charles Finney, they preached a form of perfectionism, though theirs meant not Christian deliverance from sin but realization of the divine potential in all human beings.

Except for James Marsh up in Vermont, all the Transcendentalists were either Unitarians or ex-Unitarians. Emerson's career illustrates this derivation in his own gradual transition from Christian humanism to a non-sectarian spiritual humanism. In 1829, young Waldo (as his family called him) became the assistant pastor of a Unitarian church in Boston. It seemed a logical choice of vocation for a man whose forebears included a long line of New England ministers going back to Puritan times. But after three years Emerson resigned rather than continue to administer the Lord's Supper, a rite he (like the Quakers) had come to consider an unnecessary ritual, meaningless in the modern world. He now pursued a new career as lecturer and writer, seeking to refashion for himself a role something like the one the minister had historically embodied in New England: an inspiring intellectual, spiritual, and moral leader. Instead of looking to Protestantism to define this role, he invoked the Romantic conception of the artist.[13]

After leaving the ministry, Emerson turned himself into what scholars have called a "public intellectual," meaning he was a creative thinker not operating within an academic or church setting, who sold his ideas on a wide range of issues to a general audience in the open marketplace.[14] Emerson came to earn a good living on the lecture circuit, delivering inspirational talks on many subjects including "Self-Reliance," "Experience," and "Fate," which he would later work up into publishable essays. All over America, lyceums, Mechanics' Institutes, and other voluntary associations eagerly awaited such addresses; by midcentury, in each week,

13. Lawrence Buell, *Literary Transcendentalism* (Ithaca, N.Y., 1973), 29–31, 45, 50–54.
14. Russell Jacoby, *The Last Intellectuals* (New York, 2000); Lawrence Buell, *Emerson* (Cambridge, Mass., 2003), 39–43.

something like 400,000 Americans heard someone lecture at a lyceum.[15] Emerson became so well known he could book lecture halls independently of any local host organization. His lectures rank as masterpieces of nineteenth-century American oratory alongside the sermons of Channing, the legal arguments of Webster, and the political speeches of Lincoln.

Emerson became a popular philosopher with his short book *Nature* (1836), which espoused what was essentially a new religion: idealistic, monistic, mystical, and intuitive, based on spiritual communion with nature. He summed it up (prosaically) this way: "1. Words are signs of natural facts. 2. Particular natural facts are symbols of particular spiritual facts. 3. Nature is the symbol of spirit."[16] Emerson's God (which he elsewhere named the Oversoul) was immanent in the universe. Through harmony with nature, a person achieved not merely "likeness to God" (Channing's aspiration) but participation in divinity itself. Emerson's message thus accorded self-improvement a spiritual dimension and sanction. Emerson won a hearing for these ideas because the American public felt concern about spiritual things and eagerly engaged in schemes of self-improvement. What he and his fellow Transcendentalists most valued about the their new form of spirituality was its individualism: It put every person directly in touch with the divine, without any need for tradition, a written scripture, or an institutional church. Emerson taught that all existing religious traditions represented partial visions of ultimate truth. He found Hinduism and Buddhism particularly attractive and evoked them in his poetry.

Emerson startled the American intellectual establishment of his day when he delivered an address to the graduating class at Harvard Divinity School in July 1838, challenging the harmony of reason with revelation as then understood. The prevailing orthodoxy in natural science and theology taught that both disciplines were empirical. John Locke had synthesized the Enlightenment with biblical religion in *The Reasonableness of Christianity*, where he argued that the truth of Christian theology rested on historical facts: The miracles recorded in Old and New Testaments proved Christ and the prophets indeed revealed divine truths. Emerson

---

15. Donald Scott, "The Popular Lecture and the Creation of a Public in Mid-Nineteenth-Century America," *JAH* 66 (1980): 800. See further Angela Ray, *The Lyceum and Public Culture in the Nineteenth-Century United States* (East Lansing, Mich., 2005).

16. "Nature," in *Collected Works of Ralph Waldo Emerson*, vol. I, ed. Robert Spiller (Cambridge, Mass., 1971), 7–45, quotation from 17.

challenged this orthodoxy, not by questioning whether the miracles had really occurred, but by proclaiming that religious faith came *before*, not *after*, belief in the biblical miracles. "To aim to convert a man by miracles is a profanation of the soul." People believed in the biblical miracles because they had faith, not the other way around. Faith came, according to Emerson, by immediate revelation from the divinity immanent in the universe, not "second hand," from revelations made to others thousands of years ago. Perhaps not since the trial of Anne Hutchinson in the seventeenth century had New England faced so disturbing a claim for immediate revelation.[17] Emerson not only substituted his Oversoul for the Judeo-Christian personal God, he challenged the received conception of the empirical unity of reason with revelation. Unitarian Harvard professors and Calvinist Princeton professors joined together in unusual alliance to denounce Emerson's "latest form of infidelity." Transcendentalists George Ripley, Theodore Parker, and Orestes Brownson (who would soon convert to Catholicism) rallied to defend the Emersonian position in one of the most profound intellectual debates of pre–Civil War America. In this "Miracles Controversy" the religion of the Romantic movement confronted the religion of the Protestant Enlightenment.[18]

From our standpoint in the twenty-first century, the Transcendentalist who looks the most "modern" is Margaret Fuller. Versatile and passionate, she made her impact felt on journalism, feminism, criticism (literary, music, and art), and revolution. Daughter of Timothy Fuller, a Massachusetts congressman allied with John Quincy Adams, as a precocious child Margaret had received an intensive education from her devoted father. As an adult she could draw upon a formidable fund of learning across a wide range of subjects and made herself a role model at a time when well-educated women were scarce. Aided by her friend Emerson, Fuller edited the Transcendentalists' experimental literary magazine, the *Dial*, which introduced readers to European Romanticism, criticized American bourgeois culture, and all too often fell short of its editor's grand expectations and pronouncements. Fuller, Emerson, and the other

---

17. "Divinity School Address," in *Collected Works*, I, 76–93, quotation from 83; Brooks Holifield, *Theology in America* (New Haven, 2003), 190–96; David Holland, "Anne Hutchinson to Horace Bushnell," *New England Quarterly* 8 (2005): 163–201.

18. Barbara Packer, "Transcendentalism," in *The Cambridge History of American Literature*, ed. Sacvan Bercovitch (Cambridge, Eng., 1995), II, 329–604 (on miracles, see esp. 403–13); Herbert Hovenkamp, *Science and Religion in America, 1800–1860* (Philadelphia, 1978), 79–96. For primary documents of the miracles debate, see Perry Miller, ed., *The Transcendentalists* (Cambridge, Mass., 1950), and Joel Myerson, ed., *Transcendentalism* (Oxford, 2001).

members of the Transcendentalist group sought to rescue their country from provincialism and put the American public in touch with transatlantic writers like Goethe, Coleridge, and Carlyle. America's culture derived too exclusively from Calvinism and the Enlightenment, they believed. Even though the Transcendentalists shared a debt to this inheritance (in their emphasis on literacy, individualism, and a sense of the Divine, for example), they saw these traditions as limiting and wished to press harder to explore the full range of human feelings and potential.[19]

Fuller applied Channing's humanist ideal, "self-culture," to the nurture of the female self and developed a theory of human personality as androgynous, with every person having both masculine and feminine qualities. Between 1839 and 1844, she presided over a series of "conversations" ("discussion groups," in today's terminology) intended to help women think for themselves and about themselves, and to express their ideas clearly and with confidence. Her book *Woman in the Nineteenth Century* argues that women possess the full range of human capacities ("faculties") and need to be allowed to develop their potential, rather than living only for the sake of their men. "A much greater range of occupations" must be opened to women "to rouse their latent powers," she wrote. "Let them be sea-captains, if they will."[20]

In 1844, Fuller left for New York City, where she went to work as book review editor on Horace Greeley's crusading *New York Tribune*. There her ideas reached a far wider audience. Known as the "star" of the paper, Fuller's columns typically appeared on page one, got reprinted in the *Tribune Weekly* (which had a nationwide circulation), and earned her ten dollars a week—worth about two hundred dollars after taxes in 2005 and then considered a good salary for a writer. When widespread revolution broke out in Europe in 1848, Fuller found herself defining the role of a newspaper foreign correspondent. From her vantage point in Rome, she covered such dramatic events as the first Italian efforts at democracy and national unification, and the overthrow and then the restoration of the papacy's civil authority. Meanwhile, she fell in love with a dashing Italian nobleman younger than herself, married him secretly (since his family did not approve), and bore a child. On her way back to America in 1850, the ship bearing the new marchesa d'Ossoli, her husband, and their little

19. I have written on Margaret Fuller in Daniel Howe, *Making the American Self* (Cambridge, Mass., 1997), 212–34.
20. Margaret Fuller, *Woman in the Nineteenth Century*, intro. Madeleine Stern (Columbia, S.C., 1980; facsimile of the 1845 ed.), 159, 162; David Robinson, "Margaret Fuller and the Transcendental Ethos," *PMLA* 97 (1982): 83–98.

boy ran aground in a storm off Long Island. Although within sight of land, all three perished, and Fuller's unpublished manuscript on the Italian Revolution washed out to sea. At the end of *Woman in the Nineteenth Century*, she had written, "What concerns me now is, that my life be a beautiful, powerful, in a word, a complete life in its kind." Though she was only forty when she died, the life of Margaret Fuller fulfilled her heroic aspiration.[21]

Any account of the Concord Transcendentalists must reckon with Henry David Thoreau (properly pronounced "*Thaw*-roe"). Thoreau has served as a patron saint for two movements in American life: environmentalism and civil disobedience. In actuality, Thoreau was neither a natural scientist nor a political philosopher. His genius lay in reflecting upon relatively modest experiences and turning them into great writing.

By Walden Pond, just a mile and a quarter from Concord town center, Thoreau built a one-room cabin on land owned by his friend Emerson. He stayed in it, off and on, from July 1845 to September 1847. Other Transcendentalists had experimented with living in a utopian commune called Brook Farm in West Roxbury, Massachusetts. Thoreau constructed his own one-man utopia in search of a way of life that would bypass what he found to be the distractions of social convention and material clutter. Like the Shakers and the early Quakers, like the original Christian monastics, Thoreau opted for simplicity. "I went to the woods because I wished to live deliberately, to front only the essential facts of life, and see if I could not learn what it had to teach, and not, when I came to die, discover that I had not lived." Practicing thrift as a form of spiritual discipline, Thoreau turned his back on the consumer products that his countrymen embraced so eagerly. Yet he did not scorn the industrial revolution; he felt in awe of the railroad trains that passed not far from his cabin, for they exemplified the human qualities of invention and adventure that he admired.

Why did Thoreau not go out to the frontier and build his cabin in an actual wilderness? Because he wanted to prove such a major undertaking not necessary; one could conduct a living experiment within easy reach, using few resources. If others who felt discontented with their lives wished to imitate his example, they could readily do so. The important

---

21. Charles Capper, *Margaret Fuller, The Public Years* (New York, 2007) treats the later part of her life. Fuller's newspaper accounts of the Italian Revolution have been published as *"These Sad but Glorious Days": Dispatches from Europe*, ed. Larry Reynolds and Susan Belasco Smith (New Haven, 1991).

thing was to explore one's inner state of mind, not journey long distances. As Thoreau wryly put it, "I have traveled a good deal in Concord."[22]

As for "civil disobedience," there is no evidence that Thoreau ever used the expression in his life. He spent a night in Concord jail—either the twenty-third or twenty-fourth of July 1846 (we cannot tell which)—for refusing to pay the Massachusetts state poll tax of $1.50. News traveled fast in the village, and within a few hours someone had paid the tax for him— probably his aunt Maria Thoreau, a member of the Concord Female Anti-Slavery Society like a number of other women in the Thoreau and Emerson families, who closely monitored the political stands of their menfolk.[23] So the local constable, Sam Staples, freed his friend Henry the next morning.

Henry Thoreau made this brief experience the basis of a lecture and later turned the lecture into an essay entitled "Resistance to Civil Government." He there discusses his action as a moral protest against immoral government practices: the return of escaped slaves, the war against Mexico, and the treatment of the American Indians. The essay has often been invoked by subsequent generations of protesters, including Martin Luther King, Mohandas Gandhi, and opponents of South African apartheid. Those who have cited Thoreau in this way have generally been non-violent and willing to accept punishment for their lawbreaking, but his essay makes no mention of either of those principles (and Thoreau elsewhere had repudiated non-violence). Nor, of course, did he invoke the federal Constitution to sanction his violation of a state statute. The only "higher laws" Thoreau cared about were the eternal principles of morality. Linking his act of protest with the Concord of 1775, he asserted an individual right of revolution. On the whole, Thoreau seems less concerned with disobedience as a reform tactic than as a demonstration of the moral integrity of the protester. When human law conflicted with the dictates of conscience, he did not doubt which should prevail.[24] Confident that the intuitions of conscience put everyone in touch with the same immutable moral law, neither Thoreau nor the other Transcendentalists worried about the possibility of conflicting moral principles.

22. Henry David Thoreau, *Walden*, ed. Lyndon Shanley (Princeton, 1971), quotations from 90, 4. Also see Robert D. Richardson, *Thoreau* (Berkeley, 1986), esp. 169–79.
23. See Sandra Petrulionis, "The Concord Female Anti-Slavery Society," *New England Quarterly* 74 (2001): 385–418.
24. "Resistance to Civil Government," in Henry David Thoreau, *Reform Papers*, ed. Wendell Glick (Princeton, 1973), 63–90. The commonly used title "Civil Disobedience" was invented after Thoreau's death. I discuss the essay in some detail in *Making the American Self*, 235–55.

The Concord Transcendentalists addressed two kinds of questions about American liberty in their day. One of these was what we might term the *quantitative* issue: How many people did American freedom include? In particular, did it include women and people of color? The other kind of question was *qualitative*: What should a free person's life be like? Would their freedom make Americans' lives more meaningful? On the quantitative issue, the Transcendentalists certainly supported the inclusive side. Emerson, for example, publicly protested to President Van Buren against Cherokee Removal and delivered a great address affirming black dignity on August 1, 1844, commemorating the tenth anniversary of emancipation in the British West Indies (a date widely celebrated by African Americans).[25] Margaret Fuller inspired the next generation of the women's movement. In a Transcendentalist community called Fruitlands, Bronson Alcott conducted experiments in greater equality between the sexes and respecting the autonomy of children. Theodore Parker, a Transcendentalist who unlike Emerson remained a Unitarian minister, preached a fiery blend of Transcendentalism and antislavery to overflow crowds at a converted theater in Boston; among his converts was Julia Ward Howe, future author of the "Battle Hymn of the Republic."[26]

However, the principal and uniquely profound contribution of the Transcendentalists lay in their serious exploration of the second kind of issue. What should Americans do with their freedom? The Transcendentalists endorsed Alexis de Tocqueville's warning against the danger of the tyranny of the majority. They urged Americans to introspection and integrity, to the exercise of independent judgment, to rejection of competitive display, to the realization of their full human potential, to lives in harmony with nature. The Transcendentalists saw themselves as liberating individuals from convention, conformity, and unexamined habit. Thoreau commented, "It is hard to have a southern overseer; it is worse to have a northern one; but worst of all when you are the slave-driver of yourself."[27]

As a formal religious philosophy, Transcendentalism proved evanescent; its intellectual appeal barely lasted for a single generation after Emerson's announcement of it in 1836. Yet as a literary movement, it has

---

25. "Letter to Martin Van Buren," in *The Political Emerson*, ed. David Robinson (Boston, 2004), 27–32; "Emancipation in the British West Indies," ibid., 91–119.
26. See Anne Rose, *Transcendentalism as a Social Movement* (New Haven, 1981); Dean Grodzins, *American Heretic: Theodore Parker and Transcendentalism* (Chapel Hill, 2002).
27. *Walden*, 8.

retained interest, and rightly so. The writings of the Transcendentalists affirm some of the best qualities characteristic of American civilization: self-reliance, a willingness to question authority, a quest for spiritual nourishment. Their writings, even today, urge us to independent reflection in the face of fads, conformity, blind partisanship, and mindless consumerism.

III

The Mercantile Library of Philadelphia was founded in 1821 by an association of the city's leading businessmen. A private lending library, it testified to its members' aspirations toward self-improvement and general culture while also catering to their tastes for recreational reading. In 1826, they incorporated their library and began to expand its membership; by 1844–45, they could raise enough money to construct a special building for it. Meanwhile, similar mercantile libraries had been organized in other American cities. From 1828 on, the Mercantile Library of Philadelphia sponsored lectures by prominent people.[28] In May 1841, William Ellery Channing came to give one.

Suiting his topic to his practical, worldly audience, the clerical visitor spoke on "The Present Age"—and, more particularly, on its tendency "to expansion, to diffusion, to universality." "This tendency is directly opposed to the spirit of exclusiveness, restriction, narrowness, monopoly, which has prevailed in past ages." Channing began with comments on the sciences. What struck him was not so much the new discoveries as their popularization. "Lyceums spring up in almost every village for the purpose of mutual aid in the study of natural science," he noted; "a lady gives us Conversations on Chemistry, revealing to the minds of our youth vast laws of the universe." The democratization of science fostered its practical application, "bestowing on millions, not only comforts, but luxuries which were once the distinction of a few."[29]

To Channing, the gradual democratization of politics in the United States and the rest of the world represented a consequence of the democratization of information and culture. "What is true of science is still more true of Literature. Books are now placed within reach of all." To be sure, people sometimes read for amusement (indeed, two-thirds of the books checked out in the Mercantile Library itself were novels), but Channing rejoiced that the improved printing press also provided texts for schools and Sunday schools, tracts for missions, and publications promoting

---

28. Mercantile Library Company of Philadelphia, *Essay on the History of the Mercantile Library Company of Philadelphia* (Philadelphia, 1867).
29. Channing, "The Present Age," in *Complete Works*, 131–42, quotations from 132–33.

international benevolence and reform. All understood that the venue and auspices within which Channing spoke illustrated his points. The livelihood of the members of his audience manifested analogous tendencies, he commented. Commerce too was expanding in volume, overcoming traditional trade barriers, and (illustrating the tendency to universality) reaching to farther and farther points of the globe, integrating all into one economic system and facilitating the spread of Christianity. A fearful responsibility rested with the merchants in his audience, the speaker warned, to make sure that they conveyed the virtues of Western civilization rather than its vices (exemplified at their worst in the slave trade).

Channing's observations on his age still provide useful categories for understanding it. The revolutions in communications and transportation clearly lay at the heart of his analysis, though he did not give them those modern names. Besides the transforming impact these revolutions had on political, economic, and academic life, they dramatically affected literature, the arts, and social reform as well. The improvements and economies in printing, papermaking, and distribution that multiplied newspapers, magazines, and books also had their effects on the substance of what was written. Books became not only more numerous and widely marketed but also longer, facilitating the rise of the novel as a new literary genre. Novels often appeared serialized in newspapers or magazines prior to their publication between hard covers—thus taking advantage of the low postal rates charged periodicals. Serialization especially helped rural people far from libraries or bookstores. By 1827, the North American Review could announce "the age of novel writing." The rise of the novel responded not only to improved efficiency in supply but also to expansion in demand. The audience for reading matter grew as population increased and popular education promoted literacy. By the 1840s, perhaps sooner, the United States possessed the largest literate public of any nation in world history. The reading public extended well beyond the urban middle class: Many farmers and mechanics found time to read; even some factory operatives did. It helped that people spent more time indoors, where whale oil and gas lamps shed more light than candles had. The mass production of eyeglasses, beginning in the 1830s, certainly helped. Those riding the newly built trains loved to read. Families often read aloud to each other, sitting around the fireplace, so even family members who could not read for themselves gained exposure to the printed word.[30]

30. See Nina Baym, Novels, Readers, and Reviewers (Ithaca, N.Y., 1984); the North American Review is quoted on 16. Writing as well as reading was democratized, as explained in Ronald Zboray and Mary Zboray, Literary Dollars and Social Sense (New York, 2005).

Just as Christianity responded to modern popular taste with revivalism, literature responded with the novel. In each case a popular "awakening" or "renaissance" ensued. Novels addressed the newly literate mass audience very effectively. Although fictional, they told about people with whom readers could identify in situations at least purportedly realistic. Novels did not presuppose knowledge of classical languages, ancient traditions, or epic poetry. They ranged in content from serious art to pure recreation to titillating fantasy, thus appealing to just about everyone literate who could make a little time to read. During the decade of the 1820s, U.S. publishers brought out 109 books of fiction by Americans; by the 1840s, almost a thousand. Frequently written by women, these books often dealt with women's lives and problems. Catharine Maria Sedgwick was followed by a whole school of "domestic" authors including Caroline Gilman, Susan Warner, Fanny Fern (pseudonym of Sarah Willis Farrington), and E.D.E.N. Southworth. Women wrote not only novels but history, biography, poetry, humor, drama, and melodrama. In these genres too they often dealt with domestic or moral themes, by no means necessarily accepting women's subordination to men. Literature, like religion, expressed female energy and experience sooner than politics did.[31]

In the nineteenth century, many writers and tastemakers worried about the quality of the literature (especially novels) available for public consumption—just as they would worry in more recent times about the quality of television. The same print culture that produced books produced reviews of books. Then as now, reviewers tried to encourage what they considered "serious" writing; in those days this often meant explicit didacticism. Many in the audience too shared the view that their reading habits should make them better people, not simply more cultured but more earnest and hardworking, more highly skilled, better informed citizens. The popularization of science that Channing noticed reflected a widespread attitude that all reading, fiction or nonfiction, should be "elevating" or "improving." Countless ordinary people, on farms as well as in the city, made reading a tool of self-construction. But of course, there always remained those who read for excitement, escape, and vicarious thrills.[32]

31. Michael Gilmore, *American Romanticism and the Marketplace* (Chicago, 1985), 4–7; Mary Kelley, *Private Woman, Public Stage* (New York, 1984); Nina Baym, *American Women Writers and the Work of History* (New Brunswick, N.J., 1995).

32. Ian Watt's classic *The Rise of the Novel* (London, 1957) treats England; for America, besides Baym, *Novels, Readers, and Reviewers*, see Cathy Davidson, *Revolution and the Word*, 2nd ed. (New York, 2004).

Homer Franklin ran a bookstore in New York City. In September 1840, he took an inventory that has survived. Of his 8,751 books in stock, 2,526 were Bibles or religious books, and 3,008 were educational or children's books. Both categories reflect the importance of "self-improvement" as a motive to read. The remainder included 867 professional and scientific books, 287 reference books, and 2,063 classified as "belles lettres," which included novels, poetry, and music.[33]

Channing's denomination, the Unitarians, played a distinctive and important role in the development of American literature. They had been among the first to recognize the potential of print as a means to shape public taste and morals. For centuries, Protestants had read the Bible in hope of salvation. Now, the Unitarians encouraged the reading of other "elevating" literature to foster the development of a virtuous character, which they believed more important than the sudden, all-transforming conversion experience of traditional New England Calvinism. Eager to break out of what they saw as the tyranny of Calvinist theology over American cultural life, they had created a succession of Boston literary magazines of which the most important was the *North American Review*. Founded in 1815, it became the most influential intellectual periodical in the United States for most of the nineteenth century. The Unitarian denomination would contribute a remarkably large number of prominent American writers of the mid-nineteenth century, including—besides the Transcendentalists—the novelists Nathaniel Hawthorne, Catharine Maria Sedgwick, and Lydia Maria Child, the narrative historians George Bancroft, William H. Prescott, and John L. Motley, and the poets William Cullen Bryant, Henry Wadsworth Longfellow, James Russell Lowell, and Oliver Wendell Holmes the elder (also a distinguished professor of medicine). The Unitarian denomination remained small; along with Congregationalism it underwent disestablishment in Massachusetts in 1833. Meanwhile, the political power of New England waned with the growth of the Middle Atlantic states and the trans-Appalachian West. Nevertheless, New England Unitarians could take consolation in their importance for the world of print; through it, they had found a means to exert a more subtle influence across the broad republic.[34]

33. Ronald Zboray, *A Fictive People* (New York, 1993), 141.
34. See Lawrence Buell, "The Literary Significance of the Unitarian Movement," in *American Unitarianism*, ed. Conrad E. Wright (Boston, 1989), 163–79; Marshall Foletta, *Coming to Terms with Democracy* (Charlottesville, Va., 2001), 61–70. A different interpretation is presented by Peter Field, "The Birth of Secular High Culture," *JER* 17 (1997): 575–610.

American Calvinism had long remained suspicious of novels as a waste of time and worse, encouraging the wrong kind of fantasy life, particularly among the young. But beginning in the eighteenth century, moral philosophers called the Calvinist suppositions into question. This newer psychology of art, pioneered by the Scottish moralists Francis Hutcheson and Adam Smith (the same one who also wrote on economics), taught that art could stimulate sentiments that could then be applied to real life, making the reader or viewer of sentimental art into a more morally sensitive person. Novels could serve this function, as could other artistic genres.

Responding to these ideas as the nineteenth century went by, evangelicals, Calvinist and Arminian alike, not only exploited poetry, biography, and magazine articles, but also, more cautiously, enlisted novels in the service of Christian moral sensibility. A market developed for imaginative literature that affirmed religious and moral values and thereby rebutted traditional Calvinist disapproval. Such works, demonstrating social responsibility, helped both writers and publishers legitimate their activities in the public eye. As early as 1824 the Connecticut evangelical Lydia Sigourney could comment (with some misgiving) that novels had taken over "Sunday reading" from theological works.[35] The Episcopalian Susanna Rowson and the Unitarian William Ware pioneered the biblical fiction that would reach a climax after the Civil War in Lew Wallace's *Ben-Hur*. Sigourney herself published fifty-six volumes of didactic and devout poetry and prose. Often she chose historical settings and wrote sympathetically about the American Indians. Her husband complained that she put her career ahead of her duty to him: "Were you *less of a poet*," he told her bitterly, "how much *more valuable* you would *be as a wife*." But when Charles's hardware business went bankrupt in the depression that began in 1837, Lydia's commercially successful writing supported the Sigourney family.[36]

Literature affirming the values of middle-class Christian morality reflected the aspirations of many, probably most, American readers. It provided the clearest route for a writer to combine a literary reputation with commercial success. A fine example is provided by the enormously popular poetry of Henry Wadsworth Longfellow. Longfellow made it his task as a poet to remind people of cultural and moral values, to show that there

35. Candy Brown, *The Word in the World* (Chapel Hill, 2004), 95–99; David Reynolds, *Faith in Fiction* (Cambridge, Mass., 1981), 130–44, Sigourney quotation from p. 113.
36. Melissa Teed, "A Passion for Distinction," *New England Quarterly* 77 (2004): 51–69, Charles to Lydia Sigourney (1827) quoted on 55; Baym, *American Women Writers and the Work of History*, 81–87.

was more to life than material pursuits. He sought to bring history to life with "Paul Revere's Ride" and "The Courtship of Miles Standish." He evoked sympathy for victims of injustice with his "Poems on Slavery," "The Jewish Cemetery at Newport," "The Song of Hiawatha" (which Longfellow pronounced "Hee-awatha"), and "Evangeline," treating the eighteenth-century expulsion of the French Acadians from Nova Scotia. As professor of Romance languages at Harvard, he introduced Americans to Dante by translating *The Divine Comedy*. The values Longfellow celebrated resonated with his readership. To the Victorian middle classes of America and Britain, his poetic exhortations to self-improvement seemed both relevant and inspirational. His "Psalm of Life" (1838), after rejecting a pessimistic outlook, endorses conscientious striving:

> Tell me not in mournful numbers,
>   "Life is but an empty dream,
> For the soul is dead that slumbers,
>   And things are not what they seem."
> Life is real! Life is earnest!
>   And the grave is not its goal;
> "Dust thou art, to dust returnest,"
>   Was not spoken of the soul. . . .
> Lives of great men all remind us,
>   We can make our lives sublime,
> And, departing, leave behind us
>   Footprints in the sands of time. . . .
> Let us, then, be up and doing,
>   With a heart for any fate;
> Still achieving, still pursuing,
>   Learn to labor and to wait.

After the critical reevaluation of American literature that began in the 1920s, Longfellow fell out of favor. Most literary critics now deem his didacticism and sentimentalism quaint and trite, but one suspects his poetry could still serve its original purpose of inspiring the young, if once again it were taught in schools.[37]

Not all authors aimed at the market for uplift, however. Writers such as George Lippard achieved commercial success by targeting an audience of young working-class males with sensationalism, violence (mild by our standards), social criticism, and escapism. Like the domestic fiction

---

37. "A Psalm of Life," in Henry Wadsworth Longfellow, *Poems and Other Writings*, ed. J. D. McClatchy (New York, 2000), 3–4. For a fine reevaluation of the poet's merits, see Christoph Irmscher, *Longfellow Redux* (Urbana, Ill., 2006).

aimed at women, working-class "dime novels" told about characters with whom their readers could identify. Starting in 1839, these novels would appear first serialized in weekly "story papers" and then in cheap paper-bound pamphlet editions. With their exciting adventures often set on the western frontier, such publications helped popularize imperialism, though not necessarily the expansion of slavery, among the northern working class. Dime novels confirmed the fears of Calvinists and gave cause for the concern of anxious reviewers who wanted literature to promote personal improvement.[38]

Middle-class readers throughout the Union also liked novels about frontier bloodshed, Indian wars, and the Revolution. South Carolina's William Gilmore Simms hoped to duplicate the success of New York's Fenimore Cooper in dealing with such themes. The ambitious son of a humble storekeeper, the prolific Simms worked hard at the literary profession, writing not only fiction but also poetry, history, geography, and literary criticism, lecturing on tour, and editing a series of magazines culminating in the *Southern Quarterly Review*. Nevertheless, Simms found his literary career a constant scramble and, in the end, died impoverished. Through his writing and addresses he helped create the romantic legend of the Old South (to which a number of northern writers also contributed), featuring paternal plantation owners and contented slaves. This proslavery perspective has contributed to his fall from popularity, leaving Simms in the status of a formerly famous writer.[39]

The antebellum southern author best remembered today is Edgar A. Poe (the form of his name that he preferred). Whereas both Transcendentalists and didactic Christian writers intended their art as moral and spiritual inspiration, Poe espoused the position—unusual in America at the time—that art did not need to serve some further function but was worthwhile for its own sake. He and Margaret Fuller were probably the finest American literary critics of their day. Orphaned at an early age, Poe quarreled with his guardian, developed a drinking problem, and never enjoyed a stable home life. Although he got several good jobs (notably as editor of the *Southern Literary Messenger*), he could not manage to keep

38. Michael Denning, *Mechanic Accents: Dime Novels and Working-Class Culture in America* (New York, 1987); David Reynolds, *Beneath the American Renaissance* (New York, 1988), 204–8; Shelly Streeby, *American Sensations: Class, Empire, and the Production of Popular Culture* (Berkeley, 2002), 162–69.

39. Simms is placed in his context by Eric Sundquist, "The Literature of Slavery and African American Culture," *Cambridge History of American Literature*, II, esp. 261–64; and Michael O'Brien, *Conjectures of Order* (Chapel Hill, 2004), passim.

them. His romantic relationships were tempestuous, and his young wife, Virginia, died tragically from tuberculosis. Poe's poetry and fiction reflect both his sophisticated literary theory and the agonies of his personal life. His poem "The Raven" (1844), a meticulously crafted meditation upon inconsolable grief, became an instant success and has remained among the best-known poetry of all time. Although he wrote one novel, Poe more significantly pioneered the short story and within that genre essentially invented detective fiction, which the Scotsman Arthur Conan Doyle would take up in the next generation.[40]

The difficulties Simms and Poe found in earning a living as writers were not peculiar to southerners. Emerson's Concord neighbor Nathaniel Hawthorne encountered similar problems. Starting in 1830 Hawthorne sold stories to magazines, and in 1836 collected some for publication in book form. Although well received, Hawthorne's writings generated only a modest income for him, his wife, the artist Sophia Peabody Hawthorne, and their children. He hoped that the commune started by some of his literary friends at Brook Farm would provide a way of life compatible with writing but learned otherwise and lost his financial investment in the enterprise. He got revenge by writing *The Blithedale Romance*, a thinly disguised satire on Brook Farm, Emerson, Fuller, and the Transcendentalist movement. From time to time, financial rescue came in the form of federal patronage: appointments in the Boston Custom House, the Salem Custom House, and finally as U.S. consul in Liverpool, England—all of which, however, cut into his writing time and energy. His two great novels, *The Scarlet Letter* (1850) and *The House of the Seven Gables* (1851), were written between government jobs. Despite eventually achieving recognition, if not wealth, through his work, Hawthorne always resented the competition of those he called the "damned mob of scribbling women," whose efforts sold better than his.[41]

Hawthorne tried many kinds of writing, including children's books, but the works for which we chiefly remember him deal with New England's Puritan past, combining the qualities of historical romance with psychological depth. Like Poe, Hawthorne appreciated the literary power of guilt and grief and, like him, moved away from realistic fiction into surrealism and symbolism. For this reason, he preferred to call his long works of fiction "romances" rather than "novels," a distinction generally drawn at the

---

40. See Kenneth Silverman, *Edgar A. Poe* (New York, 1991).
41. Gilmore, *Romanticism and the Marketplace*, 147. Nathaniel Hawthorne to William D. Ticknor, Jan. 19, 1855, quoted in Brenda Wineapple, *Hawthorne* (New York, 2003), 282.

time. While a Unitarian in his own religion, Hawthorne retained much of his Puritan ancestors' Calvinist sense of sin—a combination also found in John Quincy Adams, with whose politics Hawthorne disagreed.[42]

A friend and admirer of Hawthorne was the New Yorker Herman Melville. Although his parents came from distinguished families, Herman grew up in shabby gentility. A youthful rebel, he ran off to sea as a common sailor, first on a merchant ship to Liverpool in 1839, then on a whaler around Cape Horn in 1841. He jumped ship in the Pacific Islands and spent several adventurous years there before signing on with a U.S. naval vessel as a means of returning home in 1844. Back in New York, Melville turned his experiences into books, *Typee* (1846) and *Omoo* (1847), presenting a romanticized view of his Polynesian escapades that made him a controversial celebrity. Though he had achieved enough financial success now to marry the daughter of Massachusetts Chief Justice Lemuel Shaw, Melville's next three books, *Mardi*, *Redburn*, and *White Jacket*, brought him little income. Moving to the Berkshire Mountains in order to live near Hawthorne, Melville composed his giant tragic masterpiece, *Moby-Dick*, the greatest of sea stories, published in 1850 and dedicated to Hawthorne, its rhetoric redolent of Shakespeare and the King James Bible. Although it started out selling well, sales of *Moby-Dick* dried up after negative reviews appeared. Some of these, not surprisingly, objected to the book's questioning attitude toward religion. Others resulted from a defective edition published in London that omitted the epilogue and so left readers wondering how Ishmael could narrate the story when he had perished (it seemed) in the wreck of the *Pequod*. Melville's next publication, his tormented semiautobiographical *Pierre* (1851), did nothing to reassure his readership. Attempts to salvage his finances by lecture tours failed. His writing career stumbled and went into decline, while his family's security depended on his wife's inheritance and his job as a customs officer in the Port of New York, awarded after prolonged lobbying on his behalf. Only in the 1920s did literary scholars begin to recover appreciation for Melville's saga of the doomed Captain Ahab, who dares defy the incomprehensible power of the universe by his hunt for the white whale named Moby-Dick. Still more recently, readers have begun to notice the political dimension of Melville's masterpiece: Ahab the demagogue leading his followers to destruction.[43]

42. See Lawrence Buell, *New England Literary Culture* (Cambridge, Eng., 1986), 269, 279, 470.

43. Andrew Delbanco, *Melville* (New York, 2005). On the scriptural echoes in *Moby-Dick*, see Buell, *New England Literary Culture*, 177–87.

The first half of the nineteenth century witnessed publishing flourish as an industry while creative writers struggled to establish an economically viable profession in the United States. Unfortunately the interests of publishers and writers collided in the area of copyright law. The Constitution authorized copyright laws, and Congress enacted one in 1790, protecting American but not foreign authors. This law effected a massive transfer of intellectual property from British to American publishers, but it proved a very mixed benefit to American authors. In the absence of international copyright, American publishers preferred to reprint free the works of established British writers like Thackeray, Scott, Dickens, and the Brontë sisters, rather than take a chance on American writers to whom they would have to pay royalties. By our standards such reprinting constituted literary piracy, but it was not then illegal. American writers lobbied for an international copyright law to save them from this unfair competition, and found a champion in Henry Clay. The publishers declared it contrary to American national interest to pay royalties to foreign authors. They also cleverly aligned their interest with that of the reading public, arguing that free reprints kept down the price of books, and the Jacksonian Democratic Party sided with them rather than with the authors. By such means, American publishers succeeded in fending off international copyright until 1891. Ironically, the United States today strongly protects intellectual property and insists that other countries observe international copyright rules.[44]

The absence of international copyright made it harder for Americans to earn a living by writing. This helps explain why male writers often supplemented their income in other ways—lecturing, editing magazines, or seeking political patronage jobs such as Irving, Hawthorne, Melville, and James Russell Lowell obtained. Women writers found these alternatives impossible or much more difficult; this helps explain why women who wrote for a living had to concentrate so hard on making sure their publications would be commercially successful.

The connections between politics and journalism gave rise to connections between politics and literature. New York's *Democratic Review* mostly patronized Democratic authors. Whig writers more commonly appeared in the *American Whig Review*, Greeley's *Tribune Weekly*, both also originating in New York, and Boston's *North American Review*. Only

---

44. Meredith McGill, *American Literature and the Culture of Reprinting* (Philadelphia, 2003), 76–108, presents the publishers' arguments sympathetically; most other scholars sympathize with the writers. See also William St. Clair, *The Reading Nation in the Romantic Period* (Cambridge, Eng., 2004), 382–93.

occasionally did such journals run a piece by someone identified with the opposing major party, though the *Tribune Weekly* often ran pieces by radical reformers and socialists. Writers themselves sometimes befriended colleagues across party lines, as the Whig Longfellow did the Democrat Hawthorne. Margaret Fuller, active in the Whig Party despite her gender, made friends among Democratic writers of the "Young America" group in New York City. Washington Irving enjoyed good relations with both Democratic and Whig politicians; Walt Whitman started out as a Democrat but became bitterly disenchanted with the party's proslavery stance.[45]

As postcolonial peoples often do, Americans in the young republic asked themselves whether they yet possessed a distinctive national literature. The question chiefly concerned American *writers*, since American *readers* clearly inhabited a transatlantic literary world, consuming large quantities of British literature made even larger by the absence of international copyright. Conversely, a few American writers sold well in Britain (without copyright protection); the favorite poet of the English people in the nineteenth century was not Wordsworth or Tennyson but Longfellow. By midcentury the United States was just on the verge of an unparalleled explosion of literary creativity. The decade of the 1850s would witness, in addition to the great novels of Hawthorne and Melville, Emerson's *Representative Men* (1850), Thoreau's *Walden* (1854), Whitman's *Leaves of Grass* (1855), and the record-breaking best seller of the entire nineteenth century, Harriet Beecher Stowe's *Uncle Tom's Cabin* (1852). When the Association of New York Publishers met in New York's Crystal Palace (just erected in imitation of the one in London) on September 27, 1855, they could with perfect justification greet 153 of their most popular authors with the proud toast: "To American Literature!"[46]

IV

Even more than novels, the theater remained under a moral cloud in the newly independent United States. Calvinist Protestantism had disapproved of dramatic productions ever since the English Puritans had closed the theaters during the seventeenth-century interregnum. The First Continental Congress, reflecting the kind of religious fervor that imbued many in the Patriot cause, had done likewise in 1774. The influential Calvinist John Witherspoon, president of Princeton and signer of the Declaration of Independence, famously denounced the theater as an aspect of that worldly gentility and emotional indulgence which a

45. See Gilman Ostrander, *Republic of Letters* (Madison, Wisc., 1999), 218–20.
46. Zboray, *Fictive People*, 3.

well-disciplined Christian should avoid.[47] In the early decades of the nineteenth century, however, many theater owners undertook to free dramatic productions from their traditional stigma and to broaden their audiences. They presented plays with patriotic and moral themes as well as entertaining ones. Sometimes they went so far as to ban the prostitutes who had customarily plied their trade in theater galleries. And they produced lots of Shakespeare, whose plays were by no means confined to an elitist enclave. Tocqueville surely exaggerated when he wrote, "There is hardly a pioneer's hut that does not contain a few odd volumes of Shakespeare," but he had noticed something real: Americans usually read Shakespeare before seeing his plays performed. Already revered as cultural icons, the Bard's plays could be defended by theatrical producers not only as rattling good stories but also as part of a spectator's program of self-improvement. This in turn prompted many parodies of Shakespeare — not so much poking fun at the plays themselves, however, as at the use to which overly earnest playgoers put them. The parodies relied for their humor on the audience's familiarity with the original.[48]

Early nineteenth-century American theatrical performances lasted a long time. Typically, the principal production was both preceded and followed by other presentations from singers, acrobats, dancers, and comedians. Sometimes these also appeared between acts of the main play. The appropriate analogy is to the typical motion picture theater during the golden age of Hollywood, where two feature films would be accompanied by short subjects like a travelogue, a newsreel, and cartoons. Acting companies, as in Shakespeare's day, toured together, having a number of performances, major and minor, in their repertoire. By now the actors included women as well as men, and they often married each other; they were expected to sing or dance as well as act. Their productions frequently took liberties with the playwright's text. The mixture of serious and light entertainment helped draw large numbers to performances. The rowdy audiences felt free to demand their favorite musical numbers from the theater orchestra (called the "band" although it included strings).[49]

47. Ann Withington, *Toward a More Perfect Union* (New York, 1991), 11, 20–37; John Witherspoon, *A Serious Inquiry into the Nature and Effects of the Stage* (1757; New York, 1812).

48. Edwin Burrows and Mike Wallace, *Gotham* (Oxford, 1999), 483–85; John Kasson, *Rudeness and Civility* (New York, 1990), 227; Alexis de Tocqueville, *Democracy in America*, ed. Phillips Bradley (New York, 1945), II, 55; Lawrence Levine, *Highbrow/Lowbrow* (Cambridge, Mass., 1988), 13–16.

49. See Susan Porter, *With an Air Debonair* (Washington, 1991).

The distinction between "highbrow" and "lowbrow" was not then characteristic of American culture, although people distinguished between that which was "improving" and that which was not. The future poet Walt Whitman contrived to straddle the two appeals in his 1842 novel, *Franklin Evans*. Selling for a "bit" (twelve and a half cents), Whitman's story endorsed the temperance movement but included enough sensational details about urban life to attract some of the dime-novel audience.[50] Like fiction, theatrical productions could be turned into vehicles for the promotion of reform causes. On the stage, the most famous reform advocates were the Hutchinson Family Singers, who began their celebrated tours in 1842. The Hutchinsons supported not only temperance but antislavery as well. Their well-publicized appearances at reform conventions helped boost attendance.[51] After *Uncle Tom's Cabin* appeared in print, it was quickly translated into innumerable traveling stage productions.

The struggle to legitimate the theater and redeem it from opprobrium provoked conflict between the upper and middle classes on the one hand, with their aspirations to polite culture, and the urban working class, which liked the traditional theater just as it was. Working-class patrons of the old-style, nonrespectable venues in New York, like the Park Theater, resented the elegant new Astor Place Opera House, with its rules against prostitutes and its dress code appealing to the affluent. When the Astor Place scheduled the touring British actor Charles Macready to play Macbeth in May 1849, the American actor Edwin Forrest performed the same role at the Broadway. Compared to the restrained performances of Macready, Forrest's acting style was broader and his appeal more populist. The contrast between the two celebrities inflamed passions of national pride and class conflict. Forrest's fans attacked the Astor Place, and somewhere between twenty-two and thirty-one people died in the riot that ensued. Surprisingly for us, one of the most horrific incidents of class conflict in antebellum America involved culture rather than material interest—specifically, rival visions of how to present Shakespeare.[52]

The most original, popular, and distinctively American form of stage entertainment in this period was the minstrel show. Originally the word "minstrel" meant simply a traveling musician, as it did in Thomas Moore's Irish patriotic lyric "The Minstrel Boy," a favorite with Irish Americans of

50. David Reynolds, *Walt Whitman's America* (New York, 1995), 94–97.

51. See Dale Cockrell, ed., *Excelsior: Journals of the Hutchinson Family Singers* (Stuyvesant, N.Y., 1989).

52. Kasson, *Rudeness and Civility*, 227–28; Levine, *Highbrow/Lowbrow*, 63–69.

this era. Beginning in the late 1820s, white men like T. D. "Daddy" Rice applied the term to their performance of songs, dances, and comic routines with faces blackened by burnt cork. Sometimes they imitated or adapted actual African American music; sometimes they used material by white composers. Their skits and songs caricatured black people, occasionally with sympathy (as in "Old Black Joe"), more often with contempt or gross hostility. (When African Americans themselves opened a theater in New York in 1821, playing Shakespeare and other works to integrated audiences, white harassment shut it down.)[53]

The first audience for the new minstrel shows consisted of northern urban white working-class men, and that social group always remained central to defining the humor of blackface minstrel shows, even though their appeal gradually broadened. The songs that have survived from minstrel show days mostly deal with the South and plantation slavery (such as "Dixie" or "Old Folks at Home"), but in the 1840s, when minstrel shows took off in popularity, they often ridiculed the free black people of the North. Other objects of their raillery reflected other working-class male resentments: the learned professions and learning in general, the newly rich, European high culture, abolitionism, evangelical reform, and women's rights. Performance in blackface provided a convenient license for satire, since assaults on respectability could be attributed to ignorant blacks and still get laughs.[54]

In terms of party politics, minstrel shows usually sided with the Jacksonian Democracy; the most famous minstrel composer, Stephen Foster, also wrote Democratic campaign songs. Taken all in all, what minstrel show satire ultimately targeted was the ethic of self-improvement. Lampooning black people provided a vehicle for expressing contempt for self-improvement efforts, since blacks were deemed incapable of self-improvement and yet persisted in attempting it. The pretentious free Negro ("Zip Coon"), misusing big words, served as a stock comic figure in minstrel shows.[55] Blackface comedy thus provided a Jacksonian rebuttal to the contemporaneous theater of moral uplift, exemplified by Whig performers like the Hutchinson Family (although the Hutchinsons were also sometimes termed "minstrels" in the general sense of touring musicians).

53. Burrows and Wallace, *Gotham*, 487–88.

54. Robert Toll, *Blacking Up* (New York, 1974), is still useful. See also Eric Lott, *Love and Theft: Blackface Minstrelsy and the American Working Class* (New York, 1993); William Mahar, *Behind the Burnt Cork Mask* (Urbana, Ill., 1999).

55. On the minstrel show as a rejection of the ethic of self-improvement, see also Nathan Huggins, *Harlem Renaissance* (New York, 1971), 256.

Blackface minstrel shows generated such large profits that they could employ many of the most talented American composers of their age, including not only whites like Foster ("O Susannah," "The Camptown Races," "My Old Kentucky Home") but also African Americans like James A. Bland ("Carry Me Back to Old Virginny" and "Oh, Them Golden Slippers"). If imitation is the sincerest form of flattery, the minstrel shows paid African American culture the compliment of stealing ideas from it even when subjecting it to ridicule. Foster, who worked for the most successful minstrel troupe of all, Christy's Minstrels, believed that his songs promoted respect for African American music by recasting it in a form accessible to white audiences.[56]

To twenty-first-century Americans, minstrel shows constitute an awkward aspect of our national inheritance; their tunes remain catchy, but performing them can give offense. Historically, the shows' cultural importance is undeniable. They represent the American counterpart to the English music hall. They embodied not only racism but much else of the America of their time, with references to steamboats, new inventions like telegraphy, and the newly popular African American instrument, the banjo. Soldiers marched off to Mexico to the tune of "The Girl I Left Behind Me"; the forty-niners who went to California sang "O Susannah" around their camp fires. Minstrel shows remained popular for more than half a century and constituted the ancestor of the mass popular entertainment that followed.

Of course, the minstrel show would have been impossible without the authentic African American music that preceded it. Virtually everybody in America, including foreign visitors, joined in acknowledging that the most original musicians in the country were the slaves. Antislavery advocates used this as evidence of black talent; defenders of slavery pointed to it as evidence of black contentment. African American folk music took a multitude of forms both secular and sacred, to which may be traced varieties of modern music including the blues, gospel, and jazz. Its diversity bespoke its origins in diverse parts of Africa and the various New World influences to which black creativity responded, in the Caribbean and on the mainland. Music nurtured a sense of African American community. Singing could accompany work, holidays, or tragic moments like the march of newly sold slaves away from family and friends toward an unknown destination, usually westward. The most famous of African American folk songs were the spirituals, songs of Christian faith amid suffering

56. Ken Emerson, *Doo-dah! Stephen Foster and the Rise of American Popular Culture* (New York, 1998), 183.

("Nobody knows the trouble I've seen," "Were you there when they cru-
cified my Lord?"), often invoking the heroes of the Hebrew scriptures
("Joshua fit the battle of Jericho, / And the walls came tumbling down"),
multilayered in meaning, like all great art ("My Lord, what a morning
[mourning], / When the stars begin to fall"), sometimes expressing coded
longings for freedom ("When Israel was in Egypt's land, / O let my people
go!"). Although contemporary descriptions of the music of American
slaves exist, we are heavily indebted to postemancipation efforts to recon-
stitute and preserve it, such as those of the abolitionists Lucy and Wendell
Garrison, the Fisk Jubilee Singers, and the poet James Weldon Johnson.[57]

In antebellum America, white people as well as black encountered
music most often not in observing performances by professionals but
when they themselves sang, played, and danced. Free people too sang at
social events and to soothe the children. Some of their folk music we still
recognize: "The Arkansas Traveler," "She'll Be Comin' Round the Mountain," "O Shenandoah." From the American folk music of this period, often Celtic in origin, evolved what came to be called country-western.
Church worship provided one of the most common occasions for participation in music-making. By 1815, American Protestants had long since
supplemented psalm-singing with hymns as well, though organs, being
expensive, appeared only very gradually. Improvements in printing and
transportation fostered the distribution of hymnals along with other
books; thanks to increased literacy, congregations no longer had to learn
their songs by rote. Like benevolent associations, hymns were interdenominational. Their lyrics dignified the trials of everyday life with meta-
phors of Christian pilgrimage and taking up the cross.[58]

On July 4, 1831, the Sunday school children of Park Street Church in
Boston sang a new hymn with words by twenty-three-year-old Samuel
Francis Smith: "My country, 'tis of thee,/ Sweet land of liberty,/ Of thee I
sing." The conjunction of patriotism and religion seemed natural. Entitled simply "America," it was sung to the tune of "God Save the King" —
originally written in reaction against the Stuart uprising of 1745 and once
popular in the British colonies. "America" became the unofficial national
anthem, and good citizens stood up upon hearing it. (During the First
World War, Americans felt the need for a national anthem with a tune

57. Eileen Southern, *The Music of Black Americans*, 2nd ed. (New York, 1983); Dena Ep-
    stein, *Sinful Tunes and Spirituals* (Urbana, Ill., 1977); James Weldon Johnson, *The
    Books of American Negro Spirituals* (1925–26; New York, 1944).
58. Henry Wilder Foote, *Three Centuries of American Hymnody* (Cambridge, Mass.,
    1940). See also Brown, *The World in the World*, 190–242.

different from that of the British. "The Star-Spangled Banner" then re-placed "America"; Congress made this official in 1931.) Lowell Mason, the choirmaster who conducted the first performance of "America" and a collaborator with Lyman Beecher, went on to become the most influen-tial figure in the development of choirs and hymnody in antebellum U.S. Protestantism.[59]

The industrial and communications revolutions encouraged and trans-formed the performance of music at home. The former provided the piano, originally called the *pianoforte* ("soft-loud" in Italian) because unlike a harpsichord it could produce music of varied dynamic levels. Jonas Chickering, a Yankee artisan-turned-manufacturer, invented a cast-iron frame for the piano strings that withstood powerful tension. His firm pio-neered the American piano industry and the mass marketing of its product. The printing press complemented the factory-made piano by providing published sheet music. Once reserved to the wealthy elite, access to key-boards now spread as part of that polite culture to which middle-class Americans aspired. In many middle-class households, the piano replaced the fireplace as the center of home life. Family and friends gathered around the piano to sing sentimental songs like Thomas Moore's "Believe Me, If All Those Endearing Young Charms" or perhaps a simple aria from a light opera like Michael Balfe's "I Dreamt I Dwelt in Marble Halls." Learning to play the piano took hard work, which made it a prized accomplishment in a society that valued work highly. It was also a form of self-improvement considered especially suitable for women and girls.[60]

Classical music ("art music" as it is sometimes called) came slowly to the United States, since in the beginning the churches did not foster it, and no aristocracy existed to patronize it. Thomas Jefferson, who loved European classical music and played it on his violin, deplored its scarcity on the American scene. Its expansion in the nineteenth century re-sponded to the humanistic aspirations of the middle class. The cultivated bourgeoisie of Boston enjoyed singing oratorios and accordingly founded the Handel and Haydn Society in 1815 as an amateur choral group. The spread of piano-playing as a form of self-improvement greatly broadened interest in classical music, and this in turn eventually stimulated a desire to hear the best music performed by the best artists. The oldest symphony orchestra in the United States still in continuous existence, the New York

59. Ralph Branham and Stephen Hartnett, *Sweet Freedom's Song* (Oxford, 2002).
60. James Parakilas, *Piano Roles* (New Haven, 1999), 11–19; Gary Kornblith, *The Indus-trial Revolution in America* (Boston, 1998), 71–77; Craig Roell, *The Piano in America* (Chapel Hill, 1989), 1–17.

Philharmonic, was founded in 1842—the same year that P. T. Barnum took over Peale's Museum in New York and began charging admission to it. The increasing ease and frequency of transatlantic crossings put Americans in touch with European music and the musical criticism of the Romantic movement. Tours by European virtuosi, like that of the Norwegian violinist Ole Bull in 1843, proved crucial to providing classical music a foothold in the United States. Barnum, who understood how to cash in on celebrity, sponsored the wildly successful tour of Jenny Lind, "the Swedish nightingale," in 1850.

Early proponents of classical music in the United States included the Transcendentalists, especially John Sullivan Dwight and Margaret Fuller. Fuller felt a particularly powerful affinity with Beethoven's genius. In her private journal of 1843, she addressed the composer (who had died in 1827) thus: "No heavenly sweetness of Jesus, no many-leaved Raphael, no golden Plato, is anything to me, compared with thee." Her burst of Romantic feeling manifested the new attitude toward music among the nineteenth-century middle class: from music as recreation to music as spiritual uplift. For devotees like Margaret Fuller, high-quality secular music was sacred music.[61]

V

No body of literature exemplified or propagated the faith of the American Renaissance in human potential more than the writings of the men and women who had escaped from slavery. The Transcendentalist Theodore Parker called them the "one series of literary productions that could be written by none but Americans," adding that "all the original romance of America is in them."[62] While the autobiographical accounts of Henry Bibb, William Wells Brown, Sojourner Truth, and others make fascinating reading, the greatest of these accounts appeared in 1845: *Narrative of the Life of Frederick Douglass, An American Slave, Written by Himself.* A brief 125 pages, it cost 50 cents and sold a successful thirty thousand copies, emboldening its author to write two longer autobiographies later in his life. The book fell into obscurity during the first half of the twentieth century, from which it has been rescued by an outburst of attention from scholars in recent decades. They have enabled us to perceive in Douglass's narrative a paradigm of many aspects of American experience.

---

61. Mark Grant, *Maestros of the Pen* (Boston, 1998), 35–52; Margaret Fuller, Nov. 25, 1843, quoted in Bell Chevigny, *The Woman and the Myth* (New York, 1976), 61–62.
62. Theodore Parker, "The American Scholar" (1849), in his *Collected Works*, ed. Frances Cobbe (London, 1864), VII, 245.

The eight-year-old Maryland slave boy had been separated from his mother almost all his life and never knew his father's identity (but suspected his master). When his owner died in 1826 and the estate needed to be parceled out among three heirs, this virtual orphan had been allocated to Thomas Auld, the late master's son-in-law. The new owner left little Freddy with his brother and sister-in-law, Hugh and Sophia Auld of Baltimore, to serve as a companion for their young son in return for his keep. Sophia, a kindly woman and a devout Methodist, began to teach both children their ABC's and to show them how to read from the Bible (specifically, the Book of Job). Her husband put a stop to this. "If you teach that nigger how to read there would be no keeping him," he warned. "It would forever unfit him to be a slave." Frederick Bailey (as he was originally named) remembered these words uttered in his presence, and they "sank deep into my heart." Resolving to unfit himself for slavery, he determined to continue the quest for literacy in secret. He earned small change and paid it to neighbor boys to teach him; he studied discarded newspapers. Eventually he learned about the movement to abolish slavery. In 1838, at the age of twenty, Frederick Bailey escaped and made his way North. Changing his name to Frederick Douglass as a precaution against recapture, he became the most famous of many self-liberated slaves, a leader of the abolitionist movement, and a powerful voice for African American rights during and after the Civil War.[63]

Douglass's realization of the critical importance of literacy to the winning and exercise of freedom was common among members of both races. Hugh Auld's belief in the incompatibility of literacy and slavery, shared by most whites, provoked many laws throughout the southern states designed to prevent the kind of unauthorized literacy represented by Denmark Vesey, David Walker, and Nat Turner. Even in the North, the laws of several states restricted the opportunities for free Negroes to get an education, for literacy was associated with citizenship, a status that few states accorded their black residents. The published narratives of other escaped slaves besides Douglass tell of going to heroic lengths to learn how to read. After emancipation, many of the newly freed people eagerly embraced opportunities for adult education.[64]

As in Douglass's case, the first inklings of literacy often came from religious sources. In after years a former slave recalled how she picked out

63. *Narrative of the Life of Frederick Douglass, Written by Himself*, ed. David Blight (1845; Boston, 2003), 63–67.

64. Heather Williams, *Self-Taught: African American Education in Slavery and Freedom* (Chapel Hill, 2005), 7–29.

from a hymn book the words "When I can read my title clear / To mansions in the sky," by Isaac Watts. "I was so happy when I saw that I could really read, that I ran around telling all the other slaves." Among its many functions, literacy undergirded the religion that provided African Americans, whether enslaved or free, their most important sense of community. Douglass remembered his people's evocative spirituals and cautioned whites against the facile interpretation of them as signs of contentment. "Those songs still follow me, to deepen my hatred of slavery, and quicken my sympathies for my brethren in bonds."[65] At the age of fourteen he underwent a classic conversion experience in Bethel Chapel of the African Methodist Episcopal Church in Baltimore. After achieving his freedom he joined the AME Church, Zion, in New Bedford, Massachusetts, and became a lay exhorter.

In 1833 Thomas Auld had attempted to set his adolescent slave to plantation labor under an overseer with a reputation as "negro-breaker." But when this brute tried to whip him, young Frederick prevailed in a dramatic contest of physical strength and willpower. The overseer gave up rather than admit to others his embarrassing failure. This victory, Douglass recalled with satisfaction, "revived within me a sense of my own manhood." He had brought the principles of human dignity and equality from the pages where he had read about them into real life. In his autobiography Douglass returned these principles to print as an inspiration to others, an example of the triumph of human nature over animal force, a paradigm of the American Renaissance.[66]

Eventually Douglass's owner sent him back to Baltimore to learn the trade of a ship-caulker and turn over his wages. But slavery had long been declining in Baltimore, where the mixed economy and urban mobility left slaves who "hired their own time" with a measure of personal independence. The young man took full advantage of his opportunities to make friends among the city's large community of free Negroes. He joined one of their self-improvement societies, in which he met a free black woman named Anna Murray, whom he later married. Douglass's eventual escape from slavery was made possible when a free black sailor (risking severe punishment) lent him his identification papers. Like so many other talented young Americans, white as well as black, Frederick Douglass found liberation in the city, and he praised the advantages of urban life over rural in his autobiography. "Going to live in Baltimore laid

65. Janet Cornelius, *"When I Can Read My Title Clear": Literacy, Slavery, and Religion in the Antebellum South* (Columbia, S.C., 1991), vii; Douglass, *Narrative*, 51–52.

66. Ibid., 79–89.

the foundation, and opened the gateway, to all my subsequent prosperity," he wrote; "I have ever regarded it as the first plain manifestation of that kind providence which has ever since attended me."[67]

Not long after assuming his new life as a free man in Massachusetts, Douglass began attending antislavery meetings in local black churches. In August 1841, he delivered an antislavery speech on Nantucket Island that brought him to the attention of William Lloyd Garrison's abolitionist movement. The testimony of escaped slaves had proven powerful in arousing moral indignation. The American Anti-Slavery Society hired Douglass and sent him on speaking tours of northern states. Douglass's interest in oratory went back a long way. During his boyhood years in Baltimore, he had managed to get fifty cents to buy a copy of a schoolbook called *The Columbian Orator*, compiled by the antislavery editor Caleb Bingham. From it the youth imbibed stirring ideals of equal rights as well as the prevailing concepts of how to exert power through elocution, together with sample speeches from masters like Cicero, Demosthenes, Daniel Webster, and Edward Everett. It was one of the few possessions he took with him on his flight to freedom. Once free, Douglass rose to his occasion. In an age of great American oratory, Frederick Douglass made himself one of the greatest orators of all. "Speech!" he declared: "The live, calm, grave, clear, pointed, warm, sweet, melodious and powerful human voice is the chosen instrumentality" of heroic reform.[68] In his crusade against slavery, Douglass voiced the urgent concern of the American Renaissance with the dignity of human nature.

Douglass's career as author and traveling lecturer illustrates how the revolutions in communications and transportation facilitated nationwide reform movements such as antislavery. Historians have remarked on how the antislavery movement became both more insistent and more broadly based in the 1830s. This transformation was no accident. The same technological developments that permitted the formation of the new mass political parties likewise empowered other agencies for influencing public opinion. The abolitionist movement could not have flourished without the mass production of periodicals, tracts, and inexpensive books (including antislavery books for children), the circulation of petitions to Congress, the ability to gather national conferences, and convenient travel for its agents. The determination of southern postmasters to block abolitionist

---

67. Ibid., 62; Barbara Fields, *Slavery and Freedom on the Middle Ground* (New Haven, 1985), 47–57; Elizabeth McHenry, *Forgotten Readers: Recovering the Lost History of African American Literary Societies* (Durham, N.C., 2002), 13.
68. Frederick Douglass in *North Star*, November 23, 1849.

mailings recognized the importance of the distribution of information to the cause of antislavery. In a world where people communicated and traveled, the continued existence of slavery in the United States when many other countries had abolished it came to seem anomalous and embarrassing. Suddenly, there was much more reason than ever before to pay attention to the formation of public opinion on this sensitive subject. "In November 1831, the Georgia legislature offered five thousand dollars for the apprehension of William Lloyd Garrison," notes the historian Daniel Feller. "Who in Georgia, only a few years before, would have known or cared about the fulminations of an obscure Boston editor?"[69]

Meanwhile, the success that Frederick Douglass enjoyed on the lecture circuit brought its own problems. The better known Douglass became, the greater the danger that his owner would identify him and track him down. Furthermore, some incredulous hearers began to question whether he could possibly be an authentic former slave. An anxious white abolitionist advised Douglass not to seem too literate and articulate, but to "have a *little* of the plantation manner" in his speech. Douglass refused to let his well-meaning but irritating white friends control him; he insisted on being (as the historian Nathan Huggins put it) "his own man."[70]

As a solution to the problems posed by his oratory and published *Narrative*, Douglass left the United States for an extended speaking tour of the British Isles in 1845–47. There he would not be liable to recapture as a fugitive; there audiences welcomed his eloquence. After the emancipation of the slaves in the British West Indies in 1833, the British abolitionist movement had turned its attention to other countries, and especially the United States. Social reform, like literature, transcended boundaries in the English-speaking world of improved communication and transportation. Antislavery became one of many transatlantic reforms that included temperance, Sunday schools, missions to the heathen, the distribution of Bibles, and rights for women. Nineteenth-century reformers, their faith strengthened by the expectation that they worked to hasten the millennium and the Second Advent of Christ, were far more hopeful than reformers in our own chastened world. Douglass shared their confidence

69. Daniel Feller, "Rediscovering Jacksonian America," in *The State of U.S. History*, ed. Melvyn Stokes (Oxford, 2002), 79. See further Jeannine DeLombard, *Slavery on Trial: Law, Abolitionism, and Print Culture* (Chapel Hill, 2007), esp. 101–27.

70. Parker Pillsbury, quoted in James B. Stewart, *Holy Warriors*, rev. ed. (New York, 1997), 142; Nathan Huggins, *Slave and Citizen: The Life of Frederick Douglass* (Boston, 1980), 38.

that right would triumph. He got along well with British reformers and intellectuals; he reached out to the working-class Chartists and Irish nationalists; he encouraged the Calvinist Free Church of Scotland to break relations with slaveholding Calvinists in the American South. His friends raised 150 pounds sterling (then $1,250) to buy out Thomas Auld's legal claim to Frederick Bailey, so Frederick Douglass could return to the United States in safety.[71]

Welcomed back to America by his wife and children, Douglass found the abolition movement badly factionalized. Censorship of the mails had essentially frustrated the movement's attempt to convert moderate southerners; within the slave states, only Kentucky managed to sustain its own abolition movement. As a result, abolitionist efforts had more and more come to focus on a northern audience. But the abolitionists disagreed among themselves about how best to influence this audience. A serious split developed among them over questions of tactics that stemmed from different attitudes toward American society as a whole.

Those who sided with William Lloyd Garrison found American government and society thoroughly corrupt. Besides the abolition of slavery, they also supported pacifism (nonresistance to evil), anarchism, and equal rights for women—causes so unpopular that they tainted opposition to slavery with the brush of ludicrous impracticality. (The Garrisonians' professed pacifism, significantly, did nothing to reassure slaveholders, since Garrisonians were more likely, in practice, to condemn the violent suppression of slave escapes and revolts than the actions of the slaves themselves.)[72] Garrisonians also usually embraced religious views outside the evangelical mainstream. They tended to be Unitarians, Transcendentalists, Hicksite Quakers, or "come-outers" who had seceded from their original denominations. (The expression referenced the biblical injunction, "Come out of her, my people, that ye not be partakers of her sins"—Revelation 18:4.) When an international antislavery convention meeting in London in 1840 refused to accept American women as delegates and relegated them to the visitors' gallery, Garrison dramatically took a seat alongside the women instead of on the convention floor.[73]

71. David Turley, *The Culture of English Antislavery* (London, 1991); Alan Rice and Martin Crawford, eds., *Liberating Sojourn: Frederick Douglass and Transatlantic Reform* (Athens, Ga., 1999); William McFeely, *Frederick Douglass* (New York, 1991), 119–45.

72. See John McKivigan and Stanley Harrold, eds., *Antislavery Violence* (Knoxville, Tenn., 1999).

73. Kathryn Sklar, *Women's Rights Emerges within the Anti-Slavery Movement* (Boston, 2000); Henry Mayer, *All on Fire: William Lloyd Garrison and the Abolition of Slavery* (New York, 1998), 288–90.

Reacting against Garrison's broad and radical agenda, in 1840 about half of the abolitionists seceded from the American Anti-Slavery Society (AASS) that he controlled; they organized the rival American and Foreign Anti-Slavery Society (AFASS), under Lewis Tappan's leadership. Members of the AFASS considered slavery a grotesque anomaly in an otherwise relatively wholesome American society. They wanted abolitionism to function as one of the reforms within the evangelical "benevolent empire," as had the colonization movement. While supporting temperance and the evangelical religious agenda of Bibles and missions, they stayed away from Garrison's most radical "isms." Instead of "coming out" from the churches, they hoped to work within and transform them.[74] But the Garrisonians' religious beliefs generally alienated them from the Evangelical United Front that the Tappanites found congenial. In their stance toward the world, Garrisonians had more in common with members of utopian communities than with the international evangelical reform enterprise. Indeed, some utopian communities, such as those at Hopedale and Northampton, Massachusetts, had close explicit ties with Garrisonian abolitionism.[75]

The evangelical followers of Tappan were not necessarily any less bold than Garrisonians in their condemnation of slavery. Unlike the AASS, the AFASS never gave up all hope of influencing southern public opinion. In the 1840s the Tappanites sent courageous abolitionist missionaries into border and Upper South slave states, where they tried to reach blacks as well as whites, and got around postal censorship by distributing antislavery tracts in person. Although limited, their activity horrified southern politicians. (Into the Deep South, colonizationists might venture, but not abolitionists.)[76]

Perhaps surprisingly to us, not all abolitionist women joined the wing of their movement that took the strongest stand for women's rights. Women were accustomed to benevolent activity within their acknowledged "sphere" and did not necessarily rush to expand it. Some abolitionist women thought opposition to slavery a higher priority than the pursuit of their own rights and felt Garrison needlessly tactless. As a result, some local women's abolition societies affiliated with the evangelical AFASS,

---

74. Bertram Wyatt-Brown, *Lewis Tappan and the Evangelical War Against Slavery* (Cleveland, 1969), 185–204; John McKivigan, *The War Against Proslavery Religion* (Ithaca, N.Y., 1984).
75. Christopher Clark, *The Communitarian Moment* (Ithaca, N.Y., 1995), 34–49.
76. Stanley Harrold, *The Abolitionists and the South* (Lexington, Ky., 1995), 85–95, 105–6. On colonizationists, see Victor Howard, *Conscience and Slavery* (Kent, Ohio, 1990).

and some tried to mediate between the old and the new organizations. Women provided the abolitionist movement with a "great silent army" of volunteers and fund-raisers. But factionalism within the abolition movement did hamper and discourage many of the local women's societies.[77]

Actually, a number of abolitionists remained independent of both factions, notably Theodore Dwight Weld and his wife, the feminist-abolitionist Angelina Grimké. Their wedding in May 1838 brought together Garrison, Tappan, and an impressive guest list, including six former slaves of the Grimké family and representatives of all branches of reform.[78] Weld, descended from distinguished evangelical forebears including Jonathan Edwards, had agitated for black rights while a student at Lyman Beecher's Lane Seminary in Cincinnati. Converted by Charles Finney, he applied the evangelical itinerant preaching model to antislavery, recruiting a "holy band" of missionaries, who traveled, as he did, preaching immediate nationwide abolition. With the help of his wife and her sister Sarah, Weld compiled *American Slavery as It Is* (1839), a devastating documentation of the cruelties inflicted by the "peculiar institution" assembled from the testimony of eyewitnesses (sometimes former slaveholders), state legal codes, and the South's own newspaper accounts and advertisements. Although abolitionists deplored slavery as a denial of human rights, natural and Christian, even when masters behaved decently, they seized opportunities to publicize examples of brutality. Corroborating the narratives of escaped slaves, Weld's collection fed the growing public revulsion against the infliction of physical pain that manifested itself in the abolition of flogging in the armed forces and the criminal law. Within the year, the book sold one hundred thousand copies at thirty-seven cents.[79]

By adhering to the healthy diet prescribed by Sylvester Graham, Theodore Weld lived to the age of ninety-two, though his voice, overtaxed by too much public speaking, had given out many years before. In middle age, this man who had been such a firebrand in youth turned his attention away from agitation and toward another of the concerns typical of the American Renaissance, the development of children's potential. He and his wife founded an academy in 1848, devoted to

77. Amy Swerdlow, "Abolition's Conservative Sisters," in *The Abolitionist Sisterhood*, ed. Jean Yellin and John Van Horn (Ithaca, N.Y., 1994), 31–44; Julie Jeffrey, *The Great Silent Army of Abolitionism* (Chapel Hill, 1998), 105–6, 139–44. See also Carolyn Lawes, *Women and Reform in a New England Community* (Lexington, Ky., 2000).

78. Stewart, *Holy Warriors*, 88–94; Robert Abzug, *Cosmos Crumbling* (New York, 1994), 226.

79. The book was republished in 1972, abridged and edited by Richard Curry and Joanna Cowden.

cultivating the pupils' "inward unity" and preparing them for lives of service to others.[80]

Theodore Weld's collaborators, his wife, Angelina Grimké Weld, and her older sister Sarah Grimké, came from an aristocratic slaveholding family in Charleston. They moved north to join the evangelical orthodox branch of the Philadelphia Society of Friends (Quakers). Later, they embraced postmillennial abolitionism. In 1837, Angelina began to address antislavery audiences of both sexes. She did not actually set out to defy conventional gender roles thus, but men kept showing up to hear her lectures.[81] Still, American public opinion was unaccustomed to women speaking in public to "promiscuous" gatherings, the provocative term then used for groups that included both men and women. (Dorothea Dix's lecture tours yet lay in the future.) The Grimké sisters took considerable criticism for allowing women's rights to distract them from concentration on antislavery, even from people like Lydia Maria Child who agreed with their feminist principles. But other antislavery women also began to defy public opinion and speak out in public around the same time, among them Abigail Kelley and Lucretia Mott. Even when not pressing for women's rights per se, their conspicuous activity in the public sphere made an implicit feminist statement. As Angelina wrote to the black abolitionist Sarah Douglass (no relation to Frederick), "We Abolition Women are turning the world upside down."[82]

Garrison, who supported linking the causes of women and the slave, focused exclusively on moral and religious agitation and shunned politics. Moral principle took precedence over constitutional law for him, as it did for Henry David Thoreau. The constitutional guarantees for the protection of southern slavery, such as the clause mandating the return of fugitives, he called "a covenant with death and an agreement with hell," applying the terms for an unholy alliance between ancient Israel and evil Assyria (Isaiah 28:15). In the existing state of American politics, voting seemed to him not only useless but a degrading participation in an immoral system. Garrison believed women should participate fully in the crusade against slavery. (In 1833 he went so far as to declare that "the destiny of the slaves is in the hands of the American women, and complete emancipation can never take place without their co-operation.") He

80. Robert Abzug, *Passionate Liberator* (New York, 1980), 255; Norman Risjord, *Representative Americans: The Romantics* (New York, 2001), 243, 248.
81. Anna Speicher, *The Religious World of Antislavery Women* (Syracuse, N.Y., 2000), 110.
82. Quoted in Blanche Hersh, *The Slavery of Sex: Feminist Abolitionists in America* (Urbana, Ill., 1978), 29; Abzug, *Cosmos Crumbling*, 204–29.

feared that to engage in electoral politics would shunt women to the margins, since they did not have the vote.[83]

But some abolitionists came to believe that it would help their cause to organize a new political party and compete with the major parties in elections. They formed the Liberty Party. As their candidate in 1840 and 1844 they ran James G. Birney, a former Alabama plantation owner who converted to abolitionism in 1833, emancipated his slaves, and endured considerable persecution as well as financial hardship for his views. The Liberty Party's slogan was "vote as you pray and pray as you vote." Its program called for emancipation in the territories and the District of Columbia, and termination of the interstate slave trade, all of them measures that the Constitution permitted. Despite his honorable intentions, Birney secured a microscopic percentage of the popular vote in 1840 and but 2.3 percent in 1844. Historical analysis of the Liberty Party indicates that its little band of supporters came from among "middling people," such as mechanics, shopkeepers, and petty professionals, who had left the semi-subsistence farming of their parents and embraced a new way of life in the emerging commercial areas of the North, usually small towns. These people rejected not only slavery but also patriarchal family relations and valued the autonomy of the individual.[84]

The Tappanites had no objection to political activity and often enjoyed mutually supportive relations with the Liberty Party. Garrisonians, on the other hand, pointed to the party's meager achievements as confirming their own view that electoral politics did not constitute a promising arena for abolitionist activity; they also feared lest the Liberty Party be tempted to moderate its stand on slavery in the hope of picking up more votes. Probably most abolitionists drew the conclusion that it made sense to support antislavery candidates from the major parties. These were more often Whigs such as Joshua Giddings of Ohio, though there was the occasional exception like John P. Hale of New Hampshire, expelled from the state's Democratic Party in 1845 for his antislavery stands.[85]

Frederick Douglass, along with other black abolitionists, found himself in a difficult position between the quarreling groups of white abolitionists.

---

83. Mayer, *All on Fire*, 263–84; Garrison is quoted by Debra Gold Hansen in "The Boston Female Antislavery Society," in Yellin and Van Horn, *Abolitionist Sisterhood*, 59.

84. Bruce Laurie, *Beyond Garrison: Antislavery and Social Reform* (Cambridge, Eng., 2005), 7, 61; Michael Pierson, *Free Hearts and Free Homes: Gender and American Antislavery Politics* (Chapel Hill, 2003), 7.

85. Jeffrey, *Great Silent Army*, p. 163; see further in Richard Sewell, *Ballots for Freedom* (New York, 1976), 3–79.

The African American leadership included former slaves like William Wells Brown, Sojourner Truth, and Douglass himself alongside others born free like James Forten and Robert Purvis. Some had been educated at Finney's Oberlin, like John Mercer Langston. More came from the clergy than any other profession, Henry Highland Garnet and Samuel Cornish among them. A few prominent African Americans like Alexander Crummell and Martin Delaney continued to consider emigration a serious option. The black abolitionists regretted the division of the antislavery movement. They admired Garrison's courage. Douglass paid tribute to the contribution of women to abolitionism: "When the true history of the antislavery cause shall be written," he declared, "women will occupy a large space in its pages, for the cause of the slave has been peculiarly woman's cause."[86] Nevertheless, the black abolitionists had an agenda of their own, and it included getting involved in politics whenever possible. Most states, even in the North, prohibited them from voting. While black abolitionists continued to endorse self-improvement within their own community, they also turned increasingly to opposing racial discrimination in the free states. White abolitionists joined with them in protests and boycotts that sometimes succeeded in desegregating northern public facilities. The civil rights demonstrators of the 1960s could invoke the example of their antebellum precursors and called themselves "the new abolitionists."[87]

The "underground railroad"—a network of safe houses that sheltered escaped slaves—operated mostly through African Americans like William Still, though some white abolitionists participated too. One of the reasons southern members of Congress opposed emancipation in the District of Columbia so strongly was their fear that it would become a hive of rescue activity for the underground railroad—as, to some extent, it became anyway. In 1848, a well-financed mass escape of seventy-six slaves from Washington, all of whom got aboard the steamship *Pearl* bound for Philadelphia, was thwarted and most of the people sent to New Orleans for sale. The ship's white operators were sentenced to long prison terms but pardoned by Whig president Millard Fillmore in 1852.[88] As this episode indicates, slave rescue efforts became bolder as the 1840s went by. At the same time, masters found the recovery of their escapees more

86. Quoted in Jeffrey, *Great Silent Army*, xiii.
87. James B. Stewart, "Modernizing 'Difference': The Political Meanings of Color in the Free States," *JER* 19 (1999): 691–712.
88. Stanley Harrold, *Subversives: Antislavery Community in Washington, DC* (Baton Rouge, 2003); Josephine Pacheco, *The Pearl* (Chapel Hill, 2005).

difficult. A complicated decision written by Justice Story of the Supreme Court in 1842 (*Prigg v. Pennsylvania*) left northern state officials free to wash their hands of responsibility for returning fugitive slaves, and increasingly northern state legislatures instructed them to do so. Runaways found their safest asylum in Canada, though until 1850 they could feel reasonably secure in the free Negro neighborhoods of northern cities. According to one estimate, about thirty thousand escaped slaves settled in Ontario, the province where most went.[89]

Southern resentment of this situation led to passage of the Fugitive Slave Act of 1850, establishing a federal bureaucracy to enforce rendition. Abolitionists responded to the new legislation with ever more drastic rescue measures. Harriet Tubman, the most famous conductor on the underground railroad and a refugee from slavery herself, began her rescue work in the 1850s. The Transcendentalist intellectuals encouraged and endorsed resistance to the hated law. Thoreau succored an escaped slave at Walden Pond and fervently denounced the power of "Slavery in Massachusetts"; Emerson inspired Yankee abolitionists to try to free the fugitive Anthony Burns from custody in 1854; later in the 1850s, Theodore Parker even conspired with the revolutionary antislavery plot of John Brown.[90] Slavery was unpopular enough in some parts of the North (such as rural Quaker Pennsylvania and the "burned-over district" of New York) that mobs could be formed to release fugitives whom the authorities had apprehended, although only a handful of people (twenty-six, to be precise) were saved in this manner.[91]

In 1847 Frederick Douglass moved from New England to the burned-over district, where he edited a newspaper in Rochester called the *North Star*, borrowing its title from the fleeing slave's nighttime guide. Financial backing for starting up the paper came from the white philanthropist Gerrit Smith, who also donated land in upstate New York for poor black families to form the utopian community called Timbucto. Douglass and Smith associated themselves with the political wing of abolitionism, the Liberty Party.[92]

---

89. Robin Winks, *Blacks in Canada*, 2nd ed. (Montreal, 1997), 233–41. The latest account of the underground railroad is Fergus Bordewich, *Bound for Canaan* (New York, 2005).

90. See Albert von Frank, *The Trials of Anthony Burns: Liberty and Antislavery in Emerson's Boston* (Cambridge, Mass., 1998).

91. David Grimsted, *American Mobbing* (New York, 1998), 74–82.

92. On Timbucto, New York, see John Stauffer, *The Black Hearts of Men* (Cambridge, Mass., 2002), 141–58.

Douglass participated forcefully in the severe critique that abolitionists of all factions leveled at the churches for not dissociating themselves unequivocally from slavery. "I love the pure, peaceable, and impartial Christianity of Christ," he wrote in his autobiographical *Narrative*; "I therefore hate the corrupt, slaveholding, women-whipping, cradle-plundering, partial and hypocritical Christianity of this land." Likening the American churches to the Pharisees whom Jesus denounced for hypocrisy, he quoted, "They bind heavy burdens and grievous to be borne, and lay them on men's shoulders; but they themselves will not move them with one of their fingers" (Matthew 23:4).[93] As time went by, Douglass's estrangement from the mainstream churches only increased, and his personal religion came to approximate that of the Transcendentalists, a celebration of the spiritual and moral potential inherent in the human individual. But his unquenchable optimism about the future continued to manifest a kind of millennialism, such as he had heard from African American preachers. And, to the end of his life, he remained supportive of the black churches "because upon the whole, I think they contribute to the improvement and moral elevation of those who come within the reach of their influence" and advance the cause of "truth."[94]

Margaret Fuller admired Frederick Douglass as an exemplar of "the powers of the Black Race."[95] Douglass wished to see himself as a man who transcended racial differences, a "Representative Man" in the Emersonian sense of one who demonstrated the potentialities of human nature. He shared the Transcendentalists' celebration of a human nature common to all races and nationalities and, like them, hoped America would be the place where this common nature would achieve its fullest expression. As Emerson put it:

> In this continent,—asylum of all nations,—the energy of Irish, Germans, Swedes, Poles, and Cossacks, and all the European tribes,—of the Africans, and of the Polynesians will construct a new race, a new religion, a new state, a new literature.[96]

Douglass, like Emerson, put his faith in an American melting pot, out of which would spring a new humanity. Strong advocate of racial integration

---

93. Douglass, *Narrative*, 120–21.
94. David Blight, *Frederick Douglass's Civil War* (Baton Rouge, 1989), 1–25; FD to Theophilous Gould Steward, July 27, 1886, in *The Oxford Frederick Douglass Reader*, ed. William Andrews (New York, 1996), 312.
95. *New York Tribune*, June 10, 1845.
96. Quoted in Waldo Martin Jr., *The Mind of Frederick Douglass* (Chapel Hill, 1984), 223.

and equal opportunity, he scorned to take refuge in any form of black sep-aratism. One of his reasons for speaking and writing in standard nineteenth-century literary English, rather than an African American di-alect, was to underscore his message of cosmopolitan universalism.

Like Abraham Lincoln, Frederick Douglass was a self-made man in a century that cherished the ideal of self-making. When the two met for the first time in the White House during the Civil War, Douglass sensed that the president treated him with no taint of condescension and regarded him as a kindred spirit—a man who had dedicated himself, as Lincoln had, to self-improvement. Having often doubted Lincoln in the past, Douglass came away from their encounter profoundly reassured. Two more meetings later confirmed this favorable impression.[97]

VI

Southerners since the time of Jefferson had frequently apologized that slavery was not a system of their own making, but one they had inherited and of which they could only make the best. Abolitionists regarded this line of defense as an evasion; in response, they insisted upon the moral re-sponsibility of each individual under every circumstance to do right. The abolitionists strongly affirmed one of the basic premises of the American Renaissance: the power and trustworthiness of the human conscience. No more forceful statement of their moral stance exists than a poem pub-lished in December 1845 by the abolitionist James Russell Lowell, husband of Margaret Fuller's disciple Maria White Lowell. In it the poet affirms mil-lennial confidence in the long-term providence of God, while declaring that the ultimate victory of the right depends for now upon the coura-geous witness of a prophetic few.

> Once to every man and nation
> Comes the moment to decide
> In the strife of truth with falsehood,
> For the good or evil side. . . .
> Then it is the brave man chooses,
> While the coward stands aside
> Till the multitude make virtue
> Of the faith they have denied. . . .
> Though the cause of evil prosper,
> Yet 'tis truth alone is strong,
> Though her portion be the scaffold

97. Frederick Douglass, *Autobiographies*, ed. Henry Louis Gates (New York, 1994), 798; James Oakes, *The Radical and the Republican* (New York, 2007), 211, 216, 232, 242.

And upon the throne be wrong,
Yet that scaffold sways the future,
And behind the dim unknown,
Standeth God within the shadow
Keeping watch above his own.[98]

Lowell's verses, like Emerson's "Concord Hymn" and Longfellow's "Psalm of Life," evoke the heroic moral striving of the American Renaissance. Lowell entitled his poem "The Present Crisis," by which he meant the pending action by Congress to make the Republic of Texas one of the states in the American Union. Why an abolitionist believed Texas annexation presented a moral crisis requires explanation.

---

98. Excerpted from James Russell Lowell, *Poems, Second Series* (Cambridge, Mass., 1848), 53–62; orig. pub. in the *Boston Courier*, Dec. 11, 1845. The words were subsequently adapted as a hymn. For dating, I rely on Leon Howard, *Victorian Knight Errant: James Russell Lowell* (Berkeley, 1952), 214–15.

17

Texas, Tyler, and the Telegraph

On July 16, 1821, Erasmo Seguín and Stephen Austin crossed the international boundary at the Sabine River and entered Texas, then part of New Spain. They headed for the Texan capital, San Antonio de Béxar (which we call San Antonio but which their contemporaries more often called Béxar or Béjar). The two companions exemplified two peoples, Hispanic and Anglo, destined to share in shaping Texan history.[1] Seguín, the older of the two, was a merchant. Named for the Dutch writer and reformer Erasmus, he carried on a family tradition of liberal politics. He now accompanied the twenty-eight-year-old Austin because he believed in encouraging immigration from the United States into Texas. The sparsely populated region had suffered severely during fighting between Mexican rebels and the Spanish army, and critically needed skilled settlers. A liberal Spanish Cortes (parliament) in Madrid had decided to encourage such settlement, and Stephen's father, Moses Austin, had won authorization to bring colonists from the United States into Texas. But Moses suddenly died, and at Seguín's urging Stephen took up what seemed like his inherited responsibility.[2]

On August 12, the travelers heard the astonishing news that Mexico had suddenly achieved her long deferred independence from Spain. Seguín rejoiced. In due course the new government confirmed Austin's role as *empresario*, that is, colonization agent. If he could fulfill the stipulation to bring in settlers, Austin stood to make a fortune in Texas land for himself. But he also embraced Seguín's romantic vision of a prosperous Texas. To achieve this within a Mexican context, Austin learned Spanish, became a naturalized Mexican citizen, and, sometimes calling himself Esteban Austin, functioned as a mediator between the Anglo settlers and the authorities. Terms of settlement in his Mexican colony compared favorably with the $1.25 per acre the American government charged pioneers, and over the years Austin brought in about

---

1. In the usage of the southwestern United States, "Anglo" means any white English-speaker, not just those of British descent; "Hispanic," any Spanish-speaker, regardless of race.
2. Gregg Cantrell, *Stephen F. Austin* (New Haven, 1999), 88–91.

1,500 families.[3] Thus, the ink had scarcely dried on the ratifications of the Adams-Onís Treaty assigning Texas to Spain when events significantly transformed the situation on the ground: First, Mexico replaced Spain as sovereign over Texas, and second, American settlers began to move there.

Others from the United States also gained the status of *empresario*, though Austin remained the most important one. The terms the *empresarios* offered attracted many settlers from the southern and western states, adventuresome individuals as well as families hurt by the Panic of 1819 and looking to make a new life. Some of the immigrants didn't locate in any properly organized colonies but simply squatted. By 1830, the Anglos in Texas outnumbered Hispanic *tejanos* more than two to one. When, in 1829, the Mexican government moved to emancipate the slaves that Anglo colonists brought with them, Austin, although expressing grave reservations about slavery as an institution, protected the interests of his clients. The colonists pretended their workers had long-term labor contracts. Such a "contract," drawn up in Austin's colony in 1833 between Marmaduke Sandifer and Clarissa, "a girl of color," stipulated that Clarissa would "conduct & demean herself as an honest & faithful servant, renouncing and disclaiming all her right and claim to personal liberty for & during the term of ninety-nine years," in return for food, lodging, medical care, and security against disability.[4]

Colonists simply ignored the rule that they should convert to the Roman Catholic faith; even Austin himself did not do so. In practice the Church left them alone, and they tactfully refrained from building Protestant meetinghouses.[5] Besides economic benefits to Texas, the Anglos provided allies for the Hispanics in fighting the Comanches and other Indian tribes. Native Americans and African Americans, though excluded from political power, also played their parts in making Texan history.

The liberal Mexican Constitution of 1824 accorded much autonomy to the states within what it named the *Estados Unidos Mexicanos*. Texas had too few people to qualify as a Mexican state but formed a district within the state of Coahuila y Texas. The Anglo settlements enjoyed a measure of self-government and partial exemption from customs duties. In 1827,

3. The terms are described in Frederick Merk, *History of the Westward Movement* (New York, 1978), 267. On the motives prompting Americans to move to Texas, see Andrew Cayton, "Continental Politics," in *Beyond the Founders*, ed. Jeffrey Pasley (Chapel Hill, 2004), 303–27.
4. Quoted in Quintard Taylor, *In Search of the Racial Frontier* (New York, 1998), 40.
5. Paul Lack, *The Texas Revolutionary Experience* (College Station, Tex., 1992), 12.

they gained the right to trial by jury in criminal cases. Yet, from the Mexican point of view, they did not make altogether responsible use of their privileges. Highly individualistic, most of these people had little community spirit and no ties to Mexico. In December 1826, a rogue *empresario* put himself at the head of some discontented settlers and declared the independence of the "Republic of Fredonia." Austin supported the Mexican authorities, who put down the little rebellion with no difficulty.[6]

By the late 1820s, Mexican officials entertained doubts about their Texas policy. They had hoped that Texas would attract migrants from Europe and central Mexico, but although some German settlements had been established, these did not effectively counterbalance the Anglo-American settlers. Signs multiplied that the United States government and public took an unwelcome kind of interest in Texas. Spain's experience with losing the Floridas to the United States, as well as periodic unofficial military expeditions called "filibusters," launched from U.S. bases into Latin America, set a worrisome example. Two such filibusterings, in 1811 and 1819, had been directed into Texas, only to be repulsed.[7] Worst of all, U.S. diplomats kept pressing Mexico to sell Texas.

After the Mier y Terán fact-finding commission confirmed fears about U.S. intentions toward Texas in its report of 1829, the Mexican Congress passed a law suspending immigration from the United States in April 1830. Austin got an exemption from it for his own recruits, and others too found it easy to slip through the border. Mexico suffered the problem of illegal immigration from the United States until Austin's lobbying in Mexico City helped secure repeal of the ban in November 1833. Desire to promote the economic growth of Texas eventually outweighed fears for the Mexican national interest. By 1836, there were at least thirty-five thousand Anglos in Texas, now outnumbering Hispanics ten to one. "The old Latin mistake had been repeated," the historian Frederick Merk wryly observed: "admitting Gauls into the empire."[8]

In 1829, Spain made a belated attempt to recover her lost dominion and landed an army at Tampico on the Gulf of Mexico. Rallying to defend their independence, the Mexicans defeated the invasion under the leadership of General Antonio López de Santa Anna (pronounced as one word, "san-*tah*-na"), who became a national hero. Santa Anna dominated

---

6. David Weber, *The Mexican Frontier, 1821–1846* (Albuquerque, N.M., 1982), 161–66.
7. Merk, *Westward Movement*, 266.
8. Nettie Lee Benson, "Texas Viewed from Mexico," *Southwestern Historical Quarterly* 90 (1986–87): 219–91; Weber, *Mexican Frontier*, 175–77; Frederick Merk, *Slavery and the Annexation of Texas* (New York, 1972), 180.

politics in Mexico for the next generation, somewhat as another charismatic military hero, Andrew Jackson, did in the United States; Mexico, however, lacked the long Anglo-American tradition of constitutional limitation on executive power. Bold, energetic, and patriotic in his way, Santa Anna was also an opportunistic egomaniac. He saw himself as a New World Napoleon. He affiliated at first with the liberal *federalista* party that admired the constitution of the United States; middle-class intellectuals like Erasmo Seguín and his son Juan supported it. When elected president of Mexico in 1833, Santa Anna enjoyed the favor of both Anglo and Hispanic Texans. Soon, however, he betrayed his followers and embraced the *centralistas*, a conservative, clerical, and authoritarian party. He got rid of the *federalista* vice president, who had been associated with a reform program, repudiated the Constitution of 1824, and set himself up as dictator. Revolts broke out in several Mexican states where *federalistas* did not acquiesce in the *centralista* coup. The Texans observed with horror Santa Anna's bloody suppression of revolts in Zacatecas and Coahuila. Their own rebellion was triggered by conflicts over the collection of customs duties and the military presence of Mexican soldiers sent to enforce *santanista* authority. At Gonzales on 2 October 1835 Texan militia refused to return a cannon that had been lent them by the Mexican army for protection against Indians. The ensuing skirmish is considered "the Lexington of Texas," the start of the Texan Revolution.

For all the tensions over religion, culture, and slavery in Texas, none of these actually provoked the fighting. When it materialized, the Texan (or, as contemporaries called it, "Texian") Revolution broke out over economic and constitutional issues not very different from those that had provoked the American Revolution sixty years earlier. Like the American Revolution, the Texian Revolution reflected among its concerns the determination of the settlers to trade freely; neither group of colonists rested content with economic self-sufficiency. Like the British in 1775, the Mexicans could feel that theirs had been a tolerant *imperium* that had pursued a policy of "benign neglect." Like the American Patriots of 1775, who espoused the "rights of Englishmen," the Texian rebels of 1835 at first fought to restore the Mexican Constitution of 1824. At a gathering held in November, called the "Consultation," they decided to declare Texas a separate state within the Mexican Republic (that is, no longer a part of Coahuila y Texas) and appointed an acting state governor, Henry Smith. Austin and his tenants, squatters, Texians and *tejanos*: All could and did join together on such a platform. They hoped to rally *federalistas* throughout Mexico to their support; and indeed there were uprisings in other states, especially peripheral ones including Alta California, Nuevo

México, and Yucatán. The Texians noticed the parallels with the American Revolution and invoked them.[9]

Newspapers in the United States reported events in Texas in a sensational way, calculated to boost circulation. Most of them depended heavily on reprinting stories from the New Orleans papers, which got the news first, and which were eager to make Texas safe for slavery. The accounts in the press often portrayed the issue in racial terms, as simply white Americans versus Mexicans and Indians; they drew young men by the thousand from the South and West to go to Texas looking for a fight.[10] In the northern states, however, the antislavery press reported the Texan Revolution very differently. Abolitionists like Benjamin Lundy, who had spent a good deal of time in Texas, compiled evidence that the goals of the rebels included forestalling enforcement of the antislavery legislation enacted by both Mexican state and national authorities. And indeed Texan newspapers themselves warned that "the merciless soldiery" of Santa Anna came "to give liberty to our slaves, and to make slaves of ourselves."[11]

Seizing what looked like an opportunity for freedom when war broke out in October 1835, some of the slaves along the Brazos River in Austin's colony rose in rebellion, intending to redistribute the land to themselves and raise cotton for market. Anglo-Texans crushed the revolt and returned one hundred would-be free people to slavery; some were hanged or "whipd [sic] nearly to death," a report informed the empresario. Other prospective slave uprisings were nipped in the bud. Anglo-Texan men often made their top priority the security of their own communities against slave discontent, not going off to fight the Mexican army. This helps explain why so much of the burden of waging the revolutionary war fell upon the filibusterers coming in from the United States. However, many African Americans served on the Texan side of the Revolution, either voluntarily as a few free black men did or, more commonly, as enslaved laborers impressed from their masters into helping the war effort.[12]

9. James Crisp, "Race, Revolution, and the Texas Republic," in *The Texas Military Experience*, ed. Joseph Dawson (College Station, Tex., 1995), 32–48; Randolph Campbell, *An Empire for Slavery* (Baton Rouge, 1989), 48–49. For an argument that slavery was a cause of the revolution, see Taylor, *In Search of the Racial Frontier*, 39–45.

10. Merk, *Westward Movement*, 274–75.

11. Benjamin Lundy, *The War in Texas* (Philadelphia, 1836); San Felipe de Austin *Telegraph and Texas Register*, Oct. 17, 1835.

12. Paul Lack, "Slavery and the Texas Revolution," *Southwestern Historical Quarterly* 89 (1985): 181–202, quotation from 191.

The provisional government established by the Texas Consultation never worked well. Governor Smith antagonized his council; the Texan armed forces lacked effective central control; officers bickered over command; their soldiers debated whether to obey orders. Austin found that his considerable talents did not include military leadership and felt relieved to be sent off to the United States to negotiate loans and aid. The rebels captured San Antonio de Béxar in December 1835 after a siege and house-to-house combat. In terms of organizing a revolution, however, the winter of 1835–36 has been described as a descent into anarchy.[13]

Meanwhile, Santa Anna planned the subjugation of Texas to his authority, borrowing money at exorbitant interest to finance the campaign. He undertook a two-pronged offensive: General José Urrea advanced one army along the Gulf Coast while *el presidente* himself commanded another aimed at retaking San Antonio. A small Texian force at Goliad stood in Urrea's path; another one occupied an old mission nicknamed the Alamo, awaiting Santa Anna. It was symptomatic of the Texans' ineffective strategic command and control that they did not respond to the invasion by combining these forces, evacuating either position, or reinforcing them. They just waited.[14]

Although not strategically vital, the Alamo had psychological importance for both sides. Its approximately 150 defenders consisted mostly of recent arrivals from the United States, fired with zeal for the Texan cause, and led by an eloquent twenty-six-year-old lawyer named William Travis who had been in Texas since 1831. Among them were Juan Seguín, Erasmo's son and a captain in the Texas cavalry; Jim Bowie, co-commander with Travis until he fell ill, famous for the big knife with which he had killed a man; and the former Whig congressman from Tennessee, Davy Crockett. Crockett probably expected a prominent role in the Texas Revolution to help revive his political career, but he was also a man of principle and willing to take risks. He had defended Indian rights against Andrew Jackson though it cost him his seat in Congress; now he would defend Texan rights against Santa Anna at the cost of his life. Despite his status as a frontier celebrity, Crockett had a strong sense of dignity; he preferred to be called David rather than Davy, and he habitually dressed, a Texan commented, "like a gentleman and not a backwoodsman."[15]

13. Lack, *Texas Revolutionary Experience*, 53.
14. Ibid, 82.
15. Quoted in Stephen Hardin, *Texian Iliad* (Austin, Tex., 1994), 232. Crockett's political sophistication has been rescued from unjust condescension by Thomas Scruggs in "Davy Crockett and the Thieves of Jericho," *JER* 19 (1999): 481–98.

Travis and his men were no suicidal fanatics. They defended the Alamo in the belief that they had rendered it defensible until the reinforcements they had requested could arrive. Santa Anna showed up on February 22, 1836, sooner and with a larger force than they had anticipated. Travis dispatched Seguín to urge the force at Goliad to come to his aid as soon as possible. On March 5, only a handful of reinforcements having arrived, Travis recognized the hopelessness of the situation. He convened a meeting and told the occupants of the Alamo they could leave if they thought they could escape through the Mexican siege lines. Maybe he drew a line in the sand with his sword—such a dramatic gesture would not have been out of character. Santa Anna had raised the red flag that signaled no quarter. But only one man and a few of the noncombatant women took up Travis's offer.[16]

Santa Anna did not need to storm the Alamo. His biggest cannons, due to arrive soon, would readily breach its walls. His intelligence reported no reinforcements on their way to the Alamo and that the defenders, weakened by dysentery, had little food or potable water left. The dictator ordered an assault for March 6 lest a Texan surrender rob him of a glorious victory. His assault force of fifteen hundred fought their way in and killed the defenders, suffering very heavy casualties themselves. The last half dozen Texans were overpowered and taken prisoner by a chivalrous Mexican officer who intended to spare their lives. Santa Anna entered the Alamo only after the fighting had ended, when he would be safe. He ordered the prisoners killed, whereupon they were hacked to death with swords. Mexican Lieutenant José Enrique de la Peña, who admired his enemies' courage as much as he despised his own commander, noted that the men "died without complaining and without humiliating themselves before their torturers." De la Peña believed Crockett to be among this group, and historians now generally accept his testimony.[17] The defenders of the Alamo against overwhelming odds passed into the realm of heroic epic, along with the Spartans at Thermopylae and Roland at Roncesvalles.

Not quite everyone captured in the Alamo was killed. Santa Anna spared some noncombatant *tejana* women, probably in a bid for Hispanic support, two black slaves of William Travis, perhaps to encourage other bondsmen to desert his enemies, and Suzanna Dickenson, widow

---

16. Randy Roberts and James Olson, *A Line in the Sand* (New York, 2001), 154–57.

17. José de la Peña, *With Santa Anna in Texas*, trans. Carmen Perry, expanded ed. (College Station, Tex., 1997), 53; Paul Hutton, "The Alamo As Icon," in Dawson, *Texas Military Experience*, 14–31.

of a Texas officer, so she could spread the word of the horrible fate awaiting those who resisted *el presidente*. His unnecessary attack had cost his best battalions one-third of their strength. But the dictator cared so little for his soldiers that he did not bother to set up a field hospital and allowed, his secretary noted bitterly, over one hundred of his wounded to die from injuries that could have been successfully treated.[18]

At Goliad, the Texan commander James Fannin hesitated, then decided not to go to the aid of the Alamo. Goliad seemed at least as important to hold, he reasoned. But Fannin's force wound up surrounded by a much larger Mexican army and surrendered. General Urrea left his prisoners with another officer, instructed him to treat them decently, and continued his advance. Santa Anna, upon learning of their capture, sent a message commanding the execution of Goliad's defenders. On March 27, Fannin and 341 of his men were accordingly massacred; 28 managed to escape.[19] In size and circumstances, this constituted an atrocity even worse than that at the Alamo.

Up in East Texas, where most Anglos lived, many wanted to declare full independence from Mexico, and events played into their hands. The pro-independence party enjoyed its greatest strength among the most recent arrivals and among substantial slaveholders, who feared they could not continue indefinitely to get around the Mexican laws against slavery. Stephen Austin and other Anglo-Texans who had flourished under the Mexican Constitution of 1824 were less radical; the newcomers called them "Tories."[20] The outbreak of fighting produced a sudden influx of Anglo males from the United States; to these new men, the Mexican Constitution of 1824 held no meaning, and nothing but independence made any sense as a goal. Since the newcomers provided some 40 percent of the armed force Texas could put into the field, their views carried weight. The cause of Texan independence enjoyed popularity in the United States, where many viewed it as a step toward annexation. Independence would make it easier for Texas to raise men and money in the United States, just as the American Declaration of Independence in 1776 had facilitated help from France. Besides, as Stephen Austin explained, "The Constitution of 1824 is totally overturned, the social compact totally dissolved." On March 2, 1836, while the siege of the Alamo continued, a Texan Convention proclaimed independence from Mexico and issued a

18. Hardin, *Texian Iliad*, 155–57.
19. Ibid., 174.
20. Margaret Henson, "Tory Sentiment in Anglo-Texan Public Opinion," *Southwestern Historical Quarterly* 90 (1986–87): 7.

declaration carefully modeled on Jefferson's.[21] By the seventeenth, this body had drafted a national constitution modeled on that of the United States and sanctioning chattel slavery; a referendum ratified the constitution in September. The Convention also chose David Burnet first president of the Texan Republic and balanced the ticket with a Hispanic vice president, Lorenzo de Závala.

Before independence, political lines in Texas had not coincided with linguistic ones. Most Texans, Anglo and Hispanic alike, had been *federalistas*. Among the few *centralistas* there were even Anglos like Juan (originally John) Davis Bradburn, a former Kentuckian who rose high in the Mexican army. Texan independence disadvantaged *los tejanos*, putting them in the strange position of a minority group in their own land. Most of them had felt more comfortable fighting for the Constitution of 1824. Some of the *rancheros* joined with the Mexican army as it passed through their neighborhood. Other *tejanos*, including the Seguíns, embraced Texan independence and fought for it. Even so, many Anglos, especially those newly arrived, distrusted the loyalty of any Hispanic. Almost all Anglo-Texans had come from the southern section of the Union and brought with them a commitment to white supremacy. Now, many waged the revolution as a race war against a *mestizo* nation.[22]

Following their victories at the Alamo and Goliad, the Mexican armies continued their advance northward, intending to complete their destruction of the insurgency and drive whatever might be left of it across the Sabine into the United States. Now commanded by Sam Houston, the Texan army withdrew before them, as did many Anglo civilians in what they called "the Runaway Scrape." Houston continued his retreat well into East Texas, making sure that the next battle would take place on his army's familiar home ground, where the wooded environment suited his tactics better than the open country that favored the Mexican cavalry. His undisciplined soldiers complained constantly that they should stand and fight, but the outcome vindicated their commander. Santa Anna, trying to find and fix his antagonist, divided his army so that each component could search separately. In doing so he committed a classic tactical mistake, enabling Houston to attack the detachment accompanying Santa Anna with something approaching even odds. When the Texans

21. Stephen Austin to David Burnet, March 4, 1836, in Stephen Austin, *Fugitive Letters, 1829–1836*, ed. Jacqueline Tomerlin (San Antonio, Tex., 1981), 40. A contemporary broadside showing the Texan Declaration of Independence is shown in David B. Davis and Sidney Mintz, eds., *The Boisterous Sea of Liberty* (New York, 1998), 407.
22. See Lack, *Texas Revolutionary Experience*, 183–207.

intercepted a Mexican courier and found Santa Anna's troop dispositions in his saddlebags, Houston saw that his moment had arrived.

The battle occurred on 21 April 1836, inside Stephen Austin's land grant, not far from the present-day city of Houston and near a river named San Jacinto ("hah-*seen*-toe" in Spanish, but Texans say "ja-*sin*-tah"). With a negligence that equaled his immorality, Santa Anna had failed to provide local security while his tired soldiers rested. Houston's men charged, shouting "Remember the Alamo!" The surprised Mexicans fled, only to be slaughtered by Texans in no mood to take prisoners. General Houston, defying a broken ankle, along with Texas secretary of war Thomas Rusk, tried in vain to command their men to obey the laws of war; in the words of a judicious historian, "the bloodthirsty rebels committed atrocities at least as beastly as those the Mexicans had committed."[23] The next day, military order restored, those enemy soldiers lucky enough to have survived were rounded up as captives. All told, the Mexicans lost about 650 killed and 700 prisoners at San Jacinto—virtually all the men they had engaged.

Among the prisoners, Santa Anna himself turned up. Instead of treating him as a war criminal (a status not then defined), Houston shrewdly bargained with the captured dictator. In return for his life and a safe conduct, Santa Anna promised that the Mexican army would withdraw beyond the Rio Grande (also called the Rio Bravo and Rio del Norte), even though the Nueces River, 150 miles farther north, had always been the boundary of Texas in the past. Accordingly, Santa Anna sent his successor in command, General Vicente Filisola, an order to evacuate Texas. Filisola obeyed, despite the remonstrance of General Urrea and others; he had come far from his supply base, and his financially strapped government had warned that no more resources could be devoted to the campaign. As the Mexican armies withdrew, they were joined by fugitive slaves and those Hispanic civilians who did not choose to cast their lot with an independent Texas. The document forced upon Santa Anna included a provision for the restoration of runaway slaves to their Anglo owners, but it proved impossible to enforce this.[24]

The Texans considered the Velasco agreement signed by Santa Anna and Texas president David Burnet a treaty recognizing their independence; the Mexican Congress, however, refused to approve it on the

---

23. Hardin, *Texian Iliad*, 213.
24. Lack, "Slavery and the Texan Revolution," 195–96. The agreement Santa Anna signed at Velasco, Texas, including its secret provisions, can be found in Oscar Martínez, ed., *U.S.-Mexico Borderlands* (Wilmington, Del., 1996), 17–19.

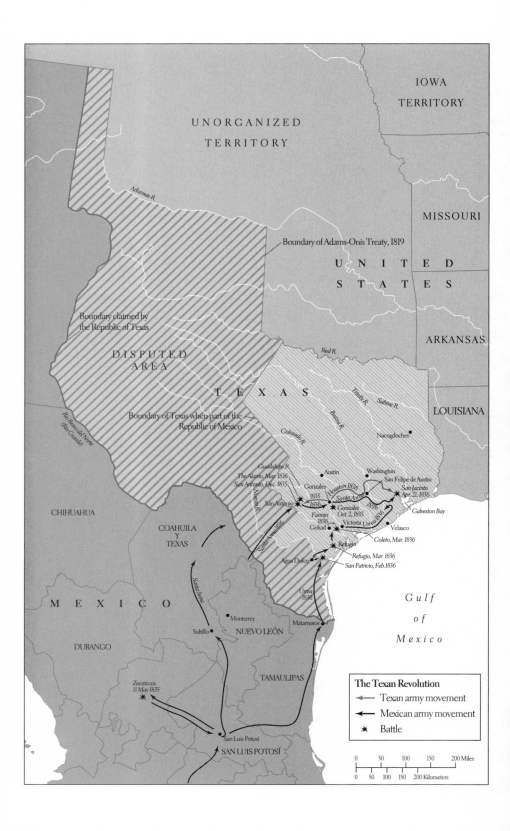

IOWA
TERRITORY

UNORGANIZED
TERRITORY

MISSOURI

Arkansas R.

Boundary of Adams-Onis Treaty, 1819

U N I T E D

S T A T E S

ARKANSAS

Boundary claimed by
the Republic of Texas

D I S P U T E D
A R E A

Red R.

LOUISIANA

T E X A S

Trinity R.

Sabine R.

Boundary of Texas when part of the
Republic of Mexico

Rio Bravo del Norte
(Río Grande)

Colorado R.

Brazos R.

Nacogdoches

CHIHUAHUA

Guadalupe R.
The Alamo, Mar. 1836
San Antonio, Dec. 1835

Austin

Washington

San Felipe de Austin

Gonzales

Houston 1836

San Jacinto
Apr. 21, 1836

Gonzales
1835
1836

Santa Anna

San Antonio

Santa Anna 1836

Nueces R.

Fannin
1836

Gonzales
Oct 2, 1835

Santa Anna

1836

Galveston Bay

COAHUILA
Y
TEXAS

Goliad

Victoria

Urrea 1836

Velasco

Coleto, Mar. 1836

Refugio

M E X I C O

Santa Anna

Agua Dulce

Refugio, Mar. 1836
San Patricio, Feb.1836

Monterrey

Urrea
1836

Matamoros

Gulf

of

Mexico

Saltillo

NUEVO LEÓN

DURANGO

TAMAULIPAS

Zacatecas
11 May 1835

The Texan Revolution

⟵ Texan army movement

◀━━ Mexican army movement

✳ Battle

San Luis Potosí

SAN LUIS POTOSÍ

0   50   100   150   200 Miles

0   50   100   150   200 Kilometers

understandable grounds that it had been extorted from a captive who had every reason to expect death if he did not consent. Intermittent warfare between Texas and Mexico continued for years. Mexican armies twice re-occupied San Antonio (in the spring and fall of 1842) but could not retain the town. The Texans tried to make good on their extravagant claim that the Rio Grande constituted their western boundary from mouth to source. They set up their national capital at Austin, rather than more log-ical places like Galveston or Houston, as a symbol of their westward aspi-rations.[25] But several expansionist Texan offensives, including attempts to capture Santa Fe in 1841 and 1843, and an expedition to Mier on the Rio Grande in 1843, all failed completely. As a result, the Nueces remained the approximate de facto limit of the independent Lone Star Republic, except for the town of Corpus Christi where the Nueces met the Gulf. (The famous Lone Star Flag of Texas, suggested by emigrants from Louisiana, derived from the flag of the 1810 Baton Rouge rebellion against Spanish West Florida, which had featured a gold star on a blue background.)[26]

In October 1836, Sam Houston won the Texan presidential election in a landslide. Stephen Austin, who also ran, already seemed a voice from the past; he died soon afterwards. Juan Seguín found himself betrayed by the Anglos he had once fought alongside. Persecuted, he and his family fled to Mexico; when the next war came, he fought on the Mexican side against the United States. Santa Anna, disgraced by his conduct in Texas, fell from power in Mexico, regained it after redeeming himself fighting a French invasion of his country in 1838–39 at the cost of one of his legs, then lost power again in 1844 to the liberal José Herrera.

In the United States, Sam Houston's longtime personal friend Andrew Jackson professed official neutrality while not actually preventing the Texans from obtaining men, munitions, and money for their cause. He also dispatched U.S. troops to the Sabine—and even across it—as an im-plied warning to Mexico that the reconquest of Texas could lead to conflict with the United States.[27] The Mexicans wrongly assumed that Jackson had fomented the rebellion; in fact, he worried that Texan independence might complicate his efforts to annex the region. They rightly perceived, however, his intention to obtain Texas for the United States. As early as

25. D. W. Meinig, *Imperial Texas* (Austin, Tex., 1969), 42.
26. Louisiana State Museum, the Cabildo, New Orleans.
27. Robert May, *Manifest Destiny's Underworld* (Chapel Hill, 2002), 9; Leonard Richards, "The Jacksonians and Slavery," in *Antislavery Reconsidered*, ed. Lewis Perry and Michael Fellman (Baton Rouge, 1979), 116.

1829, Jackson had instructed his tactless, incompetent diplomatic representative in Mexico City, Anthony Butler, to try to acquire Texas, bribing Mexican officials if necessary. Not until April 1832 did the United
States and Mexico exchange ratifications of a treaty affirming that the
border defined between the United States and Spain in 1819 would continue to apply.[28] After the Battle of San Jacinto, Jackson actually met with
the defeated Santa Anna, then eager to ingratiate himself with the Americans, and made him an offer to buy Mexico's claim to Texas for $3.5
million, but that ultimate opportunist no longer spoke for the Mexican
government.[29]

Jackson's attitude toward Texas fit with his foreign policy in general,
which was largely a projection of his personal experience. As a planter
and land speculator, he took an interest in the expansion of cotton
acreage and in securing overseas markets for agricultural staples. Indian
Removal, foreign trade agreements, and Texas annexation all reflected
these interests. A soldier renowned for his defense of New Orleans, he remained concerned with the strategic security of the Southwest and now
wanted the border pushed far beyond the Sabine (although he had favored the boundary of Adams's Transcontinental Treaty when President
Monroe asked his opinion).[30]

Jackson maintained a facade of neutrality between Texas and Mexico
out of regard for his vice president. Van Buren knew that northerners regarded Texas as an outpost of slavery they did not wish to acquire, and he
realized that the issue could complicate his election in the fall of 1836.
Once the election had safely passed, Jackson began to push hard for the
settlement of debts Mexico owed U.S. citizens. Not all the claims were
well founded, but they provided leverage to pressure the financially
strapped Mexican government into accepting some American money in
return for surrendering Texas. On his last day in office, March 3, 1837,
Old Hickory officially recognized the independence of Sam Houston's
government.

Discussions regarding Texas annexation then proceeded within the
Van Buren administration until cut short in 1838, when John Quincy

28. John Belohlavek, *Let the Eagle Soar! The Foreign Policy of Andrew Jackson* (Lincoln,
    Neb., 1985), 237–38; Hunter Miller, ed., *Treaties and Other International Acts of the
    United States* (Washington, 1933), III, 412–13.
29. Andreas Reichstein, *Rise of the Lone Star* (College Station, Tex., 1989), 94–96; Rem-
    ini, *Jackson*, III, 365.
30. Andrew Jackson to James Monroe, June 20, 1820, ms. in Monroe Papers, New York
    Public Library; Remini, *Jackson*, I, 389–90.

Adams got wind of them. Adams brought the issue to public attention, whereupon the cautious Fox backed away from a storm of northern protest.[31] Van Buren handled Texas the same way he handled the crisis across the northern border in Canada. Ontario too had attracted settlers from the United States, who also made trouble for their foreign government and talked a lot about turning over their province to their native country. But Van Buren preferred conciliation to confrontation and peace to war. He had learned the arts of regional politics in his home state, where the racist workingmen and proslavery cotton merchants of New York City had to be balanced against the antislavery sentiments upstate. Texas annexation was one concession the South did not get from Jackson's otherwise compliant successor.

II

Texas remained an independent republic for ten years. Immigration from the United States soared during the recurrent hard times that began in 1837, as southwesterners sought to escape their debts and start over in a new country where slavery had now been legalized. By 1845 the population of Texas reached 125,000, representing an increase of 75,000 in a decade. Over 27,000 of these inhabitants were enslaved, most of them imported from the United States but some from Cuba or Africa. Although the law forbade export of U.S. slaves to foreign countries, no one enforced the prohibition along the Texas/Louisiana border, either before or after Texan independence. The slave population grew even faster than the free population in the Lone Star Republic. Even if slavery did not actually trigger the Texan Revolution, the revolution's success certainly strengthened the institution in Texas.[32]

During this time the Texan government pursued a dual foreign policy. On the one hand, annexation by the United States constituted an obvious objective. It offered military security against reconquest by Mexico, as well as improved economic prospects. The decade of Texan independence included the depression years following 1837, and, like the Mexican Republic from which it separated, the Lone Star Republic suffered from a chronic shortage of capital, both public and private. Bondholders of the impecunious new entity hoped the United States could be persuaded to annex not only Texas but also the Texan national debt. Land

31. Robert Cole, *The Presidency of Andrew Jackson* (Lawrence, Kans., 1993), 266–67; William Miller, *Arguing About Slavery* (New York, 1996), 284–98.
32. Meinig, *Continental America*, 141; Campbell, *Empire for Slavery*, 54–55; Lack, "Slavery and the Texan Revolution," 202.

speculators, always influential in Texan politics, rejoiced that independence had stepped up the rate of immigration and figured (correctly) that annexation would boost it further. On the other hand, however, the dream of a strong independent Texas held attraction too, particularly if the Lone Star Republic could expand to the Pacific and become a two-ocean power. In this scenario, Britain might provide economic and military aid as a substitute for help from the United States. The emphasis in Texan foreign policy goals shifted now one way, now the other. Although the two policies envisioned alternative futures, in practice they proved quite compatible, since the prospect of an independent Texas allied with Britain alarmed U.S. authorities, encouraging them to overcome northern opposition to annexation. Even now it is by no means clear when Texan statesmen like Sam Houston were courting British aid to achieve long-term Texan independence and when they were doing it to get the attention of policymakers in Washington.

The British really did have an interest in Texas, though not so strong a one as the Texans hoped or the Americans feared. British commercial interests welcomed the prospect of trade with Texas as an alternative source of cotton imports. From a geopolitical point of view, an independent Texas sharing the North American continent might make the aggressive, troublesome United States less of a threat to the underpopulated dominions of British North America. But what shaped British policy the most was the interest of British bondholders. Since British citizens had invested in Texas and to a much greater extent in Mexico, their government hoped to promote stability and solvency in both Mexico and Texas by encouraging the two countries to make peace on the basis of Texan independence. Finally, Britain's strong antislavery movement aspired to wean the Texans away from the practice of slavery, or at least from the international slave trade, as the price of British aid.[33] This prospect considerably heightened the anxiety felt by President Tyler and certain other southern politicians.

Tyler's secretary of state, Daniel Webster, had a different perspective on Anglo-American relations. A Whig supporter of internal improvements, like most members of his party he looked upon Britain as an essential source of investment capital, particularly important in 1842 for helping the United States pull out of its depression and resume economic development.[34] To negotiate outstanding difficulties between the two countries,

33. Lelia Roeckell, "Bonds over Bondage: British Opposition to the Annexation of Texas," *JER* 19 (1999): 257–78.
34. See Jay Sexton, "Debtor Diplomacy: Finance and American Foreign Relations, 1837–1873" (D.Phil. thesis, Oxford University, 2003).

Prime Minister Robert Peel sent Lord Ashburton, retired head of the investment banking firm of Baring Brothers. Baring's had extensive experience in what the British call "the States," and Ashburton had married an American. He and Webster knew and respected each other. But the list of issues confronting them tested the resourcefulness of even these skillful and well-motivated negotiators.

The *Caroline* incident in Van Buren's administration constituted the first such issue. This conflict came back into the news when the state of New York put an alleged Canadian participant in the raid on trial for arson and murder. Fortunately for all parties, the jury acquitted him. Webster and Ashburton dealt with the *Caroline* through an exchange of letters. Webster declared that an attack on another country's territory is legitimate only when a government can "show a necessity of self-defence, [*sic*] instant, overwhelming, leaving no choice of means, and no moment for deliberation."[35] Ashburton replied that he accepted this standard and thought the circumstances had met it. He added, however, that it was too bad the British had not promptly offered an explanation and apology. Webster seized upon the word "apology" and declared American honor satisfied; he filed no claim for damages. Webster's definition of international law on the subject was cited at Nuremberg and during the Cuban Missile Crisis to define situations when preemptive strikes may or may not be justified as self-defense.[36]

Another international incident had arisen in 1841, resembling in some respects the case of the *Amistad*. This involved the American brig *Creole*, which sailed from Hampton Roads, Virginia, with a cargo of 135 slaves bound for the markets of New Orleans. On November 7, the slaves rebelled, killed one of their owners and wounded several crew members, then sailed the ship into the port of Nassau in the Bahamas, a British colony where slavery had been illegal since 1833. There they came ashore to the cheers of assembled black Bahamians. The local authorities pronounced the refugees free and decided against prosecuting anyone for murder. When the news reached Washington, the abolitionist Whig

35. *Papers of Daniel Webster: Diplomatic Papers*, ed. Kenneth Shewmaker et al. (Hanover, N.H., 1983), I, 58–68. Webster addressed the letter to Henry Fox, the British minister to the United States, but it formed the basis of his agreement with Ashburton.

36. Kenneth Stevens, *Border Diplomacy* (Tuscaloosa, Ala., 1989), 164–68; Claude Fuess, *Daniel Webster* (New York, 1930), II, 112. The present applicability of the Caroline Doctrine is debated in Timothy Kearley, "Raising the *Caroline*," *Wisconsin International Law Journal* 17 (1999): 325–46, and John Yoo, "Sinking the *Caroline*," *San Diego International Law Journal* 4 (2003): 467–90.

congressman Joshua Giddings declared the mutineers on the *Creole* had been fully justified in asserting their natural right to freedom. Formally censured for this by the House of Representatives, Giddings felt vindicated after his antislavery constituents reelected him in a landslide. Angry American slaveholders demanded their property back, and to placate them Webster had to pursue financial compensation. Ashburton agreed to refer the matter to an international commission, which in 1853 awarded the masters $110,000 from the British government.[37]

Ashburton wanted the United States to accept the right of the Royal Navy to board ships suspected of engaging in the outlawed Atlantic slave trade. So long as the United States withheld such authority, slave traders from other countries flew the Stars and Stripes to deter detection. But Lewis Cass, the ambitious Michigan Democrat who served both Van Buren and Tyler as minister to France, complained loudly that the British were trying to revive their old practice of impressing sailors on American ships; his demagogy prevented Webster from agreeing to the British proposal, although several other nations did consent. Instead, the United States promised to maintain a squadron of its own to patrol for slave traders, a commitment honored only halfheartedly by the Democratic administrations that controlled the federal government most of the time until the Civil War.[38]

The boundary dispute between the United States and Canada, stemming from the vagueness of the Treaty of 1783 and the geographical ignorance of that time, required resolution in a formal treaty. The most hotly contested portion of the boundary lay between Maine and New Brunswick. One attempt to resolve it, through Dutch mediation in 1831, had already failed. In February 1839, the militias of Maine and New Brunswick had come dangerously close to an armed clash. The intransigence of the state of Maine, which had been granted the right to veto whatever the federal government negotiated, made compromise particularly difficult. Webster worked to soften Maine's attitude by a combination of lobbying state legislators and publishing newspaper articles favoring compromise, paying for both out of secret executive funds that Congress had authorized for foreign affairs. Expending the money to influence American public opinion was something of a stretch but not forbidden by the law. To help convince key Maine individuals to accept compromise, Webster also showed them in confidence an early map assigning the

---

37. The *Creole*'s story is told in Howard Jones and Donald Rakestraw, *Prologue to Manifest Destiny* (Wilmington, Del., 1997), 71–96.
38. Don Fehrenbacher, *The Slaveholding Republic* (New York, 2001), 165–88.

whole disputed area to New Brunswick, suggesting that the American bargaining position would not bear close examination and that compromise was the only prudent course. In fact, a number of such early maps existed, showing a variety of boundaries; indeed, back in London, the foreign secretary possessed one that seemed to substantiate the American claim. The bargain that Webster and Ashburton eventually struck awarded Maine seven thousand square miles and New Brunswick five thousand square miles of the disputed area, and the states of Maine and Massachusetts (which Maine had been part of until 1820) signed off on it in return for $125,000 each from the British government.[39] The boundary as finally agreed substantially coincided with the compromise that the Dutch king had proposed back in 1831. Webster might have been able to get more territory for Maine by more diligent searching for early maps, but he judged mutual conciliation more important than any of the particular issues. As he explained to his friend, the capable U.S. minister in London, Edward Everett: "The great object is to show mutual concession and the granting of what may be regarded in the light of equivalents." History seems to have vindicated the work of Webster and Ashburton: Their peaceful compromise of the unclear boundary has proved a durable resolution.[40]

The Webster-Ashburton Treaty also demarcated the northern boundary of Minnesota more clearly. The line it drew, although the subject of less controversy at the time, proved ultimately more significant. It assigned the United States the rich iron ore, discovered many years later, of the Mesabi and Vermillion Ranges. Ashburton had no way of knowing the importance of the concession he made.[41]

The Webster-Ashburton Treaty of 1842 represented a temporary confluence of interest between Tyler and the Whigs. "His Accidency" had long been an ardent and consistent expansionist. At this moment, he wanted to resolve tensions with the British in order to minimize their opposition against his intended annexation of Texas. For their part, the Whigs wanted access to British capital for American economic recovery and development; this explains why the Whig-dominated Senate consented to

39. Norma Peterson, *The Presidencies of William Henry Harrison and John Tyler* (Lawrence, Kans., 1989), 118–22; Jones and Rakestraw, *Prologue to Manifest Destiny*, 112.
40. Daniel Webster to Edward Everett, June 14, 1842, quoted in Irving Bartlett, *Daniel Webster* (New York, 1978), 179; Francis Carroll, *A Good and Wise Measure* (Toronto, 2001), 305–6.
41. Thomas LeDuc, "The Webster-Ashburton Treaty and the Minnesota Iron Ranges," *JAH* 51 (1964): 476–81.

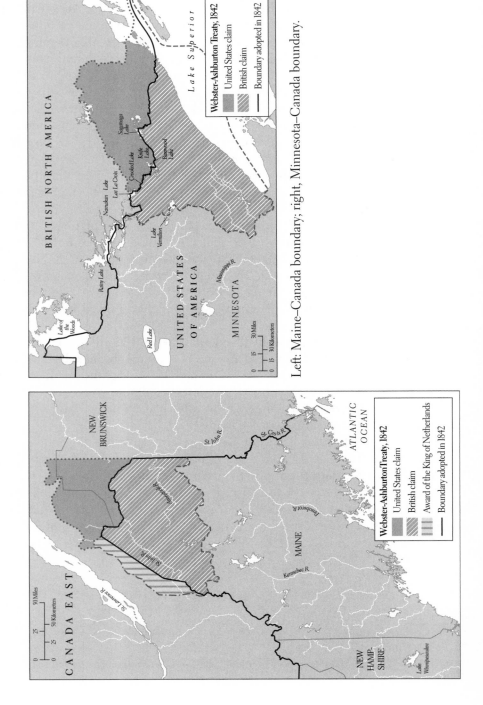

Left: Maine–Canada boundary; right, Minnesota–Canada boundary.

the treaty's ratification on August 20. While vetoing Whig plans for a third Bank of the United States, Tyler had his own project to alleviate the depression, at least for some hard-pressed southern planters. Annexing the fertile cotton lands of Texas would ensure that their slave markets stayed open and busy, bidding up the value of all slaveowners' property. The depression had also influenced the British government in its search for an accord with the United States. Responsive as usual to the interests of their bondholders, they hoped to persuade the federal government to assume the debts of states that had defaulted on their bonds. But the hope proved vain.[42]

Tyler felt encouraged by the success of the Webster-Ashburton negotiations to press for a larger accomplishment in foreign policy. Although stymied on the domestic front by congressional Whigs, the president had much more scope for achievement in foreign affairs. He sensed that the American public could be aroused to enthusiasm for westward expansion, and he determined to make Texas annexation his cause. Ideally, he could ride the issue into the White House for another term, this time in his own right. Webster's long-standing opposition to the annexation of slaveholding Texas now surfaced as a difficulty between him and Tyler, and the two parted ways. But the president had learned a lot from the somewhat devious means that Webster employed to secure approval of his treaty with Ashburton. He would resort to secrecy and government propaganda on a far more extensive scale as he manipulated public opinion regarding Texas annexation.

To succeed Webster at the State Department Tyler appointed Abel Upshur, a proslavery radical of the Calhoun school. Like many other slaveholders, John Tyler regarded Britain with deep ambivalence. The textile mills of Yorkshire and Lancashire constituted an essential customer for southern cotton. Yet Britain also headquartered the international antislavery movement. Having used Webster to resolve many of the outstanding disputes between the United States and Britain, Tyler now turned to Upshur to confront the menace of British abolitionism in Texas. Tyler hoped to win over Calhoun's faction for his presidential bid. Promoted by the Tyler administration, the issue of Texas annexation replaced state rights as the political mantra of southerners who embraced the new doctrine of the "positive good" of slavery.

The president had already sent the Calhounite newspaperman Duff Green to Europe with a kind of roving commission to spy for the White

42. Freehling, *Secessionists at Bay*, 422–24; Wilbur Jones, *The American Problem in British Diplomacy, 1841–1861* (London, 1974), 31.

House. Green's cover was that of a businessman seeking British venture capital. Green found Lewis Cass a congenial Anglophobic spirit and worked with him to frustrate British efforts for international cooperation in suppressing the Atlantic slave trade. Once Webster left the administration, no one in Washington tried to counteract the reports Green sent back about British plots to "abolitionize" Texas, that is, to guarantee payment of Texan national bonds in return for compensated emancipation. Then, Green warned, Texas would become a magnet for runaway slaves much as Florida had been before 1818, and (somehow) it would all end up with emancipation and race war in the United States. The Texan diplomatic representatives in Washington felt in no hurry to deny these rumors, sensing that they enhanced the value of Texas in the eyes of Tyler's administration. In fact, the American abolitionist Stephen Pearl Andrews was indeed in London and lobbying for British aid to Texas emancipation, but Peel's Tory ministry was not prepared to embark on any such expensive and risky adventure in altruism. Duff Green had confused the hopes of the World Antislavery Convention (which Andrews attended) with the intentions of Her Majesty's Government. The official U.S. minister to Britain, Edward Everett, tried to make the distinction clear. But Green's reports fed Upshur's preconceptions and expectations; Everett's did not.[43]

Upshur took Green's exaggerations and alarms to the American public, publishing anonymous articles in the press on the "Designs of the British Government."[44] Besides expanding the power of the United States, the annexation of Texas, they argued, would also secure southwestern slavery against the bad example of British-sponsored abolition. Arousing the latent Anglophobia of the American public was often good politics. Besides its official organ, the *Washington Madisonian*, the Tyler administration could also count on the largest-selling newspaper in the country, James Gordon Bennett's *New York Herald*, to echo Green's warnings about Britain and support American imperialism. To some extent, at least, Tyler's inner circle believed their own propaganda that slavery was under threat in Texas; Secretary Upshur privately warned a friend to remove his slaves from Texas lest he lose them to emancipation.[45]

43. David Pletcher, *The Diplomacy of Annexation* (Columbia, Mo., 1973), 119–25; Edward Crapol, *John Tyler* (Chapel Hill, 2006), 68–74.

44. Green's reports and Upshur's publications in the *Washington Madisonian* are in Frederick Merk, *Slavery and the Annexation of Texas*, 187–92, 204–5, 217–36, 245–64.

45. Thomas Hietala, *Manifest Design: Anxious Aggrandizement in Late Jacksonian America* (Ithaca, N.Y., 1985), 20–21; Abel Upshur to Beverly Tucker, March 13, 1843, printed in William Freehling, *The Reintegration of American History* (New York, 1994), 125–29.

In September 1843, Upshur initiated secret discussions with the Texan emissary Isaac Van Zandt regarding annexation. At first Texan president Sam Houston remained cool; he preferred to concentrate his diplomatic efforts on winning Mexican recognition of Texan independence, employing the good offices of Britain. The government of Texas gave no indication of fearing the British posed a threat to its system of labor exploitation, but it did worry about renewed warfare with Mexico. Only after the Mexicans had proposed a truce but no recognition did Houston assent to try negotiating annexation with the United States. In secrecy, Upshur and Van Zandt began drafting such a treaty. In January 1844, Upshur informally promised the Texan negotiator that if they signed a treaty of annexation, the U.S. president would dispatch troops to defend Texas against Mexico without waiting for congressional authorization or ratification of the treaty. This understanding proved key in reassuring the Texans.[46]

On February 28, 1844, Secretary of State Upshur, along with the secretary of the navy and several other people, were killed when a gigantic naval gun on board the USS *Princeton* exploded during a demonstration firing. A steam-powered warship (then the cutting edge of technology), the *Princeton*, with its big gun sardonically nicknamed "the Peacemaker," was the pride of the U.S. Navy. The administration had wanted to show off new weaponry prepared for any coming showdown with Mexico over Texas annexation. By the time of the accident, negotiations for annexation had largely been completed. To carry the Texas treaty forward through ratification, President Tyler appointed as his new secretary of state the ultimate Calhounite: the master of Fort Hill plantation himself.[47]

On April 12, 1844, Secretary of State Calhoun and the two Texan negotiators formally signed the treaty of annexation. It provided that Texas would become a U.S. territory eligible for admission later as one or more states. Texan public lands would be ceded to the federal government, which in return would assume up to $10 million in Texan national debt. The boundaries of Texas were not specified but left to be sorted out later with Mexico.[48]

Ten days later the treaty went to the Senate. Along with it went Calhoun's official statement of why Texas annexation was essential: a letter

---

46. Peterson, *Presidencies of Harrison and Tyler*, 199; Pletcher, *Diplomacy of Annexation*, 125–35.

47. Merk, *Slavery and Annexation*, 42–43; Freehling, *Secessionists at Bay*, 406–7.

48. "A Treaty of Annexation, Concluded between the United States of America and the Republic of Texas, at Washington, the 12th Day of April, 1844," rpt. in Merk, *Slavery and Annexation*, 271–75.

from the secretary of state to Britain's minister to the United States, Richard Pakenham, declaring that the United States acquired Texas in order to protect slavery there from British interference.[49] Although the press had finally discovered the existence of annexation negotiations a month before, the treaty's provisions remained a state secret. Tyler and Calhoun intended to make them public only after the Senate, in closed executive session, had consented to ratification.

Then the whole thing blew up in the administration's face. Senator Benjamin Tappan of Ohio, a maverick antislavery Democrat and an opponent of annexation, leaked the treaty to the newspapers on April 27. The same day, Henry Clay and Martin Van Buren, the recognized leaders of the Whig and Democratic Parties respectively, both issued statements opposing immediate annexation of Texas. The Senate censured Tappan but decided to open up much of its deliberation to the public. When Missouri's Thomas Hart Benton publicly exposed the misinformation from Duff Green on which the administration had justified its policy, he showed that even a western Jacksonian Democrat, an expansionist under most circumstances, opposed the treaty. On June 8, the Senate defeated Texas annexation by 35 to 16. A treaty needs approval by two-thirds of the Senators; this one had not even mustered one-third. The proslavery justification for Texas offered by Calhoun's letter to Pakenham immediately appealed only to slave-state Democrats, who backed the treaty 10 to 1 (Benton). Infuriated northern Whigs rejected the treaty 13 to 0. Southern Whigs stayed loyal to Clay by opposing it 14 to 1. Northern Democrats, with their strong tradition of placating the slave power, had more difficulty deciding; they split 7 to 5 against, with 1 abstention.[50]

Tyler had wanted to unite the country behind Texas annexation (and himself). What had gone wrong? Like Tyler, John C. Calhoun hoped that 1844 would be his year for the presidency. He had resigned from the Senate thinking to devote full time to campaigning. But the philosopher of state rights had not succeeded in rallying a solid South behind his candidacy and the extreme proslavery paranoia that he represented to the political community. Although some northern "doughface" Democrats came to his support, his refusal to endorse the Dorr Rebellion, popular with most northern Democratic voters, hurt him.[51] Calhoun had pulled out of the race in December 1843, without waiting for the Democratic

---

49. Excerpts rpt. in *History of U.S. Political Parties*, ed. Arthur Schlesinger Jr. (New York, 1973), 550–52.
50. Freehling, *Secessionists at Bay*, 431.
51. Sean Wilentz, *The Rise of American Democracy* (New York, 2005), 545.

National Convention. He then seized upon his appointment as Tyler's secretary of state to implement the same goal he would have pursued as president: to make the federal government explicitly proslavery. When Secretary of State Calhoun avowed the protection of slavery the primary reason for annexing Texas, this was more than most American politicians at the time were willing to swallow. Both major parties had long agreed that Texas annexation seemed too hot to handle. The prolonged secrecy surrounding the treaty proved another tactical mistake, for the northern press turned alienated and hostile when shut out from the news by which it lived.

Calhoun's presidential candidacy, which he pursued throughout 1842 and 1843, had undercut Tyler's candidacy, because of course the race had room for only one of them. Still, the Tyler and Calhoun supporters could cooperate against those who wanted to sew the nomination up for Martin Van Buren. Sometimes the lines between the Tyler and Calhoun campaigns blurred. While Tyler thought Upshur was supporting him, in reality the secretary seems to have been working for Calhoun. Very likely Calhoun, Upshur, and their friends, including Senator Robert Walker of Mississippi, played on the president's vanity, encouraging him to stay in the race to further purposes of their own without feeling any real loyalty to his cause.[52]

Having given up entirely on the Whigs, Tyler now hoped for the nomination of the Democratic Party, but that great patronage machine was not about to bestow its highest prize on an interloper. Why should the Democrats make an exception to their cherished value of party solidarity and loyalty? They benefited more by insisting that Tyler remained a Whig and that the Whigs were therefore hopelessly divided among themselves. Clinging desperately to his dream of a second term, Tyler took up the third-party option and organized a convention, consisting mostly of federal officeholders, who went through the motions of nominating him but did not provide him with a running mate.

Looking back afterwards, Tyler grumbled that his presidential bid had been hurt by the insistence of his secretary of state on making the Texas treaty an explicitly proslavery measure.[53] But, if it did Tyler's candidacy no good, Calhoun's tactic served another purpose. By identifying Texas

---

52. On the subtle relationship between Tyler and Calhoun, see John Niven, *John C. Calhoun* (Baton Rouge, 1988), 260; William J. Cooper, *The South and the Politics of Slavery* (Baton Rouge, 1978), 176–89; Charles Sellers, "Election of 1844," in *History of American Presidential Elections*, ed. Arthur Schlesinger Jr. (New York, 1985), II, 758.

53. Tyler's 1847 recollections quoted in Fehrenbacher, *Slaveholding Republic*, 125.

with slavery, Calhoun made sure that Van Buren, being a northerner, would have to oppose Texas. This, Calhoun correctly foresaw, would hurt the New Yorker's chances for the Democratic nomination. Nor did the Carolinian's ingenious strategy ultimately wreck the cause of Texas annexation. Indeed, in that respect it would turn out a brilliant success.[54]

III

The election of 1844 was one of the closest and most momentous in American history. The Whig Party met for its national convention in Baltimore on May 1. No one had the slightest doubt that the presidential nomination would go to Henry Clay, and so it did, unanimously. As a gesture of confidence in Whig judgment, the nominee allowed the convention freedom to choose his running mate. The southern delegates felt that, to balance the ticket, a northern evangelical should get the nod. The view prevailed, and the vice-presidential choice went to New Jersey's former senator, Theodore Frelinghuysen, president of the American Bible Society and the American Tract Society, befriender of the Cherokees, sabbatarian and temperance advocate, nicknamed "the Christian statesman." Clay expected his opponent to be Martin Van Buren and that the campaign would be fought along the economic lines that had emerged during the past fifteen years: the American System and a national bank versus laissez-faire and banking rules left up to the states. With Texas annexation clearly heading for defeat in the Senate, it did not seem likely to figure in the campaign. Van Buren had paid a courtesy call on Clay at Ashland in May 1842, and many people, both in their own day and since, have supposed the prospective candidates there reached an informal agreement, as Unionists and gentlemen, to leave Texas out of their contest. Very likely, however, the two reached the same conclusion independently and their simultaneous announcements were a coincidence.[55]

The Democratic convention, meeting later the same month, also in Baltimore, provided much more excitement and surprise. Ex-president Van Buren controlled a majority of the delegates but not the two-thirds Democratic rules customarily required. His support turned out to be soft. Senator Robert Walker persuaded some of Van Buren's delegates to join

54. On the motive behind Calhoun's Pakenham Letter, I accept Charles Sellers, *The Market Revolution* (New York, 1991), 413. See also Peterson, *Presidencies of Harrison and Tyler*, 213–18; William Brock, *Parties and Political Conscience* (Millwood, N.Y., 1979), 132–35.
55. Donald Cole, *Martin Van Buren* (Princeton, 1984), 393–94; Robert Remini, *Henry Clay* (New York, 1991), 613.

the South in backing reimposition of the two-thirds rule.[56] Lewis Cass of Michigan, who as Jackson's secretary of war had taken charge of Indian Removal, embraced Texas annexation and parlayed this and strident Anglophobia into a serious challenge to Van Buren. After eight ballots the two were running neck and neck. Calhoun and his followers sat in attendance, but ready to walk out and into the Tyler convention meeting across the street if they didn't get an acceptable Democratic nominee. Despite Cass's enthusiasm for Texas, the Calhounites wanted a real southern slaveholder. They opted for James Knox Polk of Tennessee, former Speaker of the House of Representatives, who had been angling for the second spot on Van Buren's ticket and who had now replaced the New Yorker as Andrew Jackson's protégé. A cabal consisting of Gideon Pillow, Benjamin Butler, and George Bancroft (who, improbably, was both an eminent historical scholar and a political wheeler-dealer) offered Polk to the convention as a way out, to prevent a Cass–Van Buren deadlock, and the delegates stampeded for him. Not having been regarded as a presidential candidate during the preceding months, Polk was the first "dark horse" candidate to win a nomination. Polk had remained technically loyal to Van Buren, and he supported an Independent Treasury. Yet on the expansion issue Polk represented, not a compromise, but an even more ambitious imperialism than Cass. After most of the tired delegates had gone home, the convention adopted a platform containing (along with the standard Democratic positions on strict construction, banking, and congressional noninterference with slavery) the following dramatic plank:

> Resolved, That our title to the whole of the Territory of Oregon is clear and unquestionable; that no portion of the same ought to be ceded to England or any other power, and that the re-occupation of Oregon and the re-annexation of Texas at the earliest practicable period are great American measures, which this Convention recommends to the cordial support of the Democracy of the Union.[57]

The Calhounites felt delighted with the outcome. "We have triumphed," Francis Pickens of South Carolina gloated. "Polk is nearer to *us* than any public man who was named. He is a large Slave holder &

---

56. Michael Morrison, "Martin Van Buren, the Democracy, and the Partisan Politics of Texas Annexation," *Journal of Southern History* 61 (1995): 695–722; Leonard Richards, *The Slave Power* (Baton Rouge, 2000), 144–45.

57. *National Party Platforms*, comp. Kirk Porter and Donald Johnson (Urbana, Ill., 1970), 4.

plants cotton—*free trade*—Texas—States rights *out & out.*"[58] Polk even obligingly promised to serve but one term, so Calhoun could continue to nurture his own obsessive presidential ambition.[59]

Robert Walker, one of the most influential southern leaders at the convention, had phrased the new plank in the Democratic platform shrewdly. To appeal to the North, it seemed to place more emphasis on Oregon than on Texas. It spoke of "re-occupation" and "re-annexation." The terms implied that the United States once enjoyed clear title to all of Oregon and Texas but had foolishly agreed to the joint occupation of the former in 1818 and surrendered the latter altogether in the Florida treaty of 1819. Expansionist Democrats claimed Texas had been included in the Louisiana Purchase and blamed John Quincy Adams for relinquishing it to Spain. Adams responded that Monroe had instructed him to do so, and that furthermore Andrew Jackson had been consulted and had consented to the boundary then drawn. Jackson indignantly denied this, and the two ex-presidents exchanged bitter recriminations. The historical record vindicates Adams's memory rather than Jackson's.[60]

By now, Jackson had removed any cloak from his aggressive imperialism. The enfeebled hero lay terminally ill at the Hermitage, but the letters he scratched out breathed his old fire against old enemies, the British and the abolitionists who stood in his way. Since Van Buren had come out against immediate annexation, Jackson wrote off his former favorite and called upon the Democratic Party to nominate someone else.[61] Although Jackson could not bring himself to admit it, his stance in 1844 aligned him with, of all people, John C. Calhoun. After the convention, Old Hickory rallied his faltering energies to endorse his Tennessee friend Polk and Texas. "Obtain it the United States must, peaceably if we can, but forcibly if we must," Jackson instructed. Polk, proud of his nickname "Young Hickory," took the old man's admonition to heart.[62]

Mississippi's Robert Walker presented the case on behalf of Texas annexation for northern audiences. Walker may have composed this remarkable

58. Francis Pickens to Henry Conner, May 29, 1844, quoted in Cooper, *Politics of Slavery*, 206.
59. For a good account of the Democratic convention, see Sellers, "Election of 1844," 747–75.
60. Michael Holt, "The Democratic Party," in Schlesinger, *History of U.S. Political Parties*, 518; Lynn Parsons, "The Last Ten Years of John Quincy Adams and Andrew Jackson," *JER* 23 (2003): 421–44, esp. 433.
61. Andrew Jackson to Francis Blair, May 11, 1844, *Correspondence of AJ*, VI, 286–87.
62. Andrew Jackson to William Lewis, April 8, 1844, ibid., VI, 278. See also Freehling, *Secessionists at Bay*, 415–17.

statement originally at John Tyler's request, but Polk's campaign used it most effectively. Walker had grown up in Pennsylvania and understood the mentality of the average northern Democrat well. He argued for Texas annexation primarily on economic grounds. Taking a leaf out of Henry Clay's book, he pointed out that Texas would enlarge the home market for American products. He also made the old Jeffersonian argument that expansion would "diffuse" the slave population into the West and make emancipation more likely in the Upper South. Looking still farther into the future, Walker predicted that when the inefficient labor of slaves had finally exhausted the soil of the Southwest, the blacks, no longer profitable to their masters, would at last be freed. Then Texas would provide a convenient conduit for the mass migration of the freedpeople into Latin America, where they would find a congenial multiracial society. Were Texas not to be annexed, he warned, emancipated slaves would probably flock northward, depressing wages and burdening northern states with their pauperism, insanity, and crime. Playing as it did on working-class fears, Walker's pamphlet, despite the perversity of its argument that Texas annexation would help get rid of slavery, had a plausible ring for northern white racists looking for reasons to believe that annexation would help the United States as a whole and not just the South. The Polk campaign distributed thousands of copies of it.[63]

All this left poor John Tyler with no distinctive campaign issue. His candidacy had forced southern Democrats to endorse Texas or watch their supporters flock over to him. Now, from the point of view of Democratic imperialists, his campaign had served its purpose. For him to stay in the race any longer would merely divide the expansionist vote. Flattering words from Jackson, together with assurances that his followers could rejoin the Democratic Party and not be excluded from patronage, smoothed the way for Tyler to withdraw his candidacy on August 20 and endorse Polk.[64] While unsuccessful, Tyler's long presidential campaign, of which his Texas treaty formed an integral part, had a huge impact on American history.

63. *Letter of Mr. Walker of Mississippi Relative to the Annexation of Texas* (Washington, 1844), rpt. in Frederick Merk, *Fruits of Propaganda in the Tyler Administration* (Cambridge, Mass., 1971), 221–52. Walker's rhetorical appeal is analyzed in Stephen Hartnett, *Democratic Dissent and the Cultural Fictions of Antebellum America* (Urbana, Ill., 2002), 103–31.

64. Michael Holt, *The Rise and Fall of the American Whig Party* (New York, 1999), 174–75.

The election of 1844 pitted two resolute, sharply defined, and closely matched party antagonists against each other. A majority of voters, perhaps a large majority, identified strongly with one party or the other and were not really open to persuasion. In the struggle to win over the undecided minority, the question of territorial expansion quickly dominated the campaign. Even without Texas or Oregon, the United States was larger than any European country except Russia. Democratic newspapers nevertheless portrayed national security as endangered by British interest in Texas. To this argument Henry Clay responded on behalf of the Whigs in his Raleigh Letter of April 17. He warned that annexation of Texas would bring war with Mexico, inflame sectional conflict within the United States, and encourage an insatiable lust for more and more land, a "spirit of universal dominion." Better the United States should cultivate friendship with both Canada (whose independence from Britain Clay foresaw) and an independent Texas.[65]

Debate over territorial expansion was by no means confined to its impact on the slavery issue, but extended to its implications for the whole future of America. Whigs preferred for the United States to concentrate its energies internally, on economic development, education, and social reform. Democrats, however, professed to find the trends in American domestic development ominous. "Our population has become comparatively dense; our new lands are exhausted," complained Orestes Brownson's Democratic *Quarterly Review*. "We are separating more and more, capital and labor, and have the beginnings of a constantly increasing operative class, unknown to our fathers, doomed always to be dependent on employment by the class who represent the capital of the country, for the means of subsistence."[66] Westward expansion, Democrats argued, would provide a safety valve and preserve America as a land of opportunity for white men. To Whigs, westward expansion seemed a recipe for continuing an undue reliance on agriculture and an inefficiently thin dispersion of population, perpetuating America's neocolonial dependence on foreign manufactures and capital.[67]

At first the Whigs felt confident of victory. James K. Polk (who had recently run for governor of Tennessee and lost) seemed too minor a figure to challenge the well-known Harry of the West. "Who's Polk?" Whig

---

65. Letter to the editors of the Washington *National Intelligencer*, April 17, 1844, *Papers of Henry Clay*, ed. Melba Hay (Lexington, Ky., 1991), X, 41–46.

66. *Brownson's Quarterly Review* 1 (Jan. 1844): 85.

67. See Michael Morrison, "Texas Annexation and the American Whig Party," *JER* 10 (1990): 221–49.

gatherings shouted in derision. But they changed their minds quickly as Polk mended his fences with the Van Buren loyalists, and the Texas issue displayed its effectiveness with the voting public. By July 27, Clay felt that his opposition to Texas annexation was hurting him so much in the South that he needed to publish a clarification. He declared that he "should be glad to see" Texas annexed—provided it could be accomplished "without dishonor, without war, with the common consent of the Union, and upon just and fair terms."[68] Obviously these conditions could not be met at the time of his writing, and indeed to list them was to restate his current objections to annexation. Nevertheless this statement disheartened some of Clay's antislavery northern supporters, while doing him little good in the South. (Van Buren had hedged his own anti-Texas stand with a similar provision for possible future annexation under changed circumstances.)

Polk had to resort to some fudging of his own position on the tariff. In a heavily publicized statement to Pennsylvania industrial workers, he declared that although he believed in a tariff for revenue only, he had no objection to "reasonable incidental protection to our home industry." Meanwhile, the Democratic nominee secretly assured southerners that he would reduce the tariff that had been raised in 1842. This behavior has been aptly characterized as "duplicitous," but it neutralized what should have been the appeal of the American System in Pennsylvania and played a key role in Polk's narrow victory there.[69]

In the South, despite the popularity of Texas, the Whig Party retained an appeal to voters in places wanting economic development and to producers of products like sugar and hemp that needed tariff protection. Townsmen and large planters continued to vote Whig because they needed a sound currency and banking system and took a dim view of the repudiation of state bonds. The extension of plantation agriculture into Texas, while it bid up the value of slaves, also had a downside from the planters' point of view: It lowered the value of their land and opened up more competition in cotton production. On the other hand, middle-sized and small cotton producers, whether slaveholders or yeomen, found westward expansion appealing because they saw in it their own best chance for upward economic mobility. Texas annexation, pitched as providing both economic opportunity and security for white supremacy, won over

---

68. Henry Clay to Thomas Peters and John Jackson, July 27, 1844, *Papers of Henry Clay*, X, 89–91. This is called Clay's "Second Alabama Letter." The First Alabama Letter, dated July 1, disavowed abolitionist support (X, 78–79).

69. Holt, *Rise and Fall of Whig Party*, 184. See also Brock, *Parties and Political Conscience*, 155.

most uncommitted southerners, especially young first-time voters, enabling Polk to run better in the South than Van Buren had done four years earlier. Clay carried only five slave states, all in the Upper South, whereas Harrison had won eight, including Louisiana, Mississippi, and Georgia.[70]

In the North the greater ethnic diversity of the electorate manifested itself in strong patterns of voting along cultural and religious lines. In many areas hard times had largely passed by the fall of 1844, so economic issues no longer seemed so urgent as they had in 1840, and ethnocultural divisions became all the more important. Territorial expansion raised moral questions involving slavery and America's role in the world, questions that different religious and cultural communities answered differently. Overall, Clay's opposition to Texas annexation helped him in most of the free states, though Polk's linkage of Texas to all of Oregon excited enthusiasm in what we now call the Midwest. The evangelical reformers rallied around Frelinghuysen as the Whig convention had intended, but his presence on the ticket also made things easier for Democratic campaign workers in Catholic neighborhoods. Relations between Catholics and Protestants had deteriorated in many places following increased Catholic immigration, Irish, German, and French-Canadian. In Philadelphia two waves of rioting, in May and July 1844, pitted the Irish Catholic and native Protestant working classes against each other and left at least twenty dead. When it came time to vote, Philadelphia Catholics went solidly for Polk. The Whigs struck a deal with the local nativist leaders but found that the Protestant workingmen, misled by Democratic claims to favor tariff protection, still cast a few votes for Polk. Although Clay won Philadelphia, it was not by a large enough margin to carry Pennsylvania.[71]

The outcome of the election hung in the balance as states voted throughout the first twelve days of November. The electoral college scored Polk 170 to Clay's 105, but this masked the closeness of the popular vote. Polk's plurality of 38,000 out of 2,700,000 votes cast gave him 49.5 percent to Clay's 48.1. The abolitionist James G. Birney, candidate of the Liberty Party, polled 62,000 votes, 2.3 percent of the total. While a small percentage, it affected the outcome; Birney took enough anti-annexation votes away from Clay to cost him New York and Michigan. If New York had gone the other way, Clay would have won the election. Massive Democratic electoral frauds also tipped the scales. In New York they

70. Holt, *Rise and Fall of Whig Party*, 199–201.
71. Sellers, "Election of 1844," 795. See also Michael Feldberg, *The Philadelphia Riots of 1844* (Westport, Conn., 1975).

voted large numbers of ineligible (noncitizen) immigrants. In the last analysis, Young Hickory may well have owed his victory less to his stand on Texas, so popular in the Deep South, than to the growing Catholic immigrant vote and the inability of Whigs like Seward to make a dent in it.[72]

It took six days for the returns from New York to reach Nashville. "I thank my god that the Republic is safe, & that he had permitted me to live to see it," declared Andrew Jackson after he learned that Polk had clinched the victory. "I can say in the language of Simeon of old 'Now let thy servant depart in peace.' "[73] Three months after Polk's inauguration, the old soldier did just that, on June 8, 1845. His commemorative eulogy was delivered in Washington by the distinguished historian George Bancroft, whom Polk had appointed secretary of the navy. We would expect a speaker on such an occasion to mention Jackson's patriotism, decisiveness, and capacity to inspire, his instinctive feeling for popular opinion. Bancroft employed romantic metaphor. He likened Old Hickory to "one of the mightiest forest trees of his own land, vigorous and colossal, sending its summit to the skies, and growing on its native soil in wild and inimitable magnificence." Jackson had embodied the principle that "submission is due to the popular will, in the confidence that the people, when in error, will amend their doings." Jackson's successful resistance to nullification meant to Bancroft "that the Union, which was constituted by consent, must be preserved by love."[74]

The chances that mutual love would preserve the Union did not look good to another learned analyst of American history and politics, John Quincy Adams. He read the election returns as evidence of the fragmentation and perversion of American republicanism. "The partial associations of Native Americans, Irish Catholics, abolition societies, liberty party, the Pope of Rome, the Democracy of the sword, and the dotage of a ruffian are sealing the fate of this nation, which nothing less than the interposition of Omnipotence can save."[75]

The consequences of the election of 1844 went far beyond Texas annexation, important as that was. If Henry Clay had won the White House, almost surely there would have been no Mexican War, no Wilmot Proviso, and therefore less reason for the status of slavery in the territories to

---

72. Holt, *Rise and Fall of Whig Party*, 203–4.
73. Jackson to Andrew Donelson, Nov. 18, 1844, *Correspondence of AJ*, VI, 329. Cf. Luke 2:29.
74. Quoted in Russel Nye, *George Bancroft* (New York, 1944), 150.
75. Jackson and Adams are quoted in Sellers, "Election of 1844," 796. By "Native Americans" Adams of course meant the nativists, not American Indians.

have inflamed sectional passions. Although he would have faced a Democratic Congress, President Clay would probably have strengthened the Whig Party through patronage and renewed its commitment to the American System. In the South, he would have encouraged moderation on the slavery issue, including the acceptance of an alternative future characterized by economic diversification and, in the long run, the gradual compensated emancipation which he advocated all his life. There might have been no reason for the Whig Party to disappear or a new Republican Party to emerge in the 1850s. After the Civil War, the great newspaper editor Horace Greeley declared that if Clay had been elected in 1844, "great and lasting public calamities would thereby have been averted." More recently, some historians have carefully examined the likely consequences of a Clay victory in 1844 and concluded that it would probably have avoided the Civil War of the 1860s.[76] We too readily assume the inevitability of everything that has happened. The decisions that electorates and politicians make have real consequences.

IV

Communication has always been a priority for empires, including the Roman, Chinese, and Incan. The messengers of the ancient Persian empire inspired the famous encomium of Herodotus, "Neither rain, nor snow, nor heat, nor gloom of night stays these couriers from the swift completion of their appointed rounds."[77] The first postal system available for public use was created in the fifteenth century by the German Emperor Maximilian I. In the 1790s, the French Revolutionary government originated, and Napoleon subsequently expanded and perfected, the fastest and most efficient communication network the world had yet seen: a system of what we would call semaphores placed about six miles apart, capable of relaying signals whenever visibility permitted. Besides facilitating political control and military operations, it typified the Enlightenment ideal of rationality. Other countries imitated the system on a smaller scale.[78]

---

76. Horace Greeley, *Recollections of a Busy Life* (New York, 1868), 168; Michael Holt, *Political Parties and American Political Development from the Age of Jackson to the Age of Lincoln* (Baton Rouge, 1992), 17–18; Gary Kornblith, "Rethinking the Coming of the Civil War: A Counterfactual Exercise," *JAH* 90 (2003): 76–105. Tom Wicker explores the related question, what if Harrison had not died in office? See his essay in *What Ifs? of American History*, ed. Robert Cowley (New York, 2003), 57–65.

77. Inscribed on the central U.S. Post Office in New York City.

78. See Daniel Headrick, *When Information Came of Age* (Oxford, 2000), 197–203.

To describe long-distance optical signaling, the word "telegraph," meaning long-distance written communication, came into the European languages. Americans too employed optical signals of various kinds, though seldom in relays; they are commemorated in innumerable "telegraph hills" and "beacon hills." By the 1820s, "telegraph" had become a popular name for newspapers, like the Jacksonian *United States Telegraph*, edited by Duff Green. The ambitious Postmaster General John McLean projected an optical telegraph relay for the United States, but capital was scarce, and a semaphore system, complete with trained operators and cryptographers to translate the signals, cost a lot. Nevertheless, by 1840, an optical telegraph line functioned between New York and Philadelphia, though only its owners were allowed to use it.[79]

In May 1844, politicians in Washington felt eager to learn news from the party conventions taking place in Baltimore, forty miles away. Help was at hand, for in March 1843 Congress had finally passed, after years of earnest lobbying, an appropriation of thirty thousand dollars for a Professor Samuel Finley Breese Morse (Finley to his family) to demonstrate an electromagnetic telegraph line between Washington and Baltimore. Morse and his team first tried laying the wire underground, but insulation problems forced them to string the lines on poles aboveground. When the Whig National Convention met on May first, the wire still stretched only about halfway to Baltimore. But Morse's associate Alfred Vail got the news from the train at Annapolis Junction and telegraphed it ahead to Washington. The information that the Whig Party had nominated Henry Clay for president and Theodore Frelinghuysen for vice president arrived an hour and fifteen minutes before the train did. By the time of the formal opening of the telegraph all the way to Baltimore on May 24, no doubt existed that it would work. From the chambers of the United States Supreme Court, Morse transmitted to Vail the famous message, WHAT HATH GOD WROUGHT.[80] When the Democratic convention began three days later, some privileged politicians huddled around Morse receiving up-to-the-minute reports, while hundreds of others outside (many of them members of Congress) tried to gain entrance or at least view the information he posted on the door. "Little else is done here but watch Professor Morse's Bulletin from Baltimore, to learn the progress of doings at Convention," a reporter for the *New York Herald*

79. Richard John, *Spreading the News: The United States Postal System from Franklin to Morse* (Cambridge, Mass., 1995), 86–89.
80. For the origin of the phrase, see the Introduction to this book.

told his paper.[81] The Democratic convention used the telegraph to offer the second spot on its ticket to Martin Van Buren's friend Silas Wright; he declined it via the same medium, and the party then turned to the Pennsylvania doughface George Dallas.

Professor Morse seemed an unlikely inventor. He was not a scientist, engineer, or mathematician but a professor of fine arts at New York University. A distinguished portrait painter, he had aspired to nurture American nationhood and shape public taste through painting historical panoramas and founding the National Academy of Design.[82] When in 1837 Congress denied him a commission to paint a historical mural for the Capitol Rotunda, Morse felt so bitterly disappointed that he gave up painting and turned his energies instead to developing an electric telegraph, a project that had engaged his attention off and on since 1832. Morse's surprising combination of artistic and technological creativity has caused him to be labeled (somewhat hyperbolically) "the American Leonardo." But two important themes provide continuity between Morse's art and telegraphy: his Calvinistic Protestantism and his American imperialism. Both of these preoccupations he had inherited from his father, Jedidiah Morse, Congregational minister and famous geographer, who prophesied that America would create "the largest Empire that ever existed."[83] If Finley Morse could not serve America's providential destiny through painting, he would help fulfill it with electromagnetic current.

A series of international scientific advances paved the way for Morse's demonstration. Alessandro Volta had invented the electric battery in 1800; Hans Christian Oersted and André Marie Ampère researched electromagnetic signals; William Sturgeon devised the electromagnet in 1824; and in 1831 the American physicist Joseph Henry announced his method for strengthening the intensity of an electromagnet so that the current could be transmitted across long distances. Leonard Gale, a professor of chemistry at NYU, called Henry's work to the attention of his colleague in fine arts and became a junior partner in Morse's enterprise. In 1837, they demonstrated the ability to send a signal through ten miles of wire. The Jackson administration, ever mindful of the Southwest, had taken an interest in the possibility of an American counterpart to the French optical telegraph to speed communication with New Orleans. The Van Buren

81. Kenneth Silverman, *Lightning Man: The Accursed Life of Samuel F. B. Morse* (New York, 2003), 233–38.
82. On Morse's career as a painter, see Paul Staiti, *Samuel F. B. Morse* (Cambridge, Eng., 1989).
83. Jedidiah Morse, *American Geography* (1789; New York, 1960), 469.

administration continued this interest. In September 1837, Morse wrote Secretary of the Treasury Levi Woodbury describing his own plan for a new kind of telegraph, based on electricity. To design the apparatus itself, Morse entered into a second partnership, one with Alfred Vail, an experienced machinist whose father owned a major ironworks and could provide some investment capital. Secretary Woodbury was impressed, but to secure financial aid from the government, Morse needed an act of Congress. When he took his project before the House Commerce Committee, chairman Francis Smith, a Maine Democrat, insisted on being made another partner in Morse's enterprise. Morse reluctantly consented, whereupon Smith enthusiastically recommended the project to Congress, making no mention of his own interest in it.[84] It proved a bad bargain. The favorable committee report did not win congressional approval for the grant, and in the years ahead Smith's shameless self-seeking would make trouble for Morse.

Morse had grown up in a New England Federalist household and retained an elitist social outlook. Nevertheless, during his time in New York he became a Democrat in politics, like his literary friends James Fenimore Cooper, Washington Irving, and William Cullen Bryant (and like so many in the New York trading community). But in spite of Morse's party affiliation, the corrupt support of Smith, and the imperial vision of Woodbury, a Democratic Congress evidently found Morse's project too much like federal aid to internal improvements to endorse. Not until the Whigs controlled Congress did the Democrat Morse get his grant approved in 1843. It carried in the House only narrowly, 89 to 83, with many abstentions.[85] Very likely Morse's vociferous anti-Catholicism, unpopular with Congress, contributed to both his failure to get the painting commission in 1837 and the later political reluctance to endorse his invention.

Morse assumed that the federal government should control the electric telegraph. "It would seem most natural," he declared, to "connect a telegraphic system with the Post Office Department; for, although it does not carry a mail, yet it is another mode of accomplishing the principal object for which the mail is established, to wit: the rapid and regular transmission of intelligence."[86] The French optical telegraph was owned by its

---

84. Paul Starr, *The Creation of the Media: Political Origins of Modern Communications* (New York, 2004), 157–61.

85. The vote is analyzed in Carleton Mabee, *The American Leonardo* (New York, 1943), 258–59.

86. S.F.B. Morse to Levi Woodbury, Sept. 27, 1837, quoted in Richard John, "Private Enterprise, Public Good?" in Pasley, *Beyond the Founders*, 339–40.

government (private persons were not even allowed to use it). With the Baltimore-Washington line having demonstrated practicality, Morse tried to get the administration to buy the rights to the electric telegraph. He persuaded Tyler's postmaster general, but not the president himself. Henry Clay wrote to Alfred Vail shortly before the election of 1844 that he believed "such an engine ought to be exclusively under the control of the government."[87] But Polk won the election, and his platform declared against aid to internal improvements. Not even Amos Kendall, Jackson's postmaster general and kitchen-cabinet member, whom Morse named president of the Magnetic Telegraph Company, could win Polk over. The administration sold off the Washington-Baltimore link, and private enterprise strung the rest of American telegraph lines.

Meanwhile bitter fights ensued between the cantankerous Morse and his partners, Morse and scientists like Joseph Henry who felt he denied them due credit, and Morse and rival companies that he accused of infringing on his patent. Those who contested his claim to have invented the telegraph included Charles T. Jackson, the same Harvard chemistry professor who also contested William Morton's claim to have developed anesthesia. Dr. Jackson had actually given advice on both projects but had pursued neither idea himself. As a result posterity has forgotten a man who played a part in both of the two greatest inventions of the 1840s. Morse, on the other hand, eventually became rich and famous, honored the world over. And he always got along with Kendall, who shared his Calvinism and his proslavery but pro-Union Democratic politics.[88] From 1866 on, the Western Union Company, in which Morse held a large interest, dominated the American telegraph network. He had consistently believed the telegraph to be what a later generation would term a natural monopoly, and it eventually became, if not a public monopoly, virtually a private one.[89]

Inventors in several nations had been at work on an electric telegraph, although most European countries needed it less than the United States because distance posed less of a problem for them. The Austrian Empire, whose autocratic and Catholic regime Morse loathed, ironically led in overseas adoption of his invention. The British already had an electric telegraph of their own, developed by the distinguished scientist Charles

---

87. Quoted in Mabee, *American Leonardo*, 163.
88. Silverman, *Lightning Man*, 259–64; 429; Albert Moyer, *Joseph Henry* (New York, 1997), 239–47; Donald Cole, *A Jackson Man: Amos Kendall* (Baton Rouge, 2004), 246–50, 301.
89. See Richard John, "The Politics of Innovation," *Daedalus* 127 (1998): 187–214.

Wheatstone, in operation since 1838 on a few lines, but Morse's system worked better, and the British gradually converted to it. The French fell into line slowly because of their commitment to the optical telegraph. Russia, like the United States, needed the telegraph to overcome giant distances, but at first the tsar refused to string the lines for fear they would facilitate political opposition.

In the United States, decades of long-term economic expansion only temporarily reversed by downturns after 1819 and 1837 encouraged the business community to accord the electric telegraph an enthusiastic reception. Investment bankers had always prized quick news. The Rothschilds in London had used carrier pigeons to learn of Wellington's defeat of Napoleon at Waterloo before anyone else did; they bought British government bonds and realized a quick profit when their value rose once the victory became widely known. Following Morse's demonstration, telegraph lines appeared rapidly in North America, chiefly in order to transmit the prices of stocks and commodities. They helped integrate financial markets so borrowers and lenders could find each other more easily. Accordingly, they first connected commercial centers: New York, Philadelphia, Boston, Buffalo, Toronto. The Philadelphia *North American* welcomed the telegraph with the pronouncement: "The markets will no longer be dependent upon snail paced mails." Remarkably, the wires reached Chicago by 1848, enabling the Chicago Commodities Exchange to open that year.[90]

Like the early railroads and steamboats, early telegraph lines were constructed in haste and as cheaply as possible—using "beanpoles and cornstalks," according to the standard joke. As a result they often malfunctioned and broke down. Data collected in 1851 identified about 70 percent of their traffic as commercial in nature, such as checking credit references from distant locations or (as one telegraph operator put it) "conveying secrets of rise and fall of markets." The wires helped validate classical economics for the Western world by making its assumption of "perfect information" among market participants more of a practical reality.[91]

---

90. See Charles Geist, *Wall Street*, rev. ed. (New York, 2004), 39; James Carey, *Communication as Culture* (Boston, 1989), 218. Quotation from the *North American*, Jan. 15, 1846, p. 2.

91. Richard DuBoff, "Business Demand and the Development of the Telegraph in the United States," *Business History Review* 54 (1980): 459–79, quotation from 468. Technical but revealing is Kenneth Garbade and William Silber, "Technology, Communication, and the Performance of Financial Markets, 1840–1975," *Journal of Finance* 33 (1978): 819–32.

Unlike the telephone, invented later in the nineteenth century, the telegraph was used much more for commercial than social purposes. But telegraph wires also carried news of sports events and lotteries for the benefit of avid gamblers. Their value to the newspapers became apparent very quickly during the war against Mexico that began in 1846. When that war started, only 146 miles of telegraph lines existed, none of them south of Richmond. With construction stimulated by the hunger for war news, the wires arrived at New Orleans in 1848, connecting it with New York sooner than the railroad did. By 1850, ten thousand miles of wire had been laid in the United States.[92]

In economic importance, the electric telegraph bears comparison with the railroad. In combination with the railroad, it facilitated nationwide commerce and diminished transaction costs. Whereas both railroads and canals had originally been envisioned as regional (typically, joining a commercial hub with an agricultural hinterland), the electric telegraph from the outset was a long-distance medium that linked commercial centers. Being cheaper to construct than railroad tracks, the telegraph lines generally realized their economic potential more quickly. One of the most dramatic practical benefits of the electric telegraph lay in its assistance to the railroads in scheduling trains and avoiding collisions on single-track lines. Surprisingly, it took several years for the railroads to recognize this.[93] In the end, the telegraph poles often paralleled railroad tracks and used the same rights-of-way.

In a broader sense, however, the spread of the electric telegraph effectively decoupled communication from transportation, sending a message from sending a physical object. The implications of this alteration in the human condition unfolded only gradually over the next several generations. But contemporaries fully realized that they stood in the presence of a far-reaching change. They valued not only the shortening of time to receive information but also the speed with which an answer could be returned; that is, conversation was possible. To call attention to its interactive potential, early demonstrations of the telegraph included long-distance chess games.[94] Of all the celebrated inventions of an age that believed in progress, Morse's

92. For more examples of the value of information to the economy, see John McCusker, "The Demise of Distance: The Business Press and the Origins of the Information Revolution in the Early Modern Atlantic World," *AHR* 110 (2005): 295–321.

93. Richard John, "Recasting the Information Infrastructure for the Industrial Age," in *A Nation Transformed by Information*, ed. Alfred Chandler and James Cortada (New York, 2000), 75, 84.

94. Menahem Blondheim, *News over the Wires: The Telegraph and the Flow of Public Information in America, 1844–1897* (Cambridge, Mass., 1994), 11–29.

telegraph impressed observers the most. They typically characterized it as "the greatest revolution of modern times." A leading New Orleans journal commented, "Scarcely anything now will appear to be impossible."[95]

The electric telegraph represented the first important invention based on the application of advanced scientific knowledge rather than on the know-how of skilled mechanics. The laboratory would begin to replace the machine shop as the site of technological innovation. For centuries, technological improvements had led to scientific discovery (the telescope and the microscope, for example). With the telegraph, this relationship reversed. Morse's recruitment of several partners and his refusal to credit others whose ideas had contributed to his technology highlighted another transition. Innovation would increasingly become a collective enterprise, pooling the knowledge of experts.[96] "Morse was only one of over fifty inventors who built some sort of an electromagnetic telegraphic device before 1840," the historian Donald Cole has pointed out. "Morse's telegraph prevailed because it was better built, less complicated, and less expensive than the others and because he was able to fight off the claims of his rivals."[97]

The telegraph associated, rightly or wrongly, with Morse proved a major facilitator of American nationalism and continental ambition. Although funding for it had to come from Whig votes in Congress, Democratic publicists seized upon the significance of the telegraph for their imperial visions: John L. O'Sullivan's *Democratic Review* rejoiced that the American empire now possessed "a vast skeleton framework of railroads, and an infinitely ramified nervous system of magnetic telegraphs" to knit it into an organic whole. A congressional committee agreed: "Doubt has been entertained by many patriotic minds how far the rapid, full, and thorough intercommunication of thought and intelligence, so necessary to the people living under a common representative republic, could be expected to take place throughout such immense bounds" as the North American continent. "That doubt can no longer exist."[98] James Gordon Bennett, editor of the *New York Herald*, was more militantly

95. "Morse's Electro-Magnetic Telegraph," *De Bow's Review* 1 (1846): 133.
96. David Hochfelder, "Taming the Lightning: American Telegraphy in a Revolutionary Technology" (Ph.D. diss., Case Western Reserve University, 1999); Paul Israel, *From Machine Shop to Industrial Laboratory* (Baltimore, 1992).
97. Cole, *Amos Kendall*, 245.
98. *Democratic Review*, quoted in William Weeks, *Building the Continental Empire* (Chicago, 1996), 85; U.S. House of Representatives, Ways and Means Committee Report, 1845, quoted in Daniel Czitrom, *Media and the American Mind* (Chapel Hill, 1982), 12.

imperialist. "Steam and electricity, with the natural impulses of a free people, have made, and are making, this country the greatest, the most original, the most wonderful the sun ever shone upon," his newspaper enthused. "Those who do not become part of this movement" of U.S. sovereignty across the continent "will be crushed into more impalpable powder than ever was attributed to the car of Juggernaut."[99] With the telegraph on America's side, who could dare oppose the acquisition of Texas?

V

John Tyler and James Polk agreed that the presidential election must be interpreted as a mandate for Texas, notwithstanding all the other factors that had entered into the result, and the plain truth that the two candidates opposed to annexation had slightly outpolled the one who favored it. Tyler felt a certain understandable resentment that Polk should have stolen his annexation issue and won with it. He was not willing, therefore, to stand aside and let Polk reap the glory of annexing Texas. The lame duck session of Congress that began in December 1844 offered the outgoing president a final chance to achieve his rightful place in the history books. Tyler seized it.

The Constitution provides that "New States may be admitted by the Congress into this Union." The friends of annexation argued that through the exercise of this power, Texas could be admitted to statehood without a treaty, even though it remained a foreign country. Such an act of Congress would require only a simple majority in each house, a much more attainable goal than the two-thirds of the Senate needed to ratify a treaty. Accordingly, the annexationists set about passage of a congressional resolution that would make Texas a state of the Union despite the failure of Tyler's treaty. Resorting to this approach had been the idea of Jackson himself, and the Democrats, under president-elect Polk's leadership, made it a party measure.[100] The substantial Democratic majority in the House of Representatives passed Texas admission handily. Passage in the Senate, with its narrow Whig majority, posed a task more difficult but not insurmountable.

Thomas Hart Benton had opposed Tyler's Texas treaty as a Van Buren loyalist. By now, Van Buren had lost, an expansionist Democrat had won, Jackson was supporting annexation ever more strongly, and the Missouri senator was feeling a lot of heat from his constituents. He needed to come

99. Quoted in Silverman, *Lightning Man*, 243.
100. Andrew Jackson to William Lewis, May 3, 1844, *Correspondence of AJ*, VI, 282.

around to support Texas. Various concessions provided an excuse for Benton and the other Van Burenites in the Senate to switch from opposition to approval of annexation. The federal government did not assume the Texas national debt, keeping the Lone Star bondholders waiting to be sure of repayment. (Later, Uncle Sam took over the responsibility for paying off the speculators as part of the Compromise of 1850.) Texas also kept what remained of its public lands after the huge grants that Spain, Mexico, and the Lone Star Republic had all made over the years. Texas received admission as a state, not a territory, with the proviso that it might later be subdivided into as many as five states. This provision, never implemented, horrified northern Whigs. Finally, the resolution stipulated that the president could exercise executive discretion, and either act upon it to admit Texas forthwith or negotiate further with Texas (and Mexico) to resolve the still-undefined boundary between them. Polk encouraged Benton and other former Van Burenites to believe he intended to return to the negotiating table; this seemed to reassure five of them in voting for the resolution.

The annexation resolution passed the Democratic-controlled House, 120 to 98. It squeaked through the Senate, 27 to 25. All Democratic senators followed their party's pro-Texas line, but three out of the fifteen southern Whigs put section ahead of party and voted for annexation. The way in which Tyler and Calhoun achieved their objective by a simple majority of each House, even though the treaty of annexation had been defeated in the Senate, infuriated John Quincy Adams; he thought it reduced the Constitution to "a menstruous [sic!] rag."[101]

Strangely enough, no one in Congress seems to have expected that Tyler would go ahead and implement the annexation resolution during the waning days of his presidency rather than leave it to Polk. But Secretary of State Calhoun felt even more eager to consummate the marriage with Texas than Tyler. On March 1, 1845, Tyler signed the joint resolution and gave his new wife, Julia Gardiner Tyler, the golden pen he had used. Wealthy, energetic, and publicity-conscious, she had lobbied hard for Texas and deserved to share in their exultation. He dispatched an envoy to offer the Texans immediate annexation without any further international negotiations. Not that it really mattered: Polk would have done the same, and he confirmed Tyler's action. The Van Burenites had been tricked.[102]

---

101. John Quincy Adams, *Memoirs*, ed. Charles Francis Adams (Philadelphia, 1874–79), XII, 171.
102. Charles Sellers, *James K. Polk, Continentalist* (Princeton, 1966), 215–20; Crapol, *John Tyler*, 220.

Calhoun's strategy for gaining Texas had triumphed. His short-term goal in identifying Texas with slavery had been to make sure that Van Buren would have to oppose Texas and thus be denied the Democratic nomination. His longer-term goals, the election of a proslavery president and the annexation of Texas, had also been achieved. The identification of Texas with slavery won over first the southern Democrats, then (through the mechanism of party loyalty) most Northern Democrats, and finally a handful of southern Whigs provided the crucial margin.[103]

After four frustrating years, John Tyler left office feeling good. The first lady threw a huge party attended by three thousand at the White House, and the outgoing president laughed as he quipped, "They cannot say *now* that I am a President *without a party*."[104] As Tyler and Calhoun intended, the annexation of Texas reassured slaveowners about the security of their distinctive form of investment and its potential for further expansion. Within twelve months of the Lone Star Republic's acceptance of annexation, the price of prime field hands on the New Orleans slave market rose 21 percent. It would continue to rise through the 1850s. And the arrival of the telegraph wires at New Orleans in 1848 integrated the cotton bales and slave pens of that city all the more effectively into the flourishing international pricing network for southern staple crops and the commodified human beings who produced them.[105]

103. See Cooper, *Politics of Slavery*, 194, 205; Freehling, *Secessionists at Bay*, 409–10.
104. Quoted in Peterson, *Presidencies of Harrison and Tyler*, 259.
105. Ulrich B. Phillips, *Life and Labor in the Old South* (1929; Boston, 1963), graph on 177.

18

Westward the Star of Empire

The fourth of March 1845: Rain fell on the inaugural parade along Pennsylvania Avenue, and when the new president arrived at the Capitol to deliver his address and take the oath of office from Chief Justice Taney, he looked out upon a sea of umbrellas. Despite the unfavorable elements, James Knox Polk made himself heard, as he would for the next four years. The speech was characteristic of the man. It rehearsed Democratic Party orthodoxies, perhaps traceable to Polk's family background in the rustic simplicity and Old School Calvinism of Mecklenburg County, North Carolina. Abolitionism and a national bank he roundly condemned in the speech.

When Jimmy Polk had been eleven, his parents moved for better economic opportunities to Middle Tennessee, where his father became a successful land speculator. The son hence grew up in a prominent and prosperous family. He too identified the acquisition of land with wealth and power, on a national as well as individual scale. Ambitious and hardworking, he graduated first in his class at the University of North Carolina and became a lawyer. Soon he went into politics, as a devoted follower of Andrew Jackson. Speaking for the producers of agricultural staples, he argued for free trade. During the Bank War, he made himself the Jackson administration's most effective congressional ally. At forty-nine the youngest president so far, Polk nevertheless had accumulated considerable leadership experience as governor of Tennessee and Speaker of the national House of Representatives. He had also recently demonstrated consummate political skills: by gaining the confidence of both the Jackson and Calhoun wings of the Democratic Party, by securing that party's nomination at the last moment, and by winning a hard-fought, close election.

Yet people found James Polk a narrow man with a dull personality, for he focused on the interests of his country and his personal advancement, caring nothing for the delights of literature, nature, or society. Even as president he made few public appearances. John Quincy Adams, a former professor of rhetoric, gave Polk low marks as a speaker; he found "no wit," "no gracefulness of delivery," "no elegance of language," "no felicitous impromptus."[1] In choosing a wife, Polk had asked Jackson's opinion;

---

1. Quoted in Sam Haynes, *James K. Polk* (New York, 1997), 18.

Old Hickory recommended the wealthy and intelligent Sarah Childress, and his follower acted on the nomination. Very much a political person too, Sarah told James she would marry him if he won a seat in the state legislature. She then became her husband's only confidante, sharing in his career goals and giving him valuable advice. The childless couple focused on James's political advancement. A staunch Presbyterian, Sarah banned dancing and card-playing in the White House but not wine, and supervised the installation of up-to-date gaslights. Meanwhile, the Polks carefully developed the cotton plantation they owned in northern Mississippi, to which they planned to retire. As president, James bought nineteen slaves for this plantation, keeping the purchases a secret because they contradicted his public image as the master of only a few inherited family retainers. The people he bought were teenagers whom his acquisition separated from their parents.[2]

In his inaugural address, the incoming president remained just as ambiguous on the tariff as he had during his campaign—occasional ambiguity being a political art James Polk understood particularly well. Then the new incumbent turned to what interested him most, his vision of continental expansion. Echoing the arguments of Robert Walker, he gave a ringing endorsement to the annexation of Texas, regardless of its impact on the slavery question. Wherever Americans chose to settle, Polk declared, the federal government should extend its protection over them, a principle he applied to both Texas and Oregon. He repeated the assertion of the Democratic platform: "Our title to the country of Oregon is clear and unquestionable." This bald affirmation went down well with those under the umbrellas, but when the text arrived across the Atlantic, it made a bad impression. "We consider we [too] have rights in this Oregon territory which are clear and unquestionable," Prime Minister Peel responded in the House of Commons. No one at the time remarked that the incoming president had left out the words "the whole of " in restating his party's Oregon platform, but their omission may have been a straw in the wind.[3]

To James Knox Polk, the imperial destiny of the United States manifested itself plainly enough. But it would be the press, not a presidential oration, that fixed the term "manifest destiny" for the American public. In the summer of 1845, one of America's most popular magazines, New

2. William Dusinberre, *Slavemaster President: The Double Career of James Polk* (New York, 2003).

3. *Presidential Messages*, IV, 381; *Hansard's Parliamentary Debates*, 3rd ser., 79 (April 1845): 199; David Pletcher, *Diplomacy of Annexation* (Columbia, Mo., 1973), 236–41.

York's Jacksonian *Democratic Review*, addressed the Texas issue. Annexation still awaited ratification by a popular vote of the Texans; in the United States, public opinion remained bitterly divided. Nevertheless, the *Review* argued, "It is time now for opposition to the annexation of Texas to cease." The integration of Texas into the Union represented "the fulfilment [*sic*] of our manifest destiny to overspread the continent allotted by Providence for the free development of our yearly multiplying millions."[4] The article, like many in nineteenth-century journalism, appeared unsigned, but historians have long believed it must have been written by the zealous partisan editor of the *Democratic Review*, John L. O'Sullivan. Recently, however, it has been argued that the ardent expansionist Jane Storm, a professional political journalist who wrote frequently for that and other periodicals, anonymously or under the gender-neutral pseudonym C. Montgomery, wrote the essay.[5] Whoever invented it, the phrase "manifest destiny" passed into the American language, an illustration of the power of the press to capture the popular imagination with a slogan in an age of communications revolution.

"Manifest destiny" served as both a label and a justification for policies that might otherwise have simply been called American expansionism or imperialism. The assumption of white supremacy permeated these policies. It never occurred to U.S. policymakers to take seriously the claims of nonwhite or racially mixed societies to territorial integrity. Antebellum Americans did not shrink from calling their continental domain an "empire." Thomas Jefferson looked forward to creating an "empire for liberty" that would include Cuba and Canada. In this empire he expected white family farming to have room to expand for generations to come, and the economic basis for Jefferson's ideal republic would be preserved against historical degeneration. Old Hickory himself drew a connection between America's democracy and imperial expansion—"extending the area for freedom," as he put it.[6] The "Young Hickory" asserted that expansion actually guaranteed American national existence. "As our boundaries have been enlarged and our agricultural population has been spread over a large surface," the Union of the states has been strengthened. "If our present population were confined to the comparatively narrow limits of the

4. "Annexation," *Democratic Review* 17 (July 1845): 5.
5. Linda Hudson, *Mistress of Manifest Destiny* (Austin, Tex., 2001), 60–62. This attribution is questioned by Robert Sampson, *John L. O'Sullivan and His Times* (Kent, Ohio, 2003), 244–45.
6. Thomas Jefferson to James Madison, April 27, 1809, *Writings of Thomas Jefferson*, ed. Andrew Lipscomb (Washington, 1905), XII, 274–77; Andrew Jackson to Aaron V. Brown, Feb. 9, 1843, in *Correspondence of AJ*, VI, 201.

original thirteen states," the incoming president warned, American institutions might be "in greater danger of overthrow." Recognizing the key role of the press in building support for territorial expansion, Polk replaced Francis Blair's *Washington Globe*, which had served Jackson and Van Buren, with a new administration newspaper, the *Washington Union*, edited by Thomas Ritchie, a more enthusiastic imperialist.[7]

National aspirations to empire could fit comfortably alongside certain conceptions of American millennialism. As the South Carolina poet William Gilmore Simms wrote in 1846:

> We do but follow out our destiny,
> As did the ancient Israelite—and strive,
> Unconscious that we work at His knee
> By whom alone we triumph as we live.[8]

If America had a divine mission to perform, to be a beacon of freedom and prepare the way for a messianic age, then perhaps increasing its extent and power would bring blessings to the whole world. "A higher than any earthly power," declared Robert Walker, propagandist for Texas whom Polk would appoint secretary of the Treasury, "still guards and directs our destiny, impels us onward, and has selected our great and happy country as a model and ultimate centre of attraction for the all nations of the world."[9] When George Bancroft, the greatest American historian of his day and an enthusiastic Jacksonian Democrat, published the first volume of his *History of the United States of America* in 1834, it appeared with this motto on the cover: "Westward the star of empire takes its way." Bancroft's history portrayed his country fulfilling a providential destiny as an example of human liberty. His epigraph makes an appropriate title for this chapter.[10]

Antebellum Americans typically linked the history of political liberty with Protestantism. Accordingly, it was possible to argue that the expansion of the United States would secure the continent for liberty and Protestantism, and save it from Catholic Mexico, whose "cruel, ambitious, and licentious priesthood," according to Robert Walker, stood ever

---

7. *Presidential Messages*, IV, 380; Joel Silbey, *Storm over Texas* (Oxford, 2005), 102.
8. William Gilmore Simms, "Progress in America," quoted in Anders Stephanson, *Manifest Destiny* (New York, 1995), 48.
9. Robert J. Walker, "Report as Secretary of the Treasury for Fiscal Year 1846–47," *Niles' Register* 73 (Dec. 18, 1847): 255.
10. Bancroft misquoted a poem by the Irish philosopher and bishop George Berkeley, "Westward the course of empire takes its way." I have taken this chapter title from Bancroft rather than Berkeley.

"ready to establish the inquisition." Despite the support Catholic voters gave the Democratic Party, anti-Catholicism was featured alongside claims of Anglo-Saxon racial superiority in the rhetoric of Jacksonian expansionists like Walker.[11]

Support for the pursuit of a "manifest destiny" came from a number of groups in American society. Western land speculators, railroad promoters, and small farmers eager for a chance to start over had obvious interests in westward expansion. Many northern workingmen saw westward expansion as guaranteeing economic opportunity and high wages; the penny press in the big cities encouraged such attitudes and celebrated American imperialism. The *New York Morning News*, edited, like the *Democratic Review*, by John L. O'Sullivan, cast westward expansion as an example of the participatory democracy of free settlers:

> To say that the settlement of a fertile and unappropriated soil by right of individual purchase is the aggression of a government is absurd. Equally ridiculous is it to suppose that when a band of hardy settlers have reclaimed the wilderness, multiplied in numbers, built up a community and organized a government, that they have not the right to claim the confederation of that society of States from the bosom of which they emanated.[12]

But the *Morning News* did not tell the whole story. It postulated a vacant continent, ignoring the prior claims of Native Americans and Mexicans. What is more, often those advocating national expansion also advocated the extension of slavery. Debate over the wisdom and morality of national expansion provoked renewed debate over the future of slavery. Expansion in one direction or another could be supported or opposed as strengthening one section at the expense of the other. Most powerfully, party politics influenced the discussion. Jackson's followers wanted to continue Jefferson's policy of extending a predominantly agrarian America across the continent. Expansionism served the Democratic Party's political interests. The pursuit of the nation's "manifest destiny" could mute conflict between native and immigrant workingmen and under favorable circumstances bridge sectional divisions, since it appealed in the Old Northwest as well as the South.

Nevertheless, American imperialism did not represent an American consensus; it provoked bitter dissent within the national polity. The

---

11. John Pinheiro, "Anti-Catholicism, All Mexico, and the Treaty of Guadalupe Hidalgo," *JER* 23 (2003): 69–96; Walker is quoted on 78.

12. *New York Morning News*, May 24, 1845, quoted in Frederick Merk, *Manifest Destiny and Mission in American History* (New York, 1963), 22–23.

Whig Party conceived of American development more in terms of qualitative economic improvement than quantitative expansion of territory. As Henry Clay wrote to a fellow Kentuckian, "It is much more important that we unite, harmonize, and improve what we have than attempt to acquire more." The historian Christopher Clark has distinguished between the two partisan goals by saying the Democrats pursued America's "extensive" development and the Whigs its "intensive" development.[13] Whigs believed in America's postmillennial role too, but interpreted it differently. They saw America's moral mission as one of democratic example rather than one of conquest. William Ellery Channing expressed a Whig view of America's empire in a famous open letter to Clay opposing the annexation of Texas: "The United States ought to provide its less fortunate sister republics with support, [and] assume the role of a sublime moral empire, with a mission to diffuse freedom by manifesting its fruits, not to plunder, crush, and destroy."[14]

Although the Whigs resisted territorial expansion through conquest, they practiced what we might consider economic and cultural imperialism through expanding trade and Christian missions. Daniel Webster, during his tenure at the State Department, put Whig principles of foreign policy into practice, not only by resolving tensions with Britain but also by extending U.S. commercial opportunities in the Pacific. New England whaling vessels had long made use of the Hawaiian Islands (then called the Sandwich Islands) as a supply base en route to the Bering Sea. Although Hawaii remained an independent native monarchy, Yankee sugar merchants and Protestant missionaries also exerted considerable influence. These American interests became alarmed when France intervened in the islands to protect Catholics, simultaneously obtaining trade concessions. Responding to their concerns, Webster persuaded the president to extend the Monroe Doctrine's opposition to European interference to include Hawaii. This statement, made in December 1842, became known as the Tyler Doctrine; it preserved U.S. economic primacy in the Sandwich Islands. When an overly zealous Royal Navy admiral annexed Hawaii to the British Empire the following spring, London disavowed his action without even waiting to receive an American

13. Henry Clay to John J. Crittenden, Dec. 5, 1843, *Papers of Henry Clay*, ed. Robert Seager II (Lexington, Ky., 1988), IX, 898; Christopher Clark, *Social Change in America: From the Revolution Through the Civil War* (Chicago, 2006), 205–6.
14. "Letter to the Hon. Henry Clay on the Annexation of Texas," Aug. 1, 1837, in William Ellery Channing, *Works* (Boston, 1847), II, 181–261.

protest; by the end of 1843 both Britain and France had promised to respect Hawaiian independence.[15]

Meanwhile, Britain had extorted by the Anglo-Chinese Opium War major trade concessions in East Asia, including a lease on Hong Kong. American (chiefly New England) shipowners and merchants worried that they would now be excluded from the lucrative China trade they had cultivated since 1784. To forestall any such development, Webster's close associate, Caleb Cushing (from Newburyport, Massachusetts, historic center of the China trade) negotiated in 1844 the Treaty of Wanghai, by which the Chinese Empire accorded the United States most-favored-nation status in trade. But congressional approval for the China mission had had to be pushed through in 1843 by Whig majorities against opposition from the Democrats.[16] The China trade, it would seem, did not involve commodities that Democratic farmers and planters marketed.

The historian Amy Greenberg has suggested that rival versions of American imperialism corresponded to different conceptions of manliness: "martial manhood," which endorsed expansion through violence, including private filibustering expeditions and war, and "restrained manhood," which preferred nonviolent forms of national expansion through commerce and missionary activity. If she is right, the violence in the lives of working-class urban young men helps explain the popularity among them of imperialism through conquest.[17]

Whether or how to pursue an imperial destiny was thus a matter of controversial public policy. The American empire did not come into existence "unconsciously," as the poet Simms alleged, or simply through the westward migration of individual families into a vacant continent. If American expansion had been truly a manifest, inevitable destiny, then it could have taken place peacefully and automatically. In practice, however, like all empires, the American one required conscious deliberation and energetic government action to bring it into being, to deal with previous occupants and competing claims to ownership. Power politics, diplomacy, and war proved as much a part of America's "manifest destiny" as covered wagons. Jacksonian Democracy, for all its disavowals of

---

15. *Presidential Messages*, IV, 211–14; Pletcher, *Diplomacy of Annexation*, 208. See further Edward Crapol, *John Tyler* (Chapel Hill, 2006), 135–55.

16. Norma Peterson, *The Presidencies of William Henry Harrison and John Tyler* (Lawrence, Kans., 1989), 140–43.

17. Amy Greenberg, *Manifest Manhood and the Antebellum American Empire* (Cambridge, Eng., 2005).

government agency, demonstrated eagerness to exploit the authority of government in expanding the American empire.[18]

II

Characteristically, James Knox Polk did not reveal his full intentions in his inaugural address. No president has ever played his cards closer to his chest. Even in his diary Polk did not let his guard down. He confided the objectives of his presidency to only one person besides his wife: George Bancroft, the New England intellectual who shared his vision of America's imperial destiny and whom he was about to name secretary of the navy. The new president slapped his thigh and avowed, "There are to be four great measures of my administration," Bancroft recalled:

> The settlement of the Oregon question with Great Britain.
> The acquisition of California and a large district on the coast.
> The reduction of the Tariff to a revenue basis.
> The complete and permanent establishment of the Constitutional Treasury, as he loved to call it, but as others had called it, "Independent Treasury."[19]

Judged by these objectives, Polk is probably the most successful president the United States has ever had. He stayed focused on these goals and achieved them all, two in foreign policy and two in domestic, while serving only a single term. Texas did not appear as a goal, for the incoming president regarded its annexation, while not yet implemented, as a fait accompli in policy. The most surprising item on the list, of course, was California. Though Texas and Oregon had been discussed in the election campaign, California had not. The president could at least claim, if not demonstrate, that he had a mandate for Texas and Oregon; certainly no mandate existed for the acquisition of California. Yet Polk's ambition for California would shape U.S.-Mexican relations more than any other issue.

Remote as it was, California experienced significant change following Mexican independence. In August 1833, the Mexican Congress secularized the Franciscan missions that had dominated Alta California for half a century. *Federalista* anticlerical liberalism motivated the action, but the *federalistas* soon fell from power, and in any case Mexico City was too distant and the government's control too tenuous for effective implementation of plans to replace the rule of the friars with self-governing Native

---

18. See Thomas Hietala, *Manifest Design: Anxious Aggrandizement in Late Jacksonian America* (Ithaca, N.Y., 1985).
19. Quoted in Charles Sellers, *James K. Polk, Continentalist* (Princeton, 1966), 213.

American *pueblos*. The actual consequences varied from mission to mission. In some cases the newly emancipated inhabitants fled back to their ancestral homes and way of life; others wound up *peones* on the *ranchos* that quickly engrossed many of the former mission lands. Land speculators rather than Indians turned out to be the chief beneficiaries of secularization.[20]

Independent Mexico eagerly broke out of the old Spanish mercantile system and opened up Alta California to the commerce of the world. She also welcomed immigrants from overseas and made naturalization easy. After the demise of the missions, enormous free homesteads could be obtained in California by those with the right combination of political connections and luck. The successful men, either Mexicans or immigrants like Johann Sutter from Switzerland, set themselves up as patriarchal landowners. With transportation and communication slow, the *rancheros* perforce pursued a measure of economic self-sufficiency, grinding their own grain and employing a variety of artisans. They hired *vaqueros* and raised cattle. When ships called at California ports, they welcomed the opportunity to trade the hides and tallow from their cattle for the products of the outside world. Richard Henry Dana's classic account of seafaring, *Two Years Before the Mast* (1840), is based on that trade; New England's new shoe factories often used leather from California. The *ranchos* yielded a good living; the climate was attractive and malaria absent. Visitors pronounced the California way of life either idyllic or decadent, characterizations that many visitors to California would repeat over the generations to come.[21]

In 1835–36, a number of outlying Mexican states rebelled against Santa Anna's imposed *centralista* regime; Juan Alvarado and Mariano Vallejo led Alta California's uprising. Their supporters included Indians and foreign immigrants as well as Mexican *rancheros*. Authorities in distant Mexico City, regarding Texas as the more serious challenge, chose conciliation with the *californios*. Alvarado and Vallejo received offices, and Alta California considerable autonomy. But the political situation remained unstable, with Monterey and Los Angeles rival power centers. The Mexican army maintained but a feeble presence in this remote region, its officers preferring assignments near the capital, where they could pursue

---

20. Gerald Geary, *The Secularization of the California Missions* (Washington, 1934); Robert H. Jackson and Edward Castillo, *Indians, Franciscans, and Spanish Colonization* (Albuquerque, N.M., 1995), 87–106.
21. See Doyce Nunis, "Alta California's Trojan Horse," *California History* 76 (1997): 299–330.

professional advancement and exert political influence. Upgrading the defenses of distant California required money that the Mexican government could never find.

Foreign powers recognized California's vulnerability. A French diplomat dispatched by his government to make a thorough inquiry reported back that California could be taken by "whatever nation chooses to send there a man-of-war and 200 men."[22] The *norteamericanos* provoked the most anxiety. In August 1841, Charles Wilkes's Pacific expedition explored San Francisco Bay and the Sacramento River; locals wondered what six vessels of the United States Navy were up to. The following year Commodore Thomas ap Catesby Jones gave their fears substance. Jones had received an alarmist message from John Parrott, U.S. consul in Mazatlán, Mexico, stating "it is highly probable there will be a war between the two countries."[23] On October 19, 1842, acting in response to this misleading intelligence and a rumor that Mexico was selling California to Great Britain, Jones's squadron demanded and received the surrender of the fort guarding Monterey, capital of Mexican California. Two days later, after going ashore to read the latest news available from Mexico City (dated August 22), the commodore realized no war existed and apologized for his mistake. His precipitous action, however, tipped the hand of the Tyler administration, which had been hoping to enlist British help in persuading the Mexicans to sell California (or at least the port of San Francisco, which was what interested Webster) to the United States. The administration relieved Jones of his command for the sake of appearances but left the provocative Parrott in post. From then on, Mexican policymakers and public, *centralistas* and *federalistas* alike, drew the conclusion that California was another Texas waiting to happen.

Besides the seaborne traders along the coast, Americans also came to California overland to settle in the interior valleys. Cheap, attractive land pulled them; hard times after 1839 pushed them. Beginning in 1841, hundreds of brave souls organized themselves into long caravans of wagons, led by professional guides. In 1842, an apprehensive Mexican Congress forbade further acquisition of California land by foreigners, but immigrants from the United States kept arriving; speculators would still sell to them, and many simply squatted. Their overland route followed the Platte River, then crossed southern Wyoming and penetrated the Rocky Mountains at South Pass. Typically, they traveled to the north of the

---

22. Quoted in Neal Harlow, *California Conquered* (Berkeley, 1982), 35.
23. John Parrott to Thomas Jones, June 22, 1842, in John Parrott, *Selected Papers*, ed. Barbara Jostes (San Francisco, 1972), 22.

Great Salt Lake and traced the Humboldt River across the Great Basin. The trip took months, and it had to be timed for crossing the Sierra Nevada into California before the snows came.[24]

A fast-talking adventurer named Lansford Hastings enticed some migrants to take what he claimed was a shortcut, going to the south of Salt Lake. Hastings would thus secure customers for his trading post on that route; in the longer term, he aimed to attract enough Americans to California to detach it from Mexico and, perhaps, rule it himself. "Hastings's Cutoff" was in fact a longer, slower, and more arduous way to California than the conventional one, as the ill-fated party led by the Donner brothers learned at great cost. Delayed by Hastings's misleading guidebook and false promises en route, they exhausted themselves in crossing the alkali desert west of Great Salt Lake, which took twice as long as he had assured them. Finally, having jettisoned many of their household goods, and with their food supplies running dangerously low, they encountered an early storm when crossing the Sierra in late October 1846. The snowbound emigrants then endured an epic of suffering, horror, death, and survival before rescue came—for some, this was not until the following April. On several occasions starving people in the last extremity had recourse to cannibalism. The worst crime occurred when two California Indians who had volunteered to help them were killed and eaten. Only forty-seven of the eighty-nine members of the party lived to reach their destination. Yet the statistics of death testify to sacrificial heroism: While more than two-thirds of the adult men perished, three-quarters of the women and children survived.[25]

III

On the Fourth of July 1836, a caravan of seventy people and four hundred animals (horses, mules, and cattle) entered the South Pass of the Rockies; it included nine wagons, for travelers had recently confirmed predictions that the pass would accommodate wheeled vehicles. Most of the party were traders representing the American Fur Company, but one group consisted of missionaries sent by the ABCFM, the American Board of Commissioners for Foreign Missions. Among the latter rode Narcissa Whitman and Eliza Spalding, the first white women to cross the Continental Divide at that point. Two days later they arrived at Green River (in

---

24. Ray Billington, *The Far Western Frontier, 1830–1860* (New York, 1956), 91–115.
25. See Will Bagley, "Lansford Warren Hastings," *Overland Trail* 12 (1994): 12–26; George Stewart, *Ordeal by Hunger* (Boston, 1960); Kristin Johnson, ed., *Unfortunate Emigrants* (Logan, Utah, 1996).

what is now Wyoming) for a *rendezvous*, a meeting with hundreds of trappers, traders, and Indians from several tribes for an annual orgy of commerce and festivities. There the female missionaries enjoyed the spectacle and the attention they received, before moving on, toward the lives of hardship and sacrifice they had chosen to spend in a remote wilderness.[26] Traders and missionaries marked the way that farming families would soon follow, in the Oregon Country as in countless other nineteenth-century frontier areas.

Upon arriving in Oregon, the women and their husbands spent time as guests at Fort Vancouver, the bustling outpost of the Hudson's Bay Company, located not at present-day Vancouver, Canada, but near the junction of the Columbia and Willamette Rivers, in what is now the state of Washington. Founded in 1670, the Hudson's Bay Company had already become one of the world's great business corporations, absorbing its chief competitor, the North-West Company, in 1821. The most powerful private organization in North America, HBC actually ruled most of Canada. The United States and Great Britain jointly occupied Oregon—which then extended all the way from California to Alaska—by an agreement first made in 1818 and extended in 1827. The British exerted their authority and influence in this vast territory almost exclusively through the Hudson's Bay Company, and what interested that company was the fur trade, a big business that connected North America with both Europe and China. HBC's Fort Vancouver had long since replaced Astoria (now deserted) as the center of the Oregon fur trade.[27]

In 1842, the medical missionary Marcus Whitman, Narcissa's husband, visited the East Coast, where he pled with the ABCFM and the federal government to take more interest in Oregon. Although historians no longer subscribe to the view that Whitman single-handedly saved Oregon for the United States, his return to the Pacific Northwest in the fall of 1843 coincided with the migration there of almost a thousand American settlers, who benefited along the way from his knowledge and advice.[28] The emigrants were fleeing economic depression and the endemic malaria of the Mississippi Valley; in the next few years more and more American farming families followed the same route. The Oregon Trail from Independence,

---

26. Julie Jeffrey, *Converting the West: A Biography of Narcissa Whitman* (Norman, Okla., 1991), 76–82.

27. See John S. Galbraith, *The Hudson's Bay Company as an Imperial Factor* (Berkeley, 1957).

28. The *New Orleans Weekly Picayune*, July 17, 1843, gave a detailed accounting of the 990 migrants and their wagons and animals.

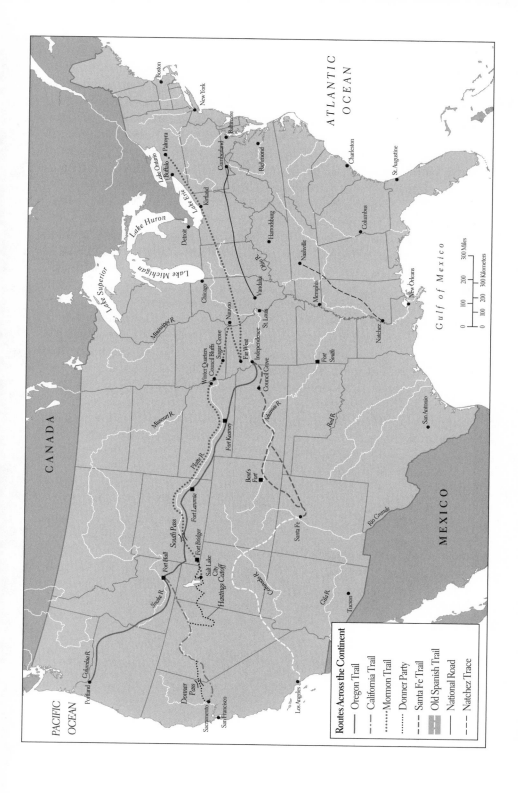

Routes Across the Continent
— Oregon Trail
-·- California Trail
······ Mormon Trail
········ Donner Party
-·- Santa Fe Trail
▦ Old Spanish Trail
— National Road
-- Natchez Trace

Missouri, coinciding much of the time with the pathway followed by migrants to California, became one of the legendary pioneer tracks across the continent. Francis Parkman further popularized it in a narrative of his 1846 journey, *The California and Oregon Trail*, serialized in the *Knickerbocker Magazine* beginning in 1847. A young New England intellectual in search of adventure, Parkman rendered a vivid account of his encounters with trappers, settlers (including Donners and Mormons), the landscape itself, and—most fascinating to him—the Ogallala Sioux.

With transportation of heavy goods upstream on the Missouri laborious and the trip around Cape Horn taking six to eight months, the practicality of maintaining U.S. control over distant Oregon had been doubted by prominent statesmen of both parties—Albert Gallatin, Daniel Webster, and Thomas Hart Benton among them. More recent developments had altered this expectation: the negotiation of the overland route with wagons, the development of the railroad, and the invention of the electric telegraph. Now it seemed that if Americans settled in the Pacific Northwest, they could remain within the United States. By the end of 1844 some five thousand Americans had relocated to Oregon—far fewer than lived in Texas but more than lived in California and enough to have an impact. By comparison, only seven hundred British subjects then lived in the condominium, most of them not permanent settlers but on temporary assignment for their employer. For thirty years the British had been more active in Oregon than the Americans; now the new arrivals tipped the balance in favor of the United States.[29]

Practically all the migrants arriving along the Oregon Trail chose to settle in the Willamette Valley, a fertile area south of the Columbia River that they felt reasonably certain would be assigned to the United States even if Oregon was eventually partitioned between the two occupying powers. There they set up an unauthorized but functioning local government of their own. During these years, many settlers also left the British Isles to pioneer colonies overseas, but they headed mainly for Australia and New Zealand. Some Canadians, retired HBC employees, had settled early in the Willamette Valley, but more recent American arrivals threatened to drive them out. These American settlers were no longer New England missionaries but mostly Missourians, a tough people little restrained by legalities, who had ruthlessly expelled the Mormons from their home state. The Americans included former trappers bitter at the HBC for its cutthroat competitive practices. The possibility of violence in

---

29. Thomas Leonard, *James K. Polk* (Wilmington, Del., 2001), 95; Meinig, *Continental America*, 105. In general see David Dary, *The Oregon Trail* (New York, 2004).

Oregon could not be ruled out.[30] Not coincidentally, relations with the Indian tribes revealed conflicting interests between the occupying powers. HBC valued the natives as customers and suppliers of otter and beaver pelts, and it willingly sold them firearms; U.S. settlers wanting to expropriate Native lands regarded such sales as an invitation to frontier warfare.

The Hudson's Bay Company tried to cultivate good relations with its new neighbors, extending them credit to purchase supplies. The settlers took the supplies and never paid for them.[31] Becoming concerned for the safety of its valuable inventories with a potentially hostile population nearby, HBC closed down Fort Vancouver in 1845 and shifted its base of operations to Fort Victoria at the site of the present city of Victoria, British Columbia. The international fur trade was beginning its decline, due to both diminishing supply and diminishing demand, and this persuaded Sir George Simpson, chief of HBC's Oregon operations, that prospective profits did not justify mounting a challenge to the American settlers. In preparation for the move northwards, the Hudson's Bay Company trapped out the southern portion of the Oregon territory, leaving the beaver there virtually extinct.[32]

The Democratic platform of 1844, with its call for the whole of Oregon, ignored the fact that the British and American governments had long assumed that Oregon would eventually be divided between them and had discussed how that division should go. The British had proposed that the existing 49th parallel boundary be extended west to the Columbia River, at which point the boundary should follow the Columbia to the sea. The Americans had proposed that the 49th parallel should simply be extended due west, all the way across Vancouver Island. Thus, of all the great Oregon Territory, only the area between the Columbia River and the 49th parallel remained in serious dispute. Historians refer to this area as "the disputed triangle," although it is only vaguely triangular. Within the disputed triangle, the Hudson's Bay Company carried on virtually all white activity.

Throughout his negotiations concerning Oregon, President Polk played a double game. While seeming to demand all of the Oregon country for the United States, in reality he revealed a willingness to compromise, provided he could get most of the core disputed triangle.

30. Frederick Merk, *The Oregon Question* (Cambridge, Mass., 1967), 234–54.
31. Peter Burnett, "Recollections of an Old Pioneer," *Oregon Historical Quarterly* 5 (1904): 93.
32. Merk, *Oregon Question*, 96.

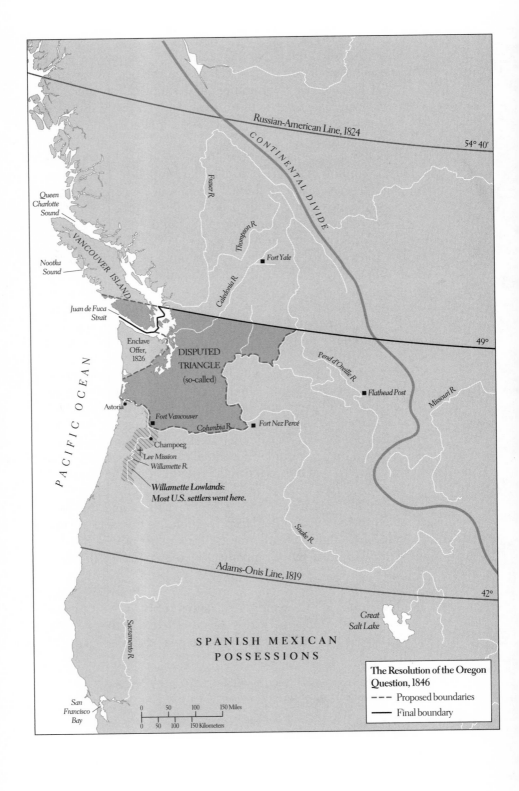

Russian-American Line, 1824

54° 40'

CONTINENTAL DIVIDE

Queen
Charlotte
Sound

Fraser R.

Thompson R.

Nootka
Sound

VANCOUVER ISLAND

Caledonia R.

Fort Yale

Juan de Fuca
Strait

49°

Enclave
Offer,
1826

DISPUTED
TRIANGLE
(so-called)

Pend d'Oreille R.

Flathead Post

Missouri R.

PACIFIC OCEAN

Astoria

Fort Vancouver

Columbia R.

Fort Nez Percé

Champoeg

Lee Mission

Willamette R.

**Willamette Lowlands:
Most U.S. settlers went here.**

Snake R.

Adams-Onis Line, 1819

42°

Great
Salt Lake

Sacramento R.

SPANISH MEXICAN
POSSESSIONS

San
Francisco
Bay

The Resolution of the Oregon Question, 1846
- - - Proposed boundaries
—— Final boundary

0   50   100   150 Miles

0   50   100   150 Kilometers

A peaceful settlement with Britain over Oregon would ensure that she would not come to Mexico's aid when he forced a showdown with that country over California. John Tyler, who had concluded the Webster-Ashburton Treaty to smooth the way for annexing Texas, provided Polk with a model: conciliating Britain facilitated getting tough with Mexico. Young Hickory attached much more importance to California than to what is now British Columbia.

Polk could not afford the political embarrassment of overtly betraying the Democratic platform of 1844, which had played such a prominent role in the campaign. The Missouri congressional delegation for a time stimulated American interest in Oregon, since their state, anchoring the east end of the Oregon Trail, provided not only many of the settlers but most of their supplies and equipment. Migration to Oregon made good business for Missouri. But the majority of the Democrats who rallied to the slogan "Fifty-four Forty or Fight" (an allusion to the latitude of the northern boundary of the Oregon condominium, which was also the southern boundary of Russian Alaska) came from the free states. To alienate them would cost Polk congressional votes he needed for the rest of his program. Northern and western Democrats had proved indispensable to the annexation of all Texas, with its vastly exaggerated boundary claims. In return many of them felt entitled to administration support for all Oregon. Polk therefore had to play his cards in such a way as to achieve a compromise over Oregon without having to accept responsibility for that compromise. In this he succeeded, although in the end the northern Democrats finally did rebel at his manipulations. One of them, Gideon Welles of Connecticut, who served as civilian head of the navy's logistics bureau during the Mexican War, concluded that Polk had "a trait of sly cunning which he thought shrewdness, but which was really disingenuousness and duplicity."[33]

Already during the Tyler administration, the capable U.S. envoy in London, Edward Everett, had suggested a compromise boundary that followed the 49th parallel except for leaving all of Vancouver Island in Canada—essentially the same line that would finally be agreed. However, Secretary of State Calhoun put the Oregon negotiations on hold while he concentrated his attention on Texas. With a continuing influx of American settlers into Oregon, he reasoned, time was on the side of the United States. President Tyler took little interest in Oregon compared

---

33. Quoted in Sellers, *Polk, Continentalist*, 219.

with Texas and would probably have been willing to accept partition of the condominium along the Columbia River line.[34]

When Polk came into office, he replaced Everett (a Webster Whig) with another experienced and knowledgeable emissary to London: Louis McLane, the successful negotiator of Jackson's commercial treaty with Britain, former secretary of state and Treasury, now president of the Baltimore & Ohio Railroad. This strong appointment signaled Polk's willingness to work toward a mutual understanding over Oregon. Lord Aberdeen, Britain's foreign secretary, sent Richard Pakenham as his emissary to Washington. A cousin of the Edward Pakenham whom Jackson had defeated at New Orleans, he proved a less happy choice of envoy than McLane. Fundamentally, the Foreign Office favored good relations with the United States. The Peel ministry intended to repeal the "Corn Laws," Britain's protective tariffs on grain; they knew that Polk too was a free trader resolved to lower the Whig tariff of 1842, and they looked forward to a mutually profitable expansion of Anglo-American trade. But, like Polk, Aberdeen had to look over his shoulder toward domestic politics when conducting diplomacy. The opposition's shadow foreign secretary, Lord Palmerston, had criticized the Webster-Ashburton Treaty and might denounce any sign of weakness in dealing with the Yankees. So Aberdeen tried to hedge. He gave Pakenham two sets of instructions, an official one to stick firmly by the British position, and an unofficial one to refer an American proposal back to London.[35]

After arriving in Washington, Pakenham received in mid-July 1845 an offer from the Polk administration to partition Oregon at the 49th parallel. Polk intended this as the opening gambit in a negotiation; he could excuse his initial failure to insist on 54° 40' by saying that the previous administration had committed the United States to offering such a compromise. Three weeks away from his government's advice, Pakenham chose to follow his official, rather than his unofficial, instructions. He rejected the American offer out of hand. It was the wrong decision. Once again the slowness of transatlantic communication played havoc with Anglo-American diplomacy; the delicately laid plans of both Polk and Aberdeen had gone awry.

34. Howard Jones and Donald Rakestraw, *Prologue to Manifest Destiny: Anglo-American Relations in the 1840s* (Wilmington, Del., 1997), 184, 187, 193; Samuel Flagg Bemis, *John Quincy Adams and the Union* (New York, 1956), 486–87; Crapol, *John Tyler*, 119–21.

35. Pletcher, *Diplomacy of Annexation*, 242–43.

Furious, Polk called upon Congress to pass an act serving Britain with one year's notice that the United States would terminate the joint occupation agreement in Oregon.[36] This would focus British attention on the need to resolve the matter somehow while according northwestern expansionists full opportunity to vent Anglophobic rhetoric. The Democratic popular press, particularly O'Sullivan's *Democratic Review,* James Gordon Bennett's *New York Herald,* and Moses Beach's *New York Sun,* beat the drums for termination as a prelude to seizing all of Oregon. Polk welcomed the bluster at this stage, hoping it would impress the British, and in the meantime he refused to negotiate with them any further over Oregon. However popular among certain Democratic voters, the president's belligerency alarmed Wall Street, and stocks fell.[37]

Passing the congressional resolution that Polk wanted proved no simple matter, due to opposition from two quarters unwilling to risk a confrontation with Britain: most Whigs, who wanted British investment capital, allied with many southern Democrats, led by Calhoun, who placed a higher value on Britain as a customer for cotton than they did on extra acreage in the Pacific Northwest inhospitable to plantation slavery. A handful of the most antislavery Whigs pressed for all of Oregon as a counterweight to slaveholding Texas.

The British now proposed arbitration, but Polk refused, knowing this would expose him to reproach from those demanding all of Oregon. Though the extremists imagined that they were on the president's side, the historian can discern indications that this inscrutable executive indulged them and exploited them to prod the British, but did not ultimately share their objective. The administration's closest collaborator on Oregon in the Senate, Thomas Hart Benton, despite his Missouri constituency, worked with the moderates to add a conciliatory amendment to the termination resolution. Louis McLane corresponded from London with Calhoun as well as Polk, but not with the expansionist chairman of the Senate Foreign Relations Committee, William Allen of Ohio. Polk certainly never seriously entertained the possibility of going to war for what is now British Columbia, since he made no military or naval preparations for it. The Peel ministry, by contrast, did prepare. (British leaders worried about having to fight the United States and France at the same

---

36. "First Annual Message to Congress" (Dec. 2, 1845), *Presidential Messages,* IV, 392–99. More recent presidents have given notice of treaty terminations on their own authority, without seeking prior congressional authorization.
37. Sellers, *Polk, Continentalist,* 357.

time just as Americans worried about having to fight both Britain and Mexico.)[38]

One perceptive contemporary saw through Polk's policy. John Quincy Adams, true to his old expansionist principles as Monroe's secretary of state, defended the title of the United States to the whole of Oregon, drawing upon his unparalleled knowledge of history and international law, confirmed by the Bible. "I want the country for our western pioneers," he told the House of Representatives. God's chosen people had been promised "the uttermost parts of the earth for thy possession" (Psalm 2:8). Yet, Adams correctly predicted, "I believe the present Administration will finally back down from their own ground."[39] (Indeed, Adams himself, as president, had approved extending the joint occupation agreement when it came up for renewal in 1827.)

After five months of debate, Congress enacted the notice of termination on April 23, 1846, with an important amendment secured by the moderates encouraging an "amicable settlement" of the Oregon Question.[40] In response, on May 19 the British proposed the 49th parallel with a detour to save them the southern tip of Vancouver Island (where, of course, the Hudson's Bay Company had built Fort Victoria). They yielded all the rest of the disputed triangle, although it contained not two dozen Americans at the time.[41] The proposal represented all Polk could reasonably hope for. Cleverly, he referred it to the Senate for "advice and consent" *before* signing a treaty rather than (as presidents customarily do) afterwards. War with Mexico having already begun by this time, most senators felt only too eager to settle the dispute with Britain, and they promptly voted 38 to 12 for acceptance. Polk immediately drew up a partition treaty in accordance with the British proposal, got it ratified, and sent it off to London on June 18. In doing so, the president could claim that he had deferred to the Senate's wishes, not broken a campaign pledge. Northern Democrats who would have held rallies to protest against the compromise received orders from party headquarters to desist. The administration's relief at having the Oregon Question satisfactorily resolved was expressed candidly if bluntly by the Democratic *New York Herald*: "We can now thrash Mexico into decency at our leisure."[42]

38. Jones and Rakestraw, *Prologue to Manifest Destiny*, 207–8, 235–37, 243.
39. *Congressional Globe*, 29th Cong., 1st sess., 157, 342.
40. Ibid., 680–83.
41. Meinig, *Continental America*, 117.
42. Sellers, *Polk, Continentalist*, 412; *New York Herald*, June 11, 1846.

The resolution of the Oregon Question stands as a monument to peaceful diplomacy. Each country received about half of the whole Oregon territory. The outcome also represented a masterpiece of domestic politics. The president had seemingly bluffed his way past both the British and the American political establishments. And just in the nick of time: Ten days after the British sent off the partition proposal that the Senate accepted, word reached London that hostilities had broken out along the Rio Grande between Mexico and the United States. If they had known the United States had involved itself in a war, the British might have tried to drive a harder bargain.

What kind of credit for the favorable settlement of the Oregon boundary should go to Polk may be questioned. His defenders, in his own time and since, have praised his firmness and quoted his words to a member of Congress: "The only way to treat John Bull was to look him straight in the eye."[43] But it seems likely that the British responded more to the presence of the American settlers, the decline of the Oregon fur trade, and their eagerness for American imports of cotton and grain than to the president's eyeballing.[44] Once the Hudson's Bay Company had decided to relocate to Vancouver Island, the die was cast, and Sir George Simpson made his decision to move before Polk even took office. The British foreign secretary would likely have settled for the boundary agreed in 1846 as early as December 1843 if the Tyler administration had followed through on Edward Everett's suggestion. Democratic rhetorical posturing on behalf of 54° 40' in fact aimed more at a domestic American audience than at a British one.[45]

Indeed, a demonstration of firmness by the British prompted Polk and his cabinet to back away from extreme demands and (secretly) invite a compromise. On February 3, 1846, McLane sent a dispatch from London that thirty warships of the Royal Navy had set sail for North American waters. Secretary of State James Buchanan received it on Saturday night, February 21, and immediately alerted the president. For several days (including Sunday) Polk and his cabinet considered what response to make. They decided not to recommend "war-like preparations" to Congress and instead instructed McLane on February 26 to assure the British that Polk would entertain a 49th parallel compromise proposal and refer it to the Senate for advice before responding. Apprised of this decision, Pakenham

43. *Diary of James K. Polk*, ed. Milo Quaife (Chicago, 1910), I, 155 (Jan. 4, 1846).
44. See David Dykstra, *The Shifting Balance of Power: American-British Diplomacy in North America, 1842–48* (Lanham, Md., 1999).
45. See Merk, *Oregon Question*, 250, 364–94.

sent a message to his government the same day stating that the flotilla had served its purpose and further preparations for war would be unnecessary. All this while the president continued to entertain visits from hawkish congressmen warning him that any retreat from 54° 40' would bring Democratic defeat at the polls.[46] If Polk is to receive a measure of credit for the peaceful resolution of the Oregon Question, it should not be for firmness but for sending a conciliatory message on February 26, 1846, instead of escalating the crisis.

Many politicians besides Polk tried to exploit the nationalistic passions of the public for political advantage in these years—among them Secretary of State Buchanan. The Pennsylvania Democrat had spoken out strongly in Congress for the whole of Oregon. Inside Polk's cabinet, however, he consistently urged compromise. Then, with the settlement finally reached, Buchanan strove to dissociate himself from it, so as to preserve his credibility with the 54° 40' extremists. "It is a great misfortune that a member of the cabinet should be an aspirant for the Presidency," Polk grumbled, "because I cannot rely upon his honest and disinterested advice." A month later the president complained that too many Democratic Senators showed less concern about "54-40" or "49" than about "48" (the coming presidential election). Considering how carefully Polk himself calculated political advantage, his witticism displayed unconscious irony.[47]

A curious red herring complicated the Oregon negotiations: whether the British should retain navigation rights on the Columbia River. Eventually, the United States granted a limited right, but the British never exercised it. The Columbia River (as insiders realized at the time), with its many rapids and a sandbar across its mouth, was actually not easily navigable to oceangoing vessels, though canoes used it. What mattered to navigation and Pacific commerce were Puget Sound and the Strait of Juan de Fuca, which the disputants ended up sharing. The real importance of the Columbia River, as only the future would reveal, lay in its capacity to generate electric power.

In November 1847, Narcissa and Marcus Whitman were martyred and their mission in eastern Oregon destroyed by members of the Cayuse tribe who resented the whites having introduced measles along with Christianity.[48] The remaining missionaries shifted their attention from the Native Americans to civilizing the rowdy white Oregonians.

---

46. Polk, *Diary*, I, 241–53 (Feb. 21–25, 1846); Paul Bergeron, *The Presidency of James K. Polk* (Lawrence, Kans., 1987), 128; Leonard, *Polk*, 117.
47. Polk, *Diary*, I, 297, 345 (March 22, April 22, 1846).
48. See Cameron Addis, "The Whitman Massacre," *JER* 25 (2005): 221–58.

IV

Joseph Smith, prophet of God escaped from a Missouri jail, crossed the Mississippi River to Illinois, where on April 22, 1839, he rejoined his family and some five thousand other recently arrived Latter-day Saints. The good people of Quincy granted a temporary haven to these refugees from religious persecution. Within a few weeks Smith had identified the site for a new stake of Zion on the left bank of the Mississippi, a hamlet called Commerce that he renamed Nauvoo, a word that he (correctly) informed his people meant "a beautiful place" in Hebrew.[49] There the faithful gathered, reinforced now by converts arriving from England via New Orleans. They drained the swampland and commenced to implement their prophet's vision of a grand city centered on a new temple. The Illinois state legislature, happy to receive an influx of hardworking migrants, granted a municipal charter allowing Nauvoo virtually complete self-rule. In practice this meant the rule of Joseph Smith: mayor of the town, commander of its militia, city planner, recorder of deeds, and chief justice of the municipal court. Unlike most frontier towns, Nauvoo aspired to economic self-sufficiency, but this was not easily achieved, particularly with a shortage of investment capital.[50] As a utopian community it impressed visitors; James Gordon Bennett's *New York Herald* called Nauvoo "a new religious civilization" based on "industry and energy," adding that it "may revolutionize the whole earth one of these days."[51] The Mormons dug up the press they had hidden and lugged it all the way from western Missouri to set it up again for a newspaper of their own: the *Times and Seasons*. For several years, Nauvoo grew even faster than Chicago and achieved a population of ten thousand by the end of 1842, making it probably the largest city in Illinois and the approximate equal of old St. Louis.[52]

Both political parties courted the Mormons in Illinois. Most U.S. male converts to the faith came from small farmer and small-town artisan backgrounds, and normally voted Democratic. In Kirtland, the Saints had voted solidly as soft-money Democrats although their part of Ohio was otherwise strongly Whig. In Missouri, however, the Democratic governor Lilburn Boggs had persecuted them and called for their "extermination."

49. R. Alcalay, *The Complete Hebrew-English Dictionary* (Tel Aviv, 1996). The pronunciation "nauvoo" is anglicized. With thanks to Rabbi Mari Chernow.

50. See Annette Hampshire, *Mormonism in Conflict: The Nauvoo Years* (New York, 1985); Richard Bushman, *Making Space for the Mormons* (Logan, Utah, 1997).

51. *New York Herald*, Jan. 19, 1842.

52. Robert Flanders, *Nauvoo, Kingdom on the Mississippi* (Urbana, Ill., 1965), 56. The population of Chicago in 1840 was 4,450.

When Smith led a delegation to Washington to ask for federal protection, Henry Clay supported them in the Senate, but President Van Buren reminded them of state rights and responded bluntly, "Your cause is just, but I can do nothing for you."[53] Accordingly, the Mormons cast their votes in 1840 for the Whig presidential electors. As a gesture toward an Illinois Democrat who had befriended them, they scratched out the last name on the Whig list of electors and wrote in that of their friend; the name they deleted: Abraham Lincoln. In spite of this, Lincoln ranked among the Illinois politicians most sympathetic to the Mormons.[54]

Democratic politicians did not give up on the Mormons, however, and when Missouri agents came to arrest Joseph Smith as a fugitive from justice, Stephen Douglas, acting in his capacity as an Illinois state judge, set the prophet free. The grateful Mormons returned to the Democratic fold in 1842. In predominantly Democratic Illinois, it seemed a safer bet. The switch infuriated the Whigs, and did not restore the Mormons' popularity with their Democratic neighbors in the nearby towns of Warsaw and Carthage. Americans were accustomed to bloc voting by ethnoreligious groups, but not to bloc voting that could go either way as directed. In May 1842 occurred an attempt on the life of Missouri's Governor Boggs, and people suspected Smith of ordering or prophesying the assassination. Illinois refused to extradite him to Missouri, but fear increased of the Saints' growing numbers and their prophet's temporal power. The gentile public once again gradually soured on the Mormons.

Early in 1844, Joseph Smith decided to run for president of the United States. If the abolitionists could field a candidate, why not the Mormons? The campaign seems to have had a place in the prophet's vision of an earthly Kingdom of God that would precede and prepare for the Second Coming of Christ. If it failed, emigration might be necessary to establish the Kingdom.[55] Such millennial expectations did not preclude policies sensible in secular terms. Smith's program included abolition of imprisonment for debt, the reestablishment of a national bank, federal protection for civil liberties abridged by states and mobs, the acquisition of not only Texas and Oregon but all of Mexico and Canada—provided the in-

53. Quoted in Leonard Arrington and Davis Bitton, *The Mormon Experience* (New York, 1979), 50.
54. Fawn Brodie, *No Man Knows My History: The Life of Joseph Smith*, rev. ed. (New York, 1972), 260, 267; Leonard Arrington, *Brigham Young, American Moses* (New York, 1985), 109.
55. Klaus Hansen, *Quest for Empire* (Lansing, Mich., 1967), 72–79; idem, "The Metamorphosis of the Kingdom of God," in *The New Mormon History*, ed. Michael Quinn (Salt Lake City, 1992), 221–46.

habitants peacefully consented— and encouragement for states to enact emancipation by providing masters compensation from federal land revenues.[56] Whatever his program's merits, Smith's campaign persuaded many gentiles that the prophet had fallen into megalomania.

Joseph Smith did not live to participate in the election. The chain of events leading up to his death began when an influential group of dissident Mormons set up a newspaper of their own, the *Nauvoo Expositor*. On June 7, 1844, the *Expositor* published its only issue. The paper accused the prophet and a few of his intimates of practicing plural marriage and teaching the existence of a plurality of gods. Both charges were essentially true and later avowed, but Smith did not yet feel ready for this. He would probably have been better advised to acknowledge the doctrines publicly and proceed immediately with the migration westward that he and his inner circle had already begun considering. Instead he had the Nauvoo city council, which he dominated, declare the new paper a "public nuisance" and destroy its press.[57] In 1837, Elijah Lovejoy had died defending his press at Alton; Illinois public opinion now regretted that episode and had resolved nothing like it would happen again. In an age of communications revolution, the Mormon assault on freedom of the press aroused unanimous condemnation from the press. Where Joseph[58] and his followers had won sympathy as victims of religious persecution, they now seemed its perpetrators. Convinced that Smith had exceeded his legal authority and become a dangerous despot, the militias assembled in Warsaw and Carthage, the centers of anti-Mormon sentiment. The militias announced their intention to restore law and order in Nauvoo by force, which, of course, exceeded their own authority. In response, Smith mobilized the Nauvoo Legion. Illinois governor Thomas Ford hastened to the scene to forestall a civil war.

Ford hoped to restore law and order through mediation rather than force. Joseph agreed to disband the Legion to avoid bloodshed. The governor demanded he also submit to arrest for the unwarranted destruction of the *Expositor*. Convinced that he faced lynching if taken into custody, Joseph's first impulse was to flee. A day later his sense of mission and

56. Joseph Smith, *Views on the Powers and Policy of the Government of the United States* (1844; Salt Lake City, 1886), 15–22.
57. *Cultures in Conflict: A Documentary History of the Mormon War in Illinois*, ed. John Hallwas and Roger Launius (Logan, Utah, 1995), 143–48 (the *Nauvoo Expositor*), 149–56 (the proceedings of the Nauvoo city council).
58. Mormons usually refer to the prophets Joseph Smith and Brigham Young by their first names, and historians also often follow this practice.

loyalty to his followers overcame his instinct of self-preservation, and he returned to face arrest and transportation to Carthage. The governor foolishly left him there guarded by the Carthage militia and went off to Nauvoo to negotiate disarmament with the Mormons. In Ford's absence, men of the disbanded Warsaw militia returned as a lynch mob. The Carthage militia, by prearrangement, made a show of defense and fled. The mob found Joseph and his brother Hirum in an unlocked cell and shot them to death on June 27, 1844. The state's press perfunctorily deplored the murders; the governor managed to secure indictments against some members of the mob, but not to convict them. The Mormons did not fight back.[59]

Mormon reaction to the assassination was well expressed by Eliza Snow, secretly a plural wife of Joseph's, later and publicly a plural wife of his successor, Brigham Young. Called a "prophetess," she contributed to Mormon theology the doctrine of a Heavenly Mother. A leader of women's organizations within the LDS Church, in later years she espoused women's suffrage for Utah Territory, achieved in 1870. Four days after the martyrdom of her prophet husband, she published her righteous anger in imagery of divine judgment:

> Never, since the Son of God was slain
> Has blood so noble flow'd from human vein
> As that which now on God for vengeance calls
> From "freedom's" ground—from Carthage prison walls!
>   Oh! Illinois! Thy soil has drunk the blood
> Of prophets martyred for the truth of God.
> Once lov'd America! What can atone
> For the pure blood of innocence thou'st sown?
>   . . .
>   Ye Saints! Be still, and know that God is just—
> With steadfast purpose in His promise trust:
> Girded with sackcloth, own His mighty hand,
> And wait His judgments on this guilty land!
> The noble Martyrs now have gone to move
> The cause of Zion in the Courts above.[60]

Among several claimants to the prophet's mantle, Brigham Young, the senior member of the Twelve Apostles, established his right to succeed Joseph as leader of the church. Where Joseph had been an imaginative, charismatic seer, Brigham was practical, decisive, and gruff. He had a

59. Kenneth Winn, *Exiles in a Land of Liberty* (Chapel Hill, 1989), 208–27.
60. Reprinted in Hallwas and Launius, *Cultures in Conflict*, 237–40.

better head for business. He received only one divine revelation, which set out the command structure for crossing the plains. The successful leader of the best organized large migration in American history, he has appropriately been called "the Moses of an American Exodus." A dissenting minority argued that the presidency should pass to the prophet's young son Joseph Smith III; they eventually established the Reorganized LDS Church, whose members (sometimes called Josephites, as distinguished from the Brighamites) have remained a separate denomination.[61] They did not join in the westward migration and did not practice polygamy.

Disillusioned with Illinois and the United States, Brigham set about planning the escape of his people to someplace else, where they could implement their theocratic vision of society and prepare for the millennium undisturbed. During Joseph's lifetime, Texas, Oregon, California, and Vancouver Island had already been considered. But the first priority remained completion of the Nauvoo temple, which was achieved by August 1845. Even before they finished construction, the Saints had begun to perform new rites there, based in part on Joseph's revision of Masonic rituals (restoring them to their ancient originals, he claimed).[62] When anti-Mormon violence resumed in September, Young promised state authorities his community would depart by the following spring. It was little enough time to ready and equip such an undertaking. To ensure Mormon departure, the state legislature voted (by wide bipartisan margins) to revoke Nauvoo's charter of self-government. By now, most gentiles saw Mormonism the way the nativists saw Roman Catholicism: as a denial of and a threat to American liberal pluralism. That opponents had to resort to illiberal measures themselves seemed to them regrettable but necessary.[63]

The exodus actually got under way early, in February 1846. With typical resourcefulness, Mormon families turned unusually cold weather to advantage, crossing the frozen Mississippi on foot. But when almost everyone in town tried to sell home and possessions at the same time, prices hit rock bottom; as in Missouri earlier, the departing Saints took a terrible financial

61. In 2000, the Reorganized LDS Church changed its name to the Community of Christ. They no longer call themselves Mormons.
62. On Mormon temple rites, see Paul Conkin, *American Originals: Homemade Varieties of Christianity* (Chapel Hill, 1997), 189–95.
63. On the conflict of political ideologies, see Marvin Hill, *Quest for Refuge* (Salt Lake City, 1989); Laurence Moore, *Religious Outsiders and the Making of Americans* (New York, 1986), 25–47; and the essays in Roger Launius and John Hallwas, eds., *Kingdom on the Mississippi Revisited* (Urbana, Ill., 1996).

beating. The Mormons did not cross the plains in a single group. During 1846, Brigham stretched out sixteen thousand people in camps all across Iowa. The circumstances taxed his leadership and the people's faith to the utmost. Having lost their savings in Nauvoo, many of the migrants needed to find temporary jobs along the way to feed their families. Persecuted, divided, impoverished, and frightened as they were, Brigham Young forged his people into a cohesive, purposeful New Israel. He enforced a military-style discipline and the pooling of resources. People would plant crops in one location and move on to another, leaving the harvest for the next company. The famous advance party—known in Utah as "the Pioneers"—left the staging area west of Winter Quarters, six miles north of present-day Omaha, on April 19, 1847, for the trek across the plains and mountains. It consisted of 143 men (3 of them the slaves of southern Mormons), 3 women (6 more women later joined the party), 2 children, 93 horses, 66 oxen, 52 mules, 72 wagons, and (since they were exploring) sextants, barometers, thermometers, telescopes, and a cannon.[64] Even in the advance party, most people did not know where they were headed.

Unlike most settler caravans, the Mormons employed no professional scouts or outfitters. Brigham chose the route west well, whether by divine guidance, careful preparation, or both. They managed good relations with all the Indian tribes except the Pawnee, who feared for the buffalo. Young admonished his people sternly to kill no more buffalo than they needed for food. On a good day the party made ten miles. The women cooked, washed, and gathered buffalo dung for fuel.[65] Much of the time they paralleled the Oregon Trail. They left messages with advice for subsequent parties. They took the Hastings Cutoff but were better prepared for it than the Donners had been. Along the way, the Pioneers could be fortified by the hymnody of one of their own number, William Clayton, written in Iowa the year before, on Brigham's order.

> Why should we mourn or think our lot is hard?
> 'Tis not so; all is right!
> Why should we think to earn a great reward,
> If we now shun the fight?
> Gird up your loins, fresh courage take,
> Our God will never us forsake.[66]

64. Stanley Kimball, *Heber C. Kimball* (Urbana, Ill., 1981), 151–54; Newell Bringhurst, *Brigham Young* (Boston, 1986), 89.
65. Ibid., 90.
66. From stanza 2 of "Come, Come Ye Saints," *Deseret Sunday School Songs* (Salt Lake City, 1909), no. 16.

On July 24, as the party emerged from Emigration Canyon in the Wasatch Mountains, the valley of the Great Salt Lake lay visible below. Brigham Young, ill inside one of the wagons, struggled up and looked out. Erastus Snow remembered him saying it: "This is the place."[67] It was isolated and barren, but those were assets, not liabilities. The Mormon leader did not want his people to settle in a place anyone else would want. Only one white person, a trader named Miles Goodyear, then made his home in the Salt Lake Valley; the Mormons bought him out.[68] As soon as Brigham had supervised building a stockade, planting crops, and beginning the irrigation system, he was off, heading back across the plains to Iowa. Along the way he greeted ten more Mormon parties coming on schedule. By the end of 1847, seventeen hundred Latter-day Saints had made their way to Utah. Until the transcontinental railroad made the trip easier in 1869, they continued to come by the thousands along the trail the Pioneers had marked out, the poorest of them, who could not afford wagons, pushing their few belongings in handcarts.

The Mormons transplanted their culture whole. Unlike so many other frontiers (Gold Rush California, for example) Utah experienced no transition from anarchy to civilization. The closest analogy in American history to the Mormon exodus would be the Great Migration of the Puritans from East Anglia to Massachusetts Bay in 1630, likewise religiously motivated, well organized, and implementing a preexisting blueprint. Brigham laid out Salt Lake City very much as Joseph had laid out Nauvoo, with wide streets at right angles, and lots distributed to faithful Mormons, all centered on a temple site. The Mormons proclaimed the State of Deseret, with generous boundaries much larger than the present state of Utah, and, like Joseph in Nauvoo, for a time Brigham united the leadership of church and state in his person. Young announced the ideal of a self-sufficient community, and this time he had geography on his side. "We do not intend to have any trade or commerce with the gentile world, for so long as we buy of them we are in a degree dependent upon them," he declared. "The Kingdom of God cannot rise independent of the gentile nations until we produce, manufacture, and make every article of use, convenience, or necessity among our own people."[69] Early Mormon Utah was the largest of American utopian communities, an example to the world but not a part of it.

67. Arrington and Bitton, *Mormon Experience*, 101.
68. Charles Kelly and Maurice Howe, *Miles Goodyear* (Salt Lake City, 1937).
69. Quoted in Arrington, *Brigham Young*, 169.

In the summer of 1848, a plague of crickets descended on the Mormons' first crop. Men, women, and children fought the horrid insects frantically. Then huge flocks of seagulls from Great Salt Lake appeared, devouring the crickets. Today, Seagull Monument in Temple Square, Salt Lake City, expresses gratitude for a providential deliverance, and Utah law forbids killing seagulls.[70]

Like the celibate Shakers and the Oneida perfectionists with their complex marriages, the Mormons had a pattern of gender relations all their own. The most distinctive feature of Mormon culture was the practice of plural marriage, or (as the gentiles called it) polygamy. Joseph Smith set out to restore the authentic religion of biblical times, and of course the patriarchs Abraham, Isaac, and Jacob took many wives. Joseph also taught that polygamous marriage constituted a step in the evolution of faithful Mormons toward godhood in the hereafter. ("As man now is, God once was: As God now is, man may be.")[71] The prophet shared his revelation commending plural marriage with a few Nauvoo intimates in 1843 while publicly denying the rumors of its practice. Careful inquiry has revealed that Joseph married between twenty-eight and thirty-three women, eleven of whom were already wives of other men. (It is not widely grasped that Joseph's plural marriages involved polyandry as well as polygyny.)[72] Among the prophet's wives was the widow of William Morgan, the Antimasonic martyr, although Joseph himself joined the Masonic Order. Brigham Young married nineteen wives in the three weeks just before leaving Nauvoo; some of these women may have been seeking to place themselves under his protection during the coming journey. In Utah, the Mormons felt freer to practice polygamy openly; Young proclaimed the doctrine publicly in 1852. By most counts, the second president of the church eventually had twenty-seven wives, who bore him fifty-six children.[73] Even in Utah, only about 10 percent of Mormon men practiced polygamy. A man was expected to support all his families, often

---

70. Only in retrospect did the Mormons attribute the seagulls' intervention to God. See William Hartley, "Mormons, Crickets, and Seagulls," *New Mormon History*, ed. Quinn, 137–52.

71. Lorenzo Snow's oft-quoted summary of the doctrine. Eliza R. Snow, *Biography and Family Record of Lorenzo Snow* (Salt Lake City, 1884), 46.

72. There are two forms of polygamy. *Polyandry* means a woman having more than one husband; *polygyny*, a man having more than one wife. See Todd Compton, *In Sacred Loneliness: The Plural Wives of Joseph Smith* (Salt Lake City, 2001); Richard Bashman, *Joseph Smith: Rough Stone Rolling* (New York, 2005), 437–46.

73. Counting the wives is complicated because Young apparently contracted a number of unconsummated marriages.

in separate establishments, which confined the practice to an economic elite. Plural marriage usually accompanied a man's advancement in the church hierarchy and showed his unreserved loyalty to the faith. Evidence of dissatisfaction with their situation among plural wives is less widespread than we might expect. Some women enjoyed their independence when their husband was living with his other families; others resented having to rear their children largely by themselves. Some felt jealous of the other wives, but sisterly affection was also common. Plural wives could divorce their husbands more readily than their husbands could divorce them; Ann Eliza Webb divorced Brigham Young.[74] After Utah became part of the United States in 1848, the Mormons claimed that the First Amendment protected their practice of polygamy as a "free exercise of religion." Eventually the Supreme Court ruled against them, and in 1890 the president of the LDS Church renounced the practice of plural marriage out of respect for the law of the land; the principle is still considered to enjoy divine sanction in the life hereafter.[75]

Ironically, the Mormons who sought to escape from the United States ended up playing a role in extending the United States. Their way of life, originally a millenarian critique of the larger society and a collectivist, authoritarian dissent from American individualistic pluralism, now impresses observers as the most "American" of all. How that transformation came about, however, is another story.

V

Sixty-eight United States dragoons commanded by Captain Seth Thornton rode out in the evening of April 24, 1846, on reconnaissance. They went to confirm intelligence that a Mexican military force had crossed the Rio Grande a few miles upstream from where Brigadier General Zachary Taylor's army encamped across the river from the Mexican town of Matamoros. The reports proved all too accurate. The next morning a superior Mexican force surprised and surrounded Thornton's soldiers at the Rancho de Carricitos. When the Americans tried to fight their way out, eleven were killed and the rest captured. The enemy allowed a wounded survivor to make his way back to Taylor bearing the news and assurances that the captives would be treated decently. (In fact, a few

---

74. For the women's perspective on plural marriage, see Lawrence Foster, *Women, Family, and Utopia* (Syracuse, N.Y., 1919), 189–98, and the essays in Claudia Bushman, ed., *Mormon Sisters*, 2nd ed. (Logan, Utah, 1997).

75. *Doctrine and Covenants of the Church of Jesus Christ of Latter-day Saints* (Salt Lake City, 1952), 256–57.

weeks later the prisoners were exchanged.) Thus inauspiciously began the war between the United States and Mexico. "Hostilities may now be considered as commenced," Taylor reported dryly to Washington. When his message reached the White House fourteen days later, the president and his cabinet responded promptly and without surprise. They had been about to recommend to Congress a declaration of war against Mexico anyway, and the little battle facilitated this task. President Polk spent all day Sunday, May 10, drafting his war message with the help of Secretary of State Buchanan and Secretary of the Navy Bancroft, taking out only enough time to go to church.[76]

Some people in the United States and elsewhere wondered what a U.S. military force was doing along the Rio Grande in the first place. The answer to this question went back more than a year. When Congress passed its joint resolution offering Texas statehood in March 1845, the president of the Lone Star Republic, Anson Jones, displayed distinct coolness to the action. Jones had an alternative vision of the Texan future; he dreamed of a powerful independent nation, stretching from sea to sea. In May 1845, the British brokered a deal by which Mexico finally offered Texas peace and recognition provided the republic remained independent. But the proposal came too late. Given the options of independence and U.S. statehood, the Texan Congress had no difficulty choosing annexation, a decision ratified by a convention in Austin on July 4, 1845. An American state constitution was approved at local community meetings throughout Texas in October; the U.S. Congress accepted it in December. But not until February 1846 would President Jones deliver a farewell address and turn legal authority in Texas over to officials of the new state government.

The Mexican minister to the United States had denounced the annexation of Texas as "an act of aggression," and in response to the statehood offer severed diplomatic relations on March 6, 1845.[77] Back in 1843, Mexico had warned the United States that annexation of Texas would mean war, but this threat was not actually carried out. Though the Mexican government considered attempting the reconquest of Texas in July 1845 after the rejection of their recognition proposal, they stopped short of it. Santa Anna's irresponsible policies had left the Mexican government at the mercy of financiers who made short-term loans at high interest rates.

76. Karl Jack Bauer, *The Mexican War* (New York, 1974), 48, 81; Pletcher, *Diplomacy of Annexation*, 376–77.

77. William Manning, ed., *Diplomatic Correspondence of the United States: Inter-American Affairs* (Washington, 1937), VIII, 699–700.

The same financial straits that precluded adequately defending California made waging war for Texas unattractive. In August 1845, President José Joaquín Herrera, a moderate *federalista* who had inherited Santa Anna's financial mess, let it be known that he would receive a U.S. emissary to discuss Texas. Herrera had a program of fiscal and domestic reform in mind, which could only be addressed if his country reconciled itself to the loss of Texas.[78]

"I regard the question of annexation as belonging exclusively to the United States and Texas," Polk had declared in his inaugural address—thereby serving notice that he would not negotiate it with Mexico.[79] But what constituted Texas? The boundary of Texas as a Mexican province had been the Nueces River, and this had remained the approximate limit of effective control by the Lone Star Republic. Nevertheless, as we have seen, Texans had repeatedly laid claim to the Rio Grande as their boundary. With annexation, the undefined boundary between Mexico and Texas became a problem between Mexico and the United States. And from the day of annexation, the Polk administration made clear to all that it considered Texas as extending to the Rio Grande.

Polk did not wait for the legal transfer of authority before trying to secure Texas, defined broadly, against Mexican reoccupation. The American diplomatic envoy to the Texan Republic, Old Hickory's nephew Andrew Jackson Donelson, pestered President Jones with the importance of military preparations against Mexican attack. Nevertheless the Polk administration did not trust Donelson to press the Texans hard enough to occupy the disputed area beyond the Nueces (since he belonged to Van Buren's faction), so they reinforced him with ardent expansionists like former Arkansas governor Archibald Yell to make the case more forcefully. In April 1845, Secretary of the Navy Bancroft ordered Commodore Robert Stockton's naval squadron to Galveston. A zealous American imperialist, Stockton there set about recruiting Texans for a military expedition into the disputed territory. Texan president Jones put a stop to it. He had reason to believe Stockton acted at Polk's direction and later complained that they had tried to "*manufacture a war*" between Texas and Mexico that the United States would then take over.[80] Stockton may have exceeded his instructions, although his activities certainly did not lose him the confidence of the administration.

78. Pletcher, *Diplomacy of Annexation*, 172–75.
79. *Presidential Messages*, IV, 380.
80. Anson Jones, *Memoranda and Official Correspondence* (New York, 1859), 46–52, quotation from 49; italics in original.

Having decided to place a U.S. military presence on the ground, on June 15, 1845, Polk ordered General Zachary Taylor across the Sabine into Texas. Later he specified that Taylor should "approach as near the boundary line, the Rio Grande, as prudence will dictate."[81] But Taylor employed the prudent discretion permitted him and stationed his force, ultimately about four thousand strong, at Corpus Christi by the mouth of the Nueces, the southernmost point under Texan control. There he spent several months intensively training his soldiers. The administration would have liked a more aggressive posture but didn't feel ready to over-rule their field commander. In August, Polk's secretary of war, William Marcy, instructed Taylor to treat any attempt by the Mexican army to cross the Rio Grande as an invasion of the United States and an act of war.[82]

Meanwhile, President Polk did not ignore President Herrera's invitation to negotiate. Polk spent much of the fall of 1845 arranging a mission to Mexico City by Congressman John Slidell of Louisiana, a fluent Spanish-speaker who had been of great help to Polk in the last election. He instructed Slidell that the annexation of Texas was nonnegotiable; he should confine himself to purchasing California and/or New Mexico and to collecting the debts Mexico owed U.S. citizens. The claims of American citizens against Mexico were badly inflated; out of some $8.5 million presented, a mixed commission had found about $2 million justified. In 1844, the financially strapped Mexican government stopped making payments on this debt, although they did not repudiate it. Polk told Slidell that at the very least, he should obtain Mexican recognition of the Rio Grande boundary in return for U.S. assumption of these debts. Beyond this, Slidell had authority to pay $5 million for New Mexico and $20 million more for California.[83] Since Mexico had already refused to sell any of its national territory, these instructions did not augur well for a resolution of outstanding differences. The United States did not occupy a strong moral position in getting tough when others fell behind in their debt payments, considering that several U.S. states had defaulted on larger sums to foreign creditors earlier in the 1840s. Complicating the mission further, Slidell's number two, William Parrott, had already been declared personally offensive and unacceptable by the Mexicans. (Parrott, the brother of the troublemaking consul in Mazatlán, made

81. Orders of June 15 and July 30, 1845, quoted in Pletcher, *Diplomacy of Annexation*, 255–56.
82. Orders of Aug. 23 and 30, 1845, quoted ibid., 260.
83. Manning, *Diplomatic Correspondence*, VIII, 172–82.

$690,000 in claims against the Mexican government that a previous U.S. envoy had described as "exaggerated in a disgusting degree"; more recently he had been exposed as a spy.)[84] Finally, although the Mexican authorities had offered to engage in negotiations over Texas, they made it clear they would not resume full diplomatic relations so long as a United States army occupied what they considered a substantial portion of their country. Polk appointed Slidell not an emissary with a particular assignment but a "minister plenipotentiary"—meaning that for Mexico to receive him would constitute a resumption of full diplomatic relations. In short, President Polk had so structured the U.S. mission that it would be extremely difficult for President Herrera even to meet the envoy, let alone negotiate with him.

Can Polk have really expected the Slidell mission to achieve a satisfactory resolution of the outstanding issues? Surviving evidence indicates that he and his advisors entertained some hope of success. From the standpoint of Mexican authorities, to sell California was as unthinkable as it would be for any U.S. administration to sell Michigan to Canada. But Polk and his circle felt no empathy with their Mexican counterparts. On the other hand, Polk did recognize the sensitive nature of Slidell's appointment as minister plenipotentiary, and he did not submit it to the Senate for confirmation.

Polk's strategy toward Mexico was precisely the converse of his strategy toward Britain. On Oregon, he wished to appear uncompromising but achieve a compromise. Regarding the issues with Mexico, however, he wished to seem reasonable and open to discussion while pressing uncompromising demands that would probably lead to war. Polk's insistence on the exaggerated Texan boundary claim, in the words of his modern biographer, "is the clearest indication of the administration's anxiety to complete annexation not only at the earliest possible moment, but also as offensively to Mexico as possible."[85] The area between the Nueces and the Rio Grande had significance not only for its own sake but also as possible cause for war with Mexico.

What lay behind Polk's provocative Mexican policy is not too difficult to discern: the acquisition of more territory, especially California. The administration's official newspaper, the *Washington Union*, proclaimed the goal as early as June 1845. "The road to California" beckoned Americans: "Who will stay the march of our western people?" Of course, the *Union*

---

84. Waddy Thompson, quoted in Sellers, *Polk, Continentalist*, 230.
85. Sellers, *Polk, Continentalist*, 223–24.

not only presented administration policy but sought to rally public support for it. If Mexico should resist the U.S. takeover of California, the paper predicted, "a corps of properly organized volunteers (and they might be obtained from all quarters of the Union) would invade, overrun, and occupy Mexico."[86] Both publicly and privately, Polk avowed a strong geopolitical interest in California, in particular a determination to deny the area to Britain. Historical investigation of the papers of the Foreign Office in London has discovered no intention to take over California, though the British would have preferred it to remain Mexican. Nevertheless, informants like Duff Green and Oliver Larkin warned Polk to fear the California ambitions of the superpower of the time. Polk portrayed himself as defending the principles of the Monroe Doctrine in California. No doubt the president also shared the characteristic Jacksonian desire to extend the area of white American agricultural settlement; his territorial ambitions, after all, included much besides California. Finally, Polk valued California for its opening onto the Pacific. "The possession of the Bay and harbor of San Francisco is all important to the United States," he instructed Slidell. "If all these [advantages] should be turned against our country, by the cession of California to Great Britain, our principal commercial rival, the consequences would be most disastrous."[87] Ironically perhaps, the congressional Whigs representing maritime New England demonstrated less eagerness than the Democratic president to obtain "an empire on the Pacific." Sometimes Democratic imperialists invoked the commercial advantages of expansion simply as a tactic to win support, as Walker had done in arguing for Texas. But Polk really does seem to have wanted to expand American power and commerce in the Pacific, manifesting once again that solicitude for American overseas trade that the Democratic Party had displayed ever since the Jackson administration.[88]

President Polk was fully prepared to persuade the Mexicans to cede California by whatever means it took. Perhaps their financially strapped government would sell territory for money, which is why Polk told Slidell to press the issue of Mexico's foreign indebtedness so hard. Jackson had done this too when he wanted to buy Texas. But in all probability, only military defeat could force this cession upon them. Such a defeat could come in either of two ways: war with the United States or a revolution in California analogous to what had happened in Texas.

86. *Washington Union*, June 2, 6, 1845.
87. Manning, *Diplomatic Correspondence*, VIII, 180.
88. See Norman Graebner, *Empire on the Pacific* (New York, 1955); and Shomer Zwelling, *Expansion and Imperialism* (Chicago, 1970).

Polk pursued all the possible routes to California—purchase, revolution, and war—simultaneously. Slidell's instructions included detailed specifications of various purchases of territory and the amounts the United States would pay for each. In October 1845, while Slidell waited in New Orleans, Polk sent Commodore Stockton off to California via Cape Horn, issued secret orders to the U.S. consul in Monterey to encourage disaffected Californians to seek U.S. annexation, and communicated these plans to Captain John C. Frémont's overland military expedition to California. Earlier orders had directed the navy's Pacific Squadron to be ready to seize San Francisco at the outbreak of war. The effect of these coordinated messages would be felt in California the following spring. But also in October, the *Washington Union* (the administration's organ) announced that on the question of whether the Mexican government would receive Slidell hung the issue of peace or war.[89] If Mexico did not rise to the challenge of the Rio Grande boundary dispute, the Slidell mission itself could provide a casus belli. Buchanan instructed Slidell, in case of failure, to let Washington know right away, while Congress was still in session, so that "prompt and energetic measures may be adopted on our part."[90] Slidell would know that meant a congressional declaration of war.

When Slidell arrived in Mexico City on December 6, 1845, he posed an excruciating difficulty for the government there. Once the terms of his appointment as plenipotentiary became known, Mexican public opinion reacted with outrage. The *federalistas* themselves divided, with *moderados* supporting President Herrera while the *puros*, left-wing populists, denounced his temporizing with foreign aggressors. Herrera's moderate foreign secretary, Manuel de la Peña y Peña, told his chief that although justice called for resistance to U.S. demands, their country's weakness counseled concession.[91] But the political left and right agreed in repudiating any willingness to negotiate with the insulting *yanquis*. Herrera fell from power before the end of the year without having received Slidell. Mariano Paredes, a *centralista* and a professional soldier, replaced him. Slidell vented his anger in his reports to Polk. "A war would probably be the best mode of settling our affairs with Mexico," he wrote.[92] After confirming that the Paredes administration would not receive him either, he

89. *Washington Union*, Oct. 2, 1845.
90. Manning, *Diplomatic Correspondence*, VIII, 183.
91. George Brack, *Mexico Views Manifest Destiny* (Albuquerque, N.M., 1975), 160–63.
92. John Slidell to James K. Polk, Dec. 29, 1845, quoted in Pletcher, *Diplomacy of Annexation*, 357.

sailed for home. In later years Slidell would embark on another famous diplomatic mission, to persuade France to help the Southern Confederacy; that too would fail.

Throughout the early months of 1846, the Oregon crisis remained unresolved and impinged on the crisis with Mexico. It stiffened the resistance of Mexican public opinion against U.S. demands by encouraging false hopes of British support. Meanwhile, American public opinion focused chiefly on the danger of war with Britain; the possibility of war with Mexico attracted much less attention. Northern Democrats in Congress provided the president solid support in his strong stand against Mexico because they still expected him to support their point of view on Oregon. Thus the existence of another simultaneous international confrontation did not moderate administration policy toward Mexico (as one might expect) but had the opposite effect. Polk's insistence that the compromise line he had secretly offered to the British in February must be publicly proposed by them first slowed down the resolution of the Oregon controversy in the spring. Perhaps he stalled on Oregon deliberately, knowing that it strengthened his hand in dealing with Mexico. Polk juggled two balls in the air at the same time. Depending on how the Oregon issue was playing out at any given moment, he slowed down or speeded up the confrontation with Mexico. In the end, the timing worked out just right for him. The British offered their Oregon compromise before learning of the fighting on the Rio Grande; Congress voted war against Mexico before northern Democratic expansionists had been disillusioned by the partition of Oregon.

In January 1846, having learned of the impending failure of the Slidell mission, the administration ordered Taylor to enforce U.S. claim to the disputed area beyond the Nueces by advancing to the Rio Grande. The nineteenth-century historian and legal scholar James Schouler called Polk's insistence on the Rio Grande as the Texan boundary "pretentious," and it has found few defenders among historians since. Even Justin Smith, the historian whose book *The War with Mexico* (1919) remains the account most sympathetic to Polk, recognized that his boundary claim was "unsound." Polk's twentieth-century biographer Charles Sellers called his insistence on the Rio Grande boundary "indefensible"—meaning it was *logically* indefensible.[93] Militarily, however, Polk resolved to defend it. If the president intended Taylor's advance simply to pressure Mexico into

---

93. James Schouler, *History of the United States* (New York, 1889), IV, 523; Justin Smith, *The War with Mexico* (New York, 1919), I, 449, n. 4 and 5; Sellers, *Polk, Continentalist*, 223.

negotiating, it seems odd that he did not order it sooner. Coming when it did, the action was more likely to provoke hostilities. Thomas Hart Benton, who had consistently favored a peaceful resolution of both the Oregon and Mexican problems, disapproved of Polk's order but did not go public with his views.[94] The Whig press publicly deplored the advance as constituting aggression.

Taylor took his time marching into the disputed territory, part of the Mexican state of Tamaulipas, for it contained some eight thousand local Mexicans. It was cattle-ranching country, with scattered villages (in the largest of which, Laredo, the U.S. Army counted 1,891 persons upon occupation).[95] Some of these civilians sold produce to Taylor's army; others fled before his coming. The *rancheros* had already suffered heavy losses to rustlers gathering herds to stock ranches up in the Texan Republic; in the coming war they would lose everything.[96] At Arroyo Colorado a Mexican military force drew up across Taylor's front, commanding him to halt; he proceeded across the arroyo anyway, and the Mexicans withdrew without firing. "Old Rough and Ready," as the American soldiers called their gruff, informal general (who often wore casual civilian clothes instead of a uniform), set up a supply base on the coast at Point Isabel and reached the site of present-day Brownsville in late March. "We have not one particle of right to be here," U.S. Lieutenant Colonel Ethan Hitchcock wrote in his diary. "It looks as if the government sent a small force on purpose to bring on a war, so as to have a pretext for taking California and as much of this country as it chooses."[97] Across the Rio Grande lay the Mexican town of Matamoros. The U.S. commander built a fort and trained his guns on the town center. The Mexican commander in Matamoros, Pedro de Ampudia, demanded the American army withdraw from the disputed territory or face military action. Taylor responded by blockading the mouth of the Rio Grande on 12 April, preventing Ampudia from receiving supplies by water and legally an act of war. Meanwhile, U.S. naval squadrons hovered by Veracruz and Mazatlán, ready to blockade Mexico's chief ports on the Atlantic and Pacific coasts respectively.

94. Polk, *Diary*, I, 375, 390 (May 3, 11, 1846); Thomas Hart Benton, *Thirty Years' View* (New York, 1856), II, 678–79.
95. Many secondary works erroneously describe the disputed area as uninhabited, but see Andres Tijerina, "Trans-Nueces," in *The United States and Mexico at War*, ed. Donald Frazier (New York, 1998), 434–35.
96. J. Frank Dobie, *The Longhorns* (Boston, 1941), 11, 28.
97. Journal entry for March 26, 1846, in Ethan Allen Hitchcock, *Fifty Years in Camp and Field*, ed. W. A. Croffut (New York, 1909), 213.

In Mexico City, the Paredes government faced a terrible dilemma. Popular sentiment and the governors of the northern states demanded a stand against what they considered a U.S. invasion. The new president had indulged these calls for firmness as his stepping stone to power. Now he realized all too well that the national treasury was bankrupt, the armed forces ill prepared for a major war, and hopes of European intervention illusory. Yet the fall of Herrera demonstrated that no Mexican government could temporize and stay in power. The *rancheros* living in the disputed area began to wage a guerrilla war of their own, ambushing U.S. soldiers who strayed too far afield. At length, on April 23, Paredes issued a proclamation blaming the United States for initiating hostilities and directing his new commander in Matamoros, Mariano Arista, to undertake "defensive" operations, yet adding that this was not a declaration of war. Paredes may have intended a resort to arms only if Taylor crossed the Rio Grande, but Arista considered the blockade sufficient provocation and notified Taylor on the twenty-fourth that "hostilities have commenced." That day he sent sixteen hundred cavalrymen over the river, where they engaged Thompson's dragoons on the twenty-fifth. Mexico drifted into war confusedly and indecisively. The Mexican Congress, with whom the constitutional power rested, never did declare war. The proclamation of resistance to invasion that Paredes finally issued on July 1 served as the functional equivalent of a war declaration.[98]

In Washington, Polk realized by early May that a compromise solution to the Oregon controversy was imminent and that when it occurred, it would hurt him with northern Democratic expansionists. A war with Mexico would help keep his party united on the basis of patriotism, but the war needed to come first, before the Oregon settlement. Northern Democrats were already asking the wrong kind of questions to suit Polk: "Why should we not compromise our difficulties with Mexico as well as with Great Britain?" demanded the *Chicago Democrat*. "If it is wicked to go to war with England for disputed territory, it is not only wicked but cowardly to go to war with Mexico for the same reason."[99] The latest reports from General Taylor indicated that he expected an attack at any time. But on Saturday, May 9, after finally having a chance to talk with John Slidell in person, Polk felt he could wait no longer. He persuaded

98. Mariano Paredes, "Proclamation," April 23, 1846, in *Origins of the Mexican War*, ed. Ward McAfee and Cordell Robinson (Salisbury, N.C., 1982), II, 134–35; Mariano Arista to Zachary Taylor, April 24, 1846, quoted in Charles Dufour, *The Mexican War* (New York, 1968), 61; Brack, *Mexico Views Manifest Destiny*, 117–18, 149, 165–66.
99. Quoted in Pletcher, *Diplomacy of Annexation*, 382.

his cabinet to support him in sending a war message to Congress immediately. (Only Bancroft voted to go on waiting for Taylor to be attacked.) The grounds on which Polk would ask Congress to declare war were refusal to receive Slidell and failure to keep up payments on acknowledged international debts. These did not constitute a strong case for war, even by nineteenth-century standards, the unmentioned real grounds being Mexico's refusal to sell territory. The president adjourned his cabinet meeting about 2:00 p.m. Four hours later the adjutant general brought to the White House Taylor's report of the fight on April 25. Now the president could compose a much stronger message:

> The cup of forbearance had been exhausted even before the recent information from the frontier of the [Rio Grande] Del Norte. But now, after reiterated menaces, Mexico has passed the boundary of the United States, has invaded our territory and shed American blood upon the American soil. . . . War exists, and, notwithstanding all our efforts to avoid it, exists by the act of Mexico herself . . . I invoke the prompt action of Congress to recognize the existence of the war, and to place at the disposal of the Executive the means of prosecuting the war with vigor, and thus hastening the restoration of peace.[100]

When presenting this war message to Congress, Polk's party managers did everything they could to stifle discussion, questions, and dissent. In the House of Representatives, they allowed only two hours for debate, then used up all but thirty minutes of this having presidential documents read aloud. The declaration of war (literally, an assertion that a state of war already existed by act of Mexico) was attached as a preamble to a bill appropriating $10 million for the troops at the front and authorizing the president to enlist fifty thousand more for defense against foreign invasion. The Whig opposition had wanted to be able to vote support for the troops without endorsing Polk's claims that Mexican aggression was to blame and that war already existed. They conceded that the executive had authority to repel an invasion (in this case meaning that Taylor's army would expel the Mexicans from the disputed area), but they wanted a thorough discussion by Congress before declaring a full-scale offensive war upon Mexico. However, with the support of the Democratic majority, the amendment attaching the preamble passed, 123 to 67. This vote reflects the actual extent of opposition to the war, rather than the tally on the combined bill, which carried 174 to 14, with 35 abstentions. "The river Nueces is the true western boundary of Texas," declared the Kentucky

---

100. *Presidential Messages*, IV, 442–43.

Whig Garrett Davis during the brief debate. "It is our own President who began this war. He has been carrying it on for months."[101] Nevertheless, Davis and most of the Whigs felt obliged to vote for war in the form the Democratic leadership had packaged it. Twenty-two Democrats abstained, which was as far as any member of the party was willing to go in expressing doubts about the president's methods. The fourteen irreconcilables, led by the venerable John Quincy Adams, were all northern Whigs with safe seats. "It is on Mexican soil that blood has been shed," explained one of them, Luther Severance of Maine, and for their "manly resistance" to U.S. invasion, the Mexicans should be "honored and applauded."[102]

In the Senate, opponents of the war included not only Whigs but John C. Calhoun. The politician who had done so much to make Polk president and to bring Texas into the Union now feared the consequences of more expansion. A striking figure in the Senate with his piercing eyes and shock of gray hair, Calhoun, now sixty-four years old, demanded time to study the situation and find out whether the Mexican government really intended war; he could not stomach Polk's executive war-making. As he put it, Calhoun "could not agree to make war on Mexico by making war on the Constitution." Fundamentally, Calhoun was not interested in territorial acquisitions unless they promised to strengthen the power of slavery. Texas certainly did, but not California and New Mexico, which the South Carolinian foresaw would provoke sectional conflict while offering little practical likelihood of slavery's extension. He worried that war with Mexico might jeopardize relations with Britain, on which cotton-growers so heavily depended. He also feared to acquire a Mexican population of mixed race that, if enfranchised, would breach the virtual monopoly of political power enjoyed by white Americans.[103]

Repeated tests of strength between the war and peace parties all produced votes of about 26 to 20 (the minority consisting of eighteen Whigs and the two senators from South Carolina). On May 12, the combined military appropriation and war declaration measure passed 40 to 2; Calhoun and two Whig senators abstained. These figures hid considerable opposition even among the Democrats. Several Van Buren Democrats, including Benton and John Dix of New York, voted for war only with great reluctance and after hard political arm-twisting. Benton pointed out

101. *Congressional Globe*, 29th Cong., 1st sess., 794.
102. Quoted in Sellers, *Polk, Continentalist*, 421.
103. Ernest Lender, *Reluctant Imperialists: Calhoun, the South Carolinians, and the Mexican War* (Baton Rouge, 1984), 6–10, 62–63.

on the Senate floor that the Mexican Congress had not declared war and the Mexican president had undertaken only defensive military actions.[104]

The unwillingness of the Whigs to oppose the war any more forcefully reflected their reading of public opinion. Polk had assessed the feelings of the popular majority accurately, at least for the moment. He had decided that imperialism was a winner with the electorate, that he could stir it up and take advantage of it politically. The exciting news from Texas and the Rio Grande would play to feelings of bellicose nationalism even more successfully than had Oregon and the Columbia River. The Whigs remembered all too well how the Federalist Party had opposed the War of 1812 and been rewarded with permanent oblivion. They resolved not to repeat that mistake.

On May 13, 1846, the president issued a proclamation announcing the state of war. The secretary of state suggested he also issue a statement that the United States had not gone to war to acquire territory; Buchanan thought this would reassure Britain and France, which might otherwise intervene to preempt the United States taking California. Polk immediately rejected the advice, as he described in his diary:

> I told him that though we had not gone to war for conquest, yet it was clear that in making peace we would if practicable obtain California and such other portion of the Mexican territory as would be sufficient to indemnify our claimants on Mexico, and to defray the expenses of the war which that power by her long continued wrongs and injuries had forced us to wage. I told him it was well known that the Mexican Government had no other means of indemnifying us. . . . I was much astonished at the views expressed by Mr. Buchanan.[105]

104. *Congressional Globe*, 29th Cong., 1st sess., 796 (Calhoun), 798 (Benton), 803–4 (votes). See also John Schroeder, *Mr. Polk's War* (Madison, Wisc., 1973), 20–26.
105. Polk, *Diary*, I, 397–99 (May 13, 1846).

19

The War Against Mexico

On the first of May 1846, before word of fighting had even reached Washington, General Taylor pulled most of the Army of Occupation (as it had been named) out of Fort Texas and, leaving only a small garrison behind, fell back toward Port Isabel to protect his supply base from the advancing Mexicans. General Arista had intended to encircle Taylor's smaller force, but a shortage of boats delayed his crossing the river until the Americans had got away. He then besieged Fort Texas and, with his main body, blocked Taylor's return to relieve it. A young U.S. second lieutenant arriving at Port Isabel on May 2 heard his first hostile gunfire, the distant booming of the Mexican cannon starting to bombard the fort. Ulysses Grant never forgot his reaction: He "felt sorry" he had joined the Army.[1]

Zachary Taylor had been born into the Virginia plantation gentry; his family were related to both James Madison and Robert E. Lee, and his daughter married Jefferson Davis of Mississippi (overcoming her father's doubts that it was a suitable match). But Taylor grew up in Kentucky, where his father had moved. He had earned his nickname, "Old Rough and Ready," during many years of service in the remote frontier areas where the Regular Army mediated between settlers and Native people. He had served with credit in the War of 1812, Black Hawk's War, and the Seminole War, and no one doubted his courage, but some wondered whether he would really be up to his present assignment. His adversary, Mariano Arista, a handsome, red-haired man who had lived in the United States, enjoyed the respect of both friend and foe.

After taking several days to strengthen the defenses of Port Isabel, Taylor commenced his return to Fort Texas with 2,288 soldiers. On May 8, at a place called Palo Alto, he encountered Arista's force of 3,270 barring his way, its flanks secure, daring him to attack. An artillery duel ensued, in which the U.S. guns inflicted heavy casualties while the Mexican ones had too short a range and lacked high explosive shells.[2] This forced Arista to do the attacking. The dense chaparral between the armies, which he

---

1. Ulysses Grant, *Personal Memoirs*, ed. Mary and William McFeely (1885; New York, 1990, 65.
2. Zachary Taylor to Thomas Butler, June 19, 1846, in Zachary Taylor, *"Old Rough and Ready" Speaks His Mind* (New Haven, 1960), 5.

had intended to hinder the *yanquis*, now deterred him from advancing his own infantry. So he repeatedly ordered his cavalry to charge. But the horsemen could not break the "hollow square" formation assumed by the U.S. infantry, and they suffered heavy losses from the surprisingly mobile U.S. field guns. At the end of the day neither army had broken through. The Mexicans had suffered worse, but the brilliant U.S. Major Sam Ringgold, who had designed the "flying artillery" that proved so successful, lay mortally wounded.

Arista decided to pick a different position and again try to force Taylor to attack him. So he withdrew a few miles and regrouped behind a *resaca*, a dry riverbed with more thick chaparral before it. The new location protected his troops from the kind of artillery fire they had endured the day before. Taylor's solution was to attack with a mixed force of infantry, cavalry, and mobile artillery, concentrating firepower at short range on the center of the Mexican line. Meanwhile, Taylor's light infantry turned Arista's left flank and got across the *resaca*. Arista himself led his lancers in a final desperate charge but could not overcome U.S. firepower. Fearing now that their line of retreat would be cut, his soldiers took off down the road. When they reached the Rio Grande, many swam across without waiting for boats, some drowning in the attempt. The Americans captured a hundred prisoners, field guns, small arms, and much ammunition the Mexicans could ill afford to lose. Taylor now relieved Fort Texas and renamed it Fort Brown, in honor of its commander, Major Jacob Brown, who had been killed during the siege. On May 18, the Americans crossed the Rio Grande and occupied Matamoros while the Mexican army silently withdrew, accompanied by a thousand women and children, to Monterrey. Matamoros became the place where Taylor received the volunteers who came streaming in during the months to come.[3]

Taylor's victory in the first major battle demonstrated a superiority in U.S. firepower that would remain a conspicuous feature of the entire war. (The Americans named each day a separate battle—Palo Alto and Resaca de la Palma—and counted them as two victories.) As at New Orleans in 1815, the Americans owed their success in large measure to their artillery—the superior range of their guns, the quality and quantity of their ammunition, and the expertise with which the gunners handled their technology. The infantry too had better equipment than their Mexican

---

3. On Palo Alto/Resaca de la Palma, see John Eisenhower, *So Far from God* (New York, 1989), 71–85; K. Jack Bauer, *The Mexican War* (New York, 1974), 49–63; Charles Dufour, *The Mexican War* (New York, 1968), 64–83; William DePalo, *The Mexican National Army, 1822–1852* (College Station, Tex., 1997), 100.

counterparts, carrying weapons that fired farther, faster, and more accurately. Though most infantrymen bore muskets, some had rifles. Samuel Colt's revolver, patented in 1835, became a commercial success a dozen years later when the inventor got a wartime contract from the U.S. Army for an improved version. What later generations would recognize as the characteristic American mode of warfare, emphasizing industry, engineering, and technological proficiency, was already appearing.[4] Though rural America, in the person of the Jacksonian President Polk, made the war, industrial-technological America won it.

War highlighted a great disparity between the economic and human resources of the combatant nations. The United States census of 1840 counted a burgeoning population of 17 million. The population of Mexico, by contrast, had declined by 10 percent during the prolonged disorders of her revolution against Spain and then leveled off; the government's calculation of 1842 (not an actual enumeration) showed 7 million Mexicans.[5] The economies of the two countries displayed an even greater inequality. The years since 1815 had not been kind to the former New Spain; plagued by political instability, independent Mexico had not realized the economic potential of her natural resources. Fierce localism and poor transportation hindered the emergence of an integrated nationwide economy even more than they did in the United States. Independent Mexico received little European immigration and had even expelled its Spanish-born people, losing their talents and skills. Mexico's gross national product fell to less than half the peak attained in 1805; not until the 1870s did it exceed that level. In the absence of financial rationalization, the Mexican government became the prisoner of foreign and domestic creditors: By 1845, 87 percent of its revenues went for debt service.[6] The republic's financial weakness severely restricted its war-making potential; the Mexican army found it easier to raise troops than to feed, clothe, arm, and pay them. Across the vast northern borderlands, tribal Indians counterattacked against Mexican settlements made in earlier generations, wreaking havoc almost with impunity. The inability of the Mexican nation to defend these areas against the Comanche, Navajo, and Kiowa en-

---

4. See Donald Houston, "The Superiority of American Artillery," in *The Mexican War*, ed. Odie Faulk and Joseph Stout (Chicago, 1973), 101–9; Waldo Rosebush, *Frontier Steel: The Men and Their Weapons* (Appleton, Wisc., 1958), 111–136.

5. Brantz Mayer, *Mexico as It Was and as It Is* (New York, 1844), 300–301.

6. David Weber, "The Spanish-Mexican Rim," in *The Oxford History of the American West*, ed. Clyde Milner et al. (New York, 1994), 73; Justin Smith, *The War with Mexico* (1919; Gloucester, Mass., 1963), II, 7.

couraged watching U.S. imperialists to judge that it would not be able to defend them against an invading army either.[7]

The war of the United States against Mexico has been called a "rehearsal" for the Civil War that began thirteen years later.[8] This is true not only in the sense that many senior officers in both Union and Confederate armies got their first experience of combat as junior officers in Mexico. In a strategic sense as well, making war on Mexico presented problems analogous to those of the Civil War. Like the Union in that later conflict, the United States needed to invade and conquer a vast country in the face of determined resistance. As in the Civil War, the U.S. Navy played a major role by blockading ports and preventing the enemy from importing munitions. Mexico, like the South later, enjoyed the benefit of interior lines of communication, which Santa Anna would exploit in the largest battle of the war, Buena Vista. Like the Confederates, the Mexicans strove to gain foreign intervention to preserve their national integrity. Finally, like the Confederacy, Mexico hoped to prolong the conflict until the invaders tired and went home without getting what they came for.

Women played a more conspicuous role with the armies in the U.S.-Mexican War than they did in the Civil War. In Mexico, the armies on both sides had women with them. For generations, armies on campaign had included women in noncombatant positions such as nurses, laundresses, and cooks; in the U.S. Army some were on the payroll, others simply drew rations. Spanish had a word for them, *soldaderas*; in English, they were called "camp followers." Traditionally, officers brought their wives with them, although the U.S. Army followed this custom only occasionally in the Mexican War. Many camp followers, however, married enlisted men. In the Revolution, camp follower "Molly Pitcher" famously took over serving a cannon when her husband was killed; the British army carried its women all the way across the Atlantic. The camp followers in Taylor's army included six-foot-tall Sarah Borginnis, admired for her strength and courage under fire.[9] Even more than their U.S. counterparts, Mexican soldiers relied for logistical support on their *soldaderas*, who sometimes brought their children. In desperate situations, women with the Mexican army assumed combat roles; a woman who led a cavalry charge by the lancers against the Americans at Monterrey earned

7. Brian Delay, "Independent Indians and the U.S.-Mexican War," *AHR* 112 (2007): 35–68.
8. Alfred Bill, *Rehearsal for Conflict: The War with Mexico* (New York, 1947).
9. Eisenhower, *So Far from God*, 72–73.

praise from her enemies as "a second Joan d'Arc."[10] Because some camp followers were prostitutes, the international evangelical revival of the nineteenth century discouraged armies from employing them. However, the presence of male civilians with the army, such as sutlers, teamsters, and newspaper reporters, continued into the Civil War.

Officers in both armies could take personal servants with them. In the U.S. Army, this meant officers from the South brought slaves. Occasionally these slaves seized an opportunity to desert to freedom on the other side.[11] Free black men were not allowed to enlist in the army, though many of them served in the U.S. Navy, as they did in the civilian merchant marine.

The outbreak of warfare along the Rio Grande underscored the need for faster communication in North America. While Andrew Jackson had won the Battle of New Orleans after the treaty of peace had been signed, Old Rough and Ready won his victory before war had been declared, and long before any of the assistance Congress had so hastily authorized could reach him. At this time only 120 miles of telegraph wire had been strung in the United States, none of it south of Richmond. The war brought Professor Morse's experiment to rapid maturity; his Washington-Baltimore line hummed for two and a half hours transmitting President Polk's war message to Congress on May 11. The eagerness of both the government and the press for news from the front stimulated rapid expansion of the telegraph system. By June 1846, the wires connected Washington with Philadelphia, New York, and Boston. War news collected at New Orleans, where the *Picayune* published it. The *Picayune*'s star reporter, George Wilkins Kendall, defined the new occupation of war correspondent. A pony express system transmitted copies of the *Picayune* to the closest telegraph line. By the end of the war the telegraph reached as far south as Charleston, and New Orleans news had been brought within three days of Washington. Even so, only one message at a time could be sent over the early wires, so bottlenecks developed. To pool telegraphed news, in 1848 six New York City papers formed the first wire service, the Associated Press.[12]

Because they underestimated the difficulty of the undertaking, President Polk and his advisors had not hesitated to force a war upon Mexico.

---

10. Elizabeth Salas, *Soldaderas in the Mexican Military* (Austin, Tex., 1990); Robert Johannsen, *To the Halls of the Montezumas* (New York, 1985), 137–41, quotation from 137.

11. James McCaffrey, *Army of Manifest Destiny* (New York, 1992), 112.

12. Kenneth Silverman, *Lightning Man* (New York, 2003), 276–79; Johannsen, *To the Halls of the Montezumas*, 17–19.

They knew that the Mexican armed forces were poorly equipped, and California and New Mexico weakly held, and that the Mexican government, essentially bankrupt, had no prospect of remedying these deficiencies. As a result, the U.S. administration anticipated that a war would be short, easy, and inexpensive. But this reflected little knowledge of Mexican geography, of the hazards of disease to an invading army, or of the Mexican people's resolve. The war had been under way only a few months when the Polk administration began trying to negotiate a peace treaty, assuming that its adversaries would quickly recognize the futility of resistance. Ironically, the winning side in this war was the side more eager to end it; bringing the Mexicans to the peace table proved difficult.

Except for one company of Texas Rangers, the small army that won at Palo Alto and Resaca de la Palma consisted of regulars, that is, professional soldiers. (The lieutenants included future Civil War generals George Gordon Meade, Ulysses Grant, and James Longstreet.) Most of the volunteers who arrived afterwards to reinforce Taylor's army came from the South and West, at first because of their proximity to the theater of operations, later because enthusiasm for the war cooled rapidly in the Northeast. Although the volunteers quickly swamped the regulars in numbers, their usefulness was limited not only by their lack of training and discipline but also by their enlistment for just one year, at the end of which they were free to leave and often did. Volunteer units were often raised by local politicians authorized to do so; they might prefer to recruit politically loyal men and close their eyes to others willing to serve. Taylor quickly concluded that the whole system of recruiting volunteers was inappropriate.[13] The short enlistment term helped fill the ranks and reflected the overconfidence of the American public and the Polk administration; eventually, however, the government realized it should ask volunteers to serve for the duration of the war. The experience of the war with Mexico revealed the value of a professional army, especially the professional officer corps; talk of abolishing the military academy at West Point ended.

The president did not welcome the improved image of the Regular Army. Most career army officers were Whigs. They expected the peacetime army, like internal improvements, to benefit from Whig strong government; indeed, the Corps of Engineers, then as now, played a prominent role in constructing internal improvements. In addition, Democratic Party Indian policies—the Removal and the Seminole War—had

---

13. Zachary Taylor to R. W. Wood, Sept. 3, 1846, *Letters of Zachary Taylor from the Battlefields* (Rochester, N.Y., 1908), 51.

become unpopular with army officers who witnessed their effects at first hand.[14] Polk needed victories, yet feared they might create another Whig military hero like William Henry Harrison. As one who knew wrote sarcastically, the president wanted "a small war, just large enough to require a treaty of peace and not large enough to make military reputations dangerous for the presidency."[15] The two most successful generals in the war, Zachary Taylor and Winfield Scott, became subject to intense jealousy and suspicion by the president because of their Whig political connections; once they had served his purposes he did all he could to disparage their accomplishments and derail their careers. Polk sought to counteract the party affiliation of the regulars in his appointments of "generals of volunteers." Every one of the thirteen generals Polk made was a Democrat, most of them former officeholders. (Other officers for the volunteer units were chosen by state governors or elected by the men they commanded.) The president even proposed that overall command of the army go to Democratic senator Thomas Hart Benton, though Congress never approved the Missourian's commission as lieutenant general, and Benton, like most Van Buren Democrats, eventually fell out completely with Polk.[16]

Mexico maintained a standing army small by European standards but substantially larger than that of the United States. Besides its war with Texas, this army had also repelled invasions by Spain and France and had subdued several domestic insurrections in the generation since independence. As a result officers often had combat experience; indeed, many of those in the higher ranks had fought for the Spanish king during the Mexican Revolution. Unfortunately many officers felt more loyalty to the army as an institution than to their civilian superiors. Within the Mexican army the cavalry constituted an elite arm, famous for superb horsemanship. The infantry included peasant conscripts even in peacetime, often *indios* with little knowledge of the Spanish language or sense of Mexican nationality, equipped with old muskets sold off by the British army as surplus after the Napoleonic Wars. The antiquated artillery was the weakest branch, a deficiency for which Mexico would pay dearly in coming battles. Although the official salary scales in the Mexican army compared favorably with U.S. ones, in practice the army often went unpaid and unsupplied, and resorted to preying upon local civilians. As the

14. Richard Winders, *Mr. Polk's Army* (College Station, Tex., 1997), 34.
15. Thomas Hart Benton, *Thirty Years' View* (New York, 1856), II, 680.
16. See Marcus Cunliffe, *Soldiers and Civilians* (Boston, 1968), 305–18; Jeffrey A. Smith, *War and Press Freedom* (New York, 1999), 94–98.

war went on, the Mexican army increasingly had recourse to untrained levies, who might go into combat never having fired their weapons. Finally, the states of the Mexican union controlled local militia, called national guard units. Although not necessarily well equipped or trained, the national guard units manifested high espirit de corps and in defense of their homes stood up firmly to U.S. firepower.[17]

In Zachary Taylor's force, immigrants made up at least half the enlisted personnel; this was typical of the composition of the regular U.S. Army. The Irish alone constituted a quarter and the Germans 10 percent. The Mexicans made strong appeals to U.S. troops to switch sides, targeting immigrants and Catholics in particular. Their broadsides emphasized the injustice of the invaders' cause in the eyes of "civilized people" and stressed what North American Catholics had in common with Mexican Catholics. Alluding to well-known riots by U.S. Protestant nativist mobs, a Mexican pamphlet asked, "Can you fight by the side of those who put fire to your temples in Boston and Philadelphia?" Mexico also offered land grants to opposing soldiers who would desert and claim them: two hundred acres for a private, five hundred for a sergeant. Together, the inducements and propaganda had an effect. The first shots in the war were fired on April 4, 1846, not between Mexican and U.S. troops, but by American sentries at an immigrant deserter swimming across the Rio Grande to the Mexican side. (The episode prompted questions in Congress.) Around three hundred U.S. deserters, the great majority of them Catholics and/or immigrants, joined the Mexican army. The Mexicans organized them into a unit of their own named St. Patrick's Battalion, for the largest single national group among the *sanpatricios* was of Irish origin.[18] In response, the U.S. Army appointed its first two Catholic chaplains (one of whom was killed in service). Most of the 9,207 deserters from the U.S. armed forces did not take up arms against their former comrades but simply disappeared. The desertion rate in the war with Mexico, 8.3 percent, was the highest for any foreign war in United States history—twice as high as that in the Vietnam War. Brutal corporal punishments, doubts about the American cause, and the prejudices of nativist

17. Josefina Zoraida Vazquez, "War and Peace with the United States," in *The Oxford History of Mexico*, ed. Michael Meyer and William Beezley (New York, 2000), 362; DePalo, *Mexican National Army*, 97, 127; Robert Ryal Miller, *Shamrock and Sword: The Saint Patrick's Battalion in the U.S.-Mexican War* (Norman, Okla., 1989), 39.
18. Peter Stevens, *The Rogue's March: John Riley and the St. Patrick's Battalion* (Washington, 1999), 83, 110, 221. My estimate of the number of U.S. deserters in the Mexican army derives from Stevens, 241–42, and Dennis Wynn, *The San Patricio Soldiers* (El Paso, Tex., 1984), 20.

officers all contributed to the desertion problem. Sometimes regular soldiers deserted to join volunteer units, in search of bounties and a more lax discipline.[19]

The conquest of Mexico by the United States turned into a longer, harder, more expensive struggle than the politicians who provoked the conflict had expected. While the size of the armies was small, their casualty rates were high. Indeed, the war against Mexico has been accurately described as the deadliest that the United States has ever fought: One American soldier out of ten died in less than two years of service, while an almost equal number were incapacitated and sent home. Disease accounted for seven-eighths of the deaths. Living in crowded, unsanitary conditions and drinking impure water, the soldiers frequently fell prey to dysentery, body lice, and communicable infections. Regulars suffered less than volunteers, for they understood the importance of clean camps and well-cooked food, and they had all been inoculated against smallpox. In the end, the war cost the United States 12,518 lives and almost one hundred million dollars.[20] Mexico lost many more lives and suffered extensive economic and social disruption. Although the total casualties look small by comparison with those of the Civil War, they did not seem small at the time, nor was the American public mollified by the fact that Mexican casualties were higher.

Taylor's early victory over a larger army that chose its ground well got his country's war with Mexico off to an impressive start. Throughout the conflict the U.S. armed forces demonstrated superb strategic planning, tactical leadership, technical skill, and courage. The occupation of so much of Mexico's vast territory by a comparatively small army in less than two years represented an astonishing feat of arms. The extent of this military achievement has never been fully appreciated, because Americans preferred to believe that their national expansion occurred automatically, as the fulfillment of an inevitable and plainly manifest destiny. Once over, the war against Mexico was conveniently forgotten, along with the bitter partisan divisions it provoked among Americans themselves.

II

Although President Polk had invoked the danger to Taylor's troops in securing a swift declaration of war from Congress, he showed little further interest in them once the war had begun. As he laid out his plans to the

---

19. Miller, *Shamrock and Sword*, 23, 159, 165, 174. Paul Foos, *A Short, Offhand, Killing Affair* (Chapel Hill, 2002), 109.

20. Winders, *Mr. Polk's Army*, 139–40.

cabinet on May 30, 1846, these called for rapid seizures of Alta California and Nuevo México, followed soon by a peace treaty on the basis of *uti possidetis*, the United States retaining permanently what its armies had occupied.[21] Of the two Mexican provinces, California was by far the more important to U.S. policymakers.

As early as June 1845, Secretary of the Navy Bancroft had sent orders to Commodore John D. Sloat of the Pacific Squadron in Honolulu to occupy San Francisco immediately upon the outbreak of war with Mexico. The same month Captain John C. Frémont led a military expedition overland westward from St. Louis. If war broke out, both navy and army would be poised for action in California.[22] Frémont's qualifications for his sensitive mission included extensive experience in the Far West; a capable, energetic wife, Jessie Benton Frémont; and the political influence of her father, Senator Thomas Hart Benton. The captain also had a strong sense of his own destiny and a talent for publicity. After crossing the Rockies and the Great Basin, he and his party startled the Mexican authorities in California, where Johann Sutter welcomed them to his estate called New Helvetia on 10 December. By the twenty-seventh, Frémont had made his way to Monterey and a conference with the U.S. consul there, Thomas Oliver Larkin. Larkin, ever an eager conspirator, got "the idea that great plans are meditated to be carried out by certain persons."[23] Frémont assured the Mexicans he was just exploring and would soon leave for Oregon. When his sixty-two heavily armed and ill-mannered visitors still remained on March 8, the suspicious authorities ordered them out. Frémont at first tried to defy the order, then moved his party very slowly northward. Along the way they massacred Indians.[24] After two months they reached Klamath Lake just over the California-Oregon border.

On April 17, 1846, a U.S. warship arrived at Monterey bearing Marine Lieutenant Archibald Gillespie with secret instructions from the State Department for both Larkin and Frémont, dated—the courier having come via Mexico City, Mazatlán, and Hawaii—the previous October. The letters appointed Larkin a confidential agent and told him to assure any potential rebels in California that "they would be received as

---

21. *Diary of James K. Polk*, ed. Milo Quaife (Chicago, 1910), I, 437–40.
22. On the planning of the two-pronged enterprise, see Russel Nye, *George Bancroft* (New York, 1944), 152.
23. Quoted in Neal Harlow, *California Conquered* (Berkeley and Los Angeles, 1982), 62.
24. Tom Chaffin, *Pathfinder: John Charles Frémont and the Course of American Empire* (New York, 2002), 291.

brethren" should they wish to follow the Texan example and seek annexation by the United States. The administration expressed particular anxiety to preempt any British intervention in California.[25]

(Polk was not the only one to think California might interest the British. Desperate for money to prepare for war with the United States, President Paredes had offered to mortgage California to Britain in return for a loan. If the British had accepted the proposal, the U.S. president's dream of acquiring California would have turned into a nightmare. Ironically, Polk's zealous pursuit of California almost lost it.)[26]

Consul Larkin eagerly accepted his new assignment, and Gillespie hurried north, catching up with Frémont on May 8. The marine delivered his packet and filled the Pathfinder in on the latest intelligence and gossip, no doubt including that Larkin had told José Castro, *comandante* at Monterey, "Our Flag may fly here in thirty days." In his *Memoirs* Frémont claimed he learned that "possession of California was the chief object of the President." At the end of the conversation Frémont concluded—as he put it—that "my hour had come."[27] He turned and headed south, back to raise up a rebellion in California. Neither Frémont's actual orders nor the other messages brought him by Gillespie have ever come to light, so we do not know whether he followed his instructions or went beyond them. Perhaps the government left things ambiguous and expected Frémont to read between the lines. The role of a headstrong military leader on the frontier operating with unclear official authorization—the role of Jackson in Florida and Robert Stockton in Texas—was repeated by Frémont in California. Contemporaries recognized the pattern. Indeed, many filibustering expeditions tried to take over foreign territory by force of arms with no U.S. government authority at all (as happened over the years in Nicaragua, Cuba, Texas, Canada, and the Floridas).[28]

In 1846, the population of Alta California numbered about fifteen thousand, not counting the much larger number of Native Americans who lived according to their own cultures and largely remained neutral in the war (though some did fight for or against Frémont). Only about

25. For an extended discussion of these orders, see Frederick Merk, *The Monroe Doctrine and American Expansionism* (New York, 1966), 111–32.

26. Ibid., 112–15; David Pletcher, *The Diplomacy of Annexation* (Columbia, Mo., 1973), 593.

27. John C. Frémont, *Memoirs of My Life* (Chicago, 1887), 489; Harlow, *California Conquered*, 83, 85.

28. See Robert E. May, *Manifest Destiny's Underworld* (Chapel Hill, 2002).

eight hundred of these people were of U.S. origin, most of them very recent arrivals.[29] With the reckless daring that characterized his whole life, young Captain Frémont expected to make a successful revolution based on those eight hundred. Although no one in California knew yet that war had broken out between the United States and Mexico, everyone knew enough to think it likely. *Comandante* Castro began to make inquiries about undocumented foreign settlers, and though he was generous with permissions to remain, some emigrants from the U.S. became fearful of eviction. Emboldened by Frémont's presence and probably encouraged by him, a band of these settlers stole a hundred or so horses intended for Castro and then on 14 June abducted a prominent landowner and retired general, Mariano Vallejo, holding him prisoner for two months despite the fact that he was the best friend the Americans had among the *californios*. The next day the rebels seized the town of Sonoma and raised a flag with a crudely pictured grizzly bear on it. After fending off Castro's militia, naming Frémont as their leader, and spiking the seventeenth-century Spanish cannons in the undefended Castillo de San Joaquín overlooking the Golden Gate, the Bear Flaggers gave themselves a celebration at Sonoma on the Fourth of July. At Frémont's insistence, they declared the independence of California, then listened to a reading of Jefferson's Declaration (an invariable feature of American celebrations of the Fourth in those days), and—being in Mexico—danced a *fandango*.[30]

The significance of this little rebellion was transformed three days later by the appearance of the United States Navy, which took possession of Monterey, as in 1842, without bloodshed. Although no official notification had reached him, Commodore Sloat had taken care to assure himself that there was a war, not wishing to repeat Commodore Jones's embarrassment. While cautious in that way, Sloat showed an astonishing presumptuousness of his own. He proclaimed not simply a wartime occupation but the permanent annexation of California to the United States, which he had no legal authority to do. The next day, July 8, Captain John B. Montgomery of the USS *Portsmouth* performed the same ceremony at Yerba Buena (renamed San Francisco in January 1847). Thus Sloat cut short the possibility of an independent California Republic. In Sonoma, the Stars and Stripes replaced the Bear Flag that had flown for three weeks. When HMS *Juno* visited San Francisco Bay on July 11, the Royal Navy could only observe an American fait accompli.[31]

29. Dufour, *Mexican War*, 138.
30. Harlow, *California Conquered*, 97–114.
31. Bauer, *Mexican War*, 172.

In the middle of the month Robert Stockton arrived, fresh from trying to "manufacture a war" in Texas, and succeeded the ailing Sloat as commander of the Pacific Squadron. Stockton managed to persuade Frémont that a naval commodore (equivalent to a brigadier general) outranked an army captain and then, recognizing a kindred spirit, delegated to him tactical command of U.S. forces on land, into which the Bear Flag rabble were incorporated. The two filibusterers, Stockton and Frémont, then went about conquering the rest of California. They acted with dispatch but also with such tactlessness that they completely alienated most of the *californios*, who, having long enjoyed considerable autonomy, might have welcomed the new regime. On August 13, Stockton occupied Los Angeles, a town of fifteen hundred that had replaced Monterey as Mexican civil capital of California. On August 17, a ship arrived at San Pedro carrying, at last, official news of the U.S. declaration of war. General Castro and Governor Pío Pico having departed with eight hundred followers, Stockton and Frémont thought the war in California over.

But in late September 1846, the *californios* rose in revolt against the U.S. occupation, using such weapons as they could find. In contrast to the ease with which the Mexican authorities had been expelled, subjugating these resolute people took hard fighting. They surrounded the U.S. garrison in Los Angeles under Lieutenant Gillespie, who then capitulated. A Swedish immigrant named Johan Braune ("Juan Flaco," or Lean John) carried news of the uprising five hundred miles north to San Francisco in five days; at one point he had to run twenty-seven miles between horses.[32] Stockton thereupon headed back south by ship. Although a naval officer, he undertook operations on land with a mixed force of army, navy, marines, and local volunteers. Meanwhile the *californios* retook Santa Barbara and San Diego and captured Oliver Larkin. Stockton proved unable to reconquer southern California and awaited reinforcements under Stephen Watts Kearny, coming across the desert from New Mexico. At San Pascual on December 6, 1846, the overconfident Kearny attacked *californios* under Andres Pico; in the ensuing battle, the improvised lances of Pico's horsemen proved at least a match for the sabers of the U.S. cavalry. It turned out that Stockton had to rescue Kearny, not the other way around. After Stockton and Kearny had joined up, however, their combined forces were able to win the Battle of Los Angeles on January 8 (shouting "New Orleans!" as they charged, since it was the anniversary of Jackson's victory) and retake the capital. A few days later Frémont's

32. William Dofflemyer, "Juan Flaco: The Paul Revere of California," *Pacific Historian* 13 (1969): 5–21.

"California Battalion" showed up, a mixture of U.S. soldiers with settler volunteers and Native American allies, having marched all the way from northern California. The now outnumbered insurgents realized the game was up. Frémont, ignoring the two senior officers, signed a regional peace treaty with the *californios* at Cahuenga on January 13, 1847, that promised them the rights of American citizens and ended fighting in Alta California.[33]

On January 19, Stockton prepared to return to sea and named Frémont "governor of the territory of California," though the commodore lacked any authority to establish civil rule.[34] Kearny actually possessed the proper authority from Washington to set up a government in California, but Stockton and Frémont refused to acknowledge this. After a month's standoff, Kearny fortunately prevailed; the erratic, contentious Frémont would not have made a good governor.[35] Stockton was replaced by Commodore Branford Shubrick; Frémont, by Colonel Richard Mason as military governor. Back east, Kearny charged Frémont with insubordination despite a long-standing friendship between the two. A court-martial attracting nationwide attention convicted Frémont, but his sentence of dismissal from the service was remitted by the president. The angry Pathfinder then resigned from the army anyway and became a popular celebrity. Polk might have acted differently if he had known that Frémont would run for president against the Democrats in 1856 on a platform favoring the restriction of slavery.[36]

III

Second only to California in importance as an object of President Polk's war was New Mexico. For this acquisition too he planned carefully and early. In 1845, Polk sent out two major military reconnaissance expeditions into the West, one to the Rockies and the other through the Indian Territory to Santa Fe. They came back with useful intelligence, both geographical and human, relating to the Native American populations of the vast region in which the army would operate in years to come.[37]

33. Lisbeth Haas, "War in California, 1846–1848," *California History* 76 (1997): 331–55.
34. Stockton's proclamation is quoted in Dale Walker, *Bear Flag Rising* (New York, 1999), 254.
35. On Frémont's personality, see Andrew Rolle, *John Charles Frémont: Character as Destiny* (Norman, Okla., 1991).
36. See Bernard DeVoto, *The Year of Decision, 1846* (Boston, 1943), 455–67.
37. William Goetzmann, *Army Exploration in the American West* (New Haven, 1959), 109–11.

Upon the declaration of war in May 1846, it did not take long for Polk to assemble what was called the Army of the West with the conquest of New Mexico its first objective. As its commander he appointed Brigadier General Stephen Watts Kearny (pronounced "Karny"), a tough, capable officer with extensive frontier experience. On June 5, Kearny's advance guard departed from Fort Leavenworth in present-day eastern Kansas. The Army of the West included 648 regulars and 1,000 Missouri volunteers, with 16 cannons and enormous supply trains consisting of 1,556 wagons, 459 horses, 3,658 mules, and 14,904 oxen and cattle. The largest military force ever seen in that part of the world, it manifested the extraordinary logistical resources available to the United States. To facilitate grazing by so many animals, the army moved in a number of separate detachments.[38] Looking ahead to the postwar period, Kearny's army included Lieutenant William Emory of the topographical engineers, assigned to map the area in the expectation of its annexation. (One of the transcontinental railroads would follow a route he suggested.) Bringing up the rear of the invading force came another 1,000 Missouri volunteers and, all the way from Council Bluffs, Iowa, the Mormon Battalion of 500 men and 70 women camp followers.[39]

The Mormon Battalion represented a bargain struck between James Knox Polk and Brigham Young. Young wanted the federal government's goodwill, especially when it began to seem likely that his intended destination would be annexed by the United States; Polk could use the troops. It was a heavy tax on the community's manpower, but the soldiers' pay would help the financially hard-pressed migration. Brother Brigham prompted men to volunteer and chose the company officers; Kearny chose Lieutenant Colonel Philip Cooke, a gentile, as the battalion commander.

In spite of the formidable nature of the forces at his command, Kearny preferred to avoid a battle. While armies usually try to keep their strength and disposition secret from the enemy, Kearny deliberately revealed his, intending to convince the *nuevomexicanos* that resistance was useless. In this he followed orders, for his civilian superiors hoped to disrupt the profitable commerce between Santa Fe and St. Louis as little as possible. In the generation since Mexico opened up her markets in 1821, the Santa Fe Trail had become the premier mercantile artery of the West, and Americans traded even as far south as Saltillo and Chihuahua. Within Santa Fe itself, some merchants, both Hispanic and Anglo, regarded a takeover by

38. Bauer, *Mexican War*, 127–34.
39. Stanley Kimball, *Heber C. Kimball* (Urbana, Ill., 1981), 151.

the United States as facilitating their commercial relations; these were called the "American party." A majority of people, however, including the Catholic clergy, regarded the prospect as an imposition of alien rule. Four thousand *nuevomexicanos* volunteered to defend Mexican sovereignty against the invaders. The governor assembled them at Apache Canyon, an ideal defensive location through which Kearny's army would have to pass to reach Santa Fe.[40]

Manuel Armijo, a self-made businessman, had been an effective governor of New Mexico. In 1841, his soldiers had captured an expedition by the Republic of Texas against Santa Fe and had marched the prisoners to Mexico City in triumph. This time, however, Kearny's army dwarfed the Texan one. On August 12, a delegation from the invaders arrived under a flag of truce. Armijo parleyed long in private with James Magoffin, Kearny's civilian agent. Within a few days Armijo disbanded his militia and fled to Chihuahua. Many Mexicans accused him of having taken a bribe from the *gringos*. Armijo did seem flush with money, and Magoffin later requested a reimbursement of fifty thousand dollars from the U.S. Treasury, of which thirty thousand was paid. Still, the governor might have decided that his volunteers with their primitive weapons could not long delay the inevitable and wanted to avoid the bloodshed. Armijo's motives, like those of Santa Anna, have long been the subject of speculation.[41]

On August 18, 1846, the Army of the West marched through Apache Canyon, entered Santa Fe without firing a shot and raised the Stars and Stripes. The soldiers had come 856 miles since June. The following Sunday General Kearny attended Mass, hoping the *santafeciños* would see it as a conciliatory gesture. The Americans built a fort with the aid of local stonemasons; two officers and a scholarly enlisted man drew up a new legal code for New Mexico. The Spanish crown had intended its northern borderlands to constitute a barrier against intrusion, but California, New Mexico, and Texas all wound up serving as gateways for it.[42]

Eighteen-year-old Susan Magoffin (sister-in-law of secret agent James) kept a diary that tells us much of what we know about life in occupied

40. Howard Lamar, *The Far Southwest* (New York, 1970), 56–65; Stephen Hyslop, *Bound for Santa Fe* (Norman, Okla., 2002) 294–310.
41. Benton, *Thirty Years' View*, II, 682–84; Daniel Tyler, "Governor Armijo's Moment of Truth," in Faulk and Stout, *The Mexican War*, 137–43; Brooke Caruso, *The Mexican Spy Company* (London, 1991), 99–100.
42. Lamar, *Far Southwest*, 63; see also Andrés Reséndez, *Changing National Identities at the Frontier: Texas and New Mexico, 1800–1850* (Cambridge, Eng., 2005).

Santa Fe and the difficulties there of sorting out true and false rumors of events elsewhere. Kearny sent detachments out to show the Apaches, Navajos, and Utes that from now on they would share their country with a more formidable white presence. It had been expected that much of the Army of the West would continue on from New Mexico to cooperate in the conquest of California. Accordingly, Kearny set out on September 25 for San Diego with the famous Kit Carson as guide, though when he heard that Stockton and Frémont had subdued California, he decided to take a mere hundred dragoons with him. Only later did Kearny realize that his expedition would have to fight the *californios*.

Before leaving, Kearny dispatched the 924 volunteers of the First Missouri Regiment under Colonel Alexander Doniphan to Chihuahua, more than five hundred miles to the south, in order to keep its trade within the orbit of Santa Fe. Three hundred wagonloads of traders and goods went with the expedition; Chihuahua would "buy American" at gunpoint. Doniphan had demonstrated his courage in Missouri as a gentile lawyer willing to stand up for Mormon rights. On this remarkable expedition he would demonstrate his qualities once again. Doniphan and his force accomplished their mission, along the way winning two battles and living off the country, to the anger of the luckless Mexican civilians in their path. His tough frontiersmen then marched another six hundred miles east to hook up with Taylor's army, and when they got home at the end of their one-year enlistments they found their exploits had become legendary, even if they had little impact on the outcome of the war.[43]

In October both the Second Missouri Regiment and the Mormon Battalion arrived in Santa Fe. The Missourians stayed as an occupying force, but, after resting for a week, most of the Mormons continued on to California, following a somewhat different route from Kearny's in order to increase geographical information, especially for a railroad route. They arrived in San Diego on January 29 and 30, 1847, ragged and footsore, a little too late to participate in the fighting. They had marched two thousand miles from Iowa and endured many hardships, particularly in the final leg of their journey, when they had to disassemble their wagons, carry them over the mountains, and put them back together again. These infantrymen were discharged in July 1847 without ever having heard a shot fired in anger. Brigham Young had promised that none of them would be lost to enemy action, and so it proved, though only 335 men and 3 women got all the way to San Diego. After discharge, some of them undertook the

43. There is a vivid account of Doniphan's exploits in DeVoto, *Year of Decision*, 382–407, a more sober assessment in Hyslop, *Bound for Santa Fe*, 404–23.

long journey back to Iowa to rejoin the Mormons there; some worked in California for a while. The great majority made their way eventually to Utah.[44]

Washington had instructed Kearny to leave as many Mexican officials as possible in office; instead, before his departure he appointed a civil government for New Mexico controlled by the "American party" merchant faction and headed by Charles Bent, the owner of Bent's Fort, who had married into a prominent Mexican family. These merchants welcomed the sudden expansion of trade with St. Louis (over $1,000,000 worth of merchandise in the first few months, triple any previous year's total).[45] Although this government included some Hispanics, the old Santa Fe elite and the Roman Catholic clergy felt marginalized, and those in all social classes who had wanted to resist the *yanquis* remained unreconciled. Undisciplined, carousing volunteer soldiers made the occupation unpopular. The Pueblo Indians, who had rebelled against Spanish and Mexican authority in the past, resented the newly imposed authority of the United States. On January 17, 1847, Pueblos and Mexicans joined together and rose against the U.S. occupation. The uprising centered in Taos, the second most important city of New Mexico and a trading center in its own right. Governor Bent, there on business, was killed along with others of the "American party" and his scalp paraded through the streets. Colonel Sterling Price, who had succeeded Kearny, moved quickly to crush the rebellion where it had broken out and nip it in the bud where it was still a conspiracy. The last group of insurgents were captured fighting in the Taos Pueblo Church, where they had taken refuge, on February 4. Instead of being treated as prisoners of war, sixteen of the captives were tried for murder and treason, convicted, and hanged. Hector Lewis Garrard, a young American who observed their trial, wrote: "I left the room, sick at heart. Justice! Out upon the word, when its distorted meaning is the warrant for murdering those who defend to the last their country and their homes." On June 26, 1847, Secretary of War Marcy ruled that the *insurrectos* could not be guilty of treason, since they owed no allegiance to the United States, but by this time all the sentences save one had been carried out.[46]

After the suppression of the uprising, New Mexico remained under an effective military dictatorship for four years until the organization of a

44. Norma Ricketts, *The Mormon Battalion* (Logan, Utah, 1996).
45. David Dary, *The Santa Fe Trail* (New York, 2000), 194.
46. James Crutchfield, *Tragedy at Taos* (Plano, Tex., 1995), 144; Hyslop, *Bound for Santa Fe*, 381–402, Garrard quoted on 400.

territorial government authorized by Congress in the Compromise of 1850. Of New Mexico's fifty to sixty thousand people in 1846, only about one thousand civilians were Anglo-American.[47] Although her population greatly exceeded that of either Texas or California at the time, New Mexico would have to wait sixty-six years for the statehood they both received promptly.

IV

Americans like to suppose that political partisanship diminishes in wartime. Whatever the general merits of this supposition, it does not apply to the war with Mexico, so highly politicized in both its origin and its conduct. Abraham Lincoln called it "a war of conquest fought to catch votes."[48] Yet the war turned out to be much less politically popular than American expansion and its slogan "manifest destiny." Notwithstanding the public appeal of imperialist braggadocio, the actual waging of war turned off many Americans outside the Southwest; the initial enthusiasm proved short-lived. Although successful on the battlefield and reaping huge territorial gains for the United States, the war with Mexico did not redound to the political advantage of either President Polk or his party.

Whig opposition to the war displayed remarkable consistency. The Whigs had taken strong exception to the assertion that even before the congressional declaration, war existed by the act of Mexico. They continued to dispute this throughout the war, arguing that President Polk, not President Paredes, bore responsibility for the resort to force; the invasion of the disputed territory and blockade of the Rio Grande, not the skirmish of April 25, marked the initiation of hostilities. "Shut your eyes to the whole course of events through the last twelve years," declared Horace Greeley's New York Tribune, "and it will become easy to prove that we are a meek, unoffending, ill used people, and that Mexico has kicked, cuffed and grossly imposed upon us. Only assume premises enough, as Polk does, and you may prove that it is New Orleans which has just been threatened with a cannonade instead of Matamoras [sic], and that it is the Mississippi which has been formally blockaded by a stranger fleet and army instead of the Rio del Norte [Rio Grande]."[49] Polk's abuse of his powers as commander in chief reminded Whigs of Andrew Jackson; once

47. Lamar, Far Southwest, 71, 82.
48. "Speech at Wilmington, Delaware" (June 10, 1848), Collected Works of AL, I, 476.
49. New York Tribune, May 13, 1846, quoted in Frederick Merk, "Dissent in the Mexican War," in S. E. Morison, F. Merk, and F. Freidel, Dissent in Three American Wars (Cambridge, Mass., 1970), 40–41.

again they took up the cudgels against executive usurpation. "No power but Congress can declare war," noted Daniel Webster, "but what is the value of this constitutional provision, if the President of his own authority may make such military movements as must bring on war?"[50] Surprisingly, American victories in battle did nothing to moderate Whig disapproval of the war. Except in Louisiana and Mississippi, southern Whigs condemned the war as vigorously as northern ones. In a series of speeches displaying eloquence and learning, Representative Alexander Stephens of Georgia decried Polk's "masked design of provoking Mexico to war" and the administration's "principle that patriotism consists in pliant subserviency to Executive will."[51]

Most of the Whig members of Congress continued to vote supplies to the armed forces while denouncing the administration for sending them into battle. They believed the soldiers and sailors entitled to the support of the government even when the government had abused their trust. Although historians have usually characterized their behavior as inconsistent, these Whig politicians accurately reflected the attitude of their Whig constituents. While Whigs disapproved of starting the war, they remained patriotic Americans, and most of them rejoiced at news of American victories. A radical minority of northern Whigs, however, refused to vote for war appropriations and demanded to bring the troops home. Joshua Giddings, the burly and outspoken radical Whig representative from the Ohio Western Reserve, invoked the example of the Whig members of Parliament who refused to vote in favor of supplies to wage an unjust war against the rebelling American colonists. Interestingly, the most defiant statement of opposition to the war came not from a radical but from a respected mainstream Whig, Senator Thomas Corwin of Ohio. Addressing the proadministration expansionists on February 11, 1847, he declared, "If I were a Mexican I would tell you, 'Have you not room enough in your own country to bury your dead men? If you come into mine we will greet you with bloody hands, and welcome you to hospitable graves.'"[52] Fourteen years later, Abraham Lincoln appointed Tom Corwin minister plenipotentiary to Mexico.

Opposition to any further territorial acquisitions from Mexico (beyond Texas) constituted a policy on which all Whigs, moderate and radical,

---

50. Daniel Webster, "Public Dinner at Philadelphia" (Dec. 2, 1846), *Writings and Speeches* (Boston, 1903), IV, 31–32.
51. *Congressional Globe*, 29th Cong., 1st sess., 15 (June 16, 1846), Appendix, 948; ibid., 2nd sess., 16 (Feb. 12, 1847), Appendix, 351.
52. *Congressional Globe*, 29th Cong., 2nd sess., Appendix, 216–17.

could agree. In principle, this represented a logical deduction from their opposition to a war of aggression. If the war was unjust, it would be immoral to use it to force Mexico to cede land to the United States. The most careful presentation of this position came from the eighty-six-year-old Jeffersonian statesman Albert Gallatin: *Peace with Mexico* (1847).[53] The policy of "No Territory" also made sense in practical terms. Whig politicians realized that a debate over whether to extend slavery into newly acquired territories would break their party wide apart across sectional lines. Never having been much enamored of the advantages of dispersing population across a vast territory, they preferred to forgo territory rather than see their party destroyed and the Union itself threatened by an argument over the spoils of war.[54]

Most Democratic politicians felt they had less to fear from expansion than the Whigs, their northern voters being less sensitive to slavery as a moral issue. Nevertheless, the Democratic Party was by no means immune to harm from the issue of slavery extension, as events would demonstrate. Indeed, some Democrats also came to oppose the war in varying degrees. Calhoun had resisted its declaration and continued to fear the consequences of the territorial acquisitions he knew Polk wanted from it. Disappointed at not being retained as secretary of state, Calhoun had reason to fear Polk as a rival for the leadership of southern sectionalism. Eventually the president gave up trying to keep Calhoun on board; he "has no patriotism," Young Hickory concluded.[55] But Democratic discontent extended to the North and West too. Some Democrats there felt they had been tricked into backing Polk's demand for all of Texas only to be betrayed by him in their own demand for all of Oregon. And some who had nursed a romantic vision of peaceful expansion found themselves embarrassed by Polk's militancy toward Mexico; these included John L. O'Sullivan, the very editor who had made the term "manifest destiny" famous. When O'Sullivan went public with his doubts about the necessity of the war, he was promptly fired from the *New York Morning News*; he then resigned from the *Democratic Review* and sold his interest in it. Without O'Sullivan, the *Democratic Review* proved unable to sustain its intellectual distinction.[56]

53. *Writings of Albert Gallatin*, ed. Henry Adams (New York, 1960), III, 555–91.
54. See Michael Morrison, "New Territory Versus No Territory," *Western Historical Quarterly* 23 (1992): 25–51.
55. Polk, *Diary*, II, 459 (April 5, 1847).
56. Robert Sampson, *John L. O'Sullivan and His Times* (Kent, Ohio, 2003), 201–4; Gilman Ostrander, *Republic of Letters* (Madison, Wisc., 1999), 220.

Other issues made for Democratic difficulties too; the administration's legislative program exposed rifts within the party. The Walker Tariff, named for the secretary of the Treasury and passed at his behest in the summer of 1846, repealed the Whig Tariff of 1842 and abandoned the principle of protection by substituting modest ad valorem rates for product-specific duties. This reaped goodwill among members of the British Liberal Party and American exporters committed to free trade, but it dismayed protectionist Pennsylvania Democrats in Congress, forcing them to choose between party loyalty and the economic interest of their constituents. The Walker Tariff only passed the Senate thanks to the votes of the two new (Democratic) senators from Texas. Meanwhile, a group of northwestern Democratic congressmen made common cause with the Whigs to pass an internal improvements bill providing federal subsidies for the dredging of rivers and harbors. Polk vetoed the measure, following the example of Jackson's Maysville Road Veto; this left its Democratic supporters feeling that the president cared nothing for their concerns. All these factors combined with the administration's general lack of candor to undermine trust, even among Democrats. Democratic senator John Dix of New York wrote Martin Van Buren that in Polk's war, "fraud is carried out to its consummation by a violation of every just consideration of national dignity, duty, and policy."[57]

In the long run, the most significant division of American opinion exacerbated by the war in Mexico was that between North and South. The doctrine of America's manifest destiny had not sprung originally from a slave power conspiracy but from policies with nationwide appeal and deep cultural roots. When James Knox Polk came into office, territorial expansion did not constitute a sectional issue but a party one. Beyond party advantage, Polk's desire for California and New Mexico seems (insofar as one can speculate about this secretive person's motives) prompted more by a geopolitical vision of national power, to make the United States dominant over North America, than by an intention to strengthen the institution of slavery. Polk did not share Calhoun's disposition to view all matters in terms of their impact on the slavery question. Nevertheless, as his term went by, his administration increasingly appeared narrowly southern in outlook. The president's imperialist objectives came to prompt a bitter sectional dispute over slavery's extension, bearing out Calhoun's foreboding.

57. Michael Holt, *The Rise and Fall of the American Whig Party* (New York, 1999), 232–37; John Dix to Martin Van Buren, May 16, 1846, quoted in John Schroeder, *Mr. Polk's War* (Madison, Wisc., 1973), 21.

What brought the simmering discontent of northern Democrats to a boil was Polk's bizarre conspiracy with Santa Anna, now exiled in Cuba. Secret discussions with a go-between named Alejandro Atocha persuaded Polk that if he arranged safe passage back to Mexico for Santa Anna, the former dictator would seize power again and then conclude a treaty of peace along the lines Polk desired. This plot had actually been laid even before the war began and helps explain Polk's confidence that it would be a short one. In August 1846, by prior arrangement, a British ship bearing Santa Anna from Cuba passed through the U.S. blockade into the port of Veracruz. Military defeats having discredited Paredes and his *centralistas*, Santa Anna exploited his old charisma and did indeed return to the presidency within a few months. But the consummate opportunist decided to betray the *gringos* rather than his countrymen. He broke whatever promise he had made to Polk, allied with the prowar wing of the *federalistas*, and set about rallying the Mexican public to support the war effort. Atocha's proposal had taken advantage of the administration's proclivity for deviousness and secrecy to help Santa Anna regain power. As Thomas Hart Benton aptly expressed it in his memoirs, "Never were men at the head of a government [in wartime] less imbued with military spirit, or more addicted to intrigue" than Polk and his cabinet. In December 1846, congressional Whigs exposed the Polk–Santa Anna conspiracy. For a time the administration denied its existence, but Polk admitted it in his Annual Message to Congress later that month. The Democratic congressional majority refused to conduct the full inquiry into the subject that Whigs demanded. Santa Anna's return animated Mexican resistance and prolonged the war. Polk finally realized that he had been duped and that Alejandro Atocha was "a great scoundrel."[58]

When he was expecting an early peace settlement with Santa Anna, Polk requested from Congress in August 1846 a $2 million appropriation for "defraying any extraordinary expenses which may be incurred in the intercourse between the United States and foreign nations." The president wanted the funds available for a quick down payment on the purchase of land from Mexico. Any Mexican government that ceded territory to the United States would risk overthrow, and this money (Polk explained in his diary) would enable it to pay the army and keep it loyal.[59] Others noticed that the money would also be available for bribes—perhaps to Santa Anna himself. The bill betrayed the administration's intention to obtain territorial concessions, though this had not yet been publicly avowed as a war aim. Whig radicals had been accusing the administration of seeking to expand the area of slavery; now, other northerners came to share this concern. When Representative Hugh White, a New York Whig, warned that Congress must prevent Polk from employing the requested money to extend slavery, a dozen northern Democratic congressmen decided to send Polk a message that he could no longer take them for granted. One of them, David Wilmot of Pennsylvania, introduced an amendment to the $2 million appropriation specifying that slavery should not be permitted in any territory acquired by it. Wilmot's famous "proviso" passed the House, 83 to 64, on a cross-party sectional vote. In the Senate, the entire appropriation, proviso and all, was filibustered[60] to death during the waning hours of the session by a prominent Whig in defense of the party's principle of No Territory.

Wilmot and his friends belonged to the Van Buren wing of the party, who had hoped to salvage some of the vast expanse of Texas for free soil and felt that Polk had manipulated and misled them on this and other matters. The Van Burenites had no representative in the cabinet and had been ignored in the distribution of patronage, even in New York. But Wilmot's proviso appealed to many besides Van Buren followers. All northern Whig Representatives and fifty-two of the fifty-six northern Democrats in the House voted for it. Polk sent his request for money to make peace with Mexico on the same day (August 8, 1846) that he submitted the Oregon Treaty to the Senate, making it at last clear to all northern Democrats that although they had supported his expansionist plans in the southwest, he would not support theirs for the 54° 40' line. Polk's disposition to compromise with Britain but not with Mexico no doubt reflected his estimate of the different power of the two countries, but contemporaries attributed it to the dominance of the South over the North in policymaking. Growing dissatisfaction among the northern electorate with southern political power had already manifested itself in the repeal of the gag rule sixteen months earlier. Now, opposition to the extension (as distinguished from the existence) of slavery proved to be a cause on which many ordinary northern voters and politicians from both major parties could join together.

Wilmot differentiated himself sharply from the abolitionist movement. He framed his measure as an appeal to the white working class, not as a humanitarian benefit to blacks. Calling his proposal the "White Man's

---

60. "Filibuster," derived from a Dutch word for "freebooter," had two distinct meanings in this period: adventurers undertaking illegal expeditions, and the obstruction of legislative action by endless debate.

Proviso," he boasted that his purpose was to "preserve for free white labor a fair country, a rich inheritance, where the sons of toil, of my own race and own color, can live without the disgrace which association with Negro slavery brings upon free labor."[61] The proviso remained an issue in the second session of the Twenty-ninth Congress in the winter of 1846–47; it passed the House again (repeatedly), but not the Senate, where the South was stronger. In the end, Polk got his appropriation (increased to $3 million) without Wilmot's amendment—and without the Whig amendment sponsored by Georgia's John Berrien, ruling out the acquisition of territory from Mexico altogether. But ten northern state legislatures adopted resolutions endorsing Wilmot's proviso in various forms, demonstrating its continued potential as an issue.[62]

The Wilmot Proviso tended to identify opposition to the war, at least in the North, with opposition to slavery and/or its extension. Abolitionists had already made the link; so had the radical land-reformers like George Henry Evans who targeted the northern working class. Opposition to the war drew strength from religious denominations that had long harbored antislavery advocates, notably New School Presbyterians, Congregationalists, Freewill Baptists, Unitarians, and Quakers, though it was by no means confined to them. A few war critics embraced the entirely pacifist position of the American Peace Society and its international movement, but more typically they objected to the particular war then being waged. (The Peace Society gave Polk credit for avoiding war with Britain, if not Mexico.) Opposition to the war and its territorial aggrandizement required at least a qualified rejection of the assumption that the spread of American civilization constituted a moral good and heralded the millennium. Abolitionists of course had long challenged acceptance of America's special virtue, though it had been commonly assumed by other evangelicals. Now, many other Protestants challenged it, all the more remarkably in a war directed at a Catholic people. "Never have I so much feared the judgments of God on us as a nation," warned James W. Alexander, an Old School Presbyterian minister and war critic.[63] An erring Israel, the United States needed prophetic voices to recall the nation to its proper (rather than its "manifest") destiny.

61. Quoted in Charles Going, David Wilmot (New York, 1924), 174.
62. Eric Foner, "The Wilmot Proviso Revisited," JAH 56 (1969), 262–79; Michael Holt, The Fate of Their Country (New York, 2004), 26; Michael Morrison, Slavery and the American West (Chapel Hill, 1997), 40–45, 72–81.
63. Richard Carwardine, Evangelicals and Politics in Antebellum America (New Haven, 1993), 143–47 quotation from 146. See also Jonathan Sassi, Republic of Righteousness (New York, 2001), 185–95.

Geographically, New England and areas of New England settlement provided the most fertile ground for radical Whiggery, as for antislavery. In Massachusetts the radicals felt strong enough to challenge the moderate Whigs, and the party split into factions, nicknamed "Conscience" Whigs and "Cotton" Whigs, that persisted until Lincoln's Republican Party reunited them. The Conscience Whigs included practically all the Transcendentalists. Posterity remembers Henry David Thoreau's lecture-turned-essay against slavery and the war upon Mexico that we call "Civil Disobedience," to which he gave a more militant title, "Resistance to Civil Government." More widely read was the poetry of Garrisonian abolitionist James Russell Lowell. Adopting the persona and dialect of a simple Yankee farmer, "Hosea Biglow," Lowell wrote:

> They may talk o' Freedom's airy
> Tell they're purple in the face,—
> It's a grand gret cemetary
>   Fer the birthrights of our race;
> They jest want this Californy
>   So's to lug new slave-states in
> To abuse ye, an' to scorn ye,
>   An' to plunder ye like sin.[64]

The administration also had its literary supporters, including Nathaniel Hawthorne and Fenimore Cooper. Walt Whitman, who still thought of himself as a Jacksonian Democrat (though he would break with the party in 1848), wrote in the *Brooklyn Eagle* soon after the war started: "What has miserable, inefficient Mexico—with her superstition, her burlesque upon freedom, her actual tyranny by the few over the many—what has she to do with the great mission of peopling the new world with a noble race? Be it ours, to achieve that mission!" The term "race" was used loosely but confidently in such assertions, with no fixed definition. "Race" provided the most common justification in the United States for expropriating land from Mexico, as it did for taking that of the Native American tribes. Captain William S. Henry very typically remarked of the disputed area along the Rio Grande, "It certainly never was intended that this lovely land should remain in the hands of an ignorant and degenerate race." Occasionally a few Americans dissented from this kind of racial presumption. Joel Poinsett, the South Carolinian who had been John Quincy Adams's minister to Mexico, understood its people perhaps

---

64. Originally published in newspapers, the collected poems then appeared as James Russell Lowell, *The Biglow Papers* (Boston, 1848), quotation from 6–7.

better than anyone else in the United States and urged his countrymen to live alongside them in friendship: "Why we are in the habit of abusing them now as a degraded race I do not understand."[65]

The midterm congressional elections, scattered, as was then the practice, through several months of 1846-47, turned against the administration, particularly in the North. From being outnumbered almost two to one (143 to 77) in the House of Representatives, the Whigs won enough seats to gain a narrow majority (115 to 108). Although the Democrats gained in the Senate, the House results significantly altered the balance of power. The results realized Van Buren's fear that the war would hurt northern Democrats because Whigs could "charge with plausibility if not truth" that it was "waged for the extension of slavery."[66] Whigs certainly regarded the outcome as a vote of no confidence in the war, even though it was by no means the only issue in the election. Fear of the Wilmot Proviso stiffened the commitment of southern Whigs to the principle of No Territory. The Walker Tariff aroused the fears of protectionists, and the Whigs gained House seats in Pennsylvania. They gained still more in New York state, where they benefited from the votes of the anti-rent movement and the split in the Democratic Party between Van Burenites (now called "Barnburners") and the administration supporters (called "Hunkers" by their critics because they "hunkered" after offices that only Washington could bestow).[67] Under the ponderous timetable of the Constitution prior to the Twentieth Amendment, the Thirtieth Congress would not take office until December 1847, by which time the major battles in Mexico had all been fought. But the elections put Polk on notice that his administration did not enjoy popularity enough to risk asking for a tax increase to finance the war during the congressional session in the winter of 1846–47. Polk devoted two-thirds of December's Annual Message to Congress to justifying the war. He complained that those who accused his administration of "aggression" would only "protract the war" and give the enemy "aid and comfort." This was a serious charge, for it used the words of the Constitution that define treason. Whig representative Daniel King of Massachusetts made this answer: "If an earnest desire to save my country from ruin and disgrace be treason, then I am a traitor."[68]

65. Whitman in the *Brooklyn Eagle*, July 7, 1846; the other quotations come from Johannsen, *To the Halls of the Montezumas*, 291, 294. See also Reginald Horsman, *Race and Manifest Destiny* (Cambridge, Mass., 1981).
66. Van Buren, quoted in Holt, *Fate of Their Country*, 18.
67. Holt, *Rise and Fall of Whig Party*, 238–45.
68. "Second Annual Message" (Dec. 8, 1846), *Presidential Messages*, IV, 471–506, quotations from 473; Daniel King quoted in Schroeder, *Mr. Polk's War*, 79.

V

Old Rough and Ready had his shortcomings as a commander. The same casual attitude he showed toward uniforms and ceremony, which made him popular with his troops, he also displayed toward hygiene. His soldiers suffered high rates of disease, especially dysentery, in Corpus Christi, Matamoros, and then in Camargo, the Mexican town where the Army of Occupation gradually moved during the sweltering months of July and August 1846. One in eight of the U.S. soldiers encamped at Camargo for six weeks that summer died there—a loss as bad as if they had fought a battle and suffered heavy casualties. "I have seen more suffering since I came out here than I could have imagined," observed Lieutenant George McClellan; "the volunteers literally die like dogs."[69] Apparently, some volunteers never learned not to fill their canteens and kettles downstream from where others washed their horses.

Taylor tolerated a certain laxity about discipline too. The young men who responded to the call to fight for America's manifest destiny brought with them the fierce individualism, propensity to violence, and racial animosity so widespread in civilian society. These rowdy volunteers fought with each other and the army's regulars. They pillaged the local Mexican civilians, sometimes murdering them in retaliation for real or imagined affronts. A Regular Army private wrote to his father, "The majority of the Volunteers sent here are a disgrace to the nation; think of one of them shooting a woman while washing on the bank of the river—merely to *test* his rifle; another tore forcibly from a Mexican woman the rings from her ears. Their officers take no notice of these outrages."[70] The Texans got an especially bad reputation for seeking to avenge wrongs committed during their revolution, but it was Arkansas volunteers who perpetrated a massacre of twenty to thirty Mexican civilians, in response to the killing of one of their own number.[71] Although many U.S. officers deplored all this, they did little to prevent it, and the administration refused to support legislation that would have helped bring the volunteers under military justice. Indeed, the ideology of American expansion seemed to legitimate the assertion of force by the strong and the destruction or expropriation of those who resisted. As the war went on, the administration actually encouraged harsh treatment of occupied areas in an effort to press the

---

69. Quoted in Milton Meltzer, *Bound for the Rio Grande* (New York, 1974), 111.
70. *Charleston Mercury*, March 2, 1847, quoted in Foos, *Short, Offhand, Killing Affair*, 116.
71. For an eyewitness account, see John Chamberlain, *My Confession*, ed. William Goetzmann (Austin, Tex., 1996; written 1855–61), 132–34.

Mexicans to sign a peace treaty ceding land. Not surprisingly, out of the sullen local populace arose guerrilla fighters, usually termed *rancheros*, who raided the *yanquis* as opportunity presented, provoking, inevitably, more reprisals.

The strategic city of Monterrey (then often spelled Monterey), population fifteen thousand, capital of the state of Nuevo León, constituted Taylor's military objective. But his army could move only slowly because of a shortage of transport. Kearny's Army of the West (to which the War Department gave priority) had taken most of the wagons immediately available, and the Polk administration both wanted and expected an inexpensive, brief war. In September Taylor substituted Mexican pack mules for wagons, and, keeping baggage to a minimum, advanced toward Monterrey with 3,200 regulars and 3,000 volunteers, leaving 4,700 behind because they were either too ill to march or had no way to transport their supplies.[72]

General Pedro de Ampudia, back in command after Arista's defeat, with 7,000 soldiers and perhaps 3,000 local irregulars, awaited the invaders approaching Monterrey from the northeast. His people had barricaded the city itself and fortified its outlying defenses. On September 19, following a council of war with his officers, Taylor sent General William Worth with 2,000 soldiers in a wide arc around the north of the city to seize the road going west to Saltillo, thereby cutting off the garrison of Monterrey from either supplies or reinforcements. Such an ambitious "turning movement" represented a risky tactic. Worth spent the twentieth getting into position and then attacked the road on the morning of September 21. Taylor's main body meanwhile created a diversion in Ampudia's front. Worth's enterprise, executed with heroism and efficiency, succeeded. The diversion, however, produced heavy U.S. casualties, perhaps because Taylor underestimated the Mexican defenders, perhaps because his subordinate commanders tried too hard to drive their attacks home instead of merely keeping the enemy busy. On the second day of the battle, Worth again made use of morning fog as cover for infantry attacks, then won an artillery duel in the afternoon sunshine. By the end of the day he had taken the Bishop's Palace, a key Mexican strongpoint. After this Ampudia pulled his forces back into the city itself.

The third day of the battle saw Worth's and Taylor's forces enter Monterrey from west and east, respectively, leading to fierce house-to-house combat that left both sides exhausted. Maria Josefa Zozaya, a Mexican woman, ministered to the intermingled wounded of the two armies until

72. Eisenhower, *So Far from God*, 111.

she was killed; the U.S. press called her "the heroine martyr of Monterrey."[73] The defenders had stored ammunition in the cathedral, but their enemies found this out and prepared to shell it. Rather than have a giant explosion devastate the city, Ampudia negotiated its surrender on the fourth day. Taylor, whose undersupplied army had little ammunition or provisions left, granted generous terms in return for the city and an end to the fighting. Having no way to deal with thousands of prisoners, he allowed Ampudia's troops to evacuate Monterrey with some of their weapons, accompanied by those civilians who preferred to abandon their homes rather than live under U.S. occupation. Lieutenant George Meade paid "a tribute of respect to the gallantry of the Mexicans, who had defended their place as long as it was in their power." But one unit in the enemy army prompted loud curses from the U.S. soldiers who watched them ride out of town: the *sanpatricios*. Forty-eight of the deserters in the battalion had been personally recruited along the Rio Grande by John Riley, a recent immigrant from Ireland, formerly a sergeant in the U.S. Army, now a captain of artillery in the Mexican one. Others switched sides in resentment at the treatment of Mexican civilians and Catholic church buildings.[74] Most immigrants in the U.S. Army demonstrated full loyalty to their adopted country and resented the *sanpatricios*.

Negotiators representing the two armies agreed to take no further military action during an eight-week armistice. Taylor felt his soldiers would not be ready for further action much sooner anyway, and most of them agreed, Lieutenant Mead and Colonel Jefferson Davis being among those who endorsed the utility of the truce. The Battle of Monterrey made Taylor and Worth heroes with the U.S. public, but not with the administration in Washington. To the president, the war consisted of tokens moved on a map like pieces on a chessboard; he could not relate to weary soldiers needing a respite from fighting. When he learned of the armistice, Polk, furious, commanded Taylor to call it off (though because of time spent in communication, the truce still lasted over six weeks). The official communication to Taylor, sent through Secretary of War Marcy, added not a word of personal praise for capturing Monterrey.[75] From that time on neither Taylor nor Polk trusted the other.

---

73. Johannsen, *To the Halls of the Montezumas*, 138.
74. Meade quoted in Meltzer, *Bound for the Rio Grande*, 128; Stevens, *Rogue's March*, 103, 143–44, 156–58.
75. Zachary Taylor to R. C. Wood, Sept. 16, 1846, *Letters from the Battlefields*, 62; William Marcy to Zachary Taylor, Oct. 13, 1846, quoted in Dufour, *Mexican War*, 163.

The rejection of U.S. peace overtures by Mexico, combined with the hard-fought Battle of Monterrey and Santa Anna's conduct since his return, convinced the administration in Washington that their original plan for a brief war and easy conquests would prove inadequate. Nothing short of a decisive defeat in the national heartland could persuade any Mexican government to consent to the loss of its vast northern patrimony. All U.S. strategists agreed, however, on the impracticality of an advance southward from Monterrey to the city of Mexico across deserts and mountains. Hence plans had to be drawn up for an invasion from the Gulf inland to the capital city and a commander designated for it. Ruling out Taylor (who had been confiding lately in Kentucky's Whig senator John Crittenden, not one of Polk's favorites), the president reluctantly made the obvious appointment of Winfield Scott, the army's senior general, to head the undertaking.[76] Although his relations with the administration had often been strained, Scott proved a superb choice, and his advance from Veracruz to Mexico City became not only the crowning achievement of his long career but a model campaign for students of military history. Even after Scott had assumed his new command, Polk continued to recommend that Congress make Senator Benton a lieutenant general with authority over Scott. (It is not clear that Polk actually desired this extraordinary commission; Secretary of War Marcy later told an interviewer that the president went through the motions to flatter Benton and retain his political support, while of course deeply offending Scott.)[77]

To mount Scott's operation required diverting troops and resources from Taylor's army. Although Scott tried to explain this to Taylor in person, he got delayed en route to northern Mexico, and the two generals missed connections. Taylor was bound to be disappointed in having the principal operations shift to another theater and another commander, and now he saw his best and most experienced units ordered away. The resentment he felt toward Scott compounded and complicated the suspicion with which he already regarded President Polk. With the armistice over, Taylor pushed ahead to Saltillo and then south to a position near a hacienda called Buena Vista.

Mexican partisans ambushed a courier bearing the plans for the transfer of units from Taylor to Scott, and thus Santa Anna became aware both of the impending attack on his capital and that Taylor now commanded a

76. Polk, *Diary*, II, 242–44 (Nov. 18, 1846); Paul Bergeron, *The Presidency of James K. Polk* (Lawrence, Kans., 1987), 92–94.

77. Parker Scammon, "A Chapter of the Mexican War," *Magazine of American History* 14 (Dec. 1885): 564–65.

shrunken force consisting almost entirely of green volunteers. A cautious general would have responded by concentrating forces to defend Veracruz and Mexico City. Instead, eager to show his people a victory, the *caudillo* amassed the largest armed force he could—about twenty thousand men plus many camp followers—and moved them north to crush Taylor's depleted army. (Raising the troops proved difficult, for only a few Mexican states supplied their full quotas; borrowing the money to fund the offensive was even harder.) Departing from his headquarters at San Luis Potosí on January 28, 1847, Santa Anna's levies marched first through winter sleet and then through desert heat, with confusion, poor logistical support, and less than half the artillery their table of organization stipulated. When they reached Taylor's vicinity, having taken three weeks to come three hundred miles, desertion and attrition had reduced their number to about fifteen thousand effectives. Warned of Santa Anna's approach by a courageous Texan scout, the Americans fell back into a valley called La Angostura (the Narrows) where the Mexican numerical superiority would count for less. Taylor had about forty-five hundred troops, only a few of them, dragoons and cannoneers, being regulars. Meanwhile, Mexican cavalry under General Urrea made common cause with local partisans to interdict Taylor's long supply line.[78]

The retreating Americans burned some supplies to prevent their falling into enemy hands, and when Santa Anna came across the fires, he jumped to the conclusion that his opponents had fled in disorder. He therefore pushed his troops, tired from their long march, forward without rest into position to attack. Santa Anna then summoned Taylor to surrender in the face of overwhelming force; Old Rough and Ready responded, "Tell Santa Anna to go to Hell!" The reply sent in Spanish used more formal language but made his refusal clear.[79] It was February 22, George Washington's Birthday, the American soldiers remembered. In preliminary fighting, the Mexicans won control of the high ground on their right flank. That chilly night, the two armies slept on their weapons, ready for further action.

The next morning, hoping to overawe his adversaries, Santa Anna staged a grand review of his army within sight of the U.S. lines (but outside of cannon range). There followed the war's largest battle, named Buena Vista in the United States and La Angostura in Mexico. Both armies consisted largely of amateur soldiers with brief training and no combat experience. Both had suffered from desertions and logistical difficulties. The

---

78. DePalo, *Mexican National Army*, 109–10.
79. Quoted in Dufour, *Mexican War*, 172.

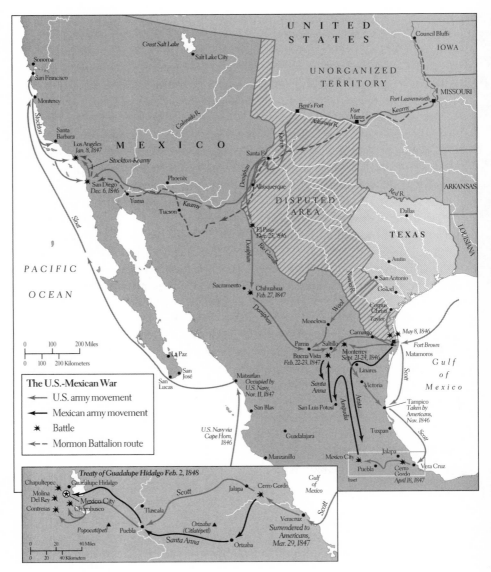

Mexicans had the advantage of numbers, the U.S. side that of tactical defense. In the morning the Mexicans renewed their assault on the defenders' left flank, and in fierce fighting drove back the volunteers from Indiana, Arkansas, and Kentucky. One fleeing deserter encountered the formidable camp follower Sarah Borginnis and cried out that the battle was lost. But she "knocked him sprawling" (in the words of an eyewitness)

and said, "You damned son of a bitch, there ain't Mexicans enough in Mexico to whip old Taylor." In fact, Old Rough and Ready had absented himself to check on his base in Saltillo; he returned at 9:00 A.M. to be told by his second in command, John Wool, "General, we are whipped." "That is for me to determine," retorted Taylor; he immediately rushed the Mississippi volunteers commanded by Jefferson Davis, whom he had brought up from Saltillo, into the breach and plugged it. The glory Davis won that day would encourage him later to take a hands-on approach to his role as commander in chief of the armies of the Southern Confederacy.[80] In the nick of time, U.S. dragoons repulsed an attempt by Mexican lancers to encircle Taylor's army. During the afternoon two more massive Mexican attacks on the American left flank halted in the face of superior U.S. firepower, notwithstanding the efforts of the *sanpatricios* manning Mexican artillery. When Taylor ordered a charge, however, his attacking units were decimated and repulsed. Cold rain fell. During the night, Taylor's small army clung to their position and received some welcome reinforcements.[81]

Santa Anna had pushed his soldiers to their limit. They were in no condition to renew their attack. Heavy fighting on top of forced marches had left them exhausted; many had scarcely had an opportunity to eat in the past two days, even though the *soldaderas* came up to the front lines to resupply them. During the night of February 23–24, the Mexican army silently withdrew, leaving campfires burning to fool their enemies. The next morning Taylor's battered soldiers could hardly believe their good fortune. It had been, as Wellington said after Waterloo, "a near run thing."[82] Santa Anna intended to renew the fight as soon as his soldiers had rested, but their heavy casualties and their commander's obvious indifference to their welfare sent the desertion rate soaring. With his army melting away, Santa Anna's officers persuaded him to begin the long march back to San Luis Potosí. The *caudillo* left behind more than two hundred of his wounded, but along the way he displayed U.S. cannons and flags his soldiers had captured early in the battle as evidence of what he claimed had been a victory. In truth, both armies had fought heroically and sustained heavy casualties: 746 on the U.S. side and about 1,600 on the Mexican. Death played no partisan favorites; American

80. Quotations from Joseph Chance, *Jefferson Davis's Mexican War Regiment* (Jackson, Miss., 1991), 98, and Eisenhower, *So Far from God*, 188.
81. On the Battle of Buena Vista, see Eisenhower, *So Far from God*, 166–91; Bauer, *Mexican War*, 206–18; Dufour, *Mexican War*, 171–84.
82. Quoted in Eisenhower, *So Far from God*, 191.

heroes killed included both Colonel Archibald Yell, former governor of Arkansas, Democrat and ardent expansionist, and Lieutenant Colonel Henry Clay Jr., son of the senator who had worked so hard for peace and who grieved that the young man had given his life in "this most unnecessary and horrible war."[83] The Battle of Buena Vista constituted a tactical draw, but in its true significance a major U.S. victory, since Santa Anna had not succeeded, despite making a supreme effort, in destroying Taylor's vulnerable force. Had Santa Anna won, he could have retaken much of northern Mexico, and the U.S. high command might well have aborted Scott's campaign against Mexico City in order to shore up the defense of the Rio Grande. Some commentators feel Santa Anna should have renewed the attack after a brief respite; certainly his army sustained losses from desertion on the march back to San Luis Potosí as heavy as those another battle would have inflicted.[84]

After the battle the Americans also withdrew. If Taylor had had more regulars available he might have tried pursuing, but instead he deemed it prudent to lead his army back to Monterrey to wait out the rest of the war. His volunteers had endured their baptism of fire and had proved themselves.

VI

Winfield Scott, one of the greatest soldiers the United States Army has ever produced, wore the stars of a general for more than fifty years, in three major wars (1812, Mexico, and the Civil War) and through several intervening frontier confrontations and campaigns, including Indian Removal and the Canadian rebellion crisis of 1837–38. Taken prisoner, exchanged, and later wounded in the War of 1812, Scott found himself celebrated for his individual exploits as well as for his judgment in command. The handsome, six-foot-four-inch Virginian became a brigadier general at the age of twenty-seven and won glory at the Battle of Chippewa in 1814, the sole American success on the Canadian–U.S. Niagara front. At the end of the War of 1812 only Andrew Jackson exceeded Scott in fame as a national hero. Both men had large egos, and not surprisingly within a few years they had developed a strong personal animosity. To the public, Jackson typified the frontiersman who took up arms when occasion required;

83. Quoted in Robert Remini, *Henry Clay* (New York, 1991), 685. Daniel Webster, another Whig critic of the war, also lost a son in it.

84. DePalo, *Mexican National Army*, 115. Santa Anna's own after-action report appears in "Letters of Santa Anna," ed. Justin Smith, *Annual Report of the American Historical Association for 1917* (Washington, 1920), 413–14.

Scott, on the other hand, typified the quintessential professional soldier, a less favorable image expressed in his unflattering nickname "Old Fuss 'n' Feathers" (an allusion to the plumes on a general's hat). Like so many others who shared his Whig political views, General Scott was a modernizer and an institution-builder. His nationalism took the form not of bellicose imperialism but of devotion to the central government and the rule of law. When the ultimate crisis came in 1861, Scott would choose not his home state but his country.

The military campaign from the Gulf to the City of Mexico represented the summit of Winfield Scott's professional career; sixty years old in 1846, he had waited long for this opportunity. The landing at Veracruz constituted the most ambitious amphibious operation the United States armed forces would conduct before D-Day in 1944. Besides the formidable string of forts protecting Veracruz, planners had to take into account the fact that the port had no proper harbor and that it was prone to severe northern winds half the year and endemic yellow fever the other half. The difficulties brought out the best in Scott: his recognition of the importance of logistics, training, and staff work, his meticulous attention to detail. A perceptive biographer has suggested that he prefigured the military "technocrat." Scott benefited from the services of Thomas Jesup, the army's experienced quartermaster general; the two had had their differences, but both were conscientious professionals. Since President Polk insisted on waging war and cutting taxes at the same time, Scott and Jesup had to scale back requests and scramble to provide troops and supplies for the operation.[85]

Invading Mexico from the Gulf required amassing an enormous flotilla of ships. The necessary cooperation between army and navy had a political as well as an interservice dimension. Beginning with Jackson, the Democratic Party had been friendly to the navy as protector of overseas commerce and international free trade, while the peacetime army had looked to the Whigs for support. (Significantly, it was Polk's Democratic administration that founded the U.S. Naval Academy.) Fortunately, Scott developed good relations with the navy's Gulf Squadron under Commodore David Conner and, after Conner's retirement, Commodore Matthew Perry. The navy had already blockaded Mexico's ports and welcomed an additional role. In November 1846, Commodore Conner occupied the Gulf port of Tampico without a fight, thanks to information

---

85. Allan Peskin, *Winfield Scott and the Profession of Arms* (Kent, Ohio, 2003), 59; Robert Smith, "The Impossible Campaign Attempted," *Military History* 10 (1993): 34–42, 92–96.

supplied by Ann Chase, who took advantage of her British citizenship to live in the city as a U.S. spy. Working with a naval officer, Scott helped design a flat-bottomed landing craft to float the invasion troops onto the Mexican beach. Scott's understanding of the potential contribution of the navy in combined operations would bear fruit again later in his "Anaconda Plan" for blockading the Southern Confederacy. Ironically, Scott succeeded less well in securing cooperation among the officers within the army itself, for his two regular subordinates, William Worth and David Twiggs, were bitter rivals, while Gideon Pillow, commanding the volunteers, was a Tennessee crony of Polk's who shared his taste for intrigue and constantly worked to undermine Scott in the president's eyes. But the general had selected a personal staff of outstanding ability, including Colonels Joseph Totten and Ethan Allen Hitchcock and Scott's own favorite, Captain Robert E. Lee.[86]

On March 9, 1847, only two weeks after Taylor had saved his army at Buena Vista, Scott's armada of over a hundred ships delivered ten thousand U.S. troops to a beach three miles south of Veracruz and beyond the reach of its batteries. Santa Anna had not had time to bring his main force from San Luis Potosí to contest the landing, and Juan Morales, commanding the Veracruz garrison of only five thousand ill-trained militia, chose not to do so either. The Mexican general put his faith in the city's stone defenses. A string of forts rendered Veracruz virtually impregnable by sea, while a wall fifteen feet high protected its landward side. Scott operated under a fixed timetable; he had to complete the reduction of Veracruz and move inland before the onset of the yellow fever season a month later. He had three options: to assault and take the city by storm, to besiege it and starve the occupants out, or to force a capitulation by bombardment. He chose the third course. Scott had long been mindful of the power of artillery; as peacetime general in chief, he had nurtured the mobile artillery that had proved so effective on the battlefields of Mexico. On March 22, Morales having declined Scott's summons to surrender, U.S. mortars commenced firing shells over the walls of Veracruz and down into the city, wreaking havoc on military targets and civilians alike. But what Scott most wanted was to pound a breach in the city's defensive wall. The government not having provided the heavy ordnance he had requested, Scott turned to his friends in the fleet. They did not care to risk their wooden ships in a firefight with the formidable seaward fortifications of Veracruz, but the navy lent Scott both guns and crews to ferry them ashore where they could batter the landward wall, the weakest point in

86. Peskin, *Winfield Scott*, 147–50.

the city's defenses. The bombardment continued day and night. Sixty-seven hundred projectiles landed in the city, starting fires and inflicting over a thousand casualties, two-thirds of them civilian, including about 180 deaths. "My heart bled for the inhabitants," commented Captain Lee, who had helped direct the cannon fire; "it was terrible to think of the women and children."[87] By March 26, with the wall breached, the hospital and post office among the buildings hit, the population feeling abandoned by their government, and the many neutral civilians in the port city terrified, a flag of truce signaled the start of surrender negotiations. Three days later the Mexican troops marched out to be paroled (that is, allowed to go home after signing a promise not to fight anymore unless exchanged for U.S. prisoners).

Eager to move most of his army inland before the yellow fever descended, Scott arranged to govern Veracruz with a skeleton force. This necessitated conciliating the local population. Unlike Taylor, Scott insisted on strict control of his occupying troops and allowed no outrages to be perpetrated on civilians. He paid for supplies his soldiers needed, instead of just commandeering them as the Polk administration had told him to do in order to save money. He reopened the port to the commerce of the world, so normal business activity could resume, but with U.S. officials collecting the customary tariff duties. And he stationed a guard by every Catholic church to protect it and its worshippers. All this happened not a moment too soon: On April 9, two deaths from yellow fever were reported.[88]

Why had Mexico's most important port and the gateway to the nation's heartland been so weakly defended? Why was there no attempt to relieve the siege of Veracruz? A revolt had broken out in Mexico City against the government. As divided as people were in the United States over political partisanship, section, and the wisdom of the war, the Mexican public was even more disunited—by region, class, and ideology. When Santa Anna went off to lead the army against Taylor, he left his vice president, Valentín Gómez Farías, in Mexico City as acting president. Gómez Farías was a *federalista puro*, prowar and anticlerical. He had been instrumental in secularizing the California missions back in 1833, and this time he had another program to seize church property for the benefit of the state. Faced with a desperate shortage of money to wage war, on January 11, 1847, Gómez Farías signed a law requisitioning 15 million pesos (a peso being worth about the same as a U.S. dollar) from the Roman Catholic

87. Quoted in John Weems, *To Conquer a Peace* (Garden City, N.Y., 1974), 338.
88. Peskin, *Winfield Scott*, 160.

Church. The church, which as Mexico's largest institutional investor often acted like a bank, had loaned money to the government in the past but was not disposed to accept confiscation of about 10 percent of its assets.[89] Ecclesiastical authorities in the capital secretly funded an uprising against the government by some upper-middle-class, proclerical national guard units stationed in Mexico City. The revolt also received encouragement from Moses Beach and Jane Storm of the *New York Sun*, ostensibly in the city on business. (Civilians traveled surprisingly freely in the nineteenth century, even between countries at war with each other.) Actually the two were on a secret mission for the U.S. government, hoping to overthrow the Mexican government and install one that would make peace.[90] Although the church commanded widespread loyalty and sympathy, the rebellion proved highly unpopular, interfering as it did with the defense of the country against invasion. It got the derisive name "revolt of the *polkos*" from the polka dance then fashionable among the city's elite. Despite being small in scope, the revolt of the *polkos* preoccupied the Mexican government, preventing aid to Veracruz. Santa Anna's return to the capital on March 21 ended the revolt but at a cost. He turned his back on those who had elected him (as he had done in 1834), rescinded the requisition, fired Gómez Farías by abolishing the vice presidency, and settled for another loan of 1.5 million pesos from the church—a pittance in relation to the government's wartime needs.[91]

Scott advanced toward Mexico City via Jalapa and Puebla, following the same route that Hernán Cortez had taken 328 years earlier, as many noticed at the time. William Hickling Prescott's vividly written *History of the Conquest of Mexico* (1843) constituted favorite reading among the intellectually inclined members of the U.S. Army (though Prescott, a New England Whig, deplored the current conquest of Mexico as "mad and unprincipled"). Promising the crowds to die fighting rather than let the enemy enter "the imperial capital of Azteca," Santa Anna came out to meet Scott's army on the border between the coastal plain and the high country, not far from his own estate, El Encero.[92] To oppose the invaders

---

89. Estimated by DePalo, *Mexican National Army*, 223, n. 113.
90. Working with only fragments of evidence, historians have given various accounts of this mission; the fullest is Anna Nelson, *Secret Agents* (New York, 1988), 72–95.
91. Michael Casteloe, "The Mexican Church and the Rebellion of the 'Polkos,'" *Hispanic American Historical Review* 46 (1966): 170–78; Pedro Santoni, *Mexicans at Arms: Puro Federalists and the Politics of War* (Fort Worth, Tex., 1996), 171–207.
92. Prescott quoted in Johannsen, *To the Halls of the Montezumas*, 245; Santa Anna quoted in Eisenhower, *So Far from God*, 271.

he gathered a force of about twelve thousand, half of them veterans of Buena Vista and the rest untrained raw recruits.

Cerro Gordo, also called Cerro Telégrafo (Signal Hill), a thousand feet high, dominated the road to Mexico City, and there Santa Anna concentrated his defense. Half a mile north of it lay another hill, La Atalaya (the Watchtower). Two Mexican engineering officers recommended placing artillery atop La Atalaya, but *el presidente* dismissed their advice, supposing that no one could get through the rough terrain and thick briars to approach from that direction.[93] In one of the most brilliant undertakings of his long and brilliant career, Robert E. Lee reconnoitered a trail that U.S. troops could cut through underbrush, bypassing the main highway where the Mexicans awaited them, and coming up on La Atalaya. At one point the daring scout had to lie motionless behind a log while Mexican soldiers sat on it and chatted only inches away. On April 17, 1847, Lee guided Twiggs's division of regulars along the route he had traced. With La Atalaya only lightly defended, the Americans captured it and that night installed heavy guns, laboriously carried along Lee's pathway, on the hilltop. At dawn the next day, this artillery supported an assault on Cerro Gordo itself, while other U.S. units struck the Mexican army at both front and rear. Santa Anna's outmaneuvered forces fled, as did their commander, leaving behind a vast amount of equipment that included virtually all their artillery, twenty thousand pesos in coin intended to meet the army's payroll, and an artificial leg Santa Anna wore to replace the one he had lost fighting the French. (Amused U.S. soldiers made up a parody of one of their favorite songs, "The Girl I Left Behind Me," entitled "The Leg I Left Behind Me.") Scott's army took some four thousand Mexican prisoners—a thousand of whom promptly escaped in all the confusion. The general and his staff soon relaxed in Santa Anna's hacienda, El Encero, where the perceptive Colonel Hitchcock noticed that all the *caudillo's* art works were foreign; none of them showed "the genius of the Mexicans."[94]

By cold logic, the Battle of Cerro Gordo should have put an end to the Mexican war effort. That it did not was due less to the Mexican government and high command than to the stubborn determination of the people themselves not to accept defeat. Scott's small army could only advance slowly, and in fact took four more months to reach the historic capital of

---

93. Carol Christensen and Thomas Christensen, *The U.S.-Mexican War* (San Francisco, 1998), 180.
94. Ethan Allen Hitchcock, journal entry for April 20, 1847, in *Fifty Years in Camp and Field*, ed. W. A. Croffut (New York, 1909), 253. The song parody can be viewed at www.ku.edu/carrie/docs/texts/mexwar.htm.

Mexican civilization. When it occupied Puebla, the second largest city in the country and one that had been a center of opposition to Santa Anna, some of the church authorities cooperated with the invaders, but ordinary Mexicans who did so exposed themselves to ostracism or worse from their fellow citizens.[95]

Scott waited in Puebla six weeks of the summer for reinforcements to replace the volunteers whose one-year enlistments expired. Only 10 percent of those whose time was up chose to reenlist. The mood of the soldiers had become one of disenchantment as the grim reality of war sank in. Captain Kirby Smith of the Regular Army wrote home to his wife about his change of attitude since the war began. "How differently I feel now with regard to the war from what I did then! *Then* vague visions of glory and a speedy peace floated through my brain." Now he felt only gloomy foreboding. "Alas, the chance is I shall never see you again!" Captain Smith would fall mortally wounded on September 8, before word of his promotion to lieutenant colonel reached him.[96] Guerrilla actions along Scott's exposed supply line, made all the more tenuous by a shortage of transport, eventually prompted the U.S. general to cut himself off from his base of operations and live off the country when he resumed his advance—an example that stuck in the mind of Lieutenant Grant, who would do the same in his campaign against Vicksburg in 1863. Grant also remembered the valor of his Mexican adversaries, even in their defeat: "I have seen as brave stands made by some of these men as I have ever seen made by soldiers," he wrote in his *Memoirs*.[97]

In June, Santa Anna hinted, through a message sent via the British, that he might make peace in return for a million-dollar bribe, with ten thousand up front. Scott and the State Department representative Nicholas Trist, who was authorized to negotiate with the Mexicans, after hesitation and discussion with the other American generals, decided to send the ten thousand. The money disappeared to no discernible purpose. Santa Anna may well have been prepared to sell out his country's interests; the Mexican Congress suspected it, and had passed a law on April 20 making unauthorized peace negotiations treason. Scott's willingness to pursue any avenue for peace, after it became known to the U.S. public and administration (probably revealed by Gideon Pillow), would come back to haunt him.[98]

95. Christensen and Christensen, *U.S.-Mexican War*, 187.
96. Emma Blackwood, ed., *To Mexico with Scott: Letters of Captain E. Kirby Smith* (Cambridge, Mass., 1917), 155, 183, and 9.
97. Grant, *Memoirs*, 115.
98. Pletcher, *Diplomacy of Annexation*, 504–11.

It took all Scott's military genius and much hard fighting by his army before the Americans reached the goal of their campaign. On August 7, 1847, 10,738 of them set out through mountain passes ten thousand feet high, undertaking to capture a metropolis of two hundred thousand people. The City of Mexico, located in the Valley of Mexico, occupied an island in the midst of marshland, approachable only along certain causeways. Santa Anna had recovered, phoenix-like, from the disgrace of defeat at Cerro Gordo and commanded the defense of his capital. Once again gathering troops and equipment, he had managed to get around the naval blockade by importing weapons through Guatemala.[99] This consummate salesman was always better at raising armies than at keeping or using them. Santa Anna assumed Scott would advance by the most direct route and constructed fortifications accordingly. But U.S. engineer officers—notably Colonel James Duncan and, once again, Captain Robert E. Lee—identified other routes, and Scott took his army via the south, a force guided by Lee even crossing the rugged bed of dried lava called the Pedregal. At Contreras on August 20, Scott's army overcame that of General Gabriel Valencia as a result of jealousy between the Mexican generals; Valencia disobeyed Santa Anna's orders in hopes of getting credit for a victory himself, whereupon Santa Anna refused to reinforce Valencia. To cover his withdrawal following the battle, Santa Anna placed some fifteen hundred local national guardsmen and *sanpatricios* in the Franciscan monastery of San Mateo, protecting a bridge over the Río Churubusco (named, appropriately, for the Aztec god of war). Scott, hoping to smash the retreating Mexicans as they crossed the Churubusco, ordered the monastery taken. What followed was one of the toughest fights of the war, a demonstration of heroism by common soldiers on both sides. Time and again the attackers charged through cornfields to be repulsed by the dogged defenders. Only after the militia had run out of ammunition were the Mexicans overcome; Santa Anna refused their pleas for resupply, having erroneously written off their case as hopeless and merely a means to buy time. The *sanpatricios* fought with a courage born of desperation, knowing the likely fate that awaited them as prisoners. In the end eighty-five of them fell into the hands of their former comrades; about sixty-five had died in the battle, and a hundred or more escaped.[100]

99. Smith, *War with Mexico*, II, 87.
100. On Churubusco, see Bauer, *Mexican War*, 296–300, and for a contemporary Mexican account, Ramón Alcaraz et al., *The Other Side*, trans. Albert Ramsey (New York, 1850), 291–98.

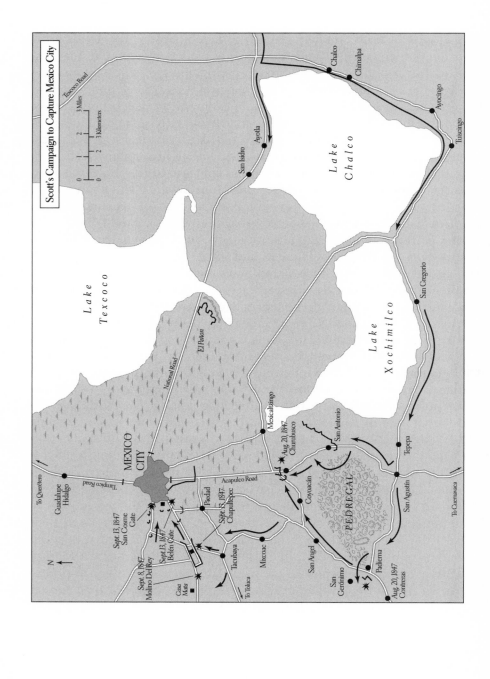

Scott's Campaign to Capture Mexico City

At this point Scott could have entered Mexico City. He chose not to, believing that his hungry troops, temporarily disorganized by battle, would pillage and burn. In such a state of disorder, he explained to the secretary of war, all Mexican government might dissolve, leaving no one with whom he could make a treaty.[101] Scott's objective was not to create an urban wasteland but to "conquer a peace" (in the phrase of the time), so he halted at the city gates and offered to negotiate. Secret messages had once again given Scott reason to hope that the unpredictable Santa Anna would come to terms. A truce commenced on August 21, but the talks it permitted led nowhere, since the Mexicans proved unwilling to cede as much territory as the U.S. negotiators demanded. Meanwhile, Santa Anna strengthened his defenses, and Scott purchased provisions from his enemies. (Rather than buy still more, he turned loose some three thousand Mexican prisoners.) By September 6, the two sides felt ready to resume the war. Santa Anna called upon the city's people to "preserve your altars from infamous violation, and your daughters and your wives from the extremity of insult."[102]

Intelligence reports reached Scott that the Mexicans were re-casting church bells into cannons at a flour mill called Molino del Rey. The general ordered a quick raid on the mill conducted in the early morning of September 8. Unfortunately Santa Anna's own intelligence warned him in time to prepare a warm reception for the attackers, and the engagement turned into a major battle. Before the Americans succeeded in destroying the site, they suffered almost eight hundred casualties, fully a quarter of their troops engaged, making it a Pyrrhic victory for an army that had only about eight thousand effectives now available for advance into the enemy capital. Worse, the intelligence on which the attack was based turned out to be faulty: The Molino contained no weapons of mass destruction.

Within sight of Molino del Rey stood the mount of Chapultepec with its castle atop it, originally built for the Viceroy of New Spain, now the Colegio Militar, the Mexican military academy. This strongpoint protected the southwest entrance to Mexico City, and Scott immediately turned his attention to its reduction. The castle loomed very formidable, and the Americans undertook its reduction with seriousness. A fourteen-hour bombardment on September 12 preceded an assault on the morning of the thirteenth. Santa Anna had not adequately garrisoned the position. The castle itself held only about two hundred Mexican soldiers, along

101. Winfield Scott to William Marcy, Aug. 18, 1847, in Bauer, *Mexican War*, 301.
102. Quoted in Otis Singletary, *The Mexican War* (Chicago, 1960), 94.

with fifty-nine cadets, ranging in age from thirteen to nineteen, who had requested permission to participate in the defense of their college. About six hundred more Mexican soldiers occupied the hill outside the building. In the van of the U.S. assault came volunteers of Franklin Pierce's brigade—although Brigadier General Pierce himself was laid up with an injury due to falling off his horse. (His absence from battle did not prevent Pierce from being elected president of the United States in 1852.) Participants in the assault included Captain Robert Anderson and Lieutenants Ulysses Grant, James Longstreet, and George Pickett, whose names would become familiar to all Americans in the coming years. With the aid of scaling ladders, the attackers climbed up into the fortress. The defenders resolved to sell their lives dearly. Those who died included six of the young cadets, who are remembered today in Mexico as Los Niños Héroes and memorialized in a monument near the Colegio Militar.

The raising of the Stars and Stripes over the castle was a glorious moment for the U.S. Army, but it sent a macabre message to thirty former *sanpatricios* captured at Churubusco and convicted by court-martial of desertion. Bound at their individual gallows, they were forced to stand and watch the castle on the skyline for four hours until the appearance of the U.S. flag signaled their execution. Twenty other *sanpatricios* had already been hanged. General Scott had, however, tempered justice with mercy when he reviewed the sentences of the court-martial. He had pardoned five of the seventy convicted and commuted the sentences of fifteen others to the lesser punishment of fifty lashes and branding with a *D* on the cheek. To the anger of many in the army, John Riley was among those whose lives the general spared. The most prominent turncoat had deserted before the declaration of war, and Scott noted that the death penalty did not apply to desertion in peacetime. Surprisingly, the well-publicized punishments meted out to the *sanpatricios* did not prevent about a hundred more U.S. soldiers from going over to the Mexicans during the remaining months of the war. Many deserters simply melted into the Mexican population; Riley himself reentered the Mexican army, wore his hair long to hide his branding scars, and after promotion to colonel retired. Neither he nor anyone else appears to have received the promised Mexican land grant. Although the U.S. Army and loyal Irish Americans in particular regarded the *sanpatricios* as a disgrace (for several decades in the later nineteenth century the War Department denied their existence), there is a monument to them, with annual commemorations, in Mexico.[103]

---

103. Stevens, *Rogue's March*, 270–76, 295–301; Miller, *Shamrock and Sword*, 178–85; Wynn, *San Patricio Soldiers*, 286.

The Americans pressed on immediately to exploit their capture of Chapultepec, moving along two causeways and overcoming stiff resistance to seize two gates on the western side of the city, Belen and San Cosme, before nightfall on the thirteenth. After conferring with his officers, Santa Anna decided to spare the historic capital destruction in house-to-house fighting, and evacuated his remaining nine thousand soldiers to Guadalupe Hidalgo north of the city. At dawn on September 14, the municipal authorities surrendered, and the flag of the United States flew over the center of Mexico City by 7:00 A.M. An hour later, Winfield Scott rode into the Zócalo, the grand plaza bordered by the National Palace, the city hall, and the cathedral, resplendent in his full dress uniform, a stark contrast to the ragged and dirty combat soldiers who lined up before him in parade formation. The conqueror, this new Cortez, dispatched a unit of U.S. Marines to secure the palace, which North Americans called the Hall of the Montezumas. (The anonymous lyrics of the Marines' Hymn commemorate the episode.) In due course Scott took up residence in the palace himself, in quarters formerly occupied by the presidents of the Mexican Republic and the viceroys of New Spain, on the site where Aztec emperors had ruled. As military governor of the city, Scott named volunteer Major General John Quitman, who had experience as governor of Mississippi.

The early days of the occupation proved harrowing even for hardened veterans. Although the city's middle class and ruling elite had acquiesced in the surrender, the poorer people, perhaps having less to lose, rose up against the intruders as people in California and New Mexico had done. Those without weapons threw stones and imprecations. After several days of fighting the mob, the army imposed order by a combination of sternness and conciliation, but *yanquis* who wandered into unfamiliar neighborhoods always did so at some risk. For the next nine months, the U.S. Army occupied Mexico City. Gradually the businesses, cafes, bars, and houses of prostitution reopened and found the strangers from faraway farms and towns to be willing customers. As early as September 30, a soldier from western Pennsylvania could write in his diary, "In the evening we went to the Theatre Nacional-De-Santa-Anna which is undoubtedly the finest building of the kind on this continent."[104] Reactions to Mexican culture, especially Catholicism, varied greatly. A lieutenant wrote to his sister, "You have no idea of the flummery that we see here every day, all of which the Mexicans call religion." But a sergeant who visited the cathedral

104. "The Journal of William Joseph McWilliams," *Western Pennsylvania Historical Magazine* 52 (1969): 388.

recorded feelings of awe in his journal. "Like the poor Indians who are kneeling around the altar, we are lost in amazement at the splendors around us."[105] Of course, the *norteamericanos* primarily perpetuated their own culture. Almost immediately, they began to publish two newspapers, the *American Star* and the *North American*, with sections in both English and Spanish.

By now widely blamed for his country's defeat, Santa Anna resigned the Mexican presidency on September 16, retaining command of the army. He made a final attempt to dislodge Scott's occupation of Mexico City by besieging Puebla, but as usual his artillery was not up to the task, and he failed to retake the city. On October 7, the new acting president, Manuel de la Peña y Peña, who as foreign minister in 1845 had tried to avoid the war, dismissed Santa Anna and ordered him to prepare for a court-martial. The *caudillo* fled and made his way to Jamaica. The Mexican government set up a temporary capital in Querétaro, some 125 miles northwest of Mexico City. The Mexican army no longer possessed the capability to conduct operations, but resistance by guerrillas continued, especially along the route between Mexico City and Veracruz, which the invaders relied on for reinforcements and the evacuation of their sick and wounded.

Winfield Scott had achieved one of the monumental military victories of the nineteenth century. He had successfully carried out a major amphibious operation, reduced the formidable fortress of Veracruz, and, overcoming shortages of heavy artillery and transportation, fought his way through difficult terrain to capture one of the world's great capitals. Along the way he set an example that Grant and Sherman would follow in the Civil War by cutting himself off from his base of operations. The army he commanded consisted largely of novices, thousands of whom departed when their enlistments expired in the middle of the campaign. He managed despite the political hostility of his president and many of the officers whom that president placed around him. The duke of Wellington, who followed Scott's campaign with close attention, called it "unsurpassed in military annals" and declared Scott "the greatest living soldier"—high praise coming from the victor of Waterloo. The military historian John Eisenhower, after reviewing Scott's whole career in three major wars, has concluded that Scott "may well have been the most

---

105. William Davis to Elizabeth Davis, Jan. 11, 1848, in *Chronicles of the Gringos*, ed. George W. Smith and Charles Judah (Albuquerque, N.M., 1968), 411; Thomas Barclay, journal entry for Sept. 27, 1847, in *Volunteers: Mexican War Journals*, ed. Allan Peskin (Kent, Ohio, 1991), 195.

capable soldier this country has ever produced"—high praise coming from the son of Dwight Eisenhower.[106]

Yet the victor of Mexico City did not remain in command of his army much longer than did the vanquished. Gideon Pillow poisoned President Polk's mind against Scott and inflamed his fear of a Whig military hero's emergence. Meanwhile, General Pillow treated his commander with insolence and publicly claimed that most of the credit for the campaign's success was due to his own efforts. Scott reminded officers in his command not to publish comments without his approval, and when Pillow and Colonel James Duncan defied the rule, he ordered them court-martialed. President Polk intervened and dismissed Scott on January 13, 1848, revoking the court-martial and setting up instead a "court of inquiry" to investigate Scott along with his subordinates. He also charged Scott with compromising military operations by an attempt to bribe Santa Anna into making peace—a peculiar accusation, considering Polk's own record of relations with Santa Anna. "To suspend a successful general in command of an army in the heart of an enemy's country, [and] to try the judge in place of the accused, is to upset all discipline," declared the astounded Robert E. Lee. The army overwhelmingly sympathized with Scott in this situation. "No general ever possessed the hearts of his troops to a greater extent than does Gen. Scott," asserted Captain George Mc-Clellan.[107] The Mexicans, with their experience of military coups, were astonished that Scott dutifully obeyed the order to relinquish command of the army when it arrived on February 18.

Polk stacked the composition of his "court of inquiry" in favor of Pillow and against Scott. Sorting through the complicated charges and counter-charges, the inquiry's inconclusive findings in July 1848 "whitewashed" Pillow and took no position on Polk's charge against Scott. The protracted hearings served Polk's political ends. They kept the conqueror of Mexico under a cloud during the critical period when the Whig party was choosing a presidential candidate for 1848. Congress, more appreciative of Scott's achievement than the president, passed a joint resolution on March 9, 1848, thanking Old Fuss 'n' Feathers for his services and directing the president to award him a medal for "his valor, skill, and judicious conduct." It was Gideon Pillow, however, who dined at the White House.[108]

106. Wellington quoted in Bauer, *Mexican War*, 322; Eisenhower, *So Far from God*, xxv.
107. Lee in a letter to his brother, Sidney Smith Lee, quoted in Dufour, *Mexican War*, 281; McClellan to his mother, March 22, 1848, in *Chronicles of the Gringos*, 440.
108. Bauer, *Mexican War*, 371–74. "Whitewashing" was Scott's term, quoted in Peskin, *Winfield Scott*, 203.

20

The Revolutions of 1848

When news of an uprising in Paris arrived in New York on March 18, 1848, Americans learned that it had broken out—appropriately, they thought—on the twenty-second of February, George Washington's Birthday. America's sense of mission, of being an example to the world, appeared justified. New York's penny press, which had celebrated manifest destiny, now sensationalized the tidings coming across the Atlantic. Within weeks, other revolutions broke out across much of Europe, promising to overthrow authoritarian regimes in the name of a variety of liberal, democratic, and ethnic-minority movements. "The finger of revolution points to us as its example, its cloud and pillar of fire!" crowed the *New York Sun* in vivid rhetoric typical of Jane Storm, the "mistress of manifest destiny," who had returned from her secret mission in Mexico. "The great principles of popular sovereignty which were proclaimed in 1776 by the immortal author of our Declaration of Independence, seem now to be in the course of rapid development throughout the world," President Polk wrote to his emissary in Paris.[1]

Like their president, most Americans assumed the United States did not need another revolution of its own. Margaret Fuller, foreign correspondent for the *New York Tribune*, drew analogies between Europe in 1848 and American political issues: "I find the cause of tyranny and wrong everywhere the same," she reported. "I listen to the same arguments against the emancipation of Italy that are used against the emancipation of our blacks; the same arguments for the spoliation of Poland as for the conquest of Mexico."[2] But only a perceptive minority of Americans saw things the way Fuller did. A "Great Demonstration" held in New York City during April typified the early, naive American enthusiasm for the European revolutions, celebrating German, French, and Italian uprisings with speeches and songs, often in the ancestral languages of the

1. *New York Sun*, May 6, 1848, attributed to Storm in Frederick Merk, *Manifest Destiny and Mission in American History* (New York, 1963), 200n.; James Knox Polk to Richard Rush, April 18, 1848, quoted in Michael Morrison, "American Reactions to European Revolutions, 1848–1852," *Civil War History* 49 (June 2003): 117.
2. Margaret Fuller, *"These Sad but Glorious Days": Dispatches from Europe*, ed. Larry Reynolds and Susan Belasco Smith (New Haven, 1991), 165.

immigrants who participated.[3] Besides confirming liberal ideology and the ethnic loyalties of immigrant groups, the revolutions overseas also provided religious omens for many Americans. Some millennialists jumped to the conclusion that the outbreaks heralded the overthrow of the papacy and the ultimate divine vindication of the Protestant Reformation. A Presbyterian minister named Alexander McGill recalculated biblical prophecies of the final destruction of Antichrist and determined that 1848 would be the year. Not surprisingly, leading American Catholics expressed a sharply different perspective on events. The country's most prominent Catholic lay theologian, Orestes Brownson, joined with New York's Bishop John Hughes to condemn the European uprisings, distinguishing them from the rational and responsible American Revolution of 1776.[4] On the other hand, the most significant attempt by Americans to intervene in Europe involved Irish Americans and the abortive Irish rebellion of 1848. A "Young Ireland" movement in New York encouraged the expectation that the Continental revolutions would spread to Ireland. Those arrested after the failure of the attempted Irish uprising included several Irish Americans. The United States had to give the British an apology to secure the release of these citizens.[5]

The two major American political parties diverged from each other in their response to the European revolutions. The Democrats' party platform, adopted in May 1848, invoked their favorite principle, "the sovereignty of the people," welcomed the erection of new republics "on the ruins of despotism in the Old World," and tendered "fraternal congratulations to the National Convention of the Republic of France" in particular.[6] Such effusive rhetoric seemed like inexpensive appeals to the immigrant voters on whom the Democratic Party relied. The Whig Party regarded the revolutions with more ambivalence. On the one hand, humanitarian reformers and supporters of universal education, strong within the party, naturally sympathized with their counterparts in Europe; the Whig *New York Tribune* displayed this attitude. Nevertheless, the Whigs felt a strong attachment to legal order, and mob rule dismayed their middle-class

3. Timothy Roberts, "The American Response to the European Revolutions of 1848" (D.Phil. thesis, Oxford University, 1997), 125–28.

4. Alexander Taggart McGill, *Popery the Punishment of Unbelief* (Philadelphia, 1848); Orestes Brownson, "Legitimacy and Revolution," in his *Essays and Reviews* (New York, 1852), 389–415; John Hughes, *The Church and the World* (New York, 1850).

5. See John Belcham, "Irish Emigrants and the Revolutions of 1848," *Past and Present* 146 (1995): 103–35.

6. Democratic Platform of 1848, *National Party Platforms*, ed. Kirk Porter and Donald Johnson (Urbana, Ill., 1966), 12.

constituency; the Washington *National Intelligencer* reflected this side of the Whig outlook.

The most conservative of American political factions, John C. Calhoun's southern Democrats, expressed grave reservations about the European revolutions from the start. "France is not prepared to become a Republic," Calhoun warned. Where others heard echoes of Jefferson's Declaration in 1848, he could only see dangerous defiance of constituted authority: "neither more nor less than Dorrism"—a reference to the Rhode Island uprising to which Chief Justice Taney refused legal recognition in a case argued before the Supreme Court in 1848. The Second French Republic's emancipation of the slaves in the French West Indies confirmed Calhoun's suspicions. His *Disquisition on Government* (written 1846–49) reflected his revulsion at the European revolutions. When German liberals, probably unaware of Calhoun's pessimism regarding their undertaking, asked his opinion on a draft constitution, the South Carolinian cautioned them to preserve state rights.[7]

Apart from its republican sympathies and sense of mission, the United States had important commercial and financial ties to Europe. Americans participated prominently, as they had ever since the restoration of international peace in 1815, in the Atlantic market economy. American business interests in Europe tended to be quite different from American ideological inclinations. Slave-grown cotton constituted the leading U.S. export to Europe. Demand for American cotton plunged in the spring of 1848 when European buyers became uncertain of the availability of credit facilities during times of turmoil. Financial markets, like the cotton market, experienced a dip during the revolutions. The American investment banking firm of Corcoran & Riggs had already found difficulty selling in Europe the U.S. government bonds issued to finance the war against Mexico. When the European revolutions broke out, demand for American securities dried up altogether. Corcoran & Riggs managed to sell only $3 million worth of bonds out of a stock of $14 million that they had acquired for resale. Only a temporary postponement of the settlement date granted by the U.S. Treasury saved the firm from bankruptcy.[8]

---

7. Calhoun quotations from Morrison, "United States and the Revolutions of 1848," 119; Taney's opinion is in *Luther v. Borden*, 48 U.S. (7 Howard) 1–88 (1849).

8. With permission of my co-author, this section reuses passages from Timothy Roberts and Daniel Howe, "The United States and the Revolutions of 1848," in *The Revolutions in Europe, 1848–49*, ed. Robert Evans and Hartmut Pogge von Strandmann (Oxford, 2000), 157–79.

Before the year 1848 had run its course, however, authoritarian regimes crushed most of the European revolutions, and the promise of reform gave way to prolonged reaction. In France the moderate regime inaugurated by the February Revolution managed to survive a little longer, until the Empire of Napoleon III put an end to the short-lived Second Republic in 1851. As the authoritarian governments reasserted their control, business confidence returned and the demand for cotton soared. On November 5, 1849, the *New York Herald* aptly commented that although Americans could not condone the brutalities of either the revolutions or their subsequent suppression, "we can console ourselves with a rise in the cotton market, [creating] as great a sensation in Wall Street and in New Orleans as the recent revolutions did among speculators in the destiny of the human race." Likewise, British and Continental financial markets rebounded as soon as the postrevolutionary reaction set in. Soon Corcoran & Riggs had no difficulty disposing of their American bonds, not only the Treasury notes but state and corporate obligations as well.[9] Whigs, always concerned for European investment in the United States, feared that the Democrats might meddle in the revolutions to cater to immigrant (especially German) voters. They need not have worried; the Democrats had enough stake in the cotton trade not to care to jeopardize it. The behavior of financial and commercial markets vindicated the decision of the United States to avoid involvement in the European revolutions and to confine expressions of sympathy to rhetoric. At least in the short run, the United States had a greater tangible stake in European stability than in European liberty.[10]

Meanwhile, 1848 would transform America in ways more lasting than the transitory revolutions in Europe. By the treaty of that year ending the war against Mexico, the United States acquired an empire on the Pacific. Along with this vast domain came the people who lived in it, many of them Hispanic in culture and Catholic in religion. The discovery of gold in 1848 produced an influx of people into California from all over the world, from Asia and Latin America as well as Europe and the eastern United States. Simultaneously another group of Catholics, even larger and exerting a greater immediate impact, was arriving in the United States: the refugees from the Irish potato famine. The presence of these diverse peoples would complicate the ethnic relationships in American

9. Roberts, "American Response," 159–65.
10. See also Richard Rohrs, "American Critics of the French Revolution of 1848," *JER* 14 (1994): 359–77; Timothy Roberts, "Revolutions Have Become the Bloody Toy of the Multitude," *JER* 25 (2005): 259–83.

society and test its commitment to democracy for generations to come. The Catholics in particular initiated a profound and prolonged transformation of America from a generically Protestant society into a religiously pluralistic one. In all these ways, 1848 marked a pivotal year for the development of American history. In the immediate future, of course, the consequences of the Mexican War were precisely what Calhoun and the Whigs had foreseen: The North and South fell to quarreling over the spoils of war. Both major political parties and many religious denominations would divide, and within a dozen years the nation tore itself apart in a Civil War. The republic as known to Andrew Jackson, John Quincy Adams, Henry Clay, and John C. Calhoun was irreversibly changed by the revolutionary developments of 1848.

II

On December 6, 1847, the Thirtieth Congress that President Polk dreaded finally met, with its House of Representatives narrowly dominated by an antiwar Whig majority. The president greeted the Congress with his Third Annual Message, a lengthy document that traversed once again the causes of the war and asserted that the Mexicans had "commenced the war," "shedding the blood of our citizens upon our own soil." To refute the Whig position that the United States should take no territory from the war, Polk argued that Mexico owed the United States an "indemnity," not only for its prewar debts but also as partial compensation for the costs of having to wage the war Mexico had started, and that the only way Mexico could pay such an indemnity was in territory. Furthermore, the weakness of Mexico's control over its northern provinces implied danger that if the United States did not take them over, some other power might do so. Thus the principle of the Monroe Doctrine, Polk claimed, dictated a substantial territorial transfer as part of any peace treaty.[11]

Polk's Annual Message justified taking territory from Mexico as an indemnity for Mexican aggression. Whigs, who wanted No Territory, responded by questioning his assertion that Mexico had in fact started the war. They held but a precarious majority in the House of Representatives: 115 Whigs, 108 Democrats, 4 others. It took three ballots to elect as Speaker the moderate Whig Robert Winthrop of Massachusetts because two northern radical and three southern imperialist Whigs refused to support him.[12] Leadership in opposing the president's rationale for the war

---

11. *Presidential Messages*, IV, 532–40.
12. John Schroeder, *Mr. Polk's War* (Madison, Wisc., 1973), 147.

and the territorial gains he wanted from it appeared in the unlikely person of a lanky congressman from Springfield, Illinois, named Abraham Lincoln. On December 22, having been in Washington only three weeks, Lincoln introduced a set of resolutions challenging Polk's claim that the war began on U.S. soil. With the logical organization characteristic of him, this freshman representative ticked off his points: The "spot" where the armed clash took place had been an acknowledged part of New Spain and Mexico since the Adams-Onís Treaty of 1819, the local population recognized no allegiance to the United States and fled before Taylor's approach, and the U.S. citizens whose blood the Mexicans shed were soldiers in an invading army. The House did not adopt Lincoln's lucid "spot resolutions," but on January 3 a party-line vote of 85 to 81 amended a resolution thanking General Taylor for his services with a statement that the war had been begun by President Polk "unnecessarily and unconstitutionally."[13] (Of course, the Democrat-controlled Senate did not agree to the amendment.)

By other actions too, the House served notice on the president that he would find it difficult to prolong the war. It refused to pass the excise tax and land-sale measures that Polk hoped would raise some money to prosecute the war, and it never acted on his two requests for more troops. The House also authorized a lower ceiling on federal borrowing than he requested. On the other hand, a radical Whig motion to call off the war unilaterally and simply bring the troops home gained support from only about half the Whig membership and went down to defeat, 41 to 137. Meanwhile, the administration pursued its own policy: the exertion of pressure on Mexico to sign a treaty yielding substantial territory by occupying the capital and the ports, depriving the Mexican government of its tariff revenues. The occupying power collected the duties but confiscated the money and used it to offset the costs of occupation. Congress had not authorized the practice; the president simply ordered it in his capacity as commander in chief of the occupying army. So far about half a million dollars had been realized this way—less than hoped, because during wartime the Mexican people did not consume as many imported goods as usual. Daniel Webster called it sheer "pillage and plunder." But making the occupation of Mexico pay for itself, at least in part, helped the administration fend off the argument that the recently lowered U.S. tariff should be raised again to generate more revenue.[14]

13. "'Spot' Resolutions in the House of Representatives," *Collected Works of AL*, I, 420–22; *Congressional Globe*, 30th Cong., 1st sess., 95.
14. *Presidential Messages*, IV, 540–49; Justin Smith, *The War with Mexico* (New York, 1919), II, 261–63; Daniel Webster, *Writings and Speeches* (Boston, 1903), IX, 269.

The administration hinted broadly that the longer the Mexicans delayed signing an acceptable treaty, the more punitive their occupation would become and the stiffer the price in territory they would have to pay as indemnity. Indeed, Polk's appetite for Mexican territory grew as time went on. By the fall of 1847, his ambitions included Baja California (invaded in July) and a right of transit to construct a canal across the Isthmus of Tehuantepec.[15] His envoy had already negotiated in 1846 such an agreement for the Isthmus of Panama with the government of New Grenada (today's Colombia), which then owned Panama. As late as April 29, 1848, when peace with Mexico had been almost finalized, the president sent a special message to Congress advocating intervention in Yucatán. There the Mayans had rebelled against the white minority. Ostensibly Polk had in mind protecting the whites and forestalling any British interference, but Democrats hoped and Whigs feared that resumption of war and the annexation of Yucatán might be on the executive agenda. In the event, the Mexican government reestablished its control over Yucatán.[16]

Two other possible scenarios for ending the war found advocates among Democrats outside the administration. Calhoun proposed withdrawing to some easily defensible line, such as that of the Rio Grande. The land north of the chosen line would be annexed, and (he argued) it would not much matter whether the rest of Mexico signed a peace treaty or not, since she would be unable to reconquer the lost provinces.[17] The administration disliked Calhoun's plan because it seemed to acquiesce in sporadic guerrilla fighting along the border, even for generations to come. The most drastic suggestion came from certain wild-eyed northern Democratic imperialists like Robert Stockton, Lewis Cass, and some editors of the northern Democratic penny press. They called for the annexation of all Mexico to the United States. Like Calhoun's plan, this one also avoided the difficulty of obtaining a peace treaty, since there would be no Mexican Republic left to sign one. Mexico's natural resources, particularly her silver mines, held considerable attraction. But most southerners abhorred the idea of "All Mexico," which by incorporating millions of Mexican people, mainly of mixed race, and presumably granting them citizenship, would seriously compromise the nature of the United States as an exclusively white republic. "Ours is the government of the white

15. Merk, *Manifest Destiny and Mission*, 128–43.
16. Frederick Merk, *The Monroe Doctrine and American Expansionism* (New York, 1966), 194–232.
17. *Congressional Globe*, 30th Cong., 1st sess., 96–100.

man," protested Calhoun in opposition to taking All Mexico.[18] The penny press propagandized the cause of All Mexico to immigrant readers who saw no difficulty in ethnic pluralism; the grandiose proposal seemed a logical consequence of the national aggrandizement the papers had touted as a manifest destiny. Several editors claimed the annexation of All Mexico by the United States would "regenerate" the Mexican people.[19] Polk had no intention of taking over the entire Mexican population, but tolerated the cause of All Mexico within the Democratic Party; it made his own plans for extensive territorial acquisitions seem modest by comparison. Within his cabinet the arch-expansionist Robert Walker sympathized with All Mexico, and James Buchanan tried to exploit the movement to promote his presidential prospects.

Mainstream Whig exasperation with the president found passionate expression in a forty-five-minute speech by Abraham Lincoln on January 12, 1848. The Texan people's right of revolution, he argued, extended only to areas where they enjoyed popular support and exerted de facto control, and this included very little southwest of the Nueces River. Polk's justification for war, Lincoln indignantly proclaimed, "is, from beginning to end, the sheerest deception." Honesty was just as indispensable to the historical Lincoln as to the Honest Abe of popular mythology. Polk should "remember he sits where Washington sat" and tell the truth about the origin of the war. "As a nation *should* not, and the Almighty *will* not, be evaded, so let him attempt no evasion—no equivocation." Addressing the president in tones worthy of the Prophet Nathan addressing King David, Lincoln declared that Polk must be "deeply conscious of being in the wrong"—that he must realize "the blood of this war, like the blood of Abel, is crying to Heaven against him." Not having been truthful about the beginnings of the war or its objectives, Polk could provide no leadership regarding its ending. Lincoln's manuscript of his speech reads:

> It is a singular omission in this message, that it, no where intimates when the President expects the war to terminate. At it's beginning, Genl. Scott was, by this same President, driven into disfavor, if not disgrace, for intimating that peace could not be conquered in less than three or four months. But now, at the end of about twenty months, during which time our arms have given us the most splendid successes . . . this same President gives us a long message, without showing us, that *as*

18. Ibid., Appendix, 51.
19. The term used by the *Boston Times*, Oct. 22, 1847, quoted in Merk, *Manifest Destiny and Mission*, 122.

to the end, he himself, has, even an immaginary conception. . . . He is a bewildered, confounded, and miserably perplexed man.[20]

Polk's perplexity and anxiety over how to end the war, which Lincoln sensed, were real enough. Faced with the implacable hostility of the Mexican people to surrendering any part of their country to the United States, how could he obtain a treaty of cession? The president told Congress that a commissioner had accompanied Scott's army, empowered to sign a peace treaty whenever the Mexicans were willing to do so, and that after the failure of negotiations in September 1847, he had recalled the commissioner. He did not tell Congress—and did not yet know himself—that the emissary refused to leave and instead resumed negotiations with the Mexican government. The same day Congress convened (December 6, 1847), Polk's diplomatic representative in Mexico City sent off to Washington a memo of sixty-five handwritten pages explaining his defiance.

III

Nicholas Trist, protégé of Thomas Jefferson, had administered the patriarch's estate and married his granddaughter Virginia Randolph. He served as private secretary to Andrew Jackson during Andrew Donelson's absence. Having spent nine years as U.S. consul in Havana for Jackson and Van Buren, Trist possessed a secure command of Spanish. He was now chief clerk of the State Department, and Secretary Buchanan trusted his loyalty implicitly, allowing him to perform as acting secretary on occasion. When President Polk decided to send a peace commissioner to Mexico, Nicholas Trist seemed a safe pair of hands.

Trist's orders, prepared in April 1847, directed him to attach himself to Winfield Scott's headquarters and encourage the Mexican government to negotiate peace with him. Elaborate instructions specified the territorial concessions he should demand and how much the United States would pay Mexico for each. Trist's mission was supposed to be a state secret, for the administration had not yet publicly admitted that it waged war for territory. Polk paid his commissioner out of executive funds and did not submit his name for Senate confirmation. Trist set out traveling under an assumed name. By the time he sailed from New Orleans, however, the newspapers had wind of his story. No one knows who blew Trist's cover, but since the leak went to Democratic, expansionist newspapers (the *New York Herald*

20. "The War with Mexico," *Collected Works*, I, 431–42; spelling, punctuation, and italics are original. See also Gabor Boritt, "Lincoln's Opposition to the Mexican War," *Journal of the Illinois State Historical Society* 67 (1974): 79–100; Mark Neely, "Lincoln and the Mexican War," *Civil War History* 24 (1978): 5–24.

and the *Boston Post*), Buchanan may have done it to ingratiate himself with the press and gain support for the next presidential nomination. Because the administration did not trust the Whig Scott, they did not fully brief him on Trist's mission and even encouraged their emissary to confide in Democratic general Gideon Pillow rather than the army commander. Unsurprisingly, Scott and Trist began quarreling as soon as Trist arrived in Veracruz on May 6, 1847. Trist wanted Scott to forward his invitation to negotiate to the Mexican minister of foreign relations, but he didn't tell Scott what the message contained. Scott, his suspicions of administration duplicity aroused, refused to do so and complained of Trist's presumptuousness. Trist enlisted the services of the neutral British to send his letter to the enemy, but matters proceeded slowly. Polk and his cabinet grumbled that the Trist-Scott alienation was hindering Trist's mission, though the origin of the problem lay in their own arrangements. Fortunately, the basic decency of Trist and Scott, together with their common dedication to winning an honorable peace, overcame their initial misunderstanding. The turning point occurred on July 6 when Trist felt sick and Scott sent him a jar of guava marmalade.[21]

During the armistice that began on August 21, following the Battle of Churubusco, Trist finally got a chance to test his government's treaty draft against the proposals of his adversaries. Polk had instructed Trist to get at least Alta California and New Mexico in addition to the Rio Grande boundary for Texas; he should also try to obtain Baja California and a canal route across the Isthmus of Tehuantepec. The Mexicans found out through their efficient intelligence network that Baja and Tehuantepec were not essential to Trist and successfully rejected his pressure for them. They conceded a willingness to sell Alta California, including San Francisco Bay, but only as far south as Monterrey. They balked at selling areas with populations loyal to Mexico, such as New Mexico and the region between the Nueces and the Rio Grande. Trist offered to refer the Texas boundary question to his government if the Mexican negotiators would refer the New Mexico question to theirs.[22] This round of negotiations ended in stalemate on September 6. Santa Anna received conflicting advice from the peace and war factions within his capital, and opted for the latter. Trist had impressed his Mexican counterparts with his courtesy and understanding for their position. His own superiors reacted with anger when his referral of the Texas boundary reached them; they could not afford to have the Rio Grande boundary questioned, since the declaration of war itself hinged upon it.

21. Wallace Ohrt, *Defiant Peacemaker* (College Station, Tex., 1997), 117.
22. Robert Drexler, *Guilty of Making Peace* (Lanham, Md., 1991), 99.

Even as these negotiations went on, however, the administration was rethinking its position. Polk decided that the U.S. military victories during the past six months justified taking more territory from Mexico than he had instructed Trist in April. The president and his cabinet agreed to put Baja and transit across Tehuantepec on the "must have" list, and that a considerable portion of what is now northern Mexico should be acquired as well, perhaps as far south as Tampico.[23] After learning that the early September negotiations had not born fruit, Polk concluded that Trist was not the man to get tough with the Mexicans and resolved to recall his commissioner. It had been a tactical mistake for the United States to appear eager to end the war, he decided. Let the Mexicans suffer under occupation a while longer, and they would come begging for peace. On October 6, 1847, a message from Secretary of State Buchanan went out ordering Trist to return to the United States "at the first safe opportunity." Buchanan did not specifically enumerate the administration's new territorial requirements, which would have been no concern of Trist's any longer.[24]

Trist's recall notice, delayed by Mexican partisan activity, took over a month getting to him. When he received it on November 16, he felt that the president, not being abreast of events in Mexico, had made a monumental mistake. Trist perceived that Mexican political realities dictated reaching an accord with the liberal *moderados* who had succeeded Santa Anna; if this were not achieved soon, power would pass to intransigents. The possibility of Mexico disintegrating into anarchy, leaving no stable government at all to negotiate, could not be ruled out. Trist wrote Buchanan on November 27 urging that a new commissioner be appointed immediately and stating his intention to remain and brief the successor. He continued to agonize over his position. Then, on December 6, Trist sent his fateful message announcing that, in violation of his orders, he had invited the Mexican government at Querétaro to negotiate a peace with him, on the basis of the instructions he had received back in April.[25]

23. *Diary of James K. Polk*, ed. Milo Quaife (Chicago, 1910), III, 161–65 (Sept. 4–7, 1847); Robert Brent, "Nicholas P. Trist and the Treaty of Guadalupe Hidalgo," *Southwestern Historical Quarterly* 57 (1954): 454–74.
24. Polk, *Diary*, III, 185–86 (Oct. 4, 5, 1847); James Buchanan to Nicholas Trist, Oct. 6, 1847, in *Diplomatic Correspondence of the United States: Inter-American Affairs*, ed. William Manning (Washington, 1937), VIII, 214–16.
25. Nicholas Trist to James Buchanan, Dec. 6, 1847, and to Edward Thornton [the British diplomat through whom Trist communicated with the Mexicans], Dec. 4, 1847, ibid., 984–1015.

Trist informed the Mexicans that his president had recalled him, and that Polk no doubt intended to impose terms even harsher than those Santa Anna had found unacceptable in early September. He offered to let them make peace on the basis of his original proposals, by which Mexico would cede Alta California, New Mexico, and Texas above the Rio Grande. Take it or leave it. The Mexican authorities took it, although reluctantly, to forestall worse. Only with peace could the *federalistas moderados* preserve the union of their states and hold free elections throughout the country. They felt heavy pressure from financiers, often representing British interests, who had lent the Mexican government money. Only with peace could their administration regain collection of the tariffs at Mexican ports from the occupying power and start to repay these loans. Mexican commissioners met with Trist throughout the month of January to settle specifics. The negotiators on both sides worried as much about getting their treaty ratified by their respective governments as they did about disagreements with each other. Trist had to work all by himself, without clerical, legal, or archival help. In defining the precise boundary, Trist gained the harbor of San Diego for the United States, but not an outlet to the Gulf of California. The negotiators relied on an inaccurate map, and not until 1963 were all the resulting boundary confusions cleared up.[26] Trist left the railroad route south of the Gila River to be acquired for $10 million in 1853 (from a restored regime of the venal Santa Anna) by what is called the Gadsden Purchase. He assumed U.S. responsibility for preventing the Indian tribes living north of the border from raiding Mexican homes south of it, a significant concession.

But Trist did not deal entirely generously with Mexico in the treaty. His original instructions actually authorized him to pay up to $20 million for the territory acquired, but he reduced the sum to $15 million, no doubt in hopes of mollifying Polk. Before the war, Slidell would have paid $25 million. Just how little $15 million represented to pay for California and New Mexico may be judged from the fact that in the summer of 1848 the United States offered Spain $50 to $100 million for its colony Cuba—and the offer was rejected.[27] The claims against Mexico by U.S. citizens were valued at no more than $3.25 million and assumed by the United States government. To the Mexicans, the terms they signed on to, stipulating the loss of almost half their territory, seemed drastic and humiliating, not moderate. The sums paid out in accordance with the treaty paled in

26. Jack Rittenhouse, *Disturnell's Treaty Map* (Santa Fe, N.M., 1965) reproduces the map and describes its problems.
27. Richard Van Alstyne, *The Rising American Empire* (Chicago, 1965), 150–54.

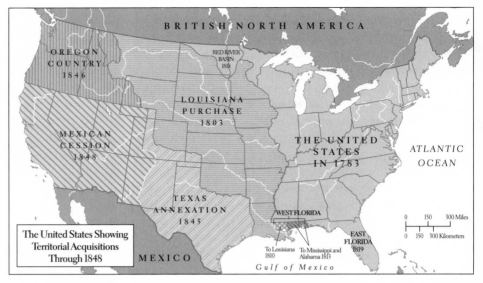

The United States Showing
Territorial Acquisitions
Through 1848

The United States as
Polk Would Have Wanted It

Above: Counting Texas, Oregon, and the Mexico Cession, Polk acquired more territory for the United States than any other president; below: This map reflects the boundary Polk wanted the peace treaty with Mexico to specify, as well as his attempts to purchase Cuba from Spain and invade Yucatan after the war was over. Other U.S. imperialists wanted to take over all of Mexico, as well as what is now British Columbia.

comparison with the estimated $100 million that it cost to wage the war, not counting pensions to veterans and widows.[28]

On February 2, 1848, the peace commissioners signed their document "In the Name of Almighty God" at Guadalupe Hidalgo, site of Mexico's national shrine to the Blessed Virgin Mary, which Trist chose as a location to impress the Mexican public with the treaty's authority.[29] Polk's order to General Butler to terminate the negotiations forcibly arrived too late to prevent the signing. Later the American diplomat revealed to his wife what had been his guiding principles.

> My object, through out was, *not* to obtain all I could, but on the contrary to make the treaty as little exacting as possible from Mexico, as was compatible with its being accepted at home. In this I was governed by two considerations: one was the iniquity of the war, as an abuse of power on our part; the other was that the more disadvantageous the treaty was made to Mexico, the stronger would be the ground of opposition to it in the Mexican Congress.

Trist wanted a treaty that could realistically end the war, capable of ratification by both sides and avoiding such outcomes as the conquest of All Mexico, that country's complete dismemberment, or the indefinite prolongation of anarchy and fighting. Privately, he also felt "shame" at his country's conduct in the war. "For though it would not have done for me to say so *there*, that was a thing for every right-minded American to be ashamed of," he remembered thinking.[30] His recognition of a moral standard higher than the unbridled pursuit of national interest was no doubt unusual in the history of diplomacy.

Trist achieved his treaty at considerable personal cost, it turned out. On January 15, 1848, President Polk received his commissioner's message of December 6. He termed it "insulting and contemptably [*sic*] base," its author "destitute of honour or principle." He hoped to punish the disobedient diplomat "severely." Polk laid much of the blame on Scott, whom he suspected (correctly, in fact) of having encouraged Trist in his course. Collaboration between Scott and Trist proved even more infuriating to

---

28. The original text, plus amendments made by the U.S. Senate and a protocol interpreting those amendments, is printed in Richard Griswold del Castillo, *The Treaty of Guadalupe Hidalgo* (Norman, Okla., 1990), 179–99.
29. Alejandro Sobarzo, *Deber y consciencia: Nicolás Trist, el negociador norteamericano* (México, 1990), 231–32.
30. Nicholas Trist to Virginia Trist, as related in a letter from Virginia Trist to [Henry?] Tuckerman, July 8, 1864, Trist Papers, University of North Carolina; quoted in Drexler, *Guilty of Making Peace*, 129.

Polk than had conflict between them.[31] When Trist evinced a determination to remain in Mexico long enough to testify on Scott's behalf before the court of inquiry, Scott's successor General Butler, following the president's orders, arrested the former peace commissioner and sent him back to the United States in custody. There he was neither indicted nor rewarded for his great achievement. Trist lived out the rest of his life in obscurity and modest financial circumstances; in 1860 the Virginian voted for Lincoln and the following year opposed secession. The Polk administration had cut off his salary and expense allowance effective November 6, 1847, the date Trist received his dismissal. Not until 1871 did Congress pass an act paying him (with interest) for the period when he negotiated the historic treaty; it did so at the behest of another statesman of conscience, Senator Charles Sumner.[32]

Trist dispatched his new treaty back to Washington with a friend, James Freaner, a reporter for the *New Orleans Delta*. Avoiding the telegraph for security reasons, this private courier made the trip in only seventeen days. (As he had promised to do, Freaner dropped off a personal letter from Nicholas to Virginia Trist before delivering the treaty to the secretary of state.)[33] Meanwhile, Scott had agreed with the Mexicans to an armistice while the two governments pondered ratification. Despite Polk's bitterness toward Trist, the president saw at once that he had no realistic alternative to submitting the treaty for the Senate's consent. The Senate Foreign Relations Committee at first called the treaty a nullity because Trist possessed no authority to make it, and urged appointment of a new commissioner to draw up another. But Polk realized that delay would play into the hands of his Whig opponents and those of the intransigent *puros* in Mexico. The House would probably vote no more supplies for war, and the United States might even end up able to secure less territory than Trist had obtained. And, after all, the treaty gave him everything from Mexico that he had originally desired.[34] The president persuaded the Senate Foreign Relations Committee to report the treaty, even with no recommendation.

When the treaty reached the Senate floor, two challenges confronted it. From the Whig side came a proposal to make peace with no territorial acquisitions at all except the port of San Francisco, which Daniel Webster

---

31. Polk, *Diary* III, 300–301 (Jan. 15, 1848).
32. Drexler, *Guilty of Making Peace*, 141.
33. Norman Graebner, "Party Politics and the Trist Mission," *Journal of Southern History* 19 (1953): 137.
34. See Polk, *Diary*, III, 344–51 (Feb. 19–21, 1847).

had coveted when he was secretary of state. The New England whaling fleet (whose shipowners were Whigs) could use the harbor. Mexico had expressed willingness to sell that part of Alta California to the United States as early as the first round of negotiations in September 1847. Eighteen of the twenty-one Senate Whigs voted for such a peace, but that was not enough. From the opposite side of the opinion spectrum, Jefferson Davis's resolution to require more extensive territorial acquisitions than Trist had secured received only eleven votes. On March 10, 1848, the Senate voted to ratify the treaty: 38 in favor, 14 opposed, with 4 abstentions. Those voting no included seven Whigs, among them Webster, whose youngest son, Edward, had died of typhoid fever on duty in Mexico ten days before the treaty was signed. The seven Democrats voting no included Benton, angry at (among other things) the administration's treatment of his son-in-law Frémont. Those voting for ratification included fourteen Whigs, whose desire for peace, in the final analysis, trumped their preference for No Territory.[35]

Horace Greeley's strongly antiwar Whig *New York Tribune* commented resignedly, "Let us have peace, no matter if the adjuncts are revolting." On the Democratic side, the papers that had trumpeted the cause of All Mexico generally accepted the end of their dream with surprisingly little complaint. Only the *New York Sun* protested strongly, calling Trist's treaty "an act of treason to the integrity, position, and honor of this Empire."[36] The speed with which most of the penny press abandoned the cause of All Mexico suggests that it may have been more an early example of sensationalism selling newspapers than a serious policy proposal.

Ratification by the two houses of the Mexican Congress was complicated by the fact that the U.S. Senate had amended the treaty to remove certain guarantees for the Roman Catholic Church and the recipients of Mexican land grants. Future Mexican president Benito Juárez, among other *puros*, argued that Mexico did not need to sign a disadvantageous peace and could prevail by waging a guerrilla war in which the invaders would inevitably tire and go home. Nevertheless, the opposition to the

---

35. The Senate considered the treaty in executive session and kept no record of its debates; later, however, it published a record of the votes on various proposals: *The Treaty Between the United States and Mexico, the Proceedings of the Senate Thereon, and Message of the President and Documents Communicated Therewith* (Washington, 1848).

36. *New York Tribune*, March 1, 1848, quoted in Michael Morrison, *Slavery and the American West* (Chapel Hill, 1997), 83; *New York Sun*, March 15, 1848, quoted in Merk, *Manifest Destiny and Mission*, 191.

treaty was overcome and the ratifications exchanged on May 30. The same day José Herrera, the moderate *federalista* who had tried to avoid war with the United States, returned to the presidency of Mexico. The evacuation of the occupying army began, and on June 12 the Mexican Tricolor replaced the Stars and Stripes over the Zócalo.[37]

Historians have overwhelmingly concluded that Trist made a courageous and justified decision in defying his orders and remaining to secure a peace treaty. Even Justin Smith, Polk's strongest defender among historians, called Trist's decision the right one, and "a truly noble act."[38] There is a strong parallel (though one not often remarked) between Polk's resolution of the Oregon Question and that of the U.S.-Mexican War. In both cases the president made extravagant demands but unhesitatingly accepted a realistic and advantageous solution when offered it. In the case of Oregon, he probably had planned the outcome all along; probably not in the case of Mexico. Yet it is interesting that Polk waited twelve days after receiving news of Trist's defiance before sending an order off to Mexico to abort whatever negotiations he might have under way. Perhaps the president secretly felt willing to give Trist a chance, provided the administration did not bear responsibility for the negotiations.[39] Indeed, Polk had earlier confided to his diary the thought that he would not mind if Moses Beach exceeded his instructions and obtained a peace treaty. "Should he do so, and it is a good one, I will waive his authority to make it, and submit it to the Senate."[40]

Even though the treaty represented the work of a man who defied him, it embodied the objectives for which Polk had gone to war. Polk had successfully discovered the latent constitutional powers of the commander in chief to provoke a war, secure congressional support for it, shape the strategy for fighting it, appoint generals, and define the terms of peace. He probably did as much as anyone to expand the powers of the presidency—certainly at least as much as Jackson, who is more remembered for doing it. The contrast with Madison's conduct of the War of 1812 could not be sharper. Wartime presidents since Polk, including Lincoln, Wilson, Franklin Roosevelt, and Lyndon Johnson, have followed in Polk's footsteps.

37. Nathan Clifford to James Buchanan, June 12, 1848, *Documentos de la relación de México con los Estados Unidos*, ed. Carlos Bosch García (México, 1985), IV, 957.
38. Smith, *War with Mexico*, II, 238. There is an unfavorable assessment of Trist's work in Jack Nortrup, "Nicholas Trist's Mission to Mexico," *Southwestern Historical Quarterly* 71 (1968): 321–46.
39. Martin Van Buren Jr. told his father he suspected as much. Graebner, "Party Politics," 156.
40. Polk, *Diary*, II, 477 (April 14, 1847).

Counting Texas, Oregon, California, and New Mexico, James K. Polk extended the domain of the United States more than any other president, even Thomas Jefferson or Andrew Johnson (who acquired Alaska). His war against Mexico did more to define the nation's continental scope than any conflict since the Seven Years War eliminated French power between the Appalachians and the Mississippi. On July 6, 1848, the president sent a message to Congress pointing with pride to the acquisition of California and New Mexico and declaring that, although they had remained "of little value" in Mexican hands, "as a part of our Union they will be productive of vast benefits to the United States, to the commercial world, and the general interests of mankind."[41] Polk conceived of the Pacific Coast empire he had achieved not as an escape into a romanticized Arcadia of subsistence family farms, but as an opening for American enterprise into new avenues of "the commercial world." For all his supporters' talk of manifest destiny, Polk had not trusted in an inevitable destiny to expand westward, but, anxious about national security and the danger of British preemption in particular, and prompted by the conviction that the American political, social, and economic order required continual room for physical expansion, he had hastily confronted both the Oregon and Mexican controversies head-on. Certain that American strength served "the general interests of mankind," he had not hesitated to adopt a bellicose tone and make extreme demands. His high-risk strategy had worked in the end because the British proved reasonable, the Mexicans disunited and bankrupt, the U.S. armed forces superbly effective, and Nicholas Trist a wise if disobedient diplomat. In each case, Polk himself knew just when to abandon truculence and settle.

In the same statement to Congress, the president described California and New Mexico as "almost unoccupied." But the people affected most immediately by the Treaty of Guadalupe Hidalgo were the residents of the domain Mexico relinquished, including some ninety thousand Hispanics and a considerably larger number of tribal Indians. By the Mexican Constitution of 1824, once again legally in force in 1848, all these persons, including the Indians, had been Mexican citizens. According to the Treaty of Guadalupe Hidalgo they were to become United States citizens unless they took action to retain their Mexican citizenship. Despite the treaty's assurances, however, the Mexican Americans found themselves generally treated like foreigners in the country where their people had lived for generations. Some individuals remained prominent under the

<hr>

41. *Presidential Messages*, IV, 589.

new regime; Mariano Vallejo participated in the California state constitutional convention and became a senator in the state legislature, though he lost most of his extensive landholdings. Vallejo's property losses were typical of the fate of most Mexican Americans, unfamiliar as they were with the English language or Anglo-American land law, and surrounded by newcomers eager to take advantage of them and obtain title to their holdings by fair means or foul. The state of California placed heavy burdens of legal proof on the owners of Mexican land grants to validate their titles, in violation of the spirit if not the letter of the Treaty of Guadalupe Hidalgo. Although state and federal courts heard many cases arising out of the treaty in decades to come, they did not consistently defend the rights of preexisting property owners as its provisions seemed to require. California did not recognize Mexican Americans as citizens until a decision by the state supreme court in 1870. In New Mexico the Hispanic population did not receive their promised full rights of citizenship until after statehood in 1912. Texas restricted the right to own land to persons of the white race, and Mexican Americans had difficulty establishing themselves as legally white. In some regions of eastern Texas, Mexican Americans were forcibly expelled.[42]

Those who suffered worst of all by the change of sovereignty were the tribal Indians of California, the people for whom the Spanish had created the mission system in the eighteenth century. While California's Hispanic landlords had valued Native Americans for their labor, the new Anglo regime saw them merely as obstacles to progress. Excluded from all rights of citizenship or property, over the next generation they were exposed to a shocking process of expropriation, disease, subjugation, and massacre that historians today sometimes call genocide. That term was not used before the twentieth century, but the great nineteenth-century compiler of the records of early California, Hubert H. Bancroft, deplored what he called "the extermination of the Indians." Indeed, in 1851, California state governor Peter Burnett predicted that "a war of extermination" would be waged "until the Indian race becomes extinct."[43] The population of the California

---

42. Griswold del Castillo, *Treaty of Guadalupe Hidalgo*, 62–86. See also Matt Meier and Feliciano Ribera, *Mexican Americans/American Mexicans* (New York, 1993), 66–78; Neil Foley, *The White Scourge: Mexicans, Blacks, and Poor Whites in Texas Cotton Culture* (Berkeley, 1997), 17–25; Vicki Ruiz, "Nuestra América: Latino History as United States History," *JAH* 93 (2006): 655–72.

43. Hubert H. Bancroft, *History of California* (San Francisco, 1890), VII, 474–94; Burnett in *California State Senate Journal*, Jan. 7, 1851, 15. See also the documents in Robert Heizer, ed., *The Destruction of the California Indians* (Santa Barbara, Calif., 1974). On the term "genocide," see Albert Hurtado, *Indian Survival on the California Frontier* (New Haven, 1988), 3–4.

Indians, a biologist has estimated, fell from 150,000 to 50,000 during the decade from 1845 to 1855. The federal government gave up on its attempt to shelter the Indians in reservations, facing strong opposition from the new state. The few remaining Natives usually eked out a living as agricultural laborers or domestic servants. Nevertheless, several tribes managed to preserve something of their integrity and culture.[44]

Contemporary judgments on Polk's imperial accomplishment varied. Democrats expressed satisfaction but showed no signs of resting content; they continued to covet Cuba as well as additional concessions in Mexico and Central America. The Whig *National Intelligencer* called Guadalupe Hidalgo "a Peace which everyone will be glad of, but no one will be proud of." The black abolitionist Frederick Douglass expressed a deeper bitterness in the *North Star*: "They have succeeded in robbing Mexico of her territory, and are rejoicing over their success under the hypocritical pretense of a regard for peace."[45] The $15 million payment, which to Democrats illustrated the essential fairness of the United States even in dealing with a defeated enemy, seemed to Whigs conscience money. As for the Mexicans, they scarcely experienced the payment at all, so quickly did it pass into the hands of their government's foreign creditors.

In the short term, President Polk's war led, as he had feared, to the election of a Whig war hero as president. In the medium term, the acquisition of an empire in the Far Southwest exacerbated the tensions over the extension of slavery that led to civil war. In the long run of history, however, in some respects, the seizure of California by the United States did work as Polk expected, for "the general interests of mankind." For example, it enabled a strong stand to be taken against the aggressions of Imperial Japan in the 1940s. God moves in mysterious ways, and He is certainly capable of bringing good out of evil.

IV

One voice that would have had something perceptive and valuable to say about the Treaty of Guadalupe Hidalgo was stilled. John Quincy Adams had voted against the declaration of war, in favor of taking no territory from Mexico, and in favor of the Wilmot Proviso in case territory should be taken. Like most Whigs, he had voted money to supply the troops in

---

44. Sherburne Cook, *The Population of the California Indians* (Berkeley, 1976), 44; Hurtado, *Indian Survival*, 100–148, 211–18.

45. Washington *National Intelligencer*, March 14, 1848; Frederick Douglass, "Peace! Peace! Peace!" *North Star*, March 17, 1848.

the field, on the grounds that soldiers obeying the nation's orders deserved support even if the orders were unwise. "The most important conclusion from all this, in my mind, is the failure of that provision in the Constitution of the United States, that the power of declaring War, is given exclusively to Congress," Adams wrote to his friend Albert Gallatin. The president had essentially made the war, and Adams feared the precedent threatened the future of American liberty.[46]

Monday morning, February 21, 1848, while Polk was explaining to his cabinet that he had received Trist's treaty and intended to send it to the Senate for ratification, Adams attended the House of Representatives. The Speaker called for a suspension of the rules to permit a vote on thanks and decorations for the generals who had led the armed forces in the victorious war against Mexico. The suspension passed overwhelmingly, but an old man's voice rang out clearly when the clerk called for those opposed. It may seem fitting that Adams's last word in Congress should have been "No!" The former president had resisted the tide in many ways: against the popular Jackson, against mass political parties, against the extension of slavery across space and time, and most recently against waging aggressive war. Yet Adams's vision was predominantly positive, not negative. He had stood in favor of public education, freedom of expression, government support for science, industry, and transportation, nonpartisanship in federal employment, justice to the Native Americans, legal rights for women and blacks, cordial relations with the Latin American Republics, and, undoubtedly, a firm foreign policy that protected the national interest.

As the clerk read the text of the resolution he opposed, Old Man Eloquent rose in his seat to seek recognition to speak. But his face reddened, and suddenly he fell into the arms of a colleague. "Mr. Adams is dying!" a member called out. The House immediately adjourned; so did the Senate and the Supreme Court as soon as they heard the news. They carried the eighty-year-old statesman to a sofa in the Speaker's office. He managed to say, "This is the end of earth, but I am composed."[47] Then he lapsed into unconsciousness until the evening of the twenty-third, when he expired. Only after several days of official mourning did the Senate Foreign Relations Committee commence its consideration of the great treaty on Monday, February 28. A railway train bore Adams's body back to

---

46. John Quincy Adams to Albert Gallatin, Dec. 26, 1847, quoted in Samuel Flagg Bemis, *John Quincy Adams and the Union* (New York, 1956), 500.
47. This version is accepted by his great biographer, Bemis, 536. Other authorities give "This is the end of earth. I am content."

Quincy, Massachusetts, the first such transportation of a dead politician and an appropriate recognition for a friend of internal improvements.[48] Of the many eloquent tributes, the most apt came from Adams's long-term political adversary, Thomas Hart Benton of Missouri. "Death found him at the post of duty; and where else could it have found him?"[49]

In due course, a young Whig colleague of Adams in the House, coming from an utterly different background both geographically and socially, would revitalize the older man's combination of commitments to national unity, the restriction of slavery, and economic modernization. Abraham Lincoln fulfilled Adams's prophecy, made at the time of the Missouri Controversy, that the slavery issue would provoke dissolution of the Union and civil war, after which: "The Union might then be reorganized on the fundamental principle of emancipation. This object is vast in its compass, awful in its prospects, sublime and beautiful in its issue. A life devoted to it would be nobly spent or sacrificed."[50]

V

Coloma, California, was a remote location in the Sierra Nevada on the South Fork of what the *californios* named the Río de los Americanos after Jedediah Smith's visit in 1827. There a carpenter named James Marshall supervised a team of Mormon Battalion veterans constructing a sawmill for local magnate Johann Sutter. On the morning of January 24, 1848, Marshall inspected the millrace (the channel for the waterwheel) they were deepening. He noticed some distinctive particles amidst the watery sand. He carried them in his hat back to the breakfasting workers and said, "Boys, I believe I have found a gold mine!" Actually, the group he addressed included a woman, Jennie Wimmer, the cook, disliked by the men because she insisted they be on time for meals. She tested Marshall's sample in her lye kettle, and the result, though not conclusive, was positive.[51] The following day, eighteen hundred miles to the south, an exhausted Nicholas Trist composed a letter to Secretary of State Buchanan reporting that he and his Mexican counterparts had completed drafting a treaty of peace; eight days later they would formally sign the document.

48. Lynn Parsons, *John Quincy Adams* (Madison, Wisc., 1998), xiv–xv.

49. Benton in *Congressional Globe*, 30th Cong., 1st sess. (Feb. 24, 1848), 389.

50. John Quincy Adams, diary entry for Feb. 24, 1820, in his *Memoirs*, ed. Charles Francis Adams (Philadelphia, 1874–79), IV, 531.

51. Quotation from Rodman Paul and Elliott West, *Mining Frontiers of the Far West*, rev. ed. (Albuquerque, N.M., 2001), 13. On Jennie Wimmer, see H. W. Brands, *The Age of Gold* (New York, 2001), 1–2; Joanne Levy, *They Saw the Elephant: Women in the California Gold Rush* (Hamden, Conn., 1990), xix–xxi.

Unknown to the negotiators in Guadalupe Hidalgo, the gigantic value of the territory Mexico was ceding away had just been demonstrated. The gold that Spanish explorers of the region had sought in vain for three hundred years had now been revealed. The discovery benefited neither Marshall nor Sutter (in fact, it ruined both of them), but the potential of the empire that Mexico had lost and the United States had won soon became dramatically apparent to all the world.

Marshall and Sutter tried and failed to keep the gold a secret. Early in May a former Mormon named Sam Brannan, hoping to promote trade at his store in New Helvetia, went through the streets of San Francisco waving a sample and shouting, "Gold! Gold! Gold from the American River!" It was one of the most sensational advertising ploys in history. By mid-June, three-quarters of the men in San Francisco had left for the gold country, some of them no doubt buying equipment from Brannan. Soldiers deserted their units and sailors their ships, leaving the abandoned vessels clogging San Francisco Bay. Oliver Larkin thought the Gold Rush introduced a strange kind of democracy, in which no one wanted to work for anyone else, and everyone in the mining camps, regardless of any new wealth, dressed alike and ate the same simple food, since no luxuries were yet available there. "A complete revolution in the ordinary state of affairs is taking place," he commented in the spring of 1848.[52]

With telegraph poles still thousands of miles away, news of the gold in California traveled faster by water than over land. It first spread around the Pacific Rim. In July gold-seekers set out from Hawaii and the Mexican west coast, especially Sonora. Over the summer, two-thirds of the white men in Oregon departed for California. Through the autumn and following winter argonauts started arriving from Chile, Peru, Australia, and the Kwangtung Province of China. In both the United States and Mexico, dislocated war veterans were especially likely to respond to the appeal of the gold fields. The people most immune to the "golden yellow fever" seemed to be the Utah Mormons. Indeed, when Brigham Young ordered them to do so in June, the Mormon veterans who had been with Marshall left the Sierra and joined the Gathering in Zion.[53]

The Atlantic world learned of the discovery more slowly and digested its import more gradually than the Pacific. On August 19, 1848, the *New*

52. Quoted in Morrison, *Slavery and the American West*, 97.
53. See Kenneth Owens, ed., *Riches for All: The California Gold Rush and the World* (Lincoln, Neb., 2002); William Greever, *The Bonanza West* (Norman, Okla., 1963), 7–8.

York Herald ran a communication from an anonymous New York volunteer soldier in California under the headline "Affairs in Our New Territory." Buried within it was this sentence: "I am credibly informed that a quantity of gold, worth in value $30, was picked up lately in the bed of a stream of the Sacramento." National attention did not focus on the discovery of gold, however, until President Polk, eager to rebut his critics and show that California had been worth a war, highlighted it in his Annual Message of December 5, 1848, sharing with the public news he had received from his military sources.[54] Underscoring the president's point, two days later there arrived in Washington a display of 230 troy ounces of gold, worth almost four thousand dollars, sent more than three months earlier by the military governor of California, Colonel Richard Mason. The secretary of war announced that the gold would be cast into medals for military heroes. After this deliberate encouragement from the political authorities, the now authenticated reports spread by the telegraph and the packets to Europe. Smaller newspapers copied, after the fashion of the time, the accounts printed in the major metropolitan dailies.[55] The great California Gold Rush in the Atlantic world ensued in 1849, though it had begun in the Pacific and the West in 1848.

One reason why the president promoted the Gold Rush was to stimulate gold coinage. His Message to Congress urged establishment of what became the U.S. Mint in San Francisco, so as to save transporting the bullion a long distance before monetizing it. By the end of 1848, $10 million in gold had been produced in California; by the end of 1851, $220 million. The value of U.S. gold coins in circulation increased by a factor of twenty.[56] This went far to alleviate the shortage of currency that had always plagued the United States and that had done so much to stimulate conflict between "hard" and "soft" money advocates. With plenty of gold in circulation, there could be no objection to the hard-money policy of the Jacksonian Democrats, and less need for a multitude of bank notes with all their problems of confusion, fraud, and counterfeiting. Polk had restored Van Buren's Independent Treasury (though this did not sever the connection between the federal government and banking; it meant the government used the Jacksonian banking firm of Corcoran & Riggs, which did not issue banknotes, to market its securities). Thanks to California gold and the generous extension of British credit in the 1850s, the

54. *New York Herald*, Aug. 19, 1848, morning ed.; *Presidential Messages*, IV, 636–37.
55. Malcolm Rohrbough, *Days of Gold* (Berkeley, 1997), 28.
56. T. H. Watkins, *Gold and Silver in the West* (Palo Alto, Calif., 1971), 40; Robert Hine and John Faragher, *The American West* (New Haven, 2000), 240.

Whigs could never again find a mandate for trying to create another national bank.[57]

People in "the States" wanting to reach California had their choice of routes. The easiest but slowest and usually the most expensive mode of travel ($300 to $700 and from four to eight months) was to sail fifteen thousand miles—often much more in order to pick up fresh water or catch the wind—around Cape Horn. The fastest option consisted of taking ship to Central America and then crossing either Panama or Nicaragua by pack mule and dugout canoe; at this point there could be an indeterminate wait for a ship to take one the rest of the way. With a good connection the whole trip could be made in five to eight weeks. When faced with a long delay between ships, frantic emigrants would pay as much as $600 for a ticket from Central America to San Francisco. This route exposed the traveler to dreaded tropical diseases. Its importance, however, prompted a wave of U.S. expansionist activity in Central America and the Caribbean during the next decade.[58] Another possibility would have been to sail to Tampico, cross Mexico and take another ship from Mazatlán. But fear of bandits and the general unpopularity of *gringos* in the aftermath of the war discouraged most North American gold-seekers from taking a Mexican route.

More than half of American migrants chose an overland route to California. This consumed at least three months of a spring and summer. Although the least expensive, it still required investment in a wagon and draft animals. Oxen were slower than mules but more tractable; most people opted for oxen. Outfitting the trip cost $180 to $200 per person, and emigrants hoped to recoup much of that by selling their animals at inflated California prices upon arrival. Of course, overland travel demanded much more in human effort than the ocean routes. Of all land emigrants, the overwhelming majority (seventy thousand in 1849–50) took the conventional pathway along the Platte and Humboldt Rivers, though some followed more southerly trails through Santa Fe and Tucson. The Gold Rush overland migration dwarfed earlier overland ones in size and included a higher proportion of town and city dwellers. Like the earlier migrants, these formed "companies," democratically organized, for their collective welfare. They found it harder, however, to hire knowledgeable guides for

57. Michael Holt, "The Market Revolution and Major Party Conflict," in *The Market Revolution in America*, ed. Melvyn Stokes and Stephen Conway (Charlottesville, Va., 1996), 246. On Corcoran & Riggs, see Henry Cohen, *Business and Politics in America from the Age of Jackson to the Civil War* (Westport, Conn., 1971).
58. See James Wall, *Manifest Destiny Denied* (Washington, 1981).

so many caravans leaving about the same time. Trails soon became littered with discarded equipment and supplies that reflected bad initial advice on what to carry. Cholera from crowded campsites and polluted water along the Platte proved as dangerous as malaria and yellow fever in Central America. Many who set out turned back.[59]

One anticipated danger on the overland trails did not usually materialize: Indian attack. To their surprise, the travelers typically enjoyed good relations with the Plains peoples through whose lands they passed. Native guides often substituted for the scarce white ones; Indian trade goods, especially horses, could be purchased when supplies ran low or animals died. After the mid-1850s, however, as the number of white migrants swelled, problems developed: The caravans competed with the bison for forage, spread disease, and sometimes killed precious game just for sport. Both on their way to California and after they got there, the gold-seekers sought anxiously to keep in touch with those they had left behind, especially wives managing a family, business, or farm in their husbands' absence. People needed to be able to send and receive not only advice but also money. Postal authorities improvised ways to provide service to California long before the famous Pony Express was established in 1860.[60]

While migrants and letter-carriers could follow any of a number of paths to California, shippers of merchandise found that the ocean route around Cape Horn provided the only practical means for sending supplies in any quantity to the burgeoning West Coast society. At the height of the Gold Rush the U.S. merchant marine almost disappeared from foreign ports, as shipowners concentrated on voyages to California.[61] Responding to the sudden demand for fast sailing vessels to navigate the Cape Horn route, the beautiful American clipper ships appeared in the 1850s. They cut the time to San Francisco to three months and proved themselves valuable for the China as well as the California trade, until eventually rendered obsolete when the British developed oceangoing steamships.

As a result of the Gold Rush, California's population increased much more rapidly than that of other Far West societies. The census of 1850 showed a population of 93,000, not counting those whose constant motion eluded the census-taker, those who had already come and gone, or

59. Brands, *Age of Gold*, 123; Rohrbough, *Days of Gold*, 65; Paula Mitchell Marks, *Precious Dust* (New York, 1994), 55–57.
60. Michael Tate, *Indians and Emigrants* (Norman, Okla., 2006), 104–20; David Henkin, *The Postal Age* (Chicago, 2006), 119–37.
61. Greever, *Bonanza West*, 21.

"Indians not taxed." Utah and Oregon, by comparison, then had about twelve thousand each. The economic effort required to supply and equip so many migrants in so brief a time has been compared to mobilizing an army in wartime. The effort in this case was made by the private, not the public, sector. Who came? Yeoman farmers, middle-class townsfolk (including a surprisingly large number of professionals), and journeyman workers—in short, those who could raise or borrow money for the trip.[62] Emigrants usually received help (financial or otherwise) from family members, even though the family was being left behind. Whole families sometimes moved within California to the gold fields in 1848, but thereafter, and among those undertaking longer journeys, about 90 percent of argonauts were men.[63] The few women who came to the early mining camps might well be as scruffy and tough as the males; they seldom actually mined but could earn as much money as the average miner (with less risk) in the traditional female occupations of washing and cooking, which were in great demand. Other entrepreneurial women set up boarding-houses in shacks.[64]

California's population expanded not only in size but also in ethnic diversity. The first participants in the Gold Rush were those already living nearby: Hispanic *californios*, the few Anglo-Americans, and the Native Americans, who, once they learned that others valued gold, used their unmatched local knowledge to advantage in finding it.[65] Then came the Pacific peoples: Native Hawaiians, Latin Americans, Asians. When migrants arrived from the United States proper—whites, free blacks, a handful of enslaved blacks—with them came Europeans: British, French, German, and Russian, sometimes failed revolutionaries. In 1848, the different varieties of newcomers got along reasonably well with each other, but in succeeding years unbridled competition among increasing numbers provoked savage ethnic violence.[66] From the start, however, the Native Americans were victimized, not permitted to stake claims either individual or tribal, and often coerced into working for others. By the end

---

62. For numbers, see Bureau of the Census, *Historical Statistics of the United States* (Washington, 1975). For class origins, see Brian Roberts, *American Alchemy: The California Gold Rush and Middle-Class Culture* (Chapel Hill, 2000), esp. 32–37.
63. Levy, *They Saw the Elephant*, xvii. This is an estimate for those who traveled overland, but it is probably appropriate overall and for all ethnic groups.
64. Paul and West, *Mining Frontiers*, 222, 265; Marks, *Precious Dust*, 354.
65. A story circulated that James Marshall actually got his first gold from a Maidu Indian named Jim. Joel Hyer, *"We Are Not Savages"* (East Lansing, Mich., 2001), 53.
66. For a vivid portrayal of this ethnic multiplicity, see Susan Johnson, *Roaring Camp: The Social World of the California Gold Rush* (New York, 2000).

of 1848 some four thousand Indians were already employed in the mines, generally at subsistence wages and sometimes in virtual slavery. In the years to come the Natives would sometimes fight back in vain, sometimes accommodate to white domination, and sometimes retreat farther into the mountains. A gold rush invariably spelled bad news for Indian tribes, as it had for the Cherokee in 1829 and as later rushes would for the Cheyenne and Sioux.[67]

The times of the California Gold Rush were turbulent, wasteful, and short. Prostitution flourished. Some women volunteered to pay for their ocean passage by indenturing their bodies for a term of six months. Other women and girls were brought involuntarily—usually from Latin America or China.[68] Gambling flourished too—not surprisingly, with prospecting for gold itself such a big gamble. Most argonauts, of whatever nationality, hoped to get rich quick and return home, not stay and build for the future. Besides wealth, they came for adventure, to participate in the great excitement ("to see the elephant," the saying went, a reference to why kids wanted to go to the circus parade). These motives did not foster prudence or public responsibility. Heedless of the environmental damage they inflicted, the migrants denuded the mountainsides of trees to get wood for their shantytowns, mines, and fuel. Even after a state government existed in Sacramento, mining camps governed themselves as informal democracies "not sharply distinguished from mob law," as the early California historian and philosopher Josiah Royce put it. Kangaroo courts dealt out rough justice to suspected offenders; notorious lynchings occurred. Personal violence became common after 1848. Royce blamed the "irresponsibility" of individual fortune-hunters plus hostility toward "foreigners" for a lack of community loyalty.[69]

The shortage of women also contributed to the temporary drop in the level of civilization among the new arrivals, mostly men in their twenties—though they had, after all, usually come from solid communities and been schooled in conventional values. The presence of respectable Anglo womanhood in California became a dream, part of an aspiration to the civilization the migrants had left behind. When her husband died in far-off San Francisco in September 1848, Eliza Farnham of New York conceived a plan to lead a shipload of virtuous, eligible young women to California to provide the new society with suitable wives and mothers.

67. Hyer, "We Are Not Savages"; Hurtado, Indian Survival, 100–124.
68. See Marks, Precious Dust, 358–63.
69. Josiah Royce, California from Conquest in 1846 to the Second Vigilance Committee, ed. Earl Pomeroy (1886; Santa Barbara, Calif., 1970), 214.

But she found only three qualified takers for her plan. She decided to go to California anyway, and operated her late husband's farm at Santa Cruz. In practice, the Gold Rush probably had as significant an impact on the status of women in the East as it did in California itself. The many married women left behind had to take on unaccustomed responsibilities, such as running the family farm or business.[70]

In 1848 and for several years thereafter, all California gold mining occurred in "placers," places where gold had been eroded out of the rocks and washed by flowing water into beds of dirt or gravel. Panning for gold in such a location required only inexpensive equipment and no great expertise, favoring the early prospectors. Some of them soon graduated to using a "rocker" or "cradle," which washed dirt more efficiently than a pan. Later arrivals would have to work harder to find gold the early ones had missed. Often they went to work for wages in hydraulic mining operations that used large amounts of water under high pressure. Eventually, excavation of quartz deposits for gold ore required both capital and specialized knowledge, and the industrial revolution came to gold mining. Mining evolved into a corporate enterprise, and the miners became unionized employees instead of amateur entrepreneurs.[71] The amount of money an individual miner could expect to make fell sharply over the years. According to the estimates of the modern expert Rodman Paul, an average miner could earn $20 a day in 1848, $16 in 1849, $5 by 1852, and $3 by 1856. Declining local prices partially offset these declining earnings. By comparison, in New York City at this time a male carpenter or printer earned on average $1.40 a day, a female milliner, about 40 cents.[72]

Quite unintentionally, President Polk dramatically exacerbated sectional conflict by his territorial acquisitions and his promotion of rapid development. The miners in California, even if Democrats or southerners, overwhelmingly opposed the introduction of black slaves—not because slavery was unsuitable for gold mining but for the very opposite reason: because employment of unfree labor conferred such a huge advantage that individual prospectors felt they would be forced out of the gold fields if large slaveholders came in. The conscripted labor of Indians had demonstrated the point, which was why the forty-niners made it their policy to kill or drive the Natives away. The same fear of the competition of cheap gang labor also appeared in the vicious persecution of Chinese

70. Rohrbough, Days of Gold, 113; Roberts, American Alchemy, 92, 233–41.

71. Paul and West, Mining Frontiers, 28–36.

72. Ibid., 35. Figures for New York come from Sean Wilentz, Chants Democratic (New York, 1984), 405 (Table 14).

"coolies" after 1852. Knowing the state of public opinion in California, and the impossibility of preventing slaves there from escaping, southern participants in the Gold Rush very seldom brought slaves with them. However, political spokesmen for the southern slaveholding interest did not readily acquiesce in its exclusion from the territories acquired from Mexico. Calhoun proclaimed the legal right of slaveholders to take their human property into all the territories as a matter of principle, fearing that legal exclusion of slavery implied moral disapproval of the institution and constituted the thin end of a wedge of eventual general emancipation. Unable to resolve the question of slavery's legality, the federal government provided no organized civilian political structures for the former Mexican territories until the great Compromise of 1850.[73] What resulted in the meantime was vigilantism in California, theocracy in Utah, and a mixture of military rule with persistent tradition in New Mexico. One of those who foresaw the bitter political fallout from the war of conquest was the Concord sage Ralph Waldo Emerson, who predicted, "The United States will conquer Mexico, but it will be as the man who swallows the arsenic which brings him down in return. Mexico will poison us."[74]

In 1837, Emerson had published his ode for the monument to commemorate the Battle of Concord: "Here once the embattled farmers stood / And fired the shot heard round the world." The memorable lines were hyperbole—the sound of the American Revolution resonated around the Atlantic but not the Pacific. James Marshall's discovery of gold in the Sierra had a better claim to triggering an event in global history. California was the first state to be settled by peoples from all over the world. (Indeed, it remains the most ethnically cosmopolitan society in existence today.) Endowing an occurrence in such a remote place with global historical consequences were the nineteenth-century developments in communication: the mass newspapers that publicized the finding, the advertisements that sold equipment and tickets, the increased knowledge of geography and ocean currents, the improvements in shipbuilding. Although the travel times to California seem long to us, the Gold Rush of 1848-49 represented an unprecedented worldwide concentration of human purpose and mobilization of human effort. To those who lived through it, the well-named "Rush" seemed a dramatic example of the individualism, instability, rapid change, eager pursuit of wealth,

73. Morrison, *Slavery and the American West*, 96–103.
74. *Journals and Miscellaneous Notebooks of Ralph Waldo Emerson*, ed. Ralph Orth and Alfred Ferguson (Cambridge, Mass., 1971), IX, 430–31. Emerson wrote this May 23, 1846, not long after the war began.

and preoccupation with speed characteristic of America in their lifetime. It also testified to the power of hope, and hope built the United States.

VI

The blight came upon Ireland suddenly. As harvest time approached in 1845, "the crops looked splendid," an emigrant remembered. "But one fine morning in July there was a cry around that some blight had struck the potato stalks." The leaves blackened, the tubers quickly rotted, and "a sickly odor of decay" spread over the land, "as if the hand of death had stricken the potato field."[75] Even today, the fungus-like spores named *Phytophthera infestans* cause hundreds of millions of dollars' worth of damage to potato and tomato crops all over the world. In 1845–51, they constituted a novel, unforeseen, and mysterious catastrophe, producing the last major famine in European history: *an gorta mór*, "the great hunger" in Irish.

Of the eight million people in Ireland at the onset of the famine, three million ate potatoes at every meal, and the poorest ones ate very little else.[76] In 1845, the blight stole about a third of the potato crop, causing serious economic hardship; in 1846, virtually the entire crop was destroyed, and famine stalked the land. By 1847, most people had eaten their seed potatoes, so only a small crop appeared; in 1848, the blight returned. Many Irish peasants had practiced "composite" agriculture, raising potatoes to eat and feed their animals, while selling the animals and other produce to pay the rent. In normal times agricultural Ireland exported linens, grain, and livestock to England. Ironically, exports of food continued during the famine; had the British government halted them, it would have provoked hunger in England. Three times as much food was imported into Ireland from the United States, including for the first time maize. (The Creek Indians, from their reservation in Oklahoma, donated a hundred thousand bushels.)[77] Prime Minister Robert Peel's repeal of the Corn Laws (the protective tariffs on grain) facilitated such importation. The maize was boiled into gruel and given away at outdoor soup kitchens by the government; in July 1847, three million Irish people got what little food they had that way. The soup kitchens, the rapid expansion

---

75. Quoted in Kerby Miller, *Emigrants and Exiles* (New York, 1985), 281.
76. On the potato diet, see Mary Daly, "Revisionism and the Great Famine," in *The Making of Modern Irish History*, ed. George Boyce and Alan O'Day (London, 1996), 78.
77. *Cambridge History of the Native Peoples of the Americas: North America*, ed. Bruce Trigger and Wilcomb Washburn (Cambridge, Eng., 1996), pt. i, 528.

of public works (chiefly road building), and relief efforts by landlords, local authorities, and religious philanthropies all fell hopelessly far short of the human need. In the decade 1846-55, over a million Irish people, perhaps a million and a half, died of starvation or diseases provoked by malnutrition such as cholera, typhus, dysentery, and typhoid fever. About two million emigrated to Britain, North America, or the Antipodes, with over half of them going to the United States. All these figures are estimates; during the Great Famine no one kept track of dying rural paupers, and because Irish people of the time enjoyed freedom to travel without passports or visas, comprehensive records of their comings and goings do not survive. The population of Ireland has never since attained its level of the 1841 census, and the Great Famine has been called an Irish holocaust.[78]

Historians conventionally distinguish between migrations prompted by "pull" and those prompted by "push." The California Gold Rush was a classic example of "pull"; the Irish Potato Famine an extreme case of "push." The years after the end of the Napoleonic Wars and before the Great Famine had already seen substantial emigration from Ireland to the United States. Although Protestants comprised only about one-fourth of the Irish population, they composed three-fourths of the Irish migrants to America before 1840. Like many others who came to the New World, these tended to be single young men, ambitious and responding to the pull of high wages for skilled labor and the chance for farmland of one's own. Whenever the U.S. economy encountered hard times, this immigration fell off.[79]

The push of the Famine significantly altered these patterns. The number of Irish emigrants soared, 90 percent of them now Catholics. The potato blight encouraged landlords to evict tenants and convert their estates to pasture for livestock, so the number of jobs in agriculture permanently declined. Hunger peaked in 1849, but emigration continued to grow as people saved their strength and money to escape what now seemed like an overpopulated rural Ireland. In 1845, 77,000 people left; in 1848, 106,000; in 1851, 250,000. Single women and families with children joined the single men in departing the blighted country. But indentured servitude no longer provided a means to pay for ocean passage; so except in a few cases, where local authorities or landlords subsidized departure, the poorest people, the ones most in danger of starving, could not afford

---

78. Miller, *Emigrants and Exiles*, 280, 201; Kevin Kenny, *The American Irish* (London, 2000), 89–90.
79. On Protestant Irish emigration to North America, see Donald Akenson, *The Irish Diaspora* (Toronto, 1996), esp. 219–30.

to emigrate. While death fell disproportionately on the very young and the very old, emigrants typically consisted of young adults in their prime. (The average age of Irish immigrants to the United States at this time was 22.3 years.) Most emigrants represented the social stratum just above destitution, that is, they were tenant peasants, either evicted or choosing to leave, or itinerant laborers and domestic servants, accustomed to moving about Ireland in search of work and now looking overseas. They benefited from the improvements in ocean transportation that led to more frequent sailings and lower transatlantic fares, which seldom now exceeded £3 10s. (the equivalent of $338 in 2005). By a combination of hard work, extreme thrift, and luck, they succeeded in saving the price of a ticket. Although unskilled, most of them knew English, not just the Irish language; indeed, many had achieved literacy and could take advantage of the newspapers and advertisements that described and compared employment opportunities available in other English-speaking countries. The communications revolution had penetrated even rural Ireland.[80] Prospective emigrants learned that getting the cheapest fares to North America often required taking a ferry to Liverpool, where the ships that brought cotton from the United States and timber from Canada welcomed passengers for the return voyage. A trip across the Irish Sea also afforded the opportunity to earn money in England to put toward the Atlantic crossing. The routes to Boston and Quebec were slightly shorter and therefore cheaper than sailing to New York; New Orleans of course cost the most. Some Irish emigrants went to Canada to take advantage of periodic British government subsidies designed to populate the empire, only to walk across the border to the United States, where better economic opportunities beckoned. American authorities did not monitor overland immigration from Canada, so their number is unknown.[81]

Ellen and Richard Holland from Kenmare in southwest Ireland were among the poorest of the immigrants. They and their three children could never have come up with passage money; their landlord, the marquess of Landsdowne, paid their way to Liverpool and thence to New York. They settled in Five Points, the most notorious slum on Manhattan, amidst other people from their home county. Richard became a day

80. Terry Coleman, *Going to America* (New York, 1972), 23; Kenny, *American Irish*, 99–104; P. J. Drudy, "Introduction," in *The Irish in America* (Cambridge, Eng., 1985), 16–19. The National School system had been introduced in 1831 with English as the sole language of instruction.

81. See Dierdre Mageean, "Nineteenth-Century Irish Emigration," in Drudy, *Irish in America*, 39–61.

laborer, and Ellen took in washing; no doubt the three children worked too. Overcrowded as it was, their urban tenement compared favorably with their cabin in the old country; it had a wooden floor rather than a dirt one, and a ceiling of plaster instead of insect-filled thatch. Amazingly, a scant thirty months after arrival, Ellen Holland deposited in the Emigrant Savings Bank $110 (equivalent to over $2,500 in 2005). Even after Richard and their eldest boy succumbed to high urban mortality, the widowed Ellen continued to save money. The historian who has traced the Hollands and other peasants relocated from the Landsdowne estate to Five Points declares her thrift not uncommon. Coming as they did from a less well developed economy, Irish immigrants had more difficulty adjusting to American life than British and German immigrants, but nevertheless they rose to the occasion. Their peasant background did not prevent the Irish immigrants from seizing the modest opportunities America presented to them.[82]

Yet emigrants from Ireland did not forget their homeland when they left it for another country. From their hard-won earnings, they sent back money to family members left behind, often enabling them to come and reunite their kin group on a new shore, a pattern known as "chain migration." Remittances from Irish Americans greatly exceeded the contributions of either the British government or private charities in tangible help to the stricken Irish countryside in the years and generations following 1845. Only one Irish immigrant in twelve left the United States to return to Ireland, compared with one in three among U.S. nineteenth-century immigrants in general who went back home.[83] The people who contrived to escape from their country's horrific ordeal and rebuild their lives elsewhere perpetuated much of Irish culture and replicated their religion in many locations thousands of miles away. These were not passive victims, uprooted prisoners of a premodern outlook (as they have sometimes been portrayed), but resourceful, courageous, indomitable fighters.[84] And fighters they needed to be, for Irish emigrants who came to the United States encountered both political hostility and economic discrimination.

82. Tyler Anbinder, "From Famine to Five Points," *AHR* 107 (2002): 351–87; Joseph Ferrie, *Yankeys Now: Immigrants in the Antebellum United States* (New York, 1999), 98, 128, 187.

83. David Fitzpatrick, *Irish Emigration* (Dublin, 1984), 20; Roger Daniels, *Coming to America*, 2nd ed. (New York, 2002), 127.

84. Contrast Oscar Handlin, *Boston's Immigrants* (Cambridge, Mass., 1941), with Akenson, *Irish Diaspora* and Drudy, *Irish in America*.

Immigration generally confers an economic benefit on the country that receives it, because the immigrants are typically adults ready to work, for whom the sending country has already born the costs of rearing. Irish immigrants played an important role in railroad and canal construction and staffing the emerging industries of the North, as well as alleviating the chronic northern shortage of domestic help. But American workers did not look upon the advent of hordes of hungry Irish as an advantage to the country; they looked upon them as competitors in the job market. Whenever real wages came under severe pressure, native-born workers naturally blamed the immigrants. Artisans who feared industrialization blamed them for the spread of the factory system. Unable to afford to move farther west, many Irish collected in the port cities of New York and Boston, where they found themselves also blamed for the congested, unhealthy, and dangerous conditions of urban life.[85]

Heavy British and German immigration also occurred in the 1840s and '50s. Germany suffered a milder version of the potato blight, provoking in April 1847 three days of rioting in Berlin that the German press termed "the Potato Revolution." The newcomers from Britain and Germany avoided much of the unpopularity of the Irish, however, partly because most of them were Protestants, and partly because more of them could afford to move beyond the port cities into the hinterland, where they took up a variety of occupations, including farming. Immigration from all sources in the decade following 1845 totaled almost three million persons, the greatest in American history relative to the resident population. The foreign-born percentage of the U.S. population increased from an estimated 8.2 in 1840 to 9.7 in 1850, the first time the census recorded it; the percentage would increase to 13.2 in 1860.[86] (The high point was 14.7 percent in 1910; in the early twenty-first century it is about 12 percent.)

The surge in immigration, particularly that of the Irish, provoked a dramatic reaction among the native born. Nativist sentiment combined economic anxieties about the new immigration with ethnic stereotyping of the Irish and long-standing religious distrust of Roman Catholicism. It could appeal to both working-class and middle-class voters. After 1846 many native-born citizens went over to what had earlier seemed the eccentric views of Samuel F. B. Morse, the fear that immigration constituted a threat to American economic and political stability. In 1850, the Order of the Star-Spangled Banner appeared, a nativist secret society

---

85. Amy Bridges, *A City in the Republic: Antebellum New York* (New York, 1984), 65, 83, 96. See also Dale Knobel, *Paddy and the Republic* (Middletown, Conn., 1986).
86. John Higham, *Send These to Me* (New York, 1975), 15, Table 2.

whose members, when questioned about it, invariably claimed to "know nothing." In derision, Horace Greeley's *New York Tribune* termed nativism the "Know-Nothing" movement, and the name stuck.

The antebellum nativist movement, unlike that of later years, did not undertake to curtail immigration itself, but to limit the political power of the immigrants, by denying the suffrage to noncitizens, extending the residency requirement for citizenship, and restricting officeholding to native-born citizens. Like the Antimasons earlier, the nativist movement transformed itself from a group of local voluntary associations into a nationwide political party in an effort to obtain its objectives. (Starting up a new political party was easier in the nineteenth century than today, because ballot access was no problem. The parties themselves printed the ballots, so any group could print its own and try to persuade voters to cast them.) In the North, the nativist "American Party" probably drew approximately equal numbers of Whig and Democratic voters into its fold; Morse himself was a Democrat. In the South, it attracted mostly Whigs.[87] Overall, the nativist movement harmed the Whig Party politically more than its rival; Catholic immigrants rallied to defend themselves against it by voting for the rousingly pro-immigrant Democratic Party. Because of the anti-antislavery stance of the Roman Catholic Church, some abolitionists and supporters of the restriction of slavery felt sympathy with nativism, although others like Seward and Wilmot firmly dissociated themselves from it. The leaders of the two national parties agreed in condemning nativism, both as a matter of principle and because they saw it as a political threat. Such apprehensions were justified, for nativism reflected discontent with the existing parties and played a major role in the demise of the second party system during the 1850s. Those Democrats who joined the nativists in the early 1850s often moved into the new Republican Party a few years later.[88]

VII

The election of 1848 marked not only a change of the party in power but a revolution of sorts in American politics: the crumbling away of the second party system. Ethnic issues made critical by soaring immigration began their rise to the forefront of politics, where they would remain for

---

87. William Gienapp, *Origins of the Republican Party* (New York, 1987), 145, 419; Robert Fogel, *The Fourth Great Awakening* (Chicago, 2000), 64.
88. William Gienapp, "Nativism and the Creation of a Republican Majority in the North," *JAH* 72 (1985): 529–59; Tyler Anbinder, *Nativism and Slavery* (New York, 1992).

several years in the 1850s. Even more importantly, the election commenced a process that led to sectional issues dominating over all others, a dominance that would then last for a generation. The economic issues that had preoccupied the America of Andrew Jackson and John Quincy Adams—banking, the tariff, internal improvements—no longer constituted the pivot around which politics moved. Polk had won a new empire for his countrymen, and now they had to decide what they wanted to do with it, and in particular whether slavery should control it. Within a few years a new party system—the one we still have—would arise in response to this challenge.

Henry Clay had been in retirement since his narrow and unexpected defeat in the election of 1844. On November 13, 1847, in a major policy address delivered in his hometown of Lexington, he announced his candidacy for 1848 on a platform of taking no territory from Mexico except for a modestly defined Texas. "The sterile lands of Mexico," he warned, "might prove a fatal acquisition, producing distraction, dissension, division, possibly disunion." The war itself he branded "unnecessary and of offensive aggression." "No earthly consideration would have ever tempted or provoked me to vote for" it, he insisted. Far from advocating the expansion of slavery, he reminded his audience that "I have ever regarded slavery as a great evil," and supported gradual emancipation and the colonization society. He called upon Congress (which now included a Whig House) to define the objectives of the war.[89] James Gordon Bennett spent five hundred dollars to run a special express train from Lexington to Cincinnati, where the telegraph connected to New York City, so Clay's speech could appear in his *New York Herald* the very next day. The penny paper editor's desire for a scoop trumped even his Democratic Party loyalty.

Despite the accuracy of his foresight, Clay lost the Whig nomination. Ratification of the Treaty of Guadalupe Hidalgo in February wiped out his No Territory platform, and his association with thirty-four years of public policy debates had become a liability. Even so sincere a Whig as Representative Lincoln felt the party needed a new face. Winfield Scott, a leading contender for the nomination based on his impressive military achievements, had been compromised by the president's accusations and some of his own ill-considered public remarks. On the fourth ballot, the Whig convention that met in June at Philadelphia nominated Zachary Taylor, the hero of Buena Vista, and ran him without a platform. Some of the issues historically associated with the Whig Party, such as currency and banking, had become passé. But one issue still alive was fear of executive

89. *The Papers of Henry Clay*, ed. Melba Hay (Lexington, Ky., 1991), X, 361–77.

usurpation, which Polk had certainly exacerbated. Historians have shaken their heads over a party running a military hero of a war they had opposed. Whigs at the time felt desperate to win, believing that Polk had so betrayed his trust that constitutional government itself was at stake. In the end, the convention shared Polk's opinion that a war hero would be the strongest of Whig candidates. Taylor, a Regular Army man who had won his biggest victory with a largely volunteer force, transcended the unpopular authoritarianism of military life (as Scott did not). The candidacy of Old Rough and Ready offered a way to repudiate Polk's presidency but not the soldiers who fought his war, while minimizing sectional tensions within the party.

The partial irrelevance of the old Whig economic program resulted in part from the success of Polk's legislative agenda. In accordance with the objectives the president had laid out to George Bancroft upon taking office, his first Congress scrapped the "pet bank" scheme in favor of the complete separation of bank and state, that is, the restoration of Van Buren's Independent Treasury. In the past, the business community had felt a need for a national bank to provide a sound but sufficiently plentiful currency. Now, however, the Irish Potato Famine so boosted American grain exports that specie flowed into the country and provided a circulating medium that satisfied Democrats and Whigs alike. In the years to come, gold from California would solve the old problem of a currency shortage until after the Civil War. The reciprocal lowering of U.S. tariffs by Congress a month after Parliament repealed the Corn Laws further stimulated international trade. Together with deficit spending on the war, this completed economic recovery from the hard times of the early forties.

To some extent the Democrats had also preempted traditional Whig economic issues. A movement within the Democratic Party called "Young America" embraced internal improvements so long as they were built by private enterprise, not mixed public-private corporations. They saw themselves as a new generation of Democrats, emphasizing nationalism and expansionism rather than currency and banking as their issues. Internal improvements seemed to them a necessary corollary of geographical expansion; they expressed eagerness to spend government money, state or federal, to subsidize transportation. The Democratic Party had always had a commercial wing, so the Young Americans were not so innovative as they imagined, but they enjoyed particular strength in the Old Northwest. Stephen A. Douglas of Illinois typified this kind of prodevelopment Democrat with his interest in railroads. From December 1844 on, Congress discussed federal land grants to a transcontinental railroad, with western Democrats eagerly competing to anchor the eastern terminus of such a route. No longer could the Whigs count on appealing to the business community with a sharp contrast between all the positions of the two parties.[90]

With the luck of world events playing into Democratic hands, Polk might have seemed a good bet to win reelection. However, he had promised to serve but one term, and felt so exhausted by the strains of his presidency, its crises and war, the bitterness of his critics and the dissension within his party, that for once he kept his word. The Democratic National Convention, meeting in Baltimore, passed over James Buchanan and bestowed its nomination on Lewis Cass of Michigan, a superimperialist especially hostile to Britain, who had been a prominent contender for the nomination in 1844. Zealous enforcer of Indian Removal as Jackson's secretary of war, Cass had wanted to annex more of Mexico and would have welcomed the chance to conquer British Columbia for the United States. He believed that an "unlimited power of expansion" constituted "our safety-valve," underwriting American economic and political democracy.[91] The European Revolutions of 1848 provided Cass an opportunity to play up to the ethnic loyalties of immigrants with truculent gestures toward Old World monarchies. As a candidate from the Old Northwest, his selection helped reconcile Democrats in that section to their party. The convention quietly shelved the Wilmot Proviso, and most northern Democrats accepted as a substitute Cass's own solution to slavery in the territories, called "popular sovereignty." According to this doctrine, slavery should be left to the white settlers in the West to decide for themselves. The attraction of this policy was that it promised to keep the explosive issue out of the halls of Congress. But the Democratic Party platform, though it commended popular sovereignty as a principle for Europeans to adopt, said nothing about it applying to the U.S. territories. And Cass himself refused to specify whether settlers could legislate against slavery before the territory was admitted to the Union. Southern Democrats, accordingly, remained free to argue that the Constitution mandated the legality of slavery in every U.S. territory unless and until the voters exercised their option to end it at the time of statehood. To a

90. Yonatan Eyal, *The Young America Movement and the Transformation of the Democratic Party, 1828–1861* (Cambridge, Eng., 2007); Michael Holt, *The Rise and Fall of the American Whig Party* (New York, 1999), 245–47; John Larson, *Internal Improvement* (Chapel Hill, 2001), 240–45.

91. Quoted in Thomas Hietala, "This Splendid Juggernaut," *Manifest Destiny and Empire*, ed. Sam Haynes and Christopher Morris (College Station, Tex., 1997), 58.

Whig like Abraham Lincoln, a Cass presidency heralded "new wars, new acquisitions of territory, and still further extensions of slavery."[92]

For all his successes as president, Polk had been much less successful as leader of his party. He had achieved his impressive legislative victories thanks to the support of northern Democrats. Vice President Dallas, although a Pennsylvania protectionist, had swallowed hard and broken a Senate tie in favor of the low Walker Tariff. Up to the time when he introduced his famous proviso, David Wilmot had been one of the most prosouthern of northern congressmen: He had defended the gag rule to the last, supported Calhoun's plan for conciliation in Oregon, and voted to reduce the tariff.[93] But in return for their loyalty, northern Democrats felt they had received little or nothing. The most disaffected of all from "Polk the Mendacious" were the followers of Martin Van Buren, who had been frozen out of the patronage. New York's electoral votes had been critical in winning the presidency for Polk, yet Van Buren's New York Democratic machine had received nothing from his administration; the only high-ranking New Yorker in it, Secretary of War Marcy, belonged to a rival party faction. When Van Buren had occupied the White House, he had accorded the slaveholding South plenty of favors; the Polk administration had not reciprocated. Finally convinced that Polk had lied to them repeatedly, the angry Van Burenites decided to break away from the Democratic Party. The party regulars gave them the contemptuous nickname "Barnburners," after the legendary New York Dutch farmer stupid enough to burn down his barn in order to drive the rats out of it.[94]

In August 1848, the Barnburners met at a third-party convention in Buffalo, New York, to negotiate an alliance with two other political elements. One consisted of "Conscience" Whigs (that is, the radical antislavery, antiwar wing of their party) who could not accept the candidacy of Zachary Taylor, hero of a war they deplored and absentee owner of a Louisiana plantation. The other group attending represented the Liberty Party, those abolitionists who engaged in politics as well as moral suasion. The convention voted Van Buren their presidential nomination in return for a platform designed to appeal to the Liberty Party and antislavery Whigs. It

---

92. "Speech in U.S. House of Representatives" (July 27, 1848), *Collected Works of AL*, V, 505. The definitive formulation of Cass's position was his letter to Alfred Nicholson, Dec. 24, 1847, reprinted in Arthur Schlesinger Jr., ed., *History of American Presidential Elections* (New York, 1971), II, 906–12.

93. Charles Sellers, *James K. Polk, Continentalist* (Princeton, 1966), 372.

94. Sean Wilentz, *The Rise of American Democracy* (New York, 2005), 583; Joel Silbey, *Storm over Texas* (Oxford, 2005), 99–111.

opposed slavery in the territories and the District of Columbia, called for free western lands to homesteaders, and endorsed internal improvements and a protective tariff. The platform concluded with the slogan "Free Soil, Free Speech, Free Labor, and Free Men!"[95]

Of course, the irony of the Free Soil movement escaped no contemporary. Van Buren, the person who legitimated political partisanship at a time when all conventional wisdom condemned it and the one who had done more than anyone else to create the national Democratic Party, now led a revolt against that party. The Free Soil convention underscored the irony by the running mate it chose for Jackson's longtime protégé: Charles Francis Adams, son of Van Buren's antagonist John Quincy Adams. Those who found the newborn party congenial included the land reformer George Henry Evans and a faction of the New York anti-renters who had become his followers; they had actually started using the term "free soil" two years earlier in 1846. Also enthusiastic were the little band of northern former Democrats whom that party had expelled for daring to criticize slavery; these included the Liberty Party's new leader, Senator John P. Hale.[96] On the other hand, a few Liberty Party members refused to stomach Van Buren and maintained their separate identity. The former president's own motivation was the protection of the Democratic machine he had built up in New York state from destruction at the hands of Polk's appointees. As a judicious biographer points out, "In 1848, Van Buren acted neither as a moral idealist nor as a revengeful cynic, but rather as the loyal New York Democrat he had always been."[97] What explained the nationwide significance of the new movement Van Buren temporarily headed was, however, the new strength of sectionalism. Twelve years later a new Republican Party, with a platform much like that of the Free Soil Party, would actually win the presidency.

November 7, 1848, witnessed the first modern presidential election; for the first time all the states chose their electors on the same day. All but South Carolina did so by popular vote. A uniform single day had been mandated by act of Congress following the notorious 1844 frauds organized on Polk's behalf by John Slidell in Louisiana, where five thousand

95. See Frederick Blue, *The Free Soilers* (Urbana, Ill., 1973); Joseph Rayback, *Free Soil: The Election of 1848* (Lexington, Ky., 1970); and for the long-term consequences, Eric Foner, *Free Soil, Free Labor, Free Men* (New York, 1970).

96. See Jonathan Earle, *Jacksonian Antislavery and the Politics of Free Soil* (Chapel Hill, 2004), esp. 58–62 on the anti-renters.

97. Donald Cole, *Martin Van Buren and the American Political System* (Princeton, 1984), 418. See also Eric Foner, *Politics and Ideology in the Age of the Civil War* (New York, 1980), 77–93.

men had cast their votes in one parish on one day and then traveled to another to vote again a day later.[98] Congress specified a Tuesday so rural voters could journey to the county seat on Monday, thus not forcing sabbatarians to travel on Sunday; November first was ruled out because Catholics went to mass on All Saints' Day. Putting all the voting on one day still did not prevent voting at more than one precinct in urban areas; in the absence of voter registration, this kind of fraud remained common enough to provoke the joking admonition, "Vote early and often." Because the telegraph network already linked much of the country in instant communication, some people worried that early reports of results in the East would affect voters in the West. (Though standard time zones still lay in the future, it was, of course, later in the day in the East than in the West.) Telegraph companies warned their employees not to divulge the contents of messages to anyone but the addressee, but the newspapers had agreed to pool information over the wires through the Associated Press in 1848. The time it took to hand-count ballots and print newspapers containing election returns mitigated the problem at this early stage of the communications revolution.[99] Later, Maine secured an exception that allowed it to hold its presidential election in September, on the grounds that the weather was often bad in Maine by November.

Counting the votes proceeded so slowly it took a week to reveal the outcome. Taylor won the election with 163 electoral votes to 127 for Cass; Old Rough and Ready carried both North and South. Polk could leave office having achieved his original goals more completely than most presidents, but the election also realized his nightmare: The war he waged created a Whig military hero who succeeded him in the White House. Van Buren's Free Soil ticket carried none of the states but came in second in New York, Massachusetts, and Vermont. Like the communications revolution, the sectional revolution in American politics was only just beginning in 1848. Both major parties had dodged the Wilmot Proviso: the Whigs by having no platform and the Democrats by running a candidate who favored popular sovereignty. Most American voters and politicians stuck with their old party loyalties. Even Van Buren's friends Benton and Francis Blair supported Cass; surprisingly enough, so did David Wilmot. On the Whig side, even such opponents of slavery extension as Lincoln

98. David Grimsted, American Mobbing (New York, 1998), 195.
99. Richard Bensel, The American Ballot Box in the Mid-Nineteenth Century (Cambridge, Eng., 2004), 156–59; Communications from Steven Bullock, Daniel Feller, and David Hochfelder to H-NET list for members of the Society for Historians of the Early American Republic, November 2000.

and Seward supported Taylor. The Free Soil Party took away enough Democratic votes in New York to give that state to Taylor; in Ohio, it took away enough Whig votes to give that state to Cass. Overall, the third party does not appear to have determined the outcome of the election, which Taylor would have won even without its intervention.[100] Yet the Free Soil Party had served notice on national politicians that a critical fraction of the northern electorate found additional slave states unacceptable. Thereafter, Congress admitted no more slave states.

After the election, Clay claimed that he too could have beaten Cass, carrying every state that Taylor did except Georgia, and he may well have been right, though Clay should perhaps also have conceded Florida and Louisiana, which Taylor carried. Whig politicians who thought Clay could not win were probably too cautious, as politicians often are. Taylor helped the Whigs only in the Deep South; in the North, Whig voters would have turned out as well or better for Clay. The Walker Tariff was deeply unpopular in protectionist Pennsylvania, a critical state that went for Taylor and presumably would have gone for Clay too. Unlike the national bank, the tariff had not died as an issue. Unlike Taylor, Clay could have held Ohio for the Whigs even with the Free Soil ticket in the field. As for Van Buren, his moment of rebellion past, he returned to the Democratic Party and remained there for the rest of his life. His caution prevailed over principle. He endorsed Pierce and Buchanan for president in the 1850s and in 1860 supported Douglas and popular sovereignty rather than Lincoln and free soil.[101]

As the United States faced the future at the close of 1848, the newly elected president from the opposition waited to assume power in March. Zachary Taylor could take a certain personal satisfaction in having beaten Lewis Cass. In 1832, Colonel Taylor, in accordance with War Department policy, evicted some white squatters from Indian land. The irate settlers sued Taylor personally. But when Taylor asked Secretary of War Cass for a deposition stating that he had obeyed orders, Cass refused. Taylor concluded that the secretary acted from "timidity, or perhaps from worse motives."[102] Although his southern supporters touted his candidacy in 1848 as that of a slaveholding planter, the outlook of Old Rough and Ready reflected more his years of national service in the army than his absentee

100. Holt, *Rise and Fall of Whig Party*, 368–81; Joel Silbey, *The Partisan Imperative* (New York, 1985), 94–95.
101. Henry Clay to Charles Fenton Mercer, Dec. 10, 1848, *Papers of Henry Clay*, X, 561–62; Donald Cole, *Martin Van Buren* (Princeton, 1984), 425, 430.
102. Willard Klunder, *Lewis Cass and the Politics of Moderation* (Kent, Ohio, 1996), 70.

ownership of a Louisiana plantation. Before an untimely death cut short his presidency, this veteran soldier would antagonize the extreme southern rights advocates by his insistence that California should become a free state and that New Mexico remain separate from Texas.

Andrew Jackson and his Democratic Party had appealed to a militant sense of egalitarianism among males of the favored race and had built a strong nation, even while keeping the role of the national state as limited as they could. The Democrats had also demonstrated a receptivity to immigration and a tolerance of cultural diversity that would prove valuable qualities for the nation in the years ahead. The extension of American sovereignty across the continent had been largely an achievement of Democrats. Yet the expansion of the economy and of educational opportunities reflected the contribution of National Republicans and Whigs. Although the Democrats had been more politically successful in the national party competition of the previous generation, on the whole the Whigs had more accurately anticipated the directions in which the country moved: toward economic diversification and industrialization, away from dependence on slavery and a uniformly agricultural economy. The leaders of the Whig Party, John Quincy Adams and Henry Clay, had both foreseen and intended the kind of empire that America would become. Adams was now dead, and Clay had lost his final try for the presidency. Still, America's future lay predominantly within the Whig vision of economic development and a stronger central government. Abraham Lincoln, admirer of Henry Clay, would apply the principles of John Quincy Adams to save the Union, purge it of slavery, and promote both education and economic expansion.

The United States over which Zachary Taylor would preside was vastly larger in area and population than it had been in 1815, richer, and more powerful. While more diverse socially, economically, and culturally, it was also much better integrated by transportation and communication. Increased speeds amazed everyone. The sailing ship *Rainbow* arrived in New York harbor on April 17, 1846, only seventy-five days after leaving Canton, China. The diarist Philip Hone commented, "Everything goes fast now-a-days; the winds, even begin to improve upon the speed which they have hitherto maintained; everything goes ahead but good manners and sound principles, and they are in a fair way to be driven from the track."[103]

Hone was by no means alone in wondering if the rapid pace of change threatened cherished values. Yet some aspects of American life

103. Philip Hone, *Diary*, ed. Bayard Tuckerman (New York, 1910), II, 276.

demonstrated uniformity and durability. Indeed, many of the innovations had been produced in response to widespread popular eagerness to participate in the market economy, and this eagerness showed no sign of abating. America's national identity had weathered crises, its economy had recovered from panics, and its political system had successfully managed repeated peaceful transfers of power. The rise of mass political parties and popular voting for presidential electors had proved compatible with stability and made the white male republic incrementally more democratic. But white male supremacy still prevailed everywhere. Only a few courageous voices demanded the abolition of slavery; even fewer ones criticized gender discrimination. The admission of Iowa and Wisconsin to statehood, balancing Texas and Florida, preserved for a little while longer the carefully contrived sectional equality that had existed in the Senate ever since the Missouri Compromise. In reality, however, North and South found themselves more divided than ever by the institution of chattel slavery, now defended more stridently than it had been in 1815. Finally, the Christian religion remained an enduring element of imponderable magnitude in American life and thought, simultaneously progressive and conservative, a source of both social reform and divisive controversy.

Finale:
A Vision of the Future

Of all the many revolutions in 1848, the most momentous for future human history was plotted by five women at Jane Hunt's tea table in Waterloo, New York, on the eleventh of July. The others present looked up to fifty-five-year-old Lucretia Coffin Mott, a well-known abolitionist speaker and traveling Quaker evangelist. Mott supported the Hicksite branch of Quakerism and sympathized with their most radical offshoot, called the Progressive Friends. She had grown up in the Nantucket whaling community where women managed affairs while their menfolk spent years at a time away at sea. Lucretia and her husband, James, a successful Philadelphia merchant who shared her commitment to humanitarian reform, had come to western New York to visit Lucretia's sister Martha Coffin Wright and to check out the Seneca Nation's first constitutional convention. Thanks partly to the support of white Quakers, the Seneca had successfully defied the process of Indian Removal and remained in western New York.[1]

The youngest of Jane Hunt's guests and the only non-Quaker in the room, a witty, energetic thirty-two-year-old, provided the spark that ignited the plan. Elizabeth Cady Stanton combined the social skills of her mother, who came from New York's landed elite, with the intellectual brilliance of her father, a distinguished judge. She felt the discontents of educated women who found the (new) role of middle-class homemaker confining. She persuaded the other four that they should call a "Women's Rights Convention" to meet on July 19 and 20 in the Wesleyan Methodist Church of nearby Seneca Falls, a venue sympathetic to radical causes. They sent announcements to the local papers, which appeared between July 11 and 14. A few days later, Cady Stanton (who made a point of preserving her maiden name along with her married one) sat at another tea table, this time in the home of Mary Ann M'Clintock (or McClintock), to lead in drafting the document for the convention to consider. This mahogany table now rests, appropriately, in the Smithsonian Institution.

1. See Margaret Hope Bacon, *Valiant Friend: The Life of Lucretia Mott* (New York, 1980).

The document produced at it brilliantly adapted Jefferson's Declaration of Independence of 1776 to the revolutionary needs of 1848, defining the program of feminism for the rest of the nineteenth century.[2]

DECLARATION OF SENTIMENTS[3]

When, in the course of human events, it becomes necessary for one portion of the family of man to assume among the people of the earth a position different from that which they have hitherto occupied, but one to which the laws of nature and of nature's God entitle them, a decent respect for the opinions of mankind requires that they should declare the causes that impel them to such a course.

We hold these truths to be self-evident: that all men and women are created equal; that they are endowed by their Creator with certain inalienable rights; that among these are life, liberty, and the pursuit of happiness; that to secure these rights governments are instituted, deriving their just powers from the consent of the governed. . . .

The history of mankind is a history of repeated injuries and usurpations on the part of man toward woman, having in direct object the establishment of an absolute tyranny over her. To prove this, let facts be submitted to a candid world.

He has never permitted her to exercise her inalienable right to the elective franchise.

He has compelled her to submit to laws, in the formation of which she had no voice. . . .

He has made her, if married, in the eye of the law, civilly dead.

He has taken from her all right in property, even to the wages she earns. . . .

He has so framed the laws of divorce, as to what shall be the proper causes, and in case of separation, to whom the guardianship of the children shall be given, as to be wholly regardless of the happiness of women—the law, in all cases, going upon a false supposition of the supremacy of man. . . .

He has monopolized nearly all the profitable employments, and from those she is permitted to follow, she receives but a scanty remuneration. . . . As a teacher of theology, medicine, or law, she is not known.

He has denied her the facilities for obtaining a thorough education, all colleges being closed against her.

---

2. Judith Wellman, *The Road to Seneca Falls* (Urbana, Ill., 2004), 183–94, 232; Ellen DuBois, *Feminism and Suffrage* (Ithaca, N.Y., 1978), 23.
3. This modest title followed the example of the statement issued at the founding of the American Anti-Slavery Society in 1833. The text of the Declaration comes from Elizabeth Cady Stanton, Susan B. Anthony, and Matilda Joslyn Gage, eds., *History of Woman Suffrage* (New York, 1881), I, 70–71.

He allows her in Church, as in State, but a subordinate position, claiming Apostolic authority for her exclusion from the ministry, and with some exceptions, from any public participation in the affairs of the Church.[4]

He has created a false public sentiment by giving to the world a different code of morals for men and women, by which moral delinquencies which exclude women from society, are not only tolerated, but deemed of little account in man. . . .

He has endeavored, in every way that he could, to destroy her confidence in her own powers, to lessen her self-respect and to make her willing to lead a dependent and abject life.

Now, in view of this entire disfranchisement of one-half the people of this country, . . . we insist that they have immediate admission to all the rights and privileges which belong to them as citizens of the United States.

The nineteenth of July dawned a bright summer day in the Finger Lakes region. Good weather had ripened the hay crop. Farms harvesting it would require the labor of all family members. Despite this and the short notice of the meeting, wagons and buggies converged on the little Methodist church. About three hundred people showed up, some of them children and men. The organizers adapted their plans and decided to let the men stay. Deferring to the custom that women did not chair meetings with men present, Lucretia Mott turned the gavel over to her husband. Discussion, spirited and conducted at a high intellectual level, followed. At a candlelight session in the evening, Lucretia Mott spoke on the relationship of women's rights to the larger reform agenda, including temperance, antislavery, and the peace movement.

The next day, Elizabeth Cady Stanton insisted that the resolutions passed at the convention, like the Declaration of Sentiments, should highlight the demand for the right to vote. Many present disagreed, feeling the suffrage cause hopeless or (as Lucretia Mott privately termed it), "ridiculous." The strongest supporters of women's rights hitherto had been Garrisonian abolitionists who believed it sinful for anyone to vote, regardless of gender. Elizabeth's own husband, Henry, though an abolitionist and a supporter of women's rights in the past, declared himself "thunderstruck" when he learned of her intention to press the suffrage issue. Perhaps fearing for his future in politics, he left town rather than attend the convention with her. On the other hand, the black abolitionist editor Frederick Douglass, who had come from Rochester, spoke strongly

4. Actually, a few women, including Lucretia Mott, had already been ordained ministers.

in favor of the suffrage demand. The resolution "that it is the duty of the women of this country to secure to themselves their sacred right to the franchise" passed by a bare majority.[5]

At the end of the two-day conference, attendees had the opportunity to sign the Declaration of Sentiments and the supporting resolutions. One hundred people — sixty-eight women and thirty-two men — did so. Lucretia Mott's name led the list. About two-thirds of the signatories were townsfolk, the rest from farming families. The signers included a nineteen-year-old farmer's daughter named Charlotte Woodward, who had driven the family wagon forty miles to come; she sewed gloves in a factory but hoped to become a typesetter in a printshop (then a male preserve) because she loved books. During the nationwide uproar that followed, when newspapers all over the country reported the women's rights convention and many of them deplored and mocked it, some of the signers came back to scratch out their names. Charlotte Woodward let hers stand. In 1920, at the first presidential election following ratification of the Nineteenth Amendment that guaranteed the right to vote regardless of sex, she alone of all the signers remained alive to cast her ballot. One who did not sign in 1848 was Amelia Bloomer, editor of the local temperance newspaper. She soon came around to support the movement, however, opened up her paper to articles by Elizabeth Cady Stanton, and designed the garments for which she became famous, intended to provide women more freedom of movement than conventional fashions permitted.[6]

Lucretia Mott felt women's ordination to the ministry a more urgent need than the suffrage; she herself had been recorded (the Quaker term) as a minister at the age of twenty-eight. Although female exhorters, deaconesses, and missionaries were not unusual, few denominations ordained women clergy.[7] Hindsight shows that women gained civic voting rights faster than they did clerical ordination. Nevertheless, Mott's sense of priority reflected the importance of religion to social reform in nineteenth-century America and the role of the churches as forums in the debates over women's rights, as in those over slavery. Early feminists tended to come from those denominations that practiced the greatest degree of gender equality — Quakers and Unitarians — and often quoted Galatians 3:28: "There is neither Jew nor Greek, there is neither bond nor

5. Wellman, *Road*, 193; Lois Banner, *Elizabeth Cady Stanton* (Boston, 1980), 42.
6. Eleanor Flexner, *Century of Struggle*, rev. ed. (Cambridge, Mass., 1975), 77; Jean Matthews, *Women's Struggle for Equality* (Chicago, 1997), 58.
7. Bacon, *Valiant Friend*, 128. Quakers, Unitarians, Methodists, and Free Will Baptists ordained a few women; the Methodists ceased doing so in 1880.

free, there is neither male nor female: for ye are all one in Christ Jesus." Lucy Stone explained away St. Paul's admonition "Let your women keep silence in the churches" (I Corinthians 14:34) as applicable only to the poorly educated women of ancient Corinth, who had been wasting the congregation's time asking questions they should have asked their husbands at home.[8] The Second Great Awakening had proclaimed that everyone, male or female, must assume responsibility for his or her own salvation, a message that could empower women. Some feminists claimed that rights for women would hasten the millennium.[9]

Disputes over slavery and women's rights disturbed several religious denominations in the Finger Lakes area. The Wesleyan Methodist Church, where the women's rights convention met, had been founded in 1843 by abolitionists who felt it impossible to continue as members of a national Methodist Church that included slaveholders. That year the abolitionist-feminist Abigail Kelley gave a controversial lecture series in Seneca Falls (starting in the home of a local merchant-politician and moving to the Baptist church) in which she encouraged people of conscience to desert churches lacking in antislavery zeal. Also in 1843 the Millerite movement arrived in town, preaching the imminent Second Coming and provoking other individual secessions. At least a quarter of the signers of the Seneca Falls Declaration belonged to the recently organized Congregational Friends Meeting, an offshoot of Hicksite Quakerism strongly committed to female equality and the abolition of slavery. Sometimes feminism accompanied a rejection of Calvinist theology; it did so in the case of Elizabeth Cady Stanton, reared in Old School Presbyterianism, attracted by Finney's revivals, but now attending Trinity Episcopal Church in Seneca Falls. In later life, she would devote considerable attention to constructing a feminist theology; her attacks on traditional male-centered religion would alienate her from more orthodox Christian women's suffragists.[10]

The Presbyterian congregation in Seneca Falls followed the doctrines of the New School; its minister, Horace Bogue, supported the American Colonization Society. This put him on a collision course with his spirited parishioner Rhoda Bement, an abolitionist. Bement attended Abby

8. Blanche Hersh, *The Slavery of Sex: Feminist-Abolitionists in America* (Urbana, Ill., 1978), 193. Modern biblical scholars have questioned the authenticity of the injunction; see *The New Oxford Annotated Bible*, ed. Michael Coogan (Oxford, 2001).

9. Sylvia Hoffert, *When Hens Crow: The Woman's Rights Movement in Antebellum America* (Bloomington, 1995), 58; Margaret McFadden, *Golden Cables of Sympathy: Transatlantic Sources of Nineteenth-Century Feminism* (Lexington, Ky., 1999), 53.

10. Banner, *Elizabeth Cady Stanton*, 155–65.

Kelley's lectures and heard her denounce Bogue's version of antislavery as sinfully inadequate. As a teetotal abstainer, Bement also refused to partake of the communion wine. After the two exchanged heated words, Bogue charged Bement with "unchristian conduct" in a church trial that tested the limits of female assertiveness. Following her conviction in January 1844, the Bements refused to repent, quit the Presbyterian Church, and joined the Wesleyan Methodists. The episode typified a time and place where competing religious views and their social implications commanded serious attention. Women's rights advocates provoked similar confrontations in other towns and other churches, asserting the primacy of individual conscience over institutional structures in ways reminiscent of the original Protestant Reformation.[11]

The Seneca Falls "convention" (as its organizers somewhat presumptuously called their local meeting) was no isolated event, but took place within a context of ferment. Even its demand for suffrage had precedent. The male abolitionist Gerrit Smith, friend and cousin of Cady Stanton, had spoken in favor of women's suffrage at a recent Liberty Party gathering in Buffalo. Samuel J. May, minister of the Unitarian church in Syracuse, had preached in favor of it as early as 1846. That same year six rural women in Jefferson County had petitioned the New York legislature for equal civil and political rights with men.[12] Two weeks after the Seneca Falls gathering, another women's rights meeting assembled at the Unitarian church of Rochester; those attending included a Hicksite Quaker named Daniel Anthony, whose daughter Susan B. would become the most famous of suffrage leaders. At Rochester, a woman presided. Other gatherings followed. At Salem, Ohio, the women enforced a rule against men speaking, collected eight thousand signatures calling for the suffrage, and dispatched them to the newly elected Ohio state constitutional convention (with no effect). The first truly national women's rights convention met in the textile mill town of Worcester, Massachusetts, in October 1850, with African Americans among the participants. Women's rights took its place as part of a nexus of causes that overlapped extensively in their support, including abolition, temperance, and opposition to Indian Removal, capital punishment, and the war with Mexico.[13]

---

11. Glenn Altschuler and Jan Saltzgaber, *Revivalism, Social Conscience, and Community in the Burned-Over District: The Trial of Rhoda Bement* (Ithaca, N.Y., 1983).

12. Lori Ginzberg, *Untidy Origins: A Story of Women's Rights in Antebellum New York* (Chapel Hill, 2005), 203.

13. On this broad context, see Nancy Isenberg, *Sex and Citizenship in Antebellum America* (Chapel Hill, 1998).

The spread of the women's rights movement following the almost im-promptu meeting at Seneca Falls provided evidence of a new conscious-ness on the part of women that was widely experienced—although one still so strange that very few women could identify it or dared voice it. By 1848, in certain parts of the United States, there had come of age a generation of women whose world was not bounded by the household and the traditional female occupations performed within it. In the nineteenth century, as in developing countries today, increased equality for women emerged in the train of economic modernization. In Seneca Falls and its vicinity, eco-nomic life had recently diversified, with commerce and manufacturing tak-ing their places alongside agriculture. The falls that gave the town its name had been circumvented in 1817 by the canal that carried its produce to mar-ket. In 1828 this canal linked up with the Erie, and the town boomed. More recently, the falls had been turned from a liability into an asset: They now powered machinery that milled flour and manufactured water pumps. When, in the mid-1840s, the town recovered from the depression of the late 1830s, manufacturing led the way. The railroad connected Seneca Falls with Rochester and Albany in 1841. The village population rose from 200 in 1824 to 2,000 in 1831 and 4,000 by 1845; that of Waterloo reached 3,600 in the latter year. Seneca County held 24,874 persons in the census of 1840.[14] The signers of the Seneca Falls Declaration included a wide variety of oc-cupations, and many of the families had connections to manufacturing. The call for women's rights at Seneca Falls reflected new conceptions of gender relations arising out of economic innovation.

As important a precursor as economic modernization was female edu-cation. Girls in New York state found secondary education widely avail-able, and those from middle-class families generally took advantage of it. The jewel in the crown of New York education for girls was Troy Female Seminary, a mixed public-private institution founded in 1821, the creation of Emma Willard with support from Governor DeWitt Clinton. There Elizabeth Cady graduated in 1833. The Declaration of Sentiments exag-gerated in claiming that "all colleges" were closed to women. Oberlin had been coeducational (and interracial) practically since its founding in 1833, and a number of women's colleges, mostly under religious auspices, served constituencies scattered from New England to Georgia.[15] Normal schools on Horace Mann's pattern, for training teachers, came to be an

14. Sandra Weber, *Women's Rights National Historical Park* (Denver, 1985), 3–12; Well-man, *Road*, 65–75.
15. On the southern women's colleges, see Michael O'Brien, *Conjectures of Order* (Chapel Hill, 2004), I, 259–60.

important component of women's higher education. Six months after the Seneca Falls convention met, an English immigrant named Elizabeth Blackwell graduated from a medical school not far away—in Geneva, New York—the first woman to do so anywhere in the modern world. The goals she set out for obtaining a medical education reflected the nineteenth-century aspiration to development of the human faculties: "The true ennoblement of woman, the full harmonious development of her unknown nature, and the consequent redemption of the whole human race."[16]

But although the ideology of self-improvement was starting to be applied to women, that of self-fulfillment had not. No professional occupation save schoolteaching had yet opened up to women. Men no longer had to follow the occupation of their fathers, and women began to wonder why they needed to follow the occupation of their mothers. Working-class women now could earn money in factories. Middle-class women, though active in religious and reform societies, found few career opportunities compatible with their relatively high level of education. They compared the constraints imposed upon them with the freedom enjoyed by their husbands and brothers.[17]

The religious organizations, philanthropic institutions, and reform movements in which women had participated for a generation proved themselves effective schools too, in the practical sense that they had taught women lessons in self-assertion, leadership, and public communication. "Those who urged women to become missionaries and form tract societies," Lydia Maria Child wrote in the *Liberator*, "have changed the household utensil to a living, energetic being."[18] Of all the benevolent causes in which women participated, probably the ones closest to direct political action were the petition campaigns to protest against Indian Removal and slavery in the District of Columbia. Of all antebellum congressional figures, John Quincy Adams probably did the most for the cause of women's rights, by presenting and defending their petitions. After the Civil War, women continued to exploit their ability to petition, using it on behalf of temperance, the suffrage, and other causes.[19]

16. Elizabeth Blackwell to Emily Collins, Aug. 12, 1848, *History of Woman Suffrage*, I, 90.
17. As Elizabeth Cady Stanton complained to Susan B. Anthony, quoted in Elisabeth Griffith, *In Her Own Right* (New York, 1984), 87.
18. Quoted in DuBois, *Feminism and Suffrage*, 33.
19. See Susan Zaeske, *Signatures of Citizenship: Petitioning, Antislavery, and Women's Political Identity* (Chapel Hill, 2003).

Having sought to help the oppressed, some women began to recognize that they themselves numbered among the oppressed. The Grimké sisters, like practically all the first generation of women's rights proponents, came to the cause through their experience with abolitionism. "The investigation of the rights of the slave has led me to a better understanding of my own," observed Angelina Grimké.[20] And like most abolitionists, the Grimké sisters came to their antislavery convictions through the experience of religious conversion. In their case, this involved an agonized spiritual migration from Episcopalianism to Presbyterianism to the Society of Friends, which led them in turn to their physical migration from Charleston to Philadelphia.[21] Garrison welcomed them into his American Anti-Slavery Society, calling abolition and women's rights two "moral reformations" bound together in "pure practical Christianity."[22]

The characteristic concerns of antebellum religious benevolence—the creation of responsible autonomy to replace external coercion, and the redemption of individuals who had not been functioning as free moral agents—carried over to the women's rights movement. Sarah Grimké's *Letters on the Equality of the Sexes* (1838), the first comprehensive exposition of feminism in America, illustrates the continuity. "God has made no distinction between men and women as moral beings," she argued, justifying her position with a logical analysis of both creation accounts in Genesis. Rejecting the idea that women and men had "separate spheres," she believed it as important for women to have equal duties as for them to gain equal rights. Like Lucretia Mott, she supported women's ordination to the ministry as well as equal pay for equal work. To fulfill their obligations as moral beings, women needed to have access to education. Nineteenth-century feminists, when they invoked the Enlightenment's language of natural rights, typically interpreted it in the light of the Second Great Awakening of religion.[23]

Historians who specialize in the anatomy of revolutions have noticed that they often occur after conditions have begun to improve. The New York state legislature had in fact started to remedy gender discrimination in its Married Women's Property Act of April 1848. This amended the

20. Quoted in O'Brien, *Conjectures of Order*, I, 273.
21. See Kathryn Kish Sklar, *Women's Rights Emerges Within the Anti-Slavery Movement* (Boston, 2000).
22. Quoted in Charles Sellers, *The Market Revolution* (New York, 1991), 406.
23. Sarah Grimké, *Letters on the Equality of the Sexes*, ed. Elizabeth Ann Bartlett (New Haven, 1988), quotation from 100. See further Alison Parker, "The Case for Reform Antecedents for the Women's Rights Movement," in *Votes for Women*, ed. Jean Baker (New York, 2002), 21–41.

common-law rule that all of a married woman's property belonged to her husband, allowing women to preserve distinct the property they brought into a marriage by means of a prenuptial agreement. In earlier years, the common-law rule had been mitigated by New York's courts of equity, headed by the eminent Chancellor James Kent; but in 1828 a statute limited equitable jurisdiction, throwing the status of married women's property in doubt. After a dozen years of agitation, the legislature responded with the new law. Among other things it protected a wife's property from her husband's creditors; like the federal bankruptcy act of 1841 it responded (belatedly) to the depression of the late 1830s. Support for it had come from three quarters: reformers who saw it as a step toward equal gender rights, reformers who wished to protect some of a bankrupt family's assets, and wealthy people wishing to preserve family estates through their daughters. But not until 1860 did New York alter the common-law rule that a wife's wages belonged to her husband. (Stanton simply ignored the New York act of 1848 when she listed married women's lack of property rights in her Declaration of Sentiments, since in many other states—especially those without courts of equity—the grievance remained unabated.)[24]

The women who met at Seneca Falls in the summer of 1848 were well aware of the European revolutions going on simultaneously. Margaret Fuller, the *New York Tribune*'s correspondent in Italy, reported fully on the revolutions in Sicily and the Papal States, emphasizing the role played by women. The London press contained vivid reports, reprinted in the United States, of the role of armed women in the Paris and Prague uprisings. In March, the daily *Voix des femmes* appeared on the streets of Paris, and the Society for the Emancipation of Women called on the French government to accord women equal rights in politics and education. In April, the new Second Republic abolished slavery in the French West Indies. In May, the Frankfort Assembly met to draw up a German national constitution, arousing the hopes of German feminists. In June, the French feminist Jeanne Deroin and the English feminist Anne Knight issued a joint call for "the complete, radical abolition of all the privileges of sex, of race, of birth, of rank, and of fortune."[25] Nevertheless, in July the women of Seneca Falls chose to model their own revolutionary appeal on

---

24. See Marylynn Salmon, *Women and the Law of Property in Early America* (Chapel Hill, 1986); Norma Basch, *In the Eyes of the Law: Women, Marriage, and Property in Nineteenth-Century New York* (Ithaca, N.Y., 1982); Richard Chused, "Married Women's Property Law, 1800–1850," *Georgetown Law Journal* 71 (1983): 1359–1423.

25. Bonnie Anderson, *Joyous Greetings: The First International Women's Movement* (Oxford, 2000), 153–78, quotation from 156.

1776, not on contemporaneous events in Europe (which, of course, proved evanescent). The choice reveals something of Americans' sense of their country's "exceptional" status as a model for the rest of the world, and corresponding reluctance to view the revolutions going on in Europe as an example for America.

The Seneca Falls convention occurred in a world undergoing a revolution in communications. Earlier statements on behalf of women's rights had attracted little attention in the United States, but now the telegraph and the newly formed Associated Press distributed the news made at Seneca Falls. Garrison's *Liberator* hailed the convention as "The Woman's Revolution." Frederick Douglass's *North Star* and Lydia Maria Child's *Anti-Slavery Standard* strongly supported women's rights. More importantly, the mainstream press accorded Seneca Falls coverage. A modern examination found 29 percent of newspaper articles on the convention favorable, 42 percent negative, and 28 percent neutral.[26] The nationally circulated *New York Tribune* of Horace Greeley generally supported women's rights and employed the feminist journalists Margaret Fuller and Jane Swisshelm. James Gordon Bennett's *New York Herald* often mocked rights for women, but his sensationalized coverage still gave the movement valuable publicity. ("By the intelligence which we have lately received, the work of revolution is no longer confined to the Old World, nor to the masculine gender," the paper's piece on Seneca Falls announced.)[27] After its founding in 1851, Henry Raymond's *New York Times* would take an intermediate position, critical of the women's movement as a whole but sometimes supporting particular reforms. Besides news of events, the printing presses also generated a vast flow of novels, religious tracts, domestic advice, and social criticism—much of it written by women authors addressing a women's audience. This output fostered greater respect for women even when not explicitly addressing legal and political issues. Without the communications revolution, it would have been much harder to change public opinion and mobilize support for a novel cause like women's rights.

In Seneca Falls itself, press opinion divided. The *Seneca Observer* had supported women's suffrage as early as 1843. But the rival newspaper, the *Seneca Democrat*, expressed the common hostile derision: "What absurd stuff is all this prattle about the 'Rights of Woman!'" If women enjoyed equal rights, "in time of war how effective would be our army and

---

26. Banner, *Elizabeth Cady Stanton*, 46; Griffith, *In Her Own Right*, 58; Wellman, *Road*, 210.
27. Hoffert, *When Hens Crow*, 74–80, quotation from *History of Woman Suffrage*, I, 805.

navy—the commander-in-chief in a delicate condition [i.e., pregnant], her officers darning stockings."[28]

In most parts of the country both major political parties, like most newspapers, opposed women's suffrage, the Democrats somewhat more vociferously than the Whigs. Women of all races, classes, and ethnic groups engaged in religious and charitable activities, but the women's rights movement involved a narrower constituency, and women's suffrage a smaller one yet. The cause of women's suffrage, like that of abolitionism, found more support among Yankees and the middle class than among other ethnic groups or the working class. Correspondingly, the Democratic Party showed less enthusiasm for women in politics than did the Whigs and their Republican successors. The greater openness of the Whig Party to the participation of women in political campaigning also reflected that party's ties to evangelical reform movements like temperance and an imitation of their faith in the moral influence of women on men. Nevertheless, it indicated an unusually enlightened attitude when Abraham Lincoln, running as a Whig for the Illinois state legislature in 1836, announced that he favored giving "the right of suffrage" to women who paid taxes.[29] The most important contribution the Whig Party made to ameliorating women's traditional subjection consisted of its support for public education and economic development.

American history between 1815 and 1848 certainly had its dark side: poverty, demagogy, disregard for legal restraints, the perpetuation and expansion of slavery, the dispossession of the Native Americans, and the waging of aggressive war against Mexico. But among its hopeful aspects, none was more encouraging than the gathering of the women at the prosperous canal town of Seneca Falls. The women who met there in 1848 set in motion, in the words of Elizabeth Cady Stanton, "a rebellion such as the world had never before seen."[30] Modern communications helped, and continues to help, this unprecedented revolution spread. "Thanks to steam navigation and electric wires," observed Fredrick Douglass, "a revolution now cannot be confined to the place or the people where it may commence, but flashes with lightning speed from heart to heart, from land to land, until it has traversed the globe."[31] The revolution proclaimed in 1848 built upon that of 1776, and would transform the lives of

28. The *Seneca Democrat*, March 23, 1843, quoted in Weber, *Women's Rights National Park*, 46–47.
29. *Collected Works of AL*, I, 48.
30. Quoted in Wellman, *Road*, 208.
31. *North Star*, April 28, 1848.

more people more profoundly. Today, its implications continue to spread over all the globe.

II

This book tells a story; it does not argue a thesis. For that reason, it does not end with a summary of an argument. The women's rights convention of 1848 highlighted several important aspects of the larger story of America's thirty-three years after 1815. It seems useful to point these out by way of conclusion.

In 1848, as in 1815, Americans still considered their country an example of democracy to the rest of the world, although that role had been embarrassed and compromised by aggressive war and the extension, rather than the contraction, of chattel slavery. The women's rights movement appealed to this democratic pride. The most important forces that had made American democracy meaningful during the years since 1815 were three. First, the growth of the market economy, facilitated by dramatic improvements in transportation, broadening the consumer and vocational choices available to most people. Second, the awakened vigor of democratically organized Protestant churches and other voluntary associations. Third, the emergence of mass political parties offering rival programs for the electorate to choose. The impact of all three of these forces had been multiplied by new developments in communications. The women's rights movement related to all three, but especially to the first two.

The struggle to win greater legal rights for women appeared when it did as an outgrowth of improvements in the economic, social, and cultural status of women in the United States. The weakening of paternal authority, the chance to earn money both within and outside the home, increased literacy, smaller family size, an expanded role for women in religious and reform activity, enhanced respect for female judgment in private life—all contributed. Many of these historical trends were themselves consequences of economic development, which transformed American life in qualitative as well as quantitative ways. Historians have often pointed out the evil consequences of industrialization—the pollution, the slums, the monotony of factory labor. We should not forget that economic development brought benefits as well, and not only in material ways. Improved transportation and communications, promoting economic diversification, widened people's horizons, encouraged greater equality within family relationships, and fostered the kind of commitments to education and the rule of law exemplified by Abraham Lincoln. Accordingly, economic development did not undercut American democracy but broadened and enhanced it—which is reassuring for developing countries today.[32] Perhaps, with aid from the federal government, economic development might also have helped alleviate the oppression of African Americans. If Henry Clay and John Quincy Adams had had their way, a program of economic modernization might have undercut the appeal of slavery in the upper South and border states.

At the close of 1848, political participation still lay in the future for women and most Americans not of the white race. White manhood democracy, on the other hand, had been firmly established in the United States—in some places after controversy over whether it should include non-property-owners, nontaxpayers, or noncitizens. As early as 1815, controversies over white male suffrage had mostly been resolved in favor of inclusion, if not always in the letter of the law then in the more important court of public opinion. Thereafter, when new states wrote their constitutions and old states rewrote theirs, they inscribed white manhood suffrage ever more firmly. Since white male democracy preceded industrialization in America, it preceded the development of a white proletariat and did not represent the kind of class conflict that it did in Europe. Only in the little state of Rhode Island had the issue provoked an insurrection, brief and almost bloodless. By 1848, only in Calhoun's South Carolina and (ironically) Jefferson's Virginia did state government remain dominated by a propertied aristocracy. In the eyes of the rest of the world, what made the United States interesting was its practical demonstration of democratic principles, with all their strengths and weaknesses. The women at Seneca Falls could take America's commitment to democracy for granted—their task was to show that democracy should not be confined to males. This is why they based their claim on Jefferson's Declaration of Independence.

The implications of both market capitalism and democratic principles unfolded gradually in the young American republic—sometimes simultaneously, as when the communications revolution facilitated both mass political parties and nationwide commercial networks. The major disputes, excitement, and violence of American history between 1815 and 1848 did not involve either a struggle to attain white male democracy or the imposition of a new "market revolution" on subsistence family farmers. Not the affirmation of democracy itself, that "all men are created equal," but attempts to broaden the legal and political definition of "men" aroused serious controversy in the United States during these

32. I am taking issue here, as elsewhere, with the argument of Charles Sellers, *The Market Revolution* (New York, 1991).

years. So clearly was voting defined as a right for white males that during the first half of the nineteenth century the suffrage was actually taken away from those few women and some of those few black men who had once been able to exercise it.[33]

If the emergence of women's rights as a cause reflected in a general way the course of economic development and the evolution of democratic principles, in a more specific way it reflected the rise of the antislavery movement. Most of the early leaders of the women's rights movement first embraced the cause of the slave and only later turned to the task of self-emancipation. The experience of gender discrimination within a movement dedicated to human liberty brought home to women like Lucretia Mott and Elizabeth Cady Stanton the urgency of calling attention to their own human rights. When the World Anti-Slavery Convention meeting in London in 1840 refused to recognize the credentials of American women delegates, it sowed the seeds of the meeting at Seneca Falls in 1848. As Abigail Kelley graphically put it, in trying to break the chains of the slave, female abolitionists had discovered "*we* were manacled *ourselves*."[34] The need to choose whether abolitionism should embrace logical consistency and support freedom for women as well as blacks, or defer women's rights in the hope of eradicating the worse form of oppression first, split the antislavery movement right down the middle.

Women's rights and antislavery both illustrate the point that some of the most important debates of the period did not take place within the arena of politics. Much of this discussion occurred within the religious communities. America's multitude of churches nurtured a variety of philosophies and value judgments, and carried on endless argument over them. In some cases, churches embraced a wider vision of democracy than political institutions did, allowing the voices of women and African Americans to be heard. Through churches, causes deliberately excluded from the halls of Congress—such as women's rights and the abolition of slavery—could still make themselves felt.

The Seneca Falls convention and the publicity following it also illustrate the changes in transportation and communications, by canals and railroads, by cheap newspapers, the telegraph, and the post office. Because of these innovations, the agendas of antislavery and women's rights could be transmitted, reinforced, and made consequential. Without these transformations, one can imagine a host of small communities arguing

33. These disfranchisements have been described above, 497–98.
34. Quoted in Henry Mayer, *All on Fire* (New York, 1998), 265.

fruitlessly, or lapsing into lethargy, with little way of knowing what was going on in the outside world. Instead, news of discoveries like gold in California, revolutions all over Europe, new proposals such as the Wilmot Proviso, and even organizations that tried to remain secret such as the so-called Know-Nothings, rapidly provoked excitement. The mass production and distribution of information, which made possible the rise of mass political parties and nationwide philanthropic organizations, also facilitated causes like women's rights. As the historian Daniel Feller has noted, "A newly functioning system of gathering and disseminating information made people aware of a larger world and gave them the power to change it."[35]

This increased "power to change" encouraged controversy and contest. Equal rights for the two human sexes was but the newest subject over which Americans divided. The disputes that raged among the people of the young republic between 1815 and 1848 cannot be reduced to a single fundamental conflict (such as the working class against the capitalists). Rancorous competition between the major political parties reflected real disagreements over policy as well as mutual distrust between their constituencies. Sharp division of economic interest provoked fierce debates over tariff levels. Sometimes confrontations resulted from rivalries between constituted authorities, as did the nullification crisis and the Bank War. Constitutional and legal ambiguities combined with fierce ambitions to produce a culture of litigation. Racial, ethnic, and religious divisions spilled over from political debate into public violence.

The most bloody conflicts, however, derived from the domination and exploitation of the North American continent by the white people of the United States and their government. If a primary driving force can be identified in American history for this period, this was it. As its most ardent exponents, the Jacksonian Democrats, conceived it, this imperialist program included the preservation and extension of African American slavery as well as the expropriation of Native Americans and Mexicans. The remarkable changes in transportation and communications facilitated it. Determination to seize more land provoked harsh expulsions of populations, wars both large and small, and argument between pro- and anti-imperialists. Above all, westward expansion rendered inescapable the issue that would tear the country asunder a dozen years later: whether to expand slavery. Ironically, after the Civil War, westward expansion would benefit women's rights. Hoping to encourage settlers, new territories and states in the Far West pioneered woman suffrage, beginning with Wyoming and Mormon Utah.

35. Daniel Feller, "Rediscovering Jacksonian America," in *The State of U.S. History*, ed. Melvyn Stokes (Oxford, 2002), 80.

"America is the country of the Future," Ralph Waldo Emerson declared to a Mercantile Library Association in 1844. "It is a country of beginnings, of projects, of vast designs and expectations."[36] Emerson rejoiced in improved transportation and expanded trade, which he believed fostered political liberty, and most of all in Americans' interest in social reforms; he called upon his audience to dream still more unconventionally. He was right, if characteristically too optimistic. Americans lived by hope for the future, but their conflicting hopes for their country and their own lives provoked dissension. Americans were continually proposing new ideas and then wrangling over them: mechanical inventions, communitarian experiments, religious sects, the reform of customs and institutions. New ideas about gender relations (which included Utah's polygamy and Oneida's "complex marriages") seemed to contemporaries the most startling of these many "isms."

Americans' aggressive imperialism manifested their preoccupation with the future rather than the present. New homes, either in the growing cities or on the frontier, constituted part of the innovative quest in which so many participated. No significant group of Americans wished to shun what all agreed was the nation's destiny to greatness. Even the critics of territorial expansion endorsed the growth of American population, productivity, and power; but they preferred to improve the quality of national life through education, economic development, and moral reform both individual and collective, rather than just expand geographically the kind of America that already existed, encumbered with the institution of slavery. The National Republicans and afterwards the Whigs, led by John Quincy Adams and Henry Clay, proposed an alternative vision to that of the Jacksonian Democrats. Their vision of government-sponsored modernization offered America a different future. Eventually, the Whig vision prevailed, but only after Abraham Lincoln had vindicated it in the bloodiest of American wars.

The transformation of the United States between 1815 and 1848 resulted from a blend of two kinds of decisions: the many private decisions made by innumerable common people in their search for a better future, and the conscious decisions of their leaders in the course of making public policy. History is made both from the bottom up and from the top down, and historians must take account of both in telling their stories. The behavior of countless families gradually moving away from patriarchal authoritarianism affected the status of women at least as directly as

36. "The Young American," in *Collected Works of Ralph Waldo Emerson*, vol. I, ed. Robert Spiller (Cambridge, Mass., 1971), 217–44, quotation from 230.

legal reforms relating to property rights and voting. Profoundly conditioning social and cultural life was the force of religion: the multitude of competing sects, some old, some brand new, with their urgent, sometimes incompatible demands. Finally, the transformation of the United States did not occur in a vacuum. It took place within a continental and global context, and the actions of peoples near and far away impinged upon it: Native Americans, Mexicans, Canadians, Irish, Africans, Chinese, and British, to mention some examples.

The complex figure of Samuel Finley Breese Morse illustrates a number of the contradictions and tensions in American society during his lifetime. Coming from a background in New England clerical Federalism, he made the apparently surprising choice to affiliate with the Jacksonian Democratic Party. With the failure of his ambition to embody his intense patriotism in historical paintings, Morse turned his considerable energy and talent to the applied science of electromagnetic telegraphy. This facilitated, even more directly than his art could have done, the growth of American empire. The twin revolutions in transportation and communications integrated the continental expansion of the United States, and no feature of these revolutions was more spectacular than the electric telegraph. Morse's technological innovation played an important part not only in the geographic expansion of the nation but also in its economic development, including the post–Civil War rise of big business.

In later years, people looked back upon Morse's demonstration of 1844 as a pivotal moment in the shaping of their world. John Quincy Adams's grandson Henry, in his retrospective autobiography published in 1918, identified the first telegraphic message between Baltimore and Washington as the time when "the old universe was thrown into the ash-heap and a new one created."[37] Even after the invention of the telephone, the telegrams of Morse's Western Union Company remained a prominent feature of life through most of the twentieth century. At the height of its business in 1929, the company sent more than 200 million telegrams all over the world. Only the rise of electronic communication finally rendered the telegraph obsolete; Western Union transmitted its last telegram on January 27, 2006.[38]

Along with its successes, Morse's career also displayed some of the defects of American democracy: its contentiousness, corruption, and ethnoreligious hostility. As late as the Civil War Morse remained an outspoken apologist for slavery. On the other hand, he strongly supported women's

---

37. *The Education of Henry Adams* (Boston, 1918), 5.
38. *New York Times*, Feb. 6, 2006.

education and became a founding trustee of Vassar College. Electric telegraphy arrived at a time of transition, innovation, injustice, aggression, turmoil, and dramatic growth. Well might Morse's contemporaries marvel but also wonder at what God had wrought in America. Like the ancient Israelites, the Americans had wrested their homeland from other occupiers, believing that this action fulfilled a divine purpose. In the biblical story that Morse's telegraph demonstration evoked, the seer Balaam, hired by the Moabite king to curse the Israelites, instead reported that God blessed them and willed them to become powerful. "Behold, the people shall rise up as a great lion" (Numbers 23:24).

In 1848, it seemed that the greatness of the American people had been shown by their extensive recent conquests across the continent. Later, that greatness could seem affirmed by the preservation of the Union, industrial might, commercial influence, scientific research, and victories over global enemies. Later still, perhaps that greatness might be seen in the extent to which the dreams of 1848 feminists and abolitionists have at length been realized. History works on a long time scale, and at any given moment we can perceive its directions but imperfectly. Like the people of 1848, we look with both awe and uncertainty at what God hath wrought in the United States of America.

Bibliographical Essay

Lengthy though it is, this essay must be highly selective. Some fine historical works have been left out, and items cited in footnotes are not necessarily repeated here. With few exceptions, I mention only books, not articles, although many articles appear in the footnotes. Where it seemed possible to do so without creating ambiguity, I have often omitted subtitles and authors' middle names.

The most influential major interpretations of this era have been those of Arthur Schlesinger Jr., *The Age of Jackson* (1945) and Charles Sellers, *The Market Revolution* (1991). Schlesinger considered the distinguishing feature of the period the spread of democracy through class conflict spearheaded by the industrial workers. Sellers argued that market capitalism was an aggressive imposition upon a reluctant population. Schlesinger's viewpoint has been updated and expanded by Sean Wilentz in *The Rise of American Democracy* (2005). All three books celebrate the Democratic Party of the time as the agent and defender of democracy against its Whig rival. I disagree with these works, but I have learned from them and admire their authors' knowledge and skill. For a discussion of Sellers's book by other historians, see Melvyn Stokes and Stephen Conway, eds., *The Market Revolution in America* (1996). Valuable general treatments of the period, concise and balanced, are John Mayfield, *The New Nation, 1800–1830*, rev. ed. (1982); Harry Watson, *Liberty and Power: The Politics of Jacksonian America* (1990); and Daniel Feller, *The Jacksonian Promise* (1995).

Older general works can retain enduring value in some respects even though dated in others; such include John Bach McMaster, *History of the People of the United States from the Revolution to the Civil War* (1895); James Schouler, *History of the United States*, rev. ed., vols. III and IV (1904); Edward Channing, *History of the United States*, vol. V (1921); and Frederick Jackson Turner, *The United States, 1830–1850* (1935). More recent works on this period include Rush Welter, *The Mind of America, 1820–1860* (1975); Edward Pessen, *Jacksonian America*, rev. ed. (1978); and Robert Wiebe, *The Opening of American Society* (1984). Marxist interpretations include William Appleman Williams, *The Contours of American History* (1961); Alexander Saxton, *The Rise and Fall of the White Republic* (1990); and John Ashworth, *Slavery, Capitalism, and Politics in the Antebellum Republic*, vol. I (1995).

Antebellum southern history has benefited from works written on a grand scale; three such monumental accomplishments are Michael O'Brien, *Conjectures of Order: Intellectual Life and the American South, 1810–1860*, 2 vols. (2004); William Freehling, *The Road to Disunion*, 2 vols. (1990–2007); and Eugene Genovese, *Roll, Jordan, Roll: The World the Slaves Made* (1974).

Diana Muir's beautifully written *Reflections in Bullough's Pond: Economy and Ecosystem in New England* (2000) emphasizes the industrial revolution. Two other fine books that should also be better known are William Brock, *Parties and Political Conscience, 1840–1850* (1979) and Major Wilson, *Space, Time, and Freedom* (1974). Two gems of narrative that reveal much social history are Patricia Cline Cohen, *The Murder of Helen Jewett* (1998) and Paul Johnson and Sean Wilentz, *The Kingdom of Matthias* (1994). For connections between religion and politics so important to American history, consult the wide-ranging book by Kevin Phillips, *The Cousins' Wars* (1999). An excellent college textbook is Pauline Maier et al., *Inventing America* (2005), vol. I. The chapters on 1815–48 were written by Merrit Roe Smith.

The millennium edition of *Historical Statistics of the United States*, ed. Susan Carter et al. (2006), became available after I had completed my research; I used the bicentennial edition (1975). Other valuable reference works include William Shade and Ballard Campbell, eds., *American Presidential Campaigns and Elections* (2003); Angus Maddison, *The World Economy: A Millennial Perspective* (2001); John Garraty and Mark Carnes, eds., *American National Biography* (1999)and *Mapping America's Past: A Historical Atlas* (1996); Arthur Schlesinger Jr. et al., eds., *Running for President: The Candidates and Their Images* (1994), *History of American Presidential Elections* (1985), and *History of U.S. Political Parties* (1973); Kenneth Martis, *Historical Atlas of Political Parties in the U.S. Congress* (1989); Donald Bruce Johnson, ed., *National Party Platforms*, rev. ed. (1978); Frank Taussig, *The Tariff History of the United States* (1910); and John J. McCusker, *How Much Is That in Real Money?* (1992).

The University of Kansas Press's American Presidency Series is excellent. I have used Robert Rutland, *The Presidency of James Madison* (1990); Noble Cunningham Jr., *The Presidency of James Monroe* (1996); Mary Hargreaves, *The Presidency of John Quincy Adams* (1985); Donald Cole, *The Presidency of Andrew Jackson* (1993); Major Wilson, *The Presidency of Martin Van Buren* (1984); Norma Peterson, *The Presidencies of William Henry Harrison and John Tyler* (1989); and Paul Bergeron, *The Presidency of James K. Polk* (1987).

Several well-written books bring to life specific years in American history: Edward Skeen, *1816: America Rising* (2003); Andrew Burstein, *America's Jubilee, 1826* (2001); Louis Masur, *1831: Year of Eclipse* (2001); and the most moving of all, Bernard DeVoto, *The Year of Decision, 1846* (1943).

A continental approach is essential for an understanding of the period between 1815 and 1848. To locate the United States in its North American geographical setting, see the wonderful work of D. W. Meinig, *The Shaping of America*; I used vol. II, *Continental America, 1800–1867* (1993). Andrew Cayton and Fred Anderson integrate the United States into North American history in *The Dominion of War: Empire and Liberty in North America, 1500–2000* (2005). Valuable context is also supplied by Lester Langley, *The Americas in the Age of Revolution* (1996); Alan Taylor, *American Colonies* (2001); and Richard White, *It's Your Misfortune and None of My Own* (1991). I was influenced by the model of Fernan Braudel's classic, *The Mediterranean and the Mediterranean World in the Age of Philip II*, trans. Sian Reynolds (1976).

On the Hispanic borderlands that became part of the United States during the period here treated, two books of David Weber are invaluable: *The Spanish Frontier in North America* (1992) and *The Mexican Frontier, 1821–1846* (1982). See also Donald Chipman, *Spanish Texas* (1992); Andrés Reséndez, *Changing National Identities at the Frontier* (2005); and Juan Gomez-Quiñones, *Roots of Chicano Politics* (1994). Works on the history of Mexico are often useful, such as Michael Meyer and William Sherman, *The Course of Mexican History* (1990) and Timothy Anna, *Forging Mexico* (1998). For Hispanic California and its missions, see Kevin Starr, *California: A History* (2005); Robert H. Jackson and Edward Castillo, *Indians, Franciscans, and Spanish Colonization* (1995); James Sandos, *Converting California* (2004); and the essays in Ramon Gutierrez and Richard Orsi, eds., *Contested Eden* (1998).

The literature on the Native American peoples is enormous and includes works of anthropology as well as history. What follows is only a representative sample of works available. For general works, see *The Cambridge History of the Native Peoples of the Americas: North America*, ed. Bruce Trigger and Wilcomb Washburn (1996); Colin Calloway, *One Vast Winter Count* (2003); Alice Kehoe, *America Before the European Invasions* (2002); Daniel Richter, *Facing East from Indian Country* (2001); Shepard Krech, *The Ecological Indian* (1999); and Linda Barrington, ed., *The Other Side of the Frontier* (1998). More specific studies include Gary Anderson, *The Indian Southwest, 1580–1830* (1999); John Ewers, *Plains Indian History and Culture* (1997); Wilbur Jacobs, *The Fatal Confrontation* (1996); Dean R. Snow, *The Iroquois* (1994); Thomas Kavanagh, *The Comanches* (1996); Robbie Ethridge, *Creek Country* (2003); L. Leitch Wright Jr., *Creeks and Seminoles* (1986); John Sugden, *Tecumseh's Last Stand* (1985); R. David Edmunds, *The Shawnee Prophet* (1983); and Peter Mancall, *Deadly Medicine: Indians and Alcohol in Early America* (1995).

For the history of the Seminoles, see J. Leitch Wright Jr., *Creeks and Seminoles* (1986); James Covington, *The Seminoles of Florida* (1993); Kevin Mulroy, *Freedom on the Border* (1993); and Kenneth Porter, *The Black Seminoles*, rev. ed. (1996). Joshua Giddings, *The Exiles of Florida* (1858) holds up well after many years. On the Florida Wars, see David and Jeanne Heidler, *Old Hickory's War* (1996); John K. Mahon, *History of the Second Seminole War*, rev. ed. (1985); Virginia Peters, *The Florida Wars* (1979); and Francis Paul Prucha, *Sword of the Republic* (1969).

The concept of a "frontier" as a place of encounter rather than a barrier is explored in Thomas Clark and John Guice, *Frontiers in Conflict: The Old Southwest, 1795–1830* (1989); Richard White, *The Middle Ground: Indians, Empires, and Republics in the Great Lakes Region* (1991); Gregory Nobles, *American Frontiers: Cultural Encounters and Continental Conquest* (1997); Andrew Cayton and Fredrika Teute, eds., *Contact Points* (1998); and Stephen Aron, *American Confluence: The Missouri Frontier* (2006). On the Great Plains, two books by Elliott West are valuable: *The Contested Plains* (1998) and *The Way to the West* (1995). See also Andrew Isenberg, *The Destruction of the Bison* (2000) and Terry Jordan, *North American Cattle-Ranching Frontiers* (1993).

Canadian-American relations can be examined in Arthur Burt, *The United States, Great Britain and British North America* (1961); Reginald Stuart, *United States Expansionism and British North America* (1988); Kenneth Bourne, *Britain and the Balance of Power in North America* (1967); and Bradford Perkins, *Castlereagh and Adams* (1964). For the diplomatic crises of Van Buren's administration, see Kenneth Stevens, *Border Diplomacy* (1989), supplemented with Albert Corey, *The Crisis of 1830–1842 in Canadian–American Relations* (1941). For the Canadian perspective, I consulted Gerald Craig, *Upper Canada, The Formative Years* (1963) and Colin Read, *The Rising in Western Upper Canada* (1982). The authoritative history of the Canadian-American boundary dispute and its resolution by the Webster-Ashburton Treaty is now Francis Carroll, *A Good and Wise Measure* (Toronto, 2001). Also see Frederick Merk, *Fruits of Propaganda in the Tyler Administration* (1971); Howard Jones, *To the Webster-Ashburton Treaty* (1977); Kenneth Stevens, *Border Diplomacy: The Caroline and McLeod Affairs* (1989); and Howard Jones and Donald Rakestraw, *Prologue to Manifest Destiny: Anglo-American Relations in the 1840s* (1997).

George Rogers Taylor, *The Transportation Revolution* (1951) is an enduring classic. The important political implications of this revolution are demonstrated in John Lauritz Larson, *Internal Improvement* (2001). Also see Louis C. Hunter, *Steamboats on the Western Rivers* (1949); Nathan Miller, *The Enterprise of a Free People: Economic Development in New York During the Canal Period* (1962); Carter Goodrich, *Government Promotion of American Canals and Railroads* (1966); Maurice Baxter, *The Steamboat Monopoly* (1972); Brooke Hindle, *Emulation and Invention* (1981); Karl Raitz, ed., *The National Road* (1996); James Dilts, *The Great Road: The Building of the Baltimore & Ohio* (1993); and John Majewski, *A House Dividing: Economic Development in Pennsylvania and Virginia Before the Civil War* (2000).

A fascinating book on the Erie Canal is Carol Sheriff, *The Artificial River* (1996). Also see Evan Cornog, *The Birth of Empire: DeWitt Clinton and the American Experience* (1998); Steven Siry, *DeWitt Clinton and the American Political Economy* (1990); Ronald Shaw, *Canals for a Nation* (1990); and Carter Goodrich, ed., *Canals and American Economic Development* (1961). Robert G. Albion, *The Rise of New York Port* (New York, 1939) is a classic. The lives of the workers who dug North American canals are described in Peter Way, *Common Labour* (1993).

On the communications revolution and its political and economic implications, Richard R. John, *Spreading the News: The American Postal System from Franklin to Morse* (1995) is a broader study than its title might suggest. Also valuable are Allan Pred, *Urban Growth and the Circulation of Information* (1973); Richard Kielbowicz, *News in the Mail* (1989); Gerald Baldasty, *The Commercialization of News in the Nineteenth Century* (1992); Richard D. Brown, *The Strength of a People: The Idea of an Informed Citizenry* (1996); and Donald Cole, *A Jackson Man: Amos Kendall* (2004). On literacy and its consequences, see William Gilmore, *Reading Becomes a Necessity of Life* (1989); Richard D. Brown, *Knowledge Is Power* (1989); and Dan Headrick, *When Information Came of Age* (2000). The cultural implications of mail are explored in David Henkin, *The Postal Age* (2006). For newspapers, see William Huntzicker, *The Popular Press* (1999); Bernard Weisberger, *The American Newspaperman* (1961); Rosalind Remer, *Printers and Men of Capital* (1996); Robert C. Williams, *Horace Greeley* (2006); and Jonathan Sarna, *Jacksonian Jew: The Two Worlds of Mordecai Noah* (1981). A fine study of the mechanization of paper-making, so important to the expansion of print, is Judith McGaw, *Most Wonderful Machine* (1987). For interaction between the communications revolution and religion see Candy Gunther Brown, *The Word in the World* (2004); Wayne Fuller, *Morality and the Mail in Nineteenth-Century America* (2003); Leonard Sweet, ed., *Communication and Change in American Religious History* (1993); David Reynolds, *Faith in Fiction* (1981); and David Paul Nord, *Evangelical Origins of Mass Media in America* (1984) and *Faith in Reading* (2004).

The best places to learn about Morse and his telegraph are: Paul Starr, *The Creation of the Media* (2004), chap. 5; Kenneth Silverman, *Lightning Man: The Accursed Life of Samuel F. B. Morse* (2003); David Hochfelder, "Taming the Lightning: American Telegraphy as a Revolutionary Technology" (Ph.D. diss., Case Western Reserve University,

1999); Menahem Blondheim, *News over the Wires: The Telegraph and the Flow of Public Information in America, 1844–1897* (1994); James Carey, *Communication as Culture* (1989), chap. 8; Richard R. John, *Spreading the News* (1995); and Jill Lepore, *A is for American* (2002), chap. 6. A lucid popular account is Tom Standage, *The Victorian Internet* (1998). Also helpful are Lewis Coe, *The Telegraph* (1993); George Oslin, *The Story of Telecommunications* (1992); Daniel Czitrom, *Media and the American Mind* (1982), chap. 1; Brooke Hindle, *Emulation and Invention* (1981), chaps. 4–6; and Robert Thompson, *Wiring a Continent* (1947). For the effects of telegraphy on accurate timekeeping, see Ian Bartky, *Selling the True Time: Nineteenth-century Timekeeping in America* (2000). An excellent work on Morse as a painter is Paul Staiti, *Samuel F. B. Morse* (1989).

Partly because of the communications revolution, nineteenth-century history throughout the Western world concerned public opinion as never before. Readers with a taste for German social theory can explore this subject through Jurgen Habermas, *The Structural Transformation of the Public Sphere*, trans. by Thomas Burger (1989; first pub. in German in 1962).

Some of the finest political history written about this period consists of state and local studies that transcend their seemingly narrow focus. Of broad interest are Lee Benson, *The Concept of Jacksonian Democracy: New York as a Test Case* (1961); Ronald Formisano, *The Birth of Mass Political Parties, Michigan, 1827–1861* (1971) and *The Transformation of Political Culture: Massachusetts, 1790s–1840s* (1983); Gerald Leonard, *The Invention of Party Politics in Jacksonian Illinois* (2002); Marc Kruman, *Parties and Politics in North Carolina* (1983); Donald Ratcliffe, *The Politics of Long Division: The Birth of the Second Party System in Ohio* (2000); Mills Thornton, *Politics and Power in a Slave Society: Alabama, 1800–1860* (1978); and Harry Watson, *Jacksonian Politics and Community Conflict: Cumberland County, North Carolina* (1981).

Other insightful works on political ideas and behavior include Marvin Meyers, *The Jacksonian Persuasion* (1960); Robert Kelley, *The Cultural Pattern in American Politics* (1979); Michael Heale, *The Presidential Quest, 1787–1852* (1982); Richard P. McCormick, *The Presidential Game* (1982); Robert Swierenga, "Ethnoreligious Political Behavior in the Mid-Nineteenth Century," in *Religion and American Politics*, ed. Mark Noll (1990); Joel Silbey, *The American Political Nation, 1838–1893* (1991); Michael Holt, *Political Parties and American Political Development* (1992); David Greenstone, *The Lincoln Persuasion* (1993); and Mark Neely, *American Political Culture in the Civil War Era* (2005). David Currie, *The Constitution in Congress: Democrats and Whigs, 1829–1861* (2005) is quirky but interesting.

Robert Remini's three-volume biography of Jackson is laudatory and thorough: *Andrew Jackson and the Course of American Empire, 1767–1821* (1977); *Andrew Jackson and the Course of American Freedom, 1822–1832* (1981); *Andrew Jackson and the Course of American Democracy, 1833–1845* (1984). There is still much useful material in James Parton, *Life of Andrew Jackson*, 3 vols. (1861). Two studies of Old Hickory's personality are James C. Curtis, *Andrew Jackson and the Search for Vindication* (1976) and Andrew Burstein, *The Passions of Andrew Jackson* (2003). For delightful anecdotes, read Marquis James, *Andrew Jackson* (1937). Richard Hofstadter's classic essay on Jackson appears in *The American Political Tradition* (1948).

Samuel Flagg Bemis's two-volume biography of John Quincy Adams is an enduring masterpiece: *John Quincy Adams and the Foundations of American Foreign Policy* (1949); *John Quincy Adams and the Union* (1956). Other treatments include Paul Nagel, *John Quincy Adams* (1997); Lynn Parsons, *John Quincy Adams* (1998); and Leonard

Richards's negative assessment of *Congressman John Quincy Adams* (1986). Robert Remini, *Henry Clay: Statesman for the Union* (1991) is thorough and workmanlike; more sympathetic are Maurice Baxter, *Henry Clay and the American System* (1995) and Clement Eaton, *Henry Clay and the Art of American Politics* (1957). Biographies of Daniel Webster include those by Robert Remini (1997) and Irving Bartlett (1978), as well as Maurice Baxter, *One and Inseparable* (1984). See also Merrill Peterson, *The Great Triumvirate: Webster, Clay, and Calhoun* (1987). Charles Wiltse, *John C. Calhoun*, 3 vols. (1944–51) has become dated. John Niven, *John C. Calhoun and the Price of Union* (1988) is sound. See also Gerald M. Capers, *John C. Calhoun: Opportunist* (1960) and Irving Bartlett, *John C. Calhoun* (1993).

The young Abraham Lincoln figures in the history of these years as state legislator and member of Congress. Of the vast literature on him, the books most useful to me were Richard Carwardine, *Lincoln* (2003); Allen Guelzo, *Abraham Lincoln, Redeemer President* (1999); David Herbert Donald, *Lincoln* (1995); Gabor Boritt, *Lincoln and the Economics of the American Dream* (1978); and Reinhard Luthin, *The Real Abraham Lincoln* (1960).

Valuable biographies of other leading political figures include Charles Sellers, *James K. Polk*, 2 vols. (1957–66); Glyndon Van Deusen, *William Henry Seward* (1967); Ralph Ketcham, *James Madison* (1971); Harry Ammon, *James Monroe* (1971); Robert Dawidoff, *The Education of John Randolph* (1979); John Niven, *Martin Van Buren and the Romantic Age of American Politics* (1983); Donald Cole, *Martin Van Buren and the American Political System* (1984); John Eisenhower, *Agent of Destiny, Winfield Scott* (1997); and Allan Peskin, *Winfield Scott and the Profession of Arms* (2003). Imaginative and readable collections of short biographies of people from varied walks of life include Joyce Appleby, ed., *Recollections of the Early Republic* (1997); Jill Lepore, *A is for American* (2002); Michael Morrison, ed., *The Human Tradition in Antebellum America* (2000), and Norman Risjord, *Representative Americans: The Romantics* (2001).

The standard account of the War of 1812 is Donald Hickey, *The War of 1812* (1989); also very helpful are Robert Quimby, *The U.S. Army in the War of 1812* (1997); J.C.A. Stagg, *Mr. Madison's War* (1983); John K. Mahon, *The War of 1812* (1972); and Anthony Pitch, *The Burning of Washington* (1998). David and Jeanne Heidler, *The War of 1812* (2002) is a handy textbook. For the impact of the war on domestic politics, see Steven Watts, *The Republic Reborn* (1987); James Banner, *To the Hartford Convention* (1970); and Linda Kerber, *Federalists in Dissent* (1970). On Jackson's great victory, see Robert Remini, *The Battle of New Orleans* (1999); Robin Reilly, *The British at the Gates* (1974); Frank Owsley Jr., *The Struggle for the Gulf Borderlands* (1981); and Wilburt Brown, *The Amphibious Campaign for West Florida and Louisiana* (1969). For what Americans made of it, see John William Ward, *Andrew Jackson, Symbol for an Age* (1955).

For the wars with the Barbary pirates, see A.B.C. Whipple, *To the Shores of Tripoli* (1991); Robert Allison, *The Crescent Obscured: The United States and the Muslim World, 1776–1815* (1995); Paul Baepler, ed., *White Slaves, African Masters: Barbary Captivity Narratives* (1993); John B. Wolf, *The Barbary Coast* (1979); and Frederick Leiner, *The End of Barbary Terror* (2006).

Christopher Clark, *Social Change in America: From the Revolution Through the Civil War* (2006) provides an excellent overview of its subject. Paul Conkin, "The American Economy in 1815," in his *Prophets of Progress* (1980), supplies a succinct starting point. Also helpful are the varied essays in Cathy Matson, ed., *The Economy of Early America* (2006). For the family farming economy, see Christopher Clark, *The Roots of Rural Capitalism*

(1990); Winifred Rothenberg, *From Market-Places to a Market Economy* (1992); David Danbom, *Born in the Country: A History of Rural America* (1995); Joyce Appleby, *Inheriting the Revolution* (2000); Allan Kulikoff, *From British Peasants to Colonial American Farmers* (2000); Martin Bruegel, *Farm, Shop, Landing: The Rise of a Market Society in the Hudson Valley* (2002); and David R. Meyer, *Roots of American Industrialization* (2003). Despite the author's preoccupation with unhelpful Marxist terminology, there is much helpful information in Allan Kulikoff, *The Agrarian Origins of American Capitalism* (1992). Rural white America in the early nineteenth century is evoked in Jack Larkin, *The Reshaping of Everyday Life, 1790–1840* (1988); Jane Nylander, *Our Own Snug Fireside* (1993); and Priscilla Brewer, *From Fireplace to Cookstove* (2000). For the roles of husbands and wives, see Nancy Osterud, *Bonds of Community* (1991); Hendrik Hartog, *Man and Wife in America* (2000); Carole Shammas, *A History of Household Government in America* (2002); and Catherine Kelly, *In the New England Fashion* (1999).

There are many fine studies of individual rural communities in preindustrial America. Examples include John Brooke, *The Heart of the Commonwealth: Society and Political Culture in Worcester County, Mass.* (1990); John Mack Faragher, *Sugar Creek: Life on the Illinois Prairie* (1986); and Randolph Roth, *The Democratic Dilemma: Religion, Reform, and the Social Order in the Connecticut Valley of Vermont* (1987). The importance of religious communities for American political thought is argued aggressively by Barry Shain, *The Myth of American Individualism* (1994).

On the origins of consumer culture, see Richard Bushman, *The Refinement of America* (1992); John Crowley, *The Invention of Comfort* (2001); Timothy Breen, *The Marketplace of Revolution* (2004); and Scott Martin, ed., *Cultural Change and the Market Revolution in America* (2005). On economic integration and convergence, see Kevin O'Rourke and Jeffrey Williamson, *Globalization and History: The Evolution of a Nineteenth-Century Atlantic Economy* (1999).

For perspectives on Americans as a seafaring people, see Daniel Vickers, *Farmers and Fishermen* (1994); Daniel Vickers and Vince Walsh, *Young Men and the Sea* (2005); Mark Kurlansky, *Cod* (1997); and Paul Gilje, *Liberty on the Waterfront* (2004). On whaling, see Lance Davis, Robert Gallman, and Karin Gleiter, *In Pursuit of Leviathan* (1997).

On the fur trade as an economic undertaking, see David Wishart, *The Fur Trade of the American West* (1979) and David Dary, *The Santa Fe Trail* (2000). For its contribution to geographical knowledge, William Goetzmann, *Exploration and Empire* (1978) and *New Lands, New Men: America and the Second Great Age of Discovery* (1986); and John Logan Allen, ed. *North American Exploration*, vol. III, *A Continent Comprehended* (1997). For the excitement of the mountain men, read Bernard DeVoto, *Across the Wide Missouri* (1947) or Dale Morgan, *Jedediah Smith and the Opening of the West* (1953).

The great historian David Brion Davis has examined the philosophy and practice of slavery and antislavery on a worldwide scale. See his *The Problem of Slavery in Western Culture* (1966), *The Problem of Slavery in the Age of Revolution* (1975), *Slavery and Human Progress* (1984), and *Challenging the Boundaries of Slavery* (2003). For more on slavery's international context, see Philip Curtin, *The Atlantic Slave Trade* (1969); Duncan Rice, *The Rise and Fall of Black Slavery* (1975); Peter Kolchin, *Unfree Labor: American Slavery and Russian Serfdom* (1987); Robin Blackburn, *The Overthrow of Colonial Slavery, 1776–1848* (1988); and Hugh Thomas, *The Slave Trade* (1997).

Life in slavery has been the subject of some of the most powerful and profound American historical writing. Kenneth Stampp, *The Peculiar Institution* (1956) created the modern understanding of the subject. Besides Eugene Genovese's *Roll, Jordan, Roll* cited above, see Lawrence Levine, *Black Culture and Black Consciousness* (1977); John Boles, *Black Southerners* (1983); Charles Joyner, *Down by the Riverside* (1984); Peter Kolchin, *American Slavery* (1993); Mark M. Smith, *Mastered by the Clock: Time, Slavery, and Freedom in the American South* (1997); Ira Berlin, *Many Thousands Gone* (1998) and *Generations of Captivity* (2003); Deborah White, *Ar'n't I a Woman?* rev. ed. (1999); and Marie Schwartz, *Born in Bondage* (2000). Claudia Goldin, *Urban Slavery in the American South* (1976) disagrees with Richard Wade, *Slavery in the Cities* (1964), but now historians tend to synthesize them. For autonomy among the slaves, see Ira Berlin and Philip Morgan, eds., *The Slaves' Economy: Independent Production by Slaves* (1991); Larry Hudson Jr., *To Have and to Hold* (1997); and John Hope Franklin and Loren Schweninger, *Runaway Slaves* (1999).

The lives and mindset of the slaveholders are portrayed in Elizabeth Fox-Genovese and Eugene Genovese, *The Mind of the Master Class* (2005); Jeffrey Young, *Domesticating Slavery* (1999); James Oakes, *The Ruling Race* (1982) and *Slavery and Freedom* (1990); Bertram Wyatt-Brown, *Southern Honor* (1982); John Boles, *The South Through Time* (1995); William Scarborough, *Masters of the Big House* (2003); and Richard Follett, *The Sugar Masters* (2005). The intertwined lives of both masters and slaves are treated in a beautiful case study, Erskine Clarke, *Dwelling Place* (2005).

That holding workers in slavery profited their masters does not seem particularly surprising, but it required massive efforts by economic historians to prove it. Alfred Conrad and John Meyer, *The Economics of Slavery* (1964) showed that slaves earned a competitive rate of return for their owners. Robert Fogel and Stanley Engerman, *Time on the Cross* (1974) made slavery seem so economically modern and efficient that critics charged they also made the system seem benign; see Paul David et al., *Reckoning with Slavery* (1976). A more widely accepted demonstration of the profitability of slavery has been Robert Fogel, *Without Consent or Contract* (1989), which is supported by three supplementary volumes of *Evidence and Methods* (1992). For the consequences of the masters' pursuit of profit, see William Dusinberre, *Them Dark Days* (1996). For a judicious historiography, see Mark Smith, *Debating Slavery* (1998).

The massive domestic commerce in slaves, local as well as interregional, is described in Steven Deyle, *Carry Me Back* (2005). The scope and horror of the interstate slave trade is portrayed in Daniel Johnson and Rex Campbell, *Black Migration in America* (1981); Michael Tadman, *Speculators and Slaves* (1989); Walter Johnson, *Soul by Soul* (2000); and Robert Gudmestad, *A Troublesome Commerce* (2003). For issues of constitutional law, see David Lightner, *Slavery and the Commerce Power* (2006). Roger Kennedy, *Mr. Jefferson's Lost Cause* (2003) and Adam Rothman, *Slave Country* (2005) treat the expansion of slavery into the Gulf states.

Slave uprisings have attracted a considerable literature. Douglas Egerton, *Rebels, Reformers, and Revolutionaries* (2002) is a collection of thoughtful essays. The most reliable accounts of the Vesey conspiracy are in Douglas Egerton, *He Shall Go Out Free*, rev. ed. (2004) and John Lofton, *Denmark Vesey's Revolt* (1983). Howard Jones, *Mutiny on the Amistad* (1987) is the best treatment of its subject. For Nat Turner, see Kenneth Greenberg, ed., *Nat Turner: A Slave Rebellion in History and Memory* (2003); Mary Kemp Davis, *Nat Turner Before the Bar of Judgment* (1999); and Stephen Oates, *The Fires of Jubilee* (1975). On the incendiary pamphleteer David Walker, see Peter Hinks, *To Awaken My Afflicted Brethren* (1997).

Not all African Americans lived in slavery; on the free black people, see Gary Nash, *Forging Freedom: The Formation of Philadelphia's Black Community* (1988); Leslie Harris,

In the Shadow of Slavery: African Americans in New York City, 1626–1868 (2003); Donald Wright, *African Americans in the Early Republic* (1993); Mary Frances Berry and John Blassingame, *Long Memory: The Black Experience in America* (1982); James Horton, *Free People of Color* (1993); James and Lois Horton, *In Hope of Liberty* (1997); and Melvin Ely, *Israel on the Appomattox* (2004).

The harshest judgment on Madison's presidency was rendered by Henry Adams in his *History of the United States During the Administrations of James Madison* (1891), the most favorable by Irving Brant in *James Madison: Commander in Chief* (1961). Judicious assessments are offered by George Dangerfield, *The Awakening of American Nationalism* (1965); Drew McCoy, *The Last of the Fathers* (1989); and Garry Wills, *James Madison* (2002). See also Norman K. Risjord, *The Old Republicans* (1965) and Lance Banning, *The Jeffersonian Persuasion* (1978).

George Dangerfield, *The Era of Good Feelings* (1952) is the classic account of that period. See also Shaw Livermore, *The Twilight of Federalism* (1962); Murray Rothbard, *The Panic of 1819* (1962); Richard Hofstadter, *The Idea of a Party System* (1969); David Waldstreicher, *In the Midst of Perpetual Fetes* (1998); Ralph Ketcham, *Presidents Above Party* (1984); Marshall Foletta, *Coming to Terms with Democracy* (2001); and Stephen Skowronek, *The Politics Presidents Make* (1993), which is particularly good on Monroe.

Dexter Perkins, *History of the Monroe Doctrine* (1963); Ernest Nay, *The Making of the Monroe Doctrine* (1965); Bradford Perkins, *Castlereagh and Adams* (1964); and Donald Dozer, ed., *The Monroe Doctrine* (1976) treat the most famous principle in American diplomacy.

Trans-Appalachian white migration into the Old Southwest is treated in Thomas Abernathy, *From Frontier to Plantation in Tennessee* (1932); Clayton James, *Antebellum Natchez* (1968); Malcolm Rohrbough, *The Trans-Appalachian Frontier* (1978); Daniel Feller, *The Public Lands in Jacksonian Politics* (1984); John Otto, *Southern Frontiers* (1989); Joan Cashin, *A Family Venture: Men and Women on the Southern Frontier* (1991); Harvey Jackson, *Rivers of History* (1995); Daniel Dupre, *Transforming the Cotton Frontier* (1997); and Samuel Hyde Jr., ed., *Plain Folk of the Old South Revisited* (1997). Two well-written books lament the passing of the frontier in Kentucky: Stephen Aron, *How the West Was Lost* (1996) and Craig Friend, *Along the Maysville Road* (2005).

The development of an economy based on slave-grown cotton is analyzed in Gavin Wright, *The Political Economy of the Cotton South* (1978); Roger Ransom, *Conflict and Compromise: The Political Economy of Slavery* (1989); and David Carlton and Peter Coclanis, *The South, the Nation, and the World* (2003). The classic account of the importance of cotton to the American economy is Douglass North, *The Economic Growth of the United States* (1961).

The industrial revolution sparked by cotton textiles marked a turning point in the history of the world. See David Jeremy, *The Transatlantic Industrial Revolution* (1981); Jonathan Prude, *The Coming of Industrial Order* (1983); Philip Scranton, *Proprietary Capitalism* (1983); Barbara Tucker, *Samuel Slater and the Origins of the American Textile Industry* (1984); Walter Licht, *Industrializing America* (1995); and Angela Lakwete, *Inventing the Cotton Gin: Machine and Myth* (2003). For copious illustrations, see Brooke Hindle and Steven Labar, *Engines of Change: The American Industrial Revolution, 1790–1860* (1991). New England's innovative role is the subject of Robert Dalzell Jr., *Enterprising Elite* (1987); Theodore Steinberg, *Nature Incorporated: Industrialization and the Waters of New England* (1991); and Naomi Lamoreaux, *Insider Lending: Banks, Personal Connections, and Economic Development in Industrial New England* (1994). For the evolution of the corporation, see Kenneth Lipartito and David Sicilia, eds., *Constructing Corporate America* (2004). Two fascinating community studies are Anthony Wallace, *Rockdale* (1978) and Thomas Dublin, *Lowell* (1992). Michael Zakim, *Ready-Made Democracy: A History of Men's Dress in the American Republic* (2003) analyzes both consumers and producers. On the cultural impact of the industrial revolution, see David Nye, *America as Second Creation* (2003).

The Old Northwest commands a growing historical literature; see James Simeone, *Democracy and Slavery in Frontier Illinois* (2000); James Davis, *Frontier Illinois* (1998); Donald Ratcliffe, *Party Spirit in a Frontier Republic* (1998); Nicole Etcheson, *The Emerging Midwest* (1996); Douglas Hurt, *The Ohio Frontier* (1996); Susan Gray, *The Yankee West* (1996); Andrew Cayton, *Frontier Indiana* (1996) and *Frontier Republic: Ohio* (1986); Andrew Cayton and Peter Onuf, *The Midwest and the Nation* (1990); and Malcolm Rohrbough, *The Land Office Business* (1968). However, Frederick Jackson Turner's *The Rise of the New West* (1906) and Richard Powers's *Planting Corn Belt Culture* (1953) are still very useful.

Robert Pierce Forbes, *The Missouri Compromise and Its Aftermath* (2007) is a profound study; I used the 1994 Yale dissertation that preceded it. See also Glover Moore, *The Missouri Controversy* (1953); William Cooper, *Liberty and Slavery* (1983); and Richard H. Brown's seminal article, "The Missouri Crisis, Slavery, and the Politics of Jacksonianism," *South Atlantic Quarterly* 65 (1966): 55–72.

The social and cultural importance of the Second Great Awakening has prompted a large body of writing. Modern interpretations include Mark Noll, *America's God* (2002); Edith Blumhover and Randall Balmer, eds., *Modern Christian Revivals* (1993); Jon Butler, *Awash in a Sea of Faith* (1990); Nathan Hatch, *The Democratization of American Christianity* (1989); Richard Carwardine, *Transatlantic Revivalism* (1978); William McLoughlin, *Revivals, Awakenings, and Reform* (1978); Scott Miyakawa, *Protestants and Pioneers* (1968); and Perry Miller's unfinished classic, *The Life of the Mind in America* (1965). Much scholarship focuses on upstate New York: Whitney Cross, *The Burned-Over District* (1950); Paul Johnson, *A Shopkeeper's Millennium* (1978); Mary Ryan, *Cradle of the Middle Class* (1981); Curtis Johnson, *Islands of Holiness* (1989); and David Hackett, *The Rude Hand of Innovation* (1991). For the South, see Christine Heyrman, *Southern Cross* (1997); John Quist, *Restless Visionaries* (1998); Randy Sparks, *On Jordan's Stormy Banks* (1994); and Donald Mathews, *Religion in the Old South* (1977). General works of much value for this period include Jon Butler et al., *Religion in American Life* (2003); Richard W. Fox, *Jesus in America* (2004); and Sydney Ahlstrom, *A Religious History of the American People*, 2nd ed. (2004).

To see how religious disestablishment paved the way for the Awakening, consult William McLoughlin, *New England Dissent, 1680–1833: The Baptists and the Separation of Church and State* (1971), 2 vols. The personalities of the evangelists can be viewed in Charles Hambrick-Stowe, *Charles G. Finney* (1996); Joseph Conforti, *Samuel Hopkins and the New Divinity Movement* (1981); Charles White, *The Beauty of Holiness: Phoebe Palmer* (1986); and Robert Abzug, *Cosmos Crumbling: American Reform and the Religious Imagination* (1994). The Beecher family has a rich historiography; on their role in the Awakening, see Marie Caskey, *Chariot of Fire* (1977); Vincent Harding, *A Certain Magnificence* (1991); and James Fraser, *Pedagogue for God's Kingdom* (1985).

Works on particular kinds of Protestantism include David Hempton, *Methodism* (New Haven, 2005); Russell Richey, *Early American Methodism* (1991); John Wigger, *Taking Heaven by Storm: Methodism and Popular Christianity* (1998); Gregory Willis, *Democratic Religion: Church Discipline in the Baptist South* (1997); Thomas Hamm,

The Transformation of American Quakerism (1988); Larry Ingle, *Quakers in Conflict* (1986); David Harrell Jr., *Quest for a Christian America: The Disciples of Christ* (1966); and Richard Hughes and Leonard Allen, *Illusions of Innocence: Protestant Primitivism in America* (1988).

For American Catholics, see Jay Dolan, *Catholic Revivalism* (1978); Ann Taves, *The Household of Faith* (1986); Charles Morris, *American Catholic* (1997); and Jay Dolan, *In Search of an American Catholicism* (2002). For controversies within the Catholic Church, see Patrick Carey, *People, Priests, and Prelates* (1987) and Dale Light, *Rome and the New Republic* (1996). For a view of Catholic relations with the Protestant majority, see Lawrence Moore, *Religious Outsiders and the Making of Americans* (1986), 48–79. Catholic attitudes toward slavery are explained (along with much else) in John McGreevy's excellent *Catholicism and American Freedom* (2003); see also Thomas Bakenkotter, *Concise History of the Catholic Church*, rev. ed. (2004), 294–302.

The active role of women in the Awakening and its philanthropy has rightly received attention from historians. See Marilyn Westerkamp, *Women and Religion in Early America* (1999); Catherine Brekus, *Strangers and Pilgrims: Female Preaching in America, 1740–1845* (1998); Nancy Hardesty, *Your Daughters Shall Prophesy* (1991); Carolyn Lawes, *Women and Reform in a New England Community* (2000); Nancy Hewitt, *Women's Activism and Social Change* (1984); Nancy Cott, *The Bonds of Womanhood*, 2nd ed. (1997); and Carroll Smith-Rosenberg, *Religion and the Rise of the American City* (1971). On the place of the Awakening in working-class history, see Jama Lazerow, *Religion and the Working Class in Antebellum America* (1995) and Teresa Murphy, *Ten Hours' Labor: Religion, Reform, and Gender in Early New England* (1992).

The Awakening occupied a prominent place in the lives of many African Americans, both free and enslaved. See Albert Raboteau, *A Fire in the Bones* (1995) and *Slave Religion* (1978); Gary Nash, *Forging Freedom* (1988); Mechal Sobel, *Trabelin' On* (1979); John Boles, ed., *Masters and Slaves in the House of the Lord* (1988); and Carol George, *Segregated Sabbaths* (1973).

For the intellectual dimension of the Awakening, see Bruce Kuklick, *Churchmen and Philosophers* (1985); Brooks Holifield, *Theology in America* (2003); Richard Steele, *"Gracious Affection" and "True Virtue"* (1994); Mark Noll, ed., *God and Mammon* (2002); Paul Conkin, *The Uneasy Center* (1995); Kenneth Startup, *The Root of All Evil* (1997); and Leo Hirrell's misnamed *Children of Wrath* (1998). Examples of the various practical consequences of the Awakening can be found in Richard Carwardine, *Evangelicals and Politics in Antebellum America* (1993); Lori Ginzburg, *Women and the Work of Benevolence* (1990); and Benjamin Thomas, *Theodore Dwight Weld* (1950). Kathleen D. McCarthy, *American Creed: Philanthropy and the Rise of Civil Society* (2003) treats social reform movements as well as organized charities.

The interlocking network of reforms in this period derived much of their impetus from religious origins, but secular changes like the communications revolution affected them too. See Ronald Walters, *American Reformers, 1815–1860* (1978); Steven Mintz, *Moralists and Modernizers* (1995); and Bruce Dorsey, *Reforming Men and Women* (2002). On the temperance movement, see W. J. Rorabaugh, *The Alcoholic Republic* (1979); Ian Tyrell, *Sobering Up* (1979); and Mark Lender and James Martin, *Drinking in America* (1987). John Rumbarger, *Profits, Power, and Prohibition* (1989) argues that temperance was imposed on workers by their employers. The international dimension of the interrelated reforms needs more study, but see, for example, Mark Noll et al., *Evangelicalism: Comparative Studies* (New York, 1994); Frank Thistlethwaite, *The Anglo-American Connection in the Early Nineteenth Century* (1959); and, of course, the works of David Brion Davis already mentioned.

P. J. Staudenraus, *The African Colonization Movement* (1961) remains useful, but historians have taken renewed interest in the enterprise. See, for example, Katherine Harris, *African and American Values: Liberia and West Africa* (1985); James Wesley Smith, *Sojourners in Search of Freedom* (1987); Amos Beyan, *The American Colonization Society and the Creation of the Liberian State* (1991); Lamin Sanneh, *Abolitionists Abroad* (1999); and Eric Burin, *Slavery and the Peculiar Solution* (2005).

Masonry and Antimasonry should be studied in conjunction. Steven Bullock treats the former well in *Revolutionary Brotherhood* (1996). Paul Goodman takes a more negative view of Antimasonry in *Towards a Christian Republic* (1988) than does William Vaughan, *The Anti-Masonic Party in the United States* (1983).

The seminal treatment of millennialism in American history is H. Richard Niebuhr, *The Kingdom of God in America* (1937); the literature that has grown up around it is enormous. The writings of James H. Moorhead provide a sound guide to postmillennialism, although they emphasize the period after 1848: *American Apocalypse* (1978) and *World Without End* (1999). The period before 1815 is treated in Ruth Bloch, *Visionary Republic* (1985) and Susan Juster, *Doomsayers* (2003). For postmillennialism in the period covered by this book, see Jonathan Sassi, *A Republic of Righteousness* (2001) and J. F. Maclear, "The Republic and the Millennium," in *The Religion of the Republic*, ed. Elwyn Smith (1971). For premillennialism and the Millerites in particular, see Ruth Doan, *The Miller Heresy, Millennialism, and American Culture* (1987); Gary Land, ed., *Adventism in America* (1986); and Ronald Numbers and Jonathan Butler, eds., *The Disappointed* (1987). Michael Barkun, *Crucible of the Millennium* (1986) usefully links millennialism and utopianism.

Amidst a very large literature on utopian communities, especially helpful are Robert Sutton, *Communal Utopias and the American Experience*, 2 vols. (2003–4); Donald Pitzer, ed., *America's Communal Utopias* (1997); Christopher Clark, *The Communitarian Moment: The Radical Challenge of the Northampton Association* (1995); Carl Guarneri, *The Utopian Alternative* (1991); and Spencer Klaw, *Without Sin: The Life and Death of the Oneida Community* (1993). On Owen and his followers, see J. F. C. Harrison, *Robert Owen and the Owenites* (1969) and Arthur Bestor, *Backwoods Utopias* (1970). Edward Deming Andrews, *The People Called Shakers* (1963) retains interest, but the authoritative work is now Stephen Stein, *The Shaker Experience in America* (1992). Sterling Delano, *Brook Farm: The Dark Side of Utopia* (2004) actually records successes as well as failures. On gender issues in utopian communities, see also Louis Kern, *An Ordered Love* (1981); Lawrence Foster, *Religion and Sexuality: Three American Communal Experiments* (1981); Carol Kolmerten, *Women in Utopia* (1990); and Suzanne Thurman, *O Sisters, Ain't You Happy?* (2002).

The comments of foreign travelers to the United States are discussed in C. Vann Woodward, *The Old World's New World* (1991). For Lafayette's tour, see Anne Loveland, *Emblem of Liberty* (1971). Lloyd Kramer, *Lafayette in Two Worlds* (1996) is a superb study, also very helpful on Tocqueville. George Pierson, *Tocqueville and Beaumont in America* (1938) is a classic; see also James Schleifer, *The Making of Tocqueville's Democracy in America* (1980) and Hugh Brogan, *Alexis de Tocqueville* (2006). R. K. Webb, *Harriet Martineau, Radical Victorian* (1960) is acute but patronizing; more sympathetic are the biographies by Valerie Pinchanick (1980) and Susan Hoecker-Drysdale (1992) and Daniel Feller's introduction to Harriet Martineau, *Retrospect of Western Travel* (2000). Also see Celia Eckhardt, *Fanny Wright* (1984).

Historical literature on Mormonism is gigantic and sometimes polemical. Insightful presentations of the Mormon religion by outsiders include Thomas O'Dea, *The Mormons* (1957); Jan Shipps, *Mormonism* (1985); and Paul Conkin, *American Originals* (1997), 162–225. The projected multivolume history by Dale Morgan was cut short by his death; what little we have appears in *Dale Morgan on Early Mormonism*, ed. John Phillip Walker (1986). Quite a few fine historians are Latter-day Saints, and some of them write about Mormon history; see, for example, Leonard Arrington and Davis Bitton, *The Mormon Experience* (1979); Klaus Hansen, *Mormonism and the American Experience* (1981); Grant Underwood, *The Millenarian World of Early Mormonism* (1993); and Richard Bushman, *Joseph Smith: Rough Stone Rolling* (2005). Additional biographies of Joseph Smith, each with its own viewpoint, include Fawn Brodie, *No Man Knows My History*, rev. ed. (1973); Robert Remini, *Joseph Smith* (2002); and Dan Vogel, *Joseph Smith: The Making of a Prophet* (2004). Mormon and gentile historians collaborate in an anthology, *The New Mormon History*, ed. D. Michael Quinn (1992). On the cultural matrix of early Mormonism, see D. Michael Quinn, *Early Mormonism and the Magic World View* (1987); John Brooke, *The Refiner's Fire* (1994); and Terryl Givens, *The Viper on the Hearth* (1997). Stephen LeSueur, *The 1838 Mormon War in Missouri* (1987) is judicious. The Mormon trek to Utah is portrayed in Leonard Arrington, *Brigham Young: American Moses* (1985); Klaus Hansen, *Quest for Empire* (1967); and Marvin Hill, *Quest for Refuge* (1989).

There are several excellent accounts of Jackson's presidency: Glyndon Van Deusen, *The Jacksonian Era* (1959); Richard Latner, *The Presidency of Andrew Jackson* (1979); and, best of all, Donald Cole, *Presidency of Andrew Jackson* (1993). For the Eaton Affair, see Catherine Allgor, *Parlor Politics* (2000); John Marszalek, *The Petticoat Affair* (2000); and Kirsten Wood, "Gender and Power in the Eaton Affair," *JER* 17 (1997): 237–75.

On the history of the "Civilized Tribes," see William McLoughlin, *Cherokee Renascence in the New Republic* (1986); Duane Champagne, *Social Order and Political Change* (1992); Michael Green, *The Politics of Indian Removal: Creek Government and Society in Crisis* (1982); and Mary Young, *Redskins, Ruffleshirts, and Rednecks* (1961). Three perspectives on the legal aspects are Tim Garrison, *The Legal Ideology of Removal* (2002); Stuart Banner, *How the Indians Lost Their Land* (2005); and Lindsay Robertson, *Conquest by Law* (2005). For Jackson's program of Indian Removal and its effects, see Anthony F. C. Wallace, *The Long, Bitter Trail* (1993); Michael Rogin, *Fathers and Children: Andrew Jackson and the Subjugation of the American Indian* (1975); and Grant Foreman's classic, *Indian Removal* (1932). A useful textbook with edited documents is Theda Perdue and Michael D. Green, *Cherokee Removal*, 2nd ed. (2005). Annie Abel, *History of Events Resulting in Indian Consolidation West of the Mississippi River* (1908) still has valuable information. On the shaping of federal Indian policy, see Ronald Satz, *American Indian Policy in the Jacksonian Era* (1975) and Bernard Sheehan, *Seeds of Extinction: Jeffersonian Philanthropy and the American Indian* (1973). Jackson's policies are defended in Francis Paul Prucha, SJ, *The Great Father: The United States Government and the American Indians* (1984), I, 179–242; and Robert Remini, *The Legacy of Andrew Jackson* (1988), 45–82; their arguments are rebutted in Donald Cole, *The Presidency of Andrew Jackson* (1993), 109–19. In his final statement Remini concedes much to Jackson's critics but reminds the reader that blame for the treatment of the Indians was widely shared: *Andrew Jackson and His Indian Wars* (2001). For white opposition to Removal, see John Andrew, *From Revivals to Removal* (1992); John G. West, *The Politics of Revelation and Reason* (1996); and Alisse Portnoy, *Their Right to Speak: Women's Activism in the Indian and Slave Debates* (2005).

On suffrage and election procedures, see Chilton Williamson, *American Suffrage, 1760–1860* (1960); James S. Chase, *Emergence of the Presidential Nominating Convention* (1973); Ronald Formisano, *The Transformation of Political Culture* (1983); and Alexander Keyssar, *The Right to Vote* (2000). Politics was strongly influenced by the mechanisms of voting and getting out the vote; see Glenn Altschuler and Stuart Blumin, *Rude Republic: Americans and Their Politics in the Nineteenth Century* (2000) and Richard Bensel, *The American Ballot Box in the Mid-Nineteenth Century* (2004).

Most of the historical writing on the "Bank War" between Jackson and Biddle dates from the period 1945 to 1975. Besides Schlesinger's *Age of Jackson* cited above, see Robert Remini, *Andrew Jackson and the Bank War* (1967); Jean Alexander Wilburn, *Biddle's Bank: The Crucial Years* (1967); Thomas Govan, *Nicholas Biddle* (1959); Bray Hammond, *Banks and Politics in America from the Revolution to the Civil War* (1957); Walter Buckingham Smith, *Economic Aspects of the Second Bank of the United States* (1953); and Fritz Redlich, *The Molding of American Banking* (1947). More recent are two books by Robert Wright, *The Wealth of Nations Rediscovered: Integration and Expansion in American Financial Markets, 1780–1850* (2002) and *The First Wall Street: Chestnut Street, Philadelphia* (2005). Ralph Catterall, *The Second Bank of the United States* (1902), full of information, remains indispensable. For the influential Democratic banking firm of Corcoran & Riggs, see Henry Cohen, *Business and Politics from the Age of Jackson to the Civil War* (1971).

William W. Freehling, *Prelude to Civil War: The Nullification Controversy in South Carolina* (1965), a model historical monograph, should now be used in conjunction with the same author's *The Road to Disunion: Secessionists at Bay, 1776–1854* (1990). For the impact of the crisis on contemporary politics, see Richard Ellis, *The Union at Risk* (1987). Much of the best scholarship on nullification is in article form. There is a brilliant assessment in Donald Ratcliffe, "The Nullification Crisis, Southern Discontents, and the American Political Process," *American Nineteenth-Century History* 1 (2000): 1–30. Also see Kenneth Stampp, "The Concept of a Perpetual Union," *JAH* 65 (1978): 5–33; Lacy K. Ford, "Inventing the Concurrent Majority," *Journal of Southern History* 60 (1994): 19–58; Richard Latner, "The Nullification Crisis and Republican Subversion," ibid. 43 (1977): 19–38; and Merrill Peterson, *Olive Branch and Sword* (1982). For nullification in the broader context of southern sectionalism, see John McCardell, *The Idea of a Southern Nation* (1979); Don Fehrenbacher, *Sectional Crisis and Southern Constitutionalism* (1995); and Peter Knupfer, *The Union as It Is* (1991).

The best book on the violence that plagued Jacksonian America is David Grimsted, *American Mobbing, 1828–1861* (1998), though it does not make pleasant reading. Also valuable are Clement Eaton, *The Freedom-of-Thought Struggle in the Old South*, rev. ed. (1964); Leonard Richards, *"Gentlemen of Property and Standing": Anti-Abolition Mobs in Jacksonian America* (1970); Dickson Bruce, *Violence and Culture in the Antebellum South* (1979); Kenneth Greenberg, *Honor and Slavery* (1996); and Paul Gilje, *The Road to Mobocracy: Popular Disorder in New York City, 1763–1834* (1987).

For the history of schools and education, see Lawrence Cremin, *American Education, The National Experience* (1980); Carl Kaestle, *Pillars of the Republic* (1983); Carl Kaestle and Maris Vinovskis, *Education and Social Change in Nineteenth-Century Massachusetts* (1980); Lee Soltow and Edward Stevens, *The Rise of Literacy and the Common School in the United States* (1981); Anne Boylan, *Sunday School* (1988); James McLachlan, *American Boarding Schools* (1970), 35–48; Theodore Sizer, *The Age of the Academies* (1964); Jonathan Messerli, *Horace Mann* (1972); Thomas Webber, *Deep like the Rivers: Education in the*

Slave Quarter Community (1978); and Janet Cornelius, *"When I Can Read My Title Clear"*: *Literacy, Slavery, and Religion in the Antebellum South* (1991).

On colleges and universities, see John Whitehead, *The Separation of College and State* (1973); Donald Tewksbury, *The Founding of American Colleges and Universities Before the Civil War* (1932); Barbara Solomon, *In the Company of Educated Women* (1985); Mark Noll, *Princeton and the Republic* (1989); D. H. Meyer, *The Instructed Conscience* (1972); and, on Harvard, Daniel Howe, *The Unitarian Conscience*, rev. ed. (1988).

The importance of the Bible to Americans in this period is attested in Nathan Hatch and Mark Noll, *The Bible in America* (1982); Paul Gutjahr, *An American Bible* (1999); James T. Johnson, ed., *The Bible in American Law, Politics, and Rhetoric* (1985); and Peter Wosh, *Spreading the Word* (1994).

The idea that the relationship between science and religion has been one of continual "warfare" has been effectively demolished; see David Lindberg and Ronald Numbers, eds., *God and Nature* (1986) and John Hedley Brooke, *Science and Religion* (1991). To capture the spirit of American science in this period, consult Herbert Hovenkamp, *Science and Religion in America, 1800–1860* (1978); Leonard Wilson, ed., *Benjamin Silliman and His Circle* (1979); Chandos Brown, *Benjamin Silliman* (1989); Margaret Welch, *The Book of Nature* (1998); John C. Greene, *American Science in the Age of Jefferson* (1984); Theodore Bozeman, *Protestants in an Age of Science* (1977); Albert Moyer, *Joseph Henry* (1997); and Hugh Slotten, *Patronage, Practice, and the Culture of American Science* (1994). A number of classic works on the relation between science and religion retain their usefulness, including Charles Gillispie, *Genesis and Geology* (1951); John C. Greene, *The Death of Adam* (1959); and A. Hunter Dupree, *Asa Gray* (1959).

For important episodes in the history of medicine, see Charles Rosenberg, *The Cholera Years* (1962; with a new afterword, 1987) and Sheldon Watts, *Epidemics and History* (1997). Martin Pernick, *A Calculus of Suffering* (1985) and Thomas Dormandy, *Worst of Evils* (2006) treat anesthesia; and Michael Sappol, *A Traffic of Dead Bodies* (2002), anatomy. On obstetrics, see Deborah McGregor, *From Midwives to Medicine* (1998) and Amelie Kass, *Midwifery and Medicine in Boston* (2002). Marie Jenkins Schwartz, *Birthing a Slave* (2006) is broader than its title might suggest. For more comprehensive accounts, see John Duffy, *From Humors to Medical Science* (1993); James Cassedy, *Medicine in America* (1991) and *American Medicine and Statistical Thinking* (1984); John S. Haller, *American Medicine in Transition* (1981); William Rothstein, *American Medical Schools and the Practice of Medicine* (1987); and G. B. Rushman et al., *A Short History of Anaesthesia* (1996). For the life of the country doctor, see Steven Stowe, *Doctoring the South* (2004); and for hospitals, Charles Rosenberg, *The Care of Strangers* (1987). The struggle between orthodox medicine and various alternatives is described in Joseph Kett, *The Formation of the American Medical Profession* (1968); Jayme Sokolow, *Eros and Modernization* (1983); and Stephen Nissenbaum, *Sylvester Graham and Health Reform* (1980). On African American folk medicine, see Sharla Fett, *Working Cures* (2002).

On the debates over slavery, see Stephen Haynes, *Noah's Curse* (2002) and Drew Faust, *A Sacred Circle* (1977) and *Southern Stories* (1992). For the relationship of southern evangelical religion to slavery, see Anne Loveland, *Southern Evangelicals and the Social Order* (1980); John Daly, *When Slavery was Called Freedom* (2002); and Elizabeth Fox-Genovese and Eugene Genovese, *The Mind of the Master Class* (2005).

On the Panics of 1837 and 1839, see Peter Temin, *The Jacksonian Economy* (1969); John McFaul, *The Politics of Jacksonian Finance* (1972); Herbert Sloan, *Principle and Interest* (1995); William Shade, *Banks or No Banks* (1972); Edwin Dodd, *American Business*

Corporations until 1860 (1954); and Douglass North, *The Economic Growth of the United States* (1961). More recent scholarship is presented in Peter Rousseau, "Jacksonian Monetary Policy, Specie Flows, and the Panic of 1837," *Journal of Economic History* 62 (2002): 457–88.

The Cambridge Economic History of the United States, ed. Stanley Engerman and Robert Gallman (Cambridge, Eng., 1996–2000), vol. II: *The Long Nineteenth Century* is an authoritative and up-to-date collection of essays. Other useful anthologies are Paul Gilje, ed., *Wages of Independence: Capitalism in the Early American Republic* (1997); Thomas Weiss and Donald Schaefer, eds., *American Economic Development in Historical Perspective* (1994); and Stanley Engerman and Robert Gallman, eds., *Long-term Factors in American Economic Growth* (1986). Stephen Usselman, *Regulating Railroad Innovation* (2002) is much broader than its title might suggest. On the growth of manufacturing, see Otto Mayr and Robert Post, eds., *Yankee Enterprise: The Rise of the American System of Manufactures* (1981); Thomas Cochran, *Frontiers of Change: Early American Industrialization* (1981); Cynthia Shelton, *The Mills of Manayunk* (1986); Ruth Schwartz Cowan, *A Social History of American Technology* (1997); Gary Kornblith, ed., *The Industrial Revolution in America* (1998); Colleen Dunlavy, *Politics and Industrialization: Early Railroads in the United States and Prussia* (1994); Peter Temin, *Engines of Enterprise* (2000); and, for its impact on American values, John Kasson, *Civilizing the Machine* (1976). Technical but rewarding are Robert Gallman and John Wallis, eds., *American Economic Growth and Standards of Living Before the Civil War* (1992) and Mary Rose, *Firms, Networks, and Business Values: The British and American Cotton Industries Since 1750* (2000).

For the history of labor, both organized and otherwise, see Walter Hugins, *Jacksonian Democracy and the Working Class* (1960); Sean Wilentz, *Chants Democratic* (1984); Herbert Gutman, *Work, Culture, and Society in Industrializing America* (1976); Alan Dawley, *Class and Community: The Industrial Revolution in Lynn* (1976); Bruce Laurie, *Artisans into Workers* (1989); Christopher Tomlins, *Law, Labor, and Ideology in the Early American Republic* (1993); Richard Stott, *Workers in the Metropolis* (1990); and Howard Rock, Paul Gilje, and Robert Asher, eds., *American Artisans* (1995). On the unskilled, see Peter Way, *Common Labour: Workers and the Digging of North American Canals* (1993). On working-class racism, see David Roediger, *The Wages of Whiteness*, rev. ed. (1999) and Anthony Gronowicz, *Race and Class Politics in New York City Before the Civil War* (1998).

Labor radicalism is treated in Paul Conkin, *Prophets of Prosperity* (1980), chap. 9; Jamie Bronstein, *Land Reform and Working-Class Experience* (1999); Jonathan Glickstein, *American Exceptionalism, American Anxiety* (2002); and Mark Lause, *Young America: Land, Labor, and the Republican Community* (2005).

On women wage-workers, see Thomas Dublin, *Women at Work: Lowell, Massachusetts*, 2nd ed. (1993) and Philip Foner's anthology, *The Factory Girls* (1977). For women as independent artisans, see Wendy Gamber, *The Female Economy: The Millinery and Dressmaking Trades* (1997). An aspect of labor often ignored is women's housework; see Jeane Boydston, *Home and Work: Housework, Wages, and the Ideology of Labor in the Early Republic* (1990) and Faye Dudden, *Serving Women: Household Service in Nineteenth-Century America* (1983).

Industrial slave labor is covered in Robert Starobin, *Industrial Slavery in the Old South* (1970); Ronald Lewis, *Coal, Iron, and Slaves* (1979); and Fred Bateman and Thomas Weiss, *A Deplorable Scarcity: The Failure of Industrialization in the Slave Economy* (1981).

For America's largest city, see Edwin G. Burrows and Mike Wallace, *Gotham: A History of New York City to 1898* (1999). Particular aspects of urban life are illuminated in

Tyler Anbinder, *Five Points* (2001); Amy Greenberg, *Cause for Alarm: The Volunteer Fire Department in the Nineteenth Century* (1998); Mary Ryan, *Civic Wars: Democracy and Public Life in the American City During the Nineteenth Century* (1997); Maureen Ogle, *All the Modern Conveniences* (1996); Timothy Gilfoyle, *City of Eros* (1992); Christine Stansell, *City of Women* (1986); and J. F. Richardson, *The New York Police* (1970).

The Whigs and Democrats of the second party system are examined in Robert Remini, *Martin Van Buren and the Making of the Democratic Party* (1959) and *The Election of Andrew Jackson* (1963); Richard P. McCormick, *The Second American Party System* (1966); Joel Silbey and Samuel McSeveney, eds., *Voters, Parties, and Elections* (1972); Daniel Howe, *The Political Culture of the American Whigs* (1979); Jean Baker, *Affairs of Party* (1983); John Ashworth, '*Agrarians*' and '*Aristocrats*' (1983); Joel Silbey, *The Partisan Imperative* (1985); Thomas Brown, *Politics and Statesmanship* (1985); Lawrence Kohl, *The Politics of Individualism* (1989); John Gerring, *Party Ideologies in America* (1998); and Daniel Feller, "Politics and Society: Toward a Jacksonian Synthesis," *JER* 10 (1990): 185–61. Michael Holt's monumental study, *The Rise and Fall of the American Whig Party* (1999), emphasizing state politics and electoral strategy, is invaluable.

Good legal history is necessarily technical, and much of it is relatively inaccessible to laypersons. I have benefited from the following: William Novak, *The People's Welfare: Law and Regulation in Nineteenth-Century America* (1996); William Nelson, *Americanization of the Common Law*, 2nd ed. (1994); Christopher Tomlins, *Law, Labor, and Ideology in the Early American Republic* (1993); Hendrick Hartog, *Public Property and Private Power* (1983); Laura Scalia, *America's Jeffersonian Experiment: Remaking State Constitutions, 1820–1850* (1999); P. S. Atiyah, *The Rise and Fall of Freedom of Contract* (1979); Peter Karsten, *Heart Versus Head: Judge-Made Law in Nineteenth-Century America* (1997); Morton Horwitz, *The Transformation of American Law* (1977); Leonard Levy, *The Law of the Commonwealth and Chief Justice Shaw* (1957); and Charles Warren, *The Supreme Court in United States History* (1923).

The momentous decisions of the Marshall Court are explained in Kent Newmyer, *John Marshall and the Heroic Age of the Supreme Court* (2001); Mark Killinbeck, *M'Culloch v. Maryland* (2006); Saul Cornell, *The Other Founders* (1999); Charles Hobson, *The Great Chief Justice* (1996); Edward White, *The Marshall Court and Cultural Change* (1988); Kent Newmyer, *Supreme Court Justice Joseph Story* (1985); and David Currie, *The Constitution in the Supreme Court* (1985). For the Supreme Court under Chief Justice Taney, see Stanley Kutler, *Privilege and Creative Destruction: The Charles River Bridge Case* (1971) and Austin Allen, *Origins of the Dred Scott Case: Jacksonian Jurisprudence and the Supreme Court* (2005).

The law of slavery is analyzed in Thomas D. Morris, *Southern Slavery and the Law* (1996); Paul Finkelman, *Slavery and the Law* (1997); Jenny Wahl, *The Bondsman's Burden* (1998); Timothy Huebner, *The Southern Judicial Tradition* (1999); Ariela Gross, *Double Character: Slavery and Mastery* (2000); and Mark Tushnet, *Slave Law in the American South* (2003).

The politics of slavery have been treated in Donald Robinson, *Slavery in the Structure of American Politics* (1971); Duncan Macleod, *Slavery, Race, and the American Revolution* (1974); William Cooper Jr., *The South and the Politics of Slavery* (1978); Richard J. Ellis, *American Political Cultures* (1993); Anthony Carey, *Parties, Slavery, and the Union in Antebellum Georgia* (1997); Don Fehrenbacher, *The Slaveholding Republic* (2001); Leonard Richards, *The Slave Power* (2001); and Matthew Mason, *Slavery and Politics in the Early American Republic* (2006).

On the anti-rent movement, see Charles McCurdy, *The Anti-Rent Era in New York Law and Politics* (2001); Reeve Huston, *Land and Freedom: Rural Society, Popular Protest, and Party Politics in Antebellum New York* (2000); and David Maldwyn Ellis, *Landlords and Farmers in the Hudson-Mohawk Region* (1946).

Too many historians have accepted the Democratic Party's characterization of William Henry Harrison as a nonentity and his election as an example of the triumph of hoopla over reason. This view is presented in Robert Gunderson, *The Log-Cabin Campaign* (1957); for a corrective, see Michael Holt, *The Rise and Fall of the American Whig Party* (1999). On the conflict between Tyler and Clay, besides William Brock, *Parties and Political Conscience*, already cited, see Dan Monroe, *The Republican Vision of John Tyler* (2003) and George Poage, *Henry Clay and the Whig Party* (1936).

Treatments of Dorr's Rebellion in Rhode Island reflect a variety of perspectives. They include Arthur Mowry, *The Dorr War* (1901); Peter Coleman, *The Transformation of Rhode Island* (1963), 218–94; Marvin Gettleman, *The Dorr Rebellion* (1973); and George Dennison, *The Dorr War* (1976).

For the role of women in electoral politics in this period, see Elizabeth Varon, *We Mean to Be Counted: White Women and Politics in Antebellum Virginia* (1998); Robert Dinkin, *Before Equal Suffrage* (1995); and Ronald Zboray and Mary Zboray, "Whig Women, Politics, and Culture in the Campaign of 1840," *JER* 17 (1997): 277–315. Sarah Josepha Hale and women's magazines are discussed in William R. Taylor, *Cavalier and Yankee* (1961) and Patricia Okker, *Our Sister Editors* (1995). For the role of petitioning in the development of women's political consciousness, and John Quincy Adams's defense of it, see Susan Zaeske, *Signatures of Citizenship* (2003). The complicated but exciting story of the Gag Rule and its repeal is told in William Lee Miller, *Arguing About Slavery* (1995) and William Freehling, *The Road to Disunion: Secessionists at Bay* (1990), 287–352.

Of the many works on William Ellery Channing, especially recommended are Madeleine Hooke Rice, *Federal Street Pastor* (1961) and Jack Mendelsohn, *Channing* (1971). For his context, see a fine anthology, Sydney Ahlstrom and Jonathan Carey, eds., *An American Reformation* (1985); as well as David Robinson, *The Unitarians and the Universalists* (1985); Anne Bressler, *The Universalist Movement in America* (2001); Conrad Wright, ed., *A Stream of Light* (1975); Conrad Edick Wright, ed., *American Unitarianism, 1805–1865* (1989); and Daniel Howe, *The Unitarian Conscience*, rev. ed. (1988).

Writings about the Transcendentalists are voluminous and mostly by literary scholars rather than historians; I mention here only a few that have most influenced me. Barbara Packer gives a superb general account: "The Transcendentalists," in *The Cambridge History of American Literature*, vol. II, ed. Sacvan Bercovitch (1995). Lawrence Buell, *New England Literary Culture from Revolution Through Renaissance* (1986) is indispensable; Francis Otto Matthiessen, *American Renaissance* (1941), an enduring classic. Perry Miller's great anthology *The Transcendentalists* (1950) should now be supplemented with that of Joel Myerson, *Transcendentalism* (2001). Charles Capper and Conrad Edick Wright, eds., *Transient and Permanent* (1999) is an outstanding essay collection. For the Transcendentalists as social rebels, see Anne Rose, *Transcendentalism as a Social Movement* (1981); Albert von Frank, *The Trials of Anthony Burns* (1998); and *Emerson's Antislavery Writings*, ed. Len Gougeon and Joel Myerson (1994). For their complex attitude toward the market revolution, see Richard Teichgraeber, *Sublime Thoughts/Penny Wisdom* (1995).

Robert Richardson Jr. has written two excellent intellectual biographies: *Henry Thoreau* (1986) and *Emerson* (1995). See also Lawrence Buell, *Emerson* (2003); Mary Cayton, *Emerson's Emergence* (1989); and Peter Field, *Ralph Waldo Emerson* (2002). Charles

Capper's two-volume biography *Margaret Fuller* (1992 and 2007) is detailed and fascinating; for more on Fuller's relationship to feminism, see Tiffany Wayne, *Woman Thinking* (2005). So far we have only the first volume of the giant two-volume biography of Theodore Parker: Dean Grodzins, *American Heretic* (2002). Norman Risjord, *Representative Americans: The Romantics* (2001) interprets the American Renaissance broadly.

The perfectibility of human nature was a central tenet of the American Renaissance. Self-improvement projects are illustrated in Daniel Howe, *Making the American Self* (1997) and Angela Ray, *The Lyceum and Public Culture in the Nineteenth-Century United States* (2005). For black people's self-improvement, see Heather Williams, *Self-Taught: African American Education in Slavery and Freedom* (2005) and Elizabeth McHenry, *Forgotten Readers: Recovering the Lost History of African American Literary Societies* (2002). On educating the most severely handicapped, see Ernest Freeberg, *The Education of Laura Bridgman* (2001) and Elisabeth Gitter, *The Imprisoned Guest* (2001). For Dorothea Dix's campaign to reform the treatment of the insane, see David Gollaher, *Voice for the Mad* (1995) and Thomas Brown, *Dorothea Dix* (1998). Stephen Rice, *Minding the Machine* (2004) interprets the ethos of self-improvement as a strategem to sustain the authority of the middle class against the working class.

Works on the American literary Renaissance are too numerous to do more than suggest some of its ramifications. William Charvat's *Literary Publishing in America* (1959) and *The Profession of Authorship in America* (1968) defined their subjects. More recent treatments of literary culture include Michael Gilmore, *American Romanticism and the Marketplace* (1985); Mary Kelley, *Private Woman, Public Stage* (1984); David Reynolds, *Walt Whitman's America* (New York, 1995); Rosalind Remer, *Printers and Men of Capital* (1996); Meredith McGill, *American Literature and the Culture of Reprinting* (2003); Ronald Zboray, *A Fictive People* (1993); and Ronald Zboray and Mary Zboray, *Literary Dollars and Social Sense* (2005). The rise of the novel is discussed in Nina Baym, *Novels, Readers, and Reviewers* (1984); Michael Denning, *Mechanic Accents: Dime Novels and Working Class Culture in America* (1987); David Reynolds, *Beneath the American Renaissance* (1988); and Cathy Davidson, *Revolution and the Word*, 2nd ed. (2004). For the connection between literature and social reform, see, for example, Jane Tompkins, *Sensational Designs* (1985) and Carolyn Karcher's biography of Maria Child, *First Woman in the Republic* (1998).

On the theater in the young republic, see John Kasson, *Rudeness and Civility* (1990); Lawrence Levine, *Highbrow/Lowbrow* (1988); Susan Porter, *With an Air Debonair* (1991); and Nigel Cliff, *The Shakespeare Riots* (2007). Minstrel shows have a substantial bibliography of their own; see Ken Emerson, *Doo-dah! Stephen Foster and the Rise of American Popular Culture* (1998); Robert Toll, *Blacking Up* (1974); Eric Lott, *Love and Theft: Black-face Minstrelsy and the American Working Class* (1993); and William Mahar, *Behind the Burnt Cork Mask* (1999).

The Cambridge History of American Music, ed. David Nicholls (1998) contains judicious essays on this period. For the music of the slaves, see, in addition to works on black culture cited earlier, Eileen Southern, *The Music of Black Americans*, 2nd ed. (1983) and Dena Epstein, *Sinful Tunes and Spirituals* (1977). Shane White and Graham White, *The Sounds of Slavery* (2005) includes recordings. The hymns of white Christians are discussed in Henry Wilder Foote, *Three Centuries of American Hymnody* (1940) and Peter Benes, ed., *New England Music: The Public Sphere* (1998).

The abolitionists are heroes to most Americans nowadays, and an extremely large body of writing pays tribute to them; what follows is a highly selective sample of it. An excellent overview is James B. Stewart, *Holy Warriors*, rev. ed. (1997). See also Stanley Harrold, *American Abolitionists* (2001); Lawrence Friedman, *Gregarious Saints* (1982); and Edward Magdol, *The Antislavery Rank and File* (1986). Two essay collections are Timothy McCarthy and John Stauffer, eds., *Prophets of Protest* (2006) and Lewis Perry and Michael Fellman, eds., *Antislavery Reconsidered* (1979). Simon Schama, *Rough Crossings* (2006) and David Brion Davis, *Inhuman Bondage* (2006) put antislavery into its international context. The best biography of Garrison is Henry Mayer, *All on Fire* (1998); for Weld, see Robert Abzug, *Passionate Liberator* (1980). Frederick Blue, *No Taint of Compromise* (2005) and Bruce Laurie, *Beyond Garrison* (2005) celebrate the political abolitionists. The growing militancy of the abolitionists is treated in Merton Dillon, *Slavery Attacked* (1990) and Stanley Harrold, *The Rise of Aggressive Abolitionism* (2004). Three historians argue about the relationship between abolitionism and capitalism in the difficult but rewarding volume entitled *The Antislavery Debate*, ed. Thomas Bender (1992).

On the schism within the abolition movement, see Aileen Kraditor, *Means and Ends in American Abolitionism* (1969); Bertram Wyatt-Brown, *Lewis Tappan and the Evangelical War Against Slavery* (1971); and John McKivigan, *The War Against Proslavery Religion* (1984). For women's resistance to the schism, see Julie Jeffrey, *The Great Silent Army of Abolitionism* (1998).

Benjamin Quarles, *Black Abolitionists* (1969) remains useful. Particular aspects of black antislavery are covered in John Stauffer, *The Black Hearts of Men* (2002) and John Ernest, *Liberation Historiography* (2004). Bruce Dain's book on race theory, *A Hideous Monster of the Mind* (2002), sheds light on African American abolitionism. A large body of writing on Frederick Douglass includes Nathan Huggins, *Slave and Citizen* (1980); William McFeely, *Frederick Douglass* (1991); and Waldo Martin Jr., *The Mind of Frederick Douglass* (1984). Nell Painter, *Sojourner Truth* (1996) is judicious.

For abolitionist feminism, see Gerda Lerner, *The Grimké Sisters from South Carolina*, rev. ed. (2004); Blanche Hersh, *The Slavery of Sex* (1978); Jean Yellin, *Women and Sisters* (1989); Jean Yellin and John Van Horne, eds., *The Abolitionist Sisterhood* (1994); Nancy Hardesty, *Women Called to Witness*, 2nd ed. (1999); Anna Speicher, *The Religious World of Antislavery Women* (2000); and Kathryn Sklar, *Women's Rights Emerges Within the Anti-Slavery Movement* (2000). Michael Pierson connects the subject to party politics in *Free Hearts and Free Homes* (2003). For the transatlantic dimension, see Clare Midgley, *Women Against Slavery* (1992), 121–53, and Kathryn Sklar and James B. Stewart, eds., *Women's Rights and Transatlantic Antislavery* (2007).

On efforts to aid escaping slaves, see Thomas Morris, *Free Men All: The Personal Liberty Laws* (1974); Stanley Harrold, *The Abolitonists and the South* (1995); David Blight, ed., *Passages to Freedom* (2004); and Fergus Bordewich, *Bound for Canaan* (2005).

There are many books on the Texan Revolution; what follows is a highly selective list emphasizing recent works. The authoritative military history is now Stephen Hardin, *Texian Iliad* (1994). For other aspects, see Gregg Cantrell, *Stephen F. Austin, Empresario of Texas* (1999); James Crisp, "Race, Revolution, and the Texas Republic," in *The Texas Military Experience*, ed. Joseph Dawson (1995), 32–48; Paul Lack, *The Texas Revolutionary Experience* (1992); Sam Haynes, *Soldiers of Misfortune: The Somervell and Mier Expeditions* (1990); Andreas Reichstein, *Rise of the Lone Star*, trans. Jeanne Willson (1989); Margaret Henson, *Juan Davis Bradburn* (1982); and Paul Hogan, *The Texas Republic* (1969). The Alamo has of course attracted particular attention: see Randy Roberts and James Olson, *A Line in the Sand* (2001); William C. Davis, *Three Roads to the Alamo* (1998); Timothy Matovina, *The Alamo Remembered: Tejano Accounts and Perspectives* (1995). Lelia

Roeckell, "British Interests in Texas, 1825–1846" (D.Phil. Thesis, Oxford University, 1993) is the most thorough treatment of its subject; for background, see also David Turley, *The Culture of English Antislavery, 1780–1860* (1991). The expulsion of the Indian tribes by Anglo settlers is the theme of Gary Anderson, *The Conquest of Texas* (2005).

Historical treatments of American imperialism in the 1840s range from celebratory to sternly critical. See William Weeks, *Building the Continental Empire* (1996); Thomas Hietala, *Manifest Design* (1985); Shomer Zwelling, *Expansion and Imperialism* (1970); Frederick Merk, *The Monroe Doctrine and American Expansionism* (1966); William Goetzman, *When the Eagle Screamed* (1966); Reginald Horsman, *Race and Manifest Destiny* (1981); Sam Haynes and Christopher Morris, eds., *Manifest Destiny and Empire* (1997); Robert F. May, *Manifest Destiny's Underworld* (2002); and Linda Hudson, *Mistress of Manifest Destiny: A Biography of Jane McManus Storm Cazneau* (2001). Concise biographies of the leading expansionist are Thomas Leonard, *James K. Polk* (2001); Sam Haynes, *James K. Polk*, 3rd ed. (2006); and John Seigenthaler, *James K. Polk* (2003). Edward Crapol, *John Tyler, the Accidental President* (2006) emphasizes his role as an expansionist.

A vivid account of the process of Texas annexation is in William Freehling, *The Road to Disunion: Secessionists at Bay* (1990), 353–452. David Pletcher, *The Diplomacy of Annexation* (1973) is detailed and solid. Frederick Merk, *Slavery and the Annexation of Texas* (1972), like everything by that meticulous historian, is still valuable. For a narrative, see Richard Winders, *Crisis in the Southwest: The United States, Mexico, and the Struggle over Texas* (2002). Joel Silbey, *Storm over Texas* (2004), treats annexation's impact on U.S. party politics.

The greatest historian of the Oregon controversy was Frederick Merk; see especially his *Manifest Destiny and Mission* (1963), *The Oregon Question* (1967), and *Fruits of Propaganda in the Tyler Administration* (1971). Also valuable are Bradford Perkins, *The Cambridge History of American Foreign Relations*, vol. I (1993) and David Dykstra, *The Shifting Balance of Power: American-British Diplomacy in North America* (1999). For the settlers, see Julie Jeffrey, *Converting the West* (1991); Michael Golay, *The Tide of Empire* (2003); and David Dary, *The Oregon Trail* (2004). On the British side, see John S. Galbraith, *The Hudson's Bay Company as an Imperial Factor* (1957) and Kenneth Bourne, *Britain and the Balance of Power in North America* (1967).

The causes of the war between the United States and Mexico are treated in Sellers, *James K. Polk, Continentalist*; Pletcher, *Diplomacy of Annexation*; Perkins, *Cambridge History of American Foreign Relations*, vol. I (all cited above); and Gene Brack, *Mexico Views Manifest Destiny* (1975). Polk's statesmanship is defended in Justin Smith's classic *The War with Mexico* (1919), vol. I, and by Seymour Connor and Odie Faulk, *North America Divided* (1971). Norman Graebner offers a judicious assessment of causality in "The Mexican War," *Pacific Historical Review* 49 (1980): 405–26. Scott Silverstone, a political scientist, analyzes how Polk provoked a war, then framed the issue so Congress would vote for it: *Divided Union: The Politics of War in the Early American Republic* (2004).

The U.S.-Mexican War has not attracted as much attention as so momentous a conflict deserves from either historians or the American public, but see Charles Dufour, *The Mexican War* (1968); Odie Faulk and Joseph Stout, eds., *The Mexican War* (1973); K. Jack Bauer, *The Mexican War* (1974); John Weems, *To Conquer a Peace* (1974); and John Eisenhower, *So Far from God* (1989). For contemporary illustrations, see Martha Sandweis et al., *Eyewitness to War* (1989) and Carol Christensen and Thomas Christensen, *The U.S.-Mexican War* (1998). On the army, see Richard Winders, *Mr. Polk's Army* (1997); James McCaffrey, *Army of Manifest Destiny* (1992); Marcus Cunliffe, *Soldiers and Civilians: The*

Martial Spirit in America, 1775–1865 (1968); and Richard Uviller and William Merkel, *The Militia and the Right to Arms* (2002). For the seamy side, see Paul Foos, *A Short, Offhand, Killing Affair* (2002). On the navy, see John Schroeder, *Shaping a Maritime Empire* (1985). On the *sanpatricios*, see Robert Ryal Miller, *Shamrock and Sword* (1989) and Peter F. Stevens, *The Rogue's March* (1999). A superb reference work is Donald Frazier, ed., *The United States and Mexico at War* (1998).

Attitudes of the U.S. public toward the war are treated in Robert Johannsen, *To the Halls of the Montezumas* (1985); John Schroeder, *Mr. Polk's War: American Opposition and Dissent* (1973); Shelley Streeby, *American Sensations: Class, Empire, and the Production of Popular Culture* (2002); and Joel Silbey, *The Shrine of Party: Congressional Voting Behavior, 1841–1852* (1967). Works in English illuminating the Mexican perspective on the war include Ramon Alcarez et al., *The Other Side*, trans. Albert Ramsey (1850); Charles Hale, *Mexican Liberalism in the Age of Mora* (1968); William DePalo, *The Mexican National Army, 1822–1852* (1997); Ruth Olivera and Liliane Crété, *Life in Mexico Under Santa Anna* (1991); and Josefina Zoraida Vázquez, "War and Peace with the United States," in *The Oxford History of Mexico*, ed. Michael Meyer and William Beezley (New York, 2000). Readers with a command of Spanish can benefit from Laura Herrera Serna, ed., *México en guerra, 1846–1848* (1997).

For the war in California, see Neal Harlow, *California Conquered* (1982); Andrew Rolle, *John Charles Frémont* (1991); Tom Chafin, *The Pathfinder: John Charles Frémont and the Course of American Empire* (2002); Dale Walker, *Bear Flag Rising* (1999); and Alan Rosenus, *General M. G. Vallejo and the Advent of the Americans* (1995). On the war in New Mexico, see Stephen Hyslop, *Bound for Santa Fe: The Road to New Mexico and the American Conquest* (2002); Howard Lamar, *The Far Southwest* (1966); Dwight Clarke, *Stephen Watts Kearny* (1961); David Lavender, *Bent's Fort* (1954); and Norma Ricketts, *The Mormon Battalion* (1996). James Crutchfield, *Tragedy at Taos* (1995) covers the uprising from the U.S. point of view. Hampton Sides, *Blood and Thunder* (2006), a novel-like history of Kit Carson and the Navajo, includes a vivid account of the U.S. conquest of the Southwest.

On Nicholas Trist and the treaty of peace, see Robert Drexler, *Guilty of Making Peace* (1991); Wallace Ohrt, *Defiant Peacemaker* (1997); Richard Griswold del Castillo, *The Treaty of Guadalupe Hidalgo* (1990); and Matt Meier and Feliciano Ribera, *Mexican Americans/American Mexicans* (1993). On the election of 1848, see Michael Morrison, *Slavery and the American West* (1997); Joseph Rayback, *Free Soil: the Election of 1848* (1971); Frederick Blue, *The Free Soilers* (1973); and Yonatan Eyal, *The Young America Movement and the Transformation of the Democratic Party* (2007).

Interest in the first year of the California Gold Rush flourishes. Recent, well-written works include Rodman Paul and Elliott West, *Mining Frontiers of the Far West*, rev. ed. (2001); H. W. Brands, *The Age of Gold* (2001); Brian Roberts, *American Alchemy: The California Gold Rush and Middle-Class Culture* (2000); Susan Johnson, *Roaring Camp: The Social World of the California Gold Rush* (2000); Malcolm Rohrbough, *Days of Gold* (1997), Paula Mitchell Marks, *Precious Dust* (1994); and Joanne Levy, *They Saw the Elephant: Women in the California Gold Rush* (1990).

Conventional historiography treats the Irish immigrants of 1845–54 as helpless victims of oppression, premodern in their worldview. See Oscar Handlin, *Boston's Immigrants* (1972; first pub. 1941) and Cecil Woodham-Smith, *The Great Hunger* (1962); a version of this interpretation can be found in Kerby Miller, *Emigrants and Exiles* (1985). Revisionist and other recent historians emphasize the resolution and resourcefulness of the migrants and the foundation they laid for the economic success of their descendants. See, for example, Donald Akenson, *The Irish Diaspora* (1996); Cormac O'Grada, *The Great Irish Famine* (1995); George Boyce and Alan O'Day, eds., *The Making of Modern Irish History* (1996); David Fitzpatrick, *Irish Emigration* (1984); and P. J. Drudy, ed., *The Irish in America* (1985). For reactions to the Irish immigrants, see Dale Knobel, *Paddy and the Republic* (1986). For illustrations, see Michael Coffey and Terry Golway, *The Irish in America* (1997). Nativism badly needs an up-to-date historical treatment. Until then, the principal account will remain Ray Billington, *The Protestant Crusade* (1938, rpt. 1964). New treatment should take account of the new Catholic history and reconceive the subject as Protestant-Catholic interaction. Nancy Schultz, *Fire and Roses* (2000) is a well-written narrative of the burning of the Charlestown convent in 1834. Mark Voss-Hubbard, *Beyond Party: Cultures of Antipartisanship in Northern Politics before the Civil War* (2002) includes a sophisticated discussion of the rise of political nativism.

The definitive account of the women's rights convention of 1848, if such a thing were possible, would be Judith Wellman, *The Road to Seneca Falls* (2004). For the context of the convention, see Nancy Isenberg, *Sex and Citizenship in Antebellum America* (1998) and Lori Ginzberg, *Untidy Origins: A Story of Women's Rights in Antebellum New York* (2005). Biographies of Elizabeth Cady Stanton include Lois Banner, *Elizabeth Cady Stanton* (1980) and Elisabeth Griffith, *In Her Own Right* (1984). Ann Gordon has edited *Selected Papers of Elizabeth Cady Stanton and Susan B. Anthony* (1997). For the larger picture, see Ellen DuBois, *Woman Suffrage and Women's Rights* (1998). The international dimension of the women's rights movement is emphasized in Margaret McFadden, *Golden Cables of Sympathy: Transatlantic Sources of Nineteenth-Century Feminism* (1999) and Bonnie Anderson, *Joyous Greetings: The First International Women's Movement* (2000).

Index